Moral Issues in Global Perspective

Moral Issues in Global Perspective

edited by

Christine M. Koggel

Broadview Press

Canadian Cataloguing in Publication Data

Main entry under title:
Moral issues in global perspective

Includes bibliographical references.
ISBN 1-55111-186-1

1. Social ethics. I. Koggel, Christine M.

HM216.M673 1999 170 C99-931323-1

The publisher has made every attempt to locate the authors of the copyrighted material or their heirs and assigns, and would be grateful for information that would allow correction of any errors or omissions in subsequent editions of the work.

BROADVIEW PRESS, LTD.
is an independent, international publishing house, incorporated in 1985

North America
Post Office Box 1243, Peterborough, Ontario, Canada K9J 7H5
3576 California Road, Orchard Park, New York, USA 14127
TEL: (705) 743-8990; FAX (705) 743-8353; E-MAIL: 75322.44@compuserve.com

United Kingdom and Europe
Turpin Distribution Services, Ltd.,
Blackhorse Rd., Letchworth, Hertfordshire, SO6 EHN
TEL: (1462) 672555; FAX: (1462) 480947; E-MAIL: turpin@rsc.org

Australia
St. Clair Press, Post Office Box 287, Rozelle, NSW 2039
TEL: (612) 818-1942; FAX: (612) 418-1923

www.broadviewpress.com

Canada

Broadview Press gratefully acknowledges the support of the Ministry of Canadian Heritage through the Book Publishing Industry Development program.

Printed in Canada

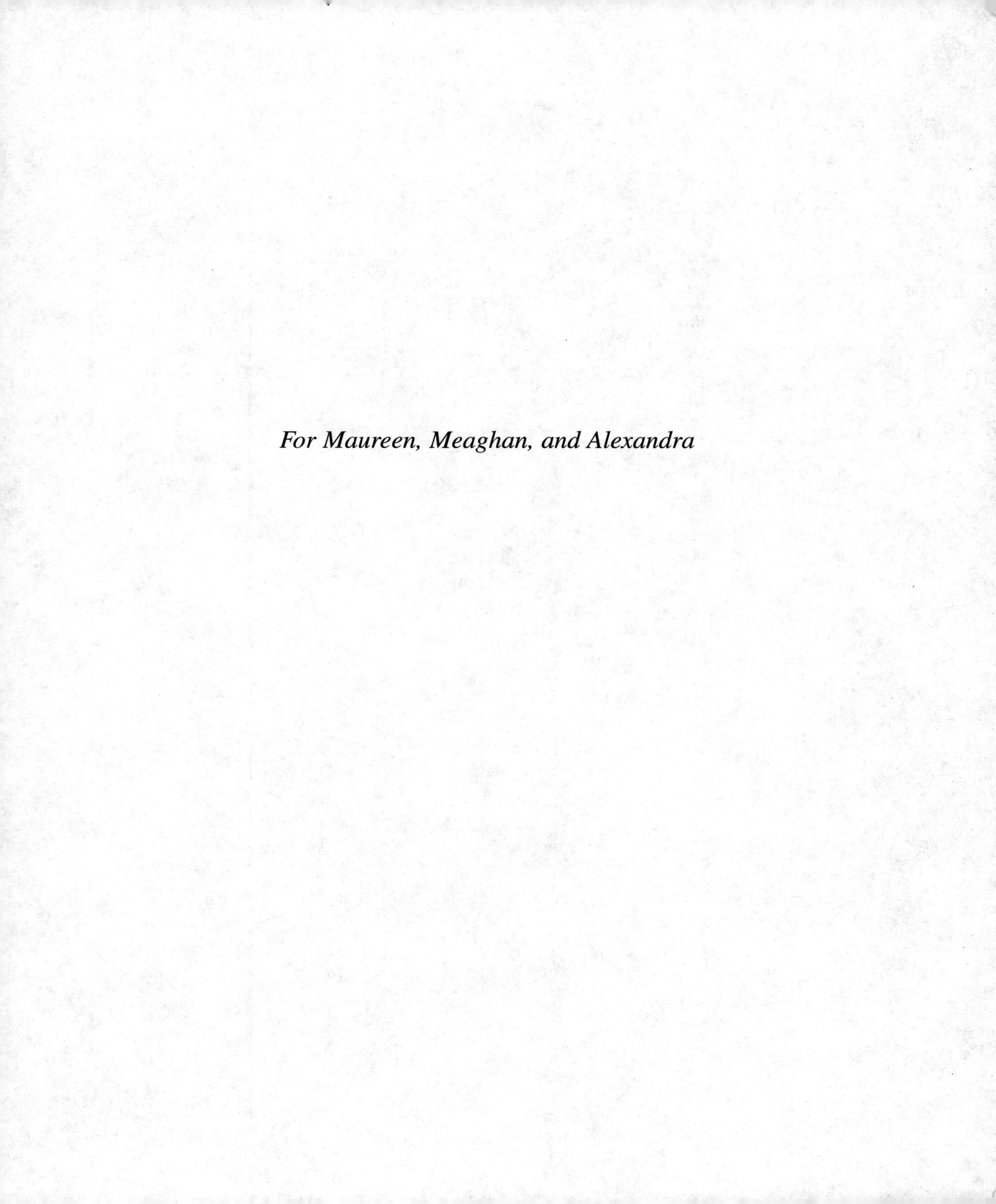

For Maureen, Meaghan, and Alexandra

Contents

PART II HUMAN DIVERSITY AND EQUALITY

Chapter Fourteen: Animals and the Environment

PREFACE

The central question in ethics is: How should we live our lives and interact with others? The motivation for this anthology is to explore answers to this question in the context of the international community or "global village" in which we now live. "Globalization" is a concept used increasingly in all sorts of contexts: in discussions of markets, international relations, economic development, human rights, the environment, labor, media, and information technology. Globalization is increasing exposure to beliefs and values very different from our own as well as communication with people from faraway places. The almost limitless access to information through television and the internet, for example, not only makes it possible for us to learn virtually instantaneously about other places, but it also makes it easy to praise or condemn people, policies, practices, and structures in other places. Globalization has universalized human rights discourse from its roots in liberal theory and has given a prominent place to international organizations that monitor human rights violations. An important effect of globalization has been to intensify our awareness of the devastating ways in which policies and practices in one area may effect not only the livelihood and choices of people in other areas, but the world as a whole.

Increased globalization not only means that no community is isolated from the world's gaze, but also that virtually no communities remain unaffected by the influx of people from other places. The latter describes the phenomenon of multiculturalism, difference and diversity *within* a community with a variety of beliefs. Multiculturalism means that we need not look across borders to find instances of the unequal treatment of and discrimination against people identified as different. It calls on us to examine the ways in which our embeddedness in particular contexts and practices shapes our associations with and perceptions of others. Multiculturalism opens the door to examining relationships and to thinking critically about our interactions with and responses to others. In making it possible to scrutinize beliefs and practices different from our own, globalization and multiculturalism ask us to critically examine the judgments we render about others both across and within borders.

These facts and effects of globalization and of multiculturalism raise questions that have become increasingly pressing to moral inquiry. This anthology assumes that these questions are relevant to the central question of how we live our lives and interact with others. Does our situatedness in a Western liberal democratic society generate problematic assumptions about what human beings are like; what we need to flourish; and what rights and responsibilities we hold? Might our commitment to the notion of the inviolability of individual liberty rights change if we learned about attitudes to rights different from those in our own social and political context? Would our understanding of what constitutes just social and political structures change if we became aware of theories that defend alternative structures, particularly by authors from societies with structures different from our own? Can social relations and policies in other contexts give us insights into ways to approach moral issues of inequality and discrimination in our own context? Does our understanding of the right way to live and of how to determine morally right action reflect the biases of Western liberal beliefs and values? Does the impact of policies in one society on the welfare and well-being of members of another society hinder us from acquiring an adequate understanding of moral, social, and political issues and of how to resolve them? In general, does our view of moral issues change when we turn our attention to the global context?

Most current collections on moral issues make it

impossible to raise these questions. They tend to feature the narrow band of agreements and disagreements of Western liberal theory and practice. *Moral Issues in Global Perspective* seeks to challenge our thinking about morality and moral issues as it has been shaped by Western liberal theory and to extend the inquiry beyond the context of North America. It includes analyses of moral issues by both liberal and non-liberal theorists from around the world, many of whom question the American understanding of human rights, social welfare, and development. It includes critiques of traditional liberal accounts of rights, justice, and moral theory, critiques that question the treatment of disadvantaged groups within liberal societies. It incorporates work by race, class, feminist, and disability theorists that challenges traditional moral theory and opens up new perspectives on issues such as reproduction, euthanasia, censorship, and environmental ethics.

This collection incorporates these kinds of perspectives into each chapter, more so than is the case with any of the textbooks on practical ethics that are currently available in North America. So, for example, we are asked to confront challenges by non-Western writers that liberal beliefs about the importance of individual rights to free speech and property may reflect a discourse about rights that has little or no application in places with traditions that uphold community values or in countries struggling to achieve economic viability, let alone stability. We may need to question our assumptions about gender when we examine the role and activities of women in places like Indonesia and Nigeria. We are asked to think about how the issue of abortion takes on a new shape in the context of Nicaragua where a strong tradition of Catholicism pulls against the aspirations of a socialist power. This anthology collects the work of some 70 authors reflecting a broad range of views from all over the world. In doing so, it attempts to show the complexity of moral issues when examined on a global scale and the richness and diversity of writing on these issues by authors outside the Western tradition.

Of course, one cannot move in new directions without a base in the familiar. Many of the readings are intended to reflect not only the wide spectrum of views among liberal theorists, but also the discussion of moral issues as it takes place in North America. With this background, we can then take up the two challenges of globalization and multiculturalism. A global context of increased awareness of human rights violations, developmental issues with respect to the environment and the lives of indigenous peoples, and the imposition of western values on other cultures challenges the notion that answers to complex moral issues can be found by focusing only on Western liberal values in a North American context. *Moral Issues in Global Perspective* stands as an illustration of how the field of moral inquiry is greatly enriched when we turn our attention to disenfranchised voices within and to contexts outside of North America.

The book is divided into three parts, each of which begins with a chapter on theory and then applies the theory to contexts and issues. Chapter One of Part I begins with discussions of the theoretical foundations for conceptions of human rights and justice, foundations that find their source in Western liberal theory. The fundamental teaching of classical liberal theory that each human being has equal moral value and deserves equal concern and respect has become the foundation for theories about how societies ought to be structured to ensure equal treatment, for accounts of what human beings need in order to flourish, and for attempts to formulate universal human rights. Yet, liberal theory has been criticized for its excessive individualism, an individualism that critics take to be apparent in the policies, structures, and kinds of human rights that liberals tend to defend. This criticism is front and center when we turn to a global context and examine theorists who challenge the very framework of individual rights that dominates debates about human rights and justice in Western liberal societies. Chapter Two of Part I applies theories of rights and justice to concrete contexts, ones in which historical and social conditions in specific parts of the world sometimes support and sometimes challenge liberal understandings of justice, human rights, and democracy.

Part II continues the exploration of the relevance of globalization and multiculturalism to moral inquiry by zeroing in on questions about human nature. Are we all the same and can we provide a list of essential human features and capabilities that generates moral imperatives for human flourishing no matter who we are or where we live? Do we operate with a set of assumptions about human beings that result in stereotypes about difference and judgments about other people's beliefs and practices? Do facts of discrimination and inequality both across and within borders shape human identity in ways that call for policies to eliminate blatant injustices? Is it possible to understand the perspectives and life experiences of members of disadvantaged groups from a vantage point of privilege or to speak for them when making judgements about them? Answers to these sorts of questions in the theory chapter that opens Part II are then followed by several chapters in which discrimination on the grounds of race and ethnicity, gender, sexual orientation, differential ability, and poverty are examined. These chapters explore moral issues raised by relationships that are shaped by the different histories, identities, and levels of power of people within and across societies.

The relationship of the individual to society tends to be central to most moral issues collections. Part III explores the relationship between the individual and society by providing accounts in traditional Western moral theory that attempt to answer the question of how individuals can determine morally right action; it then surveys some of the major critiques of those accounts. This all too brief survey of moral theories is then applied to practical issues that have acquired particular prominence in Western liberal contexts: individual choice and social responsibility at the beginning and end of human life, the value of liberty and its connection to pornography and hate speech, relations that result in sexual violence, and how we live and interact with animals and the environment. Liberal theory has tended to examine these issues in terms of the conflict between the individual and society; what, if any, restrictions to individual freedom are permissible and what sorts of moral justifications can be provided for using the power of the state to limit individual freedom? The readings in the chapters of Part III represent both defenses and critiques of this depiction of the way to resolve practical issues.

The book would not have been possible without the help and support of many people along the way. I want to begin by thanking all the authors who granted permission to reprint their work in the collection. Don LePan, president of Broadview Press, was committed to the project from its earliest stages and has provided encouragement and support throughout. The production staff, Barbara Conolly and Betsy Struthers, assisted by Margaret Hunwicks, handled this large and complex project with professionalism and enthusiasm. Their careful work on this book is greatly appreciated. I would like to thank several anonymous reviewers of early versions of the collection for their helpful suggestions concerning the organization, topics, and readings. A special thanks goes to Keith Burgess-Jackson, who demonstrated his impressive knowledge of the extensive literature in moral theory and practical issues by providing a very constructive and thorough review. His suggestions were indispensable right into the final stages of preparing the collection.

Countless people took an interest in this project, and discussions with them sometimes provided valuable advice and sometimes unearthed readings that have turned out to be key pieces in the book. In this respect, I would like to thank Claudia Card, Jay Drydyk, Lucius Outlaw, Cheshire Calhoun, Sue Campbell, Lorraine Code, Anita Kothari, Margaret Walker, and Jennifer Nedelsky. I am pleased to have been in the right places at the right times to discover important work at conferences and colloquia over the past several years. Working with these people has been a pleasure. In particular, I would like to thank Susan Babbitt, Janice Newberry, Nathan Brett, Marvin Glass, Jennifer Llewellyn, and David Crocker.

This is not the first project that Andrew Brook has taken great care to read and comment on. His help on this front is, as always, matched by his unwavering confidence in my work and his encouragement and support. Michael Krausz, Christine Overall, Raluca Munteanu, Göze Saner, Mimi Doi, Lorraine Kirschner, and Dennis Kolba influenced the project and ensured its completion in ways that only they can know. Finally, I would like to express my gratitude to the many students with inquiring minds and diverse backgrounds who made this exploration possible.

PART I

HUMAN RIGHTS AND JUSTICE

CHAPTER ONE

THEORIES AND CRITICAL ANALYSIS

As this collection is put together, the fiftieth anniversary of the United Nations Universal Declaration of Human Rights is being celebrated. It is fitting that this document opens both the book and this section. The idea underlying the Declaration is that all human beings are equal by virtue of the fact that they share basic human capacities that make them deserving of respect. They have basic needs and should be treated as equals. This idea has been enormously influential in creating a global community, one in which virtually all countries express, if not always honor, a commitment to human rights and reject discrimination based on morally irrelevant differences such as race, ethnicity, and gender. The idea of human rights has its most obvious source and development in the Western tradition beginning with classic liberal theorists such as Locke, Kant, and Mill. Yet it is well known that some of these theorists propounded equality for all people at the same time as they justified inequality and unequal treatment for some, including women and people of different ethnicity and race. It is also well-known that liberal theory has tended to emphasize the primacy of individual rights to free speech, property, and assembly, for example. The question of how human rights are conceived is important because rights articulate what human beings need to flourish and are, therefore, intricately connected with accounts of what is needed by way of political structures and institutions for meeting the demands of equality and justice.

One of the central questions to be explored in this chapter is whether the Universal Declaration of Human Rights really reflects a Western notion of human rights more than one that speaks for and meets the needs of people in all countries. A corollary to this question is whether the charge that current conceptions of human rights are predominantly Western undermines the validity or desirability of trying to formulate human rights that are *genuinely* universal. The assumption is that there is a set of rights or political structures that are valid everywhere. This has generated several tendencies discussed in Part I and examined in many chapters throughout the collection. The first is *ethnocentrism*, the disposition to judge foreign peoples or groups by the standards and practices of one's own culture or ethnic group. The term *Eurocentrism* is reserved for the particular bias in favor of the culture and values of Western liberal thinking. Second is *universalism*, the tendency to view human rights or justice ahistorically and in isolation from their social, political, and economic habitat. Often this tendency emerges from generalizing from one's own social context with specific values and political structures to all contexts and all people. Lastly, there is *essentialism*, the tendency to characterize all human beings as having the same features, capacities, and needs irrespective of social conditions, political contexts, and the particular circumstances of people's lives.

The Universal Declaration of Human Rights, the first reading in this chapter, asserts liberty rights familiar in Western liberal contexts such as freedom to own property; freedom of thought, conscience, and religion; freedom of opinion and expression; and freedom of peaceful assembly and association. These civil and political rights are often referred to as negative rights because they flow from the notion that the state should not interfere in the lives of its citizens. Those who defend negative rights and non-interference by the state argue that this context allows individuals to develop their capacities, pursue their aspirations and goals, meet their needs, and thereby flourish as human beings. Sections of the Declaration also propound positive rights such as the right to work, the right to equal pay for equal work, the right to education, and the right to a standard of living adequate for health and well-being. These positive rights are economic rights, and those who defend them justify and endorse state interference through minimum wage laws, for example, or through positive measures to ensure that basic human needs such as food and shelter are provided.

In the second reading, Adamantia Pollis and Peter Schwab examine this distinction between negative or civil/political rights and positive or economic rights and point out that the former tends to be closely aligned with Western liberal values. They argue that cultural, developmental, and ideological differences have shaped beliefs and values in non-Western countries that stand in sharp contrast with those in the West. The emphasis in the West on individuals and individual rights has little or no meaning in non-Western contexts in which the individual is conceived as an integral part of a greater whole, a whole that has primacy over the individual. They argue that because human rights originated in Western political thought and because the United Nations was dominated by the West, the Universal Declaration of Human Rights is actually the expression of legal and political thought in the West and has limited applicability in non-Western contexts. However, Pollis and Schwab do not reject the notion of human rights as such. Instead they take the realization of differing historical conditions and of a multiplicity of philosophies and ideologies to be the occasion for uncovering and discovering any universals that may exist.

In the third reading, Kenneth Inada develops the critique of human rights from a non-Western perspective and lends support to Pollis and Schwab's argument that many non-Western ideologies are holistic rather than individualistic by examining the philosophical underpinnings of the Buddhist "holistic cosmological framework." Inada argues that the tension between the tradition of Buddhism and the Western notion of rights elucidates a difference in perspective with respect to how human relationships are conceived. The Western view of human rights is based on "hard relationships" in which people are treated as separate and independent entities each having his or her own identity and self-concepts. Such relationships are exemplified in the work of modern liberal thinkers who picture people as needing to make contracts that set limits to their freedom so that liberty, security, and peaceful coexistence can be enhanced for themselves and all individuals. Inada argues that a Buddhist view of human rights emerges from recognition and knowledge of the soft side of human interaction. This is characterized by openness, depth, flexibility, and creativity and by the features of mutuality, holism, and emptiness. Together these characteristics shape relationships that emphasize virtues such as patience, trust, humility, tolerance, deference, concern, honesty, responsibility, respectfulness, and compassion. According to Inada, these virtues supersede the need for rights that define boundaries and emphasize liberty. His argument is not that human rights are meaningless in Buddhism, but rather that soft relationships are inclusive in a way that can accommodate hard relationships and allow for interaction and complementarity between these two sets of beliefs and values.

In the third reading, Jay Drydyk takes the current trend to globalization with respect to economic development and labor as an important reason for re-examining the criticism that human rights are Eurocentric constructs. He rejects Eurocentrism, but not the project of formulating a universal set of rights. He does the latter by uncovering a common ground for human rights discourse in what motivates discussions of rights and responsibilities at all. According to Drydyk, a human right to something is "calling for social protection against standard threats that exemplify a particular type of danger for humans." Such a general understanding, he argues, allows us to derive a concept of human rights from the beliefs, values and laws of both Western and non-Western countries. More importantly, it also allows us to take account of different cultural contexts and to provide a critical analysis of the accounts of danger and social protection assumed by some cultures. The emergence of a global public sphere of moral deliberation makes it possible to come up with a full set of human rights applicable on a global scale. At the center of such moral deliberation is knowledge of care, neglect, and abuse—knowledge that is specific to cultures with different conditions and circumstances that may require certain kinds of responses. Drydyk thinks there is convergence on these matters and that this should form the bedrock for ridding moral discourse of its Eurocentrism and making human rights useful for eliminating the damage caused by globalization in the areas of development and labor.

So far, the discussion in this chapter has focused on issues of the diversity and irreconcilability of beliefs across cultures and of the possibility of formulating a set of human rights applicable to all people and all places. The last two readings examine the concept of justice in the highly influential work of John Rawls. Inada takes Rawls to be an example of a modern liberal thinker who uses the notion of a social contract to generate a set of principles by which members of a community agree to abide. In *A Theory of Justice* (1971), Rawls asks us to imagine ourselves in an original position behind a veil of ignorance, a veil that conceals from us knowledge about the specific details of our lives: who we are, where we live, whether we are rich or poor, black or white. We do know that we have goals and interests that we will want to pursue, and we have general knowledge that social and political structures can determine our fate with respect to the distribution of social goods. For Rawls, these conditions enable us to reach agreement about principles of justice for shaping political structures that ensure people are treated equally and for determining the fair distribution of social goods.

Rawls's theory of justice has generated numerous critiques, some of the most serious from critics who argue that he makes assumptions about what sort of person is behind the veil of ignorance. Does Rawls already assume that people in the original position hold the beliefs and values of a liberal democratic society? If so, does his theory of justice lack proper grounding and have limited applicability to non-liberal contexts? These criticisms continue, as Xiaorong Li points out in the final reading, even in the face of revisions that Rawls has made to his theory since 1971. In his recent work, Rawls admits that his theory of justice applies to a pluralistic democratic political culture, one in which citizens are already committed to a view of themselves as free and equal and have divergent and conflicting religious, philosophical, and moral beliefs. He takes his principles of justice to be freestanding in that they are not grounded in any religious, philosophical, or moral doctrine and allow people with diverse beliefs and life plans to co-exist and co-operate in a just and stable society. Li points out that if Rawls's theory of justice presupposes liberal democratic values, then it is not freestanding after all and, consequently, lacks the foundational arguments that would make it applicable to other cultures. Without a commitment to any comprehensive moral doctrine, Rawls has little to say about why liberty and equality are superior to slavery or subjugation, for example. Li argues that Rawls fails to provide what is most promising about his theory of justice: a firm defense of liberal democratic institutions against totalitarian or authoritarian repression. As a result, his theory cannot provide a justification for transforming unjust economic conditions or political structures in places like India and China.

UNIVERSAL DECLARATION OF HUMAN RIGHTS

United Nations

The Universal Declaration of Human Rights was approved by the General Assembly of the United Nations on December 10, 1948, by forty-eight nations with eight abstentions. The Declaration is formulated as a universal standard of human rights for all nations and peoples and enumerates the rights and freedoms of individuals irrespective of "race, color, sex, language, religion, political or other opinion, national or social origin, property, birth or other status."

Whereas Member States have pledged themselves to achieve, in co-operation with the United Nations, the promotion of universal respect for and observance of human rights and fundamental freedoms.

Whereas a common understanding of these rights and freedoms is of the greatest importance for the full realisation of this pledge,

Now, therefore, the General Assembly, Proclaim this Universal Declaration of Human rights as a common standard of achievement for all peoples and all nations, to the end that every individual and every organ of society, keeping this Declaration constantly in mind, shall strive by teaching and education to promote respect for these rights and freedoms and by progressive measures, national and international, to secure their universal and effective recognition and observance, both among the peoples of Member States themselves and among the peoples of territories under their jurisdiction.

Article 1

All human beings are born free and equal in dignity and rights. They are endowed with reason and conscience and should act towards one another in a spirit of brotherhood.

Article 2

1. Everyone is entitled to all the rights and freedoms set forth in this Declaration, without distinction of any kind, such as race, colour, sex, language, religion, political or other opinion, national or social origin, property, birth or other status.
2. Furthermore, no distinction shall be made on the basis of the political, jurisdictional or international status of the country or territory to which a person belongs, whether it be independent, trust, non-self-governing or under any other limitation of sovereignty.

Article 3

Everyone has the right to life, liberty and security of person.

Article 4

No one shall be held in slavery or servitude; slavery and the slave trade shall be prohibited in all their forms.

Article 5

No one shall be subjected to torture or to cruel, inhuman or degrading treatment or punishment.

Article 6

Everyone has the right to recognition everywhere as a person before the law.

Article 7

All are equal before the law and are entitled without any discrimination to equal protection of the law. All are entitled to equal protection against any discrimination in violation of this Declaration and against any incitement to such discrimination.

Article 8

Everyone has the right to an effective remedy by the competent national tribunals for acts violating the fundamental rights granted him by the constitution or by law.

Article 9

No one shall be subjected to arbitrary arrest, detention or exile.

Article 10

Everyone is entitled in full equality to a fair and public hearing by an independent and impartial tribunal, in the determination of his rights and obligations and of any criminal charge against him.

Article 11

1. Everyone charged with a penal offence has the right to be presumed innocent until proved guilty according to law in a public trial at which he has had all the guarantees necessary to his defence.
2. No one shall be held guilty of any penal offence on account of any act or omission which did not constitute a penal offence, under national or international law, at the time when it was committed. Nor shall a heavier penalty be imposed than the one that was applicable at the time the penal offence was committed.

Article 12

No one shall be subjected to arbitrary interference with his privacy, family, home or correspondence, nor to attacks upon his honour and reputation. Everyone has the right to the protection of the law against such interference or attacks.

Article 13

1. Everyone has the right to freedom of movement and residence within the borders of each State.
2. Everyone has the right to leave any country, including his own, and to return to his country.

Article 14

1. Everyone has the right to seek and to enjoy in other countries asylum from persecution.
2. This right may not be invoked in the case of prosecutions genuinely arising from non-political crimes or from acts contrary to the purposes and principles of the United Nations.

Article 15

1. Everyone has the right to a nationality.
2. No one shall be arbitrarily deprived of his nationality nor denied the right to change his nationality.

Article 16

1. Men and women of full age, without any limitation due to race, nationality or religion, have the right to marry and to found a family. They are entitled to equal rights as to marriage, during marriage and at its dissolution.
2. Marriage shall be entered into only with the free and full consent of the intending spouses.
3. The family is the natural and fundamental group unit of society and is entitled to protection by society and the State.

Article 17

1. Everyone has the right to own property alone as well as in association with others.
2. No one shall be arbitrarily deprived of his property.

Article 18

Everyone has the right to freedom of thought, conscience and religion; this right includes freedom to change his religion or belief, and freedom, either alone or in community with others and in public or private, to manifest his religion or belief in teaching, practice, worship and observance.

Article 19

Everyone has the right to freedom of opinion and expression; this right includes freedom to hold opinions without interference and to seek, receive and impart information and ideas through any media and regardless of frontiers.

Article 20

1. Everyone has the right to freedom of peaceful assembly and association.
2. No one may be compelled to belong to an association.

Article 21

1. Everyone has the right to take part in the government of his country, directly or through freely chosen representatives.
2. Everyone has the right of equal access to public service in his country.
3. The will of the people shall be the basis of the authority of government; this will shall be expressed in periodic and genuine elections which shall be by universal and equal suffrage and shall be held by secret vote or by equivalent free voting procedures.

Article 22

Everyone, as a member of society, has the right to social security and is entitled to realisation, through national effort and international co-operation and in accordance with the organization and resources of each State, of the economic, social and cultural rights indispensable for his dignity and the free development of his personality.

Article 23

1. Everyone has the right to work, to free choice of employment, to just and favorable conditions of work and to protection against unemployment.
2. Everyone, without any discrimination, has the right to equal pay for equal work.
3. Everyone who works has the right to just and favourable remuneration ensuring for himself and his family an existence worthy of human dignity, and supplemented, if necessary, by other means of social protection.
4. Everyone has the right to form and to join trade unions for the protection of his interests.

Article 24

Everyone has the right to rest and leisure, including reasonable limitation of working hours and periodic holidays with pay.

Article 25

1. Everyone has the right to a standard of living adequate for the health and well-being of himself and of his family including food, clothing, housing and medical care and necessary social services, and the right to security in the event of unemployment, sickness, disability, widowhood, old age or other lack of livelihood in circumstances beyond his control.
2. Motherhood and childhood are entitled to special care and assistance. All children, whether born in or out of wedlock, shall enjoy the same social protection.

Article 26

1. Everyone has the right to education. Education shall be free, at least in the elementary and fundamental stages. Elementary education shall be compulsory. Technical and professional education shall be made generally available and higher education shall be equally accessible to all on the basis of merit.
2. Education shall be directed to the full development of the human personality and to the strengthening of respect for human rights and fundamental freedoms. It shall promote understanding, tolerance and friendship among all nations, racial or religious groups, and shall further the activities of the United Nations for the maintenance of peace.
3. Parents have a prior right to choose the kind of education that shall be given to their children.

Article 27

1. Everyone has the right freely to participate in the cultural life of the community, to enjoy the arts and to share in scientific advancement and its benefits.
2. Everyone has the right to the protection of the moral and material interests resulting from any scientific, literary or artistic production of which he is the author.

Article 28

Everyone is entitled to a social and international order in which the rights and freedoms set forth in this Declaration can be fully realised.

Article 29

1. Everyone has duties to the community in which alone the free and full development of his personality is possible.
2. In the exercise of his rights and freedoms, everyone shall be subject only to such limitations as are determined by law solely for the purpose of securing due recognition and respect for the rights and freedoms of others and of meeting the just requirements of morality, public order and the general welfare in a democratic society.
3. These rights and freedoms may in no case be exercised contrary to the purposes and principles of the United Nations.

Article 30

Nothing in this Declaration may be interpreted as implying for any State, group or person any right to engage in any activity or to perform any act aimed at the destruction of any of the rights and freedoms set forth herein.

HUMAN RIGHTS: A WESTERN CONSTRUCT WITH LIMITED APPLICABILITY

Adamantia Pollis • Peter Schwab

Adamantia Pollis is Professor of Political Science at the Graduate Faculty, New School for Social Research, New York. She is an area expert on Greece, Cyprus, and the Southern Mediterranean region. She has published numerous articles in various journals on topics related to these areas and on rights more generally. She is co-editor with Peter Schwab of Human Rights: Cultural and Ideological Perspectives *(Praeger, 1979) and* Toward a Human Rights Framework *(Praeger, 1982).*

Peter Schwab is Professor of Political Science at the State University of New York at Purchase. He is an area expert on Ethiopia and has published extensively on the subject of rights in numerous journals.

Pollis and Schwab claim that international documents such as the Universal Declaration of Human Rights contain strong biases that reflect Western conceptions of human rights and human dignity. As evidence for this cultural and ideological ethnocentrism, they cite the emphasis given in Western political thinking both to individual civil and political rights over economic rights and to individual freedom over social relations and community values. They question the assumption that Western-originating doctrines about human rights apply in non-Western contexts and call for greater efforts to formulate human rights that truly reflect universal values, i.e. values common to a multiplicity of philosophies and divergent beliefs in the world.

Recently there has been increasing concern that notwithstanding the Charter of the United Nations and the Universal Declaration of Human Rights, universal consensus on the concept of human rights and the content of fundamental freedoms does not exist. It is becoming increasingly evident that the Western political philosophy upon which the Charter and the Declaration are based provides only one particular interpretation of human rights, and that this Western notion may not be successfully applicable to non-Western areas for several reasons: ideological differences whereby economic rights are given priority over individual civil and political rights and cultural differences whereby the philosophic underpinnings defining human nature and the relationship of individuals to others and to society are markedly at variance with Western individualism. Consequently, application in non-Western countries of Western-originated doctrines such as the Universal Declaration of Human Rights has frequently meant that legal norms whose implementation is contingent upon the state lack the substantive meaning such rights have in the West.

If it is valid that there is no universal concurrence as to the meaning of human rights, human dignity, and freedom—and in fact there is marked diversity of opinion—then efforts to enforce the provisions of the Universal Declaration of Human Rights in states that do not accept its underlying values are bound to fail. What is needed is a rethinking of the conception of human rights; an effort must be made to distill from the multiplicity of philosophies and ideologies and their divergent values any universals that may exist. The analysis that follows is a beginning effort to deal with the problem of cultural and ideological

---

Reprinted with permission of the Greenwood Publishing Group Inc. from *Human Rights: Cultural & Ideological Perspectives*, edited by Adamantia Pollis and Peter Schwab (Westport CT: © 1979 Praeger Publishers): 1–18.

ethnocentrism in the area of human rights and human dignity.

Human Rights and the West

From the seventeenth to the twentieth centuries in England, France, and the United States, the legal and political roots of human rights were formulated. Through the philosophic and legal writings of Grotius, Locke, Montesquieu, and Jefferson a new conception of popular sovereignty and individual rights was conceived. This in turn was grounded in a new view of the nature of man, and the relationship of each individual to others and to society.[1] From these revolutionary ideas stemmed the basic premises of the Declaration of Independence and the Declaration of the Rights of Man and Citizen: "all men are created equal ... endowed ... with certain inalienable rights ... among these ... life, liberty, and the pursuit of happiness"; "Men are born and remain free and equal in rights, the aim of every political association is the preservation of the natural and imprescriptible rights of man. These rights are liberty, the ownership of property, security and the right to resist oppression." These radical concepts understood man as an autonomous being possessed of rights in nature, rights that were not dependent upon a sovereign grant or legislative statute. Liberty and democracy, therefore, were not consequences of a particular set of political institutions, but were based on natural rights that were prior to and supreme over the sovereignty of the state. The late eighteenth century revolutions in the United States and France legitimized within the context of the state the philosophical and legal justifications of natural rights. That man had certain inherent natural rights "found practical expression and legal reality in the historical documents that embodied the constitutional principles of the new American state and of revolutionary France."[2]

The seventeenth and eighteenth centuries witnessed such landmarks as the English Petition of Rights (1627), the Habeas Corpus Act (1679), the American Declaration of Independence (1776), the United States Constitution (1787), the American Bill of Rights (1791), and the French Declaration of the Rights of Man and Citizen (1789), all of which constitutionalized and institutionalized a Western standard of human rights and liberties. That standard still exists today. As Myres McDougal, Harold Lasswell, and Lung-Chu Chen wrote in 1969:

> Let it be said immediately that a certain minimum of values indispensable to a dignified human existence must be described as immune from all claims of derogation at all times. Notably among these are the right to life, freedom from torture and inhuman treatment, freedom from involuntary human experimentations, freedom from slavery, the slave trade and servitude, freedom from imprisonment for debt, freedom from retroactive application of criminal punishment, the right to recognition as a human being, and freedom of thought conscience and religion. These rights and freedoms are indispensable to a dignified human existence and remain wholly intact from derogation upon grounds of crisis. In terms of our basic postulation, it can never be necessary to encroach upon these rights and freedoms, even in times of emergency.[3]

The seventeenth—and eighteenth—century postulate that there are rights and freedoms that are not amenable to state legislation, control, or abrogation, has been carried through in the twentieth century in the conception of "minimum of values."

It is important to note that the philosophic and ideological revolution of the seventeenth and eighteenth centuries regarding the nature of man and his inalienable rights was accompanied by radical socioeconomic transformations and changing societal values. In Western Europe the communal bonds of feudalism had collapsed and extended family ties were disrupted by the Industrial Revolution—by urbanization and the factory. A capitalist system came into existence and a new industrial class rebelled against the constraints of government, demanding political participation and political freedoms and arguing the ethics of social contract. In the United States a new land was being settled where individual initiative and competition frequently were requisites for survival. Hence the new philosophic doctrines of the autonomous individual and his inherent rights were assimilated both as an explanation of and a justification for the new social order. In time such doctrines became part of the prevailing shared values of Western societies.

Whereas the seventeenth to the nineteenth centuries were eras during which the concept of natural rights was institutionalized within the context of the nation-state in the West, the twentieth century witnessed the extension of this concept and its institutionalization in regional and international organizations, particularly in the Council of Europe and the United Nations. The Universal Declaration of Human Rights, adopted by the United Nations General Assembly in 1948, for example, is based on the Jeffersonian credo, and states in its preamble that "recognition of the *inherent dignity and of the equal and inalienable rights* of all members of the human family is the foundation of freedom, justice and peace in the world ..." (our emphasis). Egon Schwelb, in his study of human rights, categorically states that the roots of the Universal Declaration of Human Rights "are in the legal and political thought of the seventeenth to twentieth centuries" in France, England, and the United States.[4]

Hence it is clear that human rights as a twentieth-century concept and as embedded in the United Nations can be traced to the particular experiences of England, France, and the United States. In turn the experiences of these states through the centuries have led directly to the concern with human rights as expressed in the Universal Declaration. It should not be forgotten that the San Francisco Conference which established the United Nations in 1945 was dominated by the West, and that the Universal Declaration of Human Rights was adopted at a time when most Third World countries were still under colonial rule. Thus to argue that human rights has a standing which is universal in character is to contradict historical reality. What ought to be admitted by those who argue universality is that human rights as a Western concept based on natural right *should* become the standard upon which all nations ought to agree, recognizing however, that this is only one particular value system. And in fact, as McDougal makes evident, this is what is really being said.[5] The critical question, however, is whether there is a universal consensus regarding the Western definition of human rights based on natural right or whether there are alternative conceptions of human rights and human dignity that merit consideration. Before discussing the extent to which individual and human rights based on Western philosophy are accepted or rejected by non-Western nations and the extent to which alternative concepts may contain significant values, it will be instructive to investigate the extent to which the rights embodied in the Universal Declaration of Human Rights are obligatory or enforceable on the states of the world.

Obligation and Enforcement of the Universal Declaration of Human Rights

On December 20, 1948 the General Assembly of the United Nations, by a vote of 48 for, none against, and eight abstentions (including the Soviet Union, South Africa, and Saudi Arabia), adopted and proclaimed the Universal Declaration of Human Rights. Although not spelled out in detail, the Declaration indicated that human rights and freedoms were related to "race, colour, sex, language, religion, political or other opinion, national or social origin, property, birth or other status" (in Article 2). A perusal of the provisions regarding rights makes it abundantly clear that the overriding philosophy underlying them is the Western concept of political liberty and democracy, inclusive of property rights in contradistinction to economic rights or egalitarianism. The rights and freedoms enumerated in the articles are life, liberty, the illegality of torture, equality before the law, prohibition against arbitrary arrest, fair trial by impartial tribunal, the right to be presumed innocent until proven guilty, freedom of travel, the right to marry freely, the right to own property, freedom of assembly, and so on. The primacy of political rights in the Declaration is clear: of the thirty articles only three, one of them dealing with property rights, can be considered as dealing with economic rights.[6] In prefacing his discussion of human rights, Moses Moskowitz articulates the extent to which the political philosophy of liberalism has dominated the conceptualization of the Universal Declaration of Human Rights over and above any other system of values or any other ideology such as socialism:

> Two hundred years ago Immanuel Kant argued that it was illusory to expect an international association to enforce peace among nations without a common moral-

> ity of democratic values. ... He asserted the rights and liberties of the individual as a condition for all true morality.[7]

The Declaration itself reads like a political "bill of rights," and according to Schwelb that is precisely how it was viewed during the drafting stage.[8]

Many authorities on human rights contend that the Declaration is not merely a recommendation to states, but a set of standards that must be applied. According to Leland Goodrich, it seems evident that at the time of adoption, although the Declaration was passed by the General Assembly without a dissenting vote, "it was not a treaty and was not intended to impose legal obligations."[9] In the words of Eleanor Roosevelt, who chaired the Commission of Human Rights, the Declaration is "not a treaty; it is not an international agreement, it is not and does not purport to be a statement of law or of legal obligation."[10] Nevertheless it is argued that subsequent international conventions have reaffirmed the Declaration's principles and consequently, regardless of the original intent of the drafters of the Universal Declaration of Human Rights, it has now become mandatory for at least the signatory states. One example cited is the Convention on the Elimination of all Forms of Racial Discrimination, adopted by the General Assembly and put into force in 1969, which states in Article 6 that "parties shall assure to everyone within their jurisdiction effective protection and remedies ... against any acts of racial discrimination which violate his human rights and fundamental freedoms. ..." Similarly the International Covenant on Economic, Social, and Cultural Rights (1966) which, in the words of its Preamble, was written in "accordance with the Universal Declaration of Human Rights," is considered a legitimizing action making the Declaration binding on member states.

Others argue that since the Declaration has been in existence for nearly 30 years it has become binding under customary law. But as J. L. Brierly explains, this is dubious.

> Custom ... is a usage felt by those who follow it to be an obligatory one. There must be present a feeling that, if the usage is departed from, some form of sanction will probably or at any rate ought to, fall on the transgressor.[11]

The Statute of the International Court of Justice specified in Article 38 that customary law can be considered binding when the alleged custom shows "evidence of a general practice accepted as law." Hence although what is customary law cannot be precisely defined, the principles of human rights do not fall within the domain of customary law and states are not bound by them. If one surveys the states that compose the international community, no general practice regarding human rights is evident and there is no feeling or expectation of sanctions if the Declaration of Human Rights or the subsequent covenant are violated.

By contrast, among states in the West, for example in the Council of Europe, some human rights are perceived as inviolate by the state under any conditions whereas others can be infringed only under extraordinary political circumstances such as a clear national emergency.[12] The European Convention on Human Rights, unlike the Universal Declaration, has a standing in law and is obligatory on the signatories. Evidence of this perception has been the relative willingness of the European states to abide by findings charging violation of rights by the European Commission of Human Rights and the European Court of Human Rights. Most striking was the action of the Council of Europe in the expulsion of Greece in 1969 for gross violations of human rights, a decision that was not implemented due to Greece's withdrawal the day prior to the vote for expulsion.[13]

To the extent that the Western European states and the United States adhere to the principles of human rights and are responsive to criticisms for their violation, it is not a consequence of the European Convention of Human Rights or the Universal Declaration of Human Rights. On the contrary, the historical experiences of both these areas had defined the issue well before 1948. Both in Western Europe and in the United States conceptions of individual human rights were assimilated over the centuries into the political cultures of these societies. The holocaust of World War II precipitated the drafting of the Universal Declaration of Human Rights which, however, was an articulation and a reinforcement of political values that had a prior existence.

It is frequently argued that many non-Western states have incorporated the values and rights of the

Universal Declaration into their own constitutions and into the charters of regional organizations such as the Organization of American States (OAS) and the Organization of African Unity (OAU), hence giving these rights a universal legal standing. But such a claim ignores several factors that vitiate these rights and make them substantively meaningless. The dominance of the United States over Latin America, particularly in 1948 when the OAS was formed, is well known. Furthermore, at the time of independence countries under colonial rule wrote constitutions in accord with and often along with former colonial administrators. For British colonies the Westminster model, including its provisions for individual rights, became practically the *sine qua non* for independence. The failure of the Westminster model is now generally accepted in light of the prevalence of military regimes that in many cases threw out colonial-inspired constitutions along with civilian regimes. Even in cases where provisions guaranteeing human rights remain in the books such as in Senegal, or where constitutions are not a direct colonial legacy, as in Greece, human rights are perceived as a grant by the state and as something that the state can give or withhold. In turn the charters of regional organizations, also written under external pressure and influence, do not necessarily bind member states to adhere to human rights. As the Organization of African Unity charter states in its preamble, it adheres "to the principles of the Charter of the United Nations and of the Universal Declaration of Human Rights as a solid foundation for peaceful and positive cooperation among states."[14] No member state is bound in any way to enforce the provisions of the Universal Declaration.

Summarizing then, in essence the Universal Declaration of Human Rights is a document whose underlying values are democratic and libertarian, based on the notion of atomized individuals possessed of certain inalienable rights in nature. These political values, as distinct from economic rights or communal rights, can be traced directly to the experiences of France, England, and the United States. The Declaration is predicated on the assumption that Western values are paramount and ought to be extended to the non-Western world. It is clear that at present the Universal Declaration of Human Rights is not binding upon states; many adhere to the International Court of Justice's interpretation of customary law implying that the Declaration is unenforceable since its functional acceptance and usage is limited. States do violate the Declaration, they do not feel bound by it, and there is little evidence that the practice of states regarding human rights follows any established norm. The discussion that follows will analyze some of the factors that account for the neglect and violation of human rights in regions other than the West.

Human Rights and the Non-Western World: Cultural, Developmental, and Ideological Differences

An interrelated and interdependent set of factors account for the limited viability and applicability of the Western concepts of human rights and human dignity in the non-Western world. Broadly speaking these factors can be divided into two categories: the cultural patterns and the developmental goals of new states including the ideological framework within which they were formulated. Traditional cultures did not view the individual as autonomous and possessed of rights above and prior to society. Whatever the specific social relations, the individual was conceived of as an integral part of a greater whole, of a "group" within which one had a defined role and status. The basic unit of traditional society has varied—the kinship system, the clan, the tribe, the local community—but not the individual. (This notion of the group defining the self, it should be mentioned, was equally valid in the West prior to the advent of individualism.) The colonial experience in the Third World did little to alter traditional conceptualizations of the social order. Regardless of specific colonial policies and political structures, all colonized peoples were subject to ultimate authority in the form of the colonial ruler, and doctrines of inalienable rights—clearly a threat to the interests of the colonial powers—were not disseminated.

With independence a multiplicity of new "sovereign" nation-states were established and at least in theory these new entities defined group membership. The notion of the primacy of the group and the submission of the individual to the group persisted, although the confines and boundaries of the group had changed to become coterminous with the state. As a consequence whatever rights an individual possesses are given to him by the state, and this state retains the right and the ability to curtail individual rights and freedoms for the greater good of the group. Inevitably constitutional government has come to be identified with a particular set of democratic political institutions but not with the doctrines of individualism or inalienable rights which constitute the philosophic underpinnings of democracy in the West.

The pervasiveness of the notion of the "group" rather than the "individual" in many cultures is evident even in concepts of property ownership. The Universal Declaration maintains in Article 17 that "everyone has the right to own property. ..." Yet in many cultures, among them the Gojami-Amhara of Ethiopia, land is owned communally and there is no "right" to individual ownership of holdings. This conception of social ownership predates by centuries any Marxist or socialist doctrines, but it is evident how such traditional conceptions can be incorporated into the different ideological frameworks of Third World countries. Furthermore, Article 16 states that the "family is the fundamental group unit of society." For many societies the nuclear family (as implied in this article) clearly is not the fundamental unit; in hunting and gathering societies the kinship group, and in China the clan, have been more "natural."[15]

The irrelevance of the Western conception of human rights founded on natural rights doctrines is not rooted solely in traditional cultural patterns, but is also a consequence of the articulated modernization goals of Third World countries. The ideology of modernization and development that has attained universal status has come to be understood primarily in terms of economic development. The colonial experience of economic exploitation gave credence to the notion of human dignity as consisting of economic rights rather than civil or political rights. Freedom from starvation, the right for all to enjoy the material benefits of a developed economy, and freedom from exploitation by colonial powers became the articulated goals of many Third World countries. The strategies that evolved for the attainment of these goals incorporated an admixture of old concepts and values frequently reinterpreted and redefined in light of contemporary realities and goals. Thus the state was to replace traditional group identities but was to retain the same supremacy as traditional groups. By the same token the state's responsibility is to free its people from colonial exploitation and to attain economic betterment. Essentially this is the conceptual framework that has structured the world view of many Third World countries and within which human rights and human dignity are understood. Democratic government is perceived as an institutional framework through which the goals of the state are to be achieved, and if it fails or becomes an impediment it can be dispensed with with impunity. Individual political rights, so revered in the West, at most take second place to the necessity of establishing the legitimacy of the new group—the state—and to the priority of economic rights that necessitate economic modernization.

It is within this context that the doctrines and policies of many African states can be understood. As early as the 1960s such leaders as Nkrumah, Toure, and Nyerere rejected democratic political institutions as undesirable for their societies. They argued forcefully that a one party state, by contrast to a multiparty state, was necessary because Ghana, Guinea, and Tanzania needed to prevent political dissension among their populations. The multiparty state was perceived as counterproductive both to the development of a nation-state and to the development of the economy; parties represented classes or ethnic or tribal groups and would foster political dissension at a time when those states had to concentrate on national unity and on social and economic change. As Nkrumah said, "the Convention People's Party (CPP) is Ghana and Ghana is the CPP."[16] Thus the CPP could do no wrong because it spoke for the entire population. With the establishment of priorities and of one-party ideologies in the new states, politically restrictive statutes were adopted.

The conjunction of a traditional culture that defined the individual in terms of group membership, the need to transpose this group identity to the nation-state level, a definition of modernization in terms of economic development, and the evolution of the notion of a one-party state as the embodiment of the people facilitated the adoption of decrees limiting freedom of speech, the adoption of preventive detention laws, the outlawing of rival political parties, the placing of the judiciary under party control, and the incorporation of all voluntary associations under the rubric of the one party. These actions were not viewed as antidemocratic but as requisites whereby ethnically diverse, extremely poor states could create the unified political framework essential for economic development. As Nkrumah and Nyerere often said, if political differences were permitted to rule the state the economy would be stymied as the unity necessary for development would be absent.[17] Social change, a process fraught with political problems, was the major priority, and its perceived importance is evident in the national leaderships' argument that "the maintenance of order becomes necessary if national goals are to be concentrated upon and achieved."[18] Democratic political institutions were to be sacrificed to some future time, while economic development was to be concentrated upon. The fact that many of these states (Ghana as a case in point) have failed to attain their articulated goals does not invalidate the conceptual framework in terms of which Third World leaders perceive their goals and the strategy of their attainment.[19]

It is perhaps instructive to keep in mind the experience of Turkey which more than 50 years ago was one of the first states to consciously and explicitly embark on a program of "westernization" (as Kemal Ataturk labeled it). Ataturk attempted to transform the Ottoman Empire into a modern Turkish nation-state. His concept of modernization did not include an ideology of individual political rights or even democratic government. In reaction to the defeat and dismemberment of the Ottoman Empire at the hands of advanced industrial states, just as African states reacted to colonial exploitation and domination, Ataturk was concerned with secularizing society, introducing a modern educational system, adopting Western technology and industry, creating new political structures, and defining Turkish nationalism.[20] On the question of even a formally democratic polity he argued that the above-mentioned goals had priority over such institutions as a multiparty system; only after Turkey had attained the goals of modernization and the unity of the state could it afford and risk a democratic political system. Ataturk, who led his revolution in the aftermath of defeat in World War I, predated the post-World War II universalization of the goal of economic growth through economic planning. Even so, he did not consider individual human rights or a multiparty system as ingredients in the modernization efforts.

The role of the state in the contemporary non-Western world can not be overemphasised. Regardless of articulated ideology the underlying conceptual framework views the state—sometimes but not always equated with the party—as the communal group through which the goals of economic development and modernization (which will provide for human dignity) will be attained. The state or party is the dispenser of all political and economic goods and economic goods have the highest priority. In fact, in the Nkrumah school of thought, democracy itself was seen as having an economic meaning: it enabled masses of poverty-stricken people to secure minimal economic liberties. The dominant role of the state and restrictions on political liberties were not consequences only of the incorporation of traditional values into a new framework and of the ideological rhetoric of socialism, but also of the empirical realities facing many new countries. The new African states were inadequate in infrastructure, had little capital for development, had extraordinarily high rates of unemployment and underemployment, were basically one-crop economies at the mercy of Western capital, and had a history of oppression through the slave trade. Colonialism left them bereft of viable political and economic structures, concurrently disrupting and distorting traditional institutions. Toure and Nkrumah saw little choice but to make the state or party the instrument of change, and economic development the primary goal. Freedom from want, from hunger, and from economic deprivation necessitated limiting political liberties that could destroy the party or state in its initial stages. Developmental success was seen as dependent on preventing opposition by those who propagated alternative political and economic models. In this context human rights were of limited importance or were directly related to the attainment of self-sufficiency, which in turn was a function of the state. In some cases this led to state capitalism, in some to state socialism. The impact of the Nkrumah ideology was widespread; even pro-Western states such as Senegal adopted a similar political framework premised on a similar conceptualization. By the 1970s African leaders generally perceived this ideology of economic statism not as pro-Western or pro-Eastern but as a specifically African solution to their monumental problems.[21]

In state constitutions and in the OAU charter, African states have given lip service to the Universal Declaration of Human Rights, and they have affixed their signatures to United Nations documents that reinforce the Declaration. It is evident from the above analysis, however, that human rights are not perceived along Western lines by African leaders. The world is seen in economic terms that are more akin to those of Karl Marx than to the classical economists and liberal political thinkers. Human rights as formulated in the West, at least in their political and legal aspects, can come into existence only after a stable economic life with a minimum of economic prosperity is assured to the African population. Furthermore, it is critical to realize that the Western-based notions of human rights, to the extent that they are articulated by Third World political elites, reflect these elites' "westernization." It cannot be assumed that the mass of people hold these concepts.

The Western conception of human rights is not only inapplicable to third World countries or to socialist states, but also to some states that profess to adhere to democratic precepts and to states that are considered part of the West. The cultural heritages of Spain, Portugal, and Greece do not include a Western conception of inalienable human rights, any more than do the African. All three countries have recently emerged from periods of dictatorial rule. Democracy is understood as a particular set of political institutions, including a multiparty system, but the philosophic underpinnings differ from those of the West. Rights are political and legal, and not attributes of individuals qua individuals. The state retains a preeminent position and has an existence other than and prior to the individuals that compose it.[22]

In fact the absence of a concept of inalienable human rights indirectly facilitated the military takeover of Greece in 1967 and the subsequent dictatorial rule. The justification that the military officers used—the threat of chaos stemming from demonstrations, strikes, and protest marches—seemed valid ground to many Greeks for the abrogation of political freedoms. Democracy is seen by the Greeks and other peoples as a set of formal institutions and individual rights that emanate from and are granted by the state, rather than being inalienable and natural. No rights exist except those specified by law, and if there is no law protecting a particular right, that right does not exist—and hence there is no question of its violation or infringement. Illustrative were the trials of torturers held after the collapse of the Greek military dictatorship in 1974. The torturers were not charged with gross violations of human rights, but with "misuse of authority"; there was and is no law specifically making torture illegal.[23] Furthermore, the absence of a notion of the autonomous individual and of individual rights, and the communal basis of traditional Greek society has led in Greece to an exalted view of the state—which is perceived as the embodiment of the Greek people.

In summary then, it is evident that in most states in the world, human rights as defined by the West are rejected or, more accurately, are meaningless. Most states do not have a cultural heritage of individualism, and the doctrines of inalienable human rights have been neither disseminated nor assimilated. More significantly the state—as a substitute for the traditional communal group—has become the embodiment of the people, and the individual has no rights or freedoms that are natural and outside the purview of the state. It is a Platonic world in that Plato "justified the ultimate right of the state to suppress dissidents since the individual owes his existence to and was a product of, the state."[24] As Indira Gandhi said, "it is not individuals who have rights but states."[25] Further limiting the significance of Third World countries of Western conceptions of human rights are the societal goals and priorities set by their leaderships. Economic development is the primary objective, for it is only through this that economic rights can be attained, and these provide for human dignity by freeing individuals from exploitation and dependence. Perhaps the best that can be expected in the political realm is what may be happening in India—the establishment of political institutions that define the rights of individuals not under the rubric of natural law but under the structure of political law.

Toward a Reevaluation of Human Rights

The cultural patterns, ideological underpinnings, and developmental goals of non Western and socialist states are markedly at variance with the prescriptions of the Universal Declaration of Human Rights. Efforts to impose the Declaration as it currently stands not only reflect a moral chauvinism and ethnocentric bias but are also bound to fail. In fact, the evidence of the last few decades shows increasing violations of the Declaration rather than increasing compliance.

The conceptualization of human rights is in need of rethinking. It should be recognized that the Western notion of human rights evolved historically, under a particular set of circumstances, in the most highly industrialized and developed areas of the world—areas that subsequently have dominated the remainder of the world. While espousing and to a great extent implementing human rights doctrines domestically, the Western industrial states nonetheless denied them to peoples they controlled for generations. In large measure both the nationalist movement—efforts to create new nations—and socialist revolutionary movements are reactions and responses to this domination and control. Hence, rather than focusing on additional legal mechanisms for imposing the West's philosophic doctrines of the individual and inalienable human rights on the non-Western world, discussion of the issue of human rights should begin with the differing historical and contemporary circumstances of non-Western societies. Given differences in historical experience and contemporary conditions, what was a "natural" evolution in the West may not appear so "natural" in the Third World.

Realization that differing historical experiences and cultural patterns have led to differing notions of human nature and to marked differences in the articulated goals of political elites should facilitate investigation and analysis of those fundamental aspects of society from which may be derived a new conceptualization of universal human rights. All societies cross-culturally and historically manifest conceptions of human dignity and human rights. If the notion of human rights is to be a viable universal concept it will be necessary to analyze the differing cultural and ideological conceptions of human rights and the impact of one on the other. There are many societies in which human dignity is culturally defined in terms of excelling in the fulfilment of one's obligation to the group, a concept that has been incorporated in a radically altered form in socialist ideology. In many states human rights are ideologically defined in terms of one's being a functionally useful member of society—through guaranteed employment and provision of the basic needs of life: food, shelter, and clothing. From this perspective, clearly, Western countries can be accused of gross violations of human rights.

In the international arena and among many human rights advocates the argument is couched in terms of political versus economic rights; which of the two has, or should have, priority. Such a simplistic categorization is reductionist and overlooks the philosophic and cultural premises underlying such a division. The Western notion of inalienable rights, whose substance is predominantly political and civil, nevertheless includes the right to private property, a right that is central to an understanding of the development of Western pluralist and capitalist societies. Similarly, despite their apparent emphasis on economic rights, socialist societies incorporate notions of political participation. Thus although the ontology and ideology of societies differ, they incorporate the totality of what is and what should be.

Despite divergences in conceptions of what constitutes the substance of human dignity there seem to be certain shared commonalities that warrant further investigation. All societies impose restraints on the use of force and violence by their members and all apply sanctions on those who, within their particular cultural or ideological context, violate their norms and values. Hence it is important to analyze both issues further. What are the societal and political limits on the use of force or violence, and to what extent and in terms of what criteria is individual or group behavior restrained? No cultural or ideological system, for example, condones arbitrary and indiscriminate destruction of life or incarceration. Thus the killings in Uganda and Ethiopia, genocide in Paraguay, and torture in Iran and Chile are not justifiable in terms of any philosophical system. Such actions, in addition to raising the basic moral question of the right to life, are arbitrary and without any specification as to the violations that lead to such extreme sanctions. If a differentiation were made in terms of the ideological or cultural context in which violations of human rights took place, then it would be easier, for example, to obtain broad African support for sanctions against Idi Amin. He would be hard pressed to justify his mass killings and torture in terms of any ideology.

Clearly there are marked differences in the specification of the areas where conformity is demanded by a polity. In the West violations of property rights are considered crimes justifying sanctions and punishment for the transgressor; in socialist societies dissent from the official ideology is considered a crime and elicits sanctions; and in many traditional societies ostracism is the consequence when norms are violated.

If a meaningful conception of human rights is to be formulated, the interrelationship between human rights and socioeconomic developments must be scrutinized. Historically Western Europe underwent an era of absolute monarchy and state building before any notion of individual human rights was extant. Given the fact that many non-Western countries are currently undergoing the process of state building—in fact attempting to form a state and a nation simultaneously—and therefore lack consensus regarding the state and the rules of the game, is a Western conception of human rights feasible? To what extent have social, political, and economic ferment eroded traditional conceptions of rights and human dignity without the formulation and implementation of alternative or reinterpreted concepts of human rights? Historical analysis of the dissemination of human rights doctrines in the West, and the question of requisites for their existence, may shed some light on the conditions prevailing in non-Western societies today.

In the contemporary world, where the legitimate order is one of sovereign nation-states, all societies regardless of ideological commitments violate their particular conceptions of human rights and human dignity under certain conditions. A more extensive investigation of the situational and empirical factors both internal and external to the state that may constrain the implementation of human rights would seem critical. In the United States for example, the perceived threat of communism was used as the justification for the infringement and violation of the civil and political rights of many individuals, particularly during the McCarthy era. Hence an investigation of the restraints, "perceived" or "real," under which Western and non-Western countries operate in implementing human rights may lead to a clarification of what societies believe constitute "emergencies" justifying restrictions of human rights however defined.

Several developments not only in third World countries but in the West itself raise fundamental issues regarding the boundaries within which doctrines of human rights are applicable. Human rights, whatever their ideological or cultural content, are largely viewed as extant within the confines of the state. The Western emphasis on individual rights vis-à-vis the state has resulted by and large in ignoring the entire question of communal rights. Yet in the West itself—in Great Britain with the resurgence of Scottish and Welsh nationalisms, in France with the movement for autonomy in Brittany, in the United States with the American Indian Movement, and in Canada with the demand for independence by the French Canadians—charges of violations of human rights are heard with increasing frequency. This challenge in the West to individual rights operative within the state to the neglect of communal rights acquires heightened importance in the Third World. A significant philosophic and empirical question is the extent to which granting legitimacy to the state has enabled central governments to diffuse and destroy the authority of traditionalism and the rights incorporated within traditional societies without providing adequate alternatives. Concomitantly the universal legitimacy accorded to the state and the demands it places on all citizens—primarily but not limited to loyalty to the state and all the attendant requisite behavior—by definition limits and restricts individual political freedoms.

The many fundamental questions that have been raised in the previous pages should be more thoroughly analyzed if the prospects for a world community geared toward enhancing human dignity are to improve. Unfortunately not only do human rights as set forth in the Universal Declaration reveal a strong Western bias, but there has been a tendency to view human rights ahistorically and in isolation from their social, political, and economic milieu. What is being advocated here is a rethinking of the conception of human rights that both takes into account the diversity in substance that exists and recognizes the need for extensive analysis of the relationship of human rights to the broader societal context. Through this process it may become feasible to formulate human rights doctrines that are more validly universal than those currently propagated.

NOTES

1. It is interesting that the modern political philosophers with the exception of John Stuart Mill in *The Subjection of Women* (1869) did not concern themselves with women. Inalienable human rights were viewed as qualities of men, not of women.
2. Alessandra Luini del Russo, *International Protection of Human Rights* (Washington, D.C.: Lerner Law Book Co., 1971), p. 11.
3. Myres McDougal, H.D. Lasswell, and Lung-Chu Chen, "Human Rights and World Public Order: A framework for Policy Oriented Inquiry," *American Journal of International Law* (1969): 237.
4. Egon Schwelb, *Human Rights and the International Community* (Chicago: Quadrangle Books, 1964), p. 12.
5. See McDougal et al., "Human Rights," pp. 237-69.
6. Articles 17, 23, and 24. Article 17 deals with private property rights; Article 23 with the right to work, equal pay for equal work, and just remuneration; and Article 24 with the right to leisure.
7. Moses Moskowitz, *The Politics and Dynamics of Human Rights* (Dobbs Ferry: Oceana Publications, 1968), p. 75.
8. Schwelb, *Human Rights*, p. 32.
9. Leland M. Goodrich, *The United Nations* (New York: Thomas Y. Crowell, 1959), p. 249.
10. United Nations General Assembly, Official Records: Third Session, First Part, Plenary, 180th Meeting (New York), p. 860.
11. J. L. Brierly, *The Law of Nations* (New York: Oxford University Press, 1963), p. 59.
12. See *Convention on the Council of Europe and Supporting Protocols. Collected Texts, European Convention on Human Rights* (Strasbourg, 1977).
13. *New York Times*, December 13, 1969.
14. For the full charter see Colin Legum, *Pan-Africanism* (New York: Praeger, 1965).
15. For an interesting and significant study on the utilization of traditional notions of small group relatedness and its reinterpretation and restructuring within a socialist ideology see Martin King Whyte, *Small Groups and Political Ritual in China* (Los Angeles: University of California Press, 1974).
16. Kwame Nkrumah, *I Speak of Freedom* (New York: Praeger, 1961). See Chapter 6, "The Party and its Progress."
17. Julius K. Nyerere, *Freedom and Socialism* (London: Oxford University Press, 1968), see Chapter 26, "The Arusha Declaration and Ujamaa"; Nyerere, *Essays on Socialism* (London: Oxford University Press, 1968), pp. 1-12. Kwame Nkrumah, *Consciencism* (New York: Monthly Review Press, 1964), see Chapter 3.
18. Peter Schwab, "Human Rights in Ethiopia," *Journal of Modern African Studies* 14 (1976): 159.
19. An analysis of the failure of African and Asian countries to achieve their economic development goals and the growing disparity between the haves and the have-nots (both within countries such as Ghana and between the industrialized countries and the Third World) is beyond the scope of this essay.
20. Lord Kinross, *Ataturk: A Biography of Mustafa Kemal, Father of Modern Turkey* (New York: Morrow, 1965), p. 518. Ataturk's famous six principles were republicanism, nationalism, populism, elitism, secularism, and revolution.
21. Nyerere, "Socialism and Rural Development," in *Essays on Socialism*.
22. Adamantia Pollis, "The Impact of Traditional Cultur-

al Patterns on Greek Politics," *The Greek Review of Social Research* 29 (1977).

23. For a criticism of Greece's failure, with the reestablishment of a parliamentary regime, to enact a law for torture see *Torture in Greece: The First Torturers' Trial 1975* (Amnesty International Publications, 1977).

24. Adamantia Pollis, "Traditional Cultural Patterns," p. 2.

25. *New York Times*, July 3, 1975.

A BUDDHIST RESPONSE TO THE NATURE OF HUMAN RIGHTS

Kenneth K. Inada

Kenneth K. Inada teaches philosophy at the State University of New York at Buffalo. He is the author of Guide to Buddhist Philosophy *(G.K. Hall, 1985), co-editor of* Buddhism and American Thinkers *(SUNY, 1984), and editor of the* Journal of Buddhist Philosophy.

Inada describes fundamental elements of Buddhism in order to identify areas of contrast and commonality between Buddhist values and Western human rights discourse. He argues that the Western notion of rights is premised on what he calls hard relationships, which are based on notions of the separateness and independence of individuals. He contrasts this with the Buddhist emphasis on soft relationships and argues that because soft relationships are more flexible, compassionate, and holistically oriented than hard relationships, Buddhist values can form the base for a conception of human rights that places less emphasis on legal remedies for settling conflicts amongst individuals than does the Western conception.

It is incorrect to assume that the concept of human rights is readily identifiable in all societies of the world. The concept may perhaps be clear and distinct in legal quarters, but in actual practice it suffers greatly from lack of clarity and gray areas due to impositions by different cultures. This is especially true in Asia, where the two great civilizations of India and China have spawned such outstanding systems as Hinduism, Buddhism, Jainism, Yoga, Confucianism, Taoism and Chinese Buddhism. These systems, together with other indigenous folk beliefs, attest to the cultural diversity at play that characterizes Asia proper. In focusing on the concept of human rights, however, we shall concentrate on Buddhism to bring out the common grounds of discourse.

Alone among the great systems of Asia, Buddhism has successfully crossed geographical and ideological borders and spread in time throughout the whole length and breadth of known Asia. Its doctrines are so universal and profound that they captured the imagination of all the peoples they touched and thereby established a subtle bond with all. What then is this bond? It must be something common to all systems of thought which opens up and allows spiritual discourse among them.

In examining the metaphysical ground of all systems, one finds that there is a basic feeling for a larger reality in one's own experience, a kind of reaching out for a greater cosmic dimension of being, as it were. It is a deep sense for the total nature of things. All this may seem so simple and hardly merits elaborating, but it is a genuine feeling common among Asians in their quest for ultimate knowledge based on the proper relationship of one's self in the world. It is an affirmation of a reality that includes but at once goes beyond the confines of sense faculties.

A good illustration of this metaphysical grounding is seen in the Brahmanic world of Hinduism. In it, the occluded nature of the self (*atman*) constantly works to cleanse itself of defilements by yogic discipline in the hope of ultimately identifying with the larger reality which is Brahman. In the process, the grounding in the larger reality is always kept intact, regardless of whether the self is impure or not. In other words, in the quest for the purity of things a

---

Reprinted with permission of Kenneth K. Inada from *Asian Perspectives on Human Rights*, ed. Claude E. Walsh and Virgina Leary (Boulder: Westview, 1990): 91–103.

larger framework of experience is involved from the beginning such that the ordinary self (*atman*) transforms into the larger Self (*Atman*) and finally merges into the ultimate ontological Brahman.

A similar metaphysical grounding is found in Chinese thought. Confucianism, for example, with its great doctrine of humanity (*jen*), involves the ever-widening and ever-deepening human relationship that issues forth in the famous statement, "All men are brothers." In this sense, humanity is not a mere abstract concept but one that extends concretely throughout the whole of sentient existence. Confucius once said that when he searched for *jen*, it is always close at hand.[1] It means that humanity is not something external to a person but that it is constitutive of the person's experience, regardless of whether there is consciousness of it or not. It means moreover that in the relational nature of society, individual existence is always more than that which one assumes it to be. In this vein, all experiences must fit into the larger cosmological scheme normally spoken of in terms of heaven, earth and mankind. This triadic relationship is ever-present and ever-in-force, despite one's ignorance, negligence or outright intention to deny it. The concept that permeates and enlivens the triadic relationship is the *Tao*. The *Tao* is a seemingly catchall term, perhaps best translated as the natural way of life and the world. In its naturalness, it manifests all of existence; indeed, it is here, there and everywhere since it remains aloof from human contrivance and manipulation. In a paradoxical sense, it depicts action based on non-action (*wu-wei*), the deepest state of being achievable. The following story illustrates this point.

A cook named Ting is alleged to have used the same carving knife for some 19 years without sharpening it at all. When asked how that is possible, he simply replied:

> What I care about is the way (*Tao*), which goes beyond skill. When I first began cutting up oxen, all I could see was the ox itself. After three years I no longer saw the whole ox. And now — now I go at it by spirit and don't look with my eyes. Perception and understanding have come to a stop and spirit moves where it wants. I go along with the natural makeup, strike in the big hollows, guide the knife through the big openings, and follow things as they are. So I never touch the smallest ligament or tendon, much less a main joint. ... I've had this knife of mine for nineteen years and I've cut up thousands of oxen with it, and yet the blade is as good as though it had just come from the grindstone.[2]

Such then is the master craftsman at work, a master in harmonious triadic relationship based on the capture of the spirit of *Tao* where the function is not limited to a person and his or her use of a tool. And it is clear that such a spirit of *Tao* in craftsmanship is germane to all disciplined experiences we are capable of achieving in our daily activities.

Buddhism, too, has always directed our attention to the larger reality of existence. The original enlightenment of the historical Buddha told of a pure unencumbered experience which opened up all experiential doors in such a way that they touched everything sentient as well as insentient. A Zen story graphically illustrates this point.

Once a master and a disciple were walking through a dense forest. Suddenly, they heard the clean chopping strokes of the woodcutter's axe. The disciple was elated and remarked, "What beautiful sounds in the quiet of the forest!" To which the master immediately responded, "You have got it all upside down. The sounds only makes obvious the deep silence of the forest!" The response by the Zen master sets in bold relief the Buddhist perception of reality. Although existential reality refers to the perception of the world as a singular unified whole, we ordinarily perceive it in fragmented ways because of our heavy reliance on the perceptual apparatus and its consequent understanding. That is to say, we perceive by a divisive and selective method which however glosses over much of reality and indeed misses its holistic nature. Certainly, the hewing sounds of the woodcutter's axe are clearly audible and delightful to the ears, but they are so at the expense of the basic silence of the forest (i.e., total reality). Or, the forest in its silence constitutes the necessary background, indeed the basic source, from which all sounds (and all activities for that matter) originate. Put another way, sounds arising from the silence of the forest should in no way deprive nor intrude upon the very source of their own being. Only human beings make such intrusions by their crude discriminate habits of perception and, consequently, suffer a truncated form of existence, unknowingly for the most part.

Now that we have seen Asian lives in general grounded in a holistic cosmological framework, we would have to raise the following question: How does this framework appear in the presence of human rights? Or, contrarily, how do human rights function within this framework?

Admittedly, the concept of human rights is relatively new to Asians. From the very beginning, it did not sit well with their basic cosmological outlook. Indeed, the existence of such an outlook has prevented in profound ways a ready acceptance of foreign elements and has created tension and struggle between tradition and modernity. Yet, the key concept in the tension is that of human relationship. This is especially true in Buddhism, where the emphasis is not so much on the performative acts and individual rights as it is on the matter of manifestation of human nature itself. The Buddhist always takes human nature as the basic context in which all ancillary concepts, such as human rights, are understood and take on any value. Moreover, the context itself is in harmony with the extended experiential nature of things. And thus, where the Westerner is much more at home in treating legal matters detached from human nature as such and quite confident in forging ahead to establish human rights with a distinct emphasis on certain "rights," the Buddhist is much more reserved but open and seeks to understand the implications of human behaviour, based on the fundamental nature of human beings, before turning his or her attention to the so-called "rights" of individuals.

An apparent sharp rift seems to exist between the Western and Buddhist views, but this is not really so. Actually, it is a matter of perspectives and calls for a more comprehensive understanding of what takes place in ordinary human relationships. For the basic premise is still one that is focused on human beings intimately living together in the selfsame world. A difference in perspectives does not mean non-communication or a simple rejection of another's view, as there is still much more substance in the nature of conciliation, accommodation and absorption than what is initially thought of. Here we propose two contrasting but interlocking and complementary terms, namely, "hard relationship" and "soft relationship."

The Western view on human rights is generally based on a hard relationship. Persons are treated as separate and independent entities or even bodies, each having its own assumed identity or self-identity. It is a sheer "elemental" way of perceiving things due mainly to the strong influence by science and its methodology. As scientific methodology thrives on the dissective and analytic incursion into reality as such, this in turn has resulted in our perceiving and understanding things in terms of disparate realities. Although it makes way for easy understanding, the question still remains: Do we really understand what these realities are in their own respective fullness of existence? Apparently not. And to make matters worse, the methodology unfortunately has been uncritically extended over to the human realm, into human nature and human relations. Witness its ready acceptance by the various descriptive and behavioural sciences, such as sociology, psychology and anthropology, On this matter, Cartesian dualism of mind and body has undoubtedly influenced our ordinary ways of thinking in such a manner that in our casual perception of things we habitually subscribe to the clearcut subject-object dichotomy. This dualistic perspective has naturally filtered down into human relationships and has eventually crystallized into what we refer to as the nature of a hard relationship. Thus, a hard relationship is a mechanistic treatment of human beings where the emphasis in on beings as such regardless of their inner nature and function in the fullest sense; it is an atomistic analysis of beings where the premium is placed on what is relatable and manipulable without regard for their true potentials for becoming. In a way it is externalization in the extreme, since the emphasis is heavily weighted on seizing the external character of beings themselves. Very little attention, if any, is given to the total ambience, inclusive of inner contents and values, in which the beings are at full play. In this regard, it can be said that postmodern thought is now attempting to correct this seemingly lopsided dichotomous view created by our inattention to the total experiential nature of things. We believe this is a great step in the right direction. Meanwhile, we trudge along with a heavy burden on our backs, though unaware of it for the most part, by associating with people on the basis of hard relationships.

To amplify on the nature of hard relationships, let us turn to a few modern examples. First, Thomas Hobbes, in his great work, *Leviathan*,[3] showed remarkable grasp of human psychology when he asserted that people are constantly at war with each other. Left in this "state of nature," people will never be able to live in peace and security. The only way out of this conundrum is for all to establish a reciprocal relationship or mutual trust that would work, i.e., to strike up a covenant by selfish beings that guarantees mutual benefits and gains, one in which each relinquishes certain rights in order to gain or realize a personal as well as an overall state of peace and security. This was undoubtedly a brilliant scheme. But the scheme is weak in that it treats human beings by and large mechanically, albeit psychologically too, as entities in a give-and-take affair, and thus perpetuates the condition of hard relationships.

Another example can be offered by way of the British utilitarian movement which later was consummated in American pragmatism. Jeremy Bentham's hedonic calculus[4] (e.g., intensity of pleasure or pain,... etc.) is a classic example of quantification of human experience. Although this is a most expedient or utilitarian way to treat and legislate behaviour, we must remind ourselves that we are by no means mere quantifiable entities. John Stuart Mill introduced the element of quality in order to curb and tone down the excesses of the quantification process,[5] but, in the final analysis, human nature and relationships are still set in hard relations. American pragmatism fares no better since actions by and large take place in a pluralistic world of realities and are framed within the scientific mode and therefore it is unable to relinquish the nature of hard relationships.

In contemporary times, the great work of John Rawls, *A Theory of Justice*,[6] has given us yet another twist in pragmatic and social contract theories. His basic concept of justice as fairness is an example of the reciprocal principle in action, i.e., in terms of realizing mutual advantage and benefit for the strongest to the weakest or the most favored to the least favored in a society. Each person exercises basic liberty with offices for its implementation always open and excess available. It is moreover a highly intellectual or rational theory. It thus works extremely well on the theoretical level but, in actual situations, it is not as practical and applicable as it seems since it still retains hard relationships on mutual bases. Such being the case, feelings and consciousness relative to injustice and inequality are not so readily spotted and corrected. That is to say, lacunae exist as a result of hard relationships and they keep on appearing until they are detected and finally remedied, but then the corrective process is painfully slow. Thus the theory's strongest point is its perpetually self-corrective nature which is so vital to the democratic process. Despite its shortcomings, however, Rawls' theory of justice is a singular contribution to contemporary legal and ethical thought.

By contrast, the Buddhist view of human rights is based on the assumption that human beings are primarily oriented in soft relationships; this relationship governs the understanding of the nature of human rights. Problems arise, on the other hand, when a hard relationship becomes the basis for treating human nature because it cannot delve deeply into that nature itself and functions purely on the peripheral aspects of things. It is another way of saying that a hard relationship causes rigid and stifling empirical conditions to arise and to which we become invariably attached.

A soft relationship has many facets. It is the Buddhist way to disclose a new dimension to human nature and behaviour. It actually amounts to a novel perception or vision of reality. Though contrasted with a hard relationship, it is not in contention with it. If anything, it has an inclusive nature that "softens," if you will, all contacts and allows for the blending of any element that comes along, even incorporating the entities of hard relationships. This is not to say, however, that soft and hard relationships are equal or ultimately identical. For although the former could easily accommodate and absorb the latter, the reverse is not the case. Still, it must be noted that both belong to the same realm of experiential reality and in consequence ought to be conversive with each other. The non-conversive aspect arises on the part of the "hard" side and is attributable to the locked-in character of empirical elements which are considered to be hard stubborn facts worth perpetuating. But at some point, there must be a break in the lock, as it were, and this is made possible by knowledge of and intimacy with the "soft" side of human endeavors. For the "soft" side has a passive nature characterized by openness, extensiveness, depth, flexibility, absorptiveness, freshness and creativity simply because it remains unencumbered by "hardened" empirical conditions.

What has been discussed so far can be seen in modern Thailand where tradition and change are in dynamic tension. Due to the onslaught of elements of modernity, Buddhism is being questioned and challenged. Buddhist Thailand, however, has taken up the challenge in the person of a leading monk named Buddhadasa who has led the country to keep a steady course on traditional values.[7]

The heart of Buddhadasa's teaching is that the Dhamma (Sanskrit, Dharma) or the truth of Buddhism is a universal truth. Dhamma is equated by Buddhadasa to the true nature of things. It is everything and everywhere. The most appropriate term to denote the nature of Dhamma is *sunnata* (Sanskrit, *sunyata*) or the void. The ordinary man considers the void to mean nothing when, in reality, it means everything—everything, that is, without reference to the self.

We will return to the discussion of the nature of the void or *sunnata* later, but suffice it to say here that what constitutes the heart of Buddhist truth of existence is based on soft relationships where all forms and symbols are accommodated and allows for their universal usage.

Robert N. Bellah has defined religion as a set of normative symbols institutionalized in a society or internalized in a personality.[8] It is a rather good definition but does not go far enough when it comes to describing Buddhism, or Asian religions in general for that matter. To speak of symbols being institutionalized or internalized without the proper existential or ontological context seems to be a bit artificial and has strains of meanings oriented toward hard relationships. Bellah, being a social scientist, probably could not go beyond the strains of a hard relationship, for, otherwise, he would have ended in a nondescriptive realm. The only way out is to give more substance to the nature of religious doctrines themselves, as is the case in Buddhism. The Buddhist Dharma is one such doctrine which, if symbolized, must take on a wider and deeper meaning that strikes at the very heart of existence of the individual. In this respect, Donald Swearer is on the right track when he says:

> the adaptation of symbols of Theravada Buddhism presupposes an underlying ontological structure. The symbol system of Buddhism, then, is not to be seen only in relationship to its wider empirical context, but also in relationship to its ontological structure. This structure is denoted by such terms as Dhamma or absolute Truth, emptiness and non-attachment. These terms are denotative of what Dhiravamsa calls "dynamic being." They are symbolic, but in a universalistic rather than a particularistic sense.[9]

Swearer's reference to an underlying ontological structure is in complete harmony with our use of the term soft relationship. And only when this ontological structure of soft relationship is brought into the dynamic tension between tradition and modernity can we give full accounting to the nature of human experience and the attendant creativity and change within a society.

Let us return to a fuller treatment of soft relationships. In human experience, they manifest themselves in terms of the intangible human traits that we live by, such as patience, humility, tolerance, deference, non-action, humaneness, concern, pity, sympathy, altruism, sincerity, honesty, faith, responsibility, trust, respectfulness, reverence, love and compassion. Though potentially and pervasively present in any human relationship, they remain for the most part as silent but vibrant components in all experiences. Without them, human intercourse would be sapped of the human element and reduced to perfunctory activities. Indeed, this fact seems to constitute much of the order of the day where our passions are mainly directed to physical and materialistic matters.

The actualization and sustenance of these intangible human traits are basic to the Buddhist quest for an understanding of human nature and, by extension, the so-called rights of human beings. In order to derive a closer look at the nature of soft relationships, we shall focus on three characteristics, namely, mutuality, holism, and emptiness or void.

Mutuality

Our understanding of mutuality is generally limited to its abstract or theoretical nature. For example, it is defined in terms of a two-way action between two parties and where the action is invariably described with reference to elements of hard relationships. Except secondarily or deviously, nothing positive is mentioned about the substance of mutuality, such as the feelings of humility, trust and tolerance that transpire between the parties concerned. Although these feelings are present, unfortunately, they hardly ever surface in the relationship and almost always are overwhelmed by the physical aspect of things.

What is to be done? One must simply break away from the merely conceptual or theoretical understanding and fully engage oneself in the discipline that will bring the feelings of both parties to become vital components in the relationship. That is, both parties must equally sense the presence and value of these feelings and thus give substance and teeth to their actions.

Pursuing the notion of mutuality further, the Buddhist understands human experience as a totally open phenomenon, that persons should always be wide open in the living process. The phrase, "an open ontology," is used to describe the unclouded state of existence. An illustration of this is the newborn child. The child is completely an open organism at birth. The senses are wide open and will absorb practically anything without prejudice. At this stage, also, the child will begin to imitate because its absorptive power is at the highest level. This open textured nature should continue on and on. In other words, if we are free and open, there should be no persistence in attaching ourselves to hard elements within the underlying context of a dynamic world of experience. The unfortunate thing, however, is that the open texture of our existence begins to blemish and fade away in time, being obstructed and overwhelmed by self-imposed fragmentation, narrowness and restriction, which gradually develop into a closed nature of existence. In this way, the hard relationship rules. But the nature of an open ontology leads us on to the next characteristic.

Holism

Holism of course refers to the whole, the total nature of individual existence and thus describes the unrestrictive nature of one's experience. Yet, the dualistic relationship we maintain by our crude habits of perception remains a stumbling block. This stunted form of perception is not conducive to holistic understanding and instead fosters nothing but fractured types of ontological knowledge taking. Unconscious for the most part, an individual narrows his or her vision by indulging in dualism of all kinds, both mental and physical, and in so doing isolates the objects of perception from the total process to which they belong. In consequence, the singular unified reality of each perceptual moment is fragmented and, what is more, fragmentation once settled breeds further fragmentation.

The Buddhist will appeal to the fact that one's experience must always be open to the total ambience of any momentary situation. But here we must be exposed to a unique, if not paradoxical, insight of the Buddhist. It is that the nature of totality is not a clearly defined phenomenon. In a cryptic sense, however, it means that the totality of experience has no borders to speak of. It is an open border totality, which is the very nature of the earlier mentioned "open ontology." It is a non-circumscribable totality, like a circle sensed which does not have a rounded line, a seamless circle, if you will. A strange phenomenon, indeed, but that is how the Buddhist sees the nature of individual existence as such. For the mystery of existence that haunts us is really the nature of one's own fullest momentary existence. Nothing else compares in profundity to this nature, so the Buddhist believes.

Now, the open framework in which experience takes place reveals that there is depth and substance in experience. But so long as one is caught up with the peripheral elements, so-called, of hard relationships one will be ensnared by them and will generate limitations on one's understanding accordingly. On the other hand, if openness is acknowledged as a fact of existence, then the way out of one's own limitations will present itself. All sufferings (*duhkha*), from the Buddhist standpoint, are cases of limited ontological vision (*avidya*, ignorance) hindered by the attachment to all sorts of elements that obsess a person.

Holism is conversant with openness since an open experience means that all elements are fully and extensively involved. In many respects, holistic existence exhibits the fact that mutuality thrives only in unhindered openness. But there is still another vital characteristic to round out or complete momentary experience. For this we turn to the last characteristic.

Emptiness

Emptiness in Sanskrit is *sunyata*.[10] Strictly speaking, the Sanskrit term, depicting zero or nothing, had been around prior to Buddhism, but it took the historical Buddha's supreme enlightenment (nirvana) to reveal an incomparable qualitative nature inherent to experience. Thus emptiness is not sheer voidness or nothingness in the nihilistic sense.

We ordinarily find it difficult to comprehend emptiness, much less to live a life grounded in it. Why? Again, we return to the nature of our crude habits of perception, which is laden with unwarranted forms. That is, our whole perceptual process is caught up in attachment to certain forms or elements which foster and turn into so-called empirical and cognitive biases. All of this is taking place in such minute and unknowing ways that we hardly, if ever, take notice of it until a crisis situation arises, such as the presence of certain obviously damaging prejudice or discrimination. Then and only then do we seriously wonder and search for the forms or elements that initially gave rise to those prejudicial or discriminatory forces.

Emptiness has two aspects. The first aspect alerts our perceptions to be always open and fluid, and to desist from attaching to any form or element. In this respect, emptiness technically functions as a force of "epistemic nullity,"[11] in the sense that it nullifies any reference to a form or element as preexisting perception or even post-existing for that matter. Second and more importantly, emptiness points at a positive content of our experience. It underscores the possibility of total experience in any given moment because there is now nothing attached to or persisted in. This latter point brings us right back to the other characteristics of holism and mutuality. Now, we must note that emptiness is that dimension of experience which makes it possible for the function of mutuality and holism in each experience, since there is absolutely nothing that binds, hinders or wants in our experience. Everything is as it is (*tathata*), under the aegis of emptiness; emptiness enables one to spread out one's experience at will in all directions, so to speak, in terms of "vertical" and "horizontal" dimensions of being. As it is the key principle of enlightened existence, it makes everything both possible and impossible. Possible in the sense that all experiences function within the total empty nature, just as all writings are possible on a clean slate or, back to the Zen story, where the sounds are possible in the silence (emptiness) of the forest. At the same time, impossible in the sense that all attachments to forms and elements are categorically denied in the ultimate fullness of experience. In this way, emptiness completes our experience of reality and, at the same time, provides the grounds for the function of all human traits to become manifest in soft relationships.

It can now be seen that all three characteristics involve each other in the selfsame momentary existence. Granted this, it should not be too difficult to accept the fact that the leading moral concept in Buddhism is compassion (*karuna*). Compassion literally means "passion for all" in an ontologically extensive sense. It covers the realm of all sentient beings, inclusive of non-sentients, for the doors of perception to total reality are always open. From the Buddhist viewpoint, then, all human beings are open entities with open feelings expressive of the highest form of humanity. This is well expressed in the famous concept of *bodhisattva* (enlightened being) in Mahayana Buddhism who has deepest concern for all beings and sympathetically delays his entrance to nirvana as long as there is suffering (ignorant existence) among sentient creatures. It depicts the coterminous nature of all creatures and may be taken as a philosophic myth in that it underscores the ideality of existence which promotes the greatest unified form of humankind based on compassion. This ideal form of existence, needless to say, is the aim and goal of all Buddhists.

As human beings we need to keep the channels of existential dialogue open at all times. When an act of violence is in progress, for example, we need to constantly nourish the silent and passive nature of nonviolence inherent in all human relations. Though nonviolence cannot counter violence on the latter's terms, still, its nourished presence serves as a reminder of the brighter side of existence and may even open the violator's mind to common or normal human traits such as tolerance, kindness and noninjury (*ahimsa*). Paradoxically and most unfortunately, acts of violence only emphasize the fact that peace and tranquillity are the normal course of human existence.

It can now be seen that the Buddhist view on human rights is dedicated to the understanding of persons in a parameter-free ambience, so to speak, where feelings that are extremely soft and tender, but nevertheless present and translated into human traits or virtues that we uphold, make up the very fiber of human relations. These relations, though their contents are largely intangible, precede any legal rights or justification accorded to human beings. In brief, human rights for the Buddhist are not only matters for legal deliberation and understanding, but they must be complemented by and based on something deeper and written in the very feelings of all sentients. The unique coexistent nature of rights and feelings constitutes the saving truth of humanistic existence.

NOTES

1. *Lu Yu* (The Analects of Confucius) VII, 29.
2. The *Complete Works of Chuang Tzu*, translated by Burton Watson (New York: Columbia University Press, 1960), pp. 50-1.
3. Thomas Hobbes, *Leviathan* (New York: Hafner, 1926).
4. Jeremy Bentham, *An Introduction to the Principles of Morals and Legislation* (New York: Hafner, 1948).
5. John Stuart Mill observed, "It is better to be a human being dissatisfied than a pig satisfied; better to be a Socrates dissatisfied than a fool satisfied." *Utilitarianism*, cited in Louis P. Pojman, *Philosophy: The Quest for Truth* (Belmont CA: Wadsworth, 1989), p. 357.
6. John Rawls, *A Theory of Justice* (Cambridge: Harvard University Press, 1971). Rawls also has a chapter on civil disobedience but it too is treated under the same concept of justice as fairness and suffers accordingly from the elements of hard relationships.
7. Donald K. Swearer, "Thai Buddhism: Two Responses to Modernity," in Bardwell L. Smith, ed., *Contributions to Asian Studies*, Volume 4: Tradition and Change in Theravada Buddhism (Leiden: E.J. Brill, 1973), p. 80. "Without reference to the self" means to uphold the Buddhist doctrine of non-self (Sanskrit, *anatman*) which underlies all momentary existence and avoids any dependence on a dichotomous self-oriented subject—object relationship. For an updated and comprehensive view on Buddhadasa's reformist's philosophy, see Donald K. Swearer, ed., *Me and Mine: Selected Essays on Bhikkhu Buddhadasa* (Albany: State University of New York Press, 1989).
8. Robert N. Bellah, "Epilogue" in Bellah, ed., *Religion and Progress in Modern Asia* (New York: Free Press, 1965), p. 173.
9. Swearer, "Thai Buddhism," p. 92.
10. Etymologically *sunyata* (in Pali, *sunnata*) means the state of being swollen, as in pregnancy, or the state of fullness of being. Thus, from the outset the term depicted the pure, open and full textured nature of experiential reality.
11. Kenneth Inada, "Nagarjuna and Beyond," *Journal of Buddhist Philosophy* 2 (1984), pp. 65-76, for development of this concept.

GLOBALIZATION AND HUMAN RIGHTS

Jay Drydyk

Jay Drydyk teaches philosophy and is currently Chair of the Philosophy Department at Carleton University in Ottawa. He is co-editor of Global Justice, Global Democracy *(Fernwood, 1997) and the author of articles in ethics, human rights, and international development.*

Drydyk critically evaluates a wide range of views on the question of whether human rights are ethnocentric and biased in favour of Western values. He argues that we can formulate human rights that avoid the Eurocentrism evident in the dominant discourse on human rights and that are sensitive to cultural contexts. He discusses two areas affected by globalization as a way of defending the need for human rights and for a reconception of them. First, the damaging effects of globalization with respect to the subcontracting and the informalization of labour calls for international labour rights, rights that can be developed from social and economic rights that are already recognized. Second, an ever growing context of a "global public sphere of moral deliberation" makes cross-cultural communication and agreement about the language of rights possible.

In the face of economic globalization, what are we to think of human rights? Globalization is a complex trend, including globalization of production processes, global capital mobility, neoliberal development agendas, and finally globalization of subcontracting and informalization of labour, as a source of competitive advantage. In much of the debate about globalization, the labour dimension—subcontracting and informalization of labour—tends to be overshadowed by the first three. My view is the opposite, that the labour dimension of globalization is the most important. In an orgy of subcontracting, employers all over the world have been eliminating jobs and shifting their work through labour contractors, nominal self-employment, and other schemes into the "informal sector," so that ever more of the work is performed by jobless workers, at low cost and with no security or regulation. As a result the movement of production to the South has not always brought *jobs*, much less prosperity.[1] The subcontracting trend, by itself, is clearly damaging to labour rights—for example, safety, equal pay for equal work, protection against unemployment, and the right to organize. Subcontracting and informalization of work also conspire with globalized production and finance to vitiate the taxation bases that nation-states need to finance their protection of social rights—for example, to subsistence, housing, health, education, social services, and welfare security.

Arguably these pressures undermine not only labour rights and social welfare rights but also civil and political rights. This argument exactly is made by Pierre Sané, the secretary-general of Amnesty International:

> The globalization of the world economy continues apace. The debt burden and the world recession exact their toll. Massive international speculation and large foreign investments chase the best returns. Millions of people move across borders in search of a better life, or any life at all....

Reprinted with permission of the Society for Socialist Studies from *Global Justice*, *Global Democracy*, edited by Jay Drydyk and Peter Penz (Halifax: Fernwood, 1997):159–178.

Everywhere, people feel powerless in the face of these global trends. And in reaction, they turn to their group for identity. Religion, race, tribe, nation—the ties of blood—all take on a new importance. ...

The nation state cannot control the global trends. It cannot easily accommodate the demands of different groups living in the same country.

And so the institution itself loses legitimacy.

The question for us, therefore, is how to develop a global countermovement to protect all the rights of all the people from the global trends that threaten to destroy the very fabric of society in many countries. [I believe that] we need a new paradigm in which "substantive participation"—at local, national and international levels—is the primary goal, not an afterthought. It should integrate the values emerging from the human rights and other social movements that are developing worldwide. It should put back the human being as the subject of history.[2]

Eurocentrism

This raises a further question for philosophers. How well can such a movement be served by current conceptions of human rights? After all, aren't the received notions of human rights Eurocentric? If so, how *could* they serve the self-understanding of a movement that is to be global, culturally pluralistic, and counter-hegemonic to Northern capital? My answer is: it is not human rights that are Eurocentric, but only certain conceptions of human rights. Properly understood, human rights are justifiable from within all cultures. Moreover, current conceptions of human rights are not as narrow as they were in 1948, when the Universal Declaration was drafted. Nearly five decades of international dialogue have transformed human rights discourse in ways that are profoundly anti-Eurocentric, and further transformations are already under way.

A wide range of views are held on the Eurocentricity of human rights:

- The *triumphalist* view is that human rights are superior, and only Western cultures can support them. Thus Jack Donnelly has argued that the concept of human rights is foreign to all but Western cultures.[3]
- The *rejectionist* view agrees that only Western cultures can support human rights, but it denies that human rights have any value. The Ayatollah Khomeini was a rejectionist, as he made perfectly clear when he said, "The Universal Declaration of Human Rights is a 'collection of mumbo-jumbo by disciples of Satan'" and "What they call human rights is nothing but a collection of corrupt rules worked out by Zionists to destroy all true religion."[4]

These two views agree that human rights concepts and beliefs are exclusively Western; they disagree as to whether human rights have any value. Alternatively, there are a number of views that both value human rights and argue for their justifiability within all existing cultures.

- *Assimilationists* argue that because we know, on independent grounds, that current international human rights standards are more or less correct, further grounds can and ought to be found within all cultures for accepting them. Once this is done, according to Abdullahi Ahmed An-Na'im, human rights will have "cultural legitimacy," and they will not be so easily portrayed as foreign impositions.[5]
- *Revisionists* argue that human rights have been understood and justified within non-Western cultures all along, and they have been understood there perfectly well. This view has been espoused by the authors of the Universal Islamic Declaration of Human Rights of 1981, who claim that "Islam gave to mankind an ideal code of human rights fourteen centuries ago."[6]
- *Transformationists* argue for the most complex position:

(i) In all cultural traditions, some people at some time or other have employed concepts of human rights that are "defective" in the sense that they limit human rights protection to in-groups, while out-groups are excluded.

(ii) Still, there are features of cross-cultural dialogue that forbid these sorts of defects—if the dialogue is not abused.

(iii) Now let us say that an "incomplete" list of

human rights is one that overlooks certain protections that people are due. These can also be found in all cultural traditions.

(iv) On the other hand, there are resources of moral and political experience, within all cultures, which argue strongly against this sort of incompleteness. Therefore, a consistent and complete knowledge of human rights can emerge cross-culturally, if the dialogue is not abused and if the relevant moral and political experience is let into the dialogue, from all quarters.

I will defend these four claims of the transformationist position in this and the next section. First, though, it will be constructive to consider what is mistaken about two of the other views: triumphalism and rejectionism.

The Western triumphalist position on human rights is represented prominently by Jack Donnelly. Typically Donnelly argues that the concept of human rights is foreign to non-Western political cultures. Depending on which culture is in question, he relies on one or another of the following arguments. (1) Some basic protections that are provided and justified in non-Western societies and cultures are not universal; only some people are protected, not all. (2) Some of these protections are conceived as grants that the community gives to people conditionally, because they accept responsibilities to and within the community. In other words, these protections are not thought of as being owed to persons just because they are persons. (3) In some non-Western contexts, basic protections are not justified as entitlements inherently belonging to individuals; rather, they are justified as other people's duties.

The latter line of argument I find particularly scandalous. It is quite right that in many cultures the political discourse of duty is far more convincing than rights talk, because it has a deeper cultural resonance. This difference is reflected in many of the regional human rights documents. For example, the document drafted in 1948 by the Ninth International Conference of American States was called the "American Declaration of the Rights *and* Duties of Man." Chapter 1 lists the Rights, and chapter 2 lists the duties. A similar format is followed in the Banjul Declaration of the Organization of African Unity: the twenty-six articles specifying rights in chapter 1 are followed by a list of duties in articles 27, 28, and 29, chapter 2. A comparable declaration for the member countries of ASEAN (Association of Southeast Asian Countries) has been proposed not by the governments but by the ASEAN Regional Council, a non-governmental organization composed of jurists and others interested in human rights. As the document title—"Declaration of the Basic Duties of ASEAN Peoples and Governments"—would suggest, each article specifies a duty. In those articles in which rights are declared, they are presented as grounded in a specific duty.

For the moment, let us pass over the fact that the ASEAN Declaration calls for more extensive protections than any Western government has ever accepted. Imagine that a Western government and an Asian government each provided its people with exactly the same basic protections against the standard threats to life and development that you wish to consider basic. Imagine, further, that these protections were justified, in the Western country, as rights. In the Asian country, imagine that the very same protections were conceived and justified as duties. Donnelly would be committed to the absurd position that the Asian country had no conception of human rights. Yet, *ex hypothesi*, they provided human rights protections identical to those provided in the West. What is scandalous about Donnelly's position is that it betrays a greater concern for how people think about human rights than for how well they protect them.

This is not only scandalous, but ironic. Donnelly takes pains to distinguish the concept of human rights from its various conceptions. Yet what he has done is to replace the core working concept of human rights with his own pet conceptions. If we want to know what the core concept of "human rights" is, then what we must want to know is what this phrase is used to refer to. The workaday world of human rights is focussed on saving people's lives, their wellness, and their basic opportunities. While there are some cultural barriers to recognizing the greatest dangers to life, wellness, and opportunity, there are not many, and they are not insurmountable. Cross-cultural understanding is not terribly difficult when we are dealing with what Henry Shue has called "the morality of the depths," where the dangers fall under commonly recognizable types, starting with threats to personal safety and threats to subsistence. Every type of danger is understood by certain standard threats that exemplify it. Standard threats vary from region to region, yet what may be a threat in one place (such as the risk of being struck by falling ice in Ottawa) can be understood as a threat elsewhere (for example, in Honduras) even though *there* it is no threat at all.

Following Shue, and indeed John Stuart Mill, I believe that calling for a human right to something is calling for social protection against standard threats that exemplify a particular type of danger for humans. The point of saying that the human right to free speech is honoured or implemented in, say, South Africa, is to say that social protection of free speech against standard threats of censorship and harassment is adequate there. The point of saying that there is a breakdown of the human right to shelter in, say, New York or London, is to say that social protection against homelessness is inadequate there. The point of saying that the human right to security was violated in East Timor is to say not only that social protection against violence failed, but also that the standard threat, here violence, against which people were to be protected, was wilfully inflicted upon them. However human rights language may be used, it must refer to the presence, absence, or violation of social protection against standard threats exemplifying some type of danger to humans.

These dangers will be recognized differently, with different language and under different descriptions, in different cultural contexts. Protections against them will also be justified differently. But as long as this kind of protection can be described within a culture, no matter how it is conceived or described, then we cannot say, as Donnelly does, that the concept of this human right is foreign to this culture. The concept of universal health care seems foreign to the minds of many Americans; shall we infer that the concept of a human right to health protection is "foreign" to them?

Another one of Donnelly's usual lines of argument targets cultures that justify extensive protection for their members, but only as the result of duties that are owed to group members in recognition of their membership. This was indeed the case in many traditional African cultures. As Kwasi Wiredu points out with reference to the Akan peoples of West Africa,

> On the face of it, the normative layer in the Akan concept of person brings only obligations to the individual. In fact, however, these obligations are matched by a whole series of rights that accrue to the individual simply because he lives in a society in which everyone has those obligations.[7]

The notion that people are entitled to these protections is not absent from Akan thought; it is simply justified in other terms, in which recognition that humans are frail, vulnerable, and dependent on one another is central. Wiredu argues:

> A number of Akan sayings testify to this conception, which is at the root of Akan commmunalism. One ... points out that to be human is to be in need of help. Literally it says simply "a human being needs help" (onipa hvia mmoa). The Akan verb hvia means "is in need of." In this context it also has the connotation of merits, "is entitled to," so that the maxim may also be interpreted as asserting that a human being, simply because he is a human being, is entitled to help from others.[8]

Nor are the rights to which a person is entitled limited in this culture to the matters of subsistence and material need. As Wiredu goes on to say,

> One finds a veritable harvest of human rights. Akan thought recognized the right of a newborn to be nursed and educated, the right of an adult to a plot of land from the ancestral holdings, the right of any well-defined unit of political organization to self-government, the right of all to have a say in the enstoolment or destoolment of their chiefs or their elders and to participate in the shaping of governmental policies, the right of all to freedom of thought and expression in all matters, political, religious, and metaphysical, the right of everybody to trial before punishment, the right of a person to remain at any locality or to leave, and so on.[9]

In response it could be argued that, in similar cultures, only members of this society who accept the culture, its responsibilities, and their place within it are recognized as persons. Thus Francis Deng, who finds similar support for human rights among the Dinka people, who live mainly in the Sudan, also observes that these commitments, like other "Dinka cultural values tend to weaken as the community widens, and they become minimal in relations with foreigners." This, however, is a different problem. The problem here is not that Dinka culture accords too little respect to individuals. The problem is that it respects too few individuals; what is missing is not individualism, but universality.

On the other hand, this lack of universality is hardly a minor problem if we are discussing a culture's supportiveness for human rights—which, after all, are meant to protect all humans. Indeed, the particularism of non-Western cultures is the feature which Donnelly seizes most firmly in arguing for their incapacity to support human rights.

Clearly one does not support human rights unless one supports their protection for everyone. Otherwise we should have to allow that General Mladic supports human rights—for Serbs only. Yet Donnelly wants to say something stronger: if a group fails to recognize that outsiders deserve basic protections no less than members, then that group has no concept of human rights. I find this claim too strong. Any group can recognize the similarities between dangers to them and dangers to outsiders. They are also capable of recognizing some cases in which general social protection against these dangers is deserved—namely, within their own group. If they had no concept of human rights, then they would be unable to pick out any communities in which such social protection is warranted. But they can pick out at least one such community, namely their own. What they cannot do so easily is to pick out others. Their knowledge of how to use the language of human rights is not absent; it is more accurate to call it "defective."

Take the case of John Locke. As we all know, Locke believed that anyone who would but consult their own Reason would conclude that behaviour threatening life, liberty or property was a danger against which social protection was warranted. Men were warranted in providing and enforcing this protection spontaneously, as required, or they could contract the work out. However, there was notoriously more male liberty and property to be protected within this view, and Locke was also the second-largest shareholder in the Royal Africa Company, "explicitly a slave trading enterprise."[10] In Locke's own thought, then, was the concept of human rights wholly lacking, or was it just horribly defective? If Donnelly wants to hold that Locke did, after all, have something to say about human rights, not just white men's rights, then he should choose the latter. To be consistent, however, he should in that case say that in certain traditional cultures—as well as in Christianity and Islam—the concept of human rights, though it may have been applied defectively, is not altogether absent.

Rejectionists hold that human rights beliefs are inconsistent with non-Western moral and political cultures—and so much the worse for human rights. The Ayatollah Khomeini was a rejectionist, as he indicated in his statements about the Universal Declaration of Human Rights being a "collection of mumbo-jumbo by disciples of Satan" and human rights being "nothing but a collection of corrupt rules worked out by Zionists to destroy all true religion."[11] There are also Western rejectionists, for example Adamantia Pollis and Peter Schwab, who claim, "It is evident that in most states in the world, human rights as defined by the West are rejected, or more accurately, are meaningless.[12] Yet on closer inspection their arguments, like Donnelly's, have more to do with favoured Western conceptions than with human rights themselves. They object to biassed construals of human rights that favour individualism over communalism, private property over group property, and nuclear over extended families, and they object to the crude and clumsy sorts of moral realism and universalism that abandon historical understanding of the variable social formations in which human rights can be implemented in favour of a simple and uniform conception of each right. On the other hand, as they themselves point out, some of the social protections to which human rights language refers can be justified in "all societies ... within their particular cultural or ideological context ... norms and values."[13]

Rejectionism, then, is better exemplified by Khomeini than by Pollis and Schwab. We can see what is wrong with Khomeini's view by examining some of the human rights debates that have occurred amongst Muslims themselves. Some Muslims have argued that a full set of human rights, comparable to those listed by the Universal Declaration, have always been prescribed by Islam. An example is the Universal Declaration of Human Rights of 1981—which, we should note, is a declaration not of any governments but rather of the Islamic Council, a private group based in London. The authors preface their Declaration with the claim that "Islam gave to mankind an ideal code of human rights fourteen centuries ago."[14] Critics of this Declaration argue that, at best, the conception of human rights it expresses is defective, because it is limited by provisions of Islamic law that deny equal rights not only to women but to all persons who are not "people of the book"—that is, Muslim, Christian, or Jewish. Nevertheless, it seems to me that the fact that this debate has occurred at all supports the following arguments.

"Believing in" a human right means believing that wide social protection against standard threats exemplifying some fundamental type of danger to humans is justified. Now, we want to be able to discuss whether each other's beliefs in human rights are defective. I want to distinguish between human rights beliefs that are "defective" and others that are "incomplete." By "defective," I mean this: while someone understands why social protection against a given type of danger is justified, that person fails to understand why this protection is justified for everyone. By "incomplete" I mean something else: while a person understands why protection against one danger is justified, she or he cannot justify protection against other dangers that are comparably serious threats to the person's life-prospects.

The debate surrounding the Islamic Declarations shows that some social protections against some basic human dangers are justifiable on the basis of Islamic beliefs. But believing that such protection is justified *is* a belief in human rights. That belief may be defective, but a defective belief in human rights is still some belief in human rights. No matter which side in this debate is right—whether it is the authors of the Islamic Declaration or their critics—it is clear that some belief in human rights is part of Islam.

In other words, the very occurrence of a revisionist position—such as that of the Islamic Council—refutes rejectionism. If human rights can be debated on Islamic grounds, then this is a debate that can occur within Islam, not between Islam and the disciples of Satan.

On the other hand, what revisionists assert—that their tradition holds a complete set of human rights—is extremely unlikely to be true. There are two general reasons for this: one is the universality of ethnocentrism, combined with the absence, until recently, of any global context for moral discourse, and the other is the historical tendency to expand the list of dangers against which social protection is deserved.

While there is indeed some concept of human rights to be found in Islam and traditional African thought as well as Lockean liberalism, these conceptions of human rights are also defective, since their arguments privilege protection of one's own group over protection of others—if, indeed, the others are recognized as persons at all. While Eurocentrism is arguably more than—and more vicious than—ethnocentrism generally, cultural history leaves little room to doubt that all cultures have ethnocentric tendencies, and therefore they have been generally unlikely to put the other on the same footing, morally, as "their own." Historically, a necessary condition for overcoming these otherwise pervasive ethnocentric tendencies is the emergence of a worldwide context for moral discussion, a global public sphere of moral deliberation, open to the participation of all. In saying this, I have in mind a specific—yet, I hope, not question—begging—conception of moral discussion. What I mean by "moral" discussion is not technical discussion about the most effective way to make something happen, nor is it negotiation, mediation or any other way of "getting your way" with others by using words. What I have in mind as "moral discussion" is typified by a mutual commitment to reach an understanding of what is the right thing to do, bringing to bear the best available resources for reaching this understanding, and seeking to reduce manipulation in the discussion as far as possible. Prior to the emergence of the United Nations and parallel international institutions, what global discussions took place were either strategic or sectarian. One might argue that previously the Christian moral discourse was global; however, it was far from all-inclusive, and it was always sectarian. One might argue that the international workers' movements were international, and had they lived up to their promise as "universal class," they might have come to create a context for global moral discourse; however, they too remained sectarian.

Admittedly, international institutions have always been arenas for strategic interactions between states and power blocs. Nevertheless, they have also created a public context in which moral discourse sporadically emerges and carries some weight, at least enough to cause minor embarrassments to governments that subordinate it to strategic manipulation, and enough to give opposition movements moral high ground from which to question the legitimacy of government policies. While global communications have made it easier to know what happens in distant parts of the world, global communications have done little to make voices from distant parts of the world audible to each other. The notion that when normative claims are put forward they can be challenged from anywhere on Earth has little currency unless there are contexts in which everyone is to some degree represented and where either one achieves mutual understanding or one courts the risk of embarrassment for defecting from a consensus that is understood by others to be plausibly justified.

We should not fool ourselves by thinking that the world public sphere, morally, has any great strength at this present time. Commitments to reaching global understandings are weak and sporadic, and their power to embarrass governments that defy or ignore them is minimal. Nevertheless, shaky though it is, a global public sphere does exist, and so we do have at least this necessary condition for moral knowledge on a global scale. This is something that all of our traditions were lacking. And therefore, I submit, it is no wonder that the understanding of human rights contained in our traditions was defective.

How a Fuller Set of Human Rights Can Be Known

I shall proceed now to the claims of transformationism, which, I think, support the sort of political goals that Sané has proposed. The first two claims are: (i) in all cultural traditions, some people at some time or other have employed concepts of human rights that are "defective" in the sense that they limit human rights protection to in-groups while excluding out-groups; (ii) still, there are features of cross-cultural dialogue that forbid these sorts of defects—if the dialogue is not abused.

Clearly the sort of understanding we want, when we want *moral understanding*, is not an agreement based on cajoling or tricking each other. In other words, a group that is committed to reaching such an understanding is thereby committed to reducing the degree of manipulation in the discussion. To such a group, not giving each other equal standing and equal consideration would be irrational: any implication that someone ought to be demoted in standing or considerability will find the force of analogical reasoning (to treat like cases alike) weighing against it; meanwhile, reasons adduced in favour of the demotion will be suspected as manipulative, self-serving ideologies. Consequently, if social protection against a basic danger to humans is warranted for some, the rationality of excluding others from this protection will always be questionable.

The next claim that transformationists make is that (iii) the lists of human rights that can be generated from received cultural norms are generally *incomplete*, by which I mean that they overlook certain protections that people are due. Three "generations" of human rights have been claimed, declared or enacted since the founding of the United Nations. In this process the United States, backed occasionally but not reliably by some of its allies, has fought a prolonged losing battle to delete or demote all but the civil and political rights from the list. Initially it succeeded in separating implementation of these "first-generation" rights from social, cultural and economic rights, which, as a result of being separated and deferred, came to be known as the "second generation" of human rights.[15] Later, once more against U.S. resistance, it was argued that both lists were formulated too abstractly, in ways that permitted equivalent protection for some groups to be ignored. On these grounds a "third generation" of rights was called for, including women's rights, rights of peoples (as distinct from states), the right to development, and others.[16] Transformationists see this trend as essentially progressive. What they claim is not only that these new rights are justified, but that (iv) the justification rests on resources for moral knowledge that exist in all cultures.

To examine this, let's begin with some second-generation rights. According to Article 25 of the Universal Declaration:

> Everyone has the right to a standard of living adequate for the health and well-being of himself and of his family, including food, clothing, housing and medical care and necessary social services, and the right to security in the event of unemployment, sickness, disability, widowhood, old age or other lack of livelihood in circumstances beyond his control.

How do we know that these things ought to be socially protected? What are the cognitive resources, available in our culture, for knowing this? They are located at two levels: moral principles that are plausible within the culture, and the knowledge of care, neglect, and abuse that informs people's treatment of each other—especially their treatment of those for whom they feel some responsibility.

First consider cultural norms. Protection of people in relation to their needs is hardly a new idea. In some traditional cultures it is justified in terms of dignity—a good example of which can be found in Francis Deng's discussion of virtue and dignity for the Dinka people of Sudan. In others, protection against need is to be rooted in the prevailing concept of personhood, as Kwasi Wiredu has shown with regard to the Akan peoples of West Africa. These cultural beliefs, then, can support recognition of human rights relating to need.

However, there are other cultural beliefs that may, in particular cases, argue for other priorities. The question, then, is whether there is any deeper resource that enables us to know that needs protection is not to be overridden by other norms or considerations. My claim is that all cultures do have such a resource, which I am calling "knowledge of care, neglect, and abuse." What this knowledge does within moral discussion is to block the use of cultural norms to justify or condone neglect or abuse. If people's common knowledge of care, neglect and abuse is allowed to prevail in a discussion, the result will be to shape the discussion. Where knowledge of care and neglect prevails, those cultural norms justifying protection against need will also prevail. One can see this influence at work particularly in the interpretation of religious traditions, such as in social Buddhism, in Christian liberation theology and among the Islamic left.

In different cultures, knowledge of care, neglect and abuse is expressed differently, and under different conditions the requirements of care will vary, as for example adequate shelter is exemplified differently in different climates. Nevertheless, when it comes to identifying the most important types of protection, and probably even to ranking the worst cases of neglect and abuse, there is remarkable convergence.[17] As a resource for moral understanding, this convergence is bedrock. Were this convergence not possible, neither would it be possible for us to know anything about human rights.

Some of the third-generation rights are supported by this same resource, social knowledge of care, neglect and abuse. This is clearly the case for the emergence of women's rights as human rights. The protections that women seek, as Charlotte Bunch and others have pointed out, include protection from domestic, sexual, and other violence that targets them as women, protection from torture and sexual abuse while in custody, subordination and sexual exploitation of women refugees, feminization of poverty, and sex discrimination. All of these could be seen as violations of already-listed first-generation and second-generation rights. Why, then, add more rights? The reason is to ensure that these will be seen as instances of human rights violations, no less serious than comparable violations that are more typically encountered by men. Moreover, our understanding of a human right is not complete without a full understanding of the *standard threats* against which this right is meant to protect people.

Consider the right to security as an example. Some male interpreters have in fact denied that the right to security includes the right of women not to be beaten by their husbands. Clearly their understanding of the broad right—of security against violence—needs to be completed by specifying that domestic violence against women by husbands is a standard threat. How do we know about these as standard threats? There is some academic study, of course, but there is also an informal basis in experience: we come to know these are standard threats through women's experiences of having to care for and protect themselves, and each other, from violence that targets them specifically as women. With this addition, our understanding of human rights is, as Bunch argues, transformed. Without it, without understanding human rights as women's rights, our understanding of human rights is incomplete.[18]

Other emerging third-generation rights rely for their justification on *political experience* of barriers to the implementation of first-generation and second-generation rights. From various histories of Southern countries we can see that not all ways of enacting civil and political rights enable nations to enact, with equal effectiveness, their social and economic rights. The last half of the twentieth century has revealed specific social and political dangers that have become standard threats to social development, and hence standard threats to the institutionalization of social and economic rights. One such threat has been the emergence of elites, which, though they may once have wished to lead their people to prosperity and development, have been unable to do so, partly because of their subordinate positioning within international economic systems. The result has been the well-known tendency towards internal repression by domestic elites. As one African writer sums it up,

> Political independence coupled with the failure of the new elites to carry out an appreciable level of socioeconomic and political transformation generated apathy, opposition, and revolutionary pressures. These pressures in turn compelled African leaders to resort to repression; the manipulation of religion and ethnicity; alliances with powerful foreign interests, particularly for support; ideological containment; and defensive radicalism.[19]

By endangering democratic development, this syndrome makes the rights of the first and second generations insecure. The solution is seen as twofold. First, international barriers to resources for development must be removed. Second, so must barriers to widespread public participation—both democratic participation and private participation—be removed, while organizations and institutions empowering people to participate in and share in control over the development process must be promoted. These are the two main elements of the third generation of human rights, which are sometimes called, "the right to development," or "peoples' rights," or, more prosaically, "peoples' rights to development." Why should this third generation of rights be recognized? One argument is that the failure to secure people's rights to development yields political structures (the repressive subaltern elite, powerless to lead development) that predictably fail to protect not only socioeconomic rights but also first-generation rights. It is argued on the basis of this political experience that enacting third-generation rights is the only process that can effectively enact first-generation and second-generation rights in Third World contexts.

In principle, then, a full list of human rights can be known. A full understanding and a complete set of human rights can be justified by moral discourse, so long as that discourse is not abused, and so long as it is open to two sorts of cognitive resources. One of these is the varied yet convergent knowledge of care, neglect and abuse that informs personal and social life in all cultures. The other is not moral but political experience of barriers to achieving social protections, including those recognized as human rights.

What we will accomplish, in struggling for the inclusion of this knowledge and experience in the moral discourse of human rights, is to rid the discourse of its former Eurocentrism and in this way render it more capable and appropriate for articulating at least some goals of the kind of world movement that Sané has called for in response to the human damage being caused by globalization. It is part of the process that South Asian feminist Corinne Kumar D'Souza has called "the Wind from the South," which fills our sails "to move outside the universal, Eurocentric, patriarchal patterns ... [and] develop a new universalism."[20]

Defending Human Rights in the Context of Globalization

Recall what labour force dualization is, and how it undermines human rights. Corporations buy the loyalty of some workers whom they employ in formal, regulated jobs, paid according to a market influenced by labour productivity and collective bargaining. On the other hand, much of the labour that the corporation requires is procured now by other means, indirectly, through subcontracting into labour pools where market conditions are far less favourable for the workers. If the labour market were unified, labour of a given type would obtain a single equilibrium price, but here, in the dual labour market, this is not the case. As long as this rift endures, "equal pay for equal work" and "just and favourable remuneration ensuring for [oneself and one's] family an existence worthy of human dignity" are protected, if at all, only for workers who continue to possess jobs in the formal sector; on the other side of the rift, these protections are only dreams—or, as well, they are seen as other workers' privileges.

One would think that once this phenomenon becomes at all widespread within a country it could also have a damaging effect on state finances. We are all familiar with the pressure on countries to strip away state spending and social protections in order to reduce budget deficits and become more "competitive" in relation to other countries. Subcontracting must be one factor contributing to this "race for the bottom." The competitive advantage that capital achieves by these means seems to be reflected in reduced earning power by workers, which must ultimately be reflected in reduced taxation power for their governments. Thus the capacity of governments to finance social rights is curtailed. It is not just labour rights that are undermined but social rights as well.

Those who are seriously committed to preserving the substance of human rights on our planet must address the problem of healing this rift in the world's workforce. The solutions, if there are any, will be complex.

To begin looking at solutions, we need to ask why it is that subcontracting gives a corporation competitive advantage. Three sources of advantage need to be distinguished. In part, there may be efficiencies of allocation: just as the "parts-on-time" system achieves economies, by analogy so too does subcontracting, as a "labour-on-time" system. For this there may be no solution; yet, at the same time, it is not clear that this aspect of subcontracting causes harm. In part—arguably the greater part—the competitive advantage comes from the kind of labour pools that capital seeks out through subcontracting. For the labour that capital was, in a previous century, able to create, infamously, through such measures as enclosures, it must now scour the earth, as the world's workforce becomes more highly educated, and more expensive. In the long term, the only solution is to increase the value of Southern labour. On the one hand, this requires social investment in education and other forms of human development. As Mahbub ul Haq has observed,

> Investing in human development has been a key strategy of economic growth in East Asia. In the Republic of Korea, labour productivity grew by 11% a year between 1963 and 1979—with only half that growth due to increased capital investment.[21]

Consequently, one part of the solution is (a) to raise the value of labour—especially at capital's new and last frontiers—by investment in human development. However, the ability of labour to realize this value, to capture the proceeds of productivity increases, depends on its bargaining power. What subcontracting allows corporations to do is reduce the cost of labour by reducing the bargaining power of labour. This is accomplished by evading labour regulation: in export processing zones, and in the informal sector (where workers are nominally entrepreneurs) there is no collective bargaining. In these two different cases—export processing zones and the informal sector—different responses are required.

(b) Export processing zones would seem to require re-regulation. This would seem easy enough to justify on human rights grounds, inasmuch as labour rights are human rights. However, the issue has been clouded by demands by France and the United States to enforce labour standards by means of trade sanctions and "social clauses" attached to trade agreements.[22]

Labour regulation is also absent from the informal sector. The informal sector is a cash economy from which regulation and taxation are largely absent. People who work it are nominally self-employed;

the earnings of many are at subsistence level, and for them this is the sector of last resort. Others manage modest accumulation, and some are able to "graduate" into formal businesses with more or less stable assets and employees. In some of the recently successful Asian economies, the graduation process has all but eliminated the informal sector.[23] Consensus among development analysts is that the best approach to the informal sector is to facilitate the graduation process, which benefits not only the entrepreneurs but workers as well—since graduation transforms jobless work into formal employment. Three requirements are generally recognized for greater chances of success by these micro-enterprises: marketing networks, credit, and business skills.[24]

(c) The task, then, is to "graduate" the informal sector. Credit and empowerment (including marketing and business skills) seem essential. All three can be called for under a new human right, a "third-generation" right: people's right to development.

In the "Declaration on the Right to Development," adopted by resolution of the General Assembly in 1986, we find a sophisticated view of the development process, of obstacles that may thwart it, and of agents that must co-ordinate their work in order to lead development through the obstacles. The conception of development that informs it is one in which welfare, autonomy, and justice are interdependent. Perhaps in order to confront exclusively welfarist conceptions of development, the document stresses from the start that individuals are to be active participants and peoples are to be self-determining in development, which is then implicitly defined as "the constant improvement of the well-being of the entire population and of all individuals, on the basis of their active, free and meaningful participation in development and in the fair distribution of the benefits resulting therefrom.[25] Major obstacles to development are identified as: lack of international co-operation; colonialism, racism, and other violations of the self-determination of peoples; violation of other human rights; threats to peace and security; and unequal access to resources—for example, by women. What the right calls for is co-ordination at all levels—local, national, and international—which promotes participatory development and surmounts these obstacles.

This is, of course, an extremely rich and powerful claim. I will discuss its justification later. For now, I want to note its consequences for the informal sector. "Graduating" the informal sector requires credit and empowerment (especially in the areas of marketing and business management). These necessities are being provided increasingly by community organizations, self-help groups, co-operatives, and similar organizations of civil society—some of them initially formed by NGOs. These popular grassroots organizations also contribute politically to participatory development by focussing demands to pry resources from a self-serving state apparatus.[26] For this and other reasons, these very organizations, which have a central role to play in the process of graduating micro-enterprises from the informal sector, have come to be interpreted as important means of realizing the right to development. The UN secretary general's report *Realizing the Right to Development*, resulting from the 1991 Global Consultation on the Right to Development as a Human Right, included these organizations within the interpretation of "participation." Thus the right to development, including participation, was seen to include the growth of these organizations.[27]

It also addresses the need for credit. Article 8 of the Declaration calls upon states to "ensure ... equality of opportunity for all in their access to basic resources," and this has been interpreted to include access to productive resources. The Global Consultation included availability of credit among its list of "criteria which might be used to measure progress" in implementing the right to development.[28]

Let us see where we stand. I began by observing that labour force dualization is a pervasive threat not only to labour rights but also to social rights generally. I have identified three types of action that will need to be taken to mend the rift in the world's workforce: (a) raising the value of Southern labour through human development investment, (b) re-regulating the EPZs, preferably through international agencies, and (c) graduating the informal sector through credit and empowerment. I have shown that the first two are justifiable under currently recognized social and economic rights, and the third can be justified on the basis of the newer human right of peoples to development. Therefore, if a global movement of the kind Sané calls for is to address this issue, its goals can be articulated and justified in terms of human rights....

NOTES

1. In a recent interview, Sandra Ramos, National Coordinator of the Movement of Working and Unemployed Women, gave the following description of conditions in Nicaragua:

   Some 70 percent of the labour force is unemployed. So jobs and the right to healthcare and education are the basic demands for women. Neo-liberalism is working towards the privatization of healthcare and education, and also to reduce the number of jobs required to produce goods.

   The Government's only alternative in terms of jobs is to go work in the *maquilas* (export-only factories). This strategy is based on the poorly paid labour of women workers. There are 20 international companies investing here—mostly Korean and Taiwanese—all producing for the North American market. The women who work here have no benefits and are entirely outside the normal labour-law requirements. Women earn an average of $70 a month—less than a third of what they need to survive. They work 10 to 15 hours a day.

   Sandra Ramos, interviewed by Richard Swift, "The NI Interview," *The New Internationalist* 279 (May 1996): 31. See also Henk Thomas, ed., *Globalization and Third World Trade Unions: The Challenge of Rapid Economic Change* (London: Zed Books, 1995).
2. Pierre Sané, "Human Rights: An Agenda for Action," *West Africa* 3978 (Dec. 20, 1993): 2294.
3. Jack Donnelly, "Human Rights and Human Dignity: An Analytic Critique of Non-Western Conceptions of Human Rights," *American Political Science Review* 76 (1982): 303-16.
4. Bassam Tibi," The European Tradition of Human Rights and the Culture of Islam," in *Human Rights in Africa: Cross-Cultural Perspectives*, ed. Abdullahi Ahmed An-Na'im and Francis M. Deng (Washington, D.C.: The Brookings Institution, 1990): 118.
5. Abdullahi Ahmed An-Na'im, "Islam, Islamic Law and the Dilemma of Cultural Legitimacy for Universal Human Rights," In *Asian Perspectives on Human Rights*, ed. Claude E. Welch Jr. and Virginia A. Leary (Boulder, Col.: Westview Press, 1990); Abdullahi Ahmed An-Na'im and Francis M. Deng, eds., *Human Rights in Africa: Cross-Cultural Perspectives* (Washington, D.C.: The Brookings Institution, 1990); Abdullahi Ahmed An-Na'im, "Problems of Universal Cultural Legitimacy for Human Rights," *in Human Rights in Africa*; Abdullahi Ahmed An-Na'im, *Human Rights in Cross-Cultural Perspectives: A Quest for Consensus* (Philadelphia: University of Pennsylvania Press, 1992).
6. Quoted by Ann Elizabeth Mayer, "Current Muslim Thinking on Human Rights," in *Human Rights in Africa*, 138.
7. Kwasi Wiredu, "An Akan Perspective on Human Rights," in *Human Rights in Africa*, p. 247.
8. *Ibid.*: p. 247.
9. *Ibid.*: p. 247.
10. Wayne Glausser, "Three Approaches to Locke and the Slave Trade," *Journal of the History of Ideas* 51 (1990): 199-216.
11. Bassam Tibi, "The European Tradition of Human Rights and the Culture of Islam," in *Human Rights in Africa*, 118.
12. Adamantia Pollis and Peter Schwab, "Human Rights: A Western Construct with Limited Applicability," in *Human Rights: Cultural and Ideological Perspectives*, ed. Adamantia Pollis and Peter Schwab (New York: Praeger, 1980): 13.
13. Pollis and Schwab, "Human Rights," 15.
14. Quoted by Mayer, "Current Muslim Thinking on Human Rights," 138. This list is extensive, including rights to life, freedom, procedural justice, political participation, free speech, religion, and association, protection of property, dignity of workers, social security, marital rights and rights of women, and rights to education, privacy, and free movement. "Universal Islamic Declaration of Human Rights," in *Human Rights Sourcebook*, ed. Albert P. Blaustein, Roger S. Clark, and Jay A. Sigler (New York: Paragon House, 1987): 917-23. However, as Tibi notes ("European Tradition," n. 4 above), the declaration stipulated that all of these rights are to be interpreted consistently with Sha'riah.
15. Virginia A. Leary, "The Effect of Western Perspec-

tives on International Human Rights," in *Human Rights in Africa*.

16. Philip Alston, "Making Space for the New Human Rights: The Case of the Right to Development," *Harvard Human Rights Yearbook* 1 (1988): 3-40.
17. I want to stress that the underlying beliefs about care, neglect, and abuse are in principle a form of *knowledge*. It is fallible and corrigible knowledge, but knowledge nonetheless. It is a form of knowledge that no culture can afford not have. Every culture—if it is going to sustain itself—must include practices of direct personal care and support. In some cases we take direct responsibility for the well-being of others—for example, our children. We also take on similar responsibilities towards adult friends and loved ones, although these responsibilites are limited by respect for their autonomy. To carry out these practices and responsibilites, people need a great deal of knowledge. Modernity has rendered some of this knowledge formal and testable, but a great deal more of the knowledge we need in order to provide each other with humane care and support is informal, a cultural reservoir of knowlege based on current and received experience. It is against this vast informal knowlege of how people are to be cared for and supported that we can also recognize neglect. Care and support are eventually concerned with providing conditions for growth and socialization, but they begin with providing protection. Consequently, those who can recognize good care can also recognize abuse.
18. Charlotte Bunch, "Women's Rights as Human Rights: Toward a Re-Vision of Human Rights," in *Applied Ethics: A Multicultural Approach*, ed. Larry May and Shari Collins Sharratt (Englewood Cliffs, N. J.: Prentice-Hall, 1994): 41-9.
19. Julius O. Ihonvbere, "Underdevelopment and Human Rights Violations in Africa," In *Emerging Human Rights: The African Political Economy Context*, ed. George W. Shepherd Jr. and Mark Anikpo (New York: Greenwood, 1990): 58.
20. Corinne Kumar D'Souza, "A New Movement, a New Hope: East Wind, West Wind, and the Wind from the South," in *Healing the Wounds: the Promise of Ecofeminism*, ed. Judith Plant (Toronto: Between the Lines, 1989): 38.
21. Mahbub ul Haq, *Reflections on Human Development* (New York: Oxford University Press, 1995).
22. See Paul Waer, "Social Clauses in International Trade," *Journal of World trade* 30 (1989): 25-42.
23. Thomas, *Globalization and Third World Trade Unions*, 50.
24. Sadig Rasheed and David Fasholé Luke, *Development Management in Africa: Toward Dynamism, Empowerment, and Entrepreneurship* (Boulder, Col.: Westview Press, 1995): 165-6, 256-7.
25. *The Realization of the Right To Development: Global Consultation of the Right To Development as a Human Right, Centre for Human Rights, Geneva* (New York: United Nations, 1991).
26. James C.N. Paul, "Participatory Approaches to Human Rights in Sub-Saharan Africa," in *Human Rights in Africa*, 213-39; George W. Shepherd Jr., "African People's Rights: The Third Generation in a Global Perspective," in *Emerging Human Rights*, 39-54.
27. *Realization of the Right to Development*, 37, 53.
28. *Ibid.*, 67, 49.

A THEORY OF JUSTICE

John Rawls

John Rawls is Professor Emeritus at Harvard University. He is the author of the well-known and path-breaking A Theory of Justice *(Harvard, 1971) and the more recent work* Political Liberalism *(Columbia, 1996).*

These excerpts from A Theory of Justice *provide a skeletal account of Rawls's project of using social contract theory to generate principles of justice for assigning basic rights and duties and determining the division of social benefits in a society. Rawls argues that the two principles that would be reached through an agreement in an original position of fairness and equality are 1) each person is to have an equal right to the most extensive basic liberty compatible with a similar liberty for others and 2) social and economic inequalities are to be arranged so that they are both a) reasonably expected to be to everyone's advantage; and b) attached to positions and offices open to all.*

---

1. The Role of Justice

Justice is the first virtue of social institutions, as truth is of systems of thought. A theory however elegant and economical must be rejected or revised if it is untrue; likewise laws and institutions no matter how efficient and well-arranged must be reformed or abolished if they are unjust. Each person possesses an inviolability founded on justice that even the welfare of society as a whole cannot override. For this reason justice denies that the loss of freedom for some is made right by a greater good shared by others. It does not allow that the sacrifices imposed on a few are outweighed by the larger sum of advantages enjoyed by many. Therefore in a just society the liberties of equal citizenship are taken as settled; the rights secured by justice are not subject to political bargaining or to the calculus of social interests. The only thing that permits us to acquiesce in an erroneous theory is the lack of a better one; analogously, an injustice is tolerable only when it is necessary to avoid an even greater injustice. Being first virtues of human activities, truth and justice are uncompromising.

These propositions seem to express our intuitive conviction of the primacy of justice. No doubt they are expressed too strongly. In any event I wish to inquire whether these contentions or others similar to them are sound, and if so how they can be accounted for. To this end it is necessary to work out a theory of justice in the light of which these assertions can be interpreted and assessed....

2. The Subject of Justice

Many different kinds of things are said to be just and unjust: not only laws, institutions, and social systems, but also particular actions of many kinds, including decisions, judgments, and imputations. We also call the attitudes and dispositions of persons, and persons themselves, just and unjust. Our topic, however, is that of social justice. For us the primary subject of justice is the basic structure of society, or more exactly, the way in which the major social institutions distribute fundamental rights and duties and determine the division of advantages from social cooperation. By major institutions I understand the

Reprinted with permission of the publisher from *A Theory of Justice* by John Rawls (Cambridge, Mass: Harvard University Press, © 1971 by the President and Fellows of Harvard College): 3–22; 60–65; 100–104; 504–507 [edited].

political constitution and the principal economic and social arrangements. Thus the legal protection of freedom of thought and liberty of conscience, competitive markets, private property in the means of production, and the monogamous family are examples of major social institutions. Taken together as one scheme, the major institutions define men's rights and duties and influence their life-prospects, what they can expect to be and how well they can hope to do. The basic structure is the primary subject of justice because its effects are so profound and present from the start. The intuitive notion here is that this structure contains various social positions and that men born into different positions have different expectations of life determined, in part, by the political system as well as by economic and social circumstances. In this way the institutions of society favor certain starting places over others. These are especially deep inequalities. Not only are they pervasive, but they affect men's initial chances in life; yet they cannot possibly be justified by an appeal to the notions of merit or desert. It is these inequalities, presumably inevitable in the basic structure of any society to which the principles of social justice must in the first instance apply. These principles, then, regulate the choice of a political constitution and the main elements of the economic and social system. The justice of a social scheme depends essentially on how fundamental rights and duties are assigned and on the economic opportunities and social conditions in the various sectors of society ...

3. The Main Idea of The Theory of Justice

My aim is to present a conception of justice which generalizes and carries to a higher level of abstraction the familiar theory of the social contract as found, say, in Locke, Rousseau, and Kant.[1] In order to do this we are not to think of the original contract as one to enter a particular society or to set up a particular form of government. Rather, the guiding idea is that the principles of justice for the basic structure of society are the object of the original agreement. They are the principles that free and rational persons concerned to further their own interests would accept in an initial position of equality as defining the fundamental terms of their association. These principles are to regulate all further agreements; they specify the kinds of social cooperation that can be entered into and the forms of government that can be established. This way of regarding the principles of justice I shall call justice as fairness.

Thus we are to imagine that those who engage in social cooperation choose together, in one joint act, the principles which are to assign basic rights and duties and to determine the division of social benefits. Men are to decide in advance how they are to regulate their claims against one another and what is to be the foundation charter of their society. Just as each person must decide by rational reflection what constitutes his good, that is, the system of ends which it is rational for him to pursue, so a group of persons must decide once and for all what is to count among them as just and unjust. The choice which rational men would make in this hypothetical situation of equal liberty, assuming for the present that this choice problem has a solution, determines the principles of justice.

In justice as fairness the original position of equality corresponds to the state of nature in the traditional theory of the social contract. This original position is not, of course, thought of as an actual historical state of affairs, much less as a primitive condition of culture. It is understood as a purely hypothetical situation characterized so as to lead to a certain conception of justice.[2] Among the essential features of this situation is that no one knows his place in society, his class position or social status, nor does anyone know his fortune in the distribution of natural assets and abilities, his intelligence, strength, and the like. I shall even assume that the parties do not know their conceptions of the good or their special psychological propensities. The principles of justice are chosen behind a veil of ignorance. This ensures that no one is advantaged or disadvantaged in the choice of principles by the outcome of natural chance or the contingency of social circumstances. Since all are similarly situated and no one is able to design principles to favor his particular condition, the principles of justice are the result of a fair agreement or bargain. For given the circumstances of the original position, the symmetry of everyone's relation to each other, this initial situation is fair between individuals as moral persons, that is, as rational beings with their own ends and capable, I shall assume, of a sense of justice. The original position is, one might say, the appropriate initial status quo, and the fundamental agreements reached in it are fair. This explains the propriety of the name "justice as fairness": it conveys the idea that the principles of justice are agreed to in an initial situation that is fair. The name does not mean that the concepts of justice and fairness are the same, any more that the phrase "poetry as metaphor" means that the concepts of poetry and metaphor are the same.

Justice as fairness begins, as I have said, with one of the most general of all choices which persons might make together, namely, with the choice of the first principles of a conception of justice which is to regulate all subsequent criticism and reform of institutions. Then, having chosen a conception of justice, we can suppose that they are to choose a constitution and a legislature to enact laws, and so on, all in accordance with the principles of justice initially agreed upon. Our social situation is just if it is such that by this sequence of hypothetical agreements we would have contracted into the general system of rules which defines it. Moreover, assuming that the original position does determine a set of principles (that is, that a particular conception of justice would be chosen), it will then be true that whenever social institutions satisfy these principles those engaged in them can say to one another that they are cooperating on terms to which they would agree if they were free and equal persons whose relations with respect to one another were fair. They could all view their arrangements as meeting the stipulations which they would acknowledge in an initial situation that embodies widely accepted and reasonable constraints on the choice of principles. The general recognition of this fact would provide the basis for a public acceptance of the corresponding principles of justice. No society can, of course, be a scheme of cooperation which men enter voluntarily in a literal sense; each person finds himself placed at birth in some particular position in some particular society, and the nature of this position materially affects his life prospects. Yet a society satisfying the principles of justice as fairness comes as close as a society can to being a voluntary scheme, for it meets the principles which free and equal persons would assent to under circumstances that are fair. In this sense its members are autonomous and the obligations they recognize self-imposed.

One feature of justice as fairness is to think of the parties in the initial situation as rational and mutually disinterested. This does not mean that the parties are egoists, that is, individuals with only certain kinds of interests, say in wealth, prestige, and domination. But they are conceived as not taking an interest in one another's interests. They are to presume that even their spiritual aims may be opposed, in the way that the aims of those of different religions may be opposed. Moreover, the concept of rationality must be interpreted as far as possible in the narrow sense, standard in economic theory, of taking the most effective means to given ends. I shall modify this concept to some extent, as explained later (§25), but one must try to avoid introducing into it any controversial ethical elements. The initial situation must be characterized by stipulations that are widely accepted.

In working out the conception of justice as fairness one main task clearly is to determine which principles of justice would be chosen in the original position. To do this we must describe this situation in some detail and formulate with care the problem of choice which it presents. These matters I shall take up in the immediately succeeding chapters. It may be observed, however, that once the principles of justice are thought of as arising from an original agreement in a situation of equality, it is an open question whether the principle of utility would be acknowledged. Offhand it hardly seems likely that persons who view themselves as equals, entitled to press their claims upon one another, would agree to a principle which may require lesser life prospects for some simply for the sake of a greater sum of advantages enjoyed by others. Since each desires to protect his interests, his capacity to advance his conception of the good, no one has a reason to acquiesce in an enduring loss for himself in order to bring about a greater net balance of satisfaction. In the absence of strong and lasting benevolent impulses, a rational man would not accept a basic structure merely because it maximized the algebraic sum of advantages irrespective of its permanent effects on his own basic rights and interests. Thus it seems that the principle of utility is incompatible with the conception of social cooperation among equals for mutual advantage. It appears to be inconsistent with the idea or reciprocity implicit in the notion of a well-ordered society. Or, at any rate, so I shall argue.

I shall maintain instead that the persons in the initial situation would choose two rather different principles: the first requires equality in the assignment of basic rights and duties, while the second holds that social and economic inequalities, for example inequalities of wealth and authority, are just only if they result in compensating benefits for everyone, and in particular for the least advantaged members of society. These principles rule out justifying institutions on the grounds that the hardships of some are offset by a greater good in the aggregate. It may be expedient but it is not just that some should have less in order that others may prosper. But there is no injustice in the greater benefits earned by a few provided that the situation of persons not so fortunate is thereby improved. The intuitive idea is that since everyone's well-being depends upon a scheme of cooperation without which no one could have a satisfactory life, the division of advantages should be such as to draw forth the willing cooperation of everyone taking part in it, including those less well situated. Yet this can be expected only if reasonable terms are proposed. The two principles mentioned seem to be a fair agreement on the basis of which those better endowed, or more fortunate in their social position, neither of which we can be said to deserve, could expect the willing cooperation of others when some workable scheme is a necessary condition of the welfare of all.[3] Once we decide to look for a conception of justice that nullifies the accidents of natural endowment and the contingencies of social circumstance as counters in quest for political and economic advantage, we are led to these principles. They express the result of leaving aside those aspects of the social world that seem arbitrary from a moral point of view....

4. The Original Position and Justification

I have said that the original position is the appropriate initial status quo which insures that the fundamental agreements reached in it are fair. This fact yields the name "justice as fairness." It is clear, then, that I want to say that one conception of justice is more reasonable than another, or justifiable with respect to it, if rational persons in the initial situation would choose its principles over those of the other for the role of justice. Conceptions of justice are to be ranked by their acceptability to persons so circumstanced. Understood in this way the question of justification is settled by working out a problem of deliberation: we have to ascertain which principles it would be rational to adopt given the contractual situation. This connects the theory of justice with the theory of rational choice.

If this view of the problem of justification is to succeed, we must, of course, describe in some detail the nature of this choice problem. A problem of rational decision has a definite answer only if we know the beliefs and interests of the parties, their relations with respect to one another, the alternatives between which they are to choose, the procedure whereby they make up their minds, and so on. As the circumstances are presented in different ways, correspondingly different principles are accepted. The concept of the original position, as I shall refer to it, is that of the most philosophically favored interpretation of this initial choice situation for the purposes of a theory of justice.

But how are we to decide what is the most favored interpretation? I assume, for one thing, that there is a broad measure of agreement that principles of justice should be chosen under certain conditions. To justify a particular description of the initial situation one shows that it incorporates these commonly shared presumptions. One argues from widely accepted but weak premises to more specific conclusions. Each of the presumptions should by itself be natural and plausible; some of them may seem innocuous or even trivial. The aim of the contract approach is to establish that taken together they impose significant bounds on acceptable principles of justice. The ideal outcome would be that these conditions determine a unique set of principles; but I shall be satisfied if they suffice to rank the main traditional conceptions of social justice.

One should not be misled, then, by the somewhat unusual conditions which characterize the original position. The idea here is simply to make vivid to ourselves the restrictions that it seems reasonable to impose on arguments for principles of justice, and therefore on these principles themselves. Thus it seems reasonable and generally acceptable that no one should be advantaged or disadvantaged by natural fortune or social circumstances in the choice of principles. It also seems widely agreed that it should be impossible to tailor principles to the circumstances of one's own case. We should insure further that particular inclinations and aspirations, and persons' conceptions of their good do not affect the principles adopted. The aim is to rule out those principles that it would be rational to propose for acceptance, however little the chance of success, only if one knew certain things that are irrelevant from the standpoint of justice. For example, if a man knew that he was wealthy, he might find it rational to advance the principle that various taxes for welfare measures be counted unjust; if he knew that he was poor, he would most likely propose the contrary principle. To represent the desired restrictions one imagines a situation in which everyone is deprived of this sort of information. One excludes the knowledge of those contingencies which sets men at odds and allows them to be guided by their prejudices. In this manner the veil of ignorance is arrived at in a natural way. This concept should cause no difficulty if we keep in mind the constraints on arguments that it is meant to express. At any time we can enter the original position, so to speak, simply by following a certain procedure, namely, by arguing for principles of justice in accordance with these restrictions.

It seems reasonable to suppose that the parties in the original position are equal. That is, all have the same rights in the procedure for choosing principles; each can make proposals, submit reasons for their acceptance, and so on. Obviously the purpose of these conditions is to represent equality between human beings as moral persons, as creatures having a conception of their good and capable of a sense of justice. The basis of equality is taken to be similarity in these two respects. Systems of ends are not ranked in value; and each man is presumed to have the requisite ability to understand and to act upon whatever principles are adopted. Together with the veil of ignorance, these conditions define the principles of justice as those which rational persons concerned to advance their interests would consent to as equals when none are known to be advantaged or disadvantaged by social and natural contingencies.

There is, however, another side to justifying a particular description of the original position. This is to see if the principles which would be chosen match our considered convictions of justice or extend them in an acceptable way. We can note whether applying these principles would lead us to make the same judgments about the basic structure of society which we now make intuitively and in which we have the greatest confidence; or whether, in cases where our present judgments are in doubt and given with hesitation, these principles offer a resolution which we can affirm on reflection. There are questions which we feel sure must be answered in a certain way. For example, we are confident that religious intolerance and racial discrimination are unjust. We think that we have examined these things with care and have reached what we believe is an impartial judgment not likely to be distorted by an excessive attention to our own interests. These convictions are provisional fixed points which we presume any conception of justice must fit. But we have much less assurance as to what is the correct distribution of wealth and authority. Here we may be looking for a way to remove our doubts. We can check an interpretation of the initial situation, then, by the capacity of its principles to accommodate our firmest convictions and to provide guidance where guidance is needed.

In searching for the most favored description of this situation we work from both ends. We begin by describing it so that it represents generally shared and preferably weak conditions. We then see if these conditions are strong enough to yield a significant set of principles. If not, we look for further premises equally reasonable. But if so, and these principles match our considered convictions of justice, then so far well and good. But presumably there will be discrepancies. In this case we have a choice. We can either modify the account of the initial situation or we can revise our existing judgments, for even the judgements we take provisionally as fixed points are liable to revision. By going back and forth, sometimes altering the conditions of the contractual circumstances, at others withdrawing our judgments and conforming them to principle, I assume that eventually we shall find a description of the initial situation that both expresses reasonable conditions and yields principles which match our considered judgments duly pruned and adjusted. This state of affairs I refer to as reflective equilibrium.[4] It is an equilibrium because at last our principles and judgments coincide; and it is reflective since we know to what principles our judgments conform and the premises of their derivation. At the moment everything is in order. But this equilibrium is not necessarily stable. It is liable to be upset by further examination of the conditions which should be imposed on the contractual situation and by particular cases which may lead us to revise our judgments. Yet for the time being we have done what we can to render coherent and to justify our convictions of social justice. We have reached a conception of the original position.

I shall not, of course, actually work through this process. Still, we may think of the interpretation of the original position that I shall present as the result of such a hypothetical course of reflection. It represents the attempt to accommodate within one scheme both reasonable philosophical conditions on principles as well as our considered judgments of justice. In arriving at the favored interpretation of the initial situation there is no point at which an appeal is made to self-evidence in the traditional sense either of general conceptions or particular convictions. I do not claim for the principles of justice proposed that they are necessary truths or derivable from such truths. A conception of justice cannot be deduced from self-evident premises or conditions on principles; instead, its justification is a matter of the mutual support of many considerations, of everything fitting together into one coherent view.

A final comment. We shall want to say that certain principles of justice are justified because they would be agreed to in an initial situation of equality. I have emphasized that this original position is purely hypothetical. It is natural to ask why, if this agreement is never actually entered into, we should take any interest in these principles, moral or otherwise. The answer is that the conditions embodied in the description of the original position are ones that we do in fact accept. Or if we do not, then perhaps we can be persuaded to do so by philosophical reflection. Each aspect of the contractual situation can be given supporting grounds. Thus what we shall do is to collect together into one conception a number of conditions on principles that we are ready upon due consideration to recognize as reasonable. These constraints express what we are prepared to regard as limits on fair terms of social cooperation. One way to look at the idea or the original position, therefore, is to see it as an expository device which sums up the meaning of these conditions and helps us to extract their consequences. On the other hand, this conception is also an intuitive notion that suggests its own elaboration, so that led on by it we are drawn to define more clearly the standpoint from which we can best interpret moral relationships. We need a conception that enables us to envision our objective from afar: the intuitive notion of the original position is to do this for us....

11. Two Principles of Justice

I shall now state in a provisional form the two principles of justice that I believe would be chosen in the original position. In this section I wish to make only the most general comments, and therefore the first formulation of these principles is tentative. As we go on I shall run through several formulations and approximate step by step the final statement to be given much later. I believe that doing this allows the exposition to proceed in a natural way.

The first statement of the two principles read as follows.

> First: each person is to have an equal right to the most extensive basic liberty compatible with similar liberty for others.
>
> Second: social and economic inequalities are to be arranged so that they are both (a) reasonably expected to be to everyone's advantage, and (b) attached to positions and offices open to all....

By way of general comment, these principles primarily apply, as I have said, to the basic structure of society. They are to govern the assignment of rights and duties and to regulate the distribution of social and economic advantages. As their formulation suggests, these principles presuppose that the social structure can be divided into two more or less distinct parts, the first principle applying to the one, the second to the other. They distinguish between those aspects of the social system that define and secure the equal liberties of citizenship and those that specify and establish social and economic inequalities. The basic liberties of citizens are, roughly speaking, political liberty (the right to vote and to be eligible for public office) together with freedom of speech and assembly; liberty of conscience and freedom of thought; freedom of the person along with the right to hold (personal) property; and freedom from arbitrary arrest and seizure as defined by the concept of the rule of law. These liberties are all required to be equal by the first principle, since citizens of a just society are to have the same basic rights.

The second principle applies, in the first approximation, to the distribution of income and wealth and to the design of organizations that make use of differences in authority and responsibility, or chains of command. While the distribution of wealth and income need not be equal, it must be to everyone's advantage, and at the same time, positions of authority and offices of command must be accessible to all. One applies the second principle by holding positions open, and then, subject to this constraint, arranges social and economic inequalities so that everyone benefits.

These principles are to be arranged in a serial order with the first principle prior to the second. This ordering means that a departure from the institutions of equal liberty required by the first principle cannot be justified by, or compensated for, by greater social and economic advantages. The distribution of wealth and income, and the hierarchies of authority, must be consistent with both the liberties of equal citizenship and equality of opportunity.

It is clear that these principles are rather specific in their content, and their acceptance rests on certain assumptions that I must eventually try to explain and justify. A theory of justice depends upon a theory of society in ways that will become evident as we proceed. For the present, it should be observed that the two principles (and this holds for all formulations) are a special case of a more general conception of justice that can be expressed as follows.

> All social values— liberty and opportunity, income and wealth, and the bases of self-respect— are to be distributed equally unless an unequal distribution of any, or all, of these values is to everyone's advantage.

Injustice, then, is simply inequalities that are not to the benefit of all. Of course, this conception is extremely vague and requires interpretation.

As a first step, suppose that the basic structure of society distributes certain primary goods, that is, things that every rational man is presumed to want. These goods normally have a use whatever a person's rational plan of life. For simplicity, assume that the chief primary goods at the disposition of society are rights and liberties, powers and opportunities, income and wealth. (Later on in Part Three the primary good of self-respect has a central place.) These are the social primary goods. Other primary goods such as health and vigor, intelligence and imagination, are natural goods; although their possession is influenced by the basic structure, they are not so directly under its control. Imagine, then, a hypothetical initial arrangement in which all the social primary goods are equally distributed: everyone has similar rights and duties, and income and wealth are evenly shared. This state of affairs provides a benchmark for judging improvements. If certain inequalities of wealth and organizational powers would make everyone better off than in this hypothetical starting situation, then they accord with the general conception.

Now it is possible, at least theoretically, that by giving up some of their fundamental liberties men are sufficiently compensated by the resulting social and economic gains. The general conception of justice imposes no restrictions on what sort of inequalities are permissible; it only requires that everyone's position be improved. We need not suppose anything so drastic as consenting to a condition of slavery. Imagine instead that men forego certain political rights when the economic returns are significant and their capacity to influence the course of policy by the exercise of these rights would be marginal in any case. It is this kind of exchange which the two principles as stated rule out; being arranged in serial order they do not permit exchanges between basic liberties and economic and social gains. The serial ordering of principles expresses an underlying preference among primary social goods. When this preference is rational so likewise is the choice of these principles in this order.

In developing justice as fairness I shall, for the most part, leave aside the general conception of justice and examine instead the special case of the two principles in serial order. The advantage of this procedure is that from the first the matter of priorities is recognized and an effort made to find principles to deal with it. One is led to attend throughout to the conditions under which the acknowledgement of the absolute weight of liberty with respect to social and economic advantages, as defined by the lexical order of the two principles, would be reasonable. Offhand, this ranking appears extreme and too special a case to be of much interest; but there is more justification for it than would appear at first sight. Or at any rate, so I shall maintain (§82). Furthermore, the distinction between fundamental rights and liberties and economic and social benefits marks a difference among primary social goods that one should try to exploit. It suggests an important division in the social system. Of course, the distinctions drawn and the ordering proposed are bound to be at best only approximations. There are surely circumstances in which they fail. But it is essential to depict clearly the main lines of a reasonable conception of justice; and under many conditions anyway, the two principles in serial order may serve well enough. When necessary we can fall back on the more general conception.

The fact that the two principles apply to institutions has certain consequences. Several points illustrate this. First of all, the rights and liberties referred to by these principles are those which are defined by the public rules of the basic structure. Whether men are free is determined by the rights and duties established by the major institutions of society. Liberty is a certain pattern of social forms. The first principle simply requires that certain sorts of rules, those defining basic liberties, apply to everyone equally and that they allow the most ex-tensive liberty compatible with a like liberty for all. The only reason for circumscribing the rights defining liberty and making men's freedom less extensive than it might otherwise be is that these equal rights as institutionally defined would interfere with one another.

Another thing to bear in mind is that when principles mention persons, or require that everyone gain from an inequality, the reference is to representative persons holding the various social positions, or offices, or whatever, established by the basic structure. Thus in applying the second principle I assume that it is possible to assign an expectation of well-being to representative individuals holding these positions. This expectation indicates their life prospects as viewed from their social station. In general, the expectations of representative persons depend upon the distribution of rights and duties throughout the basic structure. When this changes, expectations change. I assume, then, that expectations are connected: by raising the prospects of the representative man in one position we presumably increase or decrease the prospects of representative men in other positions. Since it applies to institutional forms, the second principle (or rather the first part of it) refers to the expectations of representative individuals. As I shall discuss below, neither principle applies to distributions of particular goods to particular individuals who may be identified by their proper names. The situation where someone is considering how to allocate certain commodities to needy persons who are known to him is not within the scope of the principles. They are meant to regulate basic institutional arrangements. We must not assume that there is much similarity from the standpoint of justice between an administrative allotment of goods to specific persons and the appropriate design of society. Our common sense intuitions for the former may be a poor guide to the latter.

Now the second principle insists that each person benefit from permissible inequalities in the basic structure. This means that it must be reasonable for each relevant representative man defined by this structure, when he views it as a going concern, to prefer his prospects with the inequality to his prospects without it. One is not allowed to justify differences in income or organizational powers on the ground that the disadvantages of those in one position are outweighed by the greater advantages of those in another. Much less can infringements of liberty be counterbalanced in this way. Applied to the basic structure, the principles of utility would have us maximize the sum of expectations of representative men (weighted by the number of persons they represent, on the classical view); and this would permit us to compensate for the losses of some by the gains of others. Instead, the two principles require that everyone benefit from economic and social inequalities. ...

17. The Tendency to Equality

I wish to conclude this discussion of the two principles by explaining the sense in which they express an egalitarian conception of justice. Also I should like to forestall the objection to the principle of fair opportunity that it leads to a callous meritocratic society. In order to prepare the way for doing this, I note several aspects of the conception of justice that I have set out.

First we may observe that the difference principle gives some weight to the considerations singled out by the principle of redress. This is the principle that undeserved inequalities call for redress; and since inequalities of birth and natural endowment are undeserved, these inequalities are to be somehow compensated for.[5] Thus the principle holds that in order to treat all persons equally, to provide genuine equality of opportunity, society must give more attention to those with fewer native assets and to those born into the less favorable social positions. The idea is to redress the bias of contingencies in the direction of equality. In pursuit of this principle greater resources might be spent on the education of the less rather than the more intelligent, at least over a certain time of life, say the earlier years of school.

Now the principle of redress has not to my knowledge been proposed as the sole criterion of justice, as the single aim of the social order. It is plausible as most such principles are only as a prima facie principle, one that is to be weighed in the balance with others. For example, we are to weigh it against the principle to improve the average standard of life, or to advance the common good.[6] But whatever other principles we hold, the claims of redress are to be taken into account. It is thought to represent one of the elements in our conception of justice. Now the difference principle is not of course the principle of redress. It does not require society to try to even out handicaps as if all were expected to compete on a fair basis in the same race. But the difference principle would allocate resources in education, say, so as to improve the long-term expectation of the least favored. If this end is attained by giving more attention to the better endowed, it is permissible; otherwise not. And in making this decision, the value of education should not be assessed solely in terms of economic efficiency and social welfare. Equally if not more important is the role of education in enabling a person to enjoy the culture of his society and to take part in its affairs, and in this way to provide for each individual a secure sense of his own worth.

Thus although the difference principle is not the same as that of redress, it does achieve some of the intent of the latter principle. It transforms the aims of the basic structure so that the total scheme of institutions no longer emphasizes social efficiency and technocratic values. We see then that the difference principle represents, in effect, an agreement to regard the distribution of natural talents as a common asset and to share in the benefits of this distribution whatever it turns out to be. Those who have been favored by nature, whoever they are, may gain from their good fortune only on terms that improve the situation of those who have lost out. The naturally advantaged are not to gain merely because they are more gifted, but only to cover the costs of training and education and for using their endowments in ways that help the less fortunate as well. No one deserves his greater natural capacity nor merits a more favorable starting place in society. But it does not follow that one should eliminate these distinctions. There is another way to deal with them. The basic structure can be arranged so that these contingencies work for the good of the least fortunate. Thus we are led to the difference principle if we wish to set up the social system so that no one gains or loses from his arbitrary place in the distribution of natural assets or his initial position in society without giving or receiving compensating advantages in return.

In view of these remarks we may reject the contention that the ordering of institutions is always defective because the distribution of natural talents and the contingencies of social circumstance are unjust, and this injustice must inevitably carry over to human arrangements. Occasionally this reflection is offered as an excuse for ignoring injustice, as if the refusal to acquiesce in injustice is on a par with being unable to accept death. The natural distribution is neither just nor unjust; nor is it unjust that persons are born into society at some particular position. These are simply natural facts. What is just and unjust is the way that institutions deal with these facts. Aristocratic and caste societies are unjust because they make these contingencies the ascriptive basis for belonging to more or less enclosed and privileged social classes. The basic structure of these societies incorporates the arbitrariness found in nature. But there is no necessity for men to resign themselves to these contingencies. The social system is not an unchangeable order beyond human control but a pattern of human action. In justice as fairness men agree to share one another's fate. In designing institutions they undertake to avail themselves of the accidents of nature and social circumstance only when doing so is for the common benefit. The two principles are a fair way of meeting the arbitrariness of fortune; and while no doubt imperfect in other ways, the institutions which satisfy these principles are just.

A further point is that the difference principle expresses a conception of reciprocity. It is a principle of mutual benefit. We have seen that, at least when chain connection holds, each representative man can accept the basic structure as designed to advance his interests. The social order can be justified to everyone, and in particular to those who are least favored; and in this sense it is egalitarian. But it seems necessary to consider in an intuitive way how the condition of mutual benefit is satisfied. Consider any two representative men A and B, and let B be the one who is less favored. Actually, since we are most interested in the comparison with the least favored man, let us assume that B is this individual. Now B can accept A's being better off since A's advantages have been gained in ways that improve B's prospects. If A were not allowed his better position, B would be even worse off than he is. The difficulty is to show that A has no grounds for complaint. Perhaps he is required to have less than he might since his having more would result in some loss to B. Now what can be said to the more favored man? To begin with, it is clear that the well-being of each depends on a scheme of social cooperation without which no one could have a satisfactory life. Secondly, we can ask for the willing cooperation of everyone only if the terms of the scheme are reasonable. The difference principle, then, seems to be a fair basis on which those better endowed, or more fortunate in their social circumstances could expect others to collaborate with them when some workable arrangement is a necessary condition of the good of all.

There is a natural inclination to object that those better situated deserved their greater advantages whether or not they are to the benefit of others. At this point it is necessary to be clear about the notion of desert. It is perfectly true that given a just system of cooperation as a scheme of public rules and the expectations set up by it, those who, with the prospect of improving their condition, have done what the system announces that it will reward are entitled to their advantages. In this sense the more fortunate have a claim to their better situation; their claims are legitimate expectations established by social institutions, and the community is obligated to meet them. But this sense of desert presupposes the existence of the cooperative scheme; it is irrelevant to the question whether in the first place the scheme is to be designed in accordance with the difference principle or some other criterion.

Perhaps some will think that the person with greater natural endowments deserves those assets and the superior character that made their development possible. Because he is more worthy in this sense, he deserves the greater advantages that he could achieve with them. This view, however, is surely incorrect. It seems to be one of the fixed points of our considered judgments that no one deserves his place in the distribution of native endowments, any more than one deserves one's initial starting place in society. The assertion that a man deserves the superior character that enables him to make the effort to cultivate his abilities is equally problematic; for his character depends in large part upon fortunate family and social circumstances for which he can claim no credit. The notion of desert seems not to apply to these cases. Thus the more advantaged representative man cannot say that he deserves and therefore has a right to a scheme of cooperation in which he is permitted to acquire benefits in ways that do not contribute to the welfare of others. There is no basis for his making this claim. From the standpoint of common sense, then, the difference principle appears to be acceptable both to the more advantaged and to the less advantaged individual. Of course, none of this is strictly speaking an argument for the principle, since in a contract theory arguments are made from the point of view of the original position. But these intuitive considerations help to clarify the nature of the principle and the sense in which it is egalitarian....

77. The Basis of Equality

I now turn to the basis of equality, the features of human beings in virtue of which they are to be treated in accordance with the principles of justice. Our conduct toward animals is not regulated by these principles, or so it is generally believed. On what grounds then do we distinguish between mankind and other living things and regard the constraints of justice as holding only in our relations to human persons? We must examine what determines the range of application of conceptions of justice.

To clarify our question, we may distinguish three levels where the concept of equality applies. The first is to the administration of institutions as public systems of rules. In this case equality is essentially justice as regularity. It implies the impartial application and consistent interpretation of rules according to such precepts as to treat similar cases similarly (as defined by statutes and precedents) and the like (§38). Equality at this level is the least controversial element in the common sense idea of justice.[7] The second and much more difficult application of equality is to the substantive structure of institutions. Here the meaning of equality is specified by the principles of justice which require that equal basic rights be assigned to all persons. Presumably this excludes animals; they have some protection certainly but their status in not that of human beings. But this outcome is still unexplained. We have yet to consider what sorts of beings are owed the guarantees of justice. This brings us to the third level at which the question of equality arises.

The natural answer seems to be that it is precisely the moral persons who are entitled to equal justice. Moral persons are distinguished by two features: first they are capable of having (and are assumed to have) a conception of their good (as expressed by a rational plan of life); and second they are capable of having (and are assumed to acquire) a sense of justice, a normally effective desire to apply and to act upon the principles of justice, at least to a certain minimum degree. We use the characterization of the persons in the original position to single out the kind of beings to whom the principles chosen apply. After all, the parties are thought of as adopting these criteria to regulate their common institutions and their conduct toward one another; and the description of their nature enters into the reasoning by which these principles are selected. Thus equal justice is owed to those who have the capacity to take part in and to act in accordance with the public understanding of the initial situation. One should observe that moral personality is here defined as a potentiality that is ordinarily realized in due course. It is this potentiality which brings the claims of justice into play. I shall return to this point below.

We see, then, that the capacity for moral personality is a sufficient condition for being entitled to equal justice.[8] Nothing beyond the essential minimum is required. Whether moral personality is also a necessary condition I shall leave aside. I assume that the capacity for a sense of justice is possessed by the overwhelming majority of mankind, and therefore this question does not raise a serious practical problem. That moral personality suffices to make one a subject of claims is the essential thing. We cannot go far wrong in supposing that the sufficient condition is always satisfied. Even if the capacity were necessary, it would be unwise in practice to withhold justice on this ground. The risk to just institutions would be too great.

It should be stressed that the sufficient conditions for equal justice, the capacity for moral personality, is not at all stringent. When someone lacks the requisite potentiality either from birth or accident, this is regarded as a defect or deprivation. There is no race or recognized group of human beings that lacks this attribute. Only scattered individuals are without this capacity, or its realization to the minimum degree, and the failure to realize it is the consequence of unjust and impoverished social circumstances, or fortuitous contingencies. Furthermore, while individuals presumably have varying capacities for a sense of justice, this fact is not a reason for depriving those with a lesser capacity of the full protection of justice. Once a certain minimum is met, a person is entitled to equal liberty on a par with everyone else. A greater capacity for a sense of justice, as shown say in a greater skill and facility in applying the principles of justice and in marshaling arguments in particular cases, is a natural asset like any other ability. The special advantages a person receives for its exercise are to be governed by the difference principle. Thus if some have to a preeminent degree the judicial virtues of impartiality and integrity which are needed in certain positions, they may properly have whatever benefits should be attached to these offices. Yet the application of the principle of equal liberty is not affected by these differences. It is sometimes thought that basic rights and liberties should vary with capacity, but justice as fairness denies this: provided the minimum for moral personality is satisfied, a person is owed all the guarantees of justice.

NOTES

1. As the text suggests, I shall regard Locke's *Second Treatise of Government*, Rousseau's *The Social Contract*, and Kant's ethical works beginning with the *Foundation of the Metaphysics of Morals* as definitive of the contract tradition. For all of its greatness, Hobbes's *Leviathan* raises special problems. A general historical survey is provided by J.W. Gough, *The Social Contract*, 2nd ed. (Oxford, The Clarendon Press, 1957), and Otto Gierke, *Natural Law and the Theory of Society*, trans. with an introduction by Ernest Barker (Cambridge, The University Press, 1934). A presentation of the contract view as primarily an ethical theory is to be found in G. R. Grice, *The Grounds of Moral Judgment* (Cambridge, The University Press, 1967).
2. Kant is clear that the original agreement is hypothetical. See *The Metaphysics of Morals*, pt. I (Rechtslehre), especially §§ 47, 52; and pt. II of the essay "Concerning the Common Saying: This May Be True in Theory but It Does Not Apply in Practice," in *Kant's Political Writings*, ed. Hans Reiss and trans. by H.B. Nisbet (Cambridge, The University Press, 1970), pp. 73-87. See Georges Vlachos, *La Pensée Politique de Kant* (Paris, Presses Universitaires de France, 1962) pp. 326-335; and J.G. Murphy, *Kant: The Philosophy of Right* (London, Macmillan, 1970), pp. 109-112, 133-136, for a further discussion.
3. For the formulation of this intuitive idea, I am indebted to Allan Gibbard.
4. The process of mutual adjustment of principles and considered judgments is not peculiar to moral philosophy. See Nelson Goodman, *Fact, Fiction, and Forecast* (Cambridge, Mass., Harvard University Press, 1955), pp. 65-68, for parallel remarks concerning the justification of the principles of deductive and inductive inference.
5. See Herbert Spiegelberg, "A Defense of Human Equality." *Philosophical Review*, vol. 53 (1944), pp. 101, 113-123; and D.D. Raphael, "Justice and Liberty," *Proceedings of the Aristotelian Society*, vol. 51 (1950-1951), pp. 187f.
6. See for example, Spiegelberg. pp.120f.
7. See Sidgwick, *Methods of Ethics*, p. 496.
8. This fact can be used to interpret the concept of natural rights. For one thing, it explains why it is appropriate to call by this name the rights that justice protects. These claims depend solely on certain natural attributes the presence of which can be ascertained by natural reason pursuing common sense methods of inquiry. The existence of these attributes and the claims based upon them is established independently from social conventions and legal norms. The propriety of the term "natural" is that it suggests the contrast between the rights identified by the theory of justice and the rights defined by law and custom. But more than this, the concept of natural rights includes the idea that these rights are assigned in the first instance to persons, and that they are given a special weight. Claims easily overridden for other values are not natural rights. Now the rights protected by the first principle have both of these features in view of the priority rules. Thus justice as fairness has the characteristic marks of a natural rights theory. Not only does it ground fundamental rights on natural attributes and distinguish their bases from social norms, but it assigns rights to persons by principles of equal justice, these principles having a special force against which other values cannot normally prevail. Although specific rights are not absolute, the system of equal liberties is absolute practically speaking under favourable conditions.

A CRITIQUE OF RAWLS'S "FREESTANDING" JUSTICE

Xiaorong Li

Xiaorong Li is a Research Scholar at the Institute for Philosophy and Public Policy, University of Maryland at College Park. Her research focuses on a broad range of ethical/policy issues in international/developing countries, including human rights, justice, world hunger, women's rights, economic development, population, and welfare. Her regional speciality is Asia/China.

Rawls's recent articulation of his theory of justice in Political Liberalism *(1993) carries on the contractarian approach to defining justice, which was first laid out in* A Theory of Justice *(1971). However, this approach is now characterised as "political," not metaphysical. It is intended to appeal to those who are deeply divided by cultural, religious, and moral beliefs: it is to explain how justice can be stable in a divided society. This "political" approach, nevertheless, has narrowed its appeal. Since it relies on the shared ideas in democratic societies, its appeal becomes political and cultural. Moreover, this theory's requirement of equal basic liberties for a just society calls for a relatively developed economy and social institutions. It fails to provide guidance to societies that, owing to their lesser development, cannot afford to guarantee the worth of equal basic liberties. The structural insufficiency of Rawls's "political" theory explains the failure of his continuing efforts to extend his liberal theory of justice to the international terrain. This essay analyses this insufficiency and the narrow applicability of Rawls's "political" theory of justice.*

John Rawls's *A Theory of Justice*,[1] rekindled substantive discussion in political philosophy, which had been deadened by a preoccupation with the logical analysis of philosophical language half a century ago. He advances two principles of justice that are conditions for a just society: first, social and economic inequalities must not diminish equally distributed basic liberties. Second, social and economic inequalities are permissible only if there are fair equal opportunity and benefits for the least advantaged members. These ideas have now been enunciated in *Political Liberalism*, which is essentially a continued effort of Rawls's distinct approach to defining justice, but his philosophical concerns have shifted to new emphases.

The essentially social-contract approach departs further from its classical predecessors and, to a certain degree, from Rawls's own approach in the *Theory*. Few classical liberal philosophers anticipated the fundamental changes that have reshaped human history this century. The Russian Revolution and the Holocaust have altered the lives of virtually all mankind. The rise and (partial) fall of communist totalitarian tyrannies, the eruptions of neo-fascism, racism, nationalism, and religious intolerance, mark a new era of human existence. Rawls's emphatically *political* theory of justice, which takes stock of this reality, reshapes political thinking profoundly.

Since Plato's *Republic*, philosophers have taken different approaches to defining justice. Philosophers of the Renaissance, Reformation and the early Industrial Age were preoccupied with questions of whether there should be a state, what the state ought to do, how its power should be limited, and what claims citizens have against the state. They sought a moral principle, or one set of beliefs about how life

---

Reprinted with permission of Blackwell Publishers from *Journal of Applied Philosophy* 12:3 (1995): 263–71.

should be lived, which they expected to apply to the human world universally.

Rawls zeroes in on one distinct issue: how can a just and stable society possibly be established, in which free and equal persons coexist and co-operate, when they remain divided by incompatible and irreconcilable religious, philosophical and moral doctrines? Reflecting on a diverse world that is ever more violent and out of control, Rawls's Political theory confronts the fact that the imposition of a single set of moral beliefs on political institutions is possible only by using oppressive state power, a lesson taught by the sixteenth and seventeenth century European religious wars and communist Gulags. Promoting the principle of tolerance, which emerged from the European religious wars and has since gained acceptance in Western societies, becomes the trademark of Rawls's theory of justice.

Two Problems with the "Political" Approach

Realistically speaking, can Rawls's principles unite deeply divided peoples and win their support despite the plurality of their moral doctrines? Rawls is now more concerned about this question than he was previously in the *Theory* and his answer differs from that of classical liberal thinkers, especially the contractarian theorists. He seeks to show how a just society can be stabilised *not* by organising itself according to uniformed comprehensive moral philosophical convictions about the good life. He calls his approach "freestanding" or "political."

Rawls's "political" conception of justice is worked out in a contractual procedure, where, if parties agree on a fair procedure then they will accept the end product of that procedure — i.e. they will accept the principles of justice without having to embrace any particular comprehensive religious or philosophical doctrines. As long as this idea of procedural justice is concerned, Rawls remains within the social-contract tradition of Locke, Hobbes, and Rousseau. But he departs from it by chipping away its metaphysical presuppositions about human nature and the nature of the world. He does so in order to avoid grounding his theory in any particular religious, philosophical or moral doctrine.

Rawls's hope is that reasonable members of a pluralistic democratic culture, possessing a certain level of material abundance, will converge on his principles of justice, reaching what he calls an "overlapping consensus" of reasonable but incompatible doctrines. And his conception of justice could thus be political, rallying a consensus within pluralistic societies of ideologically divided persons and groups.

But how well-equipped is Rawls's theory to achieve such an admirable goal? I think that it faces at least two problems. First, it is not entirely *freestanding*: it has presupposed some notions of moral values, namely liberal democratic political values, and second, it has limited applicability. In constructing the original position, which is a heuristic device for eliciting the principles of justice, Rawls has used the moral ideas of the person as free and equal, and of society as a fair system of co-operation. He affirms the high value of basic liberties and gives them priority over other social goods by requiring that political institutions protect basic liberties and promote pluralism.

These liberal ideas require a basis for their own support. Showing that they are part of the democratic tradition is not sufficient for their plausibility. That does not prove the superiority of liberty and equality to subjugation and slavery, since the latter could be accepted ideas in other political cultures.

The professed premises of Rawlsian theory would be either (1) too thin (lacking in moral content) to form a foundation for a conception of justice if these premises were purely rational; or (2) too shallow (lacking support) if these premises were judgments of liberal values.

If, furthermore, the liberal ideas were to be supported by some comprehensive views of the human good, then in what sense could Rawls's theory be considered "freestanding"?

This raises the second problem, which is the limited applicability of Rawls's theory. If the theory is grounded in a particular culture, i.e. the democratic political tradition, how can it be extended to other cultures, such as hierarchical authoritarian political traditions? Without a commitment to any comprehensive (or partially comprehensive) moral doctrine, a Rawlsian liberal could be said to relativise the conceptions of justice judged as acceptable by various cultural convictions. Thus, for example, a political institution that subjugates women may justify its policy by citing cultural beliefs in the inferior nature or social role of women. Surely, Rawls's principles of justice would condemn gender subjugation firmly. But if that condemnation cites its support from the belief system of democratic societies, it will not be persuasive in the face of societies where the belief system values male dominance.

If we see in Rawls's early theory a hope to address groups, nations, or societies segregated by religious bigotry, ethnic hatred, and national prejudice, his new approach may seem to have little relevance outside liberal democratic cultures. Rawls now deliberately focuses on the liberal democratic political culture, within which such bigotry, hatred, and prejudice have already been relatively contained through institutionalised protection of basic rights and liberties.

There are two ways, normally, in which we can talk about the outreach of a theory of justice designed for liberal democratic culture. One way is to reach out toward other (i.e. non-liberal-democratic) societies, and the other is toward a society of nations. The two are related in that principles governing multi-national relations need to consider the domestic characteristics of the governed nations, such as whether they are democratic or authoritarian.

The distinction between justice in international relations and justice within a nation is significant because an internally repressive regime can be law-abiding in international affairs. To ignore injustice within (other) nations is to suggest that injustice need not concern us so long as it does not affect us through international relations.

I have in mind justice within other nations when I question the applicability of the Rawlsian conception of justice to other (non-democratic) political cultures. Rawls has concerned himself with the second kind of outreach, but has hardly discussed the first. And his critics also seem to have taken steps to concern themselves with the issues of justice in international relations and global redistribution.[2]

These two problems with Rawls's approach are compounded by his own tendency to frame his discussion of domestic justice exclusively within the borders of liberal democracy. Rawls makes it clearer now that his theory addresses problems pertinent to a constitutional democracy, such as how the values of liberty and equality are best expressed in the constitutional rights of democratic citizens and the basic institutions.[3]

Rawls acknowledges that his theory does not address the more fundamental question of *why* citizens should be guaranteed basic liberties and rights. This is because his political conception of justice is founded on the basic concepts shared in a democratic political culture.[4] He has recently further suggested that a theory of justice should avoid taking positions on fundamental questions about what is a good society and what is a good human life: it should only address the problem of political justice, not that of achieving the highest good.[5] It does not refer to its conception of justice as true.[6]

These views warrant serious concern. Imagine a political culture dominated by, say, intolerant fundamentalist doctrines. Such a culture has its own shared and institutionalized value judgments. These judgements might be racist or fascist or intolerant of homosexuals. When liberal ideas begin to take root in such a culture and demand freedom and equality for all, should the more fortunate (or advantaged) who live in some distant democratic society support the liberals or deny their legitimacy in that foreign land? Rawls's approach could be construed to mean that Western liberal thinkers need not back liberal dissident movements in non-liberal cultures, since the considered, non-liberal judgments of those cultures differ from their own. Consequently, Rawls's theory of justice may espouse the relativist view that would shy away from problems of slavery, racism, and authoritarianism in certain other cultures, as these are based on those cultures' shared and deeply held judgments.

Eventually, there would seem to be no way of telling whether democracy is any more just than those practices. And if a theory of justice cannot explain why contemporary Western democracy is just, or more just than, say, authoritarian rule, then it has not really shown that such an institution (liberal democracy) is valuable.

Equal Liberties under Unfavourable Conditions

Rawls has made a unique contribution to the discussion on distributive justice, which links him to the debate on redressing global inequalities. While he is not the first to treat this topic extensively, his principles of justice entail radical solutions.

One limitation to his notion of distributive justice has, however, evaded scrutiny. His principle of distributive justice is applicable to developed countries only, where social-economic conditions are favourable to (capable of substantiating) equal basic liberties. Only under favourable conditions does Rawls's theory forcefully argue for the priority of equal basic liberties over social-economic advancement.[7] Thus, if an economically beneficial arrangement (such as an unequal distribution in order to achieve economic efficiency) infringes the basic liberties of some members in a relatively wealthy society, such an arrangement is impermissible. However, when social-economic conditions are not favourable (unable to guarantee equal basic liberties for all), as in the case of less-developed countries, Rawls is ambivalent about whether his theory would permit a trade-off of equal basic liberties for economic advancement.

Take for example India and China, two economically less-developed countries, each with a tremendously large and ethnically diverse population (especially India's). Though both societies are still largely traditional (or pre-modern), India has a democratic government, while the Chinese state remains highly authoritarian. The two have taken distinctive routes toward modernisation and have very different basic social structures.

In India, where government takes actions to democratise basic political institutions to protect liberties and equality, ethnic and religious turmoils are politically destabilising society. Social mobility and increased opportunity undermine the traditional hierarchy and caste structure, breeding envy, resentment and strife.

Just across India's northern border, China's post-Mao leaders defend a neo-authoritarian approach, credited for having brought economic miracles in Singapore, Taiwan, and South-Korea. Striving to introduce a market economy while strengthening political control, they want economic openness coupled with political repression. Indignant at the Chinese government's brutal infringement of fundamental freedoms, the West is at the same time awed by China's relative social stability and rapid economic growth.

Is Rawls's theory able to evaluate the justice (or injustice) of the Indian and Chinese development policies? It may lack appropriate tools. Will the Rawlsian [first] principle of equal basic liberty consistently (as within democratic societies) disapprove of China's infringement of basic liberties, which is justified by the regime as necessary to ensure aggregate economic advantage? To what extent can a less-developed society like India, working from Rawls's principles of justice, take away certain freedoms from its citizens in order to ease poverty and social instability? Is justice as fairness appropriate for some or all less-developed societies, in which the social-economic conditions are too poor to establish a fully adequate scheme of equal basic liberties as prescribed by Rawls's principles of justice, but not too harsh to preclude all fruitful co-operation?

The important issues of justice under unfavourable circumstances have not been directly addressed by Rawls until very recently.[8] At the heart of the above questions is the concern that justice as fairness may appear irrelevant on an economically less developed country, in which the fully adequate scheme of basic liberties required by Rawls's first principle is not immediately available. Such situations may require a compromise on basic liberties.

But justice as fairness, especially as Rawls has viewed it since the 1980s, has grown less compromising. He insists that when parties at the original position choose the priority of the first principle over the second, this "rules out exchanges ('trade-offs', as economists say) between the basic rights and liberties covered by the first principle and the social and economic advantages regulated by the difference principle."[9] From the point of view of the original position, no trade-off is allowed, period.

Rawls's ambivalence in this regard may permit critics to ponder on the defect of Rawls's assumptions and its consequences. As Thomas Pogge pointed out, Rawls's failure to address matters of justice (or injustice) in underdeveloped countries may mean that

> Rawls follows [the] tradition in treating national borders as moral watersheds. Only within a national territory and the population it defines does he view the focus on the least advantaged as appropriate. He thereby cir-

> cumvents a crucial moral question, which his theory ought to *answer*, namely whether the institutionalisation of national borders really has this magical moral force of shielding us from (or reducing the force of) the moral claims of "foreigners."[10]

To take national borders as the borders of moral responsibility could be problematic because the political institutions of states have been historically drawn and redrawn. Their legitimacy is the problem, not the criterion, of justification. Political regimes in most less-developed societies (as well as some developed ones) have contributed to the deprivations and inequalities found in these societies.

The problem here is not so much with the fact of trade-offs between individual liberties and social-economic advancement. There is no social world without loss, as Isaiah Berlin observed. Or, the two may in fact enhance each other. The difficulty lies in deciding to what extent Rawls's theory would allow liberties to be regulated if needed for economic gains in a poor country. Rawls seems to rank political liberties higher (i.e. more basic) than other basic liberties. And he of course does not regard an unchecked infringement of these liberties (such as arbitrary detention or executions) as desirable.

The conception of justice (the two principles and the priority rule) provides no clear guidance for limiting a state's power in restricting citizens' basic liberties in the name of economic well-being. The issue is complicated further by the absence of democratic representative government in most developing countries. In such circumstances of unequal political power, whose economic interest would benefit from a trade-off of citizens's basic liberties? This lack of guidance in Rawls's theory on the matter of justice in less-developed societies indicates its inapplicability to unfavourable social-economic conditions.

Extendibility: Efforts and Failures

In the *Theory*, Rawls has made an effort to "extend" his theory to the international society of nation-states. He makes further use of the device of original position. He asks us to visualise parties as representatives of different nations choosing the principles to regulate their conduct in international relations. These representatives are deprived of various kinds of information.

> ... they know nothing about the particular circumstances of their own society, its power and strength in comparison with other nations, nor do they know their place in their own society ... [They] are allowed only enough knowledge to make a rational choice to protect their interests but not so much that the more fortunate among them can take advantage of their special situation.[11]

This position is supposed to be fair and non-biased. It excludes social and historical contingencies that might affect nation-states' decisions to choose the principles of international justice. In Rawls's view, the principles that are selected under such conditions determine justice between nations. They include, among others, the "principle of equality": peoples organised as states are independent and have certain fundamental equal rights. As one consequence of this principle, they choose the principle of self-determination and the right of self-defence.[12]

However, this exercise is not at all an outreach to nations with different domestic regimes from those guided by the two principles of justice. When Rawls applies the original position at the multi-national level, he assumes that the two principles have been agreed to domestically in each of the nations at the original position. Parties in the international original position are representatives of just societies. The national interests of each of these nations have already been defined or restricted by the two principles of justice.

He assumes:

> ... we have already derived the principles of justice as these apply to societies as units and to the basic structure. Imagine also that the various principles of natural duty and of obligation that apply to individuals have been adopted. Thus the persons in the original position have agreed to the principles of right as these apply to their own society and to themselves as members of it.[13]

Restricted by the principles of justice in this manner, these nations are not eager for world power; nor are they going to wage war for purposes of economic or territorial gains; and the basic liberties of their citizens are guaranteed.

This early effort by Rawls to extend his theory thus has reached little further than the borders of his kind of just societies. This move is insufficient to demonstrate that Rawls's theory is not limited to Western liberal political culture. His theory, moreover, has not addressed the issue of why other (non-Western) cultures *should* be judged by the liberal notion of justice.

A slightly different account appears in an unpublished manuscript.[14] There, Rawls proposes that justice as fairness imposes *indirect* constraints on a non-democratic regime's domestic institutions. The selected principles of international justice impose what he calls "downward constraints" on domestic practices, meaning that, as soon as the principles of justice among states have been adopted, they put constraints on domestic violations of basic liberties and human rights. And the represented states are not required to have just domestic institutions beforehand in order to join other states to choose principles of international justice.[15] Rawls implies that it is possible that a non-democratic society, as long as it abides by certain international principles of justice (such as the principle of self-determination), could thus become domestically just. But history has not worked in favour of this hypothesis.

For any conception of international justice, there is a real need to account for international interventions in order to deliver humanitarian aid to save lives amid grave disasters and ethnic conflicts. In a recent speech, Rawls tries to confront the challenge that his political liberalism does not account for this sense of justice beyond liberal democratic societies.[16] He declares that his liberal views, if successfully clarified, can be shown to be "universal in their reach" and able to "explain how human rights hold for the domestic institutions of all societies as members in good standing in a well-ordered society of peoples." He hopes that this would remove the "worry," as shared by this author, that "these liberal views apply only to liberal democratic societies and are prejudicial to other cultures when extended further."[17] To respond to criticisms and some efforts to test the limitation of his theory,[18] Rawls now makes it clear that his conception can look "outward" to non-liberal peoples.

His effort consists in working out a case for one type of non-liberal societies — the so-called hierarchical societies — to accept "the law of peoples" (which is said to be an extension of justice as fairness to the non-liberal societies). Rawls's hierarchical societies satisfy three conditions: they are non-expansionist, legitimate in the eyes of their own people, and observant of basic human rights.[19] By "basic human rights," Rawls refers to certain "minimum rights" such as the rights to "means of subsistence and security (the right to life), to liberty (freedom from slavery, serfdom and forced occupations) and (personal) property, as well as to formal equality as expressed by the rules of natural justice (for example, that similar cases be treated similarly)."[20] Presumably, the right to freedom from slavery, serfdom and forced occupations should include political liberty to participate in political affairs, since abolishing slavery partly means equal political rights. These basic rights should also include for women the freedom from subjugation, since gender inequality often means that women are forced into certain occupations. If Rawls's "hierarchical society" could respect all these rights, such a society would hardly differ from a contemporary liberal democratic society.

The hierarchical society is selected by Rawls to be his test case, which determines whether his theory is extendable to non-liberal societies. The difficulty seems to be that societies satisfying these conditions rarely exist in reality. Perhaps, in a charitable reading, Rawls is not really interested in identifying one type of non-liberal society that can accept a set of international laws built on liberal ideas of justice (such as the ideas of equal liberties and opportunity, their priority over claims of the general good, measures assuring equal adequate means to make effective use of liberties.)[21] He seems to be testing the boundary of reasonableness: what are the conditions for a society to be reasonable, without necessarily being liberal democratic? If this is what motivates him to make the "hierarchical society" a test case, then the fact that such a "hierarchical society" is virtually non-existent does not refute his account of the extendibility of liberal ideas of justice.

Moreover, his notion of hierarchical societies can then be understood as a notion of the minimum conditions for a reasonable society. These conditions for a reasonable society are less stringent than the conditions for a liberal democratic society. And these conditions are modelled on human reason rather than on liberal ideas. If such a notion of reasonable society is plausible, then Rawls can be said to have made a case for the extendibility of his theory of justice to all reasonable societies, including liberal societies. However, for such a notion to be plausible, Rawls needs to *explain* why a minimally reasonable society has to satisfy *these* particular conditions.

Let us suppose that Rawls's theory is thus extendable beyond the borders of liberal democratic states. But how far has it been extended? What about nations that are neither liberal democratic nor "hierarchical"? For Rawls, these would be the outlaw regimes since they do not accept and abide by the law of peoples. How would Rawls's theory extend to these regimes? His solution is to form a forum of law-abiding nations (liberal and hierarchical) to condemn outlaw regimes for expansionist wars and violations of basic human rights. And this federation of peoples should also impose economic sanctions and suspend military aid. The purpose, Rawls says, is to bring outlaw regimes, eventually, into the track of the law of liberal and hierarchical peoples. Regardless of the plausibility of this new approach, Rawls can no longer be blamed for eluding questions of justice (and injustice) in the global context.

Nevertheless, Rawls remains reluctant to defend the perspective of political liberalism as better or more plausible than that of outlaw regimes. He is only willing to go so far as to say that liberal societies can judge the outlaw regimes from their own liberal point of view, for this is the view that they consider sound and satisfactory, according to their accepted criteria. Deeply entrenched in their political tradition and discourse, they will not deliberate on these issues in any other way.

If Rawls's new proposal succeeds in extending a liberal view to other nations or to the international arena, it certainly has not extended Rawls's own conceptions of justice as fairness, the blueprint for a just and stable society of free and equal persons deeply divided by their religious and philosophical beliefs. For instance if we further inquire what has presumably been extended to the hierarchical societies, we find that it is not the idea of justice as fairness, but some more general idea about the procedure of constructing justice, which is related to the idea of social contract. Nor are the two principles of justice thus extended, since the law of peoples is composed of different principles.[22] This makes it difficult to conclude that Rawls's own theory of justice *has been shown* to be extendable outward to non-liberal nations.

Moreover, when Rawls uses the contractual device to construct domestic justice, he legitimises this use by referring to the accepted ideas within the liberal democratic political culture. Now, using the contractual device to construct international justice, which will be applied to non-democratic (hierarchical) nation-states as well, he does not have a body of general liberal ideas accepted among these nations to refer to and to draw support from. How would he then legitimise the use of contractual devices at the international level?

Rawls's proposed solution to the above-mentioned problems is less than satisfactory. The main thrust of his theory are the radical projects, first, to justify a liberal constitutional democracy, or its basic structure, as it is pitted against aristocracy, slavery, one-party dictatorship, and all other forms of authoritarian regimes, and second, to present a theory that is not grounded on any particular religious, philosophical or cultural perceptions. Such a theory is expected to withstand the charge of being Western or liberally biased. This potential power, however, seemingly got lost in Rawls's often painstakingly constructed course of arguments. The perceived difficulties with the foundation and the extendibility of Rawls's theory have obscured in my view the most promising potential of Rawls's theory of justice — a firm and systematic defence of liberal democratic institutions against totalitarian or authoritarian repression, and feasible course of institutional transformation in non-democratic and less-developed societies.

NOTES

1. John Rawls (1971) *A Theory of Justice* (Harvard University Press, Cambridge, Massachusetts).

2. See Charles Beitz (1979) *Political Theory and International Relations* (Princeton University Press), Thomas Pogge (1989) *Realizing Rawls* (Cornell University Press), and Brian Barry (1989) *Theories of Justice* (University of California Press).
3. Rawls, *Political Liberalism*, (New York: Columbia University Press, 1993) p. 4.
4. *Political Liberalism*, p. 40.
5. *Political Liberalism*, p. xxvi.
6. *Political Liberalism*, p. xx.
7. This is what he calls the "priority rule," which prescribes that the first principle (equal basic liberties) has a priority over the second principle (the fair equal opportunity principle and the difference principle), and that the equal opportunity principle has a priority over the difference principle (*Theory*, pp. 243-250).
8. In "The law of peoples," in Stephen Shute and Susan Hurley, ed. (1993) *On Human Rights*, The Oxford Amnesty Lectures 1993 (New York, Basic Books), Rawls considers the case of justice *between* nations, liberal and non-liberal, but not the issue of justice within non-democratic and/or less-developed societies.
9. Rawls, "Justice as fairness": a brief statement, unpublished manuscript.
10. Pogge, op.cit., p. 10.
11. Rawls, *Theory*, p. 378.
12. Ibid., p. 378.
13. Ibid., pp. 377-38.
14. "Justice as fairness" (1989). Also see the Appendix to "Two themes: political constructivism, political liberalism," unpublished manuscript (1990).
15. "Justice as fairness," p. 151.
16. See "The law of peoples." Rawls avoided this question in previous writings. It was said to be a "separate question" that he would not consider in the theory of justice. (Fairness as Justice, p. 33).
17. *Political Liberalism*, p. xiv. Also "The law of peoples."
18. See Beitz (1979), Pt. III, Pogge (1989), Pt. III, David Richards (1971) *Reasons for Action* (Oxford, Oxford University Press), pp. 138-141, and Barry (1989).
19. "The law of peoples," pp. 2, 16-17.
20. Ibid., p. 17.
21. "The law of peoples," p. 8.
22. They include principles such as that "[p]eoples (as organised by their governments) are free and independent and their freedom and independence is to be respected by other people," and that "[p]eoples are equal parties to their own agreements."

STUDY QUESTIONS

1 What rights in The Universal Declaration of Human Rights would you take to be central to liberal societies? What sorts of rights specified in the Declaration are ones not explicitly acknowledged in the American context? Should they be? Why or why not?

2 What evidence do Pollis and Schwab provide to substantiate their claims that "the political philosophy of liberalism has dominated the conceptualization" of human rights and that human rights as defined by the West are meaningless in most states in the world?

3 Do you think Pollis and Schwab are right to suggest that we can reformulate human rights so that they truly reflect universal values underlying the multiplicity of philosophies and divergent beliefs in the world? Why or why not? What sorts of human rights would fit this requirement?

4 Like Pollis and Schwab, Inada thinks non-Western cultures tend to value the community and relationships in it over the individual rights to freedom and property emphasized in the West. According to Inada, how do soft relationships as described in Buddhist beliefs exemplify these values?

5 Explain what Inada means by hard relationships by outlining how the values underlying these kinds of relationships are evident in Western philosophical thinkers such as Hobbes and Rawls. Evaluate Inada's attempt to use the Buddhist understanding of soft relationships as a way of reconceiving the Western notion of human rights.

6 What arguments does Drydyk use to answer the claim by Pollis and Schwab that human rights are meaningless in most places in the world?

7 Drydyk takes up the challenge posed by Pollis and Schwab to reformulate human rights by making use of the notion of a "global public sphere of moral deliberation." What does he mean by this? Can it be used to avoid Eurocentrism? Why or why not?

8 Drydyk uses the phenomena of the "globalization of subcontracting and informalization of labour" not only as a call for an international movement to address the violation of labour rights, but as a way of formulating a full set of human rights that are sensitive to conditions in various social and political contexts. Is the case he presents convincing? Why or why not?

9 How does Rawls defend the idea of the primacy of justice? What is the original position? What purpose is served by the veil of ignorance? What principles of justice emerge from the original position? Do you agree that these are the principles that would be chosen in the original position? Why or why not?

10 The first principle of justice takes priority over the second and outlines the fundamental liberty rights of individuals. What are these liberty rights? What is the purpose of the second principle and what is specified in it? In your view, does the second principle support an interpretation of Rawls as a weak or strong welfare theorist? Defend your answer.

11 Is the problem of Western biases as outlined by the other authors in this chapter evident in Rawls's principles of justice? If so, does it undermine the possibility of giving Rawls's principles of justice universal application? Why or why not?

12 Explain and evaluate the two problems with Rawls's theory of justice that are identified by Xiaorong Li: 1) rather than assuming the ideas and values in a liberal democratic tradition, Rawls needs to provide arguments for his theory of justice that are "freestanding"; and 2) without these arguments, Rawls's theory of justice has limited applicability to other cultures.

13 Li does think that Rawls's principles of justice can have universal application and views it as a defect of his theory that it fails to address matters of justice in the case of human rights violations in places like India and China. Do you agree? Why or why not?

14 Take a position on the question of the possibility or moral justifiability of applying Rawls's principles of justice to non-Western settings by outlining and evaluating how the different authors in this chapter would answer that question.

SUGGESTED READINGS

Ake, Claude. "The African Context of Human Rights." *Africa Today*, v. 34, no. 142 (1987): 5-13.

An-Na'im, Abdullahi Ahmed. "Islam, Islamic Law and the Dilemma of Cultural Legitimacy for Universal Human Rights." In *Asian Perspectives on Human Rights* edited by Claude E. Welch and Virginia Leary. Boulder, CO: Westview Press, 1990.

An-Na'im, Abdullahi Ahmed and Francis M. Deng (editors). *Human Rights in Africa: Cross-Cultural Perspectives*. Washington: The Brookings Institution, 1990.

Baier, Annette C. "The Need For More Than Justice." *Canadian Journal of Philosophy*, Supplementary vol. 13 (1987): 41-56.

Bahar, Saba. "Human Rights are Women's Right: Amnesty International and the Family." *Hypatia*, v. 11, no. 1 (Winter 1996): 105-134.

Bell, Daniel A. "The East Asian Challenge to Human Rights: Reflections on an East West Dialogue." *Human Rights Quarterly*, v. 18, no. 3 (1996): 641-667.

Bunch, Charlotte. "Women's Rights as Human Rights: Toward a Re-Vision of Human Rights." *Human Rights Quarterly*, v. 12, no. 4 (1990): 486-498.

Donnelly, Jack. "Human Rights and Human Dignity: An Analytical Critique of Non-Western Conceptions of Human Rights." *The American Political Science Review*, v. 76 (1982): 303-316.

Dworkin, Ronald. "Taking Rights Seriously." In *Taking Rights Seriously*. Harvard University Press, 1978: 184-205.

Etzioni, Amitai. "Cross-Cultural Judgments: The Next Steps." *Journal of Social Philosophy*, v. XXVIII, no. 3 (Winter 1997): 5-15.

Howard, Judith A. and Carolyn Allen (editors). "Reflections on the Fourth World Conference on Women and NGO Forum '95." *Signs: Journal of Women in Culture and Society*, v. 22, no. 1 (1996): 181-226.

Li, Xiaorong. "'Asian Values' and the Universality of Human Rights." *Report from the Institute of Philosophy & Public Policy*, v. 16, no. 2 (Spring 1996): 18-23.

Nedelsky, Jennifer. "Reconceiving Rights as Relationship." *Review of Constitutional Studies*, v. 1, no. 1 (1993): 1-26.

Nielsen, Kai. "Relativism and Wide Reflective Equilibrium." *The Monist*, v. 76 (1993): 316-332.

Okin, Susan Moller. *Justice, Gender, and the Family*. New York: Basic Books, 1989.

Pollis, Adamantia. "Liberal, Socialist, and Third World Perspectives on Human Rights." In *Toward a Human Rights Framework*. New York: Praeger, 1982.

Sandel, Michael. *Liberalism and the Limits of Justice*. 2nd edition. Cambridge, England: Cambridge University Press, 1998.

Walzer, Michael. "Membership and Justice." In *Spheres of Justice*. New York: Basic Books, 1983.

Williams, Patricia. *The Alchemy of Race and Rights*. Cambridge, Mass.: Harvard University Press, 1991.

CHAPTER TWO

DEMOCRACY, JUSTICE, AND SOCIAL TRANSFORMATION

The readings in this chapter are designed to test the conceptions of human rights and justice examined in Chapter One of Part I by applying them to particular social conditions and political contexts in various parts of the world. Of course, the readings represent only a narrow range of the interesting contexts in which conceptions of human rights and justice could be explored. The ones selected raise vexing questions about human rights and justice and highlight problems presented by the tendencies of ethnocentrism, Eurocentrism, universalism, and essentialism outlined in the introduction to Chapter One. This chapter begins where the previous one ends, with the notion of democracy as understood and defended by liberal theorists.

The question of foundations for liberal democratic values is taken up by Amy Gutmann who argues that democracy does not need foundations that rest on self-evident truths about human nature, human rights, rationality, or politics. Instead, justifications can be given for why democracies as they currently exist in various non-ideal forms can provide the conditions for human flourishing. She characterizes non-ideal democracies by such features as guarantees of free speech, press, and association; the right to run for political office; the rule of law; and frequent and procedurally fair elections. She argues that because these features enhance human dignity and maximize social welfare, they justify non-ideal democracies as better than non-ideal non-democracies. However, Gutmann acknowledges that this justification does not satisfy the political philosopher's goal of articulating a democratic *ideal* that can tell us what kind of democracy is most justified. She then provides a brief outline of this ideal in her account of deliberative democracy.

Next, Chenyang Li takes China to be a good context for exploring the clash and potentially fruitful relationships between democratic and non-democratic values. Li's answer to the question of what kind of democracy is needed in China is that China needs democracy that values individual liberty, equality, and pluralism—values central to the discussion of justice and rights in Chapter One. Li answers the question of whether these values are compatible with those in the Confucian tradition that is so strong in China by examining and rejecting attempts by theorists to find compatibilities between democracy and Confucianism. He argues that Confucianism has no place for the concept of rights because there is no need for them in the society Confucius envisioned, where an emphasis on duty, loyalty, and responsibility places value on paternalism over individual liberty and autonomy. Li argues that defenses of Confucianism without democracy or democracy without Confucianism, as well as attempts to integrate the two are all misguided and threaten the integrity of each. Li maintains that both sets of values are worthwhile and desirable and proposes that they co-exist in China in the same way that the different value systems of Confucianism, Taoism, and Buddhism have co-existed in harmony in the lives of Chinese individuals.

The third reading challenges the account of democracy assumed thus far, both in the theoretical work on human rights and justice in Chapter One and in the first two readings in this chapter. Susan Babbitt argues that Western liberal accounts of democracy assume a particular conception of human rights and of liberty, a conception that is unquestioned and undefended in criticisms by Westerners that Cuba violates human rights and individual freedom. Babbitt points out that these criticisms persist even in the face of evidence that

Cuba guarantees rights to work, health, education, and social assistance in its Constitution and provides better medical care and education than do many developed countries. She argues that the negative assessment of Cuba is rooted in the philosophical assumptions that have shaped a world dominant view about what constitutes democracy, human rights, freedom, and human flourishing. These assumptions have made it possible to ignore the explanations that Cuba has offered about its history and its struggle for democracy and respect for human rights.

To understand the option presented by Cuba is to understand that its choice is to pursue a moral vision that creates new values and new possibilities for being human. Babbitt uses this account of Cuba's story to argue that that country's single party system, for example, is not in itself evidence that Cuba is undemocratic because it can be seen as providing the conditions for creating a just and humane society.

Babbitt holds that an account of the particular history, economic struggle, and dimensions of power in Cuba is essential to a proper understanding of the country. Such sensitivity to context is also important to Jennifer Llewellyn's discussion of South Africa. The specific case of South Africa provides a rare opportunity to analyze what justice demands in transitional cases, in which countries move from a past of gross injustices and violations of human rights to a future committed to building a rights-respecting culture. The system of apartheid in South Africa resulted in the systematic racial oppression of the black majority by a small but powerful white minority. Llewellyn argues that what we can learn from the dismantling of apartheid and the interpretation of justice of South Africa's Truth and Reconciliation Commission can be applied to conceptions of justice in general.

The South African Truth and Reconciliation Commission was given the mandate to deal with gross injustices of apartheid, but some critics argue that the Commission is devoid of justice because it allows amnesty for disclosure of incidences of wrongdoing. Llewellyn argues that this criticism relies on an understanding of justice as retributive, a procedure of discovering and punishing *individuals* for wrongs done in the past. Llewellyn favors a conception of justice as restorative, a conception that is particularly suited to transitional contexts, but has broad application beyond them. Restorative justice is forward-looking and relational in nature; thus, particular circumstances and contexts determine the set of practices that are appropriate for dealing with injustices on the road to restoring relationships in which all members of a community are treated equally and with respect. Llewellyn outlines the ways in which South Africa's Truth and Reconciliation Commission is modeled on a restorative conception of justice and highlights the challenges a restorative model might pose.

Another sort of context that provides a rare opportunity to examine questions of justice and rights are the claims by various nations to self-determination or secession. What conditions justify peoples in declaring themselves a nation or separating themselves from one? Omar Dahbour answers these questions by distinguishing between what he refers to as Popular Self-Determination (PSD), cases in which a population of an already existing country lacks and lays claim to self-government, and National Self-Determination (NSD), cases in which nationalities make a claim for status as independent states. The former case, argues Dahbour, is widely recognized in international law as based on the right of a people to determine their own affairs without interference from other countries. He takes the case of the latter to be less clear than the former and more problematic in international law. Those who defend NSD argue that self-determination is an attribute of nationalities constituted by an encompassing group with a common character or culture and not of peoples who are members of already existing countries. Dahbour argues that what characterizes encompassing groups is that persons do not choose to enter such groups and cannot always leave them at will. Political communities, by contrast, are characterized by their associative groups. Individuals associate for particular purposes and on the basis of mutual needs and interests. Dahbour raises several objections to NSD: it hinders the self-determination of individuals; it precludes the recognition of mutual needs and interests in existing communities; and it exacerbates international rivalries by giving legitimacy to all claims to nationhood.

DEMOCRACY, PHILOSOPHY, AND JUSTIFICATION

Amy Gutmann

Amy Gutmann is Laurance S. Rockefeller University Professor of Politics and Director of the University Center for Human Values at Princeton University. She is the author of Liberal Equality *(Cambridge, 1980) and* Democratic Education *(Princeton, 1987); co-author with Anthony Appiah of* Color Conscious: The Political Morality of Race *(Princeton, 1996); and editor of* Multiculturalism: Examining the Politics of Recognition *(Princeton, 1994).*

Gutmann answers the question "does democracy need foundations?" by clarifying what is meant by both democracy and foundations. She argues that if we think of democracy in non-ideal terms as those political institutions characterized by features such as free speech, the right to vote, competitive elections, and the rule of law, there is no need for foundations in the strong sense of features that rely on self-evident truths about human nature, human rights, or rationality. Gutmann defends a version of ideal democracy that she refers to as deliberative democracy, one that is based on moral and political argument and justification and is neither foundationalist nor anti-foundationalist.

Does democracy need foundations? We cannot adequately answer the foundationalist question without first asking how democracy is best defended. When we answer this question, however, the foundational question becomes moot. Democracy needs justifications, not foundations—at least, not foundations in the strict sense suggested by Richard Rorty and other antifoundationalists. If we cannot justify democracy, then neither can we know what kind of democracy is worth defending. If we can justify democracy, then we should not worry about whether our justification is, in the strict sense, foundationalist. Justifications need not be foundationalist or antifoundationalist. I will first suggest some reasons why this is so, and then briefly sketch a justification of deliberative democracy that is neither foundationalist nor antifoundationalist.

Foundationalism in political philosophy, if it is not to be trivially identified with any reason-giving defense of a conception of politics, is the claim that justification must rest upon truths about human nature, human rights, rationality, or politics that are self-evident, rationally incontestable, or axiomatic. Does an adequate theoretical defense of democracy need foundations in this nontrivial sense? Before answering this question, we should be clear not to confuse it with the more practical question of whether actual democracies need to rely upon philosophy in addition to, or instead of, education, elections, legislation, constitutions, and force, if necessary, in order to defend themselves against threats to their well-being that variously come from intolerance, apathy, corruption, and violent aggression. We are rather asking the theoretical question of what it takes to sustain the claim that democracy is a justified (or the most justified) form of government

First, let us consider democracy as it is often understood today to describe an increasingly common set of political institutions the world over, for which Robert Dahl coined the term "polyarchy." Polyarchies, or what we might call nonideal democ-

---

Reprinted with permission of the publisher from *Democracy and Difference: Contesting the Boundaries of the Political*, edited by Seyla Benhabib (Princeton: © 1996, Princeton University Press): 340–347.

racies, are characterized, at minimum, by guarantees of free political speech, press, association, and equal suffrage for all adults, the right of all adults above a certain age to run for political office, the rule of law, and frequent, competitive elections that are procedurally fair. How can nonideal democracy best justify itself against undemocratic forms of government?

Democracy, Winston Churchill noted, is the worst form of government except all the others. He was referring to actual, nonideal democracies and comparing them to nonideal nondemocracies. Many people today, many of whom were raised in nondemocratic societies, defend nonideal democracy on Churchillian grounds even though their nascent democratic governments are falling far short of satisfying many of their basic needs. Why are nonideal democracies better than their nonideal alternatives? Political philosophers have offered several practically compatible (yet theoretically distinct) reasons, the first having to do with the centrality of democratic liberties to human dignity, the second with the instrumental value of democratic liberties in resisting political tyranny, and the third connecting democratic liberties with the maximization of social welfare. The moral and intellectual force of these (contestable) reasons notwithstanding, the Churchillian defense of democracy is largely negative and therefore uninspiring to many citizens of nonideal democracies who take for granted the basic accomplishments of democratic government and are aspiring for something more. The Churchillian defense of nonideal democracy is also doubly inadequate to the aspirations of political philosophy. Because it stops short of articulating a full-fledged democratic ideal, it does not expect enough of democracy and also fails to tell us what *kind* of democracy is most justified. It therefore provides only a partial defense of even nonideal democracy.

Nonetheless, to say that nonideal democracy is better than the available nonideal alternatives is to say something practically and theoretically important. The Churchillian defense offers some insight into why, despite the failures of every existing democratic government to secure for all its citizens some basic goods such as an adequate income, employment, health care, and education, most citizens of nonideal democracies, including many who are deprived of these basic goods, support them over their undemocratic alternatives.

Notice that the Churchillian defense of democracy is neither foundational nor antifoundational. It is agnostic on the question of whether democracy rests on certain rationally undeniable facts about human nature and politics. (We could say the defense is foundational in the loose sense of offering reasons for defending nonideal democracies against their undemocratic alternatives but this is to confuse foundationalism with reasonableness. Antifoundationalists do not deny the need to give reasons in defense of democracy against undemocratic—or less democratic—alternatives.) Despite its lack of what we might call Cartesian foundations, the Churchillian defense of democracy is as salient in today's world as it was in Churchill's, and its force is not limited to any particular culture, or a few idiosyncratic ones.

Why should anyone think that the Churchillian position constitutes even a partial justification of nonideal democracy, as opposed to an indication of what "we democrats" just happen (without any reason) to believe in by virtue of our socialization? Ordinary people, not only political philosophers, think about whether and why they should support nonideal democratic governments rather than undemocratic ones. The theoretical question of whether nonideal democracy is justified is typically connected to a practical question: is this nonideal democracy deserving of support? Now, what else could justify the precarious support for democracy among former subjects of Soviet-style communism but the comparative advantage of nonideal democratic governments over nonideal autocratic governments? And what else but the value of civil and political liberties could account for the moral strength of nonideal democracy? The short-run economic benefits of democracy have been conspicuous by their absence. The claim that the long-run benefits of democracy outweigh its short-term costs is doubly dubious, first for sacrificing the well-being of present people for future ones, and second for its unwarranted confidence in such long-term social forecasting and calculating. Democracy needs to be justified to the people who are bound by its practices and policies. Long-term benefits may be there; yet without the basic liberties that democracy brings, those benefits would be insufficient to justify nonideal democracies to people here and now.

Consider this typical story about the extraordinary economic problems facing the new Baltic republics, featured on the front page of the *New York Times*, April 10, 1993. This story happened to be about Lithuania, whose citizens had experienced over the past year one of the worst economic situations of their lifetimes. Inflation in consumer goods was over 600 percent, and inflation in agricultural products over 700 percent. Industrial output had declined over 50 percent, and new housing had declined by over 20 percent. Unemployment was estimated at 200,000 (out of 3.7 million), an enormous shock to a citizenry completely unaccustomed to worrying about job security. Not surprisingly, Lithuanian citizens have voted out of office the more liberal president (Landsbergis) and voted in a former communist, newly turned social democratic president (Brazauskas). What is surprising is that they did not vote for a return to authoritarian rule.

The story featured an ordinary citizen, Rimantas Pirmaitis, who had, along with many of his compatriots, joined the protests of 1989-90 that led to Lithuania's democratization and independence from Soviet rule. Pirmaitis was employed under the communist regime as a construction engineer, where he made a decent living. But under the new democracy he has been reduced to selling flowers from a street stand in central Vilnius to support his family. He nonetheless remains a democrat, notwithstanding runaway inflation. "But we are past the time for marches and anthems," he says. "What we need now is something real, something we can eat and touch."

Were it not the case that the civil and political liberties of a democratic society are as real as economic benefits, the belief in a *democratic* Lithuania would be considerably less defensible. Although liberties are inedible and untouchable, they are not always overlooked by people who are struggling to survive. An appreciation of basic freedoms and their centrality to human dignity, self-respect, and well-being often makes nonideal democracy both apparently and really better than its alternatives. An understanding of the degrading experience of people living under the undemocratic alternatives to nonideal democracies may be sufficient for a nonfoundationlist defense of nonideal democracy. This defense is distinct from that of an ideal conception of democracy, but the favorable comparison with available nonideal alternatives is a strong defense nonetheless. The comparison provides reasons to people who doubt that democracy is better than the alternatives, as well as to people who are drawn to democracy but wonder why. Although much more may be said in defense of nonideal democracy, this much should suffice to show that justification, at least at the nonideal level, need not be either foundationalist or antifoundationalist to be reasonable, and useful as well.

But political philosophers aspire to something more than the defense of nonideal democracy as we now know it. We try to construct out of our inheritance, and imagine beyond it, a more fully justifiable set of social and political institutions, which we can call democracy without qualification, or at least without neologism. Political philosophers who defend a democratic *ideal* may therefore seem committed to some form of foundationalism. What else but some self-evident or rationally incontrovertible truth could support our claims for an ideal conception of democracy, which would (if democratically instituted) realize the political ideal of collective self-government? How else are we to interpret and defend such an ideal?

Suppose that a fully justified democracy authorizes all adult members of society to share, either directly or through their accountable representatives, in deliberatively shaping their collective life in a way that is consistent with respecting the basic liberties and opportunities of all individuals. Suppose also that deliberation is the give-and-take of argument in a public form (not necessarily a legislature) that aims at, and results in, provisionally justified decision-making, decisions that are respectful of the basic liberties and opportunities of all members of society. Deliberation also helps shape our understanding of basic opportunities and liberties. But if the results of democratic deliberation are to be provisionally justified, they must respect the basic liberties and opportunities of all citizens on some reasonable understanding. The arguments offered in a public forum also should be reasonable by some public standard. Deliberation at various levels of government and in different political arenas is, as far as I can discern, the most legitimate means of settling principled conflicts over social justice, conflicts that are inescapable in any free society.

This is an abbreviated outline of one interpretation of deliberative democracy. An interpretation of deliberative democracy as a political ideal, suitably expanded and more fully defended, is bound not only to be incomplete and controversial but also to be reasonably contested. Prominent among its democratic contesters are what might be called populist democracy, participatory democracy, perfectionist liberal democracy, and ultraconstitutionalist democracy. Deliberative democracy has two important advantages over these and other democratic alternatives that bear on the foundationalist question.

The first advantage of deliberative democracy is its recognition of the provisional nature of justification in politics. The empirical and moral understandings of citizens change not only over time and social space but also by virtue of deliberative interchange, the give-and-take of sometimes complementary, often conflicting, political insights and arguments (including conflicts over what counts as the political realm). Deliberative democracy therefore leaves a lot of room for "difference." Differences in practices and policies that result from deliberation among an inclusive citizenry are democratically legitimate, even if no one knows whether they are just in the strict foundational sense. Whether or not foundational claims are metaphysically possible is a moot point as far as the ideal of deliberative democratic politics is concerned. The alternative is not antifoundationalism, but fairly conducted collective deliberations that yield provisionally justified practices and policies.

A second significant advantage of deliberative democracy is its compatibility with some other conceptions of democracy, insofar as these conceptions result from democratic deliberations. Upon deliberation, citizens may decide to institute some form of perfectionist democracy. But if they decide to reject perfectionist policies, then what can philosophy divorced from democratic deliberation say in their favor? Perfectionist critics can say that the standpoint of deliberative democracy is not neutral among democratic (or undemocratic) alternatives. Of course it is not, and it need not claim to be. Critics can also say that deliberative democracy lacks incontestable foundations. Of course it does. There is neither a neutral substitute for foundationalism, as some liberal philosophers have claimed, nor a foundationalist substitute for democracy, as some perfectionist philosophers have suggested.

Defenders of deliberative democracy can offer only a moral and political argument (with the hope that it catches on). The argument, in brief, might be that the legitimate exercise of political authority requires justification to those people who are bound by it, and decision-making by deliberation among free and equal citizens is the most defensible justification anyone has to offer for provisionally settling controversial issues. This justification, once elaborated, would be compatible with respecting many moral and cultural differences within and across societies. If citizens deliberatively decide to constitute themselves as a participatory or perfectionist liberal democracy, then those forms of democracy are also provisionally justified, provided they respect the basic liberties and opportunities of all individuals and leave citizens free to deliberate in the future. (The freedom to deliberate in the future is necessary to ensure that provisional justifications are not treated as foundationalist truths.)

This defense of deliberative democracy is not an example of either foundationalism or antifoundationalism. Foundationalism tells us that we must defend democracy on the basis of human nature, natural rights, or self-evident reason; antifoundationalism tells us that reason has nothing to do with defending democracy. Both perspectives presuppose a metaphysical truth without warrant.

The foundationalist defense, sometimes attributed to Aristotle, bases deliberative democracy on an alleged truth about human nature, that human beings are rational, deliberative animals. According to this defense, only a deliberative democracy expresses the true, rational nature of individuals and offers all people the opportunity to perfect their natures through public deliberation. Every other form of government falls short of this foundational standard, because other forms of government encourage only one or a few people to deliberate on political questions, whereas all human beings are by nature deliberative beings in political as well as personal realms. Is this true? Are all people natural deliberators in politics? Maybe so, maybe not. We really do not know. The claim that people are by their very nature deliberative beings in the strong sense claimed by some Aristotelians is not self-evidently true (or false). It is subject to reasonable doubt (and defense). Far from being axiomatic, such substantive claims about human nature are reasonably contestable, and contested. This foundationalist defense of deliberative democracy does not satisfy foundationalist standards; its claims about human nature are not self-evident, rationally incontestable, or axiomatic. The claim that human beings are natural deliberators is as subject to reasonable doubt as nonfoundationalist claims about democracy. Saying that democracy is grounded in human nature cannot therefore substitute for showing that democracy gives actual people something that is valuable to them, where what is valuable includes a wide range of liberties and opportunities as well as economic well-being.

Saying that democracy needs no foundations does not leave us with anything more than a critical stance toward foundationalists, who claim or expect too much from philosophical argument. To show that democracy does not need foundations does not tell us what we need to say in its defense. We need to say something more than what is suggested by the strong antifoundationlist view, which runs roughly as follows: if we, the members of a democratic cultural community, believe in democracy but democracy happens not to satisfy the best philosophical conception of human nature or basic human needs, then so much the worse for philosophical justifications of democracy. I do not see how our widely shared belief in democracy can suffice to justify imposing a democratic government on disbelieving minorities. We need to say something to them about the political virtues of democracy. Besides, most of us believe in democracy, and in a particular kind of democracy, because we think there are good reasons to defend it against the alternatives. Our reasons will of course come from within some social understandings, but this is not to say that our reasons are therefore unnecessary, or merely a reflection of our upbringing about which we cannot critically reflect. "Our" believing in democracy is not a substitute for our offering arguments in favor of some conception of democracy. Nor is our offering good arguments a substitute for our believing in democracy. The truth in antifoundationalism is that much of what we say is going to be contestable, subject to reasonable doubt. If we take such doubt to be devastating of the philosophical case for democracy then we capitulate to critics of democracy without good cause.

All anyone can do is try to address the doubt. Few political philosophers actually argue that democracy can be defensibly dissociated from a form of deliberative self-government that secures the basic liberties and opportunities of all members of society. Most neglect the importance of deliberation. The neglect of deliberation is untenable because the defense of democracy against traditional hierarchy, enlightened autocracy, liberal perfectionism, ultraconstitutionalism, and other credible political alternatives is weakened to the extent that we imagine a democracy that does not collectively deliberate over controversial matters of political importance. Briefly and roughly, one might say that populist democracy reduces citizenship to formal political rights and majoritarian procedures; participatory democracy not only takes too many meetings but also disrespects those people who would, quite reasonably, rather be represented than represent themselves; ultraconstitutionalism identifies justice with a comprehensive set of substantive principles, as if someone could design a government that institutes the comprehensive set of just policies, known prior to deliberative decision making among citizens or their accountable representatives.

Suppose that, with regard to the many politically controversial matters that divide democratic societies, some philosophers think that they know what is just and do not need to deliberate with other citizens who see things differently in order to figure out what is just. It is quite another question, however, as to whether, in the absence of collective deliberation, their supposedly just policies, which are meant to be socially binding, can be justified to all those other people who are to be bound by them. And it is yet another question as to how a society, without deliberating, can distinguish the philosopher who really knows what is just from all those who are no less convinced that they know, but do not.

If all foundationalists claim is that democracy can be defended by publicly accessible reasons, then we are (almost) all foundationalist. If all antifoundationalists claim is that democracy cannot be deduced from self-evident truths, then we are (almost) all antifoundationalists. But if some kind of deliberative democracy is defensible, then democracy does not need either foundationalism or antifoundationalism. It needs to be liberated from this dead-end debate. Political philosophers can contribute more to both political philosophy and democracy when we stop metatheorizing and start arguing about the substantive problems that animate contemporary politics, including the continually contested question of what *kind* of democracy is most defensible.

CONFUCIAN VALUE AND DEMOCRATIC VALUE

Chenyang Li

Chenyang Li is Associate Professor in the Department of Philosophy and Religious Studies at Monmouth College, Illinois. He has taught philosophy at the University of Alaska, Fairbanks, and Beijing University. He has published articles in the areas of metaphysics, philosophy of language, and comparative philosophy.

Li uses the inevitability of the clash between democracy and Confucianism in China as an opportunity to examine the values underlying each and to explore the possibility of their mutual co-existence. He rejects various theoretical attempts to find compatibilities between democracy and Confucianism and argues that the values associated with each make them inherently incompatible. He further rejects calls for replacing Confucian beliefs and values with democratic ones. Instead Li argues that China needs both democratic and Confucian values and that Confucianism and democracy can and should co-exist independently in China.

Introduction

Samuel P. Huntington asserts that the world is now entering an age of "the clash of civilizations."[1] Specifically, the clash is between democratic Western civilizations and undemocratic civilization in the rest of the world, Confucian and Islamic civilizations in particular. Huntington also suggests that in order for democracy to take roots in a Confucian society, undemocratic elements in Confucianism must be superseded by democratic elements.[2] The purpose of this essay is to examine the future relationship between democracy and Confucianism in the part of the world where they are most likely to clash, namely, China.

1. What democracy is and what China needs

The word "democracy" has been used in so many ways that people today often disagree about exactly what it means. Many controversies about democracy concern whether it is merely a procedural method for political decisions or something more substantive that has value content.[3] Joseph Schumpeter, for example, has proposed as a minimal definition of democracy:

> the democratic method is that institutional arrangement for arriving at political decisions in which individuals acquire the power to decide by means of a competitive struggle for the people's vote.[4]

His use of "democratic method," instead of "democracy," indicates that he takes democracy primarily as a procedural form.

Francis Fukuyama has recently argued that the consolidation of democracy must occur on four levels: ideology, institutions, civil society, and finally, culture. He regards culture as the "deepest level" of democracy.[5] Many people would agree with Fukuyama in as much as democracy penetrates culture and is therefore value-loaded. Jürgen Domes, for instance, also defines democracy primarily as a value-loaded political system. In addition to its formal dimension, Domes characterizes democracy specifically by three principles: liberty, equality, and

---

Reprinted with permission of Kluwer Academic Publishers and Chenyang Li from *Journal of Value Inquiry* 31 (1997): 183–193.

pluralism.[6] This is sometimes said to characterize liberal democracy.

Without a context, it makes little sense to ask whose definition is right. The question we should ask here is, what kind of democracy does China need? I believe the answer is the kind of democracy with the values of individual liberty, equality, and pluralism. These values, as I will show, make the clash between democracy and Confucianism possible. Confucianism is no longer an institutional arrangement, and such a clash cannot take place anywhere but on the dimension of value.

Without the values of individual liberty, equality, and pluralism, democracy as a mere procedure is merely a technique of formality. This technique has been and continues to be misused in China. Unless we make explicit the values found in democracy, the misuse is likely to continue. For example, within the Chinese Communist Party (CCP), democracy as a voting procedure has been practiced. Missing, however, is the value of individual liberty. Within the CCP, members can vote, but the party leaderhip demands absolute loyalty. The value of loyalty takes the place of individual liberty in the current mainland Chinese version of democracy. Even when the voting procedure is carried through, the outcome has almost always been a unanimous decision. In *Democracy in America* Alexis de Tocqueville wrote:

> if a democratic republic, similar to that of the United States, were ever founded in a country where the power of a single individual had previously subsisted, and the effects of a centralized administration had sunk deep into the habits and the laws of the people, I do not hesitate to assert, that in that country a more insufferable despotism would prevail than any which now exists in the monarchical states of Europe; or indeed than any which could be found on this side of the confines of Asia.[7]

When democracy is taken to be merely a voting procedure, it can be counterproductive in countries like China where people have formed the habits of following a centralized administration which they may have mistakenly identified as representing their own interest and to which they habitually render unconditional loyalty. Unless individual liberty is valued, voters will not realize that they ought to feel free in choosing their representatives; and unless voters can freely choose to vote for their candidates, there cannot be true democracy. Here "free choice" does not merely mean choice without external coercion. It also means choosing candidates on the basis of individual liberty. Imagine a people in whom loyalty to their leader is such an overwhelming value that no matter what happens they will always cast their votes for their own leader. Such a so-called democracy would be no better than a tyranny. This form of government is not worth fighting for, except perhaps as a mere preliminary step from totalitarianism to real democracy. What China needs is democracy with the value of individual liberty, equality, and pluralism.[8]

While acknowledging that democracy has institutional forms, I will focus on democracy on a cultural level and consider democracy mainly as a value system which is centered on the rights of individual liberty and equality. In that value system, pluralism is also an important element. If we recognize that democracy is value-loaded, then no matter how we think about democracy and Confucianism, we have to think about how values from both sides interact.[9]

2. Is Confucianism democratic?

Among influential Confucian thinkers Mencius had a thought which is probably closest to one that might be considered democratic and is most often cited by those looking for democratic elements in traditional Chinese thought.[10] Mencius said: "(In a state) the people are the most important; the spirits of the land and grain (guardians of territory) are the next; the ruler is of slight importance."[11] This thought is often called the thought if *min-ben*, or people-rootedness. Some people think this is the model for Chinese democracy. For example, Sun Yat-sen said that Confucius and Mencius more than two thousand years ago already advocated democracy because they advocated the common good and emphasized the importance of the people.[12]

However, Mencius' thought is not democracy as defined by individual liberty and equality. First of all, Mencius' thought does not exclude having a king as the sole decision maker for social affairs. As Shu-hsien Liu properly pointed out, Mencius' idea of people-rootedness and the idea of having a good king mutually depend on each other.[13] When a king makes a decision, he should consider the well-being of the people first.[14] It would be unreasonable if we were to look for a form of government without a king in Mencius. The point here is that Mencius' form of government is what Lin Yutang has called "parental government."[15] It requires a king to treat people as he treats his children *ai min ru zi*. But even though a king considers the well-being of the people first, the form of government is not democratic. For even if a parent has the children's well-being in mind, the parent is the sole decision-maker. As the decision-making power of a parent does not come from children, a king's power comes from Heaven, not from popular free choice. In this picture there is no room for individual liberty and equality, both of which are essential for democracy. This kind of government is at most, in the phrasing of Lincoln, "for the people." It is highly questionable whether it is "of the people." It is clearly not "by the people."

Secondly, the question of whose well-being should be put first has little to do with democracy. A dictator might put the people's well-being first. The Confucian concept of government is government by gentlemen and governance by moral force. But gentlemen may be mistaken in believing that they make decisions on behalf of the people and in their best interests; or they may really represent the best interests of the people, without the people, due to lack of knowledge or wisdom, wanting them to do so. In each case the Confucian form of government would not be democratic.

Among prominent classic Confucian philosophers, Mencius' thought is considered the closest to the idea of democracy.[16] If his idea is not that of real democracy, we can conclude that democracy is not an influential value in traditional Confucianism.

While there may be practical reasons for Confucians today to make Confucianism look democratic, the claim that Confucianism is democratic is seriously flawed and, as I will show later, the move to make Confucianism democratic is misguided.

3. Are Confucianism and democracy compatible?

If democracy has not been at the heart of traditional Chinese culture, are democracy and Confucianism compatible? Liang Shuming, for example, thought that there is no room in Chinese culture for democracy. He wrote that, "it is not that China has not entered democracy, it is rather that China cannot enter democracy."[17] He believed that traditional Chinese value systems alone provide a solid foundation for a good civil society. Mou Tsung-san, a prominent contemporary New-Confucian, sees the inadequacy of traditional Confucianism and believes that through a transformation of the Confucian moral subjectivity into a cognitive subjectivity, Confucianism will provide an adequate foundation for democracy. But it is not clear how such a transformation can actually take place.[18] Mou includes liberty, equality, and human rights in democracy.[19] It is doubtful that these values can be integrated into Confucianism. Shu-hsien Liu, in contrast, sees many difficulties in grafting democracy onto Confucianism and maintains that unless politics is separated from morals, democracy will not find a home in China.[20] Liu is certainly right in thinking that democracy must take the political realm as a social institution. But what about the value content of democracy? If democratic values are to enter the culture, then we cannot ignore the relationship between democratic values and Confucian values.

There are fundamentally conflicting values between democracy and Confucianism. Democracy, as we have seen, presupposes the concept of rights. A democratic society is one in which individual rights are recognized and respected. This requires the recognition that some basic rights of individuals are inalienable. Confucianism, at least in the traditional form, has no place for the concept of rights.[21] It is, however, a serious mistake to think that Confucius left out the concept of rights by negligence. In the ideal society that Confucius envisioned, there is just supposed to be no need for rights. On the issue of whether human nature is good or bad, rights-based theories typically lean toward the view that human nature is bad or flawed. Rights are viewed as the basis for individuals to stand up for themselves.

When others impose on someone, the person can stand on a right. The Confucian social ideal is one of *jen*, which signifies humanity, compassion, and benevolence. Unlike rights-based social theories, which tend to regulate society by giving weapons to the weak to protect themselves, Confucian theory promotes the view that *jen* regulates society and protects the weak by placing moral restraints on the strong and powerful. If all people are to embody *jen* as Confucius wished, no one would inflict pain on others unjustly and everyone would be taken care of.

In Confucianism the primary concern for individuals has to do with duty, not liberty. The Confucian motto is "to return to the observance of the rites through overcoming the self constitutes benevolence (*jen*)."[22] Overcoming ourselves implies suppressing our desires of self-interest, including the desire for individual liberty. For Confucians the first order of a person's social life concerns family life, where liberty is typically not a primary concern.[23] In a family model of society, people are defined by their social roles that come with responsibilities. In Confucianism responsibilities override liberty.

Closely connected to duty is the Confucian notion of loyalty (*zhong*). Loyalty is not only a virtue of the subject to the ruler, but also a virtue among people in general. Replying to Fan Chi's question on the meaning of jen, Confucius said: "Be respectful in private life, be serious (*ching*) in handling affairs, and be loyal in dealing with others."[24] In a broad sense, a child's filial piety to parents and trust between friends are also forms of loyalty. Loyalty implies being bound to other people. As long as people have to be loyal to others, they are not really free in the liberal sense. Thus, there is an essential tension between loyalty and liberty as two values. Of course someone can freely choose to be loyal. But that does not mean that liberty and loyalty, as primary virtues, point in the same direction. Someone can freely choose to be a slave too.

Confucian loyalty becomes even more binding when it is coupled with another cardinal Confucian value, *yi*. Usually translated in English as "righteousness," *yi* has more than one meaning. In a primary sense, *yi* requires that we do not abandon friends when they are in trouble or in need of our help and that we do not let friends down even under extreme circumstances. Heavy emphasis on loyalty and *yi* as central Confucian virtues can be seen throughout history. For instance, in 1948 after Chiang Kai-shek was forced to resign from the presidency of the Republic of China, he still had almost full control of the government. The acting president, Li Tsung-jen, formally in the post, was simply unable to perform his duties without having his own people in the government. A main reason for this was that people in the government had an overwhelmingly strong sense of duty of loyalty to Chiang. The kind of loyalty he felt is almost incomprehensible to many Westerners. In contrast a democratic society such as the United States characteristically lacks for loyalty. Voters are willing to readily withdraw their support from a leader and turn to someone else at almost any time. Elected officials simply cannot count on loyalty from their voters.

As we have seen, a fundamental value for democracy is equality, whereas in Confucianism equality receives only minimal recognition. In Confucianism, while people may have equal opportunities for laboring through the role of an obedient young person to become a respected old person, there is little hope for submissive ministers to rule. Confucians believe that we are what we make ourselves to be. While everyone has the potential to make themselves a sage or superior person (*jun zi*), in practice because people are inevitably at different stages of this process, they are not on the same footing. Therefore they are not equal. To add the value of equality to Confucianism would inevitably undermine the Confucian ideal of superior person which is at its core.

Confucianism is characteristically paternalistic. Paternalism may be seen as a necessary consequence of the lack of equality within the tradition, a natural extension from the concept of *jen*, and a corollary of the Confucian ideal of meritocracy. Confucius said: "the character of a ruler (*jun zi*) is like wind and that of the people is like grass. In whatever direction the wind blows, the grass always bends."[25] Mencius advocated that those who use their minds should rule those who use their muscles.[26] A cardinal Confucian virtue for the able and wise is to direct and take care of the less able and wise. For example, it is the inescapable duty of Confucian intellectuals to speak on behalf of the masses. In contrast, in democracy, the concepts of liberty and individual rights assure that individuals are entitled to make choices for themselves even if they are wrong or unwise.[27] For that, Confucianism leaves little room. In Confucianism, under the name of common good, paternalism prevails over individual liberty and individual autonomy.

Confucians place a strong value on unity (*da yi tong*), not plurality. "Unity" here means not only political and territorial unity, but also unity in thought and ideology.[28] Confucius placed paramount importance on following the way of the Chou dynasty and thereby excluded other options.[29] While Mencius believed that the only way to settle the empire was through unity, Xun Zi advocated the idea of using a unitary principle in deciding world-affairs. The Confucian classic *Li Ji* states: "Today throughout the empire carts all have wheels with the same gauge; all writing is with the same character; and for conduct there exist the same rules."[30] This is stated with enthusiastic approval. The Kung-Yang School Confucianism almost took unity to be the only manifestation of Tao or the Way. In this tradition pluralism has no place.

The problem between Confucian and democratic values is that both sets of values are worthwhile. On the one hand, such democratic values as liberty, equality, and pluralism are desirable; and on the other, so are Confucian values like the family, duty, loyalty, and unity. Confucian values are as cherishable as democratic values. Traditional Confucian virtues such as loyalty, filial piety, paternalism, and unity are good values and ought to be retained. Just because Confucian virtues are in conflict with some democratic values, that does not mean they are less good or less valuable. The real strength of Confucianism is not in being or becoming democratic, but in the traditional virtues that are not democratic. It is a simple-minded fallacious inference that, since democracy is good, anything that is undemocratic must be bad. An argument can be made that in the United States and throughout the democratic West, healthy society has been threatened precisely by the diminishing of traditional values similar to these undemocratic Confucian values. Scholars like Samuel Huntington have made much the same mistake in thinking that because democratic values are good, undemocratic or non-democratic Confucian values must be abandoned or superseded.

At this historically critical and conceptually perplexing point, where ought China to go? Or, as the Confucian would ask, what ought Chinese intellectuals to advocate?

4. Democracy as an independent value system in China

Since Confucianism is the predominant value system in China and is not compatible with democracy in one integrated value system, will the two value systems clash with one another as democracy enters China? There are at least four possible answers to this question.

Let us call the first answer "Confucianism but not democracy." Among its proponents, besides those outrightly rejecting democracy, I include people who would want China to have minimal democracy, or democracy without pluralism or rights to individual liberty and equality. Liang Shu-ming outrightly rejected democracy. Recently Western scholars such as Henry Rosemont, Jr. also have appeared to favor the alternative of minimal democracy in China.[31] Yet since the May Fourth Movement of 1919 some people have chosen the opposing view of complete Westernization in China. Westernization may include democratization. Therefore this view may be called "democracy but not Confucianism."

Samuel Huntington provides a third answer. Pointing out the impending clash between democracy and some traditional culture in some parts of the world, Huntington writes:

> Great historic cultural traditions, such as Islam and Confucianism, are highly complex bodies of ideas, beliefs, doctrines, assumptions, writings, and behavior patterns. Any major culture, including even Confucianism, has some elements that are compatible with democracy, just as Protestantism and Catholicism have elements that are clearly undemocratic. Confucian democracy may be a contradiction in terms, but democracy in a Confucian society need not be. The question is: What elements in Islam and Confucianism are favorable to democracy, and how and under what circum-

> stances can these supersede the undemocratic elements in those cultural traditions?[32]

Huntington is evidently applying a Western hierarchical model of thinking here. For him, Confucianism can survive democratization by superseding or abandoning its undemocratic values. Admittedly, this option is not entirely impossible, just as a China with only residual Confucian values is not entirely impossible. But is that too great a price for Confucianism to pay? Can Confucianism do better than that?

I propose a fourth answer: that Confucianism and democracy independently co-exist in China. I believe that China needs both democratic and Confucian values. Because of essential tensions between democratic values and some undemocratic Confucian values, the two value systems cannot be integrated into a single system without undermining their integrity. Therefore the only way out has to be for democracy to exist in China independently of Confucianism. Chinese should not pursue a single integrated system of values, whether it is called "democratic Confucianism" or "Confucian democracy."

Because of the tensions between democratic values and some undemocratic Confucian values, the two sets of values cannot be integrated into one coherent value system without substantially sacrificing either democratic or Confucian values. Unfortunately some New-Confucians try to do just that. Any attempt to make Confucianism democratic will only make it nondescript. As a value system, Confucianism is not unchangeable. It has changed in many ways since Confucius' time, and it needs to change further. To some extent the vitality of Confucianism lies in its potentialities for change. But it does have some elements which are so central to Confucianism that it cannot survive substantially without them. Features like its emphasis on the family, filial piety, and self-cultivation and self-constraint are an indispensable part of Confucianism. Since Confucian emphases lead away from individual liberty and equality, if the emphases were to shift, how Confucian would a democratic Confucianism be? Any attempt to democratize Confucianism by superseding its traditional values would jeopardize the integrity of Confucianism. The inevitable result would be a loss to the real value of Confucianism. This kind of integration, if applied to all the non-Western world, would indeed lead to "the end of history."[33]

China should become democratic and retain its Confucian heritage. The co-existence of two value systems cannot be that of institutional Confucianism with democracy as a social institution. Confucianism as a social institution no longer exists. As value systems, democracy and Confucianism may influence each other, even as they remain independent. Confucianism and democracy may coexist in two ways. Some people are more Confucian than democratic, and value Confucian values more than democratic values, while others are more democratic than Confucian, and value democratic values more than Confucian values. Perhaps more importantly, the values of Confucianism and democracy may co-exist in the same individual. Various values that are not consistent with each other may be worth pursuing. Where that is the case, we need to achieve a delicate balance among them.

History hints at how to balance the values. The three major existing value systems in China, Confucianism, Taoism, and Buddhism, have co-existed for a long time. As Wing-Tsit Chan observed: "most Chinese follow the three systems of Confucianism, Taoism, and Buddhism, and usually take a multiple approach to things."[34] Tao Yuanming was a Taoist and a Confucian at the same time; the so-called last Confucian, Liang Shuming, remained a Buddhist throughout his life.

Thinking is not a linear process that always follows a consistent pattern. In the West, people tend to overlook this by overemphasizing a unitary rationality. People have different values, desires, and needs which can be alternately pursued. A Confucian scholar once said that Buddhism is like floating on the water, drifting wherever the current takes you, and Confucianism is like having a rudder in the boat to guide it in a certain direction. This analogy was meant to show the advantage of Confucianism over Buddhism. But if we read it from a different perspective, we can find new meanings. Is it always so bad to drift along the current? Perhaps it is better to drift for a while before using the rudder again. Sometimes it may be better to follow both ways at different times. Reading the analogy this way may help us understand how someone can adopt Confucianism along with Buddhism.[35]

Democracy may enter China similarly. The Confucian, the Taoist, and the Buddhist, who have been engaged in a dialogue for an extended period of time, may invite another participant, the democrat, to join them. Then we will see the four different value systems side by side. The primary characteristic of the dialogue should be one of harmony. When one party is too loud, it is time to shift attention to another party. For instance, the concept of rights should be voiced when there is too much emphasis on paternalism and the paternalistic practice has become oppressive; but Confucianism, Taoism, and perhaps Buddhism should be voiced when right-based talk has aroused too much individualism. Thus, despite tensions between Confucianism and democracy, the four systems can nevertheless keep themselves in balance and harmony in the same land.36

NOTES

1. Samuel P. Huntington, "The clash of civilizations," *Foreign Affairs*, 72:3 (Summer 1993), pp. 22-49.
2. *Ibid.*
3. For different versions of democracy, see C. B. Macpherson, *The Real World of Democracy* (New York: Oxford University Press, 1972).
4. Joseph A. Schumpeter, *Capitalism, Socialism, and Democracy*, 2nd edn. (New York: Harper, 1947), p. 269.
5. Francis Fukuyama, "The primacy of culture," *Journal of Democracy*, 6:1 (January 1995), pp. 7-14.
6. Jürgen Domes, "China's Modernization and the Doctrine of Democracy," in *Sun Yat-Sen's Doctrine in the Modern World*, ed. Chu-yuan Cheng (Boulder, Colo.: Westview Press, 1989), pp. 201-224.
7. Alexis de Tocqueville, *Democracy in America*, Vol. 1 (New York: Schocken Books, 1974), p. 320.
8. For some liberal views on what kind of democracy China needs, see Hua Shiping, "All roads lead to democracy: A critical analysis of the writings of three Chinese reformist intellectuals," *Bulletin of Concerned Asian Scholars*, (January-March 1992), pp. 43-58; and Yu-sheng Lin, "Reluctance to modernize: The influence of Confucianism on China's search for political modernity," in *Confucianism and Modernization: A Symposium*, ed. Joseph P. L. Jiang (Taipei, Freedom Council, 1987), pp. 21-33.
9. The relation between democracy on the one hand and Taoism and Buddhism on the other is complex and cannot be adequately dealt with in this essay. Confucianism, the predominant value system in Chinese culture, is my main concern here.
10. For the view that Confucianism is democratic, see Leonard Shihlien Hsü, *The Political Philosophy of Confucianism* (New York: Harper & Row, 1975), particularly Chapter IX: Democracy and Representation, pp. 174-197; Huang Chun-chieh and Wu Kuang-ming, "Taiwan and the Confucian aspiration: Toward the twenty-first century," in *Cultural Change in Postwar Taiwan*, ed. Stevan Harrell and Huang Chun-chieh (Boulder, Colo.: Westview Press, 1994), pp. 69-87; and more recently, Lee Teng-hui, "Chinese culture and political renewal," *The Journal of Democracy*, 6:4 (October 1995), pp. 3-8.
11. Wing-Tsit Chan, *A Source Book in Chinese Philosophy* (Princeton, N. J.: Princeton University Press, 1963), p. 81.
12. Sun Yat-sen, "First lecture on democracy," in *The Teachings of the Nation-Founding Father [Guo Fu Yi Jiao]* (Taiwan: Cultural Book Inc., 1984), Section 3. p. 70.
13. Shu-hsien Liu, *Confucianism and Modernization [Ru Jia Si Xiang Yu Xian Dai Hua]*, ed. Jing Hai-feng (Beijing: Chinese Broadcasting and TV Publishing House, 1992), p.19.
14. Female monarchs were evidently not a possibility at Mencius's time.
15. Lin Yutang, *My Country and My People* (New York: The John Day Company Books, 1939), p. 206.
16. Other liberal Confucian philosophers like Huang Zongxi (1610-1695) were much less influential in the society. For some marginal liberal elements in Confucian tradition, see Wm. Theodore de Barry, *The Liberal Tradition in China* (Hong Kong: The Chinese University Press and New York: Columbia University Press, 1983), and his "Neo-Confucianism and human rights," in *Human Rights and the World's Religions*, ed. Leroy S. Rouner (Notre Dame, Ind.: University of Notre Dame Press, 1988), pp. 183-198.
17. Liang Shu-ming, "Elements of Chinese culture [Zhong Guo Wen Hua Yao Yi]," Chapter 2, Section 5;

in *Collected Works of Liang shu-ming*, vol. 3 (Jinan, China: Shandoing People's Publishing House, 1990), p. 48.

18. Mou Tsung-san, "Preface to *Philosophy of History*," in *Reconstruction of Moral Idealism*, ed. Zheng Jiadong (Beijing: China Broadcasting TV Publishing House, 1992), pp. 128-132.
19. Ibid., p. 15.
20. Shu-hsien Liu, *op.cit.*, pp. 17-40.
21. See Henry Rosemont Jr., "Why take rights seriously? A Confucian critique," in *Human Rights and the Work Religions*, ed. Leroy Rouner (Notre Dame Ind.: University of Notre Dame Press, 1988), pp. 167-182.
22. Confucius, *Analects*, 12:1, trans. D.C. Lau (New York: Penguin Books, 1979), p. 112.
23. See Fung Yu-lan, "China's road to freedom [*Xin Shi Lun*]," Chapter 4: On the Family and State, in *Collected Work of Fung Yu-lan*, ed. Huang Kejian and Wu Xiaolong (Beijing: Qun-Yan Publishers, 1993), pp. 270-280. Also Liang Shu-min, *op. cit.*, pp.19-24.
24. Wing-Tsit Chan, *op.cit.*, p. 41.
25. *Ibid.*, p. 40.
26. *Ibid.*, p. 69.
27. See Michael Walzer, "Philosophy and Democracy," *Political Theory*, 9:3 (August 1981). pp. 379-399.
28. See Yu Rubo, "On the Confucian thought of Great Unity [*Rujia Da Yitong Sixiang Jianyi*]," *The Academic Jounal of Qilu [Qilu Xuekan]*, No. 1 (1995), pp. 51-54.
29. Confucius, *Analects* 3:14, op.cit. p. 69.
30. Quoted from Fung Yu-lan's *A History of Chinese Philosophy* Vol. 1 (Princeton: Princeton University Press, 1952), p. 370.
31. Henry Rosement, Jr., *A Chinese Mirror: Moral Reflections on Political Economy and Society* (La Salle, Ill.: Open Court, 1991).
32. Samuel P. Huntington, *The Third Wave: Democratization in the Late Twentieth Century* (Norman, Okla.: University of Oklahoma Press, 1991), p. 310.
33. Francis Fukuyama, "The end of history?" *The National Interest*, 16 (Summer 1989), pp. 3-18.
34. Wing-Tsit Chan, op.cit., pp. 184-185.
35. For a detailed account of how a person can incorporate different values, see my "How can one be a Taoist-Buddhist-Confucian?," *International Review of Chinese Religion and Philosophy*, 1 (March 1996), pp. 29-66.
36. An earlier version of this paper was presented at the Seventh East-West Philosophers' conference at the East-West Center and the University of Hawaii. I would like to thank Joel Kupperman, Charles Hayford, Craig Ihara, Ira Smolensky, Walter Benesch, Ruiping Fan, and Qingjie Wang for reading previous drafts of the paper, and the Midwest Faculty Seminar, the Center for East Asian Studies of the University of Chicago, the Center of Chinese Studies of the University of Michigan, and Monmouth College for their generous support.

FREEDOM AND DEMOCRACY IN CUBA: A PROBLEM OF UNDERSTANDING

Susan E. Babbitt

Susan E. Babbitt teaches philosophy at Queen's University in Kingston, Ontario. She is the author of Impossible Dreams: Rationality, Integrity and Moral Imagination *(Westview, 1996) and a number of articles. She is currently working on a second book on moral imagination and a three-year project (funded by a SSHRC Strategic Research Grant) on women and development in Cuba.*

"In this paper, I consider the difficulty involved in giving appropriate importance to certain facts about the Cuban situation. It is widely recognized, for instance, that Cuban children are better taken care of than in any developing country and than in many developed countries. Cuba has been praised for its accomplishments in health. Yet these accomplishments do not matter to many as much as the fact that, in some undefined sense, Cuba is not democratic and Cubans are not free. I am not concerned here with the question of whether or not Cuba is democratic, although I believe it has a better claim to democracy than some more familiar systems; rather, I am concerned with the issue of what the fair investigation of such a question involves, given that globally dominant expectations about democracy and freedom often preclude, in the case of understanding Cuba, constructive debate."

After a two-hour discussion about Cuba in a graduate seminar, a student says, without explaining what she means or to what it is relevant, "But there's no freedom," and leaves the room. At an APA conference, when I mention my interest in and passion for Cuba, someone I have not seen for a long time suggests that we must have serious disagreements. In explanation, she describes evidence of lack of freedom of expression in Cuba.

I am often impressed that freedom, in a quite undefined sense, is taken to trump any other consideration of a positive sort about Cuba. Moreover, it has this trumping role without argument. The issue about Cuba is often whether or not a certain kind of freedom or openness exists, not whether it matters and to what. In the following, I try to make some suggestions about what matters to a useful discussion of freedom and what this implies for understanding democracy in Cuba.

Expectations and Power

A Cuban newspaper tells the story of a Martian visitor who wants to understand how Earth people conceive of human rights.[1] He is taken first to the United States to know a society that respects human rights, and learns that the Constitution makes no mention of rights to work, health, education, and the rights of women and children. He sees that 59 per cent of those condemned to death are members of minority racial groups; that 5 million people are in prisons; that funding for prisons has increased 30 per cent in the past 10 years while funding for education decreased by 18 per cent during the same period; that police in New York torture and even kill those they arrest; that 78 people have been killed trying to cross the Mexican/US border; that illegal immigrants are denied medical treatment; that, according to the US President himself, 60 per cent of the children at age eight do not know how to read; that 54 per cent of the suicides of young people in developed countries take place in the US; and that social assistance has been reduced by 60 per cent. The Martian is then taken to Cuba to see what it is like in a country where human rights are not respected, to see an example of failure to respect human rights and sees that the Constitution guarantees all human rights—individual, political, and social. He sees that the Constitution guarantees rights to work, health, education, and social assistance, and he notices that it makes reference to the rights of families, children, and women. He sees that education is free at all levels, including books and materials, and that health care is free as well. And he sees that there are 54 doctors for each 10,000 citizens, an average higher than that of the much more wealthy United States. Then he learns that the United States proposes every year to the United Nations that Cuba be condemned for violation of human rights. He takes his ship and returns to Mars convinced that Earth people are both stupid and frightening.

The point of this story, I take it, is not that Cuba expresses greater respect for human rights than does the United States. Such a point does not need to be made in a Cuban newspaper. Instead, the point of the story is that it would take something like a Martian to be able to draw such conclusions. The facts mentioned in the story are common knowledge. They are widely repeated in the United States and are often in the news. It is not news, for instance, to point out that illegal immigrants are denied medical care or that those condemned to death are mostly non-white. What is not so common is to put these facts together in such a way that one draws the conclusion that many people are confused about the meaning of human rights, that there exists a general sort of erroneous thinking about human rights and their importance. What is surprising is not the information, but the conclusions that are drawn about the importance of the information, that, for instance, such thinking about human rights is frightening, as the Martian concludes. The point, I take it, is that one would have to be a Martian to see that what these facts mean is significant in a certain way. The Martian listened to the facts and fled. Many would listen to all the same facts, and even believe them, and think that nothing follows of interest for how we understand respect for human rights in general.

In the case of Cuba, it is not enough to consider empirical evidence; it is also necessary to consider the conceptual and practical background which explains the importance given to evidence. Moreover, one has to consider the fact that relevant philosophical assumptions are now very powerful, that they constitute the basis for a world view, informing the way people see themselves and interpret stories and experiences. We always interpret the world on the basis of background beliefs and traditions, and in the particular case of Cuba we have to become aware of certain beliefs and traditions, if we are to be fair.

When people talk sympathetically about Cuba, for instance, it is common to say that although Cuba is not democratic, although the Cuban government does not respect the autonomy of its people,[2] the Cuban revolution has succeeded in bringing about a social system which provides better medical care and education than many developed countries. Indeed, the statistics that generally follow the "but" which follows the claim that Cuba is not democratic indicate that in fact Cuba takes better care of its smallest and weakest citizens than probably any country in the world. One could think that this is a story about democracy, and many do. One might think that if "democracy" has to do with the people ruling themselves, and if "autonomy" has to do with individuals controlling their own destinies, it is hard to see how it can be irrelevant to democracy or autonomy what happens to people when they are in the most helpless states. But we often listen to the facts about Cuba and think somehow that recognized successes in caring generally for the weak and the sick do not *matter* to democracy, that these issues are just not the same sort of thing.

Consider the following example regarding the situation of women in Cuba. In *Sex and Revolution: Women in Socialist Cuba*, we find the following claim explaining the life of women in Cuba: "Fidel Castro marched through the public arena dressed in the uniform of the perpetual warrior," and, for three decades "life in Cuba was a succession of military emergencies, sudden campaigns and heroic efforts which disrupted the civilian economy upon which women depended."[3] Now it is true, of course, that Fidel Castro wears military uniforms most of the time and that most women in Cuba have spent a lot of time training militarily. What is interesting about this account of women in Cuba, though, is that it does not provide any explanation of why this is the case. No explanation is offered for Fidel Castro's being the "perpetual warrior" and the women's engaging in military activity. And if no information is provided in a book published by Oxford University Press, it must be because none is needed, because, perhaps, there is no surprise. This may be so either because it is assumed that everyone knows who the enemy is or because there is no enemy. But since the authors say that women "were taught to perceive [Cuba] as an embattled revolution in hostile world" (185), the missing explanation cannot be accounted for by the expectation that the enemy, or that there is an enemy, is well-known. If the women had to be taught to perceive hostility, the suggestion is that the hostility wasn't obvious to them. And since we the readers are not being taught, the expectation taken for granted must be that there is no enemy.

The authors of *Sex and Revolution* indicate that women and men in Cuba have been offered a particular explanation for the hostility directed toward Cuba in the world. Indeed, this is true. Many important documents and speeches include lengthy explanations for the hostility directed toward Cuba and what it implies. These explanations are stories, or rather, one single story, about a struggle for certain goals and values, and of the central cause of the humiliation, degradation and death endured throughout the struggle, i.e., the dominant classes of the United States. It is the story of how Cuba, the last Spanish colony, fought over a period of 30 years against the Spanish without outside help and just when the Spanish were ready to give up, the United States intervened and occupied the country, insultingly buying back the guns of the Cuban Mambises for 75 pesos each, and imposing a constitution according to which the United States had the right to intervene whenever it saw fit. It is a story of increased American investment in Cuba after 1902 until American companies owned most of the best agricultural land in Cuba and most Cubans lived a kind of slave existence, receiving coupons for their labour which they were able to exchange for goods provided by the plantation owner. It is a story of humiliating sabotage and defeat of brief revolutionary outbursts in 1933 and 1944, interludes in the succession of American supported governments some of which proclaimed openly that Cuba would be better off being a dependent colony of the United States. And it is a story of constant attempts after the 1959 revolution to liquidate the revolution and its leadership, of the most massive disinformation campaign ever, of biological warfare and of the longest and most cruel economic blockade in the history of the world.[4]

It is, in short, a history of US interest in and desire for Cuba's dependence and of Cuba's interest in and desire for independence. Now, there are those who deny that there exists a history of aggression toward Cuba by the United States. In his response to Ricardo Alarcón on Nov. 5, 1997, the representative of the United States to the United Nations said, as had the US representative in 1996, that the United States was not blockading Cuba economically, that it was only protecting its interests, and that it was justified in doing so because Cuba does not respect human rights. But since 143 countries, including the US's most powerful allies, voted on that day to condemn the US blockade of Cuba, the sixth such vote in as many years, each year with increased numbers, the claim that the United States does not have a history of aggression toward Cuba is at least not obvious.[5]

My interest here is not in discussing US policies toward Cuba. Instead, I am interested in the fact that the authors of *Sex and Revolution*, for instance, leave this story out. They point out that Cuba has been preparing itself militarily for forty years and that people are given a story about why this is so. But they do not provide the story explaining this activity. Why, when the story is offered so often by Cuba's defenders as an explanation of Cuba's position and policies, do the authors just ignore the story? It is true that Cubans are offered explanations for what is and has been happening to them as a nation. And maybe the explanation is not correct. But the authors of *Sex and Revolution* do not refute the explanation. They ignore it.

Now, one might think, in reading *Sex and Revolution*, that there is a kind of refutation of the story in the authors' allusions to the various reforms that were brought about by Cuban governments before

1959. For instance, they make reference to an "unprecedented era of democratic politics" from 1940-1952 (19) and to the Constitution of 1940 which included rights for women.

But this is not a refutation of the Cuban story. The Cuban *response* to this position is that what existed between 1940 and 1952 was *pluripartidismo*, or a system of several political parties, and *not* democracy. The story explains how these parties all represented similar expressions of the interests of the rich, that there was a lot of corruption and only a small percentage of the people showed up to vote. The Cuban story explains how *pluripartidismo* is not the same as democracy because having several parties does not amount to rule by the people, or at least it did not in Cuba in the 1940s. Moreover, the Cuban story also explains that the 1940 Constitution, while progressive in promise, did not turn out to be progressive in fact, and that this was because the constitutional reforms were not supported by progressive laws according to which such reforms could be actualized.

Smith and Padula do not refute or respond to a story that has been told repeatedly for almost half a century in Cuba explaining Cuba's aspirations for democracy and respect for human rights. Whereas almost every response by Cuban officials and spokespeople makes reference to the history of Cuba's struggle for democracy and respect for human rights, to what it means and why, as well as to the US government's commitment to undermining Cuban sovereignty, this story is often just left out of the stories told about Cuba by many who try to evaluate the Cuban Revolution from outside.

Now, one might think that there is nothing particularly interesting about this. It is simply a manifestation of ideological power. The more powerful entity does not need to tell its own story and is of course not interested in promoting the point of the view of those it wants to dominate. But I am interested in this problem as it applies to those who are sympathetic to Cuba. I am not interested in why members of the US government ignore the Cuban story; I am interested in why people who are sympathetic to Cuba—like the authors of *Sex and Revolution*—ignore the story, and what is required in order to not ignore it. I will suggest that it is an issue about the consequences of ideological power, but that it is also an issue about the nature of understanding and of the role of a particular sort of commitment and engagement in the investigation of beliefs about ideological influence: The authors of *Sex and Revolution* can leave the explanatory story out because the dominant expectations are that Cuba engages militarily *unnecessarily*. And in order to think that the explanation is important, that it must be taken seriously in order to properly appreciate empirical evidence, one must not only question relevant expectations but also think that it matters that we do so.

Philosophers of science have pointed out that when we look for explanations we look for causes that play a particular explanatory role within an investigative program generating certain cognitive needs. According to Philip Kitcher, rational decisions are those that issue from a process that has high expectations of cognitive progress, for we have to have expectations of success to generate certain directions of evaluation.[6] Causes become explanatory ones when they explain what needs to be understood. So, for instance, we wouldn't say that Smith's going to buy cigarettes explains his death on the highway, even though he would not have died if he had not gone out to buy cigarettes. Jones' drunk driving better explains Smith's death because it is the sort of action that is relevant to understanding highway deaths.[7] Drunk-driving in this case is explanatory and smoking is not because of what each contributes to a direction of understanding. The rationale is that we can pursue our concern about car crashes if we know more about drunkenness and inattention, whereas knowledge about the errands that lead people to be in the wrong place at the wrong time does not help.

Suppose we did not care about vehicular accidents. Suppose this were something that we did not see a need to try to understand or avoid. In that case, the search for an explanatory cause lacks a certain motivation, and we might well think that Smith died because he happened to like smoking late at night. Thus, certain sorts of understanding cannot be acquired or evaluated unless there is first the commitment which can generate relevant cognitive needs. This is most interestingly the case in situations in which the understanding being pursued conflicts with expectations, in which expectations need to be pursued and developed.

Speaking to the United Nations in 1960, Fidel Castro invited the audience to suppose "that a person from outer space were to come to this assembly, someone who had read neither the Communist Manifesto of Karl Marx nor UPI or AP dispatches or any other monopoly-controlled publication. If he were to ask how the world was divided up and he saw on a map that the wealth was divided among the monopolies of four or five countries, he would say, 'The world has been badly divided up, the world has been exploited'."[8] The suggestion is that without the aid of ideology or propaganda, or at least without the aid of certain ideologies and propaganda, someone from outer space might have good reason to think something is *wrong* with the way the world is divided up.

Now, it would seem that Fidel Castro's point here is not interesting primarily because it refers to a different perspective, or the suggestion of one, but rather because it refers to the difficulty of properly understanding something that is obviously true. The truth of the claim "The world is divided up badly" is hard to dispute; it's truth is somewhat obvious. But its *understanding* is difficult. It might be possible for someone from outer space to think it *matters* that the world is wrongly divided up because someone looking from outer space would not have expectations generated by how the world is currently divided up. Such a person would be reasoning without a certain set of expectations. The suggestion seems to be that someone from outer space might see differences in a different way and might indeed find certain differences irrelevant. The point in this case, however, is not that they *could* be irrelevant from another perspective but that they *are* in fact irrelevant and that the only way this might be properly understood would be from something like outer space.

The question of properly understanding certain truths may be more important in some cases than questions about their possession. Fully understanding the true statement "The world is divided up badly" requires not only a desire to understand how the world *ought* to be divided up but also, more fundamentally, a commitment according to which it *matters* that the world is divided up wrongly. The problem is not just that one has to see that there is an issue before one can appreciate the usefulness of the information. The more important problem is what is *involved* in seeing that there is an issue. Thus, it would appear that what is significant for the acquiring of understanding is not so much the discovery or identification of truth, but rather the commitment to the kinds of directions of development—particularly human development—that can make the right sorts of truths relevant. The difficulty of understanding that the world is divided up wrongly, even if one believes correctly that it is, is that such understanding requires an interest in the kind of possibilities for human existence its pursuit would make possible.

To get back to the story of the Martian visitor: What sends the Martian fleeing is the last bit of information, which is that Cuba has been condemned in the United Nations for abuse of human rights. That is, what sends the Martian fleeing in terror is not the bits of empirical evidence and what they indicate, but the information he receives about how the bits of information are assessed. What is terrifying is awareness of the context within which the results of investigation are interpreted. The Martian *flees*, presumably, not just because human rights are not respected. What sends the Martian fleeing is that it does not seem to matter that human rights are not understood.

Redefining Options

Consider the story of Sethe in Toni Morrison's *Beloved*, which I have discussed elsewhere.[9] When Sethe, an escaped slave, sees her ex slave-master coming down the road to take her and her children back to slavery, from which she had fled 28 days before, she decides, with certainty, that she should kill her children rather than let them go back to slavery. There are lots of ways in which we might think the choice a strange one. But the novel is powerful in particular because we understand Sethe's choice in terms of what becomes important to Sethe, even though that importance is not entirely articulatable. We understand Sethe's choice in terms of the awareness that Sethe acquires as she proceeds in action according to certain specific interests and needs.

Sethe tries to kill her children, succeeds in killing one, and is considered crazy by both the slave master and her own community. But Sethe has no regrets about her choice. She knew that she had to do it. Now, as Christine Korsgaard points out, the kind of normativity that most requires philosophical explanation is not that which explains why people feel compelled to choose as they do, but rather that which explains why *I* feel compelled, in other words, that which explains the first-person compulsion.[10] We might say for instance that people act morally for the sake of the continuation of the species. But this doesn't explain why *I* might feel compelled in a particular situation to do or not do something at the possible cost of my life, or the lives of others. And it seems right to say, as Korsgaard does, that an account of moral compulsion must make reference to a person's practical identity. For when someone feels compelled to act in a certain way even if the cost is death, there is an important sense in which what she feels is that to not act in a certain way is to not be the person she thinks she is.

Thus, we might say about Sethe that she decides to kill her children because if she does not act to protect their capacity for moral responsibility, she will not be able to live with herself. During her 28 days of freedom Sethe has learned that she can love her children. She has taken the risk, being a slave, of loving her children. Paul D, for instance, tells her that used-to-be-slaves should pick the smallest stars in the sky to own because dreams can be taken away and one has to be able to go on living.[11] But Sethe commits herself to sewing on a button for her daughter as if it were right that she be able to sew a garment for her daughter. So, when Sethe faces her slave master and *knows* that she cannot let her children go back to slavery, we might think that the compulsion that she tries to explain later to Paul D is that according to which she would rather be dead than go back to slavery and she would rather that her children be dead than that she allow them to go back to slavery. The moral compulsion according to which Sethe feels that she has to try to protect her children from slavery by killing them is that according to which to not do so would be to not be able to continue on as a sort of person.

But this is too simple. For Sethe's experience in the 28 days of freedom is not that of becoming a *sort* of person; it is that of becoming a person. It is not that of gaining a sort of awareness of herself and her possibilities; it is that of gaining awareness, of becoming aware of the possibility and importance of self-awareness. We might say about Sethe's compulsion that, given the person she has become and what is now important to her, the life that is offered to her under slavery is *worse* than death, as if there were a kind of comparison, a choice between discrete entities. But given that what she has become in her view *is* a person, it would seem more appropriate to say that what compels her is that what is offered to her under slavery is not offered to *her*, since she is not, under slavery, a person at all, but rather an animal.

What matters more than continuing on as a sort of person, for Sethe, is the possibility that *persons* be a sort that applies to her, and to her children. So Sethe's statement to Paul D that she absolutely could not "let all that go back to where it was"[12] is reference not just to a way of life, but more importantly, it would seem, to an orientation toward that life. What she would not let her children go back to was not just the life of slaves, but a world in which it was expected that she *ought* to be a slave because she is not a person. If Sethe were a slave and it were *wrong* that she be a slave, the situation might have been a little different. But if she is just an animal and if it is appropriate, even to those who share her experience as a slave, that she pick only the smallest stars in the sky to own, then the issue is not just about being a slave but also about how it can even be wrong that she be a slave, about the expectations according to which it is okay that she be a slave. It is important to Sethe that she be able to flee from slavery and to love her children. But what is more important, according to her, is her realization that she *ought* to be able to love her children.

To the extent that Sethe's compulsion is explained in terms of identity, it is explained in terms of expectations about and interest in a certain possibility for identity, and for the conditions that would allow such expectations and interests to be maintained, and pursued. To choose *not* to recognize expectations that she is an animal, and not human, is to choose at least the possibility, even if not fully articulatable, of an understanding of *human*, or *person*, that applies to her.

If Sethe kills her children, of course, they will not

have the possibility of realizing themselves as human beings. But if she doesn't kill them, they also do not have the possibility of realizing themselves, for they are slaves. If Sethe kills them or not, her children do not have the possibility of realizing themselves, but if she doesn't try to kill them to protect the possibility, she also risks losing the expectation of the possibility. So what Sethe chooses is not an option, or an action by itself, as much as it is a unifying perspective, a way of thinking of herself and her children in ways that generate certain expectations. What is maintained and preserved by her choice to try to protect her children from slavery is the control of the possibility of a certain (human) identity, not the identity itself, which must still be pursued in thought and action.

What seems crucial to understanding the situation of Cuba is the possibility, not the truth, of the claim that the options offered by US dominated capitalism might be wrong, that the available options for humanity rest upon mistaken liberal conceptions of what it means to be human. Understanding Cuba is not a problem in the first instance of beliefs. For one can possess all the relevant propositional beliefs about Cuba and interpret the information according to a perspective which is inadequate for attributing appropriate importance to such beliefs. This is what *Sex and Revolution* does so effectively. It presents all the relevant information but does not adequately present the story that explains, or could explain the significance of that information.

When we read the story of Sethe, we make a mistake if we ask whether or not she did the right thing when she tried to kill her children. We make a mistake because the story that she has told is one according to which she does what she does in order to be able to ask such a question. We ask the wrong question because the reason Sethe tries to kill her children is that as slaves, she and her children are not able to do right or wrong; concepts of right and wrong do not apply to them because as non-human animals, they do not possess moral responsibility. Thus, the question about the moral status of her act demonstrates failure to understand her story and what it is about, or to respect it, because the story that Sethe tells raises questions about morality itself. If it can even make sense for someone to go against morality to claim its very possibility, then to the extent that we have understood the story, we have at least to acknowledge that there is a question to be asked first about morality itself and what it involves.

The point is not that we have to believe Sethe's story. The point is that if we understand Sethe's story with a certain respect for Sethe and her situation, we have to acknowledge that there are certain difficulties in deliberating about what it is reasonable to believe. The problem here is *not* that there are different perspectives, that for instance Sethe sees slavery in a way that is different from how her neighbours see slavery, the uninteresting "now it's a duck, now it's a rabbit" insight. Instead, the problem is that there is a difficulty understanding Sethe's view because one way of thinking of slavery is not only more powerful than the other, but that it generates expectations according to which Sethe's perspective becomes implausible, and thereby difficult to articulate. Sethe's explanation of what she chooses is that she just couldn't let her children go back to "all that," by which she means a system in which they could not choose from amongst options appropriate for human beings, as a human being. So, the issue is not in the first instance one about believing or not; it is first a question about the conditions under which it becomes possible to effectively evaluate certain beliefs, or even to be able to identify what they are beliefs about.

Similarly, if there is any possibility at all that the Cuban story makes sense, then one cannot just choose between two systems. For one system and not the other defines the terms according to which the evaluation takes place. Indeed, in the theory and expression of the Cuban Revolution, it is often made explicit that there is a commitment to redefinition of options. In May, 1982, Fidel Castro said ideas do not come together easily in revolutionary situations; they cannot be expected like a ray of light, in a clear, precise, and linear fashion. But what must be linear is the commitment to action in a certain direction.[13] Action must be linear because theory cannot be, and action must be linear in order that theory *be* theory, in order that there be expectations of the sort that can make it possible to consider evidence as evidence. In May, 1982, Fidel said that commitment to direction has to have priority because ideas take their form as a result of that commitment, through development and action. Then, in October, 1997, at the Fifth Party Congress, Fidel said that what is necessary for survival in an unjust and threatening world is, in the first instance, unity and direction: "Luego una enseñanza histórica para nosotras es que hay que garantizar la dirección y que la dirección no puede fallar, el Partido no puede darse el lujo de que un día falle su dirección, porque el precio es inpagable. Esa es una idea clave: tenemos que arreglárnoslas para garantizar eso durante un largo período histórico. En los tiempos en que estamos viviendo y con el largo enfrentamiento que tenemos ante el imperialismo y el capitalismo, no es posible renunciar a la idea de la necesidad de una dirección unida y eficiente."[14]

This is a commitment to action of a certain sort, in a certain direction, as a result of which it becomes possible to maintain certain expectations. The *direction*, it is suggested, is important for unity; it is not, as is often assumed, the unity that determines the direction. Thus, there is something epistemologically, as well as politically, significant about the constant reference in the Cuban literature to the fact that there is an option to make the option that of winning or dying, that there is a choice about the choices. This was what Fidel Castro said in 1956 before a small group of people set sail from Mexico in an old yacht, in preparation for the Revolution, and it is what many in Cuba say today as the United States approves yet another amendment (the Graham Amendment declaring Cuba a security risk) and makes further suggestions about justifying military aggression.[15]

When Fidel Castro spoke at the Fifth Party Congress in October, 1997, he did not just say that the choice was between socialism or death, as he usually does. He also said that there was a choice that the choice be between socialism and death. After describing the desperate situation of the first half of 1992, when during a period of five months almost nothing arrived in the country, Fidel Castro suggested that there was an alternative that had been there for a long time. He did not propose another option, besides capitalism and death by starvation, or invasion. He proposed a reformulation of the options: "Pero también siempre hay una alternativa que ha estado presente desde el primer día...:Si no es posible vivir con honor y con justicia, si no es posible ser hombre y ser hombre libre, ¿para que queremos la vida?; es preferible la muerte.... cuando los hombres escogen el deber y el honor, cuando escogen lo que es justo, es precisamente cuando más viven, porque viven mientras viva una idea, y las ideas no mueren, las causas justas se perpetúan a lo largo de los tiempos, como se perpetuarán nuestras ideas y se perpetuará nuestra causa justa.... Y nosotros escogimos hace rato, en este dilema..."[16] In other words, the question is not about choosing between life and death, but about choosing to choose the pursuit of a certain kind of meaningful life, with a certain purpose; it is to choose to reject the meaningfulness of life as otherwise defined, to not engage with options made available by such meaningfulness.

This is not to say that there is no question about freedom. There is a burdensome question of freedom that arises within this choice, just as there is a question for Sethe about morality. But the suggestion is that there is sometimes a question about how social values and norms are defined, and how, as a result, options are made meaningful as options for life. There is a deep-seated and popular view in North American and European philosophical traditions that someone acts or chooses autonomously when she weighs her options in light of relevant information, and does or chooses that which is most likely to advance more of her aims than other options. Freedom, according to this picture, has to do, ultimately, with realization of a person's actual desires and interests. Certainly, no one would say that someone acts freely when they act upon *any* desires, since desires can be compulsive or based upon ignorance. But the popular assumption is that respecting people's autonomy involves respecting people's freedom to act on their settled values and aims, without interference other than the providing of appropriate resources.

However, when we consider the extent to which social norms and values prescribe and limit people's choices, when we consider the extent to which such norms and values constitute, as Frantz Fanon says, "a definitive structuring of the self and the world,"[17] this picture is naive. Will Kymlicka's defence of minority rights in *Liberalism, Community and Culture* involves a lengthy argument attempting to show that concern for group rights does not involve overriding individuals' essential interests in, as he puts it, living their lives "from the inside," with true beliefs.[18] Kymlicka thinks that it is uncontroversial that "no life goes better by being led from the outside according to values the person does not endorse."[19] But one might wonder why some lives might not go better if they were led by more humane values, even if these are not easy to endorse, or even to identify, as they will not be if they are not expected. To the extent that societies, or global world views can be systemically unjust, to the extent that available options are defined by norms and values that deny the humanity of some people, it *is* reasonable to think that at least some lives would indeed go better if led from the outside according to values the person involved might well not endorse, or even recognize.

Freedom has to do, among other things with identifying, understanding and being able to control forces—including one's own impulses—that would compel one to act in ways that are the result of arbitrary, unchosen aspects of one's situations. The idea that freedom is the capacity for unrestricted choice amongst available options is for some people a denial of freedom, since those available choices, and the values that explain them, are the result of arbitrary, unjust aspects of one's unchosen situation. It may be then that freedom requires above all, resistance to such choices, and the system that explains them, before one can identify what would be required to act—freely— in one's human interests.

When people approach Cuba concerned above all with the existence of a certain understanding of freedom, they are like readers who insist on concerning themselves with the morality of Sethe's choice. The question is inappropriate in the case of Sethe because Sethe does what she does in order to claim the possibility of real moral agency in a situation in which available understandings of morality are inadequate. When we insist on trying to understand her choice in terms of existing understandings of morality, we apply to Sethe's situation concepts the power and control of which Sethe struggles above all to resist, in order to be human. It may turn out to be true that human freedom depends primarily upon being able to choose from amongst many options, whatever they happen to be. And it may turn out to be true that as human beings we are incapable of transforming ourselves morally, and realizing ourselves through participation in the transformation of the social and political conditions that transform us. That is, it may be that what matters most to the realization of human worth is choice, and not the conditions under which we choose and imagine. But it's not clear that we know this yet, and if we don't we should avoid dismissing the meaningfulness of struggles the full understanding of which depends in part upon our own struggles to develop relevant expectations (for freedom and democracy) and to pursue them.

Democracy in Cuba

The single party system should be understood as the direction that is necessary for the unity (of vision), not as the unity that determines the direction and vision. This is how it is defended in the literature. What is referred to in reference to the Party is unity of direction, and it is the direction that explains the unity, not the reverse. Because Leninist parties and regimes have tended historically to become highly centralized and oligarchic, it is assumed that they were defined that way in the beginning. But the notion of the vanguard party in Antonio Gramsci's writing needs to be considered in conjunction with Lenin's and Che Guevara's ideas that socialist revolution is impossible without the bringing about of new values, new morals and new possibilities for being human. It is true that there is in Marxist-Leninist thought the idea that the moral person is a product of the superstructure. But what is important in Lenin's thought for Cuban revolutionary theory is Lenin's suggestion that the biggest mistake that could be made by the Communist Party in the Soviet Union would be to forget that the past still had to be overcome, to think that knowledge was secure and that there wasn't still a constant battle to be fought against the heritage of past traditions.[20]

The pursuit of Cuban identity—*cubanidad*—has its roots in important arguments for solidarity, for unity, in resisting the devastating consequences—psychological, ideological, political and economic—of the collapse of the Soviet Union. But liberal philosophy, especially ideas of what solidarity and unity consist of, seem to lead to a conflation in some literature and in popular conversation of the significance of moral vision with a preservation of traditional cultural values contradicting and sometimes actively undermining that vision. For instance, in an attempt to explain how it was that Cuba, despite universal predictions about its imminent collapse, not only has continued in its commitment to socialism but has begun slowly to rebuild its economy and strengthen its political system, Dario Machado lists among other factors Cuban patriotism.[21] "La patria," however, is, in the theory, a moral concept.[22] That is, it is not a notion referring to what actually or who actually exists within the Cuban nation, but rather to what *ought* to characterize the Cuban people if indeed they are to be able to go forward as an independent entity. And if "la Patria" is a normative concept, then not only is it possible to change cultural values without undermining solidarity, but in certain cases it is crucial. The unity, the solidarity, that has explained the going forward in question is unity beneath a cause.[23] Offered in explanation of how to go ahead, it is not a sharing of social and cultural characteristics; it is a shared vision. And hence the defence of that unity, the unity needed to resist, is defence not of shared qualities between people who happen to share a geographical space, but defence of a moral vision, a vision the pursuit of which may in important and painful ways, transform those shared qualities, or at least bestow a different importance to them.

The Cuban Revolution, the theory of which can be found in the writings of Che Guevara and Fidel Castro, does not express the idea that culture and moral values are a mere reflection of the superstructure and that individuals are an appendix of the economic motor, the stereotypical notion of marxist development.[24] Instead, it reflects the less orthodox, "humanist" understanding of revolution and revolutionaries that can be found in Marx's earlier writings, for instance, in the *1844 Manuscripts*,[25] and in Gramsci's *The Prison Notebooks*.[26] Che Guevara followed Gramsci in arguing for a conception of the person, and for a notion of self-realization and human growth. In the work of Gramsci, for instance, the development of awareness, of creativity, of intelligence, is both dependent upon and determining of the development of material conditions. And the unity upon which so much depends, according to this philosophy, is not imposed upon people or decreed; it cannot be. Instead, it is the result of a process characterized by the development of individuals' awareness and capacities, what Gramsci referred to as "the lifting up of simple souls."

In other words, it is not a certain sort of (structural or theoretical) unity that defines and/or determines who and what people can do and be, but rather a process of transformation of values and ways of being that makes it possible for people to be and do more than they could before, as human beings. According to Che Guevara, Marx was as interested in the spiritual repercussions of the economy as he was in the economy itself, what he called "hechos de conciencia,"[27] and Guevara thought that if communism is not interested in *los hechos de conciencia*, it can provide a method of distribution of goods but it can never be a moral revolution.[28]

The single Party system, then, has an epistemological and metaphysical justification having to do with the need for direction and organization in both the increase of understanding and the bringing about of the conditions that make such understanding desirable and possible. The argument for the Party is the following: In order to be able to control their lives people have to have the resources; they have to have the understanding and the capacity to apply it. Cuban society has a history of oppression and injustice as a result of which the values that define the society and that define the people who live in it are questionable at best and in many ways inhuman. If it is to be possible to find ways of living better, it has to be possible to examine and analyse such values, and this is a long and difficult process. A just and humane society is not a matter of decree: It must be the result of a process in which people acquire moral understanding and responsibility. What is essential to such a process is participation, and individual and social growth, moral growth. But people learn by acting and they understand through participation. So the priority is to find ways to bring about the sort of social change that makes such participation possible. The role of the Party is to find ways to do this in which people can be fully and meaningfully involved in the conditions of their own social formation. But the authority of the Party does not consist in the fact that it is a single party; instead, the Party *is* a Party in the first place to the extent that it acquires authority as a result of its capacity to respond to the interests and desires of the people.[29]

The difference between Gramsci and Guevara, and those Marxists called "historical materialists,"[30] is that Gramsci and Guevara thought that capitalism had to be overthrown, that it would not fall as a result of "objective forces." And the process according to which it would be overthrown was one of raising consciousness, of increasing awareness, of faith in human beings and what they could do and be. Yet if individuals are to take an active role in the overthrowing of capitalism, they have to be prepared to struggle also against its heritage. And Gramsci and Guevara recognized that this was a daily struggle, a struggle against values, attitudes, presuppositions, against the subjective elements. Indeed, it is primarily such a struggle. Military struggle is sometimes necessary, but it is not as important or as difficult as the struggle for ideas, and for direction.[31] For this struggle is daily and requires patience. The struggle against the *heritage* of capitalism is a constant, daily struggle in which people must be able to be involved, to participate, to bring about results and to recognize them as results. For people only learn when they can act, and people must always be *persuaded* to believe, not coerced.

The single party has an epistemological explanation in the very important suggestion that without theoretical vision, without working constantly to revise and enlarge such a vision, the freedom of individuals is limited by unexamined and unacknowledged traditions and values. And in order for people to acquire greater awareness and understanding, they must be able to participate in the bringing about of the conditions that make possible such vision. They must be able to act according to their understanding, and to recognize the results. Marx's early vision of human nature, the one that inspired Che Guevara, was that human beings realize themselves as they relentlessly strive to create the conditions that create us as certain sorts of persons. And such striving, according to Lenin, Gramsci and Guevara must be informed by the practical and theoretical education that makes it possible for people to resist certain traditional values and to assess for themselves the results.

Those who think that any argument about what happens in Cuba is trumped by tired, unimaginative remarks about freedom, are both metaphysically and epistemologically naive. For Cuba's pursuit of communism depends upon certain beliefs about human capacities for moral and personal development, beliefs which may turn out to be mistaken. The point here has been that if they are mistaken, it cannot be easy to know this, and there is no reason to think that we know it yet. To the extent that such beliefs about human development presume a different conception of human freedom, they cannot fairly be shown to be wrong on grounds that they conflict with a current conception of freedom, however powerful.

.Che Guevara made the point at the beginning of the Revolution, in response to critics who worried about the freedom of the individual, that they failed to understand the *narrow* dialectical relationship between theory and practice in a revolutionary setting.[32] By this, it seems, he was referring to the fact that the justification for the party and its direction depends upon what becomes possible for people as they participate, and as they acquire for themselves awareness of the direction in which they are painstakingly advancing. The *narrow* dialectical unity is required in situations of redefining options because understanding requires not just truth, but the development of the conditions for ascribing importance to truths, for seeing how such truths matter, or could matter.

The liberal view according to which one acts autonomously when one considers one's options on the basis of full understanding and instrumental reasoning makes sense in certain situations, as does *pluripartidismo*. It makes sense, for instance, when there is no reason to think not only that the options are inadequate but, worse, that one may easily fail to see *that* and how the options are inadequate. It makes sense, that is, where justice already exists. The problem for liberal philosophy is not just that the options offered to people by unjust societies are inadequate. The more difficult problem is that in situations in which the *explanations* for options are wrong, it is sometimes necessary to first reject the options in order to pursue conditions in which it is possible to see *how* they are wrong, or even *that* they are wrong.

Pluripartidismo might make sense if there were no struggle against and for subjective attitudes. But if there is such a struggle, developing theoretical vision requires, not just theories and analysis, but the organization and effective social change necessary for control of such a vision. It may still not be clear how best to define Cuban democracy, its merits and defects, but the fact that there is one political party involved cannot mean that there is no possibility of examining the democratic experience, without begging crucial questions about what democracy and freedom mean.

Conclusion

The theory of the Cuban Revolution is full of references to the epistemological role of the Party and to the explanation for it, but these are often ignored in discussions of democracy. Gramsci claimed that "political science, as far as both its concrete content and its logical formulation are concerned, must be seen as a developing organism."[33] It cannot be merely or mostly empirical, at least not if the object is effective criticism. The active politician, the creative intellectual, according to Gramsci, is not one who moves "in the turbid void of his own desires and dreams" but one who "applies one's will to the creation of a new equilibrium among the forces which really exist and are operative—basing oneself on the particular force that one believes to be progressive and strengthening it to help it to victory."[34] In Gramsci's view, the active theorist is one who works to change the balance, the equilibrium, and he does so relative to a vision that is being actually pursued but which may not be easily realized, even conceptually. If one does not grapple with the general vision, including the metaphysics and epistemology, one cannot rely with confidence upon what one sees and hears.

The point about the Martian story in *La Gramna* seems to be that there is a particular kind of difficulty involved in appreciating certain facts about the Cuban situation, even though it is generally recognized that these facts are true. Cubans often comment on the fact that US papers keep talking about the need for elections in Cuba, and then they ignore completely the elections in Cuba. Presumably, the reason the elections in Cuba are ignored is that they are not *like* the American elections in certain respects. This should not be a reason to think they are not elections unless one argues first for that unifying perspective according to which the participation of more than one party is an essential characteristic of an election's being what it is. Cubans point out that what happens in the US would fail to count as elections if it were stipulated that elections should involve at least an 80 per cent turn-out.[35] Again, the point here is not the issue about elections in Cuba, but the argumentative strategy that is employed, and that is able to be employed, against Cuba, specifically because of the existence of dominant expectations. It is not clear that it matters much how we think about elections, but understanding freedom and democracy certainly do matter. Thus, it is important to take seriously the possibility that there is still something to learn about what these mean and what might be implied for how we move ahead as human beings pursuing human flourishing.

AUTHOR'S NOTE

I would not have been able to write this paper without the friendship of, discussions with, and bibliographic help from Sonia Enjamio, Juscarid Morales, Inés Rodríguez, Amelia Suárez, and Ernesto Tornín. Some sections of the paper have been presented at St. Mary's University, Queen's University, and the University of Oregon, at Eugene. I am grateful to Christine Koggel for her interest in the paper and to the Social Sciences and Humanities Research Council of Canada for support during two fall semesters in Havana.

NOTES

1. Santiago Cuba Fernandez, "Derechos humanos: Ficción y realidad," *La Gramna* (La Habana, Dec. 6, 1997), p. 4.
2. E.g., Jennifer Stiff, "The Question of National Autonomy: The Case of Cuba," paper presented at North American Society for Social Philosophy conference at Queen's University, July 20, 1997.

3. Lois M. Smith and Alfred Padula, *Sex and Revolution: Women in Socialist Cuba* (New York: Oxford University Press, 1996), p. 185. References in the text are to this edition.
4. E.g., *Proyecto: El partido de la unidad, la democracia y los derechos humanos que defendemos*, V Congreso del partido comuista de Cuba, October, 1997 (Havana: Editora Política, May, 1997).
5. "¡Sexta Victoria!," *La Gramna*, Havana, Nov. 6, 1997, pp. 1, 4, 5.
6. Philip Kitcher, *The Advancement of Science* (New York: Oxford University Press, 1993). e.g. p. 193.
7. This example is from R. Miller, *Fact and Method* (Princeton: Princeton University Press, 1987), p. 93-4.
8. "The Case of Cuba is the Case of Every Underdeveloped Country," Address to the General Assembly, Sept. 26, 1960, reprinted in Fidel Castro, Che Guevara *To Speak the Truth* (New York: Pathfinder, 1992), p. 76.
9. Toni Morrison, *Beloved* (New York: Penguin Books, 1987). Discussed in *Impossible Dreams: Rationality, Integrity and Moral Imagination* (Boulder: Westview Press, 1996), esp. ch. 1.
10. Christine M. Korsgaard, *The Sources of Normativity* (Cambridge: Cambridge University Press, 1996), p. 7-18.
11. Toni Morrison, *Beloved* (New York: Penguin Books, 1987), p. 44-45.
12. *Ibid*, p. 163.
13. Discurso en la Clausura del VI Congreso del ANAP, Havana, May 17, 1982 rpt. In *Discurso en Tres Congresos* (La Habana: Editora Política, 1982), p. 153.
14. Claurura del V Congreso, *La Gramna*, Havana, Nov. 1, 1998, p. 7: "Later we learned a historical lesson, that we had to guarantee the direction, that the direction could not fail, the Party could not allow itself the luxury of failing in direction, for the price is unpayable. This is the key idea: we have to organize ourselves to guarantee direction for a long time. In the times in which we are living, and with the confrontation with imperialism and capitalism, it is not possible to renounce the idea of an efficient and united direction" (my translation).
15. Nicanor Leon Cotayo, "Enmienda Graham: Una amenaza militar contra Cuba," *La Gramna*, La Habana, # 225 (Nov. 12, 1997), p. 5.
16. *Informe Central, V Congreso, La Gramna* (Havana, Oct. 29, 1997), p. 4: "There has always been an alternative, that has been there from the beginning, that if we cannot live with honour, why do we want to live. It is better to die... when people choose duty and honour, when they choose what is just, it is when they most live, because they live with an idea, and ideas don't die, just causes continue through time, as our ideas will continue, and our just cause... and we chose a long time ago, in this dilemma...." (my translation).
17. Frantz Fanon, "The Fact of Blackness," reprinted in D. T. Goldberg, *The Anatomy of Racism* (Minneapolis: University of Minnesota Press, 1990), p. 109.
18. Will Kymlicka, *Liberalism, Culture and Community* (New York: Oxford University Press), p. 12.
19. *Ibid.*
20. V.I. Lenin, March, 1923, cited in Isabel Monal, "Tiene la palabra el camarada Lenin," *Juventud Rebelde Dominical* (La Habana, Nov. 2, 1997), p. 9.
21. See e.g. Dario L. Machado, "La coyuntura sociopolítica actual de la sociedad cubana," in *Contracorriente: Una revista cubana de pensamiento*, Ene-Feb-Mar 1996, Año 2, Número 3, p. 42-58.
22. Fidel Castro, "La Patria es inseparable del concepto de la justicia, de la dignidad, de la libertad, de la Revolución," *La Gramna*, Havana, December 17, 1996, p. 1.
23. Fidel Castro, *Unidos en una sola causa, bajo una sola bandera*" April 19, 1991 (Havana: Editora Politica, 1991).
24. See e.g. Néstor Kohan,"El Che Guevara y la filosofía de la praxis," *Debates Americanos*, No. 3 (enero-junio) 1997 La Habana, p. 55-70.
25. Karl Marx, *Economic and Philosophic Manuscripts of 1844* in Karl Marx and Frederick Engels, *Collected Works*, Vol. 3 (London: Lawrence and Wishart, 1975), p. 249-346.
26. Antonio Gramsci, *Selections from the Prison Notebooks of Antonio Gramsci*, ed. and tr. Quinton Hoare and Geoffrey Nowell-Smith (New York; International Publishers, 1971), esp. "The Intellectuals," p. 3-23.
27. "deeds of conscience" (my translation).
28. Che, "El Plan y el Hombre" en *El Socialismo y el hombre nuevo*, p. 69 rpt. in Kohan, 66.
29. *Fidel Castro: Ideología, conciencia y trabajo político, 1959-1986* (Havana; Editorial Pueblo y Educación, 1991).

30. E.g., Kohan, *op.cit.*
31. E.g., *Informe Central* of the Fifth Congress of the Cuban Communist Party, Oct. 8, 1997, rpt. In *La Gramna*, Oct. 29, 1997, p. 5.
32. Che Guevara, "El socialismo y el hombre en Cuba" in *Ernesto Che Guevara: Obras 1957-1967* (Havana: Casa de las Américas, 1970), p. 370.
33. Antonio Gramsci, "The Modern Prince," Selections from the *Prison Notebooks of Antonio Gramsci*, ed. and tr. Quinton Hoare and Geoffrey Nowell-Smith (New York; International Publishers, 1971), p. 133-4.
34. *Ibid*, p. 172.
35. E.g., Edda Diz Garcés, "Podemos medir el tamaño de nuestro pueblo por el tamaño de los obstáculos que ha tenido," *Trabajadores*, Oct. 20, 1997, p. 16.

JUSTICE FOR SOUTH AFRICA: RESTORATIVE JUSTICE AND THE SOUTH AFRICAN TRUTH AND RECONCILIATION COMMISSION

Jennifer Llewellyn

Jennifer Llewellyn is currently completing an LL.B. at the Faculty of Law, University of Toronto and will be taking up a clerkship with the Canadian Federal Court of Appeal in 1999-2000. She served as an intern with the Research Department at the South African Truth and Reconciliation Commission in 1997. A paper on Restorative Justice that she is co-authoring for the Law Commission of Canada is forthcoming in October 1998.

Llewellyn uses the South African Truth and Reconciliation Commission as a point of departure for a discussion of the nature of justice. She defends the Commission against critics who charge that it is devoid of justice by developing a conception of justice as restorative. Grounded in a relational understanding of human selves this conception of justice stands in contrast to the individualism of traditional conceptions such as retributive justice. Understood restoratively, justice is concerned with restoring relationships to the ideal of social equality — to relationships of dignity and equal concern and respect. This conception serves South Africa well in its work to make the transition from a past marred by the abuse of human rights to a peaceful and rights respecting society.

Issues of justice are particularly poignant in the South African context. The system of Apartheid introduced by the National Party government in 1948 was maintained and perpetuated by acts of manipulation, coercion and violence. The result was a country premised on lies, secrecy, and the abuse of basic human rights. South Africa endured decades of war, waged for liberation from this racial oppression. Apartheid was an all-pervasive system seemingly secure and unstoppable. Thus, it surprised even those closest to the inner workings of this system when at the opening of Parliament in 1990 F.W. De Klerk, President of the National Party government, announced the systematic dismantling of Apartheid. The living symbol of its imminent demise was the release of South Africa's most famous political prisoner – Nelson Mandela. What followed his release was transformation swifter than anyone dared to imagine. The world watched in awe as South Africa negotiated the transfer of power resulting in their first ever truly democratic elections. The magnitude of the transition will be represented forever by the results of these elections – Nelson Mandela once prisoner would now be president. He would lead a transitional government, the Government of National Unity, until the next elections in 1999.

The election of a government of national *unity* was not enough, however, to make such unity a reality. The transition from a past marred by mass human rights abuses to one based on the principles of democracy and respect for human rights could not be had simply by a transition in government. In the words of the Interim Constitution, South Africa faces the challenge of building a bridge "between the past of a deeply divided society characterized by strife, conflict, untold suffering and injustice, and a future founded on the recognition of human rights, democracy and peaceful co-existence."[1] The constitution

Published with permission of Jennifer Llewellyn.

called this the bridge of unity and reconciliation indicating the hope that a rights respecting culture would be waiting on the other side. If it is to begin construction of this bridge, South Africa, as other countries undergoing transition, must face the task of dealing with a past marked by gross human rights violations committed under Apartheid, a task placed before the first democratic government of South Africa.

Arguments for the necessity of dealing with the past arise from a common moral intuition that justice demands "something be done" to address the wrongs of the past. Traditionally the debate over how to "deal" with the past has been a debate over the two options of prosecution or impunity. It is questionable, however, whether the latter of these two qualifies as "dealing with the past" at all. Many have successfully argued that impunity, as it is generally accomplished through blanket amnesties, is tantamount to official amnesia. Impunity seems more akin to forgetting rather than dealing with the past. Thus, advocates of criminal trials argue that the only viable option for "dealing" with the past is prosecution and punishment of the guilty. Were the original terms of the debate exhaustive of all the options for dealing with the past, advocates of criminal trials might be justified in this assertion. However, a new approach has entered the picture to dissolve the all or nothing dichotomy between prosecution and impunity – namely truth commissions. While truth commissions have generally been accompanied by amnesties, their fundamental purpose has been to *prevent* the amnesia brought by traditional impunity. Contrary to the impunity resulting from blanket amnesties, truth commissions "deal" with the past by discovering and telling the truth about it.[2]

This new model for dealing with the past has been utilized in many contexts in the last decade. Current examples include South Africa, Guatemala, and Ireland and plans are underway for a Rwandan truth commission. In *Truth and Reconciliation: Obstacles and Opportunities for Human Rights*, Daan Bronkhorst notes two distinct periods since the mid 1980's marking substantially different approaches to the truth commission model. For the most part, commissions in the early period (before 1991) lacked independence and were thus little more than government puppets or propaganda agents. Bronkhorst takes the report of the Chilean Truth and Reconciliation Commission in 1991 as the line of demarcation between these two periods. According to Bronkhorst's research, "[s]ince 1991 'truth commissions' to investigate past human rights abuses have appeared in around thirty countries" and in contrast to their predecessors they have been empowered to undertake serious independent investigation.[3]

The truth commission model, as embodied in this later period, offers a conception of justice, of the 'something that must be done', that is different from that offered by advocates of criminal prosecution. Current models of truth commissions are rooted in a restorative conception of justice, a conception that deals with human rights violations of the past by working *toward* restoring a particular society to one that respects human rights. As such, this approach stands in stark contrast to the traditional alternative of criminal prosecution rooted in retributive justice, a conception centered on punishing individual wrongdoing.

In this paper, I will use the example of the South African Truth and Reconciliation Commission (TRC)[4] as a point of departure for examining the nature of justice and the mechanisms appropriate for achieving it in a transition to democracy. Through this examination, I will argue that the truth commission approach exemplified by the South African TRC is grounded in a restorative conception of justice that stands juxtaposed to the retributive approach of criminal trials; that central to restorative justice is a relational approach to dealing with the past; and that this relational approach stands in stark contrast to the individualist approach underlying a retributive conception of justice. The relational approach underlying restorative justice is better not only for addressing issues of justice in transitional contexts than approaches that are retributive in nature, but also for satisfying the demands of justice more generally. To defend the case for restorative justice, I will outline the history and structure of the South African Truth and Reconciliation Commission; introduce the justice problem in that context; outline and evaluate responses to this problem; pursue restorative justice as the conception behind the Truth and Reconciliation Commission as distinct from retributive approaches; show that the TRC is a model of restorative justice at work in South Africa; and, finally, examine some of the problems with its implementation.

South Africa and its Truth and Reconciliation Commission

South Africa, if not the clearest, is certainly one of the most familiar contemporary examples of a transitional context. After much national and international consultation and consideration,[5] the South African government chose to establish The Truth and Reconciliation Commission to fulfill the transitional imperative of dealing with the past. The Commission was charged with the difficult task of establishing "as complete a picture as possible of the causes, nature and extent of gross violations of human rights[6] which occurred between 1 March 1960 and 10 May 1994."[7] The Commission is made up of three committees with different responsibilities pertaining to this mandate:

1) *The Human Rights Violation Committee (HRV)* – is responsible for conferring victim status on those individuals who qualify under the Act[8] and come forward to the Commission to make a statement.[9] Victim status will be used to determine eligibility for government reparations. The HRV committee also holds hearings to receive public testimony on a representative number of cases. In addition, they hold special hearings concerning particular events or incidents.

2) *The Amnesty Committee* – is responsible for fulfilling the imperative contained in the Interim Constitution that "amnesty shall be granted in respect of acts, omissions and offences associated with political objectives and committed in the course of the conflicts of the past." While the Interim Constitution mandated the provision of amnesty, it left open the mechanisms, criteria and procedures by which it might be granted. By embedding the amnesty provision in the process of the TRC, the government provided accountability in amnesty rather than a blanket amnesty.[10] Thus, *individuals* must apply for amnesty in respect of *specific acts*. Such acts must have been committed in pursuit of a political objective and must have occurred before the cut-off date[11] provided for in the Act. In addition, in order to qualify for amnesty, application must be made before the deadline and individuals must offer full disclosure to the Commission. Amnesty is located in the context of the mandate of the Commission – amnesty is provided in exchange for truth.

3) *The Reparation and Rehabilitation Committee (R&R)* – is responsible for making recommendations to the government regarding the provision of reparations to and rehabilitation of victims. It is also to make recommendations concerning the prevention of future abuses and the steps necessary to create a culture of respect for human rights in South Africa. Such recommendations might include institutional, administrative, or legislative initiatives aimed at these objectives.

In addition to the work of the specific committees, the Commission itself has undertaken certain investigations and held hearings on matters related to the overall objective of establishing a picture of the past. These have included soliciting submissions from the political parties, holding hearings on the role of various institutions in upholding Apartheid (ie: the health sector, business community, legal profession)[12] and compiling chronologies and histories of particular phenomena under Apartheid (ie: massacres, commissions of inquiry, Apartheid legislation). Such work will provide the context and background for the Commission's final report, which must be submitted to the President three months after its work is finished.[13]

The South Africa commission is a part of the larger phenomenon of truth commissions as a model for dealing with the past. South Africa's experiment, however, stands apart from its predecessors in a number of ways. The South African TRC is the first of its kind to be established by an act of parliament. Other truth commissions have been either informal, unofficial or established through a decree of the head of state. The TRC is also unique in its commitment to transparency. All hearings, testimony and proceedings are open to the public and many are broadcast on public television and radio.[14] This commitment to transparency and public participation was also reflected in the Commission's selection process for its 17 Commissioners. The government undertook an open and public process, accepting public nominations for each of the positions. Members of the public could also submit questions to be put to specific candidates during the nationally televised interview process. The Commission also sets itself apart through its emphasis on victims. The TRC understands itself to be a "victim centered process" in contrast to previous commissions which have focused almost exclusively on perpetrators. These developments in the truth commission model offer guidance to other countries considering this model. Just as Chile's TRC in 1991 stands as a line of demarcation in the development of truth commission models from 'spin doctors' to serious investigative mechanisms, South Africa's commission stands poised to mark the beginning of another wave of development – toward the truth commission model as a viable option for nations reckoning with their own past.[15] These distinctive elements of South Africa's TRC fit the model of restorative justice that I shall outline and defend later.

Critics of the TRC — The "Justice Problem"

Given the preceding description, one might ask why the Commission is not simply called the 'truth' Commission. In fact, this common reference for the South African Commission may reflect a public perception that the Commission is focused on truth but has little or nothing to do with reconciliation. The Commission's slogan "Truth the road to reconciliation" might offer some explanation. The attainment of truth is seen as a *prerequisite* for reconciliation. The questions posed by one of the first witnesses to testify in front of the HRV committee are a poignant reminder of this fact. She asked: how can we forgive when we do not know whom we are to forgive and for what? The Commission attempts to provide answers to these questions. It seeks the truth about the past and *then*, truth in hand, works toward reconciliation. The Commission must be understood as *one part* of the road to reconciliation.[16]

While this answer may satisfy some who express concern that the Commission fails to offer reconciliation, it does not meet the concerns of others. A deeper concern is that the Commission itself is *harmful* to the aim of reconciliation. For example, Fred Rundle, a political analyst and member of the AWB (the militant right wing Afrikaner movement), commenting on the South African television program "Two Way," suggested that the TRC should stand for "Total Revenge Commission." Mr. Rundle, while perhaps slightly more extreme than most, is certainly not alone in this criticism. Some suggest that the Commission will simply rip open old wounds that ought to be left to heal. Others are concerned less with unleashing skeletons than with the haunting impact of the revelations on victims. At the root of all of these concerns and complaints is the perception that the Commission fails to do justice. Such concerns have lead many to suggest that justice is not only conspicuously absent from the title of the commission but from its achievements as well. Bronkhorst suggests that the consistent absence of the term "justice" from the titles of the various truth commissions may result from the fact that justice "attracts far more controversy than the other two concepts — truth and reconciliation."[17]

The South African Truth and Reconciliation Commission has certainly not managed to avoid controversy by omitting justice from its name. The perceived lack of justice in the TRC presents itself in the media, the courts, and on the street in pointed calls for "No Amnesty, No Amnesia, Just Justice." It is clear that "just justice" is a call for retributive justice. It means catch, prosecute and punish (by imprisonment or worse) the perpetrators. This position is typically an uneasy hybrid of the view that justice, in the sense of retribution, must be done regardless of the impact on the transition and of the instrumentalist view that, in fact, retributive justice is necessary to achieve the very goal of reconciliation. The Commission, it is argued, fails on both these terms to offer justice. Further, it actually *denies* justice, since by granting amnesty it robs victims of their right to seek their own justice through either the criminal or civil courts.[18] This is cutting condemnation of the TRC (and the truth commission model more generally). If the Commission is to fulfill its assigned role in the transition it seems it must find some way to respond to critics who charge that it is devoid of justice.

Possible Responses to the Justice Problem

Three responses to this justice problem seem possible. The first is to concede that justice does mean retributive justice. This option openly acknowledges that the granting of amnesty (and therefore the TRC) is unjust. The second alternative is to argue that the Commission offers "transitional justice." Transitional justice can mean one of two things: either the retributive *standard* of justice is different for transitional contexts or there is a different *kind* of justice applicable in transitional contexts. The third and final option is to re-examine our assumptions about the nature of justice. On this account, the Commission may in fact offer justice — justice understood as restorative and not retributive in nature.[19]

It is important to look at the first two options in order to understand the nature of the debate. However, it is the explanation and exploration of the third option which is the particular interest of this paper. The third option, restorative justice, not only appears to hold the most promise for offering a full response to opponents of the Commission, it may, in fact, prove a more appropriate means of conceptualizing both the ambitions of the TRC and justice more generally.

1) Retributive Justice

Advocates of "just justice" in the sense of retribution believe that criminal trials are necessary to satisfy the demands of justice. They are not alone in their belief; criminal prosecution of perpetrators has historically seemed the most obvious avenue, especially to Western human rights activists or international lawyers, for dispensing justice and dealing with the past. Currently this belief is the driving force behind the push for a World Criminal Court.

Criminal trials respond to the powerful, if not overwhelming, moral intuition that the something that must be done in the wake of gross violations of human rights is that the "monsters" responsible for the acts in question must be punished. Indeed, there is a tendency among public international lawyers to cast arguments in terms of a *duty* to prosecute and punish crimes against humanity.[20] As a result, there has been very little analysis of whether such trials actually serve the needs of a transitional society or meet the objectives behind attempts to deal with the past let alone whether they meet the demands of justice in general. This very argument — regarding a "duty" to prosecute — was invoked in the constitutional proceedings aimed at blocking South Africa's alternative approach to dealing with the conflicts of the past.

Advocates of criminal prosecutions claim that trials serve a range of purposes related to the overall goal of dealing with the past and the successful transition to democracy. First, they argue that trials promote the value of legality or the rule of law, which is crucial for a stable and lasting transition to democracy. Second, they maintain that trials allow for discovery and disclosure of what happened in the past and that this disclosure will bring with it an understanding of how such abuses could have happened — how human beings became "monsters." Third, by attributing responsibility for the worst human rights abuses committed during conflicts of the past to individuals rather than groups, it is believed that such trials can produce "closure." Fourth, it is claimed that trials allow victims an opportunity to tell their stories, to confront those who harmed them, and to begin the process of healing. Trials it is argued, present an alternative to private vendetta or vengeance. Finally, supporters of criminal prosecutions make the familiar claim that trials promote deterrence. They stand as a warning to those who might be inclined to commit such human rights violations in the future.

These are all fundamentally laudable goals. The problem is not with the content of these claims made in support of criminal trials. Rather, the problem is that criminal trials do not actually achieve what advocates claim they do. But before I examine some of the deficiencies of a retributive approach more generally, there is the pragmatic point that in the context of South Africa, the transition itself (at least in the manner and time it took place) *required* amnesty and thus precluded the possibility of criminal trials. Had criminal trials been an open possibility there is little doubt that the Apartheid government would have refused to turn over power and the country would have been plunged into civil war. The fact that even those closest to the regime were shocked by the transition and had not foreseen an end to Apartheid in the near future, makes it questionable whether the transition would have occurred (at least any time soon) through any other means than peaceful negotiation. Thus, a retributive stance would have inhibited if not prohibited transformation. It seems clear, then, given the South African realities, the raging debate over amnesty is misplaced.

However, there are general problems with a retributive conception of justice as exemplified by criminal trials, problems rooted in the inherent individualism underlying this approach to dealing with injustices of the past. Criminal trials focus on the individual as the source of the wrong and therefore as the proper subject of punishment. They "deal" with crime by "dealing" with the criminal, an objective that is achieved by extracting individual wrongdoing from the social context in which the actions occurred. There is a delinking of gross human rights violations from what Judith Shklar calls "complex social events" because, as Shklar suggests, "[a] criminal trial demands *mens rea*, and there is often no *mens rea* to be found in the development of socially complex events such as war."[21] The result is a distorted understanding of the past and, perhaps even more dangerous for transitional contexts, a complete lack of information about what political, social, and economic choices could help to avoid repeating the past.

In addition, the criminal process does not lend itself to the discovery of morally and socially relevant "truth" that can only be disclosed through the narratives of victims, perpetrators, and others. The pretence of legal objectivity actually makes it a priority of war crimes tribunals and their prosecutors to exclude or minimize such statements as highly subjective and influenced by an individual's perceptions, affiliations, and so forth. The process, Alvarez confirms, attempts to curtail precisely just such expressions, to avoid the appearance that victims are partial or are testifying in order to further the cause of one side or the other in the conflict.[22] Instead, victims are encouraged to present calm and 'dead-pan' recitation of "facts." It is hard to imagine that a process, which by its own nature and aspirations makes these demands, can permit victims to feel they have been able to express their suffering and receive understanding and sympathy for their experiences. As Nino argues, what is crucial for achieving the necessary goal of enabling "the victims of human rights abuses to recover their self-respect as holders of human rights" is not the retributivist outcome of punishment but rather "the fact that their suffering is listened to in the trials with respect and sympathy."[23] Thus, there appears to be an inherent tension between the adversarial criminal process, which is ultimately aimed at the determination of guilt of particular individuals, and the goal of a complete understanding concerning the past, an understanding that is achieved when we examine the individuals and actions in the social and political context in which they occurred.

Furthermore, criminal trials are not well-suited to exploring the margins of individual choice or to obtaining any nuanced account of moral responsibility in cases of such difficult choices as obedience to orders, passive vs. active resistance, and the perception of oneself as under threat. Even less do war crimes trials provide, generally speaking, a means of identifying and telling the stories of those who made admirable moral choices in these situations, stories that are crucial to affirming free will and demonstrating that such choices are more than hypothetical.[24] Criminal trials focus on the cases where there is no moral ambiguity. Prosecutors go after the "monsters" and leave unconsidered any sense of the range of moral choices available or operating at the time they acted. By attempting to prosecute not the "ordinary" individuals but the heroes or leaders of the various groups in conflict, criminal trials undermine their claim to affirm individual responsibility.

This brief critique makes it clear that criminal trials, owing to their individualist approach, fail to deliver on their promises for transitional contexts. The puzzle remains then, why, given these failings, theorists continue to advocate trials as the best or necessary means to dealing with the past. In other words, what is it that continues to propel people toward a solution that doesn't really work? Quite simply criminal trials, even in the face of their inadequacies, match the strong moral intuition that justice demands retribution in the sense of meting out punishment to individuals for wrong doing. If justice is understood in this retributive sense, the TRC would indeed appear to be devoid of justice. The TRC trades amnesty for disclosure about events and acts of the past. In doing so, the Commission precludes the possibility of punishment (beyond the public censure and humiliation of coming forward and admitting one's actions). Amnesty is then, by definition, unjust on a retributivist account. The TRC further fails if judged against a retributivist account as its mechanisms represent a rejection of the isolationist and individualist approach of retribution. Thus, if advocates of criminal trials are correct and justice does actually demand retribution, there is little hope of the Commission providing justice.

The first option available in response to the justice problem accepts this retributivist conception of justice and thus concedes that the TRC is unjust. Or rather, and perhaps more accurately, that *amnesty* is unjust and as a result the Commission cannot achieve justice. Such an admission, while it does render it impossible to mount a *positive* defense against the critics' charge that the commission fails to do justice, does not leave the commission altogether defenseless.[25] One might argue, in support of the TRC, that justice does not encompass the whole of the moral universe. There may be other values against which justice might be weighed in deciding what is the right thing to do. Thus, the Commission might respond to accusations that it fails to do justice by conceding this point and then claiming that its work is not about justice. The Commission might still claim that its work is *justified* because in the context of the transition, justice may need to be sacrificed to ensure instrumental goals such as peace, stability and avoidance of civil war.

2) Transitional Justice

The second option open to supporters of the TRC in their efforts to respond to the justice problem is to accept that justice ought to have some pull on the Commission. It is not acceptable, on this account, to simply claim that the TRC is not concerned with doing justice. At the same time, however, advocates of this option question the very possibility of realizing justice (i.e., "just justice" or retributive justice) in a transitional context like South Africa. This alternative is often referred to as transitional justice. "Transitional justice" as a distinct approach to justice holds that there is a different content of justice specific to transitional situations. This position varies in degree. Some advocates claim transitional justice is the same in kind as justice for other situations (that is, they claim it is retributive justice), but differs in the extent to which it is to be applied or achieved. Advocates have in mind here a compromising or tempering of justice (read: retributive justice) for transitional contexts. Other advocates of transitional justice argue, however, that such contexts demand a special and decidedly different *kind* of justice. It follows that this kind of justice would not be appropriate for other stable and established contexts.

The Chilean Truth and Reconciliation Commission employed the different standards approach (the former of the two positions).[26] It accepted that justice required retribution. It recognized, however, the need to protect the fragile process of transition. Chile's TRC attempted to strike a balance between these two goals with the claim that under the circumstances of transition one must be content with "justice to the extent possible." Recognizing that the political nature of the crimes at issue and the transitional context itself made the likelihood of "just justice" minimal at best, the Chilean Commission set itself the task of achieving justice as far as possible without threatening the transition. This version of transitional justice holds transitional contexts to a different *standard* of justice. On this account, justice is satisfied in transitional situations by the *attempt* to achieve it to the extent possible given the context.

Advocates of the other version of transitional justice make a slightly different claim. They do not suggest that one must accept a compromise of justice in transitional contexts – finding consolation in the fact that some justice is better than none. Transitional contexts, on this version, do not simply demand a variation of the standard of justice but call for a different kind of justice. Transitional justice conceived of in this way requires inquiry into the specific demands of justice in a transitional context. One can not simply apply a slightly compromised version of retributive justice to a transitional context. This does not preclude the possibility that there may be retributive aspects in this second form of transitional justice. But while it may include punishment, it is not a necessity as it is under a purely retributive conception of justice.

Thus, there is a theoretical distinction between these two understandings of transitional justice. The former accepts that justice is retributive in nature while the latter maintains that a distinct kind of justice is required for transitional contexts. Despite this difference, both versions allow that justice requires or means something different in transitional contexts. Thus, each offers the same defense of the TRC; namely, that the TRC is doing justice in a special way — it is doing transitional justice.

3) Restorative Justice

While the second option restricts its inquiry to transitional contexts, it opens the door for a third approach to the justice question. Restorative justice takes the exploration of the nature of justice a step further. By examining what we mean by justice generally rather than positing a theory of justice singularly appropriate to transitional contexts, advocates of this option provide a defense of the TRC that need not rely on the particulars of a transitional context while recognizing that the dilemmas posed by transitional contexts offer insight into the true nature of justice. The differences between the respective approaches of restorative and transitional justice in the case of transitional contexts can be highlighted in the mechanisms each would favour for achieving justice. A transitional justice perspective would maintain that if criminal trials are feasible without jeopardizing the transition or helpful in dealing with the past, they ought to occur. In contrast, a restorative justice theorist maintains that even if it were possible to have criminal trials they would not be appropriate. Restoration on this account is a first best option not simply an alternative in the face of the impossibility of retributive methods.

What Is Restorative Justice?

Tony Marshall offers a workable *description* of restorative justice in practice: "Restorative justice is a process whereby all the parties with a stake in a particular offence come together to resolve collectively how to deal with the aftermath of the offence and its implications for the future."[27] This description is very general. Its lack of specificity leaves several questions open – who is to be restored? to what are they to be restored? While Marshall is offering us a "one size fits all" description and not a theory of restorative justice, the open nature of his description holds important clues for the nature of restorative justice theory. Restorative justice does not force situations to fit theory. Rather, as a theory, it is open and flexible enough to apply on a variety of levels and to different contextual imperatives. Braithwaite argues that "restorative justice is about restoring victims, restoring offenders and restoring communities" and suggests that it is aimed at "whatever dimensions of restoration matter to the victims, offenders and communities affected by the crime."[28] In this way, restorative justice is sensitive to context and thus appropriate to a variety of situations. A restorative justice approach, on his account, is not limited to the individual level, but can be applied to the institutional level as it has been in recent programs aimed at corporations and as it is applied in the case of the TRC.

Restoring Equality – Restoring Relationships

The suggestion that justice is or ought to be restorative means it is best conceived of in relational terms. This has implications for the way in which justice is to be achieved. The mechanisms of justice must, according to this conception, be judged by their ability to restore the kind of relationships in a community that are respectful of each person's right to dignity and to equal concern and respect. Evaluated against this restorative conception of justice, the TRC, far from lacking justice or representing some compromise or special kind of justice, serves as a model of justice.

Once we understand that the concept of restoration is not that of re-establishing the *status quo ante*, that it is not aimed at restoring things to the way they were immediately before the wrong occurred, it is possible to appreciate how restoration will ultimately depend on a broad social transformation to create full equality in society among victims and perpetrators. At the same time, however, it addresses discrete offences such as gross human rights violations. Such offences may require special measures that address the *particular* way in which they disrupted the ideal possibility of victims and perpetrators living as equal members of society. In sum, restoration of social equality entails neither the *isolation* of each individual wrong as a source of disequilibrium, nor the *submergence* of each wrong to social equality more generally.[29]

Once we understand the challenge that crime poses for justice as that of restoration of *social* equality, of equality in relationship, we can begin to grasp the way in which restorative justice theory and retributive theory begin to diverge from their common goal of addressing injustice. They differ in that retributive theory imposes on the goal or purpose of restoration of social equality a particular set of historical practices (typical of a wide range of societies) often known as "punishment." It identifies the very idea of restoration with these particular practices, practices which are premised on isolating individuals from social relationships. Restorative theory, in contrast, problematizes the issue of what set of practices can or should, in a given context, achieve the goal of restoration of equality in society. Identifying these practices requires dialogue among victims, perpetrators and community and involves concrete consideration of the needs of each for restoration.[30] These practices may vary widely, from place to place and time to time—including therapy for victims, apology or acceptance of responsibility, what Braithwaite calls "reintegrative shaming,"[31] or financial compensation for victims.

Restorative justice theory preserves the intrinsically social dimension in the moral intuition that "something must be done" in response to the offence. It claims that equality or equilibrium must be restored, only it is an equality or equilibrium *in relationships within* society. Establishing equality in relationship means ensuring equal concern and respect between the parties in the relationship. This helps us then to better understand the contrast between restorative and retributive theory in terms of the social practices they justify and generate. It is not a crude contrast between punishment vs. everything else, but rather between paradigmatically isolating measures and paradigmatically reintegrative ones; between a focus on the individual isolated and abstracted from social relationship and a focus on the individual inherently embedded in relationship. What restorative justice theory asserts is not the preferability of the latter from some external point of view, such as social welfare or social self-protection. Rather, it asserts reintegrative measures as a *logical necessity* flowing from the facts of selves as inherently relational. By this claim, I do not intend to deny the individuality of selves. Rather I mean to highlight what is perhaps an obvious truth – that human selves live and develop (constitute themselves) in and through relationships with other selves. Thus, while we are each individual selves we are not wholly independent of one another, but are rather interdependent.[32] It is not enough, however, to simply assert the fact of our relationality. Not any and all relationships will serve to fulfil our needs. For human beings to flourish, there must be relationships that respect each person's right to dignity and to equal concern and respect.

The case of the South African transition is particularly stark as it is moving from a history of severe power imbalances, resulting in the systematic racial oppression of the majority of the population at the hands of the small (yet powerful) white minority. This same minority had the power to define and enforce rights. In so doing, they had the power to structure relationships to ensure inequality and disrespect for the majority. In its efforts to create a rights respecting culture, South Africa is working toward establishing relationships of equality. Restoration after such gross violations of basic human rights is the restoration of equality in all relationships; between the perpetrator of the offence and other members of society, including the victim. It is the restoration to the ideal of relationships of mutual concern and respect with which restorative justice is concerned.

Theory in Practice—Restorative Justice for South Africa?

Given the discussion of restorative justice, we are now in a position to explore how this model of justice is at work in South Africa. After decades of violent abuse of human rights, oppression and essentially civil war, South Africa needs transformation, reconciliation. Reconciliation in this context is not some idyllic notion of forgive and forget. Rather, what is sought in terms of reconciliation (as described in the South African Interim Constitution) is peaceful co-existence. This may be more difficult than it sounds. Reconciliation requires the very opposite from forgetting; it demands remembering so that each citizen can know the history of the abuses of the past and commit to live together in a different way. This notion of reconciliation seems to offer content to the idea of restoration in South Africa. In contrast to the alternative retributive model, restorative justice does not seek to avenge the wrongs of the past. Restorative justice looks backwards in order to look forward and build a different future; it is thus inherently oriented toward transformation.[33] The establishment of the TRC reflects the commitment to create a new society mindful of the lessons of the past. Such a commitment is best served by a theory of justice which is not purely retrospective or concerned with the re-establishment of the *status quo ante*.

For restorative justice, community is both subject and object; restorative justice is realized in community and is at the same time transformative of that very community. Under this model, justice can only be achieved when all those with a stake in the situation come together to collectively resolve the problem. This dimension of restorative justice has many advantages for a transitional situation like South Africa. First, much of the abuse in South Africa was perpetrated, supported and maintained in a systematic manner implicating most if not all of the population in some way. Thus, in order for any real transformation to occur, the process must include not just the individuals who were perpetrators and victims in the conventional sense, but those in their communities who were supporters, silent witnesses, and those painfully affected by particular incidences of injustice. Second, transformation by definition involves the creation or rebuilding of community, that is, the restoration of an inherently social equilibrium. Restorative justice involves different communities in coming to a resolution and requires them to assist in building the bridge to the future. Having been a part of the process, these communities have a stake in its successful outcome.[34] Lastly, through community involvement, members can learn and reconstitute themselves in a commitment to the justice process itself. Community involvement is key because in order to establish this new rights respecting society, the people must be part of the process through which it is created.[35] Restorative justice facilitates this involvement by bringing communities into the process.

Conclusion—
TRC as a Restorative Process

Archbishop Desmond Tutu, chairperson of the TRC, has explicitly stated that he understands the Commission to be an exercise in restorative justice.[36] However, as the theory developed throughout this paper has suggested, there is no single institutional model for restorative justice. Thus, it is not possible to test the TRC process against some abstract procedural ideal of restorative justice. Each restorative justice process may be fundamentally different and still be entirely restorative in nature. Thus, there might exist two restorative approaches to political transformation that are considerably different but still informed and guided by the same restorative commitments. The reason for this, as discussed in an earlier section of this paper, is that restorative justice pays attention to and is informed by context. This results in room for and indeed a necessity to develop different processes depending on context.

Underlying these various forms, however, must be common commitments; to restoration over retribution, to relational over isolating mechanisms, and to understanding communities as an integral part in the creation and solution of the social phenomenon of crime. Thus, whether it is focusing on restoring the victim, perpetrator, or the community, the focus is always broader than the individual. The focus now is on relationships. Further, these processes have a commitment to be forward looking – to look at the implications of offences for the future and to bringing together all those who have a stake in the development of that future.

It is clear, then, how the Truth and Reconciliation Commission attempts a restorative approach in dealing with South Africa's past. The Commission embeds the granting of amnesty in a process which seeks the truth of the past in order to build a different future. A comprehensive analysis of the ways in which the TRC lives out these restorative commitments is beyond the scope of this paper. However, if we return to our previous description of the TRC, we can get a picture of it as a restorative process.

First, the TRC's process implicates a wide spectrum of the society. The selection of Commissioners was a public process and driven by public nominations resulting in the appointment of individuals from several different communities and segments of society. Further, the work of the Commission is public. Sessions are open to the public and broadcast on television and radio drawing in a wider population than would be possible in person. This commitment to transparency takes the work of the Commission into the public arena for debate and discussion. It enables the community to participate in the process as a party with a great stake in the issues of transition.

Second, the Commission is clearly committed to the restoration of victims. It is by its own identification a victim centered process. The Commission attempts to listen to victims and address their needs. Such a focus enables them to ask the important question about what is required for restoration, namely, to bring the victim, perpetrator and the community together to understand the dynamics of relationships that permitted such abuse and to look for ways to restore these relationships to ones of social equality.

The Commission is also operating within a restorative model with respect to its treatment of perpetrators. Through the amnesty process, perpetrators are called to account for their actions. However, they are not removed from society, but rather left free to re-enter the community and rebuild relationships. Thus, the Commission leaves open the possibility of restoring relationships as it keeps the perpetrator in relationship with others to work toward a better future. While the amnesty provision is clearly important to the restorative approach of the TRC, it raises an interesting challenge to the TRC and restorative justice practices more generally. The challenge is that created by the need for an "axe" (or whip) to motivate people to participate in the process. There is a question about whether using punishment as this "axe" implies a retributive approach and whether it can be accommodated within restorative justice theory. It is entirely consistent with a restorative conception of justice to admit the necessity of some "axe" in order to motivate participation. Conceived of in another way, this problem asks the question: what if a person refuses to participate or for some reason cannot participate in the process of restorative justice? In short, what reason do people have to participate in the process given that the alternative is freedom?

The response must be that an "axe" is required not for justice itself but for social protection. In order to protect relationships from further disruption and to protect the restorative process itself, it is necessary to remove those who, owing to their unwillingness to participate in the restorative process, pose a threat to the achievement and stability of social equality. Even measures taken in the name of social protection must work toward bringing the perpetrator into the restorative process, a central goal evidenced in the forward-looking nature and commitment of the Commission. The Commission is focused, on a macro scale, at the restoration of communities. At its core, it is motivated by the goal of nation-building and reconciliation. Its work is done in this spirit and mindful of this goal.

Further, the focus of the Commission is not centered solely on individual responsibility, as it is in the criminal system. Rather, the TRC views individual responsibility through the context of community responsibility. It places individual acts in the context of organizational, institutional and state actions. This is clear as amnesty is granted with respect to politically motivated acts. Determinations of whether or not an act was politically motivated rest on the individual's membership or association with a political group or operation. Thus, the connection between individual and collective responsibility is clearly recognized.

Viewing the Commission through the lens of restorative justice is indeed helpful in fending off those who would condemn its lack of justice. However, this perspective also raises challenges for the way in which the Commission attempts to provide restorative justice. If the TRC is about restorative justice, then this model of justice must also serve as an evaluative tool. Thus, I want to end by highlighting one of the challenges a restorative justice model, taken seriously, might pose to the TRC.

Specific to the South African TRC (and perhaps truth commissions in general) is the problem of the lack of connection between the perpetrators and the victim. This separation causes problems for addressing the restorative needs of both. Structurally the victim and the perpetrator are dealt with separately by the TRC. The HRV committee deals with the victims and the Amnesty committee with the perpetrators. While there is some provision made for victims to face the perpetrators in an amnesty hearing, there is no room for dialogue between the two and their respective communities.[37] In fact, the question of reparations is taken out of this process altogether and has no relationship to amnesty. The rationale behind this move is that it is the state who is granting amnesty (thereby removing the victims' right to choose to seek redress through the courts as amnesty includes immunity from both criminal prosecutions and civil actions) and thus it is the state's responsibility to repay the victim. What this precludes in the process, however, is any possibility of the offender making reparation to the victim. This has implications on all levels – for the victim, perpetrator and the community. Removing reparation from the amnesty process seriously limits the connection between amnesty and restoring the victim. It restricts this connection solely to that restoration achieved through hearing and knowing the truth of the past. Practically, the victim sees the offender go free and still receives no direct reparations until the government considers proposals for reparation at some later date. As far as the perpetrator is concerned, amnesty without any way to make amends for one's actions could result in what Braithwaite refers to as a "shaming machine" serving to stigmatize rather than reintegrate perpetrators. Without at least the possibility of reparations, perpetrators are left with no way to re-enter the community and try to "make things right."[38] Further, this separation ignores the large role that reparations can play in rehabilitation. By focusing on reparations and rehabilitation only with regard to victims, the Commission forgets the importance of reintegrating perpetrators in order to heal or reconcile damaged relationships in society. The difficulty here is how far one can go and still be granting amnesty. Would a conditional amnesty have served the political purposes of facilitating the transition? It seems, however, that even if a conditional amnesty was not possible, at the very least provision for involvement in reparations or access to rehabilitation programs could have been made *available* to perpetrators. This problem might yet be addressed by the Commission through its recommendations to the President on reparations and rehabilitation.[39]

In both its strengths and weaknesses, the South African TRC stands as a compelling example of restorative justice, as a model for transitional contexts. Supporters of the TRC are able to respond to its critics who charge that it is devoid of justice. Viewed through this lens, the Truth and Reconciliation Commission does not lack justice; quite the contrary, the TRC serves as a powerful example of justice in a transitional context and offers lessons on how justice might be better achieved.

Author's Note

Jennifer Llewellyn served as an intern with the Research Department of the Truth and Reconciliation Commission. This internship was supported through CIDA's Technical Assistance Fund and a research grant from the Wright Foundation. The views expressed here are those of the author alone and do not reflect those of the Commission. The author is grateful to her colleagues at the Commission, in particular Charles Villa Vicencio, Wilhelm Verwoerd, Michelle Parleveliet, and Ronald Slye for their assistance and guidance. Special thanks is owed to Robert Howse for many discussions which provided invaluable challenge and support for the development of these ideas. The author is indebted to Christine Koggel, Jennifer Nedelsky, and Hallett Llewellyn for their insightful comments.

NOTES

1. Interim Constitution, section 232 (4).
2. For further reference, see David Crocker, "Transitional Justice and International Civil Society," National Commission on Civic Renewal, Working Paper #13; Luc Huyse "Justice after Transition: On the Choices Successor Elites Make in Dealing with the Past" (1995) *Law and Social Inquiry: Journal of the American Bar Association*; Juan E. Mendez "Accountability for Past Abuses" (1997) 19 *Human Rights Quarterly* 255; Carlos S. Nino "The Duty to Punish Past Abuses of Human Rights Put into Context: The Case of Argentina" (1991) 100 *Yale L.J.* 2619; Diane F. Orentlicher, "Settling Accounts: The Duty to Prosecute Human Rights Violations of a Prior Regime" (1991) 100 *Yale L.J.* 2537; Sam Seibert et. Al., "War Crimes: To Punish or Pardon? — Justice from Bosnia to Rwanda to Chile, a Searing Moral Debate over Amnesty" (November 21, 1994) *Newsweek* 32; M.R. Rwelamira and G. Werle (eds) *Confronting Past Injustices: Approaches to Amnesty, Punishment, Reparation and Restitution in South Africa and Germany* (Butterworths, 1996); and, Naomi Roht-Arriaza (ed) *Impunity and Human Rights in International Law and Practice* (Oxford: Oxford University Press, 1995).
3. Daan Bronkhorst, *Truth and Reconciliation: Obstacles and Opportunities for Human Rights* (Amsterdam: Amnesty International Dutch Section, 1995) at 10.
4. The Truth and Reconciliation Commission has come to be known by many names throughout its life. I tend to use several of them interchangeably for the sake of literary convenience. Most common among these is "the TRC," "the Commission," and "the Truth Commission."
5. The parliamentary bill regarding the creation of the Truth and Reconciliation Commission was the longest debated bill in the history of South Africa.
6. The Commission is not charged with the task of investigating all of the abuses, or even all of the human rights abuses committed under the Apartheid regime. The mandate of the TRC quite clearly draws the parameters of the Commission's investigations. The Commission is only concerned with "gross violations of human rights." Section 1(1) (ix) of The Promotion of National Unity and Reconciliation Act, which governs the TRC, defines gross violations of human rights as:

   ... the violation of human rights through –

   (a) the killing , abduction, torture or severe ill-treatment of any person; or

   (b) any attempt, conspiracy, incitement, instigation, command or procurement to commit an act referred to in paragraph (a),

   which emanated from the conflicts of the past and which was committed during the period 1 March 1960 to the cut-off date within or outside the Republic, and the commission of which was advised, planned, directed, commanded or ordered, by any person acting with a political motive.
7. Promotion of National Unity and Reconciliation Act, The Republic of South Africa, Act No. 34 of 1995, as amended by The Promotion of National Unity and Reconciliation Amendment Act No. 84 of 1995 (hereafter "the Act"). This act was amended to extend the latter of these two dates. The date was initially 10 December 1993, but was changed in an effort to include the events leading up to the elections in 1994.
8. Under the Act, section 1(xix), victim includes –

   (a) persons who, individually or together with one or more persons, suffered harm in the form of physical or mental injury, emotional suffering, pecuniary loss or a substantial impairment of human rights –

      (i) as a result of a gross violation of human rights; or

      (ii) as a result of an act associated with a political objective for which amnesty has been granted,

   (b) persons who, individually or together with one or more persons, suffered harm in the form of physical or mental injury, emotional suffering, pecuniary loss or a substantial impairment of human rights, as a result of such person intervening to assist persons contemplated in paragraph (a) who were in distress or to prevent victimization as may be prescribed.

   (c) Such relatives or dependents of victims as may be prescribed.
9. Given the size of the country and the conditions under which many of the victims of gross human rights live, it would have been impossible for most of them to go

to the Commission to make their statement. While the Commission does have regional offices in four locations throughout the country they were still inaccessible to many victims living in small communities, townships and homelands throughout South Africa. Thus, the HRV Committee undertook a statement taking process which involved sending statement takers throughout the country to meet with, listen to and record victim's testimony.

10. It is important to note that this is one of the unique features of the South African TRC. We will return to a discussion of the other ways in which the South African TRC stands apart from its predecessors.
11. There are two important dates with respect to the Amnesty provision. The "cut-off" date is the date that marks the period during which acts must have been *committed* to be eligible for amnesty. This date was extended by Parliament to include acts leading up to the election in 1994. The second important date is the "deadline." This is the date by which one must make *application* for amnesty in order to qualify. This date was also extended from May 10, 1997 until September 30, 1997 in order to account for the change in the cut-off date.
12. See David Dyzenhaus, *Judging the Judges, Judging Ourselves: Truth, Reconciliation and the Apartheid Legal Order* (Oxford: Hart Publishing, 1998).
13. The original legislation gave the Commission a mandate of eighteen months with a possible extension of six months at the President's discretion. An additional extension, beyond the six months contemplated in the act, was granted by an act of parliament in September 1997. The extension was granted so that the work of the Amnesty Committee could be completed during the life of the Commission and before the Commission submitted its final report to the President. The amendment calls for the extension of the Commission's mandate from its intended completion in December 1997 (final report in March 1998) to April 30 1998 (final report to be submitted by July 1998). The amendment prohibits the Commission from undertaking any new work after December 14, 1997. See Statement by Arch Bishop Desmond Tutu, Chairperson, Truth and Reconciliation Commission, September 18, 1997.
14. The only exception to this rule is under section 33 of the Act. Section 33 provides:

    Hearings of Commission to be open to public — 1 (a) Subject to the provisions of this section, the hearings of the Commission shall be open to the public.

    (b) If the Commission, in any proceedings before it, is satisfied that —

    i) it would be in the interest of justice; or

    ii) there is a likelihood that harm may ensue to any person as a result of the proceedings being open, it may direct that such proceedings be held behind closed doors and that the public or any category thereof should not be present at such proceedings or any part thereof: Provided that the Commission shall permit any victim who has an interest in the proceedings concerned, to be present.

    Such an exception is most commonly made with respect to hearings held under section 29 of the Act where individuals have been subpoenaed to appear before the Commission.
15. For further comparisons of Truth Commissions see Daan Bronkhorst, *Truth and Reconciliation: Obstacles and Opportunities for Human Rights* (*Supra* note 3); Priscilla B. Hayner "Fifteen Truth Commissions — 1974 to 1994: A Comparative Study" (1994) 16 *Human Rights Quarterly* 597; and, Michelle Parleviet "Considering Truth: Dealing with a Legacy of Gross Human Rights Violations" (1998) 16:2 *Netherlands Quarterly of Human Rights* at 141.
16. The other obvious components of the journey toward reconciliation are the Land Claims Commission, The Reconstruction and Development Plan (RDP), and the pending reparation program for victims.
17. Bronkhorst at 11.
18. This very argument was, in fact, the subject of a court challenge to the Amnesty provision in the new South African Constitutional Court. See *Azanian People's Organization (AZAPO) and Others v. President of the Republic of South Africa and Others*, 1996 (8) BCLR 1015 (CC). The challenge, brought by a few prominent victims families, failed on the grounds that the Constitution provided for the violation of their rights in the interest of national unity and reconciliation. It is interesting to note that these families are not typical of victims in South Africa. They were very prominent cases and as such might have had access to enough information to contemplate legal action. Most

victims, however, do not have any information concerning their cases and come to the commission in search of it.

19. See Charles Villa-Vicencio, "A Different Kind of Justice: The South African Truth and Reconciliation Commission" (Unpublished); and, Wilhelm Verwoerd, "Reflections from within the TRC" *Current Writing: Text and Reception in South Africa*, Vol. 8(2), October 1996, 66-85.
20. See Payam Akhavan, "Justice in the Hague, Peace in the former Yugoslavia?: A Commentary on the United Nations War Crimes Tribunal." Unpublished manuscript, the Hague; and, Carlos S. Nino, "The Duty to Punish Abuses of Human Rights Put in Context: The Case of Argentina" *Yale L.J.* Vol. 100, 1991 at 2619.
21. Judith Shklar, *Legalism: Law, Morals and Political Trials* (Cambridge Mass.:Harvard University Press, 1964) at 172.
22. José Alvarez, "The Tadic Judgement and the Nuremberg Model of Closure" unpublished manuscript, University of Michigan Law School, 1997.
23. Carlos Santiago Nino, *Radical Evil on Trial* (New Haven: Yale University Press, 1996), 147.
24. See the important work of Tzetvan Todorov, *Facing the Extreme: Moral Life in the Concentration Camps*, tr. Denner and Pollack, (New York: Henry Holt, 1996).
25. See generally Wilhelm Verwoerd *supra* note 19.
26. See Neil Kritz (ed), *Transitional Justice — Volume II: Country Studies* (Washington DC: United States Institute of Peace Press, 1995) at 487.
27. John Braithwaite, *Restorative Justice: Assessing an Immodest and a Pessimistic Theory*, 1997 (this paper is available on the World Wide Web, Australian Institute of Criminology Home Page – Http://www.aic.gov.au), at 5 (Hereafter Braithwaite 1). See also Jim Consedine, *Restorative Justice: Healing the Effects of Crime* (New Zealand: Ploughshares Publications 1995).
28. Braithwaite ch 1 at 5.
29. See Jennifer Llewellyn and Robert Howse "Dealing with the Past and the Building of a Pluralistic Society," Conference Proceedings for UNESCO International Conference on Multiculturalism and Post-Communism Tradition and Democratic Processes, Dubrovnik, Croatia, November 1997.
30. For an example of the role of dialogue in the realization of social equality, see J. Nedelsky and C. Scott "Constitutional Dialogue" in J. Bakan and D. Schneiderman, (eds) *Social Justice and the Constitution: Perspectives on a Social Union for Canada* (Ottawa: Carleton University Press, 1992) at 59.
31. John Braithwaite, *Crime, Shame, and Reintegration* (New York: Cambridge University Press, 1989) (Hereafter Braithwaite 2).
32. See generally Jennifer Nedelsky "Reconceiving Rights as Relationship" *Rev. of Constitutional Studies* 1, 1993; and, Christine Koggel *Perspectives on Equality: Constructing a Relational Theory* (Lanham, MD: Rowman & Littlefield Publishers, Inc., 1998).
33. In fact there has been some suggestion that restorative justice might be better called by the name of transformative justice. Ruth Morris, *A Practical Path to Transformative Justice* (Toronto: Rittenhouse, 1994).
34. See the evidence that there is a much higher rate of performance of reparations decided upon through restorative justice programs than those ordered by courts in Braithwaite 1.
35. See generally J. Habermas, *Between Facts and Norms*, tr. W. Rehg (Cambridge, Mass.: MIT Press 1995).
36. In conversations with the author.
37. It is important to note that the failure to make room for dialogue in the Amnesty setting is contrasted in other areas of the Commission, in particular some of the special event hearings held by the HRV committee, where dialogue and the meeting of different communities is central.
38. Consult, for example, the case of Brian Victor Mitchell who was granted amnesty with respect to the Trust Feeds Massacre — *Amnesty Application No. 2586/96*. Brian Mitchell was convicted and sentenced to death in 1992 for the murder of eleven people in the Trust Feeds area. The killings were a part of a police operation headed by Mitchell. A mistake was made and the wrong house was fired upon. The eleven people killed were not the intended victims. Mitchell was granted amnesty in 1996 and upon his release wanted to make reparation for his actions, but when he turned to the commission for assistance, there were no such programs in place. Mitchell then went back into the community where the murders took place. For over a year he would try to find ways

to give back to the community from which he took so much.

39. Although the outline for these recommendations was released October 23, 1997, and further implementation details released March 11, 1998, it gave no indication that the commission was considering a move in this direction. See "Introductory Notes to the Presentation of the Truth and Reconciliation Commission's Proposed Reparations and Rehabilitation Policies" – Truth and Reconciliation Press Release October 23, 1997; and, "Statement By Archbishop Desmond Tutu on Allocation for Reparations in the Minister of Finance's Budget" Truth and Reconciliation Commission Press Release March 11, 1998. Available at the TRC website: www.truth.org.za

SELF-DETERMINATION IN POLITICAL PHILOSOPHY AND INTERNATIONAL LAW

Omar Dahbour

Omar Dahbour teaches Philosophy at Colorado State University. He is co-editor of The Nationalism Reader *(Humanities, 1995) and editor of a special issue on "Philosophical Perspectives on National Identity" in* The Philosophical Forum *(Fall-Winter 1996-97).*

Dahbour distinguishes between the principle in international law of Popular Self-Determination (PSD) and the principle in contemporary political philosophy of National Self-Determination (NSD). PSD refers to cases in which populations of already existing countries claim the right to political sovereignty and non-interference from other states. NSD refers to cases in which nationalities without their own countries or states claim the right to self-determination in the sense of forming a nation based on claims about the shared character and culture of a group of people. Dahbour argues that NSD is philosophically less justifiable than PSD and raises several objections to NSD, arguing that it has detrimental effects for many individuals within a nation and for international relations.

While nationalism is in origin a European idea, it has spread far beyond the boundaries of Europe in the last century to become a prevalent ideology in all major regions of the world. One indication that this is the case is the increasing extent to which self-determination has become an important problem for the theory and practice of international law. It is the case, however, that self-determination has a quite different meaning in international law than it has in contemporary political philosophy.

International law posits a principle of Popular Self-Determination (PSD) that applies to cases in which populations of already existing countries lack self-government. In contrast, a number of contemporary political philosophers assert a right of National Self-Determination (NSD) that applies to nationalities without their own independent states. I argue here that the principle of PSD found in international law is *philosophically* more warranted than the right of NSD claimed by nationalists and current in political philosophy.

Reprinted with permission of Elsevier Science from *History of European Ideas* 16: 4–6 (1993): 879–884.

Self-determination as a political concept dates from the early years of this century, but its origins lie in eighteenth-and nineteenth-century philosophy. The idea of self-determination originated as a notion of the freedom of individuals to determine the conditions of their own life. Its later expansion to include the self-determination of communities as well as individuals has been characterised as a shift of concern from "personhood" to "peoplehood."[1]

The political principle of self-determination was first proclaimed by Lenin and Wilson in the aftermath of World War I. Despite the failure of the League of Nations or international jurists to acknowledge this principle in the 1920s and 30s, such proclamations inaugurated the modern advocacy of self-determination. Some measure of recognition was achieved after World War II by references to self-determination in the United Nations Charter and by the adoption of UN Resolutions 1514 and 2625 in 1960 and 1970. Despite controversy as to whether such documents constitute legitimate sources of international law, they do indicate the growing customary acceptance of some principle of self-determination.[2]

This principle has also been acknowledged in a number of state constitutions and treaties, interstate organisational charters and declarations, and decisions by the World Court. What has been recognised in most of these documents is the right or at least claim of "peoples" to self-determination. Peoples are here understood to be the inhabitants of countries—which may be and usually are multinational—rather than distinct national groups. The classic case of this principle is that of the claim of colonies to independence.[3]

More generally, self-determination in international law is regarded as the right of a people to determine their own affairs without external interference. This definition extends beyond cases of colonialism; it is a general affirmation of the principle of political sovereignty. In noncolonial cases, "sovereignty" generally means freedom from foreign interventions. I believe it is therefore appropriate to call the principle used in international law that of Popular Self-Determination in order to emphasise that it is a principle of the sovereign rule of peoples in their own countries. As a claim-right, it is applicable only to non-self-governing countries or to countries that experience interventions by foreign powers.[4]

Justifications of the principle of self-determination are usually derived from a right to self-government. In international law, self-government is equated with political sovereignty and is defined as a combination of civil rights and territorial integrity. Self-government is absent if these principles are violated; namely, if the citizenship rights of its inhabitants to political participation are denied and/or if a country and its people are governed by another sovereign country. Violations of these principles constitute prima facie evidence for a legitimate claim to PSD. Conversely, such claims have no standing when these principles are not violated.

In contemporary international law, self-determination is therefore regarded as an attribute of peoples in already existing states.[5] This definition came into general use in the period after World War II in which the United Nations was established and principles justifying anticolonial struggles for independence were formulated. But in the postcolonial period (particularly after 1960), a new concept of self-determination—here designated as National Self-Determination—has gained increasing acceptance, particularly in political philosophy, but also, to some extent, in international law.

This concept of NSD recalls in some respects the initial impetus to self-determination after World War I, when a number of nationalities in Europe carved out nation-states from the old multinational empires of Austria, Russia, and Turkey.[6] The concept of NSD challenges the prevalent view in international law that self-government is equivalent to the political sovereignty of existing states. Self-determination is regarded as an attribute of nationalities, not of peoples who are the populations of already existing countries. Nations are distinct from states in that they are, in Michael Walzer's words, "communities of character" that constitute the necessary foundation of self-government in states.[7]

From this perspective, self-government is therefore not a matter simply of determining whether a country is sovereign and whether citizenship rights exist within it. States must be coextensive with established nations in order for self-government to exist in its fullest sense. Under this definition of self-determination, claims by nations to statehood therefore constitute the core case of self-determination, not claims by non-self-governing countries to political sovereignty.

NSD is a particular reinterpretation of the core notion of self-government, as it has been developed in both philosophy and law. The basic idea is that all nations are entitled to states—that this rather than political sovereignty is the real meaning of self-government. The sovereignty of states is therefore only justifiable when they are congruent with particular nations.[8]

This view is directly contrary to the legal conception of a people (first developed in the French Revolution) as that collection of individuals who inhabit the territory of an existing state. Nationalists criticize this view because they maintain that it does not provide a convincing theory of how individuals come to have this relation to states. According to them, the distribution of membership in a community is the primary political good, without which no other goods—such as peace, justice or security—can be obtained.[9]

The nationalist criterion of membership by which

legitimacy is conferred on states is the fit of those states with nations defined as "encompassing groups."[10] This notion of encompassing groups is developed in a recent article by Avishai Margolit and Joseph Raz, who characterise such groups as having a common character and culture, along with patterns of socialisation in which individuals acquire this character and culture. The group thus exists as the primary focus of individuals' self-identification. Membership of individuals in encompassing groups is determined by the recognition or non-recognition of similarities with other members.

Margolit and Raz argue that "[t]he right to self-determination derives from the value of membership in encompassing groups." They regard NSD itself as a means to the realisation of self-government. There are three ways, they maintain, in which the nature of encompassing groups means that NSD is required for self-government.

First, individuals can only determine their own lives in their capacity as members of such encompassing groups. If self-government is justified on the basis of its realisation of individuals' freedom, it must include conditions that will guarantee this freedom—and the self-determination of encompassing groups is the primary such condition.[11]

Second, since self-government means in part the acquisition of political sovereignty, this sovereignty will be incomplete if it does not include the right of groups to decide their own conditions of membership—including whether to acquire their own state.[12] This decision can only be made given a right of self-determination. Such a right is therefore necessary for self-government.

Third, since all individuals exist within one or another nation, no one can judge the relative worth of different nations' claims to self-determination. Accordingly, all nations must be accorded equal worth in terms of their claims to states. A right of NSD cannot therefore be subordinated to the interests and demands of already existing states—it is applicable to all nations inasmuch as they assert their claims to such a right.

NSD is thus justified as an interpretation of self-government on the basis of individual freedom, political sovereignty, and the equality of nations. The legal-internationalist notion of PSD cannot, on this view, realise self-government because it is not concerned with nations as encompassing groups and gives such collectivities no consideration as political entities. The result, according to the philosophical-nationalist view, is that full self-government cannot be achieved.

The primary problem with the notion of NSD can be understood when encompassing groups are more accurately designated as "ascriptive groups." Membership in an ascriptive group is often the primary indicator of a person's identity. This identity is ascribed to them by others; they are identified by virtue of characteristics they purportedly share with other members of a group. These acts of ascribing characteristics and traits to individuals is the process by which nationalities determine their own identity.

Ascriptive groups are constitutive of individuals in that persons do not choose to enter such groups and cannot necessarily leave them at will, since they may be affected by exclusions, discrimination, or stereotyping. Such groups, according to Iris Young, "always already have specific attributes, stereotypes, and norms associated with them, in reference to which a person's identity will be formed."[13]

Political communities, by contrast, can be considered to be "associative groups" in that they are composed of individuals who associate for particular purposes. While ascriptive groups are formed in accordance with perceived and ascribed similarities or differences, associative groups are formed on the basis of mutual needs and interests. Membership in states, on this view, cannot therefore be based on nationality. The general reason for this is that basing politics on national identities undercuts the ability of associative groups to realise their common interests.

The result of the nationalist reinterpretation of self-government to mean the self-determination of ascriptive groups has three effects: (1) it *hinders* the self-determination of individuals; (2) it precludes the recognition of mutual needs and interests in existing political communities; and (3) it exacerbates international rivalries by giving just cause to all nationalist claims to statehood.

In the first case, ascriptive groups contradict the need of individuals to determine their own identities by forcing them into the predetermined mold of national stereotypes. Unlike associative groups, ascriptive groups depend for their cohesion on the subordination of individual identities to group identities. But the rejection of rigid identifications of individuals with particular groups is necessary for such individuals to meaningfully determine their own lives.[14]

NSD leads to interest in the creation, expansion, or strengthening of states, while individual self-determination leads to a concern for human rights and *restrictions* on the actions of states.[15] Despite nationalist claims that NSD is an extension of personal self-determination to the self-determination of communities, it actually impedes personal freedom and development by placing restrictions on the choices individuals can make in forming their own identities.

In the second case, ascriptive groups such as nations seek to institutionalise differences through the creation of nation-states that accord full rights of citizenship only to members of particular national groups. Nationalists advocate abandonment of the recognition of mutual needs and interests *among* nationalities for the pursuit of a politics of exclusionary identities.

The result of this espousal of nation-states is that groups end up ignoring the real ties of mutual need and dependence that characterise political communities. As Felicity Watts has written, "belief in a shared property [e.g., nationality] underlying group membership leads to a redrawing of boundaries so that the group that actually fulfils my needs is ignored and I affiliate myself with others who are like me."[16]

Finally, the nationalist claim to better realise self-government continually threatens to lead to civil and interstate conflicts since there is no objective way to determine which national groups may lay claim to which territories. Margolit and Raz maintain that there is no alternative to allowing nations to decide the justice of their own claims. Such a conclusion follows from belief in the equal political worth of all nations.

But the result of this is the all too frequent militarisation and/or internationalisation of conflicts between national groups over rival territorial claims. Though nationalists almost invariably define their nations in terms that conflict with the self-definition of rival or neighboring nationalities, there is no agreed upon way to decide the "justice" of these claims (nor can there be).

The restriction in international law of self-determination to peoples in already existing states avoids these problems.[17] The principle of PSD better realises the fundamental political good of self-government: by rejecting imposed restrictions on the free self-development of individuals, by recognising that membership in states should be a function of mutual needs, not similarities or differences, and by avoiding the problem of adjudicating rival territorial claims by national groups.

There is accordingly no warrant for replacing the principle of Popular Self-Determination with a right to National Self-Determination on the basis of the value of self-government. And since this is the primary justification given by nationalists for such a right, there is no compelling reason for a substantial modification of international law on this issue. Philosophers should begin to recognise the wisdom of jurists who continue to regard self-determination as an attribute of peoples, not nations. The claim to self-determination can in this way cease to be a potential justification for discrimination, oppression, and war, and become instead a means to secure the conditions of self-government consistent with other norms of international law.

NOTES

1. Edward M. Morgan, "The Imagery and Meaning of Self-Determination," *New York University Journal of International Law and Politics* 20 (Winter 1988), p. 359.
2. Heather A. Wilson, *International Law and the Use of Force by National Liberation Movements* (Oxford: Clarendon Press, 1988), p. 10.
3. Louis Henkin, Richard C. Pugh, Oscar Schachter, and Hans Smit, *International Law: Cases and Materials* (Saint Paul, Minn.: West Publishing co., 1980), p. 211.
4. Wentworth Ofuatey-Kodjoe, *The Principle of Self-Determination in International Law* (New York: Nellen Publishing Co., 1977), p. 156.
5. Wilson, *International Law and the Use of Force*, p. 80.

6. Rupert Emerson, "Self-Determination," *American Journal of International Law* 65 (1971), p. 463.
7. Michael Walzer, *Spheres of Justice: A Defense of Pluralism and Equality* (New York: Basic Books, 1983), p. 62.
8. Michael Walzer, *Just and Unjust Wars: A Moral Argument with Historical Illustrations* (New York: Basic books, 1977), p. 57.
9. Walzer, *Spheres of Justice*, p. 31.
10. Avishai Margolit and Joseph Raz, "National Self-Determination," *Journal of Philosophy* 87 (September 1990), pp. 439-61.
11. Lung-chu Chen, "Self-Determination: An Important Dimension of the Demand for Freedom," *American society of International Law Proceedings* 75 (1981), p. 91.
12. David Copp, "Do Nations Have the right of Self-Determination?" in Stanley G. French (ed.), *Philosophers Look at Canadian Confederation* (Montreal: Canadian Philosophical Association, 1979), pp. 86-87.
13. Iris Marion Young, "Five Faces of Oppression," *Philosophical Forum* 19 (1988), p. 274.
14. Dov Ronen, *The Quest for Self-Determination* (New Haven, Conn.: Yale University Press, 1979), p. 61.
15. Morgan, "Imagery and Meaning," p. 361.
16. Felicity Watts, "Individualism in Political Philosophy," unpublished manuscript.
17. Jeremy Brecher, "'The National Question' Reconsidered," *New Politics* 1 (1987), p. 105.

STUDY QUESTIONS

1 What does Gutmann mean by nonideal democracies and what are their defining features? What is "deliberative democracy" and how does it differ from nonideal democracies?

2 How does Gutmann answer the question with which she opens the paper: "Does democracy need foundations?" Without foundations in the strong sense is democracy undermined? Why or why not?

3 Chenyang Li's answer to the question "what kind of democracy does China need?" is "the kind of democracy with the values of individual liberty, equality, and pluralism." According to Li, what are the points of incompatibility between these values and those in Confucianism in China? Does Li succeed in undermining attempts by theorists to make democracy and Confucianism compatible? Why or why not?

4 If the values of democracy and Confucianism are truly incompatible, why does Li pursue the project of introducing democratic values in China? What solution does he propose for the problem of incompatible value systems that he identifies in China? Is this a satisfactory solution? Why or why not?

5 In Gutmann's analysis, would Babbitt count as one of the "few political philosophers [who] actually argue[s] that democracy can be defensibly dissociated from a form of deliberative self-government that secures the basic liberties and opportunities of all members of society"? If so, in what ways?

6 According to Babbitt, how do globally dominant expectations about democracy and freedom interfere with a fair investigation of and constructive debate about Cuba? What moral truths about human flourishing might we learn if we take seriously the stories told by Cubans about their aspirations for and ways of achieving human dignity and equality?

7 Does Babbitt's analysis of the situation in Cuba undermine Gutmann's and Li's accounts of what constitutes democracy? Does what we learn cast doubt on the validity of claims about the lack of freedom and democracy in Cuba? Defend your answers.

8 Llewellyn points out that the dismantling of apartheid in South Africa and its transition to a rights respecting society affords a clear opportunity to critically examine various conceptions of justice and their application to the situation in South Africa. What are some of the reasons she gives for rejecting a retributivist conception of justice as inappropriate not only for dealing with the past in transitional contexts like South Africa but also for addressing injustices more generally?

9 What is restorative justice and how does it differ from what has become identified as transitional justice? According to Llewellyn, what are some of the features of the mandate and mechanisms of the South African Truth and Reconciliation Commission that fit a conception of justice as restorative?

10 In your view, is restorative justice a better way of addressing human rights violations than a conception of justice based on retribution? Is this conception of justice limited in its application to transitional contexts or even more specifically to South Africa? Provide reasons for your answers.

11 Outline the distinction Dahbour makes between Popular Self-Determination and National Self-Determination. According to Dahbour, how does the distinction clarify the notions of sovereignty, self-determination, and nationhood?

12 Dahbour raises several objections to National Self-Determination that lead him to say that it is philosophically less justifiable than Popular Self-Determination. What are these objections? Do you agree with Dahbour's analysis? Why or why not?

13 Can insights from Dahbour's analysis of sovereignty, self-determination, and nationhood be usefully employed in the kinds of analyses of China, Cuba, or South Africa provided by the authors in this chapter?

SUGGESTED READINGS

Benhabib, Seyla. "Deliberative Rationality and Models of Democratic Legitimacy." *Constellations*, v. 1, no. 1 (1994): 26-52.

Buchanan, Allen. "Theories of Secession." *Philosophy & Public Affairs*, v. 26, no. 1 (Winter 1997): 31-61.

Buchanan, Allen. "What's So Special About Nations?" In *Rethinking Nationalism* edited by J. Couture, K. Nielsen and M. Seymour. Calgary: Calgary University Press, 1998.

Crocker, David. *Transitional Justice and International Civil Society*. Working Paper no. 13. Institute for Philosophy and Public Policy, University of Maryland: The National Commission on Civic Renewal, 1998.

Couture, J., K. Nielsen and M. Seymour (editors). *Rethinking Nationalism*. Calgary: Calgary University Press, 1998.

Dahbour, Omar. "The Nation-State as a Political Community: A Critique of the Communitarian Argument for National Self-Determination." In *Rethinking Nationalism* edited by J. Couture, K. Nielsen and M. Seymour. Calgary: Calgary University Press, 1998.

Gould, Carol C. "Diversity and Democracy: Representing Differences." In *Democracy and Difference: Contesting the Boundaries of the Political* edited by Seyla Benhabib. Princeton University Press, 1996.

Mansbridge, Jane. "Using Power/Fighting Power." *Constellations*, v. 1, no. 1 (1994): 53-73.

Mouffe, Chantal. "Democracy, Power, and the `Political'." In *Democracy and Difference: Contesting the Boundaries of the Political* edited by Seyla Benhabib. Princeton University Press, 1996.

Nielsen, Kai. "Socialism and Nationalism." *Imprints*, v. 2, no. 3 (1998): 208-222.

Rosenfeld, Michel. "Restitution, Retribution, Political Justice and the Rule of Law." *Constellations*, v. 2, no. 3 (1996): 309-332.

Sparks, Holloway. "Dissident Citizenship: Democratic Theory, Political Courage, and Activist Women." *Hypatia*, v. 12, no. 4 (Fall 1997): 74-110.

Tamir, Yael. "The Right to National Self-Determination as an Individual Right." *History of European Ideas*, v. 16, no. 4-6 (1993): 899-905.

Wellman, Christopher H. "A Defense of Secession and Political Self-Determination." *Philosophy & Public Affairs*, v. 24, no. 2 (1995): 142-171.

Yuval-Davis, Nira. "Women, Citizenship and Difference." *Feminist Review*, no. 57 (Autumn 1997): 4-27.

PART II

HUMAN DIVERSITY AND EQUALITY

CHAPTER THREE

THEORIES AND CRITICAL ANALYSIS

Part I began with theoretical accounts of human rights and justice and then moved to an examination of particular contexts and issues that both give substance to and raise questions for theory. We have learned thus far that there is virtual universal agreement about the principle of equality, the basic idea that all people are equal and ought to be treated equally. However, there is a great deal of disagreement about the basis for equality and about how the principle should be applied. People are very diverse. They differ with respect to physical features, capacities, needs, interests, and levels of ability. Differences of these sorts have been and continue to be the basis for determining the distribution of rights and privileges and of social goods such as food, education, and employment. There is now widespread consensus, exemplified in international human rights documents as well as the human rights codes and constitutions of many countries, that differences such as race, ethnicity, gender, sexual orientation, and levels of ability and wealth should not justify unequal treatment. However, these very same differences continue to be significant to the inequalities and injustices experienced by members of these groups. This is so not only all over the world, but even in liberal societies in which the belief in the inherent worth of all people is a central tenet.

Two main conceptions of equality are prominent in the liberal tradition: formal and substantive equality. Each begins with similar accounts of the importance of the human capacity to make choices and of the value of pursuing one's interests, projects, and goals. However, they arrive at different conclusions about the structures and the policies needed to promote freedom and human flourishing. Formal equality theorists argue that people are treated equally when formal and legal barriers barring people from participating in society and having the opportunities enjoyed by all are removed. Substantive equality theorists argue that sometimes equality demands that special measures be implemented so that those whose differences have been and continue to be sources of disadvantage can begin to undo the effects of a history of entrenched discrimination. Welfare measures and affirmative action programs are good examples of special treatment designed to make it possible for members of traditionally disadvantaged groups to achieve equality.

Discrimination is morally wrong when morally irrelevant differences are taken to be grounds for justifying unequal treatment. Discrimination is a moral issue because inequalities and disadvantages generated by one's mere membership in a group are morally questionable. Discrimination is also a moral issue because it represents the breakdown of moral relations: sometimes with those in one's community and sometimes with citizens of other countries. A fundamental part of living a good life is to be able to interact with and respond to others in morally appropriate ways. Questions about human diversity and equality raise issues about our moral responsibility for acquiring a proper understanding of discrimination and for attending to these relations in morally appropriate ways in our daily lives.

The first two readings of this chapter open with broad questions about human diversity and explore the universalism and ethnocentrism at the base of assessments by one country of inequalities and injustices in another country. Martha Nussbaum is critical of relativists who argue that there is no vantage point from which judgments about beliefs, practices, and values different from one's own can be rendered. She argues that in the face of the very diverse range of conditions, contexts, beliefs, and practices in the world, we can provide a list of essential human capabilities and needs that generates moral imperatives for what is required to promote human flourishing. She defends a version of essentialism that she takes to be sensitive to historical and cultural differences, inclusive with respect to members of various oppressed groups, and open to debate and reformulation. This account, argues Nussbaum, gives us the tools for criticizing practices in other cultures that disadvantage certain members or treat them unequally.

In the second reading, David Crocker returns to the dangers of ethnocentrism. Assessments about people and policies in other places, biased as they are by a strong tendency to judge others by our own standards and practices, can be particularly pernicious in relationships between Western and non-Western countries. Assumptions about the superiority of values and of models of economic development in rich and powerful North/Western and developed countries have shaped international development policies in poor South/non-Western and developing countries. Crocker develops an account of insiders and outsiders that he takes to capture the nature of people and their roles in the groups and societies to which they belong. Insiders are recognized or accepted by a group because the members share such things as beliefs, desires, memories, and hopes. Outsiders are not recognized or accepted as members of a group because they lack these shared atttributes. Crocker argues that we are all insiders and outsiders in multiple ways and with respect to a variety of groups both within and across cultures. He uses this model of insider and outsider identities to survey the advantages and disadvantages of each role in assessments of practices in foreign countries.

The rest of the readings in Chapter Three turn to questions of diversity and discrimination within countries by focusing on the North American context. Shelby Steele discusses discrimination in the context of defending what he takes to be central to liberal democracy in the United States: an emphasis on the freedom and equality of individuals. He applauds the strategies and goals of the early civil rights movements in the United States to achieve the integration of women and blacks into mainstream American society. He argues, however, that the democratic goal of integration has been abandoned in current movements that focus on collective or group entitlements rather than individual rights. These movements have shifted from democracy and integration to collective entitlements and such separatists strategies as affirmative action and the creation of black studies and women's studies departments. Steele argues that group entitlements violate the principles upon which American democracy is founded by using the arbitrary characteristics of race, ethnicity, gender, and sexual preference as the basis for identity and claims to entitlement. American democracy is based on integration, which represents the absence of arbitrary barriers to freedom and the inclusion of all citizens into the sphere of rights it espouses and the range of opportunities it promotes.

Iris Young challenges Steele's depiction of current social movements. She agrees that there has been a shift in strategy on the part of members of disadvantaged groups from removing formal barriers to freedom so that all individuals have the same rights and opportunities (formal equality) to affirming group difference and championing special treatment for disadvantaged groups (substantive equality). However, she disagrees with Steele's rejection of substantive equality. Young grants that the goal of integration has been enormously important in improving the opportunities and lives of individual members of disadvantaged groups. However, she argues that it has had little effect in unsettling the balance of economic and political power, changing the structural patterns of group privilege or making differences irrelevant to a person's life prospects. Young supports strategies of affirming group difference evident in the recovery and promotion of the language, culture, organizations, and experiences of various social groups. A politics of difference promotes group solidarity, provides perspectives from which to criticize prevailing institutions and norms, and unsettles entrenched stereotypes and self-perceptions of difference as inferiority or a liability. Young defends a relational understanding of difference, one in which difference is contextual, ambiguous, shifting, and non-essentialist.

Young's analysis undermines the idea that there is a neutral and universal vantage point from which to understand difference and the life experiences of people. Laurence Thomas explores this argument further by asking what is required of us in our relations with those who are disadvantaged or have been wronged. He argues that people who are members of well-defined diminished social categories suffer a kind of pain and misfortune that is distinguishable from that suffered by people who are victims of robberies or car accidents, for example. Being a member of a socially diminished category makes it likely that one's life will be affected by oppressive and prevailing negative attitudes and by the hostile misfortunes specific to that category. Thomas argues that because people are socially constituted by the diminished categories to which they belong and are emotionally configured by the hostile misfortunes they experience as members of a particular diminished category, their lives and experiences cannot be understood from the outside simply through reasoning about oppressive experiences or sympathizing with those who have them. People in socially diminished categories are owed moral deference by those who are not members of these categories. Moral deference is a mode of moral learning owed to those who are oppressed as a way of working toward the elimination of oppression in its various forms and manifestations.

HUMAN FUNCTIONING AND SOCIAL JUSTICE: IN DEFENSE OF ARISTOTELIAN ESSENTIALISM[1]

Martha C. Nussbaum

Martha C. Nussbaum is Professor of Law and Ethics at the University of Chicago. She is the author of numerous books including: The Fragility of Goodness: Luck and Ethics in Greek Tragedy and Philosophy *(Cambridge 1987),* The Therapy of Desire: Theory and Practice in Hellenistic Ethics *(Princeton, 1994), and* Cultivating Humanity: A Classical Defense of Reform in Liberal Education *(Harvard, 1997). She is also co-editor with Jonathan Glover of* Women, Culture, and Development: A Study of Human Capabilities *(Oxford, 1995) and with Amartya Sen of* The Quality of Life *(Oxford, 1993).*

Nussbaum defends an essentialist conception of human nature by providing a list of the most important functions that define human life. She calls her account of the human functions the "thick vague theory of the good." She argues that this account avoids the problems of a too rigid and universalist metaphysical realism by being sensitive to historical and cultural differences, inclusive with respect to members of various oppressed groups, and open to debate and reformulation.

> It will be seen how in place of the *wealth* and *poverty* of political economy come the *rich human being* and rich human need. The *rich* human being is simultaneously the human being *in need of* totality of human life-activities—the man in whom his own realization exists as an inner necessity, as *need.*
>
> —Marx,
> *Economics and Philosophical Manuscripts of 1844*

> Svetaketu abstained from food for fifteen days. Then he came to his father and said, "What shall I say?" The father said: "Repeat the Rik, Yagus and Saman verses." He replied, "They do not occur to me, Sir." The father said to him ... "Go and eat! Then wilt thou understand me." Svetaketu ate, and afterwards approached his father. And whatever his father asked him, he knew it all by heart ... After that, he understood what his father meant when he said: " Mind my son, comes from food, breath from water, speech from fire." He understood what he said, yea, he understood it.
>
> —Chandogya-Upanishad, *VI Prapathaka, 7 Kanda*

> When you love a man, you want him to live and when you hate him you want him to die. If, having wanted him to live, you then want him to die, this is a misguided judgment. "If you did not do so for the sake of riches, you must have done so for the sake of novelty."
>
> —Confucius, *Analects*, Book 12.10

Antiessentialist Conversations

I begin with three conversations, taken from my experience working in Helsinki as a research advisor at an international institute affiliated with the United Nations, which brings people from many disciplines together to work on problems connected with development economics.[2] Contemporary assaults on "essentialism" and on nonrelative accounts of human functioning have recently made a dramatic appearance there, with potential implications for public policy that I view with alarm. I have in some

---

Reprinted with permission of Sage Publications from Political Theory 20:2 (1992): 202–237 [edited].

cases conflated two separate conversations into one, but otherwise, things happened as I describe them.[3]

1. At a conference on value and technology, an American economist who has long been considered a radical delivers a paper urging the preservation of traditional ways of life in a rural area of India, now under threat of contamination from Western values. As evidence of the excellence of this rural way of life, he points to the fact that, whereas we Westerners experience a sharp split between the values that prevail in the workplace and the values that prevail in the home, here, by contrast, there exists what the economist calls "the embedded way of life." His example: just as in the home a menstruating woman is thought to pollute the kitchen and so many not enter it, so too in the workplace a menstruating woman is taken to pollute the loom and may not enter the room where looms are kept. An economist from India objects that this example is repellent rather than admirable, for surely such practices both degrade the women in question and inhibit their freedom. The first economist's collaborator, an elegant French anthropologist (who would, I suspect, object violently to a purity check at the seminar room door) addresses the objector in contemptuous tones. Doesn't he realize that there is, in these matters, no privileged place to stand? Doesn't he know that he is neglecting the radical otherness of these village people by bringing his Western essentialist values into the picture?

2. The same French anthropologist now delivers her paper. She expresses regret that the introduction of smallpox vaccination to India by the British eradicated the cult of Sittala Devi, the goddess to whom one used to pray in order to avert smallpox. Here, she says, is another example of Western neglect of difference. Someone (it might have been me) objects that it is surely better to be healthy rather than ill, to live rather than to die. The frosty answer comes back: Western essentialist medicine conceives of things in terms of binary oppositions: life is opposed to death, health to disease. But if we cast away this blinkered way of seeing things, we will comprehend the radical otherness of Indian traditions. At this point, Eric Hobsbawm, who has been listening to the proceedings in increasingly uneasy silence, rises to deliver a blistering indictment of the traditionalism and relativism that prevail in this group. He lists examples of how the appeal to tradition has been used in history to defend various types of oppression and violence. His final example is that of National Socialism. In the chaos that ensues, most of the traditionalist social scientists (above all the ones from abroad, who do not know who Hobsbawm is) demand that Hobsbawm be asked to leave the conference room. The radical American economist, covered with embarrassment at this evidence of a split between his relativism and his left-wing affiliations, convinces them, with much difficulty, to let Hobsbawm remain.

3. We shift now to another conference,[4] a philosophical conference organized by me and by the objector of my first story, the economist from India who objected to the degradation of women by menstruation taboos. (He also holds the unsophisticated view that life is opposed to death.) His paper contains much "essentialist" talk of human functioning and human capability; he begins to speak of freedom of choice as a basic human good. At this point he is interrupted by the radical economist, who points out, with the air of one in the know, that contemporary anthropology has shown that non-Western people are not especially attached to freedom of choice. His example: a new book on Japan has shown that Japanese males, when they get home from work, do not wish to choose what to eat for dinner, what to wear, and so on. They wish all these choices to be taken out of their hands by their wives.[5] A heated exchange follows about what this example really shows. I leave it to your imagination to reconstruct it; it did have some humorous dimensions. But in the end, the confidence of the radical economist is unshaken: we are both victims of bad essentialist thinking, who fail to recognize the beauty of otherness.

These examples are not unusual; I could cite many more. What we see in such cases is an odd phenomenon indeed. Highly intelligent people, people deeply committed to the good of women and men in developing countries, people who think of themselves as progressive and feminist and antiracist, are taking up positions that converge, as Hobsbawm correctly saw, with the positions of reaction, oppression, and sexism. Under the banner of their radical and politically correct "antiessentialism" march ancient religious taboos, the luxury of pampered husband, ill health, ignorance, and death. (And in my own essentialist way, I say it at the outset. I do hold that death is opposed to life in the most binary way imaginable, and slavery to freedom, and hunger to adequate nutrition, and ignorance to knowledge.)

Essentialism is becoming a dirty word in the academy and in those parts of human life that are influenced by it. Essentialism—which for these purpose I shall understand as the view that human life has certain central defining features—is linked by its opponents with an ignorance of history, with lack of sensitivity to the voices of women and minorities.[6] It is taken, usually without extended argument, to be in league with racism and sexism, with "patriarchal" thinking generally, whereas extreme relativism is taken to be a recipe for social progress. In this essay, I question these connections. I grant that some criticisms of some forms of essentialism have been fruitful and important: they have established the ethical debate on a more defensible metaphysical foundation and have redirected our gaze from unexamined abstract assumptions to the world and its actual history. But I argue that those who would throw out all appeals to a determinate account of the human being, human functioning, and human flourishing are throwing away far too much—in terms even, and especially, of their own compassionate ends.

I argue, first, that the legitimate criticisms of essentialism still leave room for essentialism of a kind: for a historically sensitive account of the most basic human needs and human functions. I then sketch such an account, which I have developed at length elsewhere, showing how it can meet the legitimate objections. I then argue that without such an account, we do not have an adequate basis for an account of social justice and the ends of social distribution. With it, on the other hand, we have—what we urgently need at this time— the basis for a global ethic and a fully international account of distributive justice...

The Assault on Essentialism

The contemporary assault on universal account of the human being and human functioning is not always accompanied by clear and explicit philosophical arguments. All too often, as in my examples, the opponents of essentialism use the word polemically as a term of abuse and with a certain air of superiority, as if they were in the know about some new and decisive discovery that removes the need for argument.[7] So, the first task for anyone who wishes to defend a position in this debate must be, it seems to me, to introduce some clarity into the picture by sorting out the varieties of antiessentialist argument and describing the train of thought that has led to the extreme relativist traditionalism exemplified in my Helsinki conversations. The attacks can, I believe, be divided into two groups: attacks that depend on a general attack on metaphysical realism and attacks that are independent of the attack on realism and might be pressed, therefore, against versions of essentialism that do not depend on realism.

Attacks on Metaphysical-Realist Essentialism

Metaphysical realism claims that there is some determinate way that the world is apart from the interpretive workings of the cognitive faculties of living beings. A description of the world is true just in case it corresponds to that independently existing structure, false insofar as it does not so correspond. Unless the metaphysical realist is also a skeptic— a combination rarely found, since it is hard to sustain confidence in realism without the belief that someone can adequately grasp reality—realism is accompanied by some related account of knowledge. Some mind or other—whether God's alone or certain human minds also—is said to be able to grasp this real structure as it is in itself; knowledge is defined in terms of this grasp. In thinking about this position, it is useful to consider the myth in Plato's Phaedrus. The gods, who have no internal impediments to understanding, march out to the rim of the heavens, and here, as the heavens turn, they see going past them the true forms or structures of the world, independent, eternal, and unchanging. Other souls, whose internal structure is more turbulent and conflicted, fail to stand serenely on the rim of heaven, and so fail to know the whole of reality. Some souls see bits and pieces of reality as they struggle upwards: these are the ones that will be human beings. Others grasp nothing of the truth— and these will be animals.

On such a view, the way the human being essentially is will be a part of the independent furniture of the universe, something the gods can see and study independently of any experience of human life and human history. The paradigms that yield knowledge of what we in our nature are, are radically independent of our actual choices, our self-understandings, our hopes and loves and fears. They are there to be discovered by experts— whether philosophical, biological, or religious— and delivered to us by those figures or intermediaries as a correct account of the way things are. This account is usually understood to have normative force: the heavenly account of what we are constrains what we may legitimately seek to be.

The common objection to this sort of realism is that this sort of metaphysical truth is not in fact available. Sometimes this is put skeptically: the independent structure may still exist, but we can know nothing of it. More often, today, doubt is cast on the coherence of the whole realist idea that there is some one determinate structure to the way things are, independent of all human interpretation. This is the objection the nonphilosophers tend to associate with Jacques Derrida's assault on the "metaphysics of presence," which he takes to have dominated the entirety of the Western philosophical tradition.[8] But it actually has a much longer and more complicated history. It begins in the Western tradition at least as early as Kant's assault on transcendent metaphysics—and perhaps far earlier, since some scholars have found a version of it in Aristotle's anti-Platonist arguments.[9] Its contemporary versions are themselves many and complex—involving, frequently, technical issues in the philosophy of science and the philosophy of language. In this sophisticated literature— whose major contributors include such outstanding philosophers as Ludwig Wittgenstein, W.V.O. Quine, Donald Davidson, Hilary Putnam, and Nelson Goodman— the arguments of Derrida are relatively minor contributions, which do not even confront a great many of the pressing questions that are at issue.[10]

The attack on metaphysical realism is far too complex to be summarized here, but its implications for essentialism are clear. If the only available (or perhaps even coherent) picture of reality is one in the derivation of which human interpretations play a part, if the only defensible conceptions of truth and knowledge hold truth and knowledge to be in certain ways dependent on human cognitive activity within history, the hope for a pure unmediated account of our human essence as it is in itself, apart from history and interpretation, is no hope at all but a deep confusion. To cling to it as a goal is to pretend that it is possible for us to be told from outside what to be and what to do, when in reality the only answers we can ever hope to have must come, in some manner, from ourselves.

Attacks on Internalist Essentialism

But one might accept these conclusions and still be an essentialist. One might, that is, believe that the deepest examination of human history and human cognition *from within* still reveals a more or less determinate account of the human being, one that divides its essential from its accidental properties. Such an account would say: take away properties X, Y, and Z (a suntan, let us say, or a knowledge of Chinese, or an income of $40,000 a year) and we will still have what we count as a human being on our hands. On the other hand, take away properties A, B, and C (the ability to think about the future say, or the ability to respond to the claims of others, or the ability to choose and act) and we no longer have a human life at all. Separating these two groups of properties requires an evaluative inquiry: for we must ask, which things are so important that we will not count a life as a human life without them? Such an evaluative inquiry into what is deepest and most indispensable in our lives need not presuppose an external metaphysical foundation, clearly: it can be a way of looking at ourselves, asking what we really think about ourselves and what holds our history together. Later on, I shall propose one version of such a historically grounded empirical essentialism—which, since it takes its stand within human experience, I shall now call "internalist" essentialism.[11] Such internalist conceptions of the human being are still vulnerable to some, if not all, of the charges brought against essentialism generally. So even though the opposition rarely makes the externalist/internalist distinction, I shall myself introduce it, mentioning three charges that I think any good internalist account will need to answer.

1. Neglect of Historical and Cultural Differences

The opposition charges that any attempt to pick out some elements of human life as more fundamental than others, even without appeal to a transhistorical reality, is bound to be insufficiently respectful of actual historical and cultural differences. People, it is claimed, understand human life and humanness in widely different ways, and any attempt to produce a list of "essential properties" is bound to enshrine certain understandings of the human and to demote others. Usually, the objector continues, this takes the form of enshrining the understanding of a dominant group at the expense of minority understandings. Such objectors usually also suggest that only an actual unanimous agreement would be sufficient to justify an essentialist conclusion. But in practice, such agreements are not forthcoming, so essentialism is bound to consist of the imposition of someone's authority on someone else.

2. Neglect of Autonomy

A different objection is pressed by liberal opponents of essentialism; usually these opponents are themselves willing to be essentialist about the central importance of human freedom and autonomy.[12] The objection is that by determining in advance what elements of human life have most importance, the essentialist is failing to respect the right of people to choose a plan of life according to their own lights, determining what is most central and what is not. Such evaluative choices must be left to each citizen. For this reason, politics must refuse itself a determinate theory of the human being and the human good.

3. Prejudicial Application

If we operate with a determinate conception of the human being that is meant to have some normative moral and political weight, we must also, in applying it, ask which beings we take to fall under the concept. Here, the objector notes that all too easily the powerless can be excluded. Aristotle himself, it is pointed out, held that women and slaves were not full-fledged human beings; and since his politics was based on his essentialism, the failure of these beings (in his view) to exhibit the desired essence led to their political exclusion and oppression. The suggestion is that renouncing the use of such a determinate conception of the human will make it easier for such people to be heard and included.

The collapse into Subjectivism

Each of these objections has some force. Later on in the essay, I ask how much force each of them has and whether there is a version of essentialism that can survive them. But what is alarming about the current debate in a variety of fields—literary theory, some parts of legal theory, and much of economic theory and development studies— is that this further inquiry has not taken place. Very often, as in my Helsinki examples, the collapse of metaphysical realism is taken to entail not only the collapse of essentialism about the human being but a retreat into an extreme relativism, or even subjectivism, about all questions of evaluation.[13]

The retreat usually takes the following form. First, an impossible demand is made say, for unmediated presentness to reality as it is in itself or for an actual universal agreement about matters of value. Next, it is claimed that this demand cannot be met. Then, without any further ado— without looking at internal realist positions, such as those of Charles Taylor and Hilary Putnam, and without asking what more moderate cognitive demands can be met— the theorist concludes that everything is up for grabs and there are no norms to give us guidance in matters of evaluation. For some theorists, evaluation then becomes a matter of power: the criterion of truth will derive from one's contingent position of social authority.[14] For others, it becomes, instead, a matter of play and self-assertion: what is good is what I (whether for reasons or arbitrarily or whimsically) choose to assert.[15] For still others, as we shall see, value collapses into utility: to judge something good is part of a transaction in which one seeks to maximize one's utility (understood as desire-satisfaction or wealth or whatever). And if you ask how come the theorist can confidently assert *that* normative theory of evaluation, the answer (as in the case of the ancient Greek skeptics) turns back on itself: what I say is itself an exercise of power or playfulness or utility-maximizing, like everything else. Let's see whether you will be influenced or play along or join in the profit-taking game.[16]

In this exercise, accounts of the human being go the way of everything else: give the one you like, and let's see who likes (or is influenced by) it. None can be said to be better than any other, except in the sense that individuals may, playing their games, assert that this or that one is better. But there are no good reasons and no rational persuasion. Furthermore, in a more general attack on distinction-making, all "binary oppositions" are frequently called into question— as if it is always both illegitimate and somehow bad to oppose one thing clearly to another, as if such distinction-making were always a preparation for some cruelty or oppression.[17] By these steps we arrive, in some cases, at the complete banishment of logic— that allegedly male patriarchal imperialist phenomenon.

Since we are talking of the collapse of distinctions, nothing is stranger than the way in which positions that take themselves to be in crucial respects distinct collapse together at this point. The proponents of these extreme antiessentialist views usually take themselves, as I said, to be politically progressive and compassionate, moved by thought about the good of women, minorities, poor, and excluded people everywhere. Much of the force of their rhetoric trades on this, suggesting that if one disagrees with them, one is thereby manifesting at best callousness, at worst racism and sexism. But consider for a moment whose company these allegedly compassionate critics are keeping. Fish says that all judgment is a matter of power—no good and bad reasons. This implies that one can never give a morally good reason for criticizing the verdicts of established authority: when one does so one is by definition just playing for power and is thus no better, morally, than one's opponent. Where the game is power, weakness is always worse. The poor are losers, and that's that. A more lighthearted deconstructionist says it is all a matter of free play. So, if I want to play around with torture and slavery and you want to stop me, nothing can be said about the moral superiority of you to me. You have your way of playing, I have mine... .

Now we are in a better position to understand why alleged radicals nearly threw Eric Hobsbawm out of the room. The commitment that he, as a Marxist, has to a determinate conception of human need and human flourishing is profoundly at odds with the new subjectivism, which takes itself to be the truly progressive and compassionate force. To this company, Hobsbawm and Amartya Sen (who was, I now reveal, the objector of my first two examples and the speaker in the third) looked like unfashionable paternalistic authorities, insensitive to the play of difference. On the other hand, Hobsbawm and Sen saw what the subjectivists did not perhaps so clearly see: that to give up on all evaluation and, in particular, on a normative account of the human being and human functioning was to turn things over to the free play of forces in a world situation in which the social forces affecting the lives of women, minorities, and the poor are rarely benign.

Confronting the Objections

...When we get rid of the hope of a transcendent metaphysical grounding for our evaluative judgments—about the human being as about anything else—we are not left with the abyss. We have everything that we always had all along: the exchange of reasons and arguments by human beings within history, in which, for reasons that are historical and human but not the worse for that, we hold some things to be good and others bad, some arguments to be sound and others not sound. Why, indeed, should the relativist conclude that the absence of a transcendent basis for judgment—a basis that, according to them, was never there anyway— should make us despair of doing as we have done all along, distinguishing persuasion from manipulation?

In fact, the collapse into extreme relativism or subjectivism seems to me to betray a deep attachment to metaphysical realism itself. For it is only to one who has pinned everything to that hope that its collapse will seem to entail the collapse of all evaluation—just as it is only to a deeply believing religious person, as Nietzsche saw, that the news of the death of God brings the threat of nihilism. What we see here, I think, is a reaction of shame—a turning away of the eyes from our poor humanity, which looks so mean and bare—by contrast to a dream of another sort. What do we have here, these critics seem to say? Only our poor old human conversations, our human bodies that interpret things so imperfectly? Well, if that is all there is, we do not really want to study it too closely, to look into the distinctions it exhibits. We will just say that they are all alike, for, really, they do look pretty similar when compared to the heavenly standard we were seeking. It is like the moment reported by Aristotle when some students arrived at the home of Heraclitus, eager to see the great sage and cosmologist. They found him—not on a hilltop gazing at the heavens but sitting in his kitchen or, perhaps, on the toilet (for there is a philological dispute at this point!). He looked at their disappointed faces, saw that they were about to turn away their eyes, and said, "Come in, don't be afraid. There are gods here too." Aristotle uses this story to nudge his reluctant students out of the shame that is preventing them from looking closely at the parts of animals. When you get rid of your shame, he says, you will notice that there is order and structure *in* the animal world.[18]

So too, I think, with realism: the failure to take an interest in studying our practices of analyzing and reasoning, human and historical as they are, the insistence that we would have good arguments only if they came from heaven—all this betrays a shame before the human. On the other hand, if we really think of the hope of a transcendent ground for value as uninteresting and irrelevant, as we should, then the news of its collapse will not change the way we do things: it will just let us get on with the business of reasoning in which we were already engaged.

And as Hilary Putnam argues,[19] the demise of realism may even boost the status of ethical evaluation. For the metaphysical realist frequently made a sharp distinction between fact and value, believing that truth of the sort the realist is after was available in the scientific realm but not in the realm of value. Bringing science inside human history makes what was already believed to be in there look better, not worse—because its claims are no longer contrasted sharply with claims that look "harder" and more "factual." Thus the polarity between scientific fact and subjective ethical value on which much of neoclassical economics rests is called into question by the collapse of realism—from the side of science, to be sure, but this reopens the whole question of the relationship between ethics and science and makes it possible to argue, as does Putnam, that ethics is no worse off than any science.

As for the objections to internalist essentialism, each of them has some force. Many essentialist conceptions have been insular in an arrogant way and neglectful of differences among cultures and ways of life. Some have been neglectful of choice and autonomy. And some have been prejudicially applied—sometimes even by their inventors (as in the cases of Aristotle and Rousseau). But none of this, it seems to me, shows that all essentialism must fail in one or more of these ways. And if one feels that there are urgent reasons why we need such an account of human functioning, one will be motivated to try to construct one that will in fact meet the objections. I now propose such an account and then return to the area of development policy, offering my reasons for thinking that we do in fact urgently need such an account.

An Essentialist Proposal: The Basic Human Functions

Here, then, is a sketch of an internal-essentialist proposal, an account of the most important functions of the human being, in terms of which human life is defined.[20] The idea is that once we identify a group of especially important functions in human life, we are then in a position to ask what social and political institutions are doing about them. Are they giving people what they need in order to be capable of functioning in all these human ways? And are they doing this in a minimal way, or are they making it possible for citizens to function well? I will consider the political implications of the account in the next section; now I must describe the account itself.

I call this account of the human functions the "thick vague theory of the good."[21] The point of this name is to insist, first of all, on the normative character of the list. We are not pretending to discover some value-neutral facts about ourselves, independently of all evaluation; instead, we are conducting an especially probing and basic sort of evaluative inquiry. The name is also chosen to contrast the account with John Rawls's "thin theory of the good," which insists on confining the list of the "primary goods" that will be used by the members of the Original Position to a group of allegedly all-purpose means that have a role in any conception of the human good whatever. By contrast, my Aristotelian conception is concerned with *ends* and with the overall shape and content of the human form of life.[22] Finally the list is "vague," and this deliberately so and in a good sense, for, as we shall see, it admits of much multiple specification in accordance with varied local and personal conceptions. The idea is that it is better to be vaguely right than precisely wrong; I claim that without the guidance offered by such a list, what we often get in public policy is precise wrongness.

This conception is emphatically not metaphysical; that is, it does not claim to derive from any source external to the actual self-interpretations and self-evaluations of human beings in history.[23] Nor is it peculiar to a single metaphysical or religious tradition. It aims to be as universal as possible, and its guiding intuition, in fact, directs it to cross religious, cultural, and metaphysical gulfs. For it begins from two facts: first, that we do recognize others as human across many divisions of time and place. Whatever the differences we encounter, we are rarely in doubt, as to when we are dealing with a human being and when we are not. The essentialist account attempts to describe the bases for these recognitions, by mapping out the general shape of the human form of life, those features that constituted a life as human wherever it is. Second, we do have a broadly shared general consensus about the features whose absence means the end of a human form of life. We have in medicine and mythology alike an idea that some transitions or changes just are not compatible with the continued existence of that being as a member of the human kind (and thus as the same individual, since species identity seems to be necessary for personal identity). This is really just another way of coming at the first question, of asking what the most central features of our common humanity are, without which no individual can be counted (or counted any longer) as human.[24]

This evaluative inquiry proceeds by examining a wide variety of self-understandings of people in many times and places. Especially valuable are myths and stories that situate the human being in some way in the universe: between the beasts, on one hand, and the gods, on the other; stories that ask what it is to live as a being with certain abilities that set it apart from the rest of the living beings in the world of nature, and with, on the other hand, certain limits that derive from our membership in the world of nature. The idea is that we do share at least a very general outline of such a conception. Frequently, we find such ideas elucidated in stories of beings who look like humans but are not recognized as human. When we ask ourselves, "Why, if these creatures resemble human beings, don't we count them as human?" we learn something about ourselves... .

The list of features that we get if we reflect in this way is, and should be, open-ended. For we want to allow the possibility that we will learn from our encounters with other human societies to recognize things about ourselves that we had not seen before, or even to change in certain ways, according more importance to something we had considered more peripheral. The list is an intuitive approximation, whose purpose is not to cut off discussion but to direct attention to certain features of importance. The list, moreover, is heterogeneous, for it contains both limits against which we press and capabilities through which we aspire. This is not surprising, since we begin from the idea of a creature who is both capable and needy. We shall return to this point, showing how it affects the political use of the list.

Here, then as a first approximation, is a story about what seems to be part of any life that we will count as a human life.

Level 1 of the Thick Vague Conception: The Shape of the Human Form of Life

Mortality. All human beings face death and, after a certain age, know that they face it. This fact shapes more or less every other element of human life. Moreover, all human beings have an aversion to death. Although in many circumstances death will be preferred to the available alternatives, the death of a loved one or the prospect of one's own death is an occasion for grief and/or fear. If we encountered an immortal anthropomorphic being or a mortal being that showed no aversion to death and no tendency to avoid death, we would judge, in both these cases, that the form of life was so different from our own that the being could not be acknowledged as human.

The human body. We live all our lives in bodies of a certain sort, whose possibilities and vulnerabilities do not as such belong to one human society rather than another. These bodies, similar far more than dissimilar (given the enormous range of possibilities), are our homes, so to speak, opening certain options and denying others, giving us certain needs and also certain possibilities for excellence. The fact that any given human being might have lived anywhere and belonged to any culture is a great part of what grounds our mutual recognitions; this fact, in turn, has a great deal to do with the general humanness of the body, its great distinctness from other bodies. The experience of the body is, to be sure, culturally shaped, but the body itself, not culturally variant in its nutritional and other related requirements, sets limits on what can be experienced, ensuring a great deal of overlap.

There is much disagreement, of course, about *how much* of human experience is rooted in the body. Here, religion and metaphysics enter the picture in a nontrivial way. Therefore, in keeping with the nonmetaphysical character of the list, I shall include at this point only those features that would be agreed to be bodily even by determined dualists. The more controversial features, such as thinking, perceiving, and emotion, I shall discuss separately, taking no stand on the question of dualism.[25]

1. *Hunger and thirst; the need for food and drink.* All human beings need food and drink in order to live; all have comparable, though varying, nutritional requirements. Being in one culture rather than another does not make one metabolize food differently. Furthermore, all human beings have appetites that are indices of need. Appetitive experience is to some extent culturally shaped, but we are not surprised to discover much similarity and overlap. Moreover, human beings in general do not wish to be hungry or thirsty (though, of course, they might choose to fast for some reason). If we discovered someone who really did not experience hunger or thirst at all, or, experiencing them, really did not care about eating and drinking, we would judge that this creature was (in Aristotle's words) "far from being a human being."

2. *Need for shelter.* A recurrent theme in myths of humanness is the nakedness of the human being, its relative susceptibility to heat, cold, and the ravages of the elements. Stories that explore the difference between our needs and those of furry or scaly or otherwise protected creatures remind us how far our life is constituted by the need to find refuge from the cold, the withering heat of the sun, from rain, wind, snow, and frost.

3. *Sexual desire.* Though less urgent as a need than the needs for food, drink, and shelter (in the sense that one can live without its satisfaction), sexual need and desire are features of more of less every human life. It is, and has been all along, a most important basis for the recognition of others different from ourselves as human beings.

4. *Mobility.* Human beings are, as the old definition goes, featherless bipeds— that is, creatures whose form of life is in part constituted by the ability to move from place to place in a certain characteristic way, not only through the aid of tools that we have made but with our very own bodies. Human beings like moving about and dislike being deprived of mobility. An anthropomorphic being who, without disability, chose never to move from birth to death would be hard to view as human.

Capacity for pleasure and pain. Experiences of pain and pleasure are common to all human life (though once again both their expression and, to some extent, the experience itself may be culturally shaped). Moreover, the aversion to pain as a fundamental evil is a primitive and, it appears, unlearned part of being a human animal. A society whose members altogether lacked that aversion would surely be judged to be beyond the bounds of humanness.

Cognitive capability: perceiving, imagining, thinking. All human beings have sense perception, the ability to imagine, and the ability to think, making distinctions and "reaching out for understanding,"[26] and these abilities are regarded as of central importance. It is an open question what sorts of accidents or impediments to individuals in these areas will be sufficient for us to judge that the life in question is not really human any longer. But it is safe to say that if we imagine a tribe whose members totally lack sense perception or totally lack imagination or totally lack reasoning and thinking, we are not in any of these cases imagining a tribe of human beings, no matter what they look like.

Early infant development. All human beings begin as hungry babies, aware of their own helplessness, experiencing their alternating closeness to and distance from that, and those, on whom they depend. This common structure to early life— which clearly is shaped in many different ways by different social arrangements— gives rise to a great deal of overlapping experience that is central in the formation of desires and of complex emotions such as grief, love, and anger. This, in turn, is a major source of our ability to recognize ourselves in the emotional experiences of those whose lives are very different in other respects from our own. If we encountered a tribe of apparent humans and then discovered that they never had been babies and had never, in consequence, had those experiences of extreme dependency, need, and affection, we would, I think, have to conclude that their form of life was sufficiently different from our own that they could not be considered part of the same kind.

Practical reason. All human beings participate (or try to) in the planning and managing of their own lives, asking and answering questions about what is good and how one should live. Moreover, they wish to enact their thought in their lives— to be able to choose and evaluate and to function accordingly. This general capability has many concrete forms and is related in complex ways to the other capabilities, emotional, imaginative, and intellectual. But a being who altogether lacks this would not be likely to be regarded as fully human in any society.

Affiliation with other human beings. All human beings recognize and feel some sense of affiliation and concern for other human beings. Moreover, we value the form of life that is constituted by these recognitions and affiliations. We live for and with others and regard a life not lived in affiliation with others to be a life not worth living. (Here, I would really wish, along with Aristotle, to spell things out further. We define ourselves in terms of at least two sorts of affiliation: intimate family and/or personal relations and social or civic relations.)

Relatedness to other species and to nature. Human beings recognize that they are not the only living things in their world, that they are animals living alongside other animals and also alongside plants in a universe that, as a complex interlocking order, both supports and limits them. We are dependent on that order in countless ways, and we also sense that we owe that order some respect and concern, however much we may differ about exactly what we owe, to whom, and on what basis. Again, a creature who treated animals exactly like stones and could not be brought to see any difference would probably be regarded as too strange to be human. So, too, would a creature who did not in any way respond to the beauty and wonder of the natural world.

Humor and play. Human life, wherever it is lived, makes room for recreation and laughter. The forms that play takes are enormously varied; yet we recognize other humans, across cultural barriers, as the animals who laugh. Laughter and play are frequently among the deepest and also the first modes of our mutual recognition. Inability to play or laugh is taken, correctly, as a sign of deep disturbance in an individual child; if it proves permanent, we will doubt whether the child is capable of leading a fully human life. An entire society that lacked this ability would seem to us both terribly strange and terribly frightening.

Separateness. However much we live with and for others, we are, each of us, "one in number," proceeding on a separate path through the world from birth to death. Each person feels only his or her own pain and not anyone else's. Each person dies without entailing logically the death of anyone else. When one person walks across the room, no other person follows automatically. When we count the number of human beings in a room, we have no difficulty figuring out where one begins and the other ends. These obvious facts need stating because they might have been otherwise. We should bear them in mind when we hear talk of the absence of individualism in certain societies. Even the most intense forms of human interaction, for example, sexual experience, are experiences of responsiveness, not of fusion. If fusion is made the goal, the result is bound to be bitter disappointment.

Because of separateness, each human life has, so to speak, its own peculiar context and surroundings—objects, places, a history, particular friendships, locations, sexual ties—that are not exactly the same as those of anyone else, and in terms of which the person to some extent identifies oneself. Although societies vary a great deal in the degree and type of strong separateness that they permit and foster, there is no life yet known that really does (as Plato wished) fail to use the words "mine" and "not mine" in some personal and nonshared way. What I use, touch, love, and respond to, I touch, use, love, and respond to from my own separate existence. And on the whole, human beings recognize one another as beings who wish to have at least some separateness of context, a little space to move around in, some special items to love or use.

As already said, the list is composed of two different sorts of items: limits and capabilities. As far as capabilities go, to call them part of humanness is to make a very basic sort of evaluation. It is to say that a life without this item would be too lacking, too impoverished, to be human at all. Obviously, then, it could not be a good human life. So, this list of capabilities is a ground-floor, or minimal, conception of the good. With the limits, things are more complicated. For we have said that human life, in its general form, consists in a struggle against these limits. Humans do not wish to be hungry, to feel pain, to die. (Separateness is highly complex—both a limit and a capability.) Yet we cannot assume that the correct evaluative conclusion to draw is that we should try as hard as possible to get rid of the limit altogether. It is characteristic of human life to prefer recurrent hunger plus eating to a life with neither hunger nor eating, to prefer sexual desire and its satisfaction to a life with neither desire nor satisfaction. Even where death is concerned, the desire for immortality, which human beings certainly seem to have, is a peculiar desire. For it is not clear that the wish to lose one's finitude completely is a desire that one can coherently wish for oneself or for someone whom one loves. That would seem to be a wish for a transition to a way of life so wholly different, with such different values and ends, that it is not clear that the identity of the individual could be preserved. So the evaluative conclusion needs to be expressed with much caution, clearly, in terms of what would be a humanly good way of countering the limitation.[27]

Things now get complicated, for we want to describe two distinct threshholds: a threshhold of capability to function, beneath which a life will be so impoverished that it will not be human at all, and a somewhat higher threshhold, beneath which those characteristic functions are available in such a reduced way that although we may judge the form of life a human one, we will not think it a good human life. The latter threshhold is the one that will eventually concern us most when we turn to public policy, for we do not want societies to make their citizens capable of the bare minimum. These are clearly, in many areas, two distinct threshholds, requiring distinct levels of resource and capability. Yet there is need for caution here. For, in many cases the move from human life to good human life is supplied by the citizens' own powers of choice and self-definition, in such a way that once society places them above the first threshhold, moving above the second is more or less up to them. This is especially likely to be so, I think, in areas such as affiliation and practical reasoning, where what we want from society and from other associations within it, such as the family, is a development of the child so that it passes the first threshhold. On the other hand, it is clear that where bodily health and nutrition, for example, are concerned, there is a considerable difference between the two threshholds, a difference made by resources over which individuals do not have full control. Clearly, there is a continuum here, and it is always going to be difficult to say where the upper threshhold, especially, should be located.

Here, then, as the next level of the conception of the human being, I now specify certain basic functional capabilities at which societies should aim for their citizens (in accordance with the political idea more fully investigated in the next section). In other words, this will be an account of the second threshhold—although in some areas, it seems to me to coincide with the first. I shall actually introduce the list as one of related capabilities rather than of actual functionings, since I shall argue that capability to function, not actual functioning, should be the goal of legislation and public planning.

Level 2 of the Thick Vague Conception: Basic Human Functional Capabilities

1. Being able to live to the end of complete human life, as far as is possible; not dying prematurely, or before one's life is so reduced as to be not worth living.
2. Being able to have good health; to be adequately nourished; to have adequate shelter; having opportunities for sexual satisfaction; being able to move from place to place.
3. Being able to avoid unnecessary and nonbeneficial pain and to have pleasurable experiences.
4. Being able to use the five senses; being able to imagine, to think, and to reason.
5. Being able to have attachments to things and persons outside ourselves; to love those who love and care for us, to grieve at their absence, in general, to love, grieve, to feel longing and gratitude.
6. Being able to form a conception of the good and to engage in critical reflection about the planning of one's own life.
7. Being able to live for and with others, to recognize and show concern for other human beings, to engage in various forms of familial and social interaction.
8. Being able to live with concern for and in relation to animals, plants, and the world of nature.
9. Being able to laugh, to play, to enjoy recreational activities.
10. Being able to live one's own life and nobody else's; being able to live one's own life in one's very own surroundings and context.

The Aristotelian essentialist claims that a life that lacks any one of these, no matter what else it has, will be lacking in humanness. So it would be reasonable to take these things as a focus for concern, in asking how public policy can promote the good of human beings. The list is, emphatically, a list of separate components. We cannot satisfy the need for one of them by giving a larger amount of another one. All are of central importance, and all are distinct in quality. This limits the trade-offs that it will be reasonable to make and thus limits the applicability of quantitative cost-benefit analysis. At the same time, the items on the list are related to one another in many complex ways. For example, our characteristic mode of nutrition, unlike that of sponges, requires moving from here to there. And we do whatever we do as separate beings, tracing distinct paths through space and time.

Among the capabilities, two—practical reason and affiliation—play a special role as architectonic, holding the whole enterprise together and making it human. All animals nourish themselves, use their senses, move about, and so forth; what is distinctive and distinctively valuable to us about the human way of doing all this is that each and every one of these functions is, first of all, planned and organized by practical reason and, second, done with and to others. Human nourishing is not like animal nourishing, nor human sex like animal sex, because human beings can choose to regulate their nutrition and their sexual activity by their very own practical reason; also because they do so not as solitary Cyclopes (who would eat anything at all, even their own guests) but as beings who are bound to other human beings by ties of mutual attention and concern.[28]

Answering the Objections

I must now try to show how the thick vague theory of the good can answer the objections most commonly made against essentialism. First of all, it should be clear by now that the list does not derive from any extra historical metaphysical conception, or rely on the truth of any form of metaphysical realism. As I have said, its guiding intuition is that we do recognize as human, people who do not share our own metaphysical and religious ideas; it aims to get at the root of those recognitions. It does so by conducting an inquiry that is, frankly, both evaluative and internal to human history. Furthermore, the conception does not even demand universal actual agreement among human beings in order to play the moral and political role that we want it to play, I have tried to arrive at a list that will command a very wide consensus, and a consensus that is fully international. Its very close resemblance to other similar lists worked out independently in parts of the world as divergent as Finland and Sri Lanka[29] gives some reason for optimism about consensus. On the other hand, unanimity is not required; for people who have not been willing to engage in the cross-cultural study and the probing evaluation that is behind the list may well refuse assent for varied reasons. Even among those who do engage in the inquiry, there may be differences of opinion. With regard to some components of the list, the very act of entering a disagreement seems to be an acknowledgment of the importance of the component: this seems true, for example, of both practical reasoning and affiliation. But with regard to others, there will be room for ongoing debate and reformulation. The aim is, simply, to achieve enough of a working consensus that we can use the list as a basis for the kind of political reflection that I describe in the next section. (We may usefully compare, at this point, John Rawls's idea of an "overlapping consensus" that is political and not metaphysical.[30]) So, the objections to essentialism that assume its dependence on realism seem to fail, in this particular case.

As for the three objections to "internalist" essentialism, each one of them is, and should remain, a central concern of the Aristotelian essentialist. For the list will command the sort of broad consensus she wishes only if these objections can be successfully met.

Concerning neglect of *historical and cultural difference*, the Aristotelian begins by insisting that the thick vague conception is vague for precisely this reason. The list claims to have identified in a very general way components that are fundamental to any human life. But it allows in its very design for the possibility of multiple specifications of each of the components. This is so in several different ways. First, the constitutive circumstances of human life, while broadly shared, are themselves realized in different forms in different societies. The fear of death, the love of play, relationships of friendship and affiliation with others, even the experience of the bodily appetites—these never turn up in simply the vague and general form in which they have been introduced here but always in some specific and historically rich cultural realization, which can profoundly shape not only the conceptions used by the citizens in these areas but their experiences themselves. Nonetheless, we do have in these areas of our common humanity sufficient overlap to sustain a general conversation, focusing on our common problems and prospects. Sometimes, the common conversation will permit us to criticize some conceptions of the grounding experiences themselves, as at odds with other things that human beings want to do and to be.[31]

When we are choosing a conception of *good* functioning with respect to these circumstances, we can expect an even greater degree of plurality to become evident. Here, the Aristotelian essentialist wants to retain plurality in two significantly different ways: what we may call the way of plural specification and the way of *local specification*.[32]

Plural specification means what its name implies. The political plan, while using a determinate conception of the good at a high level of generality, leaves a great deal of latitude for citizens to specify each of the components more concretely and with much variety, in accordance with local traditions or individual tastes.

As for local specification, Aristotelian practical reasoning is always done, when well done, with a rich sensitivity to the concrete context, to the characters of the agents and their social situation. This means that in addition to the pluralism I have just described, the Aristotelian needs to consider a different sort of plural specification of the good. For sometimes what is a good way of promoting education in one part of the world will be completely ineffectual in another. Forms of affiliation that flourish in one community may prove impossible to sustain in another. In such cases, the Aristotelian must aim at some concrete specification of the general list that suits and develops out of the local conditions. This will always most reasonably be done in a participatory dialogue with those who are most deeply immersed in those conditions. For although Aristotelianism does not hesitate to criticize tradition where tradition perpetrates injustice or oppression, it does not believe in saying anything at all without rich and full information, gathered not so much from detached study as from the voices of those who live the ways of life in question. Later, when I discuss efforts made to enhance female literacy in rural

Bangladesh, I shall give a concrete example of this sort of participatory dialogue and draw some further conclusions about this problem.

The liberal charges the Aristotelian with *neglect of autonomy*, arguing that any such determinate conception removes from the citizens the chance to make their own choices about the good life. This is a complicated issue; four points can be stressed.[33] First, the list is a list of capabilities, and not actual functions, precisely because the conception is designed to leave room for choice. Government is not directed to push citizens into acting in certain valued ways; instead, it is directed to make sure that all human beings have the necessary resources and conditions for acting in those ways. It leaves the choice up to them. A person with plenty of food can always choose to fast; a person who has access to subsidized university education can always decide to do something else instead. By making opportunities available, government enhances, and does not remove, choice.[34] Second, this respect for choice is built deeply into the list itself in the architectonic role it gives to practical reasoning. One of the most central capabilities promoted by the conception will be the capability of choosing itself, which is made among the most fundamental elements of the human essence.[35] Third, we should note that the major liberal view in this area, the view of John Rawls, does not shrink from essentialism of our internal sort in just this area. Rawls insists that satisfactions that are not the outgrowths of one's very own choices have no moral worth, and he conceives of the "two moral powers" (analogous to our practical reasoning) and of sociability (corresponding to our affiliation) as built into the definition of the parties in the original position and thus as necessary constraints on any outcome they will select.[36] In this way, the liberal view and the Aristotelian view converge more than one might initially suppose. Finally, the Aristotelian insists that choice is not pure spontaneity, flourishing independently of material and social conditions. If one cares about autonomy, then one must care about the rest of the form of life that supports it and the material conditions that enable one to live that form of life. Thus the Aristotelian claims that her own comprehensive concern with flourishing across all areas of life is a better way of promoting choice than is the liberal's narrower concern with spontaneity alone, which sometimes tolerates situations in which individuals are in other ways cut off from the fully human use of their faculties.

The Aristotelian conception can indeed by *prejudicially applied*. It is possible to say all the right things about humanness and then to deny that women or blacks or other minorities fall under the concept. How should the essentialist deal with this problem? First of all, it should be stressed that the fact that a conception can be withheld for reasons of prejudice or lack of love undermines not the conception itself but the person who withholds it. One may, looking at a minority whom one hates, speak of them as beetles or ants, and one may carry this refusal of humanity into the sphere of law and public action. Does this undermine our idea that a conception of the human being is a good basis for moral obligation? It seems to me that it does not. For what such cases reveal is the great power of the conception of the human. Acknowledging this other person as a member of the very same kind would have generated a sense of affiliation and responsibility; this was why the self-deceptive stratagem of splitting the other off from one's own species seemed so urgent and so seductive. And the stratagem of denying humanness to beings with whom one lives in conversation and some form of human interaction is a fragile sort of self-deceptive tactic, vulnerable to sustained and consistent reflection and also to experiences that cut through self-deceptive rationalization.[37]

Raul Hilberg, for example, has amassed an impressive amount of evidence concerning the psychology of such denials.[38] He argues that whenever circumstances arose that made it possible for the Nazi functionaries, whose actions depended on the denial of humanness to Jews, to sustain this denial in a particular case, what ensued was an emotional "breakthrough," in which action was indeed, at least temporarily, transformed. What were these occasions? Times, above all, when it became impossible to avoid the fact that one was interacting with a Jewish prisoner in a human manner: occasions of personal conversation or emotional connection that eluded the watchful protective mechanisms of denial. Thus one can say, I think, that focusing on the importance of the shared human functions makes it harder for prejudicial applications of the conception to take place: if we get clearer about what we are looking for in calling a being human, we will hardly avoid noticing the extent to which we acknowledge such functions, implicitly, in our dealings with others.

Any moral conception may be withheld, out of ambition or hatred or shame. But the conception of the human being seems so much more difficult to withhold than other conceptions that have been put forward as the basis for ethical obligation. The notion of the "person," for example, has sometimes been preferred to the notion of the human being as a basis for ethics, on the grounds that it is clearly a normative conception, whose connection with certain sorts of ethical obligations is especially evident. I have argued that the conception of the human being is itself, in a certain way, a normative conception, in that it involves singling out certain functions as more basic than others. And there is no getting around the fact that correct application of the concept will involve answering evaluative questions that will sometimes be difficult to answer: for a creature falls under the concept only if it possesses some basic, though perhaps altogether undeveloped, capability to perform the functions in question. It will sometimes be very difficult to say whether a certain patient with senile dementia or a certain extremely damaged infant has enough of those basic capabilities to fall under the concept. On the other hand, we have far less flexibility in the application of the concept than we do with "person," which has in history been applied and withheld extremely capriciously, more or less as the lawgiver decides to favor one group over another....With "person," the defender of equality is on uncertain ground, ground that the opponent can at any moment shift under her feet. With "human being," on the other hand, it is always open to her to say to the opponent, "Look at these beings: you cannot fail to grant that they use their senses, that they think about the future, that they engage in ethical conversation, that they have needs and vulnerabilities similar to your own. Grant this, and you grant that they are human. Grant that they are human, and you grant that they have needs for flourishing that exert a moral pull on anyone who would deny them." As I have said, it is always possible to deny such an appeal, even when looking into the face of a woman with whom one lives and bears children. On the other hand, it is impossible to do so with full and honest and consistent reflection, that is to say, at the conclusion of a fully human process of deliberation.

So far, I have focused on the higher-level (developed) human capabilities that make a life a good human life but have not spoken at length about the empirical basis for the application of the concept "human being" to a creature before us. The basis cannot, of course, be the presence of the higher-level capabilities on my list, for one of the main points of the list is to enable us to say, of some being before us, that this being might possibly come to have these higher-level capabilities but does not now have them. It is that gap between basic (potential) humanness and its full realization that exerts a claim on society and government. What, then, is to be the basis for a determination that this being is one of the human beings, one of the ones whose functioning concerns us? I claim that it is the presence of a lower-level (undeveloped) capability to perform the functions in question, such that with the provision of suitable support and education, the being would be capable of choosing these functions.[39]

There is, of course, enormous potential for abuse in determining who has these basic capabilities. The history of IQ testing is just one chapter in an inglorious saga of prejudiced capability testing that goes back at least to the Noble Lie of Plato's *Republic*. Therefore we should, I think, proceed as if every offspring of two human parents has the basic capabilities, unless and until long experience *with the individual* has convinced us that damage to that individual's condition is so great that it could never in any way, through however great an expenditure of resources, arrive at the higher capability level. (Certain patients with irreversible senile dementia or a permanent vegetative condition would fall into this category, as would certain very severely damaged infants. It would then fall to other moral arguments to decide what treatment we owe to such individuals, who are unable ever to reach the higher capabilities to function humanly. It certainly does not follow that we would be licensed to treat such individuals harshly; we simply would not aim at making them fully capable of the various functions on our list.)

Concerning individuals who can profit from education, care, and resources— and I emphasize that in practice this is to be taken to include all individuals, with the very rare exceptions just noted— the Aristotelian view observes that these basic human capabilities exert a claim on society that they should be developed. Human beings are creatures such that, provided with the right educational and material support, they can become capable of the major human functions. When their basic capabilities are deprived of the nourishment that would transform them into the higher-level capabilities that figure on my list, they are fruitless, cut off, in some way but a shadow of themselves. They are like actors who never get to go on the stage or a musical score that is never performed. The very being of these basic capabilities makes forward reference to functioning; thus if functioning never arrives on the scene, they are hardly even what they are. This basic intuition underlies the recommendations that the Aristotelian view will make for public action: certain basic and central human powers have a claim to be developed and will exert that claim on others— and especially, as Aristotle held, on government.[40]

Our Need for Essentialism in Public Policy

I have said that we urgently need a version of essentialism in public life. If we reject it, we reject guidance that is crucial if we are to construct an adequate account of distributive justice to guide public policy in many areas. It is time for me to substantiate these claims. I shall focus on the area with which I began: the assessment of the "quality of life" in developing countries, with a view to formulating policy, both within each separate country and between one country and another. The general direction of my argument should by now be clear: we cannot tell how a country is doing unless we know how the people in it are able to function in the central human ways. And without an account of the good, however vague, that we take to be shared, we have no adequate basis for saying what is *missing* from the lives of the poor or marginalized or excluded, no adequate way of justifying the claim that any deeply embedded tradition that we encounter is unjust.

Public policy analyses of the quality of life in developing countries often use measures that are extremely crude.[41] It is still common to find countries ranked in accordance with their gross national product per capita, even though this measure does not even concern itself with the distribution of resources and thus can give good marks to a country with enormous inequalities. Such an approach, furthermore, does not look at all at other human goods that are not reliably correlated with the presence of resources: infant mortality, for example, or access to education, or the quality of racial and gender relations, or the presence or absence of political freedoms. Such an approach might fail to arouse the ire of the antiessentialist because it appears to take no stand on questions of value. But, first of all, it really does take a stand, albeit a perverse one, for it assumes that the presence of more money and resources is the one important determinant of life quality. And second, insofar as it fails to take a stand on other components of the human good, such as freedom, or health, or education, it fails to offer useful guidance to the social scientist seeking to understand how countries are doing or to the policy maker seeking to make things better.

One step up in level of sophistication is an approach that measures the quality of life in terms of utility. This would be done, for example, by polling people about whether they are satisfied with their current health status or their current level of education. This approach at least has the merit of focusing on people and viewing resources as valuable because of what they do in human lives. But its narrow focus on subjective expressions of satisfaction brings with it a number of serious problems. First of all, desires and subjective preference are not always reliable indices of what a person really needs, of what would really be required to make that life a flourishing one. Desires and satisfactions are highly malleable. The rich and pampered easily become accustomed to their luxury and view with pain and frustration a life in which they are treated just like everyone else. The poor and deprived frequently adjust their expectations and aspirations to the low level of life they have known; thus their failure to express dissatisfaction can often be a sign that they really do have enough. This is all the more true when the deprivations in question include deprivation of education and other information about alternative ways of life. Circumstances confine the imagination.[42]

Thus, if we rely on utility as our measure of life quality, we most often will get results that support the status quo and oppose radical change. A poll of widowers and widows in India showed that the widowers were full of complaint about their health status; the widows, on the other hand, in most cases ranked their health status as "good." On the other hand, a medical examination showed that the widows were actually suffering far more than the males from diseases associated with nutritional deficiency. The point was that they had lived all their lives expecting that women will eat less, and the weakened health status produced in this way was second nature to them. Some years later, after a period of political "consciousness raising," the study was repeated. The utility of the women had gone down, in the sense that they expressed far more dissatisfaction with their health. (Their objective medical situation was pretty much unchanged.[43]) On the other hand, to the Aristotelian, this is progress, for their desires and expectations are now more in tune with information about what a flourishing life could be. They know what functioning they are missing. Similar results obtain in the educational sphere—where, once again, polls of women in India asking whether they are satisfied with their educational status usually produce affirmative results, so deep are the cultural forces militating against any change in this area and so little information is there concerning how education has transformed and could transform female lives.

Even if this problem were to be removed and the utility theorist were able to operate with a sophisticated view of corrected preferences, the Aristotelian would still have a number of serious questions to raise about the whole idea of utility as a basis for public policy. If utility is understood as a single thing, as in some vague sense it usually is, then the theory is implicity committed to the commensurability of values and to the idea that for any two distinct ends, we can always imagine trade-offs in purely quantitative terms. The Aristotelian is profoundly opposed to this idea. The account that she gives of the basic human functionings shows a rich plurality of distinct items, each of which must be represented in a fully human life. You cannot pay for the absence of one function by using the coin of another.[44]

Furthermore, the usual pretense of economic utilitarianism—that all this can be modeled by attaching a monetary value to the relevant human functionings—is, to the Aristotelian, especially repellent. The Aristotelian holds that money is merely a tool of human functioning and has value in human life only insofar as it subserves these functionings. More is not always better, and in general, the right amount is what makes functioning best.[45] To treat the functions themselves as commodities that have a cash value is to treat them as fungible, as alienable from the self for a price; this implicity denies what the Aristotelian asserts: that we define ourselves in terms of them and that there is no self without them. To treat deep parts of our identity as alienable commodities is to do violence to the conception of the self that we actually have and to the texture of the world of human practice and interaction revealed through this conception. As Marx put it, "Assume the human being to be the human being and its relations to the world to be a human one, then you can exchange love only for love, trust for trust, etc."[46]

Finally, utilitarianism, neglecting as it does the inalienability of certain elements of the self, neglects also the ethical salience of the boundaries between persons. As a theory of public measurement, utilitarianism is committed to the aggregation of satisfactions. Individuals are treated as centers of pleasure or pain satisfaction or dissatisfaction, and the fact of their separateness one from another is not given special weight in the theory, which proceeds by summing. But in the world we actually inhabit, it is a highly relevant fact that my pain is not yours, nor yours mine. If trade-offs between functions are problematic where a single life is concerned, they are all the more problematic when they cross the boundaries of lives, purchasing one person's satisfaction at the price of another's misery. It is easy to see what consequences this can have for policy. For the utilitarian is frequently willing to tolerate huge inequalities for the sake of a larger total or average sum. The Aristotelian's fundamental commitment, by contrast, is to bring each and every person across the threshhold into capability for good functioning. This means devoting resources to getting everyone across before any more is given to those who are already capable of functioning at some basic level. If all cannot be brought across the threshhold, to this extent the ends of public policy have not been met.

The local tradition relativism endorsed in my Helsinki examples claims to be different from prevailing economic-utilitarian views, on account of its close attention to the fabric of daily life in traditional societies. But it actually shares many of the defects of the utilitarian view, for it refuses to subject preferences, as formed in traditional societies, to any sort of critical scrutiny. It seems to assume that all criticism must be a form of imperialism, the imposition of an outsider's power on local ways. Nor does it simply claim to avoid normative judgments altogether, for it actually endorses the locally formed norms as good and even romanticizes them in no small degree. It confers a bogus air of legitimacy on these deeply embedded preferences by refusing to subject them to ethical scrutiny. So far as my other objections to utilitarianism go, it does not really avoid them either, for if some local tradition wishes to treat all values as commensurable or to commodify parts of the self (or even as often happens, whole women), the "embedded" view (associated with writers like S.A. and F.A. Marglin) must accept this result and accept it as good. The concrete consequences of this emerge clearly from the conclusions of their volume, for they end by rejecting most of what is usually called "development"—that is, most agricultural, technological, and economic change and most educational change as well—and supporting as good ways of life in which it is unlikely that they would themselves wish to dwell for more than a brief period of time, especially as a woman. One may sympathize with some of the Marglins' goals—respect for diversity, desire to protect from exploitation ways of life that seem to be rich in spiritual and artistic value—without agreeing that extreme relativism of the sort they defend is the best way to articulate and pursue these goals.

One more antiessentialist approach to questions of distributive justice must now be considered. It is by far the most powerful alternative to the Aristotelian approach, and its differences from it are subtle and complex. This is the liberal idea, defended in different forms by John Rawls and Ronald Dworkin, that distribution should aim at an equal allotment of certain basic resources (or, in the case of Rawls, should tolerate inequalities only where this would improve the situation of the worst off).[47]

The Rawlsian liberal insists on distributing basic resources without taking a stand on the human good, even in the vague way in which the "thick vague theory" has done so. The aim is to leave to each citizen a choice of the conception of the good by which he or she will live. As we have said, Rawls does take a stand on some of the components of our conception. For sociability and practical reason are treated as essential to any conception of human flourishing that can be entertained; liberty is on the list of "primary goods" as are the "social conditions of self-respect"; and in argument against utilitarianism, Rawls commits himself very strongly to the centrality of the separateness of persons.[48] On the other hand, as we have seen, the Aristotelian conception does itself insist on the fundamental role of choice and autonomy. But there are still significant differences between the two conceptions, for the Rawlsian view treats income and wealth as "primary goods" of which more is always better, independently of the concrete conception of the good. And he does define the "better off" and "worse off" in terms of quantities of these basic resources rather than in terms of functioning or capability.

To this, the Aristotelian has three replies. First, as we have said, wealth and income are not good in their own right; they are good only insofar as they promote human functioning. Rawls's view, which appears to treat them as having independent significance, obscures the role that they actually play in human life.

Second, human beings have variable needs for resources, and any adequate definition of the better off and worse off must reflect that fact. A pregnant woman has nutritional needs that are different from those of a nonpregnant woman and a child from those of an adult. The child who has exactly the same amount of protein in her diet as an adult is less well off, given her greater needs. A person whose mobility is impaired will need a significantly greater amount of resources than will a person of average mobility in order to achieve the same level of capability to move about. These are not just rare exceptions; they are pervasive facts of life. Thus the failure of the liberal theory to deal with them is a serious defect. And yet, to deal with then, we need a general conception of what functions we are trying to support.[49]

Third, the liberal, by defining being well-off in terms of possessions alone, fails to go deep enough in imagining the impediments to functioning that are actually present in many human lives. Marx argued, for example, that workers who lack control over their own activity and its products lead lives less than fully human, even if they do get adequate wages. In general, the structure of labor relations, of class relations, and of race and gender relations in a society can alienate its members from the fully human use of their faculties even when their material needs are met. It is possible to hold that a pampered middle-class housewife is well off, despite the barriers that prevent her from expressing herself fully in employment and education. What is very unclear is whether Rawls—who does indeed decide to postpone consideration of structures of power within the household—should allow himself to be in this position, given his commitment to the realization of the two moral powers for each and every citizen. At the very least, there is a tension internal to the view, which can be dispelled only by a more explicit consideration of the relationship between the two moral powers and various other human functions and their material and institutional necessary conditions.[50] With political liberty, Rawls fully seizes this problem; therefore he places liberty among the primary goods. My claim is that he needs to go further in this direction, making the list of primary goods not a list of resources and commodities at all but a list of basic capabilities of the person.

The political and economic alternative to these various antiessentialist views does exist and is in use in a variety of areas. In development economics, a position strikingly similar to the Aristotelian position has been developed by economist-philosopher Amartya Sen. Arguing that the focus of development analysis should be on human capabilities rather than on opulence or utility or resources, he has proposed ways of assessing the quality of life in developing countries that begin from a list of interrelated capabilities. His arguments for this approach and against others are closely related to the arguments of this essay. Other related approaches have been worked out by Scandinavian social scientists, by doctors measuring patients' quality of life, by teachers in a troubled society interested in laying a foundation for the peaceful resolution of conflict.[51]

Now I return to the antiessentialist stories with which I began, showing how the Aristotelian view would handle them. The case of smallpox vaccination is relatively clear-cut. The Aristotelian, while not wishing to interfere with the capability of citizens to use their imaginations and their senses for the purposes of religious expression should they choose to do so, would certainly make bodily health a top priority and would not be deterred in a program of smallpox vaccination by the likelihood that it would eradicate the cult of Sittala Devi. The Aristotelian would introduce the vaccination scheme and then leave it to the citizens to see whether they wished to continue their relationship with that goddess. Nothing would prevent them from doing so, but if they ceased to see the point in the observances, once the disease had been eradicated, the Aristotelian would weep no nostalgic tears.

As for freedom and the Japanese husband, the Aristotelian will simply remind the objector of what she means by freedom, which is the power to form a conception of the good and to select action toward its realization. She will point out that in that sense of freedom, the Japanese husband in the example has (and no doubt values) freedom; his freedom, indeed, is enhanced by having someone who will look after boring details of life. But if the freedom of one person requires pushing someone else below the threshhold of capability to exercise practical reason, the Aristotelian will call this injustice and exploitation, and will not rest content until a searching examination of gender relations in this case has shown to what extent the capabilities of women are in fact being undercut in the name of male leisure.

As for menstruation taboos, they look like a clear restriction on women's power to execute a plan of life that they have chosen. This is so even if, as is sometimes claimed, such taboos end up giving women more rest and a little more pleasure than they would have had if they were working; for some tradeoffs that diminish the power of choice, even when they result in greater comfort, are not supported by the Aristotelian view.

To conclude this part of my argument, I would now like to examine a case that is more complicated and problematic than the ones I have just related rather briefly. This case will dramatize the difference between the Aristotelian approach and its rivals in the development sphere, and will also indicate how the Aristotelian proposes to balance sensitivity to local tradition against her commitment to a theory of the human being. The case concerns a literacy campaign directed at women in rural Bangladesh. It is described in Marty Chen's excellent book, *A Quiet Revolution: Women in Transition in Rural Bangladesh.*[52]

The women in the village in which Chen worked had low status in every area, in terms of our account of human functioning. They were less well nourished than males, less educated, less free, and less respected. Let us now consider their situation with respect to just one question: the question of literacy. As I have said, polls based on the idea of utility typically show, in this and related cases, that women have no desire for a higher rate of literacy. The poll is taken; women express satisfaction; no action follows. This, of course, is not surprising, given the weight of the cultural forces pressing these women not to demand more education (and also not to feel that they want more) given, as well, the absence in their daily lives of paradigms of what education could do and be in lives similar to theirs.

The development agency with which Chen was working went into the village holding firmly to the conviction that literacy was an important basic good. At first, they tried a liberal approach, based on the distribution of resources: in cooperation with the local government, they handed out to the women of the village ample adult literacy materials, taking no stand on whether they should choose to use them. (Notice that already this approach is not really a liberal approach, in that it takes a stand on the importance of education, giving these women literacy materials rather than cash. It is also not a pure liberal approach because it singled out the women of the village, recognizing their special impediments to functioning as giving them a greater claim on resources.) The distribution had little impact on women's functioning. This was so because the development people made no attempt to perceive the women's lives in a broad or deep way or to ask what role literacy might play in those lives and what strategies of education were most suited for their particular case. Perhaps even more important, they did not ask the women to tell their own story.

The liberal project had failed. Yet the development workers did not simply drop their general conception of the good, concluding that local traditions should in each case be the arbiter of value and that belief in their own way was bound to be paternalistic. Instead, they made a transition to a more Aristotelian approach. Over a period of several years, they set up women's cooperatives in which members of the development agency joined with the local women in a searching participatory dialogue concerning the whole form of life in the village. They discussed with the women the role that literacy was currently playing in the lives of women elsewhere, showing concrete examples of transformations in empowerment and self-respect. The women, in turn, told them their own story of the special impediments to education that their traditions had given them. The result, over time, was a gradual but deep transformation in the entire shape of the women's lives. Once literacy was perceived not as a separate and highly general thing but as a skill that might be deployed in particular ways in their particular context, it became of enormous interest and led to many changes in women's lives. For example, women were able to take over the tailoring industry in the village as well as other similar functions. In this way, they began to earn wages outside the home, a circumstance that has been shown to give women a stronger claim to food and medical care when resources are scarce. On the other hand, none of these concrete transformations could have happened had the women of the development agency not held fast to their general conception, showing the women its many other concrete realizations, and proceeding with confidence that it did have some concrete realization in these particular lives. Essentialism and particular perception were not opposed: they were complementary aspects of a single process of deliberation. Had the women not been seen as human beings who shared with the other women a common humanity, the local women could not have told their story in the way they did, nor could the development workers have brought their own experiences of feminism to the participatory dialogue as if they had some relevance for the local women. The very structure of the dialogue presupposed the recognition of common humanity, and it was only with this basis securely established that they could fruitfully explore the concrete circumstances in which they were trying, in the one case, to live and in the other case, to promote flourishing human lives....

Author's Note

A version of this essay was presented at the Institute for the Humanities at the University of Chicago in May 1991; I am grateful to Norma Field for arranging the invitation and to the participants, especially David Gitomer and Chris Bobonich, for their helpful comments. I also owe thanks to Amartya Sen for many discussions, to Frédérique and Steve Marglin for challenging and provoking me, to David Crocker and Henry Richardson for valuable comments on earlier related work, and to Tracy Strong and Cass Sunstein for comments on an earlier draft.

NOTES

1. The argument of this essay is closely related to that of several others, to which I shall refer frequently in what follows: "Nature, Function, and Capability," *Oxford Studies in Ancient Philosophy*, suppl. vol. 1 (1988): 145-84 (hereafter NFC); "Non-relative virtues: An Aristotelian Approach," *Midwest Studies in Philosophy* 13 (1988): 32-53, and, in an expanded version, in *The Quality of Life*, edited by M. Nussbaum and A. Sen (Oxford: Clarendon, 1992) (hereafter NRV); "Aristotelian Social Democracy," in *Liberalism and the Good*, edited by R.B. Douglass *et al.* (New York: Routledge, 1990) 203-52 (hereafter ASD); "Aristotle on Human Nature and the Foundations of Ethics," forthcoming in a volume on the philosophy of Bernard Williams, edited by R. Harrison and J. Altham (Cambridge: Cambridge University Press, 1992) (hereafter HN); "Human Capabilities, Female Human Beings," in [*Women, Culture and Development: a Study of Human Capabilities*], ed. M. Nussbaum and J. Glover (Oxford: Clarendon, [1995]) (hereafter HC).
2. For relevant publications of the United Nations University/World Institute for Development Economics Research (WIDER), see Nussbaum and Sen, eds., *The Quality of life*, and Nussbaum and Glover, eds, [*Women, Culture and Development*].
3. Much of the material described in the examples is now published in *Dominating Knowledge: Development, Culture, and Resistance*, edited by Frédérique Apffel Marglin and Stephen A. Marglin (Oxford: Clarendon, 1990). The issue of "embeddedness" and menstruation taboos is discussed in S.A. Marglin, "Losing Touch: The Culture Conditions of Worker Accommodation and Resistance," 217-82, and related general issues are developed in S. A. Marglin, "Toward the Decolonization of the Mind," 1-28. On Sittala Devi, see S.A. Marglin, " Smallpox in Two Systems of Knowledge," 102-44; and for related arguments, see Ashis Nandy and Shiv Visvanathan, " Modern Medicine and Its Non-Modern Critics," 144-84.
4. The proceedings of this conference are published as Nussbaum and Sen, *The Quality of Life*.
5. This point is now made in S.A. Marglin, "Toward the Decolonization"; his reference is to Takeo Doi, *The Anatomy of Dependence* (Tokyo: Kedansho, 1971).
6. Because of such pervasive assumptions, in general I have not used the vocabulary of "essentialism" in describing my own (historically embedded and historically sensitive) account of the central human functions. I do so here, somewhat polemically, in order to reclaim the word for reasoned debate, and I assume that the reader will look closely at my account of what the "essentialism" I recommend, in fact, entails. For further comments on this, see HN, ASC, and HC.
7. Much of the same has been true of at least some of the opponents of relativist "antiessentialism," who speak of relativism as the source of all modern evil, without saying how they themselves would answer relativist arguments. See, for example, my criticisms of Allan Bloom's *The Closing of the American Mind* (New York: Simon & Schuster, 1987) in "Undemocratic Vistas," *The New York Review of Books*, November 5, 1987.
8. Jacques Derrida, *Of Grammatology*, translated By G. C. Spivak (Baltimore: Johns Hopkins University Press, 1977).
9. For my account of Aristotle's position, see *The*

Fragility of Goodness: Luck and Ethics in Greek Tragedy and Philosophy (Cambridge: Cambridge University Press, 1986), chap.8. Related debates in Indian philosophy are given a most illuminating discussion in B.K. Matilal, *Perception* (Oxford: Clarendon, 1985).

10. In two areas above all, the arguments familiar in the literature of deconstruction have gaps: they do not confront debates within the philosophy of science—for example, concerning the interpretation of quantum mechanics—that have great importance for the realism question, and they rarely confront in a detailed way the issues concerning reference and translation that have been debated with considerable subtlety within the philosophy of language.
11. In this category, as close relatives of my view, I would place the "internal-realist" conception of Hilary Putnam, *Reason, Truth and History* (Cambridge: Cambridge University Press, 1981), *The Many Faces of Realism* (La Salle: Open Court, 1987) and *Realism With a Human Face* (Cambridge, MA: Harvard University Press, 1990); and also Charles Taylor *Sources of the Self: The Making of Modern Identity* Cambridge, MA: Harvard University Press 1989). For my discussion of Taylor's arguments, see *New Republic*, April 1990.
12. See esp. John Rawls, *A Theory of Justice* (Cambridge, MA: Harvard University Press 1971.) Rawls's position and its relationship to the Aristotelian view is discussed in NFC, in HC and especially in ASD, with references to other later articles in which Rawls has further developed his position concerning the role of a conception on the good in his theory.
13. By relativism I mean the view that the only available standard to value is some local group or individual; by subjectivism I mean the view that the only available standard to value is some local group or individual; by subjectivism I mean the view that the standard is given by each individual's subjective preferences; thus relativism, as I understand it here, is a genus of which subjectivism is one extreme species.
14. A clear example of this view is Stanley Fish: see *Doing What Come Naturally: Change, Rhetoric, and the Practice of Theory and Legal Studies* (Durham and London: Duke University Press, 1989). I criticized Fish's position in "Sophistry About Conventions," in *Love's Knowledge: Essays on Philosophy and Literature* (New York: Oxford University Press, 1990), 220-29, and in "Skepticism About Practical Reason," a Dewey Lecture delivered at the Harvard University Law School, October 1991.
15. This is the position that Derrida appeared to take up in a number of works—for example, in *Éperons: Les styles de Nietzsche* (Paris 1979); he has more recently insisted that his position does leave room for one view to be better than another, see his Afterword to *Limited Inc.*, translated by Samuel Weber and Jeffrey Mehlmann (Evanston, IL: Northwestern University Press, 1988). Certainly, the former position is the one frequently found in the writings of followers of Derrida in literary theory and criticism.
16. I discuss the parallels to ancient skepticism in detail in "Skepticism About Practical Reason"; see also my "Therapeutic Arguments in Ancient Skepticism," *Journal of the History of Philosophy* (Fall 1991).
17. S.A. Marglin (pp. 22-23) suggests that this sort of thinking is peculiarly Western. My (entirely typical) epigraphs from non-Western traditions already cast doubt on this. Opponents of such oppositions have not explained how one can speak coherently without bounding off one thing against another, opposing one thing to another.
18. Aristotle, *Parts of Animals* 1.5, 645 a5-37. Aristotle notes that anyone who has this shame about looking at the animal world is bound to take up the same attitude to himself, since an animal is what he is.
19. See esp. *Reason, Truth and History* and also Putnam's chapter in Nussbaum and Sen, eds, *The Quality of Life*.
20. For further elaboration, see HN, ASD, and HC.
21. See ASD; for detailed argument concerning the normative character of such an inquiry into "essensce," see HN.
22. For a detailed account of this contrast, see ASD and NFC.
23. For a closely related idea, see charles Taylor, *Sources of the Self*.
24. HN discusses the relation of this idea to some debates about the end of life in contemporary medical ethics.
25. On the question of cultural variation in the construction of these basic experiences, see NRV and ASD.
26. See Aristotle, *Methaphysics* 1.1.
27. This problem is confronted in "Transcending Human-

ity," in Nussbaum, *Love's Knowledge: Essays on Philosophy and Literature* (New York: Oxford University Press, 1990).

28. For the relationship of these ideas to Marx's account of truly human functioning in the *Economics and Philosophical Manuscripts of 1844*, see NFC.
29. For Scandinavian conceptions, see the chapters by E. Allardt and R. Erikson in Nussbaum and Sen, eds., *The Quality of Life*. On capabilities in Sri Lanka, see Carlos Fonseka, *Toward a Peaceful Sri Lanka*, WIDER Research for Action series, World Institute for Developments Economics Research, Helsinki, 1990.
30. John Rawls, "The Idea of an Overlapping Consensus," *Oxford Journal of Legal Studies* 7 (1987).
31. For some examples, see NRV.
32. This is developed more fully in ASD.
33. See the longer treatment of this issue in ASD.
34. This distinction is central in the political theory of Amartya Sen. See, among others "Equality of What?" in Sen, *Choice, Welfare, and Measurement* (Oxford: Blackwell, 1982) 353-69, and *Commodities and Capabilities* (Amsterdam: North-Holland, 1985.)
35. See also Sen, *Commodities and Capabilities*.
36. See esp. Rawls, " The Priority of the Right and Ideas of the Good," *Philosophy and Public Affairs* 17 (1988); for further references and discussions, see ASD.
37. Compare the remarks on slaves in Stanley Cavell, *The Claim of Reason* (New York: Oxford University Press, 1979).
38. Raul Hilberg, *The Destruction of the European Jews* (New York: Holmes & Meier, 1985).
39. This idea is developed more fully in NFC and HC.
40. For more on this, see NFC and HC.
41. See Nussbaum and Sen, "Introduction," *The Quality of Life*.
42. For these objections, see also Sen, "Equality of What?" and *Commodities and Capabilities*. Recent utilitarian work in philosophy has to some extent addressed these objections, introducing many corrections to actual preferences, but the practice of development economists has not been much altered.
43. See Sen, *Commodities and Capabilieties*; also J. Kynch and A. Sen, "Indian Women: Well-Being and Survival," *Cambridge Journal of Economics* 7 (1983).
44. See Nussbaum, "The Discernment of Perception," in *Love's Knowledge* (1990).
45. See especially *Politics* 1.8 and 7.1.
46. Marx, *Economics and Philosophical Manuscripts of 1844*, translated by M. Milligan, in *The Marx/Engels Reader*, edited by R.C. Tucker (New York 1978). On the texture of the human work, in connection with a related criticism of utilitarianism, see Putnam, *Reason, Truth, and History*. From the debate about the adequacy of economic utilitarianism as a basis for legal judgment, see Margaret Jane Radin's outstanding article, "Market-Inalienability," *Harvard Law Review* 100 (1987) 1848ff., which criticizes Richard Posner for speaking of a woman's body as a commodity of which she may dispose in the market.
47. For a longer account of these criticisms, see ASD.
48. Rawls, *A Theory of Justice* (Cambridge, MA: Harvard University Press, 1922) 189-92.
49. See Sen, "Equality of What?"
50. On this point, see Okin, *Justice, Gender and the Family*, and my review of her in *New York Review of Books*, [October 1992].
51. See the chapters by Allardt, Erikson, and Brock in Nussbaum and Sen, eds., *The Quality of Life*; also Fonseka, *Towards a Peaceful Sri Lanka*.
52. Cambridge, MA: Schenkman, 1983. See also Chen, "A Matter of Survival: Women's Right to Work in India and Bangladesh," in Nussbaum and Glover, eds., [*Women, Culture and Development*].

INSIDERS AND OUTSIDERS IN INTERNATIONAL DEVELOPMENT

David A. Crocker

David A. Crocker is a Senior Research Scholar at the Institute for Philosophy and Public Policy and teaches in the School of Public Affairs at the University of Maryland, College Park. He is co-editor of Ethics of Consumption: The Good Life, Justice, and Global Stewardship *(Rowman & Littlefield, 1998). His current research is in the area of transitional justice and he has published a working paper, "Transitional Justice and International Civil Society," under the auspices of The National Commission on Civic Renewal. He is a founding member and the current President of the International Development Ethics Association (IDEA).*

Crocker explores answers to the question of who should engage in the moral evaluation of a country's development goals and strategies. According to Crocker, the question has been framed in terms of the debates about ethnocentrism/anti-ethnocentrism and particularism/universalism. Instead of defending a position within this framework, Crocker attempts to recast the debate by developing an account of insiders and outsiders and of the advantages and disadvantages each bring to moral inquiry about issues of development. Crocker argues that we are all insiders and outsiders to various groups, associations, and countries and that we can become more complete persons and better developmental ethicists by exploring and utilizing insider and outsider insights.

International development ethics is moral reflection on the ends and means of societal and global change.[1] Who should engage in this activity and how should it be done? We can make headway on this large question by answering some more specific questions. Should only citizens of a given nation reflect on that country's development goals and strategies? Should only a society's members morally evaluate that society's present development models, policies, and practices or advocate alternatives? Or do foreigners have a contribution to make as well?[2] Who should conduct ethical research with respect to regional and, especially, global development when regional identity is comparatively shallow and global citizenship is arguably utopian or non-existent?

I try to answer these questions in four steps. First, I briefly discuss and criticize the context in which the questions are usually framed and debated, namely the ethnocentrism/anti-ethnocentrism and particularism/universalism controversies. Second, I explain the distinction between social insiders and outsiders and argue that it is a more fruitful angle from which to address the topic of who should engage in development ethics. Foreigners can become partial insiders in an initially alien society just as citizens can be outsiders in their own societies. Third, I argue that in development ethics, as in other cross cultural activities such as sports and business, there are both advantages and disadvantages to being social insiders as well as social outsiders. In development ethics both insiders and outsiders have positive roles to play and temptations to avoid. Finally, I urge development ethicists to cultivate a mixture of insiderness/outsiderness with respect to both their own and other societies. Moreover, there are good reasons for strengthening a global community in which ethicists,

---

among others, are partial insiders. As world citizens, as well as partial insiders in other communities, ethicists can evaluate present international institutions, hammer out global norms, and forge improved international structures and relations. International norms and structures are not insignificant; they can hinder or help good national and regional development just as national and regional progress can contribute to global improvement.

I

It is widely believed, especially by those living in rich and powerful countries, that appropriate Third World and global development models, policies, and projects should reflect Northern/Western development experience. Increasingly this belief is seen, especially by those living in the Third World, as ethnocentrism. Here "ethnocentrism" means two things. First, Northern/Western ethnocentrics employ their own cultural norms in evaluating foreign practices. In this first sense, ethnocentrism is "a habitual disposition to judge foreign peoples or groups by the standards and practices of one's own culture or ethnic group." Second, these ethnocentrics employ their standards to make *invidious* comparisons. Foreign standards and practices are judged to be inferior to those of the evaluator. In this second sense, ethnocentrism is "a tendency toward viewing alien cultures with disfavor and a resulting sense of (one's own) inherent superiority."[3] Ethnocentrism is not limited to but is especially prevalent in the United States. As Ofelia Schutte remarks, "One basic difficulty with our attitude toward the rest of the world is the implicit belief that our way of life in the United States is superior to any other ... and deserves to be exported to others."[4]

Given this definition, ethnocentrism might arguably occur if a development ethicist from one culture evaluates development in another culture. The likelihood is increased when the ethicist comes from the rich North or West to assess development ends and means in the poor South or East. The ethicist is likely to judge Third World development in terms of his or her own societal norms and propose development goals and strategies to help "them" become like "us." There are three main responses to this likelihood of ethnocentrism: (1) particularist anti-ethnocentrism, (2) universalist anti-ethnocentrism, and (3) particularist anti anti-ethnocentrism.

First, particularist anti-ethnocentrism rejects the exporting of foreign development models and practices and sometimes repudiates the very idea of development.[5] Each "developing" society or region should define desirable social change according to its own "lights" (stock of ideas) and its own traditions. The particularist enjoins: "Cast your buckets where you are!"[6] Every society should be loyal to its own moral traditions and development ethic. A foreign development ethicist would have a role in an alien culture's development only if there were some overlap in the moral traditions of the two countries. The foreigner's "lights" would be shared, at least partially, by indigenous ethicists. Sometimes this kind of anti-ethnocentrism is supported on nationalistic and even ethnocentric grounds. Sometimes it is argued for on universal moral grounds: each society has the right or the duty to determine its own path and develop itself in its own way—free from foreign influence, let alone economic domination or military intervention. Schutte nicely captures (and endorses) particularist (anti-U.S.) anti-ethnocentrism:

> We should recognize that issues of national sovereignty, autonomy, and self-determination in Latin America take precedence for its inhabitants over issues related to the notion of "progress" as determined by U.S. standards of what ought to occur in the region. In philosophy, this means that there is a strong desire to preserve the legacy of Latin American thought over and against the constant incursion of U.S-backed ideas.... Latin American intellectuals tend to agree that Latin American problems need and ought to be resolved by Latin Americans and by no one else.[7]

As Schutte indicates, the more extreme versions of this position are explicitly separatist: foreigners are not welcome in a region's or a nation's development debate. Less extreme positions leave open the possibility of some general cross-cultural dialogue, but see no value and much danger in foreigners engaging in the development dialogue in and for another society.

Much of this view deserves acceptance. National

and regional self-determination should be respected. It does not follow, however, that foreigners, even from North America, cannot play a positive role in a Third World development dialogue. For as Schutte herself recognizes, this dialogue can and should take place "on no less than a perfectly equal basis."[8] But more needs to be said about the assumptions and implications of this conversational equality. Moreover, the issue is not that of foreigner versus native; for some foreigners are more a part of the "alien" society than some of that society's own members and, as we shall see, there are morally significant insider/outsider distinctions among the society's own members.

Universalist anti-ethnocentrism, a second response to ethnocentrism, seeks to get beyond all cultural bias, whether of First, Second or Third World varieties, by ascending to an ahistorical, transcendent Archimedean point.[9] From this standpoint, the timeless Truth about desirable social change can be discerned (or constructed) and then applied to societies at different stages of the one development path. Ethnocentrism is objectionable, and it should be reduced if not eliminated by replacing cultural bias with Reason.

Universalism has stronger and weaker versions depending on differences concerning how far Reason can go in reducing the plurality of development perspectives to one perspective. The weaker versions elevate national or regional self-determination and mutual tolerance to super-ethical principles and then prescribe that each society determine its own development path and be tolerant of the like effort of others. The stronger versions propose more determinate fundamental ends and basic means for *all* countries.

Common to these universalist approaches is the belief that the Truth about development can be grounded in some noncontingent source above history or deeply rooted in human nature. Rational investigators can get outside all development vocabularies, compare them with (or construct) the Truth, and rationally select the vocabulary that matches or at least best approximates the universal, transcultural Truth about what development should be. Foreigners are on an equal footing with compatriots if and when they equally transcend their cultural identity. Truth is nation-blind and region-blind, equally open to culture-transcending and knowing minds in touch with the Truth "out there" or "in here."

The trouble with the universalist critique of and alternative to ethnocentrism is that universalism (1) cannot, except by begging the question, establish itself or any non-vacuous truth; (2) provides no conclusive means of deciding among candidates for the True development model; and (3) opens the door to domination of others by those who think they have the Truth.

Finally, anti anti-ethnocentrism bites the bullet and both rejects universalism's pretensions and affirms that ethnocentrism is desirable as well as unavoidable. We cannot but evaluate by our "lights" and make invidious comparisons of our society with others. And even if we could do so, we shouldn't. Foreign development ethicists can not get outside their cultural skin and should be loyal to their own communities and moral tradition. Richard Rorty, in a passage whose length is outweighed by its verve, expresses anti anti-ethnocentrism when he characterizes pragmatism as the "accepting of the contingency of starting points" rather than "attempting to evade this contingency":

> To accept the contingency of starting-points is to accept our inheritance from, and our conversation with, our fellow humans as our only source of guidance. To attempt to evade this contingency is to hope to become a properly-programmed machine. This was the hope which Plato thought might be fulfilled at the top of the divided line, when we passed beyond hypotheses. Christians have hoped it might be attained by becoming attuned to the voice of God in the heart, and Cartesians that it might be fulfilled by emptying the mind and seeking the indubitable. Since Kant, philosophers have hoped that it might be fulfilled by finding the a priori structure of any possible inquiry, or language, or form of social life. If we give up this hope, we shall lose what Nietzsche called "metaphysical comfort," but we may gain a renewed sense of community. Our identification with our community—our society, our political tradition, our intellectual heritage—is heightened when we see this community as *ours* rather than *nature's*, *shaped* rather than *found*, one among many which men have made. In the end, the pragmatists tell us, what matters is our loyalty to other human beings clinging together

against the dark, not our hope of getting things right.[10]

A more ambitious form of anti anti-ethnocentrism affirms that "our" ethics—where "our" refers to "we relatively rich, liberal North Americans and Europeans"—is an ethic with global pretensions. Loyalty to our historical community (rather than to ahistorical Reason) requires that this society's development ethic be spread to—if not imposed on—other cultures. Thus, so the argument goes, we Northern liberals have a duty to spread our liberal development ethics to societies other than our own—even if the execution of this duty clashes with what Hegel called the other society's own "moral substance." The liberal ethic requires, however, that the clash be resolved by freedom-respecting argument rather than by coercion.

This sophisticated endorsement of ethnocentrism has much to recommend it. It rightly gives up on ahistorical grounding and recognizes that we cannot avoid evaluating by our own cultural lights. It goes too far (or in the wrong direction), however, in making these lights impervious to change and in assuming the inevitability of invidious comparison in favor of one's own society. Moreover, the ambitious forms of anti anti-ethnocentrism presume too much when they uncritically assume that what is good for one, "our development ethic," is good and relevant for all.

An approach to international development ethics is needed whereby an ethicist from a "developed" society can become convinced that a "developing" society offers some progressive ideas for the ethicist's *own* society. This better idea need not be merely a better employment of a shared ideal; it could be something new and different that substantially alters the foreigner's ethical assumptions. Each ethicist starts from but need not end with the ethics inherited from his or her society. Genuine dialogue involves a "continual reweaving" of the web of the desires and beliefs of all those involved.[11] North American and European development ethicists need to understand their activity in such a way that one upshot of international dialogue is that their own group's standards and practices might come to be seen as "bad" development or "anti-development."

Each of the three responses to ethnocentrism in development ethics has merits and deficiencies. However, instead of trying to devise a position that retains each position's strengths while avoiding its weaknesses, let us make a new start on the question.

II

Instead of focusing on the role of foreigners in a country's development debate, let us first make a distinction between the roles of social insiders and social outsiders in development ethics. What should we mean by "insider" and "outsider"? Both terms refer to persons in relation to groups rather than to persons in and of themselves. An insider is one who is counted, recognized, or accepted, by himself/herself and the other group members, as belonging to the group. One is so identified on the basis of such things as shared beliefs, desires, memories, and hopes.[12] Accordingly, one is an outsider with respect to a group just in case he or she is not counted, recognized or accepted by himself/herself and/or the group members—as belonging to the group, due to lack of these shared beliefs, desires, memories, hopes, and so forth. This insider/outsider distinction also applies to a situation as well as to a group. Some people, for example, feel "at home" in Mexican villages but alien to the streets of Mexico City.

My recognition of myself and the recognition by other group members that I too am a group member are conditions that are individually necessary and together sufficient for insiderness. If I count myself as a member of a team, and my teammates do not, I may feel like an insider but not really be one. Moreover, if my teammates recognize me as one of the team, but I do not so accept myself, my sense of myself as an outsider *makes* me an outsider.

It is important to underscore that the insider/outsider distinction does not coincide with the distinction of native/foreigner or citizen/foreigner. On the one hand, one can be outside the group formally but really be an insider. Someone can become (more or less) an insider to Mexican culture and not have been born in Mexico, reared there, or be a Mexican citizen; for example, the Guatemalan refugees's children quickly can become insiders to the Mexican culture to which their parents remain outsiders. On the other hand, one can be formally a member of a group and not (yet) be an insider, for example, a new player on the team, an adopted child, a spouse whose heart is elsewhere. Like many a Yucatecan Indian, one can be a Mexican citizen, born and reared in Mexico, and not be viewed or view oneself as a Mexican.

We are all insiders and outsiders in a multitude of ways. I am an insider in my family but an outsider in yours. I am at home in small cities but an outsider in huge metropoles, small towns, and the country. A poor Yucatecan fisherman may be an insider on the piers of Puerto Progreso yet an outsider in the nearby condos of Cancun. A Costa Rican Professor of philosophy is an insider in the University of Costa Rica but an outsider among the *vaqueros* of the Costa Rican Province of Guanacaste.

Even with respect to the same group we can be both insiders and outsiders. I identify with some of my country's values and practices and not with others. A person can be an insider in his or her family in some respects and an outsider in others. As Ruth Hubbard and Margaret Randall tell us, "insider and outsider are not mutually exclusive. We are usually both at the same time and in the same place."[13] There may be ambiguity even with regard to one and the same plan, belief, hope or memory. Hubbard suggests the "ambiguities and continuities of insider/outsiderness"[14] by the symbol of a Möbius strip:

> If you travel along it, starting at any point, say on the outside, you are shortly inside, then outside again, then inside, on and on as you go round and round. There is no demarcation or point of transition between inside and outside.[15]

So with respect to the same group we can be "quasi-insiders" and "quasi-outsiders."[16]

It follows that the insider/outsider distinction is better understood as a continuum or spectrum rather than a rigid dichotomy whose categories are mutually exclusive. Insiderness and outsiderness are differences on a continuum. You, My Costa Rican friend, are not totally an outsider or totally an insider in our family; you rightly call us your "second family." Time spent in another country can make one less an outsider to the "adopted" country and, sometimes, more an outsider to one's own country; for one can take on some of the commitments of the former and weaken or extinguish some of the latter. The result is often an exotic collage of insiderness/outsiderness, as evidenced in cities that are becoming more like (pre-Desert Storm) "Kuwaiti bazaars" than "English gentlemen's clubs."[17] Salmon Rushdie, the beleaguered Indian novelist who has lived for many years in London, observes such polychromatic mixtures in Indian immigrants living in London's Brick Lane:

> The thing you have to understand about a neighborhood like this ... is that when people board an Air India jet and come halfway across the planet, they don't just bring their suitcases. They bring everything. And even as they reinvent themselves in the new city—which is what they do—there remain these old selves, old traditions erased in part but not fully. So what you get are these fragmented, multifaceted, multicultural selves.
>
> And this can lead to such strange things.... You will find teen-age girls in this neighborhood who in so many ways are London kids: Levi 501s, Madonna T-shirts, spiky hair. They never think at all of going back to India or Pakistan, even for a visit. They might actually have been born here in London. And yet you may find among them a willingness, an eagerness in some cases, to have an arranged marriage. An arranged marriage.
>
> Or this story: In this very neighborhood, it was early in the 1980s. A Pakistani father stabbed and murdered his daughter, his only child, because he heard she had made love to a white boy. Which turned out not to be true, but that is not my point: My point is that he had brought with him this idea of honor and shame. And when I wrote about this later, I said that although I was obviously appalled—I mean, what can be more awful than murdering your own child?—I understood what had motivated him. I am a first-generation immigrant from that part of the world. I know how you can be here, and, in a way, still be there.[18]

Being a pure insider or a pure outsider would be difficult if not impossible. One would have to consider oneself (and be considered by others) as in *total* agreement, disagreement or indifference in relation to a group. One reason that pure cases of insiderness would be best construed as only a hypothetical limit is that the groups with which we identify have diverse and often antagonistic factions. And even if Alasdair MacIntyre is correct when he says that premodern societies were marked by homogeneity, he also sees that—from the point of view of its own standards—every tradition must "view itself as to some degree inadequate."[19] Another reason that pure insiderness is a conceptual limit is that we are members of different groups that pull us in different directions. Finally, in becoming *aware* of our insider status, we become something of an outsider to it. Similarly, the case of a pure outsider would be a hypothetical limit; for we find it difficult and undesirable to be completely outside human bonds. One is reminded of Sartre's dictum that "human reality ... [is] a being which is what it is not and which is not what it is."[20]

Changes occur in one's insider or outsider relations. These changes can have various reasons and causes. I just may find myself thinking more like (one type of) Costa Rican and less like a gringo. The refugee from Chilean repression found it impossible to continue identifying with a nation that had descended into barbarism. Costa Ricans and Mexicans often unthinkingly make Central American refugees into a "Them." Choice, however, is sometimes possible. There are several options here. Sometimes, the immigrant or exile, in Rushdie's words, "reinvents" himself or herself, consciously deciding to take on some of the values of the new homeland without giving up insider status in the old country. Sometimes outsiders, trying to gain acceptance as insiders, single-mindedly strive to transform themselves into fanatic representations of their new life.[21] Refugees and immigrants, however, can resist identification with the "host" country in order to keep alive insiderness with respect to the homeland. Costa Ricans decide to extend *pura vida* (the good life, Costa Rican style) to select others, such as rich gringo *pensionados* (retirees), but not others, such as refugees from Nicaraguan turmoil, Guatemalan repression, or Atlantic coast poverty.

We have seen the multiplicity of groups in relation to which one can have insider or outsider status. Are there any limits? On one extreme, one can talk—at least by metaphorical extension of oneself as a group with one member. Moral integrity is a form of insiderness. I become an outsider to myself when I violate my core values. Margaret Randall puts it well:

> I became at one and the same time more of an outsider vis-à-vis the mainstream beliefs and values of my country and more of an insider, if by that term one means someone closer to the core of her own authentic identity.[22]

What about extensions of insiderness in the other direction? In particular, can one be an insider to the biotic community or global humanity? Remember that the primary use of the insider/outsider distinction concerns human groups. Yet we find it useful to extend insiderness to non-human groups and non-groups. Suppose morality has to do with what Rorty, following Wilfred Sellars, calls "we-intentions"—with purposes that we share with others and obligations to help those who are part of the "we." Then, although the purposes I can share with non-humans may be limited, I can view myself as grateful and obligated to that biotic-natural community of which I am a part if not a member. Although "humanity" refers to an abstract class rather than to a concrete group or a common essence that binds us together, I can pledge to extend the "we" of my communities to include all persons, however distant in space and time. And just as expanding the "we" beyond the family to the tribe need not extinguish the family, so too extending our we-intentions regionally and globally need not erase—it may even nurture—our narrower group loyalties.[23]

How should we evaluate insiderness and outsiderness? There are distinctive goods and bads, opportunities and temptations, advantages and disadvantages in being outsiders as well as insiders. By virtue of one's insider and outsider status, respectively, one has different sorts of possibilities for both good and evil. The particular valuational balance will change with respect to several variables, such as the moral character and relative power of the groups from which one comes and to which one goes. Opportunities for good and temptations for evil vary with respect to the nature of the groups in relation to which one is insider and outsider. To be outside a despicable group and inside an admirable group is morally desirable.

Let us now apply this analysis of the insider/outsider distinction to our original question concerning international development ethics.

III

Suppose that a development ethicist is a member of a group and critically reflects on that group's present and future development. That group, as we have seen, may be of different kinds. In today's world, nation-states, and to a lesser extent regions, have a certain priority as development units. But the groups in which the ethicist functions range geographically from local neighborhoods, through cities/areas, to huge regions such as Central America, Latin America, the Western Hemisphere, the Third World, and the planet. Beyond political-geographical communities, the groups in which the ethicist functions can be social classes or ethnic groups as well as local, national, regional, or international enterprises. With respect to any of these groups, what opportunities and dangers does an insider-ethicist face *by virtue of being an insider?*

The advantages are at least three in number. First, by virtue of being an insider, the insider-ethicist knows what things mean to the community, for the ethicist shares in the community's practices, vocabulary, memories, hopes, and fears. This capacity is particularly important insofar as the ethicist is committed to an Aristotelian "internalist" ethics that takes into account and contributes to the community's aspirations and beliefs. Martha Nussbaum and Amartya Sen make the point well:

> Ethical inquiry, he [Aristotle] insists, must be what we might call "value-relative." That is, they are not "pure" inquiries conducted in a void; they are questions about living asked by communities of human beings who are actually engaged in living and valuing. What will count as an appropriate, and even a *true*, outcome of such inquiry is constrained, and appropriately constrained; by what human beings antecedently value and need.[24]

As part of the "we," the insider-ethicist also has the capacity not only to understand but to make himself/herself understood as a conversation partner in the group's dialogue about its identity. The insider is "one of us," literally and figuratively speaks our language; and, we presume, knows whereof he or she speaks. Development ethics should be done in a contextually sensitive way, in relation to actual facts, interpreted meanings, and shared values. As Rorty puts it, "To imagine great things is to imagine a great future *for a particular community*, a community one knows well, identifies with, can make plausible predictions about."[25] An outsider-ethicist may miss altogether the real meaning of a past event, present policy, or future option, and, hence, be in no position ethically to evaluate them.

Second, in addition to knowing the "interpreted" facts, the insider-ethicist's moral judgments about the community's past, present, and future will be in terms *accessible* to the community in question. This is not to say it will always be clear which norm to appeal to or that there will not be two communal norms in tension or conflict. But it is to say that the insider-ethicist has an advantage over the outsider in that the former can more easily appeal to an understood and presumed set of moral assumptions, even when that set involves ambiguity and inconsistency.

Third, having insider standing gives the ethicist a prima facie right to criticize the group's development path, identify costs and benefits of current development strategy, and recommend what he or she considers better alternatives for the future. By virtue of being part of the group's cooperative activity, the insider has a generally acknowledged right and responsibility to contribute to the weaving and reweaving of the group's identity. Where the relatively pure outsider's assessments may be met with, "What right have you to stick your nose into our business," the insider is accorded that right by virtue of being a member of the community. Or, I would argue, *should* be so accorded. This "right to evaluate" is based not only on the insider's contribution to the group but also on the likelihood that the insider knows the facts, as interpreted by the group, the values that inform the group, and the desires that its members express.

The advantages of insider development ethics have a flip-side; definite disadvantages and dangers also exist for insiders in development ethics. First, an insider may be oblivious to constitutive meanings in his or her community precisely because they are so omnipresent. Like a fish unaware of the water in which it continually swims, the insider-ethicist may not be cognizant of certain features of his or her tradition and community. The community may be too close to get things into the focus requisite for ethical assessment.

Second, depending on the purity and exclusivity of their insiderness, insider ethicists are more or less limited to the vocabularies and valuational resources of their group. To become more of an insider in a group, particularly when the group is a "melting pot," may require the foregoing of alternative perspectives and becoming more of an outsider to one's former allegiances. This has costs both for the group and the ethicist. The group may desperately need new ideas to replace stale ones that have been dogmatically preserved. The ethicist may find himself or herself confined to and even trapped in familiar and conventional concepts—unable to expand the horizons of the possible and desirable. The insider-ethicist may purchase "relevance" at the price of needed novelty. The danger is that the insider will give the community comforting reassurances about past achievements rather than imaginative challenges for future greatness.

Insiders in development ethics face a third limitation and related risk. To be an insider is to live in the midst of loyalties, debts, favors, obligation, promises—things which one owes to others and which one is owed. These "debts" may be owed to the group's co-members or subgroups or to other groups to which one belongs. Such debts may be compromising or corrupting. Although group membership might give one the right to criticize and propose alternatives, loyalties to co-members and debts to others may inhibit the exercise of responsibilities. In such cases the temptation may be too great; it may be too much to expect insiders to be sufficiently and properly impartial. In contrast, the outsider may be able to say what the group needs to hear, but none of the members dare say. For this reason, each university graduate committee has an "outside" member, World Cup referees come from nations different from those of the competing teams, labor arbitrators are supposedly neutral in relation to both union and management, and Costa Rican elections are monitored by an institution independent of the contending parties.

IV

Like insider-ethicists, outsider-ethicists have certain liabilities and temptations as well as advantages and opportunities. Let us first consider the negative side.

Outsiders often are ignorant about what is going on in the group, what things mean, and what the group's normative resources are. The Third World is littered with development models, policies, and projects invented by societal outsiders and properly abandoned by societal insiders. For outsiders often ignorantly assume that "what is good for us, is good for them." More specifically, outsider ethicists are often closed off from the facts, meaning, and communal values relevant for progressive social change.

Second, while the insider-ethicist is usually accorded the right to evaluate present structures and future options, doors are often closed to the outsider-ethicist, especially when this outsider comes from a "developed" and powerful group. If the group's development debate is about its own identity, only members of the group may be viewed as having a right to participate—especially if outsiders come from a dominating group. Recall, for example, Ofelia Schutte's endorsement cited earlier of particularist anti-ethnocentrism when discussing Latin America's condemnation of standards imposed by U.S. outsiders.

Supposing an invitation has been extended to an outsider-ethicist, we assume that to be effective the outsider would become "immersed," in Nussbaum's and Sen's sense, in the "alien" society:

> [Evaluation and criticism of the society] must be *immersed rather than detached* (i.e., the norm of objectivity should not be one that involves the detachment of the judging subject from the practices, the perceptions, even the emotions, of the culture), stressing, instead, that objective value judgments can be made from the point of view of experienced immersion in the way of life of a culture.[26]

Still, the outsider's temptations and liabilities are not yet eliminated. Outside-ethicists who come from the more powerful and exploitative "center" and go to the more vulnerable and dependent "periphery" tend to accord their own ideas more weight than they deserve.[27] Even more, the powerful, "developed," and "modern" outsider is tempted to assume that his or her ideas are more worthy than those of the weak, "underdeveloped," or traditional insider. Similarly, the ethicist inside a peripheral group might tend to respond to the outsider's ethics by according them more weight than they merit and even by assuming they are correct. These dangers are all the more pronounced when outsider proposals go hand-in-hand with economic inducements or when there exist strong traditions of host hospitality. The converse is also true: outsider-ethicists who go from the periphery to the center may not trust their own intuitions or principles when they clash with those of someone from the capital city, the aristocratic or educational elite, the "mother country," or the "colossus of the North." We don't have to buy the transcendental scaffolding of Habermas's theory of ideal communication to be well aware that undistorted communication and reasonable consensus require relative equality among dialogue partners. To the extent that this equality is missing, the outsider-ethicist from the "developed" center runs serious risk of having undue influence and exerting subtle coercion; the outsider-ethicist from the "less developed" periphery runs the contrary risk of being insufficiently self-reliant and bold.

Opposite dangers exist as well for both types of outsider-ethicists. Outsider-ethicists from the center and their insider hosts may practice a form of "reverse discrimination." The outsider-ethicist, aware of his or her own nation's history of cultural imperialism, may refrain from negative evaluations in favor of fawning approval of the host group's norms and practices. It is tempting to slide from an affirmation of the insider's right of self-determination to the view that the insider can't make mistakes. Similarly, the insider's justified anti-imperialism may become a dogmatic trap. Assuming a priori that nothing can be learned from an outsider, especially from the center, the insider-ethicist may close himself or herself off from new and potentially useful ideas.[28]

It must be conceded that a long-term danger of outsiders in development ethics is that peripheral communities become willingly but unfortunately dependent on outsider help, thereby failing to nurture and institutionalize their indigenous capacity for ethical reflection. Indeed, since the 1940s such Latin American philosophers as Leopoldo Zea have argued, with good reason, that Latin American thought is too imitative of and dependent upon European and North American thought.[29] The opposite consequence, however, is also a danger: peripheral groups can promote their capacity for development ethics in such a way that they overlook potential benefits of cross-cultural dialogue.

These dangers can be reduced, if not eliminated, by (1) the achievement of more equality between the various centers and their corresponding peripheries, (2) the recognition of dangers peculiar to insiders and outsiders, respectively, and (3) the promotion of appropriate kinds of insider/outsider combinations in development ethicists. Even under present, all too unequal, social circumstances, dialogue can occur that reduces the extent to which outsiders as well as insiders are either acquiescent or presumptuous.

Let us now turn to the positive contributions that outsiders can make when they reflect on an alien group's development goals and strategies. Here, outsider-ethicist strengths are the mirror image of insider-ethicist weaknesses. First, an outsider-ethicist may see and reveal things that an insider misses; we know *what-is* by contrast with *what-is-not*, and the outsider's very different experience may highlight what is hidden or obscure to the insider. Charles Taylor calls this "the language of perspicuous contrast."[30]

One way for the outsider to accomplish this is to *clarify* the debate over social identity that is taking place within that alien group. The outsider can be a sort of mirror —not a mirror to gain access to transcendental Truth but a mirror to reflect back to the group its own internal dialogue. A group is always in process. It perpetually crystallizes itself in and through dialogue about its past and future. The participants in this communal process are subgroups and individuals with more or less differing outlooks and development vocabularies. The outsider-ethicist can compare and contrast these insider traditions and perspectives. In this way, by "playing vocabularies and cultures off against each other," the insiders may see more clearly what they share with, and where they diverge from, others in their society.[31] Outsider Constantino Láscaris did this when he contrasted the everyday morality of the inhabitants of Costa Rica's four main cities, Alajuela, Cartago, Heredia, and San José, thereby helping Costa Ricans understand their differences as well as their similarities.[32] Denis Goulet's and Kwan S. Kim's recent book compares and contrasts four competing Mexican development models: growth, growth-with-redistribution, basic human needs, and development from tradition.[33]

Second, by drawing on his or her own quite different tradition, vocabulary, and experience, the outsider can inject new and sometimes needed ideas into an alien group's development deliberations. Novelty here takes several different forms and is often a matter of degree. The outsider may provide a new way of integrating prevailing commitments. Goulet and Kim for instance, have clarified and argued for a novel way of combining the best Mexican development perspectives into a model of "plural, federated development."[34] Perhaps more frequently, the outsider-ethicist will identify—on the basis of his or her own lights—beliefs already implicit in some insider practices and (partially) explicit in some insider theory. Nussbaum and Sen emphasize that outsiders, after immersion in an alien culture, can appeal to one part of the culture or tradition in order to criticize another part. Nussbaum and Sen illustrate this practice—what is sometimes called "building on the best"—when they draw on the (Asian) Indian rationalist tradition as a basis for their own affirmation of the potential importance of modern science and technology for Asian development.[35] Sometimes the progressive insider-beliefs that the outsider appeals to will have solely indigenous roots. Often, however, they will have had external origins and have been internalized at an earlier time by the culture in question.

Although Nussbaum and Sen helpfully widen the "reach" of internal critique to appeal to ideas that a culture has internalized from external sources, we also want to urge that the outsider ethicist can play a role in contributing moral ideas that are novel in two stronger senses. Drawing on the resources of his or her own tradition, the outsider ethicist can introduce moral ideas unanticipated in that society. Alternatively, outsiders and insider, in and through cross-cultural dialogue, together can create or invent novel ideas.[36]...

Rorty puts the general point well in describing what he calls the "pragmatist." Such a thinker, says Rorty, does not believe that one can get beyond or beneath vocabularies to get to the Truth "against which to test vocabularies and cultures." Rather, the pragmatist "does think that in the process of playing vocabularies and cultures off against each other, we produce new and better ways of talking and acting—not better by reference to a previously known standard, but just better in the sense that they come to *seem* clearly better than their predecessors."[37]

To come to grips with outsider ideas—be they initially unheard of or seemingly crazy or irrelevant—may prompt a beneficial reweaving of the group's beliefs and desires. The truth of particularism is that this reweaving will take place at the outset according to the group's prior stock of ideas. The truth of universalism is that the reevaluation can issue in new and better conceptions. But here the better is not measured by some historically transcendent and culturally independent standard but merely by the new lights of the community in question....

Outsiders, whether from the periphery or the center, both can criticize the status quo and propose new alternatives in and for alien social contexts. Drawing out the flip side of an earlier point, we can identify a third advantage that outsider development ethicists can have over their insider counterparts. An outsider-ethicist can be free from the insider's prior commitments and loyalties. This freedom can enhance the outsiders's ability and willingness to say what needs to be said in the comparison and assessment of development options. Sometimes, of course, such outsider activity is foolish. ("Fools rush in where wise men fear to tread.") For such "contributions" often are unwelcome or uninformed. Sometimes, however, the outsider's work is more acceptable to some subgroups than to others. In the judgment of the subgroups that agree, the outsider may have "said some things that needed saying." This positive role played by the outsider can be dramatically important when it enables a weak or repressed group to gain a voice in relation to a hegemonic and oppressive group. Exiled Chilean novelist

Ariel Dorfman, a national outsider to Argentina and a cultural outsider to indigenous cultures, spent time with the marginalized and threatened Matacos Indians in Argentina's inhospitable Gran Chaco. We expect that one result of Dorfman's visit with and writing about the Matacos' plight, will be that the Argentinean government, with some "encouragement" from foreign development agencies, will be more helpful to the Matacos as this small tribe tries to survive both economically and culturally.[38] Paula Palmer offers another such example. Initially a I outsider, for fifteen years she has immersed herself in Costa Rica's Talamanca coast and has helped the region's poor and vulnerable blacks and Indians articulate their traditions and protect their threatened way of life.[39] Ofelia Schutte formulates the general point:

> The idea ... is to open up dialogue with the repressed, silent, or excluded Other who is such relative to the power that controls the discourse in which she, he, or it is framed. ... If philosophy is the love of wisdom, then its function cannot be merely to reproduce the discourse and assumptions of the established powers. On the contrary, its function is to penetrate through to the other side and create favorable conditions for the Other to come forward and express concerns, cares, disquietudes, and aspirations. In this process of recognizing and respecting the oppressed Other, the legitimacy of the Other's discourse must first be established.[40]

How different this outsider stance is from what Bimal Krishna Matilal calls "liberal colonialism." The 19th century liberal colonialist would tolerantly but ethnocentrically accept "primitive" or "backward" societies, "barbaric" practices and all, because that was something *those* curious (and inferior) savages were wont to do. The 20th century version, often in the interest of Northern tourism, keeps the "culture of a subdued group completely separated in a protected area as a museum piece or an "endangered" zoological species."[41] Development ethicists, whether or not from dominating nations, not only can criticize the neo-colonialist societies, but, as outsiders in the "subdued" society, they also can "open up dialogue" with those subgroups that are "repressed, silent, or excluded."

V

Let us draw out a few of the implications of the above considerations for the kinds of persons we as development ethicists should be and the kind of ethics we should practice. Although I address these remarks to development ethicists, I believe they are relevant for those involved in other forms of cross-cultural and global ethics.

We development ethicists should be insider-outsider mixes in relation to the "alien" groups whose development goals and strategies become the focus of our moral reflection. We should combine insiderness and outsiderness in such a way as to accentuate the positives and reduce if not eliminate the negatives of both postures. We should be sufficiently inside so as to immerse ourselves in this different form of life, to grasp some of what is going on, and to be accepted as dialogue partners. But we should not fall into the bad faith of believing that we have become completely "one of them." We should retain and take advantage of our outsiderness so as to be able to reflect an "alien" culture pack to its insiders, call attention to the omnipresent obvious by contrasting it with our different experience, bring in new ideas, mediate between various factions, help the vulnerable gain a voice, and speak the truth made elusive by group loyalties. Yet we should not mislead ourselves or others by pretending to ascend to what is an impossible standpoint: a view of the inside from an ahistorical, transcendent, objective outside. No such "view from nowhere"[42] exists. To assume it does breeds both dominance on the part of those who think they have the Truth and servility on the part of those who long for it.

We should also cultivate a certain kind of insider-outsider mix in relation to our own groups. We must aspire to sufficient outsiderness to be able to learn from other groups. They can teach us, through the "language of perspicuous contrast," of the limitations and defects in our ways of doing things, as well as suggest better ideas that we can choose to weave into our beliefs and actions. But this outsiderness supplements an abiding insiderness which prima facie requires loyalty. Alexandrians especially are tempted to escape from the "grey in grey"[43] of their own group to the creative instability of exotic places. Our insider status not only provides a starting point for moral reflection; it also gives us the responsibility to return to our own society's ongoing debate about what it should be and how it should relate to other groups. Moreover, one does not have to be an outsider in one's own culture as long as avenues exist for social transformation with which one can identify. One can remain or become again an insider to one's self and one's group by working for desirable change in one's self and society.

We insider-outsiders in development ethics have responsibilities beyond doing moral reflection in and both our own and other groups. Without abandoning our own cultural substance, we need to help further a global community and a global ethic. We need to extend our national, ethnic, class, and gender identities to a global "we." Insofar as such a world community does not exist, we need to build it. Insofar as it does, we need to strengthen it. To guide us in these tasks as well as to help us when we cross boundaries and interact cross-culturally, we need a global ethic.

This global ethic would not be a total ethic for a *Gemeinschaft* but a "moral minimum," a basic moral charter to which most people of good will could agree, for a global *Gesellschaft*. It would be what Rawls calls an "overlapping consensus," a public and publicly-forged moral vision to which persons and groups with a variety of moral, metaphysical, and religious views could have allegiance.[44] It would provide protection for the vulnerable wherever they exist as well as enjoin respect for each group's prima facie right to hammer out its own ethics. It would give all people a common vocabulary for coping with global problems that refuse to respect national or other boundaries, as well as for resolving problems among and within nations and regions. It would guide us as we wrestle with the issue of what sort of international institutions would be good to have. These global norms and institutions are important because not only do they contribute to and partially constitute global progress, but they can promote useful development in nations and regions as well.

Although to develop the idea here is beyond the scope of this essay, I suspect that this global ethic will converge on some general cross-cultural ethical categories related in some way to certain general cross-cultural human traits and experiences that take specific forms in particular cultures. It remains to be determined whether this ethical convergence will emphasize basic human needs, capabilities, and/or rights.[45]

Like most good things, such a global community and global ethic could go bad; for rich and powerful centers could (self-deceptively) extend their domination precisely by packaging their own self-serving ethic as the new global ethic. To guard against this continual danger, we need to expand our "we intentions" beyond our groups of origin and check particularist self-serving intentions. We need to forge a global community and international ethic that celebrate regional and national differences and self-determination, and yet refuse to accept misery, oppression, and environmental degradation. We need to explore what sort of international institutions, agencies, and linkages support and are supported by such an ethic. If we are to save ourselves from global economic, ecological, and cultural disaster, our answers will need to be a good deal more robust than Rorty's model of a global Kuwaiti bazaar surrounded by exclusive national private clubs.

Such a global ethic neither eliminates nor always trumps the ethics of our narrower groups, any more than our emerging global community extinguishes or overrides groups of narrower scope. Rather, a transnational ethic requires, and is required by, the ethics of national and regional groups. Each can and should be a seed bed for and corrective of the other. The international moral minimum can both be inspired by and nurtured from good and exportable ideas invented by particular groups. In turn the global ethic can be a basis for criticizing and improving the outlooks and practices of particular traditions. Slavery as institution and ideal is a thing of the past; gender inequality is under attack throughout the world; respect for basic needs or rights and the environment are rapidly emerging as part of a global vision of "just, participatory eco-development." National development models, informed by national ethics, must be forged in relation to regional and global development models informed by international ethics. Regardless of where good ideals originated, they can move us as world citizens; and we can apply them as members of particular groups.

This is not to say that there will not be clashes between global and parochial loyalties. Unfortunately, or perhaps fortunately, we have no algorithm to adjudicate these conflicts. One of our hopes rests in the increasing number of insider-outsiders (in relation to groups of various scope) engaged in ongoing moral dialogue about good local, national, regional, and global development.

VI

Ethnocentrics and particularists begin and end inside their own groups. Universalists yearn to attain an impossible standpoint beyond all particularity. Like so many traditional philosophical problems, the particularist/universalist debate is so designed as to remain unsolved. Rather than attempting to resolve the controversy, I have elected to recast it. With the insider/outsider distinction, the theoretical problem has been transformed into a practical task. First, in doing development ethics, we must seize the opportunities and avoid the dangers of being outsiders as well as insiders in relation to various groups. Second, we development ethicists must strive to become optimal insider-outsider combinations in relation to existing groups. Third, we must promote the emergence of a world community which contributes to and is guided by a global development ethics. We must not just "think globally and act locally." As insider-outsiders we must think and act globally, regionally, nationally, and locally. We begin in our groups and return to our groups. In between, we can learn from and benefit other groups. As insider-outsiders, we can become more complete persons and better development ethicists and, thereby, help build a more desirable world.

Author's Note

The present essay is a revised and expanded English version of David A. Crocker. "Participantes internos y externos en la ética del desarrollo internacional," *Revista de la Universidad Autonoma de Yucatán*, special edition (February 1990), p. 57-71. Earlier versions of the paper were given at the V Congreso Centroamericano de Filosofía, San José, Costa Rica, May 8-12, 1989; the Second International Conference on Ethics and Development, Universidad Autónoma de Yucatán. July 3-8, 1989; and the Departments of Philosophy of the University of Florida and Colorado State University in March 1990. I have benefitted from comments by Jann Benson, Cynthia Botteron, David Freeman, Lyanda Haupt, Michael Losonsky, Ofelia Schutte, and Jerome M. Segal.

NOTES

1. For the nature, tasks, and methods of international development ethics, see David A. Crocker, "Hacia una ética del desarollo," *Revista de Filosofía de la Universidad de Costa Rica*, Vol. 25, No. 62 (December 1987) pp.129-41; "La naturaleza y la práctica de una ética del desarollo," *Revista de Filosofía de la Universidad de Costa Rica* Vol 26, No. 63-64 (December 1988), pp. 49-56: "Toward Development Ethics." World Development; "Cuatro modelos de desarrollo costarricense: Un analisis y evaluación ética," *Revista de Filosofía de la Universidad de Costa Rica*, Vol. 27, No. 66 (1989), pp. 317-32: "The Hope for Just, Participatory Ecodevelopment in Costa Rica," in J. Ronald Engel and Joan Gibb Engel, eds., *Ethics of Environment and Development: Global Challenge and International Response* (Tucson: University of Arizona Press, 1990), pp. 150-63; Denis Goulet, "Tasks and Methods in Development Ethics," *Cross Currents*, Vol. 38, No. 2 (1988) pp. 146-64, 172.
2. One finds many examples of foreigners evaluating another nation's practices and norms. Constantino Láscaris, a Spanish philosopher, wrote *El Costarricense*, 5th ed. (San José, Costa Rica: Educa, 1985), an important study of Costa Rican identity. The U.S. development ethicist Denis Goulet has evaluated development strategies in several countries, most recently those of Mexico. See Denis Goulet and Kwan S. Kim, *Estratégias de Desarrollo Para el Futuro de México* (Guadalajara: ITESCO, 1989). Jerome M. Segal, a U.S. Philosopher, offers moral and prudential arguments for a "two state" solution to the Middle-Eastern conflict. As a Jew, Segal is an outsider in relation to the PLO; as a U.S. Jew and an advocate of a Palestinian state, Segal is an outsider in relation to Israel. See Segal, *Creating the Palestinian State: A Strategy for Peace* (Chicago: Lawrence Hill Books, 1989). V.S. Naipaul, born in Trinidad of

Hindu parents, is only the most recent of a series of foreigners who have analyzed and evaluated U.S. life and institutions. See Naipaul's *A Turn in the South* (New York: Knopf, 1989). Other foreign commentators on the United States include two important European writers: The Frenchman, *Alexis de Tocqueville*, Democracy in America, trans. George Lawrence, J.P. Mayer, ed.(New York: Doubleday, Anchor Books, 1969); and the Swede, Gunnar Myrdal, *An American Dilemma: The Negro Problem and Modern Democracy* (New York and London: Harper, 1944).

3. *Webster's Third New International Dictionary*, Vol. I (Chicago: Encyclopedia Britannica, Inc. 1976), p. 781.
4. Ofelia Schutte, "Overcoming Ethnocentrism in the Philosophy Classroom," *Teaching Philosophy*, Vol. 8, No. 2 (April 1985), pp. 139-40.
5. See Howard J. Wiarda, "Toward a Nonethnocentric Theory of Development: Alternative Conceptions from the Third World," in Charles K. Wilber, ed., *The Political Economy of Development and Underdevelopment* (New York: Random House, 1984), pp. 59-82.
6. In 1895 in his "Atlanta Exposition Address," Booker T. Washington employed this metaphor to enjoin blacks to take advantage of economic and other opportunities in the U.S. South and to urge whites to have confidence in the economic productivity and loyalty of the South's blacks. See Booker T. Washington, *Up From Slavery: An Autobiography* (Williamstown, MA: Corner House Publishers, 1978). H. Odera Oruka, a Kenyan philosopher, gives the metaphor a particularist spin as he applauds a recent book by Johnny Washington, a black U.S. philosopher (H. Odera Oruka, "Forword," in Johnny Washington, *Alain Locke and Philosophy: A Quest for Cultural Pluralism* (New York: Greenwood Press, 1986), p. xiii.
7. Ofelia Schutte, "Notes on the Issue of Cultural Imperialism," *Proceedings and Addresses of the American Philosophical Association*, Vol. 59, No. 5 (June 1986), pp. 758-59. For an important statement of Latin American particularism, see Leopoldo Zea, "Identity: A Latin American Philosophical Problem," *Philosophical Forum*, Vol. 20, Nos. 1-2 (1988-89), pp. 33-42.
8. *Ibid.*, p. 759.
9. See, for example, Risiri Frondisi," Is There an Ibero-American Philosophy?" *Philosophy and Phenomenological Research*, Vol. 9 (1948-49), pp. 345-55; Onora O'Neill, "Ethical Reasoning and Ideological Pluralism," *Ethics*, Vol. 98. No. 4 (July 1988), pp. 705-22.
10. Richard Rorty, *Consequences of Pragmatism* (Minneapolis: University of Minnesota Press, 1982), p. 166. Rorty has called himself both an "ethnocentrist" and an "anti anti-ethnocentrist." In my view Rorty has either misdescribed himself, employs a different concept, or is inconsistent. For, as we shall see, Rorty recognizes—at least in his article on Roberto Unger—the way in which cross-cultural dialogue can result in the modification and even abandonment of the norms with which one starts. See Richard Rorty, "Unger, Castoriadis, and the Romance of a National Future," *Northwestern University Law Review*, Vol. 82, No. 2 (1988), pp. 335-51; "Solidarity or Objectivity," in Michael Krausz, ed., *Relativism; Interpretation and Confrontation* (Notre Dame: University of Notre Dame Press, 1989), pp. 12-13; "On Ethnocentrism: A Reply to Clifford Geertz." *Michigan Quarterly Review*, Vol. 25, No. 3 (Summer 1986), pp. 525-34. Compare with Clifford Geertz "Anti Anti-Relativism," reprinted in Krausz, ed., *Relativism*, pp. 12-34; "The Uses of Diversity," *Michigan Quarterly Review*, Vol. 25, No. 1 (1986), pp. 105-23.
11. For a description of "human life by the metaphor of a continual reweaving of a web of beliefs and desires." see Rorty, "On Ethnocentrism" p. 531.
12. Compare with Rorty's definition of a societal member: "To be part of a society is, in the relevant sense, to be taken as a possible conversational partner by those who shape that society's self-image" ("On Ethnocentrism," p. 529). The emphasis on "subjective" states should not be taken to exclude "objective" structures or public realities such as inherited vocabularies or "canonical texts," for a person's intentional states may be shaped by or have these realities as objects. Alasdair MacIntyre emphasizes the role of "canonical texts" such as the Bible or *Don Quixote* in defining a social identity; see MacIntyre,"Relativism, Power, and Philosophy," reprinted in Krausz, ed., *Relativism*, pp. 182-204.
13. Ruth Hubbard and Margaret Randall, *The Shape of Red: Outsider/Insider Reflections* (San Francisco: Cleis Press, 1988), p. 12.

14. *Ibid*, p. 26.
15. *Ibid*, p. 26.
16. *Ibid*, p. 22.
17. Clifford Geertz uses these metaphors descriptively in, "The uses of Diversity," *Michigan Quarterly Review*, Vol. 25, No. 1 (Winter 1986), p. 121. Rorty employs the metaphors normatively: "We can urge the construction of a world order whose model is a bazaar surrounded by lots and lots of exclusive private clubs" ("On Ethnocentrism." p. 533).
18. Quoted Gerald Marzorati, "Salman Rushdie: Fiction's Embattled Infidel," *New York Times Magazine*, January 29, 1989, pp. 27, 44.
19. MacIntyre, "Relativism," p. 201.
20. Jean-Paul Sartre, *Being and Nothingness: An Essay in Phenomenological Ontology*, trans. Hazel E. Barnes (New York; Philosophical Library, 1956). p. 58.
21. Rodolfo Stavenhagen reminded me of this important point.
22. Hubbard and Randall, *The Shape of Red*, p. 17.
23. See J. Baird Callicott, "Toward an Environmental Ethic," in Tom Regan, ed., *Matters of Life and Death.* 2nd ed. (New York: Random House, 1986), pp. 381-424, esp. Pp. 403-17.
24. Martha C. Nussbaum and Amartya Sen, "Internal Criticism and Indian Rationalist Traditions," in Krausz, ed., *Relativism*, p. 310. See also, Martha C. Nussbaum, *The Fragility of Goodness: Luck and Ethics in Greek Tragedy and Philosophy* (Cambridge: Cambridge University Press, 1986), esp. Part III; "Non-Relative Virtues: An Aristotelian Approach," *Mid-West Studies in Philosophy*, vol. 13 (1988), pp. 32-53; "Aristotelian social Democracy," in R. Bruce Douglass, Gerald M. Mara, and Henry S. Richardson, eds., *Liberalism and the Good* (New York: Routledge, 1990), pp. 203-52.
25. Rorty, "Unger," p. 343.
26. Nussbaum and Sen, "Internal Criticism." p. 308.
27. I use "center" to include the industrialized northern nations as well as Third world national or provincial capitals. Similarly, "peripheries" include "developing" nations as well as areas—especially rural areas—remote from Third world capitals, whether national or provincial. I assume that "center/periphery" is more than a merely economic distinction and can be characterized as a relation of unequal power as well as unequal resource flows. The center dominates the periphery, and the periphery is dependent on the center.
28. In his pronouncements, if not in his actual practice, Enrique Dussel, the Argentinean "philosopher of liberation," veers close to this geographical genetic fallacy: any idea originating from the North is thereby both incorrect and a tool of Northern domination of the South. This tendency in Dussel is sharply criticized by his fellow countryman Horacio Cerutti Guldberg in *Filosofía de la liberación latinoamericana* (México: Fondo de Cultura Económica, 1983).
29. See Schutte, "Notes on the Issue of Cultural Imperialism," and Zea, "Identity: A Latin American Philosophical Problem."
30. Charles Taylor "Understanding and Ethnocentricity," in *Philosophy and the Human Sciences*, Vol. 2 of *Philosophical Papers* (Cambridge: Cambridge University Press, 1985) p. 129.
31. Rorty, *Consequences*, p. xxxvii.
32. Láscaris, *El Costarricense*, pp. 65-74.
33. See Goulet and Kim, *Estratégias de Desarrollo*, chaps, I-III.
34. See Ibid., chaps. IV, V. See also, David Barkin, *Distorted Development: Mexico in the World Economy* (Boulder, CO.: Westview Press, 1990). For similar efforts in relation to Costa Rican development, see Crocker, "Cuatro Modelos"; The Hope for Just, Participatory Ecodevelopment"; Sheldon Annis, "Debt and Wrong Way Resource Flows in Costa Rica, "*Ethics & International Affairs*, Vol. 4 (1990). pp. 107-21.
35. Nussbaum and Sen, "Internal Criticism," esp. pp. 317-21.
36. Clifford Geertz emphasizes this in "Outsider Knowledge and Insider Criticism: What Can We Do for One Another?" (An unpublished response to Nussbaum and Sen, "Internal Criticism.")
37. Richard Rorty, *Consequences*, p. xxxvii.
38. Ariel Dorfman, "Into Another Jungle: The Final Journey of the Matacos?" *Grassroots Development: Journal of the Inter-American Foundation*, Vol. 12, No. 2 (1988), pp. 2-15.
39. See Paula Palmer, *"What Happen": A Folk-History of Costa Rica's Talamanca Coast* (San Jose, Costa Rica: Ecodesarrollos, 1977). For an important Latin American study that appreciatively evaluates Palmer's work, see Ariel Dorfman, "Bread and Burnt Rice:

Culture and Economic Survival in Latin America." *Grassroots Development: Journal of the Inter-American Foundation*, Vol. 8, No. 2 (1984). pp 3-5.

40. Schutte, "Overcoming Ethnocentrism," p. 143.
41. Bimal Krishna Matilal, "Ethical Relativism and Confrontation of Cultures," in Krausz,. ed., *Relativism*. p. 358.
42. See Thomas Nagel, *The View from Nowhere* (New York: Oxford university Press, 1986).
43. *Hegel's Philosophy of Right*, trans. R.M. Knox (Oxford: Oxford University Press, 1952) p.p. 12-13. We "Alexandrian " ethicists must guard against the temptation of believing that it is only the "exemplary instability" of the Third World (and of, at long last, the Second World) that permits and activist and socially responsible role for ethics. The "cut and dried" First World, too, has a need to be "rejuvenated."
44. John Rawl, "Justice as Fairness: Political not Metaphysical," *Philosophy and Public Affairs*, Vol. 14, no. 3 (1985), pp. 223-51; and "The Idea of an Overlapping Consensus," *Oxford Journal of Legal Studies*, Vol 7 (1987) pp. 1-25. For the possibility of a "partial convergence ... through proper confrontation and clash between culture[s], a convergence not necessarily of local moral norms, but ... of basic ethical norms," see Matilal, "Ethical Relativism," p. 358. See also Charles R. Beitz, *Political Theory and International Affairs* (Princeton: Princeton University Press, 1979); Terry Nardin, *Law, Morality and the Relations of States* (Princeton: Princeton University Press, 1983); Thomas Donaldson, "Moral Minimums for Multinationals," *Ethics & International Affairs*, Vol. 3 (1989), pp. 163-82.
45. See David Braybrooke, *Meeting Needs* (Princeton University Press, 1987); Nussbaum "Aristotelian Social Democracy"; Amartya Sen, *Resources, Values and Development* (Cambridge, MA: Harvard University Press, 1984): Henry Shue, *Basic Rights: Subsistence, Affluence, and U.S. Foreign Policy* (Princeton: Princeton University Press. 1980); David Braybrooke, "Meeting Needs: Toward a New Needs-Based Ethic"' David A. Crocker, "Functioning and Capability: the Foundations of Sen's Development Ethic"; James W. Nickel, "Rights and Development"; and G. Peter Penz, "The Priority of Basic Needs: Toward a Consensus in Development Ethics for Political Engagement." The last four papers were presented at the IDEA Montclair Workshop, entitled "Ethical Principles for Development: Needs, Capabilities, or Rights?" Montclair State College, January 24-27, 1991. The Workshop was sponsored by the Institute for Critical Thinking of Montclair State College and the International Development Ethics Association (IDEA).

THE NEW SOVEREIGNTY

Shelby Steele

Shelby Steele teaches history at San Jose State University. He is the author of The Content of Our Character: A New Vision of Race in America *(St. Martin's Press, 1990).*

Steele defends the early American civil rights movements on the basis of their goals of "democracy, integration, and developmental uplift," goals that were achieved through the removal of laws barring certain people from having the rights and range of opportunities espoused in the American ideal of democracy. He claims, however, that current social movements that are rooted in anger about a perceived lack of progress toward equality have rejected these goals in favor of demanding group or collective entitlements. In his view, collective entitlements based on race, gender, ethnicity, and other group grievances are not justified and the affirmative action measures and separatist strategies that are thereby endorsed violate the democratic ideal of integration and harmony.

In *The True Believer*, Eric Hoffer wrote presciently of this phenomenon I have come to call the New Sovereignty:

> When a mass movement begins to attract people who are interested in their individual careers, it is a sign that it has passed its vigorous state; that it is no longer engaged in molding a new world but in possessing and preserving the present. It ceases then to be a movement and becomes an enterprise.

If it is true that great mass movements begin as spontaneous eruptions of long-smoldering discontent, it is also true that after significant reform is achieved they do not like to pass away or even modify their grievance posture. The redressing of the movement's grievances wins legitimacy for the movement. Reform, in this way, also means recognition for those who struggled for it. The movement's leaders are quoted in the papers, appear on TV, meet with elected officials, write books—they come to embody the movement. Over time, they and they alone speak for the aggrieved; and, of course, they continue to speak *of* the aggrieved, adding fresh grievances to the original complaint. It is their vocation now, and their means to status and power. The idealistic reformers thus become professional spokespersons for the seemingly permanently aggrieved. In the civil rights movement, suits and briefcases replaced the sharecropper's denim of the early years, and $500-a-plate fund-raisers for the National Association for the Advancement of Colored People replaced volunteers and picket signs. The raucous bra burning of late Sixties feminism gave way to women's-studies departments and direct-mail campaigns by the National Organization of Women.

This sort of evolution, however natural it may appear, is not without problems for the new grievance-group executive class. The winning of reform will have dissipated much of the explosive urgency that started the movement; yet the new institutionalized movement cannot justify its existence without this urgency. The problem becomes one of maintaining a reformist organization after considerable reforms have been won.

To keep alive the urgency needed to justify itself, the grievance organization will do three things. First, it will work to inspire a perpetual sense of grievance in its constituency so that grievance becomes the very centerpiece of the group itself. To be black, or a women, or gay, is, in the eyes of the NAACP, NOW, or Act Up, to be essentially threatened, victimized, apart from the rest of America. Second, these organizations will up the ante on what constitutes a grievance by making support of sovereignty itself the new test of grievance. If the women's studies program has not been made autonomous, this constitutes a grievance. If the national Council of La Raza hasn't been consulted, Hispanics have been ignored. The third strategy of grievance organizations is to arrange their priorities in a way that will maximize their grievance profile. Often their agendas will be established more for their grievance potential than for the actual betterment of the group. Those points at which there is resistance in the larger society to the group's entitlement demands will usually be made into top-priority issues, thereby emphasizing the status of victim and outsider necessary to sustain the sovereign organization.

Thus, at its 1989 convention, the NAACP put affirmative action at the very top of its agenda. Never mind the fact that studies conducted by both proponents and opponents of affirmative action indicate the practice has very little real impact on the employment and advancement of blacks. Never mind, too, that surveys show most black Americans do not consider racial preferences *their* priority. In its wisdom the NAACP thought (and continues to think) that the national mood against affirmative-action programs is a bigger problem for black men and women than teen pregnancy, or the disintegrating black family, or black-on-black crime. Why? Because the very resistance affirmative action meets from the larger society makes it an issue of high grievance potential. Affirmative action can generate the urgency that justifies black sovereignty far more than issues like teen pregnancy or high dropout rates, which carry no load of collective entitlement and which the entire society sees as serious problems.....

How did America evolve its now rather formalized notion that groups of its citizens would be entitled collectively? I think it goes back to the most fundamental contradiction in American life. From the beginning America has been a pluralistic society, and one drawn to a radical form of democracy—emphasizing the freedom and equality of individuals—that could meld such diversity into a coherent nation. In this new nation no group would lord it over any other. But, of course, beneath this America of its ideals there was from the start a much meaner reality, one whose very existence mocked the notion of a nation made singular by the equality of its individuals. By limiting democracy to their own kind—white, male landowners—the Founding Fathers collectively entitled themselves and banished all others to the edges and underside of American life. There, individual entitlement was either curtailed or—in the case of slavery—extinguished.

The genius of the civil rights movement that changed the fabric of American life in the late 1950s and early 1960s was its profound understanding that the enemy of black Americans was not the ideal America but the unspoken principle of collective entitlement that had always put the lie to true democracy. This movement, which came to center stage from America's underside and margins, had as its single, overriding goal the eradication of white entitlement. And correspondingly, it exhibited a belief in democratic principles at least as strong as that of the Founding Fathers, who themselves had emerged from the (less harsh) margins of English society. In this sense the civil rights movement re-enacted the American Revolution, and its paramount leader, Martin Luther King, spoke as twentieth-century America's greatest democratic voice.

All of this was made clear to me for the umpteenth time by my father on a very cold Saturday afternoon in 1959. There was a national campaign under way to integrate the lunch counters at Woolworth stores, and my father, who was more a persuader than an intimidator, had made it a point of honor that I join him on the picket line, civil rights being nothing less than the religion of our household. By this time, age twelve or so, I was sick of it. I'd had enough of watching my parents heading off to still another meeting or march; I'd heard too many tedious discussions on everything from the philosophy of passive resistance to the symbolism of going to jail.

Added to this, my own experience of picket lines and peace marches had impressed upon me what so many people who've partaken of these activities know: that in themselves they can be crushingly boring—around and around and around holding a sign, watching one's own feet fall, feeling the minutes like hours. All that Saturday morning I hid from my father and tried to convince myself of what I longed for—that he would get so busy that if he didn't forget the march he would at least forget me.

He forgot nothing. I did my time on the picket line, but not without building up enough resentment to start a fight on the way home. What was so important about integration? We had never even wanted to eat at Woolworth's. I told him the truth, that he never took us to *any* restaurants anyway, claiming always that they charged too much money for bad food. But he said calmly that he was proud of me for marching and that he knew I knew food wasn't the point.

My father—forty years a truck driver, with the urges of an intellectual—went on to use my little rebellion as the occasion for a discourse, in this case on the concept of integration. Integration had little to do with merely rubbing shoulders with white people, eating bad food beside them. It was about the right to go absolutely anywhere white people could go being the test of freedom and equality. To be anywhere they could be and do anything they could do was the point. Like it or not, white people defined the horizon of freedom in America, and if you couldn't touch their shoulder you weren't free. For him integration was the *evidence* of freedom and equality.

My father was a product of America's margins, as were all the blacks in the early civil rights movement, leaders and foot soldiers alike. For them integration was a way of moving from the margins into the mainstream. Today there is considerable ambivalence about integration, but in that day it was nothing less than democracy itself. Integration is also certainly about racial harmony, but it is more fundamentally about the ultimate extension of democracy—beyond the racial entitlements that contradict it. The idea of racial integration is quite simply the most democratic principle America has evolved, since all other such principles depend on its reality and are diminished by its absence.

But the civil rights movement did not account for one thing: the tremendous release of black anger that would follow its victories. The 1964 Civil Rights Act and the 1965 Voting Rights Act were, on one level, admissions of guilt by American society that it had practiced white entitlement at the expense of all others. When the oppressors admit their crimes, the oppressed can give full vent to their long repressed rage because now there is a moral consensus between oppressor and oppressed that a wrong was done. This consensus gave blacks the license to release a rage that was three centuries deep, a rage that is still today everywhere visible, a rage that—in the wake of the Rodney King Verdict, a verdict a vast majority of all Americans thought unfair—fuelled the worst rioting in recent American history.

By the mid-Sixties, the democratic goal of integration was no longer enough to appease black anger. Suddenly for blacks there was a sense that far more was owed, that a huge bill was due. And for many whites there was also the feeling that some kind of repayment was truly in order. This was the moral logic that followed inevitably from the new consensus. But it led to an even simpler logic: if blacks had been oppressed collectively that oppression would now be redressed by entitling them collectively. So here we were again, in the name of a thousand good intentions, falling away from the hard challenge of a democracy of individuals and embracing the principle of collective entitlement that had so corrupted the American ideal in the first place. Now this old sin would be applied in the name of uplift. And this made an easy sort of sense. If it was good enough for whites for three hundred years, why not let blacks have a little of it to get ahead? In the context of the Sixties—black outrage and white guilt—a principle we had just decided was evil for whites was redefined as a social good for blacks. And once the formula was in place for blacks, it could be applied to other groups with similar grievances. By the 1970s more than 60 percent of the American population—not only blacks but Hispanics, women, Asians—would come under the collective entitlement of affirmative action.

In the early days of the civil rights movement, the concept of solidarity was essentially a moral one. That is, all people who believed in human freedom, fairness, and equality were asked to form a solid front against white entitlement. But after the collaboration of black rage and white guilt made collective entitlement a social remedy, the nature of solidarity changed. It was no longer the rallying of diverse peoples to breach an oppressive group entitlement. It was the very opposite: a rallying of people within a grievance group to pursue their own group entitlement. As early as the mid-Sixties, whites were made unwelcome in the civil rights movement, just as, by the mid-Seventies, men were no longer welcome in the women's movement. Eventually, collective entitlement always requires separation. And the irony is obvious: those who once had been the victims of separatism, who had sacrificed so dearly to overcome their being at the margins, would later create an ethos of their own separatism. After the Sixties, solidarity became essentially a separatist concept, an exclusionary principle. One no longer heard words like "integration" or "harmony"; one heard about "anger" and "power." Integration is anathema to grievance groups for precisely the same reason it was anathema to racist whites in the civil rights era: because it threatens their collective entitlement by insisting that no group be entitled over another. Power is where it's at today—power to set up the organization, attract the following, run the fiefdom.

But it must also be said that this could not have come to pass without the cooperation of the society at large and its institutions. Why did the government, the public and private institutions, the corporations and foundations, end up supporting principles that had the effect of turning causes into sovereign fiefdoms? I think the answer is that those in charge of America's institutions saw the institutionalization and bureaucratization of the protest movements as ultimately desirable, at least in the short term, and the funding of group entitlements as ultimately a less costly way to redress grievances. The leaders of the newly sovereign fiefdoms were backing off from earlier demands that America live up to its ideals. Gone was the moral indictment. Gone was the call for difficult, soulful transformation. The language of entitlements is essentially the old, comforting language of power politics, and in the halls of power it went down easily enough.

With regard to civil rights, the moral voice of Dr. King gave way to the demands and cajolings of poverty-program moguls, class-action lawyers, and community organizers. The compromise that satisfied both political parties was to shift the focus from democracy, integration, and developmental uplift to collective entitlements. This satisfied the institutions because entitlements were cheaper in every way than real change. Better to set up black studies and women's studies departments than to have wrenching debates within existing departments. Better to fund these new institutions clamoring for money because who knows what kind of fuss they'll make if we turn down their proposals. Better to pass laws permitting Hispanic students to get preferred treatment in college admission—it costs less than improving kindergartens in East Los Angeles.

And this way to uplift satisfied the grievance-group "experts" because it laid the ground for their sovereignty and permanency: You negotiated with us. You funded us. You shared power, at least a bit of it, with *us*.

This negotiation was carried out in a kind of quasi-secrecy. Quotas, set-asides, and other entitlements were not debated in Congress or on the campaign trail. They were implemented by executive orders and Equal Employment Opportunity Commission guidelines without much public scrutiny. Also the courts played a quiet but persistent role in supporting these orders and guidelines and in further spelling out their application. Universities, corporations, and foundations implemented their own grievance entitlements, the workings of which are often kept from the public.

Now it should surprise no one that all this entitlement has most helped those who least need it—white middle-class women and the black middle class. Poor blacks do not guide the black grievance groups. Working-class women do not set NOW's agenda. Poor Hispanics do not clamor for bilingualism. Perhaps there is nothing wrong with middle class people being helped, but their demands for entitlements are most often in the names of those less well off than themselves. The negotiations that settled on entitlements as the primary form of redress after the Sixties have generated a legalistic grievance industry that argues the interstices of entitlements and does very little to help those truly in need.

In a liberal democracy, collective entitlements

based upon race, gender, ethnicity, or some other group grievance are always undemocratic expedients. Integration, on the other hand, is the most difficult and inexpedient expansion of the democratic ideal; for in opting for integration, a citizen denies his or her impulse to use our most arbitrary characteristics—race, ethnicity, gender, sexual preference—as the basis for identity, as a key to status, or for claims to entitlement. Integration is twentieth-century America's elaboration of democracy. It eliminates such things as race and gender as oppressive barriers to freedom, as democrats of an earlier epoch eliminated religion and property. Our mistake has been to think of integration only as utopian vision of perfect racial harmony. I think it is better to see integration as the inclusion of all citizens into the same sphere of rights, the same range of opportunities and possibilities that our Founding Fathers themselves enjoyed. Integration is not social engineering or group entitlements; it is a fundamental *absence* of arbitrary barriers to freedom.

If we can understand integration as an absence of barriers that has the effect of integrating all citizens into the same sphere of rights, then it can serve as a principle of democratic conduct. Anything that pushes anybody out of this sphere is undemocratic and must be checked, no matter the good intentions that seem to justify it. Understood in this light, collective entitlements are as undemocratic as racial and gender discrimination, and a group grievance is no more a justification for entitlement than the notion of white supremacy was at an earlier time. We are wrong to think of democracy as a gift of freedom; it is really a kind of discipline that avails freedom. Sometimes its enemy is racism and sexism; other times the enemy is our expedient attempts to correct these ills.

I think it is time for those who seek identity and power through grievance groups to fashion identities apart from grievance, to grant themselves the widest range of freedom, and to assume responsibility for that freedom. Victimhood lasts only as long as it is accepted, and to exploit it for an empty sovereignty is to accept it. The New Sovereignty is ultimately about vanity. It is the narcissism of victims, and it brings only a negligible power at the exorbitant price of continued victimhood. And all the while integration remains the real work.

SOCIAL MOVEMENTS AND THE POLITICS OF DIFFERENCE

Iris Marion Young

Iris Marion Young is Professor of Public and International Affairs at the University of Pittsburgh with affiliation to Philosophy and Political Science. She is the author of Justice and the Politics of Difference *(Princeton, 1990),* Throwing Like a Girl and Other Essays in Feminist Philosophy and Social Theory *(Indiana, 1990), and* Intersecting Voices: Dilemmas of Gender, Political Philosophy and Policy *(Princeton, 1997). She is also a co-editor of* A Companion to Feminist Philosophy *(Blackwell, 1998).*

While Young applauds the progress toward equality gained through the Enlightenment and its ideal of equality as equal treatment for all people, she is critical of the goal of assimilation that is assumed in this conception of equality. She defends the positive self-definition of group difference that is evident in current social movements of oppressed groups and endorses a politics of difference as a way of reconceiving the meaning of equality. Sometimes the elimination of oppression and the inclusion of members of all groups requires not the equal treatment goal in the assimilationist model, but special or different treatment for members of disadvantaged groups.

> The idea that I think we need today in order to make decisions in political matters cannot be the idea of a totality, or of the unity, of a body. It can only be the idea of a multiplicity or a diversity. ... To state that one must draw a critique of political judgment means today to do a politics of opinions that at the same time is a politics of Ideas ... in which justice in not placed under a rule of convergence but rather a rule of divergence. I believe that this is the theme that one finds constantly in present day writing under the name "minority."
>
> —Jean-François Lyotard

There was once a time of caste and class, when tradition decreed that each group had its place, and that some were born to rule and others to serve. In this time of darkness, law and social norms defined rights, privileges, and obligations differently for different groups, distinguished by characteristics of sex, race, religion, class, or occupation. Social inequality was justified by church and state on the grounds that people have different natures, and some natures are better than others.

Then one day Enlightenment dawned, heralding a revolutionary conception of humanity and society. All people are equal, the revolutionaries declared, inasmuch as all have a capacity for reason and moral sense. Law and politics should therefore grant to everyone equal political and civil rights. With these bold ideas the battle lines of modern political struggle were drawn.

For over two hundred years since those voices of Reason first rang out, the forces of light have struggled for liberty and political equality against the dark forces of irrational prejudice, arbitrary metaphysics, and the crumbling towers of patriarchal church, state, and family. In the New World we had a head start in this fight, since the American War of Independence was fought on these Enlightenment principles, and our Constitution stood for liberty and equality. So we did not have to throw off the yokes of class and religious privilege, as did our Old World comrades. Yet the United States had its own oli-

---

Reprinted with permission of the publisher from *Justice and the Politics of Difference*, by Iris Marion Young (Princeton: © 1990, Princeton University Press):156–173.

garchic horrors in the form of slavery and the exclusion of women from public life. In protracted and bitter struggles these bastions of privilege based on group difference began to give way, finally to topple in the 1960s.

Today in our society a few vestiges of prejudice and discrimination remain, but we are working on them, and have nearly realized the dream those Enlightenment fathers dared to propound. The state and law should express rights only in universal terms applied equally to all, and differences among persons and groups should be a purely accidental and private matter. We seek a society in which differences of race, sex, religion, and ethnicity no longer make a difference to people's rights and opportunities. People should be treated as individuals, not as members of groups; their life options and rewards should be based solely on their individual achievement. All persons should have the liberty to be and do anything they want, to choose their own lives and not be hampered by traditional expectations and stereotypes.

We tell each other this story and make our children perform it for our sacred holidays—Thanksgiving Day, the Fourth of July, Memorial Day, Lincoln's Birthday. We have constructed Martin Luther King, Jr., Day to fit the narrative so well that we have already forgotten that it took a fight to get it included in the canon year. There is much truth to this story. Enlightenment ideals of liberty and political equality did and do inspire movements against oppression and domination, whose success has created social values and institutions we would not want to lose. A people could do worse than tell this story after big meals and occasionally call upon one another to live up to it.

The very worthiness of the narrative, however, and the achievement of political equality that it recounts, now inspires new heretics. In recent years the ideal of liberation as the elimination of group difference has been challenged by movements of the oppressed. The very success of political movements against differential privilege and for political equality has generated movements of group specificity and cultural pride.

In this chapter I criticize an ideal of justice that defines liberation as the transcendence of group difference, which I refer to as an ideal of assimilation. This ideal usually promotes equal treatment as a primary principle of justice. Recent social movements of oppressed groups challenge this ideal. Many in these movements argue that a positive self-definition of group difference is in fact more liberatory.

I endorse this politics of difference, and argue that at stake is the meaning of social difference itself. Traditional politics that excludes or devalues some persons on account of their group attributes assumes an essentialist meaning of difference; it defines groups as having different natures. An egalitarian politics of difference, on the other hand, defines difference more fluidly and relationally as the product of social processes.

An emancipatory politics that affirms group difference involves a reconception of the meaning of equality. The assimilationist ideal assumes that equal social status for all persons requires treating everyone according to the same principles, rules, and standards. A politics of difference argues, on the other hand, that equality as the participation and inclusion of all groups sometimes requires different treatment or the oppressed or disadvantaged groups. To promote social justice, I argue, social policy should sometimes accord special treatment to groups. I explore pregnancy and birthing rights for worker, bilingual-bicultural rights, and American Indian rights as three cases of such special treatment. Finally, I expand the idea of a heterogeneous public here by arguing for a principle of representation for oppressed groups in democratic decision-making bodies.

Competing Paradigms of Liberation

In "On Racism and Sexism" [in *Philosophy and Social Issues*, 1980], Richard Wasserstrom develops a classic statement of the ideal of liberation from group-based oppression as involving the elimination of group-based difference itself. A truly nonracist, nonsexist society, he suggests, would be one in which the race or sex of an individual would be the functional equivalent of eye color in our society today. While physiological differences in skin color or genitals would remain, they would have no significance for a person's sense of identity or how other regard him or her. No political rights or obligations would be connected to race or sex, and no important institutional benefits would be associated with either. People would see no reason to consider race or gender in policy or everyday interactions. In such a society, social group differences would have ceased to exist.

Wasserstrom contrasts this ideal of assimilation with an ideal of diversity much like the one I will argue for, which he agrees is compelling. He offers three primary reasons, however, for choosing the assimilationist ideal of liberation over the ideal of diversity. First, the assimilationist ideal exposes the arbitrariness of group-based social distinctions which are thought natural and necessary. By imagining a society in which race and sex have no social significance, one sees more clearly how pervasively these group categories unnecessarily limit possibilities for some in existing society. Second, the assimilationist ideal presents a clear and unambiguous standard of equality and justice. According such a standard, any group-related differentiation or discrimination is suspect. Whenever laws or rules, the division of labor, or other social practices allocate benefits differently according to group membership, this is a sign of injustice. The principle of justice is simple: treat everyone according to the same principles, rules, and standards. Third, the assimilationist ideal maximizes choice. In a society where differences make no social difference people can develop themselves as individuals, unconstrained by group norms and expectations.

There is no question that the ideal of liberation as the elimination of group difference has been enormously important in the history of emancipatory politics. The ideal of universal humanity that denies natural differences has been a crucial historical development in the struggle against exclusion and status differentiation. It has made possible the assertion of the equal moral worth of all persons, and thus the right of all to participate and be included in all institutions and positions of power and privilege. The assimilationist ideal retains significant rhetorical power in the face of continued beliefs in the essentially different and inferior natures of women, blacks, and other groups.

The power of this assimilationist ideal has inspired the struggle of oppressed groups and the supporters against the exclusion and denigration of these groups, and continues to inspire many. Periodically in American history, however, movements of the oppressed have questioned and rejected this "path to belonging." Instead they have seen self-organization and the assertion of a positive group cultural identity as a better strategy for achieving power and participation in dominant institutions. Recent decades have witnessed a resurgence of this "politics of difference" not only among racial and ethnic groups, but also among women, gay men and lesbians, old people, and the disabled.

Not long after the passage of the Civil Rights Act and the Voting Rights Act, many white and black supporters of the black civil rights movement were surprised, confused, and angered by the emergence of the Black Power movement. Black Power advocates criticized the integrationist goal and reliance on the support of white liberals that characterized the civil rights movement. They encouraged blacks to break their alliance with whites and assert the specificity of their own culture, political organization, and goals. Instead of integration, they encouraged blacks to seek economic and political empowerment in their separate neighborhoods. Since the late 1960s many blacks have claimed that the integration successes of the civil rights movement have had the effect of dismantling the bases of black-organized social and economic institutions at least as much as they have lessened black-white animosity and opened doors of opportunity. While some individual blacks may be better off than they would have been if these changes had not occurred, as a group, blacks are no better off and may be worse off, because the blacks who have succeeded in assimilating into the American middle class no longer associate as closely with lower-class blacks.

While much black politics has questioned the ideal of assimilation in economic and political terms, the past twenty years have also seen the assertion and celebration by blacks of a distinct Afro-American culture, both as a recovery and revaluation of an Afro-American history and in the creation of new cultural forms. The slogan "black is beautiful" pierced American consciousness, deeply unsettling the received body aesthetic which I [have] argued... continues to be a powerful reproducer of racism.

Afro-American hairstyles pronounced themselves differently stylish, not less stylish. Linguistic theorists asserted that black English is English differently constructed, not bad English, and black poets and novelists exploited and explored its particular nuances.

In the late 1960s Red Power came fast on the heels of Black Power. The American Indian Movement and other radical organizations of American Indians rejected perhaps even more vehemently than blacks the goal of assimilation which has dominated white-Indian relations for most of the twentieth century. They asserted a right to self-government on Indian lands and fought to gain and maintain a dominant Indian voice in the Bureau of Indian Affairs. American Indians have sought to recover and preserve their language, rituals, and crafts, and this renewal of pride in traditional culture has also fostered a separatist political movement. The desire to pursue land rights claims and to fight for control over resources on reservations arises from what has become a fierce commitment to tribal self-determination, the desire to develop and maintain Indian political and economic bases in but not of white society.

These are but two examples of a widespread tendency in the politics of the 1970s and 1980s for oppressed, disadvantaged, or specially marked groups to organize autonomously and assert a positive sense of their cultural and experiential specificity. Many Spanish-speaking Americans have rejected the traditional assumption that full participation in American society requires linguistic and cultural assimilation. In the last twenty years many have developed a renewed interest and pride in their Puerto Rican, Chicano, Mexican, or other Latin American heritage. They have asserted the right to maintain their specific culture and speak their language and still receive the benefits of citizenship, such as voting rights, decent education, and job opportunities. Many Jewish Americans have similarly rejected the ideal of assimilation, instead asserting the specificity and positive meaning of Jewish identity, often insisting publicly that Christian culture cease to be taken as the norm.

Since the late 1960s the blossoming of gay cultural expression, gay organizations, and the public presence of gays in marches and other forums have radically altered the environment in which young people come to sexual identity, and changed many people's perceptions of homosexuality. Early gay rights advocacy had a distinctly assimilationist and universalist orientation. The goal was to remove the stigma of being homosexual, to prevent institutional discrimination, and to achieve societal recognition that gay people are "no different" from anyone else. The very process of political organization against discrimination and police harassment and for the achievement of civil rights, however, fostered the development of gay and lesbian communities and cultural expression, which by the mid-1970s flowered in meeting places, organizations, literature, music, and massive street celebrations.

Today most gay and lesbian liberation advocates seek not merely civil rights, but the affirmation of gay men and lesbians as social groups with specific experiences and perspectives. Refusing to accept the dominant culture's definition of healthy sexuality and respectable family life and social practices, gay and lesbian liberation movements have proudly created and displayed a distinctive self-definition and culture. For gay men and lesbians the analogue to racial integration is the typical liberal approach to sexuality, which tolerates any behavior as long as it is kept private. Gay pride asserts that sexual identity is a matter of culture and politics, and not merely "behavior" to be tolerated or forbidden.

The women's movement has also generated its own versions of a politics of difference. Humanist feminism, which predominated in the nineteenth century and in the contemporary women's movement until the late 1970s, finds in any assertion of difference between women and men only a legacy of female oppression and an ideology to legitimate continued exclusion of women from socially valued human activity. Humanist feminism is thus analogous to an ideal of assimilation in identifying sexual equality with gender blindness, with measuring women and men according to the same standards and treating them in the same way. Indeed, for many feminists, androgyny names the ideal of sexual liberation—- a society in which gender difference itself would be eliminated. Given the strength and plausibility of this vision of sexual equality, it was confusing when feminists too began taking the turn to difference, asserting the positivity and specificity of female experience and values.

Feminist separatism was the earliest expression of such gynocentric feminism. Feminist separatism rejected wholly or partly the goal of entering the male-dominated world, because it requires playing according to rules that men have made and that have been used against women, and because trying to measure up to male-defined standards inevitably involves accommodating or pleasing the men who continue to dominate socially valued institutions and activities. Separatism promoted the empowerment of women through self-organization, the creation of separate and safe spaces where women could share and analyze their experiences, voice their anger, play with and create bonds with one another, and develop new and better institutions and practices.

Most elements of the contemporary women's movement have been separatist to some degree. Separatists seeking to live as much of their lives as possible in women-only institutions were largely responsible for the creation of the women's culture that burst forth all over the United States by the mid-1970s, and continues to claim the loyalty of millions of women—in the form of music, poetry, spirituality, literature, celebrations, festivals, and dances. Whether drawing on images of Amazonian grandeur, recovering and revaluing traditional women's arts, like quilting and weaving, or inventing new rituals based on medieval witchcraft, the development of such expressions of women's culture gave many feminists images of a female-centered beauty and strength entirely outside capitalist patriarchal definitions of feminine pulchritude. The separatist impulse also fostered the development of the many autonomous women's institutions and services that have concretely improved the lives of many women, whether feminists or not—such as health clinics, battered women's shelters, rape crisis centers, and women's coffeehouses and bookstores.

Beginning in the late 1970s much feminist theory and political analysis also took a turn away from humanist feminism, to question the assumption that traditional female activity expresses primarily the victimization of women and the distortion of their human potential and that the goal of women's liberation is the participation of women as equals in public institutions now dominated by men. Instead of understanding the activities and values associated with traditional femininity as largely distortions and inhibitions of women's truly human potentialities, this gynocentric analysis sought to revalue the caring, nurturing, and cooperative approach to social relations they found associated with feminine socialization, and sought in women's specific experiences the bases for an attitude toward the body and nature healthier than that predominant in male dominated Western capitalist culture.

None of the social movements asserting positive group specificity is in fact a unity. All have group differences within them. The black movement, for example, includes middle-class blacks and working-class blacks, gays and straight people, men and women, and so it is with any other group. The implications of group differences within a social group have been most systematically discussed in the women's movement. Feminist conferences and publications have generated particularly fruitful, though often emotionally wrenching, discussions of the oppression of racial and ethnic blindness and the importance of attending to group differences among women. From such discussions emerged principled efforts to provide autonomously organized forums for black women, Latinas, Jewish women, lesbians, differently abled women, old women, and any other women who see reason for claiming that they have as a group a distinctive voice that might be silenced in a general feminist discourse. Those discussions, along with the practices feminists instituted to structure discussion and interaction among differently identifying groups of women, offer some beginning models for the development of a heterogeneous public. Each of the other social movements has also generated discussion of group differences that cut across their identities, leading to other possibilities of coalition and alliance.

Emancipation Through the Politics of Difference

Implicit in emancipatory movements asserting a positive sense of group difference is a different ideal of liberation, which might be called democratic cultural pluralism. In this vision the good society does not eliminate or transcend group difference. Rather, there is equality among socially and culturally differentiated groups, who mutually respect one another and affirm one another in their differences. What are the reasons for rejecting the assimilationist ideal and promoting a politics of difference?

Some deny the reality of social groups. For them, group difference is an invidious fiction produced and perpetuated in order to preserve the privilege of the few. Others, such as Wasserstrom, may agree that social groups do now exist and have real social consequences for the way people identify themselves and one another, but assert that such social group differences are undesirable. The assimilationist ideal involves denying either the reality or the desirability of social groups.

Those promoting a politics of difference doubt that a society without group differences is either possible or desirable. Contrary to the assumption of modernization theory, increased urbanization and the extension of equal formal rights to all groups has not led to a decline in particularist affiliations. If anything, the urban concentration and interactions among groups that modernizing social processes introduce tend to reinforce group solidarity and differentiation. Attachment to specific traditions, practices, language, and other culturally specific forms is a crucial aspect of social existence. People do not usually give up their social group identifications, even when they are oppressed.

Whether eliminating social group difference is possible or desirable in the long run, however, is an academic issue. Today and for the foreseeable future societies are certainly structured by groups, and some are privileged while others are oppressed. New social movements of group specificity do not deny the official story's claim that the ideal of liberation as eliminating difference and treating everyone the same has brought significant improvement in the status of excluded groups. Its main quarrel is with the story's conclusion, namely, that since we have achieved formal equality, only vestiges and holdovers of differential privilege remain, which will die out with the continued persistent assertion of an ideal of social relations that make differences irrelevant to a person's life prospects. The achievement of formal equality does not eliminate social differences, and rhetorical commitment to the sameness of persons makes it impossible even to name how those differences presently structure privilege and oppression.

Though in many respects the law is now blind to group differences, some groups continue to be marked as deviant, as the Other. In everyday interactions, images, and decisions, assumptions about women, blacks, Hispanics, gay men and lesbians, old people, and other marked groups continue to justify exclusion, avoidance, paternalism, and authoritarian treatment. Continued racist, sexist, homophobic, ageist, and ableist institutions and behavior create particular circumstances for these groups, usually disadvantaging them in their opportunity to develop their capacities. Finally, in part because they have been segregated from one another, and in part because they have particular histories and traditions, there are cultural differences among social groups — - differences in language, style of living, body comportment and gestures, values, and perspectives on society.

Today in American society, as in many other societies, there is widespread agreement that no person should be excluded from political and economic activities because of ascribed characteristics. Group differences nevertheless continue to exist, and certain groups continue to be privileged. Under these circumstances, insisting that equality and liberation entail ignoring difference has progressive consequences in three respects.

First, blindness to difference disadvantages groups whose experience, culture, and socialized capacities differ from those of privileged groups. The strategy of assimilation aims to bring formerly excluded groups into the mainstream. So assimilation always implies coming into the game after it is already begun, after the rules and standards have already been set, and having to prove oneself according to those rules and standards. In the assimilationist strategy, the privileged groups implicitly define the standards according to which all will be measured. Because their privilege involves not recognizing these standards as culturally and experientially specific, the ideal of a common humanity in which all can participate without regard to race, gender, religion, or sexuality poses as neutral and universal. The real differences between oppressed groups and the dominant norm, however, tend to put them at a disadvantage in measuring up to these standards, and for that reason assimilationist policies perpetuate their disadvantage. Later in this chapter, I shall give examples of facially neutral standards that operate to disadvantage or exclude those already disadvantaged.

Second, the ideal of a universal humanity without social group differences allows privileged groups to ignore their own group specificity. Blindness to difference perpetuates cultural imperialism by allowing norms expressing the point of view and experience of privileged groups to appear neutral and universal. The assimilationist ideal presumes that there is a humanity in general, and unsituated group-neutral human capacity for self-making that left to itself would make individuality flower, thus guaranteeing that each individual will be different. Because there is no such instituted group-neutral point of view, the situation and experience of dominant groups tend to define the norms of such a humanity in general. Against such a supposedly neutral humanist ideal, only the oppressed groups come to be marked with particularity; they, and not the privileged groups, are marked, objectified as the Others.

Thus, third, this denigration of groups that deviate from an allegedly neutral standard often produces an internalized devaluation by members of those groups themselves. When there is an ideal of general human standards according to which everyone should be evaluated equally, then Puerto Ricans or Chinese Americans are ashamed of their accents or their parents, black children despise the female-dominated kith and kin networks of their neighborhoods, and feminists seek to root out their tendency to cry, or to feel compassion for a frustrated stranger. The aspiration to assimilate helps produce the self-loathing and double consciousness characteristic of oppression. The goal of assimilation holds up to people a demand that they "fit," be like the mainstream, in behavior, values and goals. At the same time, as long as group differences exist, group members will be marked as different—as black, Jewish, gay—and thus as unable simply to fit. When participation is taken to imply assimilation the oppressed person is caught in an irresolvable dilemma: to participate means to accept and adopt an identity one is not, and to try to participate means to be reminded by oneself and others of the identity one is.

A more subtle analysis of the assimilationist ideal might distinguish between a conformist and a transformational ideal of assimilation. In the conformist ideal, status quo institutions and norms are assumed as given, and disadvantaged groups who differ from those norms are expected to conform to them. A transformational ideal of assimilation, on the other hand, recognizes that institutions as given express the interests and perspective of the dominant groups. Achieving assimilation therefore requires altering many institutions and practices in accordance with neutral rules that truly do not disadvantage or stigmatize any person, so that group membership really is irrelevant to how persons are treated. Wasserstrom's ideal fits a transformational assimilation, as does the group-neutral ideal advocated by some feminists. Unlike the conformist assimilationist, the transformational assimilationist may allow that group-specific policies, such as affirmative action, are necessary and appropriate means for transforming institutions to fit the assimilationist ideal. Whether conformist or transformational, however, the assimilationist ideal still denies that group difference can be positive and desirable; thus any form of the ideal of assimilation constructs group difference as a liability or disadvantage.

Under these circumstances, a politics that asserts the positivity of group difference is liberating and empowering. In the act of reclaiming the identity the dominant culture has taught them to despise, and affirming it as an identity to celebrate, the oppressed remove double consciousness. I am just what they say I am—a Jewboy, a colored girl, a fag, a dyke, or a hag— and proud of it. No longer does one have the impossible project of trying to become something one is not under circumstances where the very trying reminds one of who one is. This politics asserts that oppressed groups have distinct cultures, experiences, and perspectives on social life with humanly positive meaning, some of which may even be superior to the culture and perspectives of mainstream society. The rejection and devaluation of one's culture and perspective should not be a condition of full participation in social life.

Asserting the value and specificity of the culture

and attributes of oppressed groups, moreover, results in a relativizing of the dominant culture. When feminists assert the validity of feminine sensitivity and the positive value of nurturing behavior, when gays describe the prejudice of heterosexuals as homophobic and their own sexuality as positive and self-developing, when blacks affirm a distinct Afro-American tradition, then the dominant culture is forced to discover itself for the first time as specific: as Anglo, European, Christian, masculine, straight. In a political struggle where oppressed groups insist on the positive value of their specific culture and experience, it becomes increasingly difficult for dominant groups to parade their norms as neutral and universal, and to construct the values and behavior of the oppressed as deviant, perverted, or inferior. By puncturing the universalist claim to unity that expels some groups and turns them into the Other, the assertion of positive group specificity introduces the possibility of understanding the relation between groups as merely difference, instead of exclusion, opposition, or dominance.

The politics of difference also promotes a notion of group solidarity against the individualism of liberal humanism. Liberal humanism treats each person as an individual, ignoring differences of race, sex, religion, and ethnicity. Each person should be evaluated only according to her or his individual efforts and achievements. With the institutionalization of formal equality some members of formerly excluded groups have indeed succeeded, by mainstream standards. Structural patterns of group privilege and oppression nevertheless remain. When political leaders of oppressed groups reject assimilation they are often affirming group solidarity. Where the dominant culture refuses to see anything but the achievement of autonomous individuals, the oppressed assert that we shall not separate from the people with whom we identify in order to "make it" in a white Anglo male world. The politics of difference insists on liberation of the whole group of blacks, women, American Indians, and that this can be accomplished only through basic institutional changes. These changes must include group representation in policy-making and an elimination of the hierarchy of rewards that forces everyone to compete for scarce positions at the top.

Thus the assertion of a positive sense of group difference provides a standpoint from which to criticize prevailing institutions and norms. Black Americans find in their traditional communities, which refer to their members as "brother" and "sister," a sense of solidarity absent from the calculating individualism of white professional capitalist society. Feminists find in the traditional female values of nurturing a challenge to a militarist worldview, and lesbians find in their relationships a confrontation with the assumption of complementary gender roles in sexual relationships. From their experience of a culture tied to the land American Indians formulate a critique of the instrumental rationality of European culture that results in pollution and ecological destruction. Having revealed the specificity of the dominant norms which claim universality and neutrality, social movements of the oppressed are in a position to inquire how the dominant institutions must be changed so that they will no longer reproduce the patterns of privilege and oppression.

From the assertion of positive difference the self-organization of oppressed groups follows. Both liberal humanist and leftist political organizations and movements have found it difficult to accept this principle of group autonomy. In a humanist emancipatory politics, if a group is subject to injustice, then all those interested in a just society should unite to combat the powers that perpetuate that injustice. If many groups are subject to injustice, moreover, then they should unite to work for a just society. The politics of difference is certainly not against coalition, nor does it hold that, for example, whites should not work against racial injustice or men against sexist injustice. This politics of group assertion, however, takes as a basic principle that members of oppressed groups need separate organizations that exclude others, especially those from more privileged groups. Separate organization is probably necessary in order for these groups to discover and reinforce the positivity of their specific experience, to collapse and eliminate double consciousness. In discussions within autonomous organizations, group members can determine their specific needs and interests. Separation and self-organization risk creating pressures toward homogenization of the groups themselves, creating new privileges and exclusions. But contemporary emancipatory social movements have found group autonomy an important vehicle for empowerment and the development of a group-specific voice and perspective.

Integration into the full life of the society should not have to imply assimilation to dominant norms and abandonment of group affiliation and culture. If the only alternative to the oppressive exclusion of some groups defined as Other by dominant ideologies is the assertion that they are the same as everybody else, then they will continue to be excluded because they are not the same.

Some might object to the way I have drawn the distinction between an assimilationist ideal of liberation and a radical democratic pluralism. They might claim that I have not painted the ideal of a society that transcends group differences fairly, representing it as homogeneous and conformist. The free society envisaged by liberalism, they might say, is certainly pluralistic. In it persons can affiliate with whomever they choose; liberty encourages a proliferation of lifestyles, activities, and associations. While I have no quarrel with social diversity in this sense, this vision of liberal pluralism does not touch on the primary issues that give rise to the politics of difference. The vision of liberation as the transcendence of group difference seeks to abolish the public and political significance of group difference while retaining and promoting both individual and group diversity in private, or nonpolitical, social contexts. This way of distinguishing public and private spheres, where the public represents universal citizenship and the private individual differences, tends to result in group exclusion from the public. Radical democratic pluralism acknowledges and affirms the public and political significance of social group differences as a means of ensuring the participation and inclusion of everyone in social and political institutions.

Reclaiming the Meaning of Difference

Many people inside and outside the movements I have discussed find the rejection of the liberal humanist ideal and the assertion of a positive sense of group difference both confusing and controversial. They fear that any admission by oppressed groups that they are different from the dominant groups risks justifying anew the subordination, special marking, and exclusion of those groups. Since calls for a return of women to the kitchen, blacks to servant roles and separate schools, and disabled people to nursing homes are not absent from contemporary politics, the danger is real. It may be true that the assimilationist ideal that treats everyone the same and applies the same standards to all perpetuates disadvantage because real group differences remain that make it unfair to compare the unequals. But this is far preferable to a reestablishment of separate and unequal spheres for different groups justified on the basis of group difference.

Since those asserting group specificity certainly wish to affirm the liberal humanist principle that all persons are of equal moral worth, they appear to be faced with a dilemma. Analyzing W.E.B. Du Bois's arguments for cultural pluralism, Bernard Boxill poses the dilemma this way: "On the one hand, we must overcome segregation because it denies the idea of human brotherhood; on the other hand, to overcome segregation we must self-segregate and therefore also deny the idea of human brotherhood." Martha Minow finds a dilemma of difference facing any who seek to promote justice for currently oppressed or disadvantaged groups. Formally neutral rules and policies that ignore group differences often perpetuate the disadvantage of those whose difference is defined as deviant; but focusing on difference risks recreating the stigma that difference has carried in the past.

The dilemmas are genuine, and exhibit the risks of collective life, where the consequences of one's claims, actions, and policies may not turn out as one intended because others have understood them differently or turned them to different ends. Since ignoring group differences in public policy does not mean that people ignore them in everyday life and interaction, however, oppression continues even when law and policy declare that all are equal. Thus, I think for many groups and in many circumstances it is more empowering to affirm and acknowledge in political life the group differences that already exist in social life. One is more likely to avoid the dilemma of difference in doing this if the meaning of difference itself becomes a terrain of political struggle. Social movements asserting the positivity of group difference have established this terrain, offering an emancipatory meaning of difference to replace the old exclusionary meaning.

The oppressive meaning of group difference defines it as absolute otherness, mutual exclusion, categorical opposition. This essentialist meaning of difference submits to the logic of identity. One group occupies the position of a norm, against which all others are measured. The attempt to reduce all persons to the unity of a common measure constructs as deviant those whose attributes differ from the group-specific attributes implicitly presumed in the norm. The drive to unify the particularity and multiplicity of practices, cultural symbols, and ways of relating in clear and distinct categories turns difference into exclusion.

Thus the appropriation of a universal subject position by socially privileged groups forces those they define as different outside the definition of full humanity and citizenship. The attempt to measure all against some universal standard generates a logic of difference as hierarchical dichotomy—masculine/feminine, civilized/savage, and so on. The second term is defined negatively as a lack of the truly human qualities; at the same time it is defined as the complement to the valued term, the object correlating with its subject, that which brings it to completion, wholeness, and identity. By loving and affirming him, a woman serves as a mirror to a man, holding up his virtues for him to see. By carrying the white man's burden to tame and educate the savage peoples, the civilized will realize universal humanity. The exotic orientals are there to know and master, to be the completion of reason's progress in history, which seeks the unity of the world. In every case the valued term achieves its value by its determinately negative relation to the Other.

In the objectifying ideologies of racism, sexism, anti-Semitism, and homophobia, only the oppressed and excluded groups are defined as different. Whereas the privileged groups are neutral and exhibit free and malleable subjectivity, the excluded groups are marked with an essence, imprisoned in a given set of possibilities. By virtue of the characteristics the group is alleged to have by nature, the ideologies allege that group members have specific dispositions that suit them for some activities and not others. Difference in these ideologies always means exclusionary opposition to a norm. There are rational men, and then there are women; there are civilized men, and then there are wild and savage peoples. The marking of difference always implies a good/bad opposition; it is always a devaluation, the naming of an inferiority in relation to a superior standard of humanity.

Difference here always means absolute otherness; the group marked as different has no common nature with the normal or neutral ones. The categorical opposition of groups essentializes them, repressing the differences within groups. In this way the definition of difference as exclusion and opposition actually denies difference. This essentializing categorization also denies difference in that its universalizing norms preclude recognizing and affirming a group's specificity in its own terms.

Essentializing difference expresses a fear of specificity, and a fear of making permeable the categorical border between oneself and the others. This fear is not merely intellectual and does not derive only from the instrumental desire to defend privilege, though that may be a large element. It wells from the depths of the Western subject's sense of identity, especially, but not only in the subjectivity of privileged groups. The fear may increase, moreover, as a clear essentialism of difference wanes, as belief in a specifically female, black, or homosexual nature becomes less tenable.

The politics of difference confronts this fear, and aims for an understanding of group difference as indeed ambiguous, relational, shifting, without clear borders that keep people straight—as entailing neither amorphous unity nor pure individuality. By asserting a positive meaning for their own identity, oppressed groups seek to seize the power of naming difference itself, and explode the implicit definition of difference as deviance in relation to a norm, which freezes some groups into a self-enclosed nature. Difference now comes to mean not otherness, exclusive opposition, but specifically, variation, heterogeneity. Difference names relations of similarity and dissimilarity that can be reduced to neither coextensive identity nor overlapping otherness.

The alternative to an essentializing, stigmatizing meaning of difference as opposition is an understanding of difference as specificity, variation. In this logic, as Martha Minow suggests, group differences should be conceived as relational rather than defined by substantive categories and attributes. A relational understanding of difference relativizes the previously universal position of privileged groups, which allows only the oppressed to be marked as different. When group difference appears as a function of comparison between groups, whites are just as specific as black or Latinos, men just as specific as women, able-bodied people just as specific as disabled people. Difference thus emerges not as a description of the attributes of a group, but as a function of the relations between groups and the interaction of groups with institutions.

In this relational understanding, the meaning of difference also becomes contextualized. Group differences will be more or less salient depending on the groups compared, the purposes of the comparison, and the point of view of the comparers. Such contextualized understandings of difference undermine essentialist assumptions. For example in the context of athletics, health care, social service support, and so on, wheelchair-bound people are different from others, but they are not different in many other respects. Traditional treatment of the disabled entailed exclusion and segregation because the differences between the disabled and the able-bodied were conceptualized as extending to all or most capacities.

In general, then, a relational understanding of group difference rejects exclusion. Difference no longer implies that groups lie outside one another. To say that there are differences among groups does not imply that there are not overlapping experiences, or that two groups have nothing in common. The assumption that real differences in affinity, culture, or privilege imply oppositional categorization must be challenged. Different groups are always similar in some respects, and always potentially share some attributes, experiences, and goals.

Such a relational understanding of difference entails revising the meaning of group identity as well. In asserting the positive difference of their experience, culture, and social perspective, social movements of groups that have experienced cultural imperialism deny that they have a common identity, a set of fixed attributes that clearly mark who belongs and who doesn't. Rather, what makes a group a group is a social process of interaction and differentiation in which some people come to have a particular affinity for others. My "affinity group" in a given social situation comprises those people with whom I feel the most comfortable, who are more familiar. Affinity names the manner of sharing assumptions, affective bonding, and networking that recognizably differentiates groups from one another, but not according to some common nature. The salience of a particular person's group affinities may shift according to the social situation or according to changes in her or his life. Membership in a social group is a function not of satisfying some objective criteria, but of a subjective affirmation of affinity with that group, the affirmation of that affinity by others members of the group, and the attribution of membership in that group by persons identifying with other groups. Group identity is constructed from a flowing process in which individuals identify themselves and others in terms of groups, and thus group identity itself flows and shifts with changes in social process.

Groups experiencing cultural imperialism have found themselves objectified and marked with a devalued essence from the outside, by a dominant culture they are excluded from making. The assertion of a positive sense of group difference by these groups is emancipatory because it reclaims the definition of the group by the group, as a creation and construction, rather than a given essence. To be sure, it is difficult to articulate positive elements of group affinity without essentializing them, and these movements do not always succeed in doing so. But they are developing a language to describe their similar social situation and relations to one another, and their similar perceptions and perspectives on social life. These movements engage in the project of cultural revolution I recommended in chapter [5 of *Justice and the Politics of Difference*], insofar as they take culture as in part a matter of collective choice. While their ideas of women's culture, Afro-American culture, and American Indian culture rely on past cultural expressions, to a significant degree these movements have self-consciously constructed the culture that they claim defines the distinctiveness of their groups.

Contextualizing both the meaning of difference and identity thus allows the acknowledgment of difference within affinity groups. In our complex, plural society, every social group has group differences cutting across it, which are potential sources of wisdom, excitement, conflict, and oppression. Gay men, for example, may be black, rich, homeless, or old, and these differences produce different identifications and potential conflicts among gay men as well as affinities with some straight men....

MORAL DEFERENCE

Laurence Thomas

Laurence Thomas teaches in the Department of Philosophy and the Department of Political Science at Syracuse University. He is the author of Living Morally: A Psychology of Moral Character *(Temple, 1989) and* Vessels of Evil: American Slavery and the Holocaust *(Temple, 1993).*

Thomas rejects the idea that there is a impartial vantage point from which any person can understand the morally significant experiences of others. He formulates the notion of moral deference as the kind of stance that allows one to respond in the morally appropriate way to someone who has been wronged. Moral deference is about listening to another's moral pain as a way of gaining insight into the character of the pain and how that person has been emotionally configured by it. Moral deference is owed to members of disadvantaged groups because it opens the way to understanding the social injustices they have experienced and responding in a morally appropriate way to particular injustices.

> Why is this peach-tree said to be better than that other; but because it produces more or better fruit? ... In morals, too, is not *the tree known by the fruit?*
>
> David Hume,
> *Enquiry Concerning the Principles of Morals* (V, IIn 1)

In "What Is It Like To Be a Bat?," Thomas Nagel tells us that we hardly come to know what it is like to be a bat by hanging upside down with our eyes closed.[1] That experience simply tells us what it is like to be a human behaving or attempting to behave like a bat. If bats were intelligent creatures possessing a natural language, which we could translate, surely we would have to take their word for what it is like to be a bat. If, in batese, bats—including the most intelligent and articulate ones—generally maintained that "Hanging upside down is extraordinarily like experiencing death through colors," we human beings would probably not know how to get a handle on what was being claimed, since the notion of experiencing death already strains the imagination. Just so, we would be in no position to dismiss their claim as so much nonsense because we cannot get a handle on it—because, after all, we humans experience no such thing when we engage in bat-like behavior. On this matter, bats would be owed deference.

Some people are owed deference—moral deference, that is. Moral deference is meant to stand in opposition to the idea that there is a vantage point from which any and every person can rationally grasp whatever morally significant experiences a person might have. A fundamentally important part of living morally is being able to respond in the morally appropriate way to those who have been wronged. And this ability we cannot have in the absence of a measure of moral deference. David Hume's position on the human sentiments gives us insight regarding the matter. Or so I claim in Section III. The full account of moral deference is offered in Section IV, the final section. I maintain that the attitude of moral deference is, as it were, a prelude to bearing witness to another's pain, with that person's authorization—the person's blessings, if you will.

On my view, moral deference is the bridge between individuals with different emotional category configurations owing to the injustices of society. I

Reprinted with permission of the publisher from *The Philosophical Forum* XXIV (Fall-Spring 1992–93): 233–250.

do not claim that moral deference will serve as a bridge between intelligent creatures who differ radically in their biological constitution from one another, though moral deference may nonetheless be owed. Moral deference, as I conceive of it, is not about whether individuals are innocent with respect to those who have been treated unjustly; rather, it is simply about the appropriate moral attitude to take when it comes to understanding the ways in which another has been a victim of social injustice. A person's innocence or lack thereof is irrelevant.

Social Categories

If one encounters a holocaust survivor, it would be moral hubris of the worst sort—unless one is also such a survivor—to assume that by way of rational imaginative role-taking, à la Kohlberg,[2] one could even begin to grasp the depth of that person's experiences—the hurts, pains, and anxieties of that individual's life. There is not enough good will in the world to make it possible for persons (who are not Holocaust survivors) to put themselves imaginatively in the mind of a Holocaust survivor, to do so simply as an act of ratiocination.

The slaveowners who lived among slaves and, in fact, ruled the very lives of slaves knew a great deal about slaves. In many cases, slaveowners knew more about the intimate lives of slaves than a person has the right to know about another's intimate life (unless such information is freely and voluntarily offered in a noncoercive context). Yet, for all that white slaveowners knew about black slaves, the owners did not know what it was like to be a slave. Naturally, there were slave uprisings; but no slaveowner knew what it was like to be a slave on account of being a victim of such uprisings.

If a woman has been raped, it is clear that the last thing in the world that a heterosexual man should say is, "I can imagine how you feel." A great many men can barely imagine or grasp the fear of rape that, to varying degrees, permeates the lives of women, let alone the profoundly violent act of rape itself. Few actions could be more insensitive to victims of rape than a man's supposition that via a feat of imagination he can get a grip on the pain that a victim of rape has experienced.

I am, of course, aware that heterosexual men can be raped. But given the assumption of heterosexuality, male victims of rape, unlike female victims of rape, do not in general have the awkwardness of seeking to be personally fulfilled romantically by forming a relationship with a person who belongs to the very same social category as does the person who has harmed them. Nor, in any case, do males have to contend with social attitudes—some subtle, some ever so explicit—that make them the target of sexual violence or that minimize the significance of their consent as an appropriate condition of sexual intercourse. Lesbians do not escape this latter injustice; gay men who have been raped do. Given the assumption of heterosexuality, while both a woman and a man have to recover from the mental anguish of having been violated, complete recovery for a man does not involve being able to have sex with a man again. Thus, a fortiori, complete recovery is not a matter of his being able to do so without that act conjuring up the pain of rape. By contrast, complete recovery for a woman is generally seen along precisely these lines. Hence, recovery for a heterosexual man involves nothing like the phenomenal ambivalence that it involves for a woman.

Why is it that we cannot simply imaginatively put ourselves in the shoes of a Holocaust survivor or, in the case of a man, in the shoes of a rape victim? The answer is painfully obvious: even if we had a complete description of the person's experiences, we would nonetheless not be the subject of those experiences. Nor would we have the painful memory of being the subject of those experiences. So a description, no matter how full and complete, would fail on two counts to capture the subjective element of an experience. The latter count—namely, the memories—is far from trivial, because part of the way in which experiences shape our lives is through the memories of them impressing themselves upon our lives. In fact, there are times when the impact of a bad experience upon our lives would be virtually nugatory but for the way in which our lives are affected by the memories of it.

Suppose that one has been robbed at gunpoint. The actual loss may not amount to much at all, say \$20 or \$30. Suppose one has not suffered any physical or mental abuse, since two police officers came on the scene just in time. Yet, the event may alter the way in which one lives for years to come. Of course, one will realize how lucky one was. It is just that one cannot help thinking about what might have happened but for a fluke of luck—a mode of thought that very nearly cripples one emotionally. Rehearsing an experience in one's mind can frighteningly reveal just how lucky one was. A woman who has been raped can be having sex with her male partner, which has been ever so explicitly consensual, only to find that she can no longer continue the act because she has suddenly been assailed by the painful memories of being raped.

No amount of imagination in the world can make it the case that one has the subjective imprimatur of the experiences and memories of another. And an individual's subjective imprimatur makes a very real difference. Let me tie some things together.

There can be appropriate and inappropriate responses to the moral pain of another. When a person has suffered a grave misfortune the type of moral response that will serve to help that person to recover must be sensitive to the adverse ways in which the misfortune is likely to affect her or his life. This includes not just the physical damage that has been wrought to the person's body, but the ways in which the person will be haunted by painful memories, the person's feelings of emotional and social vulnerability, and so on. For as I have noted, the bodily damage can, itself, be negligible. It is not in the damage done to the body that the horror of armed robbery necessarily lies—since there might be none—but in the damage done to the victim's sense of self. Again, while rape can certainly be physically violent, it need not be, as the idea gaining acceptance of acquaintance rape reveals.[3]

Now to be sure, there are many misfortunes, at the hands of other, which any human being can experience, and so which are independent of social categories. We may think of these as generalized misfortunes. Anyone can be robbed, or be the victim of a car accident caused by an intoxicated driver, or be hit by a stray bullet. Anyone can lose a loved one owing to a flagrant disregard for human rights. These misfortunes do not know the boundaries of social categories. And though there can be difficulties, perhaps insuperable ones in some instances, with how to individuate (events that are) misfortunes, when people have experienced generalized misfortunes of the same type, then they have considerable insight into one another's suffering. The experience of losing a leg as a teenager is perhaps qualitatively different from that of losing a leg as an adult of 50, but no doubt the two experiences are far closer qualitatively than is either to the experience of losing a parent as a teenager or as an adult of 50. And between two teenagers both of whom lose a leg, it perhaps matters if one is an athlete and one is not.[4]

To be contrasted with generalized misfortunes are misfortunes that are quite tied to diminshed social categories–misfortunes owing to oppressive, if not prevailing, negative attitudes about the members of well-defined diminished social categories. As it happens, the diminished social category may be coextensive with a natural category, as may be the case with gender.[5] I shall use the euphemism "hostile misfortunes" to refer to these misfortunes, where "hostile" is intended to capture both that the misfortune is owing to agency and that the agency, with respect to the relevant set of acts, is owing to morally objectionable attitudes regarding the diminished social category. I shall often refer to a person in such a category as a category person.

Not everyone in a diminished social category experiences all, and to the same extent, the hostile misfortunes specific to that category, but being in a diminished social category makes it exceedingly likely that one's life will be tinged with some of the hostile misfortunes specific to that diminished social category. Moreover, if one is not in that diminished social category, the likelihood of one's experiencing any of the hostile misfortunes will be virtually nil. I regard gender, ethnicity, and race as obviously involving diminished social categories of this kind, though there need not be hostile misfortunes specific to every ethnic and racial group. Although people of the same diminished social category do not all endure the same hostile experiences, the relevant experiential psychological distances between their lives will be less than such distances between their lives and the lives of those who do not belong to any diminished social category or to a very different one. Interestingly, there can be subgroups within a diminished social category, and hostile misfortunes tied to those subgroups. For instance, there are very light-complexioned blacks (some of whom are phenotypically indistinguishable from whites) and there are darker-complexioned blacks; and each subgroup has its own hostile misfortunes, in addition to those associated simply with being black. Finally, it is possible for the hostile misfortunes of two different diminished social categories to parallel one another to a considerable degree. Such may be the case with the hostile misfortunes of African-American and Hispanic-American peoples. Individuals from these groups do not experience exactly the same hostile misfortunes. But there appears to be considerable overlap. The hostile misfortunes of a diminished social category group need not be fixed. Hence, there could be less overlap between two groups at one time than at another time.

As with generalized misfortunes, though, I shall assume that when two people of the same diminished social category experience the same type of hostile misfortune, then they have considerable insight into one another's experiencing of that misfortune. Of course, the problem of individuating types of events does not disappear here. Numerous refinements are possible. However, I shall leave such matters aside. Furthermore, there is the very thorny issue of when the hostile misfortunes of two diminished social category groups are similar enough to one another that each group has some insight into the moral pains of the other. There is certainly no reason to rule this out of court on conceptual grounds; on the other hand, one of the worst mistakes that can be made is for one diminished social category group to assume, without having attended to the matter, that its suffering gives it insight into the suffering of another diminished social category group. But this issue, too, I shall leave aside.

Now, the knowledge that someone belongs to a diminished social category group does not, in and of itself, give one insight into the subjective imprimatur of that individual's experiences of and memories stemming from the hostile misfortunes tied to the category to which the person belongs. If so, then a very pressing question is: how is it possible to be morally responsive in the appropriate way to those belonging to a diminished social category if one does not belong to that category? Here is where moral deference enters into the picture, though first more needs to be said about being a member of a diminished social category.

Being Socially Constituted

David Hume observed that "Human nature cannot by any means subsist, without the association of individuals ..."[6] His point can be rendered in a contemporary vein as follows: we are constituted through others, by which I mean that the way in which we conceive of ourselves is, at least in part, owing to how others conceive of us, and necessarily so. The way in which we think of ourselves is inextricably tied to the way in which others think of us. In a fully just world, all would be constituted through others so as to be full and equal members of society. That is, each member would be constituted so as to see her or himself in this way. By contrast, in an oppressive society, the victims of oppression—diminished social category persons, I mean—are constituted, in both masterfully subtle ways and in ever so explicit ways, so as not to see themselves as full and equal members of society. I shall refer to this as downward social constitution. Each group of diminished social category persons in society experiences different forms of downward social constitution, although I have allowed that there may be overlap. Painfully, social groups that are themselves victims of downward social constitution may engage in downward social constitution of one another. Victims of sexism can be antisemitic; victims of racism can be sexist. And so on for each diminished social category group. Even worse, perhaps, there can be downward social constitution by members within a group. In an oppressive society, downward social constitution is an ongoing and pervasive phenomenon, which is not to deny that there can be pockets of relief to varying degrees. Needless to say, a society with diminished social categories will have one or more privileged social categories, the members of which are favored and have full access to the goods of society.

One of the most important ways in which downward social constitution occurs pertains to expectations. It is just assumed, often without awareness of what is being done, that this or that category person cannot measure up in an important way. The reality that we do not expect much of a person on account of her category can be communicated in a thousand and one ways. One may listen inattentively, or interrupt ever so frequently, or not directly respond to what the person actually says, or not respond with the seriousness that is appropriate to the persons concerned. Most significantly, owing to meager expectations, one may fail to five the benefit of the doubt to the diminished social category person. We often do not realize that we are participating in the downward constitution of others because communicating favorable and negative expectations with regard to others is a natural part of life. Further, behavior that contributes to the downward constitution of another may manifest itself in other contexts that have nothing to do with downward constitution. After all, one can listen inattentively simply because one is preoccupied. Or, one can fail to respond directly because one misunderstood what the person said. Accordingly, negative expectations toward a member of a diminished social category need not feel any different from negative expectations toward any other member of society, nor need the behavior bear a special mark. Except for the blatant bigot or sexist, participating in the downward social constitution of another rarely has any special phenomenological feel to it.

Thus, it is interesting that for most people the evidence that they do not engage in downwardly constituting behavior is that they do not have the appropriate feelings. It is true that if one has and sustains the appropriate feelings, then one is an X-ist (racist, sexist, and so forth), or one has acted in an X-ist way if such feelings fuel one's behavior; on the other hand, it is manifestly false that if one lacks such feelings, the X-ism is not a part of one's life.

I have said that in an oppressive society downward social constitution is an ongoing and pervasive phenomenon despite pockets of relief. Such constitution may show up in advertisement, in the casting of characters for a film (play or television program), in the assumptions about the interests (as well as professional aims and hobbies) that a person has or what such a person should be satisfied with. The list goes on. Further, an expression of downward constitution may manifest itself at almost any time in almost any context. An expression of downward constitution may come from those who are so eager to put up an appearance of caring that they deceive themselves in believing that they actually care. Such an expression may even come from those who in fact care.[7]

To be a member of a diminished social category group is invariably to have to contend with what I shall call the problem of social category ambiguity. Often enough the question will be: was that remark or piece of behavior a manifestation of downward social constitution or something else of both? It may not have been, but the very nature of the context and one's social reality as a diminished social category person does not allow one to rule out that possibility with the desired confidence. On the one hand, one does not want to accuse someone falsely; on the other, one may not want to put up with an affront owing to being a member of a diminished social category. Yet, there may be no way to inquire about the matter without giving the appearance of doing the former. Finally, there is the painful reality that one may not be able to share one's own feelings about one's social category status with those who do not belong to that category, without giving the impression of being overly concerned with such matters—even with those who regard themselves as friends. It is a reality that sometimes requires a kind of profound disassociation from one's own experiences, at least momentarily.

Together, these things all speak to a profound sense of vulnerability that comes with being a member of a diminished social category. Part of that vulnerability is owing not just to being a subject of downward social constitution, but to the memories of such experiences. Invariably, the diminished social category person will be haunted by some of these memories to varying degrees. Then there is the fact that a memory (sometimes painful, sometimes not) of an experience of downward social constitution can be triggered by any number of things, including the witnessing of another's experience of downward social constitution, or another such experience of one's own. There is a sense in which one can be assailed by the memories of past undesirable experiences. A diminished social category person is vulnerable in this way. People who are downwardly constituted socially are victims of a social claim about them—not just any old claim but the claim that they lack the wherewithal to measure up in an important social dimension. In this regard, diminished social category persons are vulnerable on several counts. First, there is the vulnerability owing to being weary of always feeling the need to prove that this social claim is a lie—if not to themselves then to others. Second, there is the vulnerability owing to the reality that there is almost nothing that diminished social category persons can do which will decisively establish the falsity of the social claim. Third, there is the vulnerability owing to the weariness of it all that stems from the feeling that one must speak up because no one else will, although one is concerned that continually speaking up will diminish one's effectiveness. Obviously, diminished social category persons cope with these vulnerabilities in a variety of different ways and with varying degrees of success. But successfully coping with a vulnerability is hardly tantamount to not being vulnerable, any more than not showing anger is tantamount to not being angry.

The remarks in the preceding two paragraphs are meant to bring out the sense of otherness that inescapably comes with being a person belonging to a diminished social category, the sense of what it means to be socially constituted as such a person. This sense of otherness is not something that a person who does not belong to one's particular diminished social category can grasp simply by an act of ratiocination. In particular, it is not something to which people belonging to privileged social categories can grasp. People who belong to a privileged social category can, of course, experience insults and affronts to their person, even at the hands of those belonging to a diminished social category. Indeed, privileged social category persons can experience these things precisely because they belong to a privileged social category. But, clearly, just as a person does not know what it is like to be a bat by hanging upside down with closed eyes, a person does not know what it is like to be a member of a diminished social category merely on account of having been affronted and insulted by diminished social category persons for being a privileged social category person. For the hallmark of a diminished social category person is that of being a person whose life has been downwardly constituted socially, with all that this implies in terms of vulnerability as noted above. A privileged social category person who has experienced affronts at the hands of diminished social category persons has no more had a downwardly constituted life on that account, with all that this implies in terms of vulnerability, than has a seventy-year-old person led a life marred by sickness for having had to spend three weeks at twenty in the hospital of exposure to meningitis and again at fifty for exposure to hepatitis.

Emotional Configuration

Hume seems to have held that if our natural capacity for sympathy and benevolence were sufficiently cultivated, we would have adequate insight into the weal and woe of others.[8] I disagree, although I think that his heart was in the right place. In a world without hostile misfortunes and diminished social category groups, and so without privileged social category groups, I think that Hume's position would, indeed, be correct or very nearly that. I hesitate only because it might be that even in a perfectly just world some differences might be impassable despite unqualified good will on all accounts. Hume's point holds given two assumptions: (a) the emotional capacities of people are essentially the same; (b) the configuration of these emotional capacities through society is essentially the same, the primary difference with respect to the latter being in their development. Thus, for Hume, Nero is simply one whose capacity for benevolence and sympathy virtually went uncultivated. By contrast, Hume thought it obvious that anyone who had benefited from some cultivation of these sentiments could not help but see that Nero's actions were criminal.[9]

Such social phenomena as downward social constitution and diminished social categories would not have occurred to Hume. Specifically, and more pointedly, it would not have occurred to him that a person's emotions could be configured along a dimension other than the extent of their cultivation, the case of gender aside.[10] So, given Hume's moral psychology, anyone whose capacity for sympathy and benevolence was properly cultivated was in a position to understand sufficiently the moral experiences of all others. I am suggesting that Hume's moral psychology must be adjusted to take into account the reality that the emotional makeup of persons can be configured along dimensions other than cultivation. There is what I shall call emotional category configuration.

In a sexist society, a politically correct male who abhors violence against females, and understands ever so well why a victim of rape would rather be comforted by a female rather than a male nonetheless does not have the emotional configuration of a female. This is because the kind of fears that he experiences when he walks alone at night do not have as their source a concern about sexual violence; whereas they do for a woman whether or not she has been raped.[11] In a sexist society, at any rate, the emotional category configuration of women and men are different. This follows from women and men being socially constituted differently.

Likewise, a white can be attacked by blacks, and that attack can be brutal and absolutely inexcusable. As a result, the person may be emotionally crippled in terms of his fear of interacting with blacks. This is painfully sad. All the same, this suffering experience does not parallel the suffering of blacks. His fear of blacks may very well be a reminder of the random brutality of some blacks and of the moral squalor in which some wallow. The experience may seal his conviction that blacks lack the wherewithal to live morally decent lives.

But for all of that, the experience will not be a reminder that he is a second-class citizen. It will not make him vulnerable to that pain. He will not have the pain of being scarred by those who in fact have power over so very much of his life. By and large, the white will not really have to concern himself with having to trust blacks who have power over him, as with a little effort and creativity the white can avoid situations of this kind; whereas for the black, having to trust whites who have power over him is a real possibility. So, whereas some physical distance from blacks, coupled with time, might serve to heal the wounds of the white, this healing route is not a genuine possibility for a black. This is yet another dimension along which the black will live with his pain in a quite different manner than the white. Certainly no innocent white should be a victim of black anger and hostility; certainly no innocent black should either. The moral wrong may be equal in either case. My point is that because the black and the white have different emotional category configurations, each will experience their respective pain in a radically different manner. While economic differences could be factored in here, I did not develop the point with such differences in mind. The force of the point is not diminished in the least if both the white and the black are quite upper middle-class people enjoying equal salaries.

A fortiori, we have a difference in emotional category configuration here rather than a difference in the cultivation of the emotions if we suppose that the black and the white went to the very same kind of schools, read many of the same books, and have overlapping interests and musical tastes. We can imagine that they have similar personalities, and have had similar maturation experiences and wrestled with many of the same issues. Nonetheless, it is most likely they will be socially constituted in different ways. In the case of the black, strangers might be surprised that he was not born poor, or wonder where he learned to speak so well. The police at the university where he has just joined the faculty might regard him with suspicion. Or, at the checkout desk at the university library, the staff person might ask him for a piece of photo-identification to confirm that he is actually the owner of the university library card (which does not have a photograph on it) that he presented. These experiences will not be a part of the white person's life.

The cumulative effect of these experiences contributes to the significant difference in the emotional category configuration of which I have been speaking. Time and time again, a well-off black must steel himself against such experiences in settings of equality, while a white need not. Ironically, some of the experiences of downward social constitution—some of the insults—that a black will encounter, the person could only encounter if she were well-off, since a black in the throes of poverty would be too far removed from such social situations in the first place.[12] A black American in the throes of poverty is not apt to experience racism in a Middle Eastern or European hotel by a white American.

Nothing that I have experienced in my entire life

had prepared me for the shock of being taken as a would-be purse snatcher in a Middle Eastern hotel by a white American who saw me enter the hotel lobby from the guest rooms. The person leapt for her pocketbook on the counter as if she had springs of her feet, although people had been sitting in the lobby all along. Worse still, she and I had been sitting in the lobby opposite one another only two days earlier. As I play back the experience in my mind, it seems so incredible surrealistic to me that I continually find myself stunned. Even granting racism, and that she had been robbed by a black man while she was in Harlem, just how reasonable under the circumstances could it have been for her to suppose that I was a poor black out to steal her purse? After all, it takes more than cab fare to get from New York, New York, to any place in the Middle East.[13] I have been called a "nigger" to my face three times in my life. One of them was in Harvard Yard between Widner and Emerson. If I were to walk around with a fear that whites might call me "nigger," I would surely be taken as mad by most of my friends and acquaintances. Or, I would be seen as having enormous and unjustified hostility against white.

Hume's moral psychology cannot account for the emotional vulnerability that comes with the above experience. This is because it would not have occurred to him that a person would be treated as anything other than a full citizen of the world on a par with all others—at least among other equally cultivated individuals—*if* the individual displayed the refinements of education and culture. It would not have occurred to him that persons displaying such refinements could be the object of hostile misfortunes. For on his view, the display of these things should suffice to elicit admiration.[14]

The Idea of Moral Deference

Moral deference is owed to persons of good will when they speak in an informed way regarding experiences specific to their diminished social category from the standpoint of an emotional category configuration to which others do not have access. The idea behind moral deference is not that a diminished social category person can never be wrong about the character of his own experiences. Surely he can, since anyone can. Nor is it that silence is the only appropriate response to what another says when one lacks that individual's emotional category configuration. Rather, the idea is that there should be a presumption in the favor of the person's account of her experiences. This presumption is warranted because the individual is speaking from a vantage point to which someone not belonging to her diminished social category group does not have access. It is possible to play a major role in helping a person to get clearer about the character of an experience delivered from the vantage point of an emotional category configuration. But helping someone get clearer is qualitatively different from being dismissive. Indeed, how a person feels about a matter can be of the utmost importance even if the individual's feelings are inappropriate, since inappropriate feelings can shed considerable light on the very appearances of things in themselves.

While I do not think that moral deference is owed only to persons of good will who are members of diminished social categories, my account begins with such persons. The assumption here is that in characterizing their feelings and experiences as diminished social category persons, those of good will do not tell an account that is mired and fueled by feelings of rancor and bitterness. This is not to suggest that persons of good will never experience tremendous anger and rage on account of experiences of downward social constitution. They sometimes do, and rightly so. Occasionally experiencing anger and rage, though, is by no means the same thing as becoming consumed by these feelings. A complete account of moral deference would have to be extended to include those who, understandably or not, have come to be full of bitterness and rancor owing to the ways in which they have been downwardly constituted socially. It becomes especially important to extend the account in this direction if one considers that oppression, itself, can render its victims so full of rancor and bitterness that the manifestation of these sentiments can blind us to their underlying cause, namely oppression itself.

Moral deference is meant to reflect the insight that it is wrong to discount the feelings and experiences of persons in diminished social category groups simply because their articulation of matters does not resonate with one's imaginative take on their experiences. Moral deference acknowledges a vast difference between the ideal moral world and the present one. In the ideal moral world there would be only one category of emotional configuration, namely the human one—or at most two, allowing for differences in the sexes. So, given adequate cultivation of emotions and feelings, everyone would be able to get an imaginative take on the experiences of others. Interestingly, this way of understanding the role of emotions in the ideal world might point to a reason for making them irrelevant entirely; for if rightly cultivated emotions would result in everyone's making the same moral judgements on the basis of them, then the emotions do not make for a morally relevant difference between people, at least not among those with rightly cultivated emotions. On this view, the emotions can only make a morally relevant difference if they are seen as a constitutive feature of what it means to be a person, and so of moral personhood. But, alas, philosophers often seem anxious to deny that the emotions have any moral relevance, in and of themselves, at the foundational conception of moral personhood.[15]

In a far from ideal moral world, such as the one we live in, which privileges some social categories and diminishes others, it stands to reason that there will be emotional boundaries between people, owing to what I have called emotional category configuration. This is one of the bitter fruits of immorality. Recall Hume's question: "In morals, too, is not the tree known by its fruits?" The idea of moral deference is true to the moral reality that the mark of an immoral society is the erection of emotional walls between persons. It is true to the reality that social immorality cannot be eliminated in the absence of a firm grasp of how it has affected its victims. It is not enough to be confident that social immorality harms. One must also be sensitive to the way in which it harms. Thus, the idea of moral deference speaks to an attitude that a morally decent person should have in an immoral society.

We can best get at what moral deference involves, and its importance, by thinking of what it means to bear witness to another's moral pain with that person's authorization. To bear witness to the moral pain of another, say, Leslie, with Leslie's authorization, is to have won her confidence that one can speak informedly and with conviction on her behalf to another about the moral pain she has endured. It is to have won her confidence that one will tell her story with her voice, and not with one's own voice. Hence, it is to have won her trust that one will render salient what was salient for her in the way that it was salient for her; that one will represent her struggle to cope in the ways that she has been in getting on with her life; that one will convey desperation where desperation was felt, and hurt where hurt was felt. And so on.

To bear witness to Leslie's pain is not to tell Leslie's story of pain as a means to explicating how her pain has affected one's own life. Accordingly, to be authorized by Leslie to bear witness to her pain is to have won her confidence that her story of pain will not take a back seat to telling one's own story of pain as caused by her story. Not that it will always be impossible for people to make reasonable inferences about how one has been affected. It stands to reason that how one has been affected will surely be obvious in some cases. Rather, whatever inferences reasonable people might be able to draw, the point of bearing witness to the moral pain of another will not be so that others can see how one has been affected by the other person's pain. Thus, to be authorized to bear witness for another is to have won her confidence that one will tell her story with a certain motivational structure.

Now, it may be tempting to think that bearing witness to the moral pain of others requires something amounting to a complete diminution of the self, to becoming a mere mouthpiece for another. But this is to think of bearing witness to the moral pain of others as something that happens to one—a state that one falls into or whatever. Perhaps there are such cases of bearing witness. I do not write with them in mind, however. Instead, as I conceive of the idea, bearing witness to the moral pain of another is very much an act of agency and, as such, it can be an extremely courageous thing to do. During the time of slavery, whites who endeavored to bear witness to the moral pain of blacks were sometimes called "nigger lovers." In Nazi Germany, some who endeavored to bear witness to the moral pain of the Jews were killed. Nowadays, those who endeavor to bear witness to the moral pain of lesbians and homosexuals are often branded as such themselves. Far from being an activity only for the faint of heart, bearing witness to the moral pain of others can require extraordinary courage and resoluteness of will.

Well, needless to say, there can be no bearing witness, as I have explicated it, to the moral pain of another without having heard his story and heard it well. One will have had to have heard the glosses on the story and the nuances to the story. One will have had to have been sensitive to the emotions that manifested themselves as the story was told, and to the vast array of nonverbal behavior with which the story was told. One will have to have heard his story well enough to have insight into how his life has been emotionally configured by his experiences. One rightly authorizes a person to bear witness to his moral pain only if these things are true.

To have such insight into another's moral pain will not be tantamount to having that person's fears or being haunted by his memories, but it will entail having a sense of the kinds of things and circumstances that will trigger his fears and memories. It will not entail being vulnerable when he is downwardly constituted on account of his diminished social category, but it will entail a sense of the kinds of social circumstances that will give rise to such vulnerability. Moreover, it will entail being appropriately moved on account of these things. To have such insight is to be in as good a position as one can be to understand while yet lacking a complete grasp of another's moral pain.

Moral deference, then, is the act of listening that is preliminary to bearing witness to another's moral pain, but without bearing witness to it. I do not see the step from moral deference to bearing witness as an easy one. A person may lack the fortitude or courage to bear witness, however well he might listen. Moral deference in not about bearing witness. It is about listening, in the ways characterized above, until one has insight into the character of the other's moral pain, and so how he has been emotionally configured by it. In any case, moral deference may be appropriate on occasions when bearing witness is not. You may not want me to bear witness to your moral pain; yet, you may be deeply gratified that I have listened well enough that I could in the ever so unlikely event that you should want me to.

Moral deference, too, is not an activity for the faint of heart. For it is a matter of rendering oneself open to another's concern, and to letting another's pain reconstitute one so much that one comes to have a new set of sensibilities—a new set of moral lenses if you will. Moral deference is rather like the moral equivalent of being nearsighted, putting on a pair of glasses for the first time, and discovering just how much out there one had been missing. Of course, one had always seen trucks, cars, people, and so forth. But there were designs on cars and trucks, and sayings on shirts, and facial expressions that people displayed, and minute movements that people made, and slight variances in colors—none of which one could see at a distance. With moral deference one acquires sensibility to the way in which a self-respecting oppressed person lives in the world. Hence, to engage in moral deference is to allow oneself to become affected in a direct interpersonal way by the injustices of this world. While not the only way in which to do this, it is a very important way in which to do this. Thus, it is a fundamentally important mode of moral learning. It is a mode of moral learning which those who have been oppressed are owed in the name of eliminating the very state of their oppression. In the absence of such learning, oppression cannot but continue to be a part of the fabric of the moral life. Indeed, the absence of such learning, the studied refusal to engage in such learning, is one of the very ways in which oppression manifests itself. Worse, such studied refusal to learn adds insult to injury.

Significantly, moral deference involves earning the trust of another—in particular, the trust of one who has been oppressed. And earning the trust of another, especially someone who is weary of trusting anyone from a different social category (diminished or privileged), is an act of great moral responsibility—something not to be taken lightly in the least. It would be morally egregious in the very worst of ways to earn such a person's trust, and then abuse it or merely withdraw from the person. If the struggle for equality is ever to be won, we must be strong enough to be vulnerable. That is, we must be strong enough to prove ourselves worthy of the trust of those whom we have oppressed. This is well-nigh impossible in the absence of moral deference given to those whom we have oppressed. Moral deference is by no means a weakness. It is quite a matter of courage, instead.

In an important essay entitled "The Need for More than Justice," Annette Baier explains the significance of departing from John Rawls's claim that justice is the first virtue of social justice.[16] One thing that is needed is the appropriate moral posture toward those who have been oppressed. Without it, we often blithely trample upon those whom we mean to help. The notion of moral deference is meant to give expression to one aspect of what that posture calls for. It is impossible to responsively help those who have been hurt if one does not understand the nature of their pain. And while it may be true that we can know what is right and wrong behavior for others without consulting them, it is simply false that, in the absence of similar experiences, we can know how others are affected by wrongdoing without consulting them.

Let me repeat a point made at the outset: the idea of moral deference helps us to understand the inadequacy of the response that one has not contributed to another's oppression. To the extent that it is true, the response does not entail that one understands another's downward social constitution. Moral innocence does not entail understanding. Neither, for that matter, does good will. Nor does either entail that one has earned the trust of one who has been downwardly constituted by society. It goes without saying that the innocence of others should never be discounted; neither should it be trumpeted for what it is not, namely understanding and the earned trust of others.

A final comment: the account of moral deference offered suggests why both those who have been downwardly constituted by society and those who have not been should think differently of one another. If, as I have argued, those who have not been should be willing to earn the trust of the downwardly constituted, then the downwardly constituted must not insist that, as a matter of principle, this is impossible. Understandably, it may be difficult to earn the trust of those who have been downwardly constituted by society. And it may, in fact, not be possible for some outside of the social category in question actually to do so. But what has to be false is that, as a matter of principle, it is impossible for anyone outside of that social category to do so.

Apart from the context of the loves of friendship and romance, there is not greater affirmation that we can want from another than that which comes in earning her or his trust. If we should be willing to accept moral affirmation from others, then surely we are more likely to treat them justly. Moral deference embodies this idea.

Author's Note

This paper owes its inspiration to my 1991 winter quarter class on the Gilligan-Kohlberg debate (which I taught while visiting at the University of Chicago); Alison M. Jaggar's, "Love and Knowledge: Emotion in Feminist Epistemology," in eds. Alison M. Jaggar and Susan R. Bordo, *Gender/Body/Knowledge: Feminist Reconstruction of Being and Knowing* (New Brunswick: Rutgers University Press, 1989); and Seyla Benhabib's "The Generalized and the Concrete Other: The Kohlberg-Gilligan Controversy and Moral Theory," in eds. Eva Feder Kittay and Diana T. Meyers, *Women and Moral Theory* (Rowman and Littlefield, 1978). I see moral deference as a way of responding to the moral significance of the concreteness of other. I received instructive comments from Norma Field, John Pittman, and Julian Wuerth. At various times, conversations with Linda Alcoff, Alan J. Richard, Michael Stocker (always a present help), and Thomas Nagel (over the penultimate draft) were very helpful. A special debt of gratitude is owed to writer Jamie Kalven whose life reveals the richness that moral deference can yield.

Some recent works on the subject of racism have been most illuminating: David Theo Goldberg, "Racism and Rationality: The Need for a New Critique," *Philosophy of the Social sciences*, Vol. 20 (1990); Adrian M.S. Piper's paper "Higher-Order Discrimination," in Owen Flanagan and Amelie Oksenberg Rorty, *Identity, Character, and Morality: Essays in Moral Psychology* (Cambridge: Massachusetts Institute of Technology Press, 1990); Elizabeth V. Spelman, *Inessential Women: Problems of Exclusion in Feminist Thought* (Beacon Press,

1988). My essay has very nearly turned out to be something of a companion piece to Michael Stocker's wonderful essay "How Emotions Reveal Value" (unpublished).

NOTES

1. In *Mortal Questions* (Cambridge University Press, 1979).
2. *The Philosophy of Moral Development* (New York: Harper & Row, 1981). See especially the essay entitled "From Is to Ought: How to Commit the Naturalistic Fallacy and Get Away with It."
3. See, for instance, "Tougher Laws Mean More Cases are Called Rape," *The New York Times*, 27 May 1991: p. 9.
4. For a very important discussion of events, and their individuation, see Judith Jarvis Thomson, *Acts and Other Events* (Cornell University Press, 1977).
5. That gender is both a biological and a social category is developed at length in my essay "Sexism and Racism: Some Conceptual Differences," *Ethics* (1980).
6. *Enquiries Concerning the Principles of Morals*: (Section IV, para. 165).
7. For an absolutely masterful discussion of these matters, see Adrian Piper, "Higher-Order Discrimination."
8. *Enquiries Concerning the Principles of Morals*: V, pt. II, pars. 183, 189; IX, pt,1, par. 220.
9. *Principles of Morals*, Appen. 1, 241.
10. For an important discussion of Hume regarding gender, see Annette Baier, *A Progress of Sentiments* (Cambridge: Harvard University Press, 1991), pp. 273-75. Hume thought that women who desired to become wives and to bear children should be held to stricter standards of chastity than men. Cf. David Hume, *Enquiries concerning the Principles of Morals*, Section V, Section VIII, par. 215 and, especially, Section VI, part I, par. 195.
11. Perhaps male child victims of male rape can approximate such fears in their own lives. Still the adult life of such males will be qualitatively different from the adult life of females, owing to great differences in the way in which society portrays women and men as sex objects. See the discussion in Section I above. This, of course, hardly diminishes the pain of having been a male victim of child rape.
12. Bernard Boxill, in a very powerful essay, "Dignity, Slavery, and the 13th Amendment," has demonstrated the deep and profound way in which slavery was insulting. His essay appears in Michael J. Meyer and William A. Parent (eds.) *Human Dignity, the Bill of Rights and Constitutional Values* (Cornell University Press, 1992).
13. I was so enraged by the experience that it was clear to me that I had better channel my rage lest I do something that I would regret. Fortunately, I had a microcassette recorder with me. I walked the streets of Tel Aviv and taped the essay "Next Life, I'll Be White," *The New York Times Op-Ed* page (13 August 1990), an expanded version of which appeared in *Ebony Magazine* (December, 1990). It is, among other things, profoundly insulting when the obvious is discounted at one's own expense.
14. *Enquires Concerning the Principles of Morals*: V, pt. II-180; VIII.
15. Cf. my "Rationality and Affectivity: The Metaphysics of the Moral Self," *Social Philosophy and Policy* 5 (1988): 154-72.
16. Morality and Feminist Theory, *Canadian Journal of Philosophy*, Supp. Vol. 13 (1987). Rawls's first sentence is "Justice is the first virtue of social institutions as truth is of systems of thought," *A Theory of Justice* (Cambridge: Harvard University Press, 1971), p. 3.

    As I was typing the final draft of this essay, Martha Minow's book, *Making all the Difference: Inclusion, Exclusion, and American Law* (Ithaca: Cornell University Press), was brought to my attention. But I did read the Afterword in which she writes: "Claiming that we are impartial is insufficient if we do not consider changing how we think. Impartiality is the guise that partiality takes to seal bias against exposure" (p. 376). This essay points to a way in which that change must go.

STUDY QUESTIONS

1 In thinking about the examples that open Nussbaum's paper, whose views would you defend: Nussbaum's or those of the people at the conference she is critical of? What is Nussbaum's version of essentialism and does it avoid charges commonly leveled against essentialism? Provide reasons for your answers.

2 Do you think that Nussbaum's list of "essential properties" or human functions, what she refers to as the "thick vague theory of the good", captures what it is to be a human being? What would you add to or remove from the list? Provide reasons for your answers.

3 How does Crocker define international development ethics and what sorts of questions does it raise about who can engage in this inquiry? What are the three main responses to ethnocentrism as outlined by Crocker? Do you find any of them satisfactory? Why or why not?

4 Outline Crocker's account of insiders and outsiders and his analysis of the advantages and disadvantages of each. Does his account answer some of the concerns raised by ethnocentrism?

5 Does Crocker's account of insiders and outsiders answer concerns that may have been raised by Nussbaum's essentialist account of human beings? Can Crocker's account of insiders and outsiders "further a global community and a global ethic"? Provide reasons for your answers.

6 What does Steele mean by "the new sovereignty"? In your view, is this a fair depiction of the current social movements for change in the United States? Why or why not?

7 Explain and evaluate Steele's claim that "in a liberal democracy, collective entitlements based upon race, gender, ethnicity, or some other group grievance are always undemocratic expedients. ... for in opting for integration, a citizen denies his or her impulse to use our most arbitrary characteristics - race, ethnicity, gender, sexual preference - as the basis for identity, as a key to status, or for claims to entitlement."

8 While Young's description of the two stages in the struggle of oppressed groups to achieve equality is similar to Steele's account, she draws conclusions quite different from his about the goal of integration and what is needed to achieve equality. How do the arguments differ? Whose account do you favor and why?

9 What does Young mean by a "politics of difference"? How does Young defend the view that a strategy of affirming group difference involves a "reconception of the meaning of equality" and a better way for achieving equality?

10 Compare and contrast Young's account of a politics of difference with Nussbaum's account of "essential properties" and Crocker's account of insiders and outsiders. Which underlying account of "human nature" do you favor and why?

11 What does Thomas mean by the term "moral deference"? Who is owed moral deference and why?

12 What sort of implications does moral deference have for the ability to speak for others; that is, to be able to understand and represent the experiences of those in a "diminished social category group" different from one's own? What implications does Thomas's account of moral deference have for the project of articulating a universal account of human nature?

SUGGESTED READINGS

Alcoff, Linda Martin. "The Problem of Speaking for Others." In *Overcoming Racism and Sexism* edited by Linda Bell and David Blumenfeld. Lanham, MD: Rowman & Littlefield, 1995.

Appiah, Kwame Anthony. "Cosmopolitan Patriots." *Critical Inquiry*, v. 23 (Spring 1997): 617-639.

Benhabib, Seyla. "Cultural Complexity, Moral Interdependence, and the Global Dialogical Community. In

Women, Culture and Development: A Study of Human Capabilities edited by Martha Nussbaum and Jonathan Glover. Oxford: Clarendon Press, 1995.

Cohen, G. A. "Equality of What? On Welfare, Goods, and Capabilities." In *Quality of Life* edited by Martha C. Nussbaum and Amartya Sen. Oxford: Clarendon Press, 1993.

Crocker, David A. "Functioning and Capability: The Foundation of Sen's and Nussbaum's Development Ethic." *Political Theory*, v. 20, no. 4 (November 1992): 584-612.

Frye, Marilyn. "Oppression." In *The Politics of Reality*. Freedom, CA: Crossing Press, 1982.

Glover, Jonathan. "The Research Programme of Development Ethics." In *Women, Culture and Development: A Study of Human Capabilities* edited by Martha Nussbaum and Jonathan Glover. Oxford: Clarendon Press, 1995.

Held, Virginia. "Reasonable Progress and Self-Respect." *The Monist*, v. 57, no. 1 (1973): 12-27.

Koggel, Christine M. *Perspectives on Equality: Constructing a Relational Theory*. Lanham, MD: Rowman & Littlefield, 1998.

Koppelman, Andrew. "Antidiscrimination Law and Social Equality." *Report from the Institute of Philosophy & Public Policy*, v. 16, no. 2 (Spring 1996): 1-7.

O'Neill, Onora. "Justice, Capabilities, and Vulnerabilities." In *Women, Culture and Development: A Study of Human Capabilities* edited by Martha Nussbaum and Jonathan Glover. Oxford: Clarendon Press, 1995.

Phillips, Anne. "Dealing with Difference: A Politics of Ideas or a Politics of Presence?" *Constellations*, v. 1, no. 1 (1994): 74-91.

Sen, Amartya. "Capability and Well-Being." In *Quality of Life* edited by Martha C. Nussbaum and Amartya Sen. Oxford: Clarendon Press, 1993.

— . "Equality of What?" In *The Tanner Lectures on Human Values* edited by S.M. McMurrin. Cambridge University Press, 1980: 195-220.

Young, Iris Marion. "Five Faces of Oppression." *Philosophical Forum*, v. 19, no. 4 (1988): 270-290.

— . "Polity and Group Difference: A Critique of the Ideal of Universal Citizenship." *Ethics* 99 (January 1989): 250-274.

CHAPTER FOUR

RACE AND ETHNICITY

One of the threads running through the readings in Chapter Three is that difference and discrimination are highly complex concepts. We may agree that discrimination is wrong when morally irrelevant differences determine how one is treated and shape one's life prospects, but there is a great deal of disagreement about what constitutes discrimination and how to eliminate it. In this and the next four chapters, this complexity is highlighted in separate discussions of the forms of discrimination that continue to be relevant and prevalent in a global context: race and ethnicity, gender, sexual orientation, differential ability and poverty. Most of the chapters in Part II include discussions of these forms of discrimination in contexts outside of North America. Many of the readings explore discrimination across borders and by North/Western countries against South/non-Western countries.They provide analyses that move the focus from individuals as such to the structures, practices, and political contexts that support conditions of disadvantage and inequality. Contributions by feminist, race, class, and disability theorists are vital to the examination of the difference that difference makes both across and within countries.

This chapter examines how race and ethnicity continue to be relevant to the perception and treatment of people even in the face of quite widespread agreement that racism is morally reprehensible. It opens with a reading by Kwame Anthony Appiah, who provides a conceptual clarification of racism as a way of exposing the underlying presuppositions to show how it works and why it continues to be prevalent. Appiah distinguishes three doctrines that fall under racism. He uses the term "racialism" to refer to the view that distinct characteristics such as morphological differences of skin color, hair type, and facial features, as well as differences in moral and intellectual capacities, divide people into a set of races. While he holds that racialism is false, he maintains that it need not be pernicious if, for example, one believes that positive moral qualities are distributed in ways that make races separate but equal. However, racialism is a presupposition of two other doctrines that have been the basis for a great deal of moral error and immoral acts.

Extrinsic racists believe that racial essence entails certain morally relevant qualities that warrant differential treatment for members of some races. Some extrinsic racists can be led out of their racism if presented with evidence, for example, that blacks are not less intelligent than whites. For an intrinsic racist, however, no amount of evidence that a member of another race is capable of great moral, intellectual, or cultural achievements offers any ground for treating that person as he or she treats someone of their own race. Appiah takes beliefs that are held about others despite overwhelming evidence to the contrary to be indicative of a cognitive incapacity, a deformation of rationality in judgment that results in racial prejudice for which training and treatment rather than reason may be appropriate. He is concerned mainly with racists who can be persuaded by reason to give up their racist beliefs, who recognize that racism violates the universal moral imperative of using only morally relevant grounds in making moral distinctions.

In the second reading, Lucius Outlaw traces what Appiah refers to as the science of racialism in the discipline of philosophy, where truth and the acquisition of it have been central topics. In Western thought, philosophers concerned with truths about human nature and human flourishing settled on the capacity to reason as the shared feature transcending accidental and arbitrary differences. However, this account of a shared capacity did not prevent the hierarchical ordering of human beings: some people, it was argued, had natures that differed with respect to the capacity to reason. While these views have been largely superceded, race continues to function in ways that order human groups both scientifically and socio-politically. Outlaw defends this grouping in current social movements that use cultural and biological characteristics as the basis of claims for social justice. He advocates a role for philosophers in developing a new form of "cosmopolitan" liberalism to replace the emphasis in universalist liberalism on truths about human nature. The goal of cosmopolitan liberalism, Outlaw argues, is not the elimination of race thinking or ethnic thinking, but the elimination of the socially divisive forms and consequences of race or ethnic thinking.

Marilyn Frye is also concerned with eliminating the socially divisive forms and consequences of racism. She recounts her own experiences of frustration and despair as a white, privileged woman trying to change attitudes. The solution, as she came to realize, was not to change her attitudes to people of color but to change what it meant for her to be white. She argues that being white is not a biological condition but a social/political category, one that holds itself together by rituals of unity and exclusion, that develops styles and attitudes of exploiting others, and that defines itself as the paradigm of humanity. Frye argues that just as masculinity and femininity are tied to certain conceptions and perceptions of what it is to be male or female, whiteliness is a deeply ingrained way of being in the world that is tied to being white-skinned. It is a way of being that is a monotonous similarity extending across ethnic, cultural, and class categories, one in which variations approximate or blend toward a norm set by elite groups of whitely people. However, whiteliness is not the same thing in the lives of women as it is in the lives of men. While whiteliness buys some respectability for women, it undermines feminist goals of women organizing to eliminate their oppression by encouraging alliances and solidarity with men.

As a social construct shaped by historical events and circumstances, whiteliness is entrenched and well-established, but Frye believes that it can be unlearned and deconstructed by practicing new ways of being in environments that nurture different habits of feeling, perception, and thought. In commenting on Frye's analysis of racism, Victoria Davion agrees that promoting white supremacy is not a matter of genetic coding but of social training and that ceasing to be racist requires more than simply believing in racial equality and consciously trying to promote it. She raises questions, however, with aspects of Frye's account of the monotonous similarity of whiteliness. Davion recognizes the characteristics of whiteliness in herself, but as a white Jew she also learned that white skin alone does not guarantee privileges. For some people, being whitely requires the erasure of ethnicity, which in turn confirms rather than challenges aspects of whiteliness that connect with other forms of racism such as anti-Semitism.

In the fourth reading, Mitsuye Yamada also explores ethnicity in the examination of issues of race and racism. She describes her experiences in the classroom to challenge the prevalent belief that Asian Americans are not oppressed and that their expressions of anger are unjustified. Yamada explains that stereotypes of Asian Americans, particularly of Asian American women as quiet, obedient, passive, and polite, contribute to these beliefs and result in a specific sort of oppression, the invisibility of Asian Americans. Invisibility, argues Yamada, has its source for Japanese Americans in their experiences of the internment camps in the United States during World War II, where conditioning shaped an attitude of resigned acceptance and beliefs that "natural disasters" such as internment camps were to be endured as inevitable and out of one's control. Invisibility continues to be a feature of the lives of Asian American women, whose protests and involvement in social movements fighting oppression are not heard or taken seriously.

The idea that perceptions of difference(s) affect how oppression is manifested and experienced is picked up in Uma Narayan's analysis of racism in the context of colonialism, the subjugation of people in distant lands by rich and powerful colonizing countries. Narayan shows how a discourse of care was used in projects of colonization to construct and perpetuate relationships of oppression between colonizers and colonized. Racists stereotypes of the colonized as childlike, inferior, and in need of guidance and rule by superiors justified the imposition of material and cultural benefits of western science, education, and economic progress as in the interests and for the good of the colonized. Narayan contends that this discourse of care resonates with contemporary debates about women and an ethic of care and shows how moral theories can be deployed in service of the ideological interests of those in power. She highlights two strategies for defeating this deployment of an ethic of care: using rights discourse to assert that the colonized and women share capacities that entitle them to the same rights as white colonizers and men and challenging the paternalistic project as based on force and exploitation rather than care. Narayan reexamines the relationships between rights and care discourses in an attempt to make both theories useful to a combined project of enforcing the claims of justice and promoting attentiveness and responsiveness to human needs. Sometimes struggles for greater justice can foster more adequate forms of care and sometimes cultivation of care can foster enhanced forms of justice.

RACISMS

Kwame Anthony Appiah

Kwame Anthony Appiah is Professor of Afro-American Studies and Philosophy at Harvard University. He is the author of In my Father's House: Africa and the Philosophy of Culture *(Oxford, 1992); co-author with Amy Gutmann of* Color Conscious: The Political Morality of Race *(Princeton, 1996); and co-editor with Henry Louis Gates, Jr. of* The Dictionary of Global Culture *(Knopf, 1997) and* Identities *(Chicago, 1995).*

Appiah argues that, while it is now commonplace to express abhorrence for racism, we lack an explicit definition and understanding of what constitutes racism. Appiah takes up our ordinary ways of thinking about race and racism in order to expose the underlying presuppositions. He defines "racialism" as the view that there are essential characteristics that allow us to classify people into distinct races, each of which shares certain traits and tendencies. He rejects this view as false, but explains that it is a presupposition for two distinct kinds of racism. Extrinsic racism takes racial essence to entail that members of particular races possess certain morally relevant qualities that thereby justify discrimination and differential treatment. Intrinsic racism is the view that the moral differentiation of races is justified irrespective of racial essence or moral characteristics. Appiah argues that both kinds of racism are theoretically and morally wrong.

If the people I talk to and the newspapers I read are representative and reliable, there is a good deal of racism about. People and policies in the United States, Eastern and Western Europe, in Asia and Africa and Latin America are regularly described as "racist." Australia had, until recently, a racist immigration policy; Britain still has one; racism is on the rise in France; many Israelis support Meir Kahane, an anti-Arab racist; many Arabs, according to a leading authority, are anti-Semitic racists;[1] and the movement to establish English as the "official language" of the United States is motivated by racism. Or, at least, so many of the people I talk to and many of the journalists with the newspapers I read believe.

But visitors from Mars — or from Malawi — unfamiliar with the Western concept of racism could be excused if they had some difficulty in identifying what racism was. We see it everywhere, but rarely does anyone stop to say what it is, or to explain what is wrong with it. Our visitors from Mars would soon grasp that it had become at least conventional in recent years to express abhorrence for racism. They might even notice that those most often accused of it — members of the South African Nationalist party, for example — may officially abhor it also. But if they sought in the popular media of our day — in newspapers and magazines, on television or radio, in novels or films — for an explicit definition of this thing "we" all abhor, they would very likely be disappointed.

Now, of course, this would be true of many of our most familiar concepts. *Sister*, *chair*, *tomato* — none of these gets defined in the course of our daily business. But the concept of racism is in worse shape than these. For much of what we say about it is, on the face of it, inconsistent.

It is, for example, held by many to be racist to refuse entry to a university to an otherwise qualified "Negro" candidate, but not to be so to refuse entry to

---

Reprinted with permission of the publisher from *Anatomy of Racism*, edited by David Theo Goldberg (Minneapolis: University of Minnesota Press, 1990): 3–17.

an equally qualified "Caucasian" one. But "Negro" and "Caucasian" are both alleged to be names of races, and invidious discrimination on the basis of race is usually held to be a paradigm case of racism. Or, to take another example, it is widely believed to be evidence of an unacceptable racism to exclude people from clubs on the basis of race; yet most people, even those who think of "Jewish" as a racial term, seem to think that there is nothing wrong with Jewish clubs, whose members do not share any particular religious beliefs, or Afro-American societies, whose members share the juridical characteristic of American citizenship and the "racial" characteristic of being black.

I say that these are inconsistencies "on the face of it," because, for example, affirmative action in university admissions is importantly different from the earlier refusal to admit blacks or Jews (or other "Others") that it is meant, in part, to correct. Deep enough analysis may reveal it to be quite consistent with the abhorrence of racism; even a shallow analysis suggests that it is intended to be so. Similarly, justifications can be offered for "racial" associations in a plural society that are not available for the racial exclusivism of the country club. But if we take racism seriously we ought to be concerned about the adequacy of these justifications.

In this essay, then, I propose to take our ordinary ways of thinking about race and racism and point up some of their presuppositions. And since popular concepts are, of course, usually fairly fuzzily and untheoretically conceived, much of what I have to say will seem to be both more theoretically and more precisely committed than the talk of racism and racists in our newspapers and on television. My claim is that these theoretical claims are required to make sense of racism as the practice of reasoning human beings. If anyone were to suggest that much, perhaps most, of what goes under the name "racism" in our world cannot be given such a rationalized foundation, I should not disagree: but to the extent that a practice cannot be rationally reconstructed it ought, surely, to be given up by reasonable people. The right tactic with racism, if you really want to oppose it, is to object to it rationally in the form in which it stands the best chance of meeting objections. The doctrines I want to discuss can be rationally articulated: and they are worth articulating rationally in order that we can rationally say what we object to in them.

Racist Propositions

There are at least three distinct doctrines that might be held to express the theoretical content of what we call "racism." One is the view — which I shall call *racialism*[2] — that there are heritable characteristics, possessed by members of our species, that allow us to divide them into a small set of races, in such a way that all the members of these races share certain traits and tendencies with each other that they do not share with members of any other race. These traits and tendencies characteristic of a race constitute, on the racialist view, a sort of racial essence; and it is part of the content of racialism that the essential heritable characteristics of what the nineteenth century called the "Races of Man" account for more than the visible morphological characteristics — skin color, hair type, facial features — on the basis of which we make our informal classifications. Racialism is at the heart of nineteenth-century Western attempts to develop a science of racial difference; but it appears to have been believed by others — for example, Hegel, before then, and many in other parts of the non-Western world since — who have had no interest in developing scientific theories.

Racialism is not, in itself, a doctrine that must be dangerous, even if the racial essence is thought to entail moral and intellectual dispositions. Provided positive moral qualities are distributed across the races, each can be respected, can have its "separate but equal" place. Unlike most Western-educated people, I believe — and I have argued elsewhere[3] — that racialism is false; but by itself, it seems to be a cognitive rather than a moral problem. The issue is how the world is, not how we would want it to be.

Racialism is, however, a presupposition of other doctrines that have been called "racism," and these other doctrines have been, in the last few centuries the basis of a great deal of human suffering and the source of a great deal of moral error.

One such doctrine we might call "extrinsic racism": extrinsic racists make moral distinctions between members of different races because they believe that the racial essence entails certain morally relevant qualities. The basis for the extrinsic racists' discrimination between people is their belief that members of different races differ in respects that *warrant* the differential treatment, respects — such as honesty or courage or intelligence — that are uncontroversially held (at least in most contemporary cultures) to be acceptable as a basis for treating people differently. Evidence that there are no such differences in morally relevant characteristics — that Negroes do not necessarily lack intellectual capacities, that Jews are not especially avaricious — should thus lead people out of their racism if it is purely extrinsic. As we know, such evidence often fails to change an extrinsic racist's attitudes substantially, for some of the extrinsic racist's best friends have always been Jewish. But at this point — if the racist is sincere — what we have is no longer a false doctrine but a cognitive incapacity, one whose significance I shall discuss later in this essay.

I say that the *sincere* extrinsic racist may suffer from a cognitive incapacity. But some who espouse extrinsic racist doctrines are simply insincere intrinsic racists. For *intrinsic racists*, on my definition, are people who differentiate morally between members of different races because they believe that each race has a different moral status, quite independent of the moral characteristics entailed by its racial essence. Just as, for example, many people assume that the fact that they are biologically related to another person — a brother, an aunt, a cousin — gives them a moral interest in that person,[4] so an intrinsic racist holds that the bare fact of being of the same race is a reason for preferring one person to another. (I shall return to this parallel later as well.)

For an intrinsic racist, no amount of evidence that a member of another race is capable of great moral, intellectual, or cultural achievements, or has characteristics that, in members of one's own race, would make them admirable or attractive, offers any ground for treating that person as he or she would treat similarly endowed members of his or her own race. Just so, some sexists are "intrinsic sexists," holding that the bare fact that someone is a woman (or man) is a reason for treating her (or him) in certain ways.

There are interesting possibilities for complicating these distinctions: some racists, for example, claim, as the Mormons once did, that they discriminate between people because they believe that God requires them to do so. Is this an extrinsic racism, predicated on the combination of God's being an intrinsic racist and the belief that it is right to do what God wills? Or is it intrinsic racism because it is based on the belief that God requires these discriminations because they are right? (Is an act pious because the gods love it, or do they love it because it is pious?) Nevertheless, the distinctions between racialism and racism and between two potentially overlapping kinds of racism provide us with the skeleton of an anatomy of the propositional contents of racial attitudes.

Racist Dispositions

Most people will want to object already that this discussion of the propositional content of racist moral and factual beliefs misses something absolutely crucial to the character of the psychological and sociological reality of racism, something I touched on when I mentioned that extrinsic racist utterances are often made by people who suffer from what I called a "cognitive incapacity." Part of the standard force of accusations of racism is that their objects are in some way *irrational*. The objection to Professor Shockley's claims about the intelligence of blacks is not just that they are false; it is rather that Professor Shockley seems, like many people we call "racist," to be unable to see that the evidence does not support his factual claims and that the connection between his factual claims and his policy prescriptions involves a series of non sequiturs.

What makes these cognitive incapacities especially troubling — something we should respond to with more than a recommendation that the individual, Professor Shockley, be offered psychotherapy — is that they conform to a certain pattern: namely, that it is especially where beliefs and policies that are to the disadvantage of nonwhite people that he shows the sorts of disturbing failure that have made his views both notorious and notoriously unreliable. Indeed, Professor Shockley's reasoning works extremely well in some other areas: that he is a Noble Laureate in physics is part of what makes him so interesting an example.

This cognitive incapacity is not, of course, a rare one. Many of us are unable to give up beliefs that play a part in justifying the special advantages we gain (or hope to gain) from our positions in the social order — in particular, beliefs about the positive characters of the class of people who share that position. Many people who express extrinsic racist beliefs — many white south Africans, for example — are beneficiaries of social orders that deliver advantages to them by virtue of their "race," so that their disinclination to accept evidence that would deprive them of a justification for those advantages is just an instance of this general phenomenon.

So too, evidence that access to higher education is as largely determined by the quality of our earlier educations as by our own innate talents, does not, on the whole, undermine the confidence of college entrants from private schools in England or the United States or Ghana. Many of them continue to believe in the face of this evidence that their acceptance at "good" universities shows them to be intellectually better endowed (and not just better prepared) than those who are rejected. It is facts such as these that give sense to the notion of false consciousness, the idea that an ideology can prevent us from acknowledging facts that would threaten our position.

The most interesting cases of this sort of ideological resistance to the truth are not, perhaps, the ones I have just mentioned. On the whole, it is less surprising, once we accept the admittedly problematic notion of self-deception, that people who think that certain attitudes of beliefs advantage them or those they care about should be able, as we say, to "persuade" themselves to ignore evidence that undermines those beliefs or attitudes. What is more interesting is the existence of people who resist the truth of a proposition while thinking that its wider acceptance would in no way disadvantage them or those individuals about whom they care — this might be thought to describe Professor Shockley; or who resist the truth when they recognize that its acceptance would actually advantage them — this might be the case with some black people who have internalized negative racist stereotypes; or who fail, by virtue of their ideological attachments, to recognize what is in their own best interests at all.

My business here is not with the psychological or social processes by which these forms of ideological resistance operate, but it is important, I think, to see the refusal on the part of some extrinsic racists to accept evidence against the beliefs as an instance of a widespread phenomenon in human affairs. It is a plain fact, to which theories of ideology must address themselves, that our species is prone both morally and intellectually to such distortions of judgment, in particular to distortions of judgment that reflect partiality. An inability to change your mind in the face of appropriate[5] evidence is a cognitive incapacity but it is one that all of us surely suffer from in some areas of belief; especially in areas where our own interests or self-images are (or seem to be) at stake.

It is not, however, as some have held, a tendency that we are powerless to resist. No one, no doubt, can be impartial about everything — even about everything to which the notion of partiality applies; but there is no subject matter about which most sane people cannot, in the end, be persuaded to avoid partiality in judgment. And it may help to shake the convictions of those whose incapacity derives from this sort of ideological defense if we show them how their reaction fits into this general pattern. It is, indeed, because it generally *does* fit this pattern that we call such views "racism"- the suffix "-ism" indicating that what we have in mind is not simply a theory but an ideology. It would be odd to call someone brought up in a remote corner of the world with false and demeaning views about white people a "racist" if that person gave up these beliefs quite easily in the face of appropriate evidence.

Real live racists, then, exhibit a systematically distorted rationality, the kind of systematically distorted rationality that we are likely to call "ideological." And it is a distortion that is especially striking in the cognitive domain: extrinsic racists, as I said earlier, however intelligent or otherwise well informed, often fail to treat evidence against the theoretical propositions of extrinsic racism dispassionately. Like extrinsic racism, intrinsic racism can also often be seen as ideological; but since scientific evidence is not going to settle the issue, a failure to see that it is wrong represents a cognitive incapacity only on controversially realist views about morality. What makes intrinsic racism similarly ideological is not so much the failure if inductive or deductive rationality that is so striking in someone like Professor Shockley but rather the connection that it, like extrinsic racism, has with the interest — real or perceived — of the dominant group.[6] Shockley's racism is in a certain sense directed *against* nonwhite people: many believe that his views would, if accepted, operate against their objective interests, and he certainly presents the black "race" in a less than flattering light.

I propose to use the old-fashioned term "racial prejudice" in the rest of this essay to refer to the deformation of rationality in judgment that characterizes those whose racism is more than a theoretical attachment to certain propositions about race.

Racial Prejudice

It is hardly necessary to raise objections to what I am calling "racial prejudice"; someone who exhibits such deformations of rationality is plainly in trouble. But it is important to remember that propositional racists in a racist culture have false moral beliefs but may not suffer from racial prejudice. Once we show them how society has enforced extrinsic racist stereotypes, once we ask them whether they really believe that race in itself, independently of those extrinsic racist beliefs, justifies differential treatment, many will come to give up racist propositions, although we must remember how powerful a weight of authority our arguments have to overcome. Reasonable people may insist on substantial evidence if they are to give up beliefs that are central to their cultures.

Still, in the end, many will resist such reasoning; and to the extent that their prejudices are really not subject to any kind of rational control, we may wonder whether it is right to treat such people as morally responsible for the acts their racial prejudice motivates, or morally reprehensible for holding the views to which their prejudice leads them. It is a bad thing that such people exist; they are, in a certain sense, bad people. But it is not clear to me that they are responsible for the fact that they are bad. Racial prejudice, like prejudice generally, may threaten an agent's autonomy, making it appropriate to treat or train rather than to reason with them.

But once someone has been offered evidence both (1) that their reasoning in a certain domain is distorted by prejudice, and (2) that the distortions conform to a pattern that suggests a lack of impartiality, they ought to take special care in articulating views and proposing policies in that domain. They ought to do so because, as I have already said, the phenomenon of partiality in judgment is well attested in human affairs. Even if you are not immediately persuaded that you are yourself a victim of such a distorted rationality in a certain domain, you should keep in mind always that this is the usual position of those who suffer from such prejudices. To the extent that this line of thought is not one that itself falls within the domain in question, one can be held responsible for not subjecting judgments that *are* within that domain to an especially extended scrutiny; and this is a fortiori true if the policies one is recommending are plainly of enormous consequence.

If it is clear that racial prejudice is regrettable, it is also clear in the nature of the case that providing even a superabundance of reasons and evidence will often not be a successful way of removing it. Nevertheless, the racist's prejudice will be articulated through the sorts of theoretical propositions I dubbed extrinsic and intrinsic racism. And we should certainly be able to say something reasonable about why these theoretical propositions should be rejected.

Part of the reason that this is worth doing is precisely the fact that many of those who assent to the propositional content of racism do not suffer from racial prejudice. In a country like the United States, where racist propositions were once part of the national ideology, there will be many who assent to racist propositions simply because they were raised to do so. Rational objection to racist propositions has a fair chance of changing such people's beliefs.

Extrinsic and Intrinsic Racism

It is not always clear whether someone's theoretical racism is intrinsic or extrinsic, and there is certainly no reason why we should expect to be able to settle the question. Since the issue probably never occurs to most people in these terms, we cannot suppose that they must have an answer. In fact, given the definition of the terms I offered, there is nothing barring someone from being both an intrinsic and an extrinsic racist, holding both that the bare fact of race provides a basis for treating members of his or her own race differently from others and that there are morally relevant characteristics that are differentially distributed among the races. Indeed, for reasons I shall discuss in a moment, *most* intrinsic racists are likely to express extrinsic racist beliefs, so that we should not be surprised that many people seem, in fact, to be committed to both forms of racism.

The Holocaust made unreservedly clear the threat that racism poses to human decency. But it also blurred our thinking because in focusing our attention on the racist character of the Nazi atrocities, it obscured their character as atrocities. What is appalling about Nazi racism is not just that it presupposes, as all racism does, false (racialist) beliefs — not simply that it involves a moral incapacity (the inability to extend our moral sentiments to all our fellow creatures) and a moral failing (the making of moral distinctions without moral differences) — but that it leads, first, to oppression and then to mass slaughter. In recent years, South African racism has had a similar distorting effect. For although South African racism has not led to killings on the scale of the Holocaust — even if it has both left South Africa judicially executing more (mostly black) people per head of population than most other countries and led to massive differences between the life chances of white and nonwhite South Africans — it *has* led to the systematic oppression and economic exploitation of people who are not classified as "white," and to the infliction of suffering on citizens of all racial classifications, not least by the police state that is required to maintain that exploitation and oppression.

Part of our resistance, therefore, to calling the racist ideas of those, such as the Black Nationalists of the 1960s, who advocate racial solidarity, by the same term that we use to describe the attitudes of Nazis or of members of the South African Nationalist party, surely resides in the fact that they largely did not contemplate using race as a basis for inflicting harm. Indeed, it seems to me that there is a significant pattern in the modern rhetoric of race, such that the discourse of racial solidarity is usually expressed through the language of *intrinsic* racism, while those who have used race as the basis for oppression and hatred have appealed to *extrinsic* racist ideas. This point is important for understanding the character of contemporary racial attitudes.

The two major uses of race as a basis for moral solidarity that are most familiar in the West are varieties of Pan-Africanism and Zionism. In each case it is presupposed that a "people," Negroes or Jews, has the basis for shared political life in the fact of being of the same race. There are varieties of each form of "nationalism" that make the basis lie in shared traditions; but however plausible this may be in the case of Zionism, which has in Judaism, the religion, a realistic candidate for a common and nonracial focus for nationality, the peoples of Africa have a good deal less in common culturally than is usually assumed. I discuss this issue at length in *In My Father's House: Essays in the Philosophy of African Culture*, but let me say here that I believe the central fact is this: what blacks in the West, like secularized Jews, have mostly in common is that they are perceived — both by themselves and by others — as belonging to the same race, and that this common race is used by others as the basis for discriminating against them. "If you ever forget you're a Jew, a goy will remind you." The Black Nationalists, like some Zionists, responded to their experience of racial discrimination by accepting the racialism it presupposed.[7]

Although race is indeed at the heart of Black Nationalism, however, it seems that it is the fact of a shared race, not the fact of a shared racial character, that provides the basis for solidarity. Where racism is implicated in the basis for national solidarity, it is intrinsic, not (or not only) extrinsic. It is this that makes the idea of fraternity one that is naturally applied in nationalist discourse. For, as I have already observed, the moral status of close family members is not normally thought of in most cultures as depending on qualities of character; we are supposed to love our brothers and sisters in spite of their faults and not because of their virtues. Alexander Crummell, one of the founding fathers of Black Nationalism, literalizes the metaphor of family in these startling words:

> Races, like families, are the organisms and ordinances of God; and race feeling, like family feeling, is of divine origin. The extinction of race feeling is just as possible as the extinction of family feeling. Indeed, a race is a family.[8]

It is the assimilation of "race feeling" to "family feeling" that makes intrinsic racism seem so much less objectionable than extrinsic racism. For this metaphorical identification reflects the fact that, in the modern world (unlike the nineteenth century), intrinsic racism is acknowledged almost exclusively as the basis of feelings of community. We can surely, then, share a sense of what Crummell's friend and co-worker Edward Blyden called "the poetry of politics," that is, "the feeling of race," the feeling of "people with whom we are connected."[9] The racism here is the basis of acts of supererogation, the treatment of others better than we otherwise might, better than moral duty demands of us.

This is a contingent fact. There is no logical impossibility in the idea of racialists whose moral beliefs lead them to feelings of hatred for other races whole leaving no room for love of members of their own. Nevertheless most racial hatred is in fact expressed through extrinsic racism: most people who have used race as the basis for causing harm to others have felt the need to see the others as independently morally flawed. It is one thing to espouse fraternity without claiming that your brothers and sisters have any special qualities that deserve recognition, and another to espouse hatred of others who have done nothing to deserve it.[10]

Many Afrikaners — like many in the American South until recently — have a long list of extrinsic racist answers to the question why blacks should not have full civil rights. Extrinsic racism has usually been the basis for treating people worse than we otherwise might, for giving them less than their humanity entitles them to. But this too is a contingent fact. Indeed, Crummell's guarded respect for white people derived from a belief in the superior moral qualities of the Anglo-Saxon race.

Intrinsic racism is, in my view, a moral error. Even if racialism were correct, the bare fact that someone was of another race would be no reason to treat them worse — or better — than someone of my race. In our public lives, people are owed treatment independently of their biological characters: if they are to be differently treated there must be some morally relevant difference between them. In our private lives, we are morally free to have aesthetic preferences between people, but once our treatment of people raises moral issues, we may not make arbitrary distinctions. Using race in itself as a morally relevant distinction strikes most of us as obviously arbitrary. Without associated moral characteristics, why should race provide a better basis than hair color or height or timbre of voice? And if two people share all the properties morally relevant to some action we ought to do, it will be an error — a failure to apply the Kantian injunction to universalize our moral judgment — to use the bare facts of race as the basis for treating them differently. No one should deny that a common ancestry might, in particular cases, account for similarities in moral character. But then it would be the moral similarities that justified the different treatment.

It is presumably because most people — outside the South African Nationalist party and the Ku Klux Klan — share the sense that intrinsic racism requires arbitrary distinctions that they are largely unwilling to express it in situations that invite moral criticism. But I do not know how I would argue with someone who was willing to announce an intrinsic racism as a basic moral idea; the best one can do, perhaps, is to provide objections to possible lines of defense of it.

De Gustibus

It might be thought that intrinsic racism should be regarded not so much as an adherence to a (moral) proposition as the expression of a taste, analogous say, to the food prejudice that makes most English people unwilling to eat horse meat, and most Westerners unwilling to eat the insect grubs that the !Kung people find so appetizing. The analogy does at least this much for us, namely, to provide a model of the way that *extrinsic* racist propositions can be a reflection of an underlying prejudice. For, of course, in most cultures food prejudices are rationalized: we say insects are unhygienic and cats taste horrible. Yet a cooked insect is no more health-threatening than a cooked carrot, and the unpleasant taste of cat meat, far from justifying our prejudice against it, probably derives from that prejudice.

But there the usefulness of the analogy ends. For intrinsic racism, as I have defined it, is not simply a taste for the company of one's "own kind," but a moral doctrine, one that is supposed to underlie differences in the treatment of people in contexts where moral evaluation is appropriate. And for moral distinctions we cannot accept that "de gustibus non est disputandum." We do not need the full apparatus of Kantian ethics to require that public morality be constrained by reason.

A proper analogy would be with someone who thought that we could continue to kill cattle for beef, even if cattle exercised all the complex cultural skills of human beings. I think it is obvious that creatures that share our capacity for understanding as well as our capacity for pain should not be treated the way we actually treat cattle — that "intrinsic speciesism" would be as wrong as racism. And the fact that most people think it is worse to be cruel to chimpanzees than to frogs suggests that they may agree with me. The distinction in attitudes surely reflects a belief in the greater richness of the mental life of chimps. Still, I do not know how I would *argue* against someone who could not see this; someone who continued to act on the contrary belief might, in the end, simply have to be locked up.

The Family Model

I have suggested that intrinsic racism is, at least sometimes, a metaphorical extension of the moral priority of one's family; it might, therefore, be suggested that a defense of intrinsic racism could proceed along the same lines as a defense of the family as a center of moral interest. The possibility of a defense of family relations as morally relevant — or, more precisely, of the claim that one may be morally entitled (or even obliged) to make distinctions between two otherwise morally indistinguishable people because one is related to one and not to the other — is theoretically important for the prospects of a philosophical defense of intrinsic racism. This is because such a defense of the family involves — like intrinsic racism — a denial of the basic claim, expressed so clearly by Kant, that from the perspective of morality, it is as rational agents *simpliciter* that we are to assess and be assessed. For anyone who follows Kant in this, what matters, as we might say, is not who you are but how you try to live. Intrinsic racism denies this fundamental claim also. And, in so doing, as I have argued elsewhere, it runs against the mainstream of the history of Western moral theory.[11]

The importance of drawing attention to the similarities between the defense of the family and the defense of the race, then, is not merely that the metaphor of family is often invoked by racism; it is that each of them offers the same general challenge to the Kantian stream of our moral thought. And the parallel with the defense of the family should be especially appealing to an intrinsic racist, since many of us who have little time for racism would hope that the family is susceptible to some such defense.

The problem in generalizing the defense of the family, however, is that such defenses standardly begin at a point that makes the argument for intrinsic racism immediately implausible: namely, with the family as the unit through which we live what is most intimate, as the center of private life. If we distinguish, with Bernard Williams, between ethical thought, which takes seriously "the demands, needs, claims, desires, and generally, the lives of other people,"[12] and morality, which focuses more narrowly on obligation, it may well be that private life matters to us precisely because it is altogether unsuited to the universalizing tendencies of morality.

The functioning family unit has contracted substantially with industrialization, the disappearance of the family as the unit of production, and the increasing mobility of labor, but there remains that irreducible minimum: the parent or parents with the child or children. In this "nuclear" family, there is, of course, a substantial body of shared experience, shared attitudes, shared knowledge and beliefs; and the mutual psychological investment that exists within this group is, for most of us, one of the things that gives meaning to our lives. It is a natural enough confusion — which we find again and again in discussions of adoption in the popular media — that identifies the relevant group with the biological unit of *genitor*, *genetrix*, and *offspring* rather than with the social unit of those who share a common domestic life.

The relations of parents and their biological children are of moral importance, of course, in part because children are standardly the product of behavior voluntarily undertaken by their biological parents. But the moral relations between biological siblings and half-siblings cannot, as I have already pointed out, be accounted for in such terms. A rational defense of the family ought to appeal to the causal responsibility of the biological parent and the common life of the domestic unit, and not to the brute fact of biological relatedness, even if the former pair of considerations defines groups that are often coextensive with the groups generated by the latter. For brute biological relatedness bears no necessary connection to the sorts of human purposes that seem likely to be relevant at the most basic level of ethical thought.

An argument that such a central group is bound to be crucially important in the lives of most human beings in societies like ours is not, of course, an argument for any specific mode of organization of the "family": feminism and the gay liberation movement have offered candidate groups that could (and sometimes do) occupy the same sort of role in the lives of those whose sexualities or whose dispositions otherwise make the nuclear family uncongenial; and these candidates have been offered specifically in the course of defenses of a move toward societies that are agreeably beyond patriarchy and homophobia. The central thought of these feminist and gay critiques of the nuclear family is that we cannot continue to view any one organization of private life as "natural," once we have seen even the broadest outlines of the archaeology of the family concept.

If that is right, then the argument for the family must be an argument for a mode of organization of life and feeling that subserves certain positive functions; and however the details of such an argument would proceed it is highly unlikely that the same functions could be served by groups on the scale of races, simply because, as I say, the family is attractive in part exactly for reasons of its personal scale.

I need hardly say that rational defenses of intrinsic racism along the lines I have been considering are not easily found. In the absence of detailed defenses to consider, I can only offer these general reasons for doubting that they can succeed; the generally Kantian tenor of much of our moral thought threatens the project from the start; and the essentially unintimate nature of relations within "races" suggests that there is little prospect that the defense of the family — which seems an attractive and plausible project that extends ethical life beyond the narrow range of a universalizing morality — can be applied to a defense of races.

Conclusions

I have suggested that what we call "racism" involves both propositions and dispositions.

The propositions were, first, that there are races (this was *racialism*) and, second, that these races are morally significant either (a) because they are contingently correlated with morally relevant properties (this was *extrinsic racism*) or (b) because they are intrinsically morally significant (this was *intrinsic racism*).

The disposition was a tendency to assent to false propositions, both moral and theoretical, about races — propositions that support policies or beliefs that are to the disadvantage of some race (or races) as opposed to others, and to do so even in the face of evidence and argument that should appropriately lead to giving those propositions up. This disposition I called "racial prejudice."

I suggested that intrinsic racism had tended in our own time to be the natural expression of feelings of community, and this is, of course, one of the reasons why we are not inclined to call it racist. For, to the extent that a theoretical position is not associated with irrationally held beliefs that tend to the *dis*advantage of some group, it fails to display the *directedness* of the distortions of rationality characteristic of racial prejudice. Intrinsic racism may be as irrationally held as any other view, but it does not *have* to be directed *against* anyone.

So far as theory is concerned I believe racialism to be false: since theoretical racism of both kinds presupposes racialism, I could not logically support racism of either variety. But even if racialism were true, both forms of theoretical racism would be incorrect. Extrinsic racism is false because the genes that account of the gross morphological differences that underlie our standard racial categories are not linked to those genes that determine, to whatever degree such matters are determined genetically, our moral and intellectual characters. Intrinsic racism is mistaken because it breaches the Kantian imperative to make moral distinctions only on morally relevant grounds — granted that there is no reason to believe that race, *in se*, is morally relevant, and also no reason to suppose that races are like families in providing a sphere of ethical life that legitimately escapes the demands of a universalizing morality.

NOTES

1. Bernard Lewis, *Semites and Anti-Semites* (New York: Norton, 1986).
2. I shall be using the words "racism" and "racialism" with the meanings I stipulate: in some dialects of English they are synonyms, and in most dialects their definition is less than precise. For discussion of recent biological evidence see M. Nei and A. K. Roychoudhury, "Genetic Relationship and Evolution of Human Races." *Evolutionary Biology*, vol. 14 (New York: Plenum, 1983) pp. 1-59; for useful background see also M. Nei and A.K. Roychoudhury, "Gene Differences between Caucasian, Negro, and Japanese Populations," *Science*, 177 (August 1972) pp. 434-35.
3. See my "The Uncompleted Argument: Du Bois and the Illusion of Race," *Critical Inquiry*, 12 (Autumn 1985); reprinted in Henry Louis Gates (eds.), *"Race" Writing, and Difference* (Chicago: University of Chicago Press, 1986) pp. 21-37
4. This fact shows up most obviously in the assumption that adopted children intelligibly make claims against their natural siblings: natural parents are, of course, causally responsible for their child's existence and that could be the basis of moral claims, without any sense that biological relatedness entailed rights or responsibilities. But no such basis exists for an interest in natural *siblings*, my sisters are not causally responsible for my existence. See "The Family Model," later in this essay .
5. Obviously what evidence should appropriately change your beliefs is not independent of your social or historical situation. In mid-nineteenth-century America, in New England quite as much as in the heart of Dixie, the pervasiveness of the institutional support for the prevailing system of racist belief — the fact that it was reinforced by religious and state, and defended by people in the universities and colleges, who had the greatest cognitive authority — meant that it would have been appropriate to insist on a substantial body of evidence and argument before giving up assent to racist propositions. In California in the 1980s, of course, matters stand rather differently. To acknowledge this is not to admit to a cognitive relativism; rather, it is to hold that, at least in some domains, the fact that a belief is widely held — and especially by people in positions of cognitive authority — may be a good prima facie reason for believing it.
6. Ideologies, as most theorists of ideology have admitted, standardly outlive the period in which they conform to the objective interests of the dominant group in a society; so even someone who thinks that the dominant group in our society no longer needs racism to buttress its position can see racism as the persisting ideology of an earlier phase of society. (I say "group" to keep the claim appropriately general; it seems to me a substantial further claim that the dominant group whose interest an ideology serves is always a class.) I have argued, however, in "The Conservation of 'Race'" that racism continues to serve the interests of the ruling classes in the West; in *Black American Literature Forum*, 23 (Spring 1989), pp. 37-60.
7. As I argued in "The Uncompleted Argument: Du Bois and the Illusion of Race." The reactive (or dialectical) character of this move explains why Sartre calls it manifestations in Négritude an "antiracist racism"; see "Orphée Noir," his preface to Senghor's *Anthologie de la nouvelle poésie nègre et malagache de langue française* (Paris: PUF, 1948). Sartre believed, of course, that the synthesis of this dialectic would be the transcendence of racism; and it was his view of it as a stage — the antithesis — in that process that allowed him to see it as a positive advance over the original "thesis" of European racism. I suspect that the reactive character of antiracist racism accounts for the tolerance that is regularly extended to it in liberal circles; but this tolerance is surely hard to justify unless one shares Sartre's optimistic interpretation of it as a stage in a process that leads to the end of all

racisms. (And unless your view of this dialectic is deterministic, you should in any case want to play an argumentative role in moving to this next stage.)

For a similar Zionist response see Horace Kallen's "The Ethics of Zionism." *Maccabaeau*, August 1906.

8. "The Race Problem in America." in Brotz's *Negro Social and Political Thought* (New York: Basic Books, 1966), p. 184.
9. *Christianity, Islam and the Negro Race* (1887; reprinted Edinburgh: Edinburgh University Press, 1967), p. 197.
10. This is in part a reflection of an important asymmetry: loathing, unlike love, needs justifying; and this, I would argue, is because loathing usually leads to acts that are *in se* undesirable, whereas love leads to acts that are largely *in se* desirable — indeed, supererogatorily so.
11. See my "Racism and Moral Pollution," *Philosophical Forum* 18, (Winter-Spring 1986-87) pp. 185-202.
12. *Ethics and the Limits of Philosophy* (Cambridge, Mass.: Harvard University Press, 1985) p. 12. I do not, as is obvious, share Williams's skepticism about morality.

PHILOSOPHY, ETHNICITY, AND RACE

Lucius Outlaw

Lucius Outlaw teaches philosophy at Haverford College. He is the author of On Race and Philosophy *(Routledge, 1996).*

Because one of philosophy's central concerns has been to provide accounts of what it is to be human in terms of reason, Outlaw explores the discourse of universal humanity that has dominated philosophy as a way of shedding light on issues of race and ethnicity. The impulse to structure the world by classifying things in it is evident in the history of attempts in philosophy and science to place people into distinct groups by providing accounts of their essential difference. While Outlaw rejects these sorts of biological accounts of group difference, he affirms the value of race and ethnicity as fundamental and positive elements of group identity and defends a cosmopolitan liberalism in which racial and ethnic diversity are respected and promoted.

Introduction

Millions of us throughout the world are living during very problematic and challenging times. The reasons are numerous and quite complex, made more so by much of what we might otherwise celebrate as milestones of human achievement in many areas: artistic creativity, material and agricultural productivity, science and technology, medicine, transportation and communication, the magnitude and velocity of knowledge and information accumulation and dispersal, and political transformations, to mention a few. A complete litany of the problems and challenges we face is unnecessary....

If we are to survive and flourish, we will, of course, have to find ways to meet the challenges and resolve the problems. However, since much of what confronts us today is made more complex and challenging by its relative uniqueness, we find ourselves without reservoirs of experience and knowledge that are directly and immediately applicable to the difficulties we encounter (for example: managing the now constant threat of conflict leading to the thermonuclear warfare and the real possibility of the elimination of virtually all of humanity). Consequently, we are compelled to forge new approaches—intellectual, moral/practical, institutional, or cultural in the larger sense—with all of the fear and trepidation, all of the risk, that such pioneering efforts embody.... And in the face of great challenges, often a near compelling strategy that is most readily available is to seek comfort in what seems to be the wisdom of sedimented knowledge and experience already at work in what we do at present. Yet doing so may well be to succumb to the inertia of the familiar but inappropriate.

Of course, we philosophers can tell the difference, can we not? For isn't this our calling: to achieve the foundational knowledge—the *wisdom*—that will make it possible for us to distinguish the *real* from the apparent, the *true* from the false, *appropriate* from inappropriate, knowledge that, in its timelessness and universality, is secure from the vagaries of historical changes? Or so we (philosophers) have said, and some of us continue to say. On this characterization of philosophy I should be able, if I am a *real* philosopher, to set forth the principles, and

---

Reprinted with permission of Quinnipiac College, Liberal Arts Department, from *Philosophy, Ethnicity and Race.* The Alfred P. Stiernotte Lectures in Philosophy (Hamden CT: Quinnipiac College, 1989) [edited].

strategies based on them, for meeting the challenges we face.

But I will not do so. First, because I am concerned only with a particular subset of challenges which are pointed to by the title of this lecture: namely, those of "race" and "ethnicity" in relation to "philosophy." I think these matters are sufficiently compelling to require at least some of our best effort, as I hope to make clear. Thus, I invite you to join me in wrestling with them. Second, precisely because I want to question this construal of philosophy as the chief executive of a timeless wisdom, particularly as it relates to the matters of race and ethnicity. The contribution of philosophy and philosophers to the successful resolution of challenges and problems is, I think, more limited, but potentially more valuable nonetheless, than keeping timeless wisdom.

Why race and ethnicity in relation to philosophy? In short, because I am convinced that we are living through a period in which race and ethnicity are so challenging to the prospect of our enjoying a future in which we can and will flourish that we are compelled to undertake a fundamental revision of some of our basic convictions regarding who we are, what our lives should be about, and how we will achieve our goals, both individual and collectively. Since such concerns have provided the motivating core for much of Western philosophy (and its sibling fields of inquiry) for more than two thousand years, and philosophy, in various incarnations, has contributed substantially to the accumulated store of knowledge that passes for wisdom with regard to these concerns, this review and revision calls, as well, for a reevaluation of philosophy itself.

Finally, there is the deeply personal dimension to my focusing on these issues, for they all come together in a poignant way to constitute my very being and to inform my daily life, and, thereby; to condition the lives of all who interact with me: I am a philosopher; I teach portions of the history of the discipline; but I do so as a person of a racial/ethnic group whose existence in America and throughout the world is marked by the holocaust of enslavement and other forms of oppression which have been rationalized by some of the "best" minds in the pantheon of Western philosophers. Thus, not only in practical living must I contend with constricting factors having to do with the politics of race and ethnicity, I must do battle, as well, inside the very citadel of reason where enlightenment leading to enhanced living is supposed to have its wellspring: in the practices and achievements of philosophy. As a person of African descent participating in the enterprise of philosophy, I have committed myself to confronting this seedy aspect of its underside and to the clearing of intellectual and social spaces in which we might come together to work and dwell in peace and harmony with justice. To this extent I take seriously the long-standing commitment of philosophy to radical critique leading to enhanced living, and seek to use this commitment against the discipline in the interest of the latter's refinement.

From "Universality" to "Particularity": The Politics of "Difference"

The challenge that is the focus of my concern is part of a much larger complex of practical and intellectual struggles, spanning many years, that recently have been grouped under the heading "the politics of difference." Examples include efforts to include persons from once excluded groups in educational, social, and occupational settings through the targeting practices of affirmative action programs; various struggles emerging from the contemporary women's movement; and, in general, the use of racial, ethnic, gender, and sexual lifestyle identifiers as the organization focus for politics and the bases for fashioning terms of justice.

What is shared by this wide range of endeavors is the attempt to revise both social-political life and intellectual domains and practices in order to facilitate the legitimate "play of differences," where difference is prized over forced homogenization—or the hegemony of one group and its values and practices over all others while masking this dominance in liberal, democratic dress. Central to this effort are two basic beliefs. First, that a full appreciation of what it means to be human requires that we take proper note of human groupings, the definitive characteristics of which (combining historically mediated physical, psychological, and cultural factors) are constitutive, in varying degrees, of the persons in the group. Second, that the principles on which we would base both the organization of sociopolitical life and those intellectual enterprises whose objects are living human beings take explicit account of these constitutive differences. Doing so, we proponents say, can and ought to lead to the acknowledged and promoted substantial enrichment of our collective life, given the wealth of messages, ideals, and practices contributed by various groups comprising our multidimensional social wholes (i.e., local, national, international). Not doing so results not only in our collective impoverishment, but, particularly when there is active opposition to those who are "different," this failure contributes directly to distortions of the cultural spaces we all occupy and to the deformation and self-deformation of members of those groups. Among the groups for whom these matters continue to be pressing issues are those constituted, at least in part, by factors termed racial and/or ethnic.

There are many aspects to the challenge posed by the advocacy of forms of political, social, cultural, and intellectual life in which the play of differences is a normative, nurtured feature. For this occasion I wish to focus primarily on what doing so requires of our basic conceptions of ourselves as individual persons and as ordered associates in sociopolitical structures and practices. And here, promoting the play of differences runs counter to some of the most basic tendencies of liberal democratic political thought and practices, and of modern Enlightenment philosophy on which it is based: namely, to look beyond what is often regarded as accidental differences, including race and ethnicity to the "substantial core" or *essence*, which, ontologically, is the definitive constitutive factor of the human species, and thus is shared by all humans. For a long time now, that essence has been identified as *reason*. Knowing and exercising this essence has been thought central to securing "universality" in epistemological matters as a foundation for unity and order in sociopolitical praxis.

For opponents of the project to give freer rein to the play of differences, emphasis on *particularity* subverts these quests and, in practical terms, threatens the always tenuous achievements of cognitive and political normativity thought to be secured by the universality of reason. The achievement and perpetuation of knowledge (in science and philosophy, for example) become exposed to the acidic effects of "relativism"; and the freedom, peace, and prosperity of political stability won through liberal (or, in today's terms, "conservative") politics are jeopardized by possibilities of drift, chaos, or, at worst, anarchy.

Such possibilities are real. Whether they are *probable* depends on a number of factors. But it is neither logically, socially, or historically *necessary* that such consequences follow from a greater play of differences. Achieving that increased play while preserving and enhancing social and intellectual life is precisely what I see as the challenge to be met in an appropriate valorization of race and ethnicity.

The Challenge to Philosophy

The challenge confronts philosophy directly. As I have noted, one of the central endeavors of Western philosophy continues to be that of attempting to provide the definitive characterization of what it is to be human (of what it is to be "man"). And, in general, the terms in which the characterizations have been and are articulated are void of any explicit references to race and ethnicity. Certainly the Enlightenment was a triumph of precisely this mode of characterizing humans. It was a triumph that made possible substantive progressive achievements in human history, won against some forces that, had they triumphed instead, would have given us a world not much to the liking of many of us, myself included.

But the victory was not without costs. At the very least, in focusing on what is shared in pursuit of unity and universality, the unique, the dissimilar, the individual, the particular is disregarded. And in doing so, a tension is created at the core of Enlightenment philosophy's view of man: between its specification of the shared and universal in the characterization of the human species that makes us all "the same" and its emphasis on the free, rational *individual*. Further, the aspirations of universalist philosophy notwithstanding, where *generally* race, ethnicity, gender, etc., were irrelevant to the formulations of key notions, the full truth of the matter discloses the ethnocentrism and racism, sexism, and class biases at the very heart of the enterprise: whether invoked in the Greek-barbarian distinction, the enslavement of non-Greeks and constraining of women when fifth and fourth century Greece was at its zenith, or in the continued oppression of women and the enslavement and oppression of African peoples during and after the modern Enlightenment.

Of course, one might argue that where we find racism, ethnocentricism, class bias, or sexism in philosophy it is due to the failure of particular thinkers to live up to the terms of humanism called for by the universalist notions of humans as rational beings—for some, created in the image of God—who are rightly worthy of respect, and that a correction of such situations requires only that the guilty parties come to be governed by the logic of these notions. Consequently, no revision of the central notions about man is required. I disagree. Not only is it necessary to extend the privileged notions to groups of persons previously excluded from coverage (e.g., women, Africans and people of African descent, other peoples of color), I hope to make a credible case that these notions, while substantive in many ways in contributing to our sense of ourselves, and thus to the organization of our individual and collective life, are also insufficient in ways that can only be corrected by revising them to include space for an appreciation of group-based particularities. We must rethink "*man*" if some of the challenges to practical life are to be overcome.

Will doing so constitute a retreat from the achievements of ancient and modern Western Enlightenments? It could, depending on how one proceeds. But it also opens us to challenging possibilities for social learning that may provide us with bases for enhanced living, for realizing futures which we otherwise might not live due to our failure to evolve. This is the possibility that I hold out to those who disagree with me and solicit, with thanks, your patience and attention as I present my case.

I shall do so by briefly rehearsing (from my perspective, of course ...) certain legacies of the enterprise of philosophy involving constructing and trusteeing the image of "man." My focus will be on the central roles of reason in these endeavors, particularly as they relate to the development of political strategies deployed in the organization and management of social life. I shall argue that at critical historical junctures reason is made a whore in service to politics when it is prostituted by fashioning and manipulating the "white mythology" of assimilated universalism through "melted" particularities as a masking apology for domination. But when those who would be melted refuse—or the politics of the situation in reality repudiate, in blatant self contradiction, their entry into the pot for the meltdown, even when they are willing to do so—we have conditions like those we are presently living through, in which the different and "unmeltable" force reconsiderations of the social project and of the understanding and the wisdom which would ground it. I will offer a modest proposal for that reconsideration.

Enlightenment through Philosophy: From Diversity to "Unity"

Philosophy: Architect and Custodian of "Man"

Certainly the narratives of Greek life and thought that have dominated philosophical discourses and provided much of the enterprise with a self-image and agenda have presented the fulfillment of the quest for wisdom as knowledge of what is beyond the merely apparent once it becomes clear that what appears to be the case may not always be so. Certainly sensory experiences cannot provide us with definitive knowledge of what is. Nor can history and tradition, or other modes of experience by way of the emotions, imagination, or spirit, provide assured guidance in practical life, across time, in a way that guarantees stability and insures that what is appropriate will always be chosen as the thing to do. The conviction of Heraclitus that all is change does not win out as the dominant philosophical orientation. Instead, it is replaced by a strategy that presumes that there is something more than the apparent, that change is a feature of some*thing* which undergoes changes, and that the goal of "true" knowledge is the uncovering or "illumination" of that something and the articulation of its character.

This strategy gives rise to other moves, one of which is particularly relevant to this discussion: namely, the gradual elaboration of a repertoire of hierarchical oppositions thought to be necessary for getting at the definitive structure of what *is* at its most fundamental level, with reason providing the means for distinguishing between them. Thus the distinctions between true/false, real/apparent, essential/accidental. Further, early in the game, a way of reading experience led to the conclusion that although there was change, all was not chaos: change, in most cases, was ordered (day/night; the seasons; the natural order of birth, development, decline, and death—and rebirth?).

The task of understanding man as a being subject to time was conditioned by this complex of intellectual strategies. From Homer onwards, speech and thinking—both referred to by the term *logos*, complemented by *nous* or "reason"—were thought by some Greek thinkers to be what distinguishes humans from other animals. These terms became integral parts of the philosophical self-image. Through these concepts and others ("truth," "goodness," "virtue," etc.), a fundamental, orienting, and *grounding* linkage was made between the microcosm of human existence and the macrocosm of the cosmos, between the divine mind and/or the governing principles and processes of the universe and the mind as the *essence* of the human. Logos was thought to be the code of being; the task of understanding (i.e., the proper and successful exercise of human logos or nous that resulted in the acquisition of knowledge) was then to grasp and decipher this code and to organize and direct human praxis, guided by the wisdom derived from the deciphering, or from the continued exercise and achievement of understanding.

Further, logos and nous were thought to be attributes that all humans share. Implied in this is the idea that humans are alike, thus are "unified" in and through logos and nous.

While this was not a generally shared notion at the time, it emerged in the thought of various persons across the years. More prevalent was the distinction between Greeks and barbarians, though the notion of a unified species that was nurtured by influential figures contributed to undermining it.[1] Among the contributors were Thucydides and the medical writers, who conceived mankind as a single species requiring rational study and did so via a biological approach which maintained humankind's unity but admitted its diversity while seeking a *reasoned* explanation of it in place of accounts supplied by tradition and prejudice. A major contributor, it turns out, was Socrates, who emerged in the period of ferment between the fifth and fourth centuries during which a number of key ideas appeared that were elaborated later:

> the notion of a single universal and permanent "human nature"; the belief that certain physical attributes are common to all men; the concept of a human unity made up of diverse elements; the rejection of traditional divisions between men as artificial and relative, not natural or absolute; the picture of "civilized man" as the human norm.[2]

Plato is perhaps the most familiar developer of these ideas in their full implications without, however, having worked out a particular treatise on the unity of mankind. Such a notion, instead, must be pulled together from his writings on the soul and other matters for which initial approaches were articulated by Socrates: namely, that the soul (psyche) is the vital part of us, the primary feature of which is logos, i.e., reason and articulate speech. Aristotle continued the exploration, making important contributions in his own right, in part by bringing together two lines of approach: on the one hand, the scientific tradition with its emphasis on the unity of the human species with egalitarian implications contributing to a disregard of accepted divisions among human beings; on the other, the idea of hierarchical gradations among persons based on defective *natures* that made for different possibilities for fulfilling the human *telos*, now identified with "rationality."[3]

Further, the task of determining all of this was assigned to philosophers by both Plato and Aristotle. On the basis of supposed certainty regarding epistemological matters, in conjunction with a particular philosophical anthropology, the Knowers were felt justified in rank-ordering groups of humans on the basis of judgments regarding their natures—a complex of generic features shared by the members of particular groups (e.g., females, children, non-Greeks, slaves). Aristotle's formulations in this area provided a powerful rationalization of Hellenistic practices.

"Reason" and Universalism: The Unity of Mankind

The Aristotelian strategy, building on Socrates, Plato, and others, who identified reason as a definitive feature of human animals, proved decisive, particularly in defining human diversity as a function of different natures. It was useful for some church thinkers during the Middle Ages and was put to work during the Enlightenment—the "Age of Reason"—even as the strategy of universalism was elaborated into explicit accounts of human nature that were to contribute to major political transformations that revolutionized Europe and what became America during the seventeenth and eighteenth centuries. A complex historical period, the Enlightenment is distinctive because of the decisive contributions of formal and popularizing thinkers—*philosophes* and philosophers[4]—to the elaboration of the ideas that became fuel for and rationalizations of the political transformations that led to decidedly new social formations. These thinkers help set the terms of and usher in modernity, an emergent historical conjunction, in part configured by social, political, economic, and cultural arrangements and developments at the core of which were a cluster of new ideas regarding reason, nature, and progress.[5]

For Enlightenment thinkers reason was a form of common sense enhanced by logical and scientific training. As with all physiological functions, reason, they thought, worked virtually the same way in all humans as products of nature's design. However, for these thinkers eighteenth century environmental conditions in the West—the wider cultural environment including church, state, social and economic class, ignorance, prejudice, superstition, poverty, and vice—had, in most humans, sufficiently corrupted reason to impede its normal and proper functioning.[6] But improvement was possible with the appropriate intervention, particularly through education, even though it might require an extended period of time. Progress—that is, historical development, orchestrated by reason, leading to the amelioration of corrupting, restricting conditions and thus to the fulfillment of human telos—would result from the reformation of social life guided by the "enlightened."

America—with its capitalist, so-called free enterprise economic order, its representative democracy structured by a host of rights, and its protected realm of civic privacy, all three resting on the universalized but privileged Enlightenment notion of man—is a paradigm of one complex form of a near successful Enlightenment project, Thomas Jefferson, a paradigmatic Enlightenment philosopher (and Ronald Reagan and George Bush claimants to trusteeship of the legacy?). Yet both America and Jefferson are also equally paradigmatic of the near self-contradicting tensions inscribed in the core of Enlightenment thought and practice: the universalist implications of the unity of mankind commitment to its philosophical anthropology anchored in its ideas regarding reason, on the one side; its attempt to manage human diversity by elaborating a hierarchy defined in terms of the purity, corruption, level of development of reason—or even the presence or absence of the ability to reason—in particular groups of persons, on the other.

The Whore of Reason: Managing Diversity through Hierarchy

Reason, Power, and the Other

For Jefferson and this nation, the enslavement of Africans was a crucible for the Enlightenment project. The institutionalization of slavery as a legitimate venture meant that a contradiction—between the universalism in the Enlightenment view of man, fueling the rationalization of the revolution and formation of the new republic guided by the principles of reason, and the rationalization of slavery, using hierarchically ranked racial distinctions—was firmly ensconced, practically and intellectually, in the heart of the great experiment called America. The compromise in behalf of solidarity among the colonies—increasingly regionalized by conflicting emerging political economies of neofeudal agricultural capitalism based on slave labor in the South and mercantile capitalism in the North and East—required a retreat from enlightened principles: reason became whore to political expediency. Or, as we might now say, the nexus of power and knowledge, with the latter serving the former, was demonstrated with brutal frankness.

But, as yet another rationalization: that is to say,

the deal was done with reason's sanction. Certainly, as noted, Aristotle had worked out a scheme in which the recognition of human diversity in terms of hierarchical ordering was in accord with reason: groups of persons differed as a function of their natures, which determined their end or telos, the most that they were capable of being when fully developed. In his words: "the nature of a thing is its end. For what each thing is when fully developed, we call its nature, whether we are speaking of a man, a horse, or a family. Besides, the final cause and end of a thing is the best.... "[7] The roles filled by persons of different groups demonstrated the practical truth of this "explanation" in Athens. Thus, it was "rational" to order social relations in such a manner that hierarchy brought the range of natures into functional relationships that were appropriate to those on each level: husband to wife; father to children; master to slave, Greek to barbarian:

> But is there any one thus intended by nature to be a slave, and for whom such a condition is expedient and right, or rather is not all slavery a violation of nature?
>
> There is no difficulty in answering this question, on grounds both of reason and of fact. For that some should rule and others be ruled is a thing not only necessary, but expedient; from the hour of their birth, some are marked out for subjection, others for rule.[8]
>
> [F]or in all things which form a composite whole and which are made up of parts, whether continuous or discrete, a distinction between the ruling and the subject element comes to light. Such a duality exists in living creatures, but not in them only; it originates in the constitution of the universe. . . .[9]

When Europeans encountered African "others," these valorizations were readily deployed in the rationalization of racial/ethnic differences into relations of superordination and subordination. Hegel, certainly one of the major figures of continental European philosophy, was quite explicit about the matter.

> Africa must be divided into three parts: one is that which lies south of the desert of Sahara—Africa proper—the Upland almost entirely unknown to us ... ; the second is that to the north of the desert—European Africa (if we may so call it) ... ; the third is the river region of the Nile....
>
> Africa proper, as far as History goes back, has remained—for all purposes of connection with the rest of the World—shut up; it is the Gold-land compressed within itself—the land of childhood, which lying beyond the day of self-conscious history, is enveloped in the dark mantle of Night.... The second portion of Africa is the river district of the Nile—Egypt; which was adapted to become a mighty centre of independent civilization, and therefore is as isolated and singular in Africa as Africa itself appears in relation to the other parts of the world.... This part was to be—must be attached to Europe....
>
> The peculiarly African character is difficult to comprehend, for the very reason that in reference to it, we must quite give up the principle which naturally accompanies all our ideas—the category of Universality. In Negro life the characteristic point is the fact that consciousness has not yet attained to the realization of any substantial objective existence—as for example, God, or Law—in which the interest of man's volition is involved and in which he realizes his own being. This distinction between himself as an individual and the universality of his essential being, the African in the uniform, undeveloped oneness of his existence has not yet attained; so that the knowledge of an absolute Being, an Other and a Higher than his individual self, is entirely wanting. The Negro, as already observed, exhibits the natural man in his completely wild and untamed state. We must lay aside all thought of reverence and morality—all that we call feeling—if we would rightly comprehend him; there is nothing harmonious with humanity to be found in this type of character....
>
> At this point we leave Africa, not to mention it again. For it is no historical part of the World; it has no movement or development to exhibit. Historical movements in it—that is in its northern part—belong to the Asiatic or European World. Carthage displayed there an important transitionary phase of civilization; but, as a Phoenician colony, it belongs to Asia. Egypt will be considered in reference to the passage of the human mind from its Eastern to its Western phase, but it does not belong to the African Spirit. What we properly understand by Africa, is the Unhistorical, Undeveloped Spirit, still involved in the conditions of mere nature, and which

had to be presented here only as on the threshold of the World's History.

Having eliminated this introductory element, we find ourselves for the first time on the real theatre of History[10]

This orientation rode the ships with the Europeans migrating to this land. It was literally made-to-order for the situation of compromise faced by the founders and had long been sanctified by various churches that worked out interpretations of the curse imposed on Adam and his progeny, as recorded in the Bible, so that one son was doomed to be forever marked by a dark stain (black skin?). In this historical case, the Other—Africans—had their difference fixed ontologically through reasoning strategies articulated by Aristotle, historically and culturally by Hegel, spiritually and biologically by the Bible, to mention just a few participants in this grand conspiracy. And "race" became a principal vehicle for this fixation. Universalism was reason-prepared, by both classical and modern Enlightenments, to handle diversity through reason-privileged hierarchy.

The Careers of "Race" and Ethnicity"

Constructing Others: "Race and the Evolutionary "Chain of Being"[11]

There is, of course, nothing more fascinating that the question of the various types of mankind and their intermixture. The whole question of heredity and human gift depends upon such knowledge; but ever since the African slave trade and before the rise of modern biology and sociology, we have been afraid in America that scientific study in this direction might lead to conclusions with which we were loath to agree; and this fear was, in reality, because the economic foundation of the modern world was based on the recognition and preservation of so-called racial distinctions. In accordance with this, not only Negro slavery could be justified, but the Asiatic coolie profitably used and the labor classes in white countries kept in their places by low wage.[12]

Race theory...had up until fairly modern times no firm hold on European thought. On the other hand, race theory and race prejudice were by no means unknown at the time when the English colonists came to North America. Undoubtedly, the age of exploration led many to speculate on race differences at a period when neither Europeans nor Englishmen were prepared to make allowances for vast cultural diversities. Even though race theories had not then secured wide acceptance or even sophisticated formulation, the first contacts of the Spanish with the Indians in the Americas can now be recognized as the beginning of a struggle between conceptions of the nature of primitive peoples which has not yet been wholly settled.... Although in the seventeenth century race theories had not as yet developed any strong scientific or theological rationale, the contact of the English with Indians, and soon afterward with Negroes, in the New World led to the formation of institutions and relationships which were later justified by appeals to race theories.[13]

For most of us, that there are different races of people is one of the most obvious features of our social worlds. The term race is thus a vehicle for beliefs and values deployed in the organization of our life-worlds and to structure our encounters and relations with persons who are significantly different from us in terms of physical features (skin color and other anatomical characteristics) and, combined with these, differences in language, behavior, ideas, and other cultural matters. In the United States especially, race is a constitutive element of our common sense, [and] thus is a key component of our "taken-for-granted valid reference schema" through which we get on in the world.[14] And, as we constantly face the need to resolve difficulties posing varying degrees of danger to the social whole in which race is the hidden or focal point of contention (or serves as a shorthand explanation for the source of contentious differences), we are reinforced in our assumption that race is self-evident. True to the prediction of W.E.B Du Bois, the twentieth century has indeed been dominated by "the problem of the color line," and is likely to be so for the remainder of the century and well into the next. In particular, we are confronted by the need to face a persistent problem within Western societies, one that, in the U.S. and other European societies in particular, makes for yet another historical conjuncture of crisis proportions: the prospects for—and the concrete configurations of—democracy in the context of historic shifts in the demographics of racial pluralism.

The centripetal, potentially balkanizing forces of racial pluralism have been intensified during the past quarter-century as political mobilization and organization often have been based on heightened racial self-consciousness, a development that displaced the constraining effects of the once dominant paradigm of "ethnicity " and the assimilationist agenda it served.[15] According to the logic of ethnicity as the paradigm for conceptualizing group differences and fashioning social policy to deal with them, the socially divisive effects of "ethnic" differences were to disappear in the social-cultural "melting pot"; or, ethnic identity would be maintained across time but would be mediated by principles of the body politic: all *individuals*, without regard to race, creed, color, or national origin, were to have an equal *opportunity* to achieve success on the basis of demonstrated achievement (i.e., merit). For assimilationists and pluralists, *group* characteristics (ethnicity) were to have no play in the determination of merit; their legitimacy was restricted to the private sphere of "culture." With this the pluralists and assimilationists are explicitly drawing off of the Enlightenment legacy of universalism.

During the past twenty years, however, race and ethnicity have been *primary* vehicles for conceptualizing and organizing around group differences with the demand that social justice be applied to persons *as members of particular groups*, and that justice be measured by *results*, not just by opportunities. With the assimilationist agenda of the ethnic paradigm no longer hegemonic, combined with the rising demographics of the "unmeltable" ethnics in the American population (and the populations of other countries) and the preponderance of "race thinking" infecting political life, race has emerged—yet again—as the focus of social conflict.

The notion of race as a fundamental component of race thinking has had a powerful career in Western history (though such thinking has not been limited to the West). Even a cursory review of this history should do much to dislodge the concept from its place as provider of access to a self-evident, obvious, even ontologically *given* characteristic of humankind. For what comes out of such a review is the recognition that though race is continually with us as an organizing, explanatory concept, what the term refers to—that is, the supposed origin and basis of racial differences—has not remained constant. The use of "race" has virtually always been in service to political agendas, beyond more "disinterested" efforts simply to "understand" the basis of perceptually obvious (and otherwise not obvious, but real nonetheless) differences among human groups.

"Race" and Science

The career of race does not begin in science but predates it and emerges from a general need to account for the unfamiliar or, simply, to classify objects of experience, and thus to organize the life-world. How—or why—it was that race came to play important classifying, organizing roles is not clear:

> The career of the race concept begins in obscurity, for experts dispute whether the word derives from an Arabic, a Latin, or a German source. The first recorded use in English of the word "race" was in a poem by William Dunbar of 1508.... During the next three centuries the word was used with growing frequency in a literary sense as denoting simply a class of persons or even things.... In the nineteenth, and increasingly in the twentieth century, this loose usage began to give way and the word came to signify groups that were distinguished biologically.[16]

This nineteenth-century development was antedated by others in preceding centuries that apparently generated a more compelling need for classificatory ordering in the social world and, subsequently, the use of race as such a device. First, there were the tensions within Europe arising from encounters among different groups of peoples, particularly "barbarians"—whether defined culturally or, more narrowly, religiously....A more basic impetus, intensified by these tensions, came from the need to account for human origins in general, for human diversity in particular. Finally, there were the quite decisive European voyages to America and Africa, and the development of capitalism and the slave trade.[17]

The authority of race as an organizing, classificatory concept was strengthened during the eighteenth century when "evidence from geology, zoology, anatomy and other fields of scientific enquiry was assembled to support a claim that racial classification would help explain many human differences . . ."[18] "Race" contributed to a form of "typological thinking"—a mode of conceptualization that was at the center of the agenda of emerging scientific praxis at the time—that facilitated the classification of human groups. As noted, Plato and Aristotle were precursors of such thinking: the former with his theory of forms; the latter via his classification of things in terms of their nature. In the modern period the science of race began in comparative morphology with its stress on pure types as classificatory vehicles....

The science of race peaked during the middle of the nineteenth century. By the end of the century, however, a variety of racial classifications had brought confusion, in part because "no one was quite sure what races were to be classified for. A classification is a tool. The same object may be classified differently for different purposes. No one can tell what is the best classification without knowing what it has to do.[19] The situation was both assisted and complicated by the work of Darwin and Mendel. Social Darwinism emerged as an effort by some (notably Herbert Spencer and Ludwig Gumplowicz) to apply Darwin's principles regarding heredity and natural selection to human groups and endeavors, thereby to provide firmer grounding for the science of race (a move Darwin was reluctant to make). Such moves were particularly useful in justifying *the* dominance of certain groups over others (British over Irish; Europeans over Africans ...).

On the other hand, however, Darwin's *Origins* shifted the terrain of scientific discourse from morphology and the stability of pure types to a subsequent genetics-based approach to individual characteristics and the effects on them of processes of change, thus to a focus on the analysis of variety....

The biology of races thus became more a matter of studying diversities within—as well as among—groups, and, of particular interest, of studying the "evolution" of groups across time and space. Joined to these efforts were contributions from the social science of race: i.e., understanding members of particular groups as sharing some distinctive biological features—though not thereby constituting the groups as biologically pure types—but with respect to which sociocultural factors are of particular importance, but in ways significantly different from the thinking of the nineteenth century theorists of racial types. For many scientists the old nineteenth century notion of "race" had become useless as a classificatory concept, and hence certainly did not support in any scientifically valid way the political agendas of racists. As noted by Livingstone, "yesterday's science is today's common sense and tomorrow's nonsense."[20] Revolutions within sciences (natural and social) conditioned transformed approaches to race, though the consequences have still not completely supplanted the popular, commonsensical notions of races as pure types, as the programs of the Ku Klux Klan, among other, indicate.

The conceptual terrain for this later, primarily twentieth-century approach to race continues to be, in large part, the notion of evolution, now understood in ways significantly conditioned by the precursive work of Mendel and Darwin, social Darwinists notwithstanding. In the space opened by this revised version of the concept it became possible at least to work at synthesizing insights drawn from natural science (genetics, biochemistry) and social science (anthropology, sociology, psychology, ethology) for a fuller understanding of "geographical races."[21] ...

But what is a race in the framework of organic evolution and the global social context of the late twentieth century? Certainly not a group of persons who are genetically homogeneous, a situation that is likely only in places where we might find a people who has remained completely isolated from other groups and hence has not been involved in intergroup sexual reproductions. On the contrary, the logics of the capitalist world system have drawn virtually all peoples into the "global village" and facilitated much "crossbreeding." But capitalism notwithstanding, "raciation"—i.e., the development of the distinctive gene pools of various groups which determine the relative frequencies of characteristics shared by their members, but generally not by them alone—has also been a function, in part, of chance....

When we classify a group as a race, then, at best we refer to generally shared characteristics derived from a "pool" of genes. Social, cultural, and geographical factors, in addition to those of natural selection, all impact on this pool to condition raciation: sometimes to sustain the pool's relative configuration (for example, by isolating the group—culturally or physically—from outbreeding); sometimes to modify it (as when "mulattoes" were produced in the U.S. in significant part through slave masters' of European descent appropriating African women for their—the "masters"—sexual pleasure). It is possible to study the evolution of a particular group over time (a case of specific evolution) with some success. The prospects for success are more limited, however, when the context of concern is *general* evolution—that is, the grouping of all of the world's peoples into ordered categories "with the largest and most heterogeneous societies in the top category and smallest and most homogeneous in the bottom."[22] In either case—general or specific evolution—the concern is with *superorganic* evolution: that is, with changes in behavior repertoires. And such changes are not determined by the genetic specificities of races.

But not all persons (or groups) think so. Though evolutionary—as opposed to typological—thinking, in some form, is at present the dominant intellectual framework for systematic reconstructions and explanations of human natural and social history, it, too, has been enlisted in the service of those who would have science pass absolution on their political agendas: to rationalize and legitimate the empowerment of certain groups, certain races, over others. Even if stripped of the more crude elements of social Darwinism's survival of the fittest, there are still those who offer us a science of race that is preoccupied with ordering human groups along an *ascending* scale, with a particular group's placement on the scale being a function of the level of their supposed development (or lack thereof) toward human perfectibility: from "primitive" to "civilized," "undeveloped" or "underdeveloped" to "developed" or "advanced."...

Race continues to function as a critical yardstick for the rank-ordering of human groups both "scientifically" and sociopolitically, the latter with support from the former. At bottom, then, "race"—sometimes explicitly, quite often implicitly—continues to be a major fulcrum of struggles over the acquisition and exercise of power and the distribution of social goods.

What is the result of this extended review of the career of "race" in science? We are left with the decisive conclusion, certainly, that race is only partially determined by biology. Biological factors provide boundary conditions and possibilities which, in complex interplay with environmental, cultural, and social factors, affect raciation and the development of geographical races.

Ethnicity

A review of the career of "ethnicity" leads to very similar conclusions, in part because it has often been used as a synonym for "race." With good reason, apparently, for the etymology of "ethnicity" reveals that the root term involved a physiological association that was retained in English: the word "ethnic" derives, via Latin, from the Greek *ethnikos*, the adjectival form of *ethnos*, a nation or race.[23] Later there were shifts from a biological (physiological) context of meaning to one that included cultural characteristics and political structures, though the shifts have been neither consistent nor unidirectional.[24] In short, definitions of "ethnic group" and "ethnicity" have been muddy.[25]

Ethnicity became paradigmatic for conceptualizing groupings of different humans during the 1920s-1930s, having successfully challenged the then prevailing biologistic approach to races which evolved after slavery to "explain" the "racial inferiority" of people of African descent—and, thereby, the "superiority" of the "white race." On one account, the rise of ethnicity to the status of reigning paradigm can be charted in its use in at least three distinct ways. First, prior to the 1930s it was an insurgent approach that challenged the biologistic view of race, an attack that was led by "progressive" scholars, activists, and policymakers for whom what has come to be called the Chicago school of sociology was a decisive institutional site. In this intellectual and social context, race was regarded as a social category and but one of a number of determinants of ethnicity or ethnic group identity. Second, during the decades spanning the 1930s through the mid-1960s, the paradigm served as the liberal/progressive "common sense" of race, a period in which assimilationism and cultural pluralism emerged as themes of discourses devoted to the articulation of strategies to guide the development of America into an "integrated" social whole in which racial/ethnic differences were "melted" away by the rationalist heat of egalitarian principles. This agenda, and the theorizing of ethnicity which was its intellectual articulation, was formed to meet the problems resulting from the migration and "culture contact" of European immigrants, hence the emphasis on—and the intellectual acceptance of the inevitability and desirability of—integration.

But the victory of the ethnicity paradigm in service to integration (that is, assimilation) was to prove hollow, in significant part because the paradigm and agenda were rooted in a framework structured so tightly around European experiences and concerns that there was a serious failure to appreciate the extent to which inequalities conditioned by biologically informed geographical raciations differed from inequalities that could be appropriately understood through the concepts of an ethnicity localized to groups of various lines of European descent. Thus, in the post-1965 period, when the Black Power movement ushered in an agenda decisively distinct from the assimilationism of the civil rights movement—and, in doing so, excited persons comprising other groups to likewise seek social justice in distributive terms referenced to their ethnic identity, not just to their being Americans—ethnicity as paradigm for integration was sharply challenged. The responses of some proponents of its continued dominance defined the paradigm's third agenda of deployment: as a defense of "conservative" egalitarianism against the "radical" assault of proponents of "group rights"—Blacks, women, ethnics who refused to be melted—that has forced a renewed focus on race, ethnicity, and the politics of difference.[26]

Beyond the "White Mythology"

We are thus in the midst of the rise of the unmeltables: that is, of social movements organized around a "new ethnicity"—new relative to the long dominance of the paradigm of assimilation—based on the use of cultural as well as biological characteristics by persons from various groups to identify *themselves* as being part of particular ethnic groups and to formulate their claims for social justice using these identifiers.

One student of this new ethnicity, Michael Novak, shares my reading of the times: this heightened awareness and articulation of ethnicity (he terms it "cultural awareness"), when politicized, makes this a major factor in global affairs, "perhaps even one of the major sources of political energy in our era."[27] Novak identifies a number of important components of the new ethnicity that are worth noting:

- it is "post-tribal," that is to say, it arises in an era when virtually every cultural group has been obliged to become aware of many others;
- it arises in an era of advanced technology that, paradoxically, liberates energies for more intense self-consciousness while simultaneously binding many cultures together in standardized technical infrastructures;
- it arises during a period of intense centripetal and homogenizing forces; and
- in some cases it involves a rebellion against forces of technical power, thus manifests a certain rebellion against the supposed moral superiority of modernity.[28]

In light of all this, combined with similar developments having to do with race, how might the challenges of race and ethnicity be met successfully?

We are in the midst of a historical conjuncture that is relatively new, one highly charged by efforts to achieve democracy in a multiethnic, multiracial society where "group thinking" is a decisive feature of social and political life. I join Novak and others in calling for a serious revision of the liberal tradition flowing out of the modern enlightenment, a tradition that has too often been a cloak for the hegemony of the complex metaphysics, ontology, and philosophical anthology of a "white mythology" which "reassembles and reflects the culture of the West: the white man takes his own mythology, Indo-European mythology, his own logos, that is, the *mythos* of his idiom, for the universal form of that he must still wish to call Reason."[29] This notion of reason, argued for—by philosophy in particular—through the classical and modern Enlightenments, must be revised in favor of a seriously reconstructed concept of universal reason and revision of the idea of philosophy, as well. In the words of Novak:

> No one would deny that there is a perfectly straightforward sense in which all human beings are members of the same human family; every human being is bound by imperatives of reasoning, justification, and communication across cultural and other boundaries; and each human being is entitled to claims of fundamental human dignity. Still, it is also widely grasped today that reason itself operates in pluralistic modes. It would be regarded as "cultural imperialism" to suggest that only one form of reasoning is valid in all matters. It would be regarded as naïve to believe that the content of human experiencing, imagining, understanding, judging, and deciding were everywhere the same.... It seems important for a liberal civilization today to thread its way philosophically between the Scylla of relativity and the Charybdis of too narrow a conception of universal reason.[30]

But philosophy has seldom taken up such a project, having been much too preoccupied with the search for the invariant structures of experience and the invariant operations of human understanding.[31] As important as this quest has been—and it has resulted in significant achievements in thought that have contributed, as well, to our practical life in very positive ways—it is not sufficient. Moreover, when it is allowed to dominate our efforts to give philosophical grounding to our collective and individual life, we sow the seeds that are harvested as the strife of renewed ethnicity and raciation, as millions are unable to locate themselves in satisfying ways or find social justice, in the terms and practices of social ordering predicated on the stifling universalism of the old liberalism.

As in previous Enlightenments, philosophers can make substantial contributions to the project suggested by Novak. But we can do so only after adopting a more critical appreciation of difference, conceived in terms of race and ethnicity, that preserves the progressive achievements of the old Enlightenments while contributing to our moving beyond them. In promoting this development I do not seek refuge in romanticism. Instead, what I desire is a new form of "liberalism," what Novak terms a *cosmopolitan* rather than *universalist* liberalism, which should rest on two pillars": firm commitment to the laborious but rewarding enterprise of full, mutual, intellectual understanding; and a respect for differences of nuance and subtlety, particularly in the area of those diversifying 'lived values' that have lain until now, in all cultures, so largely unarticulated."[32] The elaboration of this new liberalism in its possible social-political realizations would be an important contribution from philosophy, something those of us involved in the discipline have not yet worked out as fully as we might.

This elaboration must include insights gained from explorations of the "other side" of race and ethnicity: namely, the lived experiences of persons within racial/ethnic groups for whom their race or ethnicity is a fundamental and *positive* element of their identity, thus of their lifeworld. That race or ethnicity are without scientific bases in biological terms does not mean, thereby, that they are without any social value whatsoever, racism notwithstanding. Nor is that value diminished when we accept the view that what race and ethnicity mean is a function of changing historical conditions and agendas. In important cases the agendas are formed by persons who define themselves, in part, in group terms, and do so in ways that are far from detrimental to the social whole. A new liberalism that truly contributes to enlightenment and emancipation must appreciate such endeavors and appropriate the integrity of those who see themselves through the prisms of race and ethnicity, and who change their definitions of themselves. We should not err yet again in thinking that "race thinking" or "ethnic thinking" must be completely eliminated on the way to an emancipated and just society. Further, that elimination is both unlikely and unnecessary. Certainly the socially divisive forms and consequences of race thinking or ethnic thinking ought to be eliminated, to whatever extent possible. But a critical cosmopolitan liberalism which contributes to the learning and social evolution that secure democratic emancipation, in the context of racial and ethnic diversity, would be of no small consequence.

I can provide you no detailed scenario of what our

social life would look like were this project completed. As with all living, this proposal is filled with serious risk. But so is status quo. However, I invite you to join me in taking this risk, beginning with a careful review of your own experiences of the challenges and joys of successfully negotiating encounters with persons who were decidedly "different" from you, and where success did not require either of you to cease being who you were entirely. Finally, as down payment on the claim not only that the risk of forging a cosmopolitan liberalism is worth taking but that it can, in fact, be achieved, I offer incontrovertible evidence: I am here before you as an honored lecturer; you are here as honored guests granting me a most respectful hearing. I am who I am without loss; and you continue to be who you are. Furthermore, I have certainly gained from my preparation of this lecture, and from my visit to Quinnipiac College. If my contribution has been worthy of your coming, then we know, through our own direct experiences, what can be achieved, and how philosophy can make a contribution to the achievement of social relations respectful of differences that are, nonetheless, mediated by shared understanding.

NOTES

1. See H.C. Baldry, *The Unity of Mankind in Greek Thought* (Cambridge, England: Cambridge University Press, 1965).
2. *Ibid*, 52.
3. *Ibid*, 93.
4. Crane Brinton, "Enlightenment," *The Encyclopedia of Philosophy*, Vol. 2 (New York: Macmillan & Free Press, 1967), 519. Persons in the first group — *philosophes*—were popularizers, propagandists of the Enlightenment, and included men of letters, journalists, salon discussants: Voltaire, Diderot, Condorcet, Holbach; those in the second group were formal philosophers: Hobbes, Locke, Berkeley, Hume, Kant. As with such distinctions, however, this one does not provide for clean separations.
5. *Ibid*, 520.
6. *Ibid*.
7. Aristotle, *Politics*, Book 1, chapter 5, 1252B, 30-33.
8. *Ibid*, 1254A, 18-24.
9. *Ibid*, 1254A, 29-33.
10. G.W.F. Hegel, "Introduction," *The Philosophy of History* (New York: Dover Publications, 1956), 91-99. This work is produced from lectures delivered by Hegel in the winter of 1830-31, though there had been two previous deliveries in 1822-23 and 1824-25. See Charles Hegel's "Preface" to *The Philosophy of History*, xi-xiii. These ideas were expressed more than seventy years prior to the 1895 European cannibalization of Africa by a person who was to become one of Germany's and Europe's most famous philosophers, and helped to nurture a complex of ideas that rationalized European racism.
11. The discussions covering this subsection through section IV are taken from my "Towards a Critical Theory of 'Race'" in *Anatomy of Racism*, David T. Goldberg, editor, Minneapolis: University of Minnesota Press, 1990.
12. W.E.B. Du Bois, "The Concept of Race," in *Dusk of Dawn; An Essay Toward an Autobiography of a Race Concept* (New York: Schoken Books, 1968 [1940]), 103.
13. Thomas E. Gossett, *Race: The History of an Idea in America* (Dallas: Southern Methodist University Press, 1963), 16-17.
14. Alfred Schutz and Thomas Luckmann, *The Structures of the Life-World*, Richard M. Zaner and H. Tristram Engelhardt, Jr., trans. (Evanston: Northwestern University Press, 1973), 8.
15. "In contrast to biologically oriented approaches, the ethnicity-based paradigm was an insurgent theory which suggested that race was a social category. Race was but one of a number of determinants of ethnic group identity or ethnicity. Ethnicity itself was understood as the result of a group formation process based on culture and descent." Michael Omi and Howard Winant, "The dominant paradigm: ethnicity based theory," in *Racial Formation in the United States* (New York: Routledge & Kegan Paul, 1986), 14-24, 15.
16. Michael Banton and Jonathan Harwood , The Race Concept (New York: Praeger 1975), 13.
17. *Ibid.*, 14.
18. *Ibid.*, 13.
19. *Ibid.*, 38.
20. Quoted by Banton and Harwood, 58.
21. "When we refer to races we have in mind their geographically defined categories which are sometimes

called 'geographical races,' to indicated that while they have some distinctive biological characteristics they are not pure types." *Ibid.*, 62.

22. *Ibid.*, 77.
23. William Petersen, "Concepts of Ethnicity," *Harvard Encyclopedia of American Ethnic Groups* (Cambridge: Harvard University Press, 1980), 234-42, 234.
24. *Ibid.*, 234.
25. Omi & Winant, 14.
26. For a fuller discussion of the career of paradigmatic "ethnicity" see Omi & Winant, 14-16.
27. Michael Novak, "Pluralism: A Humanistic Perspective," *Harvard Encyclopedia of American Ethnic Groups* (Cambridge: Harvard University Press, 1980), 772-81, 774.
28. Novak, 774.
29. Jacques Derrida, "White Mythology: Metaphor in the Text of Philosophy," in *Margins of Philosophy*, Alan Bass, trans. (Chicago: University of Chicago Press, 1982), 207-71, 213.
30. Novak, 775.
31. *Ibid.*
32. *Ibid.*, 776.

WHITE WOMAN FEMINIST

Marilyn Frye

Marilyn Frye teaches philosophy at Michigan State University. She is the author of The Politics of Reality: Essays in Feminist Theory *(Crossing Press, 1983) and* Willful Virgin: Essays in Feminism, 1976-1992 *(Crossing Press, 1992).*

Frye describes her own struggles to understand racism as a way of conceptualizing why being white makes combating racism confounding and difficult. She begins by defending the notion that race is socially constructed and argues that like "masculine" and "masculinity," "whitely" and "whiteliness" are ways of being in the world that are learned and deeply ingrained. Frye articulates an account of whiteliness and its connections to class and gender that is designed to elucidate features of racism that make it difficult to eradicate. She calls for the unlearning of whiteliness as a way of becoming less-well assimilated members of the racial group called "white."

This essay is the latest version of something I have been (re-) writing ever since my essay "On Being White" was published in *The Politics of Reality*. In a way, this is that first essay, emerging after several metamorphoses.

"On Being White" grew out of experiences I had in my home lesbian community in which I was discovering some of what it means for a woman, a feminist, to be white. These were very frustrating experiences: they played out and revealed the ways in which the fact that I am white gave unbidden and unwanted meanings to my thought and my actions and poisoned them all with privilege.

An intermediate version of this work, delivered at various colleges and universities around 1984-86, began with the following account of my attempts to come to grips with the fact of being white in a white-supremacist racist state, and with some of the criticism my first effort had drawn.[1]

Reprinted with permission of the publisher from *Overcoming Racism and Sexism*, edited by Linda Bell and David Blumenthal (Lanham MD: Rowman & Littlefield, 1995): 113–134.

Many white feminists, myself included, have tried to identify and change the attitudes and behaviors that blocked our friendly and effective comradeship with women of color and limited our ability to act against institutional racism. I assumed at first that these revisions would begin with analysis and decision: I had to understand the problems and then do whatever would effect the changes dictated by this understanding. But as I entered this work, I almost immediately learned that my competence to do it was questionable.

The idea was put to me by several women of color (and was stated in writings by women of color) that a white woman is not in a good position to analyze institutional or personal racism and a white woman's decisions about what to do about racism cannot be authentic. About consciousness-raising groups for white women, Sharon Keller said to me in a letter,

> I think that there are things which white women working together can accomplish but I do not think that white women are in the best positions usually to know what those things are or when it is the right time to do them. It would go a long way ... for white women to take seriously their [relative] helplessness in this matter.

White women's analysis of their own racism has also often been heard by women of color as "mere psychologizing." To be rid of racism, a white woman may indeed have to do some introspecting, remembering, and verbalizing feelings, but the self-knowledge that she might achieve by this work would necessarily produce profound change, and there are many reasons why many white women may not want to change. White women's efforts to gain self-knowledge are easily undermined by the desire not to live out the consequences of getting it; their/our projects of consciousness raising and self-analysis are very susceptible to the slide from "working on yourself" to "playing with yourself." Apparently the white women herself is ill-situated for telling which is which.

All of my ways of knowing seemed to have failed me—my perception, my common sense, my good-will, my anger, honor, and affection, my intelligence and insight. Just as walking requires something fairly sturdy and firm underfoot, so being an actor in the world requires a foundation of ordinary moral and intellectual confidence. Without that, we don't know how to be or how to act; we become strangely stupid; the commitment against racism becomes itself immobilizing. Even obvious and easy acts either do not occur to us or threaten to be racist by presumptuous assumptions or misjudged timing, wording, or circumstances. Simple things like courtesy or giving money, attending a trial, working on a project initiated by women of color, or dissenting from racist views expressed in white company become fraught with possibilities of error and offense. If you want to do good, and you don't know good from bad, you can't move.[2] Thus stranded, we also learned that it was exploitive and oppressive to ask for the help of women of color in extricating ourselves from this ignorance, confusion, incompetence, and moral failure. Our racism is our problem, not theirs.[3]

Some white women report that the great enemy of their efforts to combat their own racism is their feelings of guilt. That is not my own experience, or that is not my word for it. The great enemies in my heart have been the despair and the resentment that come with being required (by others and by my own integrity) to repair something apparently irreparable, to take responsibility for something apparently beyond my powers to effect. Both confounded and angry, my own temptation is to collapse—to admit defeat and retire from the field. What counteracts that temptation, for me, seems to be little more than willfulness and lust: I *will* not be broken, and my appetite for woman's touch is not, thank goodness, throughly civilized to the established categories. But if I cannot give up and I cannot act, what do Will and Lust recommend? The obvious way out of the relentless logic of my situation is to cease being white.

The Contingency of Racedness

I was brought up with a concept of race according to which you cannot stop being the race you are: your race is an irreversible physical, indeed, ontological fact about you. But when the criteria for membership in a race came up as an issue among white people I knew, considerations of skin color and biological lineage were not definitive or decisive, or rather, they were so only when white people decided they should be, and were not when white people wanted them not to be.[4] As I argued in "On Being White."[5] white people actively legislate matters of race membership, and if asserting their right to do so requires making decisions that override physical criteria, they ignore physical criteria (without, of course, ever abandoning the ideological strategy of insisting that the categories are given in nature). This sort of behavior clearly demonstrates that people construct race actively, and that people who think they are unquestionably white generally think the criteria of what it is to be of this race or that are theirs to manipulate.[6]

Being white is not a biological condition. It is being a member of a certain social/political category, a category that is persistently maintained by those people who are, in their own and each other's perception, unquestionably in it. It is like being a member of a political party or a club or a fraternity—or being a Methodist or a Mormon. If one is white, one is a member of a continuously and politically constituted group that holds itself together by rituals of unity and exclusion, that develops in its members certain styles and attitudes useful in the exploitation of others, that demands and rewards fraternal loyalty, that defines itself as the paradigm of humanity, and that rationalizes (and naturalizes) its existence and its practices of exclusion, colonization, slavery, and genocide (when it bothers to) in terms of a mythology of blood and skin. If you were born to people who are members of that club, you are socialized and inducted into that club. Your membership in it is, in a way or to a degree, compulsory- nobody gave you any choice in the matter—but it is contingent and, in the Aristotelian sense, accidental. If you don't like being a member of that club, you might think of resigning your membership or of figuring out how to get yourself kicked out of the club, how to get yourself excommunicated.

But this strategy of "separation" is vulnerable to a variety of criticisms. A white woman cannot cease having the history she has by some sort of divorce ritual. Furthermore, the renunciation of whiteness may be an act of self-loathing rather than an act of liberation.[7] And disassociation from the race-group one was born into might seem to be an option for white folks, but it seems either not possible or not politically desirable to most members of the other groups from which whites set themselves off.[8] This criticism suggests that my thinking of disassociating from membership in the white fraternity is just another exercise (hence, another reinforcement) of that white privilege that I was finding so onerous and attempting to escape. All these criticisms sound right (and I will circle back to them at the end of the essay), but there is something very wrong here. This closure has the distinctive finality of a trap.

In academic circles where I now circulate, it has become a commonplace that race is a "social construction" and not a naturally given and naturally maintained grouping of human individuals with naturally determined sets of traits. And the recognition of race as nonnatural is presumed, in those circles, to be liberatory. Pursuing the idea of disassociating from the race category in which I am placed and from the perquisites attached to it is a way of pursuing the question of what freedom can be made of this, and for whom. But it seems to me that race (together with racism and race privilege) is *constructed* as something inescapable. And it makes sense that it would be, since such a construction would best serve those served by race and racism. *Of course* race and racism are impossible to escape; of course a white person is always in a sticky web of privilege that permits only acts that reinforce ("reinscribe") racism. This just means that some exit must be forced. That will require conceptual creativity, and perhaps conceptual violence.

The "being white" that has presented itself to me as a burden and an insuperable block to my growth out of racism is not essentially about the color of my skin or any other inherited bodily trait, even though doctrines of color are bound up with this status in some ways. The problem, then, is to find a way to think clearly about some kind of whiteness that is *not essentially* tied to color and yet has some significant relation to color. The distinction feminists have made between maleness and masculinity provides a clue and an analogy. Maleness we have construed as something a human animal can be born with; masculinity we have construed as something a human animal can be trained to—and it is an empirical fact that most male human animals are trained to it in one or another of its cultural varieties.[9] Masculinity is not a blossoming consequence of genetic constitution, as lush growths of facial hair seem to be in the males of many human groups. But the masculinity of an adult male is far from superficial or incidental, and we know it is not something an individual could shuck off like a coat or snap out of like an actor stepping out of his character. The masculinity of an adult male human in any particular culture is also profoundly connected with the local perceptions and conceptions of maleness (as "biological"), its causes and its consequences. So it may be with being white, but we need some revision of our vocabulary to say it rightly. We need a term in the realm of race and racism whose grammar is analogous to the grammar of the term "masculinity." I am tempted to recommend the neologism "albosity" for this honor, but I am afraid it is too strange to catch on. So I will introduce "whitely" and "whiteliness" as terms whose grammar is analogous to that of "masculine" and "masculinity." Being white-skinned (like being male) is a matter of physical traits presumed to be physically determined; being whitely (like being masculine) I conceive as a deeply ingrained way of being in the world. Following the analogy with masculinity, I assume that the connection between whiteliness and light-colored skin is a *contingent* connection: whiteliness can be manifested by persons who are *not* "white"; it can be absent in persons who *are*.

In the next section, I talk about whiteliness in a free and speculative way, exploring what it may be. This work is raw preliminary sketching; it moves against no such background of research and attentive observation as there is to guide accounts of masculinity. There is of course a large literature on racism, but I think that what I am after here is not one and the same thing as racism, either institutional or personal. Whiteliness is connected to institutional racism (as this discussion will show) by the fact that individuals with this sort of character are well suited to the social roles of agents of institutional racism, but it is a character of persons, not of institutions. Whiteliness is also related to individual or personal racism, but I think it is not one and the same thing as racism, at least in the sense where "racism" means bigotry/hate/ignorance/indifference. As I understand masculinity, it is not the same thing as misogyny; similarly, whiteliness is not the same thing as race hatred. One can be whitely even if one's beliefs and feelings are relatively well informed, humane, and goodwilled. So I approach whiteliness freshly, as itself, as something which is both familiar and unknown.

Whiteliness

To begin to get a picture of what whiteliness is, we need to invoke a certain candid and thoughtful reflection on the part of white people, who of course in some ways know themselves best; we also need to consider how people of color perceive white people, since in some ways they know white people best. For purposes of this preliminary exploration, I draw on material from three books for documentation of how white people are, as presented in the experience of people of color. The three are *This Bridge Called My Back*,[10] which is a collection or writings by radical women of color, *Feminist Theory: From Margin to Center*,[11] by black theorist bell hooks, and *Drylongso*,[12] which is a collection of narratives of members of what its editor calls the "core black community."[13] For white voices, I draw on my own and those I have heard as a participant/observer of white culture, and on Minnie Bruce Pratt.

Minnie Bruce Pratt, a feminist and a white southerner, has spelled out some of what I call the whitely way of dealing with issues of morality and change.[14] She said she had been taught to be a *judge*—a judge of responsibility and of punishment, according to an ethical system that countenances no rival; she had been taught to be a *preacher*—to point out wrongs and tell others what to do; she had been taught to be a *martyr*—to take all responsibility and all glory; and she had been taught to be a *peacemaker* - because she could see all sides and see how it all ought to be. I too was taught something like this, growing up in a small town south of the Mason-Dixon line, in a self-consciously Christian and white family. I learned that I, and "we," knew right from wrong and had the responsibility to see to it that right was done, that there were others who did not know right from wrong and should be advised, instructed, helped, and directed by us. I was taught that because one knows what is right, it is morally appropriate to have and exercise what I now call race privilege and class privilege. Not "might is right," but "right is might," as Carolyn Shafer puts the point.[15] In any matter in which we did not know what is right, through youth or inexpertise of some sort, we would await the judgment or instruction of another (white) person who did.

Drylongso: White people are bolder because they think they are supposed to know everything anyhow. (97)
White men look up to their leaders more than we do and they are not much good without their leaders. (99)
White people don't really know how they feel about anything until they consult their leaders or a book or other things outside themselves. (99)
White people are not supposed to be stupid, so they tend to think they are intelligent, no matter how stupidly they are behaving. (96)

Margin: The possibility [they] were not the best spokespeople for all women made [them] fear for [their] self-worth. (13)

Whitely people generally consider themselves to

be benevolent and good willed, fair, honest, and ethical. The judge, preacher, peace-maker, martyr, socialist, professional, moral majority, liberal, radical, conservative, working men and women—nobody admits to being prejudiced, everybody has earned every cent they ever had, doesn't take sides, doesn't hate anybody, and always votes for the person they think best qualified for the job, regardless of the candidate's race, sex, religion, or national origin, maybe even regardless of their sexual preferences. The professional version of this person is always profoundly insulted by the suggestion that s/he might have permitted some personal feeling about a client to affect the quality of services rendered. S/he believes with perfect confidence that s/he is not prejudiced, not a bigot, not spiteful, jealous, or rude, does not engage in favoritism or discrimination. When there is a serious and legitimate challenge, a negotiator has to find a resolution that enables the professional person to save face, to avoid simply agreeing that s/he made an unfair or unjust judgment, discriminated against someone, or otherwise behaved badly. Whitely people have a staggering faith in their own rightness and goodness, and that of other whitely people. We are not crooks.

Drylongso: Every reasonable black person thinks that most white people do not mean him well. (7)
They figure, if nobody blows the whistle, then Nothing wrong has gone down. (21)
White people are very interested in seeming to be of service. ... (4)
Whitefolks can't do right, even if there was one who wanted to. ... They are so damn greedy and cheap that it even hurts them to try to do right. (59)

Bridge: A child is trick-or-treating with her friends. At one house the woman, after realizing the child was an Indian, "quite crudely told me so, refusing to give me treats my friends had received." (47)

Drylongso: I used to be a waitress, and I can still remember how white people would leave a tip and then someone at the table, generally some white woman, would take some of the money. (8)

Bridge: The lies, pretensions, the snobbery and cliquishness. (69)
We experience white feminists and their organizations as elitist crudely insensitive, and condescending. (86)
White people are so rarely loyal. (59)

Whitely people do have a sense of right and wrong, and are ethical. Their ethics in great part an ethics of forms, procedures, and due process. As Minnie Bruce Pratt said, their morality is a matter of "ought to," not "want to" or "passionately desire to." And the "oughts" tend to factor out into propriety or good manners and abiding by the rules. Change cannot be initiated unless the moves are made in appropriate ways. The rules are often-rehearsed. I have participated in whitely women's affirming to each other that some uncomfortable disruption caused by someone objecting to some injustice or offense could have been avoided: had she brought "her" problem forth in the correct way, it could have been correctly processed. We say:

> She should have brought it up in the business meeting.
>
> She should have just taken the other woman aside and explained that the remark had offended her.
>
> She should not have personally attacked me; she should have just told me that my behavior made her uncomfortable, and I would have stopped doing it.
>
> She should take this through the grievance procedure.

By believing in rules, by being arbiters of rules, by understanding agency in terms of the applications of principles to particular situations, whitely people think they preserve their detachment from prejudice, bias, meanness, and so on. Whitely people tend to believe that one preserves one's goodness by being principled, by acting according to rules instead of according to feeling.

Drylongso: We think white people are the most unprincipled folks in the world. ...(8)
White people are some writing folks! They will write! They write every-

thing. Now they do that because they don't trust each other. Also, they are the kind of people who think that you can think about everything, about whether you are going to do, before you do that thing. Now, that's bad for them because you can't do that without wings. ...
All you can do is do what you know has got to be done as right as you know how to do that thing.
White people don't seem to know that. (88)
... he keeps changing the rules. ... Now, Chahlie will rule you to death. (16)

Authority seems to be central to whiteliness, as you might expect from a people who are raised to run things, or to aspire to that: belief in one's authority in matters practical, moral, and intellectual exists in tension with the insecurity and hypocrisy that are essentially connected with the pretense of infallibility. This pretentiousness makes a whitely person simultaneously rude, condescending, overbearing, and patronizing on the one hand, and on the other, weak, helpless, insecure, and seeking validation of their goodness

Drylongso: White people have got to bluff it out as rulers ... [they] are always unsure of themselves. (99)
No matter what Chahlie do, he want his mama to pat him on the head and tell him how cute he is. (19)
[I]n a very real sense white men never grow up. (100)
Hard on the outside, soft on the inside. (99)
Bridge: Socially ... juvenile and tasteless. (99)
No responsibility to others. (70)

The dogmatic belief in whitely authority and rightness is also at odds with any commitment to truth.

Drylongso: They won't tell each other the truth, and the lies they tell each other sound better to them than the truth from our mouths. (29)
As long as they can make someone say rough is smooth, they are happy. ...
Like I told you, white folks don't care about what the truth is. ... It's like when you lie but so much, you don't know what the truth is. (21)
You simply cannot be honest with white people. (45)
Bridge: White feminists have a serious problem with truth and "accountability." (85)

And finally, whitely people make it clear to people of other races that the last thing those people are supposed to do is to challenge whitely people's authority.

Bridge: [W]e are expected [by white women] to move, charm or entertain, but not to educate in ways that are threatening to our audiences. (71)
Margin: Though they expected us to provide first hand accounts of black experience, they felt it was their role to decide if these experiences were authentic. (11)

Often in situations where white feminists aggressively attacked individual black women, they saw themselves as the ones who were under attack, who were the victims. (13)

Drylongso: Most white people—anyways all the white people I know—are people you wouldn't want to explain Anything to. (67)

No wonder whitely people have so much trouble learning, so much trouble receiving, understanding, and acting on moral or political criticism and demands for change. How can you be a preacher who does not know right from wrong, a judge who is an incompetent observer, a martyr who victimizes others, a peacemaker who is the problem, an authority without authority, a grownup who is a child? How can those who are supposed to be running the world acknowledge their relative powerlessness in some matters in any politically constructive way? Any serious moral or political challenge to a whitely person must be a direct threat to her or his very being.

Whiteliness and Class

What I have been exploring here, and calling whiteliness, may sound to some like it is a character of middle-class white people or perhaps of middle-class people whatever their race; it may sound like a class phenomenon, not a race phenomenon. Before addressing this question more deeply, I should register that it is my impression, just looking around at the world, that white self-righteousness is not exclusive to the middle class. Many poor and working-class white people are perfectly confident that they are more intelligent, know more, have better judgement, and are more moral than black people or Chicanos or Puerto Ricans or Indians or anyone else they view as not white, and believe that they would be perfectly competent to run the country and to rule others justly and righteously if given the opportunity,

But this issue of the relationship of whiteliness to class deserves future attention.

Though I think that what I am talking about is a phenomenon of race, I want to acknowledge a close interweaving and double determination of manifestations and outcomes of race and of class, and to consider some of the things that give rise to the impression that what I am calling whiteliness may really be just "middle-classliness." One thing that has happened here is that the person who contributed to the observations assembled in the preceding section as a "participant observer" among white people (that is, the author of this analysis) is herself a lifelong member of the middle class. The whiteliness in which she has participated and about which she can write most vividly and authentically is that of her own kin, associates, and larger social group. This might, to a certain extent, bias that description of whiteliness toward a middle-class version of it.

Another reason that what I am calling whiteliness might appear to be a class character rather than a race one is that even if it is not peculiar to whites of the middle classes, it is nonetheless peculiarly suitable to them: it suits them to their jobs and social roles of managing, policing, training, disciplining, legislating, and administering, in a capitalist bureaucratic social order.

Another interesting point in this connection is that the definition of a dominant race tends to fasten on and project an image of a dominant group within that race as *paradigmatic* of the race.[16] The ways in which individual members of that elite group enact and manifest their racedness and dominance would constitute a sort of norm of enacting and manifesting this racedness to which nonelite members of the race would generally tend to assimilate themselves. Those ways of enacting and manifesting racedness would also carry marks of the class position of the paradigmatic elite within the race, and these marks too would appear in the enactments of race by the nonelite. In short, the ways in which members of the race generally enact and stylistically manifest membership in the race would tend to bear marks of the class status of the elite paradigmatic members of the race.

I do not think whiteliness is just middle-classliness misnamed. I think of whiteliness as a way of being that extends across ethnic, cultural, and class categories and occurs in ethnic, cultural, and class varieties—varieties that may tend to blend toward a norm set by the elite groups within the race. Whatever class and ethnic variety there is among white people, though, such niceties seem often to have no particular salience in the experience that people of other races have with white people. It is very significant that the people of color from whose writings and narratives I have quoted in the preceding section often characterize the white people they talk about in part by class status, bu they do not make anything of it. They do not generally indicate that class differences among white people make much difference to how people of color experience white people.

Speaking of the oppression of women, Gayle Rubin noted its "endless variety and monotonous similarity."[17] There is great variety among the men of all the nationalities, races, religions, and positions in various economies and polities, and women do take into account the particulars of the men they must deal with. But when our understanding of the world is conditioned by consciousness of sexism and misogyny, we see *also*, very clearly, the impressive and monotonous *lack* of variety among "masculinities." With my notion of whiteliness, I am reaching for the monotonous similarity, not the endless variety, in white folk's ways of being in the world. For various reasons, that monotonous similarity may have a middle-class cast to it, or my own perception of it may give it a middle class cast, but I think that what I am calling "whiteliness" is a phenomenon of race. It is integral to what constructs and what is constructed by race, and only indirectly related to class.

Feminism and Whiteliness

Being whitely, like being anything else in a sexist culture, is not the same thing in the lives of white women as it is in the lives of white men. The political significance of one's whiteliness interacts with the political significance of one's status as female or male in a male-supremacist culture. For white men, a whitely way of being in the world is very harmonious with masculinity and their social and political situation. For white women it is, of course, much more complicated.

Femininity in white women is praised and encouraged but is nonetheless contemptible as weakness, dependence, featherbrainedness, vulnerability, and so on, but whiteliness in white women is unambivalently taken among white people as an appropriate enactment of a positive status, Because of this, for white women whiteliness works more consistently than femininity does to disguise and conceal their negative value and low status as women, and at the same time to appear to compensate for it or to offset it.

Those of us who are born female and white are born into the status created by white men's hatred and contempt for women, but white girls aspire to Being and integrity, like anyone else. Racism translates this into an aspiration to whiteliness. The white girl learns that whiteliness is dignity and respectability; she learns that whiteliness is her aptitude for partnership with white men; she learns that partnership with white men is her salvation from the original position of Woman in patriarchy. Adopting and cultivating whiteliness as an individual character seems to put it in the woman's own power to lever herself up out of a kind of nonbeing (the status of woman in a male-supremacist social order) over into a kind of Being (the status of white in white-supremacist social order). But whiteliness does not save white women from the condition of *woman*. Quite the contrary. A white woman's whiteliness is deeply involved in her oppression as a woman and works against her liberation.

White women are deceived, deceive ourselves, and will deceive others about ourselves, if we believe that by being whitely we can escape the fate of being the women of the white men. Being rational, righteous, and ruly (rule-abiding and rule-enforcing) does for some of us some of the time buy a ticket to a higher level of material well-being than we might otherwise be permitted (though it is not dependable). But the reason, right, and rules are not of our own making. White men may welcome our whiteliness as endorsement of their own values and as an expression of our loyalty to them (that is, as proof of their power over us) and because it makes us good helpmates to them. But if our whiteliness commands any respect, it is only in the sense that a woman who is chaste and obedient is called (by classic patriarchal reversal) "respectable."

It is commonly claimed that the women's movement in the United States, during the past couple of decades, is a white women's movement. This claim is grossly disrespectful to the many feminists whom the label "white" does not fit. But it is indeed the case that millions of white women have been drawn to and engaged in feminist action and theorizing, and this creative engagement did *not* arise from those women's being respected for their nice whitely ways by white men: it arose from the rape, battery, powerlessness, poverty or material dependence, spiritual depletion, degradation, harassment, servitude, insanity, drug addiction, botched abortions, and murder of those very women, those women who are white.[18]

As doris davenport put it in her analysis of white feminists' racism:

> A few of us [third world women] ... see beyond the so-called privilege of being white, and perceive white wimmin as very oppressed, and ironically, invisible. ... [I]t would seem that some white feminists could [see

> this] too. Instead, they cling to their myth of being privileged, powerful, and less oppressed ... then black wimmin. .... Somewhere deep down (denied and almost killed) in the psyche of racist white feminists there is some perception of their real position: powerless, spineless, and invisible. Rather than examine it, they run from it. Rather than seek solidarity with wimmin of color, they pull rank within themselves.[19]

For many reasons it is difficult for women (of any intersection of demographic groups) to grasp the enormity, the full depth and breadth, of their oppression and of men's hatred and contempt for them. One reason is simply that the facts are so ugly and the image of that oppressed, despised, and degraded woman so horrible that recognizing her as oneself seems to be accepting utter defeat. Some women, at some times, I am sure, must deny it to survive. But in the larger picture, denial (at least deep and sustained denial) of one's own oppression cuts one off from the appreciation of the oppression of others that is necessary for the alliances one needs. This is what I think Cherríe Moraga is pointing out when she says: "Without an emotional, heartfelt grappling with the source of our own oppression, without naming the enemy within ourselves and outside of us, no authentic, non-hierarchical connection among oppressed groups can take place."[20] If white women are not able to ally with women of other races in the construction of another world, we will indeed remain defeated, in this one.

White women's whiteliness does not deliver the deliverance we were taught it would. Our whiteliness interferes with our ability to form necessary alliances both by inhibiting and muddling our understanding of our own oppression as women and by making us personally obnoxious and insufferable to many other women much of the time; it also is directly opposed to our liberation because it joins and binds us to our oppressors. By our whitely ways of being we enact partnership and racial solidarity with white men, we animate a social (if not also sexual) heterosexual union with white men, and we embody and express our possession by white men.

A feminism that boldly names the oppression and degraded condition of white women and recognizes white men as its primary agents and primary beneficiaries—such a feminism can make it obvious to white women that the various forms of mating and racial bonding with white men do not and will not ever save us from that condition. Such a feminist understanding might free us from the awful confusion of thinking that our whiteliness is dignity, and might make it possible for us to know that it is a dreadful mistake to think that our whiteliness earns us our personhood. Such knowledge can open up the possibility of practical understanding of whiteliness as a learned character (as we have already understood masculinity and femininity), a character by which we facilitate or own containment under the "protection" of white men, a character that interferes constantly and often conclusively with our ability to be friends with women of other races, a character by which we station ourselves as lieutenants and stenographers of white male power, a character that is not desirable in itself and neither manifests nor merits the full Being to which we aspire. A character by which, in fact, we both participate in and cover up our own defeat. We might then include among our strategies for change a practice of unlearning whiteliness, and as we proceed in this, we can only become less and less well-assimilated members of the racial group called "white." (I must state as clearly as possible that I do not claim that unbecoming whitely is the only thing white women need to do to combat racism. I have said that whiteliness is not the same thing as racism. I have no thought whatever that I am offering a panacea for the eradication of racism. I *do* think that *being* whitely interferes enormously with white women's attempts in general to be antiracist.)

Disaffiliation, Deconstruction, Demolition

To deconstruct a concept is to analyze it in a way that reveals its construction—both in the temporal sense of its birth and development over time and in a certain cultural and political matrix, and in the sense of its own present structure, its meaning, and its relation to other concepts.[21] One of the most impressive aspects of such an analysis is the revelation of the "contingency" of the concept, that is, the fact that it is only the accidental collaboration of various historical events and circumstances that brought that concept into being, and the fact that there could be a world of sense without that concept in it. The other impressive thing about such analyses is what they reveal of the complex and intense interplay of construction of concepts and construction of concrete realities. This interplay is what I take to be that phenomenon called the "social construction of reality."

In combination, the revelation of the historical contingency of a concept and the revelation of the intricacy of interplay between concept and concrete lived reality gives rise to a strong sense that "deconstruction" of a concept simultaneously dismantles the reality in whose social construction the evolution of the concept is so closely involved. But things do not work that way. In the first place, analyzing a concept and circulating the analysis among a few interested colleagues does not make the concept go away, does not dislodge it from the matrix of concepts in the active conceptual repertoire even of those few people, much less of people in general. In the second place, even if the deconstructive analysis so drains the concept of power for those few individuals that they can no longer use it, and perhaps their participation in the social constructions of which that concept is a part becomes awkward and halting (like tying your shoelaces while thinking directly about what you are doing), it still leaves those social constructions fully intact. Once constructed and assimilated, a social construct may be a fairly sturdy thing, not very vulnerable to erosion, decay, or demolition.[22] It is one thing to "deconstruct" a concept, another to dismantle a well-established, well-entrenched social construct. For example, Foucault's revelations about the arbitrariness and coerciveness of classifications of sexualities did not put an end to queer bashing or to the fears lesbians and gay men have of being victims of a witch-hunt.

I am interested, as I suggested earlier, in the matter of how to translate the recognition of the social-constructedness of races into some practice of the freedom these contingencies seem to promise, some way to proceed by which people can be liberated from the concrete reality of races as determined by racism. But the social-constructedness of race and races in the racist state has very different meanings for groups differently placed with respect to these categories. The ontological freedom of categorical reconstruction may be generic, but what is politically possible differs for those differently positioned, and not all the political possibilities for every group are desirable. Attempts by any group to act in this ontological freedom need to be informed by understanding of how the action is related to the possibilities and needs of the others.

I have some hope that if I can manage to refuse to enact, embody, animate this category—the white race—as I am supposed to, I can free my energies and actions from a range of disabling confinements and burdens, and align my will with the forces that eventually will dissolve or dismantle that race as such. If it is objected that it is an exercise of white privilege to dissociate myself from the white race this way, I would say that in fact this project is strictly forbidden by the rules of white solidarity and white supremacy, and is not one of the privileges of white power. It may also be objected that my adoption or recommendation of this strategy implies that the right thing to do, in general, for everyone, is to dissolve, dismantle, and bring an end to races; and if this indeed is the implication, it can sound very threatening to some of the people whose races are thus to be erased. This point is well made by Franz Fanon in a response to Jean-Paul Sartre, described by Henry Louis Gates, Jr., "Reading Sartre's account of Négritude (as an antithesis preparatory to a 'society without races,' hence 'a transition and not a conclusion'), Fanon reports: 'I felt I had been robbed of my last chance ... Sartre, in this work, has destroyed black zeal. ...'"[23] The dynamic creative claiming of racial identities (and gender identity), identities that were first imposed as devices of people's oppression, has been a politically powerful and life-enhancing response of oppressed people in modern and contemporary times. For members of oppressor groups to suddenly turn around and decide to abolish races would be, it seems, genocide, not liberation. (I have a parallel unease about the project of dismantling the category of women, which some feminists seem to favor.)

But I am not suggesting that if white women should try to abandon the white race and contribute to its demolition, then women of other races should take that same approach to their racial categorization and their races. Quite the contrary. Approaches to the matter of dismantling a dominance-subordinance structure surely should be asymmetrical—they should differ according to whether one has been molded into its category of dominance or its category of subordination. My hope is that it may contribute to the demise of *racism* if we upset the logical symmetry of race—if black women, for instance, cultivate a racial identity and a distinctive (sexually egalitarian) black community (and other women of racialized groups, likewise), while white women are undermining white racial identity and cultivating communities and agency among women along lines of affinity not defined by race. Such an approach would work toward a genuine redistribution of power.

Growing Room

The experiences of feminists' unlearning femininity and our readiness to require men to unlearn masculity show that it is thinkable to unlearn whiteliness. If I am right about all this, then, indeed, we even know a good deal about how to do it.

We know we have to inform ourselves exhaustively of its politics. We know we have to avoid, or be extremely alert in, environments in which whiteliness is particularly required or rewarded (for example, academia). We know we have to *practice* new ways of being in environments that nurture different habits of feeling, perception, and thought, and that we will have to make these environments for ourselves since the world will not offer them to us. We know that the process will be collective and that this collectivity does not mean we will blend seamlessly with the others into a colorless mass; women unlearning femininity together have not become clones of each other or of those who have been valuable models. As feminists we have learned that we have to resist the temptation to encourage femininity in other women when, in moments of exhaustion and need, we longed for another's sacrificial mothering or wifing. Similarly, white women have to resist the temptation to encourage whiteliness in each other when, in moments of cowardice or insecurity, we long for the comfort of "solidarity in superiority," or when we wish someone would relieve our painful uncertainty with a timely application of judgements and rules.

Seasoned feminists (white feminists along with feminists of other races) know how to transform consciousness. The first breakthrough is in the moment of knowing that another way of being is possible. In the matter of a white women's racedness, the possibility in question is the possibility of disengaging (on some levels, at least) one's own energies and wits from the continuing project of the social creation and maintenance of the white race, the possibility of being disloyal to that project by stopping constantly making oneself whitely. And this project should be very attractive to white women once we grasp that it is the possibility of *not being whitely*, rather than the possibility of being whitely, that holds some promise of our rescuing ourselves from the degraded condition of women in a white men's world.

NOTES

1. The working title during that period was "Ritual Libations and Points of Explosion," which referred to a remark made by Helen Wenzel in a review of my *Politics of Reality* which appeared in *The Women's Review of Books*, 1, no. 1 (October 1983). Wenzel said, "Even when white women call third world women our friends, and they us, we still agonize over 'the issue.' The result is that when we write or teach about race, racism and feminism we tend either to condense everything we have to say to the point of explosion, or, fearing just that explosion, we sprinkle our material with ritual libations which evaporate without altering our own, or anyone else's consciousness." And, coming down to cases, she continued, "Frye has fallen into both of these traps."
2. For critical reflection on "wanting to do good" and on "not knowing how to act," See "A Response to *Lesbian Ethics*: Why Ethics?" in *Willful Virgin: Essays in Feminism*, ed. Marilyn Frye (Freedom, Calif.: The Crossing Press, 1992) 138-46.
3. Actually, what I think women of color have communicated in this matter is not so harsh as that. The point is that no one can do someone else's growing for her, that white women must not expect women of color to be on call to help, and that there is a great deal of

knowledge to be gained by reading, interacting, and paying attention, which white women need not ask women of color to supply. Some women of color have helped me a great deal (sometimes in spite of me).

4. Tamara Buffalo, mixed-race Chippewa, writes: "My white husband said, 'Don't think that you have any Indian-ness, that was taken from you years ago. You speak English don't you? The way you think is white, how you dress, your ambitions, how you raise your daughter, all this is white. I know what is white and what is not white!' I told the group word for word, everything he said. Repeating it in the same flat tone he used, I was bearing witness. I was testifying against him." Tamara Buffalo, "Adopted Daughter," in *Hurricane Alice: A Feminist Quarterly* 10, no. 2 (Spring 1994). Thanks to Carolyn Shafer for bringing this statement to my attention.
5. Marilyn Frye, *The Politics of Reality* (Freedom, Calif.: The Crossing Press, 1983), 115-16.
6. It is easy for a white person who is trying to understand white privilege and white power in white supremacist states to make the mistake of (self-servingly) exaggerating that power and privilege, assuming it is total. In this case, I was making the mistake earlier of thinking that white domination means that white people totally control the definition of race and the races. Reading bell hooks's *Yearning* (Boston: South End Press, 1990), I awoke to the fact that Afro-Americans (and other racialized people) are also engaged in the definition of black (and other "race" categories); white people have the power to enforce their own definitions in many (but not all) situations, but they are not the only people determining the meanings of race categories and race words, and what they determine for themselves (and enforce) is not necessarily congruent with what others are determining for themselves.
7. I want to thank María Lugones, whose palpably loving anger on this point made me take it seriously. See María Lugones, "Hablando cara a cara/ Speaking Face to Face: An Exploration of Ethnocentric Racism," in *Making Face, Making Soul: Haciendo Caras: Critical and Creative Perspectives by Women of Color*, ed. Gloria Anzaldúa (San Francisco: aunt lute foundation press, 1990).
8. Carrie Jane Singleton, "Race and Gender in Feminist Theory," *Sage* VI, no. 1 Summer 1989):15.
9. I am not unmindful here of the anxiety some readers may have about my reliance on a distinction between that which is physically given and that which is socially acquired. I could complicate this passage immensely by shifting from the material mode of talking about maleness and skin colors to the formal mode of talking about conceptions or constructions of maleness and skin colors. But it would not make anything clearer. It is perfectly meaningful to use the term "male" and the term "white" (as a pigment word), while understanding that sex categories and color categories are "constructed" as the kinds of categories they are, that is, physical categories as opposed to social categories like "lawyer" or arithmetic categories like "ordinals."
10. Cherríe Moraga and Gloria Anzaldúa, eds., *This Bridge Called my Back: Writing By Radical Women of Color* (Brooklyn, N.Y.: Kitchen Table: Women of Color Press, 1981). I quote from writings by Barbara Cameron, Chrystos, doris davenport, and Mitsuye Yamada.
11. bell hooks, *Feminist Theory From Margin to Center* (Boston: South End Press, 1985).
12. John Langston Gewaltney, *Drylongso: A Self-Portrait of Black America* (New York: Random House, 1983). I quote from statements by Jackson Jordan, Jr., Hannah Nelson, John Oliver, Howard Roundtree, Rosa Wakefield, and Mabel Lincoln.
13. The people speaking in Drylongso were responding to questions put by an interviewer. The narratives as published do not include the questions. But the people clearly were asked in some manner to say something about how they see white people or what they think white people generally are like. Most of them, but not every one, prefaced or appended their comments with remarks to the effect that they did not think white people were "like that" by birth or blood, but by being brought up a certain way in certain circumstances.
14. Minnie Bruce Pratt, "Identity: Skin Blood Heart," in *Yours in Struggle*, ed. Elly Bulkin, Minnie Bruce Pratt, and Barbara Smith (Brooklyn: Long Haul Press, 1984).
15. For more exploration of some of the meanings of this, see Frye, "A Response to *Lesbian Ethics*: Why Ethics?"
16. Cf. Etienne Balibar, "Paradoxes of Universality,"

trans. Michael Edwards, in *Anatomy of Racism*, ed. David Theo Goldberg (Minneapolis: University of Minnesota Press, 1990), 284-85, extracted from "Racisme et nationalism," in *Race, Nation, Classe*, Etienne Balibar and Immanuel Wallerstein (Paris: Editions La Decouverte, 1988).

17. Gayle Rubin, "The Traffic in Women," in *Toward An Anthropology of Women*, ed. Rayna R. Reiter (New York: Monthly Review Press, 1975), 160.

18. Carolyn Shafer is the one who brought to my attention the fact that there is a certain contradiction in claiming both that this stage of the women's movement was created by and belongs to white women and (on the grounds of the generally better material welfare of white women, compared to women of other races in the United States) that white women are not all that badly off and don't really know what suffering is about. If white women were as generally comfortable, secure, and healthy as they might appear to some observers, they would not have participated as they have in an enormous movement the first and most enduring issues of which are bodily integrity and economic self-sufficiency.

19. doris davenport, "The Pathology of Racism: A Conversation with Third Work Wimmin," in *This Bridge Called My Back*, ed. Moraga and Anzaldúa, 89-90.

20. Moraga, *This Bridge Called My Back*, 21.

21. It will be clear to those who learned the word "deconstruction" from the writings of Jacques Derrida that I have wandered off with it in pursuit of interests other than his. They will agree, though, that he gave it up the moment he first wrote it down or uttered it.

22. My lover Carolyn was explaining what I do for a living to our coheart Keyosha, and included an account of "deconstruction." Keyosha, a welder and pipefitter in the construction trades, said that it wasn't a real word and offered "demolition" as the real word for this. Carolyn then had to admit (on my behalf) that all this deconstructing did not add up to any demolition, and a made-up abstract word was probably suitable to this abstract activity.

23. Henry Louis Gates, Jr., "Critical Remarks," in *Anatomy of Racism*, ed. David Theo Goldberg (Minneapolis: University of Minnesota Press, 1990), 325.

REFLECTIONS ON THE MEANING OF WHITE

Victoria Davion

Victoria Davion teaches philosophy at the University of Georgia, Athens. Her areas of interest are ethics, feminist philosophy, and political theory.

Davion defends Frye's argument that being white is the result of social training that can be unlearned. However, she questions Frye's tendency to think of whiteliness in universal terms and explores the ways in which ethnic differences further complicate an account of whiteliness. While Davion recognizes correspondences between being whitely and being Jewish, she also identifies some of the characteristics of being Jewish in a primarily Christian society that fail to fit Frye's account of whiteliness. She argues that ceasing to be whitely means unlearning whiteliness, but not necessarily getting rid of one's ethnicity.

Marilyn Frye is right to insist that the link between promoting white supremacy and being white skinned is contingent. Certainly white people do not have to act in ways that promote white supremacy. Acting in these ways is not a matter of genetic coding; it is a matter of social training. Frye is also right to point out that although there is only a contingent link between promoting a system based on white supremacy and having white skin, ceasing to promote white supremacy requires more than simply believing in racial equality. It requires close examination of and changes in behaviors that may not appear on the surface to promote white supremacy but in fact keep a white supremist system in place. Frye's strategy of searching for these behaviors and attitudes in both her own experiences and experiences that people of color have of white people is a good one. Thus, I want to add to this project by looking at how ethnic differences fit into this kind of analysis.

Frye's description of whiteliness is very familiar to me. It also seems very Protestant, and I am Jewish. I don't deny that white Jews and other ethnic groups engage in the kinds of behaviors she describes, but I want to make clear that many different worldviews can produce these behaviors. Whiteliness is not a particular worldview. Frye focuses on the monotonous similarity of whitely oppression, and I think she is right to do this. If, however, her analysis implies that in order to stop being whitely we must disaffiliate from our ethnic backgrounds, as a Jew I cannot accept it. I don't in fact think that ceasing to be whitely requires this, and I think it is important that this be made clear.

Frye states that whitely people trust each other. One of the quotations she cites from *Drylongso* claims just the opposite: "White people are some writing folks! They will write. They write everything. Now they do that because they don't trust each other."[1] Interestingly, I think both perceptions are right. My upbringing as a white Jew in America included education about anti-Semitism. I was raised not to trust non-Jews because they can turn on you at any time. I will return to this point shortly.

As Frye characterizes some of the other values and beliefs involved in whiteliness, these are not the values I was taught. She states: "I learned that I, and 'we,' knew right from wrong and had the responsibility to see to it right was done, that there were oth-

---

Reprinted with permission of the publisher from *Overcoming Racism and Sexism*, edited by Linda Bell and David Blumenthal (Lanham MD: Rowman & Littlefield, 1995): 135–139.

ers who did not know what is right and wrong and should be advised, instructed, helped, and directed by us. ... Not 'might is right,' but 'right is might.'"[2] As a Jew, I was taught that being right doesn't insure one any power whatsoever, and that the majority doesn't know right from wrong. Yet, because might makes right in reality, I was taught to leave the Christian majority alone to do its own thing. I was certainly not encouraged at all to spread the truth of Judaism. Rather, I was warned to shut up about all of this if I wanted to be safe.

It is in the ways that I learned how to be careful around non-Jews that I recognize much of what Frye calls whitely behaviour in myself. I learned how to tone down behaviors that might be considered stereotypical Jewish around those who might find me too loud or pushy. Although I was taught to trust and favor Jews and to hate certain groups of whites, I know how to behave as if I hate no one, trust other white people, and don't discriminate.

Why do I know how to behave in these ways? I was taught this as a survival mechanism. Although this was never stated explicitly, I now realize that I was given the message that white skin alone wouldn't guarantee me certain privileges. In addition to having white skin, I needed to be or pretend to be Christian. Often, passing for a white Christian doesn't involve doing anything. However, I learned to be sure not to call attention to the fact that I wasn't really Christian. The message was that insofar as I am white, it is safe to trust other whites in seeking white privileges. However, insofar as I am Jewish in a primarily Christian society, this isn't the case.

What does this imply about whiteliness in general and about me as a white Jew? Whiteliness is not, in my opinion, a particular worldview. Whitely behavior can be the result of a variety of worldviews. The motivation for being whitely, and also for stopping being whitely, will therefore come from a variety of sources depending on who one is. I have come to realize that in my own case, to promote the particular white-supremacist system in which we now live is at the same time to promote a system that is anti-semitic to its roots. This is why it is so important to learn the dominant behaviors and practices and to avoid acting too Jewish in public. In supporting the myth that all white people are basically the same in certain respects, which is what a white-supremacist system must do, I contribute to the fracturing of my being by being whitely. I cannot be whole in such a system.

I want to make a few things clear before going any further. I am not saying that white Jews are any less whitely or even any less racist than other whites. In fact, we may be more whitely in that the behaviors are learned as a survival mechanism. Nor am I saying that white Jews should be excused for being whitely while others should not. Supporting a white-supremacist system is wrong no matter who does it. I don't want to try to rank blame for whitely behavior. What I am saying is that as a white Jew, I have a particular motive for ceasing to be whitely. In being whitely I contribute to the erasure of myself as Jewish, and the fracturing of my identity.

If whitely behaviors are behaviors that whites from various backgrounds engage in, then getting rid of them need not mean getting rid of one's ethnicity. Rather, it will mean looking at behaviors and attitudes and rooting out the whitely ones, the ones that promote white supremacy. This brings me to a final point with regard to Frye's analysis of whiteliness. Many of the characteristics Frye names seem as if they might not be bad in themselves, but only in certain contexts. If this is true, then nobody's ethnic background is polluted to the point where it must be discarded. Instead, the strategy will be to look at the way one engages in various behaviors. Following rules is one example. Rule-following has its place. However, it is oppressive to insist that everyone follow the rules when not everyone thinks rules are appropriate for that situation to begin with, or not everyone has had the opportunity to help construct the rules. Voting for the person one thinks is best qualified for the job doesn't seem like a bad behavior in itself. It depends on what is meant by most qualified. Therefore, it is not the behaviors themselves that are the problem; it is the way that we engage in them.

Some of the other attitudes and behaviors Frye mentions are always unfortunate regardless of the context. She says:

> Many poor and working class white people are perfectly confident that they are more intelligent, know more,

> have better judgment, and are more moral than Black people or Chicanos or Puerto Ricans or Indians or anyone else they view as not white, and believe that they would be perfectly competent to run the country and to rule others justly and righteously if given the opportunity.[3]

The version of whiteliness described above sounds like racism. One of the things I find very important in Frye's project is her insistence that whitely behaviors can be manifested in people who believe in racial equality. That is, even those of us who do not think that whites are more intelligent, know more, and so on, can act in ways that promote white supremacy. This description does not seem to capture that.

I conclude that Frye is exactly right to seek something analogous to masculinity that white people are socialized into but that we can learn to stop being and doing. She is also right to listen to people of color describe the endless monotony and similarity in their experiences of race oppression. I think it is a mistake, however, to conclude that this monotony is due to any common worldview in those who behave in whitely ways (I am not saying that she does this). Many systems are at work. In addition, while I think Frye is right to look for whiteliness as she describes it abstractly, I am still not sure exactly what it is. I am not sure because some of the behaviors she mentions do not seem necessarily bad in themselves, and others seem blatantly racist. Nevertheless, her analysis has started me thinking about when and why I behave in whitely ways. It has helped me to realize that acting whitely involves affirming a framework in which behavior stereotyped as ethnically Jewish is looked down upon. Thus, in acting whitely I erase my ethnicity. Perhaps if more white people celebrated our differences publicly, the myth that whites are basically the same, a myth that is necessary for upholding a white-supremacist system, would be impossible to maintain. Thus, I regard this essay as a call for the celebration of ethnic diversity as well as a call for whites to stop acting whitely. I hope I have shown that these projects are compatible.

NOTES

1. John Langston Gewaltney, *Drylongso: A Self-Portrait of Black America* (New York: Random House, 1983), 88.
2. Marilyn Frye, "White Woman Feminist," p. 227 in this volume.
3. *Ibid.*, p. 230 in this volume.

INVISIBILITY IS AN UNNATURAL DISASTER: REFLECTIONS OF AN ASIAN AMERICAN WOMAN

Mitsuye Yamada

Mitsuye Yamada is a poet and educator. She is a Professor of English at Cypress College in Seattle, Washington and the author of Desert Run: Poems and Stories *(Kitchen Table, 1988),* Sowing Ti Leaves: Anthology *(Multicultural Women Writers, 1991) and* Camp Notes and Other Poems, *2nd edition (Kitchen Table, 1992).*

Yamada describes her own experiences in academic settings of having students and administrators fail to understand anger expressed by Asian Americans because they do not think Asian Americans constitute an oppressed group. Yamada uses the concept of invisibility to elucidate the kind of oppression experienced by Asian American women and, more specifically, by Japanese Americans. Some effects of the evacuations of Japanese Americans during World War II were the shaping of prevalent stereotypes of Asian Americans as polite, passive, and accepting and the internalization of these stereotypes by Asian Americans.

Last year for the Asian segment of the Ethnic American Literature course I was teaching, I selected a new anthology entitled *Aiiieeeee!* compiled by a group of outspoken Asian American writers. During the discussion of the long but thought-provoking introduction to this anthology, one of my students blurted out that she was offended by its militant tone and that as a white person she was tired of always being blamed for the oppression of all the minorities. I noticed several of the classmates' eyes nodding in tacit agreement.

A discussion of the "militant" voices in some of the other writings we had read in the course ensued. Surely, I pointed out, some of these other writings have been just as, if not more, militant as the words in this introduction? Had they been offended by those also but failed to express their feelings about them? To my surprise, they said they were not offended by any of the Black American, Chicano or American Indian writings, but were hard-pressed to explain why when I asked for an explanation. A little further discussion revealed that they "understood" the anger expressed by the Black and Chicanos and they "emphasized" with the frustrations and sorrow expressed by the American Indian. But the Asian Americans??

Then finally, one student said it for all of them: "It made me angry. *Their* anger made *me* angry, because I didn't even know the Asian Americans felt oppressed. I didn't expect their anger."

At this time I was involved in an academic due process procedure begun as a result of a grievance I had filed the previous semester against the administrators at my college. I had filed a grievance for violation of my rights as a teacher who had worked in the district for almost eleven years. My student's remark "Their anger made me angry ... I didn't expect their anger," explained for me the reactions of some of my own colleagues as well as the reactions of the administrators during those previous months. The grievance procedure was a time-consuming and emotionally draining process, but the basic principle was too important for me to ignore. That basic prin-

---

Reprinted with permission of Mitsuye Yamada from *This Bridge Called My Back: Writings by Radical Women of Colour*, edited by Cherrie Moraga and Gloria Anzaldua (Brooklyn NY: Kitchen Table/Women of Color Press, 1983): 35–40.

ciple was that I, an individual teacher, do have certain rights which are given and my superiors cannot, should not, violate them with impunity. When this was pointed out to them, however, they responded with shocked surprise that I, of all people, would take them to task for violation of what was clearly written policy in our college district. They all seemed to exclaim, "We don't understand this; this is so uncharacteristic of her; she seemed such a nice person, so polite, so obedient, so non-trouble making." What was even more surprising was once they were forced to acknowledge that I was determined to start the due process action, they assumed I was not doing it on my own. One of the administrators suggested someone must have pushed me into this, undoubtedly some of "those feminists" on our campus, he said wryly.

In this age when women are clearly making themselves visible on all fronts, I, an Asian American woman, am still functioning as a "front for those feminists" and therefore invisible. The realization of this sinks in slowly. Asian Americans as a whole are finally coming to claim their own, demanding that they be included in the multicultural history of our country. I like to think, in spite of my administrator's myopia, that the most stereotyped minority of them all, the Asian American woman, is just now emerging to become part of that group. It took forever. Perhaps it is important to ask ourselves why it took so long. We should ask ourselves this question just when we think we are emerging as a viable minority in the fabric of our society. I should add to my student's works, "because I didn't even know they felt oppressed," that it took this long because we Asian American women have not admitted to ourselves that we were oppressed. We, the visible minority that is invisible.

I say this because until a few years ago I have been an Asian American woman working among non-Asians in an educational institution where most of the decision-makers were men[1]; an Asian American woman thriving under the smug illusion that I was *not* the stereotypic image of the Asian woman because I had a career teaching English in a community college. I did not think anything assertive was necessary to make my point. People who know me, I reasoned, the ones who count, know who I am and what I think. Thus, even when what I considered a veiled racist remark was made in a casual social setting, I would "let it go" because it was pointless to argue with people who didn't even know their remark was racist. I had supposed that I was practicing passive resistance while being stereotyped, but it was so passive no one noticed I was resisting; it was so much my expected role that it ultimately rendered me invisible.

My experience leads me to believe that contrary to what I thought, I had actually been contributing to my own stereotyping. Like the hero in Ralph Ellison's novel *The Invisible Man*, I had become invisible to white Americans, and it clung to me like a bad habit. Like most bad habits, this one crept up on me because I took it in minute doses like Mithradates' poison and my mind and body adapted so well to it I hardly noticed it was there.

For the past eleven years I have busied myself with the usual chores of an English teacher, a wife of a research chemist, and a mother of four rapidly growing children. I hadn't even done much to shatter this particular stereotype: the middle class woman happy to be bringing home the extra income and quietly fitting into the man's world of work. When the Asian American woman is lulled into believing that people perceive her as being different from other Asian women (the submissive, subservient, ready-to-please, easy-to-get-along-with Asian woman), she is kept comfortably content with the state of things. She becomes ineffectual in the milieu in which she moves. The seemingly apolitical middle class woman and the apolitical Asian woman constituted a double invisibility.

I had created an underground culture of survival for myself and had become in the eyes of others the person I was trying not to be. Because I was permitted to go to college, permitted to take a stab at a career or two along the way, given "free choice" to marry and have a family, given a "choice" to eventually do both, I had assumed I was more or less free, not realizing that those who are free make and take choices; they do not choose from options proffered by "those out there."

I, personally, had not "emerged" until I was almost fifty years old. Apparently through a long conditioning process, I had learned how *not* to be seen for what I am. A long history of ineffectual activities had been, I realize now, initiation rites toward my eventual invisibility. The training begins in childhood; and for women and minorities whatever is started in childhood is continued throughout their adult lives. I first recognized just how invisible I was in my first real confrontation with my parents a few years after the outbreak of World War II.

During the early years of the war, my older brother, Mike, and I left the concentration camp in Idaho to work and study at the University of Cincinnati. My parents came to Cincinnati soon after my father's release from Internment Camp (these were POW camps to which many of the Issei[2] men, leaders in their communities, were sent by the FBI), and worked as domestics in the suburbs. I did not see them too often because by this time I had met and was much influenced by a pacifist who was out on a "furlough" from a conscientious objectors' camp in Trenton, North Dakota. When my parents learned about my "boy friend" they were appalled and frightened. After all, this was the period when everyone in the country was expected to be one-hundred percent behind the war effort, and the Nisei[3] boys who had volunteered for the Armed Forces were out there fighting and dying to prove how American we really were. However, during interminable arguments with my father and overheard arguments between my parents, I was devastated to learn they were not so much concerned about my having become a pacifist, but they were more concerned about the possibility of my marrying one. They were understandably frightened (my father's prison years of course were still fresh on his mind) about repercussions on the rest of the family. In an attempt to make my father understand me, I argued that even if I didn't marry him, I'd still be a pacifist; but my father reassured me that it was "all right" for me to be a pacifist because as a Japanese national and a "girl" *it didn't make any difference to anyone*. In frustration I remember shouting, "But can't you see, *I'm* philosophically committed to the pacifist cause," but he dismissed this with "In my college days we used to call philosophy, foolosophy," and that was the end of that. When they were finally convinced I was not going to marry "my pacifist," the subject was dropped and we never discussed it again.

As if to confirm my father's assessment of the harmlessness of my opinions, my brother Mike, an American citizen, was suddenly expelled from the University of Cincinnati while I, "an enemy alien," was permitted to stay. We assumed that his stand as a pacifist, although he was classified a 4-F because of his health, contributed to his expulsion. We were told the Air Force was conducting sensitive wartime research on campus and requested his removal, but they apparently felt my presence on campus was not as threatening.

I left Cincinnati in 1945, hoping to leave behind this and other unpleasant memories gathered there during the war years, and plunged right into the politically active atmosphere at New York University where students, many of them returning veterans, were continuously promoting one cause or other by making speeches in Washington Square, passing out petitions, or staging demonstrations. On one occasion, I tagged along with a group of students who took a train to Albany to demonstrate on the steps of the State Capitol. I think I was the only Asian in this group of predominantly Jewish students from NYU. People who passed us were amused and shouted "Go home and grow up." I suppose Governor Dewey, who refused to see us, assumed we were a group of adolescents without a cause as most college students were considered to be during those days. It appears they weren't expecting any results from our demonstration. There were no newspersons, no security persons, no police. No one tried to stop us from doing what we were doing. We simply did "our thing" and went back to our studies until next time, and my father's words were again confirmed: it made no difference to anyone, being a young student demonstrator in peacetime, 1947.

Not only the young, but those who feel powerless over their own lives know what it is like not to make a difference on anyone or anything. The poor know it only too well, and we women have known it since we were little girls. The most insidious part of this conditioning process, I realize now, was that we have been trained not to expect a response in ways that mattered. We may be listened to and responded to with placating words and gestures, but our psychological mind set has already told us time and again that we were born into a ready-made world into which we must fit ourselves, and that many of us do it very well.

This mind set is the result of not believing that the political and social forces affecting our lives are determined by some person, or a group of persons, probably sitting behind a desk or around a conference table.

Just recently I read an article about "the remarkable track record of success" of the Nisei in the United States. One Nisei was quoted as saying he attributed our stamina and endurance to our ancestors whose characters had been shaped, he said, by their living in a country which has been constantly besieged by all manner of natural disasters, such as earthquakes and hurricanes. He said the Nisei has inherited a steely will, a will to endure and hence, to survive.

This evolutionary explanation disturbs me, because it equates the "act of God" (i.e. natural disasters) to the "act of man" (i.e., the war, the evacuation). The former is not within our power to alter, but the latter, I should think, is. By putting the "acts of God" on par with the acts of man, we shrug off personal responsibilities.

I have, for too long a period of time accepted the opinion of others (even though they were directly affecting my life) as if they were objective events totally out of my control. Because I separated such opinions from the persons who were making them, I accepted them the way I accepted natural disasters; and I endured them as inevitable. I have tried to cope with people whose points of view alarmed me in the same way that I had adjusted to natural phenomena, such as hurricanes, which plowed into my life from time to time. I would readjust my dismantled feelings in the same way that we repaired the broken shutters after the storm. The Japanese have an all purpose expression in their language for this attitude of resigned acceptance: "Shikataganai." " It can't be helped." "There's nothing I can do about it." It is said with the shrug of the shoulders and tone of finality, perhaps not unlike the "those-were-my-orders" tone that was used at the Nuremberg trials. With all the sociological studies that have been made about the causes of the evacuations of the Japanese Americans during World War II, we should know by now that "they" knew that the West Coast Japanese Americans would go without too much protest, and of course, "they" were right, for most of us (with the exception of those notable few), resigned to our fate, albeit bewildered and not willingly. We were not perceived by our government as responsive Americans; we were objects that happened to be standing in the path of the storm.

Perhaps this kind of acceptance is a way of coping with the "real" world. One stands against the wind for a time, and then succumbs eventually because there is no point to being stubborn against all odds. The wind will not respond to entreaties anyway, one reasons; one should have senses enough to know that. I'm not ready to accept this evolutionary reasoning. It is too rigid for me; I would like to think that my new awareness in going to make me more visible than ever, and to allow me to make some changes in the "man made disaster" I live in at the present time. Part of being visible is refusing to separate the actors from their actions, and demanding that they be responsible for them.

By now, riding along with the minorities' and women's movements, I think we are making a wedge into the main body of American life, but people are still looking right through and around us, assuming we are simply tagging along. Asian American women still remain in the background and we are heard but not really listened to. Like Musak, they think we are piped into the airwaves by someone else. We must remember that one of the most insidious ways of keeping women and minorities powerless is to let them only talk about harmless and inconsequential subjects, or let them speak freely and not listen to them with serious intent.

We need to raise our voices a little more, even as they say to us "This is so uncharacteristic of you." To finally recognize our own invisibility is to finally be on the path toward visibility. Invisibility is not a natural state for anyone.

NOTES

1. It is hoped this will change now that a black woman is Chancellor of our college district.
2. Issei- Immigrant Japanese, living in the U.S.
3. Nisei- Second generation Japanese, born in the U.S.

COLONIALISM AND ITS OTHERS: CONSIDERATIONS ON RIGHTS AND CARE DISCOURSES

Uma Narayan

Uma Narayan teaches philosophy at Vassar College. She is the author of Dislocating Cultures: Identities, Traditions and Third World Feminism *(Routledge,1997) and co-editor of* Reconstructing Political Theory: Feminist Perspectives *(Penn State, 1997).*

"I point to a colonial care discourse that enabled colonizers to define themselves in relationship to 'inferior' colonized subjects. The colonized, however, had very different accounts of this relationship. While contemporary care discourse correctly insists on acknowledging human needs and relationships, it needs to worry about who defines these often contested terms. I conclude that improvements along dimensions of care and of justice often provide 'enabling conditions' for each other."

I wish to think about certain aspects of the roles played by rights and care discourses in colonial times. I shall start with the following question: How did the vast majority of people in the colonizing countries motivate themselves to participate in the large-scale phenomena of slavery and colonialism, not only embracing the idea that distant lands and peoples should be subjugated, but managing to conceive of imperialism as an *obligation*, an obligation taken so seriously that by 1914 Europe "held a grand total of roughly 85 percent of the earth as colonies, protectorates, dependencies, dominions, and commonwealths"? (Said 1993, 8).

The answer to this question forces us to attend to the self-serving collaboration between elements of colonial rights discourse and care discourse. Pervasive racist stereotypes about the negative and inferior status of enslaved or colonized Others were used both to justify denial of the rights enjoyed by the colonizers, and to construct the colonized as childish and inferior subjects, in need of the paternalistic guidance and rule of their superiors (see Said 1993). In general terms, the colonizing project was seen as *in the interests of*, *for the good of*, and *as promoting the welfare of* the colonized—notions that draw our attention to the existence of a *colonialist* care discourse whose terms have some resonance with those of some contemporary strands of the ethic of care. Particular colonial practices were seen as concrete attempts to achieve these paternalistic ends. Coercive religious conversion was seen as promoting the *spiritual* welfare of the "heathen." Inducting the colonized into the economic infrastructures of colonialism was seen as conferring the *material* benefits of western science, technology and economic progress, the *cultural* benefits of western education, and the *moral* benefits of the work ethic. There were often marked gender dimensions to these projects—colonial attempts to get "native women" to conform to victorian/Christian norms of respectable dress, sexuality, and family life were regarded as in the moral interests of the women (see Chauduri and Strobel 1992).

I am not denying there were powerful economic motivations underlying colonialism and slavery. However, justifications for colonialism and slavery in terms of crude self-interest alone seem to have been rare. These enterprises were made morally palatable by the rhetoric of responsibility and care

---

Reprinted with permission of the publisher and Uma Narayan from *Hypatia* 10:2 (1995): 133–40.

for enslaved and colonized Others. Though such justifications have often been seen as attempts to convince the dominated of the appropriateness of their domination, I would argue that the central purpose of such arguments often is to make domination morally palatable to those engaged in the infliction of domination. While much of the contemporary discourse on an ethics of care focuses on the import of one's relationships to *particular others*, thinking about care-discourse in the colonial context highlights, in contrast, the roles it has historically played in justifying relationships of power and domination between *groups of people*, such as colonizers and colonized. The paternalistic moral vision of colonialism was sustained by the discourses of religion, philosophy, science, and art—cultural practices that collaborated to make a sense of western superiority part of the collective world view of people in the colonizing countries. (A large segment of western women's movements and working class movements of the time, such as those in England, were pro-empire.)

Colonial stereotypes about the hierarchy of races had similarities to existing theories of the hierarchy of gender—where attributes such as physical "weakness," smaller craniums, deficient rationality, and moral frailty were ascribed to western women, constructing them as the "weaker sex" in need of the care, support, and guidance of western men, not unlike the colonized. However, while western women's care-taking labor, namely domestic work and childcare responsibilities, were often rendered invisible qua work by being depicted as expressions of love and care for their families, the toil and labor of exploited slaves and colonized workers were often effaced instead by depicting their products as results of the efforts of colonial capitalists. John Stuart Mill provides a vivid example in *Principles of Political Economy*:

> These [outlying possessions of ours] are hardly to be looked upon as countries, but more properly as outlying agricultural or manufacturing estates. ... Our West Indian colonies, for example, cannot be regarded as countries with a productive capital of their own, ... [but are rather] the place where England finds it convenient to carry on the production of sugar, coffee and a few other tropical commodities. All the capital employed is English capital. (Mill 1965, 693)

What does attending to the colonial context teach us about discourses of rights and care? Among the more obvious lessons is that rights discourse was only seemingly universal, not extending to the colonized, among others. Another lesson is that care discourse can sometimes function ideologically, to justify or conceal relationships of power and domination. While it has been pointed out that much of the responsibility for informal as well as institutionalized caring falls on subordinate and relatively powerless members of society—often working class and minority women (Held 1995)—I want to add that "paternalistic caring" of the sort found in colonial discourse can also be wielded as a form of control and domination by the powerful and privileged. The colonial notion of "the white man's burden" included both a sense of obligation to confer the benefits of western civilization on the colonized, and a sense of being burdened with the responsibility for doing so—an obligation and responsibility rooted in a sense of being agents who had a world-historic mission to bring the light of civilization and progress to others inhabiting "areas of darkness"!

The seemingly universal, free, equal, independent, separate, and mutually disinterested individual of contract theory and of rights discourse has been criticized as being contrary to the experiences of most women. I wish to add that the contractual focus on relationships between equals, and on agents as independent, separate and mutually disinterested was only *part* of the liberal story. Another part of the story was that these same subjects had paternalistic obligations and responsibilities to "inferior Others," whether women in their own families or distant colonial peoples. Rights-discourse was constructed during the historical time when western countries were becoming increasingly interdependent with, unseparate from, and anything but disinterested in their unfree and unequal colonies, and most liberal political theorists had no difficulty endorsing colonialism. We would be mistaken if we read liberal rights-theorists as concerned only with contractual relationships between equals, or if we focus only on notions of agency pertinent to that side of their thought, since we would be ignoring their support for colonialism, and the more "missionary" notions of agency embedded in that facet of their worldview. If we recognize that the agent of liberal rights theory was also the agent of the colonial project, its independence, separateness and disinterestedness appear to be more qualified properties than the picture of the same agent that emerges if we ignore the colonial dimensions of liberal theory.

In the colonial worldview, white women too had their own version of the "white man's burden," in which caretaking roles played a large part. Many white women went to the colonies as wives, whose presence was meant to shield their husbands from the lurking dangers of miscegenation and of "going native" (see Zlotnick 1994). White women had their own brand of paternalistic roles towards the colonized, and often shared in roles that constructed the "natives" as children.

Many aspects of the self-perceptions of the colonizers seem to have depended heavily on their relationship to the colonized. The world-view of colonialism, as well as the moral and socio-political world-views of colonialism, as well as the moral and socio-political world-views of many colonized cultures, subscribed to a picture where several large groups of people were normatively defined in terms of their relationships as inferiors and subordinates vis-a-vis members of dominant groups. To be a slave, a colonized Other, an untouchable, a woman, has often been meant as having one's entire existence defined in terms of one's "proper place" with respect to those with power, which entailed obligations to acquiesce to relationships of domination.

This suggests that strands in contemporary care discourse that stress that we are all essentially interdependent and in relationship, while important, do not go far enough if they fail to worry about the *accounts* that are given of these interdependencies and relationships. The colonizers and the colonized, for example, while both acutely conscious of their relationship to each other, had very different accounts of what the relationship and its interdependencies amounted to, and whether they were morally justified. Many social movements and struggles on the part of subordinate groups, though often couched in terms of individual rights, were also attempts to renegotiate and change the prevailing relationships between social groups.

While I do not endorse reducing the value of any moral theory to its ideological uses, I would argue that we must attend to the ideological functions served by various moral theories. Pervasive structural relationships of power and powerlessness between groups, such as those between colonizers and the colonized, tend to foster ideological justifications for the maintenance of such relationships. While aspects of care discourse have the potential virtue of calling attention to vulnerabilities that mark relationships between differently situated persons, care discourse also runs the risk of being used to ideological ends where these "differences" are defined in self-serving ways by the dominant and powerful. Notions of differences in vulnerabilities and capabilities should be recognized as *contested terrain*, requiring critical attention to who defines these differences as well as their practical implications.

Ideological pictures of the nature of Self and Others, and of one's relationship to Others are problematic pictures shared by large historically constituted groups of individuals. It is not clear to me that any moral theory is immune to such ideological deployment, nor am I convinced that there is any moral faculty or set of moral practices, neither Humean "reflexion" nor Kantian "reason," whose careful and sustained cultivation *necessarily* liberates particular individuals from the historical effects of such ideologies. It seems to me that what such ideological pictures often yield to are not primarily theoretical moral self-corrections, based either on reason or on enlarged sympathies with Others, but to political contestations and moral challenges by groups who are victimized by the status quo. To challenge the paternalisitc construction of femininity and of colonial subjectivity, western women and the colonized had to resort to insurgencies, rebellions, and protests, and had to *prove* themselves to be moral and political agents in order to make plausible their claims to such agency.

Two broad strategies were used both by western women and by the colonized in these contestations: (a) there were frequent assertions that western women or the colonized possessed the capacities and capabilities that entitled them to the same rights as white male colonizers, and (b) there were frequent re-descriptions of the "paternalistic protective project" as one based instead on force and exploitation, inflicting misery on the powerless, and brutalizing those with power. The powerful role played by rights discourse in these emancipatory movements should not lead us to ignore their concurrent critique of the paternalisitic colonial care-discourses that operated as justifications for their domination.

The alternative moral visions of the agency of women or of the colonized that developed in such political contestations, though they challenge the moral picture of the world held by the powerful, are not themselves immune to creating or reinforcing other relationships of power. A great deal has been written on how, for instance, the contemporary feminist movement has tended to be focused on the interest of middle-class white women, and about how drawing attention to the problems of women of color remains an ongoing problem. Anticolonial nationalist movements often displayed similar problems—in that nationalist discourses often constructed issues in a manner that marginalized colonized women. Several strands of Indian nationalism, for instance, associated Indian women with the preservation of Indian traditions, culture, and spirituality—a function that simultaneously gave them an *imagined function* in the nationalist agenda, but excluded them from *real participation* in many areas of work, politics, and public culture (Chatterjee 1990, 243). Thus, though I believe large-scale political movements have been historically crucial in bringing about certain forms of moral change and progress, these movements too generate problematic moral narrative. I would conclude that moral theories need to be evaluated not only in terms of their theoretical adequacy in accounting for the range of phenomena in our moral lives but also with regard to the instrumental political uses to which they lend themselves at concrete historical junctures.

I shall end with a few reflections on the relationship between rights and care discourses. The perspectives of colonialism, as well as those of many colonized cultures, and of many contemporary societies, provide several examples of what John Ladd refers to as the "Doctrine of Moral Disqualification," whereby groups with social power define members of other groups in ways that disqualify them for full membership in the moral community (Ladd 1992, 40). These definitions have been repeatedly used to justify the denial of rights to members of "disqualified" groups. These definitions have also been used to justify the failure to be genuinely attentive and responsive to the needs, interests, and welfare of the members of these groups. Dominant social definitions of what an untouchable or a slave was, did not encourage the powerful to care for the less powerful; and the same definitions were in fact inimical to the well-being of the less powerful, who were not, by these definitions, entitled to the means and opportunities for flourishing.

Justice concerns have been central to many social and political movements because asserting and gaining rights have been instrumental in transforming certain groups of people, however imperfectly, into fellow citizens whose concerns mattered, into people whose human worth mattered. However, as many slave-narratives well illustrate, much of the moral and political work that was necessary to change the "moral disqualification" inflicted on powerless groups consisted not only of claims to rights, but of attempts to call attention to the *suffering* inflicted on the powerless by the status quo. These political depictions of suffering can be seen as attempts to elicit the attentiveness and moral responsiveness of those with power, by redescribing the life situations of the powerless in ways that challenged the rationalizations of the powerful. The discourses of slave narratives, for example, make it difficult for members of dominant groups to continue to believe in the myth of happy slaves, content with their lot.

Joan Tronto may well be right in arguing that "one of the practical effects of the widespread adoption of a theory of care may be to make our concerns for justice less central" (Tronto 1995). I would like to add the converse claim, that a more serious commitment to and enforcement of the claims of justice might, at least in some cases, be a precondition for the possibility of adequately caring for and about some people. Tronto herself acknowledges that "*until* we care about something, the care process cannot begin" (Tronto 1995). Social relationships of domination often operate so as to make many who have power unable to *genuinely* care about the marginalized and powerless.

Although I am very sympathetic to the idea of a politics and of public policies that are more sensitive to needs, I am not sure we can arrive at what Tronto calls "a full account of human needs" without serious attention to considerations of justice that would enable the powerless to seriously participate in the social and political discourse where such needs are contested and defined. Once again, adequate attention to justice may, in some instances, be a precondition for adequately caring policies.

Virginia Held argues that though justice is an important moral value, much moderately good life has gone on without it, for instance, in families where there has been little justice but much care. She points out that we can have care without justice, but that, without care, there would be no persons to respect (Held 1995). I suggest that attending to what happens in some families also reveals situations in which without justice, care may fail to be provided. India, for instance, has an alarming and growing "deficit of women" in the population. Some of this is due to active acts of infanticide and female feticide. But the most significant cause seems to be what is called "the fatal neglect of female children" by their own families. In a nutshell, girl children are systematically and seemingly non-deliberately provided substantially less care—nutritional, medical, and so forth—than are boys (Sen 1990). My point is, in some families, without more justice, of a sort that changes the cultural meanings and material implications of having daughters, care will fail to be provided, and many female infants will not grow up to become adult bearers of rights.

Carol Gilligan's work suggests that rights and care perspectives provide alternative accounts of moral problems and decisions, and that shifting to a care perspective foregrounds moral issues of preserving and maintaining relationships that are often not well illuminated by a rights perspective. I understand both Tronto and Held as arguing that the care perspective is a wider or possibly more foundational framework, within which considerations of rights and justice constitute a subset—admittedly an important one.

I would like to suggest yet another possibility. Improvements along dimensions of justice and rights might, in some cases such as the issue of fatal neglect of female children, provide what I shall call "enabling conditions" for the provision of adequate care. In other cases, improvements along care dimensions, such as attentiveness to and concern for human needs and human suffering, might provide the "enabling conditions" for more adequate forms of justice. For instance, attention to the needs, predicaments and suffering of the impoverished and destitute in affluent western societies might result in social policies that institutionalize welfare rights, rights to adequate medical care, and so forth.

I suggest that this is one possible dimension of the relationships between care and justice considerations, and not an over-arching account of their relationship. I am suggesting that, in particular contexts, struggles for greater justice may foster more adequate or richer forms of care and that in others, the cultivation of a care perspective might foster enhanced forms of justice. In some situations at least, justice and care perspectives might be seen less as contenders for theoretical primacy or moral and political adequacy and more as collaborators and allies in our practical and political efforts to make our world more conducive to human flourishing.

REFERENCES

Chatterjee, Partha. 1990. The nationalist resolution of the women's question. In *Recasting women: Essays in Indian colonial history*, ed. Kumkum Sangari and Suresh Vaid. New Brunswick: Rutgers University Press.

Chaudhuri, Nupur, and Margaret Strobel, eds. 1992. *Western women and imperialism: Complicity and resistance*. Bloominton: Indiana University Press.

Held, Virginia. 1995. The meshing of care and justice. *Hypatia* 10 (2): 128-132.

Ladd, John. 1991. The idea of collective violence. In *Justice, law and violence*, ed. James A. Brady and Newton Garver. Philadelphia: Temple University Press.

Mill, John Stuart. 1965. *Principles of political economy*, Vol. 3. Ed. J. M. Robson. Toronto: University of Toronto Press.

Said, Edward. 1993. *Culture and imperialism*. New York: Alfred A. Knopf.

Sen, Amartya. 1990. More than 100 million women are missing. *New York Review of Books*, December 1990.

Tronto, Joan. 1994. Care as a basis for radical political judgements. *Hypatia* 10 (2): 141-149.

Zlotnick, Susan. 1994. Domesticating imperialism: Curry and cookbooks in Victorian England. Paper presented at the American Political Science Association meeting, New York City.

STUDY QUESTIONS

1. What does Appiah mean by racialism? What is the distinction between "extrinsic" and "intrinsic" racism meant to capture and what is the connection of each to racialism?
2. What does Appiah mean by the claim that intrinsic racism has tended to be "the natural expression of feelings of community"? Do Black Nationalists of the 1960s fit the description of intrinsic racists? Why or why not? What objections does Appiah raise against intrinsic racism?
3. Do you agree with Appiah that the right tactic for opposing racism "is to object to it rationally in the form in which it stands the best chance of meeting objections"? Do you agree with Appiah that those who hold on to their prejudices even when confronted with incontrovertible evidence that their prejudices are based on false beliefs are perhaps not morally responsible? Provide reasons for your answers.
4. According to Outlaw, what role has reason played in philosophical accounts of human nature and how have these accounts contributed to racial and ethnic discrimination?
5. Is Outlaw rejecting reason? Does his critique of reason raise concerns about Appiah's tactic of using reason to combat racism? Provide reasons for your answers.
6. Outlaw concludes his historical survey of scientific accounts of race and ethnicity by arguing that "race or ethnicity are without scientific bases in biological terms." He agrees with Appiah in this respect, but disagrees with Appiah's move toward universalism and advocates instead a "play of differences" that takes account of the "constitutive differences" of persons in a group. Compare and evaluate the respective strategies.
7. According to Outlaw, what contributions can philosophy make to the goal of an emancipated and just society? What is cosmopolitan liberalism and do you share Outlaw's view that philosophy can contribute to the achievement of this new liberalism that is not universalist? Why or why not?
8. Beginning with the idea and defense of the social construction of race, Frye invents the terms "whitely" and "whiteliness" on analogy with masculine and masculinity. What does she mean by these terms? Do you recognize whiteliness in white people? In what ways?
9. According to Frye, how do factors such as class and gender affect the account of whiteliness? Do you think that the unlearning of femininity, masculinity, or whiteliness is an effective strategy for eliminating sexism or racism? Why or why not?
10. What are some of the concerns raised by Davion about Frye's account of whiteliness? What does Davion mean by her claim that getting rid of whiteliness does not mean getting rid of one's ethnicity?
11. How does Yamada's account of student reactions to "outspoken Asian American writers" illuminate the kind of oppression experienced by Asian Americans? What does she mean by invisibility and what strategies does she propose for changing it?
12. According to Narayan, what sorts of questions are raised about the discourse of care and justice in Western liberal societies when we examine issues of colonialism?
13. According to Narayan, what can attention to the colonial context teach us about the insights of both the justice and the care approaches to morality? Does her contextual account of the relationship between justice and care provide a way to address issues of discrimination on the basis of race and ethnicity?

SUGGESTED READINGS

Alcoff, Linda Martin. "Philosophy and Racial Identity." *Radical Philosophy*, v. 75 (Jan/Feb 1996): 5-14.

Brittan, Arthur and Mary Maynard. "Primary and Secondary Oppression." In *Sexism, Racism and Oppression*. Oxford: Blackwell, 1984.

Card, Claudia. "On Race, Racism, and Ethnicity." In *Overcoming Racism and Sexism* edited by Linda Bell and David Blumenfeld. Lanham, MD: Rowman & Littlefield, 1995.

Collins, Patricia Hill. *Black Feminist Thought: Knowledge, Consciousness and the Politics of Empowerment*. Boston: Unwin Hyman, 1990.

Corlett, Angelo J. "Analyzing Racism." *Public Affairs Quarterly*, v. 12, no. 1 (January 1998): 23-50.

Du Bois, W.E.B. "The Concept of Race." In *Dusk of Dawn*. New York: Harcourt, Brace and World, 1940.

Goldberg, David Theo. "Racist Exclusions." *Philosophical Forum* (Boston), v. 26, no. 1 (Fall 1994): 1-32.

— . "The Social Formation of Racist Discourse." In *Anatomy of Racism* edited by David Theo Goldberg. University of Minnesota Press, 1990.

Lichtenberg, Judith. "Racism in the Head, Racism in the World." *Report from the Institute for Philosophy & Public Policy*, v. 12, no. 1 (Spring/Summer 1992): 3-5.

Lorde, Audre. "Age, Race, Class, and Sex: Women Redefining Difference." In *Sister Outsider*. Freedom, CA: Crossing Press, 1984: 114-123.

May, Larry. "Shared Responsibility for Racism." In *Sharing Responsibility*. University of Chicago, 1992.

Outlaw, Lucius (Jr.). *On Race and Philosophy.* New York: Routledge, 1996.

Scheman, Naomi. "Jewish Lesbian Writing: A Review Essay." *Hypatia*, v. 7, no. 4 (Fall 1992): 186-194.

Schmid, W. Thomas. "The Definition of Racism." *Journal of Applied Philosophy*, v. 13, no. 1 (1996): 31-40.

Singer, Peter. "Is Racial Discrimination Arbitrary?" *Philosophia*, v. 8, nos. 2-3 (1978): 185-205.

Thomas, Laurence. "Power, Trust, and Evil." In *Overcoming Racism and Sexism* edited by Linda Bell and David Blumenfeld. Lanham, MD: Rowman & Littlefield, 1995.

— . "What Good Am I?" In *Affirmative Action and the University: A Philosophical Inquiry* edited by Steven M. Cahn. Philadelphia: Temple University Press, 1993: 125-131.

Wasserstrom, Richard. "Racism, Sexism, and Preferential Treatment: An Approach to the Topics." *UCLA Law Review*, v. 24 (1977): 581-622.

West, Cornel. "The Black Underclass and Black Philosophers." In *Prophetic Thought in Postmodern Times*. Monroe, ME: Common Courage Press, 1993: 143-157.

CHAPTER FIVE

GENDER

At the end of the previous chapter, Narayan points to a place where racism intersects with sexism: an entrenched belief in the unequal capacities and inferior status of some human beings shapes the belief that it is in the interests of these human beings to be "cared for" by others who are superior and can confer benefits. Narayan draws parallels between relationships of colonizers and colonized as conceived by colonizers and those between men and women as conceived by men. In this chapter, we examine the latter sorts of relationships in detail. It will be useful, however, to first stop and explain the concept "feminism" already mentioned in several of the readings. Feminism is generally associated with the social movement to achieve equality for women. It also represents a huge and ever expanding body of theory, which makes it increasingly difficult to define feminism in a way that captures the diversity of feminist activists and the range of feminist theories. There are at least two elements in common: a recognition that women are oppressed and a commitment to ending that oppression. This definition leaves room for a wide variety of explanations for women's oppression and of strategies advocated for eliminating that oppression. It also leaves room for the important realization that there is no examination of women as such because there are women of different races, ethnicities, sexual orientations, and levels of ability and wealth.

The chapter opens with a reading by Susan Moller Okin, who worries that emphasizing difference(s) undermines attempts to formulate a theory of justice that can address injustices for women in poor and developing countries. Okin admits the force of the charge of essentialism from within feminism. Often it results in representing the lives and experiences of white middle- and upper-class women to the exclusion of women whose experiences reflect the affects of race, class, ethnicity, and other differences. However, she argues that this problem is less evident in the work of recent feminists and that current anti-essentialist critics lack empirical evidence to support their claims that there are no experiences shared by all women. She defends the position that Western feminist accounts of justice can be applied to the situations of poor women in many poor countries and that their experiences are "similar to ours but more so."

Okin outlines several aspects of a "generalizable, identifiable and collectively shared experience of womanhood," which she extracts through a critique of current theories of justice and of development. Both theories assume a dichotomy between a public/political sphere, to which theories of justice and development apply, and a private/domestic sphere, to which theories of justice and development do not apply. In both, it is assumed that women are caretakers of families in the private sphere, where work is invisible in data about economic development. The devaluation of women's work results in their economic dependence on men and subjection to physical and psychological abuse by men. Attention to gender, argues Okin, highlights inequalities in opportunity, access to jobs, and pay for women in the United States. These inequalities can be fatal for poor women in poor countries where power differentials between men and women are magnified, and laws and cultural norms bar women from the workforce. According to Okin, the similar situation of women in different parts of the world calls for similar strategies and solutions: challenging the dichotomization of public and private spheres and treating women as equal individuals with rights to full economic participation.

Chandra Mohanty focuses on Western feminist discourse about women in developing countries.

However, she rejects Okin's account of a generalizable, collectively shared experience of womanhood by showing that the monolithic "Third World Woman" in recent Western feminist texts fails to capture the differences that characterize the lives of third-world women. Mohanty challenges Western feminists to examine their role in producing scholarship that stands as authoritative, yet dismisses the lives and experiences of women in various developing countries. She also urges that portrayals of third-world women as a homogeneous group characterized by common dependencies, powerlessness, and victim status need to be understood in the context of relations of power between Western and developing countries.

Rather than focus on mothering or marriage or a sexual division of labor as such, Mohanty argues that we need to understand the relationships and structures within which these practices are given the meaning and value they have in particular historical contexts. A monolithic notion of gender ignores the effects of social class, ethnic identities, and cultural practices on the meaning of gender and results in a serious failure to understand the kinds of oppression experienced by women and to effectively organize to eliminate it. Mohanty does not reject generalization as such, but calls for careful historically specific generalizations that are responsive to complex realities. To erase the relevance of gender differences is to rob third-world women of their historical and political agency and to subject them to judgments about their underdevelopment and susceptibility to false consciousness about their oppression.

The idea that context is relevant to an analysis of gender is pursued by Nkiru Nzegwu, who focuses on the specific case of women in Nigeria. Nzegwu gives substance to Mohanty's claim that women in developing countries are neither a monolithic entity nor easily understood by Westerners. Like Mohanty, Nzegwu outlines factors of colonization that enter into judgments about the beliefs, practices, and values of people in developing countries. Nzegwu reconstructs Igbo traditions and values in Nigeria prior to colonization not only to highlight the virtual destruction of these by the West first through colonization and then in development projects, but to recover a picture of the place and value of women in Igbo culture that seriously challenges the Western and feminist understanding of gender.

Nzegwu describes the political culture of Igbo tradition as dual-sex, one that divided Igbo society along gender lines but accorded women respect and gave them independence through their own governing councils and power to enforce rules and regulations in specific economic domains. But development projects worked with Western assumptions about gender that devalued the female empowering institutions of Africa's indigenous cultures and left no place for women. Nzegwu advocates radical revisions to developmental approaches and policy. Instead of working with assumptions about human needs based on Western paradigms of development and models of gender roles, Nzegwu calls for greater awareness of the diverse character of different groups of women and of alternative models of knowledge and organizational skills. One such model is that offered by women's organizations that have endured in Nigeria, organizations that represent a network of women with extensive knowledge of communities, skills, practices, and needs.

In the final reading, attention is again focused closely on women in a specific context. Janice Newberry examines political structures in Indonesia from the perspectives, lives, and experiences of Indonesian women who are affected by them. Newberry describes the Indonesian government program known as PKK, a national housewives' organization institutionalized in 1973 and responsible for monitoring and maintaining health, literacy, skills training in cooking, and small business endeavors in households and communities. PKK, as Newberry explains it, is a form of state-sponsored domesticity, a structure imposed by the Indonesian government to mobilize women as unpaid community development workers with responsibility for improving the standards of living of families and communities. The rhetoric of PKK upholds the nuclear family organized around a single couple, with the woman staying at home, as the model of good households and communities. This model has its source in Indonesia's history of Dutch colonialism, both in its struggles against it and its appropriation of the Western notions of good mother and housewife that it brought.

Newberry uses the term "good terrorist" to argue that the very roles taken to be constitutive of what it is to be a good mother and housewife can and are used by Indonesian women to generate social change. Within the confines of PKK, women live lives that contest the moral order promulgated by the state. The concept of the good terrorist captures the paradoxical idea that maintaining a social order can actually be subversive as women make use of the contradictions in their daily lives through the practices and values they endorse to challenge and change the social order. Women in Indonesia, argues Newberry, are good terrorists to the extent that they comply with government directives on proper homes and domesticity, but only insofar as it serves their own ends and allows them to meet the needs of their communities. In the process, they open up a space for changing not only their own lives but the very picture of what counts as a good mother and citizen.

GENDER INEQUALITY AND CULTURAL DIFFERENCES

Susan Moller Okin

Susan Moller Okin is Martha Sutton Weeks Professor of Ethics in Society at Stanford University. She is the author of Women in Western Political Thought *(Princeton, 1979),* Justice, Gender, and the Family *(Basic, 1989) as well as of numerous articles in feminist theory and political theory more generally.*

Susan Moller Okin concedes the force of objections from within feminism that what are often presented as accounts of experiences shared by all women have excluded women whose experiences reflect the affects of race, class, ethnicity and other differences. She worries, however, that an emphasis on differences undermines attempts to formulate a theory of justice that can address injustices, particularly those suffered by women in poor and developing countries. Okin defends the idea that there is a "generalizable, identifiable and collectively shared experience of womanhood" and sets out to outline it by criticizing current theories of justice and of development that fail to consider gender altogether. Okin argues that Western feminist accounts of justice can be applied to the situations of poor women in many poor countries and that their experiences are "similar to ours but more so."

Theories of justice are undergoing something of an identity crisis. How can they be universal, principled, founded on good reasons that all can accept, and yet take account of the many differences there are among persons and social groups? Feminists have been among the first to point out that large numbers of persons have typically been excluded from consideration in purportedly universalist theories. And some feminists have gone on to point out that many feminist theories, while taking account of sexist bias or omission, have neglected racist, heterosexist, class, religious, and other biases. Yet, joining our voices with those of others, some of us discern problems with going in the direction of formulating a theory of justice entirely by listening to every concrete individual's or group's point of view and expression of its needs. Is it possible, by taking this route, to come up with any principles at all? Is it a reliable route, given the possibility of "false consciousness"? Doesn't stressing differences, especially cultural differences, lead to a slide toward relativism? The problem that is being grappled with is an important one. There can no longer be any doubt that many voices have not been heard when most theories of justice were being shaped. But how can all the different voices express themselves and be heard and still yield a coherent and workable theory of justice? This question is one I shall (eventually) return to in this essay.

Reprinted with permission of Sage Publications from *Political Theory* 22:1 (1994): 5–24.

Feminism, Difference and Essentialism

Feminists have recently had much to say about difference. One aspect of the debate has been a continuation of an old argument—about how different women are from men, what such differences may be due to, and whether they require that laws and other aspects of public policy should treat women any differently from men.[1] Another, newer, aspect of the debate is about differences among women. It is "essentialist," some say, to talk about women, the problems of women, and especially the problems of women "as such."[2] White middle- and upper-class feminists, it is alleged, have excluded or been insensitive to not only the problems of women of other races, cultures, and religions but even those of women of other classes than their own. "Gender" is therefore a problematic category, those opposed to such essentialism say, unless always qualified by and seen in the context of race, class, ethnicity, religion, and other such differences (Childers and hooks 1990; Harris 1990; hooks 1984; Lorde 1984; Minow and Spelman 1990; Spelman 1988).

The general allegation of feminist essentialism certainly has validity when applied to some work. Feminists with such pedigrees as Harriet Taylor, Charlotte Perkins Gilman, Virginia Woolf, Simone de Beauvoir, and Betty Friedan (in *The Feminine Mystique*) all seem to have assumed, for example, that the women they were liberating would have recourse to servants. With the partial exception of Woolf, who remarks briefly on the difficult lot of maids, they did not pay attention to the servants, the vast majority of whom were also, of course, women. The tendency of many white middle- and upper-class feminists in the mid-nineteenth century to think only of women of their own class and race (some were explicitly racist) is what makes so poignant and compelling Sojourner Truth's words in her famous "Ain't I a woman?" speech.[3] However, I think, and will argue, that this problem is far less present in the works of most recent feminists. But the charges of "essentialism" seem to grow ever louder. They are summed up in Elizabeth Spelman's (1988) recent claim that "the focus on women 'as women' has addressed only one group of women—namely, white middle-class women of Western industrialized countries" (p.4). This has come to be accepted in some circles as virtually a truism.

The claim that much recent feminist theory is essentialist comes primarily from three (to some extent, overlapping) sources—European-influenced postmodernist thought; the work of African-American and other minority feminist women in the United States and Britain; and, in particular, Spelman's recent book, *Inessential Woman* (hereafter *IW*). Postmodernism is skeptical of all universal or generalizable claims, including those of feminism. It finds concepts central to feminist thinking, such as "gender" and "woman," as illegitimate as any other category or generalization that does not stop to take account of every difference. As Julia Kristeva, for example, says,

> The belief that "one is a woman" is almost as absurd and obscurantist as the belief that "one is a man"... [W]e must use "we are women" as an advertisement or slogan for our demands. On a deeper level, however, a woman cannot "be"; it is something which does not even belong in the order of *being*. (Quoted in Marks and de Courtivron 1981, 137)

In the same interview, she also says that, because of the very different history of Chinese women, "it is absurd to question their lack of 'sexual liberation'" (in Marks and de Courtivron 1981, 140). Clearly, she thinks we could have no cross-cultural explanations of or objections to gender inequality.

Spelman argues that "the phrase 'as a woman' is the Trojan horse of feminist ethnocentrism" (*IW*, 13). The great mistakes of white middle-class feminists have been to exclude women different from themselves from their critiques or, even when they are included, to assume that, whatever their differences, their experience of sexism is the same. At best, she says, what is presented is "[a]n additive analysis [which] treats the oppression of a black woman in a society that is racist as well as sexist as if it were a further burden when in fact it is a *different burden*" (*IW*, 123; emphasis added).

These antiessentialist arguments, however, are often long on theory and very short on empirical evidence. A large proportion of Spelman's examples of how women's experiences of oppression are different are taken from periods of slavery in ancient Greece and, especially, in the pre-Civil War South. It is not clear, though, how relevant is the obvious contrast between the experience of white slaveholders' wives and black female slaves to most issues involving the sameness or difference of forms of gender oppression today.

Apart from the paucity of relevant evidence (which I shall return to), there seem to me to be two other related problems with Spelman's general antiessentialist argument. One is the claim that unless a feminist theorist perceives gender identity as intrinsically bound up with class, race, or other aspects of identity she ignores the effects of these other differences altogether. Spelman writes, "If gender were isolatable from other forms of identity, if sexism were isolatable from other forms of oppression, then what would be true about the relation between any man and any woman would be true about the relation between any other man and any other woman" (*IW*, 81). But this does not follow at all. One can argue that sexism is an identifiable form of oppression, many of whose effects are felt by women regardless of race or class, without at all subscribing to the view that race and class oppression are insignificant. One can still insist, for example, on the significant difference between the relation of a poor black woman to a wealthy white man and that of a wealthy white woman to a poor black man.

The second problem is that Spelman misplaces the burden of proof, which presumably affects her perception of the need for her to produce evidence for her claims. She says, "Precisely insofar as a discussion of gender and gender relations is really, even if obscurely, about a particular group of women and their relation to a particular group of men, it is unlikely to be applicable to any other group of women" (*IW*, 114). But why? Surely the burden of proof is on the critic. To be convincing, she needs to show that and how the theory accused of essentialism omits or distorts the experience of persons other than those few the theorist allegedly does take account of. This, after all, is the burden that many of the feminists Spelman considers "essentialist" have themselves taken on in critiquing "malestream" theories. One of the problems of antiessentialist feminism (shared, I think, with much of postmodernist critique) is that it tends to substitute the cry "We're all different" for both argument and evidence.

There are, however, exceptions, and they tend to come from feminists who belong to racial minorities. One of the best critiques of feminist essentialism that I know of is that by Angela Harris (1990), in which she shows how ignorance of the specifics of a culture mars even thoroughly well-intentioned feminist analyses of women's experiences of oppression within that culture. She argues, for example, that in some respects, black women in the United States have had a qualitatively rather than simply quantitatively different experience of rape than that of white women (see esp. 594, 598-601). Even here, though, I think the antiessentialist critique is only partly convincing. Although more concerned with evidence for the salience of differences than most antiessentialists seem to be, Harris raises far more empirical questions than she provides answers. She provides just one example to support her assertion that black women's experience of rape is, even now, radically different from that of white women—that it is "an experience as deeply rooted in color as in gender" (p. 598).[4] Yet she, like Spelman, is as much disturbed by white feminists' saying that black women are "just like us only more so" as she is by their marginalizing black women or ignoring them altogether. As I shall argue, this "insult[ing]" conclusion—that the problems of other women are "similar to ours but more so"—is exactly the one I reach when I apply some Western feminist ideas about justice to the situations of poor women in many poor countries.

In this essay, I put antiessentialist feminism to what I think is a reasonably tough test. In doing this, I am taking up the gauntlet that Spelman throws down. She says, referring to the body of new work about women that has appeared in many fields,

> Rather than assuming that women have something in common as women, these researchers should help us look to see whether they do.... Rather than first finding out what is true of some women as women and then inferring that this is true of all women ... , we have to investigate different women's lives and see what they have in common. (*IW,* 137)

Trained as a philosopher, she does not seem to consider it appropriate to take up the challenge of actually looking at some of this empirical evidence. Having said the above, she turns back to discussing Plato. Trained as a political scientist, I shall attempt to look at some comparative evidence. I'll put some Western feminist ideas about justice and inequality to the test (drawing on my recent book and the many feminist sources I use to support some of its arguments) by seeing how well these theories—developed in the context of women in well-off Western industrialized countries—work when used to look at the very different situations of some of the poorest women in poor countries. How do our accounts and our explanations of gender inequality stand up in the face of considerable cultural and socioeconomic difference?

Differences and Similarities in Gender Oppression: Poor Women in Poor Countries

Does the assumption "that there is a generalizable, identifiable and collectively shared experience of womanhood" (Benhabib and Cornell 1987, 13) *have* any validity, or is it indeed an essentialist myth, rightly challenged by Third World women and their spokesfeminists? Do the theories devised by First World feminists, particularly our critiques of non-feminist theories of justice, have anything to say, in particular, to the poorest women in poor countries, or to those policymakers with the potential to affect their lives for better or for worse?

In trying to answer these questions, I shall address, in turn, four sets of issues, which have been addressed both by recent feminist critics of Anglo-American social and political theory and by those development scholars who have in recent years concerned themselves with the neglect or distortions of the situation of women in the countries they study. First, why and how has the issue of the inequality between the sexes been ignored or obscured for so long and addressed only so recently? Second, why is it so important that it be addressed? Third, what do we find, when we subject households or families to standards of justice—when we look at the largely hidden inequalities between the sexes? And finally, what are the policy implications of these findings?

Why Attention to Gender Is Comparatively New

In both development studies and theories of justice, there has, until recently, been a marked lack of attention to gender—and in particular to systematic inequalities between the sexes. This point has been made about theories of justice throughout the 1980s (e.g., Kearns 1983; Okin 1989b; Crosswaite 1989). In the development literature, it was first made earlier, in pioneering work by Ester Boserup, but has lately been heard loud and strong from a number of other prominent development theorists (Chen 1983; Dasgupta 1993; Sen 1990a, 1990b; Jelin 1990). In both contexts, the neglect of women and gender seems to be due primarily to two factors. The first is the assumption that the household (usually assumed to be male-headed) is the appropriate unit of analysis. The dichotomy between the public (political and economic) and the private (domestic and personal) is assumed valid, and only the former has been taken to be the appropriate sphere for development studies and theories of justice, respectively, to attend to. In ethical and political theories, the family is often regarded as an inappropriate context for justice, since love, altruism, or shared interests are assumed to hold sway within it. Alternatively, it is sometimes taken for granted that it is a realm of hierarchy and injustice. (Occasional theorists, like Rousseau, have said both!) In economics, development and other, households until recently have simply been taken for granted as the appropriate unit of analysis on such questions as income distribution. The public/private dichotomy and the assumption of the male-headed household have many serious implications for women as well as for children that are discussed below (Dasgupta 1993; Jaquette 1982, 283; Okin 1989b, 10-14, 124-33; Olsen 1983; Pateman 1983).

The second factor is the closely related failure to disaggregate data or arguments by sex. In the development literature, it seems to appear simply in this form (Chen, Huq, and D'Souza 1981, 68; Jaquette 1982, 283-84). In the justice literature, this used to be obscured by the use of male pronouns and other referents. Of late, the (rather more insidious) practice that I have called "false gender neutrality" has appeared. This consists in the use of gender-neutral terms ("he or she," "persons," and so on), when the point being made is simply invalid or otherwise false if one actually applies it to women (Okin 1989b, esp. 10-13, 45). But the effect is the same in both literatures; women are not taken into account, so the inequalities between the sexes are obscured.

The public/domestic dichotomy has serious implications for women. It not only obscures intrahousehold inequalities of resources and power, as I discuss below, but it also results in the failure to count a great deal of the work done by women as work, since all that is considered "work" is what is done for pay in the "public" sphere. All of the work that women do in bearing and rearing children, cleaning and maintaining households, caring for the old and sick, and contributing in various ways to men's work does not count as work. This is clearly one of those instances in which the situation of poor women in poor countries is not qualitatively *different* from that of most women in rich countries but, rather, "similar but worse," for even more, in some cases far more, of the work done by women (and children) in poor countries is rendered invisible, not counted, or "subsumed under men's work." The work of subsistence farming, tending to animals, domestic crafts (if not for the market) and the often arduous fetching of water and fuel are all added to the category of unrecognized work of women that already exists in richer countries5 Chen notes that women who do all these things "are listed [by policymakers] as housewives," even though "their tasks are as critical to the wellbeing of their families and to national production as are the men's"(Chen 1983, 220; see also Dasgupta 1993; Drèze and Sen 1989, chap. 4; Jaquette 1982, citing Bourgue and Warren 1979; Waring 1989).

Why Does it Matter?

This may seem like a silly question. Indeed, I hope it will soon be unnecessary, but it isn't—yet. I therefore argue, at the outset of *Justice, Gender, and the Family*, that the omission from theories of justice of gender, and of much of women's lives, is significant for three major reasons. Each of these reasons applies at least as much to the neglect of gender in theories of development. The first is obvious: women matter (at least they do to feminists), and their well-being matters at least as much as that of men. As scholars of development have recently been making clear, the inequalities between the sexes in a number of poor countries have not only highly detrimental but *fatal* consequences for millions of women. Sen (1990a) has recently argued that as many as one hundred million fewer women exist than might normally be expected on the basis of male/female mortality rates in societies less devaluing of women—not only the Western industrialized world by much of sub-Saharan Africa, too (see also Dasgupta 1993; Drèze and Sen 1989, chap 4; Drèze and Sen 1990, Introduction, 11-14; but cf. Harriss 1990; Wheeler and Abdullah 1988). So here too we can reasonably say that the issue of the neglect of women is "similar but *much* worse."

The second reason I have raised (in the U.S. context) for the necessity for feminist critique of theories of social justice is that equality of opportunity—for women and girls—but also for increasing numbers of boys—is much affected by the failure of theories of justice to address gender inequality. This is in part due to the greater extent of economic distress in female-headed households. In the United States, nearly 25 percent of children are being raised in single female-headed households, and three-fifths of all chronically poor households with children are among those supported by single women. It has been recently estimated that throughout the world one-third of households are headed by single females, with the percentage much higher in regions with significant male out-migration (Chen 1983, 221; Jaquette 1982, 271). Many millions of children are affected by the higher rate of poverty among such families.[6] Theories of justice or of economic development that fail to pay attention to gender ignore this, too.

In addition, the gendered division of labor has a serious and direct impact on the opportunities of girls and women, which crosses the lines of economic class. The opportunities of females are significantly affected by the structures and practices of family life, particularly by the fact that women are almost invariably primary caretakers, which has much impact on their availability for full-time wage work. It also results in their frequently being overworked and renders them less likely than men to be considered economically valuable. This factor, too, operates "similarly but more so" within poor families in many poor countries. There, too, adult women suffer—often more severely—many of the same effects of the division of labor as do women in richer countries. But, in addition, their daughters are likely to be put to work for the household at a very young age, are much less likely to be educated and to attain literacy that are sons of the same households and, worst of all—less valued that their brothers—they have less chance of staying alive because they are more likely to be deprived of food or of health care (Dasgupta 1993; Drèze and Sen 1990, chap. 4; Sen 1990a; Papanek 1990).

Third, I have argued that the failure to address the issue of just distribution within households is significant because the family is the first, and arguably the most influential, school of moral development (Okin 1989b, esp. 17-23). It is the first environment in which we experience how persons treat each other, in which we have the potential to learn how to be just or unjust. If children see that sex difference is the occasion for obviously differential treatment, they are surely likely to be affected in their personal and moral development. They are likely to learn injustice by absorbing the messages, if male, that they have some kind of "natural" enhanced entitlement and, if female, that they are *not* equals and had better get used to being subordinated if not actually abused. So far as I know, this point was first made in the Western context by John Stuart Mill, who wrote of the "perverting influence" of the typical English family of his time—which he termed "a school of despotism" (Mill [1869] 1988, 88). I have argued that the still remaining unequal distribution of benefits and burdens between most parents in two-parent heterosexual families is likely to affect their children's developing sense of justice (Okin 1989b, e.g., 21-23, 97-101). In the context of poor countries, as Papanek (1990) notes, "Domestic groups in which age and gender difference confer power on some over others are poor environments in which to unlearn the norms of inequality" (pp. 163-65). She also notes that "given the persistence of gender-based inequalities in power, authority, and access to resources, one must conclude that socialization for gender inequality is by and large very successful" (p. 170). When such basic goods as food and health care are unequally distributed to young children according to sex, a very strong signal about the acceptability of injustice is surely conferred. The comparison of most families in rich countries with poor families in poor countries—where distinctions between the sexes often start earlier and are much more blatant and more harmful to girls—yields, here too, the conclusion that, in the latter case, things are not so much different as "similar but more so." Many Third World families, it seems, are even worse schools of justice and more successful inculcators of the inequality of the sexes as natural and appropriate than are their developed world equivalents. Thus there is even more need for attention to be paid to gender inequality in the former context than in the latter.

Justice in the Family

What do we find when we compare some of Anglo-American feminists' findings about justice within households in their societies with recent discoveries about distributions of benefits and burdens in poor households in poor countries? Again, in many respects, the injustices of gender are quite similar.

In both situations, women's access to paid work is constrained both by discrimination and sex segregation in the workplace and by the assumption that women are "naturally" responsible for all or most of the unpaid work of the household (Bergmann 1986; Fuchs 1988; Gerson 1985; Okin 1989b, 147-52, 155-56; Sanday 1974). In both situations, women typically work longer total hours than men:

> Time-use statistics considering all work (paid and unpaid economic activity and unpaid housework) reveal that women spend more of their time working than men in all developed and developing regions except northern America and Australia, where the hours are almost equal. (United Nations Report 1991, 81 and chap. 6 passim; see also Bergmann 1986; Hochschild 1989)

In both situations, developed and less developed, vastly more of women's work is not paid and is not considered "productive."[7] Thus there is a wide gap between men's and women's *recorded* economic participation. The perception that women's work is of less worth (despite the fact that in most places they do more, and it is crucial to the survival of household members) contributes to women's being devalued and having less power both within the family and outside the household (Blumstein and Schwartz 1983; Dasgupta 1993; Drèze and Sen 1990, chap. 4; Okin 1989b, chap. 7; Sanday 1974; Sen 1990a, 1990b). This in turn adversely affects their capacity to become economically less dependent on men. Thus they become involved in "a cycle of socially caused and distinctly asymmetric vulnerability" (Okin 1989b, 138; Drèze and Sen 1989, 56-59). The devaluation of women's work, as well as their lesser physical strength and economic dependence on men, allows them to be subject to physical, sexual, and/or psychological abuse by men they live with (Gordon 1988; United Nations Report 1991, 19-20). However, in many poor countries, as I have mentioned, this power differential extends beyond the abuse and overwork of women to deprivation in terms of the feeding, health care, and education of female children—and even to their being born or not: "of 8,000 abortions in Bombay after parents learned the sex of the foetus through amniocentesis, only one would have been a boy."(United Nations Report 1991; see also Dasgupta 1993; Drèze and Sen 1989, chap. 4; Sen 1990a).

In cross-regional analyses, both Sen and Dasgupta have found correlations between the life expectancies of females relative to males and the extent to which women's work is perceived as having economic value. Thus in both rich and poor countries, women's participation in work outside the household can improve their status within the family, but this is not necessarily assured. It is interesting to compare Barbara Bergmann's (1986) analysis of the situation of "drudge wives" in the United States, who work full-time for pay and who also perform virtually all of the household's unpaid labor, with Peggy Sanday's earlier finding that, in some Third World contexts, women who do little of the work that is considered "productive" have low status, whereas many who do a great deal of it become "virtual slaves" (Sanday 1974, p. 201; Bergmann 1986, pp. 260-73).[8]

This leads us to the issue of women's economic dependence (actual and perceived). Although most poor women in poor countries work long hours each day, throughout the world they are often economically dependent on men. This, too, is "similar to but worse than" the situation of many women in richer countries. It results from so much of their work being unpaid work, so much of their paid work being poorly paid work, and, in some cases, from men's laying claim to the wages their wives and daughters earn. Feminist critics since Ester Boserup (1970) have argued that women's economic dependency on men was in many cases exacerbated by changes that development theory and development policy makers saw only as "progressive." All too ready to perceive women as dependents, mainstream theorists did not notice that technology, geographical mobility, and the conversion from subsistence to market economies were not, from the female point of view, "unalloyed benefits, but ... processes that cut women out from their traditional economic and social roles and thrust them into the modern sector where they are discriminated against and exploited, often receiving cash incomes below the subsistence level, ... in turn increas(ing) female dependency" (Jaquette 1982; see also Boserup 1970; Rogers, in Jaquette).[9]

In both rich and poor countries, women who are the sole economic support of families often face particular hardship. However, whereas some are, not all of the reasons for this are the same. Discrimination against women in access to jobs, pay, retention, and promotion are common to most countries, with obviously deleterious effects on female-supported families. In the United States, the average full-time working woman earns a little more than two-thirds of the pay of a full-time male worker, and three-fifths of the families with children who live in chronic poverty are single female-parent families. Many such women in both rich and poor countries also suffer from severe "time poverty."

But the situation of some poor women in poor countries is different from—as well as distinctly worse than—that of most Western women today. It is more like the situation of the latter in the nineteenth century: even when they have no other means of support, they are actually *prohibited* (by religiously based laws or oppressive cultural norms) from engaging in paid labor. Martha Chen has studied closely the situation of such women in the Indian subcontinent. Deprived of the traditional economic support of a male, they are prevented from taking paid employment by rules of caste, or *purdah*. For such women, it can indeed be liberating to be helped (as they have been by outsiders like Chen) to resist the sanctions invoked against them by family elders, neighbors, or powerful social leaders. Although many forms of wage work, especially those available to women, are hardly "liberating," except in the most basic sense, women are surely distinctly less free if they are *not* allowed to engage in it, especially if they have no other means of support. Many employed women in Western industrialized countries still face quite serious disapproval if they are mothers of young children or if the family's need for their wages is not perceived as great. But at least, except in the most oppressive of families or subcultures, they are allowed to go out to work. By contrast, as Chen's work makes clear, the basic right to be *allowed* to make a much needed living for themselves and their children is still one that many women in the poorest of situations in other cultures are denied.

Here, then, is a real difference—an oppressive situation that most Western women no longer face. But to return to similarities: another that I discovered, while comparing some of our Western feminist ideas about justice with work on poor women in poor countries, has to do with the dynamics of power within the family. The differential exit potential theory that I adopt from Albert Hirschman's work to explain power within the family has recently been applied to the situation of women in poor countries (cf. Okin 1989b, chap. 7 with Dasgupta 1993 and Sen 1990b). Partha Dasgupta (1993) also uses exit theory in explaining the "not uncommon" desertion by men of their families during famines. He writes, "The man deserts [his wife] because *his* outside option in these circumstances emerges higher in his ranking than any feasible allocation within the household" (p. 329). He regards the "hardware" he employs—John Nash's game-theoretic program—as "needed if we are to make any progress in what is a profoundly complex matter, the understanding of household decisions" (p. 329). But the conclusion he reaches is very similar to the one that I reach, drawing on Hirschman's theory of power and the effects of persons' differential exit potential: any factor that improves the husband's exit option or detracts from the wife's exit option thereby gives him additional voice, or bargaining power in the relationship. Likewise, anything that improves the wife's exit option—her acquisition of human or physical capital, for example—will increase her autonomy and place her in a better bargaining position in the relationship (Dasgupta 1993, 331-33; Okin 1989b, chap.7)[10]

In the United States, recent research has shown that women's and children's economic status (taking need into account) typically deteriorates after separation or divorce, whereas the average divorcing man's economic status actually improves (McLindon 1987; Weitzman 1985; Wishik 1986). This, taken in conjunction with the exit/voice theory, implies less bargaining power for wives within marriage. In poor countries, where circumstances of severe poverty combine with a lack of paid employment opportunities for women, increasing women's dependency on men, men's power within the family—already in most cases legitimized by highly patriarchal cultural norms—seems very likely to be enhanced. Although, as Dasgupta (1993) points out, Nash's formula was not intended as a normative theory, employed in this context, the theory not only *explains* (much as does my employment of Hirschman's theory) the cyclical nature of women's lack of power within the family. It also points to the injustice of a situation in which the assumption of women's responsibility for children, their disadvantaged position in the paid workforce, and their physical vulnerability to male violence all contribute to giving them little bargaining room when their (or their children's) interests conflict with those of the men they live with, thereby in turn worsening their position relative to that of men. The whole theory, then, whether in its more or its less mathematical form, seems just as applicable to the situations of very poor women in poor countries as it is to women in quite well-off households in rich countries. Indeed, one must surely say, in this case, too, "similar but *much* worse," for the stakes are undeniably higher—no less than life or death for more than a hundred million women, as has recently been shown (Drèze and Sen 1990, chap. 4; Sen 1990a).

Policy Implications

Some of the *solutions* to all these problems, which have been suggested recently by scholars addressing the situation of poor women in poor countries, closely resemble solutions proposed by Western feminists primarily concentrating on their own societies. (By "solutions to problems" I mean to refer to both what theorists and social scientists need to do to rectify their analyses and what policymakers need to do to solve the social problems themselves.) First, the dichotomization of public and domestic spheres must be strongly challenged. As Chen (1983) writes, in the context of poor rural regions, "So long as policy-makers make the artificial distinction between the farm and the household, between paid work and unpaid work, between productive and domestic work, women will continue to be overlooked" (p. 220). Challenging the dichotomy will also point attention to the inequities that occur within households—various forms of abuse, including the inequitable distribution of food and health care. As Papanek (1990) argues, "Given a focus on socialization for inequality, power relations within the household—as a central theme in examining the dynamics of households—deserve special attention (p. 170).

Second, and following from the above, the unit of analysis both for studies and for much policy-making must be the individual, not the household.11 Noting that, given the greater political voice of men, public decisions affecting the poor in poor countries are often "guided by male preferences, not [frequently conflicting] female needs," Dasgupta (1993) concludes that

> the maximization of well-being as a model for explaining household behaviour must be rejected.... Even though it is often difficult to design and effect it, the target of public policy should be persons, not households.... Governments need to be conscious of the household as a resource allocation mechanism. (Pp. 335-36)

Especially as women are even more likely in poor countries than in richer ones to be providing the sole or principal support for their households, as Chen (1983) points out, they require as much access as men to credit, skills training, labor markets, and technologies (and, I would add, equal pay for their work) (p. 221). Policies prompting women's full economic participation and productivity are needed increasingly for the survival of their households, for women's overall socioeconomic status, and for their bargaining position within their families. As Drèze and Sen (1989) say, "important policy implications" follow from the "considerable evidence that greater involvement with outside work and paid employment does tend to go with less anti-female bias in intra-family distribution" (p. 58). Because of the quite pervasive unequal treatment of female children in some poor countries, the need for equal treatment of women by policymakers is often far more urgent than the need of most women in richer countries—but again, the issue is not so much different as "similar but more so."

Implications for Thinking About Justice

Finally, I shall speculate briefly about two different ways of thinking about justice between the sexes, in cultures very different from ours. I have tried to show that, for feminists thinking about justice, John Rawls's theory, if revised so as to include women and the family, has a great deal to be said for it, and the veil of ignorance is particularly important (Rawls 1971; Okin 1989a, 1989b). If everyone were to speak only from his or her own point of view, it is unclear that we would come up with any principles at all. But the very presence of the veil, which hides from those in the original position any particular knowledge of the personal characteristics or social position they will have in the society for which they are designing principles of justice, forces them to take into account as many voices as possible and especially to be concerned with those of the least well-off. It enables us to reconcile the requirement that a theory of justice be universalizable with the seemingly conflicting requirement that it take account of the multiple differences among human beings.

In a recent paper, Ruth Anna Putnam, arguing a strongly antiessentialist line, and accusing Rawls and myself of varying degrees of exclusionary essentialism, considers instead an "interactive" (some might call it "dialogic") feminism: "that we listen to the voices of women of color and women of a different class, and that we appropriate what we hear" (p. 21).[12] Listening and discussing have much to recommend them; they are fundamental to democracy in the best sense of the word. And *sometimes* when especially oppressed women are heard, their cry for justice is clear—as in the case of the women Martha Chen worked with, who became quite clear that being allowed to leave the domestic sphere in order to earn wages would help to liberate them. But we are not always enlightened about what is just by asking persons who seem to be suffering injustices what they want. Oppressed people have often internalized their oppression so well that they *have* no sense of what they are justly entitled to as human beings. This is certainly the case with gender inequalities. As Papanek (1990) writes, "The clear perception of disadvantages ... requires conscious rejection of the social norms and cultural ideal that perpetuate inequalities and the use of different criteria—perhaps from another actual or idealized society—in order to assess inequality as a prelude for action" (pp. 164-65). People in seriously deprived conditions are sometimes not only accepting of them but relatively cheerful—the "small mercies" situation. Deprivations sometimes become gagged and muffled for reasons of deeply rooted ideology, among others. But it would surely be ethically deeply mistaken to attach a correspondingly small value to the loss of well-being of such people because of their survival strategy.

Coming to terms with very little is no recipe for social justice. Thus it is, I believe, quite justifiable for those not thoroughly imbued with the inegalitarian norms of a culture to come forth as its constructive critics. Critical distance, after all, does not have to bring with it detachment: *committed* outsiders can often be better analysts and critics of social injustice than those who live within the relevant culture. This is why a concept such as the original position, which aims to approximate an Archimedean point, is so valuable, at least in addition to some form of dialogue. Let us think for a moment about some of the cruelest or most oppressive institutions and practices that are or have been used to "brand" women—foot binding, clitoridectomy, and purdah. As Papanek shows, "well socialized " women in cultures with such practices internalize them as necessary to successful female development. Even though, in the case of the former two practices, these women may retain vivid memories of their own intense pain, they perpetuate the cruelties, inflicting them or at least allowing them to be inflicted on their own daughters.

Now, clearly, a theory of human flourishing, such as Nussbaum and Sen have been developing, would have no trouble delegitimizing such practices (Nussbaum1992). But given the choice between a revised Rawlsian outlook or an "interactive feminist" one, as defined by Putnam, I'd choose the former any day, for in the latter, well-socialized members of the oppressed group are all too likely to rationalize the cruelties, whereas the men who perceive themselves as benefiting from them are unlikely to object. But behind the veil of ignorance, is it not much more likely that both the oppressors and the oppressed would have second thoughts? What Moslem man is likely to take the chance of spending his life in seclusion and dependency, sweltering in head-to-toe solid black clothing? What prerevolutionary Chinese man would cast his vote for the breaking of toes and hobbling through life, if he well might be the one with the toes and the crippled life? What man would endorse gross genital mutilation, not knowing *whose* genitals? And the women in these cultures, required to think of such practices from a male as well as a female perspective, might thereby, with a little distance, gain more notion of just how, rather than perfecting femininity, they perpetuate the subordination of women to men.

Martha Nussbaum (1992) has recently written of what happens when outsiders, instead of trying to maintain some critical distance, turn to what amounts to the worship of difference. Citing some examples of sophisticated Western scholars who, in their reverence for the integrity of cultures, defend such practices as the isolation of menstruating women and criticize Western "intrusions" into other cultures, such as the provision of typhoid vaccine, Nussbaum finds a strange and disturbing phenomenon:

> Highly intelligent people, people deeply committed to the good of women and men in developing countries, people who think of themselves as progressive and feminist and antiracist, ... are taking up positions that converge ... with the positions of reaction, oppression, and sexism. Under the banner of their radically and politically correct "antiessentialism" march ancient religious taboos, the luxury of the pampered husband, ill health, ignorance, and death. (P. 204)

As Nussbaum later concludes, "Identification need not ignore concrete local differences: in fact, at its best, it demands a searching analysis of differences, in order that the general good be appropriately realized in the concrete case. But the learning about and from the other is motivated ... by the conviction that the other is one of us" (p. 241).

As the work of some feminist scholars of development shows, using the concept of gender and refusing to let differences gag us or fragment our analyses does not mean that we should overgeneralize or try to apply "standardized" solutions to the problems of women in different circumstances. Chen argues for the value of a situation-by-situation analysis of women's roles and constraints before plans can be made and programs designed. And Papanek, too, shows how helping to educate women to awareness of their oppression requires quite deep and specific knowledge of the relevant culture.

Thus I conclude that gender itself in an extremely important category of analysis and that we ought not be paralyzed by the fact that there are differences among women. So long as we are careful and develop our judgments in the light of empirical evidence, it is possible to generalize about many aspects of inequality between the sexes. Theories developed in Western contexts can clearly apply, at least in large part, to women in very different cultural contexts. From place to place, from class to class, from race to race, and from culture to culture, we find similarities in the specifics of these inequalities, in their causes and their effects, although often not in their extent or severity.

Author's Note:

I am grateful to Elisabeth Friedman, Elisabeth Hansot, Robert O. Keohane, Martha Nussbaum, and Louise Tilly for helpful comments on an earlier draft of this article.

NOTES

1. This debate has been conducted mostly among feminist legal and political theorists. The legal literature is already so vast that it is difficult to summarize, and it is not relevant to this essay. For some references, see Okin (1991), ns. 1-3.
2. "Essentialism," employed in the context of feminist theory, seems to have two principal meanings. The other refers to the tendency to regard certain characteristics or capacities as "essentially" female, in the sense that they are unalterably associated with being female. Used in this second way, essentialism is very close to, if not always identical with, biological determinism. I am not concerned with this aspect of the term here.
3. In 1851, at an almost entirely white women's rights convention, Truth said,
   That man over there says women need to be helped into carriages, and lifted over ditches, and to have the best place everywhere. Nobody ever helps me into carriages, or over mud puddles, or gives me any best place. And ain't I a woman? Look at me! Look at my arm! I have ploughed, and planted, and gathered into barns, and no man could head me! And ain't I a woman? I could work as much and eat as much as a man—when I could get it—and bear the lash as well! And ain't I a woman? I have borne thirteen children, and seen most all sold off to slavery, and when I cried out with my mothers grief, none but Jesus heard me! And ain't I a woman?
4. The example is that of the many black women (and few white women) who answered Joann Little's appeal on behalf of Delbert Tibbs, a black man who had been falsely accused of raping a white woman and sentenced to death. I do not think the example clearly supports Harris's assertion that black women have "a unique ambivalence" about rape, any more than it supports the assertion she claims to refute—that their experience is similar, but different in magnitude. Black women's present experience of rape is surely similar to that of white women in several important respects: many are raped (by acquaintances as well as by strangers), they fear being raped, they sometimes modify their behavior because of this fear, and they are victimized as witnesses at the trials of their rapists. But their experience is probably also worse because, in addition to all of this, they have to live with the knowledge and experience of black men's being victimized by false accusations, harsher sentences, and, at worst, lynchings. Only empirical research that involved asking them could show more certainly whether the oppression of black men as alleged rapists (or the history of master/slave rape, which Harris also discusses) makes black women's entire contemporary experience of rape different from that of white women.

5. However, the detailed division of labor between the sexes varies considerably from culture to culture. As Jane Mansbridge (1993) has recently written, in a discussion of "gratuitous gendering":

   Among the Aleut of North America, for example, only women are allowed to butcher animals. But among the Ingalik of North America, only men are allowed to butcher animals. Among the Suku of Africa, only the women can plant crops and only the men can make baskets. But among the Kaffa of the Circum-Mediterranean, only the men can plant crops and only the women can make baskets. (P. 345).

   Her analysis is derived from data in George P. Murdoch and Caterina Provost. "Factors in the Division of labor by Sex: A Cross-Cultural Analysis." *Ethnology* 12 (1973): 203-25. However, the work done by women is less likely to be "outside" work and to be paid or valued.
6. Poverty is both a relative and an absolute term. The poorest households in poor countries are absolutely as well as relatively poor and can be easily pushed below subsistence by any number of natural, social, or personal catastrophes. Poverty in rich countries is more often relative poverty (although there is serious malnutrition currently in the United States for example and drug abuse, with all its related ills, is highly correlated with poverty). Relative poverty, although not directly life-threatening, can however be very painful, especially for children living in societies that are not only highly consumer-oriented but in which many opportunities—for good health care, decent education, the development of talents, pursuit of interests, and so on—are seriously limited for those from poor families. Single parents also often experience severe "time poverty," which can have a serious impact on their children's well-being.
7. See Dasgupta (1993) on members' perceived "usefulness" affecting the allocation of goods within poor households in poor families. Western studies as well as non-Western ones show us that women's work is already likely to be regarded as less useful—even when it is just as necessary to family well-being. So when women are really made less useful (by convention or lack of employment opportunities), this problem is compounded. Dasgupta questions simple measures of usefulness, such as paid employment, in the case of girls (1993). Where young poor women are not entitled to parental assets and their outside employment opportunities are severely restricted, the only significant "employment" for then is as child-bearers and housekeepers—so marriage becomes especially valued (even though its conditions may be highly oppressive).
8. There seems to be some conflicting evidence on this matter. See Papanek (1990, 166-68).
9. This seems similar to changes in the work and socioeconomic status of women in Western Europe in the sixteenth to eighteenth centuries.
10. I do not mean to imply here that most women, whether in developed or less developed societies, think about improving their exit options when making decisions about wage work and related issues. Indeed, in some cultures, women relinquish wage work as soon as their families' financial situation enable them to do so. But their exit option is nevertheless reduced, and their partners enhanced, thereby in all likelihood altering the distribution of power within the family.
11. This point seems to have been first explicitly made in the context of policy by George Bernard Shaw, who argues in *the Intelligent Woman's Guide to Socialism and Capitalism* (New Brunswick, NJ: Transaction books, 1984) that the state should require all adults to work and should allocate an equal portion of income to each—man, woman, and child.
12. As Joan Tronto has pointed out to me, the use of "appropriate" here is noteworthy, given Putnam's professed desire to treat these other women as her equals.

REFERENCES

Benhabib, Seyla and Drucilla Cornell. 1987. Introduction: Beyond the politics of gender. In *Feminism as critique*. Minneapolis: University of Minnesota Press.

Bergmann, Barbara R. 1986. *The economic emergence of women*. New York: Basic Books.

Blumstein, Philip, and Pepper Schwarz. 1983. *American couples*. New York: Morrow.

Boserup, Ester. 1970. *Women's role in economic development*. London: Allen & Unwin.

Chen, Lincoln C., Emdadul Huq, and Stan D'Souza. 1981. Sex bias in the family allocation of food and health care in rural Bangladesh. *Population and Development Review* 7:55-70.

Chen, Martha Alter. 1983. *A quiet revolution: Women in transition in rural Bangladesh*. Cambridge, MA: Schenkma.

— . [1995]. A matter of survival: Women's right to work in India and Bangladesh. In [*Women, Culture and Development*], edited by Nussbaum and Glover. Oxford: Oxford University Press.

Childers, Mary, and bell hooks. 1990. A conversation about race and class. In *Conflicts in feminism*, edited by Marianne Hirsch and Evelyn Fox Keller. New York: Routledge, Chapman & Hall.

Crosswaite, Jan. 1989. Sex in the original position. Unpublished manuscript, Department of Philosophy, University of Auckland.

Dasgupta, Partha. 1993. *An inquiry into well-being and destitution*. Oxford: Clarendon.

Drèze, Jean, and Amartya Sen. 1989. *Hunger and public action*. Oxford: Clarendon.

— , eds. 1990. *The political economy of hunger: Vol. 1. Entitlement and well-being*. Oxford: Clarendon.

Fuchs, Victor. 1988. *Women's quest for economic equality*. Cambridge, MA: Harvard University Press.

Gerson, Kathleen,. 1985. *Hard choices: How women decide about work, career, and motherhood*. Berkeley: University of California Press.

Gordon, Linda. 1988. *Heroes of their own lives*. New York: Viking.

Harris, Angela P. 1990. Race and essentialism in feminist legal theory. *Stanford Law Review* 42:581-616.

Harriss, Barbara. 1990. The intrafamilial distribution of hunger in South Asia. In *The political economy of hunger: Vol. 1. Entitlement and well-being*, edited by Jean Drèze and Amartya Sen. Oxford: Clarendon.

Hochschild, Arlie. 1989. *The second shift: Working parents and the revolution at home*. New York: Viking.

hooks, bell. 1984. *Feminist theory: From margin to center.* Boston: South End Press.

Jaquette, Jane S. 1982. Women and modernization theory: A decade of feminist criticism. *World Politics* 34:267-84.

Jelin, Elizabeth, ed. 1990. *Women and social change in Latin America*. London: Zed Books.

Kearns, Deborah. 1983. A theory of justice and love: Rawls on the family. *Politics (Journal of the Australasian Political Studies Association)* 18 (2): 36-42.

Lorde, Audre. 1984. An open letter to Mary Daly. In *Sister outsider*, edited by Audre Lorde. Trumansburg, NY: Crossing Press.

Mansbridge, Jane. 1993. Feminism and democratic community. In *Democratic community*, edited by John Chapman and Ian Shapiro. New York: New York University Press.

Marks, Elaine, and Isabelle de Courtivron, eds. 1981. *New French feminisms: An anthology.* New York: Schocken.

McLindon, James B. 1987. Separate but unequal: The economic disaster of divorce for women and children. *Family Law Quarterly* 12:3.

Mill, John Stuart. [1860] 1988. *The subjection of women*. Reprint. Indianapolis: Hackett.

Minow, Martha, and Elizabeth V. Spelman.1990. In context. *Southern California Law Review* 63 (6): 1597-1652.

Nussbaum, Martha. 1992. Human functioning and social justice: In defense of Aristotelian essentialism. *Political theory* 20: 202-46.

Okin, Susan Moller, 1989a. Reason and feeling in thinking about justice. *Ethics* 99 (2): 229-49.

— . 1989b. *Justice, gender, and the family*, New York: Basic Books.

— . 1991. Sexual difference, feminism and the law. *Law and Social Inquiry*.

Olsen, Frances. 1983. The family and the market: A study of ideology and legal reform. *Harvard Law Review* 96 (7).

Papanek, Hanna. 1990. To each less than she needs, from each more than she can do: Allocations, entitlements, and value. In Irene Tinker, ed., *Women and world development*. New York and London: Oxford University Press.

Pateman, Carole. 1983. Feminist critiques of the public/private dichotomy. In *Public and private in social life*, edited by Stanley Benn and Gerald Gaus. London: Croom Helm. Also in Pateman, *The disorder of women*. Stanford, CA: Stanford University Press, 1989.

Putnam, Ruth Anna. [1995] Why not a feminist theory of justice? in [*Women, Culture, and Development*], ed. Nussbaum and Glover.

Rawls, John. 1971. *A theory of justice*. Cambridge, MA: Harvard University Press.

Sanday, Peggy R. 1974. Female status in the public domain. In Michelle Zimbalist Rosaldo and Louise Lamphere, eds., *Woman, culture, and society*. Stanford, CA: Stanford University Press.

Sen, Amartya. 1990a. More than 100 million women are missing. *New York Review of Books*, December 20.

— . 1990b. Gender and co-operative conflicts. In Irene Tinker, ed., *Women and world development.* New York and London: Oxford University Press.

Spelman, Elizabeth V. 1988. Inessential woman: *Problems of exclusion in feminist thought.* Boston: Beacon.

United Nations Report. 1991. *The world's women: Trends and statistics, 1970-1990.* New York: United Nations Publication.

Waring, Marilyn. 1989. *If women counted: A new feminist economics.* San Francisco: Harper & Row.

Weitzman, Lenore. 1985. *The Divorce Revolution: The unexpected social and economic consequences for women and children.* New York: Free Press.

Wheeler, E. F., and M. Abdullah. 1988. Food allocation within the family: Response to fluctuating food supply and food needs. In I. de Garine and G. A. Harrison, *Coping with uncertainty in food supply*. Oxford: Clarendon.

Wishik, Heather Ruth. 1986. Economics of divorce: an exploratory study. *Family Law Quarterly* 20:1.

UNDER WESTERN EYES: FEMINIST SCHOLARSHIP AND COLONIAL DISCOURSES

Chandra Mohanty

Chandra Mohanty is Associate Professor of Women's Studies at Hamilton College, Clinton, New York. She is co-editor of Third World Women and the Politics of Feminism *(Indiana, 1991) and of* Feminist Genealogies, Colonial Legacies, and Democratic Futures *(Routledge, 1997).*

Mohanty is critical of the tendency in some Western feminist scholarship to understand women in non-Western countries as a monolithic group having similar identities, experiencing similar kinds of oppression and disadvantage, and needing similar strategies for addressing injustices. She provides examples of the diverse experiences, beliefs, practices, and values in different social and political contexts to challenge this tendency to generalize about women in non-Western cultures. Mohanty argues that failing to recognize the diversity amongst women has resulted in Western feminists advocating policies that are actually detrimental to the lives of women in particular non-Western countries.

It ought to be of some political significance at least that the term "colonization" has come to denote a variety of phenomena in recent feminist and left writings in general. From its analytic value as a category of exploitative economic exchange in both traditional and contemporary Marxisms (cf. particularly such contemporary scholars as Baran, Amin and Gunder-Frank) to its use by feminist women of colour in the US, to describe the appropriation of their experiences and struggles by hegemonic white women's movements,[1] the term "colonization" has been used to characterize everything from the most evident economic and political hierarchies to the production of a particular cultural discourse about what is called the "Third World."[2] However sophisticated or problematical its use as an explanatory construct, colonization almost invariably implies a relation of structural domination, and a discursive or political suppression of the heterogeneity of the subject(s) in question. What I wish to analyse here specifically is the production of the "Third World Woman" as a singular monolithic subject in some recent (western) feminist texts. The definition of colonization I invoke is a predominantly discursive one, focusing on a certain mode of appropriation and codification of "scholarship" and "knowledge" about women in the third world by particular analytic categories employed in writings on the subject which take as their primary point of reference feminist interests as they have been articulated in the US and western Europe.

My concern about such writings derives from my own implication and investment in contemporary debates in feminist theory, and the urgent political necessity of forming strategic coalitions across class, race and national boundaries. Clearly, western feminist discourse and political practice is neither singular nor homogenous in its goals, interests or analyses. However, it is possible to trace a coherence of *effects* resulting from the implicit assumption of "the west" (in all its complexities and contradictions) as the primary referent in theory and praxis. Thus, rather than claim simplistically that "western feminism" is a monolith, I would like to draw attention to the remarkably similar effects of various analytical

Reprinted with permission of Chandra Mohanty from *Feminist Review* 30 (Autumn 1998): 61–88 [edited].

categories and even strategies which codify their relationship to the Other in implicitly hierarchical terms. It is in this sense that I use the term "western feminist." Similar arguments pertaining to questions of methods of analysis can be made in terms of middle-class, urban African and Asian scholars producing scholarship on or about their rural or working-class sisters which assumes their own middle-class culture as the norm, and codifies peasant and working-class histories and cultures as Other. Thus, while this article focuses specifically on western feminist discourse on women in the third world, the critiques I offer also pertain to identical analytical principles employed by third-world scholars writing about their own cultures.

Moreover, the analytical principles discussed below serve to distort western feminist political practices, and limit the possibility of coalitions among (usually white) western feminists and working-class and feminist women of colour around the world. These limitations are evident in the construction of the (implicitly consensual) priority of issues around which apparently *all* women are expected to organize. The necessary and integral connection between feminist scholarship and feminist political practice and organizing determines the significance and status of western feminist writings on women in the third world, for feminist scholarship, like most other kinds of scholarship, does not comprise merely "objective" knowledge about a certain subject. It is also a directly political and discursive *practice* insofar as it is purposeful and ideological. It is best seen as a mode of intervention into particular hegemonic discourses (for example, traditional anthropology, sociology, literary criticism, etc.), and as a political praxis which counters and resists the totalizing imperative of age-old "legitimate" and "scientific" bodies of knowledge. Thus, feminist scholarly practices exist within relations of power—relations which they counter, redefine, or even implicitly support. There can, of course, be no apolitical scholarship.

The relationship between Woman—a cultural and ideological composite Other constructed through diverse representational discourse (scientific, literary, juridical, linguistic, cinematic, etc.)—and women—real, material subjects of their collective histories—is one of the central questions the practice of feminist scholarship seeks to address. This connection between women as historical subjects and the re-presentation of Woman produced by hegemonic discourses is not a relation of direct identity, or a relation of correspondence or simple implication.[3] It is an arbitrary relation set up in particular cultural and historical contexts. I would like to suggest that the feminist writings I analyse here discursively colonize the material and historical heterogeneities of the lives of women in the third world, thereby producing/representing a composite, singular "third-world woman"—an image which appears arbitrarily constructed but nevertheless carries with it the authorizing signature of western humanist discourse.[4] I argue that assumptions of privilege and ethnocentric universality on the one hand, and inadequate self-consciousness about the effect of western scholarship on the "third world" in the context of a world system dominated by the west on the other, characterize a sizable extent of western feminist work on women in the third world. An analysis of "sexual difference" in the form of a cross-culturally singular, monolithic notion of patriarchy or male dominance leads to the construction of a similarly reductive and homogeneous notion of what I shall call the "third-world difference"— that stable, ahistorical something that apparently oppresses most if not all the women in these countries. It is in the production of this "third-world difference" that western feminisms appropriate and colonize the constitutive complexities which characterize the lives of women in these countries. It is in this process of discursive homogenization and systematization of the oppression of women in the third world that power is exercised in much of recent western feminist writing, and this power needs to be defined and named....

Western feminist scholarship cannot avoid the challenge of situating itself and examining its role in such a global economic and political framework. To do any less would be to ignore the complex interconnections between first—and third-world economies and the profound effect of this on the lives of women in all countries. I do not question the descriptive and informative value of most western feminist writings on women in the third world. I also do not question the existence of excellent work which does not fall into the analytic traps I am concerned with. In fact I deal with an example of such work later on. In the context of an overwhelming silence about the experiences of women in these countries, as well as the need to forge international links between women's political struggles, such work is both pathbreaking and absolutely essential. However, it is both to the *explanatory potential* of particular analytical strategies employed by such writing, and to their *political effect* in the context of the hegemony of western scholarship, that I want to draw attention here. While feminist writing in the US is still marginalized (except perhaps from the point of view of women of colour addressing privileged white women), western feminist writing on women in the third world must be considered in the context of the global hegemony of western scholarship—i.e., the production, publication, distribution and consumption of information and ideas. Marginal or not, this writing has political effects and implications beyond the immediate feminist or disciplinary audience. One such significant effect of the dominant "representations" of western feminism is its conflation with imperialism in the eyes of particular third-world women.[5] Hence the urgent need to examine the *political* implications of our analytic strategies and principles.

My critique is directed at three basic analytical presuppositions which are present in (western) feminist discourse on women in the third world. Since I focus primarily on the Zed Press "Women in the Third World" series, my comments on western feminist discourse are circumscribed by my analysis of the texts in this series.[6] This is a way of focusing my critique. However, even though I am dealing with feminists who identify themselves as culturally or geographically from the "west," as mentioned earlier, what I say about these presuppositions or implicit principles holds for anyone who uses these analytical strategies, whether third-world women in the west, or third-world women in the third world writing on these issues and publishing in the west. Thus, I am not making a culturalist argument about ethnocentrism; rather, I am trying to uncover how ethnocentric universalism is produced in certain analyses. As a matter of fact, my argument holds for any discourse that sets up its own authorial subjects as the implicit referent, i.e., the yardstick by which to encode and represent cultural Others. It is in this move that power is exercised in discourse.

The first analytical presupposition I focus on is involved in the strategic location or situation of the category "women" *vis-à-vis* the context of analysis. The assumption of women as an already constituted and coherent group with identical interests and desires, regardless of class, ethnic or racial location, implies a notion of gender or sexual difference or even patriarchy which can be applied universally and cross-culturally. (The context of analysis can be anything from kinship structures and the organization of labour to media representations.) The second analytical presupposition is evident on the methodological level, in the uncritical way "proof" of universality and cross-cultural validity are provided. The third is a more specifically political presupposition, underlying the methodologies and the analytic strategies, i.e., the model of power and struggle they imply and suggest. I argue that as a result of the two modes—or, rather, frames—of analysis described above, a homogeneous notion of the oppression of women as a group is assumed, which, in turn, produces the image of an "average third-world woman." This average third-world woman leads an essentially truncated life based on her feminine gender (read: sexually constrained) and being "third world" (read: ignorant, poor, uneducated, tradition-bound, religious, domesticated, family-oriented, victimized, etc.). This, I suggest, is in contrast to the (implicit) self-representation of western women as educated, modern, as having control over their own bodies and sexualities, and the "freedom" to make their own decisions. The distinction between western feminist re-presentation of women in the third world, and western feminist self-presentation is a distinction of the same order as that made by some Marxists between the "maintenance" function of the housewife and the real "productive" role of wage-labour, or the characterization by developmentalists of the third world as being engaged in the lesser production of "raw materials" in contrast to the "real" productive activity of the first world. These distinctions are made on the basis of the privileging of a particular group as the norm or referent. Men involved in wage-labour, first-world producers, and, I suggest, western feminists who sometimes cast third-world women in terms of "ourselves undressed" (Michelle Rosaldo's term; Rosaldo, 1980:389-412, especially 392), all construct themselves as the normative referent in such a binary analytic.

"Women" as category of analysis, or: We are all sisters in struggle

By women as a category of analysis, I am referring to the crucial presupposition that all of us of the same gender, across classes and cultures, are somehow socially constituted as a homogeneous group identifiable prior to the process of analysis. The homogeneity of women as a group is produced not on the basis of biological essentials, but rather on the basis of secondary sociological and anthropological universals. Thus, for instance, in any given piece of feminist analysis, women are characterized as a singular group on the basis of a shared oppression. What binds women together is a sociological notion of the "sameness" of their oppression. It is at this point that an elision takes place between "women" as a discursively constructed group and "women" as material subjects of their own history.[7] Thus, the discursively consensual homogeneity of "women" as a group is mistaken for the historically specific material reality of groups of women. This results in an assumption of women as an always-already constituted group, one which has been labelled "powerless," "exploited," "sexually harassed," etc., by feminist scientific, economic, legal and sociological discourses. (Notice that this is quite similar to sexist discourse labelling women as weak, emotional, having math anxiety, etc.) The focus is not on uncovering the material and ideological specificities that constitute a group of women as "powerless" in a particular context. It is rather on finding a variety of cases of "powerless" groups of women to prove the general point that women as a group are powerless.[8]

In this section I focus on five specific ways in which "women" as a category of analysis is used in western feminist discourse on women in the third world to construct "third-world women" as a homogeneous "powerless" group often located as implicit victims of particular cultural and socio-economic systems. I have chosen to deal with a variety of writers—from Fran Hosken, who writes primarily about female genital mutilation, to writers from the Women in International Development school who write about the effect of development policies on third-world women for both western and third-world audiences. I do not intend to equate all the texts that I analyse, nor ignore their respective strengths and weaknesses. The authors I deal with write with varying degrees of care and complexity; however, the *effect* of the representation of third-world women in these texts is a coherent one. In these texts women are variously defined as victims of male violence (Fran Hosken); victims of the colonial process (M. Cutrufelli); victims of the Arab familial system (Juliette Minces); victims of the economic development process (B. Lindsay and the—liberal—WID school); and finally, victims of the economic basis of the Islamic code (P. Jeffery). This mode of defining women primarily in terms of the *object status* (the way in which they are affected or not affected by certain institutions and systems) is what characterizes this particular form of the use of "women" as a category of analysis. In the context of western women writing about and studying women in the third world, such objectification (however benevolently motivated) needs to be both named and challenged. As Valerie Amos and Pratibha Parmar argue quite eloquently, "Feminist theories which examine our cultural practices as 'feudal residues' or label us 'traditional' also portray us as politically immature women who need to be versed and schooled in the ethos of western feminism. They need to be continually challenged" (1984:7).

Women as victims of male violence

Fran Hosken, in writing about the relationship between human rights and female genital mutilation in Africa and the Middle East, bases her whole discussion and condemnation of genital mutilation on one privileged premise: the goal of genital mutilation is "to mutilate the sexual pleasure and satisfaction of woman" (1981:3-24, especially 11).[9] This in turn, leads her to claim that woman's sexuality is controlled, as is her reproductive potential. According to Hosken, "male sexual politics" in Africa and around the world "share the same political goal: to assure female dependence and subservience by any and all means." Physical violence against women (rape, sexual assault, excision, infibulation, etc.) is thus carried out "with astonishing consensus among men in the world" (14). Here, women are defined systematically as the *victims* of male control—the "sexually oppressed." Although it is true that the potential of male violence against women circumscribes and elucidates their social position to a certain extent, defining women as archetypal victims freezes them into "objects-who-defend-themselves," men into "subjects-who-perpetrate-violence," and (every) society into a simple opposition between the powerless (read: women) and the powerful (read: men) groups of people. Male violence (if that indeed is the appropriate label) must be theorized and interpreted *within* specific societies, both in order to understand it better, as well as in order to effectively organize to change it.[10] Sisterhood cannot be assumed on the basis of gender; it must be forged in concrete historical and political praxis.

Women as universal dependants

Beverley Lindsay's conclusion to the book, Comparative Perspectives on *Third World Women: The Impact of Race, Class and Sex* states: "Dependency relationships, based upon race, sex and class, are being perpetuated through social, educational, and economic institutions. These are the linkages among Third World Women" (1983: especially 298, 306). Here, as in other places, Lindsay implies that third-world women constitute an identifiable group purely on the basis of shared dependencies. If shared dependencies were all that was needed to bind us together as a group, third-world women would always be seen as an apolitical group with no subject status! Instead, if anything, it is the *common context* of political struggle against class, race, gender and imperialist hierarchies that may constitute third-world women as a strategic group at this historical juncture. Lindsay also states that linguistic and cultural differences exist between Vietnamese and Black American women, but "both groups are victims of race, sex and class." Again, Black and Vietnamese women are characterized and defined simply in terms of their victim status.

Similarly, examine statements like: "My analysis will start by stating that all African women are politically and economically dependent" (Cutrufelli, 1983: especially 13). Or: "Nevertheless, either overtly or covertly, prostitution is still the main if not the only source of work for African women" (Cutrufelli, 1983:33). *All* African women are dependent. Prostitution is the only work option for African women as a *group*. Both statements are illustrative of generalizations sprinkled liberally through a recent Zed Press publication, *Women of Africa: Roots of Oppression*, by Maria Rosa Cutrufelli, who is described on the cover as an "Italian Writer, Sociologist, Marxist and Feminist." In the 1980s is it possible to imagine writing a book entitled "Women of Europe: Roots of Oppression?" I am not objecting to the use of universal groupings for descriptive purposes. Women from the continent of Africa can be descriptively characterized as "Women of Africa." It is when "women of Africa" becomes a homogeneous sociological grouping characterized by common dependencies or powerlessness (or even strengths) that problems arise—we say too little and too much at the same time.

This is because descriptive gender differences are transformed into the division between men and women. Women are constituted as a group via dependency relationships *vis à vis* men, who are implicitly held responsible for these relationships. When "women of Africa" (versus "men of Africa" as a group?) are seen as a group precisely because they are generally dependent and oppressed, the analysis of specific historical differences becomes impossible, because reality is always apparently structured by divisions between two mutually exclusive and jointly exhaustive groups, the victims and the oppressors. Here the sociological is substituted for the biological in order, however, to create the same—a unity of women. Thus, it is not the descriptive potential of gender difference but the privileged positioning and explanatory potential of gender difference as the origin of oppression that I question. In using "women of Africa" (as an already constituted group of oppressed peoples) as a category of analysis, Cutrufelli denies any historical specificity to the location of women as subordinate, powerful, marginal, central or otherwise, *vis à vis* particular social and power networks. Women are taken as a unified "powerless" group prior to the historical and political analysis in question. Thus, it is then merely a matter of specifying the context *after* the fact. "Women" are now placed in the context of the family, or in the workplace, or within religious networks, almost as if these systems existed outside the relations of women with other women, and women with men.

The problem with this analytical strategy is, let me repeat, that it assumes men and women are already constituted as sexual-political subjects prior to their entry into the arena of social relations. Only if we subscribe to this assumption is it possible to undertake analysis which looks at the "effects" of kinship structures, colonialism, organization of labour, etc., on women, who are defined in advance as a group. The crucial point that is forgotten is that women are produced through these very relations as well as being implicated in forming these relations. As Michelle Rosaldo argues, "woman's place in human social life is not in any direct sense a product of the things she does (or even less, a function of what, biologically, she is) but the meaning her activities acquire through concrete social interactions" (1980:400). That women mother in a variety of societies is not as significant as the value attached to mothering in these societies. The distinction between the act of mothering and the status attached to it is a very important one—one that needs to be stated and analysed contextually.

Married women as victims of the colonial process

In Levi-Strauss's theory of kinship structures as a system of the exchange of women, what is significant is that exchange itself is not constitutive of the subordination of women; women are not subordinate because of the fact of exchange, but because of the modes of exchange instituted, and the values attached to these modes. However, in discussing the marriage ritual of the Bemba, a Zambian matrilocal, matrilineal people, Cutrufelli in *Women of Africa* focuses on the fact of the marital exchange of women before and after western colonization, rather than the value attached to this exchange in this particular context. This leads to her definition of Bemba women as a coherent group affected in a particular way by colonization. Here again, Bemba women are constituted rather unilaterally as the victims of western colonization. Cutrufelli cites the marriage ritual of the Bemba as a multi-stage event "whereby a young man becomes incorporated into his wife's family group as he takes up residence with them and gives his services in return for food and maintenance" (1983:43). This ritual extends over many years, and the sexual relationship varies according to the degree of the girl's physical maturity. It is only after the girl undergoes an initiation ceremony at puberty that intercourse is sanctioned, and the man acquires legal rights over the woman. This initiation ceremony is the most important act of the consecration of women's reproductive power, so that the abduction of an uninitiated girl is of no consequence, while heavy penalty is levied for the seduction of an initiated girl. Cutrufelli asserts that the effect of European colonization has changed the whole marriage system. Now the young man is entitled to take his wife away from her people in return for money. The implication is that Bemba women have now lost the protection of tribal laws. However, while it is possible to see how the structure of the traditional marriage contract (as opposed to the post-colonial marriage contract) offered women a certain amount of control over their marital relations, only an analysis of the political significance of the actual practice which privileges an initiated girl over an uninitiated one, indicating a shift in female power relations as a result of this ceremony, can provide an accurate account of whether Bemba women were indeed protected by tribal laws *at all times*.

However, it is not possible to talk about Bemba women as a homogeneous group within the traditional marriage structure. Bemba women *before* the initiation are constituted within a different set of social relations compared to Bemba women after initiation. To treat them as a unified group, characterized by the fact of their "exchange" between male kin, is to deny the specificities of their daily existence, and the differential *value* attached to their exchange before and after their initiation. It is to treat the initiation ceremony as a ritual with no political implications or effects. It is also to assume that in merely describing the *structure* of the marriage contract, the situation of women is exposed. Women as a group are positioned within a given structure, but there is no attempt made to trace the effect of the marriage practice in constituting women within an obviously changing network of power relations. Thus, women are assumed to be sexual-political subjects prior to entry into kinship structures.

Women and familial systems

Elizabeth Cowie, in another context (1978:49-63), points out the implications of this sort of analysis when she emphasizes the specifically political nature of kinship structures which must be analysed as ideological practices which designate men and women as father, husband, wife, mother, sister, etc. Thus, Cowie suggests, women as women are not simply located within the family. Rather, it is in the family, as an effect of kinship structures, that women as women are *constructed*, defined within and by the group. Thus, for instance, when Juliette Minces (1980: especially 23) cites *the* patriarchal family as the basis for "an almost identical vision of women" that Arab and Muslim societies have, she falls into this very trap. Not only is it problematical to speak of a vision of women shared by Arab and Muslim societies, without addressing the particular historical and ideological power structures that construct such images, but to speak of the patriarchal family or the tribal kinship structure as the origin of the socio-economic status of women is again to assume that women are sexual-political subjects prior to their entry into the family. So while on the one hand women attain value or status within the family, the assumption of a singular patriarchal kinship system (common to all Arab and Muslim societies, i.e. over twenty different countries) is what apparently structures women as an oppressed group in these societies! This singular, coherent kinship system presumably influences another separate and given entity, "women." Thus all women, regardless of class and cultural differences, are seen as being similarly affected by this system. Not only are *all* Arab and Muslim women seen to constitute a homogeneous oppressed group, but there is no discussion of the specific *practices* within the families which constitute women as mothers, wives, sisters, etc. Arabs and Muslims, it appears, don't change at all. Their patriarchal family is carried over from the times of the Prophet Muhammad. They exist, as it were, outside history.

Women and religious ideologies

A further example of the use of "women" as a category of analysis is found in cross-cultural analyses which subscribe to a certain economic reductionism in describing the relationship between the economy and factors such as politics and ideology. Here, in reducing the level of comparison to the economic relations between "developed" and "developing" countries, the question of women is denied any specificity. Mina Modares, in a careful analysis of women and Shi'ism in Iran, focuses on this very problem when she criticizes feminist writings which treat Islam as an ideology separate from and outside social relations and practices, rather than a discourse which includes rules for economic, social and power relations within society (Modares 1981: 62-82.) Patricia Jeffery's otherwise informative work on Pirzada women in purdah (1979) considers Islamic ideology as a partial explanation for the status of women in that it provides a justification for the purdah. Here, Islamic ideology is reduced to a set of ideas whose internalization by Pirzada women contributes to the stability of the system. The primary explanation for purdah is located in the control that Pirzada men have over economic resources, and the personal security purdah gives to Pirzada women. By taking a specific version of Islam as the Islam, Jeffery attributes a singularity and coherence to it. Modares notes, "'Islamic Theology' then becomes imposed on a separate and given entity called 'women.' A further unification is reached: Women (meaning *all women*), regardless of their differing positions within societies, come to be affected or not affected by Islam. These conceptions provide the right ingredients for an unproblematic possibility of a cross-cultural study of women." (1981:63)....

Women and the development process

The best examples of universalization on the basis of economic reductionism can be found in the liberal

"Women in Development" literature. Proponents of this school seek to examine the effect of development on third-world women, sometimes from self-designated feminist perspectives. At the very least, there is an evident interest in and commitment to improving the lives of women in "developing" countries. Scholars like Irene Tinker, Ester Boserup, and Perdita Huston[11] have all written about the effect of development policies on women in the third world. All three women assume that "development" is synonymous with "economic development" or "economic progress." As in the case of Minces' patriarchal family, Hosken's male sexual control, and Cutrufelli's western colonization, "development" here becomes the all-time equalizer. Women are seen as being affected positively or negatively by economic development policies, and this is the basis for cross-cultural comparison.

For instance, Perdita Huston states that the purpose of her study is to describe the effect of the development process on the "family unit and its individual members" in Egypt, Kenya, Sudan, Tunisia, Sri Lanka and Mexico. She states that the "problems" and "needs" expressed by rural and urban women in these countries all centre around education and training, work and wages, access to health and other services, political participation and legal rights. Huston relates all these "needs" to the lack of sensitive development policies which exclude women as a group. For her, the solution is simple: improved development policies which emphasize training for women field-workers, use women trainees and women rural development officers, encourage women's co-operatives, etc. Here, again women are assumed to be a coherent group or category prior to their entry into "the development process." Huston assumes that all third-world women have similar problems and needs. Thus, they must have similar interests and goals. However, the interests of urban, middle-class, educated Egyptian housewives, to take only one instance, could surely not be seen as being the same as those of their uneducated, poor maids. Development policies do not affect both groups of women in the same way. Practices which characterize women's status and roles vary according to class. Women are constituted as women through the complex interaction between class, culture, religion and other ideological institutions and frameworks. They are not "women"—a coherent group—solely on the basis of a particular economic system or policy. Such reductive cross-cultural comparisons result in the colonization of the specifics of daily existence and the complexities of political interests which women of different social classes and cultures represent and mobilize.

Thus it is revealing that for Perdita Huston women in the third-world countries she writes about have "needs" and "problems," but few if any have "choices" or the freedom to act. This is an interesting representation of women in the third world, one which is significant in suggesting a latent self-presentation of western women which bears looking at. She writes, "What surprised and moved me most as I listened to women in such very different cultural settings was the striking commonality-whether they were educated or illiterate, urban or rural—of their most basic values: the importance they assign to family, dignity, and service to others" (Huston, 1979:115). Would Huston consider such values unusual for women in the west?

What is problematical, then, about this kind of use of "women" as a group, as a stable category of analysis, is that it assumes an ahistorical, universal unity among women based on a generalized notion of their subordination. Instead of analytically *demonstrating* the production of women as socio-economic political groups within particular local contexts, this analytical move—and the presuppositions it is based on—limits the definition of the female subject to gender identity, completely bypassing social class and ethnic identities. What characterizes women as a group is their gender (sociologically not necessarily biologically defined) over and above everything else, indicating a monolithic notion of sexual difference. Because women are thus constituted as a coherent group, sexual difference becomes coterminous with female subordination, and power is automatically defined in binary terms: people who have it (read: men), and people who do not (read: women). Men exploit, women are exploited. Such simplistic formulations are both historically reductive; they are also ineffectual in designing strategies to combat oppressions. All they do is reinforce binary divisions between men and women.

What would an analysis which did not do this look like? Maria Mies's work is one such example. It is an example which illustrates the strength of western feminist work on women in the third world and which does not fall into the traps discussed above. Maria Mies's study of the lace-makers of Narsapur, India (1982), attempts to analyse carefully a substantial household industry in which "housewives" produce lace doilies for consumption in the world market. Through a detailed analysis of the structure of the lace industry, production and reproduction relations, the sexual division of labour, profits and exploitation, and the overall consequences of defining women as "non-working housewives" and their work as "leisure-time activity," Mies demonstrates the levels of exploitation in this industry and the impact of this production system on the work and living conditions of the women involved in it. In addition, she is able to analyse the "ideology of the housewife," the notion of a woman sitting in the house, as providing the necessary subjective and socio-cultural element for the creation and the maintenance of a production system that contributes to the increasing pauperization of women, and keeps them totally atomized and disorganized as workers. Mies's analyses show the effect of a certain historically and culturally specific mode of patriarchal organization, an organization constructed on the basis of the definition of the lace-makers as "non-working housewives" at familial, local, regional, statewide and international levels. The intricacies and the effects of particular power networks are not only emphasized; they also form the basis of Mies's analysis of how this particular group of women is situated at the centre of a hegemonic, exploitative world market.

This is a good example of what careful, politically focused, local analyses can accomplish. It illustrates how the category of woman is constructed in a variety of political contexts that often exist simultaneously and overlaid on top of one another. There is no easy generalization in the direction of "women" in India, or "women in the third world"; nor is there a reduction of the political construction of the exploitation of the lace-makers to cultural explanations about the passivity or obedience that might characterize these women and their situation. Finally, this mode of local, political analysis which generates theoretical categories from within the situation and context being analysed, also suggests corresponding effective strategies for organizing against the exploitations faced by the lace-makers. Here Narsapur women are not mere victims of the production process, because they resist, challenge, and subvert the process at various junctures....It is only by understanding the *contradictions* inherent in women's location within various structures that effective political action and challenges can be devised. Mies's study goes a long way towards offering such an analysis. While there are now an increasing number of western feminist writings in this tradition,[12] there is also unfortunately a large block of writing which succumbs to the cultural reductionism discussed earlier.

Methodological universalisms, or: women's oppression is a global phenomenon

Western feminist writings on women in the third world subscribe to a variety of methodologies to demonstrate the universal cross-cultural operation of male dominance and female exploitation. I summarize and critique three such methods below, moving from the most simple to the most complex methodologies.

First, proof of universalism is provided through the use of an arithmetic method. The argument goes like this: the more the number of women who wear the veil, the more universal is the sexual segregation and control of women (Deardon, 1975: 4-5). Similarly, a large number of different, fragmented examples from a variety of countries also apparently add up to a universal fact. For instance, Muslim women in Saudi Arabia, Iran, Pakistan, India and Egypt all wear some sort of a veil. Hence, this indicates that the sexual control of women is a universal fact in those countries in which the women are veiled (Deardon, 1975, 7, 10). Fran Hosken writes: "Rape, forced prostitution, polygamy, genital mutilation, pornography, the beating of girls and women, purdah (segregation of women) are all violations of basic human rights" (1981:15). By equating purdah with rape, domestic violence, and forced prostitution, Hosken asserts its "sexual control" function as the primary explanation for purdah, whatever the context. Institutions of purdah are thus denied any cultural and historical specificity and contradictions and subversive aspects are totally ruled out. In both these examples, the problem is not in asserting that the practice of wearing a veil is widespread. This assertion can be made on the basis of numbers. It is a descriptive generalization. However, it is the analytic leap from the practice of veiling to an assertion of its general significance in controlling women that must be questioned. While there may be a physical similarity in the veils worn by women in Saudi Arabia and Iran, the specific meaning attached to this practice varies according to the cultural and ideological context. In addition, the symbolic space occupied by the practice of purdah may be similar in certain contexts, but this does not automatically indicate that the practices themselves have identical significance in the social realm. For example, as is well known, Iranian middle-class women veiled themselves during the 1979 revolution to indicate solidarity with their veiled working-class sisters, while in contemporary Iran mandatory Islamic laws dictate that all Iranian women wear veils. While in both these instances similar reasons might be offered for the veil (opposition to the Shah and western cultural colonization in the first case, and the true Islamicization of Iran in the second), the concrete *meanings* attached to Iranian women wearing the veil are clearly different in the two historical contexts. In the first case, wearing the veil is both an oppositional and revolutionary gesture on the part of Iranian middle-class women; in the second case it is a coercive, institutional mandate.[13] It is on the basis of such context-specific differentiated analysis that effective political strategies can be generated. To assume that the mere practice of veiling women in a number of Muslim countries indicates the universal oppression of women through sexual segregation is not only analytically reductive, but also proves to be quite useless when it comes to the elaboration of oppositional political strategy.

Second, concepts like reproduction, the sexual division of labour, the family, marriage, household, patriarchy, etc., are often used without their specification in local cultural and historical contexts. These concepts are used by feminists in providing explanations for women's subordination, apparently assuming their universal applicability. For instance, how is it possible to refer to "the" sexual division of labour when the content of this division changes radically from one environment to the next, and from one historical juncture to another? At its most abstract level, it is the fact of the differential assignation of tasks according to sex that is significant; however, this is quite different from the meaning or value that the content of this sexual division of labour assumes in different contexts. In most cases the assigning of tasks on the basis of sex has an ideological origin. There is no question that a claim such as "women are concentrated in service-oriented occupations in a large number of countries around the world" is descriptively valid. Descriptively, then, perhaps the existence of a similar sexual division of labour (where women work in service occupations like nursing, social work, etc., and men in other kinds of occupations) in a number of different countries can be asserted. However, the concept of the "sexual division of labour" is more than just a descriptive category. It indicates the differential value placed on "men's work" versus "women's work."

Often the mere existence of a sexual division of labour is taken to be proof of the oppression of women in various societies. This results from a confusion between and collapsing together of the descriptive and explanatory potential of the concept of the sexual division of labour. Superficially similar situations may have radically different, historically specific explanations, and cannot be treated as identical. For instance, the rise of female-headed households in middle-class America might be construed as indicating women's independence and progress, whereby women are considered to have chosen to be single parents, there are increasing numbers of lesbian mothers, etc. However, the recent increase in female-headed households in Latin America,[14] where women might be seen to have more decision-making power, is concentrated among the poorest strata, where life choices are the most constrained economically. A similar argument can be made for the rise of female-headed families among Black and Chicana women in the US. The positive correlation between this and the level of poverty among women of colour and white working-class women in the US has now even acquired a name: the feminization of poverty. Thus, while it is possible to state that there is a rise in female-headed households in the US and in Latin America, this rise cannot be discussed as a universal indicator of women's independence, nor can it be discussed as a universal indicator of women's impoverishment. The *meaning* and *explanation* for the rise must obviously be specified according to the socio-historical context.

Similarly, the existence of a sexual division of labour in most contexts cannot be sufficient explanation for the universal subjugation of women in the workforce. That the sexual division of labour does indicate a devaluation of women's work must be shown through analysis of particular local contexts. In addition, devaluation of *women* must also be shown through careful analysis. In other words, the "sexual division of labour" and "women" are not commensurate analytical categories. Concepts like the sexual division of labour can be useful only if they are generated through local, contextual analyses.[15] If such concepts are assumed to be universally applicable, the resultant homogenization of class, race, religious, and daily material practices of women in the third world can create a false sense of the commonality of oppressions, interests and struggles between and amongst women globally. Beyond sisterhood there is still racism, colonialism and imperialism!...

To summarize: I have discussed three methodological moves identifiable in feminist (and other academic) cross-cultural work which seeks to uncover a universality in women's subordinate position in society. The next and final section pulls together the previous sections attempting to outline the political effects of the analytical strategies in the context of western feminist writing on women in the third world. These arguments are not against generalization as much as they are for careful, historically specific generalizations responsive to complex realities. Nor do these arguments deny the necessity of forming strategic political identities and affinities. Thus, while Indian women of different backgrounds might forge a political unity on the basis of organizing against police brutality towards women,[16] an *analysis* of police brutality must be contextual. Strategic coalitions which construct oppositional political identities for themselves are based on generalization and provisional unities, but the analysis of these group identities cannot be based on universalistic, ahistorical categories.

The subject(s) of power

This last section returns to an earlier point about the inherently political nature of feminist scholarship, and attempts to clarify my point about the possibility of detecting a colonialist move in the case of a structurally unequal first/third-world relation in scholarship....Power relations are structured in terms of a unilateral and undifferentiated source of power and a cumulative reaction to power. Opposition is a generalized phenomenon created as a response to power—which, in turn, is possessed by certain groups of people. The major problem with such a definition of power is that it locks all revolutionary struggles into binary structures—possessing power versus being powerless. Women are powerless, unified groups....

What happens when this assumption of "women as an oppressed group" is situated in the context of western feminist writing about third-world women? It is here that I locate the colonialist move. By contrasting the representation of women in the third world with what I referred to earlier as western feminisms' self-presentation in the same context, we see how western feminists alone become the true "subjects" of this counter-history. Third-world women, on the other hand, never rise above the debilitating generality of their "object" status.

While radical and liberal feminist assumptions of women as a sex class might elucidate (however inadequately) the autonomy of particular women's struggles in the west, the application of the notion of women as a homogeneous category to women in the third world colonizes and appropriates the pluralities of the simultaneous location of different groups of women in social class and ethnic frameworks; in doing so it ultimately robs them of their historical and political *agency*. Similarly, many Zed Press authors, who ground themselves in the basic analytic strategies of traditional Marxism, also implicitly create a "unity" of women by substituting "women's activity" for "labour" as the primary theoretical determinant of women's situation. Here again, women are constituted as a coherent group not on the basis of "natural" qualities or needs, but on the basis of the sociological "unity" of their role in domestic production and wage labour.[17] In other words, western feminist discourse, by assuming women as a coherent, already constituted group which is placed in kinship, legal and other structures, defines third-world women as subjects *outside* of social relations, instead of looking at the way women are constituted as women *through* these very structures. Legal, economic, religious and familial structures are treated as phenomena to be judged by western standards. It is here that ethnocentric universality comes into play. When these structures are defined as "underdeveloped" or "developing" and women are placed within these structures, an implicit image of the "average third-world woman" is produced. This is the transformation of the (implicitly western) "oppressed woman" into the "oppressed third-world woman." While the category of "oppressed woman" is generated through an exclusive focus on gender difference "the oppressed third-world woman" category has an additional attribute—the "third-world difference"! The "third world difference" includes a paternalistic attitude towards women in the third world.[18] Since discussions of the various themes I identified earlier (e.g., kinship, education, religion, etc.) are conducted in the context of the relative "underdevelopment" of the third world (which is nothing less than unjustifiably confusing development with the separate path taken by the west in its development, as well as ignoring the unidirectionality of the first/third-world power relationship), third-world women as a group or category are automatically and necessarily defined: as religious (read "not progressive"), family oriented (read "traditional"), legal minors (read "they-are-still-not-conscious-of-their-rights"), illiterate (read "ignorant"), domestic (read "backward") and sometimes revolutionary (read "their-country-is-in-a-state-of-war; they-must-fight!"). This is how the "third-world difference" is produced.

When the category of "sexually oppressed women" is located within particular systems in the third world which are defined on a scale which is normed through Eurocentric assumptions, not only are third-world women defined in a particular way prior to their entry into social relations, but since no connections are made between first- and third-world power shifts, it reinforces the assumption that people in the third world just have not evolved to the extent that the west has. This mode of feminist analysis, by homogenizing and systematizing the experiences of different groups of women, erases all marginal and resistant modes of experiences.[19] It is significant that none of the texts I reviewed in the Zed Press series focuses on lesbian politics or the politics of ethnic and religious marginal organizations in third-world women's groups. Resistance can thus only be defined as cumulatively reactive, not as something inherent in the operation of power. If power, as Michel Foucault has argued recently, can really be understood only in the context of resistance,[20] this misconceptualization of power is both analytically as well as strategically problematical. It limits theoretical analysis as well as reinforcing western cultural imperialism. For in the context of a first/third-world balance of power, feminist analyses which perpetrate and sustain the hegemony of the idea of the superiority of the west produce a corresponding set of universal images of the "third-world woman," images like the veiled woman, the powerful mother, the chaste virgin, the obedient wife, etc. These images exist in universal ahistorical splendour, setting in motion a colonialist discourse which exercises a very specific power in defining, coding and maintaining existing first/third-world connections.

To conclude, then, let me suggest some disconcerting similarities between the typically authorizing signature of such western feminist writings on women in the third world, and the authorizing signature of the project of humanism in general—humanism as a western ideological and political project which involves the necessary recuperation of the "East" and Woman" as *Others*....[I]t is only in so far as "Woman/Women"and "the East" are defined as Others, or as peripheral, that (western) Man/Humanism can represent him/itself as the centre. It is not the centre that determines the periphery, but the periphery that, in its boundedness, determines the centre. Just as feminists like Kristeva, Cixous, Irigaray and others deconstruct the latent anthropomorphism in western discourse, I have suggested a parallel strategy in this article in uncovering a latent ethnocentrism in particular feminist writings on women in the third world.[21]

As discussed earlier, a comparison between western feminist self-presentation and western feminist re-presentation of women in the third world yields significant results. Universal images of "the third-world woman" (the vieled woman, chaste virgin, etc.), images constructed from adding the "third-world difference" to "sexual difference," are predicated on (and hence obviously bring into sharper focus) assumptions about western women as secular, liberated, and having control over their own lives. This is not to suggest that western women *are* secular and liberated and have control over their own lives. I am referring to a *discursive* self-presentation, not necessarily to material reality. If this were a material reality there would be no need for feminist political struggle in the west. Similarly, only from the vantage point of the west is it possible to define the "third world" as under-developed and economically dependent. Without the overdetermined discourse that creates the *third* world, there would be no (singular and privileged) first world. Without the "third-world woman," the particular self-presentation of western women mentioned above would be problematical. I am suggesting, in effect, that the one enables and sustains the other. This is not to say that the signature of western feminist writings on the third world has the same authority as the project of western humanism. However, in the context of the hegemony of the western scholarly establishment in the production and dissemination of texts, and in the context of the legitimating imperative of humanistic and scientific discourse, the definition of "the third-world woman" as a monolith might well tie into the larger economic and ideological praxis of "disinterested" scientific inquiry and pluralism which are the surface manifestations of a latent economic and cultural colonization of the "non-western" world. It is time to move beyond the ideological framework in which even Marx found it possible to say: They cannot represent themselves; they must be represented.

Author's Note

This paper would not have been possible without S.P. Mohanty's challenging and careful critical reading. I would also like to thank Biddy Martin for our numerous discussions about feminist theory and politics. They both helped me think through and sharpen some of the arguments in this paper.

NOTES

1. See especially the essays in Moraga and Anzaldua (1983); Smith (1983); Joseph and Lewis (1981) and Moraga (1984).
2. Terms like "third" and "first" world are very problematical both in suggesting over-simplified similarities between and amongst countries labelled "third" or "first " world, as well as implicitly reinforcing existing economic, cultural, and ideological hierarchies. I use the term "third world" with full awareness of its problems, only because this is the terminology available to us at the moment. The use of quotation marks is meant to suggest a continuous questioning of the designation "third world." Even when I do not use the quotation marks, I mean to use the term critically.
3. I am indebted to Teresa de Lauretis for this particular formulation of the project of feminist theorizing. See especially her introduction to de Lauretis (1984); see also Sylvia Wynter, "The Politics of Domination," unpublished manuscript.
4. This argument is similar to Homi Bhabha's (1983) definition of colonial discourse as strategically creating a space for a subject peoples through the production of knowledges and the exercise of power.
5. A number of documents and reports on the UN International Conferences on Women, Mexico City 1975, and Copenhagen 1980, as well as the 1976 Wellesley Conference on Women and Development attest to this. Nawal el Saadawi, Fatima Mernissi and Mallica Vajarathon in "A Critical Look At The Wellesley Conference" (*Quest*, IV:2, Winter 1978, pp. 101-7), characterize this conference as "American-planned and organized," situating third world participants as passive audiences. They focus especially on the lack of self-consciousness of western women's implication in the effects of imperialism and racism in their assumption of an "international sisterhood." Amos and Parmar (1984) characterize Euro-American feminism which seeks to establish itself as the only legitimate feminism as "imperial."
6. The Zed Press "Women in the Third World" series is unique in its conception. I choose to focus on it

because it is the only contemporary series of books I have found which assumes that "women in the Third World" is a legitimate and separate subject of study and research. Since 1985, when this essay was first written, numerous new titles have appeared in the Zed "Women in the Third World" series. Thus, I suspect that Zed has come to occupy a rather privileged position in the dissemination and construction of discourses by and about third-world women. A number of the books in this series are excellent, especially those which deal directly with women's resistance struggles. In addition, Zed Press consistently publishes progressive, feminist, anti-racist and anti-imperialist texts. However, a number of texts written by feminist sociologists, anthropologists, and journalists are symptomatic of the kind of western feminist work on women in the third world that concerns me. Thus, an analysis of a few of these particular texts in this series can serve as a representative point of entry into the discourse I am attempting to locate and define. My focus on these texts is therefore an attempt at an internal critique: I simply expect and demand more from this series. Needless to say, progressive publishing houses also carry their own authorizing signatures.

7. Elsewhere I have discussed this particular point in detail in a critique of Robin Morgan's construction of "women's herstory" in her introduction to *Sisterhood is Global: The International Women's Movement Anthology* (1984) (see Mohanty) "Feminist Encounters" (pp. 30-44, especially pp. 35-7).
8. My analysis in this section of the paper has been influenced by Felicity Eldhom, Olivia Harris and Kate Young's excellent discussions (Eldhom, Harris and Young, 1977). They examine the use of the concepts of "reproduction" and the "sexual division of labour" in anthropological work on women, suggesting the inevitable pull towards universals inherent in the use of these categories to determine "women's position."
9. Another example of this kind of analysis in Mary Daly's *Gyn/Ecology*. Daly's assumption in this text, that women as a group are sexually victimized, leads to her very problematic comparison between the attitudes towards women witches and healers in the west, Chinese footbinding, and the genital mutilation of women in Africa. According to Daly, women in Europe, China, and Africa constitute a homogeneous group as victims of male power. Not only does this label (sexual victims) eradicate the specific historical realities which lead to and perpetuate practices like witch-hunting and genital mutilation, but it also obliterates the differences, complexities and heterogeneities of the lives of, for example, women of different classes, religions and nations in Africa. As Audre Lorde pointed out, women in Africa share a long tradition of healers and goddesses that perhaps binds them together more appropriately then their victim status. However, both Daly and Lorde fall prey to universalistic assumptions about "African women" (both negative and positive). What matters is the complex, historical range of power differences, commonalities and resistances that exist among women in Africa which construct African women as "subjects" of their own politics. See Daly (1978:107-312) Lorde in Moraga and Anzaldua (1983).
10. See Eldhom, Harris and Young (1977) for a good discussion of the necessity to theorize male violence within specific societal frameworks, rather than to assume it as a universal fact.
11. These views can also be found in differing degrees in collections like: Wellesley Editorial Committee, ed., *Women and National Development: The Complexities of Change* Chicago: University of Chicago Press 1977, and *Signs*, Special Issue, "Development and the Sexual Division of Labor," 7.2, (Winter 1981). For an excellent introduction to WID issues see ISIS, *Women in Development: A Resource Guide for Organization and Action* Philadelphia: New Society Publishers, 1984. For a politically focused discussion of feminism and development and the stakes for poor third-world women, see Sen and Grown, (1987).
12. See essays by Vanessa Maher, Diane Elson and Ruth Pearson, and Maila Stevens in Young, Walkowitz and McCullagh (1981); and essays by Vivian Mota and Michelle Mattelart in Nash and Safa (1980). For examples of excellent self-concious work by feminists writing about women in their own historical and geographical locations, see Lazreg (1988) on Algerian women; Gayatri Chakravorty Spivak's "A literary Representation of the Subaltern: A Woman's Text from the Third World," in Spivak (1987), and Lata Mani's essay, "Contentious Traditions: The Debate on SATI in Colonial India," *Cultural Critique* No. 7, Fall 1987, pp. 119-56.
13. See Tabari (1980) for a detailed discussion of these instances.

14. Olivia Harris in Harris (1983:4-7). Other MRG reports include Deardon (1975) and Jahan (1980).
15. See Eldhom, Harris and Young (1977) for an excellent discussion of this.
16. See Kishwar and Vanita (1984) for a discussion of this aspect of Indian women's struggles.
17. See Haraway (1985:65-108, especially 76).
18. Amos and Parmar (1984:9) describe the cultural stereotypes present in Euro-American feminist thought "The image is of the passive Asian women subject to oppressive practices within the Asian family, with an emphasis on wanting to 'help' Asian women liberate themselves from their role. Or there is the strong, dominant Afro-Caribbean woman, who despite her 'strength' is exploited by the 'sexism' which is seen as being a strong feature in relationships between Afro-Caribbean men and women." These images illustrate the extent to which *paternalism* is an essential element of feminist thinking which incorporates the above stereotypes, a paternalism which can lead to the definition of priorities for women of colour by Euro-American feminists.
19. I discuss the question of theorizing experience in my " Feminist Encounters" (1987), and in an essay co-authored with Biddy Martin in de Lauretis (1986).
20. This is one of Foucault's central points in his reconceptualization of the strategies and workings of power networks. See Foucault (1978 and 1980).
21. For an argument which demands a *new* conception of humanism in work on third-world women, see Lazreg (1988).

REFERENCES

Abdel-Malek, Anouar (1981) *Social Dialectics: Nation and revolution* Albany: State University of New York Press.

Amin Samir (1977) *Imperialism and Unequal Development*. New York: Monthly Review Press.

Amos, Valerie and Parmar, Pratibha (1984) "Challenging Imperial Feminism," *Feminist Review* No. 17.

Baran, Paul A. (1962) *The Political Economy of Growth*. New York: Monthly Review Press.

Berg, Elizabeth (1982) "The Third Woman." *Diacritic*. Summer.

Bhabha, Homi (1983) "The Other Question—The Stereotype and Colonial Discourse," *Screen* 24:6, p. 23.

Boserup, Ester (1970) *Women's Role in Economic Development*. New York: St. Martin's Press; London: Allen & Unwin.

Brown, Beverly (1983) "Displacing the Difference—Review, nature, Culture and Gender," *m/f* No. 8.

Cixous, Hélène (1981) "The Laugh of the Medusa" in Marks and de Courtivron (1981).

Cowie, Elizabeth (1978) "Woman as Sign," m/f No. 1.

Cutrufelli, Maria Rosa (1983) *Women of Africa: Roots of Oppression*. London: Zed Press.

Daly, Mary (1978) *Gyn/Ecology: The Metaethics of Radical Feminism* Boston: Beacon Press.

De Lauretis, Teresa (1984) *Alice Doesn't: Feminism, Semiotics, Cinema*. Bloomington: Indiana University Press.

— . (1986) ed. *Feminist Studies/Critical Studies*. Bloomington: Indiana University Press.

Deardon, Ann (1975) ed. *Arab Women*. London: Minority Rights Group Report No.27.

Deleuze, Giles and Guattari, Felix (1977) *Anti-Oedipus: Capitalism and Schizophrenia*. New York: Viking.

Derrida, Jacques (1974) *Of Grammatology*. Baltimore: Johns Hopkins University Press.

Eisenstein, Hester (1983) *Contemporary Feminist Thought*. Boston: G.K. Hall & Co.

Eisenstein, Zillah (1981) *The Radical Future of Liberal Feminism*. New York: Longman.

Eldhom, Felicity, Harris, Olivia and Young, Kate (1977) "Conceptualising Women," Critique of Anthropology "Women's Issue" No. 3.

Foucault, Michel (1978) *History of Sexuality Volume One*. New York: Random House.

— . (1980) *Power/Knowledge*. New York: Pantheon.

Gunder-Frank, Andre (1967) *Capitalism and Underdevelopment in Latin America*. New York: Monthly Review Press.

Haraway, Donna (1985) "A Manifesto for Cyborgs: Science, Technology and Socialist Feminism in the 1980's," *Socialist Review* No. 80.

Harris, Olivia (1983a) "Latin American Women—An Overview." in Harris (1983b)

Harris, Olivia (1983b) editor *Latin American Women* London: Minority Rights. Group Report No. 57.

Hosken, Fran (1981) "Female Genital Mutilation and Human Rights." *Feminist Issues* 1:3.

Huston, Perdita (1979) *Third World Women Speak Out*. New York: Praeger.

Irigaray, Luce (1981) "This Sex Which Is Not One" and "When the Goods Get Together" in Marks and de Courtivron (1981).

Jahan, Rounaq (1980) editor. *Women in Asia.* London: Minority Rights Group Report No. 45.

Jeffery, Patricia (1979) *Frogs in a Well: Indian Women in Purdah.* London: Zed Press.

Joseph, Gloria and Lewis, Jill (1981) *Common Differences: Conflicts in Black and White Feminist Perspectives.* Boston: Beacon Press.

Kishwar, Madhu and Vanita, Ruth (1984) *In Search of Answers: Indian Women's Voices from Manushi.* London: Zed Press.

Kristeva, Julia (1980) *Desire in Language.* New York: Columbia University Press.

Lazreg, Marnia (1988) "Feminism and Difference: the Perils of Writing as a Woman on Women in Algeria," *Feminist Issues* 14:1

Lindsay, Beverley (1983) editor *Comparative Perspectives of Third World Women: The Impact of Race, Sex and Class.* New York: Praeger.

Lorde, Audre (1983) "An Open Letter to Mary Daly," in Moraga and Anzaldua (1983).

Marks, Elaine and De Courtivron, Isobel (1981) editors *New French Feminisms.* New York: Schoken Books.

Mies, Maria (1982) *The Lace Makers of Narsapur: Indian Housewives Produce for the World Market.* London: Zed Press.

Minces, Julliette (1980) *The House of Obedience: Women in Arab Society.* London: Zed Press.

Modares, Mina (1981) Women and Shi'ism in Iran." *m/f* Nos. 5 and 6.

Mohanty, Chandra and Martin, Biddy (1986) "Feminist Politics: What's Home Got to Do With It?" in De Lauretis (1986)

Mohanty Chandra (1987) "Feminist Encounters: Locating the Politics of Experience." *Copyright* 1, "Fin de Siècle 2000."

Moraga, Cherrie and Anzaldua, Gloria (1983) editors *This Bridge Called My Back: Writings by Radical Women of Color.* New York: Kitchen Table Press.

Moraga, Cherrie (1984) *Loving in the War Years.* Boston: South End Press.

Morgan, Robin (1984) editor *Sisterhood is Global: The International Women's Movement Anthology.* New York: Anchor Press/Doubleday; Harmondsworth: Penguin.

Nash, June and Safa, Helen I.(1980) editors *Sex and Class in Latin America: Women's Perspectives on Politics, Economics and the Family in the Third World.* Massachusetts: Bergin & Garvey.

Rozaldo, M.Z. (1980) "The Use and Abuse of Anthropology: Reflections on Feminism and Cross-Cultural Understanding," *Signs* 5:3.

Said, Edward (1978) *Orientalism.* New York: Random House.

Sen, Sita and Grown, Caren (1987) *Development Crises and Alternative Visions: Third World Women's Perspectives.* New York: Monthly Review Press.

Smith, Barbara (1983) editor *Home Girls: A Black Feminist Anthology.* New York: Kitchen Table Press.

Spanos, William V. (1984) "Boundary 2 and the Polity of Interest: Humanism, the 'Center Elsewhere,' and Power." *Boundary 2* Vol. X11, No. 3/ Vol XIII, No. 1 Spring/Fall.

Spivak, Gayatri Chakravorty (1987) *In Other Worlds: Essays in Cultural Politics.* London and New York: Methuen.

Strathern, Marilyn and McCormack Carol (1980) editors *Nature, Culture and Gender*. Cambridge: Cambridge University Press.

Tabari, Azar (1980) "The Enigma of the Veiled Iranian Women." *Feminist Review* No. 5.

Tinker, Irene and Bramsen, Michelle Bo (1972) editors. *Women and World Development.* Washington DC: Overseas Development Council.

Young, Kate, Walkowitz, Carol and McCullagh, Roslyn (1981) editors *Of Marriage and the Market: Women's Subordination in International Perspective.* London: CSE Books.

RECOVERING IGBO TRADITIONS: A CASE FOR INDIGENOUS WOMEN'S ORGANIZATIONS IN DEVELOPMENT

Nkiru Nzegwu

Nkiru Nzegwu is Assistant Professor of Philosophy, Art History, Africana Studies, and Women's Studies at State University of New York at Binghamton. Her areas of research are in Aesthetics, African Philosophy, African feminist issues, and multicultural studies in Art.

Nzegwu describes the beliefs and values of the dual-sex system in Nigerian Igbo traditions prior to colonization as a way of revealing Western assumptions about the meaning of gender and of exploring the continuing detrimental effects these assumptions have for development projects in developing countries. Nzegwu builds a case for understanding the Igbo dual-sex system as non-sexist in that the separation of the duties and responsibilities of men and women did not result in differential power or inferior status for women. She describes the devastating effects of colonization on Igbo traditions and calls for a recovery of these traditions as a way of structuring development projects that can truly improve the lives of people in Nigeria.

Introduction

This paper may read to philosophers like an anthropological argument for the utilization of indigenous women's organization in development.[1] To some modernization theorists,[2] development economists, and policy makers it would sound like nativism, a romantic re-creation of a precolonial reality that is of little relevance to Africa's postcolonial condition. But viewed critically, it is a radical critique of foundational assumptions about gender that underlie current development programmes. The sociological and philosophical elements of the critique connect at points where historically constituted gender identities, social histories, and cultural norms expose the inadequacy of preconceived ideas about progress and culture that propel economic development. Though I shall argue my case through a detailed examination of Igbo women's history,[3] much of my argument has relevance to many other countries of Africa.

It is important to stress that this philosophical critique is not a point-by-point refutation of any specific development theories. Rather, it is a reading which interrogates foundational assumptions informing development wisdom. The generalist approach permits us to see how gender inequality is built into programmes. It enables us to understand the conceptual biases of the participatory-models of Non-Governmental Agencies (NGOs), and the technocratically oriented models of large development bureaucracies like the World Bank and the International Monetary Fund (IMF).

My argument proceeds in three broad moves. In the first section, I shall examine the "status of women" in Igbo political structure to determine the reasons for the apathy of modern Igbo women to political activity. In the second section, I shall describe the internal structure of one such organization and examine how the utilization of literacy as the criterion of cultural adulthood leads to designing ineffectual programmes for women. In the last section, I examine the history of development in Nigeria and explore the positive contributions indigenous women's organization could bring to development.

Reprinted with permission of the publisher from *Women, Culture and Development*, by Nkiru Nzegwu (Oxford: Oxford University Press, 1996): 444–465.

1. The Status of Women in Igbo Political Structure

Colonialism in Africa was much more than a metaphor. It was an alienating historical condition that erased and silenced the voice of women. In eastern Nigeria in general, and Igboland in particular, the British policy of indirect rule resulted in the installation of a sexist administrative structure that, despite the demise of British imperial rule, has persisted to this day. Women's disadvantaged position in southern Nigeria today, and in the eastern parts of the country in particular, could directly be traced to two important features of the colonial government: its economic and social policies that effectively marginalized women; and the asymmetrical political structure that arrogated to male officials the power to make decisions for women. This structural bias robbed women of their historical powers and relegated them to the category of dependent minors. The enforced invisibility meant that women were denied education, employment, decision-making powers, and access to resources such as credit facilities and loan schemes.[4]

Prior to colonization, the political culture of the Igbos could theoretically be described as dual-sex.[5] Under this dual-symmetrical structure, women had their own Governing Councils—*Ikporo-Onitsha, Nd'inyom*—to address their specific concerns and needs as women. The councils protected women's social and economic interests, and guided the community's development. This dual-symmetrical structure accorded immense political profile to women both in communities with constitutional monarchies (on the western side and some parts of the eastern banks of the River Niger—Onitsha, Ogbaru, and Oguta), and in the non-centralized democracies of the eastern hinterland.

Although Igbo society was divided along gender lines, antagonistic gender relations were generally avoided because the indigenous political process was primarily consensus-seeking. The socio-political structure required and depended on the active participation of women in community life. Their views were deemed critical, not because they were women, but because of the special insight they brought to issues by virtue of their spiritual, market and trading duties, and their maternal roles. In precolonial times, the Obi of Onitsha governed in consultation with the Omu (female monarch), and later with *Ikporo-Onitsha* following the demise of the Omu institution.[6] In other parts of Igboland, *Nd'inyom* governed with *ezeala* (the spiritual custodians of societal norms). The maintenance of a harmonious gender relationship was critical to the well-being of Igbo society. The consequences for destabilizing the intricate gender structure could be agonizingly severe.

For instance, men who devalued women risked being "sat on,"[7] or shunned by women who invoked constitutionally validated sanctions to restore normalcy. Scholars like Green (1964), Judith Van Allen (1976), and Monday Effiong Noah (1985) have noted that these took various forms including besieging the man in his house and singing scurrilous songs that taunt his manhood, or roughing him up and/or destroying his prized possessions. It is interesting to note that other men in the village hardly ever came to the rescue or defence of one of their own. "*Nya ma!*" (It's the persons own business), they would say. "*O kotelu okwu umunwnayi!*" (The person brought the wrath of women on himself). Green gives a telling account of an incident in Agbaja, in which women exercised this disciplinary power by killing two unpenned pigs belonging to a male neighbour, which were eating their crops. Fearing a violent response from the male owner or his male friends, Green was startled by the owner's non-aggressive response. Turning to a male informant for elucidation, she was casually informed that the owner and the other men would not take action because "it is the women who own us."[8]

In Onitsha, the same sanctionary measure was enforced in the public refusal to accord a titled offender the customary respect due a person of his rank;[9] or refusing to have him properly buried until an apology was extracted from the family.[10] In extreme cases as occurred under the reign of Omu Nwagboka in the late 1880s,[11] women withdrew *en masse* from any activity in which inter-gender relationship was implicated; and in some parts of Igboland, women collectively moved out of their villages until their demands were met.[12] Leaving men to fend for themselves and their children, impressed viscerally upon them the worth and value of women.

The social disruption that usually followed the violation of women's rights provided compelling reason for all to strive for social harmony.

Mutual gender respect thus developed, as each group had equal access to sanctionary powers and the judicial and constitutional backing to use its powers, if need be, against the other. Women who consistently and deliberately devalued the men of their marital village risked a visit from the ancestral mask of the ward. However, women's stronger group identification through their Governing Councils and their ability to work collectively in diverse associations gave them immense protection and coverage. Their networking skills enabled women to mobilize instantly across cultural, religious, and economic boundaries.[13] Since Igbo men lacked the same kind of network associations and gender identification commonly found with women, it was harder for them to enforce their decisions. Realizing that to take on one woman was to take on the whole, a situation the men were most anxious to avoid, they found it easier to lodge their complaints with the appropriate women's group rather than take action on their own.

Women's independence was fostered by cultural traditions that placed a premium on female assertiveness and collectivity, and did not define power as socially deviant. If men usually capitulated and were, or seemed politically "helpless" before the collective strength of women, it is not because they were passive or timid. It was more that they were *accustomed* to women *being* in positions of power and influence, and had consequently developed respect for their administrative skill. The indigenous structures of governance publicly validated and reinforced women in ways that normalized their presence in the judicial, economic and political spheres of life. Thus Igbo men could matter-of-factly accept the "sitting on a man" mode of conflict-expression together with its graphic imagery of "being sat on," because *in their communities* women adjudicated cases, established and enforced rules and regulations, worked in concert with Obi, *ndichie*, and *ezeala* in the administration of the community. Since women's political identity is a fact of life, and in their eyes "*nwanyibuife*" (women are of significance), there could be no shame in acknowledging and abiding by women's regulations.[14]

The theoretical significance of the social act of "sitting on a man" is that it most forcefully revealed the existence of a society in which men lacked the sort of patriarchal authority so readily presented in ethnographic literature, and assumed by development policy planners. The political significance of that sanctionary force and one which is not adequately highlighted is that it afforded women a powerful constitutional check on male excesses in society, and assured that their views were adequately factored into policy decisions.[15] Reminders of the destabilizing effects of gender conflict were used symbolically to protect and reinforce women's power. Writing in the 1930s, Green notes that at times of natural disasters, which have had a particularly great impact on women's lives (for example, when there was a higher than normal infant mortality rate, or an increased incidence of stillbirths), "women collectively ... [held] ... men and their magic responsible" and demanded propitiation.[16] This type of critical scrutiny established a framework within which men were held accountable and gender imbalances redressed.

In Igbo political tradition, representation without sanctionary powers to back it up implied non-representation, "*ewe onu okwu*" (not to have a say); its effect was social marginalization. Thus politically marginalized and reclassified as dependents under colonial rule, Igbo women, in the period between 1925 and 1935, incessantly organized protest rallies and picketed the offices and residences of colonial officials to wrest some form of representation.

In 1929 these protest movements culminated in "*Ogu Umunwanyi*" (the Women's War), in which they sought to modify the system to give them some form of representation similar to what they had in precolonial times. Appreciative of some of the benefits of colonialism such as better medical care and transportation networks, and aware of their educational handicap ("our eyes were not opened"), the women did not desire to overthrow the colonial rule as alleged.[17] Specifically, they just wanted to be consulted on the selection of Native Affairs officials, and in the formulation of policies. They wanted the prosecution of all oppressive and corrupt chiefs and court clerks, and offered to provide the necessary evidence to convict these officials. To introduce safeguards in the administrative system, they proposed that the post of warrant chiefs be limited to three years of service, and that women must be consulted in the selection of officers for those posts.[18] Most important of all, they wanted tax exemption for women.

The Women's War, which was fought to protest the imposition of taxation on women, began in Bende division of Owerri province and spread quickly throughout Owerri and Calabar provinces of eastern Nigeria. The 1929 financial crash had impacted negatively on women's produce trade, motivating them to seek assurances from the colonial government that they would not be taxed.[19] Faced with bureaucratic stonewalling, the women resolved not to pay any taxes nor have their properties assessed. So when the Warrant Chief Okugo sent an assessor to compile the figures, Nwanyeruwa Ojim refused to permit an assessment of her property. An alarm brought other women to the scene who proceeded "to sit" on Chief Okugo and the assessor, Mark Emeruwa. Messages were sent to women in other villages who, on learning of the crisis, joined the struggle. Although Chief Okugo was deposed to placate the women, the women refused to allow the dethronement to deflect them from their larger objective.

In their confrontation with the colonial administration, the women mostly employed the conflict-resolution mechanism of "sitting on a man" to signal their grievances. Unaccustomed to such militancy from women, the nervous colonial officials ordered in armed police and troops to "quell" the disturbances, which had spread over an area of 6,000 square miles. Officially 50 women were killed and another 50 wounded by the time order was restored. Despite the heavy casualties on the women's side, the end of the war did not signal the end of the protest movement and women's agitation for representation.

The profound historic importance of the 1929 Women's War consisted not simply in the courageous attempt of the women of eastern Nigeria to challenge invisibility and fight the devaluation of their personhood. It also unequivocally established that women's independence was a fact of life in precolonial times—and that these traditions could still be called upon to empower women. The fiery strong response of these women to the erosion of their rights conclusively showed not just that women *had* political roles and rights in precolonial times, but also that the political institutions through which they claimed these rights were integral parts of the political tradition in Igboland and Ibibioland. It also showed their political acumen, foresight and vision, and revealed the existence of a powerful, highly efficient political structure with networks that transcended ethnic boundaries. The women displayed an incisive grasp of the colonial agenda, and ability to perform rapid and accurate analyses of the fluid, complex situation, and a remarkable capacity for formulating and deploying appropriate strategies.

The Women's War was also important for another reason. It marked the rise of Western gender ideology, as evidenced by the non-participation in the women's action by a growing class of privileged women. Whereas in the past women had rallied in solidarity to assert their demands, the individualistic emphasis of the new ideology prevented the converts, the wives of administration officials, from participating in the political movement.[20] Their disinterest and lack of political consciousness was best explained as a rejection of Igbo gender ideology that had fostered women's independence and placed a premium on assertiveness and being outspoken. Suddenly, being assertive and having a political opinion signified the "primitive Africa"; while being cultured and civilized meant being submissive and obedient. These status-conscious wives of local officials ironically modelled themselves into the non-assertive , self-effacing, passive women that Igbos had always derisively portrayed as "*mmili oyi*" (cold water, ineffectual).

As the writings of Leith-Ross and Green show, this Western gender ideology hardly made an impact in the rural areas between the 1930s and early 1950s. To a large extent, the pattern of life of the rural and urban poor continues to this day to manifest stronger identification with traditional norms and values than with Western cultural values. With the domestication of middle-class women by the 1950s, we find a two-tiered reality: an upper-crust Westernized society, overlaying and to some extent concealing indigenous social values and practices. At the upper-tier level, educated middle-class Igbo women find themselves shackled to a sexist system that leaves them politically disadvantaged to this day.[21] In an environment where success is defined in economic terms, many women who have had to adopt a subordinate stance to their male partners do not realize that this is itself a form of oppression, regardless of the prosperity enjoyed. Meanwhile their economically disadvantaged "uneducated" sisters retain a stronger sense of their identity, and a greater degree of control over their lives.

What development planners too often ignore in designing policies is that vestiges of this cultural consciousness still remain today, albeit in a modified form. The present ambivalence of Igbo women, especially middle-class women, to political action is symptomatic, not of tradition but of an alienation from Igbo history produced by the experience of colonialism. For the urban-poor and rural women, the primary disenchantment is with the so-called "democratic" process of Western political tradition that had marginalized and stripped them of their female dignity. As early as 1929 women like Mary Onumaere were protesting against the rising power of men: "we don't wish to be oppressed by our menfolk."[22] Others like Nwato of Okpuala wondered at the internal contradictions of colonialism: "we thought that white men came to bring peace to the land . . . if this oppression continues, how are we to praise you?"[23]

Nigerian men in general benefited immensely from the inherent sexism of the system as the British officers were willing to work with them to install colonial rule, however much they despised them on racial grounds. Whereas in the past Igbo men had to share power with women, as they succeeded educationally, economically, and politically they egoistically clung to power and could not be depended upon to distribute resources equitably. The co-optation of African men into the Western gender stereotypes did incalculable damage to modern Nigerian political culture. Freed from the restraining checks and balances that had curtailed sexism, male bias was massively built into policies, programmes, and structures of the system to safeguard it for men. The results were the denial of effective representation to an inordinately large number of women; the exclusion of women's corrective influence in governance; and the creation of a politically passive female citizenry and sexist, dictatorial men.

2. Women's Organizations: The Ikporo Onitsha

In beginning with an analysis of the colonial impact on African cultural life, it might seem that I have fallen prey to what has most derisively been described as "the predilection of African intellectuals," namely the urge to "romanticize" precolonial traditions, and to unimaginatively explain away Africa's ills by blaming colonialism. It is certainly true at a superficial level that colonialism is not completely responsible for all the problems in Africa. But at a deeper level it is especially culpable, given the structures: economic, military, and bureaucratic, including gender, that it left in place.[24] Given the male bias of our colonial legacy, the female empowering institutions of Africa's indigenous cultures were devalued with no space created for the women in the new Western-derived one.

One place where this sexism is most evident in postcolonial Africa is in the field of development where projects are targeted at men and a wide disparity exists in the income-earning pattern of men over women. Barbara Rogers (1980) had argued that this income disparity derived from nonrecognition of women as producers. Citing numerous examples she showed that the underpinning conceptual bias of development militated against women in the distribution of benefits through stereotypically treating them as "dependents" of males who were treated as "principal income generators." By noting that women's labour was consistently taken for granted, Rogers showed the heavy labour-intensive demands made on women which far exceeded that made on men.

The linkage between women's self-worth and financial autonomy, which Ndiya[25] women made in 1946, is now being made by critics of development theories. Anticipating the adverse effects of a gender biased economy, Ndiya women had warned the British against the implementation of policies that would deprive women of their livelihood and self-worth. "What shall we do insofar as we know that if the mill (being introduced by the British) is *owned* and *run* by men, we will be thrown out of a *job*?"

(emphasis mine). They knew the effect of male monopoly of resources; they knew that if they became economically vulnerable and beholden to men their social worth and dignity would be severely undercut.

Zenebewoke Tadesse's (1990) analysis of women in African economy is important in that she identifies the positive impact of income-generating activities on women's self-confidence. To bring about the sort of structural changes she envisaged, women would have to be more intimately and more positively factored into development planning. It is not just that policies that accord with the *status quo* must be rejected since they reinforce the marginalized status of women. It is more that development planners should revise radically their approach if their projects are to be realistically adapted to the needs of the target group. When development planners assume that rural women must lack organizational skills, and conclude that they should devote their resources to funding "awareness workshops," they illicitly transpose the apathy of the middle-class women on to rural women who have in fact continued to be politically active; they illegitimately suppose that lack of literacy skills is equivalent to lack of organizational skills.

Observing the politics and ideological power of literacy, Pattanayak (1991) notes that when literacy is construed as the basis of modernization: "illiteracy is grouped with poverty, malnutrition, lack of education, and health care, while literacy is often equated with growth of productivity, child care, and the advance of civilization."[26] Such a classification, Pattanayak suggests, "naturalizes" literacy as the panacea for successful development even as research shows that the correlation between literacy and the adoption of improved agricultural practices is insignificant.[27] What this establishes is that literacy is not a substitute for practical skills, nor does lack of it obstruct improvement. There is no question that in today's world literacy is vital, but it must be put in a proper perspective. It does not have a propulsive force all its own to instil knowledge and experience.

Despite the lack of literacy skills, many African women are engaged in trading activities and agricultural production, and in addition possess a wide range of technical, organizational, and administrative experience gained through hands-on practical activities in numerous indigenous associations. As the Igbo Women's War showed, these experiences equip women to evaluate their economic situation and take on the challenges of mobilizing other women at the grassroot level to implement projects. But planners' devaluation of these capabilities—at the same time a devaluation of these women's personhood—has generally led to the exclusion of these valuable experiences from development programmes. Planners need to take account of the diverse character traits of different groups of women, and to be open and receptive to alternative models of experiences and organizational skills.

Therefore, guided by the belief that development assistance to grassroots women's organizations is often stalled through lack of historical knowledge, I shall follow my general account of Igbo traditions with a description of indigenous women's institutions that are deserving of development support. These associations deserve consideration for several reasons: they seek activities that have social and cultural relevance; they are advantageously positioned to channel resources to women who need more empowerment and autonomy; their existence has been obscured by hostile development policies; and their leadership is not currently in a position to articulate their demands or to argue for them in terms that officials of foreign development agencies expect and demand. My aim is not to invoke outmoded ancestral relics, but to point out enduring administrative structures that have relevance for development at the grassroot level.

I must begin by describing the organizational structure of these groups which, historically, played important social, economic, political, and spiritual roles in the community. Understanding the internal structure of an organization like *Ikporo-Onitsha*, I will show why an unswerving focus on literacy as the criterion of cultural adulthood leads to the adoption of ineffectual policies for women.

In much of former eastern Nigeria, most communities have a broad-based Women's Governing Council that has sole jurisdiction over the local affairs of women in a specific community. These councils are radically different from, and unconnected to the élitist, class-conscious, government-funded

National Council of Women's Societies with its headquarters in Lagos. Membership in these indigenous Women's Councils is open to women of a specific community regardless of their educational or class background. In fact, literacy is not a prerequisite for participation. Some of the elderly women leaders of these councils never received formal education, yet their organizational skills and leadership are widely respected.

Unlike the Western-derived National Council, the indigenous Women's Councils have an effective hold over their membership. This is so because they represent the interests of women in their community of salience, which means their home of origin, and are therefore especially responsive to these women's special interests. Regardless of a woman's social status and educational accomplishments, a council's directives are binding on her and are never treated with levity.

In Onitsha for example, such a women's council is the *Ikporo-Onitsha* (Women of Onitsha). This council has represented, and still represents, the interests of Onitsha women in Onitsha. It does not matter whether a woman lives in Lagos, Kano, Enugu, or New York, her interest is represented by the Governing Council even in her absence. No decision that has an impact on the lives or status of Onitsha women can be made without the council's knowledge and consent. Historically, this organization has played important social, economic, political, and spiritual roles in the community. To cite just a few examples, it steered women through such politically turbulent times as the resistance to colonial policies in the late 1920s and early 1930s, the 1963 to 1967 Obiship constitutional crises, and the three-year dispute with the then East Central State government in late 1973 to 1976, following that government's usurpation of Onitsha women's traditional market rights.

Prior to 1890, the *Ikporo-Onitsha* had the Omu (or female monarch) as its leader. The Omu and her Council of *otu ogene* was the female principle in governance, and complemented the male principle that was embodied in the Obi (or male monarch) and the *ndichie*.[28] Each institution was responsible exclusively for the actions and activities of members of the respective sex; their powers and privileges complemented one another. On national matters, however,[29] the two collaborated in formulating and establishing the Onitsha nation's position. This constitutionally defined consultative process ensured that the female viewpoint was well-represented in decisions affecting the whole community. At a trade negotiation in the 1870s, in which the State of Onitsha was to decide whether to permit the establishment of a European trading firm, John Whitford reported on the participation of "the old women who constituted the Board of Trade" (that was the Omu and her Council) in the decision-making process.[30]

Following the imposition of colonialism, the office of the Omu declined. The denial of recognition to the Omuship as the legitimate constitutional representative of women was politically damaging.[31] Worse still was the economic subjugation that followed. The trade and market portfolio of the Omu were gradually taken over by the British "in the interest of trade." New trading policies were promulgated[32] that tasked the women's ability to obtain operating capital, that deprived the office of the Omu of its revenue base, and in turn, stripped Onitsha women of their traditional influence over trade and market affairs. Their autonomy and powers were consequently undermined.

To survive the political erasure initiated by this economic trend, a radical transformation of the institution of the *Ikporo-Onitsha* took place. This transformation brought the organization into line with the changing reality of women's reduced economic circumstances and loss of power. To preserve the council's political role, the financially costly initiation and governance ceremonies were cut drastically. The excised constitutional powers were vested in the oldest surviving woman who, from then on, was addressed as *Onye-isi-ikporo-Onitsha* (the head of Onitsha women). Succession to this powerful office was simplified, and devolved automatically to the next oldest woman in line, once the full funeral ceremony of the predecessor was completed. Although the powers of subsequent *Onye-isi-ikporo-Onitsha* were nowhere near that of the Omu in precolonial times, the institution to this day commands immense respect and loyalty in Onitsha. The flexibility introduced by the radical restructuring gave the council new life and identity. Most importantly, its informal nature gave it a tactical advantage it never had before. This advantage was effectively deployed against the East Central State government between 1974 and 1976, to discredit and embarrass their own, Ukpabi Asika, who was then the Administrator. The police officers who were sent to track the activities of the women ran into an impenetrable thicket of elusiveness.

Today, the *Onye-isi-ikporo-Onitsha* rules through a Governing Council of 35 members: a general secretary, six to seven women leaders of opinion who advise on policy matters, and three representatives each from the nine founding villages of Onitsha. In keeping with the community's principle of equality, representation to *Ikporo-Onitsha* is on the basis of equal representation from villages, rather than population or numerical strength. Selection of representatives is based on such qualities as moral probity, strong character and charisma, articulate and fearless nature, and maturity in age. The representatives must have demonstrated leadership skills, and distinguished themselves in such other subsidiary associations. The stringent moral requirements for representatives are based on the idea that a strong moral centre is needed to deal with the tumultuous exigencies of political life. The age requirement of over 40 is not mandatory; it seems to have been put in place discretionarily to spare nurturing mothers the agony of juggling between activist community duties and child care.

The council conducts its affairs at two levels. The first is the intra-village level, in which representatives of the nine founding villages report and discuss the activities of their home constituency and vigorously represent their interests. Second is the Onitsha-national level. Here, the collective interests of Onitsha women prevail. By this I mean that issues are analysed from a gendered perspective in terms of their effect on Onitsha women as a whole. Strategies are then developed for their resolution. Because the Governing Council is a central unifying organization, its internal dynamics tend toward the promotion of shared communitarian values rather than divisive individualistic values. Except for caucus meetings, all meetings are held in an open public forum at *ilo mgbeleme* (the sacred assembly ground) where anyone can attend.

Ikporo-Onitsha branches are found in any town in Nigeria where there is a sizeable Onitsha community. These branches are seen as "international" affiliates and the members are referred to as "abroad" members. Each of these branches has an ad hoc "ambassadorial" relationship with the Governing Council in Onitsha, with which it maintains an open line of communication and to which it reports. Most of the branch membership are professional women: teachers, lawyers, doctors, engineers, retailers, and business women. Participation for abroad members is through the branch, and through village representatives when they relocate to Onitsha. Through firmly established networks and protocols, the branches are regularly kept informed of current local developments and of the official positions of the Governing Council. They receive directives from the council; and in turn send back their suggestions. Because Nigerians identify themselves primarily with their home of origin or "ethnic or cultural nation," rather than their place of domicile or "foreign land," they tend to be more interested in the progress and development of their cultural state than in the affairs of the place of domicile.

Like traditional Women's Council's elsewhere in Igboland, *Ikporo-Onitsha* has survived because of continuous organizational reviews, reevaluation of policies, timely critical responses, and adaptability to changing social conditions. Its well-developed chain of command and stringent requirement of accountability have earned it immense respect and credibility. The council's success in ensuring accountability derives from its intense monitoring system. Nothing is hidden in an environment where everyone knows the business of others. The knowledge that "everyone is their sister's keeper" means that you do only what you can publicly live with or defend. Fraud is possible, but what keeps people in check is not just the public exposure of their crimes, but the humiliating dressing-down that will be publicly meted out to them at *ilo mgbeleme*. What people dread above all is the alienating effect of ostracism which the Governing Council may pronounce on the culprit as a last resort.

Ostracism, the corrective sanction that impresses viscerally on individuals their dependency of social relations, highlights the limitations of Western notions of privacy and the primacy of the individual. The Onitsha position is that an individual's conceptualization of himself or herself as a person necessarily takes place within a social context. Only within a community of fellow beings can the idea of self-realization become intelligible. For realization implies interaction with others, establishing rites of engagement and interrelationship. Outside the border of a social realm, individuals, according to the Onitsha, become non-human, and if allowed to continue that sort of existence will break down and come to exemplify non-human tendencies. Ostracism—which bars a person from participation in family and community affairs—is a practical demonstration of the idea that humans are social beings. Living in a society and being shunned by its members definitely accords an individual his or her space, but only vividly demonstrating to them their implicit dependence on others. Since the ostracized person is, in effect, removed from the social to the natural realm, he or she enters the "land of the living dead," to live a devastatingly solitary existence. Full restoration of social rights and obligation comes from recanting and paying the stipulated fine.

It is noteworthy that this power is also applied against men. In cases where gender equilibrium is threatened profoundly, ostracism can be translated into withdrawal or disengagement of women's power from normal social interrelationship with men. This withdrawal force acts as a constitutional check, forcing men to confront their dependency on women. For instance, between 1977 and 1978, *Ikporo-Onitsha* led the whole community (men and women) in ostracizing the Obi of Onitsha Ofala Okagbue to protest his abdication of his constitutionally assigned obligation to fight for the traditional rights of Onitsha women. The same was done to the Owelle of Onitsha, the former first president of Nigeria, when his political position was defined as antagonistic to the stand *Ikporo-Onitsha* had taken officially on promoting women's welfare. Adazia Enwonwu, the Ndichi who openly taunted women for lacking significance, could not be buried as planned initially by his family, until a ritual rite of recantation was performed.

The fact that these female-centred Women's Councils have survived to this day is a testimony to both their adaptability and their resilience. They have responded progressively to the challenges of oppressive economic realities by establishing co-operatives to encourage women's trading activities.

The goals of these Women's Councils overlap with those of development agencies that are committed to grassroot development. First, the councils inculcate an ethics of community work in women, which in turn fosters a wide range of organizational, trading, and business skills. Because these skills and experiences are not abstractly named and theorized about, development officials routinely denigrate and dismiss them. Yet the hands-on administrative training that women leaders receive in the course of their service to multiple associations gives them an incisive encyclopaedic knowledge of their community. Their total understanding of cultural norms and market economics make them excellent candidates for the role of "people professionals" in the sorts of programmes that require information on local social and cultural structures.[33]

Lack of this sort of cultural knowledge has hampered development efforts in Africa in many ways. Programme evaluators too often lack the skills to carry out a comprehensive analysis of the social impact of programmes, hence they tend to rely on preconceived ideas about women and about literacy rather than "reading" the specific realities of the culture. Projects like water supply systems, food production, mechanized farming, workshops on fertilizer usage and business investment are diverted to men on the naïve assumption that men are "naturally" disposed to leadership and mechanical skills, while women are non-mechanically inclined and "naturally" disposed to a submissive role.

Numerous projects have failed for such reasons. Consider the case of water projects. Women, not men, are the traditional water managers in most African communities, and for that reason they possess all the relevant data. This came to light in a water-scheme project in northern Ghana funded by the Canadian International Development Agency (CIDA). Similar projects in other communities floundered, with the exception of one in which women were involved in the planning, implementation, and management of the project.[34] That the women co-ordinated project succeeded does not imply that men are irresponsible, but rather than they lacked the requisite knowledge about water resources to contribute effectively to the water-scheme project.

With this general moral knowledge in mind, and knowing that sustainability and accountability are the bane of development projects in Africa, let us now consider again the case of Nigerian development to determine what needs can be met by an organization like *Ikporo-Onitsha*.

3. Development Prospects: A Role for Traditional Women's Organizations

In postcolonial Nigeria, there have tended to be four main types of development projects. The first, and one that is generally given urgent national priority, is the heavy industrial type that seeks the transformation of the economy from agrarian to industrial. The second type targets male farmers in rural communities with the aim of improving their self-sufficiency through modern agricultural techniques and raising the productivity level of their cash crops. The third type of project focuses on social modernization in areas such as health care, literacy, water resources, and job training that strives to improve the general quality of life in the urban centres. Finally, the fourth category promotes self-help projects that are expected to have a far-reaching impact at grassroot levels.

In the first phase of postcolonial development in Nigeria between 1960 and 1973, the underlying model of development maintained that transformation from a communal to a capitalist economy was a prerequisite for modernization.[35] It was assumed that a technological focus, in such areas as iron and steel, road networks, bridge-building, dockyards, and agriculture was the only route to development. In line with Rostow's theory of modernization, the central assumption was that cultural development would automatically follow technological initiatives; and that the level of development of a society is determined by the number of intensive primary and secondary industries it possesses. So heavy capital-intensive projects were touted as a critical requirement for a sound economic base.

Between 1973 and 1983, the second major phase commenced. It was marked by an emphasis on technological transfer that led to an increased presence of Nigerians in the middle and upper-middle management positions. Majority shareholdership (known as indigenization) by Nigerians was another important issue. The assumption was that local ownership of industrial projects guaranteed access to technical knowledge. As in the first phase, large-scale capital-intensive projects such as iron and steel and petrochemical industries, and tangible symbols of success such as stadia, monumental office complexes, and airports were the preferred goals in development. As oil money rolled in from petroleum sales—100 billion dollars between 1973 and 1981—the need to raise agricultural productivity declined as a national priority. Earlier initiatives in agricultural development were largely abandoned as the attention shifted to the development of a manufacturing sector based solely on the assembly of semi-finished products. Social and cultural projects such as adult literacy, rural electrification and water schemes were also largely ignored and, when carried out, were haphazardly performed and monitored.

In both the first and second phases, indigenous culture was viewed as obsolete and not thought to have any significant initiating or critical role to play in industrialization. To all intents and purposes it was inert. This simplistic view of culture had devastating consequences for development, contributing to the failure of projects such as the iron and steel plant at Ajaokuta, the Aladja steel plant, the Lansat telecommunications system, and the three hi-tech incinerators in Lagos. The eventual realization that technological development presupposes a certain cultural and valuational environment led to a re-evaluation of development parameters. A different orientation exists today. The 1980s recession and the drastic decline of the economies of many African nations, coupled with the brutal effects of the Structural Adjustment Programmes insisted on by the World Bank and the International Monetary Fund have forced African nations to shift gears radically. A focus on grassroots development began in earnest in the early 1980s.

Today, development as practised by grassroot development programmes, is guided by the principle that the self-reliance of the rural and urban poor is critical to sustain cultural progress and development. At the initial stages, the NGOs programme representatives zealously approached their task with a paternalistic approach. Such an approach was counterproductive since it shut out local participation in the design of projects, with the result that local aspirations, values, priorities, and needs were excluded. The discovery that projects failed when they were not linked to the specific interests and needs of beneficiaries, brought about a change in the NGOs problemsolving techniques. To match projects to needs, participatory methodological models that stressed local participation in project design and implementation were adopted increasingly. However, a fundamental problem still remained with the models; their gender neutral emphasis ignored women.[36]

Since the attainment of independence three decades ago, Nigerian women have consistently been excluded from development. Initially, the standard argument was that development was gender neutral, and there was no need to target any specific group for programmes. Such arguments rang hollow as they masked the fact that the principal beneficiaries of development programmes were usually men. With the increasing presence of women in key decision-making positions in donor agencies, a gender perspective was added. Women, it was pointed out, constitute 70% of the workforce in agriculture in sub-Saharan Africa; so it makes sense to ask how they have benefited from massively funded agricultural projects.

But old perceptions and prejudices die hard. A telling case is that of the Washington-based African Development Foundation (ADF). In its first eight years of existence, from 1980 to 1988, only 17 per cent of grants have gone to support the efforts of local women's organizations. Yet a recent research programme and grant guideline states its support for local women management systems:

> The participation of women who are often the traditional water managers, in the design and implementation of water supply systems, is leading to improved maintenance and technological choices that are more adaptable to community needs and environmental demands. ("Perspectives on Self-Reliant Development," in *Research Programs and Grants of the African Development Foundation* (Washington, D.C.: ADF, 1989), 3-4)

In spite of such laudable statements, however, development coordinators and programme evaluators still make unwarranted assumptions about the capabilities of rural African women, and assume that their interests are served adequately in projects controlled by men. Given that a major aim of current development efforts is to facilitate grassroots development through linkages with "existing traditional, local management systems,"[37] it would seem imperative for development planners to get to know traditional women's organizations. If rural development projects fail or are non-sustainable, it could very well be that local resource organizations with an extensive pool of experienced and skilled people are being neglected.

The question really is: how relevant are indigenous Women's Councils such as *Ikporo-Onitsha* to such development initiatives and objectives? What mechanism, if any, does it have to enhance women's development, and how effectively could it respond to modern development issues? It is important, here, to see both sides of the "development divide" to know what benefits the organization can bring to rural women's development and also where planners' expectations are unrealistic. Three unrealistic expectations of planners should be briefly mentioned.

First, the expectation that rural women in Nigeria will take advantage of available funding opportunities of NGOs and private voluntary agencies is unrealistic when these agencies fail to work with indigenous organizations that are in a uniquely strong position to disseminate information. Secondly, the expectation of programme evaluators that projects will be funded on the basis of well-written project proposals stacks the deck against these women. It is like asking the women to translate their needs and experiences into the language that programme evaluators would understand without providing them with the requisite conceptual and linguistic tools. The issue at stake is not simply one of literacy, it is one of conceptual fairness. The agency that acts this way is still treating the African poor with condescension and on its own Western basis in spite of protestations that it is interested in Africa's problem. Thirdly, Africa's declining economic situation may show that evaluators' desire for self-sufficiency as a project goal is unrealistic.

Now, let's turn to the positive contributions Women's Councils could bring to development. First, the organizations have grassroots orientation and legitimacy. They have a strong community base and community focus as well as extensive knowledge of their community's values and needs. Their traditional legitimacy gives them the ability to mobilize women effectively and to guarantee women's participation in programmes. Moreover, the councils' diverse membership means that they can tap an extensive pool of professionally skilled women (and men) for advice. "Vertical linkages" between professionals and women implementors of projects match local skill to local need and help keep costs down. Professionals will view this service as part of their community service. It is noteworthy that *Ikporo-Onitsha*, for instance, used this strategem to obtain first-rate legal advice from a pool of prestigious lawyers for a four-year period without paying a dime.

Examination of the political structure of the Women's Council revealed the existence of a complex administrative structure with an effective monitoring system and inbuilt mechanisms to ensure accountability. As is well known, corruption and lack of accountability have been some of the problems that have consistently plagued development projects in Nigeria. These malpractices occur not because project managers are unqualified, but because they know that the punitive measures society will take would not undermine their social identity in the community of salience, once the booty is shared communally.[38]

Accountability, then, must be matched to the ethical motivations inherent in the cultural scheme. In the African setting, where the concept of person is tied to community validation, people will do whatever is in their power to be validated positively by their community of salience. What is significant in the account of *Ikporo-Onitsha's* sanction mechanisms is not so much the nature of the sanctions as that they are applied in ways that directly challenge the legitimacy and basis of the individual's self-identity and social validation. Such mechanisms could be used to guarantee a higher level of accountability in project implementation.

The complex, efficient administrative system of Igbo Women's Councils highlights the error in creating brand-new structures that are culturally alienated from local participants, rather than utilizing existing ones. Again what is revealed from intimate contact with Women's Councils is not their unwavering female-focus, but the leaders' incisive grasp of complex, fluid, and shifting situations, and their ability to implement their strategies.

Admittedly, the existing Women's Councils are locally limited in scope, rather than national in their orientation. This will be a point against them among those who believe in de-emphasizing ethnicity as a focus of development. But there is no evidence that "being national in outlook" (presumably, lacking a specific ethnic focus) is either necessary or sufficient for development. For one thing, the whole idea of national unity requires elaboration: what sort of unity do we wish to have, and what will be the role of ethnic plurality in it? This does not mean that development projects cannot have a national focus. But planners must be more reflective, seriously considering the conceptions they are using, and asking how indigenous ideas of nationhood and loyalty might be put to work at a trans-ethnic level.[39] To do this, they might do well to focus on the advantages that Women's Councils could bring to development.

Here is one concrete way to employ these councils. To initiate successful development projects in Onitsha, one needs to take advantage of cultural idiosyncrasies. Igbos are notoriously competitive. They care immensely for their natal communities of salience, and worry about how their progress measures up to that of rivals. Nothing will be achieved if one community is targeted for development without kindling the competitive spirit between communities. Therefore, one might suggest that a successful utilization of these Women's Councils in the role of intermediary organizations (and of their leaders as "people's professionals") must also employ three close rival communities as the experimental base for testing the utility of the councils. The competing communities should be aware that the criterion for evaluation is sustainability of projects. They should be informed that communities that perform well will receive increased funding and resources in the future.

Regular inter-community or lateral feedback is critical in the experiment. The objective is to keep the communities abreast of one another's relative performance; but feedback also allows them to compare notes on their progress, and learn from one another's strengths and weaknesses. If the competitive spirit is removed, one has removed the driving force to sustain the project to the point of self-reliance.

Can and will this work? At this stage, it is important to insist once again that the reason one hears this question is because the councils remain so unfamiliar to Western eyes, and seem so odd when held up against Western ideas of organization. The request for ironclad guarantees that one hears in such questions is really a call for reassurance before a move into unfamiliar conceptual terrain. In reality, the question cannot be answered before trying. It cannot be answered by solipsistic agony and torment. Indeed, it cannot be answered by abstract reflection at all. It can be answered only through practical engagement—by actually working with the women and their organizations. And throughout the process there must be an open mind, a mind responsive to change and flexible in change, a mind capable of perceiving and adapting to each unique situation, a mind informed by historical and cultural knowledge. That is the sort of mind—and the sort of rationality—that development planning in Africa really needs.

NOTES

1. If it does, we should see it as a manifestation of the depth in which eurocentric, colonial assumptions about knowledge have permeated scholarship. Received "critical" attitudes towards the conceptual categories of non-Western societies today, are implicit reproductions of racist prejudices and biases in which these societies have historically been cast. Materials from "other" cultures are exoticized as ethnographic literature, while the exotic materials of white-Western life is "naturalized" and presented not only as normal but as theoretically unproblematic.
2. Rostow (1960); Gino Germain, *The Sociology of Modernization: Studies on its Historical and Theoretical Aspects with Special Regard to the Latin American Case* (New Brunswick: Transaction, 1981); Josef Gugler and Williams Flanagan, *Urbanization and Social Change in West Africa* (Cambridge: Cambridge University Press, 1978).
3. The textual sources of much of that history are the works of colonial officials like D. Amaury Talbot, *Woman's Mysteries of a Primitive People: The Ibibios of Southern Nigeria* (London: Cassell, 1915); M.M. Green (1964); Sylvia Leith-Ross (1965). Recent book length studies on women have come from the following: V.C. Uchendu, *The Igbos of Southern Nigeria* (New York: Holt, Rinehart & Winston, 1965); Ify Amadiume, *Male Daughters/Female Husbands* (Zed Books, 1987). Other writers whose works include a section on Igbo women are Richard Henderson, The King in Every Man (1972); Nina Mba, *Nigerian Women Mobilized: Women's Political Activities in Southern Nigeria 1900-1965* (1982); E.E. Evans-Pritchard, *The Position of Women in Primitive Societies and other Essays in Social Anthropology* (New York: The Free Press, 1965); P. Amaury Talbot, *The Peoples of Southern Nigeria: Ethnology*, vol. 111 (London: Frank Case, 1926).
4. Since the late sixties noticeable changes have begun in the area of education. Parents are increasingly pushing for their daughters' education following the realization that women, more then men, invested more in the care of aged parents.
5. Kamene Okonjo (1976), 45-58; also Green (1964), ch. 11. Though written with colonial objectives in mind (which accounts for its much critized racist overtones), Green's book remains an incisive reading since she aims for a woman-centred view.
6. Even today, Ofala Okagbue, the Obi of Onitsha, seeks out women's stand and opinion before making policy pronouncements. This co-rulership is noted by Felicia Ekejiuba (1966:219) with respect to Omu Okwei in Ossamala; Henderson (1972) with regards to the Omu of Onitsha, and Kamene Okonjo (1976: 47-51) with respect to the Omu of Obamkpa.
7. For a detailed description of this mechanism, and how it works, see Judith Van Allen (1976:59-86); also Green (1964:174). For an account of this practice among Ibibio women see Monday Effiong Noah's description of the activities of *Iban Isong* (Ibibio women's organization) (1985:24-31).
8. Green (1964:174); also see Monday Effiong Noah's description of how men scuttle for cover when they

hear of movement of *Iban Isong* (1985:26-7); and Leith-Ross, (1939:97).

9. This was done to the Owelle of Onitsha and former President of Nigeria, Dr. Nnamdi Azikiwe, in 1976-7 when he fell out with Ikporo Onitsha. The "Owelle" is the seventh in rank of the Ndichi Ume, the highest ranking chiefs of the Obi of Onitsha's cabinet.
10. This happened to another Ndichie, Adazia Enwonwu, in 1975.
11. This is part of Onitsha oral history which Henderson documented (1972: 376, 525).
12. Interestingly, Saye women of Burkina Faso used this threat in 1981 to compel their men to build a dam. See Dankelma and Davidson (1988:35-37).
13. Mba (1982:92).
14. Barbara Rogers (1980) was undoubtedly correct when she observed that it is highly questionable that men in most precolonial cultures objectified women as passive objects (p. 29). She was also correct when she treated such theoretical intuitions as revealing more about those making the judgements (p.33). See ch. 2.
15. Many westerners including some feminists (Ann Ferguson,1991) are opposed to the idea of factoring sex into gender constructions. Catherine MacKinnon has shown that what is feared is a situation in which any possible distribution of powers necessarily reproduces sexist patriarchal roles and stereotypes. Hardliners on the issue find it difficult to comprehend how sexism can be overcome if sex differences are acknowledged. Focusing intently on the oppressive experiences women have undergone because of sex recognition, they usually forget in their fear (1) that male differences are already factored into constructions of power; (2) that factoring in female differences to displace male monopoly of the conceptual realm does not imply invoking negative stereotypical images; and (3) that sexism comes about not because biological sex is recognized, but because it is dealt with *negatively*.
16. Green (1964:176).
17. *Aba Commission of Inquiry Report* (1930:263).
18. Mba (1982:87-91). The reference on the women's war came from government documents such as *Aba Commission on Inquiry, Owerri Annual Report 1929 and 1930, Ogoja Annual Report 1929, Calabar Annual Report 1929 and 1930.* Miss Okezie's letter (*Aba District Office*, see Mba (1982), 1/21/30); from Nguru (*Owerri District Office*, see Mba (1982), 1/14/49); testimonies from Nwanyiezi of Ikefem (*Aba Commission of Inquiry Notes of Evidence* no. 148) Akulechula (ibid.: 175).
19. Ibid. 90.
20. Mba 83-5. Mba had given several reasons for the nonparticipation of middle-class women, namely pressures from husbands, non-membership in the community-based associations of the areas of protest, and adequate financial means. But these are inconclusive given that the women's action ran counter to the spirit of female consciousness in Igboland. In the rural areas, the wives and daughters of warrant chiefs and court officials led some of the revolt, so status and wealth cannot be called upon as valid explanations.
21. I have to admit that what has been described is the general trait of a class. In no way does it imply that all "educated" or "middle-class women" behaved in that manner. Exceptions like Miss Okezie, Margaret Ekpo, and Adora Ulasi could easily be found.
22. Ibid. 89. From the government document (*Aba Commission of Inquiry Notes of Evidence*) no. 805, see Mba (1982), p. 89.
23. Ibid. 92. From the government document (*Aba Commission of Inquiry Notes of Evidence*) no. 805, see Mba (1982), p. 92.
24. Femi Taiwo made this point in his paper on knowledge production which he presented at SUNY-Binghamton in March 1991.
25. Ibibio women. See Mba, 107.
26. Pattanayak (1991:105).
27. R. Shanker, "Literacy and Adoption of Improved Agricultural Practices," *Indian Journal of Adult Education* 40 (1979), 31-7.
28. For further descriptions of this see Richard Henderson (1972), Nina Mba (1982: 21-6); also see Okonjo (1976: 45-58).
29. I take here the definition of nationhood that is built on ethnicity, in which a cultural nation is equivalent to a political nation-state. This is the case in European nationalism. See B.O. Oloruntimehin, "African Politics and Nationalism, 1919-35," in Adu Boahen (ed.), *UNESCO General History of Africa: Africa under Colonial Domination 1880-1935*, vol. 7 (Los Angeles, Calif: UNESCO, 1990), 565-79.
30. Elizabeth Isichei, *Igbo Worlds: An Anthology of*

Oral Histories and Historical Descriptions (Philadelphia, Pa.: Institute for the Study of Human Issues, 1978).

31. For a more detailed account of this development see Mba 1982: 25-6, 49); Okonjo (1976:45-58).
32. The one-shilling produce inspection test was introduced in 1928 to regulate the quality of palm oil.
33. Lawrence Salmen used the term in another context, to describe local experts who are unaffiliated to development agencies, but who provide technical advice. My use differs only in the sense that I am treating the cultural advice to agencies as technical. See Lawrence E. Salmen, *Listen to the People: Participant-Observer Evaluation of Development Projects* (New York: Oxford University Press, 1987).
34. This successful project was evaluated by a female consultant Theodora Carroll Foster. She met with stiff opposition from the male area co-ordinator who felt that the local women had nothing to contribute.
35. This is Rowtow's model (1960), in which modernization defined the point of "take-off." It is assumed that industrialization, education, population, and labour are the necessary factors for sustained growth.
36. It is instructive to mention that this attitude occurs even with female programme officials. Being female does not imply that one is aware of the presence and complex nature of the gender stereotypes inherent in programmes.
37. *ADF Guidelines* (1989),6.
38. Although I find Harman's (1986) generalizations rather sweeping at times, he identified correctly this linkage between corrupt officials and their communities as the bane of development in Nigeria. See Harman(1986).
39. Policymakers who consider development as a vehicle for "natural unity" should bear in mind that Nigerians tend to view their place of domicile as a "foreign land," and are in turn viewed as "strangers" by the indigenes. This belief has had negative implications for development projects. In the politically volatile climate of Nigeria, where appointments are made on the basis of nepotism, workers will lack commitment to projects that are not located in their areas of salience.

BIBLIOGRAPHY

Arnold, Guy (1979). "Development Problems and Multilateral Aid," in *Aid in Africa*. London: Kogan Page.

Chapin, Mac (1990). "The Seduction of Models: Chinampa Agriculture in Mexico," *Grassroot Development*, 12, 8-17.

Dankelma, Irene, and Davidson, Joan (1988). *Women and Environment in the Third World: Alliance for the Future*. London: Earthscan Publications.

Ekejiuba, Felicia (1966). "Omu Okwei: The merchant Queen of Ossomari" *Nigeria*, Sept. 90, 213-20.

Ferguson, Ann (1991). *Sexual Democracy*. Boulder, Colo.: Westview Press.

Green, M.M. (1964). *Ibo Village Affairs*. New York: Praeger.

Harman, Nicholas (1986). "After the Ball: A Survey of Nigeria," *The Economist*, 3 May, 1- 42.

Henderson, Richard (1972). *The King in Every Man*. New haven, Conn." Yale University Press.

Leith-Ross, Sylvia (1965). *African Women: A Study of the Ibo of Nigeria*. London: Routledge & Kegan Paul, 1939, 2nd edn.

MacKinnon, Catharine (1987). "Difference and Dominance: On Sex Discrimination," in *Feminism Unmodified*. Cambridge, Mass.: Harvard University Press, 32-45.

Mba, Nina (1982). *Nigerian Women Mobilized: Women's Political Activities in Southern Nigeria*, 1900-1965. Berkeley, Calif.: University of California Press.

Noah, Monday Effiong (1985). "The Role, Status and Influence of Women in Traditional Times: The Example of the Ibibio of Southeastern Nigeria," *Nigeria*, 53, 24-31.

Okonjo, Kamene (1976). "The Dual-Sex Political System in Operation: Igbo Women and Community Politics in Midwestern Nigeria," in Hafkin and Bay (eds). *Women in Africa*. Stanford, Calif.: Stanford University Press, 45-58.

Pattanayak, D.P. (1991). "Literacy: an Instrument of Oppression," in Olson and Torrance (eds.), *Literacy and Orality*. New York: Cambridge University Press, 105-8.

Rogers, Barbara (1980). *The Domestication of Women: Discrimination in Developing Societies*. London: Tavistock.

Rostow, Walt Whitman (1960). *The Stages of Economic Growth.* Cambridge: Cambridge University Press.

Salmen, Lawrence (1987). *Listen to the People: Participant-Observer Evaluation of Development Projects.* New York: Oxford University Press.

Tadesse, Zenebewoke (1990). "Coping with Change: An Overview of Women and the African Economy," in *The Future For Women in Development: Voices From the South*. Ottawa: the North-South Institute, 44-62.

Thurow, Lester C. (1983). *Dangerous Currents: The State of Economics.* New York: Random House.

Van Allen, Judith (1976). "Aba Riots" or Igbo "Women's War?": "Ideology, Stratification , and the Invisibility of Women," in Hafkin and Bay (eds.), *Women in Africa*. Stanford Calif.: Stanford University Press, 59-85.

THE GOOD TERRORIST: DOMESTICITY AND THE POLITICAL SPACE FOR CHANGE

Janice Newberry

Janice Newberry received her Ph.D. in Anthropology from the University of Arizona in 1997. She currently is Coordinator for Undergraduate Internships and Research Activities at Bryn Mawr College, and is acting chair and visiting professor in the Anthropology Department at Haverford College (1998-99).

In this paper, Newberry uses the metaphor of the good terrorist to explore how the daily domestic practices of urban working-class women in a Javanese neighborhood illustrate that state-mandated domesticity has practical uses in the lives of local women. The making of the bourgeois home in Europe organized around the domestic angel is described, along with its extension to the colonies and then its reworking during national independence. In Indonesia, despite the poor fit between women's working lives and the imagined role of housewives, working-class women reproduce a version of the housewife as they work to accomplish other mundane tasks. Consequently, the denigrated national housewives organization takes on new meaning, and state rule and moral order is reproduced even as it is reformed.

Something was clearly afoot. Neighborhood women leaned longer at the fence, talking to one another. Glances were cast at the house of Pak Wayang, the puppet maker, and then heads came together. Slower to understand neighborhood gossip than others, I did not know at first what the trouble was. In fact, it wasn't until the drama was over that I came to hear the story of the trouble at our end of the street. The only hint I had that something had changed in the neighborhood's view of Pak Wayang[1] and his family was when Bu Sae sniffed dismissively that Bu Wayang didn't keep good house and worst of all did not cook for herself. Indexed in her disdain for Bu Wayang's housekeeping skills was an accusation about the family's moral standing. Her failure as an *ibu rumah tangga* (housewife) was surely a sign that theirs was not a good home.

This incident, detailed from my ethnographic work in a working-class Javanese neighborhood or *kampung*[2] came late in my fieldwork and confirmed what I had come to suspect already. That is, the disparaged government program known as PKK (from *Pembinaan Kesejahateraan Keluarga*, or Support for the Prosperous Family) was more meaningful for local Javanese women than was generally acknowledged. While it was true that this national housewives organization, a quasi-public structure that includes all adult[3] women in Indonesia, was denigrated in local conversation, the central features of this program, a mother/wife who takes care of her family and hence her community, had become a resource in the local value system that was invoked when Bu Sae categorized Bu Wayang as a bad housewife. That is, although PKK was often called *Perempuan Kurang Kerja*, or Women without Enough Work to Do, indeed, the gender values at its very center were actually used by local women to manage their own communities. And this is so despite the fact that the category of housewife is a relatively recent one in Indonesia (Tiwon 1996).

My research in a working-class, urban Javanese *kampung*, or neighborhood, shows that what might be considered the retrograde social role of housewife, which has been fostered by the Indonesian

---

Published with permission of Janice Newberry.

government at least since it institutionalized PKK in 1973, has come to be used by residents in their daily lives. Consequently, the category not only gains meaning, it becomes a resource for shaping local, and simultaneously, national politics. In this paper I examine the structure and practice of PKK to show how the social category of housewife, commonly perceived as conservative, has the potential for generating social change, and moreover, how the quotidian use of the category in working-class women's lives illustrates the cultural process of state formation. That is, the political order that is the state and its social reproduction are related to the daily practices of citizens, and further, the formation of the state may properly and profitably be understood as the negotiation of state structures in everyday life. From this perspective then, the state is less a set of elite institutions, legal codes, and political instrumentalities than it is the accretion of myriad daily acts of conformation and contestation that constitute a particular moral order.

After reviewing the sources of the various inflections of women's domestic roles and spaces in Java, I will consider how the resources provided by PKK are used by women to render credible accounts of themselves as housewives to meet and manage social obligations on a local level. These daily negotiations and investments are what animate and make real the social category of housewife, despite its ambivalent fit in women's lives. In this way, I hope to show that the formation of a moral state order is comprised in part in the everyday practice of female subject-citizens, and the power associated with reproduction in an expanded sense has volatile political potential when wielded by these *good terrorists*.

PKK: State-Sponsored Domesticity

> The government will support PKK which we hope will be a spearhead for the development of society from below, 'motored' by women. I ask that the various activities programmed at the national level be channeled through PKK. We can have many programs for women to enhance the role of women in development. But it should not be forgotten that these programs are aimed and to be implemented by women in the villages, whether in the urban or rural areas. If there are too many organizations, it is not in accordance with their simple desires and way of thinking, and will only serve to confuse them (Presidential meeting on the occasion of the National Working Meeting of P2W-KSS, 2 March 1981, cited in Suryakusuma 1991:57).

The structure of the Indonesian government is a pyramid that reaches from the office of the president in an unbroken hierarchy that reaches at its lowest level to the unpaid, popularly selected representatives of blocks of 10-20 households. This smallest division is known as the *RT* for *Rukun Tetangga* or Harmonious Neighbors. Six of these small units are comprised within a single *RW*, *Rukun Warga* or Harmonious Citizens. These lowest two levels of governance are unpaid positions, and all levels above are considered civil service. The leadership structure of PKK is a mirror image of the predominantly male administrative structure; that is, the titular head of PKK is the wife of the president of Indonesia, and the local head of PKK is the wife of the Bapak RT. Thus the Pak RT and Bu RT are the married couple who represent the government's regulation of local community and who mediate local residents' relationship to the state apparatus (as do the Pak and Bu RW for the larger neighborhood grouping at the next level up). The base membership of PKK, however, is every adult woman in Indonesia.

The activities of PKK are synopsized in the 10 important programs of PKK (*10 Program Pokok PKK*) which appear in the form of plaques and signs at the entrance to most villages and *kampung* in Java. These programs include support for the government's ideology of *Pancasila*,[4] mutual self-help, clothing and food, skills training, health, developing cooperation, preservation of the neighborhood, and health planning. In their administration, these programs translate into, among other things, monthly baby weighings to monitor their health, literacy programs for older women, mosquito reduction as well as cooking demonstrations and fashion shows.

In essence, the Indonesian government uses PKK to mobilize women as unpaid community development workers, who through their efforts improve the standards of living of their families and communities. On the face of it, such a program seems an efficient way for a lower income country to provide necessary social services in a low cost manner. Most of the community projects are self-funded or receive very small amounts of government cash. Yet, the basis for this program is the nuclear family organized around a single couple, with the woman staying at home, a description that arguably does not fit the majority of Indonesian families. In fact, in my own small sample, only two families out of 47 families conform to this ideal.

The use of state-sponsored domesticity to organize social welfare by the Indonesian government is related to the government's promotion of a specific form of community organization and governance. Despite a complicated history of pre-colonial, Dutch colonial, Japanese occupational, and nationalist influences, the ideal community is presented rhetorically as that essential rural *Javanese* social form—the cooperative peasant village.[5] The discursive work of (re)instantiating these forms of community and cooperation is accomplished in part through PKK, and the connections made between women, the ideal family and community are quite clear in government publications:

> The objective of the PKK movement is to materialize family welfare, which covers mental, spiritual, and physical wellbeing. The target of the programmes is the family. Since the mother performs the central role in the family the programmes are mostly focused on her. In this context the woman is viewed as an individual, a mother, a wife, often co-breadwinner, and a fellow citizen... (Ministry of Home Affairs 1983).

Or as another government publication puts it, PKK is "aimed at establishing a healthy prospering family in order to create a welfaring community" (Department of Information 1984:31). Indeed, women's participation is built into the very structure of community administration, and women are positioned as the point of articulation between the family and the state, and between the family and the community.

Yet, the rhetoric of PKK not only tries to persuade women to stay at home and raise good citizens and keep good house and community, it also encourages them to search for supplemental income. That is, women are encouraged to begin cottage-type industries in their homes and neighborhoods so that they may work for extra cash without entering the formal waged economy. Such efforts are supported in various ways by the government of Indonesia, which offers loans, classes, and various incentives to women to begin such businesses. Enterprises include sewing for others, cooking for sale, handicraft industries such as making shoes, handbags, and other small-scale work. Home-based or community-based small-scale enterprises and multiple occupations have long been used by families to supplement general income, the difference is now the government officially supports these efforts.

As a consequence, Indonesia's low-cost labor is reproduced, chronic male under-employment is masked and subsidized, and the bottleneck of educated, unemployed youths who spend a long period finding employment is ameliorated. That is to say, the simultaneous increase in state intervention in the agricultural sector which led to the dis-employment of female labor through changing technological and social relations along with the appearance of PKK programs aimed at encouraging women to stay home and support their families appears more than coincidental.[6] The scale of PKK, once it was nationalized in the early 1970s, suggests its importance to the government: "when one considers that there is a PKK in each one of the nearly 700,000 villages in Indonesia, and that two-thirds of government funds for women in Indonesia are allotted to PKK, the implications are great" (Suryakusuma 1991:55). It could be argued that the government's desire for national development of human and productive resources could logically have lead to the structural unemployment as well as the emergence of PKK, and indeed, no hypothesis of a governmental conspiracy is offered here. Instead, the near simultaneity of the release of female labor and the institution of programs aimed at domesticity likely has many causes along with multiple effects.

Still, the benefits of PKK for the Indonesian government seem indisputable. In a situation of surplus labor, the informal sector and family labor of women serves to keep households afloat while it removes women from competition for jobs with the male unemployed. While the official stance towards women in formal sector employment appears proactive, the practices of the government work to encourage women to stay home and work in the informal sector. And up to this point, the informal sector appears to be infinitely absorptive. The work of women not only supports the young and educated in the period before they attain employment, it also serves to support the family in the face of low male employment. Thus, the institution and continuation of PKK is overdetermined by the various needs of the Indonesian state—crucially, the reproduction of a large reserve army of labor and willing low-wage workers. Working class women are not only encouraged to reproduce and support this army of reserve labor, but to do so under the guise of correct moral guidance and service to the Republic of Indonesia as good managers of homes and communities.

What is of concern to me here is the effect of these programs in the everyday lives of Javanese women and how the domestic and political space that is created through PKK and its programs can be used to contest, affirm, and sometimes change the social formation of the state. As the preceding discussion suggests, reproduction has several aspects and women's roles must be considered in terms of all three: the biological reproduction of humans, the reproduction of socialized humans, and the reproduction of the social relations that sustain the state structure, i.e., state formation (cf. Moore 1994). It is the centrality of women's roles in this expanded sense of reproduction, the very thing that makes them so useful to the state, that makes them ideally suited to be *good terrorists*.[7]

Good Terrorists

The "Good Terrorist" is a reference to a book of the same name by Doris Lessing (1985). I use the idea of the Good Terrorist to challenge the position of housewives in official Indonesian rhetoric and in popular Western culture alike, because although the idea of resistance has come to stand for the limited political space of the down-trodden (and is too often understood as discourse alone), in fact, the housewife and her domestic space offer the opportunity for room for movement.

Lessing's novel concerns a half-baked group of would-be terrorists who call themselves the Communist Centre Union, and it charts their development from a bunch of unemployed marginal "radicals" to their eventual, almost accidental, bombing of a crowded street in London. At the center of the novel is a character Alice Mellings who works assiduously not only to be a good radical but to create a comfortable house for the radicals. Alice "is strong, emotionally intuitive, and sympathetic, brave, warm-hearted, hard-working, and generous—the sort of woman whose domestic skills and maternal sympathy have traditionally held the world together..." (*New York Times Book Review*, December 19, 1985). Alice is also a committed radical, working with a cell of nascent terrorists who squat in an abandoned house while they lay plans. It is Alice who cleans, paints, finds furniture, and persuades local authorities to restore utility services, and it is Alice who comforts the other squatters and cooks healthy soups and stews for them. It is Alice who confronts her bourgeois parents and demands money to pay for the politics of her little band—made necessary by her parent's middle class life—and it is Alice who recreates the comforts of home for her compatriots. As one review noted, it is "one of the most disturbing ironies of this disturbing novel that Alice's best qualities, her domestic genius, her generosity and sympathy and energy, are ultimately responsible for the transformation of a collection of dissatisfied radicals into a terrorist gang" (*New York Times Book Review*, December 19, 1985).

The appeal of the Good Terrorist is that it puts together the idea of maintaining a social order, in Alice's case the bourgeois refinements of home, with the idea of subversion and social change. Alice Mellings illustrates nicely two issues significant in a consideration of domesticity: that the work of cooking and cleaning must always be done—even for disenfranchised radicals—and that the figure of the housewife, often taken to be one associated with conservatism, can actually be an agent of change. These two features follow necessarily from the centrality of reproductive work to human life. Yet, this very centrality entails room for significant contradictions, and hence the paradox of the "Good Terrorist." How can housekeeping, its second term implying "keeping" things as they are, have anything to do with subversion and transformation? How can conservation and change occupy the same political space?

As the next sections of this paper will show, the critical importance of reproduction has prompted governments, colonial and nationalist, to try and control women and the moral power of domestic space. Yet the contradictions implied in the emergence of the housewife as a key social figure from the colonial and nationalist eras shows that the contents of such social categories are volatile, and the uses of such categories and resources may differ from their official conceptions. In contemporary Indonesia, for example, the "cult of domesticity" with its ideal housewife and mother/citizen figures prominently in developmentalist ideology and government programs to raise standards of living and improve local infrastructure. Paradoxically, this emphasis on the good mother and housewife has worked to provide working class women with the resources needed to challenge and change local conditions. Although the creation of the home and the housewife can be said to be inherently oppressive to women—this is after all, Engels' world historic defeat of women (1942[1902])—it is also the case, as my own work suggests, that new political spaces are created that have the potential to help women improve and expand their lives.

Domestic Angels or Cult Followers

> Social historians now observe as commonplaces (1) that the emergence of a developed "domestic domain"—associated with women, unwaged housework, and child raising, and the "private"—was a corollary of industrial capitalism ...; (2) that "domesticity" was integral to the cult of "modernity" at the core of bourgeois ideology; and (3) that, far from being a natural or universal social institution, it grew to maturity with the rise of the factory system, which entailed the reconstruction of relations of production, of personhood and value, of class and gender (Comaroff and Comaroff 1992 :38).

The literature on the emergence of the ideology of home as the domestic haven, seat of filial piety, of sentiment, of family values, and the habitat of the domestic angel has been analyzed predominantly by social historians and feminist historians as the peculiar result of the emergence of the bourgeois nation-state in England and parts of Europe.

During the age of empire in nineteenth-century Victorian Europe, evolutionary histories, Social Darwinism, and laissez-faire capitalism were at their height. The "Victorian debate on women" ramified in the lives of both European women and indigenous, colonized women. In the metropole, middle and upper class women were being consigned to the domestic sphere as distinct from the public, a feat made possible by the contemporaneous consignment of lower class women to the domestic sphere of elite women's kitchens, not to mention the very public, industrial labor force. Although it was the experience of middle and upper class women that would inform bourgeois ideology, as Maria Mies, who coined the term housewifization (1986), suggests, it would result in all women being socially defined as housewives, dependent on their husbands, whether they were or not. In this way, the class specific outlines of the domestic sphere were extended to all women and inequality was masked. Others have noted the equivalence of the process of domestication or "housewifization"as a protracted historical process "comparable with and closely related to proletarianization" (Bennholdt-Thomsen 1988:159).

A suite of meanings associated with the Victorian ideal of private home life emerged alongside the transformation of social relations that accompanied the deepening of industrial capitalism.[8] The separation of women away from the world created the moral space of the home which became the dominant model for domestic life, even for those women who earned their wage inside the domestic haven of others. The moral dimensions of the Victorian home are clear in its descriptions, such as that offered by Ruskin:

> "It is a place of Peace; the shelter, not only from all injury, but from all terror, doubt, and division ... a sacred place." He concludes the romantic image of the domestic angel with a telling profile of her qualities: "she must be enduringly, incorruptibly good; instinctively, infallibly, wise—wise, not for self-development, but for self renunciation" (cited in Callaway 1987:33).

The creature at the center of the Victorian home, the domestic angel, has turned out to be remarkably resilient across cultures in every succeeding generation, despite the fact that she was the product of a very particular phase of industrial capitalism in one part of the world. Part of the resiliency of the "housewife" and "good mother" is her association with what appear to be essentially feminine qualities such as nurturing of the young, care, and loving sacrifice, all of which were understood to be the surface manifestations of her biologically determined role as mother. And as Olivia Harris notes, "since the human body is ideologically presented as a natural given, outside of history ..., it is easy to slide into treating domestic labour as a natural activity, also outside the scope of historical analysis" (Harris 1984:148).

Morality and Domestic Space in the Colonies

The persistence of the dual spheres of male and female endlessly reiterated through the distinctions public:private, culture:nature, material:spiritual and their apparent "naturalness" provided the motive force behind the effective extension of this signifying system and its attendant social forms to the colonies and subsequently its use by post-colonial nationalist and revolutionary movements. The physical enclosure of middle-class women within the single family home was accompanied by their capture within an ideological space that served to exclude not only the dirty world of money and manufacture but the poor, the racially degenerate, and by extension to the colonies, the native. The physical space of the home became wedded with the moral space associated with appropriate sexuality, proper child rearing, and correct social behavior.

Purity of race and questions of racial degeneracy, when combined with presumptions of appropriate home life, marriage, sex, and family, were a powerful means to control social hierarchy in the colonies. In the early stages of colonialism in the Dutch East Indies, for example, reproductive work, including sexual intercourse, was performed by the native *nyai*, who served as a housekeeper and bedmate to the lonely Dutch man. The VOC (East Indies Company) would not allow Dutch women to join their husbands without special dispensation (Stoler 1985; Gouda 1995; Taylor 1983), although after 1652, "men above the ranks of soldier and assistant in the civilian hierarchy" were allowed to bring out their families (Taylor 1983:29). In the early years of colonialism, social and sexual relationships were relatively fluid: children born of Dutch-Javanese unions were recognized as Dutch, and Dutch Indies society included many Eurasians. Over time, as the colonial presence deepened, Dutch women were allowed to emigrate and what had previously been a situation of fluid social arrangements between colonials and the indigenes became rigid.

The policing of this social distance often fell to women, whose position as reproducers of empire's children and culture obscured their commonalities with other subordinate classes. Colonial discourse on both race and gender concealed the issues of stratification within the empire, both at home and in the colonies. *Nyais* were replaced by proper Dutch wives whose children may have been raised by native *baboes*, but whose parents were purely Dutch.

The arrival of white women in colonies as diverse as Sumatra, Fiji, Nigeria, and the Solomon Islands[9] corresponded to the fixing of social and physical space within the colony in imitation of the metropole. Remarkably, despite their place on lower rungs of civilization's evolutionary ladder, European women were thought to exemplify both the best and worst of the national identity of the European metropoles; engendering a civilized response from their European men while exciting native men almost beyond control and inscribing social distance so effectively that they were accused of being bigots worse than the imperially dispatched patriarch of the household. Frances Gouda describes how "incorporated" European wives were the "foot soldiers—either willingly or with moral qualms—who were in charge of defending an elaborate colonial pecking order that placed indigenous women at the bottom and classified white men at the top." In their daily domestic routines, Dutch women gave concrete expression to a male-defined imperial agenda and knowingly contributed to "the ideological work of gender" (Gouda 1995:162-3).

The literature on European women in the colonies

suggests that they were the bearers of a metropolitan moral tradition, based on nineteenth century scientific racism and laissez-faire economics, rather than any primordial female character. Subsequently, during reactions to colonialism, women again provided the moral symbol and force to be manipulated by a male, nationalist leadership to rally opposition to the empire.

Neutralizing Popular and Sexual Power

Caught between the desire to modernize their countries along the lines of European technologic and economic excellence and the desire to assert independence, nationalist discourses in many parts of the Third World made use of an invented tradition that privileged women as a sign of distant and glorious pre-colonial past.[10] Thus, the very logic of separate spheres that had emerged in the metropole and been used to secure colonial dominance through racial and sexual purity and separation was used in reverse to justify a nationalist independence that preserved what was taken to be *authentic* culture—embodied in women. Paradoxically then, nationalist movements often served to conserve the Western division of male and female spheres, using women again to defend a particular moral order and frequently domesticating Third World women in all too familiar ways. For nationalist Indonesia, the power of an early radical women's movement led to its subsequent capture by the new Indonesian state within programs such as PKK. This appropriation of the momentum to change women's roles by the state illustrates not only the potential volatility of women's moral power, but also how it may be secured by the state.

During the nationalist period in what would become Indonesia, the domestic needs of women became a rallying cry for GERWANI (*Gerakan Wanita*, Women's Movement), one of many vigorous women's organizations that emerged during the early 1900s. As Saskia Wieringa suggests, PKK and GERWANI were initially nearly identical in many of their goals. The activities of GERWANI included "credit groups, kindergartens, consumer cooperatives, literacy courses, assistance to women with marriage problems, handicraft courses, campaigns to lower the prices of staple foodstuffs" (Wieringa 1993:20). GERWANI, however, offered assistance to leftist organizations like the Indonesian Communist Party (PKI, *Parti Komunis Indonesia*), although it addressed "a group of women the PKI never paid any attention to: housewives" (Wieringa 1993). The difference between GERWANI and PKK was the political connotation of each, as should be clear from the reference to the Indonesian Communist Party above. It was during the crack-downs after the alleged attempted Communist coup of 1965 that GERWANI was banned while PKK became the focus of the government's goals regarding women. This shift was part of a larger attempt to de-politicize the successful grassroots organizations associated with the Indonesian nationalist revolution while capturing their momentum for change.

One explanation for how this was accomplished is offered by Wieringa (1993; see also 1988), who discusses the persistent story that members of GERWANI were involved in the genital mutilation and torture deaths of the generals associated with the alleged coup attempt in 1965 that led to the New Order regime of Suharto. Despite evidence that this did not in fact occur (Anderson 1987), the myth continues, presumably because of its power to discourage women's active participation in politics. Campaigns to construct "an image of GERWANI members as whores and sexually perverted women" were orchestrated, while PKK members were "extolled as good ibus [mothers] and dutiful and respectable citizens" (Wieringa 1993:17). In the early years of the new republic following the revolution Indonesian women engaged in a genuine suffrage movement, but with the coming of the New Order all of that changed. After the coup of 1965, the government "opted pragmatically simply to coopt women in the organization structure of their husbands" (Suryakusuma 1996:100). The new developmentalist regime used programs such as PKK to specify women's roles in the developmental process, but this was accomplished by structuring women's participation as part of a "non-political women's movement," while still using elements of older women's associations and groups (Gerke 1992:30, n.17).

The difference between PKK and GERWANI was

not just who controlled their structure but in their apparent potential for radical social change. GERWANI was an independent women's organization; PKK is an arm of the government. It is significant that the rhetoric used to discredit GERWANI was overtly sexual; that is, not only were its members communists but they were whores and prostitutes as well. Here we have the good terrorist in another guise. Women were to remain important "motors" for social change, but through a structure thoroughly de-politicized by the Indonesian state. The transmogrification of organizations such as GERWANI from a group of sexually perverse and dangerous subversives working to topple the government to good terrorists working for social change at the behest of the government—and importantly without the taint of unrestrained sexuality—resonates with the earlier colonial obsession with proper sexual conduct and right culture. The successful depoliticization of PKK in the government's eyes is clear since currently "PKK is the only organization allowed to work at the village grass-roots level" (Wieringa 1993:24).

The gutting of the nationalist era women's movement and the retention of the general form of these organizations to be used in state development is only one of the many contradictions embedded within the organization of PKK. There is, more critically perhaps, an inherent contradiction in the linking of the maintenance of healthy families and communities to the work of stay-at-home mothers. Javanese women, particularly rural Javanese women, have long been economically active and engaged in a variety of income-generating activities that take them out of their homes. If indeed the model of rural community is embraced as a national ideal, as the Indonesian government declares, then it would immediately contradict the PKK ideal of women at home. In fact, the PKK stay-at-home mom is an artifact of the particular history of change in the Javanese countryside matched with Dutch notions of middle class women and their place (Carey and Houbens 1987; Gouda 1995; Taylor 1983). This is not to say that women in Java have not been involved in the management and support of communities and families, but that this was done in addition to work outside the home.

Power and Morality's Mother

The association of women with right morals, whether those of the colonial metropole or those of the nationalist revolution, persists in modern politics in ways that continue the linked association of domestic and moral space. Indeed, women's roles in producing good citizens has proved (and continues to prove) to be a particularly powerful way for women to affect public policy. The "mother" as somehow outside or beyond political guile has great symbolic and practical political power. The protests by the mothers of the disappeared in Argentina, the so-called *Plaza de Mayo Madres*, proved to be such a powerful protest to the ruling junta as they marched day after day holding the pictures of their disappeared children and wearing embroidered diapers on their heads to signify their domestic roles *because* they were *just mothers* (Schirmer 1994; Perelli 1994). Other women have used the role of mother to win political office, offering the differing politics of the domestic as an alternative to politics as usual; for example, Violetta Chamorro who ran successfully for the presidency of Nicaragua on the basis of her experience as *mother*. Yet the symbolic power of the mother and her practical work may be captured for less happy causes. Claudia Koonz (1987) documents the role of Nazi women in a fascist regime that sought to end women's electoral privileges as it sanctified their roles as reproducers of the master race (see also De Grazia 1992 on Italian fascism and its effects for women). Nazi women reproduced a pleasant home place for their families even while they worked to prevent that haven for those who were racially unworthy.

The political power of the Mother, or the *Ibu*, is also evident in Indonesia. Djajadiningrat-Nieuwenhuis coined the term *ibuism* to refer to the combination of elite *priyayi*[11] values with those of the Dutch petit-bourgeois that produces an ideology that sanctions any action taken by a mother on the part of family, class, or country without asking for anything in return (1987:44). *State ibuism* has been used subsequently by Suryakusuma to suggest the New Order government's role in promoting such self sacrifice for state goals. PKK is a prime example of this state-sponsored domestic cult. The moral power of the role of mother, devolving from colonial, nationalist, and developmentalist histories, has been fully captured within the rhetoric of the Indonesian state. For example, *Hari Ibu* (Mother's Day)[12] was inaugurated officially in 1953 along with the Mother's Day Banner.

> The banner shows the Melati flower as the symbol of pure motherhood, while its buds symbolize the natural unity and relation between the Mother as the source of love and her children. The five petals of the stylised Melati flower stand for Pancasila, the Five Principles of the state philosophy. The slogan on the banner reads "Merdeka melaksanakan Dharma," meaning "Free to do one's social duties" (Department of Information 1984:10-11).

During my fieldwork, the mutual ideological constitution of good mothers, wives, and citizens was made abundantly clear in a banner promoting breast feeding: *Aku Sayang Ibu*, *Aku Sayang Istri*, *Aku Sayang Indonesia*, or I love my mother, I love my wife, I love Indonesia.

Women's roles as defenders of the moral order, whether colonial or nationalist, has granted them some political space and authority such that the Indonesian government has tried to control it. Yet the political space opened for women as mothers can be used to mobilize for local change in homes and communities. Once appropriated, the moral power of the good mother provides room for acts of terrorism.

Kampung Space

The movement from the cult of domestic angels, to the colonial architecture of proper domestic life, to the construction of the nationalist home as site of authentic culture describes an arc that is general enough to capture the experience in many different parts of the world. Yet, the specific curvature in any particular place requires some adjustment. To understand the particular effects of PKK, current, local practice of morality must be considered. The daily dramas of *kampung* life that I observed and participated in illustrate not only the value and salience of community for *kampung* inhabitants, but the key role of women in its functioning. More importantly here, the programs, practices, and propaganda of PKK have now become resources to be used in the negotiation of community and morality by *kampung* dwellers.

In taking seriously the daily use of PKK in *kampung* women's lives, their roles as managers of household accounts become significant. The women I worked and lived among in the *kampung* managed not only the financial and domestic accounts of their households, but their social and moral accounts as well. Ethnomethodologists make use of the concept of *accountability* in a similar way; for example, Harold Garfinkel (1967:1) speaks of situated practices of "looking-and-telling" that allow members of a group or community to be held accountable. Behaviors that are "observable-and-reportable" to other community members necessitate attempts to render credible accounts of oneself as a good neighbor, citizen, or in this instance, housewife. This idea of accountability not only dovetails nicely with the ethnomethodologist's "theme of tacit or 'taken for granted' understandings" (Giddens 1995:237), but it also offers a micro-level tool for understanding the connection between state structure and everyday action. To suggest that PKK is an ideological instrument of the Indonesian state is not a sufficient explanation for how it becomes real in the lives of Javanese housewives. My ethnographic fieldwork in a working class *kampung* showed that women used PKK as a resource to render credible accounts of themselves in their daily lives, thus reproducing a particular state and moral order even while opening up room for change.

Raising good children and keeping good house are used as barometers of social character not only in the macrocosm of colonial society and nationalist rhetoric but in the microcosm of the *kampung*, and so it was with the family of the puppet maker from my earlier example. Pak Wayang appeared to be a good addition to the neighborhood at first, at least to the nearby Cipto family who never turned down a good time. Not only did his puppet making industry provide job opportunities, but at night the men would gather in the open area that earlier had been filled with workers to play *keroncong* music (the Javanese equivalent to country-western music that is derived from Portuguese songs; Ferzacca 1997). The men would typically sit up until late in the night drinking *jamu*, a traditional health tonic, in this case bolstered with beer or wine. These late night gatherings often led to card games.

Over time, in a fashion so subtle that I almost missed it, local *kampung* sentiment begin to shift against Pak Wayang and his family. What began as whispered conversations among women as they swept their front steps and the narrow street or *gang* in front of their houses each day in the *sore* (early evening), soon became a full-fledged lobbying effort on the part of women to do something about the situation at Pak Wayang's. Apparently the gambling had become a problem. Bu Apik's ne'er-do-well husband was taking money from her purse to gamble and was losing. Other men were losing money too. Since women typically control family finances, neighborhood wives were immediately aware of the peril posed by this new gambling problem. To make matters worse for Bu Sae, who lived next door practically, her youngest son had taken to spending his nights there as well.

I began to hear stories about the troubles at Pak Wayang's. As already mentioned, his wife, who was never much involved in *kampung* affairs anyway, was described as being a poor housekeeper. This whispered campaign centered around Bu Sae and Bu Apik, the two women most unhappy about what was happening. In *kampung* cases such as this the plaintiffs typically seek out the Pak RT, who as the most local representative of the government is charged with keeping order, to ask for his counsel and intervention in what is perceived as a threat to *kampung* security. Unfortunately, the Pak RT had become one of the cohort of regular gamblers at Pak Wayang's. As a result, the women sought the help of one of the local neighborhood's other moral bulwarks, Pak Hormat. While the impetus for change was the product of the lobbying of women who felt the threat first, they looked to a male patron to take direct action. In the case of Pak Wayang's deviance from *kampung* norms, Pak Hormat was apparently asked to approach him. Not long after, the gambling stopped.

This example of moral control in the *kampung* illustrates the role of women in keeping accounts and monitoring one another's behavior, particularly that of other women. After all, the first reports I heard were about Bu Wayang's poor housekeeping skills. It also illustrates the indirect power of women in mobilizing support, while leaving direct action to a male. The moral force of good housekeeping and good community is also evident. After all, Bu Sae and Bu Apik were just keeping good house and good community. Elizabeth Fox-Genovese noted this extension of women's domestic roles to community politics in Anglo-American history: "women presented many of their most impressive accomplishments as 'social housekeeping' and justified them in the name of prescribed domestic responsibilities" (Fox-Genovese 1991:37).

Yet another example of community morality mobilized for what might conventionally be considered a private concern actually happened a year or so before we arrived in the *kampung*, although based on what residents said, it remained fresh in people's memories. The fullest telling of the incident came from Bu Apik herself, who was at the center of the story. According to Bu Apik, her husband was bewitched by a woman who lived at the other end of our street, in the far eastern section of the adjoining RT. Her magic had led him to begin an affair with her. It had to be bewitchment, according to Bu Apik, because the woman in question was not blessed in looks or temperament. This affair between a man and a woman at opposite ends of the narrow street that stretched between the two extreme ends of the adjoining RT apparently became a cause for public scandal, because a community meeting was convened in an attempt to solve the problems. At the meeting, Bu Apik's husband was asked to choose between the two women—publicly. This meeting was a painful event in Bu Apik's life, because her handsome, troublesome husband chose to stay with his lover at that time. When we arrived in the *kampung*, Bu and Pak Apik had been reunited, and although I never heard how that happened, I heard repeatedly about their earlier troubles.

It is perhaps inconceivable to an American audience that a neighborhood meeting would be called to settle an instance of marital infidelity, but different codes of behavior and community conduct were at play in the *kampung*. The tacit agreement to play by the rules is part of the responsibility of living in such a close and closed community. This agreement is made clear daily in the *kampung*, especially as new challenges to its logic arise.

Bu Apik and her continuing troubles provide a counterpart to Bu Sae's life and her role in the family and *kampung*. Bu Sae was a lightning rod for *kampung* morality. She represented not only the generation of working class families whose children were doing better, she personally was an example of a successful PKK ibu. In her income-generating activities, Bu Sae fit the PKK ideal. Not only had she and the other women of the PKK shop where she worked pursued government funds to open it, she further added to her family's income by cooking peanuts to order and selling the ice from her refrigerator. Her husband was gainfully employed as were her two oldest children. Bu Sae was an active member of PKK, and she and her husband had served a long tenure as Bapak and Ibu RT. The back room of her house had a large cupboard that was still filled with the plates, cutlery, and glasses necessary for hosting the various meetings associated with serving as Bu RT. Yet, Bu Sae was a problematic figure in the *kampung*. Despite her successful identification with the goals and roles of PKK, Bu Sae was perceived by her neighbors to be haughty, withholding of resources, and condescending to those who couldn't match her high moral standards. She lived within a dense network of kin, not all of whom were on good terms with her. Nonetheless, Bu Sae used PKK to better herself and her family, and she did serve as a moral arbiter for the community.

Bu Apik and Bu Sae provide an interesting contrast in terms of their use of PKK as a resource and its effects for their standing in the community. Bu Sae was not well liked by many of her close neighbors and family because they believed she had gotten above herself (a clear *kampung* taboo). Still Bu Sae and her family were considered to be very respectable, and her active involvement in PKK enhanced that reputation. On the other hand, Bu Apik, despite involvement in several levels of community governance and PKK work (she was the local birth control officer, for example), could not redeem her disreputable family. More popular than Bu Sae, Bu Apik nonetheless struggled to improve her family's reputation. The experiences of Bu Sae and Bu Apik illustrate both the power of PKK and its local limitations.

Kampung morality is not disconnected from the state-sponsored forms of appropriate domesticity and citizenry. Although *kampung* morality hinges on more than the behavior of women, women are—just as the PKK cant would have it—a critical point of articulation between individual households and the community. Javanese housewives, in their roles as mediators in community and national development, in effect mirror social relations to the state apparatus but also serve to refract state directives to the local community. These two levels of experience are related in ways that light up the connection between the personal and the public. *Kampung* dwellers use the sentiments of harmonious community and of proper domestic conduct on a daily basis. This is not to say that everyone subscribes to these beliefs wholeheartedly. As already demonstrated, many women and *kampung* folk have a very developed sense of irony about some of the contortions required in state rhetoric. Still, every time an official transgression is noted and acted upon and every time a woman or family seeks status through official service they are indexing these ethics and making them real. Moreover, whether women agree with PKK or not, it is often true that to give a credible account of oneself within *kampung* community may mean making use of the resources of PKK. Those women unable to give credible accounts of themselves as household managers, as well as PKK workers, suffered not just the sting of gossip but the very real cut of not receiving mutual aid and community support.

Still, PKK offers more than a way for women to police other women and their own communities. In my time in the *kampung*, I saw women using PKK as a different kind of resource. Many of the women in the two RTs where I did most of my fieldwork work for wages, both inside and outside of the home, and as a consequence, they often experienced the monthly PKK meetings as an onerous demand on their time. Even those not involved in the higher levels of PKK administration needed to attend as many as four regular meetings a month, plus help with the specific activities of PKK, such as the baby weighings, hospital visits, and other neighborhood obligations. It is not surprising that *kampung* women view PKK with some ambivalence; not only does the very idea of stay-at-home mother contradict their working lives in many cases, it also poses yet another demand on their limited time. It is all the more interesting then that PKK is now being used by these women to accomplish community social reproduction in ways that lighten their loads. A good example of this are the activities of the PKK group in my RT associated with Ramadan, the Muslim month of fasting.

Before the month of fasting begins, each family is obligated to send a meal to neighbors, relatives, and close friends. This meal typically includes *apem*, a rice flour griddle cake, as well as a sweet cassava dish. In the past, each family fulfilled this obligation on its own, requiring large amounts of labor on the part of the women of the family. What has happened in recent years is that the women of PKK organize a communal cooking session to produce a single boxed meal for everyone in the neighborhood, thereby greatly reducing the labor for the individual women. The use of the PKK organization to solve a community responsibility results not from government planning but from the redirection of government structure for local practice. The effects for community maintenance are contradictory. While community obligations are met and women's workloads are decreased, individual family responsibility for social obligations is also attenuated.

The use of PKK and its offices to meet community-wide social obligations suggests several things. First, it shows that community obligation still has valence, and this is reinforced by the community support that goes on within *and without* government administrative units. The use of PKK to solve local problems reveals not only the continuing importance of community cooperation, it also suggests the importance of women in this work. It is women who visit hospitals, who collect social funds, who cook communally, and who make certain that family obligations to community are met. Moreover, the adaptation of PKK to meet these needs indexes not only women's increased workloads but shows that the structure provided by the government may be used for different ends. Thus, the organization founded around the ideal of the stay-at-home mom actually serves to help women who work outside the home meet *kampung* obligations.

Political Space for Change

> Drawing on past legacies, contemporary black women can begin to reconceptualize ideas of homeplace, once again considering the primacy of domesticity as a site for subversion and resistance (hooks 1990:48).

Taking the ethnomethodologist's emphasis on accountability, on giving credible accounts through daily practices of living and telling, and using it to understand *kampung* morality returns our gaze to reproduction. Passing as a good PKK housewife means, necessarily, the reproduction of a particular gendered experience. The contortions of *kampung* women as they fit themselves around PKK womanhood are the micro-technology of adjustment to an international division of labor, a national developmentalist regime, and a local culture of common sense. Henrietta Moore notes that in reproducing a set of social relations the experience of these social relations is also reproduced: "These conventional understandings can be seen as local theories of entitlement, and such theories are always bound up with ideologies and with unequal power relations" (Moore 1994:104). Simultaneously, the introduction of new resources and the changes in use of old resources offers a means to change. And as Moore suggests, shifts in meaning can often follow from a "reordering of practical activities...., such as putting something in the wrong place or placing it in relation to something else from which it is normally kept separate" (Moore 1994:83).

When Bu Sae and Bu Apik approached Pak Hormat to put an end to the gambling threatening their families and community they might be said to have engaged a long-standing set of ideas about appropriate community conduct, but these ideas coincide with a governmental view of women as the upholders of community morality. When Bu Apik takes on more and more roles within PKK she may be responding to personal family problems, but she is also activating the power of state-sponsored domesticity to improve her own status as well as that of her community. By calling on the resources of the PKK ideal of womanhood in their own lives, women make the policy manifest. And when women feel compelled to acknowledge this discourse or to gesture to it by acknowledging its credibility in their daily accounts it enters the realm of common sense and the daily life of culture (Goffman 1959). That is, PKK becomes real in everyday life when *kampung* women feel embarrassed about their non-attendance or non-conformity to the extent that they maintain their reputation by apologizing, temporizing or avoiding the behavior in the first place. Most importantly, when women take the resources intended to bolster women's roles within the family and community and use them to make short-work of these duties, the original intent of the program can be said to have been misplaced, consequently changing PKK , its relationship to women, and their relationship to the state, however subtly. It matters less here whether *kampung* dwellers are imagining that they are involved in "traditional" patterns of *gotong-royong* (mutual self-help) or that the state perpetuates imagined ideals of community and motherhood. The effect is the same. Women and community are reproduced through the local-level use of state resources and state rule is reproduced through the action of women in giving credible accounts of themselves. The result of this zig-zag between the state and the local is what constitutes state formation, and it is an eminently *cultural* process that belies the "non-political" character of PKK in the government's eyes.

I am arguing here that my Javanese neighbors are good terrorists. They comply with government directives on appropriate homes and domesticity only insofar as it serves their own ends. And they often "misplace" these directives, ideas and programs by using them to suit other local, *kampung* needs. In so doing, *kampung* members subvert—at least partially—the government's attempts to structure lives in a particular way and instead make the programs their own. This might be understood as resistance to the degree that *kampung* dwellers fail to comply with government programs in the strict sense they were intended, but it is more profitable to see that by accepting and reforming these programs within their own lives, *kampung* dwellers not only live the state but change it.

So the Javanese women with whom I worked were placed in the role of housewives as a consequence of a long history of colonial intervention and by a nationalist, developmentalist government seeking to deal with unemployment and other structural issues in the economy, but these women took up PKK when it served their own ends. They are quite capable of cynicism about their roles in the organization known as "women without enough work to do" while effectively fulfilling their positions in the organization, and thereby reproducing the category of community-oriented housewife, and as I have suggested, producing a new type of gendered subject position in modernizing Indonesia: the underemployed female as mother of the country. Yet, by using the goals and rhetoric of PKK within their families and communities as justification and moral code, they make this government program real within their lives. And when they misplace the rhetoric of PKK to deal with their own community issues they open up a space for change. They are good women insofar as they work to support their families and communities, but they are terrorists as they reform government directives to suit their own ends.

Author's Note

This paper is based on doctoral fieldwork supported by grants from the Southeast Asia Council (SEAC) and the University of Arizona Graduate School. I would like to thank the *Lembaga Ilmu Pengetahuan Indonesia* (LIPI) for permission to conduct this research, and the American-Indonesian Exchange Foundation (AMINEF) for all their support. I would also like to thank Steve Ferzacca and Mei Sugiarti for their research assistance.

NOTES

1. *Pak* is the shortened form of the male honorific *Bapak*, or father, which is used for all of equal or higher status than the speaker. *Bu* is the shortened form of the female honorific *Ibu*. All the names provided here are pseudonyms.
2. *Kampung* refers to a specific type of community, circumscribed both spatially and socially. The term has meant variously ethnic enclave, guild neighborhood, and urban or rural village community. Current meanings for *kampung* vary by social position. From within, *kampung* are described as home community with

a sense of cohesion, cooperation and intimate social relations; from without, *kampung* are frequently described as urban slums (cf. Sullivan 1992).

3. Adult is defined here as being married or having children or being the sole or main breadwinner of a household.
4. Pancasila comprises the five basic principles of the Republic of Indonesia: belief in one God, a just and civilized humanity, the unity of all of Indonesia, a democracy guided by wise and representative deliberation, and social justice for all Indonesians.
5. Any implied isomorphism between the small island of Java, where the largest percentage of population resides, and the Republic of Indonesia, which comprises many different islands and ethnic groups, is problematic. Still, the experience of Java, which is the focus of this paper, has likewise been central to definitions of what is Indonesia, as programs such as PKK illustrate.
6. Drastic changes in the Indonesian economy took place in the years between 1965-85 with the introduction of Green Revolution technologies and related economic restructuring. The introduction of high yielding varieties (HYV) of rice and related technology to the countryside eventually moved Indonesia to being a net exporter of rice. In the process, there was rapid release of labor, especially female labor, in the agricultural sector. For example, the replacement of the small hand knife, or *ani-ani*, used by female rice harvesters, with the sickle, used by men, reduced labor requirements in harvesting by up to 60 percent (Wolf 1992; Collier et al. 1973; Hart 1986), and the introduction of the mechanized rice huller meant estimated job losses "as high as 1.2 million in Java alone and as high as 7.7 million in all of Indonesia" (Cain 1981:134).
7. I use the term "terrorist" here to be provocative. Its use is not intended to minimize the reality and violence of terrorist acts nor their effects on the lives of those who have experienced it, nor does its use here imply a sustained discussion of what constitutes terrorism—a worthy goal beyond the scope of this paper. I use it here, particularly in contrast with the adjective "good," to challenge the conventional and essentialized characteristics of women as housewives.
8. See for example Boris and Bardaglio 1983; Corrigan and Sayer 1985; Davidoff and Hall 1987; Oakley 1974; Scott and Tilly 1975; Williams 1961.
9. See Boutilier 1982; Callaway 1987; Knapman 1986; Stoler 1989a, 1989b, 1996. See also Chatterjee 1989; Strobel 1993; and White 1990.
10. Jayawardena's discussion of Third World feminisms (1986), like Chatterjee's classic piece (1989) on Indian nationalism, highlight the gendered effects of nationalist revolutions (see also Rowbotham 1972). Such revolutions are not just confined to the so-called Third World. The American Revolution saw similar effects on women's roles (see Matthews 1987; Cott 1977).
11 *Priyayi* refers to the bureaucratic elites made up of old court retainers and the bureaucrats who worked for the Dutch.
12. In Indonesia, Mother's Day is actually *Hari Ibu Kartini* or *Mother Kartini Day*. Princess Kartini is known in Indonesia for her advocacy of girl's education in domestic skills. In a famous series of letters to her Dutch benefactor, Kartini described how she longed for the life of a young Dutch girl and the freedom to pursue her education (Kartini 1920). Although associated with Mother's Day, Kartini did not long for the role of mother. She died in childbirth at the age of 25 after an arranged marriage she resisted.

REFERENCES

Anderson, Benedict. 1987. How did the Generals Die? *Indonesia* 43:109-13.

Bennholdt-Thomsen, Veronika. 1988. Why do housewives continue to be created in the third world too? In *Women: The last colony*, ed. Maria Mies, Veronika Bennholdt-Thomsen, and Claudia von Werlhof. London: Zed Books.

Boris, Eileen and Peter Bardaglio. 1983. The transformation of patriarchy: The historic role of the state. In *Families, politics, and public policy*, ed. Irene Diamond. New York: Longman.

Boutilier, James. 1982. European women in the Solomon Islands, 1900-1942: Accommodation and change on the Pacific frontier. In *Rethinking women's roles: Perspectives on the Pacific*, ed. Denise O'Brien and Sharon Tiffany. Berkeley: University of California Press.

Cain, Melinda. 1981. Java, Indonesia: The introduction of rice processing technology. In *Women and technologi-*

cal change in developing countries, ed. R. Dauber and M. Cain. Boulder, CO: Westview.

Callaway, Helen. 1987. *Gender, culture and empire: European women in colonial Nigeria*. Oxford, UK: Macmillan Press.

Carey, Peter and Vincent Houben. 1987. Spirited Srikandhis and Sly Subbadras: The social, political and economic role of women at the central Javanese courts in the 18th and early 19th centuries. In *Indonesian woman in focus: Past and present notions*, ed. Elsbeth Locher-Scholten and Anke Neihof. Dordrecht, Holland: Foris Publications.

Chatterjee, Partha. 1989. Colonialism, nationalism and colonised women: The contest in India. *American ethnologist* 16(4):622-633.

Collier, W., Gunawan Wiradi and Soetono. 1973. Recent changes in rice harvesting methods. *Bulletin of Indonesian economic studies* 9(2):36-45.

Comaroff, Jean and John Comaroff. 1992. Home-made hegemony: Modernity, domesticity, and colonialism in South Africa. In *African encounters with domesticity*, ed. Karen Tranberg Hansen. New Brunswick, NJ: Rutgers University Press.

Corrigan, Philip and Derek Sayer. 1985. *The great arch: English state formation as cultural revolution* Oxford, UK: Basil Blackwell.

Cott, Nancy. 1977. *The bonds of womanhood: "Woman's sphere" in New England, 1780-1835*. New Haven: Yale University Press.

Davidoff, Leonore and Catherine Hall. 1987. *Family fortunes: Men and women of the English middle class.* Chicago: University of Chicago Press.

de Grazia, Victoria. 1992. *How fascism ruled women: Italy, 1922-1945.* Berkeley: University of California Press.

Department of Information. 1984. *The women of Indonesia.* Second Print. Republic of Indonesia.

Djajadiningrat-Nieuwenhuis, Madelon. 1987. Ibuism and priyayization: Path to power? In *Indonesian woman in focus: Past and present notions*, ed. Elsbeth Locher-Scholten and Anke Neihof. Dordrecht, Holland: Foris Publications.

Engels, Friedrich. 1942[1902]. *The origin of the family, private property and the state, in the light of the researches of Lewis H. Morgan.* New York: International Publishers.

Ferzacca, Steve. 1997. Keroncong music in a Javanese neighborhood: Rehearsals with spirits of the popular. Paper given to Society for Ethnomusicology, 42nd Annual Meeting, Pittsburgh, PA, October 24.

Fox-Genovese, Elizabeth. 1991. *Feminism without illusions: A critique of individualism.* Chapel Hill, NC: University of North Carolina Press.

Garfinkel, Harold. 1967. *Studies in ethnomethodology.* Englewood Cliffs, NJ: Prentice-Hall.

Gerke, Solvay. 1992. *Social change and life planning for rural Javanese women.* Saarbrucken: Verlag Breitenbach Publishers.

Giddens, Anthony. 1995. *Politics, sociology and social theory: Encounters with classical and contemporary social thought.* Stanford: Stanford University Press.

Goffman, Erving. 1959. *The presentation of self in everyday life.* Garden City, NY: Doubleday.

Gouda, Frances. 1995. *Dutch culture overseas: Colonial practice in the Netherlands Indies, 1900-1942.* Amsterdam: Amsterdam University Press.

Harris, Olivia. 1984. Households as natural units. In *Of marriage and the market: Women's subordination internationally and its lessons*, ed. by K. Young, C. Wolkowitz, and R. McCullagh. London: Routledge, Kegan Paul.

Hart, Gillian. 1986. *Power, labor, and livelihood: Processes of change in rural Java.* Berkeley: University of California Press.

hooks, bell. 1990. *Yearning: Race, gender, and cultural politics.* Boston, MA: South End Press.

Jayawardena, Kumari. 1986. *Feminism and nationalism in the third world.* London: Zed Books.

Kartini, Raden Adjeng. 1920. *Letters of a Javanese princess.* Translated by Agnes Louise Symmers. New York: Alfred Knopf.

Knapman, Claudia. 1986. *White women in Fiji, 1985-1930: The ruin of empire?* Sydney: Allen and Unwin.

Koonz, Claudia. 1987. *Mothers in the fatherland: Women, the family and Nazi politics.* New York: St. Martin's.

Lessing, Doris. 1985. *The good terrorist.* New York: Knopf.

Matthews, Glenna. 1987. *"Just a housewife": The rise and fall of domesticity in America.* New York: Oxford University Press.

Mies, Maria. 1986. *Patriarchy and accumulation on a world scale: Women in the international division of labour.* London: Zed Books.

Ministry of Home Affairs. 1983. The family welfare movement in Indonesia: PKK. Directorate General of Rural Development. Mimeograph.

Moore, Henrietta. 1994. *A passion for difference: essays in anthropology and gender.* Bloomington, IN: Indiana University Press.

New York Times Book Review. 1985. Bad housekeeping. December 19:8-9.

Nugent, Daniel. 1993. *Spent cartridges of revolution: An anthropological history of Namiquipa, Chihuahua.* Chicago: University of Chicago Press.

Oakley, Ann. 1974. *Woman's work: The housewife, past and present.* New York: Pantheon.

Perelli, Carina. 1994. *Memoria de sangre:* Fear, hope, and disenchantment in Argentina. In *Remapping memory: The politics of TimeSpace*, ed. Jonathon Boyarin. Minneapolis: University of Minnesota Press.

Rowbotham, Sheila. 1972. *Women, resistance, and revolution; a history of women and revolution in the modern world.* New York: Pantheon Books.

Schirmer, Jennifer. 1994. The claiming of space and the body politic within national-security states: The Plaza de Mayo madres and the Greenham Common women. In *Remapping memory: The politics of TimeSpace*, ed. Jonathon Boyarin. Minneapolis: University of Minnesota Press.

Scott, Joan and Louis Tilly. 1975. Woman's work and the family in nineteenth-century Europe. In *The family in history*, ed. Charles Rosenberg. Philadelphia: University of Pennsylvania Press.

Stoler, Ann Laura. 1985. *Capitalism and confrontation in Sumatra's plantation belt, 1870-1979.* New Haven: Yale University Press.

— . 1989a. Making empire respectable: The politics of race and sexual morality in 20th-century colonial cultures. *American ethnologist* 16(4):643-660.

— . 1989b. Rethinking colonial categories: European communities and the boundaries of rule. *Comparative studies in society and history* 31:134-61.

— . 1996. A sentimental education: Native servants and the cultivation of European children in the Netherlands Indies. In *Fantasizing the feminine in Indonesia*, ed. Laurie Sears. Durham, SC: Duke University Press.

Strobel, Margaret. 1993. Gender, sex, and empire. In *Islamic and European expansion: The forging of a global order*, ed. Michael Adas. Philadelphia, PA: Temple University Press.

Sullivan, John. 1992. *Local government and community in Java: An urban case-study.* Singapore: Oxford University Press.

Suryakusuma, Julia. 1991. State Ibuism: The social construction of womanhood in the Indonesian New Order. *New Asian visions* 6(2):46-71.

— . 1996. The state and sexuality in New Order Indonesia. In *Fantasizing the feminine in Indonesia*, ed. Laurie Sears. Durham, NC: Duke University Press.

Taylor, Jean Gelman. 1983. *The social world of Batavia: European and Eurasian in Dutch Asia.* Madison, WI: University of Wisconsin Press.

Tiwon, Sylvia. 1996. Models and maniacs: Articulating the female in Indonesia. In *Fantasizing the feminine in Indonesia*, ed. by Laurie Sears. Durham, NC: Duke University Press.

White, Luise. 1990. *The comforts of home: Prostitution in Colonial Nairobi.* Chicago, IL: University of Chicago Press.

Wieringa, Saskia. 1988. Aborted feminism in Indonesia: A history of Indonesian socialist feminism. In *Women's struggles and strategies*, ed. S. Wieringa. Aldershot, UK: Gower.

— . 1993. Two Indonesian women's organizations: Gerwani and the PKK. *Bulletin of concerned Asian scholars* 25(2).

Williams, Raymond. 1961. *The long revolution.* New York: Columbia University Press.

Wolf, Diane. 1992. *Factory daughters: Gender, household dynamics, and rural industrialization in Java.* Berkeley: University of California Press.

STUDY QUESTIONS

1. Do you think that Okin provides a convincing case for her argument that the experiences of oppression by poor women in poor countries are similar to those of white middle-class women in Western countries "only more so"? Why or why not?
2. Mohanty argues that there is a tendency in western feminist writing to present "third world woman" as a "monolithic subject." In your view, does Okin's account of gender fall prey to these charges? Why or why not?
3. What sorts of evidence does Mohanty provide that might cast doubt on Okin's defence of a "generalizable, identifiable, and collectively shared experience of womanhood"? Do you agree with Okin that the debate about differences amongst women in various parts of the world undermines attempts to address issues of injustice? Formulate your answer to this question by discussing at least one example from each of the Okin and Mohanty papers.
4. According to Mohanty, western feminist assumptions and methodologies contribute to the misrepresentation of the lives and experiences of women in developing countries and to the generation of policies that have a detrimental effect on their lives. Evaluate this claim by explaining what Mohanty means by western feminist assumptions and methodologies.
5. Outline the features of the dual-sex system that Nzegwu describes as part of the Igbo tradition in Nigeria prior to colonization. According to Nzegwu, how did colonialism undermine this dual-sex system and thereby worsen conditions for women in Nigeria?
6. How do Igbo values differ from those in the West? Is this system free of sexism? What challenges, if any, do these values present for accounts of gender by other authors in this chapter?
7. What lessons can be learned from Nzegwu's analysis of Igbo traditions and political structures with respect to increasing the effectiveness of developmental projects in Africa today?
8. According to Newberry, how have accounts of the proper housewife and of domesticity in Indonesia been shaped by Dutch colonialization and current government directives?
9. What does Newberry mean by the term "good terrorist"? Does the particular situation of women in Indonesia afford a good opportunity for exploring the notion of the good terrorist? Why or why not?
10. Newberry argues that the roles of reproduction in the extended sense of reproducing children, socializing them into citizens, and reproducing social relations are used by women in Indonesia not only to create and sustain society, but also to subvert and change the restricted aspects of state sponsored domesticity. Is the case she presents convincing? Can these insights about the subversive aspects of roles of reproduction be applied to women in general? Provide reasons for your answers.
11. Do you think that women in Indonesia lead lives that are subversive and conducive to generating social and political change and that eliminate the oppressive aspects of these roles? Give reasons for your answer.

SUGGESTED READINGS

Accad, Evelyne. "Sexuality and Sexual Politics: Conflicts and Contradictions for Contemporary Women in the Middle East." In *Third World Women and the Politics of Feminism* edited by Chandra Mohanty, Ann Russo, Lourdes Torres. Indiana University Press, 1991: 237-250.

Annas, Julia. "Women and the Quality of Life: Two Norms or One?." In *Quality of Life* edited by Martha Nussbaum and Amartya Sen. Oxford: Clarendon Press, 1993: 279-296.

Burgess-Jackson, Keith. "On the Coerciveness of Sexist Socialization." *Public Affairs Quarterly*, v. 9, no. 1 (January 1995): 15-27.

Chen, Martha. "A Matter of Survival: Women's Right to Employment in India and Bangladesh." In *Women, Culture and Development: A Study of Human Capabilities* edited by Martha Nussbaum and Jonathan Glover. Oxford: Clarendon Press, 1995.

Cindoglu, Dilek. "Virginity Tests and Artificial Virginity in Modern Turkish Medicine." *Women's Studies International Forum*, v. 20, no. 2 (1997): 253-261.

Clatterbaugh, Kenneth. "Are Men Oppressed?" In *Rethinking Masculinity: Philosophical Explorations in Light of Feminism*. 2nd edition. Edited by Larry May, Robert Strikwerda, and Patrick D. Hopkins. Lanham, MD: Rowman & Littlefield, 1996.

Cudd, Ann E. "Oppression By Choice." *Journal of Social Philosophy*, 25th Anniversary Special Issue (1994): 22-44.

Davis, Angela Y. "Radical Perspectives on the Empowerment of Afro-American Women: Lessons for the 1980s." *Harvard Educational Review*, v. 58, no. 3 (August 1988): 348-353.

Friedman, Marilyn. "Multicultural Education and Feminist Ethics." *Hypatia*, v. 10, no. 2 (Spring 1995): 56-68.

Frye, Marilyn. "Sexism." In *The Politics of Reality*. Freedom, CA: Crossing Press, 1982.

Gilligan, Carol. *In a Different Voice: Psychological Theory and Women's Development.* Cambridge, Mass.: Harvard University Press, 1982.

Hirschmann, Nancy J. "Revisioning Freedom: Relationship, Context, and The Politics of Empowerment." In *Revisioning The Political: Feminist Reconstructions of Traditional Concepts in Western Political Theory.* Edited by Nancy J. Hirschmann and Christine De Stefano. Boulder CO: Westview, 1996.

Holmstrom, Nancy. "Do Women Have a Distinct Nature?" *Philosophical Forum* (Boston), v. 14, no. 1 (Fall 1982): 25-42.

Li, Xiaorong. "Gender Inequality in China and Cultural Relativism." In *Women, Culture and Development: A Study of Human Capabilities* edited by Martha Nussbaum and Jonathan Glover. Oxford: Clarendon Press, 1995.

Lucas, J. R. "Because You Are a Woman." *Philosophy*, v. 48 (1973): 161-171.

Minow, Martha and Mary Lyndon Shanley. "Relational Rights and Responsibilities: Revisioning the Family in Liberal Political Theory and Law." *Hypatia*, v. 11, no. 1 (Winter 1996): 4-29.

Nussbaum, Martha. "Human Capabilities, Female Human Beings." In *Women, Culture and Development: A Study of Human Capabilities* edited by Martha Nussbaum and Jonathan Glover. Oxford: Clarendon Press, 1995.

Sen, Amartya. "Gender Inequality and Theories of Justice." In *Women, Culture and Development: A Study of Human Capabilities* edited by Martha Nussbaum and Jonathan Glover. Oxford: Clarendon Press, 1995.

Sumner, L.W. "Positive Sexism." *Social Philosophy and Policy*, v. 5, no. 1 (1987): 204-222.

Valdés, Margarita, M. "Inequality in Capabilities Between Men and Women in Mexico." In *Women, Culture and Development: A Study of Human Capabilities* edited by Martha Nussbaum and Jonathan Glover. Oxford: Clarendon Press, 1995.

Warren, Mary Anne. "Secondary Sexism and Quota Hiring." *Philosophy & Public Affairs*, v. 6, no. 3 (Spring 1977): 240-261.

Williams, Joan C. "Dissolving the Sameness/Difference Debate: A Post-Modern Path Beyond Essentialism in Feminist and Critical Theory." *Duke Law Journal* (1991): 296-323.

CHAPTER SIX

SEXUAL ORIENTATION

In the final reading of the previous chapter, Newberry directed our attention to a global context in which European colonization gave prominence to the model of women's proper domain in a private sphere as mother, housewife, and caretaker. This chapter connects this model to sexual orientation: the caretaker of the private sphere is a woman married to, having sexual relations with, and bearing the children of a man who is the breadwinner, public actor, and political decision-maker. Issues of sexual orientation bring to the fore the question of proper sexual relations and the values and virtues considered appropriate to the people in them. Yet, while there are similarities and intersections between discrimination on the basis of gender and of sexual orientation, there are also differences. In the diversity of views on gender in the previous chapter, there seemed to be a consensus about what makes gender a moral issue. Gender is or becomes a moral issue when the roles assigned on the basis of being a male or a female result in the devaluation of women and inequalities in women's life prospects. In this chapter, we will examine whether the injustices associated with discrimination on the basis of sexual orientation are similar in this respect. We shall also explore the relevance of the social construction of identities and self-identities in the context of sexuality and sexual practices.

The chapter opens with a reading from Jeffrey Jordan, who explores these questions: Is homosexual sex on a moral par with heterosexual sex? Is it wrong to discriminate against homosexuals by treating them in less favorable ways than one does heterosexuals? Jordan sets out to answer these questions by outlining two sets of arguments: the "parity thesis" holds that there are no morally relevant differences between heterosexuality and homosexuality that justify a difference in treatment; the "difference thesis" holds that there are morally relevant differences that permit different treatment. Jordan defends the difference thesis in the case of same-sex marriage by developing an account of the moral impasse and public dilemma generated by homosexuality.

Moral impasses arise out of moral disputes in which there are conflicting beliefs regarding the moral status of a particular issue or act. When many people hold conflicting views, the moral impasse can have policy implications that bring it into the public domain. Public dilemmas are moral impasses that have public policy ramifications. Jordan turns to religious views to show that a deeply entrenched position on the immorality of homosexual acts supports the difference thesis, at least for acts in the public domain such as same-sex marriage. He argues that the state should, as far as possible, be neutral with regard to the disputing parties in a public dilemma. Otherwise, the state risks forcing people to live under a government that tolerates and promotes activities that many find immoral. If the state were to sanction same-sex marriage in a context of prohibitions against them, it would be taking sides in the impasse and sanctioning that which religion-based opponents find seriously immoral. Jordan argues that accommodation can be made by allowing homosexual activity to be personal choices in a private realm, but not by sanctioning same-sex marriage in the public realm.

In the second reading, Christine Overall can be said to challenge a premise foundational to Jordan's argument: his claim that "it is clear that heterosexual unions merit the state recognition known as marriage, along with all the attendant advantages." Overall describes heterosexuality as a pervasive characteristic of the human condition, so much a part of human relationships as to be invisible and yet appear natural and unquestionable. Heterosexuality, argues Overall, is an institution of contemporary Western cultures that embodies a set of social standards, customs, and expected practices that regulate relationships in ways that enforce heterosexuality. She then provides a feminist critique of the differential impact of the institution of heterosexuality on men and women, one that highlights the unequal power relations between men and women that are perpetuated and endorsed by heterosexuality.

Radical feminists argue that heterosexuality is enforced through social practices, religion, education, culture, and the law in ways that benefit men and present costs for women in the violence, degradation, and exploitation that it condones and the separation of women from their allies and each other that it promotes. Overall argues, however, that this analysis raises two questions. First, if social pressure to be heterosexual is enforced and failure to conform is punished, can a woman be said to *choose* heterosexuality? Second, if talk about choice is meaningful here, *should* a woman choose non-heterosexuality as a way of undermining the institution of heterosexuality? Overall rejects the portrayal of women as victims or the objects of false consciousness implied by the argument that women do not choose heterosexuality. While the institution of heterosexuality is oppressive, not all heterosexual relationships are. By choosing heterosexuality, a woman can be said to be rejecting the view that male sexuality is inevitably and innately violent and exploitative and to be engaged in the project of understanding the power and limits of the heterosexual institution so as to challenge and change it.

Cheshire Calhoun is skeptical that we can arrive at an adequate understanding of discrimination on the basis of sexual orientation through an analysis of the discrimination experienced by racial minorities and women. To understand gender injustice, for example, is to understand the place of women in socio-economic structures and practices, the disadvantages of occupying those places, and the factors that keep women in those places. Here socialization, the structure of the family, the devalued status of domestic-reproductive labor, the distinction between public and private spheres, and the normalization of violence toward women are relevant. Calhoun argues that there are substantial differences in form between sexuality injustice and gender and racial injustice. Gay men and lesbians do not constitute a social group in the same way that women do because homosexuals are not readily distinguishable from heterosexuals, homosexuality can be deliberately concealed, and the presumption that persons are heterosexual allows homosexuals to be treated as members of the social group "heterosexuals." Gay men and lesbians evade statistical concentration because they are everywhere and are not located in the structural places of the private sphere, urban ghettoes, menial jobs, the sex industry, poverty zones, or "pink collar" jobs that racial minorities and women are. Sexual orientation does not make the kind of difference to one's material conditions that gender or race does.

Calhoun identifies the particularities of sexuality injustice through an examination of the history of laws, policies, and practices in the Western tradition that enforce and support heterosexuality and displace gays and lesbians to the outside of civil society. This displacement is central to Calhoun's analysis of sexuality injustice. It is apparent in the requirement that all citizens either have a heterosexual identity or adopt a pseudonymous one as a condition of access to the public sphere. Laws may entitle individuals to *be* lesbian or gay in public spaces but not to *represent* themselves as lesbian or gay in the public sphere. Policies intervene in restricting gay and lesbian parenting, employment in child care, and participation in early education and child service organizations. Cultural images and perceptions that mark homosexual activity as immoral and gay men and lesbians as criminals perpetuate stereotypes of them as untrustworthy and deny them equal standing to participate in legal, social, and moral debates about the place of gay and lesbian identity in the public and private spheres. All of these factors maintain the displacement of gay men and lesbians to the outside of civil society and constitute sexuality injustice.

Calhoun does not advocate strategies or recommend policies for alleviating the injustice experienced by gay men and lesbians, but her analysis of displacement implies policies of inclusion in civil society. In the reading that follows, Claudia Card raises questions about whether equal rights strategies in liberal societies in areas such as same-sex marriage are appropriate or adequate for addressing sexuality injustice. She argues that those who identify as lesbian or gay should be reluctant to campaign for legal equity with heterosexuals in marriage and in parenting because these institutions are deeply flawed as they currently exist and should be neither emulated nor reproduced. Card is not opposed to long-term relationships or to forming bonds between adults and children or to guiding, educating, and caring for children, but wonders if the interests and needs of people in these important relationships are best met by the institutions of marriage and motherhood.

Benefits such as affordable health and dental insurance, social securities, inheritance, visitation rights, and workers' compensation pressure people into marrying. The financial burdens of divorce and the lack of state protection against violent spouses act as disincentives for leaving bad marriages. While marriage may seem to provide an important environment for rearing children, the model of parenting evident in laws that grant the status of parent to at most two persons at a time is not the only or best model and is being challenged by gay and lesbian parenting and by communities where there is collective responsibility for childrearing and many people have roles as caretakers for many children. Every society, argues Card, would benefit from an attentiveness to the experiences of children, the relationships of children to adults, and the conditions under which children grow into adulthood. Such attentiveness should undermine the model of mothers as primary caretakers and the institution of marriage within which mothering takes place.

Like other feminist and lesbian theorists, Card advances the notion that gay men and lesbians have relationships and live lives that not only challenge a status quo of heterosexuality, but present new ways of being with others and of caring for others. Elisabeth Däumer extends this reasoning in her argument that bisexuality also contributes to the project of devising alternative, non-oppressive ways of relating and responding to others. She understands bisexuality not as an identity that integrates heterosexual and homosexual orientations, but as an ambiguous position that can challenge notions of fixed sexual identities, lead to an appreciation of difference, and open up a range of choices that resist heterosexism. A queer ethics, argues Däumer, would stress the interrelatedness of different and conflicting communities and emphasize the need to forge new bonds and alliances for fighting both homophobia and sexism.

"IS IT WRONG TO DISCRIMINATE ON THE BASIS OF HOMOSEXUALITY?"

Jeffrey Jordan

Jeffrey Jordan teaches philosophy at the University of Delaware, Newark, Delaware. He specializes in metaphysics and the philosophy of religion and has interests in the area of individual rights.

Jordan argues that there is a moral impasse in the United States about the wrongness or rightness of homosexuality. He defends the principle that the state ought to be neutral as far as possible about moral impasses that constitute public dilemmas and uses this principle to justify discriminating against homosexuals in certain public matters such as marriage. He argues that state sanctioning of same-sex marriage is not a neutral policy for those who have religious objections to homosexuality. Jordan leaves open the possibility that discriminating against homosexuals in contexts that affect private matters is not justified.

Much like the issue of abortion in the early 1970s, the issue of homosexuality has exploded to the forefront of social discussion. Is homosexual sex on a moral par with heterosexual sex? Or is homosexuality in some way morally inferior? Is it wrong to discriminate against homosexuals—to treat homosexuals in less favorable ways than one does heterosexuals? Or is some discrimination against homosexuals morally justified? These questions are the focus of this essay.

In what follows, I argue that there are situations in which it is morally permissible to discriminate against homosexuals because of their homosexuality. That is, there are some morally relevant differences between heterosexuality and homosexuality which, in some instances, permit a difference in treatment. The issue of marriage provides a good example. While it is clear that heterosexual unions merit the state recognition known as marriage, along with all the attendant advantages—spousal insurance coverage, inheritance rights, ready eligibility of adoption—it is far from clear that homosexual couples ought to be accorded that state recognition.

The argument of this essay makes no claim about the moral status of homosexuality per se. Briefly put, it is the argument of this essay that the moral impasse generated by conflicting views concerning homosexuality, and the public policy ramifications of those conflicting views justify the claim that it is morally permissible, in certain circumstances, to discriminate against homosexuals.[1]

1. The Issue

The relevant issue is this: does homosexuality have the same moral status as heterosexuality? Put differently, since there are no occasions in which it is morally permissible to treat heterosexuals unfavorably, whether because they are heterosexual or because of heterosexual acts, are there occasions in which it is morally permissible to treat homosexuals unfavorably, whether because they are homosexuals or because of homosexual acts?

A negative answer to the above can be termed the "parity thesis." The parity thesis contends that homosexuality has the same moral status as heterosexuality. If the parity thesis is correct, then it would be immoral to discriminate against homosexuals because of their homosexuality. An affirmative

Reprinted with permission from *Journal of Social Philosophy* 26:1 (Spring 1995): 39–52.

answer can be termed the "difference thesis" and contends that there are morally relevant differences between heterosexuality and homosexuality which justify a difference in moral status and treatment between homosexuals and heterosexuals. The difference thesis entails that there are situations in which it is morally permissible to discriminate against homosexuals.

It is perhaps needless to point out that the difference thesis follows as long as there is at least one occasion in which it is morally permissible to discriminate against homosexuals. If the parity thesis were true, then on no occasion would a difference in treatment between heterosexuals and homosexuals ever be justified. The difference thesis does not, even if true, justify discriminatory actions on every occasion. Nonetheless, even though the scope of the difference thesis is relatively modest, it is, if true, a significant principle which has not only theoretical import but important practical consequences as well.[2]

A word should be said about the notion of discrimination. To discriminate against X means treating X in an unfavorable way. The word "discrimination" is not a synonym for "morally unjustifiable treatment." Some discrimination is morally unjustifiable; some is not. For example, we discriminate against convicted felons in that they are disenfranchised. This legal discrimination is morally permissible even though it involves treating one person unfavorably different from how other persons are treated. The difference thesis entails that there are circumstances in which it is morally permissible to discriminate against homosexuals.

2. An Argument for the Parity Thesis

One might suppose that an appeal to a moral right, the right to privacy, perhaps, or the right to liberty, would provide the strongest grounds for the parity thesis. Rights talk, though sometimes helpful, is not very helpful here. If there is reason to think that the right to privacy or the right to liberty encompasses sexuality (which seems plausible enough), it would do so only with regard to private acts and not public acts. Sexual acts performed in public (whether heterosexual or homosexual) are properly suppressible. It does not take too much imagination to see that the right to be free from offense would soon be offered as a counter consideration by those who find homosexuality morally problematic. Furthermore, how one adjudicates between the competing rights claims is far from clear. Hence, the bald appeal to a right will not, in this case anyway, take one very far.

Perhaps the strongest reason to hold that the parity thesis is true is something like the following:

1. Homosexual acts between consenting adults harm no one. And,
2. respecting persons' privacy and choices in harmless sexual matters maximizes individual freedom. And,
3. individual freedom should be maximized. But,
4. discrimination against homosexuals, because of their homosexuality, diminishes individual freedom since it ignores personal choice and privacy. So,
5. the toleration of homosexuality rather than discriminating against homosexuals is the preferable option since it would maximize individual freedom. Therefore,
6. the parity thesis is more plausible than the difference thesis.

Premise (2) is unimpeachable: if an act is harmless and if there are persons who want to do it and who choose to do it, then it seems clear that respecting the choices of those people would tend to maximize their freedom.[3] Step (3) is also beyond reproach: since freedom is arguably a great good and since there does not appear to be any ceiling on the amount of individual freedom—no "too much of a good thing"—(3) appears to be true.

At first glance, premise (1) seems true enough as long as we recognize that if there is any harm involved in the homosexual acts of consenting adults, it would be harm absorbed by the freely consenting participants. This is true, however, only if the acts in question are done in private. Public acts may involve more than just the willing participants. Persons who have no desire to participate, even if only as spectators, may have no choice if the acts are done in public. A real probability of there being unwilling participants is indicative of the public realm and not the private. However, where one draws the line between private acts and public acts is not always easy to discern; it is clear that different moral standards apply to public acts than to private acts.[4]

If premise (1) is understood to apply only to acts done in private, then it would appear to be true. The same goes for (4): discrimination against homosexuals for acts done in private would result in a diminishing of freedom. So (1)—(4) would lend support to (5) only if we understand (1)—(4) to refer to acts done in private. Hence, (5) must be understood as referring to private acts; and, as a consequence, (6) also must be read as referring only to acts done in private.

With regard to acts which involve only willing adult participants, there may be no morally relevant difference between homosexuality and heterosexuality. In other words, acts done in private. However, acts done in public add a new ingredient to the mix; an ingredient which has moral consequence. Consequently, the argument (1)—(6) fails in supporting the parity thesis. The argument (1)—(6) may show that there are some circumstances in which the moral status of homosexuality and heterosexuality are the same, but it gives us no reason for thinking that this result holds for all circumstances.[5]

3. Moral Impasses and Public Dilemmas

Suppose one person believes that X is morally wrong, while another believes that X is morally permissible. The two people, let's stipulate, are not involved in a semantical quibble; they hold genuinely conflicting beliefs regarding the moral status of X. If the first person is correct, then the second person is wrong; and, of course, if the second person is right, then the first must be wrong. This situation of conflicting claims is what we will call an "impasse." Impasses arise out of moral disputes. Since the conflicting parties in an impasse take contrary views, the conflicting views cannot all be true, nor can they all be false.[6] Moral impasses may concern matters only of a personal nature, but moral impasses can involve public policy. An impasse is likely to have public policy ramifications if large numbers of people hold the conflicting views, and the conflict involves matters which are fundamental to a person's moral identity (and, hence, from a practical point of view, are probably irresolvable) and it involves acts done in public. Since not every impasse has public policy ramifications, one can mark off "public dilemma" as a special case of moral impasses: those moral impasses that have public policy consequences. Public dilemmas, then, are impasses located in the public square. Since they have public policy ramifications and since they arise from impasses, one side or another of the dispute will have its views implemented as public policy. Because of the public policy ramifications, and also because social order is sometimes threatened by the volatile parties involved in the impasse, the state has a role to play in resolving a public dilemma.

A public dilemma can be actively resolved in two ways.[7] The first is when the government allies itself with one side of the impasse and, by state coercion and sanction, declares that side of the impasse the correct side. The American Civil War was an example of this: the federal government forcibly ended slavery by aligning itself with the Abolitionist side of the impasse.[8] Prohibition is another example. The Eighteenth Amendment and the Volstead Act allied the state with the Temperance side of the impasse. State mandated affirmative action programs provide a modern example of this. This kind of resolution of a public dilemma we can call a "resolution by declaration." The first of the examples cited above indicates that declarations can be morally proper, the right thing to do. The second example, however, indicates that declarations are not always morally proper. The state does not always take the side of the morally correct; nor is it always clear which side is the correct one.

The second way of actively resolving a public dilemma is that of accommodation. An accommodation in this context means resolving the public dilemma in a way that gives as much as possible to all sides of the impasse. A resolution by accommodation involves staking out some middle ground in a dispute and placing public policy in that location. The middle ground location of a resolution via accommodation is a virtue since it entails that there are no absolute victors and no absolute losers. The middle ground is reached in order to resolve the public dilemma in a way which respects the relevant views of the conflicting parties and which maintains social order. The Federal Fair Housing Act and, perhaps, the current status of abortion (legal but with restrictions) provide examples of actual resolutions via accommodation.[9]

In general, governments should be, at least as far as possible, neutral with regard to the disputing parties in a public dilemma. Unless there is some overriding reason why the state should take sides in a public dilemma—the protection of innocent life, or abolishing slavery, for instance—the state should be neutral, because no matter which side of the public dilemma the state takes, the other side will be the recipient of unequal treatment by the state. A state which is partial and takes sides in moral disputes via declaration, when there is no overriding reason why it should, is tyrannical. Overriding reasons involve, typically, the protection of generally recognized rights.[10] In the case of slavery, the right to liberty; in the case of protecting innocent life, the right involved is the negative right to life. If a public dilemma must be actively resolved, the state should do so (in the absence of an overriding reason) via accommodation and not declaration since the latter entails that a sizable number of people would be forced to live under a government which "legitimizes" and does not just tolerate activities which they find immoral. Resolution via declaration is appropriate only if there is an overriding reason for the state to throw its weight behind one side in a public dilemma.

Is moral rightness an overriding reason for a resolution via declaration? What better reason might there be for a resolution by declaration than that it is the right thing to do? Unless one is prepared to endorse a view that is called "legal moralism"—that immorality alone is a sufficient reason for the state to curtail individual liberty—then one had best hold that moral rightness alone is not an overriding reason. Since some immoral acts neither harm nor offend nor violate another's rights, it seems clear enough that too much liberty would be lost if legal moralism were adopted as public policy.[11]

Though we do not have a definite rule for determining a priori which moral impasses genuinely constitute public dilemmas, we can proceed via a case by case method. For example, many people hold that cigarette smoking is harmful and, on that basis, is properly suppressible. Others disagree. Is this a public dilemma? Probably not. Whether someone engages in an imprudent action is, as long as it involves no unwilling participants, a private matter and does not, on that account, constitute a public dilemma.[12] What about abortion? Is abortion a public dilemma? Unlike cigarette smoking, abortion is a public dilemma. This is clear from the adamant and even violent contrary positions involved in the impasse. Abortion is an issue which forces itself into the public square. So, it is clear that, even though we lack a rule which filters through moral impasses designating some as public dilemmas, not every impasse constitutes a public dilemma.

4. Conflicting Claims on Homosexuality

The theistic tradition, Judaism and Christianity and Islam, has a clear and deeply entrenched position on homosexual acts: they are prohibited. Now it seems clear enough that if one is going to take seriously the authoritative texts of the respective religions, then one will have to adopt the views of those texts, unless one wishes to engage in a demythologizing of them with the result that one ends up being only a nominal adherent of that tradition.[13] As a consequence, many contemporary theistic adherents of the theistic tradition, in no small part because they can read, hold that homosexual behavior is sinful. Though God loves the homosexual, these folk say, God hates the sinful behavior. To say that act X is a sin entails that X is morally wrong, not necessarily because it is harmful or offensive, but because X violates God's will. So, the claim that homosexuality is sinful entails the claim that it is also morally wrong. And, it is clear, many people adopt the difference thesis just because of their religious views: because the Bible or the Koran holds that homosexuality is wrong, they too hold that view.

Well, what should we make of these observations? We do not, for one thing, have to base our moral conclusions on those views, if for no other reason than not everyone is a theist. If one does not adopt the religion-based moral view, one must still respect those who do; they cannot just be dismissed out of hand.[14] And, significantly, this situation yields a reason for thinking that the difference thesis is probably true. Because many religious people sincerely believe homosexual acts to be morally wrong and many others believe that homosexual acts are not morally wrong, there results a public dilemma.[15]

The existence of this public dilemma gives us reason for thinking that the difference thesis is true. It is only via the difference thesis and not the parity thesis, that an accommodation can be reached. Here again, the private/public distinction will come into play.

To see this, take as an example the issue of homosexual marriages. A same-sex marriage would be a public matter. For the government to sanction same-sex marriage to grant the recognition and reciprocal benefits which attach to marriage would ally the government with one side of the public dilemma and against the adherents of religion-based moralities. This is especially true given that, historically, no government has sanctioned same-sex marriages. The status quo has been no same-sex marriages. If the state were to change its practice now, it would be clear that the state has taken sides in the impasse. Given the history, for a state to sanction a same-sex marriage now would not be a neutral act.

Of course, some would respond here that by not sanctioning same-sex marriages the state is, and historically has been, taking sides to the detriment of homosexuals. There is some truth in this claim. But one must be careful here. The respective resolutions of this issue whether the state should recognize and sanction same-sex marriages do not have symmetrical implications. The asymmetry of this issue is a function of the private/public distinction and the fact that marriage is a public matter. If the state sanctions same-sex marriages, then there is no accommodation available. In that event, the religion-based morality proponents are faced with a public, state-sanctioned matter which they find seriously immoral. This would be an example of a resolution via declaration. On the other hand, if the state does not sanction same-sex marriages, there is an accommodation available: in the public realm the state sides with the religion-based moral view, but the state can tolerate private homosexual acts. That is, since homosexual acts are not essentially public acts; they can be, and historically have been, performed in private. The state, by not sanctioning same-sex marriages is acting in the public realm, but it can leave the private realm to personal choice.[16]

5. The Argument from Conflicting Claims

It was suggested in the previous section that the public dilemma concerning homosexuality, and in particular whether states should sanction same-sex marriages, generates an argument in support of the difference thesis. The argument, again using same-sex marriages as the particular case, is as follows:

7. There are conflicting claims regarding whether the state should sanction same-sex marriages. And,
8. this controversy constitutes a public dilemma. And,
9. there is an accommodation possible if the state does not recognize same-sex marriages. And,
10. there is no accommodation possible if the state does sanction same-sex marriages. And,
11. there is no overriding reason for a resolution via declaration. Hence,
12. the state ought not sanction same-sex marriages. And,
13. the state ought to sanction heterosexual marriages. So,
14. there is at least one morally relevant case in which discrimination against homosexuals, because of their homosexuality, is morally permissible. Therefore,
15. the difference thesis is true.

Since proposition (14) is logically equivalent to the difference thesis, then, if (7)-(14) are sound, proposition (15) certainly follows.

Premises (7) and (8) are uncontroversial. Premises (9) and (10) are based on the asymmetry that results from the public nature of marriage. Proposition (11) is based on our earlier analysis of the argument (1)-(6). Since the strongest argument in support of the parity thesis fails, we have reason to think that there is no overriding reason why the state ought to resolve the public dilemma via declaration in favor of same-sex marriages. We have reason, in other words, to think that (11) is true.

Proposition (12) is based on the conjunction of (7)-(11) and the principle that, in the absence of an overriding reason for state intervention via declaration, resolution by accommodation is the preferable route. Proposition (13) is just trivially true. So, given the moral difference mentioned in (12) and (13), proposition (14) logically follows.

6. Two Objections Considered

The first objection to the argument from conflicting claims would contend that it is unsound because a similar sort of argument would permit discrimination against some practice which, though perhaps controversial at some earlier time, is now widely thought to be morally permissible. Take mixed-raced marriages, for example. The opponent of the argument from conflicting claims could argue that a similar argument would warrant prohibition against mixed-race marriages. If it does, we would have good reason to reject (7)-(14) as unsound.

There are three responses to this objection. The first response denies that the issue of mixed-race marriages is in fact a public dilemma. It may have been so at one time, but it does not seem to generate much, if any, controversy today. Hence, the objection is based upon a faulty analogy.

The second response grants for the sake of the argument that the issue of mixed-race marriages generates a public dilemma. But the second response points out that there is a relevant difference between mixed-race marriages and same-sex marriages that allows for a resolution by declaration in the one case but not the other. As evident from the earlier analysis of the argument in support of (1)-(6), there is reason to think that there is no overriding reason for a resolution by declaration in support of the parity thesis. On the other hand, it is a settled matter that state protection from racial discrimination is a reason sufficient for a resolution via declaration. Hence, the two cases are only apparently similar, and, in reality, they are crucially different. They are quite different because, clearly enough, if mixed-race marriages do generate a public dilemma, the state should use resolution by declaration in support of such marriages. The same cannot be said for same-sex marriages.

One should note that the second response to the objection does not beg the question against the proponent of the parity thesis. Though the second response denies that race and sexuality are strict analogues, it does so for a defensible and independent reason: it is a settled matter that race is not a sufficient reason for disparate treatment; but, as we have seen from the analysis of (1)-(6), there is no overriding reason to think the same about sexuality.[17]

The third response to the first objection is that the grounds of objection differ in the respective cases: one concerns racial identity; the other concerns behavior thought to be morally problematic. A same-sex marriage would involve behavior which many people find morally objectionable; a mixed-race marriage is objectionable to some, not because of the participants' behavior, but because of the racial identity of the participants. It is the race of the marriage partners which some find of primary complaint concerning mixed-race marriages. With same-sex marriages, however, it is the behavior which is primarily objectionable. To see this latter point, one should note that, though promiscuously Puritan in tone, the kind of sexual acts that are likely involved in a same-sex marriage are objectionable to some, regardless of whether done by homosexuals or heterosexuals.[18] So again, there is reason to reject the analogy between same-sex marriages and mixed-race marriages. Racial identity is an immutable trait and a complaint about mixed-race marriages necessarily involves, then, a complaint about an immutable trait. Sexual behavior is not an immutable trait and it is possible to object to same-sex marriages based on the behavior which would be involved in such marriages. Put succinctly, the third response could be formulated as follows; objections to mixed-race marriages necessarily involve objections over status, while objections to same-sex marriages could involve objections over behavior. Therefore, the two cases are not strict analogues since there is a significant modal difference in the ground of the objection.

The second objection to the argument from conflicting claims can be stated so: if homosexuality is biologically based—if it is inborn[19]—then how can discrimination ever be justified? If it is not a matter of choice, homosexuality is an immutable trait which is, as a consequence, morally permissible. Just as it would be absurd to hold someone morally culpable for being of a certain race, likewise it would be absurd to hold someone morally culpable for being a homosexual. Consequently, according to this objection, the argument from conflicting claims "legitimizes" unjustifiable discrimination.

But this second objection is not cogent, primarily because it ignores an important distinction. No one could plausibly hold that homosexuals act by some sort of biological compulsion. If there is a biological component involved in sexual identity, it would incline but it would not compel. Just because one naturally (without any choice) has certain dispositions, is not in itself a morally cogent reason for acting upon that disposition. Most people are naturally selfish, but it clearly does not follow that selfishness is in any way permissible on that account. Even if it is true that one has a predisposition to do X as a matter of biology and not as a matter of choice, it does not follow that doing X is morally permissible. For example, suppose that pyromania is an inborn predisposition. Just because one has an inborn and, in that sense, natural desire to set fires, one still has to decide whether or not to act on that desire.[20] The reason that the appeal to biology is specious is that it ignores the important distinction between being a homosexual and homosexual acts. One is status; the other is behavior. Even if one has the status naturally, it does not follow that the behavior is morally permissible, nor that others have a duty to tolerate the behavior.[21]

But, while moral permissibility does not necessarily follow if homosexuality should turn out to be biologically based, what does follow is this: in the absence of a good reason to discriminate between homosexuals and heterosexuals, then, assuming that homosexuality is inborn, one ought not discriminate between them. If a certain phenomenon X is natural in the sense of being involuntary and nonpathological, and if there is no good reason to hold that X is morally problematic, then that is reason enough to think that X is morally permissible. In the absence of a good reason to repress X, one should tolerate it since, as per supposition, it is involuntary. The argument from conflicting claims, however, provides a good reason which overrides this presumption.

7. A Second Argument for the Difference Thesis.

A second argument for the difference thesis, similar to the argument from conflicting claims, is what might be called the "no-exit argument." This argument is based on the principle that:

> A. no just government can coerce a citizen into violating a deeply held moral belief or religious belief.

Is (A) plausible? It seems to be since the prospect of a citizen being coerced by the state into a practice which she finds profoundly immoral appears to be a clear example of an injustice. Principle (A), conjoined with there being a public dilemma arising over the issue of same-sex marriages, leads to the observation that if the state were to sanction same-sex marriages, then persons who have profound religious or moral objections to such unions would be legally mandated to violate their beliefs since there does not appear to be any feasible "exit right" possible with regard to state sanctioned marriage. An exit right is an exemption from some legally mandated practice, granted to a person or group, the purpose of which is to protect the religious or moral integrity of that person or group. Prominent examples of exit rights include conscientious objection and military service, home-schooling of the young because of some religious concern, and property used for religious purposes being free from taxation.

It is important to note that marriage is a public matter in the sense that, for instance, if one is an employer who provides health care benefits to the spouses of employees, one must provide those benefits to any employee who is married. Since there is no exit right possible in this case, one would be coerced, by force of law, into subsidizing a practice one finds morally or religiously objectionable.[22]

In the absence of an exit right, and if (A) is plausible, then the state cannot morally force persons to violate deeply held beliefs that are moral or religious in nature. In particular, the state morally could not sanction same-sex marriages since this would result in coercing some into violating a deeply held religious conviction.

8. A Conclusion

It is important to note that neither the argument from conflicting claims nor the no-exit argument licenses wholesale discrimination against homosexuals. What they do show is that some discrimination against homosexuals, in this case the refusal to sanction same-sex marriages, is not only legally permissible but also morally permissible. The discrimination is a way of resolving a public policy dilemma that accommodates, to an extent, each side of the impasse and, further, protects the religious and moral integrity of a good number of people. In short, the arguments show us that there are occasions in which it is morally permissible to discriminate on the basis of homosexuality.[23]

NOTES

1. The terms "homosexuality" and "heterosexuality" are defined as follows. The former is defined as sexual feelings or behavior directed toward individuals of the same sex. The latter, naturally enough, is defined as sexual feelings or behavior directed toward individuals of the opposite sex.

   Sometimes the term "gay" is offered as an alternative to "homosexual." Ordinary use of "gay" has it as a synonym of a male homosexual (hence, the common expression, "gays and lesbians"). Given this ordinary usage, the substitution would lead to a confusing equivocation. Since there are female homosexuals, it is best to use "homosexual" to refer to both male and female homosexuals, and reserve "gay" to signify male homosexuals, and "lesbian" for female homosexuals in order to avoid the equivocation.
2. Perhaps we should distinguish the weak difference thesis (permissible discrimination on some occasions) from the strong difference thesis (given the relevant moral differences, discrimination on any occasion is permissible).
3. This would be true even if the act in question is immoral.
4. The standard answer is, of course, that the line between public and private is based on the notion of harm. Acts which carry a real probability of harming third parties are public acts.
5. For other arguments supporting the moral parity of homosexuality and heterosexuality, see Richard Mohr, *Gays/Justice: A Study of Ethics, Society and Law* (NY: Columbia, 1988); and see Michael Ruse, "The Morality of Homosexuality" in *Philosophy and Sex*, eds. R. Baker and F. Elliston (Buffalo, NY: Prometheus Books, 1984), pp. 370-390.
6. Perhaps it would be better to term the disputing positions "contradictory" views rather than "contrary" views.
7. Resolutions can also be passive in the sense of the state doing nothing. If the state does nothing to resolve the public dilemma, it stands pat with the status quo, and the public dilemma is resolved gradually by sociological changes (changes in mores and in beliefs).
8. Assuming, plausibly enough, that the disputes over the sovereignty of the Union and concerning states' rights were at bottom disputes about slavery.
9. The Federal Fair Housing Act prohibits discrimination in housing on the basis of race, religion, and sex. But it does not apply to the rental of rooms in single-family houses, or to a building of five units or less if the owner lives in one of the units. See 42 U.S.C. Section 3603.
10. Note that overriding reasons involve generally recognized rights. If a right is not widely recognized and the state nonetheless uses coercion to enforce it, there is a considerable risk that the state will be seen by many or even most people as tyrannical.
11. This claim is, perhaps, controversial. For a contrary view see Richard George, *Making Men Moral* (Oxford: Clarendon Press, 1993).
12. This claim holds only for smoking which does not affect other persons—smoking done in private. Smoking which affects others, second-hand smoke, is a different matter, of course, and may well constitute a public dilemma.
13. See, for example, Leviticus 18:22, 21:3; and Romans 1:22-32; and Koran IV:13.
14. For an argument that religiously-based moral views should not be dismissed out of hand, see Stephen Carter, *The Culture of Disbelief: How American Law and Politics Trivialize Religious Devotion* (NY: Basic Books, 1993).
15. Two assumptions are these: that the prohibitions

against homosexuality activity are part of the religious doctrine and not just an extraneous addition; second, that if X is part of one's religious belief or religious doctrine, then it is morally permissible to hold X. Though this latter principle is vague, it is, I think, clear enough for our purposes here (I ignore here any points concerning the rationality of religious belief in general, or in particular cases).

16. This point has implications for the moral legitimacy of sodomy laws. One implication would be this: the private acts of consenting adults should not be criminalized.

17. An *ad hominem* point: If this response begs the question against the proponent of the parity thesis, it does not beg the question any more than the original objection does by presupposing that sexuality is analogous with race.

18. Think of the sodomy laws found in some states which criminalize certain sexual acts, whether performed by heterosexuals or homosexuals.

19. There is some interesting recent research which, though still tentative, strongly suggests that homosexuality is, at least in part, biologically based. See Simon LeVay, *The Sexual Brain* (Cambridge, MA: MIT Press, 1993), pp. 120-122; and J.M. Bailey and R.C. Pillard, "A Genetic Study of Male Sexual Orientation," *Archives of General Psychiatry* 48 (1991) 1089-1096; and C. Burr, "Homosexuality and Biology," *The Atlantic* 271/3 (March 1993) 64; and D. Hamer, S. Hu, V. Magnuson, N. Hu, A. Pattatucci, "A Linkage Between DNA Markers on the X Chromosome and Male Sexual Orientation," *Science* 261 (16 July 1993) 321-327; and see the summary of this article by Robert Pool, "Evidence for Homosexuality Gene," *Science* 261 (16 July 1993) 291-292.

20. I do not mean to suggest that homosexuality is morally equivalent or even comparable to pyromania.

21. Even if one were biologically or innately impelled to do X, it clearly does not follow that one is thereby impelled to do X in public. Again, the public/private distinction is morally relevant.

22. Is the use of subsidy here inappropriate? It does not seem so since providing health care to spouses, in a society where this is not legally mandatory, seems to be more than part of a salary and is a case of providing supporting funds for a certain end.

23. I thank David Haslett, Kate Rogers, Louis Pojman, and Jim Fieser for helpful and critical comments.

HETEROSEXUALITY AND FEMINIST THEORY

Christine Overall

Christine Overall is a Professor of Philosophy and Associate Dean, Faculty of Arts and Science, at Queen's University, Kingston. She is the author of Ethics and Human Reproduction: A Feminist Analysis *(Allen & Unwin, 1987),* Human Reproduction: Principles, Practices, Policies *(Oxford, 1991), and* A Feminist I: Reflections from Academia *(Broadview, 1998). She also writes a weekly feminist column, "In Other Words," for the* Kingston Whig-Standard.

Overall examines the phenomenon of heterosexuality as an institution of contemporary Western culture, one that reflects the systematized set of social standards, customs, and expected practices that both regulate and restrict romantic and sexual relationships between men and women. She argues that the tremendous social pressure toward heterosexuality has differential impacts on men and women in the areas of benefits, reproduction, law, education, and levels of violence. Overall raises questions about the possibility of a feminist heterosexuality and uses the notion of a continuum to argue that feminists can choose to be heterosexual and at the same time undermine the institution of heterosexuality by being aware of its effects and by changing its oppressive nature for women.

Heterosexuality, which I define as a romantic and sexual orientation toward persons not of one's own sex, is apparently a very general, though not entirely universal, characteristic of the human condition. In fact, it is so ubiquitous a part of human interactions and relations as to be almost invisible, and so natural-seeming as to appear unquestionable, indeed, the 1970 edition of *The Shorter Oxford English Dictionary* defines "heterosexual" as "pertaining to or characterized by the *normal* relation of the sexes."[1]

In this respect heterosexuality is strikingly different from the romantic and sexual orientation toward persons of one's own sex, or what I shall call, for the sake of brevity, non-heterosexuality.[2] I caution that the use of the term "non-heterosexuality" could be misleading, since it falsely suggests a uniformity among other sexual orientations comparable to that of heterosexuality. There are many significant differences among lesbianism, male homosexuality, and both male and female bisexuality. But what I am concerned with is not those differences, significant and far-ranging as they are, but rather the general contrast they collectively provide to heterosexuality.

Historically, for example, there has been a tendency to investigate the causes of forms of non-heterosexuality, but not of heterosexuality; to consider whether non-heterosexuality, but not heterosexuality, can be spread through a sort of contagion effect;[3] to ask whether non-heterosexuality is unnatural, but not to contemplate whether heterosexuality in any sense could be. If we make any assumption about a person's sexual orientation, it is almost always the assumption that the person is heterosexual. Ordinarily most parents seldom wonder whether their offspring will grow up to be heterosexual, and, compared to the ubiquitous depictions of heterosexual relations, there are very few widely available cultural images of non-heterosexuality. If one is not heterosexual, one may have the choice to pass as heterosexual; one may, that is, attempt for purposes of self-protection to assimilate into the dominant cul-

---

Reprinted with permission from *Canadian Journal of Philosophy* 20:1 (March 1990): 1–18.

ture. But except within the context of the very specific non-heterosexual culture, we would not usually speak of someone as passing as non-heterosexual. To be a sexual being, in our culture, is just to be heterosexual. Moreover, heterosexual expression is defined as *real* sex in particular, sexual intercourse is the standard of 'having sex' by reference to which all other sexual stages and activities—e.g., "virginity," "foreplay," etc.—are defined.

This is, then, the first of what I shall refer to as the paradoxes of heterosexuality: As an expected, supposedly normal characteristic of adult and even pre-adult life, it is so pervasive that it melts into our individual lives; its invisibility as a social condition makes it seem to be just a matter of what is personal, private, and inevitable. Heterosexuality is simultaneously the only "real" form of sexuality, and yet (for that very reason) very difficult to perceive. Heterosexuality is transparent, in the way that a piece of plastic wrap is transparent. Yet, like plastic wrap, it has the ability to hold things in place, to keep things down, and to provide a barrier to prevent other things from coming in contact with that which it seems to be protecting.

I The Institution of Heterosexuality

It is this transparent, virtually invisible, yet very powerful condition that I wish to subject to examination. But I am not primarily concerned with *individual* heterosexual relationships: who loves whom, who is attracted to or turned on by whom, or who does what to whom. Although, of course, what happens in those individual heterosexual relationships is not at all irrelevant to the understanding of heterosexuality, nevertheless it is not individual practices in and of themselves which interest me here. Instead, it is heterosexuality as an *institution* of contemporary western culture which is the focus of my examination. Although this institution is not the only cultural influence upon human sexuality, it is one of the most significant. By the institution of heterosexuality, or what I shall call for short the heterosexual institution, what I mean is the systematized set of social standards, customs, and expected practices which both regulate and restrict romantic and sexual relationships between persons of different sexes in late twentieth-century western culture.

The heterosexual institution by definition involves both men and women. But, given the constraints imposed by patriarchal society, in which oppression for the fact of being female is often both accepted and promoted, it cannot be expected that the heterosexual institution will say and do the same things to women as it does to men, or that it will be experienced in the same way by women and by men. As Marilyn Frye points out, "institutions *are* humanly designed patterns of access—access to persons and their services."[4] It is important to be aware of the ways in which access is patterned differently for women and for men. As a feminist, what I therefore want to discuss is the reality of the heterosexual institution *for women*: that is, its effects on women, its meanings for women, what it says to and about women. I shall first describe some main features of the heterosexual institution, and then turn to a discussion of the place of heterosexuality in women's lives and its interpretation by feminist theory. I cannot accomplish any of this without saying a fair amount about men, but I think that an examination of the heterosexual institution as it is experienced by men would be an endeavour quite different from this one.[5]

In referring to heterosexuality as an institution, I am rejecting an essentialist or reified view of sexual orientations. Human sexuality is culturally constructed, that is, it is "a social, not [only] a biological phenomenon."[6] There is no reason to suppose that sexual activity and expression are more immune to the effects of enculturation than are other apparently "natural" human activities such as caring for children, or eating. Of course, the fact that sexuality is culturally constructed does not entirely preclude the possibility that some form of sexual expression is innate or "natural," or that we have "biological inclinations" toward some form of sexual activity. But it does imply both that the evidence for such a natural sexuality will be virtually impossible to detect, and that the stronger hypothesis is that there is no such natural sexuality. One cannot even refer to primordial feelings or irresistible passions as natural, since enculturation processes, including the heterosexual institution, help to define what feelings we do and do not, or ought and ought not to have.

I shall therefore assume that there is no "fixed sexual, 'essence' or 'nature' that lies buried beneath layers of social ordering"[7] in any of us. In particular, I deny that most human beings are "naturally" or innately heterosexual; if sexual desire and activity are socially constructed, then one sort of orientation is no more natural, innate, or inevitable than another. Nor do I make the somewhat more fashionable (these days) assumption that human beings are "naturally" bisexual. Bisexual is no more what we *really* are than is heterosexual.[8] In other words, if the heterosexual institution somehow did not exist, I see no more (and no less) reason to suppose that individuals would therefore be romantically and sexually oriented to persons of both sexes than to suppose that individuals would be romantically and sexually oriented to persons of only one sex or the other. Neither of these seems to be more natural or inevitable than the other. In fact, the only useful interpretation of the claim some have made that we are "really" bisexual is just that we all have the physical capacity for sexual interactions with members of both sexes. And no one would dispute that, for the reason that it is not a very interesting or controversial claim; and it certainly tells us nothing whatsoever about a person's "real" or "natural" sexual orientation.

But, for the purposes of this paper, nothing much depends upon the assertion that no sexual orientation is innate. For, whatever our inherent proclivities may or may not be, there is undeniably tremendous social pressure toward heterosexuality. This pressure is a part of the heterosexual institution. Indeed, I wonder why, if heterosexuality is innate, there are so many social voices telling us, ad nauseum, that is what we should be. These voices include the ideology that surrounds heterosexual romance, "dating," and marriage; the mythology of falling in (and out of) heterosexual love, of flings, crushes, affairs, passions, and helpless attractions; the cultural apparatus that purports to assist women to be heterosexually attractive, to be coy, alluring, "sexy," and flirtatious, in order to "find true love" or to "catch a man," and then to maintain his interest once he's caught; the psychotherapies and medical treatments, together with literature ranging from self-help manuals to scholarly treatises, that claim to prescribe the nature and forms of and adjustment to healthy female heterosexuality and the cures or panaceas for its dysfunctions; the cultural images, in popular music, paintings, dance crazes, novels, stories, advice columns, films, videos, plays, and advertising, that interpret human sexuality and love exclusively in terms of two by two heterosexual pairing; and the predominant instruments of western social life—the bars, dances, parties, clubs—that recognize only the heterosexual couple. Why is there so much insistence, via these intensive socialization mechanisms, that all women be heterosexual and *learn* to be heterosexual, if that is what we are all naturally inclined to be anyway? So the presence of that strong social insistence upon heterosexuality is, to my mind, one very large piece of evidence that heterosexuality is not innate. But, whether it is or it is not, it is the heterosexual institution that is the subject of discussion in this paper.

II The Politics of Heterosexuality

To examine the heterosexual institution is to raise questions not only about sex but about the nature of love, passion, loyalty, and trust between men and women. These are, at least at first glance, moral questions, about human responsibility, obligation, and commitment. But, since the heterosexual institution involves connections between unequals, they are also political questions, concerned with the uneven distribution of power between members of two groups which have been socially constructed to be very different. Hence, a feminist discussion of heterosexuality requires the consideration of questions about allegiances and affiliations, about separatism, and about political choices and strategies.

To arrive at a better understanding of the political nature of the heterosexual institution, it is helpful to consider one aspect of the dictionary definition of "institution." The *Shorter Oxford English Dictionary* defines "institution" as "an establishment, organization, or association instituted for the *promotion of some object*, especially one of public utility, religious, charitable, educational, etc."[9] This definition raises the question, what object is promoted by the heterosexual institution?

In asking about the object of the heterosexual institution, I am not of course assuming that there is any consciously chosen goal of heterosexuality. No person or power, no god or father nature, created the heterosexual institution, and I am not asking a teleological question here. The easy answer, that the object of the heterosexual institution is the facilitation of human reproduction, seems not to be the whole story, for it overlooks the institution's historically variant features. Although there is undeniably some connection between heterosexual behaviour and reproduction, that connection is becoming more tenuous, with the availability of contraception on the one hand and new reproductive technologies on the other.

In fact, a number of observations count against the claim that the object of the heterosexual institution is reproduction. First, not all heterosexual activity, even when unconstrained by deliberate use of contraception and abortion, results in procreation—consider the case of heterosexually active individuals who are too young or too old to reproduce, or who are, for other reasons, infertile, or who engage in non-reproductive sexual behaviour. Such persons may be just as interested in heterosexual activity as those who do wish to reproduce, and that interest is fostered by the heterosexual institution quite independently of their willingness or ability to reproduce. Second, it is remarkable that women who are celibate, whether by choice or through force of circumstance, are usually still thought of as being heterosexual; the presumption of heterosexuality operates in the absence of reproductive activity. Third, heterosexual desire is not at all the same as the desire to reproduce; one may have either one without the other[10] and there is no longer much pressure in western culture to promote or to evaluate heterosexual desire by reference to reproductive goals. Fourth, the heterosexual institution continues to operate at full force even in places where, one would think, the needs of reproduction are already amply or even excessively filled. Finally, seeing reproduction as the object of the heterosexual institution simply "portrays men and women as the dupes of their own physiology and considers eroticism as a mere cover-up for Nature's reproductive aims."[11] Hence, although heterosexual activity and reproduction are sometimes causally connected, the latter is not the object, or at least not the only object, of the former. The heterosexual institution does not exist merely to further procreation; it has some other important function or functions.

My question about the object of the heterosexual institution is akin to questions about the object of other institutions such as the state, the family, the educational systems, or religion. And one way of starting to answer such questions is by looking to see what individuals or groups of individuals benefit from the institution, what the benefits are, how those benefits are created and distributed, and at whose cost the benefits are acquired.

For the past two decades, radical feminists have offered disturbing answers to these questions. They have argued, first, that the heterosexual institution primarily benefits men, not women; and that it affords men easy sexual gratification and material possession of women, as well as reproduction of themselves and their offspring. Second, these benefits are created and distributed through what Adrienne Rich and others have described as the compulsory nature of heterosexuality: female heterosexual desire and activity must be enforced and coerced, through a myriad of social practices in the family, in culture, in religion, education, and law.[12] This process has been described as the deliberate recruitment of women into active participation in heterosexuality.[13] Mariana Valverde states,

> [G]iven the enormous social weight of heterosexism, one cannot accurately describe heterosexuality as merely a personal preference, as though there were not countless social forces pushing one to be heterosexual. People do not generally choose heterosexuality out of a number of equally valid, equally respected lifestyles.
>
> ... As long as certain choices are punished while others are presented as natural, as the norm, it is naive to describe the complicated process of the construction of conformity and/or deviance by reference to a consumer-type notion of personal preference.[14]

Third, whatever its rewards may be (and they are more than amply celebrated in romantic fiction, films, songs, and everyday mythology) the costs for women of providing the benefits of female heterosexuality for men are of two types: First, violence, degradation, and exploitation of women's bodies and women's sexuality, through such practices as prostitution, rape and other forms of sexual assault, woman battering, pornography, and incest; and second, the deliberately cultivated separation of women from their allies, each other. The operation of the heterosexual institution is a very successful demonstration of the political maxim that to keep a subject group down, it is important to keep its members divided, to prevent them from developing loyalties to each other, and to direct their trust and commitment to members of the oppressor group. In short, the heterosexual institution is the strongest arm and most powerful manifestation of patriarchy; and therefore one of its most important objects is the oppression of women.

As an agent of patriarchal oppression, the heterosexual institution generates a second paradox in heterosexuality: the conjunction of heterosexual privilege and heterosexism. On the one hand, the heterosexual institution grants a certain privilege to heterosexual women that is not possessed by non-heterosexual women. A heterosexual woman is validated for having (or at least wanting) men in her life: the presence of a boyfriend or husband—or even the search for a male partner—confirms that the woman is a "real woman"; that (some) men (sometimes) find her attractive; that, whatever else she might be or feel or think, she is not (so the assumption goes) a "manhater" and therefore beyond the moral pale (even though woman hating is considered a fairly normal part of human civilization). A woman's heterosexuality, visibly demonstrated, shields her from the vicious attacks reserved for non-heterosexual women.

At the same time, heterosexual privilege is coupled with heterosexism, that is, discrimination on grounds of non-heterosexual orientation. Hence, heterosexual privilege has its price: strict conformity to the standards and requirements of heterosexual behaviour and appearance. On the one hand, deviations, even apparent ones, are usually noticed and punished, through verbal and even physical violence, ostracism, and the threatened loss of employment, reputation, peace and safety, home, children, or financial security. In many instances to be a feminist (regardless of one's sexual activities) is to invite heterosexist vituperation; many people, including some feminists as well as non-feminists, are inclined to regard the word "lesbian" as a dangerous term whose application to oneself undermines one's credibility and acceptability. Yet on the other hand, successful conformity to heterosexual standards of behaviour and appearance may also be painful, and necessitate contortions, self-abasement, and continual self observation in order to regulate one's feelings, speech and behaviour to fit the image of the heterosexual woman. Hence, not only are there tremendous costs for the person who is non-heterosexual, but also the heterosexual woman is in a classic double-bind situation: to avoid the damages of non-conformity, she must incur the damages of conformity.

III Heterosexuality and Choice

In one of my favourite cartoons, a young woman asks her tough and savvy feminist mother, "Ma, can I be a feminist and still like men?""Sure," replies the mother, "Just like you can be a vegetarian and like fried chicken." When I recounted this joke in an introduction to a feminism course, my young female students were disturbed rather than amused. And this is not surprising. To some, the mother's reply may seem to be a *reductio ad absurdum* of combining feminism and heterosexuality. A good vegetarian, one might think, just does not like fried chicken; or she certainly *ought* not to like it. And if, in a moment of weakness, she does consume fried chicken, then she is either not a good, moral, consistent vegetarian, or, worse still, she is not a vegetarian at all. So also with the feminist. While many of my students hoped that it would be both logically and empirically possible to be a feminist and still like men, or even to love them, they also saw considerable tension in being both heterosexual and feminist. Some feminists who love men have expressed both doubt and guilt about the legitimacy of their lives, and some non-heterosexual feminists have encouraged those feelings. For some women, for example,

> feminism has made them sharply aware of how male power is used, abused and reproduced in personal relationships, to the point where they despair of ever achieving equality. They begin to question their attachment to men and wonder if it is really men's bodies they

desire, or if they are merely addicted to their power ... [To be heterosexual seems like a weakness, like a] chink in [one's] feminist armour.[15]

Is, then, a "feminist heterosexuality" possible?[16] To answer that question, it is necessary first to consider the nature of choice. If, as some feminists have argued, heterosexuality in women is coerced, it would seem that no woman chooses to be heterosexual. When there are not several recognized and legitimate options, when there are so many pressures to be heterosexual, and when failure to conform is so heavily punished, it is difficult to regard heterosexuality as the genuine expression of a preference. In fact, as one (heterosexual) woman remarked to me, given the damning indictment of heterosexuality which has been presented by some feminists, it might seem that any woman would be heterosexual only if it were *not* a choice.

But this is not all that can be said about the possibility of choosing heterosexuality. For, first, a single-minded focus on the coercive aspects of the heterosexual institution absolves heterosexual women of any responsibility for their sexual practice in a way that seems inappropriate, at least in the case of feminist women, who have had some opportunities to reflect upon the role of heterosexuality in patriarchal oppression. The idea that all heterosexual women (unlike non-heterosexual women) just can't help themselves and are somehow doomed to love and be attracted to men gives too much weight to the view of women as victims, and too little credit to the idea that women can act and make decisions on their own behalf. Moreover, it implicitly imputes to all heterosexual women a sort of false consciousness. Most such women will not see themselves as victims of coercion. Although they may not think of heterosexual practice as a choice they have made, they also do not necessarily feel like helpless victims of the heterosexual institution. But if no woman can choose to be heterosexual, then all heterosexual women either fail to correctly understand their own sexuality, or they can correctly understand their sexuality only be seeing themselves as helpless victims.

On the contrary, I would argue, it is a mistake to summarily dismiss *all* heterosexual women's experience as a failure to understand their own sexuality. Indeed, it is possible that some such women may

have actively chosen, rather than fallen into, a life of heterosexual marriage and children ... and that in their heterosexual relationships, they have control over their own sexuality and share equally in the enjoyment of and participation in their sexual relationships.[17]

I am not saying here only that some heterosexual women may lead exceptional lives in the sense that their relationship with their man (or men) is experienced as egalitarian and uncoercive; I am saying that there is an important sense in which a woman can genuinely and even sanely choose to be heterosexual, although the conditions and opportunities for that choice may be fairly rare. Beyond the claim that heterosexuality is innate (which seems to be an insufficiently grounded essentialist claim) and the claim that heterosexuality is coerced (which seems true in regard to the heterosexual institution as a whole) there is a third possibility: that heterosexuality is or can be chosen, even—or especially!—by feminists.

If it is possible to choose *not* to be heterosexual—and most radical feminists have argued that it is—then it is possible to actively choose to be heterosexual. To some degree, each of us is able to make ourselves into the kinds of sexual beings we are, through a process of interpretation and reinterpretation of our past and present experiences and of our feelings and emotions, and through active interaction with other persons, not just passive receptivity to their influence. By choosing one's heterosexuality I mean not merely acquiescing in it, or benefiting from heterosexual privilege, but actively taking responsibility for being heterosexual. Admittedly, most apparently heterosexual women never make, and never have an opportunity to make, such an active conscious choice. In what cases, then, might it be correct to say that a woman has genuinely chosen her heterosexuality? The following remark by Charlotte Bunch provides a crucial insight into the paradoxical answer to that question:

Basically, heterosexuality means men first. That's what it's all about. It assumes that every woman is heterosexual; that every woman is defined by and is the property of men. Her body, her services, her children belong to men. If you don't accept that definition, you're a queer—no matter who you sleep with. ...[18]

For a heterosexual woman, to start to understand the institution of heterosexuality and the ideology of heterosexism is already to start to leave standard heterosexuality behind. For part of what is customarily meant by the ascription of heterosexuality is its unconscious "perfectly natural" character. Persons who are non-heterosexual never have the luxury of accepting their sexuality in this way. As Mariana Valverde has pointed out, even those non-heterosexuals who feel driven by their sexual needs and desires, and compelled to seek sexual partners of the same sex,

> are forced at some point to define themselves, and ask how and why they have come to have such desires.... Since we all "naturally" grow up to be heterosexual, it is only the deviations that call out for an explanation; the norm appears as natural, and few heterosexual people ever wonder whatever caused them to be heterosexual.[19]

Anne Wilson Schaef claims that in general, women do not view the world in sexual terms:

> First, we do not categorize individuals and situations according to their sexuality. Second, we do not assume that each and every relationship must be sexual, nor do we view everything we do and everyone we meet as having some sexual significance. In fact, women do not define the world in sexual terms.[20]

Sometimes, however, instead of being enlightened, as Schaef seems to assume, this refusal or inability to categorize in sexual terms may be a form of blindness. Marilyn Frye has pointed out that in discussions of sexual prejudice and discrimination one may often hear a statement such as "I don't think of myself as heterosexual"—presumably said by a person who engages in heterosexual activity.[21] Heterosexuals ordinarily extend to others the somewhat dubious privilege of assuming that everyone is like them; since to be sexual is to be *hetero*sexual, "[t]he question often must be *made* to arise, blatantly and explicitly, before the heterosexual person will consider the thought that one is lesbian or homosexual."[22] On the other hand, such persons often perceive non-heterosexuals as being unnecessarily preoccupied with their sexuality, unable to stop talking about it and "flaunting" it to the world. But, Frye suggests,

> Heterosexual critics of queers' "role-playing" ought to look at themselves in the mirror on their way out for a night on the town to see who's in drag. The answer is, everybody is. Perhaps the main difference between heterosexuals and queers is that when queers go forth in drag, they know they are engaged in theater—they are playing and they know they are playing. Heterosexuals usually are taking it all perfectly seriously, thinking they are in the real world, thinking they *are* the real world. [23]

The person whose sexual practice is heterosexual and who honestly and innocently states that she does not think of herself as heterosexual shows herself most clearly to be heterosexual in the standard sense. Paradoxically, then, for a woman to firmly and unambiguously affirm her heterosexuality may already be to begin to leave it behind, that is, to cease to be heterosexual in the unthinking unconscious way she once was: She ceases to participate wholeheartedly in the heterosexual institution, and begins the process of disaffiliation from it.[24] When that sort of reflection takes place, I believe, the woman is beginning genuinely to choose her heterosexuality; and she is choosing heterosexual practice without a concomitant endorsement of the heterosexual institution.

Of course, for such a woman, heterosexuality is still something which is enforced, in Rich's sense; that is, persistent cultural pressures strive to ensure her conformity, and deviance from heterosexuality is penalized, often severely. No amount of awareness of the heterosexual institution can, by itself, change the compulsory nature of heterosexuality, and disaffiliation by one woman will not rock the institution.

Nevertheless, that awareness can make a difference, for the previously unawarely heterosexual woman, in the dimensions of her own sexuality: She can begin the process of shaping her own sexuality, by making decisions and choices based upon an understanding of the power and the limits of the heterosexual institution. For she can explore her own personal history and determine how and when her sense of the erotic became separated from women and connected to men.[25] In so doing, she can no longer regard her heterosexual orientation as something over which she has no power or control, as something which just dominates her sexual feelings and practices. Instead, she can distinguish between sexual passion and attraction, on the one hand, and dependence, need, fear, and insecurity on the other. She can become aware of her feelings about women's and men's bodies, and discover whether and/or to what degree she has internalized a socially validated revulsion toward the female body. She can genuinely ask herself whether sexual activity with men is something she wants, or merely something in which she engages. (For, of course, we cannot assume that all women whose sexual practice is heterosexual also enjoy their sexual activities.)

If the answer is no, it is not something she wants, she then has the prospect of choosing to be non-heterosexual. On the other hand, if the answer is yes, she can, in a way, begin to come out as a heterosexual: not in the heterosexist fashion by which almost all heterosexuals, male and female, ordinarily mark their heterosexuality, but rather in terms of an informed and self-aware feminist evaluation of her life as a heterosexual,[26] renouncing as far as possible the privilege accorded by heterosexuality,[27] and recognizing both the different varieties of oppression non-heterosexuals undergo and also the affinities she shares with non-heterosexual women. She can support non-heterosexual women, validate their relationships, and refuse any longer to be complicitous in the erasures they often undergo. She thereby chooses to be heterosexual as a matter of sexual practice, but not as a matter of the exclusive heterosexist alignment or orientation of her life.

Nevertheless, although it may now seem that heterosexuality can be genuinely chosen by women, for some feminists the question may still remain whether it *ought* to be chosen, whether it is ever a good choice, a choice a feminist could responsibly make. Although some heterosexual feminists pride themselves on their "exceptional" heterosexual relationships, relationships which are, apparently, non-oppressive and egalitarian, still, whatever the particular relationship is like, it nonetheless remains *possible* for the man to take advantage of his potential power. All that stands in the way of his using that power is his own good will, while he is not similarly dependent on the woman's good will. And he still benefits, however indirectly, from male hegemony, and "even the advantages that he is in a position to refuse are waiting for him if he changes his mind."[28]

> [C]hanging our expectations will [not] by itself change the unequal power relationship. It does not, for instance, change the expectations and behaviour of the man. Neither does it remove the institutional power vested in the male in heterosexual relationships.[29]

Moreover, the woman in such a relationship is still giving her energies very largely to a man, consorting intimately with a member of an oppressor group, and hence, indirectly withholding her energies from a woman. For any woman, heterosexual orientation seems to mean putting men, or at least a man, first. And even while rejecting the heterosexual institution, such a woman also still benefits from heterosexual privilege. Thus, no matter how idyllic her relationship, it seems to fail of its very nature to challenge the status quo, and to reinforce the apparent exclusive loyalty of a woman to her man. Together, the two persons in the relationship still appear to participate in and contribute to the perpetuation of an institution which is oppressive of women, particularly of non-heterosexual women and unattached women of any orientation, as well as of heterosexual women in abusive relationships.[30] And of course having an exceptional relationship does not in any way spare a woman from the worst excesses of the heterosexual institution as they may be visited upon her by men other than her immediate sexual partner(s).

The foregoing observations appear to call into question the *legitimacy* of a woman's deliberately deciding to be heterosexual, and I have only very tentative responses to them. The first involves taking seriously the distinction between the institution of heterosexuality on the one hand, and on the other hand, specific heterosexual relations and the persons who become involved in them. This is the same sort of distinction made by Adrienne Rich in her discussion of motherhood. Rich has urged us to recognize that while motherhood itself is an oppressive institution, mothering particular children may be a delightful, worthwhile, valuable human activity.[31] Similarly, while heterosexuality is an oppressive institution, not all heterosexual relationships are valueless as a result. Glimpsing this possibility might also encourage feminists to make a distinction between what could be called the *institution* of manhood, on the one hand, and individual men on the other. It must have been some such distinction that I had implicitly in mind years ago when I complained to a male friend at some length about masculine behaviour. After he mildly pointed out that he was a man (and therefore, presumably, a counterexample to some of the generalizations I was inclined to make), I spontaneously patted his hand and replied, "But Bob, I don't think of you as a man!"

In regard to this distinction between being male and being "a man," or masculine, Marilyn Frye writes,

> I have enjoined males of my acquaintance to set themselves against masculinity. I have asked them to think about how they can stop being men, and I was not recommending a sex change operation.[32]

This answer, by itself, has of course all the weaknesses of any "individual solution" to problems of oppression. For it depends upon a commitment of the man in the relationship not to avail himself of the power of his position. And so, it must be said, for a woman to actively choose to be heterosexual is an act of faith—faith first of all in the fundamental humanity of the men whom she chooses to love. By actively choosing to be heterosexual, a feminist woman is rejecting the view that male sexuality is inevitably and innately violent and exploitive, and that men are hopelessly fated to engage only in aggressive and oppressive relationships. Although members of the two sexes acquire very different roles, men just as much as women learn to participate in the heterosexual institution. And it is a lesson which men can reject. The heterosexual institution is a social artifact that can be changed, and men themselves may be the allies of women in changing it.

A woman who deliberately chooses to be heterosexual is also expressing her faith in her own individual power and strengths, her belief that a woman in a heterosexual relationship can be something far more than a helpless victim. She is rejecting the invidious all-or-nothing fallacies that restrict what she is and can be. She is recognizing that she is not, or need not be, only a sexual being; that she is not, or need not be, only heterosexual. Joanna Russ points out that in the late nineteenth century the new focus on sexuality as an indicator of the "health" of one's personality led to the invention of a new kind of person: "The Homosexual."[33] Similarly, I think, some recent feminist theory has resulted in the invention of "The Heterosexual," seen as a woman entirely defined by her sexual orientation to men. Both moves, though they originate from very different sources and agendas, hypothesize the existence of an entire personality and political affiliation on the basis of a species of sexual activity. But while we can easily recognize the power and ubiquity of the heterosexual institution, we need not thereby conclude that that institution subsumes entire personalities. To describe a woman as heterosexual (or as not heterosexual) in no way provides an exhaustive description of that woman's activities, beliefs, values, attitudes, or temperament.

There are, moreover, degrees of heterosexuality. Heterosexual orientation need not mean the exclusion of loyalty to, attraction toward, and love for women. Women who are heterosexual can develop intimate relationships with women, and value them at least as much as they value their relationships with men. Adrienne Rich has spoken movingly of what she calls "the lesbian continuum." She defines it as

> [the full] range—through each woman's life and throughout history—of women–identified experience; not simply the fact that a woman has had or consciously desired genital sexual experience with another woman. [The lesbian continuum] embrace[s] many more forms of primary intensity between and among women, including the sharing of a rich inner life, the bonding against male tyranny, [and] the giving and receiving of practical and political support....[34]

Sometimes, unfortunately, the concept of the lesbian continuum is appealed to by some feminists rather prematurely as a way of foreclosing on confrontation and acrimony between heterosexual and non-heterosexual women. Nevertheless, provided the differences between heterosexual and non-heterosexual woman in culture, experience, oppression, and privilege are not glossed over, the concept of the lesbian continuum is a powerful source of insight for women who have chosen to be heterosexual, and a reminder that they are not or need not be only heterosexual. So far, under patriarchal conditions, what women's sexuality is and can be has scarcely been explored; but in a non-patriarchal society there would be no limitations on life-promoting human relationships.

AUTHOR'S NOTE

An earlier version of this paper was first presented at the Queen's University Philosophy Department Colloquium, and I am grateful for the suggestions which I received. I am particularly indebted to Michael Fox for his detailed and thoughtful commentary.

NOTES

1. *Shorter Oxford English Dictionary*, Addenda (1970), my emphasis.
2. Frances Giberson has pointed out to me that celibacy could also be thought of as a type of non-heterosexuality, indeed, a rejection of the heterosexual institution. In men, the absence of heterosexual behaviour is usually taken as prima facie evidence of homosexuality; whereas in women, the absence of heterosexual behaviour is often taken to mean the woman is celibate. Unfortunately, there is not space in this paper to explore further the important issues connected with celibacy.
3. See Christine Overall, "Sexuality, Parenting, and Reproductive Choices," *Resources For Feminist Research/Documentation sur la recherche féministe* 16 (September 1987) 44.
4. Marilyn Frye, "Some Reflections on Separatism and Power," in her *The Politics of Reality: Essays in Feminist Theory* (Trumansburg, NY: The Crossing Press 1983) 106-7, Frye's emphasis.
5. And it has been done. See, for example, Howard Buchbinder's "Male Heterosexuality: The Socialized Penis Revisited," in Howard Buchbinder et al., eds., *Who's On Top? The Politics of Heterosexuality* (Toronto: Garamond Press 1987) 63-82.
6. Carole S. Vance and Ann Barr Snitow, " Toward a Conversation About Sex in Feminism: A Modest Proposal," *Signs* 10 (1984) 127.
7. Ruth Bleier, *Science and Gender: A Critique of Biology and Its Theories on Women* (New York: Pergamon Press 1984) 166.
8. Mariana Valverde, *Sex, Power and Pleasure* (Toronto: Women's Press 1985) 113-14.
9. *Shorter Oxford English Dictionary*, my emphasis.
10. Alan Soble, "Preface: Changing Conceptions of Human Sexuality," in Earl E. Shelp, ed., *Sexuality and Medicine: Conceptual Roots* (Boston: D. Reidel 1987) xiii.
11. Valverde, 50.
12. Adrienne Rich, "Compulsory Heterosexuality and Lesbian Existence," in Catharine R. Stimpson and Ethel Spector Person, eds., *Women: Sex and Sexuality* (Chicago: University of Chicago Press 1980) 62-91.
13. Beatrix Campbell, "A Feminist Sexual Politics: Now You See It, Now You Don't" in The Feminist Review, ed., *Sexuality: A Reader* (London: Virago Press 1987) 23.
14. Valverde, 114.
15. Ibid., 62-3.
16. The question is taken from the title of Angela Hamblin's article, "Is a Feminist Heterosexuality Possible?," in Sue Cartledge and Joanna Ryan, eds., *Sex and Love: New Thoughts on Old Contradictions* (London: The Women's Press 1983) 105-23.
17. Bleier, 182-3. Cf. Ann Ferguson, "Patriarchy, Sexual Identity, and the Sexual Revolution," in Nannerl O. Keohane, Michelle Z. Rosaldo, and Barbara C. Gelpi, eds., *Feminist Theory: A Critique of Ideology* (Chicago: University of Chicago Press 1982) 159.
18. Charlotte Bunch, "Not For Lesbians Only," in Charlotte Bunch et al., eds., *Building Feminist Theory: Essays From Quest* (New York: Longman 1981) 69.
19. Valverde, 114-15.
20. Anne Wilson Schaef, *Women's Reality: An Emerging Female System in a White Male Society* (Minneapolis: Winston Press 1985) 47.

21. Marilyn Frye, "Lesbian Feminism and the Gay Rights Movement: Another View of Male Supremacy, Another Separatism," in the *Politics of Reality*, 147. Michael Ramberg has pointed out to me that to say "I don't think of myself as heterosexual" could also mean "I am not *only* heterosexual" or "I will not always be heterosexual."
22. Marilyn Frye, "On Being White: Toward A Feminist Understanding of Race and Race Supremacy," in *The Politics of Reality*, 116, her emphasis.
23. Marilyn Frye, "Sexism," in *The Politics of Reality*, 29, her emphasis.
24. Frye, "On Being White," 127.
25. Marilyn Frye, "A Lesbian Perspective on Women's Studies," in Margaret Cruikshank, ed., *Lesbian Studies: Present and Future* (Old Westbury, NY: The Feminist Press 1982) 197.
26. See Katherine Arnup, "Lesbian Feminist Theory," *Resources for Feminist Research/Documentation sur la recherche feministe* 12 (March 1983) 55.
27. Amy Gottlieb, "Mothers, Sisters, Lovers, Listen," in Maureen Fitzgerald, Connie Guberman, and Margie Wolfe, eds., *Still Ain't Satisfied! Canadian Feminism Today* (Toronto: Women's Press 1982) 238-9.
28. Sara Ann Ketchum and Christine Pierce, "Separatism and Sexual Relationships," in Sharon Bishop and Marjorie Weinzweig, eds., *Philosophy and Women* (Belmont, CA: Wadsworth 1979) 167-168.
29. Hamblin, 117.
30. See Lees Revolutionary Feminist Group, "Political Lesbianism: The Case Against Heterosexuality," in *Love Your Enemy? The Debate Between Heterosexual Feminism and Political Lesbianism* (London: Onlywomen Press 1981) 5-10.
31. Adrienne Rich, *Of Woman Born: Motherhood as Experience and Institution* (New York: Bantam Books 1976).
32. Frye, "On Being White," 127.
33. Joanna Russ, *Magic Mommas, Trembling Sisters, Puritans and Perverts* (Trumansburg, NY: The Crossing Press 1985) 67.
34. Rich, "Compulsory Heterosexuality and Lesbian Existence," 81.

SEXUALITY INJUSTICE

Cheshire Calhoun

Cheshire Calhoun is Associate Professor of Philosophy at Colby College, Waterville, Maine. She works at various intersections of ethics, feminist philosophy, philosophy of emotion, and gay/lesbian studies. "Sexuality Injustice" is part of a forthcoming book tentatively titled Centering Sexual Orientation Politics.

"Sexuality injustice differs significantly in form from racial and gender injustice. Because persons who are gay or lesbian can evade being publicly identified and treated as gays or lesbians, sexuality injustice does not consist, as racial and gender injustice does, in the disproportionate occupation of disadvantaging and highly exploitable places in the socio-economic structure. Instead, sexuality injustice consists in the displacement of homosexuality and lesbianism to the outside of society. I examine, in particular, (1) the production of society as heterosexual through the requirement that all citizens adopt a real or pseudonymous heterosexual identity as a condition of access to the public sphere; (2) the reproduction of heterosexual society through legal, psychiatric, educational, and familial practices whose aim is to prevent future generations of lesbian and gay people; and (3) the legitimation of heterosexual society through the construction of criminalizing stereotypes of gay and lesbian identity."

It was while reading Susan Okin's *Justice, Gender, and the Family* that it occurred to me to wonder if there was a *sexuality* injustice comparable to the gender injustice that has been the target of feminist critique.

The language of "gay and lesbian rights," following as it does on the heels of the civil rights and women's rights movements, suggests that there is indeed an analogy between the political position of gay men and lesbians on the one hand and of women and racial minorities on the other. At first glance, affinities are not hard to find. Lesbians and gays face a formidable array of discriminatory policies and practices that limit their liberty and opportunity. Legally, we are in much the same position as racial minorities and women were prior to the civil rights act—unprotected against informal discrimination and subject to differential treatment under the law.

But the feminist notion of gender injustice goes well beyond the thought that women confront legal inequities. Over the past several decades, feminists have carefully developed the idea that gender injustice is a matter of oppression, not just legal inequities.[1] That is, the devaluation of women is systematically built into the ways that we, as a society, live and think. The consequence *and evidence* of this systematic devaluation is that women are disproportionately clustered in opportunity-limiting and highly exploitable places. So for instance, the private sphere, pink collar jobs, domestic labor, the sex industry, the roster of welfare clients, and the poverty zone are all places disproportionately inhabited by women. To understand gender injustice is to understand the *places* that women occupy in socio-economic structures and practices, the disadvantaging *effects* of occupying those places, and the factors (including the law) that systematically keep women *in place*.

What I want to understand is the presumably analogous injustice to which gay men and lesbians are

---

Reprinted with permission of Cheshire Calhoun from *Notre Dame Journal of Law, Ethics & Public Policy* 9:1 (1995): 241–274.

subject. What content can be given to the idea of a *sexuality* injustice comparable to gender injustice?[2] A central difficulty in developing this notion of sexuality injustice is that lesbians and gay men, unlike women, do not appear to be located in any particular social structural places. This is largely because, unlike women or racial minorities, gays and lesbians often can evade having their sexual orientation recognized. The social presumption that persons are heterosexual unless there is clear evidence to the contrary helps to conceal gay men and lesbians. Moreover, like criminal identity, sexual identity can be deliberately concealed by adopting, in James Woods's term, a counterfeit heterosexual identity. As a result, persons who *are* lesbian or gay are often treated *as* heterosexuals. Thus anti-gay ideology and discriminatory policies and practices do not have the necessary consequence of *systematically* undermining gays' and lesbians' material conditions or access to opportunities. Consider, for example, the substantially different impact of the military policy barring women from combat and its policy of barring gay men and lesbians from military service. The former effectively bars all women from combat. The latter does not effectively bar gays and lesbians from service; it only bars the *identifiably* gay or lesbian. So long as they pass as heterosexual, gays and lesbians will occupy virtually the same location in the opportunity structure as heterosexuals.

Thus it seems that sexuality injustice is *not* closely analogous to gender or racial injustice. In particular, sexuality injustice does not materialize in a disadvantaging *place* in which gays and lesbians are disproportionately concentrated. Organizations on the religious right, such as Lou Sheldon's Traditional Values Coalition have capitalized on this fact, coming to the conclusion that there is no such thing as sexuality injustice and thus that gay and lesbian rights must be special rights.

What I want to suggest instead is that sexuality injustice consists in the systematic *dis*-placement of gays and lesbians to the outside of civil society so that lesbians and gays have no legitimized place—not even a disadvantaged one. One mechanism for displacing lesbians and gays is the requirement that all citizens have an apparent heterosexual identity as a condition of access to the public sphere. This means that gays and lesbians must adopt a pseudonymous heterosexual identity in order to gain full access to the public sphere. As a result, gay and lesbian *identities* are effectively displaced from the public sphere. A second mechanism for displacing lesbians and gays is the institutionalization of legal, psychiatric, educational, and familial practices whose aim is to prevent future generations of lesbian and gay people. So for example, both anti-gay child custody decisions and anti-gay educational policies are aimed at reproducing heterosexuality and thus displacing homosexuality and lesbianism from our social future. This heterosexualization of society is then legitimized through the social construction of criminalizing stereotypes of lesbian and gay identity that undermines the claim of lesbians and gays to full civic status. I will consider both mechanisms of displacements in turn, concluding with some comments about the criminalization of lesbian and gay identity.

I. Displacing Gay and Lesbian Identities from the Public Sphere

In discussing the displacement of gay and lesbian identities from the public sphere, I will begin with some brief observations about the legal construction of same-sex sexuality as the publicly *unmentionable* crime. I will then turn to a discussion of the way that military policy, employment practice, and court decisions work to displace gay and lesbian *identities*, though not the persons themselves, from the public sphere. I will conclude this first part with some reasons why I think that the First Amendment does not adequately secure lesbians' and gays' entitlement to represent their identities publicly.

Sodomy has a long, distinctive history, as the unmentionable crime. Prior to the secularization of sodomy prohibitions in the 1500s, "sodomy had been defined in strictly ecclesiastical terms as one of the gravest sins against divine law whose name alone proved such an affront to God that it was often named only as the unnameable." Throughout the 1600s, sodomy continued to be referred to within British law as the crime that among Christians is not to be mentioned, and a century later, William Blackstone uses this same (non)description in his *Commentaries on the Laws of England*. He remarks,

> I will not act so disagreeable a part, to my readers as well as myself, as to dwell any longer upon a subject, the very mention of which is a disgrace to human nature. It will be more eligible to imitate in this respect the delicacy of our English law, which treats it, in its very indictments, as a crime not fit to be named.

In the United States, some state statutes still refuse to name what they prohibit, instead referring with vague decency to "crimes against nature."[3] And in his concurring opinion in *Bowers v. Hardwick*, Justice Burger recalled the words of Blackstone, pronouncing sodomy "a heinous act 'the very mention of which is a disgrace to human nature,' and 'a crime not fit to be named.'"[4]

The history of laws prohibiting sodomy and acts of gross indecency between men is thus simultaneously a history of the linguistic taboo on publicly naming and describing same-sex sexuality. It is the history of laws that not only render privately performed sex a matter of public concern but that *also* privatize public acts of linguistic representation. That dual history ultimately has the dual effect of undercutting the claim of gays and lesbians to have a private sphere where their sexual, affiliational, and familial relations are protected from public intrusion *and* of denying them any entitlement to represent themselves in the public sphere as lesbians and gays. The unmentionability of homosexuality and lesbianism in the *public* sphere effectively displaces gay and lesbian identities to the outside of civil society.

By contrast, unlike this love that dare not speak its name, heterosexuality is the love whose name is continually spoken in the everyday routines and institutions of public social life. Heterosexuals move about in the public sphere as heterosexuals, and that identity is by no means a private matter. Public social interaction and the structure of public institutions are pervaded with the assumption that public actors are heterosexual and with opportunities to represent themselves as such. Humor, formal and informal dress codes, corporate benefits policies, "scripts" for everyday conversation about personal life, public display of family pictures, and so on presuppose that public persons *are* heterosexual. They also enable individuals to publicly represent themselves *as* heterosexuals.[5]

This double standard for heterosexual versus homosexual self-representation is based on the assumption that heterosexuality is and ought to be constitutive of what it means to be a public actor, a citizen. The equation of 'public actor' with 'heterosexual actor' is in part sustained by regarding homosexual identity as a private, behind-closed-doors matter. It is also sustained by requiring that lesbians and gays adopt a pseudonymous heterosexual identity as a condition of access to the public sphere, and by instituting a set of discriminatory practices and policies that penalize individuals for publicly representing themselves as gay or lesbian. Military policy is a case in point.

Military policy has in the past implicitly invoked,[6] and now explicitly invokes, a distinction between status and conduct. Supposedly, that distinction is critical to framing a policy that does not discriminate on the basis of who one *is* yet still grants the military authority to regulate what its members *do*. In reality, the distinction is critical to controlling the identities that are allowed to appear in the military's public space.

Prior to 1994, military policy prohibited not only sexual activity between persons of the same sex, it also prohibited making one's homosexuality known.[7] Publicly stating "I am a lesbian" warranted discharge no less than did private lesbian sexual acts. In discussing the proposed new policy, revealingly dubbed "don't ask, don't tell," Sam Nunn, affirmed that avowing one's homosexuality or lesbianism *is* conduct and ought to be prohibited.[8] Although the policy that actually went into effect in 1994 does not make self-identifying statements automatic grounds for dismissal, it does make them grounds for starting an investigation, "and once such an investigation is started, the service member would have to prove that he had not engaged in homosexual acts."[9] In controlling public identity, not just sexual acts, both old and new policies require that the persons who are to be exempted from status-discrimination adopt a pseudonymous heterosexual identity.[10]

Courts have also invoked the status-conduct distinction to the same end of controlling public identity. In *Singer v. United States Civil Service Commission*,[11] for example, the Court concluded that the Civil Service Commission had not acted improperly in firing John F. Singer. Singer was a clerk typist for the Seattle Office of (ironically) the EEOC. He had been fired by the Civil Service Commission for "flaunting" and "broadcasting" his homosexuality and for receiving "wide-spread publicity in this respect in at least two states."[12] The Commission noted that Singer had kissed a male in front of the building elevator and in the company cafeteria, had applied with another man for a marriage license, had "homosexual advertisements" on the windows of his car, was on the Board of Directors of the Seattle Gay Alliance, showed by his "dress and demeanor" that he intended to continue his homosexual activity, and he had received television, newspaper, radio, and magazine publicity.[13] The Commission denied that Singer was discharged because of his status. Instead, it claimed that Singer's "repeated flaunting and advocacy of a controversial lifestyle"[14] would undermine public confidence in, and thus the efficiency of, the Civil Service. The Court agreed, noting that this case differed from *Norton v. Macy*. In *Norton v. Macy*, the D.C. Circuit Court ruled that NASA could not discharge an employee for being gay. What made Singer's case different was that Singer had not attempted, as Norton had, to keep his homosexuality private.[15] In the eyes of both the EEOC and the Court, Singer brought discredit on his employer by publicly occupying a discredited identity.

What both the military in its new policy, and the Courts in *Norton* and *Singer*, acknowledge is that the presence of persons who *are* gay or lesbian need not "contaminate" the heteronormativity of public space. Public actors may *be* gay or lesbian. What they may not do is make those identities known by *representing* themselves as lesbian or gay. Instead, both military policy and government employment practice in effect require lesbians and gays to adopt pseudonymous heterosexual identities in their public lives.

Briefly considering what the gender analog to status-conduct distinguishing policies would look like brings the problem into sharper focus. Imagine, for example, a military service policy that, while claiming not to discriminate against persons who *are* women, proceeded to ban all "conduct" that made women publicly identifiable *as* women. Women would be subject to discharge both for engaging in womanly activities (say, joining the National Organization for Women or wearing women's clothing) and for making the self-identifying statement "I am a woman." Avowing their womanhood and flaunting or carelessly displaying their unorthodox gender in public would constitute a breach of acceptable military conduct.[16] While not discriminating on one level (one may *be* a woman), this fictional policy clearly discriminates on another. It would burden women with the task of managing their public identities so that they appear to be men. And it would prohibit women from doing what men may do, namely, represent themselves as having the identities that they do have.[17]

It is tempting to argue that these restrictions on public self-representation violate First Amendment rights to freedom of speech and association. This is exactly what Judge Edwards and later Justice Brennan did argue in dissenting opinions concerning *Rowland v. Mad River Local School District*. Marjorie Rowland was a high school counselor. She disclosed her bisexuality to several fellow school employees, and was subsequently asked to resign. When she refused, she was suspended, then transferred to a position with no student contact, and then not rehired after her contract expired. The Sixth Circuit Court deemed Rowland's disclosure merely personal, not the public speech of a citizen speaking on a matter of public concern and debate. It thus refused to grant first amendment protections to her disclosure.

Both Judge Edwards and Justice Brennan took issue with this classification of Rowland's identity-statement as merely personal. The Circuit Court had argued that "[t]here was absolutely no evidence of any public concern in the community or at Stebbins High with the issue of bisexuality among school personnel when [Rowland] began speaking to others about her own sexual preference."[18] Taking a larger view of the public, both Judge Edwards[19] and Justice Brennan[20] argued that public debate about the rights of homosexuals was in fact currently ongoing (even if not at Stebbins High), and thus "[t]he fact of petitioner's bisexuality, once spoken, necessarily and ineluctably involved her in that debate."[21]

However tempting invoking first amendment protections in this way may be, there is something odd about classifying representations of one's identity as *either* public or private speech. Consider, first, the fictional gender policy. Is discharging a person for stating "I am a woman" best criticized as a violation of rights to speech, expression, and association? Is one's gender, like one's political views, simply a possible subject of speech or basis of association? Or is it instead constitutive of being a speaker? In our social world, gender is such a fundamental social category that it is the first thing people want to know about the persons with whom they interact. Furthermore, in our social world the psychological process of becoming gendered is part of the process of becoming a self, a subject, an 'I'. In short, speakers enter into the world of speech and expression as gendered subjects. Thus gender is better viewed as a feature of being a speaker rather than simply something one might wish to express to others. To prohibit a particular gendered self-representation in the public world is, then, to do much more than restrict what a speaker may say or with whom she may associate. It is to deny that a particular subject may speak at all. Under the fictional gender policy, women may not speak. Only men, real and pseudonymous, may.

Like gender, sexuality is a fundamentally constitutive feature of our social world and of the persons who inhabit it. For better or worse, we have inherited a view of sexuality as something that, like gender, pervades the entire personality and orients persons in the social world. Persons enter the adult world of speech and expression as sexual subjects. Unlike gender, however, the pressure to know others' and make clear one's own sexuality is relieved, for heterosexuals at least, by the presumption of universal heterosexuality. That presumed heterosexuality, however, is better viewed as a presumption about what it means to be a speaker rather than a presumption about what speakers might wish to express. As in the case of gender, prohibiting a particular sexual self-representation in the public world not only restricts the content of speech, but more importantly denies that lesbian, gay, or bisexual subjects may speak at all. Only heterosexuals, real and pseudonymous, may.

The upshot of the Court's decision in *Rowland* was precisely to deny that a bisexual subject may speak. Although denying that Rowland could be penalized simply for her status as a bisexual, it affirmed that it was permissible for the school to discipline her for making statements about her sexual preference.[22] In a social context like ours, where speakers' heterosexuality is presumed, this amounts to ruling that employers may penalize their employees for refusing to speak as (presumed) heterosexual subjects.

In sum, neither status-based anti-discrimination policies nor first amendment protections of speech adequately guarantee lesbians and gays that they may dare speak their names. First, status-based policies—like the military's or the EEOC's—may simply entitle individuals to *be* lesbian or gay in public space, but not to *represent* themselves as lesbian or gay in public space. Second, the first amendment protects speech, guaranteeing that some things *may be said*. It does not protect speakers, guaranteeing that some sorts of speakers *may do the saying*. When Marjorie Rowland announced "I am a bisexual," she specified who was doing the saying.

II. Preventing Future Generations of Gay and Lesbian Persons

I turn now to the displacement of lesbians and gays from our social future. I will begin with some historical remarks about the psychiatric distinction between true and situational homosexuality. Then I will turn to considering how this distinction has affected psychiatric, legal, educational, and familial practices whose aim is to prevent future generations of lesbians and gays.

From the first emergence of "sexual inversion" in psychiatric taxonomies of the late 1800s, the distinctions between congenital and acquired conditions, between personality type and behavior, and between cross-genderization and same-sex conduct were central to understandings of the forms that homosexuality and lesbianism could take. For turn of the century sexologists, Havelock Ellis and Richard von Krafft-Ebing–both of whom played a central role in establishing sexual inversion as a psychiatric condition—"true" inverts came by their homosexuality congenitally; and their distinguishing feature was not the orientation of their desire, but their cross-genderization, that is, their apparent constitution as a unique personality type—the "third sex."[23] True, congenital inversion was contrasted with acquired, situational inversion. Situational factors were thought to be capable of turning "true" heterosexuals into persons who, though not significantly cross-gendered, sexually desired others of the same sex. Those situational factors included childhood masturbation, confinement to same-sex environments in prisons, convents, and boarding schools, participation in the women's movement, and the seductive advances of true inverts. While congenital inversion was, perhaps, incorrigible, acquired inversion was, on this view, both curable and preventable by manipulating situational factors and inculcating proper sexual habits.

The "true" versus "acquired" distinction affected and continues to affect policy concerning gay men and lesbians in this century. During World War II, for example, motivated partly by psychiatric insistence on the difference between true homosexuality and mere homosexual conduct, and partly by the practical need to retain military personnel, the military attempted to distinguish "true" from "salvageable" homosexuals.[24] Current military policy continues to distinguish between true and situational homosexuals, with the burden of proof falling on those charged with homosexual conduct to demonstrate that they are "truly" heterosexuals.[25]

In the 1990s, the search for a gay gene continues the tradition of equating true homosexuality with a congenital condition. Arguments for gay-tolerant policies based on the claim that gays and lesbians are "born that way" fall squarely in line with turn of the century arguments for social acceptance of the congenital invert.[26] However, given a pervasive cultural distinction between true and situational homosexuals, such arguments are doomed from the outset to be ineffective against a broad band of social policies whose aim is not so much the differential treatment of truly and incorrigibly gay or lesbian as the prevention of new gay and lesbian persons.

In an essay ironically titled "How to Bring Your Kids up Gay," Eve Sedgwick argues that increasing tolerance of adult gay persons has gone hand in hand with the attempt to prevent new gay persons from coming into being.[27] She notes that in the same year that the American Psychiatric Association depathologized homosexuality, it added a new category—Gender Identity Disorder of Childhood—to its Diagnostic and Statistical Manual's roster of pathological conditions.[28] Boys become susceptible to this diagnosis if, in addition to expressing distress about being a boy, they display a "preoccupation with female stereotypical activities as manifested by a preference for either cross-dressing or simulating female attire, or by a compelling desire to participate in the games and pastimes of girls."[29] The revised edition, DSM-III-R, adds "...and rejection of male stereotypical toys, games, and activities."[30] Similarly, girls become susceptible to this diagnosis if, in addition to expressing distress about being a girl, they show a "persistent marked aversion to normative feminine clothing and insistence on wearing stereotypical masculine clothing, e.g., boys' underwear and other accessories."[31] Harkening back to sexologists' equation of true inversion with cross-genderization, this new disorder appears to be as much about the early detection and prevention of lesbianism and homosexuality as about control of gender deviance. The message of DSM-III, in Sedgwick's view, is that while *existing adult* homosexuals deserve dignified treatment at the hands of psychiatric professionals, psychiatrists may intervene in the lives of proto-gay *children* to prevent new lesbian and gay persons from coming into being.[32]

Gay preventative measures have been framed not only as matters of gender health, but matters also of parental rights and duties. One of the psychiatrists Sedgwick critiques, for example, invokes the theory of parental dominion to justify parental intervention in proto-gay children's lives. He remarks: "the rights of parents to oversee the development of children is a long-established principle. Who is to dictate that parents may not try to raise their children in a manner that maximizes the possibility of a heterosexual outcome?"[33] Others construe intervention as obligatory. For example, in her article advocating gay access to surrogacy, Sharon Elizabeth Rush moves swiftly from sanctioning adult homosexuality to condemning the creation of new gay persons. She says,

> Many heterosexual parents may be quite tolerant and accepting of homosexuality, and many homosexual parents may be quite proud to be homosexual. Nevertheless, given the social reprobation that at present attaches to being homosexual in the United States, and given the love and affection that most parents feel toward their children, I find it unbelievable that any parents—heterosexual or homosexual—would teach their children to be homosexual.[34]

However legitimated—whether on grounds of psychological health, parental rights, or parental obligation—the goal of preventing kids from turning out gay underlies policy that restricts gay and lesbian parenting, gay and lesbian employment in child care, early education, and child service organizations (such as the Boy Scouts), as well as the sexual content of school curricula.

For instance, one of the University of Missouri's principal reasons for refusing to recognize the student group Gay Lib was that "[w]hat happens to a latent or potential homosexual from the standpoint of his environment can cause him to become or not to become a homosexual."[35] In the university's and dissenting Judge Regan's view, the university had a responsibility to protect potential homosexuals from becoming overt homosexuals.[36] And that, in their view, meant protecting them from being influenced by their fellow (overtly) gay and lesbian students.

This goal of preventing new gay and lesbian persons also figured centrally in the court ruling on the New Hampshire adoption law that "prohibits any person who is homosexual from adopting any person, from being licensed as a member of a foster family, and from running day care centers."[37] When asked for a judicial opinion on the constitutionality of this law, the New Hampshire Supreme Court ignored any criteria of fitness to parent other than capacity to raise children to be heterosexual. In its view, "the legislature can rationally act on the theory that a role model can influence the child's developing sexual identity,"[38] and thus can legitimately regard gay and lesbian persons as unfit for adoptive and foster parenting.

Gay prevention also underlies attempts to outlaw the so-called "promotion" of homosexuality. In 1988, Britain passed Clause 28 of the Local Government Act which stipulated that "A local authority shall not—(a) intentionally promote homosexuality or publish material with the intention of promoting homosexuality; (b) promote the teaching in any maintained school of the acceptability of homosexuality as a pretended family relationship."[39] In a similar vein, a 1992 Oregon ballot measure would have amended the state constitution to prohibit the use of state facilities to "promote, encourage, or facilitate homosexuality." It would also have required that the Oregon Department of Higher Education and the public schools, "assist in setting a standard for Oregon's youth that recognizes homosexuality ... as abnormal, wrong, unnatural and perverse and that these behaviors are to be discouraged and avoided."[40] Both "no promo homo" policies, as legal theorist Nan Hunter calls them, were antedated by the (failed) 1978 California Briggs Initiative under which any school employee could be fired for "advocating, soliciting, imposing, encouraging or promoting of private or public homosexual activity directed at, or likely to come to the attention of schoolchildren and/or other employees."[41]

Heterosexual control over standards of child mental health, over blood, adoptive, and foster parenting, and over the socialization of children in public institutions facilitates the reproduction of heterosexual society. It ensures that adult gay men and lesbians will have little say in what kinds of persons future generations will be. And even if it is not possible to make proto-gay children turn out heterosexual, gay preventative socialization practices can go some way toward ensuring that the next generation of lesbians and gays will accept as reasonable both the requirement of adopting a pseudonymous heterosexual identity as a condition of access to the public sphere and their exclusion from any socially legitimated, "nonpretended" private sphere of marriage, parenting, and the family.

It is tempting to respond to these various gay preventative strategies by arguing that pathologizing gender deviance in childhood makes little sense in a psychiatric scheme that depathologizes homosexuality; that in point of fact the children of lesbians and gays are just as likely to grow up heterosexual as are the children of heterosexuals; and that "no promo homo" policies involve censorship and the legal underwriting of one set of moral values. Though having a place, such arguments miss the deeper issue. That deeper issue concerns whether heterosexuals as a social group may legitimately claim for themselves exclusive entitlement to determine the character of future generations.

III. Constructing Gay and Lesbian Persons as Unnatural Criminals

I turn now to the stereotype of lesbians and gays as criminals which legitimizes the displacement of gays and lesbians from civil society. Again, I will begin with some historical comments about the social construction of this criminalizing identity. I will then turn to considering the effects that it has had on gays and lesbian civic status.

The moral prohibition on sodomy, understood as a crime against nature and sin against God, dates from the Middle Ages when it was part of a more general prohibition on nonreproductive sexual acts.[42] Prior to the late 1800s the prohibition on sodomy did not presuppose a special sort of actor (the homosexual), nor was sexual object choice the determinant of who counted as a sinner.[43] But with the social construction in the late 1800s of a special sort of sexual actor—the homosexual— sodomy shifts from being simply a forbidden act, like abortion or adultery, to being one among many indicators of an underlying psycho-sexual personality structure. The invention of the homosexual—the pervert, the degenerate, the sexual psychopath—opened the doors for the invention of the person for whom moral depravity and criminality were constitutive of his or her nature. Criminality and immorality come to reside less in *what* one does than *who* one is.

In *Morrison v. State Board of Education*, judicial discussion of Morrison's same-sex activity was mediated by assumptions about who Morrison was.[44] When Marc Morrison's week-long sexual relationship with a fellow teacher, Fred Schneringer, came to light, the California State Board of Education charged Morrison with immoral and unprofessional conduct, and revoked his licenses to teach secondary school and exceptional children. The court argued that the board's interpretation of "immoral conduct" was overly broad, unconnected to considerations of employees' fitness to teach, and threatened "arbitrarily [to] impair the right of the individual to live his private life, apart from his job, as he deems fit."[45] Moreover, there was no evidence that Morrison had sought improper relations with students, had failed to convey to them correct principles of morality, or that his relationship with co-workers had been affected by the incident; in short, there was no evidence of his unfitness to teach.[46] However, the particular facts that the court chose to highlight in *Morrison* do not support this line of reasoning. Instead those facts suggest that Morrison was not really a homosexual, even if he had engaged in same-sex sex. The court repeatedly stressed the "limited" nature of Morrison's homosexual relationship and observed that Morrison and Schneringer were suffering severe emotional stress at the time, that Morrison had suggested women whom Schneringer might date, that with the exception of the Schneringer incident Morrison had not had any "homosexual urges" in a dozen years, and that there was no evidence of "abnormal activities or desires" since that incident.[47] Here the court seems less interested in ascertaining whether Morrison's private conduct affected his public work performance than in ascertaining *who* Morrison really is. Is he really a homosexual, that is, a morally suspect kind of person, whose fitness to teach might reasonably be doubted? Or is he more innocently just a heterosexual performer of homosexual acts?

The image of lesbians and gays as morally depraved and prone to criminal conduct fully flowered in the McCarthy era's programs to purge the military and civil service of all "sexual perverts." Gay men and lesbians were, by their very nature, a threat to national security, an inherently subversive element in society, and "generally unsuitable" for government employment.[48] They were declared to be so by an executive order, which commanded their dismissal from all branches of government service.[49] And in 1952, Congress officially closed the national borders to immigrants with "psychopathic personalities," i.e., gays and lesbians.[50]

Because of this equation, consolidated in the 1950s, of *being* gay or lesbian with criminality and immorality, the normative status of the identities 'gay' and 'lesbian' ends up *preceding* and infecting the normative status of their acts. What makes same-sex touching, kissing, hand holding, knee-squeezing, cohabitation, and marriage wrong is neither so much their same-sexedness nor their likely eventuation in sodomy. Rather, it is their being done by a kind of person, that is, their being *homosexual* or *lesbian* acts —not just their same-sexedness. This is perhaps nowhere more clearly evident than in military policy itself. Army Regulations exempt from automatic discharge soldiers who have engaged in same-sex sex but who can prove that same-sex sexuality was a departure from customary behavior, is unlikely to recur, and is undesired.[51] As Judge Norris nicely summarizes Army policy in *Watkins v. U.S. Army*,

> If a straight soldier and a gay soldier of the same sex engage in homosexual acts because they are drunk, immature or curious, the straight soldier may remain in the Army while the gay soldier is automatically terminated. In short, the regulations do not penalize soldiers for engaging in [same-sex] acts; they penalize soldiers who have engaged in [same-sex] acts only when the Army decides that those soldiers are actually gay.[52]

The distinction between an act of same-sex sex (which can be done by either heterosexuals or non-heterosexuals) and a specifically *homosexual* act (which can only be done by homosexuals) is here out in the open. It is also out in the open in New Hampshire's statute against gay and lesbian adoption, which distinguishes between "true" homosexuals and those who have engaged in same-sex sex but can claim a heterosexual identity.[53]

The combined effect of equating homosexuality with criminality but *only* statutorily forbidding sodomy is the production of a novel civic status: the citizen-criminal. Almost everything that lesbians and gays might consider constitutive of or connected to their being lesbian or gay is legal: nonsodomitical sex practices, kissing, holding hands, membership in gay organizations, going to gay bars, holding a marriage ceremony, providing AIDS and safe sex education, publishing books about being lesbian or gay, lobbying for AIDS research funding and against anti-gay initiatives, and so on. Given the legality not just of *being* gay (viewed as some inner "tendency") but also of conducting one's life as a lesbian or gay man, anyone who is gay or lesbian might naturally conclude that they have the same citizenship status that any heterosexual has. However, because all things gay or lesbian are routinely coupled, in legal and lay imaginations, with sodomy (or child abuse, or solicitation, or some other category of illegality), nothing one does *as* a gay or lesbian person is untainted by the specter of criminality. Everything one does becomes an act of promoting criminality or immorality. And every gay-positive statement metamorphoses into an endorsement of crime or immorality.

Constructed as citizen-criminals, gay men and lesbians occupy a shadowy territory neither fully outside nor fully inside civil society. Unlike the criminally insane, whose inability to tell right from wrong disqualifies them from civic status, gays and lesbians formally possess civic status. But unlike heterosexual citizens, whose relation to crime is presumed to be merely contingent (they might or might not violate the law), gays and lesbians are presumed to be inherently implicated in criminal activity.

This citizen-criminal status gives discriminatory policies against gays and lesbians a distinctive flavor. While racial and gender discrimination are largely predicated on *inferiorizing* stereotypes, sexuality discrimination is largely predicated on *criminalizing* stereotypes whose ultimate suggestion is not that gays and lesbians are *incompetent*, but that they are *untrustworthy* members of civil society. Socially constituted as beings whose very nature it is to commit crimes against nature, God, and state, lesbians and gays, insofar as they publicly claim those identities, speak under a pall of guilt. Unlike their presumed "innocent" and civic-minded heterosexual counterparts, they cannot represent themselves as lesbian or gay without undermining their standing in the public sphere. That includes their standing to challenge conventional moral and legal norms. Heterosexuals have, for example, been extremely successful in decriminalizing heterosexual "crimes against nature," which include use of birth control, abortion, adultery, and heterosexual sodomy. Heterosexuals have also been reasonably successful in pluralizing acceptable family arrangements—divorce, single-parenting, egalitarian gender arrangements, separate husband and wife domiciles. As presumed trustworthy members of civil society, heterosexuals have the standing to claim that they simply have different moral opinions about the permissibility of "alternative" sexual and familial practices and thus have the standing to request that law and social practices recognize differences of opinion. As presumed untrustworthy members, lesbians' and gays' expression of different, disagreeing moral opinions is continuously vulnerable to being reconstituted as promotion of immorality, if not also criminality.

IV. Conclusion

To conclude: Sexuality injustice is not best understood as a matter of confining persons who are gay or lesbian to subordinate, disadvantaging, exploitable places within sexuality-structured public and private hierarchies. Thus specific measures, such as extending privacy rights and anti-discrimination protection to gay men and lesbians, should not be seen as primarily aimed at remedying systematic inequities in their material condition and access to opportunities.

Instead, sexuality injustice is, I think, better understood as a matter of displacing gays and lesbians to the "outside" of civil society, and thus denying a place for gays and lesbians within both public and private spheres. First, gay and lesbian *identities* are displaced from workplaces, streets, the military, markets, schools, and other public spaces by requiring lesbians and gays to adopt pseudonymous heterosexual identities as a condition of access to those public spaces. Displacing gay and lesbian identities from the public sphere in this way amounts to reserving the public sphere for heterosexuals only. Second, homosexuality and lesbianism are displaced from our social future via legal, educational, psychiatric, and familial practices that are aimed at insuring the heterosexuality of future generations. This institutionalization of gay preventative and heterosexual productive measures amounts to reserving for heterosexuals only exclusive entitlement to determine the character of future generations. Finally, the displacement of lesbians and gays from civil society is legitimized by equating being gay or lesbian with criminality, immorality, and untrustworthiness as a citizen. Defined as citizen-criminals, gays and lesbians are denied equal standing to participate in legal, social, and moral debates, including most importantly debates over the place of gays and lesbians in the public and private spheres.

NOTES

1. Marilyn Frye gives a classic definition of oppression: "The experience of oppressed people is that the living of one's life is confined and shaped by forces and barriers which are not accidental or occasional and hence avoidable, but are systematically related to each other in such a way as to catch one between and among them and restrict or penalize motion in any direction." *The Politics of Reality* 4 (1983).
2. I have made up the term "sexuality injustice." I would have preferred the less cumbersome term "sexual injustice," but this has long been used synonymously with "gender injustice." The only other available terms—"homophobia" and "heterosexism"—bear, like "gynophobia" and "sexism," overly strong attitudinal connotations and thus are ill-suited for describing social, structural, and conceptual features.
3. Massachusetts (Mass. Gen. L. ch. 272 §34 (1986)), Tennessee (Ten. Code Ann. §39-2-612 (1980)), Florida (Fla. Stat. §800.02 (1987)), Mississippi (Section 97-29-59, Mississippi Code of 1972).
4. 478 US at 194.
5. James D. Woods & Jay H. Lucas, *The Corporate Closet: The Professional Lives of Gay Men in America* (1993), generally, gives a thorough account of the heterosexualization of corporate life.
6. The Army at least *claimed* in *Watson* that it discriminated only on the basis of conduct not status. Judge Norris argued that Army policy could not reasonably be interpreted as drawing a conduct-status distinction (infra pp. 40-41).
7. One of the bases for separation was the fact that "[t]he member has stated that he or she is a homosexual or bisexual...." 32 *Code of Federal Regulations* Pt. 41, App. A, part 1, H.1.c.2 (1992).
8. Pat Towell, "Nunn Offers a Compromise: 'Don't Ask/Don't Tell,'" *Cong. Q. Weekly Rep.*, May 15, 1993, at 1240.
9. Michael R. Gordon, "Pentagon spells out rules for ousting homosexuals" *New York Times* Dec. 23, 1993, at A14.

10. Revealingly, General Norman Schwarzkopf testified that "homosexuals have served in the past and done a great job serving their country, and I feel they can in the future" but "it's *open* homosexuality in a unit that causes this breakdown in unit cohesion." Quoted in Anne B. Goldstein, "'Reasoning about Homosexuality: A Commentary on Janet Halley's 'Reasoning about Sodomy: Act and Identity In and After *Bowers v. Hardwick*,'" *Virginia Law Review* 1781, 1803 n.115 (1993) (emphasis added) (quoting Norman Schwarzkopf).
11. 530 F. 2d 247 (9th Cir. 1976).
12. Ibid. at 250 (quoting Civil Service Commission letter to Singer).
13. Ibid. at 249 (summarizing Commission letter to Singer).
14. Ibid. at 251.
15. Ibid. at 255.
16. Although some women would find it easier than others to conceal their gender and adopt a pseudonymously male identity (just as some gay men and lesbians find it easier than others to adopt a pseudonymous heterosexual identity), the status-conduct distinction would permit the military or any other institution that adopted such a policy to claim that it was not discriminating against persons who are women, but only against womanly conduct.
17. The example is not entirely fictional. While claiming not to discriminate against persons because they are women or black, employers may penalize employees for not exhibiting sufficiently masculine or white traits. The disanalogy between gay men and lesbians on the one hand and women and blacks on the other is perhaps best understood as one of degree.
18. *Rowland* 730 F.2d at 449.
19. Ibid. at 452-453.
20. *Rowland* 470 U.S. at 1012.
21. Ibid.
22. *Rowland*, 730 F.2d at 450.
23. Havelock Ellis, *Studies in the Psychology of Sex, Vol. II: Sexual Inversion* (1928). Richard von Krafft-Ebing, *Psychopathia Sexualis: A Medico-Forensic Study* (1947).
24. Allan Bérubé, *Coming Out Under Fire: A History of Gay Men and Women in World War II* 136-138 (1990) [hereafter Bérubé].
25. 32 *Code of Federal Regulations* Pt. 41, App. A, part 1, H.1.c.1 (1992).
26. John Lauritsen and David Thorstad, *The Early Homosexual Rights Movement, 1864-1935* (1974) [hereafter Lauritsen].
27. Eve Kosofsky Sedgwick, "How to Bring Your Kids up Gay," in *Fear of a Queer Planet: Queer Politics and Social Theory* (Michael Warner ed. 1993) 69.
28. American Psychiatric Association, *Diagnostic and Statistical Manual of Mental Disorders*, (3rd ed., 1980) (DSM-III). The American Psychiatric Association de-pathologized homosexuality in 1973, although DSM-III was not published until 1980.
29. Ibid. at 266.
30. American Psychiatric Association, *Diagnostic and Statistical Manual*, 73 (3rd revised ed., 1987), (DSM-III-R).
31. Ibid.
32. Dignified treatment of gay men and lesbians within psychiatry has not, of course, always been the norm. Efforts to "cure" gay men and lesbians reached their peak during the 1950s and 1960s. For an autobiographical account, see Martin Duberman, *Cures: A Gay Man's Odyssey* (1992).
33. Sedgwick supra note 27, at 78.
34. Sharon Elizabeth Rush, "Breaking with Tradition: Surrogacy and Gay Fathers," in *Kindred Matters: Rethinking the Philosophy of the Family* 102, 119 (Diana Tietjens Meyers, Kenneth Kipnis, and Cornelius F. Murphy eds., 1993).
35. *Gay Lib v. University of Missouri* 558 F.2d 848, 852 (1977) (summarizing the Board of Curators of the University of Missouri's resolution).
36. Ibid. at 859.
37. Quoted in *Opinion of the Justices*, Supreme Court of New Hampshire, 530 A.2d 21, 23 (N.H. 1987).
38. Ibid. at 25.
39. Quoted in Jeffrey Weeks, "Pretended Family Relationships," in *Against Nature: Essays on History, Sexuality, and Identity* 134, 137 (1991). Weeks also provides a socio-historical analysis of why the family became a focus of British legal attention.
40. Timothy Egan, "Oregon Measure Asks State to Repress Homosexuality," *New York Times*, August 16, 1992, at A34.
41. Cal. Proposition 6, § 3(b)(2) (1978). Quoted in Nan D. Hunter, "Identity, Speech, and Equality," 79 *Virginia Law Review* 1695 (1993) at 1703. She gives a detailed account of the full range of no promo homo policies.

42. John Boswell, "Categories, Experience and Sexuality," in *Forms of Desire: Sexual Orientation and the Social Constructionist Controversy* 157-158 (Edward Stein ed., 1990).
43. Ibid. at 159.
44. 461 P.2d 375 (Cal. 1969).
45. Ibid. at 394.
46. Ibid. at 392.
47. Ibid. at 377-378.
48. *Employment of Homosexuals and Other Sex Perverts in Government*, Interim Report by the Subcomm. for Comm. on Expenditure in the Exec. Dep'ts, S. Doc. 24, 81st Cong., 2d Sess. (1950), 3.
49. Executive Order 10,450. 18 *Fed. Reg.* 2489 (1953).
50. Immigration and Nationality Act, Pub. L. No. 82-414, 66 Stat. 163 (1952). For an historical account of the McCarthy era purge of homosexuals, see Bérubé supra note 24.
51. Lauritsen supra note 26.
52. 875 F.2d 699, 715 (9th Cir. 1989) (Judge Norris, concurring). For clarity, I have substituted "same-sex" for "homosexual" in the original text.
53. *Opinion of the Justices* 530 A.2d at 24.

AGAINST MARRIAGE AND MOTHERHOOD

Claudia Card

Claudia Card teaches in the Philosophy Department as well as in Women's Studies and Environmental Studies at the University of Wisconsin, Madison. She is the author of Lesbian Choices *(Columbia, 1995) and* The Unnatural Lottery: Character and Moral Luck *(Temple, 1996) and the editor of* Adventures in Lesbian Philosophy *(Indiana, 1994),* Feminist Ethics *(Kansas, 1991), and* Feminist Ethics at the Turn of the Millennium *(Kansas, 1999).*

This essay argues that current advocacy of lesbian and gay rights to legal marriage and parenthood insufficiently criticizes both marriage and motherhood as they are currently practiced and structured by Northern legal institutions. Instead we would do better not to let the State define our intimate unions and parenting would be improved if the power presently concentrated in the hands of one or two guardians were diluted and distributed through an appropriately concerned community.

The title of this essay is deliberately provocative, because I fear that radical feminist perspectives on marriage and motherhood are in danger of being lost in the quest for equal rights. My concerns, however, are specific. I am skeptical of using the institution of motherhood as a source of paradigms for ethical theory. And I am skeptical of legal marriage as a way to gain a better life for lesbian and gay lovers or as a way to provide a supportive environment of lesbian and gay parents and their children. Of course, some are happy with marriage and motherhood as they now exist. My concern is with the price of that joy borne by those trapped by marriage or motherhood and deeply unlucky in the company they find there. Nevertheless, nothing that I say is intended to disparage the characters of many magnificent women who have struggled in and around these institutions to make the best of a trying set of options.

Reprinted with permission of the publisher and Claudia Card from *Hypatia* 11:3 (Summer 1996): 1–23.

Backgrounds

My perspective on marriage is influenced not only by other's written reports and analyses but also by my own history of being raised in a lower-middle-class white village family by parents married (to each other) for more than three decades, by my first-hand experiences of urban same-sex domestic partnerships lasting from two and one half to nearly seven years (good ones and bad, some racially mixed, some white, generally mixed in class and religious backgrounds), and by my more recent experience as a lesbianfeminist whose partner of the past decade is not a domestic partner. My perspective on child rearing is influenced not by my experience as a mother, but by my experience as a daughter reared by a full-time mother-housewife, by having participated heavily in the raising of my younger siblings, and by having grown to adulthood in a community in which many of the working-class and farming families exemplified aspects of what bell hooks calls "revolutionary parenting" (hooks 1984, 133-46).

bell hooks writes, "Childrearing is a responsibility that can be shared with other childrearers, with people who do not live with children. This form of parenting is revolutionary in this society because it takes place in opposition to the idea that parents, especially mothers, should be the only childrearers. Many people raised in black communities experienced this type of community-based child care" (hooks 1984, 144). This form of child rearing may be more common than is generally acknowledged in a society in which those whose caretaking does not take place in a nuclear family are judged by those with the power to set standards as unfortunate and deprived. Although bell hooks continues to use the language of "mothering" to some extent in elaborating "revolutionary parenting," I see this revolution as offering an alternative to mothering as a social institution.

Because it appears unlikely that the legal rights of marriage and motherhood in the European American models of those institutions currently at issue in our courts will disappear or even be seriously eroded during my lifetime, my opposition to them here takes the form of skepticism primarily in the two areas mentioned above: ethical theorizing and lesbian/gay activism. I believe that women who identify as lesbian or gay should be reluctant to put our activist energy into attaining legal equity with heterosexuals in marriage and motherhood—not because the existing discrimination against us is in any way justifiable but because these institutions are so deeply flawed that they seem to me unworthy of emulation and reproduction.

For more than a decade, feminist philosophers and lesbian/gay activists have been optimistic about the potentialities of legal marriage and legitimated motherhood. This should be surprising, considering the dismal political genealogies of those institutions, which have been generally admitted and widely publicized by feminist thinkers. Yet, in the project of claiming historically characteristic life experiences of women as significant data for moral theory, many are turning to women's experiences as mothers for ethical insight. Not all focus on marriage and motherhood. Feminist philosophers are taking as valuable theoretical paradigms for ethics many kinds of caring relationships that have been salient in women's lives. Marilyn Friedman, for example, has explored female friendship in *What Are Friends For?* (1993). Sarah Hoagland (1988) offers value inquiry based on experiences of lesbian bonding in many forms. *Mothering*, edited by Joyce Trebilcot (1983), includes essays representing critical as well as supportive stances regarding motherhood. These works, however, are exceptions to a wider trend of theorizing that draws mainly positive inspiration from the experiences of women as mothers. Thus, Sara Ruddick's *Maternal Thinking* (1989), which acknowledges the need for caution, is devoted to developing ethical ideas based on experiences of mother-child relationships. Nel Noddings's *Caring* (1984) and Virginia Held's *Feminist Morality* (1993) likewise take inspiration from the experience of "mothering persons" and other caregivers, and to some extent, Annette Baier does likewise in *Moral Prejudices* (1994). These last four philosophers urge an extension of mothering values to more public realms of activity.

In *Black Feminist Thought* Patricia Hill Collins also speaks of "a more generalized ethic of caring and personal accountability among African-American women who often feel accountable to all the Black community's children" (1991, chap.6). Her models for an "ethic of caring and personal accountability," however, differ significantly from the models characteristic of the work of so many white feminists in that her models already involve a wider community that includes "othermothers" as well as "bloodmothers," models elaborated by bell hooks as instances of "revolutionary parenting" (hooks 1984, 133-46). My skepticism is not aimed at such "revolutionary parenting" which I find has much to recommend it. Yet "parenting" by a wider community is a form of child care not currently enshrined in Northern legal systems. It is not the model guiding lesbian and gay activists currently agitating for equal rights before the law. For more communal child care, the language of "mothering" and even "parenting" is somewhat misleading in that these practices are not particularly "mother-centered" or even "parent-centered" but are centered on the needs of children and of the community.

Audre Lorde, who wrote about her relationship with her son (1984, 72-80), has left us with reflections on yet another model of parenting, that of a lesbian relationship struggling against the models of heterosexual marriage and patriarchal motherhood in her social environment. Nevertheless, she does not attempt to generalize from her experience or to treat it as a source of inspiration for ethical theory.

When confronted with my negative attitudes toward marriage and motherhood, some recoil as though I were proposing that we learn to do without water and oxygen on the ground that both are polluted (even killing us). Often, I believe, this reaction comes from certain assumptions that the reader or hearer may be inclined to make, which I here note in order to set aside at the outset.

First, my opposition to marriage is not an opposition to intimacy, nor to long-term relationships of intimacy, nor to durable partnerships of many sorts.[1] I understand marriage as a relationship to which the State is an essential third party. Also, like the practices of footbinding and suttee, which, according to the researches of Mary Daly (1978, 113-52), originated among the powerful classes, marriage in Europe was once available only to those with substantial social power. Previously available only to members of propertied classes, the marriage relation has come to be available in modern Northern democracies to any adult heterosexual couple neither of whom is already married to someone else. This is what lesbian and gay agitation for the legal right to marry is about. This is what I find calls for extreme caution.

Second, my opposition to motherhood is neither an opposition to the guidance, education, and caretaking of children nor an opposition to the formation of many kinds of bonds between children and adults.[2] Nor am I opposed to the existence of homes, as places of long-term residence with others of a variety of ages with whom one has deeply committed relationships. When "the family" is credited with being a bulwark against a hostile world, as in the case of many families in the African and Jewish disaporas, the bulwark that is meant often consists of a variety of deeply committed personal (as opposed to legal) relationships and the stability of caring that they represent, or home as a site of these things. The bulwark is not the legitimation (often precarious or nonexistent) of such relationships through institutions of the State. The State was often one of the things that these relationships formed a bulwark against.

Marriage and motherhood in the history of modern patriarchies have been mandatory for and oppressive to women, and they have been criticized by feminists on those grounds. My concerns, however, are as much for the children as for the women that some of these children become and for the goal of avoiding the reproduction of patriarchy. Virginia Held, one optimist about the potentialities of marriage and motherhood, finds motherhood to be part of a larger conception of family, which she takes to be constructed of noncontractual relationships. She notes that although Marxists and recent communitarians might agree with her focus on noncontractual relationships, their views remain uninformed by feminist critiques of patriarchal families. The family from which she would have society and ethical theorists learn, ultimately, is a postpatriarchal family. But what is a "postpatriarchal family"? Is it a coherent concept?

"Family" is itself a family resemblance concept. Many contemporary lesbian and gay partnerships, households, and friendship networks fit no patriarchal stereotypes and are not sanctified by legal marriage, although their members still regard themselves as "family."[3] But should they? Many social institutions, such as insurance companies, do not honor such conceptions of "family." Family, as understood in contexts where material benefits tend to be at stake, is not constituted totally by noncontractual relationships. At its core is to be found one or more marriage contracts. For those who work to enlarge the concept of family to include groupings that are currently totally noncontractual, in retaining patriarchal vocabulary there is a danger of importing patriarchal ideals and of inviting treatment as deviant or "second class" at best.

"Family," our students learn in Women's Studies 101, comes from the Latin familia, meaning "household," which in turn came from *famulus*, which according to the OED, meant "servant." The ancient Roman *paterfamilias* was the head of a household of servants and slaves, including his wife or wives, concubines, and children. He had the power of life and death over them. The ability of contemporary male heads of households to get away with battering, incest, and murder suggests to many feminists that the family has not evolved into anything acceptable yet. Would a household of persons whose relationships with each other transcended (as those families do) sojourns under one roof continue to be rightly called "family" if no members had significant social support for treating other members abusively? Perhaps the postpatriarchal relationships envisioned by Virgina Held and by so many lesbians and gay men should be called something else, to mark that radical departure from family history. But it is not just a matter of a word. It is difficult to imagine what such relationships would be.

In what follows, I say more about marriage than about motherhood, because it is legal marriage that sets the contexts in which and the background against which motherhood has been legitimated, and it defines contexts in which mothering easily becomes disastrous for children.

Lesbian (or Gay) Marriage?

A special vantage point is offered by the experience of lesbians and gay men, among whom there is currently no consensus (although much strong feeling on both sides) on whether to pursue the legal right to marry a same-sex lover (Blumenfeld, Wolfson, and Brownworth, all 1996). When heterosexual partners think about marriage, they usually consider the more limited question whether they (as individuals) should marry (each other) and if they did not marry, what the consequences would be for children they might have or raise. They consider this in the context of a State that gives them the legal option of marriage. Lesbians and gay men are currently in the position of having to consider the larger question whether the legal option of marriage is a good idea, as we do not presently have it in relation to our lovers. We have it, of course, in relation to the other sex, and many have exercised it as a cover, as insurance, for resident alien status, and so forth. If it is because we already have rights to marry heterosexually that right-wing attackers of lesbian or gay rights complain of our wanting "special rights," we should reply that, of course, any legalization of same-sex marriage should extend that "privilege" to heterosexuals as well.

The question whether lesbians and gay men should pursue the right to marry is not the same as the question whether the law is wrong in its refusal to honor same-sex marriages. Richard Mohr (1994, 31-53) defends gay marriage from that point of view as well as I have seen it done. Evan Wolfson develops powerfully an analogy between the denial of marriage to same-sex couples and the antimiscegenation laws that were overturned in the United States just little more than a quarter century ago (Wolfson 1996). What I have to say should apply to relationships between lovers (or parents) of different races as well as to those of same-sex lovers (or parents). The ways we have been treated are abominable. But it does not follow that we should seek legal marriage.

It is one thing to argue that others are wrong to deny us something and another to argue that what they would deny us is something we should fight for the right to have. I do not deny that others are wrong to exclude same-sex lovers and lovers of different races from the rights of marriage. I question only whether we should fight for those rights, even if we do not intend to exercise them. Suppose that slave-owning in some mythical society were denied to otherwise free women, on the ground that such women as slave-owners would pervert the institution of slavery. Women (both free and unfree) could (unfortunately) document empirically the falsity of beliefs underlying such grounds. It would not follow that women should fight for the right to own slaves, or even for the rights of other women to own slaves. Likewise, if marriage is a deeply flawed institution, even though it is a special injustice to exclude lesbians and gay men arbitrarily from participating in it, it would not necessarily advance the cause of justice on the whole to remove the special injustice of discrimination.

About same-sex marriage I feel something like the way I feel about prostitution. Let us, by all means, *decriminalize* sodomy and so forth. Although marriage rights would be *sufficient* to enable lovers to have sex legally, such rights should not be necessary for that purpose. Where they *are* legally necessary and also available for protection against the social oppression of same-sex lovers, as for lovers of different races, there will be enormous pressure to marry. Let us not pretend that marriage is basically a good thing on the ground that durable intimate relationships are. Let us not be eager to have the State regulate our unions. Let us work to remove barriers to our enjoying some of the privileges presently available only to heterosexual married couples. But in doing so, we should also be careful not to support discrimination against those who choose not to marry and not to support continued state definition of the legitimacy of intimate relationships. I would rather see the state *de*regulate heterosexual marriage than see it begin to regulate same-sex marriage.

As the child of parents married to each other for thirty-two years, I once thought I knew what marriage meant, even though laws vary from one jurisdiction to another and the dictionary, as Mohr notes, sends us around in a circle, referring us to "husband" and "wife," in turn defined by "marriage." Mohr argues convincingly that "marriage" need not presuppose the gendered concepts of "husband" and "wife" (1994, 31-53). I will not rehearse that ground here. History seems to support him. After reading cover to cover and with great interest John Boswell's *Same-Sex Unions in Premodern Europe* (1994), however, I no longer feel so confident that I know when a "union" counts as a "marriage." Boswell, who discusses many kinds of unions, refrains from using the term "marriage" to describe the same-sex unions he researched, even though they were sanctified by religious ceremonies. Some understandings of such unions, apparently, did not presuppose that the partners were not at the same time married to someone of the other sex.

Mohr, in his suggestions for improving marriage law by attending to the experience of gay men, proposes that sexual fidelity not be a requirement (1994, 49-50). What would remain without such a requirement, from a legal point of view, sounds to me like mutual *adoption*, or guardianship. Adoption, like marriage, is a way to become next-of-kin. This could have substantial economic consequences. But is there any good reason to restrict mutual adoption to two parties at a time? If mutual adoption is what we want, perhaps the law of adoption is what we should use, or suitably amend. And yet the law of adoption is not without its problematic aspects, some similar to those of the law of marriage. For it does not specify precisely a guardian's rights and responsibilities. Perhaps those who want legal contracts with each other would do better to enter into contracts the contents of which and duration of which they specifically define.

As noted above, my partner of the past decade is not a domestic partner. She and I form some kind of fairly common social unit which, so far as I know, remains nameless. Along with such namelessness goes a certain invisibility, a mixed blessing to which I will return. We do not share a domicile (she has her house; I have mine). Nor do we form an economic unit (she pays her bills; I pay mine). Although we certainly have fun together, our relationship is not based simply on fun. We share the sorts of mundane details of daily living that Mohr finds constitutive of marriage (often in her house, often in mine). We know a whole lot about each other's lives that the neighbors and our other friends will never know. In times of trouble, we are each other's first line of defense, and in times of need, we are each other's main support. Still, we are not married. Nor do we yearn to marry. Yet if marrying became an option that would legitimate behavior otherwise illegitimate and make available to us social securities that will no doubt become even more important to us as we age, we and many others like us might be pushed into marriage. Marrying under such conditions is not a totally free choice.

Because of this unfreedom, I find at least four interconnected kinds of problems with marriage. Three may be somewhat remediable in principle, although if they were remedied, many might no longer have strong motives to marry. I doubt that the fourth problem, which I also find most important, is fixable.

The first problem, perhaps easiest to remedy in principle (if not in practice) is that employers and others (such as units of government) often make available only to legally married couples benefits that anyone could be presumed to want, married or not, such as affordable health and dental insurance, the right to live in attractive residential areas, visitation rights in relation to significant others, and so forth. Spousal benefits for employees are a significant portion of many workers' compensation. Thus married workers are often, in effect, paid more for the same labor than unmarried workers (Berzon 1988, 266; Pierce 1995, 5). This is one way in which people who do not have independent access to an income often find themselves economically pressured into marrying. Historically, women have been in this position oftener than men, including, of course, most pre-twentieth century lesbians, many of whom married men for economic security.

The second problem is that even though divorce by mutual consent is now generally permitted in the United States, the consequences of divorce can be so difficult that many who should divorce do not. This to some extent is a continuation of the benefits problem. But also, if one partner can sue the other for support or receive a share of the other's assets to which they would not otherwise have been legally entitled, there are new economic motives to preserve emotionally disastrous unions.

The third issue, which would be seriously troublesome for many lesbians, is that legal marriage as currently understood in Northern democracies is monogamous in the sense of one *spouse* at a time, even though the law in many states no longer treats "adultery" (literally "pollution") as criminal. Yet many of us have more than one long-term intimate relationship during the same time period. Any attempt to change the current understanding of marriage so as to allow plural marriage partners (with plural contracts) would have economic implications that I have yet to see anyone explore.

Finally, the fourth problem, the one that I doubt is fixable (depending on what "marriage" means) is that the legal rights of access that married partners have to each other's persons, property, and lives makes it all but impossible for a spouse to defend herself (or himself), or to be protected against torture, rape, battery, stalking, mayhem, or murder by the other spouse. Spousal murder accounts for a substantial number of murders each year. This factor is made worse by the presence of the second problem mentioned above (difficulties of divorce that lead many to remain married when they should not), which provide motives to violence within marriages. Legal marriage thus enlists state support for conditions conducive to murder and mayhem.

The point is not that all marriages are violent. It is not about the frequency of violence, although the frequency appears high. The points are, rather, that the institution places obstacles in the way of protecting spouses (however many) who need it and is conducive to violence in relationships that go bad. Battery is, of course, not confined to spouses. Lesbian and gay battery is real (see Renzetti 1992; Lobel 1986; Island and Letellier 1991). But the law does not protect unmarried batterers or tend to preserve the relationships of unmarried lovers in the way that it protects husbands and tends to preserve marriages.

Why, then, would anyone marry? Because it is a tradition, glorified and romanticized. It grants status. It is a significant (social) mark of adulthood for women in patriarchy. It is a way to avoid certain hassles from one's family of origin and from society at large—hassles to oneself, to one's lover (if there is only one), and to children with whom one may live or whom one may bring into being. We need better traditions. And women have long needed other social marks of adulthood and ways to escape families of origin.

Under our present exclusion from the glories of legal matrimony, the usual reason why lesbians or gay men form partnerships and stay together is because we care for each other. We may break up for other kinds or reasons (such as one of us being assigned by an employer to another part of the country and neither of us being able to afford to give up our jobs). But when we stay together, that is usually because of how we feel about each other and about our life together. Consider how this basic taken-for-granted fact might change if we could marry with the State's blessings. There are many material benefits to tempt those who can into marrying, not to mention the improvement in one's social reputation as a reliable citizen (and for those of us who are not reliable citizens, the protection against having a spouse forced to testify against us in court).

Let us consider each of these four problems further. The first was that of economic and other benefits, such as insurance that employers often make available only to marrieds, the right of successorship to an apartment, inheritance rights, and the right to purchase a home in whatever residential neighborhood one can afford. The attachment of such benefits to marital status is a problem in two respects. First, because the benefits are substantial, not trivial, they offer an ulterior motive for turning a lover relationship into a marriage—even for pretending to care for someone, deceiving oneself as well as others. As Emma Goldman argued in the early twentieth century, when marriage becomes an insurance policy, it may no longer be compatible with love (1969). Second, the practice of making such benefits available only to marrieds discriminates against those who, for whatever reason, do not marry. Because of the first factor, many heterosexuals who do not fundamentally approve of legal marriage give in and marry anyhow. Because of the second factor, many heterosexual feminists, however, refuse legal marriage (although the State may regard their relationships as common law marriages).

Now add to the spousal benefits problem the second difficulty, that of the consequences of getting a divorce (for example, consequences pertaining to shared property, alimony, or child support payments and difficulties in terms of access to children), especially if the divorce is not friendly. Intimate partnerships beginning from sexual or erotic attraction tend to be of limited viability, even under favorable circumstances. About half of all married couples in the United States at present get divorced, and probably most of the other half should. But the foreseeable consequences of divorce provide motives to stay married for many spouses who no longer love each other (if they ever did) and have even grown to hate each other. Staying married ordinarily hampers one's ability to develop a satisfying lover relationship with someone new. As long as marriage is monogamous in the sense of one *spouse* at a time, it interferes with one's ability to obtain spousal benefits for a new lover. When spouses grow to hate each other, the access that was a joy as lovers turns into something highly dangerous. I will return to this.

Third, the fact of multiple relationships is a problem even for relatively good marriages. Mohr, as noted, argues in favor of reforming marriage so as not to require sexual exclusiveness rather than officially permitting only monogamy. Yet he was thinking not of multiple *spouses* but of a monogamous marriage in which neither partner expects sexual exclusiveness of the other. Yet, one spouse per person is monogamy, however promiscuous the spouses may be. The advantages that Mohr enumerates as among the perks of marriage apply only to spouses, not to relationships with additional significant others who are not one's spouses. Yet the same reasons that lead one to want those benefits for a spouse can lead one to want them for additional significant others. If lesbian and gay marriages were acknowledged in Northern democracies today, they would be legally as monogamous as heterosexual marriage, regardless of the number of one's actual sexual partners. This does not reflect the relationships that many lesbians and gay men have or want.

Boswell wrote about same-sex unions that did not preclude simultaneous heterosexual marriages (1994). The parties were not permitted to formalize unions with more than one person of the same sex at a time, however. Nor were they permitted to have children with a person of the other sex to whom they were not married. Thus, in a certain restricted sense, each formal union was monogamous, even though one could have both kinds at once.

Christine Pierce argues, in support of the option to legalize lesbian and gay marriages, that lesbian and gay images have been cast too much in terms of individuals—*The Well Of Loneliness* (Hall 1950), for example—and not enough in terms of relationships, especially serious relationships involving long-term commitments (Pierce 1995, 13). Marriage gives visibility to people "as couples, partners, family, and kin," a visibility that lesbians and gay men have lacked and that could be important to dispelling negative stereotypes and assumptions that our relationships do not embody many of the same ideals as those of many heterosexual couples, partners, family, and kin (Pierce 1996). This is both true and important.

It is not clear, however, that legal marriage would offer visibility to our relationships as they presently exist. It might well change our relationships so that they became more like heterosexual marriages, loveless after the first few years but hopelessly bogged down with financial entanglements or children (adopted or products of turkey-baster insemination or previous marriages), making separation or divorce (at least in the near future) too difficult to contemplate, giving rise to new motives for mayhem and murder. Those who never previously felt pressure to marry a lover might confront not just new options but new pressures and traps.

My views on marriage may surprise those familiar with my work on the military ban (Card 1995). For I have argued against the ban and in favor of lesbian and gay access to military service, and I argued that even those who disapprove of the military should object to wrongful exclusions of lesbians and gay men. In the world in which we live, military institutions may well be less dispensable than marriage, however in need of restraint military institutions are. But for those who find legal marriage and legitimate motherhood objectionable, should I be moved here by what moved me there—that it is one thing not to exercise an option and another to be denied the option, that denying us the option for no good reason conveys that there is something wrong with us, thereby contributing to our public disfigurement and defamation, and that these considerations give us good reasons to protest being denied the option even if we never intend to exercise it? I am somewhat but not greatly moved by such arguments in this case. The case of marriage seems to me more like the case of slavery than like that of the military.

Marriage and military service are in many ways relevantly different. Ordinarily, marriage (like slavery) is much worse, if only because its impact on our lives is usually greater. Marriage is supposed to be a lifetime commitment. It is at least open-ended. When available, it is not simply an option but tends to be coercive, especially for women in a misogynist society. For those who choose it, it threatens to be a dangerous trap. Military service is ordinarily neither a lifetime nor open-ended commitment; one signs up for a certain number of years. During war, one may be drafted (also for a limited time) and, of course, even killed, but the issue has not been whether to draft lesbians and gay men. Past experience shows that gay men will be drafted in war, even if barred from enlistment in peace. When enlistment is an option, it does not threaten to trap one in a relationship from which it will be extremely difficult to extricate oneself in the future. There is some analogy with the economically coercive aspect for the marriage "option." Because those who have never served are ineligible for substantial educational and health benefits, many from low- (or no-) income families enlist to obtain such things as college education and even health and dental insurance. However, the service one has to give for such benefits as an enlistee is limited compared to spousal service. Being killed is a risk in either case.

In such a context, pointing out that many marriages are very loving, not at all violent, and proclaim to the world two people's honorable commitment to each other, seems to me analogous to pointing out, as many slave-owners did, that many slave-owners were truly emotionally bonded with their slaves, that they did not whip them, and that even the slaves were proud and honored to be the slaves of such masters.

Some of the most moving stories I hear in discussions of gay marriage point out that the care rendered the ill by families is a great service to society and that the chosen families of gay AIDS patients deserve to be honored in the same way as a family based on a heterosexual union. The same, of course, applies to those who care for lesbian or gay cancer patients of for those with severe disabilities or other illnesses. But is this a service to society? Or to the State? The State has a history of depending on families to provide care that no human being should be without in infancy, illness, and old age. Lesbians and gay men certainly have demonstrated our ability to serve the State in this capacity as well as heterosexuals. But where does this practice leave those who are not members of families? Or those who object on principle to being members of these unions as sanctified by the State?

To remedy the injustices of discrimination against lesbians, gay men, and unmarried heterosexual couples, many municipalities are experimenting with domestic partnership legislation. This may be a step in the right direction, insofar as it is a much more voluntary relationship, more specific, more easily dissolved. Yet, partners who are legally married need not share a domicile unless one of them so chooses; in this respect, eligibility for the benefits of domestic partnership may be more restrictive than marriage. And the only domestic partnership legislation that I have seen requires that one claim only one domestic partner at a time, which does not distinguish it from monogamous marriage (see Berzon 1988, 163-82).

Whatever social unions the State may sanction, it is important to realize that they become State-defined, however they may have originated. One's rights and privileges as a spouse can change dramatically with one's residence, as Betty Mahmoody discovered when she went with her husband to Iran for what he had promised would be a temporary visit (Mahmoody with Hoffer 1987). She found after arriving in Iran that she had no legal right to leave without her husband's consent, which he then denied her, leaving as her only option for returning to the United States to escape illegally (which she did). Even if a couple would not be legally recognized as married in a particular jurisdiction, if they move from another jurisdiction in which they *were* legally recognized as married, they are generally legally recognized as married in the new jurisdiction, and they are held to whatever responsibilities the new jurisdiction enforces. The case of Betty Mahmoody is especially interesting because it involves her husband's right of access. Spousal rights of access do not have the same sort of contingency in relation to marriage as, say, a right to family rates for airline tickets.

Marriage is a legal institution the obligations of which tend to be highly informal—i.e., loosely defined, unspecific, and inexplicit about exactly what one is to do and about the consequences of failing. In this regard, a marriage contract differs from the contract of a bank loan. In a legal loan contract, the parties' reciprocal obligations become highly formalized. In discharging the obligations of a loan, one dissolves the obligation. In living up to marriage obligations, however, one does not dissolve the marriage or its obligations; if anything, one strengthens them. As I have argued elsewhere, the obligations of marriage and those of loan contracts exhibit different paradigms (Card 1988, 1990). The debtor paradigm is highly formal, whereas the obligations of spouses tend to be relatively informal and fit better a paradigm that I have called the trustee paradigm. The obligations of a trustee, or guardian, are relatively abstractly defined. A trustee or guardian is expected to exercise judgment and discretion in carrying out the obligations to care, protect, or maintain. The trustee *status* may be relatively formal—precisely defined regarding dates on which it takes effect, compensation for continuing in good standing, and the consequences of losing the status. But consequences of failing to do this or that specific thing may not be specified or specifiable, because what is required to fulfill duties of caring, safekeeping, protection, or maintenance can be expected to vary with circumstances, changes in which may not be readily foreseeable. A large element of discretion seems ineliminable. This makes it difficult *to hold a trustee accountable for abuses* while the status of trustee is retained, and it also means that it is difficult to prove that the status should be terminated. Yet the only significant sanction against a trustee may be withdrawal of that status. Spousal status and parental status fit the trustee model, rather than the debtor model, of obligation. This means that it is difficult to hold a spouse or a parent accountable for abuse.

Central to the idea of marriage, historically, has been intimate access to the persons, belongings, activities, even histories of one another. More important than sexual access, marriage gives spouses physical access to each other's residences and belongings, and it gives access to information about each other, including financial status, that other friends and certainly the neighbors do not ordinarily have. For all that has been said about the privacy that marriage protects, what astonishes me is how much privacy one gives up in marrying.

This mutual access appears to be a central point of marrying. Is it wise to abdicate legally one's privacy to that extent? What interests does it serve? Anyone who in fact cohabits with another may seem to give up similar privacy. Yet, without marriage, it is possible to take one's life back without encountering the law as an obstacle. One may even be able to enlist legal help in getting it back. In this regard, uncloseted lesbians and gay men presently have a certain advantage—which, by the way, "palimony" suits threaten to undermine by applying the idea of "common law" marriage to same-sex couples (see, e.g., Faulkner with Nelson 1993).

Boswell argued that, historically, what has been important to marriage is consent, not sexual relations. But, consent to what? What is the point of marrying? Historically, for the propertied classes, he notes, the point of heterosexual marriage was either dynastic or property concerns or both. Dynastic concerns do not usually figure in arguments for lesbian or gay marriage. Although property concerns do, they are among the kinds of concerns often better detached from marriage. That leaves as a central point of marriage the legal right of cohabitation and the access to each other's lives that this entails.

It might still be marriage if sexual exclusivity, or even sex, were not part of it, but would it still be marriage if rights of cohabitation were not part of it? Even marrieds who voluntarily live apart retain the *right* of cohabitation. Many rights and privileges available to marrieds today might exist in a real relationship that did not involve cohabitation rights (for example, insurance rights, access to loved ones in hospitals, rights to inherit, and many other rights presently possessed by kin who do not live with each other). If the right of cohabitation is central to the concept of legal marriage, it deserves more critical attention that philosophers have given it.

Among the trappings of marriage that have received attention and become controversial, ceremonies and rituals are much discussed. I have no firm opinions about ceremonies or rituals. A far more important issue seems to me to be the marriage *license*, which receives hardly any attention at all. Ceremonies affirming a relationship can take place at any point in the relationship. But a license is what one needs to initiate a legal marriage. To marry legally, one applies to the state for a license, and marriage, once entered into, licenses spouses to certain kinds of access to each other's persons and lives. It is a mistake to think of a license as simply enhancing everyone's freedom. One person's license, in this case, can be another's prison. Prerequisites for marriage licenses are astonishingly lax. Anyone of a certain age, not presently married to someone else, and free of certain communicable diseases automatically qualifies. A criminal record for violent crimes is, to my knowledge, no bar. Compare this with other licenses, such as a driver's license. In Wisconsin, to retain a drive's license, we submit periodically to eye exams. Some states have more stringent requirements. To obtain a driver's license, all drivers have to pass a written and a behind-the wheel test to demonstrate knowledge and skill. In Madison, Wisconsin, even to adopt a cat from the humane society, we have to fill out a form demonstrating knowledge of relevant ordinances for pet-guardians. Yet to marry, applicants need demonstrate no knowledge of the laws pertaining to marriage nor any relationship skills nor even the modicum of self-control required to respect another human being. And once the marriage exists, the burden of proof is always on those who would dissolve it, never on those who would continue it in perpetuity.

Further disanalogies between drivers' and marriage licenses confirm that in our society there is greater concern for victims of bad driving than for those of bad marriages. You cannot legally drive without a license, whereas it is now in many jurisdictions not illegal for unmarried adults of whatever sex to cohabit. One can acquire the status of spousehood simply by cohabiting heterosexually for several years, whereas one does not acquire a driver's license simply by driving for years without one. Driving without the requisite skills and scruples is recognized as a great danger to others and treated accordingly. No comparable recognition is given the dangers of legally sanctioning the access of one person to the person and life of another without evidence of the relevant knowledge and scruples of those so licensed. The consequence is that married victims of partner battering and rape have less protection than anyone except children. What is at stake are permanently disabling and life-threatening injuries, for those who survive. I do not, at present, see how this vulnerability can be acceptably removed from the institution of legal marriage. Measures could be taken to render its disastrous consequences less likely than they are presently but at the cost of considerable state intrusion into our lives.

The right of cohabitation seems to me central to the question whether legal marriage can be made an acceptable institution, especially to the question whether marriage can be envisaged in such a way that its partners could protect themselves, or be protected, adequately against spousal rape and battery. Although many states now recognize on paper the crimes of marital rape and stalking and are better educated than before about marital battering, the progress has been mostly on paper. Wives continue to die daily at a dizzying rate.

Thus I conclude that legalizing lesbian and gay marriage, turning a personal commitment into a license regulable and enforceable by the state, is probably a very bad idea and that lesbians and gay men are probably better off, all things considered, without the "option" (and its consequent pressures) to obtain and act on such a license, despite some of the immediate material and spiritual gains to some of being able to do so. Had we any chance of success, we might do better to agitate for the abolition of legal marriage altogether.

Nevertheless, many will object that marriage provides an important environment for the rearing of children. An appreciation of the conduciveness of marriage to murder and mayhem challenges that assumption. Historically, marriage and motherhood have gone hand in hand—ideologically, although often enough not in fact. That marriage can provide a valuable context for motherhood—even if it is unlikely to do so—as an argument in favor of marriage seems to presuppose that motherhood is a good thing. So let us consider next whether that is so.

Why Motherhood?

The term "mother" is ambiguous between a woman who gives birth and a female who parents, that is, rears a child—often but not necessarily the same woman. The term "motherhood" is ambiguous between the experience of mothers (in either sense, usually the second) and a social practice the rules of which structure child rearing. It is the latter that interests me here. Just as some today would stretch the concept of "family" to cover any committed partnership, household, or close and enduring network of friends, others would stretch the concept of "motherhood" to cover any mode of child rearing. That is not how I understand "motherhood." Just as not every durable intimate partnership is a marriage, not every mode of child rearing exemplifies motherhood. Historically, motherhood has been a core element of patriarchy. Within the institution of motherhood, mother's primary commitments have been to father and only secondarily to his children. Unmarried women have been held responsible by the State for the primary care of children they birth, unless a man wished to claim them. In fact, of course, children are raised by grandparents, single parents (heterosexual, lesbian, gay, asexual, and so on), and extended families, all in the midst of patriarchies. But these have been regarded as deviant parentings, with nothing like the prestige or social and legal support available to patriarchal mothers, as evidenced in the description of the relevant "families " in many cases as providing at best "broken homes."

Apart from the institution of marriage and historical ideals of the family, it is uncertain what characteristics mother-child relationships would have, for many alternatives are possible. In the good ones, mother-child relationships would not be as characterized as they have been by involuntary uncompensated caretaking. Even today, an ever-increasing amount of caretaking is being done contractually in day-care centers, with the result that a legitimate mother's relationship to her child is often much less a caretaking relationship than her mother's relationship to her was. Nor are paid day-care workers "mothers" (even though they may engage briefly in some "mothering activities"), because they are free to walk away from their jobs. Their relationships with a child may be no more permanent or special to the child than those of a babysitter. Boswell's history *The Kindness of Strangers* (1988) describes centuries of children being taken in by those at whose doorsteps babies were deposited, often anonymously. Not all such children had anyone to call "Mother." Children have been raised in convents, orphanages, or boarding schools rather than in households. Many raised in households are cared for by hired help, rather than by anyone they call "Mother." Many children today commute between separated or divorced parents, spending less time in a single household than many children of lesbian parents, some of whom, like Lesléa Newman's Heather, have two people to call "Mother" (Newman 1989). Many children are raised by older siblings, even in households in which someone else is called "Mother."

My point is not to support Newt Gingrich by glorifying orphanages or other hired caretakers but to put in perspective rhetoric about children's needs and about the ideal relationships of children to mothers. Much ink has been spilled debunking what passes for "love" in marriage. It is time to consider how much of the "love" that children are said to need is no more love than spousal attachments have been. Children do need stable intimate bonds with adults. But they also need supervision, education, health care, and a variety of relationships with people of a variety of ages. What the State tends to enforce in motherhood is the child's access to its mother, which guarantees none of these things, and the mother's answerability for her child's waywardness, which gives her a motive for constant supervision, thereby removing certain burdens from others but easily also endangering the well-being of her child if she is ill supplied with resources. Lacking adequate social or material resources, many a parent resorts to violent discipline in such situations, which the State has been reluctant to prevent or even acknowledge. This is what it has meant, legally, for a child to be a mother's "own": her own is the child who has legal rights of access to her and for whose waywardness she becomes answerable, although she is largely left to her own devices for carrying out the entailed responsibilities.

By contrast, children raised by lesbian or gay parents today are much more likely to be in relationships carefully chosen and affirmed by their caretakers.[4] Even though that would no doubt continue to be true oftener of the children of lesbian and gay parents in same-sex marriages than of the children of heterosexual parents, marriage would involve the State in defining who really had the status of "parent." The State has been willing to grant that status to at most two persons at a time, per child. It gives the child legal rights of access to at most those two parties. And it imposes legal accountability for the child's waywardness on at most those two parties. Under the present system that deprives lesbian and gay parents of spousal status, many lesbian and gay couples do their best anyway to emulate heterosexual models, which usually means assuming the responsibilities without the privileges.[5] Others I have known, however, attempt to undermine the assumption that parental responsibility should be concentrated in one or two people who have the power of a child's happiness and unhappiness in their hands for nearly two decades. Children raised without such models of the concentration of power may be less likely to reproduce patriarchal and other oppressive social relationships.

The "revolutionary parenting" that bell hooks describes (1984) dilutes the power of individual parents. Although children retain special affectional ties to their "bloodmothers," accountability for children's waywardness is more widely distributed. With many caretakers (such as "othermothers"), there is less pressure to make any one of them constantly accessible to a child and more pressure to make everyone somewhat accessible. With many caretakers, it is less likely that any of them will get away with prolonged abuse, or even be tempted to perpetrate it.

In my childhood, many adults looked out for the children of my village. I had, in a way, a combination of both kinds of worlds. My parents, married to each other, had the legal rights and the legal responsibilities of patriarchal parents. Yet, some of those responsibilities were in fact assumed by "othermothers," including women (and men) who never married anyone. Because it could always be assumed that wherever I roamed in the village, I would never be among strangers, my parents did not think they always needed to supervise me, although they were also ambivalent about that, as they would be legally answerable for any trouble I caused. I used to dread the thought that we might move to a city, where my freedom would probably have been severely curtailed, as it was when we lived in a large, white middle-class urban environment during World War II. In the village, because everyone assumed (reasonably) that someone was watching us, we children often escaped the intensity of physical discipline that I experienced alone with my mother amid the far larger urban population.

There are both worse and better environments that can be imagined for children than stereotypical patriarchal families. Urban environments in which parents must work away from home but can neither bring their children nor assume that their children are being watched by anyone are no doubt worse. Children who have never had effective caretakers do not make good caretakers of each other, either. Feminism today has been in something of a bind with respect to the so-called postpatriarchal family. If both women and men are to be actively involved in markets and governments and free to become active members of all occupations and professions, when, where, and how is child care going to be done? The solution of many feminists has been, in practice, for two parents to take turns spending time with the children. There is an increasing tendency today for parents who divide responsibilities for the children to pay others to do the child care, if they can afford it, when their turn comes. To the extent that this works, it is evidence that "mothering" is not necessary for child care. Children who have had effective caretakers may be better at taking care of themselves and each other, with minimal supervision to protect them against hazards to life and health, than is commonly supposed. Charlotte Perkins Gilman's solution in *Women and Economics* (1966) and *Herland* (1992) was twofold. On one hand, she would turn child care into one of the professions that everyone with the requisite talents and motivations is free to enter. At the same time, she would *make the public safe* even for children, by an ethic that incorporated aspects of good caretaking. Virginia Held's *Feminist Morality* also suggests the latter strategy. A danger of this strategy, of course, is instituting paternalism among adults but spelled with an *m* instead of a *p*. Still, the idea of improving the safety of the public environment is compelling. If it were improved enough, there might be no need for motherhood—which is not to say that children would not need to bond with and be supervised by adults.

In *Feminist Morality* Virginia Held maintains that the mother-child relationship is the fundamental social relationship, not in a reductive sense but in the sense that so much else depends on one's relationships to primary caretakers (Held 1994, 70). This idea, also urged by Annette Baier (1994), seems to me in a certain sense incontrovertible and its general appreciation by philosophers long overdue. The sense in which it seems to me incontrovertible is that when one does in fact have a primary caretaker who has, if not the power of life and death, then the power of one's happiness and unhappiness in their hands for many years in the early stages of one's life, the influence of that experience on the rest of one's life is profound. It seems, for example, to affect one's ability to form good relationships with others in ways that are extremely difficult to change, if they are changeable at all. Yet, there is another sense in which the observation that the mother-child relationship is fundamental may be misleading. It may be misleading if it suggests that everyone really needs a single primary caretaker (or even two primary caretakers) who has the power of one's happiness and unhappiness in their hands for many years during the early stages of ones' life. Perhaps people need that only in a society that refuses to take and share responsibility collectively for its own consciously and thoughtfully affirmed reproduction. In such a society, conscientious mothers are often the best protection a child has. But if so, it is misleading to say that such a relationship as the mother-child relationship is the, or even a, fundamental social relationship. It has been even less fundamental for many people, historically, than one might think, given how many children have been raised in institutions other than households or raised by a variety of paid caretakers with limited responsibilities.

Because mothers in a society that generally refuses to take collective responsibility for reproduction are often the best or even the only protection that children have, in the short run it is worth fighting for the right to adopt and raise children within lesbian and gay households. This is emergency care for young people, many of whom are already here and desperately in need of care. There is little that heterosexual couples can do to rebel as individual couples in a society in which their relationship is turned into a common law relationship after some years by the State and in which they are given the responsibilities and right of parents over any children they may raise. Communal action is what is required to implement new models of parenting. In the long run, it seems best to keep open the option of making parenting more "revolutionary" along the lines of communal practices such as those described by bell hooks. Instead of encouraging such a revolution, legal marriage interferes with it in a state that glorifies marriage and takes the marriage relationship to be the only truly healthy context in which to raise children. Lesbian and gay unions have great potentiality to further the revolution, in part because we *cannot* marry.

If motherhood is transcended, the importance of attending to the experiences and environments of children remains. The "children" if not the "mothers" in society are all of us. Not each of us will choose motherhood under present conditions. But each of us has been a child, and each future human survivor will have childhood to survive. Among the most engaging aspects of a major feminist treatise on the institution of motherhood, Adrienne Rich's *Of*

Woman Born, are that it is written from the perspective of a daughter who was mothered and that it is addressed to daughters as well as to mothers. This work, like that of Annette Baier, Virginia Held, bell hooks, Patricia Hill Collins, and Sara Ruddick, has the potential to focus our attention not entirely or even especially on mothers but on those who have been (or have not been) mothered, ultimately, on the experience of children in general. Instead of finding that the mother-child relationship provides a valuable paradigm for moral theorizing, even one who has mothered might find, reflecting on both her experience as a mother and her experience of having been mothered, that mothering should not be necessary, or that it should be less necessary than has been thought, and that it has more potential to do harm than good. The power of mothers over children may have been historically far more detrimental to daughters than to sons, at least in societies where daughters have been more controlled, more excluded from well-rewarded careers, and more compelled to engage in family service than sons. Such a finding would be in keeping with the project of drawing on the usually unacknowledged historically characteristic experiences of women.

In suggesting that the experience of being mothered has great potential for harm to children, I do not have in mind the kinds of concerns recently expressed by political conservatives about mothers who abuse drugs or are sexually promiscuous. Even these mothers are often the best protection their children have. I have in mind the environments provided by mothers who in fact do live up to contemporary norms of ideal motherhood or even exceed the demands of such norms in the degree of attention and concern they manifest for their children in providing a child-centered home as fully constructed as their resources allow.

Everyone would benefit from a society that was more attentive to the experiences of children, to the relationships of children with adults and with each other, and to the conditions under which children make the transition to adulthood. Moral philosophy might also be transformed by greater attention to the fact that adult experience and its potentialities are significantly conditioned by the childhoods of adults and of those children's relationships to (yet earlier) adults. Whether or not one agrees with the idea that motherhood offers a valuable paradigm for moral theorizing, in getting us to take seriously the significance of the child's experience of childhood and to take up the standpoint of the "child" in all of us, philosophical work exploring the significance of mother-child relationships is doing feminism and moral philosophy a great service.

AUTHOR'S NOTE

Thanks to Harry Brighouse, Vicky Davion, Virginia Held, Sara Ruddick, anonymous reviewers for *Hypatia*, and especially to Lynne Tirrell for helpful comments and suggestions and to audiences who heard ancestors of this essay at the Pacific and Central Divisions of the American Philosophical Association in 1995.

NOTES

1. Betty Berzon claims that her book *Permanent Partners* is about "reinventing our gay and lesbian relationships" and "learning to imbue them with all the *solemnity* of marriage without necessarily imitating the heterosexual model" (1988, 7), and yet by the end of the book it is difficult to think of anything in legal ideals of the heterosexual nuclear family that she has not urged us to imitate.
2. Thus I am not an advocate of the equal legal rights for children movement as that movement is presented and criticized by Purdy (1992), namely, as a movement advocating that children have exactly the same legal rights as adults, including the legal right not to attend school.
3. See, for example, Weston (1991), Burke (1993), and Slater (1995). In contrast, Berzon (1988) uses the language of partnership, reserving "family" for social structures based on heterosexual unions, as in chap. 12, subtitled "Integrating Your Families into Your Life as a Couple."
4. An outstanding anthology on the many varieties of lesbian parenting is Arnup (1995). Also interesting is the anthropological study of lesbian mothers by Lewin (1993). Both are rich in references to many resources on both lesbian and gay parenting.
5. Lewin (1993) finds, for example, that lesbian mothers

tend to assume all caretaking responsibilities themselves, or in some cases share them with a partner, turning to their families of origin, rather than to a friendship network of peers, for additionally needed support.

REFERENCES

Arnup, Katherine, ed. 1995. *Lesbian parenting: Living with pride and prejudice.* Charlottetown, P.E.I.: Gynergy Books.

Baier, Annette C. 1994. *Moral prejudices: Essays on ethics.* Cambridge: Harvard University Press.

Berzon, Betty. 1988. *Permanent partnerships: Building lesbian and gay relationships that last.* New York: Penguin.

Blumenfeld, Warren J. 1996. Same-sex marriage: Introducing the discussion. *Journal of Gay, Lesbian and Bisexual Identity* 1 (1): 77.

Boswell, John. 1988. *The kindness of strangers: The abandonment of children in Western Europe from late antiquity to the Renaissance.* New York: Pantheon.

— , 1994. *Same-sex unions in premodern Europe.* New York: Villard.

Brownworth, Victoria A. 1996. Tying the knot or the hangmans's noose: The case against marriage. *Journal of Gay, Lesbian, and Bisexual Identity* 1(1): 91-98.

Burke, Phyllis. 1993. *Family values: Two moms and their son.* New York: Random House.

Card, Claudia. 1988. Gratitude and Obligation. *American Philosophical Quarterly* 25 (2): 115-27.

— , 1990. Gender and Moral Luck. In *Identity, character, and morality: Essays in moral psychology*, ed. Owen Flanagan and Amelie Oksenberg Rorty, Cambridge: MIT Press.

— , 1995. *Lesbian choices.* New York: Columbia University Press.

Collins, Patricia Hill. 1991. *Black feminist thought: Knowledge, consciousness, and the politics of empowerment.* New York: Routledge.

Daly, Mary. 1978. *Gyn/Ecology: The metaethics of radical feminism.* Boston: Beacon.

Faulkner, Sandra, with Judy Nelson. 1993. *Love match: Nelson vs. Navratilova.* New York: Birch Lane Press.

Friedman, Marilyn. 1993. *What are friends for? Feminist perspectives on personal relationships and moral theory.* Ithaca: Cornell University Press.

Gilman, Charlotte Perkins. 1966. *Women and economics: The economic factor between men and women as a factor in social evolution*, ed. Carl Degler. New York: Harper.

— ,1992. Herland. In *Herland and selected stories by Charlotte Perkins Gilman*, ed. Barbara H. Solomon. New York: Signet.

Goldman, Emma. 1969. Marriage and Love. In *Anarchism and other essays.* New York: Dover.

Hall, Radclyffe. 1950. *The well of loneliness.* New York: Pocket Books. (Many editions; first published 1928).

Held, Virginia. 1993. *Feminist morality: Transforming culture, society, and politics.* Chicago: University of Chicago Press.

Hoagland, Sarah Lucia. 1988. *Lesbian ethics: Toward new value.* Palo Alto, CA: Institute of Lesbian Studies.

hooks, bell. 1984. *Feminist theory from margin to center.* Boston: South End Press.

Island, David, and Patrick Letellier. 1991. *Men who beat the men who love them: Battered gay men and domestic violence.* New York: Harrington Park Press.

Lewin, Ellen. 1993. *Lesbian mothers.* Ithaca: Cornell University Press.

Lobel, Kerry, ed. 1986. *Naming the violence: Speaking out about lesbian battering.* Seattle: Seal Press.

Lorde, Audre. 1984. *Sister outsider: Essays and speeches.* Trumansburg: Crossing Press.

Mahmoody, Betty, with William Hoffer. 1987. *Not without my daughter.* New York: St. Martin's.

Mohr, Richard D. 1994. *A more perfect union: Why straight America must stand up for gay rights.* Boston: Beacon.

Newman, Leslea. 1989. *Heather has two mommies.* Northampton, MA: In Other Words Publishing.

Pierce, Christine. 1995. Gay marriage. *Journal of Social Philosophy* 28 (2): 5-16.

Purdy, Laura M. 1992. *In their best interest? The case against equal rights for children.* Ithaca: Cornell University Press.

Renzetti, Clair M. 1992. *Violent betrayal: Partner abuse in lesbian relationships.* Newbury Park, CA: Sage Publications.

Rich, Adrienne. 1976. *Of woman born: Motherhood as experience and as institution.* New York: Norton.

Ruddick, Sara. 1989. *Maternal thinking: Toward a politics of peace.* Boston: Beacon.

Slater, Suzanne. 1995. *The lesbian family life cycle.* New York: Free Press.

Trebilcot, Joyce, ed. 1983. *Mothering: Essays in feminist theory.* Totowa, N.J.: Rowman and Allanheld.

Weston, Kath. 1991. *Families we choose.* New York: Columbia University Press.

Wolfson, Evan. 1996. Why we should fight for the freedom to marry: The challenges and opportunities that will follow a win in Hawaii. *Journal of Lesbian, Gay, and Bisexual Identity* 1 (1): 79-89.

QUEER ETHICS; OR, THE CHALLENGE OF BISEXUALITY TO LESBIAN ETHICS

Elisabeth D. Däumer

Elisabeth D. Däumer is Director of Graduate Studies in English at Eastern Michigan University, where she also teaches in Women's Studies and Literary Theory. She is a co-editor of The Feminist Teacher Anthology: Pedagogies and Classroom Strategies *(Teacher's College Press, 1998).*

Due to its problematic political and social position between two opposed sexual cultures, bisexuality has often been ignored by feminist and lesbian theorists both as a concept and a realm of experiences. The essay argues that bisexuality, precisely because it transgresses bipolar notions of fixed gendered and sexed identities, is usefully explored by lesbian and feminist theorists, enhancing our effort to devise an ethics of difference and to develop nonoppressive ways of responding to alterity.

In her recent book *Lesbian Ethics: Toward New Value*, Sarah Hoagland affirms that lesbian existence, because it "challenges the social construction of reality," holds a promise for a transformation of consciousness: "the conceptual, material possibility of female agency not defined in terms of an other" (Hoagland 1988, 6). Concerned with nourishing this promise, Hoagland offers a wealth of strategies for creating values that would enhance lesbian capacity to separate from heterosexualism—"a way of living," in Hoagland's words, "that normalizes the dominance of one person and the subordination of another" (7)—and to respond to differences among lesbians in ways that do not replicate forms of domination but enable moral agency and authentic choice. That the experiences and views of bisexual women are absent from a book on lesbian ethics might surprise only a few of its readers. In this essay, however, I shall propose that an exploration of bisexuality—as an experience as much as a moral, social, and epistemological point of view—contributes significantly to feminist and lesbian theorizing, and especially to the endeavor, so admirably advanced in Hoaglands's work, of devising alternative, nonoppressive ways of responding to alterity.

Beginning with a poetic rendition of experiences and fitful reflections of a fictitious woman named Cloe, I will, in the second part of the essay, explore the theoretical implications and transformative promise of Cloe's ostensibly missing or indeterminate sexual identity for a feminist antihomophobic understanding of sexuality and gender.[1] Finally, I will show how a serious examination of bisexuality draws out the implications of recent work on lesbian ethics, most fully developed in Hoagland's book, for a "queer ethics": an ethics dedicated to creating values that would nourish the queer in all of us and help us—whether we are male or female, gay- or lesbian-identified, bisexual, heterosexual, or undecided—separate from straightness or, as Hoagland terms it, heterosexualism. I do not anticipate a grand conclusion to the medley of voices and perspectives that I am here assembling. But I do hope to contribute to the burgeoning dialogue on what is still a strangely repressed and uncomfortable subject—the instability and fracturedness of our gendered, sexed, social and political selves—by showing its centrality to our attempt at developing an ethics of difference.[2]

Reprinted with permission of the publisher and Elisabeth Daümer from *Hypatia* 7:4 (Fall 1992): 91–105, [edited].

I.

> We are increasingly aware that sexuality is about flux and change, that what we call "sexual" is as much a product of language and culture as of nature. But we earnestly strive to fix it, stabilize it, say who we are by telling of our sex—and the lead in this conscious articulation of sense of self has been taken by those radically disqualified for it by the sexual tradition. (Weeks 1985, 186)

In an age of constructed sexualities a new type of constructed being is claiming our attention. She identifies as female. Let us call her, like earlier heroines of feminist history, Cloe. Neither straight of gay, Cloe is also not bisexual, at least not in the traditional, still current, sense of the word—pregenderized, polymorphously perverse, or simply sexually undecided, uncommitted, and hence untrustworthy. Cloe can make up her mind; but she would be so much better at explaining how indeed she is making up her mind, if others—her lesbian friends worried about her relapse into an inevitably heterosexist heterosexualism, her straight friends enchanted or disquieted by her exoticism—if many of these well-meaning friends wouldn't try to make up her mind for her.

To be historically exact, Cloe owes much of her existence to the valiant struggles of lesbian feminists who established oases of political and sexual sisterhood, which despite certain censorious tendencies allowed women like Cloe to move away from straightness, to explore their sexuality, their emotional, sexual attraction to other women in a welcoming environment—an environment quite different from that which older lesbians had faced and many other lesbians are still struggling with. Thus Cloe is deeply grateful to these women who weathered homophobic ostracism and enabled their younger—i.e., newer—sisters to explore their "deviancy" joyfully, often playfully, safe from the twin specters of internalized guilt and external ostracism.

Of course, these differences in experience invariably produced tension and at times division. While Cloe no longer feels straight (i.e., heterosexual), indeed is passionately nonstraight, she also does not, if the truth be told, feel that she ever came out of the closet. There had been for her no closet to begin with. Rather, her experience of being closeted coincided with her coming out as a lesbian or, to be more accurate, with her first female lover, whose hand she dared not hold in public, whose presence she needed to explain—not once, but again and again—to friends, family, colleagues, who, until then, had had no reason to assume she was not heterosexual, like them.

Like other women coming to feminism in the 1970s and 1980s, Cloe fell in love with women not out of a deep-seated sense of sexual orientation but in the course of political bonding and passionate intellectual conversations. Nor was it sexual or social aversion to men that drove her to women, but something positive—enchantment and delight with the company of people who excited her intellectually, emotionally, then sexually, who did not expect, like men she had known, nonreciprocal access to her at all times. Over the months and years, Cloe simply preferred being with women; and it seemed to her a small, and natural, step from intellectual passion to sexual intimacy.

Nevertheless, when she took that step she was deeply startled by the difference it made. Nothing had prepared her for the sweetness of a woman's mouth, the mystery of a woman's breast. Nor could she have described how she changed. Falling from her old sense of self, she was reborn into a new way of experiencing her body, her sexuality, her femininity. She could not even say that her new way of being in the world was *truer*. On the contrary, she walked about like a stranger, newly alive to what had appeared to her a familiar world, a familiar body, a familiar self. But most of all, she felt enlarged, filled with wonder at her ability to give abundantly and to receive joyfully. And to her mother, who could not help observing the flowering of confidence and well-being in her daughter, Cloe said that now, for the first time in her life, she felt she had a choice—a choice about whom to love, a choice in creating and re-creating her sexuality.

Cloe soon found out, however, that choosing to love a particular woman was not, for her, the same as affirming a specific sexual identity. Not that she didn't try to become a lesbian. She did. But after a brief and enthusiastic effort at making herself into a real sister, when Cloe lovingly invested herself with all the paraphernalia of lesbian feminism and fell in and out of love with a small-boned dark-haired woman, after what should perhaps be described as a second adolescence, Cloe began to wonder: Could it be possible to relate to men and women, or the creatures answering to these names, not as men and women, as straight or gay, but—and her she would whisper to herself embarrassedly—as *humans*? Of course, she was wise and self-resisting enough not to voice such deluded, liberal gibberish.

Nevertheless, she could not help dreaming. She would see herself at a table with a beloved—was she male, he female, she a celibate androgyne, he a lesbian mother?—with whom, over glasses of deep red wine, she could engage in beautiful, deliciously double- or triple-voiced conversations. She was dreaming not of a genderless, sexless creature, nor of an androgynous one (although this was closer to her vision), but of somebody with whom she was not primarily a woman, a lesbian, or a misrecognized heterosexual. Navigating questions of identity in a postmodern age, Cloe dreamed not of instability or indecidability so much as of an intimacy not regulated through positionings in ostensibly stable sexual identities. Cloe longed for people with whom she could create herself anew, again and again, and for whom she could do the same.

What delusions, we might say. Poor Cloe! After a brief relapse with a man, closely monitored by her lesbian sisters, the question of her sexual identity became pressingly imminent. She refused, passionately, to return to straightness, but neither could she in good conscience call herself a dyke. So why not say she was bisexual, as some sympathetic friends had tentatively suggested? Yet somehow Cloe wasn't happy with that label, even if in terms of her sexual and emotional experience it seemed closest to the truth. After all, she had loved men in her life and she had loved women, and she could not imagine ceasing to love either. But to assume that label of bisexuality? That gave her pause. A host of little comments, brief remarks, as well as her own assumptions made this a less than savory, and hardly political, identity: it seemed one was bisexual by default, for lack of commitment and the ability to make up one's mind. True, a male friend—now homosexual, formerly married, and in both apparently happy—had remarked that bisexuals have the best of both worlds. A lesbian friend disagreed. To her it seemed a bisexual had the worst of both worlds: who, she asked, would your friends be?

And Cloe agreed with her. For even if her heterosexual or hetero-identified friends tended to view bisexuality with tolerant, sometimes condescending, curiosity, the lesbian community—as community—expressed above all suspicion, even contempt, for women "who went back to men," women who were "ac-dc," on the fence. The threat of AIDS has only exacerbated such suspicion, leading many lesbians to view bisexual women as potential AIDS–carriers. Inherently contaminated, they endanger lesbian purity. Moreover, because such women might refuse to assume either a clearly lesbian or heterosexual identity, they carry the taint of promiscuity, as if they were floundering, promiscuously and opportunistically, back and forth between people of either gender—exploiting heterosexual privilege on the one hand, while savoring, unrightfully, the honey of lesbian sisterhood on the other. And while Cloe was careful not to minimize the social ostracism endured by gays, she could not help but feel that those who dared to call themselves bisexual were also subjected to a sort of ostracism, not only by the larger society but by lesbians as well.

II.

> It is rather amazing fact that, of the very many dimensions along which the genital activity of one person can be differentiated from that of another (dimensions that include preference for certain acts, certain zones or sensations, certain physical types, a certain frequency, certain symbolic investments, certain relations of age or power, a certain species, a certain number of participants, etc. etc. etc.), precisely one, the gender of object choice, emerged from the turn of the century, and has remained, as *the* dimension denoted by the now ubiquitous category of "sexual orientation." (Sedgwick 1990, 8)

Prompted by my reading of Sedgwick's *Epistemology of the Closet*, from which the above quotation is taken, I recently argued during a dinner with friends that we ought to problematize more stringently the relations between sexual acts, sexual identity, politics, and gender. Inspired by Sedgwick's dazzling description of the infinite multitude of ways in which sexuality could be defined were we not as exclusively fixated on riveting it to the gender of whom we are attracted to or sexual with, I impersonated Cloe and wondered if it was possible for a woman and a man to engage in a lesbian relationship. After all, if, as some lesbian theorists like Monique Wittig have suggested, a lesbian is "outside the categories of sex (woman and man), because the designated subject (lesbian) is *not* a woman, either economically, or politically, or ideologically" (Wittig 1981, 53), why, then, could it not be possible for a man to resist his designated gender (including the relations of domination embodied within it) and assume a lesbian identity?[3] On a theoretical level, at least, Sedgwick's observations add a twist to Wittig's construction of lesbian that gives rise to exciting—or disturbing—questions and possibilities: How would we define the relationship between a female lesbian and a gay man, who, like a character in Caryl Churchill's *Cloud Nine* wants to be a lesbian? Would their relationship be heterosexual, even though neither partner views her/himself as straight? Could such a union not be called "lesbian" in the utopian feminist sense of the term? Both partners, after all, insist on being *not* a woman and *not* a man; and for both, gender identification is secondary to, or entirely determined by, their commitment to establishing a relationship that resists the domination of heterosexually gendered positions.

One of my friends immediately pinpointed what was to her most problematic about this proposition. It would, she said, efface her own identity as a lesbian, and, by stretching the term beyond any intelligible, useful boundaries, perpetuate lesbian invisibility in new and dangerous ways. She also asked, disbelievingly, who—i.e., what woman, what man—would want to define their relationship in this manner, and how would the concept of heterosexual privilege fit into this scheme? Since these are serious charges, I'd like to respond to them in some detail.

Let us start with the second. In light of Cloe's desultory attempt to fashion for herself a sexual identity from the startling dearth of currently available options (hetero, homo, or bi), we ought not be surprised that she would think up something as improbable as a lesbian relationship between a woman and a man. Since she herself feels no longer straight, she wonders, of course, how to name her current relationship to a man. Is it heterosexual just because it implies certain sexual practices—namely, penetration—that can or cannot be performed? Is it heterosexual because clearly she is a woman, at least anatomically, and he a man? Is it heterosexual because it conforms to the dominant idea of a "normal" relationship—and thus also reaps the benefits of heterosexual privilege—despite the fact that the individual members in this relationship might view themselves as "queer"?

Cloe is not oblivious to the sociopolitical connotations of engaging in what to most would look like a heterosexual relationship. Nor is she unaware of the privileges conferred upon this relationship: social endorsement and a certain visibility; legal and financial benefits; relative safety from homophobia (she is also affected by homophobia, if differently from a woman who is lesbian-identified and lives in a relationship with another woman).[4] Cloe would not, moreover, seriously insist on describing either herself or her relationship as lesbian. Yet her half-mischievous proposal to do so reflects her increasingly dizzying awareness of the many possible sexual and gendered selves, the many passions and attractions, fantasies and relationships—whether sexual, erotic, affectional or intellectual—that remain frustratingly silenced, unspoken in the discourses of sexuality currently available to us. Her own sense of the fissures and contradictions (between sexual and political identities, political and personal, emotional commitments, etc.) that attend her way of being in the world has produced in her a hunger for language differentiated enough to capture the wealth of contradictions that pervades the efforts of individual men and women to subvert or modify dominant constructions of gender and sexuality.

I have so far resisted calling Cloe "bisexual" because it seems to me that the term "bisexuality," rather than broadening the spectrum of available sexual identifications, holds in place a binary framework of two basic and diametrically opposed sexual orientations. Contributors to a recent anthology on this subject, *Bi Any Other Name*, affirm that bisexuality, when made visible, disrupts a "monosexual framework" by challenging "assumptions about the immutability of people's sexual orientations and society's supposed divisions into discrete groups" (Hutchins and Kaahumanu 1991, 3).[5] Yet the various efforts chronicled in this anthology to construct a bisexual identity—distinct from heterosexual and homosexual identities while comprising aspects of both—do not always bear out the radical potential of its affirmation.[6]

Some of the contributors, for instance, view themselves as divided between homosexual and heterosexual orientations; thus Loraine Hutchins, one of the editors, describes her struggle to "[accept] myself as the 70-percent straight person I probably really am," while "constantly [fighting] to have the 30 percent lesbian side not be ridiculed or misunderstood" (xv). Others think of themselves as integrating both orientations and thus, as one of the editors, quoting Robin Morgan, maintains, "[sacrificing] nothing except false categories and burned-out strategies" (xxiv). Yet such tropes of bisexuality as either neatly divided between or integrating heterosexuality and homosexuality threaten to simplify bisexuality: on the one hand, they retain a notion of sexuality—and sexual identity—based exclusively on the gender of object choice, thus implying that a bisexual woman, for instance, would be heterosexually involved with a man, homosexually involved with a woman. (Cloe, for one, finds it impossible to say, with the absolute certainty that such definitions of bisexuality imply, that she loves men and women differently; and although she finds it equally impossible to say that she loves them the same, she is reluctant to ascribe the difference in these encounters—whether imaginary or real—to gender alone. Is it really always that easy, she wonders, to keep straight whom one was loving and how? What if, by mistake, one forgot that the person holding one's hand was a man—or a woman—and if one, equally by mistake, were to slip into a heterosexual relationship with a woman, a lesbian relationship with a man?)

On the other hand, in their tendency to reduce bisexuality to a third sexual orientation (or a mixture of orientations), these tropes of bisexuality simplify its sociopolitical implications. Bisexuality is not merely a problem of an unrecognized or vilified sexual preference that can be solved, or alleviated, through visibility and legitimation as a third sexual option. The problems of bisexuals are social and political ones, resulting, as Lisa Orlando, one of the contributors to the anthology, points out, "from [our] ambiguous position ... between what currently appear as two mutually exclusive sexual cultures, one with the power to exercise violent repression against the other" (224-225).

To be sure, the affirmation of an integrated, unified bisexual identity, fostered within supportive bisexual communities, might boost the psychological well-being of many bisexual people. It remains to be seen, however, if and how such increased visibility would contribute to our struggle against homophobia, sexism, and heterosexism—the forces that have made the formation of an oppositional sexual culture necessary in the first place. Put differently, as long as there are two mutually exclusive sexual cultures, and as long as it is politically essential to maintain oppositional cultures—based on sexuality as much as on gender—the effort to disambiguate bisexuality and elevate it into a sign of integration might counteract the subversive potential of bisexuality as a moral and epistemological force, as well as obscure its contribution to current discussions among feminist and lesbian theorists on the limitations of identity politics and the urgent need to respect differences among women.

I propose, therefore, that we assume bisexuality, not as an identity that integrates heterosexual and homosexual orientations, but as an epistemological as well as ethical vantage point from which we can examine and deconstruct the bipolar framework of gender and sexuality in which, as feminists and lesbian feminists, we are still too deeply rooted, both because of and despite our struggle against homophobia and sexism.

What are the advantages of assuming bisexuality as a perspective? I can think of many:

1. Because bisexuality occupies an ambiguous position *between* identities, it is able to shed light on the gaps and contradictions of all identity, on what we might call the difference *within* identity. This

ambiguous position, while it creates painful contradictions, incoherences, and impracticalities in the lives of those who adopt it, can also lead to a deep appreciation of the differences among people—whether cultural, sexual, gendered—since any attempt to construct a coherent identity in opposition to another would flounder on the multiplicity of at times conflicting identifications generated by the bisexual point of view.

2. Because of its nonidenticalness, bisexuality exposes the distinctive feature of all politicized sexual identities: the at times radical discontinuities between an individual's sexual acts and affectional choices, on the one hand, and her or his affirmed political identity, on the other. By doing so, bisexuality reactivates the gender and sexuality destabilizing moment of all politicized sexual identities, at the same time that it can help us view contradiction, not as a personal flaw or a danger to our communities, but as a source of insight and strength, as a basis for more incluse "we's" that enable rather than repress the articulation of difference.

3. Because of its ambiguous position between mutually exclusive sexual cultures, bisexuality also urges us to problematize heterosexuality in ways that distinguish more clearly between the institution of compulsory heterosexuality and the efforts of individual men and women to resist heterosexualism within and without so-called heterosexual relationships. Thus as feminist and lesbian theorists we need to inquire more intently into the possibility of antiheterosexist heterosexual relationships and describe such relationships in ways that neither obscure how they are impacted by heterosexualism nor collapse them univocally with heteropatriarchy. Marilyn Frye took an important step in this direction in a speech delivered at the 1990 National Women's Studies Association conference, "Do You Have to Be a Lesbian to Be a Feminist?" In this speech, which was published later that year in *off our backs*, Frye firmly asserted that we do not but that we need to be "virgins" in the radically feminist lesbian sense—i.e., women "in creative defiance of patriarchal definitions of the real, the meaningful" (Frye 1990, 23). A series of letters to *off our backs* in response to Frye's speech revealed, however, that many non-lesbian-identified or heterosexual women understood her to affirm the opposite—that you need to be a lesbian to be a feminist. This misreading on the part of the respondents reflects, perhaps, their sense that many lesbian feminists, because they tend to equate the difficulty of being a feminist in relation to a man with its impossibility, are unable to be curious about, or respectful of, the antipatriarchal, antiheterosexist struggle waged by many non-lesbian-identified women and mothers. Of course, heterosexually identified feminists need, on their part, to embrace more emphatically feminism as a sign of sexual ambiguity and refuse to disavow the destabilizing "queer" force of feminism by, for instance, publicly dissociating themselves from lesbianism.

4. Because the bisexual perspective enacts within itself the battle of contradictory sexual and political identifications, it can also serve as a bridge between identifications and communities, and thus strengthen our ability temporarily to "forget" entrenched and seemingly inevitable differences—especially those of race, gender, and sexuality—in order to focus on what we might have in common.

III.

> It is the queer in me that empowers—that lets me see those lines and burn to cross them; that lets me question the lies we all were told about who women are, who men are, how we may properly interact ... what nice girls do and don't do. The queer in all of us clamors for pleasure and change, will not be tamed or regulated, wants a say in the creation of a new reality. (Queen 1991, 20-21)

Cloe, as I mentioned previously, fell from straightness—from an assumption of heterosexuality as natural and, at least for herself, unavoidable—within her group of lesbian-feminist friends. In this close-knit circle of friends, Cloe began to conceive of loving another woman erotically and sexually. But neither her dreams and fantasies nor her actual experience of falling in love with a woman could entirely convince her that now a truer, more authentic self had surfaced within her. Instead she experienced the exhilaration of being offered a choice that she had not known—or felt—to exist: the choice to explore her sexuality and the complex depth of her bonds to women, the choice to act in resistance to institutionalized compulsions, to her own socialization, to her fear of familial rejection and social ostracism.

Making that choice did not, for Cloe, automatically eliminate other options—e.g., the option to love a man. Rather, Cloe entered a new perceptual framework—what I would like to call a "queer universe"—in which the fluctuations and mutabilities of sexuality, the multitude of different, changing, and at times conflicting ways in which we experience our sexual, affectional and erotic proclivities, fantasies, and practices can be articulated and acknowledged. In the queer universe, to be queer implies that not everybody is queer in the same way. It implies a willingness to enable others to articulate their own particular queerness.

Yet if, in Cloe's experience, the lesbian-feminist community had opened up this vision of queerness by enabling her to explore her difference, she often felt that the same community and culture had also restricted her own and other women's self-exploration for the sake of communal cohesion and self-protection. Thus, although many lesbian theorists insist on attributing lesbianism to a political choice against heterosexualism and urge heterosexual feminists to realize that they, too, do not simply follow a natural calling but choose to be, or at least to remain, heterosexual, few of these theorists have displayed any curiosity about the whole range of choices that might be opened by such initial resistance against heterosexualism. A recent example of such lack of curiosity is Bette S. Tallen's "How Inclusive is Feminist Political Theory? Questions for Lesbians," in which she asserts that "non-lesbian feminists, to the degree that they refuse to separate from men and masculine values and identify with lesbian existence, participate in the maintenance of patriarchal order" (Tallen 1990, 250). Not only does such affirmation uncritically collapse heterosexuality with the maintenance of heteropatriarchy, on the one hand, and lesbianism with resistance to patriarchy, on the other, but Tallen's article also displays no interest in other possible ways of resisting patriarchy and straightness. It demands that nonlesbian women identify with the "L-word," while demonstrating no reciprocal concern for the struggles of bisexual or other nonstraight women against heteropatriarchy.

Although there is no evidence to suggest that Hoagland would not agree with analyses such as Tallen's, *Lesbian Ethics* proffers a needed and exciting antidote to the tendency of some lesbian thinkers to place the needs of lesbian identity and unity over the articulation of differences, a tendency that ultimately works to contradict the centrality of choice and individual moral agency in feminist and lesbian ethics. Believing that "if we are to form an enduring community, it will not be on the basis of outside threats ... of a rich tradition nor of what we find here ... but on the basis of the values we believe we can enact here" (Hoagland 1988, 154), Hoagland maintains that we can only foster moral agency in others and ourselves if we are willing to acknowledge differences between ourselves and others. Indeed, her whole book is dedicated to the creation of a new ethic that would nourish lesbian connection but not at the expense of suppressing differences. In pursuit of this aim, she proposes alternative ways of thinking about alterity, designed to enhance our capacity, as a group and as individuals, to respond affirmatively to forces that have often been experienced as threatening to lesbian identity and community—the tensions, ambiguities, and contradictions arising from differences of race, class, age, able-bodiedness, as much as from differences of sexual, affectional, and intellectual choices.

The strength of Hoagland's ethical model lies in its conceptualization of moral agency according to which we choose to act with a full awareness of what constrains our ability to choose. "Choice," Hoagland affirms, "is at the very core of the concept of 'moral agency.' *It is not because we are free and moral agents that we are able to make moral choices. Rather, it is because we make choices, choose from among alternatives, act in the face of limits, that we decare ourselves moral beings*" (231). From the vantage point of this revisionary concept of moral agency, Hoagland takes a close and critical look at the way in which lesbian notions of choice are still, and often destructively, rooted in traditional ethics, which assume "that to be ethical we must be able to control external forces or, at the very least, that a proper moral choice would be one in which there were no constraints on us, no limits" (198). As a result, she explains, the focus of traditional ethics is exclusively "on whether we can blame or praise others for what they have done and whether we can be blamed or praised for what we have done" (198). Pointing to the implications of such ethical notions—for instance, the belief that it is always easy to distinguish between good and bad choices, since good choices have only good consequences and will not harm anyone—Hoagland proposes instead that we direct our energies to making our choices "intelligible" and to understanding the "complexity" emerging from them (220-28).

Although this conceptualization of agency raises compelling questions about bisexuality as a moral choice, the experiences and views of bisexual women and lesbians are, as I mentioned previously, absent from Hoagland's work. Since her study draws on the narratives of U.S. lesbians from a variety of communities, we might, of course, conclude that there were no bisexual women in these communities. Equally likely is the possibility that, if there were such women, they did not speak up about their experiences, silenced both by their own sense of disloyalty and by fear of not being understood, of not being able to make themselves, or to be viewed as, "intelligible." Certainly, Hoagland's own references to women whose experiences imply a certain measure of bisexuality do not reflect an interest in the complexity of their existence. Once, for instance, a married heterosexual woman is mentioned who "keeps trying to get closer to [her lesbian friend] and start something even though she just got pregnant and so is situating herself in a way that will make it much harder to leave her husband" (218). My quarrel is not with the fact that Hoagland's attention is in this case centered on the lesbian friend and her difficult choices, but with her manner of describing the other woman as "heterosexual," a designation that reduces the complexity of her being and even seems to imply that her desire for another woman is somehow less legitimate than that of a self-identified lesbian.

From a bisexual vantage point, however, what is promising in *Lesbian Ethics* is that Hoagland's apparent indifference to choices that challenge notions of fixed sexual identities (whether lesbian or heterosexual) coexists with her insistence *not* to define "lesbian." To do so, she explains, is to "succumb to a context of heterosexualism. No one ever feels compelled to explain or define what they perceive as the norm. If we define 'lesbianism,' we invoke a context in which it is not the norm" (8). In addition, her refusal to define lesbianism indicates a reluctance to make identity simply and unproblematically the cornerstone of lesbian ethics. In a compellingly "universalizing" or "queer" gesture, Hoagland equates lesbianism with support of female agency not defined in relation to man, on the one hand, and separation from heterosexualism on the other.[7] Thus, while retaining a notion of lesbian that is necessarily rooted in dominant categories of gender, even as it resists those (only a woman can refuse to belong to the category "woman"), Hoagland drives a wedge between the automatic linking of sexuality and gender, thereby opening her inquiry to an awareness of both the actual permeability of sexual identity and the plurality of ways in which people of all genders and sexualities resist straightness. In its universalizing force, then, lesbianism is not only separation from men (i.e., defined in terms of the gender of object choice) but also "a challenge to heterosexualism." Heterosexualism, in turn, by designating "a way of living that normalizes the dominance of one person and the subordination of another," is not confined to the relations between men and women but includes as well other, not specifically gender-based, relations: "the 'protective' relationship between imperialists and colonized, the 'peace-keeping' relationship between democracy (U.S. capitalism) and threats to democracy" (8). ...

Hoagland's universalizing impulse ought not to be confused with an endeavor to be more inclusive, for while the latter sustains a conceptual framework of identifiable essences constituted in reference to an outside that serves as a foil to the communities internal boundaries, a universalizing gesture undercuts this framework by challenging the belief in immutable categories of gender and sexuality itself. Thus Hoagland is aware that our capacity to respond affirmatively to differences within a community is enhanced not necessarily through a call for more inclusivity but rather through a rethinking of the ways in which a community defines itself. Letting go of the "urge to define" the borders of lesbian community, and thus of "the metaphor of a fortress which requires defending from invasion," Hoagland begins to reenvision community in terms of a shared focus of attention, a "ground of lesbian be-ing, a ground of possibility" (9). Moreover, given this universalizing or queer impulse of her work, there is no intrinsic reason for Hoagland's exclusion of the moral choices of bisexuals from lesbian ethics. On the contrary, since bisexuals transgress boundaries of sexually identified communities and thus are always both inside and outside a diversity of conflicting communities, a serious consideration of their experiences and moral choices would help us develop the insight that I find so promisingly Implied in Hoagland's *Lesbian Ethics*—that our ability to respond to diversity within lesbian community is linked to our capacity to articulate and reimagine the complex relations and interactions, as well as the shifting boundaries and allegiances, between communities.

Hence, as a sign of transgression, ambiguity, and mutability, bisexuality also provides a necessary theoretical link between lesbian theory and the rapidly expanding field of queer theory, on the one hand, and lesbian ethics and queer ethics, on the other. In its current usage, "queer," as Teresa de Lauretis explains, is intended "to mark a certain critical distance" from the designations "lesbian" and "gay," and a desire to "transgress and transcend them—or at the very least problematize them" (de Lauretis 1991, v). Among other things, queer theory is dedicated to opening up differences that, in de Lauretis's words, "are, paradoxically, elided, because taken for granted, in 'lesbian and gay' " (vi). A queer ethics, as I have briefly and provisionally proposed at the beginning of this essay, would support and nurture the queer in all of us—both by questioning all notions of fixed, immutable identities and by articulating a plurality of differences among us in the hope of forging new bonds and allegiances. In doing so, queer ethics poses a creative challenge to lesbian ethics, which need neither supercede nor undercut such ethics but can further its aim of enabling female agency and authentic choice through separation from heterosexualism. In addition, however, a queer ethics would stress the interrelatedness of different, and at times conflicting, communities and thus emphasize the need to combine forces in our various antihomophobic and antisexist endeavors.

NOTES

1. The first part of this essay served as an introduction to my presentation "Feminist Biphobia; or, What Does Sexuality Have to Do with Gender?" delivered at the 1991 North Central Women's Studies Association conference in Athens, Ohio. I would like to thank Sandra Runzo and Kate Mehuron for their helpful and challenging responses to the present, extended version of this presentation.
2. For recent work problematizing sexuality and gender, see especially Butler (1990), Sedgwick (1990), Fuss (1989 and 1991), de Lauretis (1991).
3. Diana Fuss asks a similar question when she points to Monique Wittig's and Adrienne Rich's problematic attitude to male homosexuality: "given the way in which gay men, in their social and sexual practices, radically challenge the current notions of masculinity and the 'naturalness' of heterosexual desire, one would think that they, too, disrupt and disable the logic of the straight mind (or what Rich prefers to call the 'institution of compulsory heterosexuality')" (Fuss 1989, 47).
4. In the welcome and useful anthology *Bi Any Other Name: Bisexual people speak out*, which I will discuss in more detail below, the painful difficulties of bisexual passing are compared, by a number of contributors, to the problems of multiracial people. Indeed, in her review of the anthology, Aurora Levins Morales points out that "bisexuality and mixed racial heritage feel so similar because they pose the same kind of challenge to society. Both represent a claim to a complex humanity that undermines deeply held ideas of category: the societal belief in immutable, biologically based groupings of human beings" (Morales 1992, 24).
5. According to the editors of *Bi Any Other Name*, "*Monosexual* is a term coined by the bisexual movement to mean anyone (gay or heterosexual) who is attracted to just one sex, their own or the opposite one" (Hutchins and Kaahuman 1991, 10).
6. By saying this I wish in no way to question the tremendous usefulness and timeliness of this anthology. Apart from reassuring me that my own thoughts and experiences were shared by many other people, the anthology has also provided an important starting point for the present study of bisexuality and lesbian ethics.

7. I take the term "universalizing" from Sedgwick's useful distinction between "minoritizing" and "universalizing" understandings of homo/heterosexual definition. According to the first view, homo/heterosexual definition is "an issue of active importance primarily for a small, distinct, relatively fixed homosexual minority"; from the latter perspective, it is an "issue of continuing, determinative importance in the lives of people across the spectrum of sexualities" (Sedgewick 1990, 1). My linkage between "universalizing" and "queer" is one that emerges clearly within recent work in queer theory. Thus, to Michael Warner, the preference for the term "queer" over "lesbian" and "gay" "represents, among other things, an aggressive impulse of generalization; it rejects a minoritizing logic of toleration or simple political interest-representation in favor of a more thorough resistance to regimes of the normal. The universalizing utopianism of queer theory does not entirely replace more minority-based versions of lesbian and gay theory—nor could it, since normal sexuality and the machinery of enforcing it do not bear down equally on everyone" (Warner 1991, 16).

REFERENCES

Butler, Judith, 1990. *Gender Trouble*. New York: Routledge.

Churchill, Caryl. 1985. *Plays*. London: Methuen.

Däumer, Elisabeth. 1991. Feminist biphobia; or, what does sexuality have to do with gender? Paper presented at North Central Women's Studies Association conference, 19 October, Athens, Ohio.

de Lauretis, Teresa, ed. 1991. Special issue of *Differences: A Journal of Feminist Cultural Studies* 3 (2).

Frye, Marilyn. 1990. Do you have to be a lesbian to be a feminist? *off our backs* August/September.

Fuss, Diana. 1989. *Essentially speaking*. New York: Routledge.

— . Ed. 1991. *inside/out: Lesbian theories, gay theories*. New York: Routledge.

Hoagland, Sarah Lucia. 1988. *Lesbian ethics: Toward new value.* Palo Alto: Institute of Lesbian Studies.

Hutchins, Loraine, and Lani Kaahumanu, eds. 1991. *Bi any other name: Bisexual people speak out.* Boston: Allyson Publications.

Morales, Aurora Levins. 1992. First but not least. Review of *Bi any other name: Bisexual people speak out*, ed. Loraine Hutchins and Lani Kaahumanu. *Women's Review of Books* 9 (6): 23-24.

Orlando, Lisa. 1991. Loving whom we choose. In *Bi any other name*. See Hutchins and Kaahumanu.

Queen, Carol A. 1991. The queer in me. In *Bi any other name*. See Hutchins and Kaahumanu.

Sedgwick, Eve Kosofsky. 1990. *Epistemology of the closet.* Berkeley: University of California Press.

Tallen, Bette S. 1990. How inclusive is feminist political theory? Questions for lesbians. In *Lesbian philosophies and cultures*, ed. Jeffner Allen. Albany: State University of New York Press.

Warner, Michael. 1991. Introduction: Fear of a queer planet. *Social Text* 29: 3-17.

Weeks, Jeffrey. 1985. *Sexuality and its discontents.* London: Routledge and Kegan Paul.

Wittig, Monique. 1981. One is not born a woman. *Feminist Issues* 1 (2): 47-54.

STUDY QUESTIONS

1. What does Jordan mean by moral impasses? What does he mean by public dilemmas? What is it about homosexuality that has Jordan conclude that this is a case of a moral impasse that constitutes a public dilemma about which the state can only remain neutral if it does not sanction same sex marriage? Do you agree? Why or why not?
2. While Jordan argues that discrimination against homosexuals in the case of allowing them to marry is justified, he leaves open the possibility that discrimination against homosexuals is impermissible in other cases. What might these cases be? Would it include allowing homosexuals to adopt children or enter the army? Make use of Jordan's account of the "parity thesis" to answer these questions.
3. Does Overall's analysis of heterosexuality as an institution that is "transparent, virtually invisible, yet very powerful" undermine Jordan's argument that the state can only remain neutral if it does not sanction same sex marriage? Why or why not?
4. What evidence does Overall provide to support her argument that women and men are differentially affected by the institution of heterosexuality and the social pressures to be heterosexual?
5. If heterosexuality is enforced in the ways described by Overall, can women *choose* heterosexuality? Can a feminist be heterosexual? Does Overall's use of the notion of a "lesbian continuum" help to answer these questions? According to Overall, what sorts of feminist strategies would challenge or undermine the institution of heterosexuality?
6. Calhoun differentiates the sorts of inequality and oppression experienced by gays and lesbians from that experienced by racial minorities and women. What are the main differences she outlines as constituting what she refers to as "sexuality injustice"? Does her account challenge Overall's feminist analysis of heterosexuality? Why or why not?
7. What does Calhoun mean when she claims that sexuality injustice consists in the displacement of homosexuality and lesbianism to the outside of society? Outline and evaluate the three main arguments Calhoun uses to support this claim.
8. Card gives reasons very different from those given by Jordan for questioning the legitimacy of institutionalizing same-sex marriage. What are they? Whose account do you favor and why?
9. Why does Card also raise doubts about the institution of motherhood and how are these doubts connected to her scepticism about supporting same-sex marriage?
10. Däumer argues that lesbians and feminists need not be as disapproving and distrustful of bisexuals as they have tended to be. What reasons does she offer for the distrust and what arguments does she provide in defence of bisexuality?
11. According to Däumer, how can bisexuality contribute to the goals of devising an ethics of difference and developing nonoppressive ways of responding to difference? Compare and contrast this strategy for undermining the institution of heterosexuality with strategies advocated by the other authors in this chapter.

SUGGESTED READINGS

Abelove, Henry et. al. (editors). *The Lesbian and Gay Studies Reader.* New York: Routledge, 1993.
Allison, Dorothy. *Skin: Talking about Sex, Class, & Literature.* Ithaca, NY: Firebrand Books, 1994.
Almaguer, Tomás. "Chicano Men: A Cartography of Homosexual Identity and Behavior." *differences: A Journal of Feminist Cultural Studies*, v. 3, no. 2 (1991): 75-100.

Austin, Andrea and Adrian Alex Wellington. "Outing: The Supposed Justifications." *The Canadian Journal of Law & Jurisprudence*, v. 8, no. 1 (1995): 83-105.

Bedecarré, Corrinne. "Swear by the Moon." *Hypatia*, v. 12, no. 3 (Summer 1997): 189-197.

Butler, Judith. "Imitation and Gender Insubordination." In *Inside/Out: Lesbian Theories, Gay Theories* edited by Diana Fuss. New York: Routledge, 1991.

Card, Claudia. *Lesbian Choices.* New York: Columbia University Press, 1995.

Clarke, Cheryl. "Lesbianism: An Act of Resistance." In *This Bridge Called my Back: Writings by Radical Women of Color* edited by Cherree Moraga, Gloria Anzalduá. New York: Kitchen Table, Women of Color Press, 1983: 128-137.

Eskridge, William N. Jr. "Beyond Lesbian and Gay 'Families We Choose'." In *Sex, Preference, and Family: Essays on Law and Nature* edited by David M. Estlund and Martha Nussbaum. Oxford University Press, 1996.

Frye, Marilyn. *Willful Virgin: Essays in Feminism.* Freedom, CA: The Crossing Press, 1992.

Hale, Jacob. "Are Lesbians Women?" *Hypatia*, v. 11, no. 2 (Spring 1996): 94-121.

Halperin, David. "Is There a History of Sexuality?" *History and Theory*, v. 28 (1989): 257-274.

Heldke, Lisa. "In Praise of Unreliability." *Hypatia*, v. 12, no. 3 (Summer 1997): 174-182.

Hoagland, Sarah. *Lesbian Ethics: Toward New Value.* Palo Alto, CA: Institute of Lesbian Studies, 1988.

O'Connor, Peg. "Warning! Contents Under Heterosexual Pressure." *Hypatia*, v. 12, no. 3 (Summer 1997): 184-188.

Rich, Adrienne. "Compulsory Heterosexuality and Lesbian Existence" *Signs: Journal of Women in Culture and Society*, v. 5, no. 4 (1980): 631-660.

Rubin, Gayle. "Thinking Sex: Notes for a Radical Theory of the Politics of Sexuality." In *Pleasure and Danger: Exploring Female Sexuality* edited by Carole Vance. New York: Routledge, 1984.

Ruse, Michael. "Is Homosexuality Bad Sexuality?" In *Homosexuality*. Oxford: Blackwell, 1988.

Wellington, Adrian Alex. "Why Liberals Should Support Same Sex Marriage." *Journal of Social Philosophy*, v. 26, no. 3 (Winter 1995): 5-32.

CHAPTER SEVEN

DIFFERENTIAL ABILITY

By now a very clear picture should have started to take shape in thinking about issues of diversity and equality, a picture of the highly complex nature of kinds of discrimination that are now taken to be morally wrong. Many of the chapters in Part II highlight the role that stereotypes play in shaping perceptions and self-perceptions of members of disadvantaged groups in ways that affect their lives and life prospects. For example, stereotypes of racial minorities and women as intellectually inferior have resulted in their exclusion from power. One result of stereotypes of gay men and lesbians as engaged in immoral activity is their exclusion from debates about policies regarding sexuality, marriage, parenting, childcare, and education. While there are similarities in the ways in which forms of discrimination are manifested and in the inequalities that result, there are also significant differences as well as places where intersections result in the creation of new issues and problems. As we move to questions about the difference that levels of ability make to a person's life prospects, it is a good idea to keep this complexity in mind.

The World Health Organization distinguishes three concepts related to differential ability. *Impairments* are physiological, psychological, or anatomical abnormalities or losses as described by biomedical scientists. *Disabilities* are restrictions or lack of ability to perform an activity in the manner or range *considered* normal. Disabilities can be the result of impairments, but not all impairments result in disabilities. *Handicaps* are disadvantages created by how the disabilities or impairments are perceived and received. If I am an amputee in a wheelchair, my impairment is the loss of my legs and my disability means that I cannot walk, but I am handicapped by a social environment that does not provide ramps to let me into buildings. The conceptual clarification is meant to capture the idea that disadvantages experienced by persons with disabilities arise from the interaction of their impairments with the social environment and not from biology or social practice alone.

David Wasserman discusses changes to perceptions of and policies with respect to disability by examining the Americans with Disabilities Act (ADA) enacted by the US Congress in 1990. The ADA acknowledges that people with disabilities were bypassed by early civil rights movements and that individuals experiencing discrimination on the basis of disability had no legal recourse to address such discrimination. Wasserman argues that the ADA's anti-discrimination framework serves several functions: it emphasizes similarities between the treatment of people with disabilities and the treatment of other minorities; it encourages society to find the source of disadvantages in its own attitudes and practices rather than in the disabilities themselves; and it supports the notion that accommodating people with disabilities is a matter of justice and not charity. The ADA's "reasonable accommodation" requirement supports a conception of equality that demands more than the removal of legal barriers to opportunities in its recommendations for reconstructing the social world itself to accommodate the *full* range of human abilities. The requirement serves functions similar to forced busing and affirmative action measures in that it compensates for the effects of past and ongoing injustice and it undermines stereotypes that have kept people with disabilities out of the workforce and mainstream society in general. Wasserman supports the framework of the ADA and its policies, but argues that it offers little guidance on how much accommodation justice requires in the face of limited resources and severe disabilities.

Anita Silvers also examines the Americans with Disabilities Act and in the process raises a few questions about Wasserman's analysis. Silvers agrees with Wasserman that the ADA reconceptualizes disability as an issue that is not to be located in the physical or mental state of a minority of society's members, but in the way society is organized and structured so as to disadvantage this minority. She argues, however, that Wasserman does not fully grasp the conceptual shift advanced by the ADA and thereby implicitly accepts the devaluing stereotypes that the ADA opposes and attempts to dislodge. At the bottom of these devaluing stereotypes of persons with disabilities as deviant, disgusting, beyond cure by modern science, and in need of care-givers is the standard medical model that treats persons with disabilities as biologically inferior and incapable of moral agency. Silvers holds that the assumptions underlying the standard medical model can also be found in a model of care as it applies to perceptions and treatment of persons with disabilities. Care, she argues, promotes dependency and undermines agency by assuming that a "normal" able-bodied person can understand what it is like to be in a disabled person's place. The goal of the ADA, argues Silvers, is not the medical model one of making the disabled whole or of caring for them, but of eliminating social practices that implicitly or explicitly favor the non-disabled. The ADA requires that persons with disabilities be treated as fully equal. This goes much further than does the medical model and philosophical theories of care that emerge from it.

In the third reading, Nirmala Erevelles situates her analysis of a care model in the discussion of a voluntary organization in South India, DOST, that cares for disabled children. Erevelles identifies a point of disagreement between feminists and disability activists to turn our attention to how the intersections of class/caste, race, gender, and disability are shaped by the exploitative economic conditions of capitalism. Feminists have argued that community care for persons with disabilities relocates the burden of informal care on women, who are expected to care for people not cared for by the state. Disability activists contend that these arguments by feminists undermine the right of disabled persons to live meaningful lives within the community by continuing to relegate them to institutional settings. For Erevelles, the category of disability is embedded with information about who gets to work, who deserves the privileges of social welfare, and who is exempt from certain obligations of citizenship. As such, it permits a critical analysis of capitalism and the welfare state, an analysis she provides by describing DOST in India. The care-givers in DOST have the same levels of social and economic deprivation as the disabled children they care for. They are as destitute and exploited as those in their charge, relegated to these caring roles, and considered only marginally useful in the labor market of mainstream society. Erevelles uses this discussion to argue that relocating domestic labor in the capitalist market will not mitigate the exploitative conditions of the social division of labor, a division that cuts across race, gender, and class/caste and is evident in the discourse of disability and the caring work associated with it.

The final reading in this chapter brings the discussion of issues of disability into a global context by exploring the relationship between poverty and disability. Peter Beresford points out that people with disabilities are grossly over-represented among poor people, that they experience levels of economic and social deprivation rarely encountered by other groups, and that the majority of disabled people live in developing countries where they receive little or no resources. He argues that accounts of poverty fail to address the urgent issue of the relationship between poverty and disability and are based on the perspectives, ideologies, and interests of rich North/Western countries. *Absolute poverty* is the lack of basic necessities for life. *Relative deprivation* is the inability to live according to the customs and values of one's society. The absolute definition is taken as an objective scientific measure and provides no account of individual, occupational, cultural, or ethnic differences. The relative definition is tied to existing patterns of consumption and associated with dominant customs, values, and patterns of living not shared or accepted by everyone. Both rely on paternalistic attitudes and emphasize material goods as standards for measuring human flourishing.

Beresford maintains that an examination of the overlapping perspectives of people who live in poverty and people with disabilities can offer insights for understanding the relation between poverty and disability. Like anti-poverty groups, disabled people's organizations have challenged their exclusion from the discourse and conceptualization of poverty. Beresford defends a rights-based approach, one that can offer a framework for persons with disabilities in the North and South to pursue their goals and objectives while acknowledging their political, cultural, social, and economic differences.

DISABILITY, DISCRIMINATION, AND FAIRNESS

David Wasserman

David Wasserman is a Research Scholar at the Institute for Philosophy and Public Policy at the University of Maryland, College Park. His research focuses on criminal law and legal practice, ethical and policy issues in genetic research and technology, justice for people with disabilities, and various issues in procedural and distributive justice. In addition to numerous articles and book chapters, he has written A Sword for the Convicted: Representing Indigent Defendants on Appeal *(Greenwood, 1990) and co-authored* Disability, Difference, Discrimination: Perspectives on Justice in Bioethics and Public Policy *with Anita Silvers and Mary Mahowald (Rowman & Littlefield, 1998).*

Wasserman provides a critical examination of the Americans with Disabilities Act (ADA) enacted by Congress in 1990. He argues that the ADA serves the important functions of emphasizing similarities between the treatment of people with disabilities and the treatment of other disadvantaged groups, encouraging society to find the source of the disadvantages in its own attitudes and practices rather than in the disabilities, and defending the view that accommodating persons with disabilities is a matter of justice, not charity. Yet, Wasserman argues, the ADA's injunction against discrimination and its requirement of equal opportunity offers little practical guidance about what justice requires when society is faced with limited resources and severe disabilities.

It is widely agreed that people with disabilities are treated unfairly in our society: that they are the victims of pervasive discrimination, and that they have been denied adequate accommodation in areas ranging from housing construction to hiring practices to public transportation. As Congress declared in enacting the Americans with Disabilities Act (ADA) in 1990:

> [I]ndividuals with disabilities are a discrete and insular minority who have been faced with restrictions and limitations, *subjected to a history of purposeful unequal treatment*, and relegated to a position of political powerlessness in our society. ...[emphasis added]

Reprinted with permission of the publisher and David Wasserman from *Report from the Institute for Philosophy & Public Policy* 13:4 (Fall 1993): 7–12.

Yet people with disabilities were largely bypassed by the civil rights revolution of the past generation. Congress found that "unlike individuals who have experienced discrimination on the basis of race, color, sex, national origin, religion, or age, individuals who have experienced discrimination on the basis of disability have often had no legal recourse to redress such discrimination."

The ADA is intended to provide that legal recourse. It requires employers, transit systems and public facilities to modify their operations, procedures, and physical structures so as to make reasonable accommodation for people with disabilities. The ADA recognizes broad exceptions in cases where these modifications would result in "undue hardship" or pose risks to third parties. But in principle, the statute treats the failure to ensure that people with disabilities have an "equal opportunity to benefit" from a wide range of activities and services as a form of discrimination.

The ADA's anti-discrimination framework serves several important functions. It emphasizes similarities between the treatment of people with disabilities and the treatment of other minorities. It encourages society to find the source of the disadvantages experienced by people with disabilities in its own attitudes and practices, rather than in the disabilities themselves, and it supports the proposition that accommodating people with disabilities is a matter of justice, not charity.

But the anti-discrimination model offers little guidance on how much accommodation justice requires in the face of limited resources and severe disabilities. Its requirement of equal opportunity to benefit is ambiguous, and its emphasis on remedial action by private individuals and organizations overlooks our collective responsibility for constructing a more accommodating environment. The difficult problems of social justice raised by disabilities cannot be resolved by a simple injunction against discrimination.

The Civil Rights Analogy

The ADA has obvious similarities with recent civil rights legislation. It is designed to protect members of a group long subject to exclusion and prejudice, and it does this by removing barriers to the employment and accommodation of that group. The ADA recognizes that people with disabilities have suffered from false beliefs about their capacities, just as blacks and women have, and that their exclusion has been insidiously self-perpetuating, denying them the experience needed to overcome such biases.

The tendency to devalue those with "visible differences" goes beyond overt prejudice. A recent study of the impact of disability on neo-natal treatment decisions found that doctors and parents were both more likely to decline treatment for premature infants in cases involving a disability, while denying that the disability played any role in their decisions. The researchers saw this as "testimony to the insidious depths to which social stigmas associated with disability can embed themselves in individual consciousness."

Like earlier civil rights law, the ADA recognizes that such deeply embedded prejudice will work its way into the design of social structures and practices, and that stringent measures may be necessary to root it out. The enduring and pervasive impact of prejudice has long prompted the courts to give close scrutiny to "facially neutral" policies with an adverse impact on mistreated and disfavored groups. If public officials, for example, decide that children should attend schools in their own neighborhoods, this may appear to be a neutral basis for school assignment, but in fact it perpetuates the effects of residential covenants and other discriminatory practices that have kept minority families out of affluent suburban communities. Forced busing is not intended to achieve racially diverse schools *per se*, but to undo the enduring effects of those practices. Similarly, affirmative action is not designed to achieve demographic representativeness so much as to surmount the barriers to employment left by generations of exclusion.

The ADA's requirement of "reasonable accommodation" serves many of the same remedial functions, helping to overcome the enduring effects of conscious and unconscious discrimination. As Gregory Kavka notes, the rationales for affirmative action under earlier civil rights law are equally applicable to reasonable accommodation under the ADA: to establish the kinds of role models and "old-boy" networks that dominant groups now enjoy; to correct for the systematic errors in evaluation that result from stereotyping and over-generalization; and to compensate for the effects of past and ongoing injustice, such as exclusion from relevant training.

On the other hand, the assumption that any adverse impact can be traced to prejudice, hatred, contempt, or devaluation—to what Ronald Dworkin has called "invidious discrimination"—is clearly less tenable for disability than for race or ethnicity. The ADA itself recognizes that the physical endowment of people with disabilities contributes to their disadvantage: the statute defines disability as "physical or mental impairment" that "substantially limits [the impaired person's] pursuit of major life activities." Thus, while the ADA rightly holds the attitudes and practices of the larger society responsible for much of the limitation experienced by people with disabilities, it also recognizes an objective category of biological impairment; a person whose major life activities were limited *only* by other people's attitudes or practices would be "disabled" only in a derivative sense. The disadvantages experienced by people with disabilities arise from the interaction of their physical conditions and their social environment; those disadvantages can rarely be attributed to biology *or* social practice alone.

But this understanding of disability raises a critical question about the meaning of "equal opportunity to benefit" under the ADA. In one obvious sense, we assure equal opportunity by removing *legal* barriers to entry or access. (Keep in mind that legal barriers have, in the not-too-distant past, been oppressive and pervasive: in an era when one of the great liberal Supreme Court justices could declare that "three generations of imbeciles in enough," people with disabilities were often forbidden to work, to marry, to have children, or even to be seen in public.) Yet equal opportunity conceived as freedom from legal restriction is clearly inadequate to encompass the kind of accommodations to which people with disabilities seem entitled. A more demanding notion of equal opportunity would require us to undo the effects of invidious discrimination, past and present, de jure and de facto. But even this would fail to address the severely constricted opportunities available to many people with disabilities.

A much stronger sense of equal opportunity is suggested by the ADA's mandate to eliminate "architectural barriers" and other structural impediments to access and mobility. In order to provide equal opportunity in this sense, we must remove not only barriers imposed intentionally by law and prejudice, but also barriers imposed incidentally by designs and structures that ignore the needs of people with disabilities. We must reconstruct the social world to better accommodate the range of abilities of those who inhabit it.

Structural Accommodation and Equal Opportunity

This stronger conception of equal opportunity emerges from the feminist critique of earlier civil rights laws, with their focus on invidious discrimination. Many feminists argue that the design of physical structures and social practices to accommodate one group—able-bodied males—denies equal opportunity to everyone else. The structures and practices of our society embody a dominant norm of healthy functioning, just as they embody a dominant norm of male functioning. As Susan Wendell argues:

> In North America at least, life and work have been structured as though no one of any importance in the public world ... has to breast-feed a baby or look after a sick child .... Much of the world is also structured as though everyone is physically strong ... as though everyone can walk, hear and see well....

The public world provides stairs to the able-bodied so that they can overcome the force of gravity; it is less consistent about providing ramps so that paraplegics can do the same. To build stairs for the one group without building ramps for the second denies the latter equal opportunity to benefit.

This position was anticipated a generation ago by Jacobus tenBroek, who argued that the right of people with disabilities "to live in the world" required comprehensive changes in our physical and social order: not just in the design of buildings and public spaces, but in the duties of care owed by "abled" pedestrians, drivers, common carriers, and property owners to people with disabilities as they travel in public spaces. The refusal to make these changes denies people with disabilities their right to live in the world—the same right that was denied to blacks and women when they were excluded from public facilities.

However, providing equal opportunity for people with disabilities involves a more ambiguous and problematic commitment than the example of stairs and ramps might suggest. Ramps cost little more than stairs and are useful for people of widely varying abilities. The same is true for most of the design standards mandated by the ADA. These standards were developed more than 30 years ago, when tenBroek was writing, and their prompt implementation at that time would have probably brought about dramatic improvements in mobility and access at very slight cost.

But other opportunities to benefit do not come so cheaply. Technology sometimes offers considerable benefits, but only at enormous cost: one thinks of the devices that allow Stephen Hawking to "speak."

More often, perhaps, the benefits of costly technology are slight or uncertain. Does the failure to provide quadriplegics with the latest advances in robotics deny them equal opportunity? We could spend indefinitely more on robotic research and equipment, but no matter how much we spent, the opportunities of some quadriplegics would remain severely constricted.

More broadly, we cannot reasonably expect to raise all people with disabilities to a level of functioning where they can receive the same benefit from facilities and services as able-bodied people. There are many areas of employment, transit, and public accommodation where it would be impossible to achieve absolute equality in the opportunity to benefit, and where significantly reducing inequalities in the opportunity to benefit would exhaust the resources of those charged with the task of equalization.

In addressing the issue of how much a decent society should spend to improve the opportunities of people with disabilities, an equal opportunity standard is either hopelessly ambiguous or impossibly demanding. Within the ADA, moreover, there is an unresolved tension between the equal opportunity standard it affirms and the degree of inequality that will remain acceptable under its regulatory guidelines. For example, although the public transit provisions of the statute speak of equal opportunity, the accompanying regulations will leave most people with disabilities with a far greater burden of mobility than most able-bodied people. Perhaps the regulations should require more. But however much they required, they would fall short of assuring equal mobility.

The fact of biological impairment, recognized by the ADA in its definition of disability, makes the notion of "equal opportunity to benefit" problematic. This is a serious defect in a statute that treats the denial of such opportunity as a form of discrimination.

Disability and Biological Misfortune

Recognizing impairments as biological disadvantages raises the question of the extent to which a decent society must accommodate natural misfortune. Such misfortune matters greatly in determining fair treatment within the smaller unit of the family. Consider, for instance, the father's dilemma presented by Thomas Nagel:

> Suppose I have two children, one of which is quite normal and quite happy, and the other of which suffers from a painful handicap.... Suppose I must decide between moving to an expensive city where the second child can receive special medical treatment and schooling, but where the family's standard of living will be lower and the neighbourhood will be unpleasant and dangerous for the first child—or else moving to a pleasant semi-rural suburb where the first child ... can have a free and agreeable life.... [Suppose] the gain to the first child of moving to the suburb is substantially greater than the gain to the second child of moving to the city. After all, the second child will also suffer from the family's reduced standard of living and the disagreeable environment. And the educational and therapeutic benefits will not make [the second child] happy but only less miserable. For the first child, on the other hand, the choice is between a happy life and a disagreeable one.

Because the second child is worse off, his interests have a greater urgency than those of the first child. Moving to the city would be the more egalitarian decision, and, if the difference in benefit to the two children is only slight, the fairer decision. But the urgency of the second child's interests does not give them absolute priority; we would think it unfair to the first child to reduce him to the same level of misery as the second for very slight gains in the second child's well-being.

This dilemma is writ large in the allocation of educational resources for children with learning disabilities. Special education is very expensive, and many financially strapped school systems find that providing more than minimal benefit to severely disabled children would require drastic cutbacks in other programs, such as honors classes for gifted students. Yet the Education for All Handicapped Children Act of 1975 (EHA) mandates "free appropriate education" for all children, regardless of ability. This mandate has been variously interpreted to mean that children with disabilities must receive "some educational benefit," that they must receive benefit "commensurate" with that accorded to normal children, or that they must receive the "maximum possible" benefit.

William Galston makes a powerful argument for a commensurate benefit standard:

> In spite of profound differences among individuals, the full development of each individual—however great or limited his or her natural capacities—is equal in moral weight to that of every other.... [A] policy that neglects the educable retarded so that they do not learn how to care for themselves and must be institutionalized is, considered in itself, as bad as one that deprives extraordinary gifts of their chance to flower.

But technology makes "natural capacity" and "full development" very elastic notions, and this raises serious problems for a standard of equal opportunity that requires a comparison of actual and potential development.

If a society were a family, some loss of educational benefit to the most gifted students might seem justified in a school system intent upon enhancing opportunity for students with disabilities. But even in that case, an allocation that left the most gifted at the same low level of educational development as the most grievously disabled would seem grossly unfair. And it is not clear that even the modest sacrifices that would be appropriate within a family would be appropriate for the larger society; perhaps one feature that distinguishes families from larger, impersonal social units is a greater concern for the welfare of each member than for each one's share of external resources.

Clearly, biological misfortune raises issues about the meaning of fair treatment that the ADA's anti-discrimination framework gives us little guidance in resolving. That framework also limits the social response to disabilities by imposing the costs of accommodation primarily on individuals. As we saw in the case of special education, the larger society may not always be able to bear such costs. But in other cases, burdens that would be excessive for an individual or agency may well be reasonable for a city or state. An individual should not have to plead undue hardship in order to avoid costs properly imposed on the community; a person with disabilities should not be denied accommodation because it imposes an undue hardship on an individual employer.

A recent analysis of the employment provisions of the ADA predicted that its anti-discrimination framework would have the effect of confining its benefits to a "disability elite"—those workers "who have the least serious disabilities and the strongest education, training, and job skills." Because employers have to bear the costs of accommodation, they will "skim the 'cream' of the population with disabilities," bypassing those with more severe and debilitating conditions. In order to help those with the most serious and pervasive disabilities, the government must significantly increase its investments in welfare, employer subsidies, and job training. But such measures are matters of distributive justice, and the fact that they are not among the remedies mandated by the ADA suggests the limitations of the anti-discrimination model upon which the current law rests.

Nevertheless, the specific provisions of the ADA on employment, transit, and public accommodation reflect, in Chief Justice Earl Warren's famous phrase, "the evolving standards of decency that mark the progress of a maturing society." To say that the question of fair treatment for people with disabilities does not have an obvious or final answer is not to say that we cannot reach a consensus on what fairness requires at our level of affluence and technological development. The ADA represents a major step towards achieving such a consensus.

REFERENCES

Amundson, Ron. "Disability, Handicap, and the Environment," *Journal of Social Philosophy*, vol. 23, no.1 (1992).

Burkhauser, Richard V. "Beyond Stereotypes: Public Policy and the Doubly Disabled," *The American Enterprise* (September/October 1992).

Dworkin, Ronald. *Taking Rights Seriously* (Harvard University Press, 1977).

Evans, Daryl. "The Psychological Impact of Disability and Illness on Medical Treatment Decisionmaking," *Issues in Law and Medicine*, vol. 5 No. 3 (1989).

Galston, William. *Liberal Purposes: Goods, Virtues, and Diversity in the Liberal State* (Cambridge University Press, 1991).

Kavka, Gregory S. "Disability and the Right to Work," *Social Philosophy & Policy*, vol. 9, No. 1 (1992).

Nagel, Thomas. "Equality," in *Readings in Social and Political Philosophy*, edited by Robert M. Stewart (Oxford University Press, 1986).

Rebell, Michael A."Structural Discrimination and the Disabled," *Georgetown Law Journal*, vol. 74 (1986).

tenBroek, Jacobus. "The Right to Live in the World: The Disabled in the Law of Torts," *California Law Review*, vol. 54 (1966).

Trouwers-Crowley, S. *ADA Primer: A Concise Guide to The Americans With Disabilities Act of 1990* (Prentice Hall, 1990).

Wendell, Susan. "Toward a Feminist Theory of Disability," *Hypatia* vol. 4, no. 2 (1989).

(IN) EQUALITY, (AB) NORMALITY, AND THE AMERICANS WITH DISABILITIES ACT

Anita Silvers

Anita Silvers teaches philosophy at San Francisco State University. She has written extensively on the philosophy of art, ethics, and public policy. She is co-editor with Margaret Battin and Rosamond Rhodes of Physician Assisted Suicide: Expanding the Debate *(Routledge, 1998) and co-author with David Wasserman and Mary Mahowald of* Disability, Difference, Discrimination: Perspectives on Justice in Bioethics and Public Policy *(Rowman & Littlefield, 1998).*

The 1990 Americans with Disabilities Act enacted a conceptual shift in the meaning of "disability." Rather than defining "disability" as a disadvantageous physical or mental deficit of persons, it codifies the understanding of "disability" as a defective state of society which disadvantages these persons. In contrast, the standard medical model incorrectly conceptualizes disabled persons as biologically inferior, and thus confines them to the role of recipients of benevolence or care. Turning to an ethic of caring yields counter-intuitive results that conflict with the conceptual apparatus of the ADA. It is argued that in order to liberate social thought from this medical model and thus move the disabled from being socially marginalized to being socially enabled, one must re-conceptualize current practice by adopting the ADA's conceptual framework.

I. The Americans with Disabilities Act

The United States Constitutions's Fourteenth Amendment codifies the protection that no State shall "deny any person within its jurisdiction the equal protection of the laws." In 1990, congress enacted the Americans with Disabilities Act (ADA), public law 101-336, which extends equal protection to individuals whose physical or mental impairments substantially limit one or more life functions. Congress cited a history of isolation and discrimination to explain the need for this law.

> Historically, society has tended to isolate and segregate individuals with disabilities, and despite some improvements, such forms of discrimination ... continue to be a serious problem.... Individuals with disabilities are a discrete and insular minority who have been faced with restrictions and limitation, subjected to a history of purposeful unequal treatment, and relegated to a position of political powerlessness in our society based on characteristics that are beyond the control of such individuals and resulting from stereotypic assumptions not truly indicative of the individual ability of such individuals to participate in, and contribute to society (ADA, 1990).

While the ADA contains no explicit references to health care delivery, its requirements reach to the core of medical thought because through it Congress legislates a reconceptualization of the meaning of "disability." The ADA codifies into law the understanding that a disabling condition is a state of society itself, not a physical or mental state of a minority of society's members, and that it is the way society is organized rather than personal deficits which disadvantages this minority.

Reprinted with permission of the publisher from *The Journal of Medicine and Philosophy* 21 (1996): 209–224.

In striking contrast, the standard medical model[1] conceptualizes the disabled as biologically inferior, and in so conceiving confines such individuals to the role of recipients of benevolence rather than as persons with social and moral agency. This model assumes that uncompromised and unimpaired physical and mental status is the standard of "normalcy" for both medical practice and social policy.

In this paper I will argue that shifting the locus of disability from immutable personal shortcoming to remediable public failure liberates disabled individuals from the encroachment of the medical model. The ADA reformulates disabled persons' moral status, casting them in positive roles as responsible agents. Concomitantly, the ADA liberates society from having any special charitable duties to the disabled. I will begin the argument by laying out some of the conceptual history of the medical model which informs the attitudes of many physicians and other health care workers. My argument will proceed then in three parts. First, I will argue that the medical model pervasively infects typical medical rationing schemes, such as the Oregon Plan. Second, to its detriment, much philosophical discussion assumes the medical model. Third, turning to an ethic of caring has counter-intuitive results and conflicts with the ADA's conceptual framework. In sum, perceiving individuals with impairments as needing care subordinates them to care givers; when viewed as perpetual patients rather than as persons, their equality is limited.

II. A Conceptual History

To fully grasp the impact of the ADA, one must comprehend the ingrained historical categories of repression to which the disabled have been subjected. It is but a short slippery slide from thinking of a disability as a misfortune or a shame to considering it to be shameful. When we see a disabled person it is our practice to look away. This "etiquette" is an example of that which Charles Taylor terms the oppressive withholding of recognition (1992, p. 36). Until relatively recently the invisibility of disabled people even had legal sanction. For example, testimony supporting the passage of the ADA referenced a Chicago municipal ordinance that barred maimed, mutilated or otherwise deformed individuals from public ways or other public places. And the Wisconsin Supreme Court upheld the exclusion of a boy with cerebral palsy from school because he "produce(d) a depressing and nauseating effect on the teachers and school children." Personal testimony to the Congress was filled with narratives about how disabled citizens were expelled from public events because they were "disgusting to look at," from theaters because the manager did "not want her in here," from a zoo because an official believed the disabled individual would "upset the chimpanzees," and from being an account holder in a bank because the disabled customer "did not fit the image the bank wished to project" (ADA, 1989).

That we withhold social recognition from individuals with disabilities by not even looking at, let alone seeing, them has a long social history. In the thirteenth and fourteenth centuries the disabled began to be treated as a deviant social group. With the breakdown of the feudal system, laborers gained geographical mobility, however the need for place bound laborers remained pressing. Consequently, laws were enacted which forbade able-bodied workers from traveling between towns without special authorization. Disabled individuals, on the other hand, were encouraged to travel among towns to afford the able-bodied relief from their protracted presence. This mechanism effectively expelled the disabled from the ranks of the laboring class.

Persons with disabilities were grouped into a single inferior social class. It is this institutionalizing process from which sprang the concept of the disabled as a minority of persons whose physical and mental impairments disadvantage them in society. By the seventeenth century, the virtue of according charitable benevolence to those in need clashed outright with the fear of creating a class of drones. To combat this fear there emerged the concept of the deserving poor, a class which was reserved for those who would have worked if it were not for their unfortunate impairments.

Members of the deserving poor were carefully distinguished from the undeserving, willfully malfunctioning poor. However, careful attention to appropriate character was necessary if a disabled person was to avoid slipping into the undeserving class. With the advent of the medical model of disability, those with impairments were urged to submit themselves regularly to curative processes as proof of their dissatisfaction with their defective state. Because these often failed, the medical model rendered disability a state not only involuntary but immutable, one beyond redemption by modern science.

As a social class, the disabled were required, by definition, to be non-productive, and thus were considered incapable of responsible use of the goods which charity bestowed. Thus there emerged the social class of care-givers whose profession it was to channel and administer charity for the disabled. The role assigned to the disabled in this scheme magnified mere malfunctioning into an incapacity to shoulder responsibility and make a contribution. It is against this historical backdrop that the ADA would make its first decisive stand against the medical model.

III. The ADA'S First test: The Oregon Plan

In 1992, the Oregon Plan's rationing system for health care included language which legislated existing or potential disabilities as reasons for disallowing or diminishing medical treatment.[2] The Plan denied persons with existing or potential disabilities equal treatment under the law, and thus federal legal assessment concluded that the proposal violated the civil rights of the disabled.

Oregon's policies grew out of a telephone survey in which nondisabled individuals were asked to rank a variety of treatments and health care levels in various life circumstances. Physical or mental impairment of a kind which defied medical restoration was ranked lower than able-bodiness and thus Medicaid coverage for individuals with certain types of impairments was ranked lower than other types of coverage. The rankings assumed a conceptual framework in which to be physically or mentally impaired meant to live a life of an inferior quality. For instance, the Oregon commission ranked liver transplants for alcoholics much lower than liver transplants for persons without this debilitating condition. This ranking reflects the stereotypical belief that liver transplants must have poorer outcomes in alcoholic patients. No such data exist (Forman, 1993). The commission failed to dis-ambiguate between alcoholics who continue to imbibe large quantities of alcohol and those who have ceased. Only those who continue to drink have an increased chance of recurring liver disease.

Taken as a group, alcoholics may have a greater probability of recurring liver disease. Nevertheless, it is a fallacy to conclude that the higher probability attributable to the group as a whole applies equally to each member of the group. If such a mistake is made in association with withholding medical treatments for persons with disabilities, the ADA classifies it as a violation of the law. Thus, in so far as alcoholism can be classified as a disability, the ADA considers it a violation to bar a recovered alcoholic, who no longer drinks alcohol, from life saving treatment available to non-alcoholics. Assigning a lower priority for health care to persons in virtue of some debilitating condition is in direct conflict with the ADA's representation of a disability as a condition that does not diminish an individual's right to be recognized and cared for as a fully equal person.

In part the Oregon Plan's problems arose through the use of quality adjusted life year (QALY) calculations. The Oregon Health Services Commission designated that three factors—cost of the treatment, years of life saved, and amount of improvement in quality of life—be considered in rank-ordering a comprehensive list of medical services. Rationing based on QALY calculations incorporates the medical model; it assumes that an un-compromised, unimpaired physical and mental status is the desideratum which should guide the expenditure of health care dollars. QALY calculations cut across the conceptual distinctions of the ADA in that they generally assign a lower value to saving disabled persons with life threatening medical problems than to able-bodied persons with identical medical problems.

IV. The Persistence of Disability Discrimination

The medical model has intruded its influence into policy analyses. In a report on the ADA commissioned for the Report from the Institute for Philosophy and Public Policy, David Wasserman contended that nature makes persons with disabilities less equal than other persons (1993, pp. 7-12). He maintains that there are biological differences which constitute the definitive characteristics of the class protected by the ADA. Such properties, according to Wasserman, render the class's members irreparably inferior in respect to claims to fair or equitable treatment.

> ... [The ADA] also recognizes an objective category of biological impairment; a person whose major life activities were limited only by other people's attitudes or practices would be "disabled" only in a derivative sense (p. 9).

And later,

> [t]he fact of biological impairment, recognized by the ADA in its definition of disability, makes the notion of "equal opportunity to benefit" problematic. This is a serious defect in a statute that treats the denial of such opportunity as a form of discrimination (p.10).

However, the ADA neither mentions nor otherwise refers to biological impairment. While meticulously inclusive in its coverage of both physically and cognitively impaired persons, the ADA does not legislate that disability is biological in origin. In any case, although some impairments have a genetic or chemical origin, many are the result of traumatic injury, which is a mechanical rather than a biological process.

Conceiving of disability as essentially biological has the effect of explaining the social exclusion visited upon the disabled as "natural" or as ascribable to a non-social source. Policy makers who naturalize the isolation of the disabled have denied that society has any obligation to correct the social disadvantage which burdens individuals with disabilities. As Ron Amundson argues:

> (I)f handicaps are natural consequences (rather than social consequences) of disabilities, the victim's loss of opportunity can be thought of as beyond the resources, or at least beyond the responsibility of society to remedy. Someone whose disadvantage comes from a natural disaster may be an object of pity, and perhaps of charity.... Someone whose disadvantage occurs as a result of social decision has a more obvious claim for social remediation (1991, p. 113).

Those who suffer disadvantage as a result of social oppression may be owed rectification, while those whose disadvantage is of natural origin may be due only pity or charity. Suggestions that a social explanation of the disabled's isolation and disadvantage is not as objective as a biological explanation are spurious. This line of argument only functions as an apology to absolve society from responsibility for remedying the adverse impact of socially sanctioned exclusionary practices.

Wasserman also fails to recognize the conceptual shift inherent in the ADA's understanding of disability. He argues that

> (t)he ADA itself recognizes that the physical endowment of people with disabilities contributes to their disadvantage: the statute defines disability as "physical or mental impairment" that "substantially limits (the impaired person's) pursuit of major life activities" (p. 8).

The ADA, however, does not cite any direct causal connection between physical or mental state and disadvantage. The term "disadvantage" occurs in its text only in Finding 6, which argues that empirical research demonstrates that people with disabilities "occupy an inferior status in our society, and (are) severely disadvantaged socially, vocationally, economically, and educationally" (ADA, 1990). Thus, the law explicitly conjoins the disadvantaged state of disabled persons with the social status to which they have been consigned. This demonstrates the conceptual shift. "Disability" is not a physical or mental state of persons. Rather, the ADA codifies disability as a state of society which disadvantages persons. *As such, it is a problem which occurs as a result of social decision and is therefore subject to social correction.*

Moreover, while an impairment may not be an advantage, it does not logically follow that it must be a disadvantage. Disadvantages are heavily context dependent and relative to the ends or goals of an individual. In an age of corrective lenses and supermarkets, nearsightedness is not the disadvantage that it was to a Neanderthal hunter.

Informed by the historical perspective outlined above, and the medical model which grew out of it, Wasserman views the ADA as a mandate for charitable rather than equitable treatment. Without fully comprehending the conceptual shift, it is impossible to understand that *equal opportunity* rather than *exceptional treatment* is the ADA's legislative objective. For instance, the ADA's preface sets out the goal of remedying inequalities of opportunity which handicap citizens with disabilities.

> The continuing existence of unfair and unnecessary discrimination and prejudice denies people with disabilities the opportunity to compete on an equal basis ... (ADA, 1990).

Wasserman finds it impossible for individuals with disabilities to compete on an equal basis with the able-bodied. His report interprets the ADA's standard as guaranteeing equal outcomes, and argues that such a warrant is absurd.

> More broadly, we cannot reasonably expect to raise all people with disabilities to a level of functioning where they can receive the same benefits from facilities and services as able bodied people ... (p. 10).

This argument interposes a straw man.[3] Neither the ADA nor any disabled advocacy group proposes identity of outcomes as the test that people with disabilities are being treated equally. The goal is not to make the disabled whole, but rather to eliminate social practices which implicitly or explicitly favor the non-disabled. Benefiting equally from public transportation, for example, means having the opportunity to travel the same public routes with approximately the same time and expenditure as nondisabled individuals.

The ADA does not try to render mobility-impaired individuals fully mobile. Wasserman's criticism that the regulation would still "leave most people with disabilities with a far greater burden of mobility than most able-bodied people" (p. 10) is at best irrelevant. It mistakenly imputes to the ADA the medical notion of the disabled as patients to be either made whole or cared for.

Wasserman confounds and obscures the distinction between two quite different questions. First, a medical question: whether a departure from normal physical or mental status is correctable. Second, a social question: whether society ought to ignore, repair, or adapt to a person's physical or mental impairment. To confound these two issues is tantamount to accepting the devaluing stereotypes which it is the ADA's avowed purpose to oppose. Thus Wasserman condemns the ADA by adopting the flawed social perspective it was designed to dislodge.

V. The Model of Caring

One philosophical response to Wasserman's criticisms is to turn to an ethics of care, in which moral relations are defined as taking place among unequals. In this type of moral framework being abnormal does not result in being morally marginalized. As Laurence Blum insists, it is not by reasoning about whether defective individuals are equal, but rather by feeling about their situations as they do themselves, that we can conduct ourselves morally towards them (1991).

Blum's diagnosis grows out of a conviction that logic driven judgments fail in situations where agents must behave ethically toward persons less advantaged than themselves. Rather than attempting to judge impartially or categorically, agents should respond so sensitively that their perception of the particularities of any situation match the perceptions of those with whom they are interacting.

Consider a case in which a worker debilitated by distress is treated callously by a supervisor, who refuses to adjust her standards to his impaired performance. Blum argues that it is natural to recognize the reality of another's pain, even if one cannot imagine one's self being in such pain. The pain of another is invisible only to the morally blind. Utilizing this moral schema, Blum argues that certain types of emotional responses impair moral vision in such a way that threatening aspects of reality are blocked out. Able-bodied persons dread beholding damaged persons out of a fear that they, themselves, might someday be impaired (1991, p. 718). Blum concludes that it is the supervisor's impaired moral perception which blocks her from accepting the pained person's estimation of the incapacitating impact of his pain, and his assessment of what the supervisor owes him with regard to it.

But Blum's assessment of this case is not accurate. To condemn the supervisor's moral proficiency in this manner has bizarre implications. A common experience among disabled individuals who have adapted to their impairments is to regret that there was an initial period of debilitating panic and self abdication. Regret of this sort is recounted again and again in anecdotal autobiographical material. On Blum's schema, though, persons who are now reconciled to their disabilities must be guilty of moral insensitivity toward their earlier despondent selves. This result is absurd. A disabled person does not owe it to his earlier self to regard prior self pity as credible. If such reasoning is absurd intra-personally, why should it be valid inter-personally? Concomitantly, there is a logical flaw in thinking that the supervisor owes a debilitated worker acceptance of the worker's own assessment of the quality of his life.

On the other hand, it is also not the case that a disabled individual ought necessarily to accept an able-bodied person's assessment of the disabled person's situation. Recognizing this point requires a rejection of the stereotypes stubbornly embedded in our social perceptions. As Amundson observes:

> The "sick role" ... relieves a person of normal responsibilities, but carries other obligations with it. The sick person is expected to ... regard his or her condition as undesirable. These requirements resonate with the attitudes of society toward disabled people.... One interesting correlation is that able-bodied people are often offended by disabled people who appear satisfied or happy with their condition (1992, pp. 114,118).

Society expects its projected image of regret to be in evidence. It is this expectation which places the disabled into the role of the sick to whom care must be given.

Proponents of the ethics of caring argue that social intimacy, originating from the natural affection of parents for their young, is the foundation of moral interaction. Within a functional family, defects in persons cause them to be cared for rather than condemned; it is this model that proponents attempt to apply to all moral interaction. Notice that this model is potentially limited if tender feelings for familial dependents are not largely extendible to total strangers.[4]

Functionally, a dependent stance is advantageous only if genuine; that is, if the putative dependent truly requires dependency status. In social systems which erect social and physical barriers to the disabled, and in which caring-for is the primary manner in which the able-bodied relate to the disabled, it becomes socially incumbent upon the latter to possess dependency status, even if they are more competent than the former.

Unfortunately, this type of moral framework lends itself to harming the putative dependent. It can lead to a requirement that the putative dependent accept lesser quality care than they would administer to themselves. There is no obligation that some individuals ought to allow themselves to be harmed simply to afford others with opportunities to be virtuous. Is it reasonable for a moral framework to make it virtuous to be poor simply so that the rich have the opportunity to act charitably? Analogously, this framework typecasts the disabled as subordinate, encouraging them to be vulnerable so that others may care for them.

To his credit, Blum recognizes that (dis)advantage and (mis)fortune are anchored to particular points of view. Consequently, his proposal to remediate inequality between the positions of moral agents assigns moral priority to the manner in which whomever is *disadvantaged* desires to be treated. Individuals with disabilities are allowed to designate appropriate conduct advanced toward themselves, and thus potentially equalize their relationship vis-à-vis the advantaged agent. Privileging the perspective of disabled individuals, however, is no improvement over disregarding their perspectives. *Such a framework merely assumes that it is the disabled which are subordinate and thus disadvantaged.* If forbearance for subordinates, rather than respect for equals, motivates moral conduct, then if disabled persons abandon the compliant behavior which mark them as subordinate, they dissolve the moral binds which link them to others. Thus, modeling morality on caring appears to make such self-sacrificing compliant behavior obligatory. This result is counter-intuitive in the extreme.

VI. Equality

What impedes persons with disabilities from commanding the respect due to equals? Why should a disabled person not count as fully in moral deliberation as someone unimpaired? The unreflective reaction to this question seems to be that being unable to perform some major life activity thoroughly devastates an individual's capacity for responsible performance and destroys the person's potential for all of life. Were this bleak depiction a fact instead of an over-reaction, no familiar moral criteria would afford individuals with disabilities equal moral weight. Amundson's critique of Amartya Sen's view of the disabled is worth repeating here to illustrate how the attribution of a physical or mental impairment may exclude an individual from the general application of consequentialist principles.[5]

> Sen criticizes utilitarian moral theory on the grounds that it would distribute income unfairly, as for example in "a case where one person A derives exactly twice as much utility as person B from any given level of income, say, because B has some handicap, e.g., being a cripple" (Sen, 1973). Sen apparently sees the "incapacitation" of cripples to be so global as to affect even their capacity for enjoyment—or at least their capacity to experience increases in personal utility from increases in resources proportional to those experienced by able-bodied people. This is a profoundly mistaken and destructive stereotype (1992, p. 114).

Similarly, Charles Taylor, commenting on the extent to which egalitarianism characterizes modern moral thought, exaggerates the impact of a disability and thus blocks equitable access to categorical moral principles affirming that humans generally deserve respect. Taylor identifies "the basis for our intuitions of equal dignity" as "an universal human potential, a capacity that all humans share." But, he continues, "our sense of the importance of potentiality reaches so far that we extend this protection even to people who through some circumstance that has befallen them are incapable of realizing their potential in the normal way—handicapped people ... for instance" (1992, pp. 42-42). This manner of explicating matters intimates that "handicapped" people are equal only by extension or derivation or fiction because they really do not possess the essentially human capacity to fulfill their potential "normality."

Yet reflection exposes the flaw in purporting to delineate normal from abnormal, or restricted, realization of human potential in this matter. Every person, equally, has potentials and whether these could have been fulfilled "in the normal way," and whether any loss accrues in not realizing them "in the normal way" is merely speculative. We would not dream of declaring that an athletically gifted person, who cannot realize his potential as a boxer because he wants to play the violin, is equal only in some extended sense. So, why place an artistically gifted person such as Itzhak Perlman, who for different reasons is not a boxer, in an inferior category?

Ethical thinking is obstructed because reasoning responds to the common, rather than the deviant. Modern moral thought has not construed disability as being like other particularities which differentiate moral agents from each other. While modern moral thought commonly dismisses differences between persons as contingent and external, and thus as inessential to a person's moral being, disability unmistakably has been embraced as *a morally essential attribute*; one which assigns the disabled to the borderline of moral worth. It is curious that modern thought, with its emphasis on inferiority and its disregard of external variation, fails to accept disability as inessential. But, as I have argued, the continuing influence of the medical model springs from social and historical prejudices which deny individuals with disabilities this acceptance.

The moral status of individuals with disabilities is impaired because society's stereotype defeats a condition imposed by most, perhaps all, rational moral systems, namely, that reasons for action must not be opaque to normal adults. For a moral reason to have motivating power, agents must at least understand the reason. However, a "normal" able-bodied individual is physically and socially blocked from accurately grasping what it is like to be in a "damaged" individual's place (as was evident in the Oregon health Plan's flawed telephone survey). Truths about how one would want to be treated if one were disabled are likely to be opaque to "normal" individuals and thus unable to motivate them morally. Far from extending protection so that it cloaks even individuals with disabilities, modern moral thought tends to magnify the influence of the medical model, with the result, inexorably, of excluding these individuals from normal moral recognition. The compulsion to dismiss them as abnormal—that is, as being in a state unthinkable for one's self—renders all appeals to what one would wish done, if one were to be in the other's place, ineffective.

Is inequality, cast as an intractable aspect of a person's experience, an essential human condition, or merely the artifact of an inequitable social arrangement? In the everyday life of persons mobilizing in wheelchairs, their experience of inequality, and their inequality in the eyes of others, manifests itself not only in the inability to walk but also in exclusion from bathrooms, from theaters, from transportation, from places of work, and from life-saving medical treatment. In keeping with this reality, it is the strategy of the ADA to require that whomever operates a facility or program must accommodate individuals with disabilities unless doing so would constitute an undue hardship, as measured against the overall financial resources of the facility or program. What informs this mandate is recognition that accessibility would be a commonplace, not a novelty, were the majority, not the minority, of the population disabled.

To conclude that physical or mental impairment, a contingent individual state, entails a moral deficit neglects the extent to which structural social arrangement permeates particular experience. Particularists like Blum, who legitimately focus on the experiential uniqueness of moral situations, tend to ground the possibility of interpersonal moral agreement in the existence of an "objective" moral reality, equally experientially accessible to all moral agents alike. They thereby discount the influence of the generalized social, political, and economic environment in composing experience, at most appealing to it to explain moral deviance, blockage, or blindness. In addition, they tend to discount the power of environmental reform to transfigure moral experience; including whether we can think of others, or ourselves, as equal. Likewise, essentialists who focus on universal human properties discount the extent to which social organization influences how we conceptualize or define ourselves.

Suppose that most persons used wheelchairs? Would we continue to build staircases rather than ramps? Suppose most were deaf? Closed-captioning would have been the standard for television manufacture long before July 1, 1993. By counter-factualizing about what society would do were persons with disabilities dominant rather than suppressed, it becomes evident that systematic exclusion of the disabled is a consequence not of their natural inferiority but of their minority social status.

VII. Conclusion

Very recently, it has become fashionable in philosophy, even commonplace, to challenge the theoretical transition from imagining one's self in others' places to accepting others as equivalent to one's self, which is the basis modern social thought has used since the enlightenment for assigning moral and social equality. It is argued that particularities of attachment, or of race or gender, exercise such substantial positive moral impact that to conceive of moral agents as fundamentally interchangeable strips away crucial moral features. In other words, abstracting from the features which differentiate persons is no longer thought to be necessary—indeed, is considered potentially counterproductive—to affording them equal moral recognition.

Heretofore, the particularities of disability have been impervious to this reform. And it remains to be seen whether particularizing, or, instead, universalizing, moral thinking better advances recognition of the moral agency of individuals with disabilities. I am inclined to have greater confidence in the latter approach, as my discussion in this essay makes manifest, but only if the social adjustments the ADA demands suffice to compel an understanding of equality which does not conflate being equal with being normal. On the other hand, were social practice to be reformed to expunge the influence of the medical model of disability, perhaps we could recognize how normal it is to be an individual with a disability and could accept such persons as fully rather than fictionally equal.

NOTES

1. In speaking of the "medical model," I refer to assumptions embedded deeply in current health care practice. I do not intend to stereotype all health care practitioners as accepting these assumptions. Nor do I contend that the relationships governed by these conceptions are injurious in every instance. Rather, my argument is that individuals with disabilities are confined to these relationships by the medical model.
2. Obtaining equitable health care is a widespread problem for individuals with disabilities (Evans, 1989).
3. In this part of his report, Wasserman appears to import Sen's metric of "capability" (Sen, 1980). However, Sen advances the goal of equality of capability as an alternative to equality of welfare, not as an alternative to equality of opportunity. Sen's concept of the responsibility of society to prefer individuals with disabilities as compensation for their deficits is not the ADA's assignment of responsibility not to discriminate against individual's with disabilities.
4. David Hume depicts these extended trust relationships as an "artificial contrivance for the convenience and advantage of society" and as requiring constant education and effort to maintain (1975).
5. Amundson somewhat misses Sen's point, which is that capability, not enjoyment, should be the metric of egalitarian distribution.

REFERENCES

Americans With Disabilities Act (ADA) 42 U.S.C., Sec 12101-12213 (Supp. II, 1990).

Americans With Disabilities Act (ADA) Record of Senate Hearing, 1989.

Amundson, R.: 1992, "Disability, handicaps and the environment," *Journal of Social Philosophy*, Vol. 23, no. 1, pp. 105-119.

Blum, L.: 1991, "Moral perception and particularity," *Ethics*, 101 (4), pp. 701-725.

Constitution of the United States, Fourteenth Amendment.

Evans, D.: 1989, "The psychological impact of disability and illness on medical treatment decision-making," *Issues in Law & Medicine*, Vol. 5, no. 3, pp. 295-6.

Forman, J.: 1993, "Defining basic benefits: Oregon and the challenge of health care reform," *Report from the Institute of Philosophy and Public Policy*, Winter/Spring, pp. 12-18.

Kolata, G.: 1992, "Ethical struggles with judgment of 'the value of life,'" *New York Times*, November 24, pp. B5, B7.

Mollat, M.: 1986, *The Poor in the Middle Ages: An Essay in Social History*, A. Goldhammer (trans.) New Haven: Yale University Press.

Sen, A.: 1973, *On Economic Inequality*, Oxford: Oxford University Press.

Sen, A.: 1980, "Equality of what?" *Tanner Lectures on Human Value*, S. McMurrin (ed.), Cambridge: Cambridge University Press.

Silvers, A.: 1994, "Defective' agents: Equality, difference and the tyranny of the normal," *The Journal of Social Philosophy*, June 1994.

Silvers, A.: 1995, "Damaged goods: Does disability disqualify people from just health care?" *The Mount Sinai Journal of Medicine*, Vol. 62, No. 2, pp. 102-111.

Taylor, C. *et al.*: 1992, *Multiculturalism and "The Politics of Recognition,"* Princeton: Princeton University Press.

Wasserman, D.: 1993, *Report for the Institute of Philosophy and Public Policy*, vol 13, No. 1/2, Winter/Spring.

DISABILITY AND THE DIALECTICS OF DIFFERENCE

Nirmala Erevelles

Nirmala Erevelles is currently a Graduate Student in the School of Education at Syracuse University.

"This paper re-theorises disability by asking the following question: within what historical, social, economic and political conditions does disability as an analytic of difference get constructed in a dialectical relationship with gender, class, caste and race? To respond to this question, I will first offer a materialist reading of the category of disability. I will then situate this discussion in an ethnographic study of a voluntary organisation in South India which provides residential as well as rehabilitational services for disabled children. Finally, I will discuss the politics of gendered "caring work" and its implications for the continued production of marginalised difference. In doing this, I will thus demonstrate how disability can be re-understood as an ideological condition which is also structured by the same exploitative material conditions of capitalism as are race, caste, class and gender."

Within the current theoretical context, disability discourses that continue to privilege physiological/biological models indicate an outmoded intellectual framework. In fact, the more prevalent discourses on disability draw upon the "Social Model of Disability," which argues that it is not the physical and/or mental impairment that disables an individual, but the "handicapping" effects of a society whose interests are geared toward an "able-bodied" population (Biklen and Bogdan, 1977; Bogdan and Taylor, 1977; Finkelstein, 1980; Abberley, 1987; Oliver, 1990; Morris, 1991; Lloyd, 1992). It is through such "handicapist" practices that disabled persons often find themselves excluded from mainstream lifestyles, relegated to the margins of society. Over the last decade, an increasing number of disabled individuals have refused to accept these marginal locations and through an active Disability Rights Movement have demanded the right to be regarded as valued participants within mainstream society (Abberley, 1987; Scotch, 1988; Oliver, 1990). However, notwithstanding the many gains this movement has won for disabled people, in recent years, the cohesiveness of this movement itself has been challenged, particularly by those disabled persons who have also faced "simultaneous" or "multiple" discrimination on the basis of their race, class, gender or sexual orientation (Fine and Asch, 1988; Lonsdale, 1990; Morris, 1991; Deegan, 1991; Begum, 1992; Lloyd, 1992; Priestley, 1995). They have argued that the all-encompassing category of "handicapism"—the systematic discrimination against people labelled as disabled—has been inadequate in effectively describing the complexities of the experiences of disabled people who face discrimination on multiple fronts. Thus, the new challenges that disability advocates now face is to critically reconceptualise disability within a specific and interlocking context that can also account for their experiences of oppression on the basis of race, class, caste, gender and sexual orientation.

There have been many attempts to address this challenge of the simultaneity of oppression by claiming that the collective experience of marginality can be construed as the common thread linking

---

Reprinted with permission of Carfax Publishing from *Disability and Society* 11:4 (1996): 519–522, 526–537.

these axes of difference together (Fine & Asch, 1988; Morris, 1991; Lloyd, 1992; Begum, 1992; Priestley, 1995). However, I am arguing here that it is more important to move beyond this obvious commonality and treat disability as a critical theoretical category—one that can also effectively account for the challenge posed by the other constructs of difference. In fact, rather than asking how the theoretical discourses of race, class and gender can incorporate/accommodate disability within their analyses, I wish to shift the focus and ask a different question. In what ways can we, from the vantage point of disability, (re)write the theoretical terrain occupied by the other axes of difference such as race, class and gender?

The particular context in which I choose to make this argument is one where the politics of class/caste, race, gender and disability intersect—the context of care-giving where disabled children/adults receive both paid/unpaid services from their care-givers who are mostly women within both institutional and community settings. This context has been one that is rife with contestation, because both feminist scholars and disabled activists have viewed these relationships as often antagonistic to their specific political interests. Feminists have argued that "community care" relocates the burden of informal care on women—a burden that has been placed on them as a result of the sexual division of labour, which has been historically maintained through the patriarchal institution of the family (Finch & Grove, 1983; Ungerson, 1987; Dalley, 1988; Graham, 1991; Parker, 1993). Disability activists on the other hand claim that such arguments by feminists would in fact undermine the right of disabled persons to live meaningful lives within the community by continuing to relegate them to the oppressive confines of institutional settings (Morris, 1995). Thus, I am going to use this space of contestation as the point of departure so as to (re)theorise both disability and gender as well as draw out its implications for race, class and caste. To do this, I will first offer a (re)theorisation of the category of disability. I will then ground this theoretical discussion in the context of an ethnographic study of a voluntary organisation in South India which provides residential as well as rehabilitative services for poor disabled children. I will focus on one particular aspect of this study—the politics of the gendered "caring work" that is involved in providing services for disabled children within this organisation. By reading, dialectically, the material relationships between the female carers and their disabled clients, I will thus demonstrate how disability can be re-understood as an ideological discourse which is also produced by the same exploitative economic conditions of capitalism and structures the discourses of race, caste, class, gender and sexual orientation along the axes of disability.

In Search of the Disabled Subject

The argument I am putting forward is this. The construct of "disability" or what has otherwise been commonly understood as "deviant" difference has been historically used as an ideological tool in order to justify as "natural" the social hierarchies produced and maintained within capitalist societies. In arguing for this thesis I am treating disability as a conceptual category rather than a biological condition. This is in stark contrast to dominant understandings of disability, like the following official definition produced by the World Health Organisation

> In the context of health experience, disability is any restriction or lack (resulting from an impairment) of ability to perform an activity in the manner or within the range considered normal for a human being. (1980, p. 143.)

Such understandings presume disability to be a biological constant made readily apparent by "nature" and assumed to be outside of all historical frames of understanding that condition modes of normality. Therefore, the history of disability has always been seen as a history of irrelevance to global affairs, except of course in the area of social welfare where it enjoys a specious prominence.

Furthermore, even radical theories of difference that have sought to denaturalise and historicise the construction of the categories of race, class, gender and sexual orientation, have done so at the expense of the category of disability which they often tend to reify. These theories have critiqued dominant ideologies that have habitually drawn upon biological/

physiological arguments to justify the exploitation and/or exclusion of specific social groups in their participation within the capitalist marketplace. They have challenged the conservative argument that the exploitative and oppressive life situations of the unemployed, the homeless, poor women, people of different colours, gays and lesbians, and third world people have been the result of their inferior/deviant/different physiological/psychological make-up. They have contested such allegations by active assertions of their own normality, and have instead placed the onus of their oppression on attitudes, language, and/or the historical, social, political and economic conditions of social life. In other words, these groups have argued that these differences notwithstanding, they can still compete on equal footing with those subjects not marked by biological difference.

This stance posits disability in an uneasy relationship with the other political categories of difference. For example, in the most recent argument around the bell-curve and its connection to racial differences pertaining to intelligence and ability, critiques of Charles Murray's and Richard Hernstein's racist book the "Bell Curve," which links IQ with geneticism in the United States, have argued that race is a construct derived mainly from perceptions conditioned by events of recorded history and it has no basic biological reality. However, I would argue that notwithstanding the progressive critique, this rejection of the biological criteria is not, in fact, a rejection, but only a re-inscription, because the discourses of biology are still centred, only this time they are re-interpreted so as to satisfy the demands of "normality" made by the dominant ideologies—a demand which still excludes severely disabled people. This is because in revoking the alleged claims of biological difference and in (re)asserting a biological wholeness, subjects marked by race, class, caste, gender and/or sexual orientation assume without question the basic premises of humanism; something that would be difficult for disabled people to do. By not challenging the very premises of humanism, such discourses, thereby, continue to maintain an ideological distance from disability. Thus, in yet another example, the Marxist John Molyneux (1994), in an article entitled: "Is 'human nature' a barrier to socialism?" makes the following assertion:

> This physical nature (biology) endows beings with common needs and capacities which are the foundation of human nature ... the capacities include the five senses, a large brain, the ability to walk upright, a hand which allows precise manual operations, vocal chords which permit speech and so on. *It is the way in which these capacities are used to meet needs that make humans different from all other species.* (My emphasis.)

In making such claims, Molyneux excludes from his revolutionary socialist vision all persons with both physical and/or mental handicaps. Thus, when even those who espouse radical discourses seem unable to reconceptualise an alternative world without being locked into the political constructions of what constitutes appropriate humanness, then it becomes apparent that the disability movement has a task that goes above and beyond merely extending the boundaries of the discourses that celebrate humanism and instead needs to focus its energy on re-theorising itself...

Capitalism, Social Welfare, and the Indian State

The purpose of the welfare state is to provide services to those members of its citizenry who are deemed unable to support themselves within the prevailing conditions of the market. However, in an economy where participation in the labour force is the primary guarantor of citizenship, there needs to be some means by which the state can decide which of its citizens can be excluded from this participation without loosing their rights to citizenship. Stone (1984) has argued that it is here that disability has become a useful "administrative" category—one which can verify which members are entitled to privileges in the form of social aid as well as to exemptions from certain obligations of citizenship. In other words, the one context where the category of disability assumes a centrality is in the area of social welfare, where its "realness" is validated by the "neutral" mechanism of clinical judgment, and thus, it becomes the primary arbitrator between the deserving and the undeserving poor.

Unlike in Europe or in the United States, capitalism in India has not heralded the birth of a new society based on the destruction of pre-capitalist forms.

Instead, for reasons of survival, capitalism in India has been dependant on pre-capitalist forms of social inequality, e.g. the division of labour on the basis of the caste system (Hasan, 1989). Thus the structure of capitalism has been erected on the prevailing social divisions and differentiations which continue to propagate the uneven distribution of economic development (Hasan, 1989; Rao, 1989). In response to these anomalies, the Indian State has both a developmentalist as well as an interventionist thrust to its policies. In its developmentalist stance, it is pursuant of a capitalist mode of production so as to stimulate economic growth for competition within the world markets and in its interventionist role its activities are directed towards a redressal of both the historical inequalities of the pre-capitalist past that still persist as well as the more recent disparities that the current system of capitalism have produced (Hasan, 1989). However, rather than moving towards a more egalitarian re-distribution of resources in a move to transform Indian society, the Indian State seeks to humanise capitalism, by providing a social welfare system for those excluded from the economic enterprise.

The Indian State, given its own precarious economic position, has sought increasingly through its Five Year Plans to shift the major responsibilities of social welfare to voluntary organisations, offering them grants-in-aid to partially subsidize their efforts. Over the last few years, the field of disability has become increasingly visible on the national agenda in Social Welfare where the government has set up National Institutes, as training and resource centres that will offer voluntary organisations technical know-how in the area of rehabilitation and educational services for almost all conditions of disability. However, both the monetary and technical support from the State, though valuable is often inadequate and thus voluntary organisations for disabled persons have to depend on larger funding agencies, as well as volunteer work in order to provide the minimal possible services particularly for the urban and the rural poor.

With economic restructuring going on in India, and the Indian State being forced to pull back in the area of Social Welfare to focus more on economic growth, voluntary organisations are facing a decrease in monetary resources from the state. Given that the surplus allocated for the provision of such services is very limited, voluntary organisations, are forced to promote an "ethic of service" in order to attract voluntary workers who would freely offer their services for the needy and the suffering. However, this "ethic of service" that typifies the work performed within a voluntary organisation is itself an idealistic concept, because at this historical moment, the pool of workers "able" or "willing" to offer their labour power for no wage is very small. Therefore, there is the need to allocate some part of capitalism's surplus to pay the wages of these workers. However, given the limited resources in the service sector, and its status as non-profit, there is plenty of justification for providing a "nominal wage" and "minimal" work related benefits as compared to other institutions/ organisations which are aimed at profit maximisation.

Contradictions of Caring: A Case Study

At this point, I would like to move my argument to a voluntary organisation, DOST, that provides residential, educational and rehabilitational services for very poor disabled children in a large city in Tamil Nadu, South India. DOST is run by Sister Benedict, a European nun, who is the founder of the organisation. Within its premises are a clinic that caters to the medical needs of the residents at DOST as well as the neighbourhood, a special school for both day scholars and residents a dormitory section for resident children, a home economic unit for girls and young women, a carpentry section for boys and men, and a manufacturing unit for artificial limbs. In order to support all these activities, DOST depends heavily on donations from international aid agencies, individual foreign donors, the catholic church in India, the state and central governments in India, and to a minor extent, from fees collected from its clients. The reason DOST depends primarily on donations rather than fees from its clients is because most of the children who attend DOST come from economically destitute backgrounds in both urban and rural settings, where supporting a disabled child is an economic burden on the family, unless the child is able to contribute to the family's income. This is because the labour of every member of the household is necessary for economic survival, even the labour of the non-disabled children, who are forced to forego their own education in order to work. These families are usually involved in casual labour that pays daily wages based on the availability of work and for which they earn a monthly income of about Rs. 600 (approximately $20). On account of the abject poverty within which these families live and the non-availability of supportive services, particularly, in rural Tamil Nadu, these families find it almost impossible to provide for the daily care of their disabled children. They are thus forced to turn to voluntary organisations like DOST that charge little money for the institutional care of their children.

In this study my focus was on the meanings of disability as produced by the every day practices, motivations and belief systems of all the participants. This paper, however, focuses only on the personal care-givers/dormitory workers at DOST. These dormitory workers were assigned in pairs to care for 18 children in each of four dormitory rooms. Their primary task was to assist the children, many of whom were dependant on their caregivers for their daily living needs, on account of their moderate to severe disabilities. In my initial interviews, almost all the dormitory workers assigned a special status to this task of care-giving—sometimes thinking of it as a divine calling to a work that was humbling and yet, at the same time, ennobling. Thus, Sushila, a 22-year-old dormitory worker, a recent convert to Christianity, explains her calling for this work as follows:

> I did not wish to work in this kind of job. I am a Christian. I pray to Jesus and read the Bible. So God said: Remember Jesus used to work with the lepers. They had so many troubles ... Then God told me: You are a Christian. You are supposed to love all people. Why do you view this job as difficult? He spoke like that to me. Then, I came for the job, and started first of all by being humble. First I did not like the job. Then I kept speaking to God. And now I took the job and after that I am able to do it well.

Similarly, Palani, another dormitory worker, who has worked for 3 years at DOST saw her own interest in this work maintained through the relationships she developed with the children she cared for. As she explains:

> Sometimes, I think I should really leave this place and the next minute I would get a job. It is only my interest that is keeping me here. If I tell the children I am leaving, they will say don't go *Akka* [big sister], please don't go. For with all these persons the amount of affection I get I will not find anywhere else. I, too, have a lot of affection for these children.

It is not surprising that the entire staff at DOST, not just the dormitory workers considered their decision to work at DOST as voluntary, motivated by an ethic of service offered to a group of individuals whom they considered society's most unfortunate members. In conjunction with the dominant paradigm of disability, they therefore constructed the disabled children they cared for as perpetual victims dependent on their benevolence. Ironically, however, these initial assertions of benevolence towards disability were soon disrupted by a brutal politics that at the same moment also produced them as victims of gendered, class and caste hierarchies. In listening to these women closely, I soon became aware of another sub-text that constantly haunted their dogged assertions of dutiful and affectionate service. In the course of the interviews, I discovered that all these women, even while talking about the unfortunate situations of disabled people, at the same time often alluded to oppressive conditions in their own lives that seemingly had greater detrimental effects on themselves than the disabled children they cared for.

First of all, contrary to their initial assertions of freely choosing to be voluntaristic agents, most of the dormitory workers coming from poor, lower caste backgrounds were not there by choice, but because the material circumstances of their lives offered them no other alternative. Most of them were unmarried, had not completed high school, were economically destitute and did not wish to work as domestic servants in middle class households. For some, because this position offered room and board, this was the only option they had that would keep them from starvation or sexual exploitation. Thus, Rita, a 19-year-old dormitory worker describes the conditions that led her to work here in the following way:

> Before coming to DOST, I used to stay in a hostel and work in a sports company. Then I was not able to pay the fees for the hostel. And they said, "Don't stay here. Go to another hostel." And so I moved ... But I did not know where else to go. I had no friends. No family. I did not even have a guardian. I did not know what to do. Then somebody said, "Go to DOST. Go and see it." I was in a lot of trouble, so I went. They talked to sister and I got the job. So I have been here for two years.... I do not like this job.... When I fist came to this hostel, I did not know about any of these children who had no brains. I thought that there were only children here who could not walk—They would be able to dress themselves... Take care of themselves ... However, with these children who have no intelligence, taking care of them became a problem. That is why I think this job is very difficult. May be I should leave and go somewhere else. But they said, "No. You stay here. Otherwise what else will you do? Stay here. We'll see what else we can do for you. We will find someone to marry you." So I said, "Ok, I will stay."

Such observations, like Rita's decision to work at DOST, made amidst the pressures of social and economic deprivation destabilised the liberal humanist notions of agency by free, rational, philanthropic subjects—a notion that these workers had also bought into. This observation, thereby pointed me to conditions that had to be taken into account that extended above and beyond the fenced boundaries of this voluntary organisation, DOST, and of course pertained to the material realities of these women's lives.

Secondly, the levels of social and economic deprivation that the disabled children faced were not very different from the levels of deprivation experienced by these same staff members. In fact, many of these care-givers came from similar social class backgrounds as the families of these children and therefore also experienced a limited education in very poorly resourced educational institutions. Furthermore, unlike the schools that educate the Indian bourgeoisie, schooling for the poor emphasises the functionality of basic skills that will prepare them for the unskilled and semi-skilled positions in the labour force, therefore leaving little room for encouraging creative development or enjoyable leisure activities. Interestingly enough, special education for disabled children does not accentuate academic skills, but places emphasis on creative and leisure activities as the means to learn daily living skills. Therefore, for example, the living and learning environment that was offered to these young children with disabilities, was an environment that these dormitory workers had never ever experienced throughout their childhood and young adult years. They had very little knowledge of how to use educational aids or how to organise play time for their young charges. Thus, these dormitory workers seemed particularly needy even in the most simple of creative activities and often were excited when they learned skills at the same time as their disabled charges. In one of my interviews, Marika, made painfully aware of the shortcomings of her own education is grateful to the Australian and British volunteers at DOST for teaching her new skills. She says:

> It is useful when foreigners come here for social work ... If I do not know something, they will show me how to do it. These foreigners have a lot of activities to offer. Hand work. Paper cutting. Design house. Flower. Dog. Different kinds of art ... Games. Skittles. Skittles was a new method that the foreigners used at DOST. I did not even know what skittles was. Simply I would tell them to throw a ball. Then they showed me that you put the skittles in a line. Then give each child three chances. That's what they taught me.

What gets poignantly highlighted once again in her words is that the social deprivation of disabled children was similar to that of non-disabled individuals who lived under similar social conditions of poverty and deprivation.

Furthermore, the regular working day for these women, who had to do the "dirtiest" work of cleaning after children who were incontinent, ill, and difficult extended from six in the morning to midnight. For doing this work, they received free room and board, and an annual salary of Rs. 2400 (equivalent to $80). Often the administration justified these low salaries by claiming that this was work that needed no new skills—only motivation and a dedication to serve others—qualities that they claimed these women seldom exhibited. This lack of motivation was exacerbated by the devalued status ascribed to those who perform this labour— a legacy of the caste system that used this as means of social stratification and oppression. As a result of such ascriptions, Sushila goes out of her way to keep the details about her work at DOST from her family:

> They [her family] do not know much about this [her work]. I have not told them about it at all.... My grandmother always asks me about this. She will scold me: Why are you doing this sort of work at all? What are you going to gain from all of this?... So they have called me home.... They think that good work is in being a teacher. Or some office work. Like a typist. Those kind of jobs they like a lot. But this kind of work they do not want. You too will become sick like them. Then what will happen?... Even now I do not tell them a lot. I do not tell them that they make kaka [feces]. That they get dirty. All that I do not tell them. Just that I simply look after the children ... that I teach them. I have told them not to come here. When my brothers and sisters have come to visit, I have made them sit outside and talked to them.... Just showed them the children. I have not told them what kind of help these children really need.

However, notwithstanding her family's optimism, the options for finding an alternative job outside of DOST are remote. Given the long work hours and the real impossibility of saving any money, there are hardly any opportunities for these workers to acquire skills in more lucrative professions in mainstream society. Thus, these women had no other choice but to wait their time out at DOST. If these service providers themselves were caught in their own webs of destitution and super-exploitation that excluded them from participating as "productive" workers within mainstream society, then perhaps we can assume that the alienation they experienced could have some links with how the disabled subject is also constructed as an alienated subject.

Finally, the manner in which rehabilitation is understood within the voluntary organisation presumes that there is a client and a service provider, who attempts to move the client from his/her marginalised position to a more central location within mainstream society (i.e. the rhetoric of integration an of social work). However, given the alienation that these service providers already experienced, rehabilitation that is also couched within a benevolent voluntarism on the part of service providers seemed as much a service that they themselves also desperately needed. Sister Benedict, the administrator, realises this anomaly when she says:

> They [dormitory workers] come in because they have no money, are starving, and they have no possibility of looking after themselves and anyone else. Sometimes it works out good. Sometimes it's a big pain in the neck. We can't send them anywhere because they have nowhere to go... Some of them, I think, are looking for attention. And haven't had enough love and attention showered on them themselves. Therefore, they can't give what they haven't got. The young ones are too young. They are just beginning now after three years to relate and be with children. Personally, I think that they themselves have been deprived of family and love and therefore they cannot give it.

It thus seemed that notwithstanding the differences in their states of destitution both service providers and clients shared a commonality in the socio-political-economic alienation they experienced in mainstream society.

The Social Division of Labour and the Politics of Difference

I have argued earlier that capitalist markets only absorb as wage labourers those who through their labour power can in the most efficient way expedite the maximum extraction of surplus for the capitalist. Thus, contrary to the claims of a liberal democracy (an ideology that is essential for validating the capitalist enterprise), the construction of disability, as defined earlier, can be used as an objective criteria to justify why certain subjects can be denied their rights to participate in a free market. Many of them because they have no access to accumulated capital, therefore, become the clients of the social welfare system—now labelled as "delinquent," "physically and mentally handicapped," "problem families, " etc., and bear the stigma of being unproductive as a result of their non-participation in the market. In addition, the deviance attributed to these clients is treated as physiological and thereby a scientific certainty, and virtually ignores the class context of poverty, inequality and powerlessness that inform these conditions in the first place. Instead of mitigating the economic conditions that have produced this deviance in the first place, under the rubric of the welfare state, rehabilitation becomes the means of transforming the labour power of this deviant population into an industrial reserve army from which the capitalist economy can draw upon in its hour of need.

However, there are specific populations that offer rehabilitation its most stringent challenges. Jones (1984) identifies them as follows:

> To be old or handicapped in a capitalist society is extremely problematic for those who have few independent resources and no wealth. For both categories of people their chances of work are virtually non-existent. Their labour power has either been exhausted or is regarded, in the case of many handicapped people, as being too difficult to exploit and extract (p. 24).

It is this population then that requires personal and individualised care offered either in the residential institutions or in the community—and care that will not impose any major financial burden on the state. This caring work which includes, but is not limited to the tasks of tending disabled children and adults who need to be washed, fed, toiletted, dressed, lifted, and loved has historically been "naturalized" as women's work through the sexual division of labour. As a result, the technicality of caring seldom is an issue, because simply by virtue of being female, it is assumed that the only skills that are needed would be a caring attitude, maternal instincts and sound common sense. Therefore, the personal care provided to disabled people is performed mostly by women in both the private sphere of the family or the public sphere of the market.

Many feminist scholars (Finch and Groves, 1983; Ungerson, 1987; Dalley, 1988; Graham, 1991; Parker, 1993; Morris 1995) have critiqued the biological determinism that pervades the caring work that women perform for disabled people through the sexual division of labour. Most of their analyses are located within the private domain of the family, referring to the unpaid domestic labour women perform for those with whom they have kinship ties through birth and marriage (Ungerson, 1987; Graham, 1991; Thomas, 1993; Parker 1993). Their arguments stem from marxist feminist critiques of the sexual division of labour that produces the false dichotomy of public waged labour as productive labour and non-waged reproductive labour as non-productive (Fox, 1980; Mies, 1986; Waring, 1988). These feminists have argued that through the daily chores of domestic labour, women replenish the labour force for yet another work day and therefore contribute as productive workers to the capitalist enterprise. Most marxist feminists would agree that treating domestic labour as non-productive and therefore as non-waged labour, even though it is essential for capitalist accumulation, contributes to the continued exploitation of all women. However, what they have found difficult to concur on is whether this domestic labour can be theorised as producing use value (value produced to satisfy need) or as producing exchange value (value produced for profit). To critically examine the issues on both sides of this debate are beyond the scope of this paper. However, the main issue that is pertinent to our discussion is that these analyses expose the biological determinism that haunts most of women's domestic labour (e.g. caring work) as an ideological operation that is utilized to justify the continued appropriation of female labour without wages within capitalism's stratified labour market on the basis of gendered difference.

These critiques of the sexual division of labour have led feminists to take issue with the new community care policies that have moved disabled people out of institutions and into the community (Finch and Groves, 1983; Ungerson 1987; Dalley, 1988; Graham 1991; Parker 1993). The institution of these community care policies have been the result of the tireless work by disabled activists who have argued that institutionalisation is tantamount to "social death" (Morris, 1995). However, some feminists see this move as antagonistic to feminist interests. They are critical of the interpretation of community—

where "community" in bureaucratic terms has often been synonymous with "family". Given the sexual division of labour that has been historically maintained within the family, feminists have accused policy-makers of cutting welfare costs under the guise of community care policies by exploiting the non-waged labour of caring that women have performed with in the institution of the family (Nakano-Glenn, 1992). They have therefore argued that the provision of such services be moved from the private sphere of the family into the public space of the market where at least those who perform that labour would receive a wage. However, what if such labour was moved out into the market? In what ways would the exploitative conditions surrounding the sexual division of labour be mitigated? Who then would perform this labour and what value would be placed on this labour? Moreover, in what ways can this work, centred as it is on disabled individuals whose labour power has very little value in the economy, be deemed as productive; given that it can do little to replenish the labour force as other reproductive labour has been able to do?

What these feminist critiques are blind to is that relocating domestic labour in the capitalist market will not mitigate the exploitative conditions of the sexual division of labour for all women. In fact, as my own study has pointed out, this labour has been assigned to lower class/caste women who are poor, young, unmarried, uneducated and unskilled except in their "natural" work, i.e. their reproductive labour. Since these women, because of the exploitative conditions of the economy (denied access to material resources that can offer them alternative opportunities) are assigned very little value to their labour power, they thus come to comprise the reserve army that is physically and mentally able, but socially, educationally and economically disabled, and who can only circumvent the rehabilitation cycle by locating their services precisely within that area taking on the only jobs that are offered them. In other words, the exploitation produced by the sexual division of labour is now placed on the shoulders of those women located on the lowest rungs of the social hierarchy. Furthermore, as a result of the oppression these women face, the material conditions under which they live has more in common with their disabled charges than with their bourgeois sisters.

This analysis is substantiated by Nakano-Glenn's (1992) study of paid service work within the United States. In her study, this paid reproductive labour under the rubric of service jobs (e.g. nurses aides) is performed by mostly poor coloured women, most of them new immigrants, who also experience the exploitation of low wages and poor working conditions. Furthermore, Nakano-Glenn points out that this labour is able to relieve bourgeois women from the drudgery of caring work to perform productive labour for the capitalist economy. Therefore, these studies illustrate that what gets re-instituted within this sexual division of labour are other social divisions of labour based on class, caste and race. By highlighting these other social divisions of labour, what becomes apparent is how difference itself becomes a dialectical category that has differential effects on different individuals based on their specific location within the social divisions of labour produced by capitalism.

Conclusion: Bodies That Do Not Matter

Nakano-Glenn's historical analysis of service work within US society points to the fact that analyses of gender are always imbricated within analyses of race and class. She does this by effectively demonstrating how the unpaid reproductive labour of bourgeois white women within the private sphere of the home is inextricably bound to the paid reproductive labour of poor women of colour within the public sphere of the market. Thus, according to her, a struggle against gender hierarchies would require that a simultaneous struggle be waged against class, race and caste hierarchies. Notwithstanding this ground-breaking work, Nakano-Glenn, nevertheless, falls into the same trap as other feminists when it comes to the issue of disability, by treating disabled individuals as dependant entities with no political stakes in her otherwise critical analyses. In highlighting the exploitative nature of caring work and its implications on race, caste, class and gender, such analyses place disabled persons, who are of course central to this debate, as antagonistic to the interests of the class, caste and gender politics. On the other hand, how would our analyses be transformed if disability is conceptualised not as an alien category, among the other categories of difference, but as structured by and upholding the same exploitative material conditions that have produced oppression on the basis of race, class, caste and gender?

In stepping back from my data for a moment and looking across individuals, across institutions and across national boundaries, what becomes apparent is that the class of people who are generally associated with these organisations (either as clients or as service providers) have personal histories that have constructed them as extremely marginal subjects. Furthermore, these locations of extreme marginality (lack of education, restricted access to material resources, institutionalised exclusionary practices) render them only marginally useful to the capitalist enterprise since the market has very little use for their labour power. It is here then that institutions organised around disability become the most benign tools that are utilised as an effective means of separating the "favorables" from the "unfavorables." Under the rhetoric of welfare, and in this particular case, "rehabilitation", it appears to be the most useful way of constructing a division of labour that is broader than the divisions that have historically been described in sociological theory. In fact, I am arguing here that this division of labour draws upon other historicised divisions of labour along the axes of class, gender, race, caste and sexual orientation to produce subjects who are bound to live within boundaries that mark them as separate from those who are considered productive in the mainstream society. In fact, such institutions can now become the newest forms of institutionalising difference under the guise of social welfare.

Such conclusions force us to move beyond theorisations of biology that at some point or the other continue to re-inscribe nature as the central determinant of our lives, even while we claim a distance from such theorisations and calls us to construct the terms of the debate on different more radical grounds. These radical grounds need to be materially constituted as opposed to being biologically overdetermined and thereby provides us with some agency to change our world. In doing this, we can thus see how the marginal discourse of disability and the caring work associated with it is not, in fact, something that is peripheral to our social order. Instead, it marks the point at which the relations of capital, class, caste, race, gender and disability intersect, and it should therefore be the place where we begin and not end our analysis of modern society.

Acknowledgements

I would like to acknowledge the contributions of Robert M. Young, whose careful readings of many drafts and energetic discussions have helped me conceptualise many difficult parts of this paper. My thanks also goes to Priti Ramamurthy, Aarti Saihjee and Corri Zoli.

REFERENCES

Abberley, P. (1987) The concept of oppression and the development of a social theory of disability, *Disability, Handicap and Society*, 2, pp. 5-19.

Begum, N. (1992) Disabled women and the feminist agenda, *Feminist Review*, 40, pp. 70-84.

Biklen, D. and Bogdan, R. (1977) Handicapism in America, in: B. Blatt, D. Biklen and R. Bogdan (Eds). *An Alternative Text Book In Special Education: People, Schools, and Other Institutions* (Colorado, Love Publishing Company).

Bogdan, R. and Taylor, S. (1977) *Inside Out: The Social Meaning of Mental Retardation* (Toronto, University of Toronto Press).

Dalley, G. (1988) *Ideologies of Caring* (London, Macmillan Education).

Deegan, M. J. (1981) Multiple minority groups: a case study of physically disabled women, *Journal of Sociology and Social Welfare*, 8, pp. 274-297.

Ehrenreich, B. (1987) The new right attack on social welfare, in: F. Block, R. Ploward, B. Ehrenreich and F. Piven (Eds) *The Mean Season: the Attack on the Welfare State* (New York, Pantheon Books).

Finch, D. and Groves, D. (1983) *A Labour of Love: Women, Work, and Caring* (Boston, Routledge and Kegan Paul).

Fine, M. and Asch, A. (Eds) (1988) *Women with Disabilities: Essays in Psychology, Culture, and Politics* (Philadelphia, Temple University Press).

Finkelstein, V. (1980) *Attitudes and Disabled people: Issues for Discussion* (New York, World Rehabilitation Fund, Inc).

Fox, B. (Ed.) (1980) *Hidden in the Household: Women's Domestic Labor under Capitalism* (Toronto, The Women's Press).

Fox, N. J. (1994) *Postmodernism, Sociology, and Health* (Toronto, University of Toronto Press).

Graham, H. (1991) The concept of caring in feminist research: the case of domestic service, *Sociology*, 25, pp. 61-77.

Hasan, Z. (1989) Introduction: state and identity in modern India, in: Z. Hasan, S. N. Jha and R. Khan (Eds) *The State, Political Processes, and Identity Reflections on Modern India* (Delhi, Sage Publications).

Jones, C. (1984) *State Social Work and the Working Class* (London, The Macmillan Press).

Lloyd, M. (1992) Does she boil eggs?—towards a feminist model of disability, *Disability, Handicap, and Society*, 7, pp. 207-221.

Lonsdale, S. (1990) *Women with Disability: The Experience of Physical Disability among Women* (New York, St. Martins Press).

Mies, M. (1986) *Patriarchy and Accumulation on a World Scale: Women in the International Division of Labour* (New Jersey, Zed Books).

Molyneux, J. (1991) *Arguments for a Revolutionary Socialism* (Chicago, Bookmarks.)

Morris, J. (1991) *Pride against Prejudice: Transforming Attitudes to Disability* (Philadelphia, New Society Publishers).

Morris, J. (1995) Creating a space for absent voices: disabled women's experience of receiving assistance with daily living activities. *Feminist Review*, 51, pp. 68-93.

Murray, C. (1993) The coming white underclass, *Wall Street Journal*, Oct 29.

Nakano-Glenn, E. (1992) From servitude to service work: historical continuities in the racial division of paid reproductive labour, *Signs: Journal of Women in Culture and Society*, 18, pp. 1-42.

Parker, G. (1993) *With This Body: Caring and Disability in Marriage* (Philadelphia, Open University Press).

Priestley, M. (1995) Commonality and difference in the movement: an "Association of Blind Asians" in Leeds, *Disability and Society*, 10, pp. 157-169.

Oliver, M. (1990) *The Politics of Disablement* (New York, St. Martins Press).

Rao, K. R. (1989) Understanding the Indian state: a historical materialist exercise, in: Z. Hasan, S. N. Jha and R. Khan (Eds) *The State, Political Processes, and Identity Reflections on Modern India* (Delhi, Sage Publications).

Scotch, R. (1988) Disability as the basis for a social movement: advocacy and the politics of definition, *Journal of Social Issues*, 44, pp. 159-172.

Stone, D. (1984) *The Disabled State* (Philadelphia, Temple University Press).

Thomas, C. (1993) De-constructing concepts of care, *Sociology*, 27, pp. 649-669.

Ungerson, C. (1987) *Policy is Personal: Sex, Gender and Informal Care* (New York, Tavistock Publications).

Waring, M. (1988) *If Women Counted: A New Feminist Economics* (San Francisco, Harper and Row Publishers).

World Health Organisation (1980) *International Classification of Impairments, Disabilities, and Handicaps* (Geneva, World Health Organization).

Zavarzadeh, M. (1989) Theory as resistance, *Rethinking Marxism*, 2, pp. 49-70.

POVERTY AND DISABLED PEOPLE: CHALLENGING DOMINANT DEBATES AND POLICIES

Peter Beresford

Peter Beresford is a Professor in the Department of Social Work at Brunel University in England. He has associations with and has done work for Open Services Project, Citizen's Commission on the Future of the Welfare State, and the UK Coalition Against Poverty. He has published numerous reports and articles in the areas of welfare, disability, and poverty.

This article explores the relationship between poverty, disability and impairment in a global context. It challenges dominant critiques of poverty and disability, and explores the critiques, policy proposals and developments of the disabled people's movement to combat poverty. It offers an international perspective including the experience of both the North and South.

The relationship between poverty and disability is close, complex and multi-facetted. It has changed over time, with industrialisation, and varies in different parts of the world, notably between the North and the South. The nature of this relationship has been a longstanding concern of the disabled people's movement. Disabled people and their organisations have sought to challenge dominant interpretations of it.

Disabled people's organisations call into question assumptions that impairment is inextricable from poverty and that if you have an impairment you have to be poor. Impairment is not only a function of poverty and it is not restricted to disabled people. An analysis of disability based solely on poverty is both inaccurate and misleading.

At the same time, by all definitions of poverty, disabled people are grossly over-represented among poor people. This is true for all groups who are disabled, including people with physical and sensory impairments, people with learning difficulties and where included, people labelled as mentally ill. They experience levels of economic and social deprivation rarely encountered by other sections of the population (Barnes and Mercer, 1995). In Britain and the US over 60% of disabled people live below the poverty line (*New Internationalist*, 1992, p. 18). It is generally accepted that the majority of disabled people live in developing countries (Barnes and Mercer, 1995) yet they get less resources (*New Internationalist*, 1992, p. 18). In a statement presented to the United Nations World Summit on Social Development in 1995 on behalf of Disabled People's International, Liisa Kauppinen, General Secretary of the World Federation of the Deaf said:

> We are the poorest of the poor in most societies.... Two thirds of disabled people are estimated to be without employment. Social exclusion and isolation are the day-to-day experience of disabled people. (Kauppinen, 1995)

The issue of poverty and disabled people is a heavily contested one because it relates to two dominant discourses which disabled people and their organisations have challenged: the poverty and disability discourses. It will be helpful to begin by examining these discourses and their ramifications for disabled people, before moving on to explore the

---

Reprinted with permission of Carfax Publishing from *Disability and Society* 11:4 (1996): 553–567.

disabled people's movement's own approaches to the analysis and reduction of the poverty which is a central feature of people's disablement. In this way we can see how dominant debates and policies have contributed to the problems of poverty facing disabled people and how alternatives from disabled people's organisations offer a feasible strategy for change.

The Conventional Poverty Debate

While the gap between rich and poor in the world is growing (United Nations, 1996) the prevailing debate about poverty has long been a narrow and eurocentric one. It has mainly been based on the perspectives, ideologies, and interests of non-poor and non-disabled experts and politicians, and reflected their concerns and commitments.

There are two other broad points it is helpful to make about poverty discourse. First, the dominant western debate has been based on a social administration approach which has long failed to integrate "race," disability, age, sexual orientation and gender into its analysis, instead treating them as separate, discrete issues. Secondly, there has so far been relatively little research done outside this tradition on the relationship between poverty and disability, and this issue requires urgent attention. As Oliver states, so far "there have been very few international studies of the lives of disabled people" (Oliver, 1996, p 114).

Poor and disabled people continue to be marginalised in debates and developments around poverty. In 1995, the Joseph Rowntree Foundation published *Income and Wealth*, which acted as a major focus for renewed public and political discussion of poverty in the UK (Barclay, 1995; Hills, 1995). Yet people with experience of poverty were not involved in the process of its production or included in the membership of the inquiry group whose findings and recommendations it reported. It had little to say on disability (Beresford and Green, 1996).

The 1995 United Nations World Summit on Social Development brought together heads of state to discuss poverty, unemployment and exclusion. However, "very little happened ... disability was on the agenda (but it was) not seen as a priority ... The people concerned were effectively silenced, and no group more so than disabled people" (Disability Awareness In Action, 1995a, p. 1). Both disabled people and poor people were marginalised at the summit and denied effective access to it.

There has been a tendency to isolate and lump people together indiscriminately as poor, without examining the disparate causes of their social and economic exclusion, and to stereotype them as dangerous or dependent. The effect has been to obscure both people's differences and their shared oppressions. While people with sensory and physical impairments have generally been presented as dependent, people with intellectual impairments or labelled as mentally ill, are frequently presented as both dependent and dangerous.

The poverty debate has long been narrowly focused on two competing definitions of poverty; the absolute definition, related to a notion of the lack of basic necessities for life and the relative deprivation definition, based on not being able to live in accordance with the customs and values of the society in which the person is located. While these two definitions are frequently polarised politically against each other, social scientists now increasingly acknowledge their overlaps (Alcock, 1993, p. 62). Both also come from the same paternalistic tradition, with poor people playing little or no part in their formulation. While absolute poverty is most often associated with the developing world, both absolute and relative poverty are identified in western countries like the United Kingdom (Oppenheim, 1993; Oppenheim and Harker, 1996).

Both definitions of poverty are defective. The problems with the absolute definition have long been documented. It does not take adequate account of individual, occupational, cultural or ethnic differences; people's social and cultural needs, dietary, housing and other changes over time, and it is presented as an objective scientific measure, when it is actually based on externally imposed normative judgements (Alcock, 1993, pp. 58-66).

The relative definition of poverty is tied to existing patterns of consumption and associated with the increasing commodification of goods and services—

that is, the conversion of needs into goods and services which have to be purchased—and the resultant expansion of consumerism. It is generally associated with dominant customs, values and patterns of living which may not be shared or accepted by everyone. This underplays the diversity within and between societies, and has led to criticism of this model for being eurocentric. While the relative definition of poverty is rooted in an idea of equality and redistribution, in practice there is an emphasis on material standards.

This materialist approach has wider ramifications, particularly when the debate is opened up to include developing countries. As Coleridge says:

> Poverty will never be "abolished" by a system that is run only on materialist principles; indeed "development" based on the notion of acquiring more material benefits will always enrich some and impoverish others. (Coleridge, 1993, p. 10)

Poverty and Rights

More recently, another more helpful approach to understanding poverty has emerged: the rights-based approach. This highlights the way in which civil, political and social rights are undermined by poverty. It also emphasises the interrelationship of rights. The full and effective exercise of legal and political rights requires a firm base of social and economic rights. Poverty undermines the ability of many millions to fulfil either their private or social obligations (Lister, 1990). It restricts people's right to travel, to free association and political participation. Poverty like other consequences of institutionalised discrimination facing disabled people restricts their rights. There are constructive links to build upon between the rights approach to poverty and the concern of the disabled people's movement with civil rights, to which we shall return later.

There are two key sources of insight for understanding the relation between disability and poverty, both of which, as we have seen, have been marginalised in dominant discussions. These insights come from the overlapping perspectives of people with experience of poverty and the disabled people's movement.

The Perspective of People with Experience of Poverty

Poor people and organisations of people who are poor organised around their poverty have had minimal involvement in anti-poverty policy and campaigning in societies like Britain. In the UK, for example, virtually none of the major campaigning anti-poverty organisations are controlled by poor people. People with experience of poverty are also under-represented in their membership. While many organisations of poor people have developed, like claimants' unions and unemployed workers' centres, their organisations have generally been ignored, excluded and devalued in the development of anti-poverty policy. Their experience of exclusion from debates and developments which concern them has mirrored that of disabled people in many ways. This approach to debates and developments has also been exported by the North to the South.

Poor people have rarely been asked their views about poverty and anti-poverty action. They have been marginalised in anti-poverty discussions (Beresford and Croft, 1995). However, this is now beginning to change. There are now examples in Europe and in Britain of poor people coming together to develop their ideas and proposals (Croft, 1989; Croft and Beresford, 1990). What is beginning to emerge from this, is that many people don't like being labelled as poor or being lumped together under this stigmatising label. Many see it as an unhelpful basis for action and conceive of poverty as about much more than material deprivation. They also see it as about the denial of rights, emotional insecurity, and the inability to maintain responsibilities as individuals, parents and citizens (Lister and Beresford, 1991).

The Challenge from Disabled People's Organisations

Disabled people's organisations have called into question both the conceptualisation of poverty and traditional anti-poverty campaigning. They have challenged their exclusion from the discourse, demanding full involvement in the discussion and development of policy (Disability Awareness In

Action, 1995a, p. 1; Rowland and Elissalde, 1994). In Britain, from the 1970s, the Union of the Physically Impaired Against Segregation challenged the philosophy, strategy and objectives of conventional anti-poverty action. They provided a detailed critique of its key characteristics (UPIAS and Disability Alliance, 1976). The Union argued that such campaigning didn't involve disabled people, focused on poverty and income in isolation from other social conditions disabling people, concentrated on "parliamentary pressure" at the expense of grassroots involvement and initiatives, and that non-disabled people set themselves up as experts. The Union rejected a model by which non-disabled "experts" collected information to educate the public and achieve reform as ineffective and undemocratic. The Union felt that organising groups of non-disabled experts "to speak for disabled people ... can only entrench the disability of physically impaired people."

Disabled people's organisations internationally argue instead that they must be fully involved in campaigning and that poverty should be seen as one expression of the institutional discrimination disabled people face. What are described as the "racialisation" and "feminisation" of poverty represent further expressions of poverty as a consequence of institutional discrimination facing other overlapping oppressed groups. Disabled activists have mainly opted for campaigning through their own organisations around disability rather than under the heading of poverty.

Poverty and the Medical Model of Disability

Poverty has conventionally been seen as an expression of the inherent dependence of disabled people. This analysis has been associated with the medicalisation of disability, linked with both collective welfare and charitable responses. This structures disabled people as economically dependent through reliance on state benefits, charitable giving or individual begging.

The disabled people's movement challenges all the links in this chain of dependence. It rejects both collective welfare and organised charity which makes disabled people economically dependent. Both are condemned in principle and practice. They are not what many disabled people want. They deny disabled people the social and economic choices and opportunities open to others. In the UK, for example, according to Barnes:

> the overwhelming majority of disabled people and their families are disproportionately reliant upon social security arrangements for their livelihood and experience extreme economic deprivation as a result. The evidence shows that for disabled people the price of living on welfare is a systematic erosion of personal autonomy and excessive bureaucratic regulation and control. (Barnes, 1991)

State income support systems generally perpetuate people's poverty, keeping them at or below socially-defined poverty lines, rather than lifting them out of poverty. They reflect the pre-occupation of the social administration approach to poverty with welfare solutions. Such systems are not viable for poorer countries. Their future at existing levels is also uncertain in western societies—although the economic arguments for this are disputed (Oppenheim, 1994)—with demographic change resulting in higher numbers of very old people, ideological shifts away from state intervention, long term recession and changed patterns of employment. Economic and ideological changes also mean that reliance on welfare is being made increasingly oppressive, with welfare benefits being fixed at lower levels and made more difficult to get. In the UK this has been reflected in the introduction of "incapacity benefit," and the increasingly punitive treatment of disabled people seeking or receiving benefit.

Pre-occupation with a medical response to impairment has been at the expense of addressing disabled people's opportunities for economic independence (Oliver, 1990). Psychiatric system survivors evidence how people's capacities are reduced by chemical and mechanical medical "treatments" for their distress (Weitz, 1994).

Disabled activists challenge the charity model of meeting disabled people's needs, both where it is applied within countries, as in western societies like Britain and the US, and where it is exported from the North to the South, as an alternative to economic equalisation, development and support for self-help (Coleridge, 1993). Reliance on international charity confirms the social and economic status quo. Individual reliance on charity is personally demeaning, inadequate and unreliable. It is out of people's control, inherently patronising and substitutes personal dependence for disabled people's individual and collective rights. In the South, disabled people increasingly argue that disability is a development, not a welfare issue (Haque, 1994).

Most important, disabled people's organisations dismiss the analysis on which such dependency-based policies rest. The disabled people's movement has rejected an individual or medical model of disability and instead developed the social model, in which "impairment" is defined as functional limitation within the individual caused by physical, mental or sensory impairment (Barnes, 1991) and "disability" as socially imposed restriction (Oliver, 1983) associated with "the complex system of constraints imposed on people with impairments" by discriminatory societies (Barnes and Mercer, 1995).

Poverty and Disemployment

The analysis of the disabled people's movement of the relationship between disability and poverty is part of a coherent theory of disability. The poverty of disabled people is seen as an expression of the institutionalised discrimination which they face. It is one manifestation of a disabling society. Central to this, is disabled people's greatly restricted access to employment. "A very high percentage of unemployment" is seen as "one of the central problems facing disabled people....In the developing world, the extremely high percentage of unemployment among disabled people means they are forced to beg to survive" (Disability Awareness In Action, 1995b, p. 1). Disabled people's high level of unemployment are linked with their inferior and segregated education, and restricted access to training and further education, which disadvantage disabled people in the labour market; inaccessible and inflexible employment which reduces opportunities; and the prejudice disabled people face, stereotyping them as incapable and unreliable. In the UK and USA, for example, 67% of disabled people aged 15-64 are unemployed compared with 32% of the non-disabled population of the same age. In Tunisia, 85% of disabled people of comparable age are unemployed and in Zimbabwe, less than 1% of disabled people are formally contributing to the economy of the country (Disability Awareness In Action, 1995b, p. 1). For many employed disabled people, paid work does not offer a route out of poverty because a disproportionate number of disabled people are confined to less secure, lower paid employment (Barnes, 1991, pp. 62-97). The few disabled people who do get jobs in the South "must accept very low levels of pay unrelated to their productivity" (Disability Awareness In Action, 1995b, p. 1).

Meeting the Additional Costs of Impairment

The impoverishment of disabled people is exacerbated by the frequent failure to recognize and address the additional cost of living expenses of impairment. These include costs for extra heating, special diet, special clothing, laundry, medication and transport. Disabled people require higher incomes than non-disabled people to maintain the same living standard, yet most have lower incomes. These expenses do not diminish when disabled people are in employment. "This additional financial burden must be seen in relation to income. The combination of disproportionately low wages and the added costs if impairments forces a great many disabled people out of the labour market altogether" (Barnes, 1991).

Disabled People's Diverse Experience of Poverty

While poverty is widely experienced among disabled people, there are also significant differences in their experience which should be recognised. Distinctions need to be drawn, for example, between the particular problems facing disabled children in poor families, the need for training and support for recently disabled people to live independently, and the needs of adults disabled from infancy.

Disabled women are doubly disadvantaged. They have much lower rates of employment and receive lower pay (*New Internationalist*, 1992, p. 19). "The disabled woman is still the worst victim of ignorance, poverty and disease and is placed at the lowest rung of the social ladder" (Shah, quoted in Barnes and Mercer, 1995). In Tunisia, for example, disabled women find it four times harder than disabled men to get work, and are more likely to be low-paid and unskilled (Disability Awareness In Action, 1995b, p. 1). In Western societies like Britain, black people face disproportionate problems of poverty and disabled black people experience complex patterns of discrimination. The chances of being poor are far higher for people from ethnic minorities than for white people, and the way in which poverty is experienced is often compounded by discrimination and exclusion (Amin and Oppenheim, 1992). Ageism and heterosexism also compound disabled people's problems of poverty.

Disability is an issue common to both the rich North and the poor South, but there are differences in the nature and causes of impairment, and different solutions are demanded. Eighty per cent of disabled people live in Asia and the Pacific, but they receive just 2% of resources allocated to disabled people. Less than 2% of disabled people in developing countries are reported to have access to any kind of services (Disabled People's International, 1992). In poorer societies, disabled people are among the most destitute (Barnes and Mercer, 1995). According to Joshua Malinga, Chair of the Disabled People's International: "While people in the rich world are talking about Independent Living and improved services, we are talking about survival" (quoted in Baird, 1992). The particular economic conditions in the South have led disabled activists to emphasise a different strategy in their struggle for emancipation—notably, the significance of community-based initiatives for economic participation and equality (Barnes and Mercer, 1995; Disability Awareness In Action, 1995b, p. 2).

Disability and Rights

Differences between North and South have also led to questioning of the relevance of a rights approach to disability in the South, with concern expressed about the eurocentrism of the concept. In Western societies like the UK and USA, disabled people's organisations have based their struggles very deliberately on ideas of and struggles to achieve their civil and human rights. There has been an emphasis on achieving anti-discrimination legislation and the equal treatment of disabled people. While there is a strong citizenship discourse which excludes on grounds of "race," gender and disability, there is also an emerging citizenship debate concerned with inclusion, participation and difference (Critical Social Policy, 1989). While it is important to recognise the particular social and economic circumstances which face disabled people in the South and their concern to develop their own proposals and strategies to deal with them, this is not an argument for conceiving of their rights and citizenship as inferior. As Coleridge argues:

> The crucial distinction that has to made is between universal rights and individual needs. Charity is about attending to individual needs; what disabled people want is for their rights as ordinary citizens to be recognised. (Coleridge, 1993, p. 48)

This discussion of rights in relation to North and South mirrors discussions about relative poverty. Right wing politicians and policy makers draw divisive distinctions between poverty in the North and South. They dismiss evidence of poverty in countries like the UK as reflecting no more than inequality, and only accept as poverty the extremes of hunger, famine and lack of shelter which they associate with the South. In 1996, the UK social security secretary, Peter Lilley, refusing to take measures to counter poverty in response to the UN world summit on social development, wrote that he regarded it as a matter for "underdeveloped countries" and that Britain already had the mechanisms "to prevent poverty" (Brindle, 1996).

The idea of rights can offer both a framework and a benchmark for disabled people to pursue their goals and objectives in North and South, while acknowledging their political, cultural, social and economic differences.

Rejecting Eugenic Policies

There is now increased interest in eugenic policies to deal with disability. As Shakespeare observes:

> The background to the current discussion is two-fold. Firstly, biological determinist understandings of disability have only recently been effectively challenged and are still predominant within medial discourses ...Secondly, a renewed biological determinism is evident at the current time, with a genetically-based reductionism fuelling a reactionary common sense, exploited and encouraged by mass media interest. (Shakespeare, 1995, pp. 22-23)

This is reflected in the west in genetic research to screen out conditions associated with physical and sensory impairments, as well as mental distress and learning difficulties. In China legislation now requires women to have genetic tests and abortions if their foetuses are judged abnormal (Croft and Beresford, 1994; Life, Death and Rights, 1994). As Morris says, "The explicit motivation ...is the notion that physical or intellectual impairment means a life which is not worth living. The hidden motivation is actually that disabled people are not deemed productive and constitute a high economic cost" (Morris, 1992). Such genetic policies are advanced as a remedy for both individual and societal impoverishment caused by impairment. Their significance is that they offer a new collective "solution" to the "problem" of "impairment" based on a traditional individualistic analysis. As Shakespeare says: "One of the original drives behind eugenics was to prevent the breeding of inferior social strata" (Shakespeare, 1995, p 32). The impoverishment of disabled people and the high rates of unemployment which they experience make them very vulnerable to such thinking. Eugenic arguments are damaging and devaluing to disabled people; they do not offer an acceptable or effective way of breaking the link between poverty and disability, and should be challenged and rejected. The demands of disabled people's organisations for independent living and inclusion in the labour market, and rejection of welfare solutions to their disablement offer an effective strategy to do this.

Policies for Alleviating and Reducing Poverty

Disabled activists argue that action to alleviate and reduce the poverty of disabled people needs to be based on a social model of disability. The discussion here has already highlighted some of the implications of a social model of disability for alleviating and reducing the poverty of disabled people. It points to a number of policies. It will be helpful to examine these in more detail. They include:

1. The full involvement of disabled people in the conceptualisation, analysis and discussion of poverty

Without this involvement, disabled people's experience and the effects of institutionalised discrimination which they face are likely to be ignored or distorted. There are distinct issues around the nature and causes of disabled people's poverty which should be recognised. It is also likely to be helpful for disabled people's organisations to have discussions and develop alliances with other groups experiencing poverty, including older people, lone parents and low paid workers, both because of their overlaps with disabled people and the insights, support and strength such discussions and contacts can offer.

2. The economic inclusion of disabled people

At the heart of most disabled people's poverty is their restricted access to the labour market. To overcome this, a four track approach is needed. This includes: increased education and employment training opportunities for disabled people; encouraging flexible and accessible employment; meeting the additional costs of impairment, and challenging prejudice against disabled people in employment by providing accurate information about their abilities. In this way, disabled people will be transformed from a group treated as dependent and a drain on societies' economies, to a group which is economically productive and can contribute socially, politically and culturally to its fullest ability.

3. The re-allocation of resources

The prevailing charitable and medical response to disability has been the establishment of institutions. These are expensive, inappropriate and ineffective and beyond the resources of poorer economies. Disability is a political, social and economic issue, not a medical or charitable one. Resources should be shifted away from medical technologies and institutions and non-disabled "expert" salaries, and in the South directed to nutrition and support for indigenous, low-tech strategies to minimise disability and to cushion its impact.

4. The full involvement of disabled people and their organisations in the development of (anti-poverty) policy

There are now a growing number of social action and community-based disability initiatives, based on disabled people's self-advocacy, participation, expertise and involvement in decision-making, in many parts of the world. As Joshua Malinga says: "We want to be involved in the development process and not treated as charity cases" (New Internationalist, 1992, p. 13). A social model in which disabled people play a full part in development decision-making is a realistic and achievable goal and offers perhaps the only viable way of extending opportunities for rehabilitation and decent lives to as many disabled people as possible (Coleridge, 1993, p. 6).

5. Supporting disabled people's organisations and countering their impoverishment

There has been a considerable growth in disabled people's organisations at local, regional and national levels around the world. The Disabled People's International now includes members from over 100 countries. Poverty does not just disproportionately affect disabled people as individuals. It also affects their organisations. These are chronically underfunded. They generally receive far less governmental and public support than organisations for disabled people (Barnes, 1991, pp. 134-135). Funding is particularly difficult to secure in developing countries. There needs to be a redirection of resources from organisations for disabled people to organisations of disabled people.

Poverty and dependence prevent people having control over their lives. They make people feel bad about themselves. Poverty restricts people's access to information, education and knowledge. Disabled people's organisations have a crucial part to play in reaching and involving disabled people, increasing their confidence and skills, and supporting them to break out of this vicious circle. As Venkatesh, Director of Action on Disability and Development (ADD) India, says, "If people feel good about themselves, they can start to created change" (Coleridge, 1993, p. 17).

6. A changed role for state and government

In western societies, the main governmental response to disability has been the creation of social welfare policies based on income maintenance and segregated services. This has been challenged by disabled people's organisations for perpetuating poverty and dependency. Because disability is a social not an individual issue, the state has a central role to play in recognising and supporting the rights of disabled people. This does not mean taking on a traditional role as welfare service provider. Rather, it means providing a legal framework to support disabled people's equal rights and integrating disability into mainstream policies. In the US, the Americans With Disabilities Act has begun to challenge the social exclusion and impoverishment of disabled people. By contrast Conservative administrations in the UK consistently opposed anti-discrimination legislation for disabled people on the unsubstantiated grounds it would be too costly, effectively arguing for the impoverishment of disabled people as the cheaper public policy option, before finally introducing weak legislation based on a medical model of disability.

Instead of seeing the rights and needs of disabled people as different, separate or of less priority than mainstream domestic, overseas and aid policy, they should become an inherent part of all policies, including employment, land, income support, health and child care policies.

7. Aid, development and disability

There are many similarities in the way in which international aid policy and domestic charity address disability. Disabled activists argue that governments and non-government agencies should base aid policy and practice on a development, not charity model, working to involve and empower disabled people (Coleridge, 1993). Aid policy should include specific components, identified by disabled people, addressing the rights and needs of disabled people. It is also crucial to decouple aid from the disabling arms trade.

Addressing the Two-way Relationship Between Poverty and Disability

The relationship between poverty and disability is a two-way one. As Liisa Kaupinnen said at the World Summit on Social Development: "Disability increases poverty and poverty increases disability"(Kauppinen, 1995). As well as disabling policies and practice generating poverty among disabled people, notably through disabled people's marginalisation by and exclusion from the labour market, poverty generates ill health and impairment. This is true in both rich and poor societies. Poverty generates impairment by reducing intellectual abilities, causing immediate physical damage and leading to early onset of frailty. Research in the UK confirms the strong link between economic inequality, ill-health and early death (Davy Smith *et al.*, 1990).

This relationship is true of inequalities both within and between societies. People in poverty in Britain are more likely to be affected by illness and disability (Oppenheim, 1993, p. 85). In one UK study of families living on income support, almost two-thirds of families reported long-term illness or disability (Cohen *et al.*, 1992).

Malnutrition produces one in five impairments in the world today (Abberley, 1987). More than 90% of infant impairments is due to social causes such as poverty and disease (Rioux, 1992). "Malnutrition, mothers weakened by frequent childbirth, inadequate immunisation programmes, accidents in over-crowded homes, all contribute to an incidence of disability among poor people that is higher than among people living in easier circumstances" (Coleridge, p. 64).

If they are to be effective, policies for poverty reduction and alleviation need to have a twin focus. They must be concerned with the economic inclusion and income needs of disabled people, and they must challenge the broader creation of impairment through poverty. Policy is needed to address both the rights and needs of disabled people, and the social and economic creation of impairment to break the link between poverty and disability.

Combating the Broader Causes of Poverty and Impairment

It is helpful to make a distinction between disabling policies and impairment-creating policies, operating at both domestic and international levels, as a starting point for combating both. The wider social, economic and political causes of disability must also be taken into account if poverty alleviation and reduction is to start at source. The creation of impairment and the impoverishment of disabled people cannot be understood in isolation from these causes. Physical abuse, industrial accidents, unsafe environments and environmental pollution, stress and exhaustion, war and violence are significant causes of impairment (Abberley, 1987). For example, an estimated 100,000 Cambodians have been disabled by landmines (Vietnam Veterans of America Foundation, 1992).

In the long term, fundamental changes are required to alter the global economic order which forces poor countries to export their food and resources at low prices (Coleridge, 1993). "Without some major realignment in the balance of economic power between the North and the South, the prospects for further change, particularly in developing societies, remains bleak" (Barnes and Mercer, 1995, p. 11). The increasing "globalisation" of the economy, the shift in the North to insecure, part-time, low wage economies, and the political and financial pressures placed on the South to adopt and maintain unrestricted market economies, work to the particular disadvantage and economic exclusion of disabled people. There is a need for a different kind of economics in harmony with human need and the environment (Ekins and Max-Neef, 1992).

As might be expected, a critical analysis of poverty and disability highlights the structural relationships underpinning both policy and discourse at national and international levels. It is important to make these broader connections between poverty and disability, and not be offput by their far-reaching implications. It is a further challenge to conventional assumptions that disability is an individual issue, amenable to individual solution, and provides a marker for action for the future. Disabled activists in developing countries are already focusing on nutrition, land rights, training and income generation to tackle these broader issues. In the fight against poverty internationally, disabled people have learned key lessons. Local issues, circumstances and strategies may be different, but there are common themes and common struggles to unite round for the future.

Acknowledgments

This paper is a revised, extended and updated version of a paper which was adopted as the Disabled People's International's Elaborate Paper on Poverty Alleviation and Reduction for the World Summit on Social Development, United Nations 1995.

I have many people to thank for their help in writing this paper. I would particularly like to thank Colin Barnes of the British Council of Disabled People's Research Unit, Leeds University, Rachel Hurst of the Disabled People's International, Jennifer Delaney of New Internationalist, Peter Coleridge and Paula Browning of Oxfam, Bob Peckford of the British Deaf Association, and Sally Kneeshaw and Theresa Stansbury of the Royal National Institute for the Blind.

REFERENCES

Abberley, P. (1987) The concept of oppression and the development of a social theory of disability. *Disability, Handicap and Society*, 2, pp. 5-20.

Alcock, P. (1993) *Understanding Poverty* (London, Macmillan).

Amin, K. with Oppenheim, C. (1992) *Poverty in Black and White: Deprivation and Ethnic Minorities* (London, Child Poverty Action Group Ltd., in association with The Runnymede Trust).

Baird, V. (1992) Difference and defiance. *New Internationalist*, No. 233, July, pp. 4-7.

Barclay, P. (Chair), (1995) *Joseph Rowntree Inquiry Into Income and Wealth, Volume 1, Report of the Inquiry*, February (York, Joseph Rowntree Foundation).

Barnes, C. (1991) *Disabled People in Britain and Discrimination: a Case for Anti-discrimination Legislation* (London, Hurst).

Barnes. C. and Mercer, G. (1995) Disabled people and community participation, in: G. Craig and M. Mayo (Eds) *Community Participation and Empowerment* (London, Zed Books).

Beresford, P. and Croft, S. (1995) It's our problem too: challenging the exclusion of poor people from poverty discourse. *Critical Social Policy*, Issue 44/45, Autumn, pp. 75-95.

Beresford, P. and Green, D.A. (1996) Income and wealth: an opportunity to reassess the UK poverty debate? *Critical Social Policy*, Issue 46, Vol. 16 (2) February, pp. 95-109.

Brindle, D. (1996) Charities' UN Protest Over British Poverty: Ministers "fail to honour social pledges." *Guardian*, 22 May, p. 7.

Cohen, R., Coxall, J., Craig, G. and Sadiq-Sangester, A. (1992) *Hardship Britain: being poor in the 1990s* (London, Child Poverty Action Group Ltd., in association with Family Service Units).

Coleridge, P. (1993) *Disability, Liberation And Development* (Oxford, Oxfam in association with Action Disability and Development).

Critical Social Policy (1989) Special Issue: Citizenship And Welfare, Issue 26, Autumn.

Croft, S. (1989) Sharing the wider issues of poverty. *Social Work Today*, 16 February, p. 39.

Croft, S. and Beresford, P. (1990) Involving poor people in poverty research. *Benefits Research*, Issue five, Benefits Research Unit, University of Nottingham, April, Nottingham, pp. 20-23.

Croft, S. and Beresford, P. (1994) User views. Changes, *An International Journal of Psychology and Psychotherapy*, 12, March, No. 2.

Davy Smith, G., Bartly, M. and Blane, D. (1990) The Black Report on socioeconomic inequalities in health: 10 years on. *British Medical Journal*, 301, August, pp. 1-25.

Disability Awareness in Action (1995a) World Summit on Social Development, *Disability Awareness In Action Newsletter*, 25, March.

Disability Awareness in Action (1995b) Employment special. *Disability Awareness In Action Newsletter*, 27 May.

Disabled People's International (1992) *Equalisation of*

Opportunities: Proceedings of the Third World Congress of Disabled People's International (Winnipeg, Disabled People's International).

Ekins P. and Max-Neef, M. (Ed) (1992) *Real-Life Economics: Understanding Wealth Creation* (London, Routledge).

Haque, S. (1994) Disability is not a welfare, but a development issue. *Disability Awareness in Action Newsletter*, 22 November/ December, p. 9.

Hills, J. (1995) *Joseph Rowntree Inquiry into Income And Wealth, Volume 2: A Summary of the Evidence*, February (York, Joseph Rowntree Foundation).

Kauppinen, L. (1995) Statement on behalf of the World Federation of the Deaf, the World Blind Union, the International League of Societies for Persons with Mental Handicap, Rehabilitation International and Disabled People's International. *Disability Awareness In Action Newsletter*, 25, March, p. 2.

Life, Death And Rights (1994) An occasional news sheet on eugenics and euthanasia. *Disability Awareness In Action*, No. 2, November.

Lister, R. (1990) *The Exclusive Society: Citizenship and the Poor* (London, Child Poverty Action Group).

Lister, R. and Beresford, P. (1991) *Working Together Against Poverty: Involving Poor people in Action Against Poverty* (London, Open Services Project/ Department of Applied Social Studies, University of Bradford).

Morris, J. (1992) Tyrannies of perfection. *New Internationalist*, July, pp. 16-17.

New Internationalist (1992) Disabled Lives: Difference and defiance, Special Issue, No. 233, July.

Oliver, M. (1983) *Social Work with Disabled People* (London, Macmillan).

Oliver, M. (1990) *The Politics of Disablement* (London, Macmillan).

Oliver, M. (1996) *Understanding Disability: From Theory to Practice* (London, Macmillan).

Oppenheim, C. (1993) *Poverty The Facts*, revised and updated edn. (London, Child Poverty Action Group Ltd.).

Oppenheim, C. (1994) *The Welfare State: Putting the Record Straight* (London, Child Poverty Action Group Ltd).

Oppenheim, C. and Harker, L. (1996) *Poverty The facts*, revised and updated 3rd edn. (London, Child Poverty Action Group).

Rioux, M. (1992) Paper delivered at *Independence* 92, April, Vancouver.

Rowland, W. and Elissalde, E. (1994) *World Summit on Social Development, Declaration on behalf of the Word Blind Union*, Infama, South African Council for the Blind's Newsletter, June.

Shakespeare, T. (1995) Back to the future?: new genetics and disabled people. *Critical Social Policy*, Issue 44/45, Autumn, pp. 22-35.

UPIAS (The Union of The Physically Impaired Against Segregation) and The Disability Alliance (1976) *Fundamental Principles of Disability* (London, UPIAS and The Disability Alliance).

United Nations (1996) *The Human Development Report*, 1996, 7th edn. (New York, United Nations Development Programme).

Vietnam Veterans of America Foundation (1992) *Report* (USA, VVAF).

Weitz, D. (1994) Ev'rybody must get stoned. *Changes, An International Journal of Psychology and Psychotherapy*, 12 (1), March, pp. 50-59.

STUDY QUESTIONS

1. According to Wasserman, what is the anti-discrimination framework adopted by the Americans with Disabilities Act (ADA) that allows us to understand it as a significant departure from previous conceptions of equal opportunity for persons with disabilities? According to Wasserman, what important functions are served by the ADA?
2. In your view, is there a cohesiveness amongst people with disabilities that allows us to attribute group identity to or endorse group politics for persons with disabilities? Formulate your answer by explaining how the Americans with Disabilities Act would answer these questions and by comparing discrimination based on differential abilities with the kinds of discrimination examined in previous chapters.
3. Outline and evaluate the problems with and the limitations of the ADA as identified by Wasserman.
4. Silvers agrees with Wasserman that the ADA represents a significant shift in policy with respect to persons with disabilities. She argues, however, that Wasserman does not grasp fully the conceptual shift reflected in the ADA. What objections does Silvers raise against Wasserman's analysis of differential ability and of his critique of the ADA's approach and policy?
5. Why does Silvers reject an ethic of care approach to issues of differential ability? From what you have learned about an ethic of care so far (more to follow in Chapter 9), is Silvers's account of an ethic of care and her application of it to issues of disability accurate or fair? Provide reasons for your answer.
6. Do you agree with Silvers that "a 'normal' able-bodied individual is physically and socially blocked from accurately grasping what it is like to be in a 'damaged' individual's place"? Why or why not? If true, what effect does this have on policies with respect to persons with disabilities?
7. While both Silvers and Erevelles are critical of the role of care and care givers with respect to treatment of persons with disabilities, they raise different objections. Compare and evaluate their respective accounts by paying attention to the contexts within which they provide their critiques.
8. Does Erevelles's discussion of a voluntary organization for disabled children in South India lend support to her argument that disability is "structured by the same exploitative material conditions of capitalism as are race, caste, class and gender?" Why or why not?
9. Outline Erevelles's employment of the category of disability as a critical tool for analyzing capitalism and the welfare state. Can this analysis be applied to contexts other than that of India? Why or why not?
10. People with disabilities are over-represented among poor people. According to Beresford, how has conventional discourse around poverty contributed to the failure to perceive this connection between disability and poverty? How have welfare policies contributed to the phenomenon?
11. According to Beresford, what are some of the differences in conditions and policies for persons with disabilities in the rich North and poor South? How does Beresford defend his argument that the "idea of rights can offer both a framework and a benchmark for disabled people to pursue their goals and objectives in North and South, while acknowledging their political, cultural and economic differences." Does he succeed? Why or why not?

SUGGESTED READINGS

Bickenbach, Jerome E. *Physical Disability and Social Policy.* Toronto: University of Toronto Press, 1993.

Connors, Debra. "Disability, Sexism and the Social Order." In *With the Power of Each Breath: A Disabled Women's Anthology* by Susan Browne, Debra Connors and Nancy Stern. Pittsburgh: Cleis Press, 1985: 92-106.

Friesen, Bonita Janzen. "Bangladeshi Disabled Women Find Hope." In *Imprinting our Image: an International Anthology by Women with Disabilities* by Diane Driedger and Susan Gray. Gynergy Books, 1992.

Kopelman, Loretta M. "Ethical Assumptions and Ambiguities in the Americans with Disabilities Act." *Journal of Medicine and Philosophy*, v. 21 (1996): 187-208.

McMahon, Jeff. "Cognitive Disability, Misfortune, and Justice." *Philosophy & Public Affairs*, v. 25, no. 1 (1996): 3-35.

Meekosha, Helen and Leanne Dowse. "Enabling Citizenship: Gender, Disability and Citizenship in Australia. *Feminist Review* 57 (Autumn 1997): 49-72.

Silvers, Anita. "'Defective' Agents: Equality, Difference and the Tyranny of the Normal." *Journal of Social Philosophy.* 25th Anniversary Special Issue (1994): 154-174.

— . "Reconciling Equality to Difference: Caring (F)or Justice for People with Disabilities." *Hypatia*, v. 10, no. 1 (Winter 1995): 30-55.

Stummer, T. Christina F. "The ABCs of Disability." In *Imprinting our Image: an International Anthology by Women with Disabilities* by Diane Driedger and Susan Gray. Gynergy Books, 1992.

Tremain, Shelley. "Dworkin on Disablement and Resources." *Canadian Journal of Law and Jurisprudence*, v. IX, no. 2 (July 1996): 343-359.

Wendell, Susan. *The Rejected Body: Feminist Philosophical Reflections on Disability.* New York: Routledge, 1996.

— . "Toward a Feminist Theory of Disability." *Hypatia*, v. 4, no. 2 (1989): 104-124.

CHAPTER EIGHT

POVERTY AND WELFARE

The final reading in the previous chapter introduced poverty as it exists in a global context, is effected by relations between the rich North and poor South, and manifests itself in connection with other forms of discrimination. Being poor is linked with one's membership in groups disadvantaged by factors of race, ethnicity, and gender as well as disability. Being poor results in diminished life prospects, declining living conditions, and unequal opportunities. In some ways, then, the moral issues underlying poverty bring us full circle to the theoretical issues that opened Part II. Poverty asks us to consider whether all people ought to be provided with the material resources to meet basic human needs. And it asks the more difficult question of how resources can be provided in a world with problems of overpopulation and starving populations. We have observed the important role that liberal theory has played in an understanding of equality, a role evident in the stated commitments to human rights in countries all over the world. We have also outlined the centrality of liberty in liberal accounts of human rights and examined the two conceptions of formal and substantive equality prominent in the liberal tradition. In this chapter, we begin our examination of poverty as it exists and is discussed in liberal societies and use this as a base for examining poverty on a global scale.

In the first reading, Jeremy Waldron examines the ideology of American liberalism with respect to poverty. He discusses the particular issue of homelessness to uncover a tension between liberal accounts of the primacy of freedom and its justifications for private property. He distinguishes between private, collective, and common property rules to show how these rules determine who is allowed and not allowed to be in a given place. One way to describe the homeless is to say that there is no place governed by private property rules that they are allowed to be unless they are invited in, in which case they are at the mercy of the owner and can be excluded. In an ideal libertarian society, where all land might be held as private property, there would be no place where a homeless person was allowed to be. But in the United States, where some territory is held as collective property and made available for common use, the homeless are allowed to be in places such as streets, parks, and under bridges. Waldron argues that the increasing interest in regulating streets, parks, and other public places and restricting the activities that can be performed there results in severe limitations to such basic freedoms as where the homeless can sleep, cook, eat, use bathroom facilities, and be. The liberal values of freedom of speech or freedom of religion are meaningless to a person who lacks the elementary necessities of life. The freedoms that matter here are those that allow one to satisfy basic needs such as food, shelter, and clothing. Waldron argues that in a society with an economic system that allows homelessness, we need to ask whether we are willing to allow those in this predicament to have the freedom to look after their own needs in public spaces.

Waldron identifies and raises objections to various counter arguments defending property rules and tolerating homelessness. One of these arguments is that the homeless are responsible for their condition and have the same opportunity as anyone else to change it. Such accounts of equality of opportunity and of desert are the focus of attention in the third reading by G.A. Cohen. Cohen uses the specific example of the reduction of income tax rates in Britain in the late 1980s, which had the effect of increasing disparities of wealth between the rich and the poor, to examine arguments justifying inequalities in wealth. Some theorists argue that rich people are either entitled to or deserve their wealth because they produced it themselves or it was transferred to them voluntarily. Others defend the utilitarian argument that inequality is justified because it has the effect of expanding the gross national product and thereby increasing the sum of human happiness. Cohen is interested in a particular argument by substantive liberals like Rawls that inequalities are justified if they improve the condition of the least well-off. The justification is based on the incentive argument: high levels of income act as incentives for productive people to produce more and thereby make those who are relatively poor better off than they would be in a more egalitarian society. Cohen argues that when the incentive argument is isolated from all references to desert or entitlement, it generates an argument for inequality that violates the spirit of justice itself as defended by theorists like Rawls.

Justifications for particular policies need to be comprehensive in that they must pass what Cohen refers to as the interpersonal test and stand as justified when uttered by any member of society to any other member. The incentive argument seems reasonable in its usual presentation in third person impersonal form, but the argument undergoes a devaluation when it is pronounced in first person interpersonal terms. The statement, "because I, a talented rich person, will not work as hard unless I have incentives such as greater wealth, you, the poor, will be worse off," puts background issues of equality, obligation, and justice in the foreground. On the lips of the talented rich and presented to the poor, the incentive argument fails to explain why the talented rich will not work as hard and thereby worsen the condition of the less well-off unless there are inequalities in wealth. In failing to offer justifications for the behavior for which they ought to be accountable, the talented rich show themselves to be out of community with the poor with respect to the economic dimension of their lives. Justice would seem to demand that all members of a community are owed justifications for decisions by some members that affect the welfare of the whole. Cohen argues that Rawls's defense of a well-ordered society, where members are motivated by a sense of justice, actually calls for the condemnation of incentives. If conditions that actually obtain in liberal societies dictate that we need inequalities to encourage productivity, then it might be foolish not to have them. It does not follow, argues Cohen, that they can be justified as just.

The readings in the chapter thus far highlight possible tensions between liberal accounts of equality of opportunity, merit, desert, liberty, justice, and community and actual inequalities in wealth characteristic of liberal societies. In the third reading, Garrett Hardin explores moral obligations between communities by examining the question of whether rich countries have an obligation to provide aid to poor countries. He argues that a Marxian ideal of "from each according to his ability, to each according to his needs" calls on rich countries to meet the needs of poor populations without considering how this policy contributes to the crisis of overpopulation. In the face of the complexity of the need to determine the consequences of policies, Hardin contends that it is instructive to invert a question like "How can we help India?" to "How can we harm India?" He answers this question by saying that we do harm by sending India food year after year. He argues that this policy generates political and economic consequences of distributional problems, political corruption, and disincentives for food production and development. He adds that sending food also increases such things as unemployment, demands for materials and resources that require energy, environmental problems to meet demands for energy, and revolutions and civil disorder. Hardin concludes that we can never help India by sending food only and that a program of sending food and energy would be just as harmful because it hastens the crisis of overpopulation and a depletion of energy resources.

The belief, supported by Hardin, that overpopulation has reached crisis proportions is questioned by Amartya Sen in the final reading. Sen argues that neither the position of impending doom nor that of optimism and complacency on the issue of world population provides a genuine understanding of the nature of the population problem. He situates his analysis in the context of large increases in population in developing countries and the myths and fears that are thereby generated in the rich North/Western countries toward poor South/non-Western countries. Sen provides a critical analysis of two rival approaches to dealing with the population problem. The *override* approach, based on alarmist views, recommends forceful measures to coerce people in the South to have fewer children. Those who defend these measures point to the success of China's "one child policy" in reducing population growth. Force can be in the form of imposing birth control or tying population policies to economic policies and can be imposed by governments within or outside particular countries. The *collaborative* approach does not rely on legal restrictions or economic coercion but on the rational decisions of men and women. This approach does not mean lack of government involvement, but rather involvement in expanding educational facilities, health care, and economic well being so that the choices and security of people are enhanced.

Sen provides data to disprove the prevailing presumption that economic and social development only encourages people to reproduce. Regions in Africa, for example, that have lagged behind in economic and social development are the ones that fail to reduce birth rates significantly. He ends by comparing attitudes and policies in China and India, which show that collaborative policies in specific areas of India like Kerala have resulted in reduced rates of population growth similar to that in China. Sen argues that the cost of severe limitations of freedom and choice in the lives of women in China is a social loss with its own harmful social consequences.

HOMELESSNESS AND THE ISSUE OF FREEDOM

Jeremy Waldron

Jeremy Waldron is in the School of Law at Columbia University. He is the author of Liberal Rights: Collected Papers, 1981-1991 *(Cambridge, 1993) and* The Right to Private Property *(Oxford, 1988) and the editor of* Theories of Rights *(Oxford, 1984).*

Waldron examines liberal assumptions about the connection between property rights and freedom and builds a case for considering homelessness as a kind of violation of a person's freedom. Waldron explores the role of private property in Western societies in giving people the freedom to perform basic human functions such as sleeping and using a washroom and argues that these functions cannot be performed freely in the public spaces in which homeless people exist. He claims that moves to restrict even further what public spaces can be occupied and used by homeless people should be understood as placing severe limits on a person's freedom.

Introduction

There are many facets to the nightmare of homelessness. In this essay, I want to explore just one of them: the relation between homelessness, the rules of public and private property, and the underlying freedom of those who are condemned by poverty to walk the streets and sleep in the open. Unlike some recent discussions, my concern is not with the constitutionality of various restrictions on the homeless (though that, of course, is important).[1] I want to address a prior question—a more fundamental question—of legal and moral philosophy: how should we think about homelessness, how should we conceive of it, in relation to a value like freedom?

The discussion that follows is, in some ways, an abstract one. This is intentional. The aim is to refute the view that, on abstract liberal principles, there is no reason to be troubled by the plight of the homeless, and that one has to come down to the more concrete principles of a communitarian ethic in order to find a focus for that concern. Against this view, I shall argue that homelessness is a matter of the utmost concern in relation to some of the most fundamental and abstract principles of liberal value. That an argument is abstract should not make us think of it as thin or watery. If homelessness raises questions even in regard to the most basic principles of liberty, it is an issue that ought to preoccupy liberal theorists every bit as much as more familiar worries about torture, the suppression of dissent, and other violations of human rights. That the partisans of liberty in our legal and philosophical culture have not always been willing to see this (or say it) should be taken as an indication of the consistency and good faith with which they espouse and proclaim their principles.

I. Location and Property

Some truisms to begin with. Everything that is done has to be done somewhere. No one is free to perform an action unless there is somewhere he is free to perform it. Since we are embodied beings, we always have a location. Moreover, though everyone has to be somewhere, a person cannot always choose any location he likes. Some locations are physically inac-

---

Reprinted with permission of the publisher and Jeremy Waldron from *UCLA Law Review* 39 (1991): 295–324 [edited].

cessible. And, physical inaccessibility aside, there are some places one is simply not allowed to be.

One of the functions of property rules, particularly as far as land is concerned, is to provide a basis for determining who is allowed to be where. For the purposes of these rules, a country is divided up into spatially defined regions or, as we usually say, places. The rules of property give us a way of determining, in the case of each place, who is allowed to be in that place and who is not. For example, if a place is governed by a private property rule, then there is a way of identifying an individual whose determination is final on the question of who is and who is not allowed to be in that place. Sometimes that individual is the owner of the land in question, and sometimes (as in a landlord-tenant relationship) the owner gives another person the power to make that determination (indeed to make it, for the time being, even as against the owner). Either way, it is characteristic of a private ownership arrangement that some individual (or some other particular legal person) has this power to determine who is allowed to be on the property.

The actual rules of private property are, of course, much more complicated than this and they involve much besides this elementary power of decision.[2] However, to get the discussion going, it is enough to recognize that there is something like this individual power of decision in most systems of private ownership. Private ownership of land exists when an individual person may determine who is, and who is not, allowed to be in a certain place, without answering to anyone else for that decision. I say who is allowed to be in my house. He says who is to be allowed in his restaurant. And so on.

The concept of *being allowed* to be in a place is fairly straightforward. We can define it negatively. An individual who is in a place where he is not allowed to be may be removed, and he may be subject to civil or criminal sanctions for trespass or some other similar offense. No doubt people are sometimes physically removed from places where they are allowed to be. But if a person is in a place where he is not allowed to be, not only may he be physically removed, but there is a social rule to the effect that his removal may be facilitated and aided by the forces of the state. In short, the police may be called and he may be dragged away.

I said that one function of property rules is to indicate procedures for determining who is allowed and not allowed (in this sense) to be in a given place, and I gave the example of a private property rule. However, not all rules of property are like private property rules in this regard. We may use a familiar classification and say that, though many places in this country are governed by private property rules, some are governed by rules of collective property, which divide further into rules of state property and rules of common property (though neither the labels nor the exact details of this second distinction matter much for the points I am going to make).[3]

If a place is governed by a *collective* property rule, then there is no private person in the position of owner. Instead, the use of collective property is determined by people, usually officials, acting in the name of the whole community.

Common property may be regarded as a sub-class of collective property. A place is common property if part of the point of putting it under collective control is to allow anyone in the society to make use of it without having to secure the permission of anybody else. Not all collective property is like this: places like military firing ranges, nationalized factories, and government offices are off-limits to members of the general public unless they have special permission or a legitimate purpose for being there. They are held as collective property for purposes other than making them available for public use. However, examples of common property spring fairly readily to mind: they include streets, sidewalks, subways, city parks, national parks, and wilderness areas. These places are held in the name of the whole society in order to make them fairly accessible to everyone. As we shall see, they are by no means unregulated as to the nature or time of their use. Still, they are relatively open at most times to a fairly indeterminate range of uses by anyone. In the broadest terms, they are places where anyone may be.

Sometimes the state may insist that certain places owned by private individuals or corporations should be treated rather like common property if they fulfill the function of public places. For example, shopping malls in the United States are usually on privately owned land. However, because of the functions such places serve, the state imposes considerable restrictions on the owners' powers of exclusion (people may not be excluded from a shopping mall on racial grounds, for example) and on their power to limit the activities (such as political pamphleteering) that may take place there.[4] Though this is an important development, it does not alter the analysis I am developing in this Essay, and for simplicity I shall ignore it in what follows.

Property rules differ from society to society. Though we describe some societies (like the United States) as having systems of private property, and others (like the USSR—at least until recently) as having collectivist systems, clearly all societies have some places governed by private property rules, some places governed by state property rules, and some places governed by common property rules. Every society has private houses, military bases, and public parks. So if we want to categorize whole societies along these lines, we have to say it is a matter of balance and emphasis. For example, we say the USSR is (or used to be) a collectivist society and that the USA is not, not because there was no private property in the USSR, but because most industrial and agricultural land there was held collectively whereas most industrial and agricultural land in the United States is privately owned. The distinction is one of degree. Even as between two countries that pride themselves on having basically capitalist economies, for example, New Zealand and Britain, we may say that the former is "communist" to a greater extent (i.e. is more a system of common property) than the latter because more places (for example, all river banks) are held as common property in New Zealand than are held as common property in Britain. Of course, these propositions are as vague as they are useful. If we are measuring the "extent" to which a country is collectivist, that measure is ambiguous as between the quantitative proportion of land that is governed by rules of collective property and some more qualitative assessment of the importance of the places that are governed in this way.[5]

II. Homelessness

Estimates of the number of homeless people in the United States range from 250,000 to three million.[6] A person who is homeless is, obviously enough, a person who has no home. One way of describing the plight of a homeless individual might be to say that there is no place governed by a private property rule where he is allowed to be.

In fact, that is not quite correct. Any private proprietor may invite a homeless person into his house or onto his land, and if he does there *will* be some private place where the homeless person is allowed to be. A technically more accurate description of his plight is that there is no place governed by a private property rule where he is allowed to be whenever *he* chooses, no place governed by a private property rule from which he may not at any time be excluded as a result of someone else's say-so. As far as being on private property is concerned—in people's houses or gardens, on farms or in hotels, in offices or restaurants—the homeless person is utterly and at all times at the mercy of others. And we know enough about how this mercy is generally exercised to figure that the description in the previous paragraph is more or less accurate as a matter of fact, even if it is not strictly accurate as a matter of law.[7]

For the most part the homeless are excluded from *all* of the places governed by private property rules, whereas the rest of us are, in the same sense, excluded from *all but one* (or maybe all but a few) of those places. That is another way of saying that each of us has at least one place to be in a country composed of private places, whereas the homeless person has none.

Some libertarians fantasize about the possibility that *all* the land in a society might be held as private property ("Sell the streets!").[8] This would be catastrophic for the homeless. Since most private proprietors are already disposed to exclude him from their property, the homeless person might discover in such a libertarian paradise that there was literally *nowhere* he was allowed to be. Wherever he went he would be liable to penalties for trespass and he would be liable to eviction, to being thrown out by an owner or dragged away by the police. Moving from one place to another would involve nothing more liberating than moving from one trespass liability to another. Since land is finite in any society, there is only a limited number of places where a person can (physically) be, and such a person would find that he was legally excluded from all of them. (It would not be entirely mischievous to add that since, in order to exist, a person has to be *some*where, such a person would not be permitted to exist.)

Our society saves the homeless from this catastrophe only by virtue of the fact that some of its territory is held as collective property and made available for common use. The homeless are allowed to be—provided they are on the streets, in the parks, or under the bridges. Some of them are allowed to crowd together into publicly provided "shelters" after dark (though these are dangerous places and there are not nearly enough shelters for all of them). But in the daytime and, for many of them, all through the night, wandering in public places is their only option. When all else is privately owned, the sidewalks are their salvation. They are allowed to *be* in our society only to the extent that our society is communist.

This is one of the reasons why most defenders of private property are uncomfortable with the libertarian proposal, and why that proposal remains sheer fantasy.[9] But there is a modified form of the libertarian catastrophe in prospect with which moderate and even liberal defenders of ownership seem much more comfortable. This is the increasing regulation of the streets, subways, parks, and other public places to restrict the activities that can be performed there. What is emerging—and it is not just a matter of fantasy—is a state of affairs in which a million or more citizens have no place to perform elementary human activities like urinating, washing, sleeping, cooking, eating, and standing around. Legislators voted for by people who own private places in which they can do all these things are increasingly deciding to make public places available only for activities other than these primal human tasks. The streets and subways, they say, are for commuting from home to office. They are not for sleeping; sleeping is something one does at home. The parks are for recreations like walking and informal ball-games, things for which one's own yard is a little too confined. Parks are not for cooking or urinating; again, these are things one does at home. Since the public and the private are complementary, the activities performed in public are to be the complement of those appropriately performed in private. This complementarity works fine for those who have the benefit of both sorts of places. However, it is disastrous for those who must live their whole lives on common land. If I am right about this, it is one of the most callous and tyrannical exercises of power in modern times by a (comparatively) rich and complacent majority against a minority of their less fortunate fellow human beings.

III. Locations, Actions and Freedom

The points made so far can be restated in terms of freedom. Someone who is allowed to be in a place is, in a fairly straightforward sense, free to be there. A person who is not allowed to be in a place is unfree to be there. However, the concept of freedom usually applies to actions rather than locations: one is free or unfree to do X or to do Y. What is the connection, then, between freedom to be somewhere and freedom to do something?

At the outset I recited the truism that anything a person does has to be done somewhere. To that extent, all actions involve a spatial component (just as many actions involve, in addition, a material component like the use of tools, implements, or raw materials). It should be fairly obvious that, if one is not free to be in a certain place, one is not free to do anything at that place. If I am not allowed to be in your garden (because you have forbidden me) then I am not allowed to eat my lunch, make a speech, or turn a somersault in your garden. Though I may be free to do these things somewhere else, I am not free to do them there. It follows, strikingly, that a person who is not free to be in any place is not free to do anything; such a person is comprehensively unfree. In the libertarian paradise we imagined in the previous section, this would be the plight of the homeless. They would be simply without freedom (or, more accurately, any freedom they had would depend utterly on the forbearance of those who owned the places that made up the territory of the society in question).

Fortunately, our society is not such a libertarian paradise. There are places where the homeless may be and, by virtue of that, there are actions they may perform; they are free to perform actions on the streets, in the parks, and under the bridges. Their freedom depends on common property in a way that ours does not. Once again, the homeless have freedom in our society only to the extent that our society is communist.

That conclusion may sound glib and provocative. But it is meant as a reflection on the cold and awful reality of the experience of men, women, and children who are homeless in America. For them the rules of private property are a series of fences that stand between them and somewhere to be, somewhere to act. The only hope they have so far as freedom is concerned lies in the streets, parks, and public shelters, and in the fact that those are collectivized resources made available openly to all.

It is sometimes said that freedom means little or nothing to a cold and hungry person. We should focus on the material predicament of the homeless, it is said, not on this abstract liberal concern about freedom. That may be an appropriate response to someone who is talking high-mindedly and fatuously about securing freedom of speech or freedom of religion for people who lack the elementary necessities of human life.[10] But the contrast between liberty and the satisfaction of material needs must not be drawn too sharply, as though the latter had no relation at all to what one is free or unfree to do. I am focusing on freedoms that are intimately connected with food, shelter, clothing, and the satisfaction of basic needs. When a person is needy, he does not cease to be proccupied with freedom; rather, his preoccupation tends to focus on freedom to perform certain actions in particular. The freedom that means most to a person who is cold and wet is the freedom that consists in staying under whatever shelter he has found. The freedom that means most to someone who is exhausted is the freedom not to be prodded with a nightstick as he tries to catch a few hours sleep on a subway bench.

There is a general point here about the rather *passive* image of the poor held by those who say we should concern ourselves with their needs, not their freedom.[11] People remain agents, with ideas and initiatives of their own, even when they are poor. Indeed, since they are on their own, in a situation of danger, without any place of safety, they must often be more resourceful, spend more time working out how to live, thinking things through much more carefully, taking much less for granted, than the comfortable autonomous agent that we imagine in a family with a house and a job in an office or university. And—when they are allowed to—the poor do find ways of using their initiative to rise to these challenges. They have to; if they do not, they die.

Even the most desperately needy are not always paralyzed by want. There are certain things they are physically capable of doing for themselves. Sometimes they find shelter by occupying an empty house or sleeping in a sheltered spot. They gather food from various places, they light a fire to cook it, and they sit down in a park to eat. They may urinate behind bushes, and wash their clothes in a fountain. Their physical condition is certainly not comfortable, but they are *capable* of acting in ways that make things a little more bearable for themselves. Now one question we face as a society—a broad question of justice and social policy—is whether we are willing to tolerate an economic system in which large numbers of people are homeless. Since the answer is evidently, "Yes," the question that remains is whether we are willing to allow those who are in this predicament to act as free agents, looking after their own needs, in public places—the only space available to them. It is a deeply frightening fact about the modern United States that those who have homes and jobs are willing to answer "Yes" to the first question and "No" to the second.

A. Negative Freedom

...To say—as I have insisted we should say—that property rules limit freedom, is not to say they are *eo ipso* wrong.[12] It is simply to say that they engage a concern about liberty, and that anyone who values liberty should put himself on alert when questions of property are being discussed. (The argument I have made about the homeless is a striking illustration of the importance of our not losing sight of that.)

Above all, by building the morality of a given property system (rights, duties, and the current distribution) into the concept of freedom, the moralizing approach precludes the use of that concept as a basis for arguing about property. If when we use the words "free" and "unfree," we are already assuming that it is wrong for A to use something that belongs to B, we cannot appeal to "freedom" to explain why B's ownership of the resource is justified. We cannot even extol our property system as the basis of a "free" society, for such a boast would be nothing more than tautological. It is true that if we have independent grounds of justification for our private property system, then we can say that interfering with property rights is wrong without appealing to the idea of freedom. In that case, there is nothing question-begging about the claim that preventing someone from violating property rights does not count as a restriction on his freedom. But the price of this strategy is high. It not only transforms our conception of freedom into a moralized definition of positive liberty (so that the only freedom that is relevant is the freedom to do what is right), but it also excludes the concept of freedom altogether from the debate about the justification of property rights. Since most theorists of property do not want to deprive themselves of the concept of freedom as a resource in that argument, the insistence that the enforcement of property rules should not count as a restriction on freedom is, at the very least, a serious strategic mistake.

B. General Prohibitions and Particular Freedoms

I think the account I have given is faithful to the tradition of negative liberty. One is free to do something only if one is not liable to be forcibly prevented from or penalized for doing it. However, the way I have applied this account may seem a little disconcerting. The issue has to do with the level of generality at which actions are described.

The laws we have usually mention general types of actions, rather than particular actions done by particular people at specific times and places. Statutes do not say, "Jane Smith is not to assault Sarah Jones on Friday, November 24, on the corner of College Avenue and Bancroft." They say, "Assault is prohibited," or some equivalent, and it is understood that the prohibition applies to all such actions performed by anyone anywhere. A prohibition on a general type of action is understood to be a prohibition on all tokens of that type. Jurists say we ought to value this generality in our laws; it is part of what is involved in the complex ideal of "The Rule of Law." It makes the laws more predictable and more learnable. It makes them a better guide for the ordinary citizen who needs to have a rough and ready understanding (rather than a copious technical knowledge) of what he is and is not allowed to do as he goes about his business. A quick checklist of prohibited acts, formulated in general terms, serves that purpose admirably.[13] It also serves moral ideals of universalizability and rationality: a reason for restraining any particular act of the same type, unless there is a relevant difference between them (which can be formulated also in general terms).[14]

All that is important. However, there is another aspect of "The Rule of Law" ideal that can lead one into difficulties if it is combined with this insistence on generality. Legal systems of the kind we have pride themselves on the following feature: "Everything which is not explicitly prohibited is permitted." If the law does not formulate any prohibition on singing or jogging, for example, that is an indication to the citizen that singing and jogging are permitted, that he is free to perform them. To gauge the extent of his freedom, all he needs to know are the prohibitions imposed by the law. His freedom is simply the complement of that.[15]

The difficulty arises if it is inferred from this that a person's freedom is the complement of the general prohibitions that apply to him. For although it is possible to infer particular prohibitions from prohibitions formulated at a general level ("All murder is wrong" implies "This murder by me today is wrong"), it is not possible to infer particular permissions from the absence of any general prohibition. In our society, there is no general prohibition on cycling, but one cannot infer from this that any particular act of riding a bicycle is permitted. It depends (among other things) on whether the person involved has the right to use the particular bicycle he is proposing to ride.

This does not affect the basic point about complementarity. Our freedoms *are* the complement of the prohibitions that apply to us. The mistake arises from thinking that the only prohibitions that apply to us are general prohibitions. For, in addition to the general prohibitions laid down (say) in the criminal law, there are also the prohibitions on using particular objects and places that are generated by the laws of property. Until we know how these latter laws apply, we do not know whether we are free to perform a particular action.

It is *not* a telling response to this point to say that the effect of the laws of property can be stated in terms of a general principle—"No one is to use the property of another without his permission." They *can* so be stated; but in order to apply that principle, we need particular knowledge, not just general knowledge.[16] A person needs to know that *this* bicycle belongs to him, whereas those bicycles belong to other people. He needs that particular knowledge about specific objects as well as his general knowledge about the types of actions that are and are not permitted.

At any rate, the conclusions about freedom that I have reached depend on taking the prohibitions relating to particular objects generated by property laws as seriously as we take the more general prohibitions imposed by the criminal law. No doubt these different types of prohibition are imposed for different reasons. But if freedom means simply the absence of deliberate interference with one's actions, we will not be in a position to say how free a person is until we know everything about the universe of legal restraints that may be applied to him. After all, it is not freedom in the abstract that people value, but freedom to perform particular actions. If the absence of a general prohibition tells us nothing about anyone's concrete freedom, then we should be wary of using only the checklist of general prohibitions to tell us how free or unfree a person or a society really is.

These points can readily be applied to the homeless. There are no general prohibitions in our society on actions like sleeping or washing. However, we cannot infer from this that anyone may sleep or wash wherever he chooses. In order to work out whether a particular person is free to sleep or wash, we must also ask whether there are any prohibitions of *place* that apply to his performance of actions of this type. As a matter of fact, all of us face formidable battery of such prohibitions. Most private places, for example, are off-limits to us for these (or any other) activities. Though I am a well-paid professor, there are only a couple of private places where I am allowed to sleep or wash (without having someone's specific permission): my home, my office, and whatever restaurant I am patronizing. Most homeless people do not have jobs and few of them are allowed inside restaurants. ("Bathrooms for the use of customers only.") Above all, they have no homes. So there is literally no private place where they are free to sleep or wash.

For them, that is a desperately important fact about their freedom, one that must preoccupy much of every day. Unlike us, they have no private place where they can take it for granted that they will be allowed to sleep or wash. Since everyone needs to sleep and wash regularly, homeless people have to spend time searching for non-private places—like public restrooms (of which there are precious few in America, by the standards of most civilized countries) and shelters (available, if at all, only at night)—where these actions may be performed without fear of interference. If we regard freedom as simply the complement of the general prohibitions imposed by law, we are in danger of overlooking this fact about the freedom of the homeless. Most of us can afford to overlook it, because we have homes to go to. But without a home, a person's freedom is his freedom to act in public, in places governed by common property rules. That is the difference between our freedom and the freedom of the homeless.

C. Public Places

What then are we to say about public places? If there is anywhere the homeless are free to act, it is in the streets, the subways and the parks. These regions are governed by common property rules. Since these are the only places they are allowed to be, these are the only places they are free to act.

However, a person is not allowed to do just whatever he likes in a public place. There are at least three types of prohibition that one faces in a place governed by rules of common property.

(1) If there are any general prohibitions on types of action in a society, like the prohibition on murder or the prohibition on selling narcotics, then they apply to all tokens of those types performed anywhere, public or private. And these prohibitions apply to everyone: though it is only the homeless who have no choice but to be in public places, the

law forbids the rich as well as the poor from selling narcotics, and *a fortiori* from selling narcotics on the streets and in the parks.

(2) Typically, there are also prohibitions that are specific to public places and provide the basis of their commonality. Parks have curfews; streets and sidewalks have rules that govern the extent to which one person's use of these places may interfere with another's; there are rules about obstruction, jaywalking, and so on. Many of these rules can be characterized and justified as rules of fairness. If public places are to be available for everyone's use, then we must make sure that their use by some people does not preclude or obstruct their use by others.

(3) However, some of the rules that govern behavior in public places are more substantive than that: they concern particular forms of behavior that are not to be performed in public whether there is an issue of fairness involved or not. For example, many states and municipalities forbid the use of parks for making love. It is not that there is any general constraint on lovemaking as a type of action (though some states still have laws against fornication). Although sexual intercourse between a husband and wife is permitted and even encouraged by the law, it is usually forbidden in public places. The place for that sort of activity, we say, is the privacy of the home.

Other examples spring to mind. There is no law against urinating—it is a necessary and desirable human activity. However, there is a law against urinating in public, except in the specially designated premises of public restrooms. In general, it is an activity which, if we are free to do it, we are free to do it mainly at home or in some other private place (a bathroom in a restaurant) where we have an independent right to be. There is also no law against sleeping—again a necessary and desirable human activity. To maintain their physical and mental health, people need to sleep for a substantial period every day. However, states and municipalities are increasingly passing ordinances to prohibit sleeping in public places like streets and parks.[17] The decision of the Transit Authority in New York to enforce prohibitions on sleeping in the subways attracted national attention a year or two ago.[18]

Such ordinances have and are known and even intended to have a specific effect on the homeless which is different from the effect they have on the rest of us. We are all familiar with the dictum of Anatole France: "[L]a majestueuse égalité des lois ... interdit au riche comme au pauvre de coucher sous let ponts. ..."[19] We might adapt it to the present point, noting that the new rules in the subway will prohibit anyone from sleeping or lying down in the cars and stations, whether they are rich or poor, homeless or housed. They will be phrased with majestic impartiality, and indeed their drafters know that they would be struck down immediately by the courts if they were formulated specifically to target those who have no homes. Still everyone is perfectly well aware of the point of passing these ordinances, and any attempt to defend them on the basis of their generality is quite disingenuous. Their point is to make sleeping in the subways off limits to those who have nowhere else to sleep.[20]

Four facts are telling in this regard. First, it is well known among those who press for these laws that the subway is such an unpleasant place to sleep that almost no one would do it if they had anywhere else to go. Secondly, the pressure for these laws comes as a response to what is well known to be "the problem of homelessness." It is not as though people suddenly became concerned about *sleeping* in the subway as such (as though that were a particularly dangerous activity to perform there, like smoking or jumping onto a moving train). When people write to the Transit Authority and say, "Just get them out. I don't care. Just get them out any way you can," we all know who the word "them" refers to.[21] People do not want to be confronted with the sight of the homeless—it is uncomfortable for the well-off to be reminded of the human price that is paid for a social structure like theirs—and they are willing to deprive those people of their last opportunity to sleep in order to protect themselves from this discomfort. Thirdly, the legislation is called for and promoted by people who are secure in the knowledge that they themselves have some place where they are permitted to sleep. Because they have some place to sleep which is not the subway, they infer that the subway is not a place for sleeping. The subway is a place where those who have some other place to sleep may do things besides sleeping.

Finally, and most strikingly, those who push for these laws will try to amend them or reformulate them if they turn out to have an unwelcome impact on people who are not homeless. For example, a city ordinance in Clearwater, Florida, prohibiting sleeping in public, was struck down as too broad because it would have applied even to a person sleeping in his car.[22] Most people who have cars also have homes, and we would not want a statute aimed at the homeless to prevent car owners from sleeping in public.

Though we all know what the real object of these ordinances is, we may not have thought very hard about their cumulative effect. That effect is as follows.

For a person who has no home, and has no expectation of being allowed into something like a private office building or a restaurant, prohibitions on things like sleeping that apply particularly to public places pose a special problem. For although there is no *general* prohibition on acts of these types, still they are effectively ruled out altogether for anyone who is homeless and who has no shelter to go to. The prohibition is comprehensive in effect because of the cumulation, in the case of the homeless, of a number of different bans, differently imposed. The rules of property prohibit the homeless person from doing any of these acts in private, since there is no private place that he has a right to be. And the rules governing public places prohibit him from doing any of these acts in public, since that is how we have decided to regulate the use of public places. So what is the result? Since private places and public places between them exhaust all the places that there are, there is nowhere that these actions may be performed by the homeless person. And since freedom to perform a concrete action requires freedom to perform it at some place, it follows that the homeless person does not have the freedom to perform them. If sleeping is prohibited in public places, then sleeping is comprehensively prohibited to the homeless. If urinating is prohibited in public places (and if there are no public lavatories) then the homeless are simply unfree to urinate. These are not altogether comfortable conclusions, and they are certainly not comfortable for those who have to live with them....

V. Freedom and Important Freedoms

I have argued that a rule against performing an act in a public place amounts *in effect* to a *comprehensive* ban on that action so far as the homeless are concerned. If that argument is accepted, our next question should be: "How serious is this limitation on freedom?" Freedom in any society is limited in all sorts of ways: I have no freedom to pass through a red light nor to drive east on Bancroft Avenue. Any society involves a complicated array of freedoms and unfreedoms, and our assessment of *how free* a given society is (our assessment, for example, that the United States is a freer society than Albania) involves some assessment of the balance in that array.

Such assessments are characteristically qualitative as well as quantitative. We do not simply ask, "How may actions are people free or unfree to perform?" Indeed, such questions are very difficult to answer or even to formulate coherently.[23] Instead we often ask qualitative questions: "How important are the actions that people are prohibited from performing?" One of the tasks of a theory of human rights is to pick out a set of actions that it is thought particularly important from a moral point of view that people should have the freedom to perform, choices that it is thought particularly important that they should have the freedom to make, whatever other restrictions there are on their conduct.[24] For example, the Bill of Rights picks out things like religious worship, political speech, and the possession of firearms as actions or choices whose restriction we should be specially concerned about. A society that places restrictions on activities of these types is held to be worse, in point of freedom, than a society that merely restricts activities like drinking, smoking, or driving.

The reason for the concern has in part to do with the special significance of these actions. Religious worship is where we disclose and practice our deepest beliefs. Political speech is where we communicate with one another as citizens of a republic. Even bearing arms is held, by those who defend its status as a right, to be a special assertion of dignity, mature responsibility, civic participation, and freedom from the prospect of tyranny. And people occasionally disagree about the contents of these lists of important freedoms. Is it really important to have the right to bear arms, in a modern democratic society? Is commercial advertising as important as individual political discourse? These are disputes about which choices have this high ethical import, analogous to that attributed, say, to religious worship. They are disputes about which liberties should be given special protection in the name of human dignity or autonomy, and which attacks on freedom should be viewed as particularly inimical to the identity of a person as a citizen and as a moral agent.

On the whole, the actions specified by Bills of Rights are not what are at stake in the issue of homelessness. Certainly there would be an uproar if an ordinance was passed making it an offense to pray in the subway or to pass one's time there in political debate.[25] There has been some concern in America about the restriction of free speech in public and quasi-public places[26] (since it is arguable that the whole point of free speech is that it take place in the public realm). However, the actions that are being closed off to the homeless are, for the most part, not significant in this high-minded sense. They are significant in another way: they are actions basic to the sustenance of a decent or healthy life, in some cases basic to the sustenance of life itself. There may not seem anything particularly autonomous or self-assertive or civically republican or ethically ennobling about sleeping or cooking or urinating. You will not find them listed in any Charter. However, that does not mean it is a matter of slight concern when people are prohibited from performing such actions, a concern analogous to that aroused by a traffic regulation or the introduction of a commercial standard.

For one thing, the regular performance of such actions is a precondition for all other aspects of life and activity. It is a precondition for the sort of autonomous life that is celebrated and affirmed when Bills of Rights are proclaimed. I am not making the crude mistake of saying that if we value autonomy, we must value its preconditions in exactly the same way. But if we value autonomy we should regard the satisfaction of its preconditions as a matter of importance; otherwise, our values simply ring hollow so far as real people are concerned.

Moreover, though we say there is nothing particularly dignified about sleeping or urinating, there is certainly something deeply and inherently *un*dignified about being prevented from doing so. Every torturer knows this: to break the human spirit, focus the mind of the victim through petty restrictions pitilessly imposed on the banal necessities of human life. We should be ashamed that we have allowed our laws of public and private property to reduce a million or more citizens to something approaching this level of degradation.

Increasingly, in the way we organize common property, we have done all we can to prevent people from taking care of these elementary needs themselves, quietly, with dignity, as ordinary human beings. If someone needs to urinate, what he needs above all as a dignified person is the *freedom* to do so in privacy and relative independence of the arbitrary will of anyone else. But we have set things up so that either the street person must *beg* for this opportunity, several times every day, as a favor from people who recoil from him in horror, or, if he wants to act independently on his own initiative, he must break the law and risk arrest. The generous provision of public lavatories would make an immense difference in this regard—and it would be a difference to freedom and dignity, not just a matter of welfare.

Finally we need to understand that any restriction on the performance of these basic acts has the feature of being not only uncomfortable and degrading, but more or less literally *unbearable* for the people concerned. People need sleep, for example, not just in the sense that sleep is necessary for health, but also in the sense that they will eventually fall asleep or drop from exhaustion if it is denied them. People simply cannot bear a lack of sleep, and they will do themselves a great deal of damage trying to bear it. The same, obviously, is true of bodily functions like urinating and defecating. These are things that people simply have to do; any attempt voluntarily to refrain from doing them is at once painful, dangerous, and finally impossible. That our social system might in effect deny them the right to do these things, by prohibiting their being done in each and every place, ought to be a matter of the gravest concern.[27]

It may seem sordid or in bad taste to make such a lot of these elementary physical points in a philosophical discussion of freedom. But if freedom is important, it is as freedom for human beings, that is, for the embodied and needy organisms that we are. The point about the activities I have mentioned is that they are both urgent and quotidian. They are urgent because they are basic to all other functions. They are actions that have to be performed, if one is to be free to do anything else without distraction and distress. And they are quotidian in the sense that they are actions that have to be done every day. They are not actions that a person can *wait* to perform until he acquires a home. Every day, he must eat and excrete and sleep. Every day, if he is homeless, he will face the overwhelming task of trying to find somewhere where he is allowed to do this.

VI. Homes and Opportunities

That last point is particularly important as an answer to a final objection that may be made. Someone might object that I have so far said nothing at all about the fact that our society gives everyone the *opportunity* to acquire a home, and that we are all—the homeless and the housed—equal in *this* regard even if we are unequal in our actual ownership of real estate.

There is something to this objection, but not much. Certainly a society that denied a caste of persons the right (or juridical power) to own or lease property would be even worse than ours. The opportunity to acquire a home (even if it is just the juridical power) is surely worth having. But, to put it crudely, one cannot pee in an opportunity. Since the homeless, like us, are real people, they need some real place to be....

In the final analysis, whether or not a person really has the *opportunity* to obtain somewhere to live is a matter of his position in a society; it is a matter of his ability to deal with the people around him and of there being an opening in social and economic structures so that his wants and abilities can be brought into relation with others'.[28] That position, that ability, and that opening do not exist magically as a result of legal status. The juridical fact that a person is not legally barred from becoming a tenant or a proprietor does not mean that there is any realistic prospect of that happening. Whether it happens depends, among other things, on now he can present himself, how reliable and respectable he appears, what skills and abilities he can deploy, how much time, effort, and mobility he can invest in a search for housing, assistance, and employment, and so on.

Those are abstract formulations. We could say equally that it is hard to get a job when one appears filthy, that many of the benefits of social and economic interaction cannot be obtained without an address or without a way of receiving telephone calls, that a person cannot take *all* his possessions with him in a shopping cart when he goes for an interview but he may have nowhere to leave them, that those who have become homeless become so because they have run out of cash altogether and so of course do not have available the up-front fees and deposits that landlords require from potential tenants, and so on.

Everything we call a social or economic opportunity depends cruelly on a person's being able to *do* certain things—for example, his being able to wash, to sleep, and to base himself somewhere. When someone is homeless he is, as we have seen, effectively *banned* from doing these things; these are things he is *not allowed* to do. So long as that is the case, it is a contemptible mockery to reassure the victims of such coercion that they have the opportunity to play a full part in social and economic life, for the rules of property are such that they are prohibited from doing the minimum that would be necessary to take advantage of that opportunity.[29]

Conclusion

Lack of freedom is not all there is to the nightmare of homelessness. There is also the cold, the hunger, the disease and lack of medical treatment, the danger, the beatings, the loneliness, and the shame and despair that may come from being unable to care for oneself, one's child, or a friend. By focusing on freedom in this essay, I have not wanted to detract from any of that.

But there are good reasons to pay attention to the issue of freedom. They are not merely strategic, though in a society that prides itself as "the land of the free," this may be one way of shaming a people into action and concern. Homelessness is partly about property and law, and freedom provides the connecting term that makes those categories relevant. By considering not only what a person is allowed to do, but where he is allowed to do it, we can see a system of property for what it is: rules that provide freedom and prosperity for some by imposing restrictions on others. So long as everyone enjoys some of the benefits as well as some of the restrictions, that correlativity is bearable. It ceases to be so when there is a class of persons who bear all of the restrictions and nothing else, a class of persons for whom property is nothing but a way of limiting their freedom.

Perhaps the strongest argument for thinking about homelessness as an issue of freedom is that it forces us to see people in need as agents. Destitution is not necessarily passive; and public provision is not always a way of compounding passivity. By focusing on what we allow people to do to satisfy their own basic needs on their own initiative, and by scrutinizing the legal obstacles that we place in their way (the doors we lock, the ordinances we enforce, and the night-sticks we raise), we get a better sense that what we are dealing with here is not just "the problem of homelessness," but a million or more persons whose activity and dignity and freedom are at stake.

AUTHOR'S NOTE

An earlier version of this essay was presented at faculty workshops at Cornell University and at Boalt Hall. I am grateful to all who participated in those discussions, but particularly to Gary Gleb, Carol Sanger, and Henry Shue for the very detailed suggestions they have offered.

NOTES

1. See, e.g., Siebert, "Homeless People: Establishing Rights to Shelter," 4 *Law & Inequality* 393 (1986) (no constitutional guarantee of adequate housing); Comment, "The Unconstitutionality of 'Antihomeless' Laws: Ordinances Prohibiting Sleeping in Outdoor Public Areas as a Violation of the Right to Travel," 77 *Calif. L. Rev.* 595 (1989) (authored by Ades) (arguing that laws that proscribe sleeping in outdoor public areas violate the right to travel).
2. The best discussion remains Honoré, "Ownership," in *Oxford Essays in Jurisprudence* 107 (A.G. Guest ed. 1961); *see also* S. Munzer, *A Theory of Property* 21-61 (1990); J. Waldron, *The Right to Private* Property 15-36 (1988).
3. See J. Waldron, note 2 (above), at 40-42; Macpherson, "The Meaning of Property," in *Property: Mainstream and Critical Positions* 1, 4-6 (C. Macpherson ed. 1978).
4. In *Pruneyard Shopping Center v. Robins*, 447 U.S. 74 (1980), the United States Supreme Court held that the California courts may reasonably require the owners of a shopping mall to allow persons to exercise rights of free speech on their premises under the California Constitution, and that such a requirement does not constitute a taking for the purposes of the Fifth Amendment to the Constitution of the United States.
5. For a more complete discussion, see J. Waldron, note 2 (above), at 42-46.
6. Diluliu, "There But For Fortune," *New Republic*, June 24, 1991, at 27, 28.
7. But this ignores the fact that a large number of people with no home of their own are kept from having to wander the streets only by virtue of the fact that friends and relatives are willing to let them share their home, couches, and floors. If this generosity were less forthcoming, the number of "street people" would be much greater.
8. See, e.g., M. Rothbard, *For a New Liberty* 201-2 (1973).
9. Herbert Spencer was so disconcerted by the possibility that he thought it a good reason to prohibit the private ownership of land altogether....A. Reeve, *Property* 85 (1986) (quoting H. Spencer, *Social Statics* 114-15 (1851)).
10. For a useful discussion, see I. Berlin, "Introduction," in *Four Essays on Liberty* i, xlv-lv (1969).
11. See also Waldron, "Welfare and the Images of Charity," 36 *Phil. Q.* 463 (1986).
12. It is not even to deny that they may enlarge the amount of freedom overall. Isaiah Berlin put the point precisely: "Every law seems to me to curtail *some* liberty, although it may be a means to increasing another. Whether it increases the total sum of attainable liberty will of course depend on the particular situation."

I. Berlin, note 10 (above), at xlix no. 1 (emphasis in original).

13. For the connection between generality, predictability, and the rule of law, see F. Hayek, *The Constitution of Liberty* 148-61 (1960).
14. See R. Hare, *Freedom and Reason* 10-21 (1963).
15. For example, Dicey puts forward the following as the first principle of "the rule of law": "no man is punishable or can be lawfully made to suffer in body or goods except for a distinct breach of law established in the ordinary legal manner before the ordinary courts of the land." A. Dicey, *Introduction to the Study of the Law of the Constitution* 188 (10th ed. 1959).
16. For a discussion of how a lay person applies the rules of property, see B. Ackerman, *Private Property and the Constitution* 116-18 (1977).
17. Here are some examples. The City Code of Phoenix, Arizona provides: "It shall be unlawful for any person to use a public street, highway, alley, lane, parkway, [or] sidewalk ... for lying [or] sleeping ... except in the case of a physical emergency or the administration of medical assistance." A St. Petersburg, Florida ordinance similarly provides that: "No person shall sleep upon or in any street, park, wharf or other public place." I am indebted to Paul Ades for these examples. Comment, note 1 (above), at 595 n. 5, 596 n. 7 (quoting *Phoenix, Ariz., City Code* § 23-48.01 (1981); *St. Petersburg, Fla., Ordinance* 25.57 (1973)).
18. And New Yorkers have grown tired of confronting homeless people every day on the subway, at the train station and at the entrances to supermarkets and apartment buildings.

    Lynette Thompson, a Transit Authority official who oversees the outreach program for the homeless in the subway, said there had been a marked change this year in letters from riders.

    "At the beginning of last year, the tenor of those letters was, 'Please do something to help the homeless,'" Ms. Thompson said. " But since August and September, they've been saying: 'Just get them out. I don't care. Just get them out any way you can.' It got worse and people got fed up."

    "Doors closing as Mood on the Homeless Sours," *N.Y. Times*, Nov. 18, 1989; at 1, col.2, 32, col.1, col.2.
19. A. France, *Le Lys rouge* 117-18 (rev. ed. 1923) ("The law in its majestic equality forbids the rich as well as the poor to sleep under the bridges.").
20. See M. Davis, *City of Quartz: Excavating the Future in Los Angeles* 232-36 (1990) for an excellent account of similar devices designed to render public spaces in downtown Los Angeles "off-limits" to the homeless, as well as Davis's "Afterword—A logic Like Hell's: Being Homeless in Los Angeles," 39 *UCLA L. Rev.* 325 (1991).
21. See note 18 (above).
22. Bracing for the annual influx of homeless people fleeing the Northern cold, the police here [in Miami, Florida] have proposed an emergency ordinance that would allow them to arrest some street people as a way of keeping them on the move....

    The new measure would replace a century-old law against sleeping in public that was abandoned after a similar statute in Clearwater, Fla., was struck down by Federal courts in January. The courts said the statute was too broad and would have applied even to a person sleeping in his car.

    The new proposal seeks to get around the court's objection by being more specific. But it would also be more far-reaching than the original law, applying to such activities as cooking and the building of temporary shelters.

    Terry Cunningham, a 23-year-old who lives on the steps of the Federal Courthouse, asked of the police, "Where do they expect me to sleep?"

    City and county officials had no answer. "That's a good question," Sergeant Rivero of the Police Department said. "No one is willing to address the problem."

    "Miami Police Want To Control Homeless by Arresting Them," *N.Y. Times*, Nov. 4, 1988, at A1, col.1. A16, col.4.
23. For a critique of the purely quantitative approach, see Taylor, "What's Wrong with Negative Liberty?" in *The Idea of Freedom*, (A. Ryan, ed. 1979), at 183.
24. Cf. R. Dworkin, *Taking Rights Seriously* 270-72 (rev. ed. 1978) (discussion of the theory that a right to certain liberties can be derived from the "special character" of the liberties).
25. The failure of First Amendment challenges to restrictions on panhandling does not bode well for the survival of even these protections. See *Young v. New York City Transit Auth.*, 903 F. 2d 146 (2d Cir.), cert. denied, 111 S. Ct. 516 (1990). But see Hershkoff and

Cohen, "Begging to Differ: The First Amendment and the Right to Beg," 104 *Harv. L. Rev.* 896 (1991) (arguing that begging is protected speech).

26. See note 4 (above).
27. I hope it will not be regarded as an attempt at humor if I suggest that the Rawlsian doctrine of "the strains of commitment" is directly relevant here. J. Rawls, *A Theory of Justice* 175-76 (1971). If the effect of a principle would be literally unbearable to some of those to whom it applies, it must be rejected by the parties in Rawls's contractarian thought-experiment, known as the "original position."
28. This idea is sometimes expressed in terms of "social citizenship." See King and Waldron, "Citizenship, Social Citizenship, and the defense of Welfare Provision," 18 *Brit. J. Pol. Sci.* 415 (1988); see also R. Dahrendorf, *The Modern Social Conflict: An Essay on the Politics of Liberty* 29-47 (1988).
29. And this is to say nothing about the appalling deprivation of ordinary opportunity that will be experienced by those tens of thousands of *children* growing up homeless in America. To suggest that a child sleeping on the streets or in a dangerous crowded shelter, with no place to store toys of books, and no sense of hope or security, has an opportunity equal to that of anyone in our society is simply a mockery.

INCENTIVES, INEQUALITY, AND COMMUNITY

G.A. Cohen

G.A. Cohen is Chichele Professor of Social and Political Theory and Fellow of All Soul's College at Oxford. He is the author of Self-Ownership, Freedom, and Equality *(Cambridge, 1995),* History, Labour, and Freedom: Themes from Marx *(Oxford, 1988), and numerous articles in political theory.*

Cohen examines the fairly pervasive belief in liberal theory that inequalities of wealth serve as an incentive for talented people to work harder than they would if everyone had the same amount of material goods, which in turn generates the kind of wealth and opportunities that allow everyone to benefit. Cohen mounts a case against the incentive argument on the grounds that it violates a condition of community. To be part of a community, citizens need to be able to provide what Cohen refers to as "comprehensive justifications," justifications for policies that stand as reasonable and acceptable to all its members. Cohen argues that it becomes apparent that the incentive argument fails this test when it is presented in first person interpersonal terms rather than the third person impersonal terms in which it is usually presented. The statement, "because I, a talented rich person, will not work as hard unless I have incentives such as greater wealth, you, the poor, will be worse off," makes issues of responsibility, justice, and community evident. According to Cohen, while it may be prudent for the poor to accept inequalities in wealth in contexts in which beliefs in incentives prevail, this sidesteps the issue of what is just. Cohen applies his analysis of the incentive argument to Rawls's theory of justice and argues that the difference principle not only assumes the incentive argument in its justification for inequalities, it also violates the spirit of an agreement supposedly based on what is fair and just.

> ... the rulers of mankind ... maintain side by side two standards of social ethics, without the risk of their colliding. Keeping one set of values for use, and another for display, they combine, without conscious insincerity, the moral satisfaction of idealistic principles with the material advantages of realistic practice.
>
> — H. Tawney, *Equality*

I. The Incentive Argument, the Interpersonal Test, and Community

1.

In March of 1988, Nigel Lawson, who was then Margaret Thatcher's chancellor of the exchequer, brought the top rate of income tax in Britain down, from 60 to 40 percent. That cut enlarged the net incomes of those whose incomes were already large, in comparison with the British average, and, of course, in comparison with the income of Britain's poor people. Socialists hated the tax cut, and a recent policy document says that the Labour party would, effectively, restore the pre-1988 rate.[1]

How might the Lawson tax cut be defended? Well, economic inequality is no new thing in capitalist society, so there has been plenty of time for a lot of arguments to accumulate in favor of it. We hear, from the political right, that rich people are entitled to their wealth: to part of it because they produced it themselves—but for them, it would not have existed—and to the rest of it because it was transferred to them voluntarily by others who were themselves entitled to it because they produced it, or because

Reprinted with permission of the publisher from *The Tanner Lectures on Human Values*, Vol. 13, ed. Grethe B. Peterson (Salt Lake City: The University of Utah Press, 1992) 261-329 [edited].

they received it as a gift or in voluntary trade from others who were themselves entitled to it because ... (and so on). (Some who hold that view also think that it is because it establishes moral desert that production justifies title, while others find the entitlement story compelling even when the idea of desert plays no role in it.) And then there is the utilitarian proposition, affirmed not only on the right but in the center, that inequality is justified because, through dynamizing the economy, it expands the gross national product and thereby causes an increase in the sum of human happiness.

Left-wing liberals, whose chief representative in philosophy is John Rawls, reject these arguments for inequality: they do not accept the principles (entitlement, desert, and general utility) which figure in their major premises.[2] But the right and center sometimes offer an additional argument for inequality, to the major premise of which the liberals are friendly. That major premise is the principle that inequalities are justified when they render badly off people as well off as it is possible for such people to be.[3] In one version of this argument for inequality—and this version of it is the topic of these lectures—their high levels of income cause unusually productive people to produce more than they otherwise would; and, as a result of the incentives enjoyed by those at the top, the people who end up near the bottom are better off than they would be in a more equal society. This was one of the most politically effective justifications of the unequalizing policy of Thatcher Conservatism. We were ceaselessly told that movement contrary to that policy, in a socialist egalitarian direction, would be bad for badly off people, by advocates of a regime which seems itself to have brought about the very effect against which its apologists insistently warned.[4]

Left-wing liberals deny the factual claim that the vast inequalities in Britain or America actually do benefit the badly off, but they tend to agree that if they did, they would be justified, and they defend inequalities that really are justified, in their view, by the incentive consideration. That is a major theme in John Rawls's work. For Rawls, some people are, mainly as a matter of genetic and other luck, capable of producing more than others are, and it is right for them to be richer than others if the less fortunate are caused to be better off as a result.[5] The policy is warranted by what Rawls calls the difference principle, which endorses all and only those social and economic inequalities that are good for the worst off, or, more generously, those inequalities that either make the worst off better off or do not make them worse off: in this matter there is a certain ambiguity of formulation in Rawls, and in what follows I shall take the difference principle in its more generous form, in which it allows inequalities that do not help but also do not hurt the worst off.

Back now to the socialist egalitarians, who did not like the Lawson tax cut. Being to the left of left-wing liberals, socialist egalitarians are also unimpressed by the desert, entitlement, and utility justifications of inequality. But it is not so easy for them to set aside the Rawlsian justification of inequality. They cannot just dismiss it, without lending to their own advocacy of equality a fanatical hue which they could not themselves on reflection find attractive.

Socialist egalitarians say that they believe in equality. We might well think that they count as egalitarians because equality is their premise. But the structure of that premise is too simple to accommodate the thought that gets them going politically, which is: why should some people be badly off, when other people are so *well* off? That is not the same as the colorless question, Why should some people be better off than others? For in that question there is no reference to absolute levels of condition, hence no reference to anyone being badly off, as opposed to just *less* well off than other people are. Maybe some egalitarians would maintain their zeal in a world of millionaires and billionaires in which no one's life is hard, but the politically engaged socialist egalitarians that I have in mind have no strong opinion about inequality at millionaire/billionaire levels. What they find wrong is that there is, so they think, unnecessary hardship at the lower end of the scale. There are people who are badly off and who, they believe, would be better off under an equalizing redistribution. The practically crucial feature of the situation is that the badly off are worse off than anyone needs to be, since an equalizing redistribution would enhance their lives.

For these egalitarians, equality would be a good thing because it would make the badly off better off.

They do not think it a good thing about equality that it would make the well off worse off. And when their critics charge them with being willing, for the sake of equality, to grind everyone down to the level of the worst off, or even lower, they do not say in response: well, yes, let us grind down if necessary, but let us achieve equality on a higher plane if that is possible. Instead, what they say is somewhat evasive, at the level of principle; they just deny that it is necessary, for the sake of achieving equality, to move to a condition in which some are worse off and none are better off than now. Were they more reflective, they might add that, if leveling down were necessary, then equality would lose its appeal. Either it would make the badly off worse off still, in frustration of the original egalitarian purpose, or it would make the badly off no better off, while others are made worse off to no evident purpose. Relative to their initial inspiration, which is a concern about badly off people, an inequality is mandatory if it really is needed to improve the condition of the badly off, and it is permissible if it does not improve but also does not worsen their condition.

Accordingly, these egalitarians lose sight of their goal, their position becomes incoherent or untrue to itself, if, in a world with badly off people, they reject the difference principle and cleave to an egalitarianism of strict equality. (Given the priorities and emphases that I have attributed to them, they should, strictly speaking, affirm as fundamental neither equality nor the difference principle but this complex maxim: make the badly off well off, or, if that is not possible, make them as well off as possible. But, on a modestly demanding interpretation of what it means to be well off, and on a realistic view of the world's foreseeable resource prospects, the practical consequences of the complex maxim are those of the difference principle.) We might conclude that the socialist egalitarians that I have in mind should not be called "egalitarians," since (if I am right) equality is not their real premise. But that conclusion would be hasty, and I shall say more about the property of the name "egalitarian" in a moment.

For my part, I accept the difference principle, in its generous interpretation (see above), but I question its application in defense of special money incentives to talented people. Rawlsians think that inequalities associated with such incentives satisfy the principle. But I believe that the idea that an inequality is justified if, through the familiar incentive mechanism, it benefits the badly off is more problematic than Rawlsians suppose; that, at least when the incentive consideration is isolated from all reference to desert or entitlement, it generates an argument for inequality that requires a model of society in breach of an elementary condition of community. The difference principle can be used to justify paying incentives that induce inequalities only when the attitude of talented people runs counter to the spirit of the difference principle itself: they would not need special incentives if they were themselves unambivalently committed to the principle. Accordingly, they must be thought of as outside the community upholding the principle when it is used to justify incentive payments to them....

2.

I return to Rawls and the difference principle in Part III of these lectures. Right now I want to focus on Nigel Lawson's tax cut, and on the incentive case against canceling it, the case, that is, for maintaining rewards to productive people at the existing high level. And I shall consider that case only with respect to those who, so it is thought, produce a lot by exercising skill and talent, rather than by investing capital. Accordingly, the argument I shall examine applies not only to capitalist economies but also to economies without private ownership of capital, such as certain forms of market socialism. Of course, there also exists an incentive argument for high returns to capital investment, but I am not going to address that argument in these lectures.

Proponents of the incentive argument say that when productive people take home modest pay, they produce less than they otherwise do, and, as a result, relatively poor and badly off people are worse off than they are when the exercise of talent is well rewarded. Applied against a restoration of the top tax to 60 percent, the argument runs as follows:

> Economic inequalities are justified when they make the worst off people materially better off. [Major, normative premise]
>
> When the top rate of tax is 40 percent, (*a*) the talent-

ed rich produce more than they do when it is 60 percent, and (*b*) the worst off are, as a result, materially better off. [Minor, factual premise]

Therefore, the top tax should not be raised from 40 percent to 60 percent.

It is immaterial to present concerns how the circumstance alleged to obtain in part *a* of the minor premise of the argument is supposed to occasion the result described in part *b*. One possibility is that the rich work so much harder when the tax rate goes down that the tax take goes up, and more is available for redistribution. Another is that, when the rich work harder, they produce, among other things, (better) employment opportunities for badly off people.

I am going to comment negatively on the incentive argument, but my criticism of it will take a particular form. For I shall focus not, directly, on the argument as such, but on the character of certain utterances of it. Accordingly, I shall not raise questions about the validity of the argument, or about the truth of its premises, save insofar as they arise (and they do) within the special focus just described. And I shall not, in particular, pursue possible doubts about the minor, factual, premise of the argument. I shall question neither claim a, that the supposedly talented rich are more productive when they are more generously rewarded, nor claim b, that the badly off benefit from the greater productivity of the well off affirmed in a. I do not aim to show that the minor premise of the incentive argument is false.

The critique that follows is not of everything that could be called an incentive, but only of incentives that produce inequality and which are said to be justified because they make badly off people better off. I raise no objection against incentives designed to eliminate a poverty trap, or to induce people to undertake particularly unpleasant jobs. It is not constitutive of those incentives that they produce inequality. My target is incentives conferring high rewards on people of talent who would otherwise not perform as those rewards induce them to do. I believe that the familiar liberal case for incentives of that kind has not been thoroughly thought through.

3.

I said that I would criticize the incentive argument be focusing on certain utterances of it. For I believe that, although the argument may sound reasonable when it is presented, as it usually is, and as it was above, in blandly impersonal form, it does not sound so good when we fix on a presentation of it in which a talented rich person pronounces it to a badly off person. And the fact that the argument undergoes this devaluation when it occurs in that interpersonal setting should affect our assessment of the nature of the society that the incentive justification by implication recommends.

A normative argument will often wear a particular aspect because of who is offering it and/or to whom it is being addressed. When reasons are given for performing an action or endorsing a policy or adopting an attitude, the appropriate response by the person(s) asked so to act or approve or feel, and the reaction of variously placed observers of the interchange, may depend on who is speaking and who is listening. The form, and the explanation, of that dependence vary considerably across different kinds of case. But the general point is that there are many ways, some more interesting than others, in which an argument's persuasive value can be speaker-audience-relative, and there are many reasons of, once again, different degrees of interest, why that should be so.

Before describing a form of dependence (of response on who is addressing whom) that operates in the case of the incentive argument, and in order to induce a mood in which we think of arguments in their contexts of delivery, I list a few examples of the general phenomenon:

(*a*) I can argue that the driver over there should not be blamed for just now making a right turn on a red light, since he does not know that the rules are different outside California. But he cannot, at the moment, make that very argument, entirely sound thought it may be.

(*b*) You want the fishing rod for recreation, and I need it to get my next meal. I know that you are so unstoical that you will be more upset if you do not get to fish than I will be if I do not get to eat. So I let you have the rod, and I cite your hypersensitivity to disappointment as my reason. It would be a lot less good for you to give that as a reason why you should have the rod.

(*c*) I might persuade my fellow middle class friend that, because my car is being repaired, and I consequently have to spend hours on the buses these days, I have a right to be grumpy. The same conclusion, on the same basis, sounds feeble when the audience is not my friend but a careless fellow bus passenger who is forced to endure these slow journeys every day.

(*d*) As designers of advertisements for charitable causes know, our ordinary self-serving reasons for not giving much (we need a new roof, I'm saving for my holiday, I'm not actually *very* rich) sound remarkably lame when we imagine them being presented to those for whom our lack of charity means misery and death.[6]

(*e*) And such quotidian reasons also sound feeble when they are presented to people whose sacrifice for the cause is much larger than the one the speaker is excusing himself from offering.[7]

(*f*) Since the pot should not call the kettle black, an employee may be unimpressed when a routinely tax-evading well-heeled superior dresses him down because of his modest appropriations from petty cash.

The examples show that arguments vary in their capacity to satisfy because of variations in people's epistemic (a) or moral (e, f) or social (c) position, or because of issues of tact and embarrassment (c, d, e) and immediacy (d), or because being generous is more attractive than being grabby (b). I shall not here attempt a systematic taxonomy of ways that arguments subside in different sorts of interpersonal delivery. Instead, I pass to a type of case which is of special interest here, since the incentive argument belongs to it.

4.

In this type of case, an argument changes its aspect when its presenter is the person, or one of the people, whose choice, or choices, make one or more of the argument's premises true. By contrast with other presenters of the same argument, a person who makes, or helps to make, one of its premises true can be asked to justify the fact that it is true.[8] And sometimes he will be unable to provide a satisfying justification.

For a dramatic example of this structure, consider the argument for paying a kidnapper where the child will be freed only if the kidnapper is paid. There are various reasons for not paying. Some concern further consequences: maybe, for example, more kidnapping would be encouraged. And paying could be thought wrong not only in some of its consequences but in its nature: paying is acceding to a vile threat. You will nevertheless agree that, because so much is at stake, paying kidnappers is often justified. And the argument for paying a particular kidnapper, shorn of qualifications needed to neutralize the countervailing reasons mentioned a moment ago, might run as follows:

> Children should be with their parents.
> Unless they pay him, this kidnapper will not return this child to its parents.
> So, this child's parents should pay this kidnapper.

Now, that form of the argument is entirely third-personal: in that form of it, anyone (save, perhaps, someone mentioned in the argument) might be presenting it to anyone. But let us now imagine the kidnapper himself presenting the argument, to, for example, the child's parents. (What will matter here is that he is doing the talking, rather than that they are doing the listening: the latter circumstance achieves prominence in section 11 below.) The argument that follows is the same as that given above, by an unimpeachable criterion of identity for arguments: its major premise states the same principle and its minor premise carries the same factual claim:

> Children should be with their parents.
> I shall not return your child unless you pay me.
> So, you should pay me.

Notice, now, that despite what we can assume to be the truth of its premises and the validity of its inference, discredit attaches to anyone who utters this argument in the foregoing interpersonal setting, even though uttering the same argument in impersonal form is, in most cases,[9] an innocent procedure. And there is, of course, no mystery about why the argument's presenter attracts discredit in the exhibited interpersonal case. He does so because the fact to which he appeals, which is that you will get your child back only if you pay, is one that he deliberately causes to obtain; he makes that true, and to make that true is morally vile.

When he presents the argument, the kidnapper shows himself to be awful, but it is hardly necessary for us to reflect on his utterance of the argument to convince ourselves that he merits disapproval. Independently of any such reflection, we amply realize that the kidnapper's conduct is wrong, and we need not be particularly scandalized by his frank avowal of it. Indeed, in certain instances a kidnapper's presentation of the argument will be a service to the parents, because sometimes his utterance of the argument's minor premise will, for the first time, put them in the picture about how to get their child back. One can even imagine a maybe slightly schizoid kidnapper suddenly thinking, "Omigod, I've forgotten to tell the kid's parents!" and experiencing some concern for them, and for the child, in the course of that thought.

Yet although what is (mainly) bad about the kidnapper is not his voicing the argument, but his making its minor premise true, he should still be ashamed to voice the argument, just because he makes that premise true. The fact that in some cases he would do further ill not to voice the argument does not falsify the claim that in all cases he reveals himself to be ghastly when he does voice it.

In the kidnapper argument, there are two groups of agents, the kidnapper and the parents, both referred to in the third person in the initial presentation of the argument, and referred to in the first and second persons in its revised presentation. Consider any argument that refers to distinct groups of people, A and B. There are many different ways in which such an argument might be presented. It might be uttered by members of A or of B or of neither group, and it might be addressed to members of either group or of neither. And all of that applies to the incentive argument, with the groups being talented rich people on the one hand and the worst off on the other. In my treatment of the incentive argument I shall mainly be interested in the case where a talented rich person puts it forward, sometimes no matter to whom and sometimes where it matters that poor people are his audience; and at one point I shall consider the opposite case, where a poor person addresses the argument to a talented rich one.

The incentive argument has something in common with the kidnapper argument, even though there are major differences between withholding a hostage and withholding labor until one gets the money one desires. But before looking more carefully at similarities and contrasts between the kidnapper and incentive arguments, I want to explain why the word "community" appears in the title of these lectures.

5.

In its familiar use, "community" covers a multitude of conditions, and I shall introduce the particular condition that I have in mind by relating it to the concept of a *comprehensive justification*.

Most policy arguments contain premises about how people will act when the policy is, and is not, in force. Schemes for housing, health, education, and the economy typically operates by altering agents' feasible sets, and their justifications usually say what agents facing those sets can be expected to choose to do.

Consider, then, a policy, *P*, and an argument purportedly justifying it, one of whose premises says that a subset, *S*, of the population will act in a certain fashion when *P* is in force. We engage in what might be called *comprehensive assessment* of the proffered justification of *P* when we ask whether the projected behavior of the members of *S* is itself justified. And *comprehensive justification* of *P* obtains only if that behavior is indeed justified.[10]

"We should do *A* because they will do *B*" may justify our doing *A*, but it does not justify it comprehensively if they are not justified in doing *B*, and we do not provide a comprehensive justification of our doing *A* if we set aside as irrelevant the question whether they are justified in doing *B*. Thus, insofar as we are expected to treat the incentive argument as though no question arises about the justification of the behavior of the talented rich that its minor premise describes, what we are offered may be a justification, but it is not a comprehensive justification, of the incentives policy.

Now, a policy argument provides a comprehensive justification only if it passes what I shall call the *interpersonal test*. This tests how robust a policy argument is, by subjecting it to variation with respect to who is speaking and/or who is listening when the argument is presented. The test asks whether the argument could serve as a justification of a mooted policy when uttered by any member of society to any other member. So, to carry out the test, we hypothesize an utterance of the argument by a specified individual, or, more commonly, by a member of a specified group, to another individual, or to a member of another, or, indeed, the same, group. If, because of who is presenting it, and/or to whom it is presented, the argument cannot serve as a justification of the policy, then whether or not it passes as such under other dialogical conditions, it fails (*tout court*) to provide a comprehensive justification of the policy.

A salient way that arguments fail, when put to this test, and the only mode of test failure that will henceforth figure in these lectures, is that the speaker cannot fulfill a demand for justification that does not arise when the argument is presented by and/or to others. So, to anticipate what I shall try to show, the incentive argument does not serve as a justification of inequality on the lips of the talented rich, because they cannot answer a demand for justification that naturally arises when they present the argument, namely, *why* would you work less hard if income tax were put back up to 60 percent? The rich will find that question difficult no matter who puts it to them, but I shall often focus on the case where their interlocutors are badly off people, because in that setting the question, and the difficulty the rich have with it may lead to further dialogical development that carries further illumination.

When the justification of policies that mention groups of people is presented in the usual way, with exclusively third-person reference to groups and their members, the propriety of the question why various people are disposed to act as they do is not always apparent. It becomes evident when we picture the relevant people themselves rehearsing the argument, and sometimes more so when the audience is a strategically selected one. The test of interpersonal presentation makes vivid that the justification of policy characteristically depends on circumstances that are not exogenous with respect to human agency.

And so to community. I began by observing that there is more than one kind of community, and I must now specify the kind that is relevant to present concerns. First, though, a few points about the semantics of the word "community."

Like "friendship," "community" functions both as a count noun and as a mass noun. It is a count noun when it denotes sets of people variously bound or connected (the European community, London's Italian community, our community) and it is a mass noun when we speak of how much community there is in a certain society, when we say that some action enhances or reduces, or some attitude honors or violates, community, and so on.

A community, one could say, is a set of people among whom there is community: that is how the count-notion and the mass-notion are linked. "Community" is in this respect like "friendship": a friendship is a relationship in which friendship obtains. Notice that friends can do and feel things that are inconsistent with friendship without thereby dissolving their friendship. There can be a lapse of friendship in a friendship without that friendship ceasing to be. But there cannot (enduringly) be *no* friendship in a friendship. And all that is also true of community: there can be violations and lapses of community in a community, but there cannot be no community in a community.

In addition to community in the adjectivally unqualified sense where it is analogous not only in form but also in content to friendship, there are specific types of community, some of which do, while others do not, contribute to community in the just denoted sense. And types of community (mass-wise) distinguish types of community (count-wise). Linguistic community, or community of language, constitutes a linguistic community as such; community of nationality establishes a national community; and community of interest in stamps binds the philatelic community.

The form of community that concerns me here, which I shall call *justificatory community*, prevails in justificatory communities. And justificatory community, though something of a concocted notion, contributes to community *tout court*, that is, to community in the full (adjectivally unqualified) sense sketched a moment ago. A justificatory community is a set of people among whom there prevails a norm (which need not always be satisfied) of comprehensive justification. If what certain people are disposed to do when a policy is in force is part of the justification of that policy, it is considered appropriate to ask them to justify the relevant behavior, and it detracts from justificatory community when they cannot do so. It follows that an argument for a policy satisfies the requirement of justificatory community, with respect to the people it mentions, only if it passes the interpersonal test. And if all arguments for the policy fail that test, then the policy itself evinces lack of justificatory community, whatever else might nevertheless be said in its favor.

Now, an argument fails the interpersonal test, and is therefore inconsistent with community, if relevant agents *could* not justify the behavior the argument ascribes to them. What if the agents are actually asked to justify their stance and, for one reason or another, they refuse to do so? Then the argument in question does not necessarily fail the test, for it might be that they could justify their stance. But if their reason for refusing to justify it is that they do not think themselves accountable to their interrogators, that they do not think that they *need* provide a justification, then they are forswearing community with the rest of us in respect of the policy issue in question. They are asking us to treat them like a set of Martians in the light of whose predictable aggressive, or even benign, behavior it is wise for us to take certain steps, but whom we should not expect to engage in justificatory dialogue.

To employ the interpersonal test and to regard its failure as indicative of a lack of community is to presuppose nothing about which particular collections of people constitute communities in the relevant sense. Some may think that there is no reason why there should be community between rich and poor in a society, and they may therefore regard failure of the test as uninteresting, or, if interesting, then not because it shows lapse of community. Others, by contrast, might think that community ought to obtain among all human beings, so that it would stain a policy argument advanced by rich countries in North-South dialogue if it could not pass muster in explicit I-thou form. The thesis associated with the interpersonal test is that, if a policy justification fails it, then anyone proposing that justification in effect represents the people it mentions as *pro tanto* out of community with one another. Whether they should be in community with one another is a separate question. That depends on a doctrine, not to be articulated here, about what the proper boundaries of a community are. In my own (here undefended) view, it diminishes the democratic character of a society if it is not a community in the present sense, since we do not make policy *together* if we make it in the light of what some of us do that cannot be justified to others.

It is often said that it is unrealistic to expect a modern society to be a community, and it is no doubt inconceivable that there should be a standing disposition of warm mutual identification between any pair of citizens in a large and heterogeneous polity. But community here is not some soggy mega-*Gemeinschaftlichkeit*. Instead, my claim about the incentive justification is that, to appropriate a phrase of Rawls's, it does not supply "a public basis in the light of which citizens can justify to one another their common institutions" and that the justification is therefore incompatible with what Rawls calls "ties of civic friendship."[11]

Now some examples of the battery of concepts introduced above.

Under the premiership of Harold Wilson, some economic policies were justified by reference to the intentions of the so-called "gnomes of Zurich," the international bankers who, it was said, would react punitively to various government decisions. It was a mark of their *foreign* status that economic policy had to *placate* those bankers, and although it might have been thought that they should behave differently, it would not have been considered appropriate for the British government to call upon them to do so. But such a call would surely be appropriate in the case of people conceived as belonging to our own community. Nor should members of our own community need to be *placated* by our community's policies: when justified, their demands should be satisfied, but that is a different matter.

An example that for some readers may be close to home: the policy argument that rates of pay to British academics should be raised, since otherwise they will succumb to the lure of high foreign salaries. We can suppose that academics are indeed disposed to leave the country because of current salary levels. The issue of whether, nevertheless, they should emigrate is pertinent to the policy argument when they are regarded as fellow members of community who owe the rest a justification for decisions that affect the welfare of the country. And many British academics with an inclination to leave who put the stated policy argument contrive to avoid that issue by casting the minor premise of the argument in the third person. They say: "Academics will go abroad," not: "We'll go abroad." ...

6.

The interpersonal test focuses on an utterance of an argument, but what it tests, through examination of that utterance, is the argument itself. If lack of community is displayed when the rich present the incentive argument, then the argument itself (irrespective of who affirms it) represents relations between rich and poor as at variance with community. It follows, if I am right, that the incentive argument can justify inequality only in a society where interpersonal relations lack a communal character, in the specified sense.

Sometimes, as, for example, in the kidnapper case, the interpersonal test will be a roundabout way of proving an already evident point (in the kidnapper case, that there is significant lack of community between the kidnapper and the parents). But in other cases the test will illuminate, and I believe that the incentive argument is one of them. The argument is generally presented in throughly third-personal terms and, relatedly, as though no question arises about the attitudes and choices of the rich people it mentions. When, by contrast, we imagine a talented rich person himself affirming the argument, then background issues of equality and obligation come clearly into view, and, if I am right, the rich are revealed to be out of community with the poor in respect of the economic dimension of their lives. So we see more deeply into the character of the incentive argument when we cast it in the selected I-thou terms.

Now, and important qualification. I say that the incentive argument shows itself to be repugnant to community when it is offered *on its own* by well-off people. I insert that phrase because the present case against the argument lapses when the argument appears in combination with claims about desert, and/or with Nozick-like claims about a person's entitlements to the reward his or her labor would command on an unfettered market. I do not myself accept that sort of compound justification of incentive inequality, but I do not here contend that it fails the interpersonal test. My target here is the unadorned or naked use of the incentive justification. It is often used nakedly, and with plenty of emphasis that it is being used nakedly. That emphasis occurs when advocates say it is an advantageous feature of the incentive justification that it employs no controversial moral premises about desert or entitlement. (Notice that, since John Rawls rejects use of desert and entitlement to justify inequalities, the Rawlsian endorsement of incentives takes what I call a naked form.)

The sequence of claims that I make goes as follows: The talented rich cannot justify the fact that the minor premise of the (naked) incentive argument is true. If they cannot justify the truth of its minor premise, then they cannot use the argument as a justification of inequality. If they cannot use it as a justification of inequality, then it cannot be used as a justification within community. If it cannot be used as a justification within community, then anyone who uses it (in effect) represents society as at variance with community when he does so....

II. Testing the Incentive Argument

So imagine, now, a set of highly paid managers and professionals addressing poorly paid workers, unemployed people, and people indigent for various personal and situational reasons, who depend on state welfare. The managers are lobbying against a rise in tax from 40 to 60 percent, and this is what they say:

> Public policy should make the worst off people (in this case, as it happens, you) better off.
>
> If the top tax goes up to 60 percent, we shall work less hard, and, as a result, the position of the poor (your position) will be worse.
>
> So, the top tax on our income should not be raised to 60 percent.

Although these argument-uttering rich may not, for one or other reason, count as *threatening* the poor, they remain people of superior income and form of life who could continue to work as now if the tax rose to 60 percent, and thereby bring more benefit to the poor, while still being much better off than they are, but who would refuse to do that. They say, in effect: we are unwilling to do what we could do to make you better off and yet still be much better off, ourselves, than you are. We realize that, at the present level of fuel allowance, many of you will be very cold this winter.[12] If the tax went up to 60 percent and we worked no less hard in response, revenue for fuel expenditure could rise, and some of you would be more comfortable. But in fact we would work less, and you would be worse off, following such a tax rise.

Having presented their argument, the rich are not well placed to answer a poor person who asks: "Given that you would still be much better off than we are if you worked as you do now at the 60 percent tax, what justifies your intention to work less if the tax rises to that level?" For these rich people do not say that they deserve a lot because of their prodigious effort, or merit more because of their higher contribution to production. There is in their approach no appeal to such controversial moral premises, and many of them would think that, being free of such premises, their argument is consequently less vulnerable. And they cannot respond by saying that the money inequality which they defend is necessary to make the poor better off, since it is they who make it necessary, and the question put by the poor asks, in effect, what their justification is for making it necessary.

The incentive argument does furnish the poor with a reason to accept the inequality that it recommends. For the poor can take it as given that the rich are determined to sustain the intentions that make the argument work. But the argument cannot operate like that for the rich themselves: since they cannot treat their own choices as objective data, they cannot take it as given that the minor premise of the argument is true. Correspondingly, and unlike the poor, they need a justification not for accepting but for imposing the inequality that the argument defends.

But it might be said that the rich can indeed respond convincingly to the poor, and without advancing the controversial claims about desert and entitlement that are here ruled out. They can say: "Look, it simply would not be worth our while to work that hard if the tax rate were any higher, and if you were in our shoes you would feel the same way."[13] Would that not be a good answer to the question the poor pose?

As I shall presently allow, there is some power in this answer. But its rhetorical cast makes it seem more powerful than it is.

Notice, to begin with, that the first part ("Look ... higher") of the quoted plea has no independent interest, no interest, that is, which is independent of the associated claim that the poor, if better placed, would feel (and act) as the rich now do. For it is a presupposition of the challenge the poor put to the rich that the latter do prefer, and intend, to work less hard if the tax goes up, and in speaking of what is "worth their while" the rich can only be reminding the poor of those preferences and intentions: they cannot mean, for example, that they are paid nothing, or paid badly, if they work hard at a 60 percent rate of tax.

So the burden of the rhetorically presented justificatory move is that a typical poor person would have to behave just as the rich, on the whole, do. But there is something that the poor person can say in reply. He can say: "Neither of us really knows how I would behave. Not all rich people market maximize as a matter of course, and I hope that, if I were rich, I would not belong to the vast majority that do, especially if I retained a lively sense of what it is like to be in the condition I am now actually in." (A slave need not be impressed when a master says: "Had you been born into the slaveholder class, you too would have lived well and treated your slaves like slaves.") Such counterfactual predictions do not show that what people at a certain social level typically choose to do is justifiable.[14]

Suppose, now, that the rich abandon the vivid but problematic "you'd do the same in my shoes" style of justification. Suppose they just say that, even when desert and entitlement are set aside, only an extreme moral rigorist could deny that *every person has a right to pursue self-interest to some reasonable extent* (even when that makes things worse than they need be for badly off people).

I do not wish to reject the italicized principle, which affirms what Samuel Scheffler has called an "agent-centered prerogative."[15] But a modest right of self-interest seems insufficient to justify the range of inequality, the extremes of wealth and poverty, that actually obtain in the society under discussion. Entitlement or desert might justify vast differences between rich and poor: no limit to the inequality they might endorse is inscribed in them. This is particularly clear in the case of the entitlement principle that I am absolute owner of my own labor power. Whey my power to produce is conceived as fully private property, I may do with it as I will and demand what I may for its use. A proportionately greater attention to one's own interest, as opposed to that of others, is more limited in its justificatory reach, and it seems unlikely to justify the existing contrast of luxury and want.

Now, it might be objected that, in characterizing the position of the less well off as one of deprivation or want, I am unfairly tilting the balance against the incentive argument. To such an objection I have three replies.

First, I am in this part concerned with a real political use of the incentive argument. Reference to real circumstances is therefore entirely appropriate.

Second, the incentive argument is quite general. It should therefore apply no matter how badly off the badly off are, both absolutely and relatively to the well off. Accordingly, it is methodologically proper to focus on particularly dramatic cases of its application.

And it is precisely when the condition of the badly off is especially wretched that the *major* premise of the incentive argument can pass as compelling. Where the worst off are not too badly off, it looks more fanatical to assign absolute priority to their claims. But the stronger the case for ameliorating the situation of the badly off is, the more discreditable (if I am right) the incentive argument is on the lips of the rich. So the argument is most shameful where, at first sight, it is most apt.

Now, a world that implements John Rawls's *two* principles of justice will not display the degree of inequality that characterizes contemporary Britain. Accordingly, the foregoing attempt to neutralize the agent-prerogative defense of the incentive argument in its common use will not serve to defeat it as a defense of the Rawlsian use of the argument, and more will be said about that later....

11.

The incentive argument is not problematic (in the particular way that I say it is) when it is thought acceptable to view the rich as outside the community to which the poor belong. But sometimes, in Britain, anyway, many of the rich themselves are eager to invoke community, when, for example, they react with (real or fake) horror to militant agitation among the poor. (Maybe some of the rich think that "belong to the same community as" denotes a non-symmetrical relation.)

Of course, particular talented people can affirm the incentive argument without difficulty, by declaring that they personally lack the disposition attributed to members of their class in the argument. But if the argument is going to pass muster as a justification of unequal reward within community, then putting it forward in the first person, and without such disavowal, should not be problematic.

In the third person, the minor premise of the argument just predicts how the rich will behave, and it can show misunderstanding of the speaker's message to demand a justification of that behavior: the speaker is not responsible for it, and he might himself be disposed to condemn it. But to affirm the minor premise of the argument with full first-person force is to declare, or, what suffices for present purposes, to manifest, an intention, and a demand for justification is therefore in order. Observe the difference between these two interchanges, each of which follows assertion of the minor premise of the argument to a poor person, in the first case *by* a poor person, or by some third party.

> Poor person: But they, the rich, should not demand so much.
>
> Reply: That has nothing to do with me. The fact is that they do.

That is a valid reply to the poor person's lament. But now consider an analogous interchange following a first-person presentation of the premise:

> Poor person: But you, the rich, should not demand so much.
>
> Reply: That has nothing to do with me. The fact is that we (I, and the others) do.

Here the very incoherence of the reply confirms the aptness of the challenge against which it strains.

Finding it difficult to provide a convincing reply, the rich may represent their own optional attitudes and decisions *as* given facts. They might say to the poor, "Look, we all have to accept the reality of the situation." Yet it is not an exogenous reality which they are asking the poor to recognize. In this rhetoric of the rich, a declaration of intention masquerades as a description of something beyond choice: the rich present *themselves* in third-personal terms, in alienation from their own agency.[16]

For an analogous self-misrepresentation, consider how absurd it would be for the kidnapper to say: "Gee, I'm sorry, but the fact is that unless you pay I will not release your child." If he says that in factual style, and not as a piece of macabre humor, his remark expresses an estrangement from his own intention which means that he is crazy.

And I believe that there is also something weird going on when the will of a class is depicted by its members as *just* a sociological fact. The rich man sits in his living room, and he explains, in a detached style that says that *his* choices have nothing to do with the matter, why the poor should vote against higher taxes on the rich. Here, too, there is alienation, but, because it is less obvious than the alienation of the single kidnapper that I just portrayed, you do not have to be completely crazy to slip into it. It is easy to slip into *this* alienation because each rich person's individual choice lacks salience, lost as it is among the millions of similar choices typical of members of his class: he participates in a practice so familiar that it gets treated as part of, or on a par with the course of nature. In a reflective moment he might be appalled by the situation of the badly off, but he reifies the intentions of rich people (his own included), which frustrate their claim to priority, into hard data which social policy must take as parametric. He is unalive to the fact that his own decisions contribute to the condition he describes, a condition which is the upshot of a vast number of personal choices, but which he describes in the impersonal discoursed of sociology or economics.

Recall the crazy kidnapper, who says, "Gee, I'm sorry." The child's parents might display a corresponding craziness. They do so if they treat the kidnapper's intention as an objective fact not only for them but even for him. And then they think of his demand as just what they happen to have to pay to get their child back, and maybe one of them says to the kidnapper, as to a possibly sympathetic bystander: "Well, £5000 *is* a lot of money, as I'm sure you'll agree, but it's less, after all, than what it cost to have Sally's adenoids removed, and, as you've pointed out, it is her *life* that's at stake."

And these reflections also have a bearing on the incentive argument. I have said that the incapacity of that argument to serve as a justification of inequality when the rich present it to the poor shows that the argument presupposes a lack of community between them. And I have just now also said that when the rich deliver it in a certain cast or tone, they imply that they do not qualify as choosing human agents. In considering that second point, it may be instructive to contemplate a presentation of the incentive argument that we have not yet considered, one in which a poor person addresses a set of rich ones. Now the minor premise will say: if the top tax rises to 60 percent, *you* will work less hard, and we shall consequently be worse off. If the poor speaker says that in an objective tone of voice, his rich listeners might, as a result, feel the weirdness that comes when someone predicts your behavior as though you have no control over it. Some of the listeners might even protest: "Hey, wait a minute. We would like at least to *try* not to work less if the tax rises." And the poor speaker might counter: "You're not likely to stick to that resolution. *Please* vote against the tax rise." In his insistence on the truth of the incentive argument's minor premise, this poor person would be setting his face against community, or against the capacity for agency of his listeners, or against both.

III. Incentives and the Difference Principle

12.

I have thus far scrutinized a defense of the inequalities of an actually existing capitalist society (Great

Britain) that occurs in ordinary political discourse. I now leave the vernacular context and turn to a text-based examination of John Rawls's difference principle. It is certain that Rawls would not endorse the particular inequalities that prevail in Britain. But his own defense of inequality has significant elements in common with the case for Lawson's tax cut, and much of my criticism of the latter also bears against Rawls's views.

It is usually supposed, and it is evidently supposed by Rawls himself, that his affirmation of the difference principle is consistent with his endorsement of the inequalities that come with special incentives to people of talent. But I shall argue that, when true to itself, Rawlsian justice condemns such incentives, and that no society whose members are *themselves* unambivalently committed to the difference principle need use special incentives to motivate talented producers....

It is very important in the present connection that Rawls's theory describes what he calls a well-ordered society, one, that is, whose citizens display full and willing compliance with the demands of justice. In a well-ordered society each person acts out of a sense of justice informed by the principles of justice not merely at the ballot box but as he goes about his daily business.

So much is clear from many passages in Rawls's writings. We are told not only that "everyone accepts, and knows that others likewise accept, the same first principles of right and justice," which might, by itself, be consistent with a ballot box view of their commitment, but also that the parties "in everyday life ... affirm and act from [those] first principles of justice.[17] Full compliance with the principles means that they act *from* them, in everyday life, "in the course," as Rawls also puts it, "of their daily lives."[18] And their "full autonomy is achieved" partly through "acting *from* these principles as their sense of justice dictates."[19] Citizens are strongly committed to acting that way. They "have a highest-order desire, their sense of justice, to *act* from the principles of justice."[20] They "have a desire to express their nature as free and equal moral persons, and this they do most adequately by acting *from* the principles that they would acknowledge in the original position. When all strive to comply with these principles and each succeeds, then individually and collectively their nature as moral persons is *most* fully realized, and with it their individual and collective good."[21]

Now, such statements seem to me to imply that the economic motivation of Rawlsian citizens is influenced by the difference principle. How could they act like maximizing incentive seekers if in "*their daily lives*" they act "*from*" a principle which directs primary concern for the badly off? Can we say that they act *from* such a principle in their daily lives just because they support taxation which is shaped by the principle and which aims to modify the results of their acting *from* maximizing motives? Such support might show that you respect the claim of the principle against you, but it surely does not suffice as proof of your being inspired by it as part of a sense of justice on which you operate in your daily life.[22] How could your "nature as [a] moral person" count as "*most* fully realized" when you go for as much as you can get in your own market choices,[23] and merely endorse application of the principle by the government in imperfect moderation of the inequality which the choices of people like you tend to cause?

Consider this passage from *A Theory of Justice*: "by abstaining from the exploitation of the contingencies of nature and social circumstances within a framework of equal liberty, persons express their respect for one another in the very constitution of their society."[24] If that is so, then it seems to me that in the Rawlsian society there will not be incentive seekers, since they do exploit their contingent talent and social advantages, and the passage says that people who do that show a lack of respect for other people that the constitution of their society requires. If you deny that the passage has this implication, then you must make one or other of two implausible claims. You must claim either that (1) despite what the passage says, Rawlsianly just talented people might exploit the contingency of their superior talent, or that (2) contrary to what seems evident, talented market-maximizers do not engage in such exploitation.[25]

Think about it this way. On a Rawlsian view, there is no reason of basic principle why the talented should earn more than the untalented. It is merely that things (supposedly) fall out that way, when the difference principle is applied. So imagine that we address the talented rich people, and we ask them why they do not give the above-average parts of their incomes to people of below-average income, when, *ex hypothesi*, they would have compliantly accepted the resulting post-giveaway incomes had the difference principle happened to mandate them. What could they say? They certainly could not say that they were abstaining from exploitation of their talent advantages, and we could not say that they live under "a conception of justice that nullifies the accidents of natural endowment and the contingencies of social circumstance as counters in the quest for...economic advantage...."[26]

17.

Rawls says that "a person in the original position would concede the justice of [the] inequalities [required for incentives]. Indeed, it would be short-sighted of him not to do so."[27] Now, the phrasing of this contention is curious, since we normally think of short-sightedness as poor perception not of justice but of one's own interests[28] And I point out this infelicity in the formulation because I believe that it reflects an unresolved tension in the Rawlsian architectonic, one that underlies the difficulties exposed in these lectures. That underlying tension is between a *bargaining* conception and a *community* conception of social relationships. (There are conceptions which fall between those two, with elements of each, but, as I read Rawls, both of them appear in his work, in relatively pure forms.)

But let us ignore the infelicitous phrasing in the passage, and concentrate on the implied claim that it would be a mistake not to concede the justice of incentive inequalities. My reply to that claim, a reply that by now is entirely predictable, is that, *if* we are talking within the assumption of full compliance, then we need not and should not concede either that incentive inequalities are required to motivate performance or that they are just. Let us now, however, retire the heady assumptions of full compliance and a widespread sense of justice. Consider, instead, a society like the United States, where fortunate people learn to expect more than they would get when the difference principle prevails in a comprehensive way. In that case, we might agree that it would be a mistake not to concede incentive inequalities. If we need inequalities to "encourage effective performance"[29] then it might be folly not to have them, but it does not follow that having them is a requirement of basic justice, where a *basic* principle of justice is one that has application in a society where, as in Rawls's, everyone always acts justly.

Although his primary topic is justice under full compliance, Rawls also treats his principles as standards for assessing actually existing society.[30] In my view, the difference principle, conceived as one that would govern a just society, condemns as unjust those existing inequalities which are necessary to benefit the worst off where that necessity reflects the intentions of the talented rich; but, given that the inequalities are necessary, albeit for the stated reason, to remove them would be reckless. If we are concerned about the badly off, then we should sometimes concede incentives, just as we should sometimes satisfy even a kidnapper's demands. We are not then acting on the difference principle in its strict interpretation, in which it is a principle of justice governing a society of just people who are inspired by it. We are acting on the lax version of the difference principle, which endorses incentives and which has application in societies of the familiar unjust kind. On the assumption that they are indeed unavoidable, incentive payments may be justified, but it does not follow that no injustice occurs when they are provided. (One might say, to a child's guardian: the kidnapper is unjustly threatening the safety of the child, and justice to the child therefore demands that you pay him. And one might say, to legislators in a structurally unequal society: the talented are unjustly indifferent to the plight of the poor, and justice to the poor therefore demands that you do not impose very high taxation.)

The policy of paying productive people plenty to get them to produce so that badly off people will be better off is rational when productive people are resolved to serve only if they are richly rewarded. But their stance is then unjust by the very standard which the difference principle itself sets. Accordingly, on a strict view of Rawlsian justice, the difference principle in its lax interpretation, which does mandate the incentives policy, is not a basic principle of justice but a principle for handling people's injustice.

It is not a basic principle of justice, since it confers benefit on market maximizers who offend against justice. We might call it a principle of damage limitation in the field of justice.

When doing so limits the damage, it is wise to run society on lax difference principle lines, but it is also wise to recognize that society is not then based on justice. A related and more general point is that one should not suppose that, as Rawls says in *A Theory of Justice*, "justice is *the* first virtue of social institutions," where that means that "laws and institutions ... must be reformed or abolished if they are unjust."[31] For sometimes justice is unattainable, and we do well to settle for something else....

18.

My principal contention about Rawls is that (potential) high fliers would forgo incentives properly so-called in a full compliance society governed by the difference principle and characterized by fraternity and universal dignity. I have not rejected the difference principle in its lax reading as a principle of public policy: I do not doubt that there are contexts where it is right to apply it. What I have questioned is its description as a principle of (basic) justice, and I have deplored Rawls's willingness to describe those at the top end of a society governed by it as undergoing the fullest possible realization of their moral natures. My own socialist-egalitarian position was nicely articulated by John Stuart Mill in his *Principles of Political Economy*. Contrasting equal payment with incentive-style payment according to product ("work done"), Mill said that the first

> appeals to a higher standard of justice, and is adapted to a much higher moral condition of human nature. The proportioning of remuneration to work done is really just, only in so far as the more or less of the work is a matter of choice; when it depends on natural difference of strength or capacity, this principle of remuneration is in itself an injustice: it is giving to those who have; assigning most to those who are already most favored by nature. Considered, however, as a compromise with the selfish type of character formed by the present standard of morality, and fostered by the existing social institutions, it is highly expedient; and until education shall have been entirely regenerated, is far more likely to prove immediately successful, than an attempt at a higher ideal.[32]

Rawls's lax application of his different principle means "giving to those who have." He presents the incentive policy as a feature of the just society, whereas it is in fact, and as Mill says, just "highly expedient" in society as we know it, a sober "compromise with the selfish type of character" formed by capitalism.[33] Philosophers in search of justice should not be content with an expedient compromise. To call expediency *justice* goes against the regeneration to which Mill looked forward at the end of this fine passage.

AUTHOR'S NOTE

Many friends and colleagues commented helpfully, and in some cases at magnanimous length, on earlier versions of the material forming these lectures. For perceptive admonitions at various Oxford meetings I thank Ronald Dworkin, Susan Hurley, Thomas Nagel, Derek Parfit, Thomas Scanlon, Samuel Scheffler, and Joseph Raz. For (often voluminous) letters of criticism, I thank Richard Arneson, John Baker, Annette Barnes, Gerald Barnes, Christopher Bertram, Akeel Bilgrami, Giacomo Bonanno, Joshua Cohen, Gerald Dworkin, Jon Elster, Keith Graham, Daniel Hausman, Ted Honderich, Will Kymlicka, Andrew Levine, Kasper Lippert-Rasmussen, Murray MacBeath, John McMurtry, David Miller, Michael Otsuka, Derek Parfit, Philip Pettit, Thomas Pogge, Janet Radcliffe-Richards, John Roemer, Amelie Rorty, Miles Sabin, Robert Shaver, William Shaw, Seana Shiffrin, Hillel Steiner, Joseph Stiglitz, Robert Ware, Martin Wilkinson, Alan Wertheimer, Andrew Williams, Joseph Wolff, and Erik Wright. My greatest debt is to Arnold Zuboff, who devoted countless hours to arguing with, and correcting, me, and I am particularly grateful to Samuel Scheffler for his incisive criticism at the seminar following the lectures. I should add that some of the argumentation of the lectures is anticipated in these articles about Rawls: Thomas Grey, "The First Virtue," *Stanford Law Review* 25 (January 1973); Jan Narveson, "A Puzzle about Economic Justice in Rawls' Theory," *Social Theory and Practice* 4, no. 1 (1976); and Joseph

Carens, "Rights and Duties in an Egalitarian Society," *Political Theory* 14, no. 1 (February 1986).

NOTES

1. Strictly speaking, the top tax would be raised to 50 percent, but the ceiling on National Insurance contributions would be removed, and the effect of the two measures would be the same as that of raising the income tax to 59 percent and leaving National Insurance alone.
2. To be more precise, they reject those principles *at the relevant fundamental level*. The qualification is necessary because left-wing liberals recognize desert and entitlement as (derivative) rules of legitimate reward in schemes of contribution and compensation which are not *grounded* in notions of desert and entitlement. (See John Rawls, *A Theory of Justice* [Cambridge: Harvard University Press, 1971], pp. 103, 310-15; and Thomas Scanlon, "The Significance of Choice," in *The Tanner Lectures on Human Values*, Vol. 8 [Salt Lake City: University of Utah Press, 1988], pp, 188, 203. For a recent statement of nuanced views on desert and entitlement, see John Rawls, *Justice as Fairness: A Briefer Restatement* [Cambridge: Harvard University, 1989, manuscript], pp. 54 sec. 2, and 57 n. 34; I do not understand the doctrine presented in the latter place).
3. For extensive use of this principle, see F. A. Hayek, *The Constitution of Liberty* (Chicago: University of Chicago Press, 1960), chap. 3, and esp. pp. 44-49.
4. Strong support for that charge comes from *Punishing the Poor: Poverty under Thatcher*, by Kay Andrews and John Jacobs (London: Macmillan, 1990).
5. See Rawls, *A Theory of Justice*, pp. 15, 102, 151, 179, 546; Rawls, *Justice as Fairness*, pp. 57, 89.
6. "How do you tell a person dying of hunger that there's nothing you can do?" (*Action Aid* leaflet, 1990).
7. An exploitation of (inter alia) this particular relativity occurred in an advertisement of 1943 whose purpose was to promote the purchase of war bonds. In March 1944 the advertisement won a prize for its contribution to the war effort.

   The top third of the ad's space pictures an American prisoner of war in a bleak cell. Below the picture, we find the following text:

   WILL YOU WRITE A LETTER to a Prisoner of War ... tonight?

   Maybe he's one of Jimmie Doolittle's boys. Perhaps he was left behind when Bataan fell. Anyway, he's an American, and he hasn't had a letter in a long, long time.

   And when you sit down to write, tell *him* why you didn't buy your share of War Bonds last pay day.

   "Dear Joe," you might say, "the old topcoat was getting kind of threadbare, so I ... "

   No, cross it out. Joe might not understand about the topcoat, especially if he's shivering in a damp Japanese cell.

   Let's try again. "Dear Joe, I've been working pretty hard and haven't had a vacation in over a year, so ... "

   Hell, better cross that out, too. They don't even get vacations where Joe's staying.

   Well, what are you waiting for? Go ahead, write the letter to Joe. *Try* to write it, anyhow.

   But mister, if somehow you find you can't finish that letter, will you, at least, do this for Joe? Will you up the amount of money you're putting into War Bonds and keep buying your share from here on in? (1945 *Britannica Book of the Year [A Record of the March of Events* of 1944] [Chicago: Encyclopaedia Britannica, 1945], p. 22).

   A word about the form of this ad, and about the sources of its motivating power (if it did the motivating it should have done to deserve the prize it won). The ad is directed not, of course, at one person but at a large set of people, all the people in the condition of material life and personal intention of the civilian that the ad sketches. Yet the ad speaks as though to one person and it has that single person address a single member of the set of POWs. The content of the ad implies that civilians as such have some kind of obligation to POWs as such. But the ad aims to convey the obligation falling on many by selecting one individual from each of the two groups and figuring forth an encounter between them. Notice, moreover, that the ad would have sacrificed little or nothing of its purpose and power if its personal references had been pluralized, if, that is, the civilian had spoken of *our* threadbare coats, run-down sheds, and lacks of vacation, to an imagined *assembly* of POWs. (Compare first-person plural presentation of the incentive justification, by a rich person, or by all of them in unison, to all the poor people).

The ad makers thought that they could expose the insufficiency of the reasons civilians give themselves for not buying bonds by portraying a civilian offering them to Joe. And they were right that it is easier to face yourself when you decide for the stated reasons not to buy bonds if you do not have to face Joe at the same time.

The power of the ad to move the reader is multiply determined, mingling elements that go into types *c*, *d*, and *e* above. The ad simulates an immediacy between the civilian and Joe, such immediacy being one rhetorical effect of casting an argument in interpersonal form. And then, immediacy having been secured, there are two or three separable things, mixed here in a powerful cocktail, on which the ad relies: that Joe and I are members of the same community, and he is suffering; that Joe and I are coparticipants in an immensely important enterprise in which at least the *quality* of my life and that of the members of my family is at stake; and that Joe is a moral hero—look what he has given, for the sake of the mentioned enterprise, compared with the modest thing that I resist giving. These considerations combine to make me feel answerable to Joe. The ad says that although it sounds quite reasonable for a person to choose a new coat before buying more bonds, the burden of wearing a threadbare coat carries no justificatory weight when it is compared with the burden Joe carries: that, so the ad implies, explains the shame a civilian would feel in telling Joe that his threadbare coat was a good reason for not buying more bonds.

Finally, a comment on the role of immediacy, which, so I noted, is one source of the advertisement's power. Immediacy can contribute to persuasion in cases where what is rendered immediate is not a person (or a group) that is addressed. We do not speak to animals, but arguments justifying their use in certain experiments might be hard to deliver in the lab while those experiments are in train. We also do not speak to trees, but it might be harder to justify the size of the Sunday edition of the *New York Times* when one is standing in a majestic forest. So: having to face a person when uttering an argument is a special case of immediacy, not part of its general form, and it is perhaps not crucial to the ad's power that the POW is *addressed* as opposed to just on scene when the argument is presented.

8. As opposed to the claim that it is true, which every presenter of the argument can be asked to justify.
9. I express myself in that cautious way because, apart from the case, if you want to allow it, in which the kidnapper himself uses the impersonal form of the argument, referring to himself as "he," there is the case of a person who puts it forth and conveys (for example, by his tone) that he is quite insensitive to the countervailing (if properly overridden) considerations, and/or that he sees nothing untoward in the kidnapper's threat, and/or that he sees human dealings on the model of interaction of impersonal forces.
10. It follows, harmlessly, that penal policies adopted to reduce the incidence of crime lack comprehensive justification. The very fact that such a policy is justified shows that all is not well with society.
11. John Rawls, "Kantian Constructivism in Moral Theory," *Journal of Philosophy* 77, no. 9 (September 1980): 561; Rawls, *A Theory of Justice*, p. 536.
12. According to Robin Cook, MP, Labour spokesman on health, in the severe winter of 1991 there were 4,000 more deaths of old people than are usual in such a period.
13. This piece of dialogue comes from Samuel Scheffler's seminar commentary on these lectures. Sheffler pressed the challenge to which the rest of this section is a response.
14. I have always thought that the right reply to a white South African who says, to an anti-Apartheid advocate, "You would see things differently if you were in my position," is: "Quite: I'm sure it does blind one's vision"
15. See his *Rejection of Consequentialism* (Oxford: Clarendon Press, 1982).
16. This is not a rerun of the inability claim, which we left behind at the end of section 7. That claim acknowledges that the rich form and/or execute certain alternative ones. In the motif of alienation, the very fact of intentional agency is concealed, or at least obscured.
17. Rawls, "Kantian Constructivism," p. 521.
18. *Ibid.*, p. 528. Cf. Rawls, *A Theory of Justice*, p. 253: they "knowingly act on the principles of justice in the ordinary course of events."

19. Rawls. "Kantian Constructivism," p. 528, emphasis added.
20. *Ibid.*, p. 532, emphasis added.
21. Rawls, *A Theory of Justice*, p. 528, emphases added.
22. Rawls says that "citizens have a normally effective sense of justice, that is, one that enables them to understand and to apply the principles of justice, and for the most part to act from them as their circumstances require (*Justice as Fairness*, p.154). Why would they have to apply the principles themselves to their own circumstances if just behavior consisted in obeying laws designed to effect an implementation of those principles?
23. How does the economic behavior of a maximizer who is committed to the lax difference principle differ from that of a maximizer who is not? It might be said that, unlike the latter, the former is willing to maximize only when and because the principle is in force. But that is not necessarily true: people who believe that the lax difference principle should be instituted may have various views about what they should do in a society in which it is not. And even if our believer would indeed behave nonmaximizingly if the principle were not in force, that hardly shows that he "strive[s] to comply with" the difference principle in his "daily life."
24. Rawls, *A Theory of Justice*, p. 179, and see, generally, pp. 72-75.
25. It has been claimed, against my interpretation of the quoted passage, that it speaks of an expression of mutual respect when persons choose their constitution and not, as I have supposed, when they act in the society it constitutes. But there is no scope of "abstaining from the exploitation of the contingencies of nature and social circumstance" at the stage of constitutional choice, since, at that point, no one knows what those contingencies are. This and other phrases (not quoted above) in the paragraph from which the passage is drawn establish that the objection is misguided, that Rawls is here commenting on people's choices in real life rather than in the original position. He is speaking about how things are "when society follows these principles" (ibid., p. 179).
26. Rawls, *A Theory of Justice*, p. 15.
27. *Ibid.*, p. 151.
28. A person in the original position does not, in any case, ask himself what is *just*. He asks himself what, given his ignorance, is the best choice from the point of view of his interests.
29. Rawls, *A Theory of Justice*, p. 151.
30. See *ibid.*, pp. 245-46.
31. *Ibid.*, p. 3, my emphasis.
32. John Stuart Mill, *Principles of Political Economy*, book 2, chap. 1, sec. 4, in J. M. Robson, ed., Collected Works of John Stuart Mill, vol. 2 (Toronto: University of Toronto Press, 1965), p. 210. In chapter 5 of his *Utilitarianism Mill* argues, at great length, that justice is a species of expediency. But here the selfsame principle of remuneration is, under the stated conditions, both "highly expedient" and "an injustice." It is a nice question whether that conjunction of designations is compatible with everything that Mill says in *Utilitarianism*.
33. For sapient criticism of Rawls along these lines, see Allen Buchanan, *Marx and Justice* (Totowa, N.J.: Rowman and Littlefield, 1982), pp. 127-28. According to Mill, "the deep-rooted selfishness which forms the general character of the existing state of society is so deeply rooted only because the whole course of the existing institutions tends to foster it" (*Autobiography* [New York: New American Library, 1965], pp. 168-69). See, for further pertinent references, Richard Ashcraft, "Class Conflict and Constitutionalism in J. S. Mill's Thought," in Nancy Rosenblum, ed., *Liberalism and the Moral Life* (Cambridge: Harvard University Press, 1989), pp. 117-18.

CARRYING CAPACITY AS AN ETHICAL CONCEPT

Garrett Hardin

Garrett Hardin is Professor Emeritus of Biological Sciences at the University of California at Santa Barbara. He is the author of numerous publications in the areas of human ecology, population, and evolution.

Hardin uses the notion of the tragedy of the commons to raise questions about the moral justifiability of giving aid. He argues that more needs to be known about the consequences of providing foreign aid to poor countries or to people starving in other countries. He claims that foreign aid to developing countries can do more harm than good because it can contribute to the problem of overpopulation, worsen political and economic strife within the developing country, and magnify problems of unemployment and environmental degradation in these countries.

Lifeboat ethics is merely a special application of the logic of the commons.[1] The classic paradigm is that of a pasture held as common property by a community and governed by the following rules: first, each herdsman may pasture as many cattle as he wishes on the commons; and second, the gain from the growth of cattle accrues to the individual owners of the cattle. In an underpopulated world the system of the commons may do no harm and may even be the most economic way to manage things, since management costs are kept to a minimum. In an overpopulated (or overexploited) world a system of the commons leads to ruin, because each herdsman has more to gain individually by increasing the size of his herd than he has to lose as a single member of the community guilty of lowering the carrying capacity of the environment. Consequently he (with others) overloads the commons.

Even if an individual fully perceives the ultimate consequences of his actions he is most unlikely to act in any other way, for he cannot count on the restraint *his* conscience might dictate being matched by a similar restraint on the part of *all* the others. (Anything less than all is not enough.) Since mutual ruin is inevitable, it is quite proper to speak of the *tragedy* of the commons.

Tragedy is the price of freedom in the commons. Only by changing to some other system (socialism or private enterprise, for example) can ruin be averted. In other words, in a crowded world survival requires that some freedom be given up. (We have, however, a choice in the freedom to be sacrificed). Survival is possible under several different politico-economic systems—but not under the system of the commons. When we understand this point, we reject the ideal of distributive justice stated by Karl Marx a century ago. "From each according to his ability, to each according to his needs."[2] This ideal might be defensible if "needs" were defined by the larger community rather than by the individual (or individual political unit) *and if "needs" were static*.[3] But in the past quarter-century, with the best will in the world, some humanitarians have been asserting that rich populations must supply the needs of poor populations even though the recipient populations increase without restraint. At the United Nations conference on population in Bucharest in 1973 spokesmen for the poor nations repeatedly said in effect: "We poor people have the right to reproduce

---

Reprinted with permission from *Soundings* 59:1 (1976): 120–137.

as much as we want to; you in the rich world have the responsibility of keeping us alive."

Such a Marxian disjunction of rights and responsibilities inevitably tends toward tragic ruin for all. It is almost incredible that this position is supported by thoughtful persons, but it is. How does this come about? In part, I think, because language deceives us. When a disastrous loss of life threatens, people speak of a "crisis," implying that the threat is temporary. More subtle is the implication of quantitative stability built into the pronoun "they" and its relatives. Let me illustrate this point with quantified prototype statements based on two points of view.

Crisis analysis: "These poor people (1,000,000) are starving, because of a crisis (flood, drought, or the like). How can we refuse *them* (1,000,000)? Let us feed *them* (1,000,000). Once the crisis is past those who are still hungry are few (say 1,000) and there is no further need for our intervention."

Crunch analysis: "*Those* (1,000,000) who are hungry are reproducing. We send food to *them* (1,010,000). *Their* lives (1,020,000) are saved. But since the environment is still essentially the same, the next year *they* (1,030,000) ask for more food. We send it to *them* (1,045,000); and the next year *they* (1,068,000) ask for still more. Since the need has not gone away, it is a mistake to speak of a passing crisis: it is evidently a permanent crunch that this growing "they" face—a growing disaster, not a passing state of affairs."

"They" increases in size. Rhetoric makes no allowance for a ballooning pronoun. Thus we can easily be deceived by language. We cannot deal adequately with ethical questions if we ignore quantitative matters. This attitude has been rejected by James Sellers, who dismisses prophets of doom from Malthus[4] to Meadows[5] as "chiliasts." Chiliasts (or millenialists to use the Latin-derived equivalent of the Greek term) predict a catastrophic end of things a thousand years from some reference point. The classic example is the prediction of Judgment Day in the year 1000 anno Domini. Those who predicted it were wrong, of course; but the fact that this specific prediction was wrong is no valid criticism of the use of numbers in thinking. Millenialism is numerology, not science.

In science, most of the time, it is not so much exact numbers that are important as it is the relative size of numbers and the direction of change in the magnitude of them. Much productive analysis is accomplished with only the crude quantitation of "order of magnitude" thinking. First and second derivatives are often calculated with no finer aim than to find out if they are positive or negative. Survival can hinge on the crude issue of the sign of change, regardless of number. This is a far cry from the spurious precision of numerology. Unfortunately the chasm between the "two cultures," as C.P. Snow called them,[6] keeps many in the nonscientific culture from understanding the significance of the quantitative approach. One is tempted to wonder also whether an additional impediment to understanding may not be the mortal sin called Pride, which some theologians regard as the mother of all sins.

Returning to Marx, it is obvious that the *each* in "to each according to his needs" is not—despite the grammar—a unitary, stable entity: "each" is a place holder for a ballooning variable. Before we commit ourselves to saving the life of *each* and every person in need we had better ask this question: "*And then what?*" That is, what about tomorrow, what about posterity? As Hans Jonas has pointed out,[7] traditional ethics has almost entirely ignored the claims of posterity. In an overpopulated world humanity cannot long endure under a regime governed by posterity-blind ethics. It is the essence of ecological ethics that it pays attention to posterity.

Since "helping" starving people requires that we who are rich give up some of our wealth, any refusal to do so is almost sure to be attributed to selfishness. Selfishness there may be, but focusing on selfishness is likely to be non-productive. In truth, a selfish motive can be found in all policy proposals. The selfishness of *not* giving is obvious and need not be elaborated. But the selfishness of giving is no less real, though more subtle.[8] Consider the sources of support for Public Law 480, the act of Congress under which surplus foods were given to poor countries, or sold to them at bargain prices ("concessionary terms" is the euphemism). Why did we give food away? Conventional wisdom says it was because we momentarily transcended our normal selfishness. Is that the whole story?

It is not. The "we" of the above sentence needs to

be subdivided. The farmers who grew the grain did not give it away. They sold it to the government (which then gave it away). Farmers received selfish benefits in two ways: the direct sale of grain, and the economic support to farm prices given by this governmental purchase in an otherwise free market. The operation of P.L. 480 during the past quarter-century brought American farmers to a level of prosperity never known before.

Who else benefited—in a selfish way? The stockholders and employees of the railroads that moved grain to seaports benefited. So also did freight-boat operators (U.S. "bottoms" were specified by law). So also did grain elevator operators. So also did agricultural research scientists who were financially supported in a burgeoning but futile effort "to feed a hungry world."[9] And so also did the large bureaucracy required to keep the P.L. 480 system working. In toto, probably several million people personally benefited from the P.L. 480 program. Their labors cannot be called wholly selfless.

Who *did* make a sacrifice for P.L. 480? The citizens generally, nearly two hundred million of them, paying directly or indirectly through taxes. But each of these many millions lost only a little: whereas each of the million or so gainers gained a great deal. The blunt truth is that *philanthropy pays*—if you are hired as a philanthropist. Those on the gaining side of P.L. 480 made a great deal of money and could afford to spend lavishly to persuade Congress to continue the program. Those on the sacrificing side sacrificed only a little bit per capita and could not afford to spend much protecting their pocketbooks against philanthropic inroads. And so P.L. 480 continued, year after year.

Should we condemn philanthropy when we discover that some of its roots are selfish? I think not, otherwise probably no philanthropy would be possible. The secret of practical success in large-scale public philanthropy is this: see to it that the losses are widely distributed so that the per capita loss is small, but concentrate the gains in a relatively few people so that these few will have the economic power needed to pressure the legislature into supporting the program.

I have spent some time on this issue because I would like to dispose once and for all of condemnatory arguments based on "selfishness." As a matter of principle we should always assume that selfishness is *part* of the motivation of every action. But what of it? If Smith proposes a certain public policy, it is far more important to know whether the policy will do public harm or public good than it is to know whether Smith's motives are selfish or selfless. Consequences ("ends") can be more objectively determined than motivations ("means"). Situational ethics wisely uses consequences as the measure of morality. "If the end does not justify the means, what does?" asked Joseph Fletcher.[10] The obsession of older ethical systems with means and motives is no doubt in part a consequence of envy, which has a thousand disguises.[11] (Though I am sure this is true, the situationist should not dwell on envy very long, for it is after all only a motive, and as such not directly verifiable. In any case public policy must be primarily concerned with consequences.)

Even judging an act by its consequences is not easy. We are limited by the basic theorem of ecology, "We can never do merely one thing."[12] The fact that an act has many consequences is all the more reason for deemphasizing motives as we carry out our ethical analyses. Motives by definition apply only to intended consequences. The multitudinous unintended ones are commonly denigrated by the term "side effects." But "The road to hell is paved with good intentions," so let's have done with motivational evaluations of public policy.

Even after we have agreed to eschew motivational analysis, foreign aid is a tough nut to crack. The literature is large and contradictory, but it all points to the inescapable conclusion that a quarter of a century of earnest effort has not conquered world poverty. To may observers the threat of future disasters is more convincing now than it was a quarter of a century ago—and the disasters are not all in the future either.[13] Where have we gone wrong in foreign aid?

We wanted to do good, of course. The question, "How can we help a poor country?" seems like a simple question, one that should have a simple answer. Our failure to answer it suggests that the question is not as simple as we thought. The variety of contradictory answers offered is disheartening.

How can we find our way through this thicket? I suggest we take a cue from a mathematician. The great algebraist Karl Jacobi (1804-1851) had a simple stratagem that he recommended to students who found themselves butting their heads against a stone wall. *Umkehren, immer umkehren*—"Invert, always invert." Don't just keep asking the same old question over and over: turn it upside down and ask the opposite question. The answer you get then may not be the one you want, but it may throw useful light on the question you started with.

Let's try a Jacobian inversion of the food/population problem. To sharpen the issue, let us take a particular example, say India. The question we want to answer is, "How can we help India?" But since that approach has repeatedly thrust us against a stone wall, let's pose the Jacobian invert, "How can we *harm* India?" After we've answered this perverse question we will return to the original (and proper) one.

As a matter of method, let us grant ourselves the most malevolent of motives: let us ask, "How can we harm India—*really* harm her?" Of course we might plaster the country thermonuclear bombs, speedily wiping out most of the 600 million people. But, to the truly malevolent mind, that's not much fun: a dead man is beyond harming. Bacterial warfare could be a bit "better," but not much. No: we want something that will really make India suffer, not merely for a day or a week, but on and on and on. How can we achieve this inhumane goal?

Quite simply: by sending India a bounty of food, year after year. The United States exports about 80 million tons of grain a year. Most of it we sell: the foreign exchange it yields we use for such needed imports as petroleum (38 percent of our oil consumption in 1974), iron ore, bauxite, chromium, tin, etc. But in the pursuit of our malevolent goal let us "unselfishly" tighten our belts, make sacrifices, and do without that foreign exchange. Let us *give* all 80 million tons of grain to the Indians each year.

On a purely vegetable diet it takes about 400 pounds of grain to keep one person alive and healthy for a year. The 600 million Indians need 120 million tons per year; since their nutrition is less than adequate presumably they are getting a bit less than that now. So the 80 million tons we give them will almost double India's per capita supply of food. With a surplus, Indians can afford to vary their diet by growing some less efficient crops; they can also convert some of the grain into meat (pork and chickens for the Hindus, beef and chickens for the Moslems). The entire nation can then be supplied not only with plenty of calories, but also with an adequate supply of high quality protein. The people's eyes will sparkle, their steps will become more elastic; and they will be capable of more work. "Fatalism" will no doubt diminish. (Much so-called fatalism is merely a consequence of malnutrition.) Indians may even become a bit overweight, though they will still be getting only two-thirds as much food as the average inhabitant of a rich country. Surely—we think—surely a well-fed India would be better off?

Not so: *ceteris paribus*, they will ultimately be worse off. Remember, "We can never do merely one thing." A generous gift of food would have not only nutritional consequences: it would also have political and economic consequences. The difficulty of distributing free food to a poor people is well known. Harbor, storage, and transport inadequacies result in great losses of grain to rats and fungi. Political corruption diverts food from those who need it most to those who are more powerful. More abundant supplies depress free market prices and discourage native farmers from growing food in subsequent years. Research into better ways of agriculture is also discouraged. Why look for better ways to grow food when there is food enough already?

There are replies, of sorts, to all the above points. It may be maintained that all these evils are only temporary ones; in time, organizational sense will be brought into the distributional system and the government will crack down on corruption. Realizing the desirability of producing more food, for export if nothing else, a wise government will subsidize agricultural research in spite of an apparent surplus. Experience does not give much support to this optimistic view, but let us grant the conclusions for the sake of getting on to more important matters. Worse is to come.

The Indian unemployment rate is commonly reckoned at 30 percent, but it is acknowledged that this is a minimum figure. *Under*employment is rife. Check into a hotel in Calcutta with four small bags and four bearers will carry your luggage to the room—with another man to carry the key. Custom, and a knowledge of what the traffic will bear, decree this practice. In addition malnutrition justifies it in part. Adequately fed, half as many men would suffice. So one of the early consequences of achieving a higher level of nutrition in the Indian population would be to increase the number of unemployed.

India needs many things that food will not buy. Food will not diminish the unemployment rate (quite the contrary); nor will it increase the supply of minerals, bicycles, clothes, automobiles, gasoline, schools, books, movies, or television. All these things require energy for their manufacture and maintenance.

Of course, food is a form of energy, but it is convertible to other forms only with great loss; so we are practically justified in considering energy and food as mutually exclusive goods. On this basis the most striking difference between poor and rich countries is not in the food they eat but in the energy they use. On a per capita basis rich countries use about three times as much of the primary foods—grains and the like—as do poor countries. (To a large extent this is because the rich convert much of the grain to more "wasteful" animal meat.) But when it comes to energy, rich countries use ten times as much per capita. (Near the extremes Americans use 60 times as much per person as Indians.) By reasonable standards much of this energy may be wasted (e.g., in the manufacture of "exercycles" for sweating the fat off people who have eaten too much), but a large share of this energy supplies the goods we regard as civilized: effortless transportation, some luxury foods, a variety of sports, clean space-heating, more than adequate clothing, and energy-consuming arts—music, visual arts, electronic auxiliaries, etc. Merely giving food to a people does almost nothing to satisfy the appetite for any of these other goods.

But a well-nourished people is better fitted to try to wrest more energy from its environment. The question then is this: Is the native environment able to furnish more energy? And at what cost?

In India energy is already being gotten from the environment at a fearful cost. In the past two centuries millions of acres of India have been deforested in the struggle for fuel, with the usual environment degradation. The Vale of Kashmir, once one of the garden spots of the world, has been denuded to such an extent that the hills no longer hold water as they once did, and the springs supplying the famous gardens are drying up. So desperate is the need for charcoal for fuel that the Kahsmiri now make it out of tree leaves. This wasteful practice denies the soil of needed organic mulch.

Throughout India, as is well known, cow dung is burned to cook food. The minerals of the dung are not thereby lost, but the ability of dung to improve soil tilth is. Some of the nitrogen in the dung goes off into the air and does not return to Indian soil. Here we see a classic example of the "vicious circle": because Indians are poor they burn dung, depriving the soil of nitrogen and make themselves still poorer the following year. If we give them plenty of food, as they cook this food with cow dung they will lower still more the ability of their land to produce food.

Let us look at another example of this counterproductive behavior. Twenty-five years ago western countries brought food and medicine to Nepal. In the summer of 1974 a disastrous flood struck Bangladesh, killing tens of thousands of people, by government admission. (True losses in that part of the world are always greater than admitted losses.) Was there any connection between feeding Nepal and flooding Bangladesh? Indeed there was, and is.[14]

Nepal nestles amongst the Himalayas. Much of its land is precipitous, and winters are cold. The Nepalese need fuel, which they get from trees. Because more Nepalese are being kept alive now, the demand for timber is escalating. As trees are cut down, the soil under them is washed down the slopes into the rivers that run through India and Bangladesh. Once the absorption capacity of forest soil is gone, floods rise faster and to higher maxima. The flood of 1974 covered two-thirds of Bangladesh, twice the area of "normal" floods—which themselves are the consequence of deforestation in preceding centuries.

By bringing food and medicine to Nepal we intend only to save lives. But we can never do merely one thing, and the Nepalese lives we saved created a Nepalese energy famine. The lives we saved from starvation in Nepal a quarter of a century ago were paid for in our time by lives lost to flooding and its attendant evils in Bangladesh. The saying, "Man does not live by bread alone," takes on new meaning.

Still we have not described what may be the worst consequence of a food-only policy: revolution and civil disorder. Many kindhearted people who support food aid programs solicit the cooperation of "hard-nosed" doubters by arguing that good nutrition is needed for world peace. Starving people will attack others, they say. Nothing could be further from the truth. The monumental studies of Ancel Keys and others have shown that starving people are completely selfish.[15] They are incapable of cooperating with others; and they are incapable of laying plans for tomorrow and carrying them out. Moreover, modern war is so expensive that even the richest countries can hardly afford it.

The thought that starving people can forcefully wrest subsistence from their richer brothers may appeal to our sense of justice, *but it just ain't so.* Starving people fight only among themselves, and that inefficiently.

So what would happen if we brought ample supplies of food to a population that was still poor in everything else? They would still be incapable of waging war at a distance, but their ability to fight among themselves would be vastly increased. With vigorous, well-nourished bodies and a keen sense of their impoverishment in other things, they would no doubt soon create massive disorder in their own land. Of course, they might create a strong and united country, but what is the probability of that? Remember how much trouble the thirteen colonies had in forming themselves into a United States. Then remember that India is divided by two major religions, many castes, fourteen major languages and a hundred dialects. A partial separation of peoples along religious lines in 1947, at the time of the formation of Pakistan and of independent India, cost untold millions of lives. The budding off of Bangladesh (formerly East Pakistan) from the rest of Pakistan in 1971 cost several million more. All these losses were achieved on a low level of nutrition. The possibilities of bloodletting in a population of 600 million well-nourished people of many languages and religions and no appreciable tradition of cooperation stagger the imagination. Philanthropists with any imagination at all should be stunned by the thought of 600 million well-fed Indians seeking to meet their energy needs from their own resources.

So the answer to our Jacobian questions, "How can we harm India?" is clear: send food *only*. Escaping the Jacobian by reinverting the question we now ask, "How can we *help* India?" Immediately we see that we must never send food without a matching gift of non-food energy. But before we go careening off on an intoxicating new program we had better look at some more quantities.

On a per capita basis, India uses the energy equivalent of one barrel of oil per year; the U.S. uses sixty. The world average of all countries, rich and poor, is ten. If we want to bring India only up to the present world average, we would have to send India about 9 x 600 million bbl. of oil per year (or its equivalent in coal, timber, gas or whatever). That would be more than five billion barrels of oil equivalent. What is the chance that we will make such a gift?

Surely it is nearly zero. For scale, note that our total yearly petroleum use is seven billion barrels (of which we import three billion). Of course we use (and have) a great deal of coal too. But these figures should suffice to give a feeling of scale.

More important is the undoubted psychological fact that a fall in income tends to dry up the springs of philanthropy. Despite wide disagreements about the future of energy it is obvious that from now on, for at least the next twenty years and possibly for centuries, our per capita supply of energy is going to fall, year after year. The food we gave in the past was "surplus." By no accounting do we have an energy surplus. In fact, the perceived deficit is rising year by year.

India has about one-third as much land as the United States. She has about three times as much population. If her people-to-land ratio were the same as ours she would have only about seventy million people (instead of 600 million). With the forested and relatively unspoiled farmlands of four centuries ago, seventy million people was probably well within the carrying capacity of the land. Even in today's India, seventy million people could probably make it in comfort and dignity—provided they didn't increase!

To send food only to a country already populated beyond the carrying capacity of its land is to collaborate in the further destruction of the land and the further impoverishment of its people.

Food plus energy is a recommendable policy; but for a large population under today's conditions this policy is defensible only by the logic of the old saying, "If wishes were horses, beggars would ride." The fantastic amount of energy needed for such a program is simply not in view. (We have mentioned nothing of the equally monumental "infrastructure" of political, technological, and educational machinery needed to handle unfamiliar forms and quantities of energy in the poor countries. In a short span of time this infrastructure is as difficult to bring into being as is an abundant supply of energy.)

In summary, then, here are the major foreign-aid possibilities that tender minds are willing to entertain:

a. Food plus energy—a conceivable, but practically impossible program.

b. Food alone—a conceivable and possible program, but one which would destroy the recipient.

In the light of this analysis the question of triage shrinks to negligible importance. If *any* gift of food to overpopulated countries does more harm than good, it is not necessary to decide which countries get the gift and which do not. For posterity's sake we should never send food to any population that is beyond the realistic carrying capacity of its land. The question of triage does not even arise....

NOTES

1. Garrett Hardin, 1968: "The Tragedy of the Commons," *Science*, 162: 1243-48.
2. Karl Marx, 1875: "Critique of the Gotha program." (Reprinted in *The Marx-Engels Reader*, Robert C. Tucker, editor. New York: Norton. 1972).
3. Garrett Hardin and John Baden, 1977: *Managing the Commons*. (San Francisco: W.H. Freeman).
4. Thomas Robert Malthus, 1798: *An Essay on the Principle of Population, as It Affects the Future Improvement of Society*. (Reprinted, inter alia, by the University of Michigan Press, 1959, and The Modern Library, 1960).
5. Donella H. Meadows, Dennis L. Meadows, Jorgen Randers, and William H. Behrens, 1972: *The Limits to Growth* (New York: Universe Books).
6. C.P. Snow, 1963: *The Two Cultures; and a Second Look*. (New York: Mentor).
7. Hans Jonas, 1973: "Technology and Responsibility: Reflections on the New Task of Ethics," *Social Research*, 40:31-54.
8. William and Paul Paddock, 1967: *Famine—1975* (Boston: Little, Brown & Co.)
9. Garrett Hardin, 1975: "Gregg's Law," *BioScience*, 25:415.
10. Joseph Fletcher, 1966: *Situation Ethics* (Philadelphia: Westminster Press).
11. Helmut Schoeck, 1969: *Envy* (New York: Harcourt, Brace & World).
12. Garrett Hardin, 1972: *Exploring New Ethics for Survival* (New York: Viking).
13. Nicholas Wade, 1974: "Sahelian Drought: No Victory for Western Aid," *Science*, 185:234-37.
14. Erik P. Eckholm, 1975: "The Deterioration of Mountain Environments," *Science*, 189:764-70.
15. Ancel Keys, et al., 1950: *The Biology of Human Starvation*. 2 vols. (Minneapolis: Unversity of Minnesota Press).

POPULATION: DELUSION AND REALITY

Amartya Sen

Amartya Sen is Principal of Trinity College, Cambridge. He received the 1998 Nobel Prize for Economics. He is the author of Commodities and Capabilities *(Elsevier, 1985) and* Inequality Reexamined *(Cambridge, 1992) and co-editor with Martha Nussbaum of* The Quality of Life *(Oxford, 1993).*

Sen argues that the predictions of impending doom with respect to world population and the arguments on which they are based deserve serious scrutiny because they encourage the tendency to search for emergency solutions that treat people in overpopulated countries as in need of strong social discipline rather than as reasonable beings or allies facing a common problem. Sen rejects both the too optimistic and the too pessimistic accounts of world population and distinguishes two approaches to the population problem. The first is a collaborative approach and involves voluntary choice and a collaborative solution and the second is an override approach and involves overriding voluntary choice through legal or economic coercion. Sen raises objections to the moral justifiability and practicality of the override approach by examining the successes and failures of policies for controlling population in China and India.

1.

Few issues today are as divisive as what is called the "world population problem." With the approach this autumn of the International Conference on Population and Development in Cairo, organized by the United Nations, these divisions among experts are receiving enormous attention and generating considerable heat. There is a danger that in the confrontation between apocalyptic pessimism, on the one hand, and a dismissive smugness, on the other, a genuine understanding of the nature of the population problem may be lost.[1]

Visions of impending doom have been increasingly aired in recent years, often presenting the population problem as a "bomb" that has been planted and is about to "go off." These catastrophic images have encouraged a tendency to search for emergency solutions which treat the people involved not as reasonable beings, allies facing a common problem, but as impulsive and uncontrolled sources of great social harm, in need of strong discipline.

Such views have received serious attention in public discussions, not just in sensational headlines in the popular press, but also in seriously argued and widely read books. One of the most influential examples was Paul Ehrlich's *The Population Bomb*, the first three sections of which were headed "Too Many People," "Too Little Food," and "A Dying Planet."[2] A more recent example of a chilling diagnoses of imminent calamity is Garrett Hardin's *Living within Limits*.[3] The arguments on which these pessimistic visions are based deserve serious scrutiny.

If the propensity to foresee impending disaster from overpopulation is strong in some circles, so is the tendency, in others, to dismiss all worries about population size. Just as alarmism builds on the recognition of a real problem and then magnifies it, complacency may also start off from a reasonable belief about the history of population problems and fail to see how they may have changed by now. It is

Reprinted with permission from *The New York Review of Books* (22 September 1994): 62–71.

often pointed out, for example, that the world has coped well enough with fast increases in population in the past, even though alarmists had expected otherwise. Malthus anticipated terrible disasters resulting from population growth and a consequent imbalance in "the proportion between the natural increase of population and food."[4] At a time when there were fewer than a billion people, he was quite convinced that "the period when the number of men surpass their means of subsistence has long since arrived." However, since Malthus first published his famous *Essay on Population* in 1798, the world population has grown nearly six times larger, while food output and consumption per person are considerably higher now, and there has been an unprecedented increase both in life expectancies and in general living standards.[5]

The fact that Malthus was mistaken in his diagnosis as well as his prognosis two hundred years ago does not, however, indicate that contemporary fears about population growth must be similarly erroneous. The increase in the world population has vastly accelerated over the last century. It took the world population millions of years to reach the first billion, then 123 years to get to the second, 33 years to the third, 14 years to the fourth, 13 years to the fifth billion, with a sixth billion to come, according to one UN projection, in another 11 years.[6] During the last decade, between 1980 and 1990, the number of people on earth grew by about 923 million, an increase nearly the size of the total world population in Malthus's time. Whatever may be the proper response to alarmism about the future, complacency based on past success is no response at all.

Immigration and Population

One current worry concerns the regional distribution of the increase in world population, about 90 percent of which is taking place in the developing countries. The percentage rate of population growth is fastest in Africa—3.1 percent per year over the last decade. But most of the large increases in population occur in regions other than Africa. The largest absolute increases in numbers are taking place in Asia, which is where most of the world's poorer people live, even though the rate of increase in population has been slowing significantly there. Of the worldwide increase of 923 million people in the 1980s, well over half occurred in Asia—517 million in fact (including 146 million in China and 166 million in India).

Beyond concerns about the wellbeing of these poor countries themselves, a more self-regarding worry causes panic in the richer countries of the world and has much to do with the current anxiety in the West about the "world population problem." This is founded on the belief that destitution caused by fast population growth in the third world is responsible for the severe pressure to emigrate to the developed countries of Europe and North America. In this view, people impoverished by overpopulation in the "South" flee to the "North." Some have claimed to find empirical support for this thesis in the fact that pressure to emigrate from the South has accelerated in recent decades, along with a rapid increase in the population there.

There are two distinct questions here: first, how great a threat of intolerable immigration pressure does the North face from the South, and second, is that pressure closely related to population growth in the South, rather than to other social and economic factors? There are reasons to doubt that population growth is the major force behind migratory pressures, and I shall concentrate here on that question. But I should note in passing that immigration is now severely controlled in Europe and North America, and insofar as Europe is concerned, most of the current immigrants from the third world are not "primary" immigrants but dependent relatives—mainly spouses and young children—of those who had come and settled earlier. The United States remains relatively more open to fresh immigration, but the requirements of "labor certification" as a necessary part of the immigration procedure tend to guarantee that the new entrants are relatively better educated and more skilled. There are, however, sizable flows of illegal immigrants, especially to the United States and to a lesser extent to southern Europe, though the numbers are hard to estimate.

What causes the current pressures to emigrate? The "job-worthy" people who get through the immigration process are hardly to be seen as impoverished and destitute migrants created by the sheer pressure of population. Even the illegal immigrants who manage to evade the rigors of border control are typically not starving wretches but those who can make use of work prospects in the North.

The explanation for the increased migratory pressure over the decades owes more to the dynamism of international capitalism than to just the growing size of the population of the third world countries. The immigrants have allies in potential employers, and this applies as much to illegal farm laborers in California as to the legally authorized "guest workers" in automobile factories in Germany. The economic incentive to emigrate to the North from the poorer Southern economies may well depend on differences in real income. But this gap is very large anyway, and even if it is presumed that population growth in the South is increasing the disparity with the North—a thesis I shall presently consider—it seems unlikely that this incentive would significantly change if the Northern income level were, say, twenty times that of the Southern as opposed to twenty-five times.

The growing demand for immigration to the North from the South is related to the "shrinking" of the world (through revolutions in communication and transport), reduction in economic obstacles to labor movements (despite the increase in political barriers), and the growing reach and absorptive power of international capitalism (even as domestic politics in the North has turned more inward-looking and nationalistic). To try to explain the increase in immigration pressure by the growth rate of total population in the third world is to close one's eyes to the deep changes that have occurred—and are occurring—in the world in which we live, and the rapid internationalization of its cultures and economies that accompanies these changes.

Fears of Being Engulfed

A closely related issue concerns what is perceived as a growing "imbalance" in the division of the world population, with a rapidly rising share belonging to the third world. That fear translates into worries of various kinds in the North, especially the sense of being overrun by the South. Many Northerners fear being engulfed by people from Asia and Africa, whose share of the world population increased from 63.7 percent in 1950 to 71.2 percent by 1990, and is expected, according to the estimates of the United Nations, to rise to 78.5 percent by 2050 AD.

It is easy to understand the fears of relatively well-off people at the thought of being surrounded by a fast growing and increasingly impoverished Southern population. As I shall argue, the thesis of growing impoverishment does not stand up to much scrutiny; but it is important to address first the psychologically tense issue of racial balance in the world (even though racial composition as a consideration has only as much importance as we choose to give it). Here it is worth recollecting that the third world is right now going through the same kind of demographic shift—a rapid expansion of population for a temporary but long stretch—that Europe and North America experienced during their industrial revolution. In 1650 the share of Asia and Africa in the world population is estimated to have been 78.4 percent, and it stayed around there even in 1750.[7] With the industrial revolution, the share of Asia and Africa diminished because of the rapid rise of population in Europe and North America; for example, during the nineteenth century while the inhabitants of Asia and Africa grew by about 4 percent per decade or less, the population of "the area of European settlement" grew by around 10 percent every decade.

Even now the combined share of Asia and Africa (71.2 percent) is considerably below what its share was in 1650 or 1750. If the United Nations' prediction that this share will rise to 78.5 percent by 2050 comes true, then the Asians and the Africans would return to being proportionately almost exactly as numerous as they were before the European industrial revolution. There is, of course, nothing sacrosanct about the distributions of population in the past; but the sense of a growing "imbalance" in the world, based only on recent trends, ignores history and implicitly presumes that the expansion of Europeans earlier on was natural, whereas the same process happening now to other populations unnaturally disturbs the "balance."

Collaboration versus Override

Other worries involving the relation of population growth to food supplies, income levels, and the environment reflect more serious matters.[8] Before I take up those questions, a brief comment on the distinction between two rival approaches to dealing with the population problem may be useful. One involves voluntary choice and a collaborative solution, and the other overrides voluntarism through legal or economic coercion.

Alarmist views of impending crises tend to produce a willingness to consider forceful measures for coercing people to have fewer children in the third world. Imposing birth control on unwilling people is no longer rejected as readily as it was until quite recently, and some activists have pointed to the ambiguities that exist in determining what is or is not "coercion."[9] Those who are willing to consider—or at least not fully reject—programs that would use some measure of force to reduce population growth often point to the success of China's "one child policy" in cutting down the national birth rate. Force can also take an indirect form, as when economic opportunities are changed so radically by government regulations that people are left with very little choice except to behave in ways the government would approve. In China's case, the government may refuse to offer housing to families with too many children—thus penalizing the children as well as the dissenting adults.

In India the policy of compulsory birth control that was initiated during the "emergency period" declared by Mrs. Gandhi in the 1970s was decisively rejected by the voters in the general election in which it—along with civil rights—was a major issue. Even so, some public health clinics in the northern states (such as Uttar Pradesh) insist, in practice, on sterilization before providing normal medical attention to women and men beyond a certain age. The pressures to move in that direction seem to be strong, and they are reinforced by the rhetoric of "the population bomb."

I shall call this general approach the "override" view, since the family's personal decisions are overridden by some agency outside the family—typically by the government of the country in question (whether or not it has been pressed to do so by "outside" agencies, such as international organizations and pressure groups). In fact, overriding is not limited to an explicit use of legal coercion or economic compulsion, since people's own choices can also be effectively overridden by simply not offering them the opportunities for jobs or welfare that they can expect to get from a responsible government. Override can take many different forms and can be of varying intensity (with the Chinese "one child policy" being something of an extreme case of a more general approach).

A central issue here is the increasingly vocal demand by some activists concerned with population growth that the highest "priority" should be given in third world countries to family planning over other public commitments. This demand goes much beyond supporting family planning as a part of development. In fact, proposals for shifting international aid away from development in general to family planning in particular have lately been increasingly frequent. Such policies fit into the general approach of "override" as well, since they try to rely on manipulating people's choices through offering them only some opportunities (the means of family planning) while denying others, no matter what they would have themselves preferred. Insofar as they would have the effect of reducing health care and educational services, such shifts in public commitments will not only add to the misery of human lives, they may also have, I shall argue, exactly the opposite effect on family planning than the one intended, since education and health care have a significant part in the *voluntary* reduction of the birth rate.

The "override" approach contrasts with another, the "collaborative" approach, that relies not on legal or economic restrictions but on rational decisions of women and men, based on expanded choices and enhanced security, and encouraged by open dialogue and extensive public discussions. The difference between the two approaches does not lie in government's activism in the first case as opposed to passivity in the second. Even if solutions are sought through the decisions and actions of people themselves, the chance to take reasoned decisions with more knowledge and a greater sense of personal security can be increased by public policies, for example, through expanding educational facilities, health care, and economic wellbeing, along with providing better access to family planning. The central political and ethical issue concerning the "override" approach does not lie in its insistence on the need for public policy but in the ways it significantly reduces the choices open to parents.

The Malthus-Condorcet Debate

Thomas Robert Malthus forcefully argued for a version of the "override" view. In fact, it was precisely this preference that distinguished Malthus from Condorcet, the eighteenth-century French mathematician and social scientist from whom Malthus had actually derived the analysis of how population could outgrow the means of living. The debate between Condorcet and Malthus in some ways marks the origin of the distinction between the "collaborative" and the "override" approaches, which still compete for attention.[10]

In his *Essay on Population*, published in 1798, Malthus quoted—extensively and with approval—Condorcet's discussion, in 1795, of the possibility of overpopulation. However, true to the Enlightenment tradition, Condorcet was confident that this problem would be solved by reasoned human action: through increases in productivity, through better conservation and prevention of waste, and through education (especially female education) which would contribute to reducing the birth rate.[11] Voluntary family planning would be encouraged, in Condorcet's analysis, by increased understanding that if people "have a duty toward those who are not yet born, that duty is not to give them existence but to give them happiness." They would see the value of limiting family size "rather than foolishly ... encumber the world with useless and wretched beings."[12]

Even though Malthus borrowed from Condorcet his diagnosis of the possibility of overpopulation, he refused to accept Condorcet's solution. Indeed, Malthus's essay on population was partly a criticism of Condorcet's enlightenment reasoning, and even the full title of Malthus's famous essay specifically mentioned Condorcet. Malthus argued that

> there is no reason whatever to suppose that anything beside the difficulty of procuring in adequate plenty the necessaries of life should either *indispose* this greater number of persons to marry early, or *disable* them from rearing in health the largest families.[13]

Malthus thus opposed public relief of poverty: he saw the "poor laws" in particular as contributing greatly to population growth.[14]

Malthus was not sure that any public policy would work, and whether "overriding" would in fact be possible: "The perpetual tendency in the race of man to increase beyond the means of subsistence is one of the great general laws of animated nature which we can have no reason to expect will change."[15] But insofar as any solution would be possible, it could not come from voluntary decisions of the people involved, or acting from a position of strength and economic security. It must come from overriding their preferences through the compulsions of economic necessity, since their poverty was the only thing that could "indispose the greater number of persons to marry early, or disable them from rearing in health the largest families."

Development and Increased Choice

The distinction between the "collaborative" approach and the "override" approach thus tends to correspond closely to the contrast between, on the one hand, treating economic and social development as the way to solve the population problem and, on the other, expecting little from development and using, instead, legal and economic pressures to reduce birth rates. Among recent writers, those such as Gerard Piel[16] who have persuasively emphasized our ability to solve problems through reasoned decisions and actions have tended—like Condorcet—to find the solution of the population problem in economic and social development. They advocate a broadly collaborative approach, in which governments and citizens would together produce economic and social conditions favoring slower population growth. In contrast, those who have been throughly skeptical of reasoned human action to limit population growth have tended to go in the direction of "override" in one form or another, rather than concentrate on development and voluntarism.

Has development, in fact, done much to reduce population growth? There can be little doubt that economic and social development, in general, has been associated with major reductions in birth rates and the emergence of smaller families as the norm.

This is a pattern that was, of course, clearly observed in Europe and North America as they underwent industrialization, but that experience has been repeated in many other parts of the world.

In particular, conditions of economic security and affluence, wider availability of contraceptive methods, expansion of education (particularly female education), and lower mortality rates have had—and are currently having—quite substantial effects in reducing birth rates in different parts of the world.[17] The rate of world population growth is certainly declining, and even over the last two decades its percentage growth rate has fallen from 2.2 percent per year between 1970 and 1980 to 1.7 percent between 1980 and 1992. This rate is expected to go steadily down until the size of the world's population becomes nearly stationary.[18]

There are important regional differences in demographic behavior; for example, the population growth rate in India peaked at 2.2 percent a year (in the 1970s) and has since started to diminish, whereas most Latin American countries peaked at much higher rates before coming down sharply, while many countries in Africa currently have growth rates between 3 and 4 percent, with an average for sub-Saharan Africa of 3.1 percent. Similarly, the different factors have varied in their respective influence from region to region. But there can be little dispute that economic and social development tends to reduce fertility rates. The regions of the third world that lag most in achieving economic and social development, such as many countries in Africa, are, in general, also the ones that have failed to reduce birth rates significantly, Malthus's fear that economic and social development could only encourage people to have more children has certainly proved to be radically wrong, and so have all the painful policy implications drawn from it.

This raises the following question: in view of the clear connection between development and lower fertility, why isn't the dispute over how to deal with population growth fully resolved already? Why don't we reinterpret the population problem simply as a problem of underdevelopment and seek a solution by encouraging economic and social development (even if we reject the oversimple slogan "development is the most reliable contraceptive")?

In the long run, this may indeed be exactly the right approach. The problem is more complex, however, because a "contraceptive" that is "reliable" in the long run may not act fast enough to meet the present threat. Even though development may dependably work to stabilize population if it is given enough time, there may not be, it is argued, time enough to give. The death rate often falls very fast with more widely available health care, better sanitation, and improved nutrition, while the birth rate may fall rather slowly. Much growth of population may meanwhile occur.

This is exactly the point at which apocalyptic prophecies add force to the "override" view. One claim, then, that needs examination is that the world is facing an imminent crisis, one so urgent that development is just too slow a process to deal with it. We must try right now, the argument goes, to cut down population growth by drastic and forceful means if necessary. The second claim that also needs scrutiny is the actual feasibility of adequately reducing population growth through these drastic means, without fostering social and economic development.

2.

Population and Income

It is sometimes argued that signs of an imminent crisis can be found in the growing impoverishment of the South, with falling income per capita accompanying high population growth. In general, there is little evidence for this. As a matter of fact, the average population of "low-income" countries (as defined by the World Bank) has been not only enjoying a rising gross national product (GNP) per head, but a growth rate of GNP per capita (3.9 percent per year for 1980-1992) that is much faster than those for the "high-income" countries (2.4 percent) and for the "middle-income" ones (0 percent).[19]

The growth of per capita GNP of the population of low-income countries would have been even higher had it not been for the negative growth rates of many countries in sub-Saharan Africa, one region in which a number of countries have been experiencing economic decline. But the main culprit causing this state of affairs is the terrible failure of economic production in sub-Saharan Africa (connected particularly with political disruption, including wars and military rule), rather than population growth, which is only a subsidiary factor. Sub-Saharan Africa does have high population growth, but its economic stagnation has contributed much more to the fall in its per-capita income.

With its average population growth rate of 3.1 percent per year, had sub-Saharan Africa suddenly matched China's low population growth of 1.4 percent (the lowest among the low-income countries), it would have gained roughly 1.7 percent in per-capita GNP growth. The real income per person would still have fallen, even with that minimal population growth, for many countries in the region. The growth of GNP per capita is *minus* 1.9 percent for Ethiopia, *minus* 1.8 percent for Togo, *minus* 3.6 percent for Mozambique, *minus* 4.3 percent for Niger, *minus* 4.7 percent for Ivory Coast, not to mention Somalia, Sudan, and Angola, where the political disruption has been so serious that no reliable GNP estimates even exist. A lower population growth rate could have reduced the magnitude of the fall in per capita GNP, but the main roots of Africa's economic decline lie elsewhere. The complex political factors underlying the troubles of Africa include, among other things, the subversion of democracy and the rise of combative military rulers, often encouraged by the cold war (with Africa providing "client states"—from Somalia and Ethiopia to Angola and Zaire—for the superpowers, particularly from the 1960s onward). The explanation of sub-Saharan Africa's problems has to be sought in these political troubles, which affect economic stability, agricultural and industrial incentives, public health arrangements, and social services—even family planning and population policy.[20]

There is indeed a very powerful case for reducing the rate of growth of population in Africa, but this problem cannot be dissociated from the rest of the continent's woes. Sub-Saharan Africa lags behind other developing regions in economic security, in health care, in life expectancy, in basic education, and in political and economic stability. It should be no great surprise that it lags behind in family planning as well. To dissociate the task of population control from the politics and economics of Africa would be a great mistake and would seriously mislead public policy.

Population and Food

Malthus's exact thesis cannot, however, be disputed by quoting statistics of income per capita, for he was concerned specifically with food supply per capita, and he had concentrated on "the proportion between the natural increase of population and food." Many modern commentators, including Paul Ehrlich and Garrett Hardin, have said much about this, too. When Ehrlich says, in his *Population Bomb*, "too little food," he does not mean "too little income," but specifically a growing shortage of food.

Is population beginning to outrun food production? Even though such an impression is often given in public discussions, there is, in fact, no serious evidence that this is happening. While there are some year-to-year fluctuations in the growth of food output (typically inducing, whenever things slacken a bit, some excited remarks by those who anticipate an impending doom), the worldwide trend of food output per person has been firmly upward. Not only over the two centuries since Malthus's time, but also during recent decades, the rise in food output has been significantly and consistently outpacing the expansion of world population.[21]

But the total food supply in the world as a whole is not the only issue. What about the regional distribution of food? If it were to turn out that the rising ratio of food to population is mainly caused by increased production in richer countries (for example, if it appeared that US wheat output was feeding the third world, in which much of the population expansion is taking place), then the neo-Malthusian fears about "too many people" and "too little food" may have some plausibility. Is this what is happening?

In fact, with one substantial exception, exactly the opposite is true. The largest increases in the production of food—not just in the aggregate but also per person—are actually taking place in the third world, particularly in the region that is having the largest absolute increases in the world population, that is, in Asia. The many millions of people who are added to the populations of India and China may be constantly cited by the terrorized—and terrorizing—advocates of the apocalyptic view, but it is precisely in these countries that the most rapid rates of growth in food output per capita are to be observed. For example, between the three-year averages of 1979-1981 and 1991-1993, food production per head in the world moved up by 3 percent, while it went up by only 2 percent in Europe and went down by nearly 5 percent in North America. In contrast, per capita food production jumped up by 22 percent in Asia generally, including 23 percent in Asia generally, including 23 percent in India and 39 percent in China.[22] (See Table 1.)

TABLE 1 Indices of Food Production Per Capita

	1979-1981 Base Period	1991-1993
World	100	103
Europe	100	102
North America	100	95
Africa	100	94
Asia	100	122
including		
India	100	123
China	100	139

Source: *FAO Quarterly Bulletin of Statistics*

During the same period, however, food production per capita went down by 6 percent in Africa, and even the absolute size of food output fell in some countries (such as Malawi and Somalia). Of course, many countries in the world—from Syria, Italy, and Sweden to Botswana in Africa—have had declining food production per head without experiencing hunger or starvation since their economies have prospered and grown; when the means are available, food can be easily bought in the international market if it is necessary to do so. For many countries in sub-Saharan Africa the problem arises from the fact that the decline in food production is an integral part of the story of overall economic decline, which I have discussed earlier.

Difficulties of food production in sub-Saharan Africa, like other problems of the national economy, are not only linked to wars, dictatorships, and political chaos. In addition, there is some evidence that climatic shifts have had unfavorable effects on parts of that continent. While some of the climatic problems may be caused partly by increases in human settlement and environmental neglect, that neglect is not unrelated to the political and economic chaos that has characterized sub-Saharan Africa during the last few decades. The food problem of Africa must be seen as one part of a wider political and economic problem of the region.[23]

The Price of Food

To return to "the balance between food and population," the rising food production per capita in the world as a whole, and in the third world in general, contradicts some of the pessimism that characterized the gloomy predictions of the past. Prophecies of imminent disaster during the last few decades have not proved any more accurate than Malthus's prognostication nearly two hundred years ago. As for new prophecies of doom, they cannot, of course, be contradicted until the future arrives. There was no way of refuting the theses of W. Paddock and P. Paddock's popular book *Famine—1975!*, published in 1968, which predicted a terrible cataclysm for the world as a whole by 1975 (writing off India, in particular, as a basket case), until 1975 actually arrived. The new prophets have learned not to attach specific dates to the crises they foresee, and past failures do not seem to have reduced the popular appetite for this creative genre.

However, after noting the rather dismal forecasting record of doomsayers, we must also accept the general methodological point that present trends in output do not necessarily tell us much about the prospects of further expansion in the future. It could, for example, be argued that maintaining growth in food production may require proportionately increasing investments of capital, drawing them away from other kinds of production. This would tend to make food progressively more expensive if there are "diminishing returns" in shifting resources from other fields into food production. And, ultimately, further expansion of food production may become so expensive that it would be hard to maintain the trend of increasing food production without reducing other outputs drastically.

But is food production really getting more and more expensive? There is, in fact, no evidence for that conclusion either. In fact, quite the contrary. Not only is food generally much cheaper to buy today, in constant dollars, than it was in Malthus's time, but it also has become cheaper during recent decades. As a matter of fact, there have been increasing complaints among food exporters, especially in the third world, that food prices have fallen in relation to other commodities. For example, in 1992 a United Nations report recorded a 38 percent fall in the relative prices of "basic foods" over the last decade.[24] This is entirely in line with the trend, during the last three decades, toward declining relative prices of manufactured goods. The World Bank's adjusted estimates of the prices of particular food crops, between 1953-1955 and 1983-1985, show similarly steep declines for such staples as rice (42 percent), wheat (57 percent), sorghum (39 percent), and maize (37 percent).[25]

Not only is food getting less expensive, but we also have to bear in mind that the current increase in food production (substantial and well ahead of population growth, as it is) is itself being kept in check by the difficulties in selling food profitably, as the relative prices of food have fallen. Those neo-Malthusians who concede that food production is now growing faster than population often point out that it is growing "only a little faster than population," and they are inclined to interpret this as evidence that we are reaching the limits of what we can produce to keep pace with population growth.

But that is surely the wrong conclusion to draw in view of the falling relative prices of food, and the current difficulties in selling food, since it ignores the effects of economic incentives that govern production. When we take into account the persistent cheapening of food prices, we have good grounds to suggest that food output is being held back by a lack of effective demand in the market. The imaginary crisis in food production, contradicted as it is by the upward trends of total and regional food output per head, is thus further debunked by an analysis of the economic incentives to produce more food.

Deprived Lives and Slums

I have examined the alleged "food problem" associated with population growth in some detail because it has received so much attention both in the traditional Malthusian literature and in the recent writings of neo-Malthusians. In concentrating on his claim that growing populations would not have enough food, Malthus differed from Condorcet's broader presentation of the population question. Condorcet's own emphasis was on the possibility of "a continual diminution of happiness" as a result of population growth, a diminution that could occur in many different ways—not just through the deprivation of food, but through a decline in living conditions generally. That more extensive worry can remain even when Malthus's analysis of the food supply is rejected.

Indeed, average income and food production per head can go on increasing even as the wretchedly deprived living conditions of particular sections of the population get worse, as they have in many parts of the third world. The living conditions of backward regions and deprived classes can decline even when a country's economic growth is very rapid on the average. Brazil during the 1960s and 1970s provided an extreme example of this. The sense that there are just "too many people" around often arises from seeing the desperate lives of people in the large and rapidly growing urban slums—*bidonvilles*—in poor countries, sobering reminders that we should not take too much comfort from aggregate statistics of economic progress.

But in an essay addressed mainly to the population problem, what we have to ask is not whether things are just fine in the third world (they obviously are not), but whether population growth is the root cause of the deprivations that people suffer. The question is whether the particular instances of deep poverty we observe derive mainly from population growth rather than from other factors that lead to unshared prosperity and persistent and possibly growing inequality. The tendency to see in population growth an explanation for every calamity that afflicts poor people is now fairly well established in some circles, and the message that gets transmitted constantly is the opposite of the old picture postcard: "Wish you weren't here."

To see in population growth the main reason for the growth of over-crowded and very poor slums in large cities, for example, is not empirically convincing. It does not help to explain why the slums of Calcutta and Bombay have grown worse at a faster rate than those of Karachi and Islamabad (India's population growth rate is 2.1 percent per year, Pakistan's 3.1), or why Jakarta has deteriorated faster than Ankara or Istanbul (Indonesian population growth is 1.8 percent, Turkey's 2.3), or why the slums of Mexico City have become worse more rapidly than those of San José (Mexico's population growth rate is 2.0, Costa Rica's 2.8), or why Harlem can seem more and more deprived when compared with the poorer districts of Singapore (US population growth rate is 1.0, Singapore's is 1.8). Many causal factors affect the degree of deprivation in particular parts of a country—rural as well as urban—and to try to see them all as resulting from over-population is the negation of social analysis.

This is not to deny that population growth may well have an effect on deprivation, but only to insist that any investigation of the effects of population growth must be part of the analysis of economic and political processes, including the effects of other variables. It is the isolationist view of population growth that should be rejected.

Threats to the Environment

In his concern about "a continual diminution of happiness" from population growth, Condorcet was a pioneer in considering the possibility that natural raw materials might be used up, thereby making living conditions worse. In his characteristically rationalist solution, which relied partly on voluntary and reasoned measures to reduce the birth rate, Condorcet also envisaged the development of less improvident technology: "The manufacture of articles will be achieved with less wastage in raw materials and will make better use of them"[26]

The effects of a growing population on the environment could be a good deal more serious than the food problems that have received so much attention in the literature inspired by Malthus. If the environment is damaged by population pressures this obviously affects the kind of life we lead, and the possibilities of a "diminution in happiness" can be quite considerable. In dealing with this problem, we have to distinguish once again between the long and the short run. The short-run picture tends to be dominated by the fact that the per-capita consumption of food, fuel, and other goods by people in third world countries is often relatively low; consequently the impact of population growth in these countries is not, in relative terms, so damaging to the global environment. But the problems of the local environment can, of course, be serious in many developing economies. They vary from the "neighborhood pollution" created by unregulated industries to the pressure of denser populations on rural resources such as fields and woods.[27] (The Indian authorities had to close down several factories in and around Agra, since the façade of the Taj Mahal was turning pale as a result of chemical pollution from local factories.) But it remains true that one additional American typically has a larger negative impact on the ozone layer, global warmth, and other elements of the earth's environment than dozens of Indians and Zimbabweans put together. Those who argue for the immediate need for forceful population control in the third world to preserve the global environment must first recognize this elementary fact.

This does not imply, as is sometimes suggested, that as far as the global environment is concerned, population growth in the third world is nothing to worry about. The long-run impact on the global environment of population growth in the developing countries can be expected to be large. As the Indians and the Zimbabweans develop economically, they too will consume a great deal more, and they will pose, in the future, a threat to the earth's environment similar to that of people in the rich countries today. The long-run threat of population to the environment is a real one.

3.

Women's Deprivation and Power

Since reducing the birth rate can be slow, this and other long-run problems should be addressed right now. Solutions will no doubt have to be found in the two directions to which, as it happens, Condorcet pointed: (1) developing new technology and new behavior patterns that would waste little and pollute less, and (2) fostering social and economic changes that would gradually bring down the growth rate of population.

On reducing birth rates, Condorcet's own solution not only included enhancing economic opportunity and security, but also stressed the importance of education, particularly female education. A better-educated population could have a more informed discussion of the kind of life we have reason to value; in particular it would reject the drudgery of a life of continuous child bearing and rearing that is routinely forced on many third world women. That drudgery, in some ways, is the most immediately adverse consequence of high fertility rates.

Central to reducing birth rates, then, is a close connection between women's well-being and their power to make their own decisions and bring about changes in the fertility pattern. Women in many third world countries are deprived by high birth frequency of the freedom to do other things in life, not to mention the medical dangers of repeated pregnancy and high maternal mortality, which are both characteristic of many developing countries. It is thus not surprising that reductions in birth rates have been typically associated with improvement of women's status and their ability to make their voices heard—often the result of expanded opportunities for schooling and political activity.[28]

There is nothing particularly exotic about declines in the birth rate occurring through a process of voluntary rational assessment, of which Condorcet spoke. It is what people do when they have some basic education, know about family planning methods and have access to them, do not readily accept a life of persistent drudgery, and are not deeply anxious about their economic security. It is also what they do when they are not forced by high infant and child mortality rates to be so worried that no child will survive to support them in their old age that they try to have many children. In country after country the birth rate has come down with more female education, the reduction of mortality rates, the expansion of economic means and security, and greater public discussion of ways of living.

Development versus Coercion

There is little doubt that this process of social and economic change will over time cut down the birth rate. Indeed the growth rate of world population is already firmly declining—it came down from 2.2 percent in the 1970s to 1.7 percent between 1980 and 1992. Had imminent cataclysm been threatening, we might have had good reason to reject such gradual progress and consider more drastic means of population control, as some have advocated. But that apocalyptic view is empirically baseless. There is no imminent emergency that calls for a breathless response. What is called for is systematic support for people's own decisions to reduce family size through expanding education and health care, and through economic and social development.

It is often asked where the money needed for expanding education, health care, etc., would be found. Education, health services, and many other means of improving the quality of life are typically highly labor-intensive and are thus relatively inexpensive in poor countries (because of low wages).[29] While poor countries have less money to spend, they also need less money to provide these services. For this reason many poor countries have indeed been able to expand educational and health services widely without waiting to become prosperous through the process of economic growth. Sri Lanka, Costa Rica, Indonesia, and Thailand are good examples, and there are many others. While the impact of these social services on the quality and length of life have been much studied, they are also major means of reducing the birth rate.

By contrast with such open and voluntary developments, coercive methods, such as the "one child policy" in some regions, have been tried in China, particularly since the reforms of 1979. Many commentators have pointed out that by 1992 the Chinese birth rate has fallen to 19 per 1,000, compared with 29 per 1,000 in India, and 37 per 1,000 for the average of poor countries other than China and India. China's total fertility rate (reflecting the number of children born per woman) is now at "the replacement level" of 2.0, compared with India's 3.6 and the weighted average of 4.9 for low-income countries other than China and India.[30] Hasn't China shown the way to "solve" the population problem in other developing countries as well?

4.

China's Population Policies

The difficulties with this "solution" are of several kinds. First, if freedom is valued at all, the lack of freedom associated with this approach must be seen to be a social loss in itself. The importance of reproductive freedom has been persuasively emphasized by women's groups throughout the world.[31]

The loss of freedom is often dismissed on the grounds that because of cultural differences, authoritarian policies that would not be tolerated in the West are acceptable to Asians. While we often hear references to "despotic" Oriental traditions, such arguments are no more convincing than a claim that compulsion in the West is justified by the traditions of the Spanish Inquisition or of the Nazi concentration camps. Frequent references are also made to the emphasis on discipline in the "Confucian tradition"; but that is not the only tradition in the "East," nor is it easy to assess the implications of that tradition for modern Asia (even if we were able to show that discipline is more important for Confucius than it is for, say, Plato or Saint Augustine).

Only a democratic expression of opinion could reveal whether citizens would find a compulsory system acceptable. While such a test has not occurred in China, one did in fact take place in India during "the emergency period" in the 1970s, when Indira Gandhi's government imposed compulsory birth control and suspended various legal freedoms. In the general elections that followed, the politicians favoring the policy of coercion were overwhelmingly defeated. Furthermore, family planning experts in India have observed how the briefly applied programs of compulsory sterilization tended to discredit voluntary birth control programs generally, since people became deeply suspicious of the entire movement to control fertility.

Second, apart from the fundamental issue of whether people are willing to accept compulsory birth control, its specific consequences must also be considered. Insofar as coercion is effective, it works by making people do things they would not freely do. The social consequences of such compulsion, including the ways in which an unwilling population tends to react when it is coerced, can be appalling. For example, the demands of a "one-child family" can lead to the neglect—or worse—of a second child, thereby increasing the infant mortality rate. Moreover, in a country with a strong preference for male children—a preference shared by China and many other countries in Asia and North Africa—a policy of allowing only one child per family can easily lead to the fatal neglect of a female child. There is much evidence that this is fairly widespread in China, with very adverse effects on infant mortality rates. There are reports that female children have been severely neglected as well as suggestions that female infanticide occurs with considerable frequency. Such consequences are hard to tolerate morally, and perhaps politically also, in the long run.

Third, what is also not clear is exactly how much additional reduction in the birth rate has been achieved through these coercive methods. Many of China's longstanding social and economic programs have been valuable in reducing fertility, including those that have expanded education for women as well as men, made health care more generally available, provided more job opportunities for women, and stimulated rapid economic growth. These factors would themselves have reduced the birth rates, and it is not clear how much "extra lowering" of fertility rates has been achieved in China through compulsion.

For example, we can determine whether many of the countries that match (or outmatch) China in life expectancy, female literacy rates, and female participation in the labor force actually have a higher fertility rate than China. Of all the countries in the world for which data are given in the *World Development Report 1994*, there are only three such countries: Jamaica (2.7), Thailand (2.2), and Sweden (2.1)—and the fertility rates of two of these are close to China's (2.0). Thus the additional contribution of coercion to reducing fertility in China is by no means clear, since compulsion was superimposed on a society that was already reducing its birth rate and in which education and jobs outside the home were available to large numbers of women. In some regions of China the compulsory program needed little enforcement, whereas in other—more backward—regions, it had to be applied with much severity, with terrible consequences in infant mortality and discrimination against female children. While China may get too much credit for its authoritarian measures, it gets far too little credit for the other, more collaborative and participatory, policies it has followed, which have themselves helped to cut down the birth rate.

China and India

A useful contrast can be drawn between China and India, the two most populous countries in the world. If we look only at the national averages, it is easy to see that China with its low fertility rate of 2.0 has achieved much more than India has with its average fertility rate of 3.6. To what extent this contrast can be attributed to the effectiveness of the coercive policies used in China is not clear, since we would expect the fertility rate to be much lower in China in view of its higher percentage of female literacy (almost twice as high), higher life expectancy (almost ten years more), larger female involvement (by three quarters) in the labor force, and so on. But India is a country of great diversity, whose different states have very unequal achievements in literacy, health care, and economic and social development. Most states in India are far behind the Chinese provinces in educational achievement (with the exception of Tibet, which has the lowest literacy rate of any Chinese or Indian state), and the same applies to other factors that affect fertility. However, the state of Kerala in southern India provides an interesting comparison with China, since it too has high levels of basic education, health care, and so on. Kerala is a state within a country, but with its 29 million people, it is larger than most countries in the world (including Canada). Kerala's birth rate of 18 per 1,000 is actually lower than China's 19 per 1,000, and its fertility rate is 1.8 for 1991, compared with China's 2.0 for 1992. These low rates have been achieved without any state coercion.[32]

The roots of Kerala's success are to be found in the kinds of social progress Condorcet hoped for, including among others, a high female literacy rate (86 percent, which is substantially higher than China's 68 percent). The rural literacy rate is in fact higher in Kerala—for women as well as men—than in every single province in China. Male and female life expectancies at birth in China are respectively 67 and 71 years; the provisional 1991 figures for men and women in Kerala are 71 and 74 years. Women have been active in Kerala's economic and political life for a long time. A high proportion do skilled and semi-skilled work and a large number have taken part in educational movements.[33] It is perhaps of symbolic importance that the first public pronouncement of the need for widespread elementary education in any part of India was made in 1817 by Rani Gouri Parvathi Bai, the young queen of the princely state of Travancore, which makes up a substantial part of modern Kerala. For a long time public discussions in Kerala have centered on women's rights and the undesirability of couples marrying when very young.

This political process has been voluntary and collaborative, rather than coercive, and the adverse reactions that have been observed in China, such as infant mortality, have not occurred in Kerala. Kerala's low fertility rate has been achieved along with an infant mortality rate of 16.5 per 1,000 live births (17 for boys and 16 for girls), compared with China's 31 (28 for boys and 33 for girls). And as a result of greater gender equality in Kerala, women have not suffered from higher mortality rates than men in Kerala, as they have in the rest of India and in China. Even the ratio of females to males in the total population in Kerala (above 1.03) is quite close to that of the current ratios in Europe and America (reflecting the usual pattern of lower female mortality whenever women and men received similar care). By contrast, the average female to male ratio in China is 0.94 and in India as a whole 0.93.[34] Anyone drawn to the Chinese experience of compulsory birth control must take note of these facts.

The temptation to use the "override" approach arises at least partly from impatience with the allegedly slow process of fertility reduction through collaborative, rather than coercive, attempts. Yet Kerala's birth rate has fallen from 44 per 1,000 in the 1950s to 18 by 1991—not a sluggish decline. Nor is Kerala unique in this respect. Other societies, such as those of Sri Lanka, South Korea, and Thailand, which have relied on expanding education and reducing mortality rates—instead of on coercion—have also achieved sharp declines in fertility and birth rate.

It is also interesting to compare the time required for reducing fertility in China with that in the two states in India, Kerala and Tamil Nadu, which have done most to encourage voluntary and collaborative reduction in birth rates (even though Tamil Nadu is well behind Kerala in each respect).[35] Table 2 shows the fertility rates both in 1979, when the one-child policy and related programs were introduced in China, and in 1991. Despite China's one-child policy and other coercive measures, its fertility rate seems to have fallen much less sharply than those of Kerala and Tamil Nadu. The "override" view is very hard to defend on the basis of the Chinese experience, the only systematic and sustained attempt to impose such a policy that has so far been made.

TABLE 2 Fertility Rates in China, Kerala, and Tamil Nadu

	1979	1991
China	2.8	2.0
Kerala	3.0	1.8
Tamil Nadu	3.5	2.2

Sources: For China, Xizhe Peng, *Demographic Transition in China* (Oxford University Press, 1991), Li Chengrui, *A Study of China's Population* (Beijing: Foreign Language Press, 1992), and *World Development Report 1994*. For India, *Sample Registration System: Fertility and Mortality Indicators 1991* (New Delhi: Ministry of Home Affairs, 1993).

Family Planning

Even those who do not advocate legal or economic coercion sometimes suggest a variant of the "override" approach—the view, which has been getting increasing support, that the highest priority should be given simply to family planning, even if this means diverting resources from education and health care as well as other activities associated with development. We often hear claims that enormous declines in birth rates have been accomplished through making family planning services available, without waiting for improvements in education and health care.

The experience of Bangladesh is sometimes cited as an example of such success. Indeed, even though the female literacy rate in Bangladesh is only around 22 percent and life expectancy at birth no higher than 55 years, fertility rates have been substantially reduced there through the greater availability of family planning services, including counseling.[36] We have to examine carefully what lessons can, in fact, be drawn from this evidence.

First, it is certainly significant that Bangladesh has been able to cut its fertility rate from 7.0 to 4.5 during the short period between 1975 and 1990, an achievement that discredits the view that people will not voluntarily embrace family planning in the poorest countries. But we have to ask further whether family planning efforts may themselves be sufficient to make fertility come down to really low levels, without providing for female education and the other features of fuller collaborative approach. The fertility rate of 4.5 in Bangladesh is still quite high—considerably higher than even India's average rate of 3.6. To begin stabilizing the population, the fertility rates would have to come down closer to the "replacement level" of 2.0, as has happened in Kerala and Tamil Nadu, and in many other places outside the Indian sub-continent. Female education and the other social developments connected with lowering the birth rate would still be much needed.

Contrasts between the records of Indian states offer some substantial lessons here. While Kerala, and to a smaller extent Tamil Nadu, have surged ahead in achieving radically reduced fertility rates, other states in India in the so-called "northern heartland" (such as Uttar Pradesh, Bihar, Madhya Pradesh, and Rajasthan), have very low levels of education, especially female education, and of general health care (often combined with pressure on the poor to accept birth control measures, including sterilization, as a qualifying condition for medical attention and other public services). These states all have high fertility rates—between 4.4 and 5.1. The regional contrasts within India strongly argue for the collaborative approach, including active and educated participation of women.

The threat of an impending population crisis tempts many international observers to suggest that priority be given to family planning arrangements in the third world countries over other commitments such as education and health care, a redirection of public efforts that is often recommended by policymakers and at international conferences. Not only will this shift have negative effects on people's well-being and reduce their freedoms, it can also be self-defeating if the goal is to stabilize population.

The appeal of such slogans as "family planning first" rests partly on misconceptions about what is needed to reduce fertility rates, but also on mistaken beliefs about the excessive costs of social development, including education and health care. As has been discussed, both these activities are highly labor intensive, and thus relatively inexpensive even in very poor economies. In fact, Kerala, India's star performer in expanding education and reducing both death rates and birth rates, is among the poorer Indian states. Its domestically produced income is quite low—lower indeed in per capita terms than even the Indian average—even if this is somewhat deceptive, for the greatest expansion on Kerala's earnings derives from citizens who work outside the state. Kerala's ability to finance adequately both educational expansion and health coverage depends on both activities being labor-intensive; they can be made available even in a low-income economy when there is the political will to use them. Despite its economic backwardness, an issue which Kerala will undoubtedly have to address before long (perhaps by reducing bureaucratic controls over agriculture and industry, which have stagnated), its level of social development has been remarkable, and that has turned out to be crucial in reducing fertility rates. Kerala's fertility rate of 1.8 not only compares well with China's 2.0, but also with the US's and Sweden's 2.1, Canada's 1.9, and Britain's and France's 1.8.

The population problem is serious, certainly, but neither because of "the proportion between the natural increase of population and food" nor because of some impending apocalypse. There are reasons for worry about the long-term effects of population growth on the environment; and there are strong reasons for concern about the adverse effects of high birth rates on the quality of life, especially of women. With greater opportunities for education (especially female education), reduction of mortality rates (especially of children), improvement in economic security (especially in old age), and greater participation of women in employment and in political action, fast reductions in birth rates can be expected to result through the decisions and actions of those whose lives depend on them.

This is happening right now in many parts of the world, and the result has been a considerable slowing down of world population growth. The best way of dealing with the population problem is to help to spread these processes elsewhere. In contrast, the emergency mentality based on false beliefs in imminent cataclysms leads to breathless responses that are deeply counterproductive, preventing the development of rational and sustainable family planning. Coercive policies of forced birth control involve terrible social sacrifices, and there is little evidence that they are more effective in reducing birth rates than serious programs of collaborative action.

NOTES

1. This paper draws on my lecture arranged by the "Eminent Citizens Committee for Cairo '94" at the United Nations in New York on April 18, 1994, and also on research supported by the National Science Foundation.
2. Paul Ehrlich, *The Population Bomb* (Ballantine, 1968). More recently Paul Ehrlich and Anne H. Ehrlich have written *The Population Explosion* (Simon and Schuster, 1990).
3. Garrett Hardin, *Living within Limits* (Oxford University Press, 1993).
4. Thomas Robert Malthus, *Essay on the Principle of Population As It Affects the Future Improvement of Society with Remarks on the Speculation of Mr. Godwin, M. Condorcet, and Other Writers* (London: J. Johnson, 1798), Chapter 8; in the Penguin classics edition, *An Essay on the Principle of Population* (1982), p. 123.
5. See Simon Kuznets, *Modern Economic Growth* (Yale University Press, 1966).
6. Note by the Secretary-General of the United Nations to the Preparatory Committee for the International Conference on Population and Development, Third Session, A/Conf. 171/PC/5, February 18, 1994, p. 30.
7. Philip Morris Hauser's estimates are presented in the National Academy of Sciences publication *Rapid*

Population Growth: Consequences and Policy Implications, Vol.1 (Johns Hopkins University Press, 1971). See also Simon Kuznets, *Modern Economic Growth*, Chapter 2.

8. For an important collection of papers on these and related issues see Sir Francis Graham-Smith, F.R.S., editor, *Population: The Complex Reality: A Report of the Population Summit of the World's Scientific Academies*, issued by the Royal Society and published in the US by North America Press, Golden, Colorado. See also D. Gale Johnson and Ronald D. Lee, editors, *Population Growth and Economic Development, Issues and Evidence* (University of Wisconsin Press, 1987).
9. Garrett Hardin, *Living within Limits*, p. 274.
10. Paul Kennedy, who has discussed important problems in the distinctly "social" aspects of population growth, has pointed out that this debate "has, in one form or another, been with us since then," and "it is even more pertinent today than when Malthus composed his Essay," in *Preparing for the Twenty-first Century* (Random House, 1993), pp. 5-6.
11. On the importance of "enlightenment" traditions in Condorcet's thinking, see Emma Rothschild, "Condorcet and the Conflict of Values," in *The Historical Journal*.
12. Marie Jean Antoine Nicholas de Caritat Marquis de Condorcet's *Esquisse d'un Tableau Historique des Progrès de l'Esprit Humain*, Xe Epoque (1795). English translation by June Barraclough, *Sketch for a Historical Picture of the Progress of the Human Mind*, with an introduction by Stuart Hampshire (Weidenfeld and Nicolson, 1955), pp. 187-192.
13. T.R. Malthus, *A Summary View of the Principle of Population* (London: John Murray, 1830); in the Penguin classic edition (1982), p. 243; italics added.
14. On the practical policies, including, criticism of poverty relief and charitable hospitals, advocated for Britain by Malthus and his followers, see William St. Clair, *The Godwins and the Shelleys: A Biography of a Family* (Norton, 1989).
15. Malthus, *Essay on the Principle of Population*, Chapter 17; in the Penguin Classics edition, *An Essay on the Principle of Population*, pp. 198-199. Malthus showed some signs of weakening in this belief as he grew older.
16. Gerard Piel, *Only One World: Our Own to Make and to Keep* (Freeman, 1992).
17. For discussions of these empirical connections, see R.A. Easterlin, editor, *Population and Economic Change in Developing Countries* (University of Chicago Press, 1980); T. P. Schultz, *Economics of Population* (Addison Wesley, 1981); J.C. Caldwell, *Theory of Fertility Decline* (Academic Press, 1982); E. King and M.A. Hill, editors, *Women's Education in Developing Countries* (Johns Hopkins University Press, 1992); Nancy Birdsall, "Economic Approaches to Population Growth" in *The Handbook of Development Economics*, edited by H.B. Chenery and T. N. Srinivasan (Amsterdam: North Holland, 1988); Robert Cassen, et. al., *Population and Development: Old Debates, New Conclusions* (New Brunswick: Overseas Development Council/Transaction Publishers, 1994).
18. World Bank, *World Development Report 1994* (Oxford University Press, 1994), Table 25, pp. 210-211.
19. World Bank, *World Development Report 1994*, Table 2.
20. These issues are discussed in my joint book with Jean Drèze, *Hunger and Public Action* (Oxford University Press, 1989), and the three volumes edited by us, *The Political Economy of Hunger* (Oxford University Press, 1990), and also in my paper "Economic Regress: Concepts and Features," *Proceedings of the World Bank Annual Conference on Development Economics 1993* (World Bank, 1994).
21. This is confirmed by, among other statistics, the food production figures regularly presented by the United Nations Food and Agricultural Organization (see the *FAO Quarterly Bulletin of Statistics*, and also the *FAO Monthly Bulletins*).
22. For a more detailed picture and references to data sources, see my "Population and Reasoned Agency: Food, Fertility and Economic Development," in *Population, Economic Development, and the Environment*, edited by Kerstin Lindahl-Kiessling and Hans Landberg (Oxford University Press, 1994); see also the other contributions in this volume. The data presented here have been slightly updated from later publications of the FAO.
23. On this see my *Poverty and Famines* (Oxford University Press, 1981).

24. See UNCTAD VIII, Analytical Report by the UNCTAD Secretariat to the Conference (United Nations, 1992), Table V-S, p. 235. The period covered is between 1979-1981 to 1988-1990. These figures and related ones are discussed in greater detail in my paper "Population and Reasoned Agency," cited earlier.
25. World Bank, *Price Prospects for Major Primary Commodities*, Vol. II (World Bank, March 1993), Annex Tables 6, 12, and 18.
26. Condorcet, *Esquisse d'un Tableau Historique des Progrès de l'Esprit Humain*; in the 1968 reprint, p. 187.
27. The importance of "local" environmental issues is stressed and particularly explored by Partha Dasgupta in *An Inquiry into Well-Being and Destitution* (Oxford University Press, 1993).
28. In a forthcoming monograph by Jean Drèze and myself tentatively called "India: Economic Development and Social Opportunities," we discuss the importance of women's political agency in rectifying some of the more serious lapses in Indian economic and social performance—not just pertaining to the deprivation of women themselves.
29. See Jean Drèze and Amartya Sen, *Hunger and Public Action* (Oxford University Press, 1989), which also investigates the remarkable success of some poor countries in providing widespread educational and health services.
30. World Bank, *World Development Report 1994*, p. 212; and *Sample Registration System: Fertility and Mortality Indicators 1991* (New Delhi: Ministry of Home Affairs, 1993).
31. See the discussions, and the literature cited, in Gita Sen, Adrienne German, and Lincoln Chen, editors, *Population Policies Reconsidered: Health, Empowerment, and Rights* (Harvard Center for Population and Development Studies/International Women's Health Coalition, 1994).
32. On the actual processes involved, see T.N. Krishnan, "Demographic Transition in Kerala: Facts and Factors," in *Economic and Political Weekly*, Vol. 11 (1976), and P.N. Mari Bhat and S.I. Rajan, "Demographic Transition in Kerala Revisited," in *Economic and Political Weekly*, Vol. 25 (1990).
33. See, for example, Robin Jeffrey, "Culture and Governments: How Women Made Kerala Literate," in *Pacific Affairs*, Vol. 60 (1987).
34. On this see my "More Than 100 Million Women Are Missing," *New York Review of Books*, December 20, 1990; Ansley J. Coale, "Excess Female Mortality and the Balance of the of the Sexes: An Estimate of the Number of 'Missing Females'" *Population and Development Review*, No. 17 (1991); Amartya Sen, "Missing Women," *British Medical Journal*, No. 304 (March 1992); Stephan Klasen, "'Missing Women' Reconsidered," *World Development*.
35. Tamil Nadu has benefited from an active and efficient voluntary program of family planning, but these efforts have been helped by favorable social conditions as well, such as a high literacy rate (the second highest among the sixteen major states), a high rate of female participation in work outside the home (the third highest), a relatively low infant mortality rate (the third lowest), and a traditionally higher age of marriage. See also T.V. Antony, "The Family Planning Programme: Lessons from Tamil Nadu's Experience," *Indian Journal of Social Science*, Volume 5 (1992).
36. World Bank and Population Reference Bureau, *Success in a Challenging Environment: Fertility Decline in Bangladesh* (World Bank, 1993).

STUDY QUESTIONS

1. What are the distinctions between private, collective, and common property as outlined by Waldron? What does Waldron mean when he claims that every society has private, collective, and common property and that property rules differ from society to society with respect to determining the balance and degree of each? How is this account of property relevant to his analysis of the issue of homelessness?
2. How does Waldron's examination of the plight of the homeless undermine liberal assumptions about the connection between property rights and freedom? What particular restrictions on freedom does Waldron identify with respect to the homeless? What implications does his account have for policies with respect to the homeless?
3. Before reading Cohen, did you share the prevalent belief that inequalities in wealth are justifiable and necessary because they serve as incentives? Did your views about incentives and the justification for them undergo a change as he switched from the third person impersonal to the first person interpersonal presentation of the incentive argument? Why or why not?
4. What are comprehensive justifications? What is a justificatory community? Why, according to Cohen, are these important to an analysis of the incentive argument?
5. Does Cohen succeed in strengthening his case for socialist egalitarianism and for eliminating inequalities in wealth? Give reasons for your answer.
6. What is the "tragedy of the commons"? Do the Waldron and Cohen critiques of property and the unequal distribution of wealth lend support to the notion of the tragedy of the commons or do they challenge the notion or solve the problem of the tragedy of the commons? Provide reasons for your answer.
7. Why does Hardin think that a useful way to address questions about foreign aid is to invert the question of how we can help India to how we can harm India? Outline and evaluate the answers he comes up with for how we can harm India.
8. In what ways does Sen's analysis of the "world population problem" contradict Hardin's account? What implications does this have for Hardin's evaluation of the consequences of foreign aid and his case against helping the poor in other countries?
9. Does Sen's analysis of the tensions and differences between the North and South undermine prevalent myths and fears of the North concerning the South? Does the analysis shed light on policies with respect to overpopulation?
10. Sen provides a critical evaluation of the two main approaches to population control by comparing the cases of China and India. What are the two approaches? How do the cases in these two countries differ and is this significant in formulating policies for population control?

SUGGESTED READINGS

Arthur, John. "Rights and the Duty to Bring Aid." In *World Hunger and Moral Obligation* edited by William Aiken and Hugh LaFollette. Englewood Cliffs, NJ: Prentice Hall, 1977.

Barry, Brian. "Humanity and Justice in Global Perspective." In *Nomos XXIV: Ethics, Economics and the Law* edited by J.R. Pennock and J. W. Chapman. New York University Press, 1982: 219-252.

Coole, Diana. "Is Class a Difference that Makes a Difference?" *Radical Philosophy*, v. 77 (May/June 1996): 17-25.

Commoner, Barry. "Population and Poverty." In *Making Peace with the Planet*. New York: Pantheon Books, 1990.

Fraser, Nancy. "Women, Welfare, and the Politics of Need Interpretation." In *Unruly Practices: Power, Discourse, and Gender in Contemporary Social Theory*. University of Minnesota Press, 1989.

Fraser, Nancy and Linda Gordon. "'Dependency' Demystified: Inscriptions of Power in a Keyword of the Welfare State." *Social Politics*, v. 1 (1994): 4-31.

Govier, Trudy. "The Right to Eat and the Duty to Work." *Philosophy of the Social Sciences*, v. 5 (1975): 125-143.

Kahn, Herman. "The Confucian Ethic and Economic Growth." In *The Gap Between Rich and Poor* edited by Seligson. Boulder, CO: Westview Press, 1984.

Marin, Peter. "Helping and Hating the Homeless." *Harper's Magazine* (Jan. 1987)

Nicholson, Linda J. "Affirmative Action, Education and Social Class." *Philosophy of Education* (1983): 233-242.

Peckham, Irvin. "Complicity in Class Codes: The Exclusionary Function of Education." In *This Fine Place So Far From Home: Voices of Academics from the Working Class* edited by C. L. Barney Dews and Carolyn Leste Law. Philadelphia: Temple University Press, 1995.

Sen, Amartya. "Property and Hunger." *Economics and Philosophy*, v. 4 (1988): 57-68.

Singer, Peter. "Famine, Affluence, and Morality." *Philosophy & Public Affairs*, v. 1, no. 3 (1972): 229-243.

PART III

INDIVIDUAL AUTONOMY AND SOCIAL RESPONSIBILITY

CHAPTER NINE

THEORIES AND CRITICAL ANALYSIS

How do we determine what actions we ought to perform and what responsibilities we have to others? Is the whole of morality captured by the notion that there is a formula or set of principles that we can discover and should follow? Is the notion that morality emerges from the rational capacities of individual agents permeated with Western liberal assumptions about autonomy, agency, and responsibility? What does responsibility mean in a context in which the actions of individuals and the practices and policies of various societies have an increasing impact on other people, societies, and the world as a whole? Does the primacy of individual freedom with respect to the consumption or production of pornography have an impact on the role and treatment of women in our society? What sorts of dimensions of power are at work in incidences of sexual violence and how do these dimensions work in a global context? Does the liberal framework for debate about practical issues such as reproduction, euthanasia, health care, pornography, free speech, sexual violence, and animals and the environment change when we learn about concrete practices in non-Western contexts or in places outside North America? Do the policies in place for dealing with these issues in particular contexts have a differential impact on members of traditionally disadvantaged groups? Part III explores answers to these kinds of questions in the context of examining a range of moral theories and practical issues.

Immanuel Kant is an important figure in the development of moral theory in the Western tradition. His approach is referred to as deontological, a theory that derives an account of rights and duties independently of the consequences. Kant's deontological rights based approach to morality is evident in the kinds of arguments found in the practical issues we shall examine in Part III. He begins by characterizing morality in terms of distinct capacities possessed by human beings. Human beings are differentiated from non-human entities in having a will: "the will is a faculty of choosing only that which reason, independently of inclinations, recognizes as being practically necessary, i.e., as good." Reason tells us what actions we ought to perform and sets them as imperatives that command categorically. Kant argues that the categorical imperative is distinctive of moral action and that there is only one: "Act only according to that maxim whereby you can at the same time will that it should become a universal law." The categorical imperative can be viewed as a formula for determining one's moral duties. Kant shows how the formula works in practice by applying it to four examples.

The possession of a will gives human beings absolute worth, which is to be contrasted with conditional worth in that the latter is characteristic of non-human entities that have value only insofar as humans give them value. The absolute worth of human beings means that human beings exist as ends in themselves and can never be used merely as a means by another. This leads Kant to the second formulation of the categorical imperative: "Act in such a way that you treat humanity, whether in your own person or in the person of another, always at the same time as an end and never simply as a means." Kant returns to his examples to show the application of this version of the categorical imperative. He argues that the practical necessity of acting according to duty and not feelings, impulses, and inclinations makes each human being a legislating member in a society of self-legislating beings.

Kant provides a formula for determining the moral actions that it is one's duty to perform irrespective of inclinations, circumstances, and contexts. Consequentialists argue that inclinations and desires are relevant and that morally right action should be assessed in terms of the consequences of possible actions on oneself and others. Mill's Utilitarianism is an example of consequentialist theory. For Utilitarians, pleasure and pain are the only things desirable as ends, and morally right action is that which results in promoting the good consequences of maximizing pleasure. Mill differentiates his version of Utilitarianism from previous accounts by defending happiness rather than pleasure as such. Some pleasures are more desirable and valuable than others; namely, pleasures associated with human capacities and distinctive to human beings. Pleasures such as those of the intellect, of feelings and imagination, and of moral sentiments are qualitative ones that have a higher value than mere bodily and quantitative pleasures.

According to the greatest happiness principle, the ultimate end for the sake of which all other things are desirable is an existence as exempt as possible from pain and as rich as possible in pleasure, both quantitative and qualitative. Mill adds the important qualification that the standard for right conduct is not the agent's own happiness but that of all concerned. For Mill, morally right action is that which results in the greatest happiness for the greatest number of people affected by the particular action. Mill responds to Kant's depiction of morality as necessarily motivated by duty by claiming that what is important is not the motive but following the rule that promotes the general interest and performing the action that results in the greatest happiness for the greatest number of people.

Both Kant and Mill emphasize capacities that make individual human beings capable of determining what actions are morally right and performing those actions. In the third reading, Jennifer Nedelsky follows feminists and communitarians in raising concerns about the individualism at the base of liberalism and traditional Western moral theory. To be autonomous is to be "governed by one's own law," but, argues Nedelsky, autonomy can only develop in the context of relationships with significant people, such as parents, teachers, and friends, who nurture this capacity. Moreover, the content of one's own law is only comprehensible with reference to shared norms, values, and concepts. Such an account would seem to generate a tension between the idea of autonomy as originating with oneself and as being shaped by one's social context. Nedelsky defends the view that we need to retain the value of freedom but reconceive autonomy so that social contexts and the centrality of relationships in constituting the self are taken seriously in moral and political inquiry.

Nedelsky rejects the idea that autonomy can flourish if individuals are left alone and boundaries are erected to protect freedom. This prevailing conception identifies autonomy with individual independence and security from collective power and sets up a false dichotomy of either admitting collective control or preserving autonomy. Nedelsky acknowledges the tension, but argues that the collective is not simply a potential threat to individuals but constitutive of them and thus a source of autonomy as well as a danger to it. The way to think of autonomy is in terms of the social relations that could enhance autonomy for many people and allow it to develop and flourish. What is required, she argues, is an understanding of the practices that foster autonomy so that citizens can ask whether the actions or institutions proposed in their collective decision-making are consistent with the autonomy of all.

Margaret Walker pursues the discussion of individualism. She examines Carol Gilligan's work on an ethic of care, an ethic that is contrasted with the ethic of justice taken to be characteristic of Western moral theory. Gilligan's *In a Different Voice* has generated debate and controversy in its apparent endorsement of the claim that care and justice are orientations to morality characteristically adopted by women and men respectively. Gilligan has persistently rejected this interpretation and argues that the different voice of care offers a distinct moral perspective embodying conceptions of self, relationship, and responsibility that challenge the traditional justice approach to morality. Walker explores Gilligan's claim by pursuing questions about whether the ethic of care is a unified perspective, what that perspective is, and whether it offers an important addition or correction to prevailing philosophical views.

Walker locates two distinct themes in Gilligan's characterization of care as a responsibilities rather than a rights based justice approach. The *care and response orientation* tells us what morality is about and takes sensitivity to the needs of others, concern with relationships and responsibility, attachment and compassion to be central moral concerns. Caring for others requires minute attention, identification in thought and feeling, precise communication, and sensitivity to rich circumstantial detail and history. The contextual-deliberative picture tells us how we must think about morality and marks the distinction between justice and care in terms of method, approach, and standards for defining and solving moral problems. Whereas justice is moral reasoning that abstracts from interpersonal contexts, prioritizes rules, and arrives at universal formulas, the care perspective rejects this notion of moral decision as a deductive operation and takes concrete information about the particular case to be relevant to moral decisions. The care orientation rotates the focus so that the particular is always first and the application of generalized standards is derivative and degenerate. The debate about care as a woman's voice can now be seen in a different light. Because women's roles require the majority of them to initiate new members into the moral community, their perspectives on caring relationships are vantage points contributing to an understanding of what moral concern requires.

GROUNDING FOR THE METAPHYSICS OF MORALS

Immanuel Kant

Immanuel Kant was born in Germany and lived from 1724-1804. His significant contributions to all major areas of philosophy has made him one of the most important philosophers of all time. Some of his most important works include: Critique of Pure Reason, Critique of Practical Reason, Prolegomena to All Future Metaphysics, *and the book from which this reading is taken,* Grounding for the Metaphysics of Morals.

Kant defines moral action as that which human beings have a duty to perform irrespective of particular motives, desires, and inclinations. Human beings are the kind of rational and self-legislating entities that make it possible for them to determine morally right action in accordance with the dictates of the supreme rule of the categorical imperative. Kant provides several formulations of the categorical imperative, the first and most well-known of which is: act only on that rule that one would be willing to make into a universal law for everyone to follow.

... Everything in nature works according to laws. Only a rational being has the power to act according to his conception of laws, i.e., according to principles, and thereby has he a will. Since the derivation of actions from laws requires reason, the will is nothing but practical reason. If reason infallibly determines the will, then in the case of such a being actions which are recognized to be objectively necessary are also subjectively necessary, i.e., the will is a faculty of choosing only that which reason, independently of inclination, recognizes as being practically necessary, i.e., as good. But if reason of itself does not sufficiently determine the will, and if the will submits also to subjective conditions (certain incentives) which do not always agree with objective conditions; in a word, if the will does not in itself completely accord with reason (as is actually the case with men), then actions which are recognized as objectively necessary are subjectively contingent, and the determination of such a will according to objective laws is necessitation. That is to say that the relation of objective laws to a will not thoroughly good is represented as the determination of the will of a rational being by principles of reason which the will does not necessarily follow because of its own nature.

The representation of an objective principle insofar as it necessitates the will is called a command (of reason), and the formula of the command is called an imperative.

All imperatives are expressed by an *ought* and thereby indicate the relation of an objective law of reason to a will that is not necessarily determined by this law because of its subjective constitution (the relation of necessitation). Imperatives say that something would be good to do or to refrain from doing, but they say it to a will that does not always therefore do something simply because it has been represented to the will as something good to do. That is practically good which determines the will by means of representations of reason and hence not by subjective causes, but objectively, i.e., on grounds valid for every rational being as such. It is distinguished from the pleasant as that which influences the will only by means of sensation from merely subjective causes, which hold only for this or that person's senses but do not hold as a principle of reason valid for everyone.

A perfectly good will would thus be quite as much

Reprinted with permission of Hackett Publishing Co. Inc. from *Grounding for the Metaphysics of Morals*, trans. and ed. by James A. Ellington (Indianapolis: Hackett, 1993): 23-44 [edited].

subject to objective laws (of the good), but could not be conceived as thereby necessitated to act in conformity with law, inasmuch as it can of itself, according to its subjective constitution, be determined only by the representation of the good. Therefore no imperatives hold for the divine will, and in general for a holy will; the *ought* is here out of place, because the *would* is already of itself necessarily in agreement with the law. Consequently, imperatives are only formulas for expressing the relation of objective laws of willing in general to the subjective imperfection of the will of this or that rational being, e.g., the human will.

Now all imperatives command either hypothetically or categorically. The former represent the practical necessity of a possible action as a means for attaining something else that one wants (or may possibly want). The categorical imperative would be one which represented an action as objectively necessary in itself, without reference to another end.

Every practical law represents a possible action as good and hence as necessary for a subject who is practically determinable by reason; therefore all imperatives are formulas for determining an action which is necessary according to the principle of a will that is good in some way. Now if the action would be good merely as a means to something else, so is the imperative hypothetical. But if the action is represented as good in itself, and hence as necessary in a will which of itself conforms to reason as the principle of the will, then the imperative is categorical.

An imperative thus says what action possible by me would be good, and it presents the practical rule in relation to a will which does not forthwith perform an action simply because it is good, partly because the subject does not always know that the action is good and partly because (even if he does know it is good) his maxims might yet be opposed to the objective principles of practical reason.

A hypothetical imperative thus says only that an action is good for some purpose, either possible or actual. In the first case it is a problematic practical principal; in the second case an assertoric one. A categorical imperative, which declares an action to be of itself objectively necessary without reference to any purpose, i.e., without any other end, holds as an apodeictic practical principle.

Whatever is possible only through the powers of some rational being can be thought of as a possible purpose of some will. Consequently, there are in fact infinitely many principles of action insofar as they are represented as necessary for attaining a possible purpose achievable by them. All sciences have a practical part consisting of problems saying that some end is possible for us and of imperatives telling us how it can be attained. These can, therefore, be called in general imperatives of skill. Here there is no question at all whether the end is reasonable and good, but there is only a question as to what must be done to attain it. The prescriptions needed by a doctor in order to make his patient thoroughly healthy and by a poisoner in order to make sure of killing his victim are of equal value so far as each serves to bring about its purpose perfectly. Since there cannot be known in early youth what ends may be presented to us in the course of life, parents especially seek to have their children learn many different kinds of things, and they provide for skill in the use of means to all sorts of arbitrary ends, among which they cannot determine whether any one of them could in the future become an actual purpose for their ward, though there is always the possibility that he might adopt it. Their concern is so great that they commonly neglect to form and correct their children's judgment regarding the worth of things which might be chosen as ends.

There is, however, one end that can be presupposed as actual for all rational beings (so far as they are dependent beings to whom imperatives apply); and thus there is one purpose which they not merely can have but which can certainly be assumed to be such that they all do have by a natural necessity, and this is happiness. A hypothetical imperative which represents the practical necessity of an action as means for the promotion of happiness is assertoric. It may be expounded not simply as necessary to an uncertain, merely possible purpose, but as necessary to a purpose which can be presupposed a priori and with certainty as being present in everyone because it belongs to his essence. Now skill in the choice of means to one's own greatest well-being can be called prudence in the narrowest sense. And thus the imperative that refers to the choice of means to one's own happiness, i.e., the precept of prudence, still remains hypothetical; the action is commanded not absolutely but only as a means to a further purpose.

Finally, there is one imperative which immediately commands a certain conduct without having as its condition any other purpose to be attained by it. This imperative is categorical. It is not concerned with the matter of the action and its intended result, but rather with the form of the action and the principle from which it follows; what is essentially good in the action consists in the mental disposition, let the consequences be what they may. This imperative may be called that of morality....

If I think of a hypothetical imperative in general, I do not know beforehand what it will contain until its condition is given. But if I think of a categorical imperative, I know immediately what it contains. For since, besides the law, the imperative contains only the necessity that the maxim should accord with this law, while the law contains no condition to restrict it, there remains nothing but the universality of a law as such with which the maxim of the action should conform. This conformity alone is properly what is represented as necessary by the imperative.

Hence there is only one categorical imperative and it is this: Act only according to that maxim whereby you can at the same time will that it should become a universal law.

Now if all imperatives of duty can be derived from this one imperative as their principle, then there can at least be shown what is understood by the concept of duty and what it means, even though there is left undecided whether what is called duty may not be an empty concept.

The universality of law according to which effects are produced constitutes what is properly called nature in the most general sense (as to form), i.e., the existence of things as far as determined by universal laws. Accordingly, the universal imperative of duty may be expressed thus: Act as if the maxim of your action were to become through your will a universal law of nature.

We shall now enumerate some duties, following the usual division of them into duties to ourselves and to others and into perfect and imperfect duties.

1. A man reduced to despair by a series of misfortunes feels sick of life but is still so far in possession of his reason that he can ask himself whether taking his own life would not be contrary to his duty to himself. Now he asks whether the maxim of his action could become a universal law of nature. But his maxim is this: from self-love I make as my principle to shorten my life when its continued duration threatens more evil than it promises satisfaction. There only remains the question as to whether this principle of self-love can become a universal law of nature. One sees at once a contradiction in a system of nature whose law would destroy life by means of the very same feeling that acts so as to stimulate the furtherance of life, and hence there could be no existence as a system of nature. Therefore, such a maxim cannot possibly hold as a universal law of nature and is, consequently, wholly opposed to the supreme principle of all duty.

2. Another man in need finds himself forced to borrow money. He knows well that he won't be able to repay it, but he sees also that he will not get any loan unless he firmly promises to repay it within a fixed time. He wants to make such a promise, but he still has conscience enough to ask himself whether it is not permissible and is contrary to duty to get out of difficulty in this way. Suppose, however, that he decides to do so. The maxim of his action would then be expressed as follows: when I believe myself to be in need of money, I will borrow money and promise to pay it back, although I know that I can never do so. Now this principle of self-love or personal advantage may perhaps be quite compatible with one's entire future welfare, but the question is now whether it is right. I then transform the requirement of self-love into a universal law and put the question thus: how would things stand if my maxim were to become a universal law? He then sees at once that such a maxim could never hold as a universal law of nature and be consistent with itself, but must necessarily be self-contradictory. For the universality of a law which says that anyone believing himself to be in difficulty could promise whatever he pleases with the intention of not keeping it would make promising itself and the end to be attained thereby quite impossible, inasmuch as no one would believe what was promised him but would merely laugh at all such utterances as being vain pretenses.

3. A third finds in himself a talent whose cultivation could make him a man useful in many respects. But he finds himself in comfortable circumstances and prefers to indulge in pleasure rather than to bother himself about broadening and improving his fortunate natural aptitudes. But he asks himself further whether his maxim of neglecting his natural gifts, besides agreeing of itself with his propensity to indulgence, might agree also with what is called duty. He then sees that a system of nature could indeed always subsist according to such a universal law, even though every man (like South Sea Islanders) should let his talents rust and resolve to devote his life entirely to idleness, indulgence, propagation, and, in a word, to enjoyment. But he cannot possibly will that this should become a universal law of nature or be implanted in us as such a law by a natural instinct. For as a rational being he necessarily wills that all his faculties should be developed, inasmuch as they are given him for all sorts of possible purposes.

4. A fourth man finds things going well for himself but sees others (whom he could help) struggling with great hardships; and he thinks: what does it matter to me? Let everybody be as happy as Heaven wills or as he can make himself; I shall take nothing from him nor even envy him; but I have no desire to contribute anything to his well-being or to his assistance when in need. If such a way of thinking were to become a universal law of nature, the human race admittedly could very well subsist and doubtless could subsist even better than when everyone prates about sympathy and benevolence and even on occasion exerts himself to practice them but, on the other hand, also cheats when he can, betrays the rights of man, or otherwise violates them. But even though it is possible that a universal law of nature could subsist in accordance with that maxim, still it is impossible to will that such a principle should hold everywhere as a law of nature. For a will which resolved in this way would contradict itself, inasmuch as cases might often arise in which one would have need of the love and sympathy of others and in which he would deprive himself, by such a law of nature springing from his own will, of all hope of the aid he wants for himself.

These are some of the many actual duties, or at least what are taken to be such, whose derivation from the single principle cited above is clear. We must be able to will that a maxim of our action become a universal law; this is the canon for morally estimating any of our actions. Some actions are so constituted that their maxims cannot without contradiction even be thought as a universal law of nature, much less be willed as what should become one. In the case of others this internal impossibility is indeed not found, but there is still no possibility of willing that their maxim should be raised to the universality of a law of nature, because such a will would contradict itself. There is no difficulty in seeing that the former kind of action conflicts with strict or narrow [perfect] (irremissible) duty, while the second kind conflicts only with broad [imperfect] (meritorious) duty. By means of these examples there has thus been fully set forth how all duties depend as regards the kind of obligation (not the object of their action) upon the one principle.

If we now attend to ourselves in any transgression of a duty, we find that we actually do not will that our maxim should become a universal law—because this is impossible for us—but rather that the opposite of this maxim should remain a law universally. We only take the liberty of making an exception to the law for ourselves (or just for this one time) to the advantage of our inclination. Consequently, if we weighed up everything from one and the same standpoint, namely, that of reason, we would find a contradiction in our own will, viz., that a certain principle be objectively necessary as a universal law and yet subjectively not hold universally but should admit of exceptions. But since we at one moment regard our action from the standpoint of a will wholly in accord with reason and then at another moment regard the very same action from the standpoint of a will affected by inclination, there is really no contradiction here. Rather, there is an opposition (*antagonismus*) of inclination to the precept of reason, whereby the universality (*universalitas*) of the principle is changed into a mere generality (*generalitas*) so that the practical principle of reason may meet the maxim halfway. Although this procedure cannot be justified in our own impartial judgment, yet it does show that we actually acknowledge the validity of the categorical imperative and (with all respect for it) merely allow ourselves a few exceptions which, as they seem to us, are unimportant and forced upon us.

We have thus at least shown that if duty is a concept which is to have significance and real legislative authority for our actions, then such duty can be expressed only in categorical imperatives but not at all in hypothetical ones. We have also—and this is already a great deal—exhibited clearly and definitely for every application what is the content of the categorical imperative, which must contain the principle of all duty (if there is such a thing at all.) But we have not yet advanced far enough to prove a priori that there actually is an imperative of this kind, that there is a practical law which of itself commands absolutely and without any incentives, and that following this law is duty....

The will is thought of as a faculty of determining itself to action in accordance with the representation of certain laws, and such a faculty can be found only in rational beings. Now what serves the will as the objective ground of its self-determination is an end; and if this end is given by reason alone, then it must be equally valid for all rational beings. On the other hand, what contains merely the ground of the possibility of the action, whose effect is an end, is called the means. The subjective ground of desire is the incentive; the objective ground of volition is the motive. Hence there arises the distinction between subjective ends, which rest on incentives, and objective ends, which depend on motives valid for every rational being. Practical principles are formal when they abstract from all subjective ends; they are material, however, when they are founded upon subjective ends, and hence upon certain incentives. The ends which a rational being arbitrarily proposes to himself as effects of this action (material ends) are all merely relative, for only their relation to a specially constituted faculty of desire in the subject gives them their worth. Consequently, such worth cannot provide any universal principles, which are valid and necessary for all rational beings and, furthermore, are valid for every volition, i.e., cannot provide any practical laws. Therefore, all such relative ends can be grounds only for hypothetical imperatives.

But let us suppose that there were something whose existence has in itself an absolute worth, something which as an end in itself could be a ground of determinate laws. In it, and in it alone, would there be the ground of a possible categorical imperative, i.e., of a practical law.

Now I say that man, and in general every rational being, exists as an end in himself and not merely as a means to be arbitrarily used by this or that will. He must in all his actions, whether directed to himself or to other rational beings, always be regarded at the same time as an end. All the objects of inclinations have only a conditioned value; for if there were not these inclinations and the needs founded on them, then their object would be without value. But the inclinations themselves, being sources of needs, are so far from having an absolute value such as to render them desirable for their own sake that the universal wish of every rational being must be, rather, to be wholly free from them. Accordingly, the value of any object obtainable by our action is always conditioned. Beings whose existence depends not on our will but on nature have, nevertheless, if they are not rational beings, only a relative value as means and are therefore called things. On the other hand, rational beings are called persons inasmuch as their nature already marks them out as ends in themselves, i.e., as something which is not to be used merely as means and hence there is imposed thereby a limit on all arbitrary use of such beings, which are thus objects of respect. Persons are, therefore, not merely subjective ends, whose existence as an effect of our actions has a value for us; but such beings are objective ends, i.e., exist as ends in themselves. Such an end is one for which there can be substituted no other end to which such beings should serve merely as means, for otherwise nothing at all of absolute value would be found anywhere. But if all value were conditioned and hence contingent, then no supreme practical principle could be found for reason at all.

If then there is to be a supreme practical principle and, as far as the human will is concerned, a categorical imperative, then it must be such that from the conception of what is necessarily an end for everyone because this end is an end in itself it constitutes an objective principle of the will and can hence serve as a practical law. The ground of such a principle is this: rational nature exists as an end in itself. In this way man necessarily thinks of his own existence; thus far is it a subjective principle of human actions. But in this way also does every other rational being think of his existence on the same rational ground that holds also for me; hence it is at the same time an objective principle, from which, as a supreme practical ground, all laws of the will must be able to be derived. The practical imperative will therefore be the following: Act in such a way that you treat humanity, whether in your own person or in the person of another, always at the same time as an end and never simply as a means. We now want to see whether this can be carried out in practice.

Let us keep to our previous examples.

First, as regards the concept of necessary duty to oneself, the man who contemplates suicide will ask himself whether his action can be consistent with the idea of humanity as an end in itself. If he destroys himself in order to escape from a difficult situation, then he is making use of his person merely as a means so as to maintain a tolerable condition till the end of his life. Man, however, is not a thing and hence is not something to be used merely as a means; he must in all his actions always be regarded as an end in himself. Therefore, I cannot dispose of man in my own person by mutilating, damaging, or killing him. (A more exact determination of this principle so as to avoid all misunderstanding, e.g., regarding the amputation of limbs in order to save oneself, or the exposure of one's life to danger in order to save it, and so on, must here be omitted; such questions belong to morals proper.)

Second, as concerns necessary or strict duty to others, the man who intends to make a false promise will immediately see that he intends to make use of another man merely as a means to an end which the latter does not likewise hold. For the man whom I want to use for my own purposes by such a promise cannot possibly concur with my way of acting toward him and hence cannot himself hold the end of this action. This conflict with the principle of duty to others becomes even clearer when instances of attacks on the freedom and property of others are considered. For then it becomes clear that a transgressor of the rights of men intends to make use of the persons of others merely as a means, without taking into consideration that, as rational beings, they should always be esteemed at the same time as ends, i.e., be esteemed only as beings who must themselves be able to hold the very same action as an end.

Third, with regard to contingent (meritorious) duty to oneself, it is not enough that the action does not conflict with humanity in our own person as an end in itself; the action must also harmonize with this end. Now there are in humanity capacities for greater perfection which belong to the end that nature has in view as regards humanity in our own person. To neglect these capacities might perhaps be consistent with the maintenance of humanity as an end in itself, but would not be consistent with the advancement of this end.

Fourth, concerning meritorious duty to others, the natural end that all men have is their own happiness. Now humanity might indeed subsist if nobody contributed anything to the happiness of others, provided he did not intentionally impair their happiness. But this, after all, would harmonize only negatively and not positively with humanity as an end in itself, if everyone does not also strive, as much as he can, to further the ends of others. For the ends of any subject who is an end in himself must as far as possible be my ends also, if that conception of an end in itself is to have its full effect in me.

This principle of humanity and of every rational nature generally as an end in itself is the supreme limiting condition of every man's freedom of action. This principle is not borrowed from experience, first, because of its universality, inasmuch as it applies to all rational beings generally, and no experience is capable of determining anything about them; and, secondly, because in experience (subjectively) humanity is not thought of as an end of men, i.e., as an object that we of ourselves actually make our end which as a law ought to constitute the supreme limiting condition of all subjective ends (whatever they may be); and hence this principle must arise from pure reason [and not from experience]. That is to say that the ground of all practical legislation lies objectively in the rule and in the form of universality, which (according to the first principle) makes the rule capable of being a law (say, for example, a law of nature). Subjectively, however, the ground of all practical legislation lies in the end; but (according to the second principle) the subject of all ends is every rational being as an end in himself. From this there now follows the third practical principle of the will as the supreme condition of the will's conformity with universal practical reason, viz., the idea of the will of every rational being as a will that legislates universal law.

According to this principle all maxims are rejected which are not consistent with the will's own legislation of universal law. The will is thus not merely subject to the law but is subject to the law in such a way that it must be regarded also as legislating for itself and only on this account as being subject to the law (of which it can regard itself as the author)....

When we look back upon all previous attempts that have been made to discover the principle of morality, there is no reason now to wonder why they one and all had to fail. Man was viewed as bound to laws by his duty; but it was not seen that man is subject only to his own, yet universal, legislation and that he is bound only to act in accordance with his own will, which is, however, a will purposed by nature to legislate universal laws. For when man is thought as being merely subject to a law (whatever it might be), then the law had to carry with it some interest functioning as an attracting stimulus or as a constraining force for obedience, inasmuch as the law did not arise as a law from his own will. Rather, in order that his will conform with law, it had to be necessitated by something else to act in a certain way. By this absolutely necessary conclusion, however, all the labor spent in finding a supreme ground for duty was irretrievably lost; duty was never discovered, but only the necessity of acting from a certain interest. This might be either one's own interest or another's, but either way the imperative had to be always conditional and could never possibly serve as a moral command. I want, therefore, to call my principle the principle of the autonomy of the will, in contrast with every other principle, which I accordingly count under heteronomy.

The concept of every rational being as one who must regard himself as legislating universal law by all his will's maxims, so that he may judge himself and his actions from this point of view, leads to another very fruitful concept, which depends on the aforementioned one, viz., that of a kingdom of ends.

By "kingdom" I understand a systematic union of different rational beings through common laws. Now laws determine ends as regards their universal validity; therefore, if one abstracts from the personal differences of rational beings and also from all content of their private ends, then it will be possible to think of a whole of all ends in systematic connection (a whole both of rational being as ends in themselves and also of the particular ends which each may set for himself); that is, one can think of a kingdom of ends that is possible on the aforesaid principles.

For all rational beings stand under the law that each of them should treat himself and all others never merely as means but always at the same time as an end in himself. Hereby arises a systematic union of rational beings through common objective laws, i.e., a kingdom that may be called a kingdom of ends (certainly only an ideal), inasmuch as these laws have in view the very relation of such beings to one another as ends and means.

A rational being belongs to the kingdom of ends as a member when he legislates in it universal laws while also being himself subject to these laws. He belongs to it as sovereign, when as legislator he is himself subject to the will of no other.

A rational being must always regard himself as legislator in a kingdom of ends rendered possible by freedom of the will, whether as member or as sovereign. The position of the latter can be maintained not merely through the maxims of his will but only if he is a completely independent being without needs and with unlimited power adequate to his will.

Hence morality consists in the relation of all action to that legislation whereby alone a kingdom of ends is possible. This legislation must be found in every rational being and must be able to arise from his will, whose principle then is never to act on any maxim except such as can also be a universal law and hence such as the will can thereby regard itself as at the same time the legislator of universal law. If now the maxims do not by their very nature already necessarily conform with this objective principle of rational beings as legislating universal laws, then the necessity of acting on that principle is called practical necessitation, i.e., duty. Duty does not apply to the sovereign in the kingdom of ends, but it does apply to every member and to each in the same degree.

The practical necessity of acting according to this principle, i.e., duty, does not rest at all on feelings, impulses, and inclinations, but only on the relation of rational beings to one another, a relation in which the will of a rational being must always be regarded at the same time as legislative, because otherwise he could not be thought of as an end in himself. Reason, therefore, relates every maxim of the will as legislating universal laws to every other will and also to every action toward oneself; it does so not on account of any other practical motive or future advantage but rather from the idea of the dignity of a rational being who obeys no law except what he at the same time enacts himself.

In the kingdom of ends everything has either a price or a dignity. Whatever has a price can be replaced by something else as its equivalent; on the other hand, whatever is above all price, and therefore admits of no equivalent, has a dignity.

Whatever has reference to general human inclinations and needs has a market price; whatever, without presupposing any need, accords with a certain taste, i.e., a delight in the mere unpurposive play of our mental powers, has an affective price; but that which constitutes the condition under which alone something can be an end in itself has not merely a relative worth, i.e., a price, but has an intrinsic worth, i.e., dignity.

Now morality is the condition under which alone a rational being can be an end in himself, for only thereby can he be a legislating member in the kingdom of ends. Hence morality and humanity, insofar as it is capable of morality, alone have dignity. Skill and diligence in work have a market price; wit, lively imagination, and humor have an affective price; but fidelity to promises and benevolence based on principles (not on instinct) have intrinsic worth. Neither nature nor art contain anything which in default of these could be put in their place; for their worth consists, not in the effects which arise from them, nor in the advantage and profit which they provide, but in mental dispositions, i.e., in the maxims of the will which are ready in this way to manifest themselves in action, even if they are not favored with success. Such actions also need no recommendation from any subjective disposition or taste so as to meet with immediate favor and delight; there is no need of any immediate propensity or feeling toward them. They exhibit the will performing them as an object of immediate respect; and nothing but reason is required to impose them upon the will, which is not to be cajoled into them, since in the case of duties such cajoling would be a contradiction. This estimation, therefore, lets the worth of such a disposition be recognized as dignity and puts it infinitely beyond all price, with which it cannot in the least be brought into competition or comparison without, as it were, violating its sanctity.

What then is it that entitles the morally good disposition, or virtue, to make such lofty claims? It is nothing less than the share which such a disposition affords the rational being of legislating universal laws, so that he is fit to be a member in a possible kingdom of ends, for which his own nature has already determined him as an end in himself and therefore as a legislator in the kingdom of ends. Thereby is he free as regards all laws of nature, and he obeys only those laws which he gives to himself. Accordingly, his maxims can belong to a universal legislation to which he at the same time subjects himself. For nothing can have any worth other than what the law determines. But the legislation itself which determines all worth must for that very reason have dignity, i.e., unconditional and incomparable worth; and the word "respect" alone provides a suitable expression for the esteem which a rational being must have for it. Hence autonomy is the ground of the dignity of human nature and of every rational nature....

We can now end where we started in the beginning, viz., the concept of an unconditionally good will. That will is absolutely good which cannot be evil, i.e., whose maxim, when made into a universal law, can never conflict with itself. This principle is therefore also its supreme law: Act always according to that maxim whose universality as a law you can at the same time will. This is the only condition under which a will can never be in conflict with itself, and such an imperative is categorical. Inasmuch as the validity of the will as a universal law for possible actions is analogous to the universal connection of the existence of things in accordance with universal laws, which is the formal aspect of nature in general, the categorical imperative can also be expressed thus: Act according to maxims which can at the same time have for their object themselves as universal laws of nature. In this way there is provided the formula for an absolutely good will.

Rational nature is distinguished from the rest of nature by the fact that it sets itself an end. This end would be the matter of every good will. But in the idea of an absolutely good will—good without any qualifying condition (of attaining this or that end)—complete abstraction must be made from every end that has to come about as an effect (since such would make every will only relatively good). And so the end must here be conceived, not as an end to be effected, but as an independently existing end. Hence it must be conceived only negatively, i.e., as an end which should never be acted against and therefore as one which in all willing must never be regarded merely as means but must always be esteemed at the same time as an end. Now this end can be nothing but the subject of all possible ends themselves, because this subject is at the same time the subject of a possible absolutely good will; for such a will cannot without contradiction be subordinated to any other object. The principle: So act in regard to every rational being (yourself and others) that he may at the same time count in your maxim as an end in himself, is thus basically the same as the principle: Act on a maxim which at the same time contains in itself its own universal validity for every rational being. That in the use of means for every end my maxim should be restricted to the condition of its universal validity as a law for every subject says just the same as that a subject of ends, i.e., a rational being himself, must be made the ground for all maxims of actions and must thus be used never merely as means but as the supreme limiting condition in the use of all means, i.e., always at the same time as an end.

Now there follows incontestably from this that every rational being as an end in himself must be able to regard himself with reference to all laws to which he may be subject as being at the same time the legislator of universal law, for just this very fitness of his maxims for the legislation of universal law distinguishes him as an end in himself. There follows also that his dignity (prerogative) of being above all the mere things of nature implies that his maxims must be taken from the viewpoint that regards himself, as well as every other rational being, as being legislative beings (and hence are they called persons). In this way there is possible a world of rational beings (*mundus intelligibilis*) as a kingdom of ends, because of the legislation belonging to all persons as members. Therefore, every rational being must so act as if he were through his maxim always a legislating member in the universal kingdom of ends. The formal principle of these maxims is this: So act as if your maxims were to serve at the same time as a universal law (for all rational beings). Thus a kingdom of ends is possible only on the analogy of a kingdom of nature; yet the former is possible only through maxims, i.e., self-imposed rules, while the latter is possible only through laws of efficient causes necessitated from without. Regardless of this difference and even though nature as a whole is viewed as a machine, yet insofar as nature stands in a relation to rational beings as its ends, it is on this account given the name of a kingdom of nature. Such a kingdom of ends would actually be realized through maxims whose rule is prescribed to all rational beings by the categorical imperative, if these maxims were universally obeyed. But even if a rational being himself strictly obeys such a maxim, he cannot for that reason count on everyone else's being true to it, nor can he expect the kingdom of nature and its purposive order to be in harmony with him as a fitting member of a kingdom of ends made possible by himself, i.e., he cannot expect the kingdom of nature to favor his expectation of happiness. Nevertheless, the law: Act in accordance with the maxims of a member legislating universal laws for a merely possible kingdom of ends, remains in full force, since it commands categorically. And just in this lies the paradox that merely the dignity of humanity as rational nature without any further end or advantage to be thereby gained—and hence respect for a mere idea—should yet serve as an inflexible precept for the will; and that just this very independence of the maxims from all such incentives should constitute the sublimity of maxims and the worthiness of every rational subject to be a legislative member in the kingdom of ends, for otherwise he would have to be regarded as subject only to the natural law of his own needs....

From what has just been said, there can now easily be explained how it happens that, although in the concept of duty we think of subjection to the law, yet at the same time we thereby ascribe a certain dignity and sublimity to the person who fulfills all his duties. For not insofar as he is subject to the moral law does he have sublimity, but rather has it only insofar as with regard to this very same law he is at the same time legislative, and only thereby is he subject to the law. We have also shown above how neither fear nor inclination, but solely respect for the law, is the incentive which can give an action moral worth. Our own will, insofar as it were to act only under the condition of its being able to legislate universal law by means of its maxims—this will, ideally possible for us, is the proper object of respect. And the dignity of humanity consists just in its capacity to legislate universal law, though with the condition of humanity's being at the same time itself subject to this very same legislation.

UTILITARIANISM

John Stuart Mill

John Stuart Mill, a British philosopher, lived from 1806-1873. He is most well-known for his works On Liberty *and* Utilitarianism, *both of which have been highly influential in moral and political theory.*

Mill argues that morally right action is that which results in the greatest amount of happiness for the greatest number of people. There are several elements important to Mill's version of utilitarianism. Mill promotes happiness rather than pleasure and holds, for example, that the quality of intellectual pleasures ranks higher than the quantity of bodily pleasures; the former are distinctive of and important to human happiness. Morally right action is determined by calculating the amount of happiness and unhappiness in terms of quality rather than mere quantity and in the lives of each person affected by the action.

What Utilitarianism Is

... The creed which accepts as the foundation of morals "utility" or the "greatest happiness principle" holds that actions are right in proportion as they tend to promote happiness; wrong as they tend to produce the reverse of happiness. By happiness is intended pleasure and the absence of pain; by unhappiness, pain and the privation of pleasure. To give a clear view of the moral standard set up by the theory, much more requires to be said; in particular, what things it includes in the ideas of pain and pleasure, and to what extent this is left an open question. But these supplementary explanations do not affect the theory of life on which this theory of morality is grounded—namely, that pleasure and freedom from pain are the only things desirable as ends; and that all desirable things (which are as numerous in the utilitarian as in any other scheme) are desirable either for pleasure inherent in themselves or as means to the promotion of pleasure and the prevention of pain.

Now such a theory of life excites in many minds, and among them in some of the most estimable in feeling and purpose, inveterate dislike. To suppose that life has (as they express it) no higher end than pleasure—no better and nobler object of desire and pursuit—they designate as utterly mean and groveling, as a doctrine worthy only of swine, to whom the followers of Epicurus were, at a very early period, contemptuously likened; and modern holders of the doctrine are occasionally made the subject of equally polite comparison by its German, French, and English assailants.

When thus attacked, the Epicureans have always answered that it is not they, but their accusers, who represent human nature in a degrading light, since the accusation supposes human beings to be capable of no pleasures except those of which swine are capable. If this supposition were true, the charge could not be gainsaid, but would then be no longer an imputation; for if the sources of pleasure were precisely the same to human beings and to swine, the rule of life which is good enough for the one would be good enough for the other. The comparison of the Epicurean life to that of beasts is felt as degrading, precisely because a beast's pleasures do not satisfy a human being's conceptions of happiness. Human beings have faculties more elevated than the animal appetites and, when once made conscious of them, do not regard anything as happiness which does not include their gratification. I do not indeed, consider

---

From *Utilitarianism* (White Plains NY: Longman's, 1907).

the Epicureans to have been by any means faultless in drawing out their scheme of consequences from the utilitarian principle. To do this in any sufficient manner, many Stoic, as well as Christian, elements require to be included. But there is no known Epicurean theory of life which does not assign to the pleasures of the intellect, of the feelings and imagination, and of the moral sentiments a much higher value as pleasures than to those of mere sensation. It must be admitted, however, that utilitarian writers in general have placed the superiority of mental over bodily pleasures chiefly in the greater permanency, safety, uncostliness, etc., of the former—that is, in their circumstantial advantages rather than in their intrinsic nature. And on all these points utilitarians have fully proved their case; but they might have taken the other and, as it may be called, higher ground with entire consistency. It is quite compatible with the principle of utility to recognize the fact that some kinds of pleasure are more desirable and more valuable than others. It would be absurd that, while in estimating all other things quality is considered as well as quantity, the estimation of pleasure should be supposed to depend on quantity alone.

If I am asked what I mean by difference of quality in pleasures, or what makes one pleasure more valuable than another, merely as a pleasure, except its being greater in amount, there is but one possible answer. Of two pleasures, if there be one to which all or almost all who have experience of both give a decided preference, irrespective of any feeling of moral obligation to prefer it, that is the more desirable pleasure. If one of the two is, by those who are competently acquainted with both, placed so far above the other that they prefer it, even though knowing it to be attended with a greater amount of discontent, and would not resign it for any quantity of the other pleasure which nature is capable of, we are justified in ascribing to the preferred enjoyment a superiority in quality so far outweighing quantity as to render it, in comparison, of small account.

Now it is an unquestionable fact that those who are equally acquainted with and equally capable of appreciating and enjoying both do give a most marked preference to the manner of existence which employs their higher faculties. Few human creatures would consent to be changed into any of the lower animals for a promise of the fullest allowance of a beast's pleasures; no intelligent human being would consent to be a fool, no instructed person would be an ignoramus, no person of feeling and conscience would be selfish and base, even though they should be persuaded that the fool, the dunce, or the rascal is better satisfied with his lot than they are with theirs. They would not resign what they possess more than he for the most complete satisfaction of all the desires which they have in common with him. If they ever fancy they would, it is only in cases of unhappiness so extreme that to escape from it they would exchange their lot for almost any other, however undesirable in their own eyes. A being of higher faculties requires more to make him happy, is capable probably of more acute suffering, and certainly accessible to it at more points, than one of an inferior type; but in spite of these liabilities, he can never really wish to sink into what he feels to be a lower grade of existence. We may give what explanation we please of this unwillingness; we may attribute it to pride, a name which is given indiscriminately to some of the most and to some of the least estimable feelings of which mankind are capable; we may refer it to the love of liberty and personal independence, an appeal to which was with the Stoics one of the most effective means for the inculcation of it; to the love of power or to the love of excitement, both of which do really enter into and contribute to it; but its most appropriate appellation is a sense of dignity, which all human beings possess in one form or other, and in some, though by no means in exact, proportion to their higher faculties, and which is so essential a part of the happiness of those in whom it is strong that nothing which conflicts with it could be otherwise than momentarily an object of desire to them. Whoever supposes that this preference takes place at a sacrifice of happiness—that the superior being, in anything like equal circumstances, is not happier than the inferior—confounds the two very different ideas of happiness and content. It is indisputable that the being whose capacities of enjoyment are low has the greatest chance of having them fully satisfied; and a highly endowed being will always feel that any happiness which he can look for, as the world is constituted, is imperfect. But he can learn to bear its imperfections, if they are at all bearable; and they will not make him envy the being who is indeed unconscious of the imperfections, but only because he feels not at all the good which those imperfections qualify. It is better to be a human being dissatisfied than a pig satisfied; better to be Socrates dissatisfied than a fool satisfied. And if the fool, or the pig, are of a different opinion, it is because they only know their own side of the question. The other party to the comparison knows both sides.

It may be objected that many who are capable of the higher pleasures occasionally, under the influence of temptation, postpone them to the lower. But this is quite compatible with a full appreciation of the intrinsic superiority of the higher. Men often, from infirmity of character, make their election for the nearer good, though they know it to be the less valuable; and this no less when the choice is between two bodily pleasures than when it is between bodily and mental. They pursue sensual indulgence to the injury of health, though perfectly aware that health is the greater good. It may be further objected that many who begin with youthful enthusiasm for everything noble, as they advance in years, sink into indolence and selfishness. But I do not believe that those who undergo this very common change voluntarily choose the lower description of pleasures in preference to the higher. I believe that, before they devote themselves exclusively to the one, they have already become incapable of the other. Capacity for the nobler feelings is in most natures a very tender plant, easily killed, not only by hostile influences, but by mere want of sustenance; and in the majority of young persons it speedily dies away if the occupations to which their position in life has devoted them, and the society into which it has thrown them, are not favorable to keeping that higher capacity in exercise. Men lose their high aspirations as they lose their intellectual tastes, because they have not time or opportunity for indulging them; and they addict themselves to inferior pleasures, not because they deliberately prefer them, but because they are either the only ones to which they have access or the only ones which they are any longer capable of enjoying. It may be questioned whether anyone who has remained equally susceptible to both classes of pleasures ever knowingly and calmly preferred the lower, though many, in all ages, have broken down in an ineffectual attempt to combine both.

From this verdict of the only competent judges, I apprehend there can be no appeal. On a question which is the best worth having of two pleasures, or which of two modes of existence is the most grateful to the feelings, apart from its moral attributes, and from its consequences, the judgment of these who are qualified by knowledge of both, or, if they differ, that of the majority among them, must be admitted as final. And there needs be the less hesitation to accept this judgment respecting the quality of pleasures, since there is no other tribunal to be referred to even on the question of quantity. What means are there of determining which is the acutest of two pains, or the intensest of two pleasurable sensations, except the general suffrage of those who are familiar with both? Neither pains nor pleasures are homogeneous, and pain is always heterogeneous with pleasure. What is there to decide whether a particular pleasure is worth purchasing at the cost of a particular pain, except the feelings and judgment of the experienced? When, therefore, those feelings and judgment declare the pleasures derived from the higher faculties to be preferable *in kind*, apart from the question of intensity, to those of which the animal nature, disjoined from the higher faculties, is susceptible, they are entitled on this subject to the same regard.

I have dwelt on this point as being part of a perfectly just conception of utility or happiness considered as the directive rule of human conduct. But it is by no means an indispensable condition to the acceptance of the utilitarian standard; for that standard is not the agent's own greatest happiness, but the greatest amount of happiness altogether; and if it may possibly be doubted whether a noble character is always the happier for its nobleness, there can be no doubt that it makes other people happier, and that the world in general is immensely a gainer by it. Utilitarianism, therefore, could only attain its end by the general cultivation of nobleness of character, even if each individual were only benefited by the nobleness of others, and his own, so far as happiness is concerned, were a sheer deduction from the benefit. But the bare enunciation of such an absurdity as this last renders refutation superfluous.

According to the greatest happiness principle, as above explained, the ultimate end, with reference to and for the sake of which all other things are desirable—whether we are considering our own good or that of other people—is an existence exempt as far as possible from pain, and as rich as possible in enjoyments, both in point of quantity and quality; the test of quality and the rule for measuring it against quantity being the preference felt by those who, in their opportunities of experience, to which must be added their habits of self-consciousness and self-observation, are best furnished with the means of comparison. This, being according to the utilitarian opinion the end of human action, is necessarily also the standard of morality, which may accordingly be defined "the rules and precepts for human conduct," by the observance of which an existence such as has been described might be, to the greatest extent possible, secured to all mankind; and not to them only, but, so far as the nature of things admits, to the whole sentient creation....

I must again repeat what the assailants of utilitarianism seldom have the justice to acknowledge, that the happiness which forms the utilitarian standard of what is right in conduct is not the agent's own happiness but that of all concerned. As between his own happiness and that of others, utilitarianism requires him to be as strictly impartial as a disinterested and benevolent spectator. In the golden rule of Jesus of Nazareth, we read the complete spirit of the ethics of utility. "To do as you would be done by," and "to love your neighbor as yourself," constitute the ideal perfection of utilitarian morality. As the means of making the nearest approach to this ideal, utility would enjoin, first, that laws and social arrangements should place the happiness or (as, speaking practically, it may be called) the interest of every individual as nearly as possible in harmony with the interest of the whole; and, secondly, that education and opinion, which have so vast a power over human character, should so use that power as to establish in the mind of every individual an indissoluble association between his own happiness and the good of the whole, especially between his own happiness and the practice of such modes of conduct, negative and positive, as regard for the universal happiness prescribes; so that not only he may be unable to conceive the possibility of happiness to himself, consistently with conduct opposed to the general good, but also that a direct impulse to promote the general good may be in every individual one of the habitual motives of action, and the sentiments connected therewith may fill a large and prominent place in every human being's sentient existence. If the impugners of the utilitarian morality represented it to their own minds in this its true character, I know not what recommendations possessed by any other morality they could possibly affirm to be wanting to it; what more beautiful or more exalted developments of human nature any other ethical system can be supposed to foster, or what springs of action, not accessible to the utilitarian, such systems rely on for giving effect to their mandates.

The objectors to utilitarianism cannot always be charged with representing it in a discreditable light. On the contrary, those among them who entertain anything like a just idea of its disinterested character sometimes find fault with its standard as being too high for humanity. They say it is exacting too much to require that people shall always act from the inducement of promoting the general interest of society. But this is to mistake the very meaning of a standard of morals and confound the rule of action with the motive of it. It is the business of ethics to tell us what are our duties, or by what test we may know them; but no system of ethics requires that the sole motive of all we do shall be a feeling of duty; on the contrary, ninety-nine hundredths of all our actions are done from other motives, and rightly so done if the rule of duty does not condemn them. It is the more unjust to utilitarianism that this particular misapprehension should be made a ground of objection to it, inasmuch as utilitarian moralists have gone beyond almost all others in affirming that the motive has nothing to do with the morality of the action, though much with the worth of the agent. He who saves a fellow creature from drowning does what is morally right, whether his motive be duty or the hope of being paid for his trouble; he who betrays the friend that trusts him is guilty of a crime, even if his object be to serve another friend to whom he is under great obligations. But to speak only of actions done from the motive of duty, and in direct obedience to principle: it is a misapprehension of the utilitarian mode of thought to conceive it as implying that people should fix their minds upon so wide a generality as the world, or society at large. The great majority of good actions are intended not for the benefit of the world, but for that of individuals, of which the good of the world is made up; and the thoughts of the most virtuous man need not on these occasions travel beyond the particular persons concerned, except so far as is necessary to assure himself that in benefiting them he is not violating the rights, that is, the legitimate and authorized expectations, of anyone else. The multiplication of happiness is, according to the utilitarian ethics, the object of virtue: the occasions on which any person (except one in a thousand) has it in his power to do this on an extended scale—in other words, to be a public benefactor—are but exceptional; and on these occasions alone is he called on to consider public utility; in every other case, private utility, the interest or happiness of some few persons, is all he has to attend to. Those alone the influence of whose actions extends to society in general need concern themselves habitually about so large an object. In the case of abstinences indeed—of things which people forbear to do from moral considerations, though the consequences in the particular case might be beneficial—it would be unworthy of an intelligent agent not to be consciously aware that the action is of a class which, if practiced generally, would be generally injurious, and that this is the ground of the obligation to abstain from it. The amount of regard for the public interest implied in this recognition is no greater than is demanded by every system of morals, for they all enjoin to abstain from whatever is manifestly pernicious to society.

The same considerations dispose of another reproach against the doctrine of utility, founded on a still grosser misconception of the purpose of a standard of morality and of the very meaning of the words "right" and "wrong." It is often affirmed that utilitarianism renders men cold and unsympathizing; that it chills their moral feelings toward individuals; that it makes them regard only the dry and hard consideration of the consequences of actions, not taking into their moral estimate the qualities from which those actions emanate. If the assertion means that they do not allow their judgment respecting the rightness or wrongness of an action to be influenced by their opinion of the qualities of the person who does it, this is a complaint not against utilitarianism, but against any standard or morality at all; for certainly no known ethical standard decides an action to be good or bad because it is done by a good or bad man, still less because done by an amiable, a brave, or a benevolent man, or the contrary. These considerations are relevant, not to the estimation of actions, but of persons; and there is nothing in the utilitarian theory inconsistent with the fact that there are other things which interest us in persons besides the rightness and wrongness of their actions. The Stoics, indeed, with the paradoxical misuse of language which was part of their system, and by which they strove to raise themselves above all concern about anything but virtue, were fond of saying that he who has that has everything; that he, and only he, is rich, is beautiful, is a king. But no claim of this description is made for the virtuous man by the utilitarian doctrine. Utilitarians are quite aware that there are other desirable possessions and qualities besides virtue, and are perfectly willing to allow to all of them their full worth. They are also aware that a right action does not necessarily indicate a virtuous character, and that actions which are blamable often proceed from qualities entitled to praise. When this is apparent in any particular case, it modifies their estimation, not certainly of the act, but of the agent. I grant that they are, notwithstanding, of opinion that in the long run the best proof of a good character is good actions; and resolutely refuse to consider any mental disposition as good of which the predominant tendency is to produce bad conduct. This makes them unpopular with many people, but it is an unpopularity which they must share with everyone who regards the distinction between right and wrong in a serious light; and the reproach is not one which a conscientious utilitarian need be anxious to repel.

If no more be meant by the objection than that many utilitarians look on the morality of actions, as measured by the utilitarian standards, with too exclusive a regard, and do not lay sufficient stress upon the other beauties of character which go toward making a human being lovable or admirable, this may be admitted. Utilitarians who have cultivated their moral feelings, but not their sympathies, nor their artistic perceptions, do fall into this mistake; and so do all other moralists under the same conditions. What can be said in excuse for other moralists is equally available for them, namely, that, if there is to be any error, it is better that it should be on that side. As a matter of fact, we may affirm that among utilitarians, as among adherents of other systems, there is every imaginable degree of rigidity and of laxity in the application of their standard; some are even puritanically rigorous, while others are as indulgent as can possibly be desired by sinner or by sentimentalist. But on the whole, a doctrine which brings prominently forward the interest that mankind have in the repression and prevention of conduct which violates the moral law is likely to be inferior to no other in turning the sanctions of opinion against such violations. It is true, the question "What does violate the moral law?" is one on which those who recognize different standards of morality are likely now and then to differ. But difference of opinion on moral questions was not first introduced into the world by utilitarianism, while that doctrine does supply, if not always an easy, at all events a tangible and intelligible, mode of deciding such differences.

It may not be superfluous to notice a few more of the common misapprehensions of utilitarian ethics....

We not uncommonly hear the doctrine of utility inveighed against a *godless* doctrine. If it be necessary to say anything at all against so mere an assumption, we may say that the question depends upon what idea we have formed of the moral character of the Deity. If it be a true belief that God desires, above all things, the happiness of his creatures, and that this was his purpose in their creation, utility is not only not a godless doctrine, but more profoundly religious than any other. If it be meant that utilitarianism does not recognize the revealed will of God as the supreme law of morals, I answer that a utilitarian who believes in the perfect goodness and wisdom of *God* necessarily believes that whatever God has thought fit to reveal on the subject of morals must fulfill the requirements of utility in a supreme degree. But others besides utilitarians have been of opinion that the Christian revelation was intended, and is fitted, to inform the hearts and minds of mankind with a spirit which should enable them to find for themselves what is right, and incline them to do it when found, rather than to tell them, except in a very general way, what it is; and that we need a doctrine of ethics, carefully followed out, to *interpret* to us the will of God. Whether this opinion is correct or not, it is superfluous here to discuss; since whatever aid religion, either natural or revealed, can afford to ethical investigation is as open to the utilitarian moralist as to any other. He can use it as the testimony of God to the usefulness or hurtfulness of any given course of action by as good a right as others can use it for the indication of a transcendental law having no connection with usefulness or with happiness....

Again, defenders of utility often find themselves called upon to reply to such objections as this—that there is not time, previous to action, for calculating and weighing the effects of any line of conduct on the general happiness. This is exactly as if anyone were to say that it is impossible to guide our conduct by Christianity because there is not time, on every occasion on which anything has to be done, to read through the Old and New Testaments. The answer to the objection is that there has been ample time, namely, the whole past duration of the human species. During all that time mankind have been learning by experience the tendencies of actions; on which experience all the prudence as well as all the morality of life are dependent. People talk as if the commencement of this course of experience had hitherto been put off, and as if, at the moment when some man feels tempted to meddle with the property or life of another, he had to begin considering for the first time whether murder and theft are injurious to human happiness. Even then I do not think that he would find the question very puzzling; but, at all events, the matter is now done to his hand. It is truly a whimsical supposition that, if mankind were agreed in considering utility to be the test of morality, they would remain without any agreement as to what *is* useful, and would take no measures for having their notions on the subject taught to the young and enforced by law and opinion. There is no difficulty in proving any ethical standard whatever to work ill if we suppose universal idiocy to be conjoined with it; but on any hypothesis short of that, mankind must by this time have acquired positive beliefs as to the effects of some actions on their happiness; and the beliefs which have thus come down are the rules of morality for the multitude, and for the philosopher until he has succeeded in finding better. That philosophers might easily do this, even now, on many subjects; that the received code of ethics is by no means of divine right; and that mankind have still much to learn as to the effects of actions on the general happiness, I admit or rather earnestly maintain. The corollaries from the principle of utility, like the precepts of every practical art, admit of indefinite improvement, and, in a progressive state of the human mind, their improvement is perpetually going on. But to consider the rules of morality as improvable is one thing; to pass over the intermediate generalization entirely and endeavor to test each individual action directly by the first principle is another. It is a strange notion that the acknowledgment of a first principle is inconsistent with the admission of secondary ones. To inform a traveler respecting the place of his ultimate destination is not to forbid the use of landmarks and direction-posts on the way. The proposition that happiness is the end and aim of morality does not mean that no road ought to be laid down to that goal, or that persons going thither should not be advised to take one direction rather than another....

Whatever we adopt as the fundamental principle of morality, we require subordinate principles to apply it by; the impossibility of doing without them, being common to all systems, can afford no argument against any one in particular; but gravely to argue as if no such secondary principles could be had, and as if mankind had remained till now, and always must remain, without drawing any general conclusions from the experience of human life is as high a pitch, I think, as absurdity has ever reached in philosophical controversy.

The remainder of the stock arguments against utilitarianism mostly consist in laying to its charge the common infirmities of human nature, and the general difficulties which embarrass conscientious persons in shaping their course through life. We are told that a utilitarian will be apt to make his own particular case an exception to moral rules, and, when under temptation, will see a utility in the breach of a rule, greater than he will see in its observance. But is utility the only creed which is able to furnish us with excuses for evil-doing and means of cheating our own conscience? They are afforded in abundance by all doctrines which recognize as a fact in morals the existence of conflicting considerations, which all doctrines do that have been believed by sane persons. It is not the fault of any creed, but of the complicated nature of human affairs, that rules of conduct cannot be so framed as to require no exceptions, and that hardly any kind of action can safely be laid down as either always obligatory or always condemnable. There is no ethical creed which does not temper the rigidity of its laws by giving a certain latitude, under the moral responsibility of the agent, for accommodation to peculiarities of circumstances; and under every creed, at the opening thus made, self-deception and dishonest casuistry get in. There exists no moral system under which there do not arise unequivocal cases of conflicting obligation. These are the real difficulties, the knotty points both in the theory of ethics and in the conscientious guidance of personal conduct. They are overcome practically, with greater or with less success, according to the intellect and virtue of the individual; but it can hardly be pretended that anyone will be the less qualified for dealing with them, from possessing an ultimate standard to which conflicting rights and duties can be referred. If utility is the ultimate source of moral obligations, utility may be invoked to decide between them when their demands are incompatible. Though the application of the standard may be difficult, it is better than none at all; while in other systems, the moral laws all claiming independent authority, there is no common umpire entitled to interfere between them; their claims to precedence one over another rest on little better than sophistry, and, unless determined, as they generally are, by the unacknowledged influence of consideration of utility, afford a free scope for the action of personal desires and partialities. We must remember that only in these cases of conflict between secondary principles is it requisite that first principles should be appealed to. There is no case of moral obligation in which some secondary principle is not involved; and if only one, there can seldom be any real doubt which one it is, in the mind of any person by whom the principle itself is recognized.

RECONCEIVING AUTONOMY: SOURCES, THOUGHTS, AND POSSIBILITIES

Jennifer Nedelsky

Jennifer Nedelsky is Professor of Law and Political Science at the University of Toronto. In addition to her book Private Property and the Limits of American Constitutionalism *(Chicago, 1990), she has published numerous articles in the areas of constitutional history and interpretation, feminist theory, and comparative constituencies.*

Nedelsky raises questions about the individualist conceptions of the self and of autonomy prevalent in the liberal tradition. While she agrees that autonomy in the sense of an individual having the freedom to pursue his or her life goals is valuable and needs to be embraced by feminists, she rejects two assumptions of liberal theory: that autonomy is possible in isolation from others and that it is promoted through non-interference from others. Nedelsky argues that we need to reconceive autonomy as shaped in and through relationships; it can flourish or be harmed by particular sorts of relationships.

I. Feminism and the Tensions of Autonomy

A. *Feminist Guidance*

Feminism requires a new conception of autonomy. The prevailing conception stands at the core of liberal theory and carries with it the individualism characteristic of liberalism. Such a conception cannot meet the aspirations of feminist theory and is inconsistent with its methodology.[1] The basic value of autonomy is, however, central to feminism. Feminist theory must retain the value, while rejecting its liberal incarnation.

Feminism is not, of course, alone in its rejection of liberal individualism. The individualistic premises of liberal theory (and their inadequacies) have become an important subject of debate in contemporary political and legal theory.[2] Feminism offers us a particularly promising avenue for advancing this debate, not because it provides a fully articulated alternative to liberal theory, but because feminist concerns so effectively capture the problems such an alternative must address.

Feminism appears equivocal in its stance toward liberalism because it simultaneously demands a respect for women's individual selfhood and rejects the language and assumptions of individual rights that have been our culture's primary means of expressing and enforcing respect for selfhood. This apparent equivocation is not the result of superficiality or indecision. On the contrary, it reflects the difficulties inherent in building a theory (and practice) that adequately reflects both the social and the individual nature of human beings. Feminist perspectives and demands can guide the inquiry: they point to dangers, define aspirations, and indicate the contours of an approach that transcends the limitations of liberal theory while fostering its underlying values. This article is part of that process: an inquiry into the meaning of autonomy, guided by feminist objectives.

B. *Self-Determination and Social Construction*

The notion of autonomy goes to the heart of liberalism and of the powerful, yet ambivalent, feminist

Reprinted with permission from *Yale Journal of Law and Feminism* 1:7 (Spring 1989): 7–36 [edited].

rejection of liberalism. The now familiar critique by feminists and communitarians is that liberalism takes atomistic individuals as the basic units of political and legal theory and thus fails to recognize the inherently social nature of human beings. Part of the critique is directed at the liberal vision of human beings as self-made and self-making men (my choice of noun is, of course, deliberate). The critics rightly insist that, of course, people are not self-made. We come into being in a social context that is literally constitutive of us. Some of our most essential characteristics, such as our capacity for language and the conceptual framework through which we see the world, are not made by us, but given to us (or developed in us) through our interactions with others.

The image of humans as self-determining creatures nevertheless remains one of the most powerful dimensions of liberal thought.[3] For all of us raised in liberal societies, our deep attachment to freedom takes its meaning and value from the presupposition of our self-determining, self-making nature: that is what freedom is for, the exercise of that capacity. No one among the feminists or communitarians is prepared to abandon freedom as a value, nor, therefore, can any of us completely abandon the notion of a human capacity for making one's own life and self. Indeed, feminists are centrally concerned with freeing women to shape our own lives, to define who we (each) are, rather than accepting the definition given to us by others (men and male-dominated society, in particular). Feminists therefore need a language of freedom with which to express the value underlying this concern. But that language must also be true to the equally important feminist precept that any good theorizing will start with people in their social contexts. And the notion of social context must take seriously its constitutive quality; social context cannot simply mean that individuals will, of course, encounter one another.[4] It means, rather, that there are no human beings in the absence of relations with others. We take our being in part from those relations.

The problem, of course, is how to combine the claim of the constitutiveness of social relations with the value of self-determination.[5] The problem is common to all communitarians but is particularly acute for feminists because of women's relations to the traditions of theory and of society. It is worth restating the problem in terms of these complex and ambivalent relations. Feminists angrily reject the traditions of liberal theory that has felt so alien, so lacking in language and ability to comprehend our reality, and that has been so successful in defining what the relevant questions and appropriate answers are.[6] Anyone who has listened closely to academic feminists will have heard this undercurrent of rage at all things liberal.[7] Yet liberalism has been the source of our language of freedom and self-determination. The values we cherish have come to us embedded in a theory that denies the reality we know: the centrality of relationships in constituting the self.

That knowledge has its own ironies: women know this centrality through experience, but the experience has been an oppressive one. One of the oldest feminist arguments is that women are not seen and defined as themselves, but in their relations to others. The argument is posed at the philosophical level of de Beauvoir's claim that men always experience women as "Other" (a perverse, impersonal form of "relationship") and in the mundane, but no less important, form of objections to being defined as someone's wife or mother. We need a language of self-determination that avoids the blind literalness of the liberal concept.[8] We need concepts that incorporate our experience of embeddedness in relations, both the inherent, underlying reality of such embeddedness and the oppressiveness of its current social forms.[9] I think the best path to this end is to work towards a reconception of the term "autonomy."

C. *Finding One's Own Law*

The word "autonomy" is so closely tied to the liberal tradition that it is often treated as symbolizing the very individualism from which I am trying to reclaim it. Among critics of liberalism one can hear the phrase "autonomous individuals" uttered with the contempt meant to express the absurdity of conceiving of individuals in isolation from one another. But one also hears the word used with approbation, usually in the context of the problem of achieving true autonomy (as opposed to the false liberal autonomy). I think the word itself carries with it the complexity of the issue. The literal meaning of the word is to be "governed by one's own law." To become autonomous is to come to be able to find and live in accordance with one's own law.

I speak of "becoming" autonomous because I think it is not a quality one can simply posit about human beings. We must develop and sustain the capacity for finding our own law, and the task is to understand what social forms, relationships, and personal practices foster that capacity. I use the word "find" to suggest that we do not make or even exactly choose our own law. The idea of "finding" one's law is true to the belief that even what is truly one's own law is shaped by the society in which one lives and the relationships that are a part of one's life. "Finding" also permits an openness to the idea that one's own law is revealed by spiritual sources, that our capacity to find a law within us comes from our spiritual nature.[10] From both perspectives, the law is one's own in the deepest sense, but not made by the individual; the individual develops it, but in connection with others; it is not chosen, but recognized. "One's own law" connotes values, limits, order, even commands just as the more conventional use of the term does. But these values and demands come from within each person rather than being imposed from without. The idea that there are commands that one recognizes as one's own, requirements that constrain one's life, but come from the meaning or purpose of that life, captures the basic connection between law and freedom[11]—which is perhaps the essence of the concept of autonomy. The necessary social dimension of the vision I am sketching comes from the insistence, first, that the capacity to find one's own law can develop only in the context of relations with others (both intimate and more broadly social) that nurture this capacity, and second, that the "content" of one's own law is comprehensible only with reference to shared social norms, vales, and concepts.

This concept has inherent tensions between the idea of autonomy as both originating with oneself *and* being conditioned and shaped by ones's social context. Those tensions are the tensions of feminism, and they come from feminism's recognition of the nature of human beings. The word "autonomy" is thus a suitable vehicle for achieving feminist objectives. It is capable of carrying the full dimensions of feminist values and perspectives. And sticking with the word, working toward reconceiving it, has the further virtue of rescuing not only a term, but a basic value, from the confines of liberalism. That is the project of this article.

D. *The Objective: Understanding and Overcoming Pathology*

So far we have only a general sense of what some of the ingredients of autonomy must be. I have already mentioned the (problematic) notion of self-determination. I think comprehension, confidence, dignity, efficacy, respect, and some degree of peace and security from oppressive power are probably also components. (Note that these ingredients are both characteristics of individuals and states of being which presuppose certain conditions in intimate and social-structural relationships.) But we have as yet no full or integrated articulation of the values and perspectives I have mentioned. There are many different ways of trying to come to the articulation of a new value or, as in the case of autonomy, to help that value emerge from the process of transforming an old one. Here I want to focus on a particular dimension of our current conception of autonomy that stands in the way of the necessary transformation: the dichotomy between autonomy and the collectivity.

This dichotomy is grounded in the deeply ingrained sense that individual autonomy is to be achieved by erecting a wall (of rights) between the individual and those around him. Property (as I will discuss more fully later) is, not surprisingly, the central symbol for this vision of autonomy, for it can both literally and figuratively provide the necessary walls. The most perfectly autonomous man is thus the most perfectly isolated.[12] The perverse quality of this implicit ideal is, I trust, obvious. This vision of the autonomous individual as one securely isolated from his threatening fellows seems to me to be a pathology that has profoundly affected western societies for several centuries.[13]

If we ask ourselves what actually enables people to be autonomous, the answer is not isolation, but relationships—with parents, teachers, friends, loved ones—that provide the support and guidance necessary for the development and experience of autonomy. I think, therefore, that the most promising model, symbol, or metaphor for autonomy is not property, but childrearing. There we have encapsulated the emergence of autonomy through relationship with others. We see that relatedness is not, as our tradition teaches, the antithesis of autonomy, but a literal precondition of autonomy, and interdependence a constant component of autonomy. This model of what actually sustains autonomy is, appropriately, the opposite of the isolated, distancing symbol of property. We may, in fact, have more to learn about the nature of autonomy by thinking about childrearing than by the sort of inquiry into law and bureaucracy that I undertake here. But there are advantages to avoiding the problems of extrapolating from intimate relationships to large-scale ones. And some of the relationships which either foster or undermine autonomy are not of an intimate variety, but rather are part of the more formal structures of authority (which include employment relations as well as the officially "public" sphere I deal with here). Ultimately, I think the different approaches (and I plan eventually to pursue both) will complement each other.

Here I will focus on how the pathological conception of autonomy as boundaries against others has played itself out in some of the central public institutions of the United States. This approach has the virtue of addressing immediate problems while at the same time moving toward a fuller conception of autonomy. The approach is also suggested by my belief that abstract theorizing alone is not likely to get us where we want to go. If we want to understand the social forms that foster autonomy, we need first to look at actual practices of collective organization that can reveal for us the possibilities of a new understanding of autonomy and help us understand the nature and sources of the limitations of the prevailing conception. Let me turn therefore to the particular problems of autonomy in the American bureaucratic state.

II. Bureaucracy, Collectivity, and Autonomy

The American bureaucratic state threatens individual autonomy because it threatens to transform the objects of its action from citizens to subjects—dependent, passive, helpless before the power of the collective. This threat is not peculiar to American forms of bureaucracy. Whenever a democratic society assumes collective responsibility for individual welfare, it faces the task of implementing this responsibility in ways that foster rather than undermine citizens' sense of their own competence, control, and integrity. The traditional American conception of autonomy impedes this task and thus limits our understanding of the problem and the potential for its solution. The tradition of American political thought sets individual autonomy in opposition to collective power.[14] This opposition now distorts our perceptions. The characteristic problem of autonomy in the modern state is not, as our tradition has taught us, to shield individuals from the collective, to set up legal barriers around the individual which the state cannot cross, but to ensure the autonomy of individuals when they are *within* the legitimate sphere of collective power. The task is to render autonomy compatible with the interdependence which collective power (properly used) expresses.

The problem of interdependence, individual autonomy, and collective power takes its characteristic modern form in the relations between citizens and administrative bodies.[15] The dependence of citizens on those who apply policy to their particular cases poses a problem distinct from the traditional issues of democracy. The extent to which the policies administered are formulated by bodies (e.g., elected legislatures) which citizens have democratic access to and control over continues to be an important issue. But it is no longer the only one.

Even if legislative policy-making were democratically optimal, citizens in the modern state would still be subject to the decisions of administrators. People's knowledge that the policies behind these decisions were made in some distant way with their consent may do little to ease their sense of dependence and helplessness. (The distant quality of consent seems likely to prevail in any large-scale society, even when the forms of democracy make citizen participation active, widespread, and effective.) The nature of people's interactions with bureaucratic decision-making may be as important as the nature of legislative policy-making[16] in determining whether citizens are autonomous members of a democratic society or dependent subjects of collective control.

The objective of making the direct exercise of collective power conducive to the autonomy of those subject to it requires more than a shift in focus from legislation to administration. We also need to see that our traditional focus on protecting the individual from the collective has given us a distorted image of the problem of autonomy and of alternative visions of society. The prevailing conception of autonomy sets alternatives in the context of a false choice: when autonomy is identified with individual independence and security from collective power, the choice is posed between admitting collective control and preserving autonomy in any given realm of life. It is as though the degree of collective responsibility for, say, the material needs of citizens must result in a corresponding decrease in the autonomy of those receiving the benefits. Such a dichotomy between autonomy and collective power forecloses a whole range of social arrangements—at least to anyone who values autonomy. A classic example of a choice premised on this dichotomy is the claim that a free press is possible only if newspapers are privately owned. This claim rests on a notion of what the law can and cannot do which is unfounded. It assumes, first, that the law can protect property against the power of the collective and that this protection will provide the necessary insulation and foundation for freedom of expression. At the same time, the claim assumes that the law cannot provide comparable *direct* protection of this freedom by legal limits on the power of the state to control expression. The implicit conclusion is that if there were public rather than private ownership of the press, those wishing to express their views would require the (virtually uncontrollable) "permission" of the state.

This conclusion denies the possibility of structuring the relations between citizen and public press, their corresponding rights and powers, in a way compatible with freedom of expression. But we need no more assume that the relationship would take the form of "asking permission" to use the press than we assume the necessity of asking permission to use public schools, parks, or water. There is nothing in the nature of the legal protections themselves, (as I shall return to later) nor in our experience of public resources to justify the stark dichotomy between freedom founded on private property and tyranny produced by collective control.[17]

State control of resources always poses problems, but the American legal system has found ways of distinguishing control from caprice, of rendering dependence upon state services (imperfectly) compatible with freedom and autonomy. Were the dichotomy between state power and autonomy exhaustive and inevitable, we would be forced either to give up on autonomy in large spheres of our lives or to advocate a vast limitation on state power, which would be incompatible both with modern economic and political realities and with aspirations for a more communal and equitable society. This choice is not necessary. Despair about individual freedom in the face of collective power reflects a poverty of imagination about the possibilities for protection and control.

Belief in the false choice between autonomy and collective power is the product of a powerful tradition of political thought. Paradoxically, the tradition (mis)shapes the perception of the problem while pointing in the direction of solutions....

We can examine some of the directions the tradition points to, some of the problems it alerts us to in the effort to reconceive autonomy.

The first is that while the stark opposition between autonomy and collectively presumed in the American tradition is misleading, that opposition also reflects a basic truth. There is a real and enduring tension between the individual and the collective, and any good political system will recognize it. The problem with our tradition is that it not only recognizes, but highlights the tension, and has a limited view of the non-oppositional aspects of the relation and of the social dimension of human beings. There is thus a twofold objective in reconceiving autonomy: (1) to recognize that the irreducible tension between the individual and the collective makes choices or trade-offs necessary; and (2) at the same time, to move beyond a conception of human beings which sees them exclusively as separate individuals and focuses on the threat of the community. The collective is not simply a potential threat to individuals, but is constitutive of them, and thus is a source of their autonomy as well as a danger to it.[18] For some purposes it makes sense to talk about the separate constructs of "the individual" and "the community." But those constructs are misleading[19] if they obscure the fact that people do not exist in isolation, but in social and political relations. People develop their predispositions, their interests, their autonomy—in short, their identity—in large part out of these relations. The very way one experiences and perceives the world, for example, is shaped by the social constructions of language. The task, then, is to think of autonomy in terms of the forms of human interactions in which it will develop and flourish.[20] And the starting point of this inquiry must be an attention both to the individuality of human beings and to their essentially social nature. The hope is that a society with such an outlook could escape some of the problems of our more limited perspective and could structure relations of community which also fostered autonomy.

The tradition warns us, however, that there is probably an inevitable trade-off between collective cohesion and responsibility on the one hand, and individual freedom and autonomy on the other—at least as we currently understand these concepts. The individualism of liberal capitalism has never actually provided all citizens with its proclaimed values of freedom and independence. But our system has made comparatively few demands on its citizens and has left a wide scope for individual choice. American democratic capitalism has neither demanded nor fostered excellence, virtue, commitment, social or civic responsibility (which is not, of course, to say that none of these ever emerged). A society which seeks to promote these characteristics will have a far greater interest in the values its members hold, the relationships they form, and the way they choose to spend their time and their talents. Such a society will almost certainly be more demanding and constraining in those areas, leaving fewer spheres of action to private choice.

Ultimately, the objective is to find the optimal relation between individual and collective and, more particularly, to understand the core of human autonomy and the forms and scope of collective activity that will foster it. We can take from the tradition a recognition that the new forms of autonomy within collectivity will involve choices, even trade-offs. But the limitations of our current conceptions should lend us confidence that to choose new forms of autonomy is to reconstitute it, not abandon it.

The tradition also offers us a way of grasping the essence of autonomy. An understanding of the powerful associations between property, security, and autonomy is likely to provide a better sense of the nature of autonomy and the requirements for it. (This despite the fact that autonomy in a collective state will be quite different from the individualistic, oppositional model associated with property.)

The rhetorical, even mythical power of the identification of property with freedom goes beyond the literal power and advantages of property under liberal capitalism. And the experience of the rights of property as qualitatively different from and more secure than other legal rights cannot be accounted for by the legal history of property rights. Property rights have in fact been subject to a great deal of state interference and to redefinition which amounted to destruction.[21] As I argued earlier, there is nothing intrinsic about legal rights of property which make them a more promising basis for freedom than other legal rights. Property rights, like all legal rights, take their formal meaning from definitions and guarantees provided by the state. The security which property provides rests, on an institutional level, on the state's power to protect what it defines as property. And the forms and means of defining and protecting property are, at root, indistinguishable from those of other legal rights.

What then accounts for the enduring associations between property and autonomy? Two striking and distinguishing characteristics of property are its concreteness and the relative unobtrusiveness of the state power which lies behind it.[22] The concreteness of property makes it an effective symbol. It is easy for people to see the relationship between owning property and autonomy, and it seems (deceptively) easy to know what property is and when it is violated. And most people do not think of their ownership of property as in any way involving the state; it is simply theirs. It is not granted to them by the state or administered by the state. Most property rights can be exercised most of the time without the obvious intervention of the state. The fact that property rights only have meaning when backed by the power of the state seems an abstraction that students have a hard time grasping, many sophisticated theorists ignore entirely, and the general population has no idea about. Due process, by comparison with property, is abstract rather than concrete and clearly requires official action. If these are the characteristics which make the association of property with freedom so compelling, we should be alerted to the probable limitations of due process as an alternative source, symbol, or protector of autonomy.

Finally, my comments about property reflect a more general approach to the problem of autonomy and to what tradition and current practices can teach us about it. Autonomy is an elusive problem in part because it is practically inseparable from an experience or feeling.[23] In an earlier version of this article I added the qualification that "It would, of course, seriously distort any political analysis of autonomy to treat it as a 'mere' feeling. One can evaluate the degree of autonomy an individual is actually capable of exercising, and there can be disparities between experience and reality." This qualification was an effort to meet the objection that people may be deluded about what provides them with autonomy.[24] In fact, I think people may be very wrong in their opinions about the relation between autonomy and institutions or practices. But I doubt that it makes sense to say they could actually feel autonomous and not be so.[25] However, just as we need to develop a new conception of autonomy, probably most of us need to learn what real autonomy feels like.

Our actual experiences of autonomy—those rare moments when we feel that we are following an inner direction rather than merely responding to the pushes and pulls of our environment—are so fleeting that it is often difficult to know or remember what it is like to live by one's own law. And our society misleads us about the very nature of autonomy as well as the conditions for it. We not only learn, as I noted above, that the essence of autonomy is the power to close out others; we are also taught that money is power and power is freedom—and the power is from and over others, not inner power.[26] We are taught that the capacity to manipulate our environment is the power of freedom. A participant at the Yale Legal Theory Workshop, where an earlier version of this article was presented, suggested that those who feel autonomous are those who believe that their actions generate predicted and desired results, as opposed to those who feel powerless to control their lives, who feel buffeted about by forces beyond their control. (This notion of autonomy, he pointed out, has the virtue of being measurable.) In fact, many people learn to "play the game" effectively, to do what is wanted of them, and to confidently reap the rewards handed out for compliance. This counts as success and generates the feeling he described. It is not autonomy. Playing someone else's game well is not defining the path of one's own life.

These perverse messages about autonomy contain a germ of truth: powerlessness is destructive of autonomy. And the question of power points to the ways autonomy entails, but does not consist in, a feeling. Autonomy is a capacity, but it is unimaginable in the absence of the feeling or experience of being autonomous. The capacity can be destroyed by being subjected to the arbitrary and damaging power of others.[27] Power relations are, in that sense, an external, "objective" reality. To be autonomous a person must feel a sense of her own power (which does not mean power over others), and that feeling is only possible within a structure of relationships conducive to autonomy. But it is also the case that if we lose our feeling of being autonomous, we lose our capacity to be so. Autonomy is a capacity that exists only in the context of social relations that support it and only in conjunction with the internal sense of being autonomous.

Although I define autonomy as a capacity and not a feeling, I insist upon the feeling of autonomy as an inseparable component of the capacity for several reasons. First, I think the capacity does not exist without the feeling. Second, I think the feeling is our best guide to understanding the structure of those relationships which make autonomy possible. Third, focusing on the feelings of autonomy defines as authoritative the voices of those whose autonomy is at issue. Their autonomy is then not a question that can be settled for them by others. The focus on feeling or internal experience defines whose perspective is taken seriously,[28] and by turning our attention in the right direction it enhances our ability to learn what fosters and constitutes autonomy. For the purpose of evaluating institutions, one can generate a list, or at least a sense, of the components or dimensions of autonomy and then try to identify the practices that seem to foster some or all of those components. To that extent one would be engaged in an "objective" inquiry. But the underlying concern would be the actual experience of autonomy. We cannot understand or protect, much less reconceive, autonomy unless we attend to what gives citizens a sense of autonomy, to what makes them feel competent, effective, able to exercise some control over their lives, as opposed to feeling passive, helpless, and dependent.[29]

But this ingredient of subjectivity introduces an added complication. The institutions, social practices, and relations that foster the feeling of autonomy may vary considerably across cultures and over time within a culture.[30] These variations raise the question of whether one form and experience of autonomy (and the institutions that sustain it) can be judged to be superior to another. (Such a judgment is, of course, implicit in this article.) Recognizing subjective experience as an essential component of autonomy invites all the much debated problems of objectivity and universal truths—which are beyond the scope of this article. Here I want only to draw attention to feelings as a basic dimension of the abstract concept of autonomy, and to note that feminist theory is becoming increasingly practiced in dealing with these issues.

Recognizing the subjective element of autonomy is also important because the very fact that autonomy is in part a feeling may make people particularly resistant to changes in its form. Bruno Bettelheim, for example, suggests that the ancient nomads, as they watched society shifting to agriculture, may have responded with anxiety and contempt as they saw their fellows give up "for greater economic ease and security, a relative freedom to roam."[31] In this instance, Bettelheim is willing to make a tacit judgment that the new settled life was not, in fact, a diminished one. But he does suggest that real accommodations had to be made. Because, as I argued above, trade-offs are probably inevitable, hostility to new approaches to autonomy may be based on real perceptions of loss. Perhaps it is even likely that the new approach will draw the contempt Bettelheim mentions. Perhaps all alternatives to what has been perceived as the essence of freedom are likely to be cast by anxious critics in terms of the basic (and base) needs, as libertarians, for example, dismiss as mere envy or greed claims that economic equality is a precondition of autonomy....

Autonomy should be contrasted with democratic values in the following related senses: democracy is not itself sufficient to ensure autonomy; autonomy is a substantive value which can be threatened by democratic outcomes, even though the democratic process is itself a necessary component of autonomy; and the outcomes of democratic processes should respect the autonomy of all citizens and should be held accountable for doing so.

The confusion and correspondence between democracy and autonomy do not, of course, rest with prevailing legal theories alone; the correspondence between the two is real. Participation seems central to both. Its importance to democracy is obvious. It has been my basic point here that citizens who participate directly[32] in the decisions affecting them are less likely to relinquish their autonomy as they accept the benefits or control of the state. But participation here is a means to autonomy, not its substantive content. The fact that the means of protecting autonomy may primarily be forms of participation should not lead to the confusion that autonomy can be subsumed under democracy. We should not collapse democracy and autonomy into a single value, despite their close connection.

The perfection of democracy thus cannot alone assure protection of autonomy. To believe that it can is to believe that a democratically organized collective would never do violence to the autonomy of any of its members. That seems to me implausible. What is required is an understanding of the substance of autonomy and of the practices that foster it so that citizens can ask whether the actions or institutions proposed in their collective decision-making are consistent with the autonomy of all. We must, for example, ask whether official action in any particular circumstance denies clients basic respect or treats them in ways that makes them less able to understand what is happening to them, less able to participate effectively in the decision affecting their lives, less able to define and pursue their own goals—in short, in ways that undermine rather than foster their capacity to find and live by their own law.

It may be that if such failings are found, increased participation will be a partial remedy. Or the client may need information or support. Or the outlook of the official (e.g., seeing parents as time-consuming sources of trouble rather than as participants valued for their information and judgment) may be the source of the problem. Or it may be that the interaction, such as intrusive home visits, is inherently incompatible with the autonomy of the client and can only be justified under exceptional circumstances (e.g., the sort of probable cause needed for a warrant). And impasses such as that over home visits may be evidence that the whole relationship between client and authority must be restructured if it is to foster the client's autonomy.

Further, some mechanism would probably be needed to encourage and facilitate the posing of questions about institutional compatibility with autonomy. In other words, there must be means of measuring the content of collective decisions against the (separate and substantive) value of autonomy. Such means would include appropriate institutions, language, and habits of inquiry through which citizens and representatives of some kind (including judges) could check whether the laws, rules, or patterns of official behavior fostered or undermined autonomy. Such an inquiry is only possible if we have a concept of autonomy that is distinct from the democratic processes which may threaten it.

It is important to distinguish the above (somewhat vague and awkwardly stated) ideas from the conventional liberal understanding of individual rights, and of autonomy in particular. First, the wordy awkwardness arises from a deliberate effort to avoid the neat and pithy claim that autonomy should be a substantive limit to democratic outcomes. That powerful vision of rights-as-limits no longer seems to me the best way of thinking about or trying to institutionalize the notion that in any society there will be competing values and that groups of people exercising democratic power may be inclined to override even basic values. What seems important is the clear articulation of the values a society considers basic (surely an ongoing process), together with the idea that democratic outcomes are not (at least in the first instance) dispositive of the meaning of those values or what counts as a violation of them. But that is a long way from saying that rights are trumps. A society should, as I argued above, acknowledge the inherent tension between the collective and the individual and find means of mediating as well as sustaining the tension. I say "sustaining" because the values of neither the individual nor the collective should be collapsed into the other. Treating rights as limits on democracy is one way of maintaining both distinct values; but it is a method that throws its weight too heavily to the side of the individual.

There is a second distinction that is best put as an answer to the following challenge: You started by saying that you were going to break down the conventional dichotomies, but aren't we right back in the conventional choices and conflicts between collective goods and individual rights? Aren't you just restating the old liberal argument that, of course, rights (including autonomy) sometimes have to be balanced against the public good—only without the willingness to guarantee rights against collective oppression? How is this a new conception of autonomy?[33] The answer is that in measuring and weighing collective choices against the value of autonomy, the meaning of autonomy will be different. The autonomy I am talking about does remain an individual value, a value that takes its meaning from the recognition of (and respect for) the inherent individuality of each person. But it takes its meaning no less from the recognition that individuality cannot be conceived of in isolation from the social context in which that individuality comes into being. The value of autonomy will at some level be inseparable from the relations that make it possible; there will thus be a social component built into the meaning of autonomy. That is the difference. But the presence of a social component does not mean that the value cannot be threatened by collective choices; hence the continuing need to identify autonomy as a separate value, to take account of its vulnerability to democratic decision-making, and to find some way of making those decisions "accountable" to the value of autonomy.

V. Conclusion

This inquiry has been prompted more by an interest in future possibilities than by hopes for the perfection of autonomy under the current American legal system. Forms of bureaucratic decision-making—however participatory or otherwise optimal—cannot change basic power relations and structures of inequality. These more than anything determine the potential for autonomy for all citizens, for subordination and powerlessness are incompatible with autonomy. But even in a quite imperfect society, experiments with forms of collective (bureaucratic) power and with the relations between those implementing it and those dependent upon it can give us insight into what optimal forms and relations would look like. What I have tried to do is suggest a framework which we can use to help extract what is useful out of current experiments—since I believe that a new conception of autonomy is not likely to spring full-blown from theory.

I see the development of such a conception as essential for working out alternatives to our present system. The alternatives which seeem compelling to me all involve a far greater role for collective power and responsibility than does our current system. Those who aspire to such alternatives must be able to persuade themselves as well as their critics that such changes need not diminish, though they will certainly change, autonomy. More importantly, we must have language that adequately captures our highest goals, in terms that reflect both the individual and the social dimensions of human beings. That language will take some time to emerge, but in the meantime we cannot cede to liberal convention a monopoly on the value of autonomy.

AUTHOR'S NOTE

This project began when I was a postdoctoral fellow at the Russell Sage Foundation. The Foundation provided a wonderful community of scholars, who gave me many helpful comments and suggestions. I am particularly grateful to Robert Merton for his encouragement, probing questions, and general assistance with this and related projects. Circulating the draft I wrote at Russell Sage first introduced me to the exciting range of overlapping projects other feminist scholars are engaged in. I received encouraging and helpful responses from Drucilla Cornell, Kathy Ferguson, and Susan Sherwin. I would also like to thank the participants in the Yale Legal Theory Workshop for their questions and comments. Finally, I owe a special thanks to my colleague Hudson Janisch, who first planted the seed of my interest in administrative law and who has helped me in the area since. Naturally, any errors are mine alone.

NOTES

1. Among the many discussions of feminist theory and methodology are: Alison Jagger, *Feminist Politics and Human Nature* (Totowa, N.J.: Rowman & Allanheld, 1983); Lorraine Code, Sheila Mullett, and Christine Overall, eds., *Feminist Perspectives: Philosophical Essays on Method and Morals* (Toronto: University of Toronto Press, 1988); Sandra Harding, ed., *Feminism and Methodology: Social Science Issues* (Bloomington: Indiana University Press, 1987); Carol Gilligan, *In a Different Voice: Psychological Theory and Women's Development* (Cambridge: Harvard University Press, 1982); Tronto, "Beyond Gender Difference to a Theory of Care," 12 *Signs* 644 (1987) (applying Gilligan's work to political theory); MacKinnon, "Feminism, Marxism, Method, and the State: Toward Feminist Jurisprudence," 8 *Signs* 635 (1983); Scales, "The Emergence of Feminist Jurisprudence: An Essay," 95 *Yale L.J.* 1373 (1986).
2. Among the best known critics of liberal individualism are Alasdair MacIntyre, *After Virtue: A Study in Moral Theory* (Notre Dame, Ind: University of Notre Dame Press, 1981); Michael J. Sandel, *Liberalism and the Limits of Justice* (Cambridge: Cambridge University Press, 1982); Charles Taylor, *Philosophy and the Human Sciences* (Cambridge: Cambridge University Press, 1985), particularly Ch. 7, "Atomism." Michael Sandel has edited an excellent collection of essays on this debate entitled *Liberalism and Its Critics* (New York: New York University Press, 1984).
3. Charles Taylor provides a particularly compelling statement of the importance of this vision in the origins and enduring power of liberal thought. Taylor, "Justice After Virtue," paper presented at Legal The-

ory Workshop Series, University of Toronto Faculty of Law, 23 October 1987. See also "Atomism," *supra* note 2.

4. I once heard (an otherwise) thoughtful liberal theorist dismiss with exasperation the critique that liberal theory fails to take seriously the social nature of human beings. "Of course it does," he said. "Liberal theory is all about the proper rules governing the interaction among people, so, of course it recognizes their social nature." This observation completely misses the point. Drawing boundaries around the sphere of individual rights to protect those individuals from the intrusions of others (individuals or the state) naturally takes for granted the existence and interaction of others. Such an assumption, however, has nothing in common with the claim that a person's identity is in large part constituted by her interactions with others. On this view there is, in an important sense, no "person" to protect within a sphere protected from all others, for there is no pre-existing, unitary self in isolation from relationships.
5. The parallel with old theological debates about the freedom of man and the omnipotence of God is really quite striking. Taylor comments on the relevance of these debates to the emergence of liberalism. "Justice After Virtue," *supra* note 3.
6. It is, of course, not some disembodied Theory, but those who practice it who arouse these feelings. The convention is, however, to indulge in the more polite (and safer) sounding reification.
7. Excepting, of course, liberals who think of themselves as feminists. They take their theoretical framework from liberalism and thus are not part of the enterprise of developing a distinctive feminist theory.
8. The fact that contemporary liberals know all about "social conditioning" doesn't seem to change the structure of their concepts. It may mean that they, too, face similar dilemmas but do not choose to make them central to their theoretical inquiries.
9. In developing such concepts, feminists have an advantage in avoiding one of the pitfalls of challenges to liberal individualism: women's experience of relationships as oppressive as well as essential has the virtue of making us less likely to be romantic about the virtues of community as such.
10. Indeed, it may be that the idea of one's own law, as opposed to one's own wishes, presupposes some transcendent, spiritual order of which we are a part. Such a notion need not, of course, be anything like Kant's categorical imperative with its exclusive reliance on man's rationality. See Immanuel Kant, *Groundwork of the Metaphysic of Morals*, trans. H.J. Paton (New York: Harper & Row, 1964).
11. There is a passage in Ursula K. Le Guin's novel, *The Beginning Place* (New York: Harper & Row, 1980), which expresses this connection: "There was no boundary. It was all his country. But this time, this was far enough: he would go no further now. Part of the pleasure of being here was that he could listen for and obey such impulses and commands coming from within him, undistorted by external pressures and compulsions. In that obedience, for the first time since early childhood, he sensed the headiness of freedom, the calmness of power" (p. 27).

    Of course this connection is played out in the political realm as well, and entails the same paradox: in a democracy, limited government means self-limiting government. The people must limit themselves. The fictions of constitutionalism try to obscure the paradox: a constitution spells out the limits the people have placed on themselves; those limits once set need not be reconsidered (except in the exceptional circumstances of amendments). The fiction works particularly nicely in the United States, where the Constitution was written so long ago. The reality is, of course, that the limits must be constantly reinterpreted. The "people," in the form of their representatives in the judiciary, must constantly set and reset the limits that they will treat as clear, fixed, and unquestioned. Within these self-defined limits, the collective finds its own law, which is an essential element of collective freedom. I discuss the paradox of self-limiting government more fully in "American Constitutionalism and the Paradox of Private Property," in *Constitutionalism and Democracy*, J. Elster and R. Slagstad, eds. (Cambridge: Cambridge University Press, 1988), 241-273.
12. There is an interesting corroboration of my view of property-based independence as isolation in J. G.A. Pocock's analyses of the relationship between property and autonomy in 17th century liberal thought: "The point about freehold in this context is that it involves its proprietor as little as possible in dependence upon or *even in relations with other people* and

so leaves his free for the full austerity of citizenship in the classical sense" (emphasis added). J.G.A. Pocock, *Politics, Language, and Time: Essays on Political Thought and History* (New York: Atheneum, 1971), 91.

13. For a brilliant discussion of the western conception of the separate self, see Catherine Keller, *From a Broken Web: Separation, Sexism, and Self* (Boston: Beacon Press, 1986). She also points to another connection between feminism and the reconception of autonomy: men's fear of women is tied to their fear of the collective. She begins her book (p.1) with a telling quotation from C.S. Lewis's *Surprised by Joy*: "You may add that in the hive and the anthill we see fully realized the two things that some of us most dread for our own species—the dominance of the female and the dominance of the collective."
14. This focus on American political thought provides specificity in looking at how the problem of autonomy fits within a larger framework of political theory. The American treatment of autonomy is particularly focused on boundaries (as we shall see later), but it is not unique. On the contrary, I think it helps us understand a problem characteristic of all liberal thought.
15. In the course of my discussion I will use both the terms "state power" and "collective power." I am addressing the broad problem of the tension between individual autonomy and the power of the collective. In our political system that power is ordinarily exercised by the state, and thus in most contexts it is appropriate to refer to state or governmental power; but part of my argument is that the tension will endure however collective power is organized. The analysis therefore should be relevant both to alternative political systems and to the non-governmental power exercised by such "private" entities as corporations.
16. The legislative and bureaucratic "models" of democratic citizenship are in some ways in tension with one another. If the legislature managed to make all policy decisions, if it were possible to formulate rules which neutral, efficient bureaucrats could apply mechanically (i.e., without evil degrees of discretion), citizens would be spared the sense of being subject to arbitrary control. But they would also have little scope for participation in the decisions on their own cases. While this may be advantageous from one point of view, it may seriously undermine the autonomy of citizens directly subject to governmental action over which they feel they have no control.
17. The example of airwaves, of course, points to the complexity of government control. The government has assumed a much larger role in regulating the electronic than the written media, on the grounds of regulating a finite public resource. One need not be sanguine about the history of this regulation to see that public control can take a wide range of forms.
18. The childrearing model is helpful here: parents are both a source of a child's autonomy and a potential threat to it. It is easy to see that the powerful relationship of dependency children have with their parents is a necessary foundation for the child's autonomy. But the relationship can also be structured in ways that undermine autonomy, that maintain dependence. It is probably the case that all relationships necessary for autonomy can easily be perverted to undermine it.
19. In our current discourse it is hard to avoid such misleading language. The concept of "self-determination" which I described as central to autonomy, carries the tension implicit in the problem itself. Few people in our culture believe that people are truly self-determining. It is commonly accepted that people are shaped to a great extent by their culture and genetic make-up. Yet self-determination remains an important value and aspiration. The new conception of autonomy must give force to the aspiration while incorporating a recognition of interdependence.
20. Bruno Bettelheim offers a brief but fascinating discussion of the kinds of relations which foster autonomy. In his account they are direct and personal rather than large scale, anonymous, or abstract. If his views are correct, we can both understand something about why autonomy has been associated with the private sphere and see that the relevant characteristics are possible in spheres not conventionally considered private. Bettelheim offers as examples both the relation to parents and to teachers. Bruno Bettelheim, *The Informed Heart: Autonomy in a A Mass Age* (Glencoe, Ill: Free Press, 1960), 95-97.
21. *See* Scheiber, "Property Law, Expropriation, and Resource Allocation by Government in the United States, 1789-1910," 33 *J. Econ. Hist.* 232 (1973).

22. This argument is elaborated in J. Nedelsky, *supra* note 11.
23. It is important to avoid a misunderstanding about the "mere subjectivity" of feelings. In my view, feelings have two dimensions not commonly associated with the word: (1) There is a truth about feelings. One can be right or wrong about them. Thus while they are subjective in the sense that only the person having the feeling is "authoritative" on whether she feels something, her true feelings are not simply whatever impression, or experience, or sensation she has at the moment. A person must inquire internally to determine her true feelings. They may be hard to discern, there may be confusion, but there is in the end a right answer to what she really feels. (2) The related point is that feelings are, at least in our culture, not always immediately ascertainable. There is a commonplace association between the word "feeling" and something like the experience of a pin prick. One feels pain. No inquiry is necessary. The experience is immediate and obvious. The perception is instantaneous and (under normal circumstances, excluding states of hypnosis or delusion) infallible. But this association is misleading. Even a feeling like anger is by no means always obvious. Only the "feeler's" statements are authoritative, but she can be mistaken. In our culture most people seem to need to learn to recognize the signs by which one can tell the truth of a feeling.
24. I think the qualification was also, less consciously, a response to the sense that taking subjectivity seriously was unacceptable in academic theorizing about law and politics. And, indeed, despite the disclaimer, a commentator on the paper wittily objected that, "If autonomy is a feeling, there are pharmacological solutions to the problem." I think that is clever, but wrong. Perhaps I have too little faith in modern technology and/or too little experience with drugs, but I can imagine a drug making one feel euphoric, maybe even happy, but not autonomous.
25. Of course, to ascertain someone's feeling of autonomy, it would be necessary to communicate effectively about the content of the value and the experience, not simply ask for a response to a term, "autonomy."
26. The distinction between power over others and empowerment, a power from within, is discussed in Starhawk, *Truth or Dare: Encounters With Power, Authority, and Mystery* (San Francisco: Harper & Row, 1987).
27. Bettleheim's *The Informed Heart*, *supra* note 20, is a study of the extreme case of such destruction in concentration camps.
28. I owe this insight to Lucinda Finley.
29. A government's efforts to encourage its subjects to feel autonomous when they are not is obviously a perversion. The recent history of administrative hearings may provide evidence of the relation between the actual effectiveness of citizen-participation and the way hearings make participants feel about the process, the decision, and their role in it. See Handler, "Justice for the Welfare Recipient: Fair Hearings in AFDC: The Wisconsin Experience," 43 *Soc. Serv. Rev.* 12 (1969); Hammer and Hartley, "Procedural Due Process and the Welfare Recipient: A Statistical Study of AFDC Fair Hearings in Wisconsin," 1978 *Wis. L.Rev.* 145.
30. For example, the much vaunted freedom of mainstream North-American life seems to many Native Americans to entail patterns of work with such extreme regimentation as to be incompatible with freedom or autonomy. (Brian Slattery of Osgoode Hall Law School provided me with this example from his work with Native peoples.) Of course, this observation leaves open the question whether the participants in the mainstream patterns of life actually experience their lives as autonomous.
31. Bettelheim, *supra* note 20, at 45.
32. As noted earlier, I do not think that the more general form of participation in elections of democratic bodies can substitute for direct participation in administrative decision-making.
33. My thanks to my colleague Alan Brudner for posing this challenge.

WHAT DOES THE DIFFERENT VOICE SAY?: GILLIGAN'S WOMEN AND MORAL PHILOSOPHY

Margaret Urban Walker

Margaret Urban Walker teaches philosophy at Fordham University. She is the author of Moral Understandings: A Feminist Study in Ethics *(Routledge, 1998) as well as numerous articles in the areas of moral theory and feminist ethics.*

Walker examines Gilligan's account of an ethic of care as a characteristically female voice distinct from an ethic of justice in order to explore answers to questions about whether the ethic of care presents a unified perspective on morality and, if so, whether it represents an important addition or corrective to prevailing philosophical views on morality. She argues that there are two distinct and mutually independent themes in the care perspective: a substantive one that is a "care and response orientation" and a methodological one that is a "contextual-deliberative picture" of moral thinking. Together these themes make it possible to think of the care perspective as a unified approach distinct from and even challenging traditional accounts of morality.

Many want to see psychologist Carol Gilligan as advancing the view that there are "male" and "female" moral voices, a view which she disclaims early on in *In A Different Voice*[1] and in later writings.[2] Gilligan does advance the hypothesis that the different voice—or "care perspective"—is "characteristically a female phenomenon in the advantaged populations that have been studied" and holds that this hypothesis receives support from studies other than her own (R, p. 330). But she continues to maintain that what makes this voice different is that it offers "a moral perspective different from that currently embedded in psychological theories and measures" (R, p. 327), one which embodies distinctive conceptions of self, relationship, and responsibility (R, p. 326).

Much discussion of Gilligan's work has centered on whether she has adequate evidence for the claim of significant gender-related differences in moral thinking. I pursue another set of questions here, because the interest of the different voice for moral philosophy lies primarily in *what* it expresses, perhaps some significant part of moral truth.[3] My questions are: whether the differences in moral thinking she outlines amount to a unified perspective on morality; what that perspective is; and whether this (*possibly* more characteristically "feminine") viewpoint represents an important or interesting addition or correction to prevailing philosophical views.[4]

In section I, I distinguish two themes apparently characteristic of the different voice, and in Section II show how plausible versions of each may appear separately in already well-known types of moral views. In Section III I consider two ways in which versions of the themes might be internally related to produce a view which is both unified and distinctive. One of these interpretations is found superior as a rendering of Gilligan's subjects' views; it is also a plausible moral outlook which significantly challenges standard philosophical conceptions about morality. In conclusion (IV) I remark that while the existence and significance of a different moral voice remains in question, women's voices surely matter for moral philosophy in any case.

Reprinted with permission of Kluwer Academic Publishers and Margaret Urban Walker from *The Journal of Value Inquiry* 23 (1989): 123–143.

I

Gilligan holds that the different voice is "characterized not by gender but theme" (p. 2). The characterizing theme is referred to by her variously as "care," "responsibility," or "response" (in contrast to the alternative theme of "justice" or "fairness" or "reciprocity"). But in reviewing her presentation of and commentary on those particular quoted voices which are held to exemplify the care perspective, one hears not one theme but *two*, and these two themes appear not only distinct, but mutually independent.

One focal description of the care and justice perspectives which comes early on in *In A Different Voice* makes the two themes readily apparent:

> In this [care] conception, the moral problem arises from conflicting responsibilities rather than from competing rights and requires for its resolution a mode of thinking that is contextual and narrative rather than formal and abstract. This conception of morality as concerned with the activity of care centers moral development around the understanding of responsibility and relationships, just as the conception of morality as fairness ties moral development to the understanding of rights and rules (p. 19).

This passage touches on both the *substance* of moral concern in the alternative visions, and on the *method* of definition and construction appropriate to the solutions of moral problems. Both strains recur throughout the book's discussion, sometimes intertwined, sometimes discretely. I will call the substantive one a *care and response orientation*, the methodological one a *contextual-deliberative picture* of moral thinking.[5]

Often Gilligan seems to identify the different voice in terms of a kind of *value* orientation, i.e. what it sees as calling for moral concern. For example:

> The moral imperative that emerges repeatedly in interviews with women is an injunction to care, a responsibility to discern and alleviate the "real and recognizable trouble" of this world. For men, the moral imperative appears rather as an injunction to respect the rights of others and thus to protect from interference the rights to life and self-fulfillment (p. 100).

The care orientation resides in "sensitivity to the needs of others and the assumption of responsibility for taking care," (p. 16); it is concerned with "equity" in light of persons' very different needs (p. 164). An "overriding concern with relationships and responsibilities" (pp. 16-17) makes connection and attachment (pp. 19, 45, 48), compassion (p. 71) and intimacy (p. 17) central moral concerns. As little girls are reported to terminate their games rather than threaten the continuance of their relationships (p. 10), so adult women recognize "the continuing importance of attachment in the human life cycle" (p. 23); it "creates and sustains the human community" (p. 156).

Sometimes Gilligan's characterizations are ambiguous between caring as instrumental to the goods of need-fulfillment or non-violence, and caring as itself the object or attainment of moral endeavor. But these are not exclusive alternatives, and often enough Gilligan seems to be saying, and is heard by others as saying, that women care specially *for* relationships or attachments as themselves fundamental goods of our lives. Jean Grimshaw, for example, in a searching consideration of the idea of a "female ethic" concedes: "There is evidence, both from common experience and from the work of Carol Gilligan and others, that women often perceive the maintenance of relationships as very important in their lives, and see it as a moral priority."[6] In a care and response orientation, then, caring relationships and the responsive attitude which sustains them are particularly morally valued, whether as means, ends, or both.

Gilligan, however, understands these women to be describing and exemplifying a different structure of moral understanding as well as a certain set of concerns. Here the difference between care and justice is marked by method, approach, and the standards for defining and solving moral problems. Here thinking that is "contextual and narrative" contrasts with thinking that "abstracts the moral problem from the interpersonal situation" (p. 32) so that a "formal logic" of fairness can take hold (p. 73). The justice perspective drives toward classification of cases at a high level of generality so that antecedently ordered rules and formulas can do their work in deciding the particular case. The different voice, however, strains against schematically depicted situations toward further concrete information about the particular case (pp. 100-101). It is mistrustful about the relevance of prior, abstract moral orderings (p. 101). And it does not necessarily expect moral dilemmas to yield to resolution without remainder on which "all rational men can agree"[7] and no conflicting claims retain authority. This contextual deliberative view rejects a top-down, nomological picture of moral decision as a deductive operation, it views typifications of actions and situations as only, at best, heuristic, and it leaves room for moral remainders. For it a moral problem is not "a math problem with humans" (p. 28) and there is no moral decision procedure, no guarantee of neat closure. Instead, a "narrative of relationships that extends over time" (p. 28) may supply materials for a context-sensitive adjudication of claims.

Here are the two themes, consonant but seemingly addressed to different questions: one to *what* we must think about morally, one to *how* we must do so. This seems not simply an ethic of care nor simply a context-sensitive, particularistic ethic, but instead a *contextualist ethic of care*. Is this *one* thing, or *two* things contingently juxtaposed?

II

It is not difficult to see how a care and response orientation and a contextual deliberative view might be separate commitments. A contextualist, after all, could have many other value orientations than the care and response one. She might believe that what matters morally is self-realization, or eudaimonia, or something else. She might think many things matter—courage, wisdom, integrity, dignity, gratitude—and each in several ways. She might think care matters too, but not see it as a specially dominant or highest-ranked value. But her way of structuring moral deliberation and achieving resolution will not be a logical deduction or computation defined in advance by a strict formal program, but a minute and concrete exploration of the particulars. She might like "Sharon" in Gilligan's book "try to be as awake as possible, to try to know the range of what you feel, to try to consider all that's involved" (p. 99) and then, to borrow a phrase, let the decision rest with perception.[8] But her perception might be informed by more than considerations of care and response, and perhaps by other kinds of considerations entirely. Aristotelians, ethical individualists, Bradleyian self-realizationists, and Christian agapeists can be (although may not be in every version) contextualists in the relevant sense.

In turning to the reverse case, of an ethic of care that is not particularistic, but is principled and rigorously logical in carrying theory into practice, consider classical utilitarianism (and many contemporary variants) which could lay claim to being the ultimate in case perspectives.[9] The utilitarian sees the world in terms of a single value, happiness, where that is specified in terms of fulfillment, contentment, satisfaction, pleasure, or preference, i.e., the well-being of others in their own terms.[10] But utilitarians are not content to let the concern for well-being play itself out in the commonplace and parochial ways, and so insist on unqualified and impartial commitment to caring—caring for all, counting each for one and no more. When joined to the positive injunction to produce the greatest aggregate amounts of well-being possible, the strenuousness of this caring seems hard to outdo. Further, full-blooded act utilitarians are known for their mitigated commitment to justice: in the face-off between care and justice that is one recurring motif of Western ethical thought,[11] utilitarians know what side they are on.[12]

Utilitarianism thus can see itself as raising on the ground of human interdependence and fellow-feeling a system for responding to human want without compromise and for extending the care of each over the whole human community, and perhaps over the wider community of all feeling, needing beings.[13] Utilitarians also sometimes claim for their view the virtue of sensitivity to context, inasmuch as rights and wrongs are reckoned afresh case by case. But they are reckoned rigorously, by a procedure laid out in advance, one which allows no competitors and which promises decisive resolution where applicable at all. The narrative of relationships could only matter in providing data for prediction of outcomes and payoffs. Utilitarian moral decision making *is* a math problem with humans.

Is the different voice then whole in some way other than being the sum of these two separable parts? Does it matter? Before proceeding to the first question, I touch here briefly on the second.

I think the unity of the different voice does matter. For Gilligan, it must have mattered originally in a special way in her critique of Kohlbergian developmental theory. In laying down the gauntlet on page one of her book, Gilligan claimed that the two ways of speaking about morality, self, and other which she discerned were an ongoing contrapuntal structure of moral life rather than "steps in a developmental progression," i.e., that the ordering of these ways as higher or lower stages à la Kohlberg was a mistake. But his challenge itself takes the view that these perspectives on morality are equally *like* Kohlbergian stages—internally differentiated but "logically unified, functionally *holistic* structures"[14] of moral thought—at the *same* level. For the different voice to have been a fragment of a view or worse an unordered set of moral *apercus* would have made a lame case, in Kohlbergian terms.

The interests of moral philosophy are not those of Kohlbergian theory, and moral philosophy is properly eager for any pieces of moral insight with claim to intuitive entrenchment. Still, what seems *exciting* about the different voice for moral philosophy is that it might reveal or suggest a unified and comprehensive view of moral life—one might say a "moral vision"—which is genuinely alternative in important ways to those which are prevalent philosophically. It would not be negligible, although it would not be so exciting, I think, if the news were that women tended to align, say, with Mill on value but with Aristotle on method.

III

The consideration of utilitarianism as a care-ethic provides a useful comparison case in seeking a picture of the different voice whole. Utilitarians are fully committed to caring about welfare, about the "well-being of others in their own terms," about assessing the particular, present situation, and do not traffic in advance ordering of different values (for there is only one) but in reckoning actual consequences. These are all marks of the care perspective Gilligan describes (e.g., pp. 78, 101). But clearly, Gilligan has not meant that women have a bent for utilitarian thinking. This would leave out the emphasis of the different voice on care focused in terms of relationship, intimacy, attachment, and "natural bonds" (pp. 17, 19, 32, 48, 132). Magnification of the "impartial viewpoint" has put both utilitarianism and Kantian ethical views under suspicion of unwisely demoting or neglecting just the special caring bonds on which the different voice dwells.[15] Seeing care in terms of relationship is a clue to understanding how care and contextualism may be more than accidentally conjoined.

I see two different ways of bringing the care-orientation and the contextual-deliberative view into more intimate union. Both turn on an identification of care primarily with the loving attention characteristic of specific personal bonds. This identification joins them in common cause against the utilitarian ideal of uniform, generalized benevolence—"administrative care" one might call it, as it undertakes the task of reckoning in common terms the satisfactions of persons close by and familiar alongside those who may be any, distant, and unknown. The emphasis on personal bonds also provides each of these ways with a clear basis for finding universalism and legalism either inappropriate or derivative as views about the structure of moral reasoning and resolution. But these two ways part company decisively over a fundamental issue. On one, the creation and maintenance of caring relations is *itself* the human good; on the other, caring relations are a necessary condition for the practice within which varied human goods might emerge and flourish. The first way is neater, but it is also more reductive about the direction and point of moral life than is the second way. The divergence corresponds to the ambiguity noted earlier in Gilligan's own descriptions of women's valuation of caring.

The first way is represented lucidly and without compromise by Nel Noddings. In *Caring: A Feminine Approach to Ethics and Moral Education*[16] Noddings anchors morality in the human affective response of natural sympathy and its characteristic issue of natural caring, transformed reflectively into a moral ideal of oneself as one-caring. The caring this ideal demands consists in direct relations in which loving attention and minute recognition flow toward the one cared for, who completes the caring by responding in ways which show its nurturant and supportive power (C, pp. 79-84). Such relations can arise only in actual encounters. Since this is so and since the acts constituting care are determined by close perceptions of individuals, the only appropriate methods of moral thought and resolution are those which embody as much concrete detail as possible and which represent as specific a response as can be mustered. Subsuming people's "cases" under generalization and treating them by rule would be not simply inadequate, but a denial of the very nature of the moral demand and a foreclosure of the achievement of the only moral value. Noddings makes this clear. "Rule-bound responses in the name of caring lead us to suspect that the claimant wants most to be credited with caring" (C, p. 24). A care-ethic of this kind is necessarily contextualist because of the value it demands be realized morally (a completed instance of a specific caring relation) and the nature of human beings who participate in its realization (psychologically non-interchangeable individuals whose ways of wanting, needing, perceiving, and receiving may be very different). Legalistic reasoning and impartial computations are wholly inapplicable on this view, and the respect or generalized benevolence which are their attitudinal correlates—their "carings"—are found counterfeit, period. On Noddings's view caring is just one thing, and it is, morally speaking, the *only* thing. The presence, ordering, and extent of moral obligations for her varies with encounters and the possibility of completion, but the object of obligations is invariable; care is both ground and object of the demands morality places upon us.

Noddings's view is one candidate for a consistent systematization of what the different voice is saying. It suggests that women, including Gilligan's subjects, tend to care, ultimately, *about* caring; that is what they seek to initiate or complete in their lives, or at least what they feel (in Noddings's view correctly) obligated to realize. It also suggests that if care as a specific relation is itself what is valued, then caring will be kept close to home, since direct encounters, and primarily those embedded in a prior history of relationship, are the only obligating occasions. Generalized concern—whether benevolence or that yet more astringent attitude, respect—and its concomitant sense of obligation are on this view illusory (C, pp. 18, 29, 90). It is in just these respects that I find Noddings's view less than satisfactory either as a rendering of what resides in Gilligan's subjects' voices, or as a moral vision on its own feet.[17]

Are Gilligan's women properly described as caring about care itself? It seems not; different of the different voices invoke, as decisive or central grounds for moral choice, such values as equality (p. 64), honesty (p. 65), authenticity (p. 52), growth (p. 159), safety from danger and hurt (p. 129), self-preservation (p. 111). Further, a striking feature of a number of cited responses is a tendency to extend the scope of concern very widely indeed. One woman feels strongly "responsible to the world" and obligated to better it if only on a small scale (p. 21). Another finds mundane practical decisions open onto agonizing vistas of others' poverty, unknown children in need, and a world full of trouble and headed for "doom"; and it is clear that she does not dismiss the claim this seems to make on her (p. 99). "Claire" articulates the sweeping view positively: other people are "*part of you*," so that link by link is formed a "giant collection of people that you are connected to" (p. 160). A number of Gilligan's women seem not at all hesitant to generalize concern and to ponder, troubled, the overwhelming implications. What they seem *not* to do is to generalize the *other persons*, to view them abstractly as generalizable kinds of cases (p. 11). The distinction is important and is needed to make sense of a certain kind of strain in these voices. A different way of modelling the moral sensibility at work here captures this.[18]

On this second way, an ethic of care might be seen as affirming the *generative* role of caring relations in morality. Caring relations initiate new human beings into the kind of interpersonal acknowledgement that full moral concern requires: of the separate reality of other persons, of the complex and precarious process of communicating and understanding. Ongoing opportunities to care and be cared for continue the education of those dispositions and capacities which allow us to know how it is with another and to make ourselves known as well. Caring relationship provides a *paradigm* of the understanding that determines full and appropriate response to persons: it must be direct, personal, and specific; it requires minute attention, identification in thought and feeling, precise communication. It will be, among other things, "contextual and narrative," that is, defined by reference to rich circumstantial detail, to the history of the episode, and ideally to the history of the person. This understanding carried through to appropriate action, on this view, *is* caring. But to carry through to *appropriate* action requires more. It requires a *conception of human good*, a picture of what's worth aiming at; there is no reason to think that this cannot be a rich and varied conception in which many important goods (intrinsic, internal, contributory) are complexly related. Care itself, this attentive relation of acknowledgement and understanding, will no doubt reappear *within* this conception of value. It is one of those things worth spending the hard-won understanding of care on reproducing. Care plays a very special role in moral life, on this view, but not that of sole or even dominant end. Care appears instead as a condition for the fullest and most direct pursuit of such goods as there may be.[19]

Full, minute, and sensitive attention is a paradigm of how the materials for the exercise of moral concern are had. It is a *paradigm* because it represents the *best* case: it is in this way I know "fully and directly" to what and to whom I am responding. Yet many cases are not, cannot be, of the best type. Connection may be attenuated, access blocked. If I am not in a position to care in the paradigmatic way I may be reduced to applying incomplete versions of care, or even resorting to surrogates: general benevolence, respect, fair consideration may be the best I can do. It is, I think, important to let this way remain open. The different voice need not be seen as denying any role to generalized concern, but as marking its incompleteness. This truly rotates the usual order of philosophical precedence 180°, saying that the particular is always first, and the application of rules or generalized standards to someone as a kind of "case" is not just a derivative, but in fact a degenerate instance. The conviction that *moral adequacy falls off in the direction of generality* seems to be one of the plaintive notes in this style of moral discourse. The note struck is plaintive because it is understood that this kind of inadequacy is recurrent and inevitable. What is condemnable from this perspective, then, is *not* doing one's inadequate best where that is all one can do, but denying or ignoring how far the principled, universalistic view may be from adequate moral response in many situations, and how much responsibility one has evaded in adopting it. This is our situation when truly personal understanding eludes us. Gilligan's recent work, interestingly, is more concerned with different understandings of the nature of persons, and with questions of adequate knowledge and disclosure than with particular structures of moral judgement.[20]

The combination of indefinite openness to responsibility and of the particularistic paradigm of understanding persons accounts for a certain kind of strain I discern in these voices. The fact of human connectedness that makes for endless vistas of responsibility (both with respect to *any* person and with respect to *all*) runs up against the inescapable arbitrariness and *ad hoc* limitations of actual connections and the moral possibilities they underwrite and exclude. The moral situation appears to these moral agents entangling, compromising, and permanently unwieldy.[21]

IV

These two versions of the different voice rendered unified are, of course, energetic reconstructions and idealizations. One would not expect a view "systematic" in the philosopher's sense to spring full-blown from any survey of opinion. It must be admitted, finally, that perhaps these reconstructions are too energetic. It may be that similar things many women have to say about morality and responsibility are only contingently related by the fact of women's common situation and social training, and not by some deep conceptual structure a moral philosopher might strive (or contrive) to find. It might be that women's preoccupation with care and relationship and their propensity for concrete over abstract are, if a fact, simply each orientations of thought and feeling which serve their traditional social roles of nurturers, helpers, and keepers of the homely but indispensable material conditions of life. It is this possibility that accounts for much of the ambivalent or hostile reaction to

Gilligan's work.[22] It can appear as further depressing adumbration of the apparatus which keeps women in their subservient and private places.[23]

Even if the concerns of the different voices are artifacts of an objectionably limiting social assignment, this does not discredit the view (or views) from that particular set of windows on moral reality. This is not only because any human experience yields matter for moral reflection, nor only because the task of enabling the continuance of human life, to which women's traditional roles and the values these embody are so deeply bound, has now on a global scale become precarious and urgent in ways it has not been for human beings before. It is also because women's social assignments, whatever the local variations, involve the majority of them intimately in quite a special endeavor from the viewpoint of morality: initiation of new members into the moral community. A position of social disadvantage may, on the topic of moral education and moral competence, be one of some epistemic privilege.[24] These voices should be heard, whether they have some large thing to say or many smaller ones.[25]

NOTES

1. (Cambridge: Harvard University Press, 1982), p. 2. All page references in the text are to this work unless otherwise marked.
2. "Reply," (p. 324) in L. Kerber, C. Greeno and E. Maccoby, Z. Luria, C. Stack and C. Gilligan, "On *In a Different Voice*: An Interdisciplinary Forum," *Signs* 11 (1986):304-333, hereafter cited in the text as R. See also Carol Gilligan and Grant Wiggins, "The Origins of Morality in Early Childhood Relationships," in *The Emergence of Morality in Early Childhood*, ed. Jerome Kagan and Sharon Lamb (Chicago: University of Chicago Press, 1987) for closer discussion of both findings on distribution of moral orientations and their significance.
3. I don't claim that questions about whether certain moral views are significantly gender-related are of no consequence to moral philosophy. They may well be theoretically, methodologically, and sociologically consequential. But one does need to know what those views are before these sorts of consequence may be seriously explored.
4. Since this paper was written a valuable set of papers in response to or occasioned by Gilligan's work has appeared which includes a number of discussions whose aim, like mine, is conceptual exploration of what this work suggests for moral theory. See Eva Feder Kittay and Diana T. Meyers (eds.), *Women and Moral Theory* (Totowa, NJ: Rowman and Littlefield, 1987).
5. Marilyn Friedman, "Abraham, Socrates, and Heinz: Where Are the Women? (Care and Context in Moral Reasoning)," also distinguishes two themes in the different voice. Friedman sees "contextual relativism" as a concern with concrete detail detachable from a relationship orientation, and interprets relationship orientation as special concern with and for relationship as a value or source of norms. For her these features are separable as well as distinct. I find both of these elements more complex and the matter of their connection more puzzling than she does. Neither of the two interpretations I entertain below is identical with her understanding, which she uses to develop a strong criticism of Kohlbergian assumptions and results. In *Moral Dilemmas*, ed. Carol Gibb Harding (Chicago: Precedent Publishing, Inc. 1985), pp. 25-41.
6. *Philosophy and Feminist Thinking* (Minneapolis: University of Minnesota Press, 1986), p. 210. While Grimshaw finds the claim about distinctive values tolerable subject to critical refinement, she rejects any claim that the structure of women's moral thinking is distinctive as confused and dangerous (pp. 204-215).
7. Carol Gilligan, "Woman's Place in Man's Life Cycle," *Harvard Educational Review* 49 (1979):444.
8. Trenchant critiques (from an Aristotelian viewpoint) of legalistic pictures of moral deliberation in favor of context-sensitive ones are: John McDowell, "Virtue and Reason," *The Monist* 62 (1979):331-50, and David Wiggins, "Deliberation and Practical Reason," in *Practical Reasoning*, ed. Joseph Raz (New York: Oxford University Press, 1978), pp. 144-152.
9. One thinks also of a certain kind of rigoristic, impersonal Christian agapeism that takes a dim view of all partiality and special affection. An echo of this resonates in Kant's famous distinction between practical and pathological love. See Gene Outka's *Agape* (New Haven: Yale University Press, 1972), Chapter One,

for a discussion of variants of agapeistic care on the issue of love for others.

10. I deliberately use Gilligan's own phrase here for what women are "talking about" from "The Conquistador and the Dark Continent: Reflections on the Psychology of Love," *Daedulus* 113 (1984): 78.
11. Gilligan often invokes this duality, e.g., in "Conquistador" (pp. 77-78) and *In A Different Voice* (p. 69). In "Remapping the Moral Domain: New Images of the Self in Relationship" in *Reconstructing Individualism*, ed. Thomas C. Heller et al. (Palo Alto: Stanford University Press, 1986), pp. 241-256, she suggests briefly that this duality reflects universal experiences, in childhood, of inequality and attachment. For a fuller treatment, see Gilligan and Wiggins "Origins ... " (note 2, above).
12. See J.S. Mill on expediency over justice in chapter 5 of *Utilitarianism* (New York: New American Library, 1962), pp. 320-321. (Subsequent references to Mill are to this edition.) For a more wistful admission that justice might have to go, see J.J.C. Smart, *Utilitarianism for and against*, with Bernard Williams (Cambridge: Cambridge University Press, 1973). pp. 69-74.
13. It is not cant when Mill says "In the golden rule of Jesus of Nazareth, we read the complete spirit of the ethics of utility. To do as you would be done by, and to love your neighbor as yourself, constitute the ideal perfection of utilitarian morality" (*Utilitarianism*, Chapter 2, 268). Mill's belief in the "powerful natural sentiment" (p. 284) and "contagion" (p. 285) of sympathy are important grounds of his defense of utilitarianism.
14. Bill Puka, "An Interdisciplinary Treatment of Kohlberg," *Ethics* 92 (1982):469. Puka provides a clear statement of the basic commitments of "cognitive-developmentalism" in morality.
15. Mill responded early on to criticisms of the demandingness and coldness of utilitarianism (*Utilitarianism*, chapter 2, pp. 269-272). Contemporary critiques on this score include: Bernard Williams, "Persons, Character, and Morality," in *Moral Luck* (Cambridge: Cambridge University Press, 1981), pp. 1-19; Michael Stocker, "The Schizophrenia of Modern Ethical Theories," *The Journal of Philosophy* 73 (1976):453-466. See also, Linda Nicholson, "Women, Morality, and History," *Social Research* 50 (1983):514-536, especially 524-525, on how both utilitarianism and Kantianism reflect the same historical location and social organization that yield a certain version of the public vs. private split.
16. (Berkeley and Los Angeles: University of California Press, 1984), hereafter cited in the text as C.
17. Noddings does not put her view forward as a representation of Gilligan's different voice, but does identify her view with Gilligan's at points or recruits Gilligan's view in support of hers (e.g., C, pp. 8, 96).
18. See Seyla Benhabib's excellent "The Generalized and The Concrete Other: The Kohlberg-Gilligan Controversy and Moral Theory" in Kittay and Meyers, pp. 154-171.
19. Owen Flanagan, "Virtue, Sex, and Gender: Some Philosophical Reflections on the Moral Psychology Debate," *Ethics* 92 (1982):499-512, claims Gilligan's "contextualism" is really just a general kind of cognitive sophistication, that of making subtle discriminations (p. 511). But this fails to consider that the cognition central to care is understanding persons; I do not think intellectual subtlety in, say, mathematics or philosophy indicates cognitive sophistication we should expect to carry over to interpersonal perceptiveness. Nor can Gilligan's claim that the care and justice orientations are "fundamentally incompatible," like two ways of seeing a puzzle picture ("Remapping ... ," pp. 242, 246), be evaluated if the grounding of these two views in different representations of interpersonal relationship and understanding are not fully explored. Yet without considering these different representations at length or in detail, Flanagan and Kathryn Jackson in "Justice, Care and Gender: the Kohlberg-Gilligan Debate Revisited," *Ethics* 97 (1987): 622-637, argue that it is possible to "integrate" perceptions aligned with each into the same episode of moral deliberation (p. 626).
20. See "Remapping the Moral Domain" (note 11, above) and Carol Gilligan and Eve Stern, "The Riddle of Femininity and the Psychology of Love," in *Passionate Attachments*, ed. Willard Gaylin and Ethel Person (New York: Free Press, 1988).
21. Sharon Bishop, "Connections & Guilt," *Hypatia* 2 (1987):7-23, explores the implications of a Gilligan-like ethics of responsibility for the inevitability of moral conflict and the resulting affective binds which require working through over time and may leave intelligible but only partly expungeable remainders of guilt.

22. The *Signs* forum (note 2, above) illustrates this amply; beyond criticism, there is resentment, frustration, and distress. I don't mean to imply, of course, there is no basis for dispassionate criticism.
23. Grimshaw, op. cit., expresses this reservation about "women's viewpoint" theories generally. But even so, exposing "female" morality to view may open a mine of insight into the hidden presuppositions and agendae of "male" (read, public) moralities. See, e.g. Annette Baier, "Poisoning the Wells," in *Postures of the Mind* (Minneapolis: University of Minnesota Press, 1985), pp. 263-291, especially pp. 273-276.
24. Sara Ruddick's excellent studies, "Maternal Thinking," and "Preservative Love and Military Destruction" are exemplars for examining the intelligent structure of "women's work ." In Joyce Trebilcot (ed.), *Mothering* (Totowa, NJ: Rowman and Allanheld, 1984), pp. 213-230, 231-262. In a related vein, see Virginia Held, "Feminism and Moral Theory," in Kittay and Meyers, pp. 111-128, on the understanding of human relationship that grows out of the mothering experience.
25. I am grateful for the opportunity to present a shorter version of this paper at the American Philosophical Association Central Division Meeting in April, 1987, in sessions on Carol Gilligan's work sponsored by the American Society for Value Inquiry, organized by Nancy Tuana. In addition to a number of members of that audience, I thank Carol Gilligan, Celeste Schenck, and Arthur Walker for critical comments and encouragement both. I am grateful to Fordham University for a Faculty Fellowship in 1986-87 which provided the time and support that enabled me to write this paper. This author has previously published under the name Margaret Urban Coyne.

STUDY QUESTIONS

1. According to Kant, what is the difference between a hypothetical and a categorical imperative and why is the latter distinctive of morality?
2. Kant gives several formulations of the categorical imperative. What are they? Explain how these formulations are taken to be equivalent by applying the different formulations to at least one of Kant's examples of moral dilemmas.
3. What is the principle of utility? Why does Mill distinguish between quantity and quality of pleasures? Does the distinction capture an account of human nature that is, in the end, similar to Kant's account of the dignity of human beings? Why or why not?
4. How does Mill answer the kind of objection that Kant would make that morality has to do with determining one's duty and not with maximizing happiness either for the individual or for the greatest number of individuals?
5. When deciding what is morally right, is the best way to calculate consequences and maximize happiness or to determine one's duty in accordance with universal moral laws? Formulate your answer to this question by exploring cases that present problems for one or the other kind of moral theory.
6. What is meant by Nedelsky's claim that the account of autonomy at the core of liberalism is individualistic? Is this individualism evident in the discussion of autonomy in Kant's moral theory? Is it evident in Mill's defence of Utilitarianism? Provide reasons for your answers.
7. Why, according to Nedelsky, is an individualist conception of autonomy inconsistent with feminist methodology and incapable of meeting the aspirations of feminist theory?
8. Nedelsky retains the goal of enhancing autonomy, but argues that the liberal ideal of autonomy needs to be reconceived. How does she reconceive autonomy? What implications does this relational conception of autonomy have for social policies concerned with enhancing individual autonomy?
9. In what ways does Kant's moral theory fit the description of an ethic of justice as described in Walker's account of Gilligan's work on justice and care? In what ways is a care perspective similar to and different from Utilitarianism?
10. Do you think that women tend to adopt an ethic of care? Is this question relevant to an evaluation of care as a way of thinking about morality and resolving moral issues? Why or why not?
11. Outline the two themes that Walker identifies in a care orientation. Does Walker's strategy of bringing the care-orientation and contextual-deliberative view together work to capture the differences between an ethic of care and an ethic of justice? Does it succeed in showing how an ethic of care challenges traditional accounts of morality and enriches moral theory? Provide reasons for your answers.

SUGGESTED READINGS

Aja, Egbeke. "Changing Moral Values in Africa: An Essay in Ethical Relativism." *Journal of Value Inquiry*, v. 31 (1997): 531-543.

Annas, Julia. "Virtue and Eudaimonism." *Social Philosophy & Policy*, v. 15, no. 1 (Winter 1998): 37-55.

Bok, Sissela. "What Basis for Morality? A Minimalist Approach." *The Monist*, v. 76 (1993): 349-359.

Calhoun, Cheshire. "Responsibility and Reproach." *Ethics*, v. 99 (January 1989): 389-406.

Dillon, Robin S. "Self-Respect: Moral, Emotional, Political." *Ethics* 107 (January 1997): 226-249.

Friedman, Marilyn. "Feminism and Modern Friendship: Dislocating the Community." *Ethics*, v. 99 (1989): 275-290.

Hekman, Susan. "Moral Voices, Moral Selves: About Getting it Right in Moral Theory." *Human Studies*, v. 16 (1993): 143-162.

Jackson, W. M. "Rules Versus Responsibility in Morality." *Public Affairs Quarterly*, v. 3, no. 2 (April 1989): 27-40.

Louden, Robert. "Some Vices of Virtue Ethics." *American Philosophical Quarterly*, v. 21 (1984): 227-236.

Isaacs, Tracy. "Cultural Context and Moral Responsibility." *Ethics*, v. 107 (July 1997): 670-684.

Manning, Rita C. *Speaking From the Heart: A Feminist Perspective on Ethics.* Lanham, MD: Rowman & Littlefield, 1992.

Matilal, Bimal Krishna. "Ethical Relativism and Confrontation of Cultures." In *Relativism: Interpretation and Confrontation* edited by Michael Krausz. Notre Dame, IN: University of Notre Dame Press, 1989.

Moody-Adams, Michele. "Culture, Responsibility, and Affected Ignorance." *Ethics*, 104 (January 1994): 291-309.

Nussbaum, Martha and Amartya Sen. "Internal Criticism and Indian Rationalist Traditions." In *Relativism: Interpretation and Confrontation* edited by Michael Krausz. Notre Dame, IN: University of Notre Dame Press, 1989.

Rorty, Richard. "Solidarity or Objectivity?" In *Anti-Theory in Ethics and Moral Conservatism* edited by Stanley G. Clarke and Evan Simpson. Albany, NY: SUNY Press, 1989.

Sher, George. "Ethics, Character, and Action." *Social Philosophy & Policy*, v. 15, no. 1 (Winter 1998): 1-17.

Sherman, Nancy. "Concrete Kantian Respect." *Social Philosophy & Policy*, v. 15, no. 1 (Winter 1998): 119-148.

Slote, Michael. "The Justice of Caring." *Social Philosophy & Policy*, v. 15, no. 1 (Winter 1998): 171-195.

Walker, Margaret Urban. *Moral Understandings: A Feminist Study of Ethics.* New York: Routledge, 1998.

Wolf, Susan. "Moral Saints." *Journal of Philosophy*, v. 79 (1982): 419-439.

Wong, David B. *Moral Relativity.* Berkeley: University of California Press, 1984.

CHAPTER TEN

REPRODUCTIVE ISSUES

In Chapter Nine, we observed how Kant's account of human beings as ends in themselves, as entities whose worth is absolute, generates moral imperatives about how human beings ought to be treated. A fairly uncontroversial principle that emerges from the idea of the absolute value of human beings is that it is wrong to end the life of a human being or, in to put it in positive terms, that human beings have a right to life. This principle has played a large role in the contested and controversial debate on abortion as it takes place in traditional Western moral theory and continues to play a role in new dilemmas in the area of reproduction. Advances in medical technology have created possibilities for terminating, correcting, and extending human life at the very earliest stages of development. These advances have expanded the debates from the issue of the moral justifiability of abortion to a complex set of issues raised by reproductive technologies that provide new methods for creating human life.

A question that has dominated the debate on abortion in North American and Western contexts is the issue of the moral status of the fetus. Kant intended his account of absolute worth to cover entities with a will, human beings who could reason, act to fulfill or reject particular inclinations and desires, and perform the moral duties dictated by reason. None of these characteristics appear to be possessed by human beings who are not yet born or, some would argue, even by human beings in the early years of their lives. Some theorists have captured this distinction between human beings with developed capacities and those without by referring to the first as persons and to the second as human beings and reserving the right to life for persons. Others argue that the question of the status of the fetus and its right to life is neither the only issue nor the most important one in the debate on abortion and that there are competing rights that carry moral weight and need to be taken into account.

The value accorded individual autonomy generates an account of the right to make choices about one's own life and one's own body that some take to be moral justification for abortion. Some defend the right to choose as absolute, arguing that a woman should be able to evaluate her own goals and aspirations and make decisions that affect her life. Some argue that the right to choose is outweighed by the interests of the state in protecting fetuses who are sufficiently like persons in the later stages of pregnancy. Others argue that only certain cases such as rape justify exercising the right to choose in the case of abortion. In all these cases, the issues and arguments are taken to reflect what was identified in the previous chapter as a justice approach to morality and moral problems: the identification of competing values, the prioritizing and universalizing of rules, the abstraction from the concrete details of contexts and lives, and the application of general principles to cases. In recent years, this approach to abortion has been challenged by feminists, some of whom defend an ethic of care approach. We will examine these challenges as well as policies on reproductive issues in other places and thereby raise questions about discussions in the North American context.

In the first reading, Don Marquis develops the argument that abortion is in the same moral category as killing an innocent adult human being and is, therefore, seriously immoral. He bases his argument on what he takes to be a central premise in the debate on abortion: that the question of whether or not abortion is morally permissible stands or falls on whether the fetus is the sort of entity whose life it is seriously wrong to end. Marquis argues that this question has resulted in a standoff between anti-abortionists and pro-choice advocates. The anti-abortionist defends a moral principle about the wrongness of killing that is broad in scope and covers fetuses even at the earliest stages, but this embraces too much and cannot explain why it is not wrong to destroy a living human cancer cell or why mere possession of the human genetic code is morally relevant. The pro-choicer finds a moral principle about the wrongness of killing that is narrow in scope so that fetuses do not fall under it, but this does not embrace enough and cannot explain why it is wrong to kill infants or the severely mentally disabled.

Marquis holds that a way out of the standoff is to provide a more complete account of the wrongness of killing. What makes killing wrong, argues Marquis, is that "the loss of one's life deprives one of all the experiences, activities, projects, and enjoyments that would otherwise have constituted one's future." Killing fetuses is wrong because they have futures including a set of experiences, projects, and activities that are identical to the futures of adult human beings. Because the category is "future like ours" and not personhood, Marquis claims that his argument avoids equivocations on concepts like human life, human being, or person as well as difficulties encountered in moves by anti-abortionists that the fetus has the potential to become a person. Marquis ends by raising several possible objections to his account and reaffirming his argument that the property of value of a future like ours is one that can settle the central question about the moral status of the fetus.

Ann Cudd's short critique of Marquis's essay rebuts what she takes as his initial assumption: that the central question for settling the issue of abortion is that of the moral status of the fetus. Cudd charges that Marquis conflates two questions: 1) Is the fetus the sort of thing that could have any rights and toward which we could have obligations? and 2) Are these rights or obligations absolute? She maintains that whatever we decide about the status of the fetus, there remain important questions about the bundle of rights held by the woman carrying the fetus. Cudd argues that taking this bundle of rights seriously is precisely what many of the authors that Marquis wrongly depicts as focusing on the question of the status of the fetus do. Some of these authors argue that the fetus's lack of personhood is a sufficient but not necessary condition for abortion to be morally permissible, and others argue that the woman's right to life or her serious loss of well-being overrides the rights of the fetus. Cudd argues that even if we agree that the fetus is the sort of thing whose killing is so morally wrong as to overwhelm completely a woman's rights to privacy, health, medical care, and even life, the point needs argument and not assertion.

Elisabeth Porter questions the very framework reflected in the arguments about rights to life and choice in the first two readings, a framework illustrating a justice approach to issues of reproduction. Porter questions whether abortion is best understood as a woman's right to choose and calls for a re-evaluation of liberal goals of equality, rights, and choice. She highlights the deficiencies when the two approaches of formal and substantive equality in the liberal tradition are applied to the issue of abortion. The formal equality approach of removing differential treatment so that everyone is treated equally assumes women are actually the same as men in all respects and they are not with respect to reproductive capacities. The substantive equality approach takes account of actual differences to generate a justification for special rights, but general abstract rights do not address specific social relations, particular needs, and concrete social requirements. In the case of abortion, the right to choose conceals interrelated needs such as sex education, contraception, childcare, housing, and daily maintenance. The right to choose also accentuates the notion of an entitlement possessed independently of social conditions and circumstances and in isolation from the social factors that influence choice.

Porter concurs with these critiques of rights as abstract, ahistorical, and individualistic. She suggests that an examination of the dialectical relationship between claims of rights and the social contexts in which the struggle for an assertion of rights occurs can highlight the interdependence of rights and responsibilities. Abortion is not just a private issue and choice, but takes place in social relations in which history, social divisions, differential access to power and resources, cultural interpretations of sexuality and reproduction, and social and material conditions shape women's choices. Abortion is not simply an individual right but a social right, one that takes access to reproductive rights as including both abortion needs and conditions that allow children to flourish such as policies regarding maternity leave, income supplements, health care, child support, housing, nutrition, and education. The right to choose is a social right that does not lead to unlimited, unprincipled abortion claims, but to a critical analysis of factors in particular social and political contexts that shape an understanding of individual rights and social responsibilities.

Social factors are also relevant to the analysis of new reproductive technologies that Dorothy Roberts provides. Roberts challenges the common perception that new reproductive technologies such as in virtro fertilization (IVF), embryo donation, and contract pregnancy enhance freedom by expanding procreative options for individuals. Roberts agrees with those feminists who argue that these technologies are more conforming than liberating because they reinforce traditional patriarchal roles. Their availability is restricted to heterosexual married women, and they objectify women's procreative capacity. Roberts examines how new reproductive technologies also work to reflect and reinforce racial hierarchy in the United States.

Reproductive technologies are used almost exclusively by white people. The profile of people most likely to use IVF is the opposite of those likely to be infertile: people who are older, poorer, Black, and poorly educated. Roberts argues that the reasons for racial disparity in use center around financial barriers, cultural preferences, and deliberate professional manipulation. She considers three possible responses to new reproductive technologies. The liberal response is to acknowledge that race influences the use of these technologies, but to hold that this does not justify interfering with an individual's freedom to use them. The distributive solution is to work to ensure equal access by reducing costs or including the procedures in insurance plans. There is a third solution: to show that these technologies are harmful and to discourage their use. Roberts argues that we can no longer avoid considerations of social costs of procedures that are grossly expensive in comparison to policies such as improving conditions that lead to infertility. Expanding these technologies or improving their distribution will not solve the problems created by racial disparity. She argues that restrictions imposed by government and through moral persuasion may be more successful in eradicating group oppression than policies that protect the reproductive choices of the most privileged.

In the fourth reading, Maxine Molyneux turns to Nicaragua, where an advanced record on political issues of pluralism, democracy, and the death penalty contrast with a conservative position on reproductive rights. Although Nicaragua's Sandinista government has pledged a commitment to women's emancipation and has implemented policies and legal reforms designed to establish greater equality, it has retained the 1974 Criminal Code legislation regarding abortion. The legislation specifies that the request must originate not from the woman, but from a spouse or next of kin and must be considered by a three-member medical panel. The effect of this legislation in a country with a shortage of medical goods is that abortions are performed illegally and at great cost to the lives of women. Molyneux does not think an abstract proclamation of rights is the solution and argues that women's reproductive rights need to be appropriate to the political, social and economic constraints faced by a country like Nicaragua.

While the Nicaraguan government has achieved success in improving women's socio-economic position, extending their rights within the family and workplace, and promoting participation in economic development, the Catholic Church's considerable power makes the extension of women's rights to reproductive self-determination an explosive issue. Molyneux concedes that the argument by the government that full reproductive rights would magnify problems of underpopulation and labor shortage has force, but argues that pronatalist polices are not incompatible with reproductive rights and can be pursued with sensitivity to women's needs and preferences. Women's reproductive rights need to be matched by a concrete attainment of political and subjective conditions for the implementation of these rights. In Nicaragua, this requires an understanding of the relation between women and the Catholic Church, programs of education for women to mobilize and organize for reform, and decisive and united action by the revolutionary state.

WHY ABORTION IS IMMORAL

Don Marquis

Don Marquis is Professor of Philosophy at the University of Kansas, Lawrence. He has published numerous articles in the areas of ethics and medical ethics.

Marquis claims that the debate on abortion is based on a major assumption that he accepts; that the question of whether abortion is morally permissible stands or falls on the issue of the status of the fetus. He argues that we can best answer questions about the status of the fetus by asking what makes killing us wrong. His answer is that it is wrong because we are deprived of "the experiences, activities, projects, and enjoyments that would otherwise have constituted one's future." Because the fetus possesses this valuable property of having a "future-like-ours," abortion is immoral and in the same moral category as killing an innocent human being or wantonly killing innocent animals. He concludes that abortion is seriously immoral in the great majority of cases.

The view that abortion is, with rare exceptions, seriously immoral has received little support in the recent philosophical literature. No doubt most philosophers affiliated with secular institutions of higher education believe that the anti-abortion position is either a symptom of irrational religious dogma or a conclusion generated by seriously confused philosophical argument. The purpose of this essay is to undermine this general belief. This essay sets out an argument that purports to show, as well as any argument in ethics can show, that abortion is, except possibly in rare cases, seriously immoral, that it is in the same moral category as killing an innocent adult human being.

The argument is based on a major assumption. Many of the most insightful and careful writers on the ethics of abortion—such as Joel Feinberg, Michael Tooley, Mary Anne Warren, H. Tristram Engelhardt, Jr., L. W. Sumner, John T. Noonan, Jr., and Philip Devine[1]—believe that whether or not abortion is morally permissible stands or falls on whether or not a fetus is the sort of being whose life it is seriously wrong to end. The argument of this essay will assume, but not argue, that they are correct.

Also, this essay will neglect issues of great importance to a complete ethics of abortion. Some anti-abortionists will allow that certain abortions, such as abortion before implantation or abortion when the life of a woman is threatened by a pregnancy or abortion after rape, may be morally permissible. This essay will not explore the casuistry of these hard cases. The purpose of this essay is to develop a general argument for the claim that the overwhelming majority of deliberate abortions are seriously immoral.

I

A sketch of standard anti-abortion and pro-choice arguments exhibits how those arguments possess certain symmetries that explain why partisans of those positions are so convinced of the correctness of their own positions, why they are not successful in convincing their opponents, and why, to others, this issue seems to be unresolvable. An analysis of the

---

Reprinted with permission of the publisher and Don Marquis from *The Journal of Philosophy* 86:4 (1989): 183–202 [edited].

nature of this standoff suggests a strategy for surmounting it.

Consider the way a typical anti-abortionist argues. She will argue or assert that life is present from the moment of conception or that fetuses look like babies or that fetuses possess a characteristic such as a genetic code that is both necessary and sufficient for being human. Anti-abortionists seem to believe that (1) the truth of all of these claims is quite obvious, and (2) establishing any of these claims is sufficient to show that abortion is morally akin to murder.

A standard pro-choice strategy exhibits similarities. The pro-choicer will argue or assert that fetuses are not persons or that fetuses are not rational agents or that fetuses are not social beings. Pro-choicers seem to believe that (1) the truth of any of these claims is quite obvious, and (2) establishing any of these claims is sufficient to show that an abortion is not a wrongful killing.

In fact, both the pro-choice and the anti-abortion claims do seem to be true, although the "it looks like a baby" claim is more difficult to establish the earlier the pregnancy. We seem to have a standoff. How can it be resolved?

As everyone who has taken a bit of logic knows, if any of these arguments concerning abortion is a good argument, it requires not only some claim characterizing fetuses, but also some general moral principle that ties a characteristic of fetuses to having or not having the right to life or to some other moral characteristic that will generate the obligation or the lack of obligation not to end the life or a fetus. Accordingly, the arguments of the anti-abortionist and the pro-choicer need a bit of filling in to be regarded as adequate.

Note what each partisan will say. The anti-abortionist will claim that her position is supported by such generally accepted moral principles as "It is always prima facie seriously wrong to take a human life" or "It is always prima facie seriously wrong to end the life of a baby." Since these are generally accepted moral principles, her position is certainly not obviously wrong. The pro-choicer will claim that her position is supported by such plausible moral principles as "Being a person is what gives an individual intrinsic moral worth" or "It is only seriously prima facie wrong to take the life of a member of the human community." Since these are generally accepted moral principles, the pro-choice position is certainly not obviously wrong. Unfortunately, we have again arrived at a standoff.

Now, how might one deal with this standoff? The standard approach is to try to show how the moral principles of one's opponent lose their plausibility under analysis. It is easy to see how this is possible. On the one hand, the anti-abortionist will defend a moral principle concerning the wrongness of killing which tends to be broad in scope in order that even fetuses at an early stage of pregnancy will fall under it. The problem with broad principles is that they often embrace too much. In this particular instance, the principle "It is always prima facie wrong to take a human life" seems to entail that it is wrong to end the existence of a living human cancer-cell culture, on the grounds that the culture is both living and human. Therefore, it seems that the anti-abortionist's favored principle is too broad.

On the other hand, the pro-choicer wants to find a moral principle concerning the wrongness of killing which tends to be narrow in scope in order that fetuses will *not* fall under it. The problem with narrow principles is that they often do not embrace enough. Hence, the needed principles such as "It is prima facie seriously wrong to kill only persons" or "It is prima facie wrong to kill only rational agents" do not explain why it is wrong to kill infants or young children or the severely retarded or even perhaps the severely mentally ill. Therefore, we seem again to have a standoff. The anti-abortionist charges, not unreasonably, that pro-choice principles concerning killing are too narrow to be acceptable; the pro-choicer charges, not unreasonably, that anti-abortionist principles concerning killing are too broad to be acceptable.

Attempts by both sides to patch up the difficulties in their positions run into further difficulties. The anti-abortionist will try to remove the problem in her position by reformulating her principle concerning killing in terms of human beings. Now we end up with: "It is always prima facie seriously wrong to end the life of a human being." This principle has the advantage of avoiding the problem of the human cancer-cell culture counterexample. But this advantage is purchased at a high price. For although it is clear that a fetus is both human and alive, it is not at all clear that a fetus is a human *being*. There is at least something to be said for the view that something becomes a human being only after a process of development, and that therefore first trimester fetuses and perhaps all fetuses are not yet human beings. Hence, the anti-abortionist, by this move, has merely exchanged one problem for another.[2]

The pro-choicer fares no better. She may attempt to find reasons why killing infants, young children, and the severely retarded is wrong which are independent of her major principle that is supposed to explain the wrongness of taking human life, but which will not also make abortion immoral. This is no easy task. Appeals to social utility will seem satisfactory only to those who resolve not to think of the enormous difficulties with a utilitarian account of the wrongness of killing and the significant social costs of preserving the lives of the unproductive.[3] A pro-choice strategy that extends the definition of "person" to infants or even to young children seems just as arbitrary as an anti-abortion strategy that extends the definition of "human being" to fetuses. Again, we find symmetries in the two positions and we arrive at a standoff.

There are even further problems that reflect symmetries in the two positions. In addition to counterexample problems, or the arbitrary application problems that can be exchanged for them, the standard anti-abortionist principle "It is prima facie seriously wrong to kill a human being," or one of its variants, can be objected to on the grounds of ambiguity. If "human being" is taken to be a biological category, the anti-abortionist is left with the problem of explaining why a merely *biological* category should make a moral difference. Why, it is asked, is it any more reasonable to base a moral conclusion on the number of chromosomes in one's cells than on the color of one's skin?[4] If "human being," on the other hand, is taken to be a *moral* category, then the claim that a fetus is a human being cannot be taken to be a premise in the anti-abortion argument, for it is precisely what needs to be established. Hence, either the anti-abortionist's main category is a morally irrelevant, merely biological category, or it is of no use to the anti-abortionist in establishing (noncircularly, of course) that abortion is wrong.

Although this problem with the anti-abortionist position is often noticed, it is less often noticed that the pro-choice position suffers from an analogous problem. The principle "Only persons have the right to life" also suffers from an ambiguity. The term "person" is typically defined in terms of psychological characteristics, although there will certainly be disagreement concerning which characteristics are most important. Supposing that this matter can be settled, the pro-choicer is left with the problem of explaining why *psychological* characteristics should make a *moral* difference. If the pro-choicer should attempt to deal with this problem by claiming that an explanation is not necessary, that in fact we do treat such a cluster of psychological properties as having moral significance, the sharp-witted anti-abortionist should have a ready response. We do treat being both living and human as having moral significance. If it is legitimate for the pro-choicer to demand that the anti-abortionist provide an explanation of the connection between the biological character of being a human being and the wrongness of being killed (even though people accept this connection), then it is legitimate for the anti-abortionist to demand that the pro-choicer provide an explanation of the connection between psychological criteria for being a person and the wrongness of being killed (even though that connection is accepted).[5]

Feinberg has attempted to meet this objection (he calls psychological personhood "commonsense personhood"):

> The characteristics that confer commonsense personhood are not arbitrary bases for rights and duties, such as race, sex or species membership; rather they are traits that make sense out of rights and duties and without which those moral attributes would have no point or function. It is because people are conscious; have a sense of their personal identities; have plans, goals, and projects; experience emotions; are liable to pains, anxieties, and frustrations; can reason and bargain, and so on—it is because of these attributes that people have values and interests, desires and expectations of their own, including a stake in their own futures, and a personal well-being of a sort we cannot ascribe to unconscious or nonrational beings. Because of their developed capacities they can assume duties and responsibilities and can have and make claims on one

another. Only because of their sense of self, their life plans, their value hierarchies, and their stakes in their own futures can they be ascribed fundamental rights. There is nothing arbitrary about these linkages (*op.cit.*, p. 270).

The plausible aspects of this attempt should not be taken to obscure its implausible features. There is a great deal to be said for the view that being a psychological person under some description is a necessary condition for having duties. One cannot have a duty unless one is capable of behaving morally, and a being's capability of behaving morally will require having a certain psychology. It is far from obvious, however, that having rights entails consciousness or rationality, as Feinberg suggests. We speak of the rights of the severely retarded or the severely mentally ill, yet some of these persons are not rational. We speak of the rights of the temporarily unconscious. The New Jersey Supreme Court based their decision in the Quinlan case on Karen Ann Quinlan's right to privacy, and she was known to be permanently unconscious at that time. Hence, Feinberg's claim that having rights entails being conscious is, on its face, obviously false.

Of course, it might not make sense to attribute rights to a being that would never in its natural history have certain psychological traits. This modest connection between psychological personhood and moral personhood will create a place for Karen Ann Quinlan and the temporarily unconscious. But then it makes a place for fetuses also. Hence, it does not serve Feinberg's pro-choice purposes. Accordingly, it seems that the pro-choicer will have as much difficulty bridging the gap between psychological personhood and personhood in the moral sense as the anti-abortionist has bridging the gap between being a biological human being and being a human being in the moral sense.

Furthermore, the pro-choicer cannot any more escape her problem by making person a purely moral category than the anti-abortionist could escape by the analogous move. For if person is a moral category, then the pro-choicer is left without the resources for establishing (noncircularly, of course) the claim that a fetus is not a person, which is an essential premise in her argument. Again, we have both a symmetry and a standoff between pro-choice and anti-abortion views.

Passions in the abortion debate run high. There are both plausibilities and difficulties with the standard positions. Accordingly, it is hardly surprising that partisans of either side embrace with fervor the moral generalizations that support the conclusions they preanalytically favor, and reject with disdain the moral generalilizations of their opponents as being subject to inescapable difficulties. It is easy to believe that the counterexamples to one's own moral principles are merely temporary difficulties that will dissolve in the wake of further philosophical research, and that the counterexamples to the principles of one's opponents are as straightforward as the contradiction between A and O propositions in traditional logic. This might suggest to an impartial observer (if there are any) that the abortion issue is unresolvable.

There is a way out of this apparent dialectical quandary. The moral generalizations of both sides are not quite correct. The generalizations hold for the most part, for the usual cases. This suggests that they are all *accidental* generalizations, that the moral claims made by those on both sides of the dispute do not touch on the *essence* of the matter.

This use of the distinction between essence and accident is not meant to invoke obscure metaphysical categories. Rather, it is intended to reflect the rather atheoretical nature of the abortion discussion. If the generalization a partisan in the abortion dispute adopts were derived from the reason why ending the life of a human being is wrong, then there could not be exceptions to that generalization unless some special case obtains in which there are even more powerful countervailing reasons. Such generalizations would not be merely accidental generalizations; they would point to, or be based upon, the essence of the wrongness of killing, what it is that makes killing wrong. All this suggests that a necessary condition of resolving the abortion controversy is a more theoretical account of the wrongness of killing. After all, if we merely believe, but do not understand, why killing adult human beings such as ourselves is wrong, how could we conceivably show that abortion is either immoral or permissible?

II.

In order to develop such an account, we can start from the following unproblematic assumption concerning our own case: it is wrong to kill *us*. Why is it wrong? Some answers can be easily eliminated. It might be said that what makes killing us wrong is that a killing brutalizes the one who kills. But the brutalization consists of being inured to the performance of an act that is hideously immoral; hence, the brutalization does not explain the immorality. It might be said that what makes killing us wrong is the great loss others would experience due to our absence. Although such hubris is understandable, such an explanation does not account for the wrongness of killing hermits, or those whose lives are relatively independent and whose friends find it easy to make new friends.

A more obvious answer is better. What primarily makes killing wrong is neither its effect on the murderer nor its effect on the victim's friends and relatives, but its effect on the victim. The loss of one's life is one of the greatest losses one can suffer. The loss of one's life deprives one of all the experiences, activities, projects, and enjoyments that would otherwise have constituted one's future. Therefore, killing someone is wrong, primarily because the killing inflicts (one of) the greatest possible losses on the victim. To describe this as the loss of life can be misleading, however. The change in my biological state does not by itself make killing me wrong. The effect of the loss of my biological life is the loss to me of all those activities, projects, experiences, and enjoyments which would otherwise have constituted my future personal life. These activities, projects, experiences, and enjoyments are either valuable for their own sakes or are means to something else that is valuable for its own sake. Some parts of my future are not valued by me now, but will come to be valued by me as I grow older and as my values and capacities change. When I am killed, I am deprived both of what I now value which would have been part of my future personal life, but also what I would come to value. Therefore, when I die, I am deprived of all of the value of my future. Inflicting this loss on me is ultimately what makes killing me wrong. This being the case, it would seem that what makes killing *any* adult human being prima facie seriously wrong is the loss of his or her future.[6]

How should this rudimentary theory of the wrongness of killing be evaluated? It cannot be faulted for deriving an "ought" from an "is," for it does not. The analysis assumes that killing me (or you, reader) is prima facie seriously wrong. The point of the analysis is to establish which natural property ultimately explains the wrongness of the killing, given that it is wrong. A natural property will ultimately explain the wrongness of killing, only if (1) the explanation fits with our intuitions about the matter and (2) there is no other natural property that provides the basis for a better explanation of the wrongness of killing. This analysis rests on the intuition that what makes killing a particular human or animal wrong is what it does to that particular human or animal. What makes killing wrong is some natural effect or other of the killing. Some would deny this. For instance, a divine-command theorist in ethics would deny it. Surely this denial is, however, one of those features of divine–command theory which renders it so implausible.

The claim that what makes killing wrong is the loss of the victim's future is directly supported by two considerations. In the first place, this theory explains why we regard killing as one of the worst of crimes. Killing is especially wrong, because it deprives the victim of more than perhaps any other crime. In the second place, people with AIDS or cancer who know they are dying believe, of course, that dying is a very bad thing for them. They believe that the loss of a future to them that they would otherwise have experienced is what makes their premature death a very bad thing for them. A better theory of the wrongness of killing would require a different natural property associated with killing which better fits with the attitudes of the dying. What could it be?

The view that what makes killing wrong is the loss to the victim of the value of the victim's future gains additional support when some of its implications are examined. In the first place, it is incompatible with the view that it is wrong to kill only beings who are biologically human. It is possible that there exists a different species from another planet whose members have a future like ours. Since having a future like that is what makes killing someone wrong, this theory entails that it would be wrong to kill members of such a species. Hence, this theory is opposed to the claim that only life that is biologically human has great moral worth, a claim which many anti-abortionists have seemed to adopt. This opposition, which this theory has in common with personhood theories, seems to be a merit of the theory.

In the second place, the claim that the loss of one's future is the wrong-making feature of one's being killed entails the possibility that the futures of some actual nonhuman mammals on our own planet are sufficiently like ours that it is seriously wrong to kill them also. Whether some animals do have the same right to life as human beings depends on adding to the account of the wrongness of killing some additional account of just what it is about my future or the futures of other adult human beings which makes it wrong to kill us. No such additional account will be offered in this essay. Undoubtedly, the provision of such an account would be a very difficult matter. Undoubtedly, any such account would be quite controversial. Hence, it surely should not reflect badly on this sketch of an elementary theory of the wrongness of killing that it is indeterminate with respect to some very difficult issues regarding animal rights.

In the third place, the claim that the loss of one's future is the wrong-making feature of one's being killed does not entail, as sanctity of human life theories do, that active euthanasia is wrong. Persons who are severely and incurably ill, who face a future of pain and despair, and who wish to die will not have suffered a loss if they are killed. It is, strictly speaking, the value of a human's future which makes killing wrong in this theory. This being so, killing does not necessarily wrong some persons who are sick and dying. Of course, there may be other reasons for a prohibition of active euthanasia, but that is another matter. Sanctity-of-human-life theories seem to hold that active euthanasia is seriously wrong even in an individual case where there seems to be good reason for it independently of public policy considerations. This consequence is most implausible, and it is a plus for the claim that the loss of a future of value is what makes killing wrong that it does not share this consequence.

In the fourth place, the account of the wrongness of killing defended in this essay does straightforwardly entail that it is prima facie seriously wrong to kill children and infants, for we do presume that they have futures of value. Since we do believe that it is wrong to kill defenseless little babies, it is important that a theory of the wrongness of killing easily account for this. Personhood theories of the wrongness of killing, on the other hand, cannot straightforwardly account for the wrongness of killing infants and young children.[7] Hence, such theories must add special ad hoc accounts of the wrongness of killing the young. The plausibility of such ad hoc theories seems to be a function of how desperately one wants such theories to work. The claim that the primary wrong-making feature of a killing is the loss to the victim of the value of its future accounts for the wrongness of killing young children and infants directly; it makes the wrongness of such acts as obvious as we actually think it is. This is a further merit of this theory. Accordingly, it seems that this value of a future-like-ours theory of the wrongness of killing shares strengths of both sanctity-of-life and personhood accounts while avoiding weaknesses of both. In addition, it meshes with a central intuition concerning what makes killing wrong.

The claim that the primary wrong-making feature of a killing is the loss to the victim of the value of its future has obvious consequences for the ethics of abortion. The future of a standard fetus includes a set of experiences, projects, activities, and such which are identical with the futures of adult human beings and are identical with the futures of young children. Since the reason that is sufficient to explain why it is wrong to kill human beings after the time of birth is a reason that also applies to fetuses, it follows that abortion is prima facie seriously morally wrong.

This argument does not rely on the invalid inference that, since it is wrong to kill persons, it is wrong to kill potential persons also. The category that is morally central to this analysis is the category of having a valuable future like ours; it is not the category of personhood. The argument to the conclusion that abortion is prima facie seriously morally wrong proceeded independently of the notion of person or potential person or any equivalent. Someone may wish to start with this analysis in terms of the value of a human future, conclude that abortion is, except perhaps in rare circumstances, seriously morally wrong, infer that fetuses have the right to life, and then call fetuses "persons" as a result of their having the right to life. Clearly, in this case, the category of person is being used to state the *conclusion* of the analysis rather than to generate the *argument* of the analysis.

The structure of this anti-abortion argument can be both illuminated and defended by comparing it to what appears to be the best argument for the wrongness of the wanton infliction of pain on animals. This latter argument is based on the assumption that it is prima facie wrong to inflict pain on me (or you, reader). What is the natural property associated with the infliction of pain which makes such infliction wrong? The obvious answer seems to be that the infliction of pain causes suffering and that suffering is a misfortune. The suffering caused by the infliction of pain is what makes the wanton infliction of pain on me wrong. The wanton infliction of pain on other adult humans causes suffering. The wanton infliction of pain on animals causes suffering. Since causing suffering is what makes the wanton infliction of pain wrong and since the wanton infliction of pain on animals causes suffering, it follows that the wanton infliction of pain on animals is wrong.

This argument for the wrongness of the wanton infliction of pain on animals shares a number of structural features with the argument for the serious prima facie wrongness of abortion. Both arguments start with an obvious assumption concerning what it is wrong to do to me (or you, reader). Both then look for the characteristic or the consequence of the wrong action which makes the action wrong. Both recognize that the wrong-making feature of these immoral actions is a property of actions sometimes directed at individuals other than postnatal human beings. If the structure of the argument for the wrongness of the wanton infliction of pain on animals is sound, then the structure of the argument for the prima facie serious wrongness of abortion is also sound, for the structure of the two arguments is the same. The structure common to both is the key to the explanation of how the wrongness of abortion can be demonstrated without recourse to the category of person. In neither argument is that category crucial.

This defense of an argument for the wrongness of abortion in terms of a structurally similar argument for the wrongness of the wanton infliction of pain on animals succeeds only if the account regarding animals is the correct account. Is it? In the first place, it seems plausible. In the second place, its major competition is Kant's account. Kant believed that we do not have direct duties to animals at all, because they are not persons. Hence, Kant had to explain and justify the wrongness of inflicting pain on animals on the grounds that "he who is hard in his dealings with animals becomes hard also in his dealing with men."[8] The problem with Kant's account is that there seems to be no reason for accepting this latter claim unless Kant's account is rejected. If the alternative to Kant's account is accepted, then it is easy to understand why someone who is indifferent to inflicting pain on animals is also indifferent to inflicting pain on humans, for one is indifferent to what makes inflicting pain wrong in both cases. But, if Kant's account is accepted, there is no intelligible reason why one who is hard in his dealings with animals (or crabgrass or stones) should also be hard in his dealings with men. After all, men are persons: animals are no more persons than crabgrass or stones. Persons are Kant's crucial moral category. Why, in short, should a Kantian accept the basic claim in Kant's argument?

Hence, Kant's argument for the wrongness of inflicting pain on animals rests on a claim that, in a world of Kantian moral agents, is demonstrably false. Therefore, the alternative analysis, being more plausible anyway, should be accepted. Since this alternative analysis has the same structure as the anti-abortion argument being defended here, we have further support for the argument for the immorality of abortion being defended in this essay.

Of course, this value of a future-like-ours argument, if sound, shows only that abortion is prima facie wrong, not that it is wrong in any and all circumstances. Since the loss of the future to a standard fetus, if killed, is, however, at least as great a loss as the loss of the future to a standard adult human being who is killed, abortion, like ordinary killing, could be justified only by the most compelling reasons. The loss of one's life is almost the greatest misfortune that can happen to one. Presumably abortion could be justified in some circumstances, only if the loss consequent on failing to abort would be at least as great. Accordingly, morally permissible abortions will be rare indeed unless, perhaps, they occur so early in pregnancy that a fetus is not yet definitely an individual. Hence, this argument should be taken as showing that abortion is presumptively very seriously wrong, where the presumption is very strong—as strong as the presumption that killing another adult human being is wrong.

III.

How complete an account of the wrongness of killing does the value of a future-like-ours account have to be in order that the wrongness of abortion is a consequence? This account does not have to be an account of the necessary conditions for the wrongness of killing. Some persons in nursing homes may lack valuable human futures, yet it may be wrong to kill them for other reasons. Furthermore, this account does not obviously have to be the sole reason killing is wrong where the victim did have a valuable future. This analysis claims only that, for any killing where the victim did have a valuable future like ours, having that future by itself is sufficient to create the strong presumption that the killing is seriously wrong....

IV.

...A different strategy for avoiding these anti-abortion consequences involves limiting the scope of the value of a future argument. More precisely, the strategy involves arguing that fetuses lack a property that is essential for the value-of-a-future argument (or for any anti-abortion argument) to apply to them.

One move of this sort is based upon the claim that a necessary condition of one's future being valuable is that one values it. Value implies a valuer. Given this one might argue that, since fetuses cannot value their futures, their futures are not valuable to them. Hence, it does not seriously wrong them deliberately to end their lives.

This move fails, however, because of some ambiguities. Let us assume that something cannot be of value unless it is valued by someone. This does not entail that my life is of no value unless it is valued by me. I may think, in a period of despair, that my future is of no worth whatsoever, but I may be wrong because others rightly see value—even great value—in it. Furthermore, my future can be valuable to me even if I do not value it. This is the case when a young person attempts suicide, but is rescued and goes on to significant human achievements. Such young people's futures are ultimately valuable to them, even though such futures do not seem to be valuable to them at the moment of attempted suicide. A fetus's future can be valuable to it in the same way. Accordingly, this attempt to limit the anti-abortion argument fails....

...Paul Bassen[9] has argued that, even though the prospects of an embryo might seem to be a basis for the wrongness of abortion, an embryo cannot be a victim and therefore cannot be wronged. An embryo cannot be a victim, he says, because it lacks sentience. His central argument for this seems to be that, even though plants and the permanently unconscious are alive, they clearly cannot be victims. What is the explanation of this? Bassen claims that the explanation is that their lives consist of mere metabolism and mere metabolism is not enough to ground victimizability. Mentation is required.

The problem with this attempt to establish the absence of victimizability is that both plants and the permanently unconscious clearly lack what Bassen calls "prospects" or what I have called "a future life like ours." Hence, it is surely open to one to argue that the real reason we believe plants and the permanently unconscious cannot be victims is that killing them cannot deprive them of a future life like ours; the real reason is not their absence of present mentation.

Bassen recognizes that his view is subject to this difficulty, and he recognizes that the case of children seems to support this difficulty, for "much of what we do for children is based on prospects." He argues, however, that, in the case of children and in other such cases, "potentiality comes into play only where victimizability has been secured on other grounds" (*ibid.*, p. 333).

Bassen's defense of his view is patently question-begging, since what is adequate to secure victimizability is exactly what is at issue. His examples do not support his own view against the thesis of this essay. Of course, embryos can be victims: when their lives are deliberately terminated, they are deprived of their futures of value, their prospects. This makes them victims, for it directly wrongs them.

The seeming plausibility of Bassen's view stems from the fact that paradigmatic cases of imagining someone as a victim involve empathy, and empathy requires mentation of the victim. The victims of food, famine, rape, or child abuse are all persons with whom we can empathize. That empathy seems to be part of seeing them as victims.[10]

In spite of the strength of these examples, the attractive intuition that a situation in which there is victimization requires the possibility of empathy is subject to counterexamples. Consider a case that Bassen himself offers: "Posthumous obliteration of an author's work constitutes a misfortune for him only if he had wished his work to endure" (*op cit.*, p. 318). The conditions Bassen wishes to impose upon the possibility of being victimized here seem far too strong. Perhaps this author, due to his unrealistic standards of excellence and his low self-esteem, regarded his work as unworthy of survival, even though it possessed genuine literary merit. Destruction of such work would surely victimize its author. In such a case, empathy with the victim concerning the loss is clearly impossible.

Of course, Bassen does not make the possibility of empathy a necessary condition of victimizability; he requires only mentation. Hence, on Bassen's actual view, this author, as I have described him, can be a victim. The problem is that the basic intuition that renders Bassen's view plausible is missing in the author's case. In order to attempt to avoid counterexamples, Bassen has made his thesis too weak to be supported by the intuitions that suggested it.

Even so, the mentation requirement on victimizability is still subject to counterexamples. Suppose a severe accident renders me totally unconscious for a month, after which I recover. Surely killing me while I am unconscious victimizes me, even though I am incapable of mentation during that time. It follows that Bassen's thesis fails. Apparently, attempts to restrict the value of a future-like-ours argument so that fetuses do not fall within its scope do not succeed.

V.

In this essay, it has been argued that the correct ethic of the wrongness of killing can be extended to fetal life and used to show that there is a strong presumption that any abortion is morally impermissible. If the ethic of killing adopted here entails, however, that contraception is also seriously immoral, then there would appear to be a difficulty with the analysis of this essay.

But this analysis does not entail that contraception is wrong. Of course, contraception prevents the actualization of a possible future of value. Hence, it follows from the claim that futures of value should be maximized that contraception is prima facie immoral. This obligation to maximize does not exist, however; furthermore, nothing in the ethics of killing in this paper entails that it does. The ethics of killing in this essay would entail that contraception is wrong only if something were denied a human future of value by contraception. Nothing at all is denied such a future by contraception, however.

Candidates for a subject of harm by contraception fall into four categories: (1) some sperm or other, (2) some ovum or other, (3) a sperm and an ovum separately, and (4) a sperm and an ovum together. Assigning the harm to some sperm is utterly arbitrary, for no reason can be given for making a sperm the subject of harm rather than an ovum. Assigning the harm to some ovum is utterly arbitrary, for no reason can be given for making an ovum the subject of harm rather than a sperm. One might attempt to avoid these problems by insisting that contraception deprives both the sperm and the ovum separately of a valuable future like ours. On this alternative, too many futures are lost. Contraception was supposed to be wrong, because it deprived us of one future of value, not two. One might attempt to avoid this problem by holding that contraception deprives the combination of sperm and ovum of a valuable future like ours. But here the definite article misleads. At the time of contraception, there are hundreds of millions of sperm, one (released) ovum and millions of possible combinations of all of these. There is no actual combination at all. Is the subject of the loss to be a merely possible combination? Which one? This alternative does not yield an actual subject of harm either. Accordingly, the immorality of contraception is not entailed by the loss of a future-like-ours argument simply because there is no nonarbitrarily identifiable subject of the loss in the case of contraception.

VI.

The purpose of this essay has been to set out an argument for the serious presumptive wrongness of abortion subject to the assumption that the moral permissibility of abortion stands or falls on the moral status of the fetus. Since a fetus possesses a property, the possession of which in adult human beings is sufficient to make killing an adult human being wrong, abortion is wrong. This way of dealing with the problem of abortion seems superior to other approaches to the ethics of abortion, because it rests on an ethics of killing which is close to self-evident, because the crucial morally relevant property clearly applies to fetuses, and because the argument avoids the usual equivocations on "human life," "human being," or "person." The argument rests neither on religious claims nor on Papal dogma. It is not subject to the objection of "speciesism." Its soundness is compatible with the moral permissibility of euthanasia and contraception. It deals with our intuitions concerning young children.

Finally, this analysis can be viewed as resolving a standard problem—indeed, *the* standard problem—concerning the ethics of abortion. Clearly, it is wrong to kill adult human beings. Clearly, it is not wrong to end the life of some arbitrarily chosen single human cell. Fetuses seem to be like arbitrarily chosen human cells in some respects and like adult humans in other respects. The problem of the ethics of abortion is the problem of determining the fetal property that settles this moral controversy. The thesis of this essay is that the problem of the ethics of abortion, so understood, is solvable.

NOTES

1. Feinberg, "Abortion," in *Matters of Life and Death: New Introductory Essays in Moral Philosophy*, Tom Regan, ed. (New York: Random House, 1986), pp. 256-293; Tooley, "Abortion and Infanticide," *Philosophy and Public Affairs*, II, 1 (1972) 37-65; Tooley, Abortion and Infanticide (New York: Oxford, 1984); Warren, "On the Moral and Legal Status of Abortion," *The Monist*, I.VII, 1 (1973); 43-61; Engelhardt, "The Ontology of Abortion," *Ethics*, I. XXXIV, 3 (1974): 217-234; Sumner, *Abortion and Moral Theory* (Princeton: University Press, 1981); Noonan, "An Almost Absolute Value in History," in *The Morality of Abortion: Legal and Historical Perspectives*, Noonan, ed. (Cambridge: Harvard, 1970); and Devine, *The Ethics of Homicide* (Ithaca: Cornell, 1978).
2. For interesting discussions of this issue, see Warren Quinn, "Abortion: Identity and Loss," *Philosophy and Public Affairs*, XIII. 1 (1984): 24-54; and Lawrence C. Becker, "Human Being: the Boundaries of the Concept," *Philosophy and Public Affairs*, IV, 4 (1975): 334-359.
3. For example, see my "Ethics and The Elderly: Some Problems," in Stuart Spicker, Kathleen Woodward and David Van Tassel, eds., *Aging and the Elderly: Humanistic Perspectives in Gerontology* (Atlantic Highlands, NJ: Humanities, 1978): pp. 341-355.
4. See Warren, *op.cit.*, and Tooley, "Abortion and Infanticide."
5. This seems to be the fatal flaw in Warren's treatment of this issue.
6. I have been most influenced on this matter by Jonathan Glover, *Causing Death and Saving Lives* (New York: Penguin, 1977), ch. 3; and Robert Young, "What is So Wrong with Killing People?" *Philosophy*, LIV, 210 (1979): 515-528.
7. Feinberg, Tooley, Warren, and Engelhardt have all dealt with this problem.
8. "Duties to Animals and Spirits," in *Lectures on Ethics*, Louis Infeld, trans. (New York: Harper, 1963), p. 239.
9. "Present Sakes and Future Prospects: The Status of Early Abortion," *Philosophy and Public Affairs*, XI, 4 (1982): 322-326.
10. Note carefully the reasons he gives on the bottom of p. 326.

SENSATIONALIZED PHILOSOPHY: A REPLY TO MARQUIS'S "WHY ABORTION IS IMMORAL"

Ann E. Cudd

Ann E. Cudd teaches philosophy at the University of Kansas, Lawrence. Her main areas of interest include philosophy of social science and social and political philosophy. Her published work focuses on decision theory and applications of it to feminist and other social issues.

Cudd identifies what she takes to be a fundamental flaw in Marquis's argument against abortion. She rejects his claim that the moral justifiability of abortion stands or falls on the issue of the moral status of the fetus as well as his claim that philosophers on both sides of the debate accept this claim. Even if we grant that the fetus has moral status, there are other values and rights that justifiably enter the debate on abortion.

In a recent article, Don Marquis[1] claims to show "Why Abortion is Immoral." The title is, as I shall show, much bolder than what is warranted by his argument. This essay simply rebuts Marquis's initial assumption: that the only important question for settling the abortion issue is the moral status of the fetus, and the corroboration for this claim which he alleges to exist in the abortion literature. I mean this as only a partial reply,[2] and I do not claim to add to the positive argument here. In fact, I would not add to the thousands of pages written on this topic if I did not feel morally compelled to rebut what I see as a sensationalized and erroneous treatment of an issue of utmost current political importance.

In the beginning of his article, Marquis explicitly makes the assumption that "whether or not abortion is morally permissible stands or falls on whether or not a fetus is the sort of being whose life it is seriously wrong to end" [539]. There are two issues that arise in assessing this claim: (1) Is the fetus the sort of thing that could have any rights or toward which we could have obligations? (2) Are these rights or obligations prima facie or absolute? Marquis's claim seems to conflate the two issues, assuming that whatever rights of, or obligations to, fetuses there are, they must be absolute.

The assumption that any obligations we have to fetuses are absolute, presented without argument, is philosophically (and politically) irresponsible. It is as if fetuses were things growing out in the garden, and the question of abortion were whether one may decide to till them under rather than let them come to fruition. The question of abortion inextricably involves (at least) two lives and a compelling bundle of rights on the side of the woman carrying the fetus, whatever we decide about the status of the fetus. Ignoring these rights makes about as much sense as considering the issue of the moral permissibility of killing adult, fully-conscious humans without considering the justification of self-defense. If no countervailing rights or other moral considerations were to be allowed to figure into the judgment, the criterion on which Marquis claims that abortion is impermissible, having a "future-like-ours," would also rule out killing in self-defense. He makes no exceptions to his claim that abortion is immoral. Thus, it seems that to be consistent he would also have to reject any self-defense plea in killing any human being.

The only justification Marquis provides for the dubious assumption that a fetus's right to its future is

---

Reprinted with permission of the publisher and Ann E. Cudd from *The Journal of Philosophy* 87:5 (1990): 262–264.

absolute and overriding is an appeal to his favorite authors on abortion. He writes:

> Many of the most insightful and careful writers on the ethics of abortion ... believe that whether or not abortion is morally permissible *stands or falls* on whether or not the fetus is the sort of being whose life it is seriously wrong to end ([183], emphasis mine).

The list of authors Marquis provides is quite impressive. The claim he makes about their arguments here is false, however. They all consider rights (and other moral concerns) of the pregnant woman, and find cases in which her rights or concerns override any considerations in favor of the fetus.[3] The authors cited can be divided into two categories: those who argue that abortions are permissible because the fetus is not the sort of being whose life it is seriously wrong to end,[4] and those who argue that abortions are impermissible in most (but not all) cases because the fetus is such a being.[5]

With regard to the first group, it is an obvious logical mistake to infer from:

> (A) Since the fetus is not the sort of being whose life it is seriously wrong to end, it is morally permissible to abort.

that therefore,

> (B) If it were the case that the fetus is the sort of being whose life it is seriously wrong to end, then it would be morally impermissible to abort.

The writers in the first group hold (A), but they make no claims like (B). That is, these writers merely claim that the fetus's lack of personhood is a sufficient, though not necessary, condition for abortion to be morally permissible. Marquis's phrase "stands or falls" requires it to be both a necessary and sufficient condition on the permissibility of abortion.

In the second group, both authors deny (A), but allow that, in cases in which the mother's life is in danger, or, perhaps, the woman was a victim of rape, abortion is morally permissible, thus denying (B) as well. In these cases, they reason, the woman's right to life or her serious loss of well-being overrides the rights of the fetus. Thus, they regard the woman's rights as a relevant issue in deciding the moral permissibility of abortion, and so could hardly be said to argue that the moral permissibility of abortion stands or falls with the issue of whether it is wrong to kill fetuses.

Even if we might ultimately agree that the fetus is the sort of thing whose killing is so morally wrong as to overwhelm completely a woman's rights to privacy, health, medical care, and even life, the point surely needs argument. Nothing that has been said in the abortion debate to date has come close to settling this issue against the woman. So *at most* Marquis can claim to have shown "Why Abortion is Killing a Being-Like-Us." When one recalls that persons may legitimately be killed for many reasons, this title has not the same moral urgency of Marquis's.

AUTHOR'S NOTE

I would like to thank Neal Becker, Jack Bricke, Tony Genova, Leslie Jones and JoAnn Reckling for helpful comments. I, alone, am responsible for any remaining errors.

NOTES

1. [*The Journal of Philosophy*] LXXXVI, 4 (April 1989): 183-202.
2. This is only part of what was originally a longer reply, which is available on request from the author.
3. Mary Anne Warren, "On the Moral and Legal Status of Abortion," *The Monist*, LVII, 1 (1973): 43-61: "The immorality of abortion is no more demonstrated by the humanity of the fetus, in itself, than the immorality of killing in self-defense is demonstrated by the fact that the assailant is a human being" (p. 46). H.T. Engelhardt, Jr., "The Ontology of Abortion," *Ethics*, LXXXIV, 3 (1974): 217-234: "The rights of the mother regarding abortion are paramount. After all, she is the only actual person involved....Consequently, it is to her that one owes overriding obligations." (p. 233). Michael Tooley, "Abortion and Infanticide." *Philosophy and Public Affairs*, II, 1 (1972): 37-65. Tooley claims that the argument is settled by the fact that the fetus is not a person, and endorses Judith Jarvis Thomson's general claims about what would be the case if the fetus were a person, namely, that the woman's rights over-

ride. Joel Feinberg, "Abortion," in *Matters of Life and Death: New Introductory Essays in Moral Philosophy*, Tom Regan, ed. (New York: Random, 1986), pp. 256-293: "Even if we grant that the fetus is a moral person and thus has a valid claim to life, it does not follow that abortion is always wrong" (p.233). J.T. Noonan, Jr., *Private Choice* (New York: Free Press, 1979). Noonan urges the reversal of Roe v. Wade, but on many grounds, including the rights of the family and the poor, as well as his view that fetuses are the sorts of beings that it is seriously wrong to kill. Philip Devine, *The Ethics of Homicide* (Ithaca: Cornell 1978). Devine allows that there are cases when abortion is not morally impermissible, see esp. Ch. III. It also seems that one cannot legitimately ignore Thomson, "A Defense of Abortion," *Philosophy and Public Affairs*, I, 1 (1971): 47-66, as being among the most insightful writers on abortion. Her view is quite clearly opposed to Marquis's; the legal, if not in each case moral, permissibility of abortion stands on the rights of women to refuse to donate their bodies to others.

4. Warren, Engelhardt, Tooley, and Feinberg.
5. Noonan and Devine.

ABORTION ETHICS: RIGHTS AND RESPONSIBILITIES

Elisabeth Porter

Elisabeth Porter teaches sociology and feminist theory at the University of Ulster at Coleraine. She is the author of Women and Moral Identity *(Unwin, 1991).*

"Abortion considerations require deep reflection on law, convention, social mores, religious norms, family contexts, emotions, and relationships. I have three arguments. First, a liberal "right to choose" framework is inadequate because it is based on individualist notions of rights. Second, reproductive freedoms should be extended to all women. Third, abortion ethics involves a dialectical interplay between rights and responsibilities, and between social, cultural, and particular contexts, and is best understood in terms of moral praxis."

I. Liberal Rights

In dealing with reproductive control, the women's liberation movement of the 1960s and 1970s imbibed liberal individual goals of equality, rights, and choice. These goals often translated into thinking of equality as sameness to men, of rights as self-preference, and of free choice as a negative freedom from interference by others. A reevaluation of these goals questions whether abortion is best understood as a "woman's right to choose." It is worth summarizing the bases of these interrelated goals and why a reevaluation is necessary.

Equal Rights

The dominant liberal view of equality extends to equal rights, opportunities, respect, and impartial treatment and procedures. It has an implicit ethic of justice, that to treat people fairly means to treat people as equals. As applied to women's rights, this view has historical roots in the writings of J.S. Mill, who saw women as having complementary talents that should be equally valued. Adherents of this liberal view still maintain that once differential treatment of women is removed, equality will quickly follow. Linda Krieger points to two problematic assumptions behind this argument. First, she notes what is problematic about the assumption that there are no "real" differences between men and women. Second, she argues against the idea that there are no characteristics unique to one sex. To highlight what is wrong with these assumptions, she uses the 1982 example of *Fritz v. Hagerstown Reproductive Health Services*, in which a husband is seen to have an equal right to decide on a continuation or termination of his wife's pregnancy. In Krieger's terms, this treats maternity and paternity as if they are the same (1987, 53). They are not the same, and the substantial differences matter, as I explore shortly.

There are theoretical and practical constraints in applying an equal treatment principle to all. First, at a theoretical level, we need to consider the political tradition of individual rights, where the founding fathers of Western democracies articulate political and civil citizenship rights of men, and natural and social responsibilities of women. The idea that women as equals have rights, presupposes they are equal heirs to the tradition of political liberty that grants rights of choice to persons of moral autonomy, who are considered to be capable of being held responsible to that choice. This presupposition is his-

---

Reprinted with permission of the publisher and Elisabeth Porter from *Hypatia* 9:3 (Summer 1994): 66–87.

torically dubious. A formal equality that assumes sameness crystallizes power networks. Second, practical constraints in applying an equal treatment principle abound, given the realities of unequal practices, inequalities of opportunity, and the injustice of being treated differently because of one's sex. As Elizabeth Kingdom usefully differentiates, equality includes a moral principle of gender equality, a formal legal equality, and a substantive equality, the latter incorporating actual domestic, economic, financial, and political relations between men and women (1991, 119). The discrepancy between having formal legal equality but not being taken seriously as a person capable of moral decisions has led some theorists to argue for a redefinition of equality in a legislative combination of equal rights and special rights.

Special Rights

Equal rights are basic rights, accruing to all, but special rights are often created to guarantee the possibility of exercising these equal rights. The rationale behind special rights is to take account of actual differences, circumstances and contexts; so special rights have a pragmatic dimension. As Paul Green asks, "What morally relevant differences among groups are sufficient to trigger the creation of a special right?" (1987, 69). Any response in terms of natural differences has a particular appeal to questions of reproduction. Elizabeth Wolgast certainly argues that there are natural sex differences, and so treating people equally means treating these differences respectfully (1980, 1989). Special rights thus depend on individual features that distinguish people. Men do not become pregnant, so, as Wolgast writes, "some rights are simply different" (1989, 160), like differential rights for pregnant women. To use another of her examples, we have no problem with the idea that disabled persons in wheelchairs need special rights to have equal rights. Such persons are unable to exercise equal rights, like the right to employment, unless special ramps to places of employment are provided (1980, 51).

As Kingdom points out, the use of a concept of special rights restores meaning to people's ordinary experiences by permitting differences to be properly acknowledged in law and institution (1991, 123). Yet she argues forthrightly that Wolgast is mistaken in thinking that special rights are a solution to equal rights. Rather, Kingdom maintains, they merely describe the problem. "People ought to be treated equally except in those cases where they ought to be treated specially" (1991, 128). Kingdom intimates the dilemmas of jurisprudence in needing to decide on the criteria for determining valid exceptions, that is, when do special rights need to be created? She also warns against reducing policy to philosophic quibbles that may deflect attention from the material social conditions and the practical dilemmas to be resolved (1991, 129). While this warning needs to be heeded, the reduction is not inevitable. Indeed, what is needed is a merging of both moral principles and material practices. For example, if we accept that "sometimes gender should be relevant in claiming rights" (Markowitz 1990, 3), we must consider both why it is relevant and how rights are situated in gendered material power relations. In attempting to consider principles and practices, Lizbeth Hasse offers a radical critique of "the rule-of-law equal treatment analysis [that] requires men and women to be *similarly situated* before the equal treatment challenge will be triggered" (1987, 288). Where a similar social and power situation does not occur, Hasse suggests that a reconstruction of the law is needed to reflect women's moral values institutionally, irrespective of whether differences have occurred naturally or historically. As a lawyer, her worry is understandably about implementation of forums to judge moral issues. Clearly, feminist concepts of equality must recognize special needs, yet they should not allow these needs to ground inconsistencies. For example, feminists often reject gender-specific practices based on naturalistic assumptions of maternity, while persistently defending gender-specific needs, such as abortion. Needs emerge from material contexts. While laws, constitutions and practices often masquerade as gender-neutral but imply the male body, gender-specific differences of needs will be ignored or will involve discrimination. Hence, in addressing special rights, "specificity is now a needed corrective" (Eisenstein 1991, 108). This is not an easy task.

Freedom as the Right to Choice

So what place should abortion ethics give to interpreting specificity as the freedom of choice? In the history of the abortion rights movement, the politically powerful slogan "a woman's right to choose" expressed real needs for women who had no choice, but now diverse groups are troubled at the adversarial nature of campaigns based solely on this slogan. Let me extend Rosalind Pollack Petchesky's argument, that the principles underlying the slogan are insufficient and problematic in that they evade "moral questions about when, under what conditions, and for what purposes reproductive decisions should be made" (1986, 7). A simple assertion that women should decide tells us nothing pragmatically normative "about the moral and social values women ought to bring to this decision, *how* they should decide" (Petchesky 1980, 100). The message behind the slogan is vulnerable to the liberal individualist abstract assumptions of equal individual rights discussed above. General abstract rights accruing to all do not address specific social relations and sexual divisions. We need rights, but rights emerge from particular needs; they necessarily take into account specific, concrete social requirements. As I argue later, some women "need" the "special right" of an abortion.

So, does the "right to choose" argument accommodate this need? In asking "What's wrong with rights?" Kingdom highlights three points relevant for this discussion. First, abortion is but one of a number of interrelated reproductive rights that need to be situated in "a framework which recognizes the complexity of women's needs in the sphere of reproduction" (1991, 51). These needs cover the gamut of sex education, contraception, antenatal care, childcare, and economic considerations of diet, housing, warmth, and daily maintenance. Second, the slogan under critique "accentuates the notion of a right as inhering in an individual, as the moral entitlement of an individual human being which is possessed independently of prevailing social conditions" (1991, 54). Any inference that a pregnant woman stands in isolation understates the ways in which actual social factors influence moral choice. All our choices are made in contexts of our religion, ethnicity, social status and past experiences. Third, Kingdom suggests that "appeals to a woman's right to choose are notoriously vague in their meaning" (1991, 59), that is, they skate over complex issues of deciding on specific proposals and strategies, and thus these appeals obstruct serious engagement with legal issues. In summary, a simplistic "right to choose" framework is inadequate on at least three major levels. It is premised on abstract notions of rights, debatably assumed to apply to all. It has individualistic connotations, rights that need not take into account other relationships and social contexts. It leaves the individual as the sole moral arbiter, providing no assistance with how individuals should choose or how law should incorporate such rights.

Rashmi Luthra presents a challenging argument regarding the limitations of "choice" in the abortion rights movement. She argues that in racist, classist societies, issues of forced sterilization, and high infant and maternal mortality are part of the social reality for working-class women of color. "In the absence of access to abortion services, decent health care, decent childcare, acceptable life options for their children, 'choice' is a hollow and abstract concept" (1993, 44). Luthra reminds us that for women of color, "the 'choice to be a mother' is as important as the choice of whether to abort or not" (1993, 45). She challenges us also to evaluate morally a typical white Western feminist opposition to the selective abortion of female fetuses where there is extreme preference for sons, while we leave the choice of the selective abortion of disabled fetuses open. Her agenda is to redirect the focus to appropriate broad structural changes, whether eugenics, racism, poverty, illiteracy, or health care.

II. Reproductive Rights

How then can we take seriously some women's "need" of the "special right" of an abortion and yet avoid the abstract, ahistorical, individualistic connotations of liberal rights? While the critique of rights as formal, abstract, and divorced from context is valid, what I want to address is the dialectical relationship between claims of rights and the social contexts in which the struggle for an assertion of rights occurs. The political philosophic justification for rights that accrue to moral beings interacts with the social practices that prompt the necessity for rights—there is a dialectical relationship between theories of rights and practices of claims of rights that can be understood through the concept of praxis. I am using praxis in the sense Elizabeth Schneider uses it, as "the active role of consciousness and subjectivity in shaping both theory and practice and the dynamic interrelationship that results" (1990, 229). The following discussion of abortion ethics is situated within the praxial process of rights and responsibilities. In part three, I summarize the nature of moral praxis for abortion ethics. This second part prepares the ground for establishing the interdependence of rights and responsibilities by first establishing the legitimacy of reproductive rights, and then by showing the need to deal adequately with seemingly conflicting reproductive rights, particularly those of mother versus fetal rights. My goal is to demonstrate the importance of individual rights within a context of community responsibilities. I am extending issues raised in Alison Jaggar's earlier important work (1976), that moral philosophic questions of if or when an abortion can be justified often predominate over social and political questions concerning the responsibility for applying such reflections to particular women. Jaggar suggests moving the focus from individual rights to fulfilling human needs. One way to explore this suggestion is to look to broader reproductive freedoms.

Reproductive Freedoms

Reproductive rights are part of reproductive freedoms that affirm ideals of equality and autonomy. Given women's body, sexuality, and reproductive potential, reproductive rights affirm equality as an extension of the principle of bodily integrity, and self-determination. Given the social position of women, a defense of autonomy is important. Insofar as women are not only responsible for pregnancy but also usually for the care of children, women must be the ones who ultimately decide on contraception, abortion, and childbearing. This is certainly the argument Jaggar proposed in 1976. Equality is rooted in individual generalized rights, autonomy in socially determined particular needs. Petchesky's argument, which I am extending, "is that reproductive freedom ... is irreducibly social and individual at the same time; that is, it operates 'at the core of social life' as well as within and upon women's individual bodies" (1980, 94; 1986, 2). An important part of this struggle to achieve reproductive freedom is realizing this dual nature of citizenship as moral identities: we are individuals and we are social (Porter 1991). Platforms conducted solely on women's right to choose, or, as I expand shortly, on individual privacy, cannot incorporate this dual emphasis. While reproductive liberty sounds an enticing idea, within an individualistic framework, as Jeanne Schuler warns, "it signals a new level of alienated sexuality," a view of freedom without a vision of community, family, or social being, where "what happens to me is overwhelmingly up to me" (1987-88, 130). This is not the type of reproductive freedom I am discussing.

My reconceptualizing reproductive rights to include particularities, responsibilities, and social needs exposes the limitations of the supposedly free, unencumbered liberal citizen. So, what does it mean to call women's choice in reproductive matters, a "liberty right" (Smith 1984, 270)? More specifically, is the right to abortion a "democratic right?" If it is, can we resist reading rights discourse as if these rights accrue to humans irrespective of their particularity? The answers to these questions hinge on a more inclusive focus on reproductive rights, rather than just on abortion rights. Zillah Eisenstein argues that reproductive rights are democratic rights that "are located in this space *in between*: between our rights and our access to them, between our reproductive specificity and our universal human claims" (1991, 12). The beauty of this balance between individuality and commonality is that it permits a theory and practice that has as its starting point "*both* the individual (her specificity) and her right to reproductive freedom (which is universal)" (1991, 120). As Eisenstein argues, this balance has important implications for coalition politics. Once the democratic right is established, the nature of the specificity can be contested, that is, what are this or that woman's actual needs that require a resolution?

Working through specificity necessitates negotiation with privileged, dominant discourses to destabilize rigid meanings or unspecified abstract rights.

For example, exposure to the rights of "a pregnant woman of color" urges rights discourse to be inclusive, indicating possible differences race, ethnicity, and class make, not only to possessing rights but also to having access to them. With individual differences, women may have the right to abort, but not the finances to cover the costs. Other women might not legally possess the right—access is restricted—so desperate measures are taken. This feminist rights discourse is situating the individuality of reproductive need within the context of shared needs of women. The universality of rights discourse is a prerequisite. It acts as a safety measure, ensuring that everyone is granted rights equally and enabling those who don't enjoy these rights to struggle to claim them personally. This principle of reproductive freedom needs to apply to all women as potential mothers, and it is justified in terms of specifically determinate needs. Viewed in these terms, reproductive freedom is more than individual rights, it is a social principle.

Collective Rights

Does the analysis of collective rights facilitate our understanding of the social nature of this principle? Douglas Sanders shows how groups suffering discrimination often draw on rights discourse to assert a collective identity, of, say, "the gay community" or "Afro-American writers." Diversity and cultural pluralism is part of the contemporary political rhetoric. But, he notes, "International human rights law continues to stress the individual" (1991, 376). This is understandable. Individual and collective rights are not the same. Individual rights accrue to individuals. Collective rights seek to protect cultural characteristics, particularly language, religion, legal norms, and culturally important activities (Article 27 of the Covenant on Civil and Political Rights, in Sanders 1991, 382). Individual and collective rights are distinctive, and they are sustained through cultural communities. For example, the right to freedom of religion affirms an individual right to personal belief and a collective right to public worship and cultural practices. Yet when conflict between individual and collective rights develops, the resolution requires evaluating the conflict. Who is to do the balancing? The UN Human Rights Committee provides guidelines on a general interest level, but much of the balancing is left to courts and legislatures. If the right to sexual equality as part of reproductive freedoms is not seen as a legitimate right to which all women are entitled, then the attempt to claim collective rights of women to full citizenship is problematic. In this political controversy, the fundamental issue is not the rights of women as separate, isolated individuals, or the rights of women as a collectivity, who share identical needs or social-sexual position. The fundamental issue that a notion of collective rights misses is that of affirming the common rights of individual women whose specificity varies.

Conflicting Rights: Fetal or Mother Rights?

Having established the legitimacy of reproductive freedoms, I move now to the task of dealing with seemingly conflicting reproductive rights. The hope that abstract, general, impartial rights could generate a just society is noble, but as noted, the outcome is often a privileging of perspectives, the protection of rights of privileged citizens. Furthermore, within a liberal paradigm, rights are individualizing. Competing rights are seen as part of the structures of "oppositional, hierarchical entitlements" (Lee and Morgan 1991, 9). These competing rights emerge in extreme forms in debates concerning a pregnant woman versus a fetus, often presented as a seemingly intractable moral-legal dilemma. Let us examine then the extreme impasse between those who believe the woman has an exclusive right to choose whether or not to terminate a pregnancy and those who believe the fetus has a right to life on the basis of human status, and hence whose destruction should be prohibited by law. These are competing rights, "seen to be in conflict, in the sense that one cannot be granted without withholding the other"(Smith 1984, 265). A woman's right to choose means that the fetus's right to life is threatened. A fetus's right to life prevents women from having any choice. The conundrum has been solved in the past by prioritizing one right over the other, or by declaring it to be insoluble, as if one decision is as arbitrary as another. As competing rights, the conundrum does appear insoluble, for both positions are "logically defensible if one accepts certain premises" (Clarke 1991, 155) about the personhood or nonpersonhood of fetuses. In wanting to develop a feminist morality of abortion, I do not accept that one decision is as arbitrary as another, or that the premises on which they are based are equally supportive. Yet nor do I want to view this rights discourse as a competitive win-lose situation, but rather I seek to develop some ideas that are responsive to women's autonomy and to the moral significance of pregnancy and birth.

First, let us explore some of the premises behind the pitting of rights in debates concerning fetal versus mother rights. Talk of fetal rights is couched in issues of moral status, human potential, and the relationship to a pregnant woman. Regarding the species and potentiality principles, Judith Areen asks us to consider what is more influential, our prior concept of a "person" or "human being," or our moral view of abortion, to which this concept is then adapted? (1989, 111). Agreement on the status of the fetus does not itself exhaust moral inquiry. Does personhood start with conception, brain life, quickening, lung development, birth, personality or rational choice? Again, there are a range of plausible responses. "Just as *brain death* is now generally accepted as marking the ending of life so *brain life* marks the beginning of personhood" (Brazier 1988, 13). This occurs at about ten weeks. In common law, the killing of the child in the womb constituted only a misdemeanor, a lesser offense than murder, but it was taken more seriously after quickening (about eighteen weeks) given the presumed ensoulment. Even Catholic doctrine disputes the precise moment at which the fetus is animated with a soul. Petchesky argues that the concept of fetal personhood is offensive because it ignores the distinctiveness of human beings, namely our capacity for consciousness and sociability. She makes her point through a stark example that an assumption of fetal personhood places the death of Holocaust victims on the same level as aborted fetuses, and this demeans the moral value of human consciousness (1986, 341).

There are important qualitative differences in degrees of consciousness, yet even when the fetus is not regarded as a person in the full sense, "it is not nothing, and important questions will still remain as to what sort of being it is and how it ought to be treated" (Overall 1987, 41). What is the moral status of the fetus? Some answer this both in view of "what it is" and "what it might become," that is, the potential to become a full human being, confirming the moral importance and inviolability of fetuses. Questions of potentiality are particularly important in establishing guidelines for research on embryos. The Warnock Report (1985) decided on a limit of fourteen days beyond fertilization. In objecting to potentiality arguments, John Harris reminds us that acorns are not oak trees, and that while part of our humanity is the reality of death, we do not regard this as a good reason for treating people as if they were already dead (1991, 90-91). He contends that "If the potentiality argument is sound, then human potential is present quite as much before 14 days as it is after that limit" (1991, 93). Also, if the moral rationales that might justify abortion are sound, then research on experimentation up to this upper limit are also sound. In my reckoning, potentiality arguments need to consider the present state and the possible state.

So does the fetus have rights? None the law recognizes. Most Western abortion acts give a right to doctors to assess whether an abortion is medically justified. For legal rights the fetus must first be born and be a child. As May Ann Warren expresses it: "There is room for only one person with full and equal rights inside a single human skin. That is why it is birth, rather than sentience, viability, or some other prenatal milestone that must mark the beginning of legal parenthood" (1989, 63), and of legal personhood. Yet it is important to qualify that "the embryo has a recognised status worthy of legal protection" (Brazier 1988, 12). That is, "unlike an individual egg or sperm cell, an embryo may become a person, and it is therefore different from mere body parts" (Overall 1987, 75). An abortion is not the same as having a tooth pulled out, or even having a limb amputated. Christine Overall (1987) argues that no one, not even a genetic parent has an automatic entitlement to destroy an embryo. Yet similarly, the embryo has no automatic right to occupy a mother's uterus. Compulsion to nourish a fetus is itself a moral issue (Petchesky 1986, 327). Overall's claim is a specific application of a more general principle, that no one has the right to the use of anyone else's body (1987, 77). This is precisely what makes rape, incest, and slavery wrong. Maintaining bodily integrity is essential to self-respect and moral identity. As Judith Jarvis Thomson argues, "The issue is not should the mother be prevented from destroying the embryo, but shall the law compel her to sustain its life and growth for the nine months from fertilization to birth?" (1973, 112). In a similar vein, Sally Markowitz posits her "impossible sacrifice principle" (1990, 7). In a situation of structurally imbalanced power relations, to require oppressed groups to make sacrifices that might exacerbate oppression is morally impermissible. To insist that pregnant women never assert their need for an abortion is to insist on an "impossible sacrifice principle." However, even if the fetus has no immediate right of occupancy, this does not imply it is never wrong to terminate, particularly where a woman has incurred a degree of responsibility. Overall uses the examples of where a mother has a well-advanced fetus, or she is tired, is a careerist, or where the fetus is not the preferred sex.

Abortion ethics must take into account both the well-being of the fetus and a respect for a woman's autonomy. This view takes seriously the idea that moral personhood emerges in relation to others, in specific social contexts. It rejects the prevalent fetal imagery that adopts a Hobbesian view of people "as disconnected, solitary individuals, paradoxically helpless and autonomous at the same time" (Petchesky 1986, xi). As Petchesky points out, even the medical concept "viability," with its images of younger, tinier fetuses being saved, reinforces this idea that the fetus's identity is separate and autonomous, waiting for scientific medical expertise to present as the saviour. The point I am reinforcing is that there is a direct interdependence between a woman and her fetus, though the relationship is asymmetrical. It is the fetus who is completely dependent on the woman for its "welfare-right" (Smith 1984, 270). This is, as Janet Farrell Smith puts it, the right to well-being that requires duties of nurture of a particular woman. She argues that asserting a fetus's "right to life" to be "in conflict with a woman's right to choose is incoherent when the 'right to life' depends on and only makes sense in terms of that very woman's nurture and sustaining of the pregnancy" (1984, 268). Her point is that while there is a crucial interdependence between the woman and her fetus, there are serious difficulties in imposing a conflict of rights construction, given the asymmetrical relationship, where the woman can live independent of the fetus, but the fetus is totally dependent on the woman for sustenance. The fetus needs the woman in a way that the woman does not need the fetus. "A conflict of rights presumes independent beings capable of making countervailing claims upon one another" (1984, 268); it presumes social agents in decision-making contexts. In Smith's terms, this is nonsensical when the conflict is between fetal versus mother rights because impasses prevail. I agree with Faye Ginsburg that "there is a tragic dimension to the polarization around the abortion issue" (1989, 79), for both grassroots pro-life and pro-choice women struggle to enhance women's position in cultural systems that place motherhood and wage labor in competition. The polarization of goals and strategies masks the common vision of liberating women.

Privacy Rights versus Social Rights

The core of the liberal argument for abortion is not in resolving conflicting rights debates, but in defending privacy rights—particular rights of property inherent in personhood, including bodies as possessing private rights. So the Supreme Court in the United States decided in the landmark 1973 *Roe v. Wade* case that the right to choose an abortion is a woman's private decision, that rights of privacy belong to pregnant women. Although privacy is generally included in concepts of autonomy, arguments based on a respect for autonomy are more far-reaching, acknowledging individuality in democratic pluralism. In a positive way, privacy rights affirm the importance of a respect for autonomy and uncoerced decision making in ethical life, protecting personal choices from arbitrary interference or state intervention. In a negative way, privacy rights leave us alone to grapple over personal dilemmas, and this occurs in cultures of isolation, where "truly the individual is left on her own" (Eisenstein 1991, 101). As Elizabeth Schneider contends, articulating women's rights to reproductive freedoms as a matter of privacy is problematic, "because it reinforces and legitimizes the public and private dichotomy that historically has been damaging to women" (1990, 241). Rather than seeing the right to abortion as part of the collective freedom of women as equal citizens, privacy rights leaves the decision in the domestic sphere.

Within the larger context of the politics of abortion, an emphasis on privacy rights makes individual freedom of choice and self-preference the moral arbiter. Choice is important, but as Alisdair MacIntyre bemoans, the "privatization of good" diminishes the scope of morality and contributes to the sterility of public debate on issues such as abortion, which are admitted to the public realm. He is criticizing the fragmentary nature of moral discourse where issues are abstracted from their contexts, privatized, and treated in isolation from related social practices. This privatization obscures the larger context, of which he notes the point and purpose of family life, the place of upbringing of children in that life, and the relationship of family ties to other social ties (MacIntyre 1990, 353). Michael Sandel similarly points to the difficulties of bracketing moral judgments from law. What we need rather is a "keener appreciation of the role of substantive moral discourse in political and constitutional argument" (1989, 522). To demonstrate these difficulties, he reflects back to *Roe v. Wade* and the Court's claim to neutrality. He shows how a minimalist liberalism proposes bracketing controversial moral issues in order to secure some cooperation in view of disagreement about ends. Where there is massive disagreement about "the good," attempts to achieve social cooperation of some sort is understandable. But as an ultimate goal, neutrality or minimalism offers no grounds for moral choice. As Sandel argues, in attempts to bracket moral controversies for the sake of cooperation, it might not be clear what is being bracketed. Resolving that confusion "requires either a substantive view about the moral and religious interests at stake or an autonomous conception of the person" (1989, 533), and both of these solutions deny a minimalist liberalism its neutrality. Rather, they implicate particular political conceptions in the moral commitments they seek to avoid. Ironically, "the tendency to bracket substantive moral questions makes it difficult to argue for toleration in the language of the good" (1989, 538).

In support of this need for substantive public debates, how then can we approach the relationship between individual liberty and the community morality debates? Morris Kaplan suggests that it "is not simply the striking of a balance" (1991, 203), but rather reformulating the terms of both the coercive apparatus of state enforcement of homogeneous practices and the nature of individual autonomy and community consensus. In many ways, the law implements the moral standards of a community. Law is concerned with the pursuit of dignified living. Hart (1963) insists on the need of societies to deploy critical moral standards in order to evaluate social norms. But Kaplan writes, "such standards of critical morality must themselves be defined within the context of the moral practices of specific historical communities" (1991, 203). The ethos of Western democracy embodies "constitutional morality" institutionalized in the judiciary, but the basis of this moral discourse must be frequently evaluated. It cannot simplistically be identified with majority sentiment. Kaplan argues that the respect for individual autonomy requires both a "moral pluralism and a political neutrality" (1991, 209). His justification is that the enforcement of a particular morality by coercive political authorities violates individual autonomy. I ask, *Is* neutrality really a precondition for a lack of coercion? Or can we, through public dialogue and rigorous open debate, discover a range of "public goods" to accommodate moral diversity, and to keep us evaluating shared values?

III. Abortion, Contexts, and Social Responsibilities

To answer questions on abortion that relate to public goods and moral diversity, let us situate abortion in a broad social context, namely one in which there are significant discrepancies between legal norms, public morality, and the toleration of moral practices. Abortion is on a spectrum of contested issues regarding relationships between the individual, the family, the state, and society. I now link together social and relational contexts to show the interrelation of rights and responsibilities, and how abortion law can combine individuality with community in a workable moral praxis.

Social and Relational Contexts

To grant substance to the idea that abortion is not just a private issue, theorists talk of the "social relations of reproduction" (Petchesky 1980, 104; O'Brien 1983, 23; Himmelweit 1988, 53), which emphasize history, conflict, agency, social divisions, differentiated access to power and resources, cultural interpretations of sexuality and reproduction, and the social and material conditions under which choices are made. The situation of a financially secure career woman who finds herself with an unplanned pregnancy is drastically different from that of a teenage girl, a rape/incest victim, a single mother unsure of her new partner, or a woman who has more mouths to feed than she can cope with. A stress on social context pushes rights discourse to articulate its terms. That is, talk of abortion as a mere "privacy right" is empty without social content. Rights are not exercised in a social vacuum; they gain meaning in specific communities (Greschner 1989, 148). Even where the "right" is legally established, there are economic and social impediments to abortion access. Furthermore, given conservative drifts, there is talk of "medical necessity" versus women's autonomy. This line ignores familial or economic reasons that might lead to a justified abortion need. Where the state restricts the availability of abortion, it affirms the value of the unborn. It thus has a responsibility to assist those who through mishap or choice have children. Family policies do not always reflect this responsibility.

An emphasis on social context confronts policy practices regarding maternity leave, income supplements to families, public health, child support, childcare, housing, nutrition, and education. Access to reproductive rights includes both abortion needs and the conditions to raise flourishing children. This access is fundamental to citizenship and to moral agency. It involves a major structural challenge that "moves beyond defending 'privacy' as some abstract good to enunciate a discourse of *public* morality, one that acknowledges abortion access as a *social right* of women if they are to function as full persons in the public domain" (Petchesky 1986, xiv). With this challenge in mind, Petchesky argues "abortion is not simply an 'individual right' (civil liberty) or even a 'welfare right' (for those 'in need') but a 'social right'" (1986, 387) in that the real availability of abortion is a prerequisite to women's well-being and self-determination, even if women never have the need to avail themselves of this social right. Calling abortion a social right is one thing, but it requires also the enabling conditions outlined here to make rights actually realizable. So rights must apply to women regardless of color, race, occupation, status, and wealth. The underlying principle of a feminist morality of abortion is an affirmation of the self-autonomy of social beings. This is not the liberal autonomous "leave me alone." Rather, the decisions that affect our bodies, personhood, and citizenship are influenced by and influence our participation in the social community. Understanding what it means to be social beings involves understanding the social, relational basis of our moral being, that we are selves-in-relations (Porter 1991).

Contemplation of abortion occurs within relational contexts. For many women in most cultures, the primary identification of women is relational: their identity is defined by reference to families, partners, and children. Matters of the womb often define women's status so that women who evade this destiny are often damned as both selfish and sinful. In many cultures, abortion is seen as a sin against God, a defiance of women's nature; hence women are considered morally culpable. Patriarchal ideology ensures the almost neurotic preoccupation of many women with being socially acceptable mothers and for these women, abortion is abnormal, unnatural, a defiance of feminine purpose. Where fetal personhood is paramount, motherhood is not only taken as a moral duty but as a passive biological state, stripped of its broader context. As Carol Gilligan discovered, women, in considering whether to abort a pregnancy, generally approach this decision as one "that affects both self and others and engages directly the critical moral issue of hurting" (1983, 71). The decision calls on questions of responsibility and choice. Yet this presupposes women have been considered, and consider themselves, persons with moral autonomy, the ability to make decisions, to be accountable for their choices and to be socially responsible, as opposed to merely being defined relationally, as daughter, sister, spouse, mother, grandmother. Now while O'Brien (1983) links women's consciousness about mothering to the enormous amount of caring knowledge acquired through practice, Petchesky maintains, that it is not this motherliness alone that justifies responsibility for deciding on an abortion but that "control over decisions ought to be exercised by those whose works and concern have been most consistently involved in the activity in question" (1986, 377). Theorists have built on Jaggar's earlier views on abortion which involves two principles: first, that "the right to life ... means the right to a full human life" (1976, 351), by which she means the requirements for full development as a human; and second that the ultimate decision should rest with those most affected, that "the potential mother ... should have the ultimate responsibility for deciding whether or not an abortion should be performed" (1976, 353). Jaggar's point is that women's right to decide is not absolute but is contingent on women's situation in society where generally mothers are the prime nurturers of children, and where society rarely facilitates this responsibility. Recognizing gender-specific needs, such as possible abortions, acknowledges the responsibility of women's social contribution without reverting to simplistic naturalistic assumptions about maternalism.

Interdependence of Rights/Responsibilities

To consider fully the social and relational contexts in which abortion needs arise, we need to consider the interdependence of social rights and responsibilities. This is nowhere more conspicuous than in pregnancy, where there is a clear connection, with no way out of acting without consequence to self and other. If a pregnant woman smokes heavily, drinks to excess, is exhausted, or relaxes to music, the possibility of effects to another exists. As noted, this interconnection is not always appreciated; indeed, conflicts between women's right to choose and fetal rights are often presented as insoluble moral dilemmas. Given the manner in which the special circumstances of pregnancy affect a fetus's right to life, Smith reconceptualizes abortion as a moral construct "of care, nurture, and responsibility, rather than a conflict of rights" (1984, 265). She recasts the abortion question as a conflict of responsibilities. Smith's position is that because of women's special reproductive capacities, pregnant women have a special duty to consider their capacity for sustaining pregnancy, childbirth, and child-rearing. Bringing another human into the world is a morally serious consideration that overrides any absolute duty to remain pregnant. It adjusts "the imperative to sustain life to the necessity for care and nurture to be undertaken responsibly" (1984, 271). Of course this adjustment does not guarantee responsible action, but it is a clear attempt to reconceptualize rights as responsibilities. Smith's view ties in comfortably with Gilligan's abortion study, where she discovered that women typically construct the moral problem "as a problem of care and responsibility in relationships rather than as one of rights and rules" (1983, 73). In discussing moral conflicts, judgments of possible choices and eventual decisions, Gilligan found a reiterative use of the words "selfish" and "responsible"; women saw the dilemmas in terms of conflicting responsibilities. So whereas an ethic of rights balances the claims of other and self, an ethic of responsibility arises from the multiple experiences of connection with others, relationships, and social contexts, and rests on the problem of inclusion, and minimizing hurt, and maximizing compassion and care.

I argue that moral judgments rarely, if ever, call on an either/or option. Rather, moral rights and responsibilities interact in a dynamic dialectical fashion. Caring relationships provide the moral ideal; a respect for rights provides the moral floor, "a minimum protection for individuals which remains morally binding even where appropriate caring relationships are absent or have broken down" (Warren 1989, 47). It is interesting to note that this interdependence of rights and responsibilities is not reducible to mere egg, uterus, labor or even birth, a recognition Warren points us to in claiming the moral significance of birth, which ends one relationship and begins a new existence as a rights-bearing socially responsive community member. The moral significance lies in the emerging relations. The point I am trying to make here is not that all women experience the idea or practice of abortion similarly, as an interdependence of rights and responsibilities, or even as morally significant, but that "the signification attached to abortion provides each side with different but interrelated paradigms" (Ginsburg 1989, 79) for reconstituting visions of being a woman that are true to different life narratives. Such paradigms allow for a rich morality that synthesises what have been considered as oppositional dualisms of self/other, rights/responsibilities, and individuals/ communities. This creative synthesis transforms the moral construct, self-identity, one's relationships and moral choice. With this synthesis, abortion ethics remains an emotionally intense issue, but it is transformed from a narrow rigid dilemma to a dynamic moral construct.

Abortion Law, Individuality, and Community

Viewing rights and responsibilities as an interdependent relationship brings out the dialectical nature of a moral praxis of individuality and community. To make this relationship explicit in a political way, I conclude by comparing family laws in Western, individualistic democracies with certain European communitarian emphases. Glendon (1989, 292) provides us with an important historical context for the transformation of family law. She writes that at the turn of the twentieth century, Western family law systems shared common, unitary conceptions of the family as marriage-centered, determining social status of spouses and children, and patriarchal, with a husband/father as authoritarian figure and breadwinner, and the wife/mother as domestic laborer and nurturer, bound by exclusive sex relations. The emphasis was on family solidarity rather than on individual personalities and interests. In the light of individualistic, egalitarian, and secularizing trends, not one of these basic assumptions has survived unchanged. What is pervasive is the tendency for sociolegal programs to break the family down into component parts, to treat the family members as separate and independent. In the Nordic and Anglo-American-Australian worlds, the shift of legal emphasis is from the family as a unit to individual family members. In the name of toleration, democratic pluralism, and neutrality about the good, modern family law relinquishes overt attempts to promote particular sets of ideas about family life. As argued earlier, the moral good is privatized, and public values are lost. Despite these prevailing currents toward personal definitions of the good, there are countercurrents, stronger in the Romano-Germanic world, which seek a closer alliance between individual and social interpretations of the good. In Continental civil law, "Rights tend to be seen as naturally paired with responsibilities. The individual is more often envisioned in a social context" (Glendon 1989 , 298). Take, for example, the right of privacy, the right of an individual to be free from unwarranted government intrusion. This right emphasizes the isolated individual. More communitarian views of privacy articulate privacy rights as ultimately social in that they are necessarily limited in their conception by the rights of others' moral codes, and the social bonds of the community. Thus privacy rights are part of a broader view of autonomy that values interdependence and connections with others.

These contrasts emerge starkly in assumptions influencing abortion law. While the right to privacy pervades much of the West, German Basic law protects the "right to life," emphasizing "the character of this right as a value of the community rather than as something that belongs to the fetus" (Glendon 1987, 38). The concern is with the state's obligation to promote public values rather than any rights these values might give to individuals. Indeed rights discourse can "affirm the creative, expressive, and connective possibilities of rights" (Schneider 1990, 237). The emphasis is on connections among the women, the developing life, and the larger community. Similarly, under the Spanish Constitution, the courts state that unborn life is a public good, and so it is necessarily protected. In these examples, we see not a balancing of individual rights, but an emphasis on a noncoercive commitment to an order of values that allows diverse life-styles and opinions and acts as a safety check to such diversity.

I have three final questions. What is involved in this contrast? What is at stake in a commitment to political neutrality? Why is a vision of value-ordered polity necessary? First, the contrasts are between an isolated, sovereign individual and an individual aware of a dynamic interplay between individuality and community. Donald Kommers (1985) contrasts Roe's emphasis on the individual woman, her privacy and autonomy, with the Continental, civil, substantive position on societies' interest not just in abortion, but in the entire gamut of beliefs and attitudes about human life. Glendon also remarks that these European laws do not just tell pregnant women that abortion is a serious moral consideration, but they communicate to fathers also that producing a child is a serious commitment, "and communicate to both that the welfare of each child is a matter in which the entire society is vitally interested" (1987, 58). The contrast is between an emphasis on individual rights and an emphasis on social obligations, a contrast between individualistic and communitarian values.

Second, a commitment to political neutrality and the privatization of the good leaves the nature of public debate on issues like abortion ambiguous. The difference in the contrasts discussed above is not just that one legal structure imposes a certain version of morality on pregnant women while another leaves the moral decision up to the individual woman herself. "The notion that abortion is an individual and private decision is itself a moral notion" (Glendon 1987, 35-36). Endorsing other theorists (Sandel 1984), Glendon states a position that I am supporting: it is becoming less clear why we should prefer the values of absolute toleration and freedom of choice when other important values are also at stake. I suggest that these values are concerned with public discourse on ethics, the range of moral goods, and strategies to create communities with social bonds capable of resisting individualistic fragmentation. Similarly, Julia Tao, writing of the Chinese moral ethos, criticizes the weakness of a rights-based morality for its emphasis on individuation and failure to recognize intrinsic value in collective goods. She defines these goods as "fundamental moral duties grounded in respect for the values which give meaning to human life" (1990 , 126). Her point is that the choice of whether to abort involves more than the pragmatic choosing, it involves the reasons and values that prompt our choice. I agree with Glendon that "the impossibility of identifying a single widely shared notion of virtue or the common good in modern societies does not mean that modern law can remain resolutely neutral on all controversial questions involving moral issues" (1987, 139). Admittedly, there are many ambiguities in communal conventions. The commitment to pluralism that is central to modern politics entails the acceptance of conflicting collective norms and practices, but it also entails exciting models of individuality that provide scope for replacing notions of the isolated, individualist self with notions of selfhood that consider others in situated, concrete, historical, social, and familial settings.

Third, a vision of a value-ordered polity is necessary to ensure that the liberal state is "undergirded by a moral vision that rejects the agnosticism of liberalism," and despite rival moral traditions, it enables "a common core of agreement with respect to the meaning of the good" (Kommers 1990, 367). As Kommers says, in the files of constitutional adjudication "we have a golden opportunity to combine, in a new synthesis, a constitutionalism of rights with a constitutionalism of virtue" (1990, 368). Many legal, liberal, and feminist theorists are interested in increasing the meaningfulness of public discourse through forms of moral praxis like Habermas's (1979) "communicative action" and MacIntyre's (1982) "socially embodied argument." For MacIntyre, this social dialogue incorporates an Aristotelian insight that it is through our action and ways of knowing that we create our sociopolitical standing. It is through our moral praxis that we exhibit our commitment to creating ethical communities. Social discourse on controversial issues often involves misunderstandings, but the process of exploring worthy social ends is healthy. We have the capacity to be good citizens, but I suggest that it is our actual moral praxis that we need to evaluate, as individuals within various communities.

Yet what are women to do, when they are placed in societies where the social consensus, the idea of common good, is pitted against minority demands? Our exercise of rights is dependent on our given social structures. Take the Republic of Ireland, where "the social consensus is constructed through a dialectic composed in part of ideas of monetarism mitigated by social justice; of a conservative Catholic morality mitigated by pragmatic compassion" (Riddicks 1990, 14). What this means in practice is that the Irish social mores agree that abortion should be illegal, but, as Ruth Riddicks summarizes typical attitudes, "we are disturbed that women in crisis might be forcibly restrained from seeking (lawful) abortion abroad. While we are unshakeable in our belief that the act of abortion is a grievous sin, we forgive, privately and in religious confession, the woman who has been driven to such an unfortunate action" (1990, 14). These considerations are difficult to incorporate into a moral praxis, for what is at stake is the merging of law, religion, the state, social convention, familial expectation, personal beliefs, and the need to choose, often in a crisis context. These are real dilemmas, not hypothetical moral dramas. In response to these dilemmas, what does it mean to incorporate abortion decisions into a moral praxis?

Moral Praxis

Moral praxis takes on our embodied selves, our social consciousness, and our subjectivity in our historical and cultural contexts. Theory, ideology, and law interact dynamically with specific needs, moral self-reflection, and the choices we make. Clearly the abortion debate, remaining on the public, political agenda, is a crucial part of this moral praxis. Public opinion polls indicate little support for making all abortions illegal or for unrestricted freedom of choice. In fact they show that majorities oppose elective abortion, or a total ban on abortion, but believe that the law should specify permissible circumstances (Glendon 1987, 41). Between 92 percent and 96 percent of abortions occur in the first trimester, with more than half in the first eight weeks (U.S. data in Petchesky 1986, 347). These data confirm the sense of developmental differences that correspond to differences in relationship and thus obligations to the fetus. Similarly, miscarriage often takes on a different meaning if it occurs in the early months, or the later months. And the meaning is often different if a child is stillborn, or a neonate dies. In this vein, the public distinguishes between early and later stages of gestation, and the state and the medical profession distinguish between first, second, and third trimesters, but there remains significant uncertainty about the cut-off points. This is not indifference or moral relativism. Rather it is in the nature of moral praxis that we deliberate, reflect, weigh options, equivocate, and eventually decide, sometimes realizing in retrospect the mistakes of our choice. The process of self-reflection and choice are complex.

This complexity is evident in later abortions, frequently those of teenagers who have procrastinated in telling relevant authority figures. Religious beliefs also add to the complexity, but curiously Catholics in the United States get abortions just as frequently as non-Catholics (Petchesky 1986, 366). This fact should not be interpreted to mean that religion does not influence women's choice; rather it reflects an immediacy and attentiveness to the practical demands of concrete constraints. Indeed, the Irish Republic has the most restrictive abortion laws in the Western world, but this does not prevent many women from going outside Ireland, mainly to England for abortions. If other countries did not accept Irish women for abortions, their plight would be more extreme. Many women cannot afford to travel elsewhere. Similarly, women from Latin America, the Caribbean, Asia, Africa, and the Pacific have in excess of 38 million abortions annually, more than half of these illegally. These are women who usually have several children and cannot reasonably provide for more. "Restrictive legislation leads not to the reduction of the abortion incidence, but instead to bad practice" (Ketting and van Praag 1986, 157), to the exportation of the problem, to backyard abortions; young women flee their homes and often suffer extreme, lifetime guilt. Given these consequences, total legal restriction appears naive. Even the Catholic church with its tight moral codes, distinguishes between "to kill" and "to murder," relative to particular situations. Rigid absolutes like total restrictions on abortion do not include people's changing situations.

Being aware of the historical particularity of moral concepts allows us to adopt a healthy caution about absolutist positions and to question ongoing moral debate. Difficult decisionmaking involves multiple negotiations between social structures, ideologies, immediate social contexts, and particular desires; rationales shift according to changing needs. Moral praxis involves deep grappling that draws on all of our resources, religious beliefs, moral frameworks, and personal experiences. Women's training in the consideration of others has taught women how to exercise care in regard to vulnerable lives. Their decisions are likely to be morally informed. Thus the "morality" of abortion is intimately connected to the social practices of care, nurture, and responsibility for others. Riddicks offers a useful notion of this moral choice as "a dialectic where the pragmatic is informed by the altruistic" (1990, 15). Retaining a notion of the ambiguity of much of our moral praxis, Glendon concludes, "perhaps it is fitting that abortion law at present should mirror our wonder as well as our ignorance about the mystery of life, our compassion for women who may be frightened and lonely in the face of a major crisis, and our instinctive uneasiness at terminating a form of innocent human life, whether we call it a fetus, an embryo, a baby, or an unborn child" (1987, 46). She presents divorce laws as analogous: we preserve the notion that society has an interest in the institution of marriage by permitting a termination where there is an irretrievable breakdown.

In conclusion, abortion needs are real. To claim the social right to abortion is to say it is more than an individualistic right to choice. The basis of its social claim lies in the integration of a particular rights claim as a woman, and a general human rights claim for autonomous bodily self-determination. This social right does not lead to unlimited, unprincipled abortion claims, but to an agonizing, morally acute dilemma that involves reflecting on the dialectical interplay between rights and responsibilities, in view of personal life narratives, and making a choice based on one's social, cultural, and personal contexts. Abortion ethics prompts a sensitive incorporation of both individual rights and social responsibilities.

REFERENCES

Areen, Judith. 1989. Limiting procreation. In *Medical Ethics*, ed. Robert Veatch. Boston: Jones and Bartlett.

Brazier, Margaret. 1988. Embryo's "rights": Abortion and research. In *Medicine, ethics and the law*, ed. M.D.A. Freeman. London:Stevens and Sons.

Clarke, Linda. 1991. Abortion: A rights issue? In *Birthrights: Law and ethics at the beginning of life*, ed. Robert Lee and Derek Morgan. London: Routledge.

Eisenstein, Zillah. 1991. Privatizing the state: Reproductive rights, affirmative action, and the problem of democracy. *Frontiers* 12 (1): 98-125.

Fox-Genovese, Elizabeth. 1991. *Feminism without illusions: A Critique of individualism.* Chapel Hill: University of North Carolina Press.

Gilligan, Carol. 1983. *In a different voice: Psychological theory and women's development.* Cambridge: Harvard University Press.

Ginsburg, Faye. 1989. Dissonance and harmony: The symbolic function of abortion in activists' life stories. In *Interpreting women's lives: Feminist theory and personal narratives*, ed. Personal Narratives Group. Bloomington: Indiana University Press.

Glendon, Mary Ann. 1987. *Abortion and divorce in western law.* Cambridge: Harvard University Press.

— . 1989. *The transformation of family law: State, law, and family in the U.S. and western Europe.* Chicago: University of Chicago Press.

Green, Paul. 1987. The logic of special rights. *Hypatia* 2 (1): 67-70.

Greschner, Donna. 1989. Feminist concerns with the new communitarians: We don't need another hero. In *Law and the community: The end of individualism?* Ed. Allan C. Hutchinson and Leslie Green. Toronto: Carswell.

Habermas, Jurgen. 1979. *Communication and the evolution of society.* Translated by Thomas McCarthy. London: Heinemann.

Harris, John. 1991. Should we experiment on embryos? In *Birthrights: Law and ethics at the beginnings of life*, ed. Robert Lee and Derek Morgan. London: Routledge.

Hart, H.L.A. 1963. *Law, liberty and morality.* Stanford, CA: Stanford University Press.

Hasse, Lizbeth. 1987. Legalizing gender-specific values. In *Women and moral theory*, ed. Eva Feder Kittay and Diana T. Meyers. New Jersey: Rowman and Littlefield.

Himmelweit, Susan. 1988. More than "a woman's right to choose"? *Feminist Review* 29: 38-55.

Jaggar, Alison. 1976. Abortion and a woman's right to decide. In *Women and philosophy: Toward a theory of liberation*, ed. Carl C. Gould and Marx W. Wartofsky. New York: G.P. Putnam's Sons.

Kaplan, Morris B. 1991. Autonomy, equality, community: The question of lesbian and gay rights. *Praxis International* 11 (2): 195-213.

Ketting, Evert and Philip van Praag. 1986. The marginal relevance of legislation relating to induced abortion. In *The new politics of abortion*, ed. Joni Lovenduski. London: Sage.

Kingdom, Elizabeth. 1991. *What's wrong with rights?*

Problems for feminist politics of law. Edinburgh: Edinburgh University Press.

Kommers, Donald. 1985. Liberty and community in constitutional law: The abortion cases in comparative perspective. *Brigham Young University Law Review* 371: 399-409.

— . 1990. Comment on MacIntyre. *Review of Politics* 52: 364-68.

Krieger, Linda. 1987. Through a glass darkly: Paradigms of equality and the search for a woman's jurisprudence. *Hypatia* 2 (1): 45-61.

Lee, Robert and Derek Morgan, eds. 1991. *Birthrights: Law and ethics at the beginnings of life.* London: Routledge.

Luthra, Rashmi. 1993. Toward a reconceptualization of "choice": Challenges by women at the margins. *Feminist Issues* 13 (1): 41-54.

MacIntyre, Alisdair. 1982. *After virtue: A study in moral theory.* London: Duckworth.

— . 1990. The privatization of good: An inaugural lecture. *Review of Politics* 52: 344-61.

Markowitz, Sally, 1990. Abortion and feminism. *Social Theory and Practice.* 16 (1): 1-17.

O'Brien, Mary. 1983. *The politics of reproduction.* Boston: Routledge and Kegan Paul.

Overall, Christine. 1987. *Ethics and human reproduction: A feminist analysis.* Boston: Allen and Unwin.

Petchesky, Rosalind Pollack. 1980. Reproductive freedom: Beyond "a woman's right to choose." In *Women, sex and sexuality*, ed. Catherine R. Stimpson, and Ethel Spector Person. Chicago: University of Chicago Press.

— . 1986. *Abortion and woman's choice: The state, sexuality, and reproductive freedom.* London: Verso.

Porter, Elisabeth. 1991.*Woman and moral identity.* Sydney: Allen and Unwin.

Riddicks, Ruth. 1990. *The right to choose: Questions of feminist morality.* Dublin: Attic Press.

Sandel, Michael. 1984. Morality and the liberal ideal. *The New Republic* 7:15.

Sanders, Douglas. 1991. Collective rights. *Human Rights Quarterly* 13: 368-86.

Schneider, Elizabeth M. 1990. The dialectic of rights and politics: Perspectives from the women's movement. In *Women, the state, and welfare*, ed. Linda Gordon. Wisconsin: University of Wisconsin Press.

Schuler, Jeanne. 1987-88. Baby M and the politics of gender. *Telos* 74: 126-33.

Smith, Janet Farrell. 1984. Rights-conflict, preg-nancy and abortion. In *Beyond domination: New perspectives on women and philosophy*, ed. Carol Gould. New Jersey: Rowman and Allanheld.

Tao, Julia. 1990. The Chinese moral ethos and the concept of individual rights. *Journal of Applied Philosophy* 7(2): 119-27.

Thomson, Judith Jarvis. 1973. A defense of abortion. In *The problem of abortion*, ed. Joel Feinberg. Belmont, CA: Wadsworth.

Warnock, Mary. 1985. *A question of life: The Warnock report on human fertilisation and embryology.* Oxford: Basil Blackwell.

Warren, Mary Ann. 1989. The moral significance of birth. *Hypatia.* 4 (3): 46-65.

Wellman, Carl. 1989. Doing justice to rights. *Hypatia* 3 (3): 153-58.

Wolgast, Elizabeth. 1980. *Equality and the rights of women.* Ithaca: Cornell University Press.

— . 1989. A reply to Carl Wellman. *Hypatia* 3 (3): 159-61.

RACE AND THE NEW REPRODUCTION

Dorothy E. Roberts

Dorothy E. Roberts is Professor at Rutgers University School of Law, Newark, NJ. Her main research interests are feminist legal theory, critical race theory, the reproductive rights of women of color, and the politics of motherhood. She is the author of Killing the Black Body: Race, Reproduction and the Meaning of Liberty *(Pantheon, 1997) and numerous articles and essays in books, journals, and newspapers.*

Roberts agrees with feminists who challenge the prevalent belief in Western liberal societies that new reproductive technologies expand procreative options and thereby enhance human freedom. She extends the feminist critique that new reproductive technologies enforce traditional patriarchal roles and conventional family norms by examining how they also reflect and reinforce racial hierarchy in America. Even though blacks have higher rates of reproductive problems of infertility, Roberts argues that because of financial barriers, cultural preferences, and professional manipulation, the new methods of reproduction are used almost exclusively by white people. Roberts rejects responses to this situation that merely defend individual freedom or advocate policies to ensure greater access to these technologies. Instead she calls for an analysis of the harms of these technologies and more restrictive policies on the use and development of them.

Introduction[1]

New means of procreating are heralded by many legal scholars and social commentators as inherently progressive and liberating. In this view, in vitro fertilization (IVF), embryo donation, and contract pregnancy expand the procreative options open to individuals and therefore enhance human freedom. These innovations give new hope to infertile couples previously resigned to the painful fate of childlessness. In addition, this view holds that the new reproduction creates novel family arrangements that break the mold of the traditional nuclear family. A child may now have five parents: a genetic mother and father who contribute egg and sperm, a gestational mother who carries the implanted embryo, and a contracting mother and father who intend to raise the child.[2] A proponent of new means of reproduction, John Robertson opens his book *Children of Choice* by proclaiming that these "powerful new technologies" free us from the ancient subjugation to the "the luck of the natural lottery" and "are challenging basic notions about procreation, parenthood, family, and children."[3]

My impression of these technologies, however, is that they are more conforming than liberating: they more often reinforce the status quo than challenge it. True, these technologies often free outsiders from the constraints of social convention and legal restrictions. They have helped single heterosexual women, lesbians, and gay men, whom society regards as unqualified to raise children, to circumvent legal barriers to parenthood.[4] Informal surrogacy arrangements between women, for example, may provide a means of self-help for women who wish to have children independently of men; moreover, they have the advantage of requiring no government approval, medical intervention, or even sexual intercourse.[5]

But these technologies rarely serve to subvert conventional family norms. Most often they complete a traditional nuclear family by providing a married couple with a child.[6] Rather than disrupt the stereo-

Reprinted with permission of the publisher from *Hastings Law Journal* 47:4 (April 1996): 25–39.

typical family, they enable infertile couples to create one. Most IVF clinics only accept heterosexual married couples as clients,[7] and most physicians have been unwilling to assist in the insemination of single women.[8] The new reproduction's conservative function is often imposed by courts and legislatures, as well. Laws regulating artificial insemination contemplate use by a married woman and recognition of her husband as the child's father,[9] and recent state legislation requiring insurance coverage of IVF procedures applies only when a wife's eggs are fertilized using her husband's sperm.[10] On the other hand, as Martha Field observes, courts have been willing to grant parental rights to sperm donors "when no other man is playing the role of father for the child," such as when the mother is a lesbian or unmarried.[11]

Feminists have powerfully demonstrated that the new reproduction enforces traditional patriarchal roles that privilege men's genetic desires and objectify women's procreative capacity.[12] They make a convincing case that IVF serves more to help married men produce genetic offspring than to give women greater reproductive freedom.[13] In this essay I will explore how these technologies reflect and reinforce the racial hierarchy in America. I will focus primarily on in vitro fertilization because it is the technology least accessible to Black people and most advantageous to those concerned about genetic linkages.[14] The salient feature of in vitro fertilization that distinguishes it from other means of assisted reproduction is that it enables an infertile couple to have a child who is genetically-related to the husband.[15]

I. The Role of Race in the New Reproduction

A. *Racial Disparity in the Use of Reproductive Technologies*

One of the most striking features of the new reproduction is that it is used almost exclusively by white people. Of course, the busiest fertility clinics can point to some Black patients; but they stand out as rare exceptions.[16] Only about one-third of all couples experiencing infertility seek medical treatment at all; and only 10 to 15 percent of infertile couples use advanced techniques like IVF.[17] Blacks make up a disproportionate number of infertile people avoiding reproductive technologies.

When I was recently transfixed by media coverage of battles over adopted children, "surrogacy" contracts, and frozen embryos, a friend questioned my interest in the new methods of reproduction. "Why are you always so fascinated by those stories?" he asked. "They have nothing to do with Black people."[18] Think about the images connected with reproduction-assisting technologies: They are almost always of white people. And the baby in these stories often has blonde hair and blue eyes—as if to emphasize her racial purity. A "Donahue" show featured the family of the first public surrogacy adoption. Their lawyer Noel Keane describes the baby, Elizabeth Anne, as "blonde-haired, blue-eyed, and as real as a baby's yell."[19] He concludes, "The show was one of Donahue's highest-rated ever and the audience came down firmly on the side of what Debbie, Sue, and George had done to bring Elizabeth Anne into the world."[20]

In January, 1996, *The New York Times* launched a prominent four-article series entitled "The Fertility Market," and the front page photograph displayed the director of a fertility clinic surrounded by seven white children conceived there while the continuing page featured a set of beaming IVF triplets, also white.[21]

When we do read news accounts involving Black children created by these technologies they are always sensational stories intended to evoke revulsion at the technologies' potential for harm. In 1990, a white woman brought a lawsuit against a fertility clinic which she claimed had mistakenly inseminated her with a Black man's sperm, rather than her husband's, resulting in the birth of a Black child.[22] Two reporters covering the story speculated that "if the suit goes to trial, a jury could be faced with the difficult task of deciding the damages involved in raising an interracial child."[23] Although receiving the wrong gametes was an injury in itself, the fact that the gametes were of the wrong race added a unique dimension of harm to the error.

In a similar, but more bizarre, incident in the Netherlands in 1995, a woman who gave birth to twin boys as a result of IVF realized when the babies were two months old that one was white and one was Black.[24] A *Newsweek* article subtitled "a Fertility Clinic's Startling Error" reported that "while one boy was as blonde as his parents, the other's skin was darkening and his brown hair was fuzzy."[25]

It is easy to conclude that the stories displaying blond-haired blue-eyed babies born to white parents are designed to portray the positive potential of the new reproduction, while the stories involving the mixed-race children reveal its potential horror.

These images and the predominant use of IVF by white couples indisputably reveal that race in some way helps to shape both the use and popularity of IVF in America. What are the reasons underlying this connection between race and the new reproduction?

First, the racial disparity in new reproduction has nothing to do with rates of infertility. Married Black women have an infertility rate one and one-half times higher than that of married white women.[26] In fact, the profile of people most likely to use IVF is precisely the opposite of those most likely to be infertile. The people in the United States most likely to be infertile are older, poorer, Black and poorly educated.[27] Most couples who use IVF services are white, highly educated, and affluent.[28]

Besides, the new reproduction has far more to do with enabling people (mostly men) to have children who are genetically related to them than with helping infertile people to have children.[29] The well-known "surrogacy" cases such as Baby M and Anna J. involved fertile white men with infertile wives who hired gestational mothers in order to pass on their own genes. Moreover, at least half of women who undergo IVF are themselves fertile, although their husbands are not.[30] These women could conceive a child far more safely and inexpensively by using artificial insemination although the child would not be genetically-related to the husband. Underlying their use of IVF, then, is often their husbands' insistence on having a genetic inheritance. In short, use of reproduction-assisting technologies does not depend strictly on the physical incapacity to produce a child.

Instead, the reason for the racial disparity in fertility treatment appears to be a complex interplay of financial barriers, cultural preferences, and more deliberate professional manipulation. The high cost of the IVF procedure places it out of reach of most Black people whose average median income falls far below that of whites. The median cost of one procedure is about $8,000; and, due to low success rates, many patients try several times before having a baby or giving up.[31] Most medical insurance plans do not cover IVF, nor is it included in Medicaid benefits.[32] IVF requires not only huge sums of money, but also a privileged lifestyle that permits devotion to the arduous process of daily drug injections, ultrasound examinations and blood tests, egg extraction, travel to an IVF clinic, and often multiple attempts—a luxury that few Black people enjoy. As Dr. O'Delle Owens, a Black fertility specialist in Cincinnati explained, "For White couples, infertility is often the first roadblock they've faced—while Blacks are distracted by such primary roadblocks as food, shelter and clothing."[33] Black people's lack of access to fertility services is also an extension of their more general marginalization from the health care system.

There is evidence that some physicians and fertility clinics may deliberately steer Black patients away from reproductive technologies. For example, doctors are more likely to diagnose white professional women with infertility problems such as endometriosis than can be treated with in vitro fertilization.[34] In 1976, one doctor found that over 20 percent of his Black patients who had been diagnosed as having pelvic inflammatory disease, often treated with sterilization, actually suffered from endometriosis.[35]

Screening criteria not based specifically on race tend to exclude Black women, as well. Most Black children in America today are born to single mothers, so a rule requiring clients to be married would work disproportionately against Black women desiring to become mothers. One IVF clinic addresses the high cost of treatment by offering a donor oocyte program that waives the IVF fee for patients willing to share half of their eggs with another woman.[36] The egg recipient in the program also pays less by forgoing the $2,000 to $3,000 cost for an oocyte donor.[37] I cannot imagine that this program would help many Black patients, since it is unlikely that the predominantly white clientele would be interested in donation of their eggs.

The racial disparity in the use of reproductive technologies may be partially self-imposed. The myth that Black people are overly fertile may make infertility especially embarrassing for Black couples.[38] One Black woman who eventually sought IVF treatment explained, "Being African-American, I felt that we're a fruitful people and it was shameful to have this problem. That made it even harder."[39] Blacks may find it more emotionally difficult to discuss their problem with a physician, especially considering the paucity of Black specialists in this field. Blacks may also harbor a well-founded distrust of technological interference with their bodies and genetic material at the hands of white physicians.

Finally, Blacks may have an aversion to the genetic marketing aspect of the new reproduction. Black folks are skeptical about any obsession with genes. They know that their genes are considered undesirable and that this alleged genetic inferiority has been used for centuries to justify their exclusion from the economic, political and social mainstream. Only last year Richard Herrnstein & Charles Murray's *The Bell Curve* was a national bestseller, and it reopened the public debate about racial differences in intelligence and the role genetics should play in social policy.[40]

Blacks have understandably resisted defining personal identity in biological terms. Blacks by and large are more interested in escaping the constraints of racist ideology by defining themselves apart from inherited traits. They tend to see group membership as a political and cultural affiliation. Their family ties have traditionally reached beyond the bounds of the nuclear family to include extended kin and nonkin relationships.

My experience has been that fertility services simply are not a subject of conversation in Black circles, even among middle-class professionals. While I have recently noticed stories about infertility appearing in magazines with a Black middle-class readership such as *Ebony* and *Essence*, these articles conclude by suggesting that childless Black couples seriously consider adoption.[41] Black professional women I know are far more concerned about the assault that recent welfare reform efforts are inflicting on our poorer sisters' right to bear children—an assault that devalues all Black women and children in America.[42]

Moreover, Black women are also more concerned about the higher rates of sterilization in our community, a disparity that cuts across economic and educational lines. One study found that 9.7 percent of college-educated Black women had been sterilized, compared to 5.6 percent of college-educated white women.[43] The frequency of sterilization increased among poor and uneducated Black women. Among women without a high school diploma, 31.6 percent of Black women and 14.5 percent of white women had been sterilized.[44]

B. The Importance of the Genetic Tie

Race also influences the importance we place on IVF's central aim—having genetically-related children.

Of course sharing a genetic tie with children is important to people of different races and in racially homogeneous cultures. Most parents I know take great satisfaction in having children who "take after them." It seems almost natural for people to want to pass down their genes to their children, as if they achieve a form of immortality by continuing their "blood line" into future generations.

Yet we also know that the desire to have genetically-related children is influenced, if not created, by our culture. A number of feminists have advocated abandoning the genetic model of parenthood because of its origins in patriarchy and its "preoccupation with male seed."[45] We should add to these concerns the tremendous impact that the inheritability of race has had on the meaning of the genetic tie in American culture.

The social and legal meaning of the genetic tie helped to maintain a racial caste system that preserved white supremacy through a rule of racial purity.[46] The contradiction of slavery existing in a republic founded on a radical commitment to liberty required a theory of racial hierarchy. Whites took the hereditary trait of race and endowed it with the concept of racial superiority and inferiority;[47] they maintained a clear demarcation between Black slaves and white masters by a violently enforced legal system of racial classification and sexual taboos.[48]

The genetic tie to a slave mother not only made the child a slave and subject to white domination; it also passed down a whole set of inferior traits. Children born to a slave, but fathered by a white master, automatically became slaves, not members of the master's family. To this day, one's social status in America is determined by the presence or absence of a genetic tie to a Black parent. Conversely, the white genetic tie—if free from any trace of blackness—is an extremely valuable attribute entitling a child to a privileged status, what Cheryl Harris calls the "property interest in whiteness."[49]

For several centuries a paramount objective of American law and social convention was keeping the white bloodline free from Black contamination. It was only in 1967 that the United States Supreme Court in *Loving v. Virginia*[50] ruled antimiscegenation laws unconstitutional. Thus, ensuring genetic relatedness is important for many reasons, but, in America, one of those reasons has been to preserve white racial purity.

C. *Value of Technologically Created Children.*

Finally, the new reproduction graphically reflects and reinforces the disparate values placed on members of social groups.

The monumental effort, expense and technological invention that goes into the new reproduction marks the children produced as especially valuable. It proclaims the unmistakable message that white children are precious enough to devote billions of dollars towards their creation. Black children, on the other hand, are the primary object of welfare reform measures designed to discourage poor women from procreating.

II. Implications for Policy Regarding the New Reproduction

What does it mean that we live in a country in which white women disproportionately use expensive technologies to enable them to bear children, while Black women disproportionately undergo surgery that prevents them from being able to bear any? Surely this contradiction must play a critical part in our deliberations about the morality of these technologies. What exactly does race mean for our own understanding of the new reproduction?

Let us consider three possible responses. First, we might acknowledge that race influences the use of reproductive technologies, but decide this does not justify interfering with individuals' liberty to use them. Second, we could work to ensure greater access to these technologies by lowering costs or including IVF in insurance plans. Finally, we might determine that these technologies are harmful and that their use should therefore be discouraged.

A. *The Liberal Response: Setting Aside Social Justice*

The Liberal response to this racial disparity is that it stems from the economic and social structure, not from individuals' use of reproductive technologies. Protection of individuals' procreative liberty should prohibit government intervention in the choice to use IVF, as long as that choice itself does not harm anyone.[51] Currently, there is little government supervision of reproduction-assisting technologies, and many proponents fear legal regulation of these new means of reproduction. In their view, financial and social barriers to IVF are unfortunate but inappropriate reasons to interfere with the choices of those fortunate enough to have access to this technology. Nor, according to the liberal response, does the right to use these technologies entail any government obligation to provide access to them. And if for cultural reasons Blacks choose not to use these technologies, this is no reason to deny them to people who have different cultural values.

Perhaps we should not question infertile couples' motives for wanting genetically-related children. After all, people who have children the old-fashioned way may also practice a form of genetic selection when they choose a mate. The desire to share genetic traits with our children may not reflect the eugenic notion that these particular traits are superior to others; rather, as Barbara Berg notes, "these characteristics may simply symbolize to the parents the child's connection to past generations and the ability to extend that lineage forward into the future."[52] Several people have responded to my concerns about race by explaining to me, "White couples want white children not because of any belief in racial superiority, but because they want children who are like them."

Moreover, the danger of government scrutiny of people's motives for their reproductive decisions may override my concerns about racism. This danger leads some feminists who oppose the practice of using abortion as a sex selection technique, for example, nevertheless to oppose its legal prohibition.[53] As Tabitha Powledge explained:

> To forbid women to use prenatal diagnostic techniques as a way of picking the sexes of their babies is to begin to delineate acceptable and unacceptable reasons to have an abortion.... I hate these technologies, but I do not want to see them legally regulated because, quite simply, I do not want to provide an opening wedge for legal regulation of reproduction in general.[54]

It would be similarly unwise to permit the government to question the individuals' reasons for deciding to use reproduction-assisting technologies.

B. The Distributive Solution

The distributive solution does not question individuals' motives in order to question the societal impact of a practice.[55] This approach to procreative liberty places more importance on reproduction's social context than does the liberal focus on the fulfillment of individual desires.[56] Policies governing reproduction not only affect an individual's personal identity; they also shape the way we value each other and interpret social problems. The social harm that stems from confining the new reproduction largely to the hands of wealthy white couples might be a reason to demand equalized access to these technologies.

Obviously the unequal distribution of wealth in our society prevents the less well off from buying countless goods and services that wealthy people can afford. But there may be a reason why we should be especially concerned about this disparity when it applies to reproduction.

Reproduction is special. Government policy concerning reproduction has tremendous power to affect the status of entire groups of people. This is why the Supreme Court in *Skinner v. Oklahoma* declared the right to bear children to be "one of the basic civil rights of man."[57] "In evil or reckless hands," Justice Douglas wrote, the government's power to sterilize "can cause races or types which are inimical to the dominant group to wither and disappear."[58] This explains why in the Casey opinion Justices O'Connor, Kennedy, and Souter stressed the importance the right to an abortion had for women's equal social status. It is precisely the connection between reproduction and human dignity that makes a system of procreative liberty that privileges the wealthy and powerful particularly disturbing.

Procreative liberty's importance to human dignity is a compelling reason to guarantee the equal distribution of procreative resources in society. Moreover, the power of unequal access to these resources to entrench unjust social hierarchies is just as pernicious as government interference in wealthy individuals' expensive procreative choices. We might therefore address the racial disparity in the use of reproductive technologies by ensuring through public spending that their use is not concentrated among affluent white people. Government subsidies, such as Medicaid coverage of IVF, and legislation mandating private insurance coverage of IVF would allow more diverse and widespread enjoyment of the new reproduction.

C. Should We Discourage the New Reproduction?

If these technologies are in some ways positively harmful, will expanding their distribution in society solve the problem? The racial critique of the new reproduction is more unsettling than just its exposure of the maldistribution of fertility services. It also challenges the importance that we place on genetics and genetic ties.

But can we limit individuals' access to these technologies without critically trampling our protection of individual freedom from unwarranted government intrusion? After all, governments have perpetrated as much injustice on the theory that individual interests must be sacrificed for the public good as they have on the theory that individual interests must be sacrificed for the public good as they have on the theory that equality must be sacrificed for individual liberty. This was the rationale justifying eugenic sterilization laws enacted earlier in this century.[59]

Even for liberals, individuals' freedom to use reproductive technologies is not absolute. Most liberals would place some limit on their use, perhaps by defining the legitimate reasons for procreation.[60] If a core view of reproduction can limit individuals' personal procreative decisions, then why not consider a view that takes into account reproduction's role in social arrangements of wealth and power? If the harm to an individual child or even to a core notion of procreation can justify barring her parents from using the technique of their choice, then why not the new reproduction's potential for worsening group inequality?

Some have concluded that the harms caused by certain reproduction-assisting practices justify their prohibition. In 1985, for example, the United Kingdom passed the Surrogacy Arrangements Act banning commercial contract pregnancy arrangements and imposing fines and/or imprisonment on the brokers who negotiate these agreements.[61] Some Marxist and radical feminist agree that paid pregnancy contracts should be criminalized to prevent their exploitation and commodification of women and children.[62]

On the other hand, the government need not depart at all from the liberal noninterference model of rights in order to discourage or refuse to support practices that contribute to social injustice.[63] Even the negative view of liberty that protects procreative choice from government intrusion leaves the state free to decide not to lend assistance to the fertility business or its clients.

We may therefore question a practice that channels millions of dollars into the fertility business, rather than spending similar amounts on programs that would provide more extensive benefits to infertile people. *New York Times* writer Trip Gabriel describes IVF clinics as "[a] virtually free-market branch of medicine, the $350 million-a-year business has been largely exempt from government regulation and from downward pressure on costs that insurance companies exert."[64]

Indeed, we can no longer avoid these concerns about the social costs and benefits of IVF. Such calculations are now part of the debate surrounding the advisability of state laws requiring insurance companies to include the cost of fertility treatment in their coverage. A study recently reported in the *New England Journal of Medicine* calculated the real cost of IVF at approximately $67,000 to $114,000 per successful delivery.[65] The authors concluded that the debate about insurance coverage must take into account these economic implications of IVF, as well as ethical and social judgments about resource allocation.[66]

Black women in particular would be better served by a focus on the basic improvement of conditions that lead to infertility, such as occupational and environmental hazards, diseases, and complications following childbirth and abortion.[67]

Taking these social justice concerns more seriously, then, might justify government efforts to reallocate resources away from expensive reproductive technologies.

Conclusion

These are thorny questions. It is extremely difficult to untangle white couples' reasons for using reproduction-assisting technologies and Black couples' reasons for avoiding them. Evidence is hard to come by: what doctor or fertility clinic will admit (at least publicly) to steering Black women away from their services? Few people seem to want to confront the obvious complexion of this field. Moreover, the problems raised by the racial disparity in the use of these technologies will not be solved merely by attempting to expand their distribution. Indeed, the concerns I have raised in this essay may be best addressed by placing restrictions on the use and development of the technologies, restrictions imposed by the government or encouraged by moral persuasion. This possibility is met by a legitimate concern about protection of our private decisions from government scrutiny. Indeed, Black women are most vulnerable to government efforts to control their reproductive lives.

Nonetheless, we cannot ignore the negative impact that the racial disparity and imagery of the new reproduction can have on racial inequality in America. Our vision of procreative liberty must include the eradication of group oppression, and not just a concern for protecting the reproductive choices of the most privileged. It must also include alternative conceptions of the family and the significance of genetic relatedness that truly challenge the dominant meaning of family.

NOTES

1. Dorothy Roberts, Professor, Rutgers University School of Law—Newark. B.A. 1977, Yale college; J.D. 1980, Harvard Law School. This is a written version of a talk presented at Rutgers University's Center for the Critical Analysis of Culture and University of California, Hastings College of the Law; I am grateful to the participants for their comments. Portions of this article are adapted from Dorothy E. Roberts, "The Genetic Tie," 62 *University of Chicago Law Review* 62 (1995): 209.
2. See generally John L. Hill, "What Does It Mean To Be a 'Parent'?: The Claims of Biology as the Basis for Parental Rights," *New York University Law Review* 66 (1991): 353, 355; Andrea E. Stumpf, Note, "Redefining Mother: A Legal Matrix for New Reproductive Technologies," *Yale Law Journal* 96 (1986): 187, 192-94.
3. John Robertson, *Children of Choice: Freedom and the New Reproductive Technologies* (Princeton: Princeton University Press, 1995): 3. [See Robertson, pp. 556-587].
4. See Nancy D. Polikoff, "This Child Does Have Two Mothers: Redefining Parenthood to Meet the Needs of Children in Lesbian-Mother and Other Nontraditional Families," *Georgetown Law Journal* 78 (1990): 459, 466; Sharon E. Rush, "Breaking with Tradition: Surrogacy and Gay Fathers," *Kindred Matters: Rethinking the Philosophy of the Family*, eds. Diana Tietjens Meyers, et al. (Ithaca, NY: Cornell University Press, 1993): 102, 132-133.
5. Juliette Zipper and Selma Sevenhuijsen, "Surrogacy: Feminist Notions of Motherhood Reconsidered," *Reproductive Technologies: Gender, Motherhood and Medicine*, ed. Michelle Stanworth (Minneapolis: University of Minnesota Press, 1987): 118, 137-138. Under this arrangement, a fertile woman would informally promise an infertile woman who wants a child to impregnate herself with a man's sperm and to give the baby to the infertile woman for adoption.
6. Robertson, *supra* note 3, at 145 (noting that assisted reproduction furthers the "primary aim to provide a couple with a child to live and rear in a two-parent family").
7. Thomas A. Shannon, "In Vitro Fertilization: Ethical Issues," *Embryos, Ethics, and Women's Rights: Exploring the New Reproductive Technologies*, eds. Elaine Hoffman Baruch et al. (New York: Harrington Press, 1988): 155,163.
8. Daniel Wikler and Norma J. Wikler, "Turkey-baster Babies: The Demedicalization of Artificial Insemination," *Milbank Quarterly* 69 (1991): 5, 13-16.
9. Bartha M. Knoppers and Sonia LeBris, "Recent Advances in Medically Assisted Conception: Legal, Ethical and Social Issues," *American Journal of Law and Medicine* 17 (1991): 329, 332-33, 346-47; Lisa C. Ikemoto, "Destabilizing Thoughts on Surrogacy Legislation," *University of San Francisco Law Review* 28 (1994): 633, 636-37.
10. See, e.g., *Md. Code Ann.* (West 1995): Art. 48a, 354 DD (3); *Haw. Rev. Stat.* (West 1995) 431: 10A-116.5 (3).
11. Martha Field, *Surrogate Motherhood: The Legal and Human Issues* (Cambridge: Harvard University Press, 1988):116.
12. See, e.g., Janice G. Raymond, *Women as Wombs: Reproductive Technologies and the Battle Over Women's Freedom* (New York: Harper Collins 1993); Barbara Katz Rothman, *Recreating Motherhood: Ideology and Technology in a Patriarchal Society* (New York: Norton, 1989); *Reproduction, Ethics, and the Law: Feminist Perspectives*, ed. Joan C. Callahan (Bloomington, IN: Indiana University Press, 1995).
13. See , e.g., Susan Sherwin, *No Longer Patient: Feminist Ethics and Health Care* (Philadelphia: Temple University Press, 1992):127.
14. I capitalize the "B" in Black Americans because I believe that Black Americans consider themselves to be an ethnic group, like Asian-Americans, whereas I believe that white Americans do not see themselves in that way.
15. As I explain below, many women who could conceive through artifical insemination prefer the more expensive and risky IVF because it can produce a baby with a genetic link to their husband. See *infra* note 29 and accompanying text.

16. See Lori B. Andrews and Lisa Douglass, "Alternative Reproduction," *Southern California Law Review* 65 (1991): 623, 646; F.P. Haseltine et al., "Psychological Interviews in Screening Couples Undergoing In Vitro Fertilization," *Annals of the New York Academy of Science* 442 (1985): 504, 507; Martha Southgate, "Coping with Infertility," *Essence* (September 1994):28.
17. Office of Technology Assessment, *Infertility: Medical and Social Choices* (OTA-BA-358, 1988): 7, 49-60.
18. I first recounted this story in Roberts, *supra* note 1 at 209.
19. Noel P. Keane and Dennis L. Breo, *The Surrogate Mother* (New York: Everest House, 1981):96.
20. Id.
21. Trip Gabriel, "High-Tech Pregnancies Test Hope's Limit," *The New York Times* 07 January 1996: A1, A10.
22. Robin Schatz, "'Sperm Mixup' Spurs Debate: Questioning Safeguards, Regulations," *New York Newsday*, 11 March 1990: 3; Ronald Sullivan, "Mother Accuses Sperm Bank of a Mixup," *The New York Times*, 9 March 1990:B1.
23. Barbara Kantrowitz and David A Kaplan, "Not the Right Father," *Newsweek*, 19 March 1990:50.
24. Dorinda Elliott and Friso Endt, "Twins—With Two Fathers; The Netherlands: A Fertility Clinic's Startling Error," *Newsweek*, 03 July 1995: 38.
25. Id.
26. Laurie Nsiah-Jefferson and Elaine J. Hall, "Reproductive Technology: Perspectives and Implications for Low-Income Women and Women of Color," *Healing Technology: Feminist Perspectives*, eds. Kathryn Strother Ratcliff et al. (Ann Arbor: University of Michigan Press, 1989): 93, 108.
27. Sevgi O. Aral and Willard Cates, Jr. "The Increasing Concern with Infertility: Why Now?," *The Journal of the American Medical Association* 250 (1983): 2327.
28. Andrews and Douglass, *supra* note 16, at 646.
29. Joan C. Callahan, "Introduction to Reproduction, Ethics and the Law: Feminist Perspectives," *supra* note 12, at 24-25.
30. Raymond, *supra* note 12, at 6; Judith Lorber, "Choice, Gift, or Patriarchal Bargain?: Women's Consent to In Vitro Fertilization in Male Infertility," *Feminist Perspectives in Medical Ethics*, eds. Helen Bequaert Holmes and Laura M. Purdy (Bloomington: Indiana University Press, 1992): 169, 172.
31. Gabriel, *supra* note 21, at 10-11.
32. Annetta Miller et al., "Baby Makers Inc.," *Newsweek*, 29 June 1992: 38, 38; Gabriel, *supra* note 21, at 10; George J. Annas, "Fairy Tales Surrogate Mothers Tell," *L. Ed. Health Care* 16 (1988): 27,28. Only 10 states require insurance coverage of IVF. Gabriel, *supra* note 21, at 10.
33. Monique Burns, "A sexual Time Bomb: The Declining Fertility Rate of the Black Middle Class," *Ebony* (May 1995): 74, 76.
34. Lisa C. Ikemoto, "Destabilizing Thoughts on Surrogacy Legislation,"*U.S. F.L. Rev.* 28 (19): 633, 639.
35. Donald L. Chatman, "Endometriosis in the Black Woman," *American Journal of Obstetrics and Gynecology* 125 (1976): 987 (1976).
36. Cooper Center for IVF, "Cooper Center for IVF Responds to 'The Fertility Market,'" *The New York Times*, 14 January 1996: 16 (advertisement).
37. Id.
38. Martha Southgate, "Coping with Infertility," *Essence* (September 1994):28.
39. Id.
40. See Richard J. Herrnstein and Charles Murray, *The Bell Curve: Intelligence and Class Structure in American Life* (New York: Free Press, 1994).
41. See, e.g., Burns, *supra* note 33, at 148; Southgate, *supra* note 38, at 28.
42. See Dorothy E. Roberts, "Welfare and the Problem of Black Citizenship," *Yale Law Journal* 105 (1996): 1563, 1582 (book review).
43. Levin and Taub, "Reproductive Rights," *Women and the Law*, ed. C. Lefcourt (1989): sec. 10A.07 [3] [b], 10A-28.
44. Id.
45. Joan C. Callahan, "Introduction," *Reproduction, Ethics, and the Law: Feminist Perspectives*, *supra* note 12, at 1, 11. See, e.g, Rothman, *supra* note 12, at 39; Christine Overall, *Ethics and Human Reproduction: A Feminist Analysis* (Boston: Allen & Unwin, 1987): 149 (noting that "the need for a genetic connection with one's offspring seems to be of particular importance to men").
46. Roberts, *supra* note 1, at 223-30.
47. See Stephen Jay Gould, *The Mismeasure of Man* (New York: Norton, 1981).

48. Barbara K. Kopytoff and A. Leon Higginbotham, Jr., "Racial Purity and Interracial Sex in the Law of Colonial and Antebellum Virginia," *Georgetown Law Journal* 77 (1989): 1967, 1967-68.
49. Cheryl L. Harris, "Whiteness as Property" *Harvard Law Review* 106 (1993): 1707, 1713.
50. U.S. 1 (1967): 388.
51. See generally Robertson, *supra* note 3, at 22-42.
52. Barbara J. Berg, "Listening to the Voices of the Infertile," *Reproduction, Ethics, and the Law: Feminist Perspectives*, *supra* note 12, at 80, 82
53. Joan C. Callahan, "Introduction, Part II: Prenatal and Postnatal Authority," *Reproduction, Ethics, and the Law: Feminist Perspectives*, *supra* note 12, at 133-134.
54. Tabitha M. Powledge, "Unnatural Selection: On Choosing Children's Sex," *The Custom-Made Child?: Women-Centered Perspectives*, eds. Helen B. Holmes et al. (Clifton, NJ: Humana Press, 1981): 193, 197.
55. See Overall, *supra* note 45, at 17-39.
56. For a more extended critique of the liberal approach to reproduction-assisting technologies, see Dorothy E. Roberts, "Social Justice, Procreative Liberty, and the Limits of Liberal Theory: Robertson's *Children of Choice*," *Law and Social Inquiry* 20 (1995): 601; Joan C. Callahan and Dorothy E. Roberts, "A Feminist Social Justice Approach to Reproduction-Assisting Technologies: A Case Study on the Limits of Liberal Theory," *Kentucky Law Journal* 84 (1996).
57. U.S. 316 (1942): 535, 541.
58. Id.
59. See Mark H. Haller, *Eugenics: Hereditarian Attitudes in American Thought* (New Brunswick, NJ: Rutgers University Press, 1963).
60. See, e.g., Robertson, *supra* note 3, at 167 (positing "a core view of the goals and values of reproduction" that limits an individual's right to shape offspring characteristics).
61. Rosemarie Tong, "Feminist Perspectives on Gestational Motherhood: The Search for a Unified Focus," *Reproduction, Ethics, and the Law: Feminist Perspectives*, *supra* note 12, at 55, 58 (citing "Surrogacy Arrangements Act," 1985, United Kingdom, Chapter 49, p. 2 (1) (a) (b) (c).
62. Id. At 64-68.
63. Callahan and Roberts, *supra* note 56.
64. Gabriel, *supra* note 21, at 10. [See Gabriel, p. 587].
65. Peter J. Neuman et al., "The Cost of a Successful Delivery with In Vitro Fertilization," *New England Journal of Medicine* 331 (1994): 239, 239. Unlike the $8,000 cost per IVF cycle mentioned above, the figures quoted in this study refer to the cost involved in the birth of at least one live baby as a result of an IVF cycle.
66. Id.
67. See Nadine Taub, "Surrogacy: A Preferred Treatment for Infertility?" *Law, Medicine & Health Care* 16 (1988):89.

THE POLITICS OF ABORTION IN NICARAGUA: REVOLUTIONARY PRAGMATISM — OR FEMINISM IN THE REALM OF NECESSITY?

Maxine Molyneux

Maxine Molyneux is a Senior Lecturer in Sociology at the Institute of Latin American Studies, University of London, School of Advanced Studies. She has published widely on communist and post communist states including the book, State, Gender and Institutional Change in Cuba's 'Special Period': the Federación de Mujeres Cubanas *(London, 1966).*

While Nicaragua's government presents itself as having a progressive socialist commitment to women's emancipation, Molyneux explains that a strong tradition of Catholicism as well as under population and a labour shortage continue to succeed in suspending the implementation of women's right to reproductive self-determination. She argues that the unresolved problem of reproductive rights in Nicaragua reflects the tension between feminist visions of women's emancipation and the practical realities and policies of socialist governments. The successful implementation of reproductive rights requires social reform and education that is sensitive to the particular social and political conditions in Nicaragua.

> Abortion is an incredibly complex subject here. This is a Catholic country, and we all know the position of the Church on abortion. It has always been condemned here as a criminal act except where the woman is clearly at risk. Most abortions are illegal and are done by unqualified people, the result is often haemorrhage and infection.... Peasant women have a historical role, and that's having children. They see abortion as murder. For them, God sends children and you have to have them—seven, eight or ten children. City women are different: they're more involved in defence and production and see that a lot of children can be a "problem" for them, a limitation. So they use contraception and if necessary abortion.... But it's being discussed all over the place—it's a big issue now. (Susana Veraquas, Natural Childbirth Centre, Esteli, 1987)[1]

> One way of depleting our youth is to promote the sterilization of women in Nicaragua ... or to promote a policy of abortion. (President Daniel Ortega, 1987)[2]

Reprinted with permission of the publisher and Maxine Molyneux from *The Feminist Review* 29 (May 1988): 114–132.

Nicaragua is an anomaly among socialist states.[3] Its comparatively advanced record on general political issues—pluralism, democracy, abolition of the death penalty—contrasts with a surprisingly conservative position on reproductive rights.[4] Since coming to power in 1979 Nicaragua's revolutionary government has pledged itself to women's emancipation and has implemented a range of policies and legal reforms designed to establish greater equality between the sexes. However, it has not legalized abortion, and nor has it amended the pre-revolutionary *Somozista* codes. Abortion was declared illegal under the Criminal Code of 1974, and, while "therapeutic" terminations can be obtained, the grounds must be of a strictly medical nature. Worse still, under this legislation the woman herself cannot ask for the permission: the request must originate from her spouse or next of kin, who is in addition required to give formal permission. Requests for abortion have to be considered by a three-member medical panel: its members are, in the normal course of events, men.

In 1988, nearly a decade after the triumph of the revolution, the options open to the majority of Nicaraguan women who want an abortion are the same as they were under the Somoza dictatorship: these are limited to self-abortion or to seeking out illegal operatives. Both courses of action are dangerous and the latter is expensive, costing the equivalent of five months' wages for an average (urban) woman worker.[5] Most back-street abortions are performed in squalid and dangerous conditions, but even for those women who can afford a safer termination the risks are high. Illegal operatives have inadequate facilities, and cannot usually maintain the necessary standards of hygiene. Nicaragua's acute shortage of medical goods—equipment, drugs and sterilizing fluids—compound the risks. Even in hospitals operations such as caesarians and hysterectomies are on occasion performed without anaesthesia (Angel and Macintosh, 1987).

The social and medical costs of such legislation are high, to say nothing of the toll in human misery. Nicaragua has a high maternal death rate, 3 per thousand compared with 0.5 in most developed countries. Many of these deaths are due to botched abortions. These are estimated to account for some 60 per cent of admissions into the main women's hospital in Managua. Research carried out between March 1983 and June 1985 found that 8,752 women were admitted to this hospital with complications arising from abortions, equivalent to an average of ten women every day. In the sample group 10 per cent died, and 26 per cent required hysterectomies, of whom 16 per cent had not yet had children. According to one doctor, it is likely, for a variety of economic, social and demographic reasons, that the abortion rate has gone up since the revolution rather than down.[6]

How then, do the Sandinistas reconcile their support for women's emancipation with facts such as these? An answer to this question, inevitably tentative as it must be, can help illumine not only some of the paradoxes of the Nicaraguan revolution, but also some of the political difficulties encountered by a certain radical feminist position on reproductive rights. Some feminists have argued, for example, that abortion is "the feminist issue of our times" and have proceeded to judge both feminist consciousness in certain countries, and government legislation in terms of these somewhat absolutist and ethnocentric criteria. The Nicaraguan case allows of no easy conclusions in this regard and sensitizes those who follow the fortunes of its revolution to the complexities of the issue. Precisely because of the central place of the abortion issue in relations of gender power, all campaigns in support of it meet deeply entrenched resistance. An abstract proclamation of women's rights has to be matched by a concrete attainment of the conditions, both political and subjective, for the implementation and vigilant defence of those rights. This has proved as true in Europe and the United States as it is in Nicaragua today.

Sandinista policy

In the more than eight years since the Somoza dictatorship was overthrown, the Sandinistas have made a considerable effort to promote improvements in women's socio-economic position: women have seen an extension of their rights within the family and in the workplace through legal reform; they have been more involved in the political life of the country than ever before; and they have been encouraged to participate in the defence and development efforts, entering various kinds of economic activity in large numbers.[7] Despite these advances, however, the majority of women still lack the means to control their fertility safely, and the termination of unwanted pregnancies has always been regarded as a problem for which there is no clear policy solution.

Since 1979 there have been a variety of shifts in official thinking about the related issues of abortion and women's rights. Each change in legislation directed at improving the social and legal position of women has aroused considerable, sometimes stormy, public debate. There have been advances and retreats, but a number of important gains overall.

During most of this time, particularly in the last few years, the FSLN has devoted an unexpected amount of time and energy to debating women's issues within the Party itself; unexpected that is, given its parlous economic situation and the ever-present and deepening effects of the *contra* war. As far as abortion is concerned the Party has yet to clarify its position, but it appears to be broadly in favour of some change in the law and health provisions.

Some members of the leadership have at times publicly acknowledged support for women's right to reproductive self-determination. In 1982 the then Minister of Health, Lea Guido (now head of the women's organization AMNLAE),[8] explained the FSLN's position thus: "While we don't have a problem of over-population (far from it), abortion and contraception are a human right. We want to make these available but since there is opposition to it, we must be careful how we proceed" (Molyneux, 1985b). Doris Tijerino, who has won the status of comandante through her role in the struggle against Somoza, and is acting Chief of Police, has adopted a similar position:

> I am for abortion—not just as a woman, but also as a police officer. The current law restricts the civil rights of the woman by denying her the right to freely determine maternity. But this law should not just be changed by decree. Discussion and education must first take place among the broad masses of women. (Barricada, 1985)

Research carried out into the abortion issue by the Women's Office of the National Directorate, has recently concluded: "The studies show quite clearly that penalizing abortion has negative effects on women's health, raises maternal mortality and hospital costs, and contradicts state policies aimed at improving health conditions" (Oficina de la Mujer, 1986).

The organized opposition to legalizing abortion has come largely from the hierarchy of the Catholic Church and from the political parties and groups to the right of the FSLN. However, many Catholic supporters of the Sandinistas and some members of the Party are themselves reluctant on religious grounds to endorse abortion, and some oppose it. Many radical priests and nuns, adherents of the "theology of liberation," even find contraception a difficult issue, advocating at most the "scientific rhythm method," that is, the use of charts in an effort to identify the so-called "safe" period in what is at best an unpredictable biological process.[9] Popular attitudes among both men and women bear the influence of Catholicism which retains considerable institutionalized power within Nicaragua. The situation on mainland Nicaragua is not analogous to that in Cuba, a Caribbean island, where for a variety of historical reasons Catholicism did not have a significant hold over the population at the time of the revolution. Abortion is legal there, and is available virtually on demand and at negligible cost. Cuba shares with the United States and Uruguay the most liberal position in the Americas on abortion. Nicaragua's position is, by contrast, even less liberal than that of a number of other Latin American states, including neighbouring Honduras and Costa Rica, as well as Bolivia and Venezuela, all of which allow abortions on social as well as medical grounds.

The FSLN, itself divided over the issue and fearful of a political backlash organized on religious grounds, has therefore chosen to pursue a cautious policy with respect to women's reproductive rights. This has entailed leaving the old law intact for the time being while trying to alleviate its effects in three main ways. Firstly, the FSLN has ensured that nobody is prosecuted for having or performing illegal abortions, unless gross violations of medical practice are brought to the attention of the authorities. Secondly, efforts are made to ensure that contraceptives are more widely available than hitherto—both through medical and market outlets. Thirdly, a sex education programme has been set in train to increase public awareness of the "facts of life" and, in theory, to prevent unwanted pregnancies. This has been policy since 1985 when a commission funded by the United Nations agreed to promote a national programme of sex education aimed largely at teachers and young people.

Despite the good intentions behind them, such measures can do little to increase the realm of real freedom available to Nicaraguan women. The anomalous situation of abortion's semi-legality may be preferable to repressive controls in the absence of any alternative, but at the same time it hinders controls of genuine abuses as well as state-led initiatives to provide safe methods of terminating pregnancies (among them the vacuum method).

As far as reducing the necessity for abortions through more widespread use of fertility control is concerned, this has met with limited success. Nicaragua has a very low rate of contraceptive usage and availability. In 1983 only 9 per cent of the relevant section of the population was estimated to be using prophylactics—chiefly IUDs and the contraceptive pill (World Bank, 1985). Contraception is regarded as almost exclusively women's responsibility and there is very little uptake of condoms which Latin American men tend to see as emasculating. Overall, the availability of contraceptives has remained too restricted to constitute a reliable form of fertility control and supplies, all of which have to be imported, have become even scarcer since 1985 as a result of growing economic difficulties. There are, in addition to these practical questions of supply, the problems of widespread ignorance of how to use contraceptive methods, real and imagined fears about their effects, and, especially important in Nicaragua, men's resistance to fertility control. The cults of *machismo* and *hombria* (manliness) place considerable store on being able to father large numbers of children, biologically if not socially. At the same time, women who use contraceptives are suspected of infidelity, and often have to resort to secrecy. The Church, too, weighs in with its admonitions against contraception, and its more zealous clerics have not been above refusing confession to women with IUDs or who are on the pill. Sex and reproduction remain bound together by belief and necessity. The issue of contraceptive use and of fertility control more generally is therefore indissolubly linked to power relations between the sexes, and to the ideological control of religion, neither of which can be addressed if the problem is defined simply as one of supply.

The Sandinistas, aware of this, have placed their hopes on sex education, an initiative which is to be welcomed for addressing at least some of the problems. It has, however, proved to be a highly charged issue. One example will suffice, that of a biweekly series called *Sex and Youth* which was shown on national television. The twelve programmes took up a wide range of sensitive issues including sexually transmitted diseases, birth control, homosexuality (male and female), abortion and masturbation. The series caused something of a furore. Criticism came from a variety of quarters, with the material being accused among other things of being "too realistic." As a result, a three-man review committee was established and some of the programmes were duly censored. Among these was a discussion of female masturbation and a scene showing childbirth—one of the censors apparently fainted at the showing of the latter. The programme was eventually rescheduled from a daytime showing to late at night when few people would be able to watch it. As these responses show, Catholic attitudes have helped to keep Nicaragua a socially conservative country and the Government will have to allocate substantial resources, time and energy to fund and sustain such campaigns directed at altering public attitudes.

Inadequate though these measures were, they at least responded to some of the problems and represented some gain for women. In their own terms, too, they would have been more effective in a country which had not had its economy destroyed and its human resources depleted by the US backed *contra* war. They also have to be seen in their internal political context. In essence, they represented a compromise on the part of the Sandinista Government not only with Catholic sensibilities but also with members of the growing feminist[10] lobby which developed within and around the women's organization, AMNLAE. This latter comprised legal advisers, educationalists, health-workers, journalists and activists among others, whose position gathered strength in 1985. This was an important year, one in which the popularity of the Sandinista Government was put to the test in the free elections of November. The preparation for this event, and analysis of its aftermath, made party activists more aware of, and take more seriously, the hopes and aspirations of different sections of the population. Women's views were canvassed and their vote counted (and found to be numerically more important than men's). In the midst of all this, Nicaraguan feminists were posing fundamental questions to the FSLN, such as, how far had the Party addressed the real concerns of women during its period of rule? Women had participated in the revolution and had been mobilized in fulfilment of its goals, but it was not clear to what extent they had seen their own specific needs addressed. A debate opened up within the FSLN and within the women's organization, which had important consequences at the policy level.

At this juncture in the mid-decade, AMNLAE was generally felt to be in the doldrums. Since 1979 it had pursued what is now described as an "integrationist" policy, that is, one which sought to mobilize women into the main tasks of the revolution—such as defence, employment, education, and the like (Vilas, 1986). AMNLAE had made some progress in the legislative sphere, in particular in its attempt to equalize rights between men and women in the family. It had also improved women's access to basic needs, and participated in a variety of campaigns aimed at extending access to education and health. Nevertheless, it was increasingly felt by many women and, indeed, by the FSLN leadership itself, that the organization had not realized its potential as a vehicle either for mobilizing women or promoting women's emancipation. In 1985, in response to growing dissatisfaction with AMNLAE's role, and in preparation for its Second National Congress, a major debate on policy developed both within the organizations directly concerned and in the public realm. Six hundred open "assemblies" were held in Managua alone with more than 40,000 women meeting in small groups to debate issues and priorities. AMNLAE activists were reportedly surprised to discover how critical their constituency was of their failure to address such issues as domestic violence, machismo, rape, contraception and even abortion (Angel and Macintosh, 1987).

There were a number of positive outcomes of these developments. In the first place the issue of abortion finally came into the open as a policy matter. In November 1985 a public debate began in the pages of the party newspaper *Barricada* on whether to legalize abortion. The first item to be published was the findings of the report on the hospital admissions of women suffering from the effects of abortions. Other articles voiced different views pro and con, with the newspaper making its own position clear: legal abortion and safe contraception were necessary for women's health. This public debate did not last long; it was considered to be too explosive an issue. However, discussion continued both within the Party and outside it over the following year.

A second outcome was a reorganization and limited radicalization of the women's organization itself. A new agenda was drawn up in which women's issues were treated with more seriousness, were investigated, analysed and discussed. In its 1986 submission to the commission set up to draft a new constitution, AMNLAE included various suggestions previously considered to be "too feminist." Among these was a proposal to leave the possibility open for the future legalization of abortion, and a more egalitarian divorce law. When the draft of the new Constitution was debated in the National Assembly, the abortion issue was one of several to occasion bitter disputes. Article 24 of the Constitution guarantees the right to life, and during the debate anti-abortionists argued that this clause should be expanded to specify the outlawing of abortion. Members of the Conservative Party wanted life to be defined as beginning with conception. This move was eventually defeated, with the help of arguments presented by delegates acting as AMNLAE's legal advisers. The new Constitution, signed into law on January of 1987, established equality between the sexes for the first time, and while the Constitution guarantees the right to life, it does not specify where precisely life is deemed to have begun.

The third outcome of the 1985-6 debate was a shift in the overall public stance of the FSLN towards "the woman question." At AMNLAE's Third Congress in 1987, the FSLN presented a policy document which placed the struggle for women's liberation on a new footing (FSLN, 1987). It stated that the struggle against what it called "women's discrimination" would not be "put off" or separated from the defence of the revolution. Machismo and other forms of discrimination against women had to be combatted now, because they "inhibited the development of the whole society." This was seen by some of the feminist campaigners as a positive indication that women's issues had been given overt support by the Party, a view given further public affirmation by the presence at AMNLAE's Third Congress of four of the nine members of the (all-male) National Directorate, the nearest equivalent in Nicaragua to a Politburo.[11] At the same time and with more debatable objectives, AMNLAE was reorganized. It acquired a new executive and the status of "movement" was again confirmed to distinguish it from "organization."[12] Its brief was to work more closely at the regional level within mass organizations such as the trade unions, Sandinista Youth, the agrarian workers co-operative movement and the neighbourhood-based Sandinista Defence Committees. It was further emphasized that men and women should work together to achieve common goals, and the document rejected tendencies that held the emancipation of women to result from struggles against men or saw it as the exclusive preserve of women (FSLN, 1987).

So where did all this leave abortion? The situation had apparently not worsened but nor had it improved. At the official level there continued to be concern about the problem, with no clear commitment to reform even on the part of the reorganized women's movement. In July 1987 Silvia McEwan, one of the members of AMNLAE's new National Directorate, explained where things stood:

> Abortion is a serious social problem and merits a profound analysis to help formulate a law which will both benefit woman and respect her dignity as a mother. AMNLAE has not taken a position with respect to abortion, but it considers that there now exist the conditions to have a wide discussion about it. (Quoted in *Perspectiva Mundial*, 1987:18)

By spring 1988 there was still no statement. Nicaragua was in the grip of severe economic crisis and facing the prospects of a continuation of the *contra* war.

Some observers are hopeful that the abortion legislation will be tackled in due course; others see few indications of meaningful change in the Government's attitude of defensive compromise with the opposition. There are signs that the leadership remains divided over the issue and in some quarters attitudes against reform have hardened. In September 1987 at a "face the people" meeting called to mark the 10th anniversary of the founding of AMNLAE, more than a thousand women gathered to meet President Ortega and the Minister of Health, Dora Maria Téllez. Among the issues which were raised from the floor were sterilization, birth control and abortion. A worker at a shoe factory reminded the leadership that for many women sterilization was just as important an issue as abortion when she complained that not only were sterilizations very difficult to get, but that they even required the husband's permission. To prolonged applause from the meeting she asked, "Are we our husbands' property?" and went on to propose that women with three or more children should have an automatic right to sterilization without "consulting anybody." The Minister of Health promised to do something straightaway about the requirement of husbands' authorization. Another delegate said she wanted to raise a problem that was regarded as a "touchy issue" and one which was often labelled as a "petty bourgois concern," namely abortion. She noted that the Government was prepared to take on *other* difficult issues such as confiscating property through land reform; as for the supposed class character of the issue, abortion was in fact a more serious problem for the poor because they suffered most from the consequences of illegality. In their concluding speeches to the gathering, the President and Minister of Health indicated that they saw the issues in rather different terms. Téllez said she thought the solution was "not to defend the right to abortion, but to prevent abortions." This was being tackled by simultaneously improving the availability of birth-control devices and by maintaining public education campaigns.

President Ortega reportedly caused concern in the audience with his remarks on sterilization and abortion. These issues, he said, had to be seen in the context of US government policy towards colonial and semi-colonial countries. Rather than carry out a just distribution of wealth, US policy had been to "freeze the population growth in these countries, to avoid the risk of an increase in the population that could threaten a revolutionary change." Nicaragua, he argued, had a small population and was subject "to a policy of genocide" through the US-sponsored *contra* war: "The ones fighting in the front lines against this aggression are grown men"; "One way of depleting our youth is to promote the sterilization of women in Nicaragua ... or to promote a policy of abortion"; "The problem is that the woman is the one who reproduces. The man can't play that role." He said that some women, "aspiring to be liberated," decide not to bear children. Such a woman "negates her own continuity, the continuity of the human species" (*Militant*, 1987)

While not representative of FSLN thinking in general, Ortega's speech has none the less sent a wave of disapproval through feminist circles in both Nicaragua and beyond. Ortega is a man who lives the war every day, and his off-the-cuff remarks reflect a pragmatic, political attitude towards what he sees, above all, as an issue of national interest. Yet some have seen a suggestion of moralism in his formulations in the implication that women have been passive bystanders in the revolutionary process and must now therefore discharge their debt to the nation by having babies. The implicit denial of women's place in the world of men, a common cultural trope in Latin America, is at odds with Nicaragua's policies promoting gender equality, and women's public roles in the defence of the nation and in employment. What annoyed many women was the fact that Ortega saw fit to use the authority and discourse of the revolution and the war against the *contras* to attack and demobilize the campaigners and supporters of women's reproductive choice.

Inconsistencies in the speech were also noted: in particular that it was delivered in happier times, when peace not war seemed to be on the agenda, amidst the autumn euphoria of the Central American peace accord. This was seen by FSLN leaders and newspapers as heralding the ebbing if not the ending of the war. However, many in the FSLN viewed the problems of peace as possibly even more insuperable than the problems of war. Bayardo Arce, a member of the National Directorate, expressed the disquiet thus: "Peace may have other costs. We are facing an emotional and provocative mood on the right in this country.... We must prepare for the political struggle which will become more intense when we achieve peace" (*Barricada International*, 1987). Such fears were well founded with respect to the political fortunes of the FSLN; and peace, although deeply desired, could have certain negative implications for the women of Nicaragua. The advent of peace to the region would entail two immediate consequences for women. First, an estimated 70,000 soldiers would return from the armed forces and expect jobs—in many cases ones which women in their thousands had occupied for the duration of the *contra* war. Secondly, the sense of social and political solidarity that typifies nations at war would be prone to weakening during peacetime, with an attendant rise in social and political tensions. In such circumstances governments are forced to compromise with the opposition, and in Nicaragua the Catholic hierarchy is a powerful, cynical and intransigent force to bargain with. Peace, in the short term at least, could adversely affect the prospects for progress in the more difficult areas of reproductive rights such as abortion or sterilization. If Ortega's remarks are indicative of views held more widely within the Party, then even legal reforms of a relatively minor kind will not be won without a prior internal struggle.

Sandinista reservations

The case against establishing full reproductive rights from within the FSLN has always drawn on three main arguments: that, as Ortega expressed it, Nicaragua is underpopulated and suffers from a labour shortage; that "the people" are against any change on religious grounds; and that the issue is itself so explosive that to tackle it would lend support to the opposition. There is some validity to each of these arguments but the issues are far from clear-cut and nor do they necessarily justify the status quo.

The population issue is an especially sensitive one within Third World countries, many of whose governments feel that the problem of underdevelopment is largely externally generated by imperialism and that the issue of population growth is merely a diversion, something confected by the advanced capitalist countries to obscure the underlying causes of global power imbalances. However, this view has been changing over recent years, and many Third World countries—China, most notably—are now seeing the benefits of lower rates of population growth. However, intervention by foreign powers through population control measures has a long and bitter history in Latin America and Ortega's emotive remarks on "genocide" would have been well understood by his audience (Mass, 1975). From a Latin American feminist perspective these are difficult questions to deal with but the issue becomes less one of why fertility control should be encouraged than, especially for women, how and by what means, and with what degree of choice this control can come about.

As far as the population issue is concerned, Nicaragua does have a lower population density than its neighbouring Latin American countries. This has been compounded by the heavy losses it suffered both in the struggle to overthrow Somoza and in the US-backed *contra* war. An estimated 50,000 died in the former and 40,000, from both sides, in the latter, in a country with a population of around only three million. However, whether there is, as a result, a shortage of labour and of population is a matter which economists and demographers are best able to decide and, even then, these matters are open to interpretation. If shortages do exist, they can be dealt with by adopting a variety of different strategies. Within the range of planning options available, limiting women's access to safe abortions, or even to voluntary sterilizations, comes rather low on the list, and certainly cannot remedy the current problem of labour shortages. Children conceived over the next year will not be available for work until the year 2000.

At least two factors could mitigate any scarcity in the short term. If peace comes to the region, or if there is a significant reduction in *contra* forces, many of the people in the army would be released for other work, while at the same time, Nicaragua would regain access to labour reserves elsewhere in the region, from which the country has drawn in the past, especially for its seasonal labour. In the longer term, assuming there is no change in Nicaragua's demand for labour through technological innovations, the problem of labour shortages could be offset by its high rates of natural reproduction. Nicaragua has one of the highest birthrates in the world, with a total fertility rate of 6.3 and a natural rate of population growth of 3 per cent per annum (World Bank, 1985). It could therefore well be expected over time to make up such absolute deficiencies as may exist. Indeed, if the population issue is paramount then it could reasonably be argued that the unsafe abortions currently carried out, leading to involuntary sterility, premature later births and spontaneous abortions, illness and death, are themselves a major brake on Nicaragua's natural birthrate.

If, as seems likely, the military threat continues, and pro-natalist policies are indeed the only answer to the problem of labour supply, this does not constitute an argument against extending the realm of women's choice in matters concerning reproduction. As many FSLN members themselves argue, it is not as if the moral claims of labour supply planning should, even if valid, prevail over those of women's health. Pro-natalist policies can, in any case, be pursued with some degree of sensitivity to women's needs and preferences.[13] As some other Third World countries (South Yemen, for example, with its high rates of out-migration) have found, pro-natalist policies can coincide with extending reproductive rights to women. The adoption of spaced birth policies, which aim to maintain high birthrates but make it possible for women to plan their fertility be leaving a few years between pregnancies, has been shown to have positive health effects for both women and children, reducing maternal and child morbidity and mortality. Such programmes depend upon an acceptance of the principle of providing access to fertility control including, if necessary, abortion for social as well as medical reasons. It is evident that if reform in the law is to occur at all, health arguments such as these will occupy a critical place in the debate.

The second and third arguments concerning "popular" opposition and the threat of a political backlash carry more weight, although they are less amenable to empirical investigation, let alone practical resolution. They are of course linked; if the people are against any change on religious grounds, then the issue is likely to be explosive and any real change to the laws would be used to political advantage by the opposition. In Nicaragua as in southern Ireland, that redoubt of conservative clergy, the organized power and cultural hegemony of Catholicism has proven an effective opponent of reform because of its resonance within the population. In Ireland, unlike Nicaragua, the Constitution specifically outlaws abortion (as it does divorce), thus making any attempt at legal reform a complicated process (Mahon, 1987). However, even in such resilient contexts, some progress can be made through public campaigns directed at mobilizing support for realistic goals, that is, those that will be carefully argued within the cultural context of what is acceptable and can be treated as a first step in a longer campaign. Reproductive rights and especially abortion have never been "popular issues" anywhere in the world, and especially in societies which are deeply religious or socially conservative in character. With the exception of state socialist societies, in every case where reform or repeal of abortion laws occurred, this did not occur without bitter struggles carried out by feminists and their supporters. In Nicaragua a public campaign around reproductive rights has not been organized by the FSLN or by AMNLAE, and nor have feminists been encouraged to form a movement in support of reform. Without gaining some measure of public popular support and neutralizing the opposition, any radical legal reform would entail clear political risks. At the same time the FSLN fears the consequences of allowing such a campaign to take place. It is not clear how much research has been undertaken in Nicaragua to canvass views on the matter; certainly not enough information exists to justify the view that "the people" as a whole uniformly oppose reform of any kind. In this, as in every case, the people are likely to be divided along lines of sex, class and age, politics and belief. Abortion is no simple matter even, or especially, for women; in Catholic countries where women's identification with motherhood is positive and particularly strong, many women may oppose it on principle despite the fact that they may have had recourse to it.[14] Moreover one Nicaraguan feminist explained:

> The losses of the war have strengthened rather than diminished the emotional significance of motherhood. There are 11,000 women in Managua alone who are mothers of soldiers who have died in the fighting. Abortion in such a context is associated with more death; for some women it's unthinkable.

Abortion on demand is therefore a remote prospect in Nicaragua, as is its full legalization. It is, moreover, important to recognize that even if legality were achieved by some miracle tomorrow, it would make little difference to women's range of choice on its own. The scarcity of facilities, equipment and qualified personnel to perform abortions would continue and the backstreet operator would therefore still thrive. For the State to meet existing demand, far-reaching changes in the health system would be required, involving training, resource allocation and new equipment. In the straitened circumstances of contemporary Nicaragua very strong arguments would have to be made to convince the authorities that abortion had priority over other areas of health provision. It is for these reasons, both political and practical, that more moderate reforms, such as the decriminalization of the law, allowing social reasons for terminations and removing the legal sanctions over women's fertility practised by spouses, are more likely to be on the agenda.

Conclusions

This difficult and unresolved problem of reproductive rights encapsulates the tension between feminist visions of women's emancipation and the practical realities and policies of socialist governments. Two points should, however, be clear from the foregoing discussion and can help to guard against any simple attribution of the causes of slow progress on women's rights primarily to acts of bad faith by men in positions of power, anxious to retain the privileges of their sex. The first is that the FSLN itself is not of one mind on this question, let alone on how it defines its support for women's emancipation. While no one is against some form of women's emancipation, the conceptions of what constitutes this emancipation vary considerably, from a limited, traditional "protection" of women, and mobilization of them behind certain national campaigns (employment, defence of the revolution, mass education and health), to policies informed by feminism which see an alteration of gender relations and the full implementation of reproductive rights as the goal towards which the revolution should be moving. The debate is, therefore, not only about whether or not the FSLN supports women's emancipation, but what the definition of that emancipation is, and how much of a priority it is, given other demands on resources.

The second point which the Nicaraguan case underlines is that all campaigns for women's rights have to take account of the objective as well as the subjective conditions for their implementation. The point is illustrated if reform of women's position is compared with other social reforms of a kind that post-revolutionary regimes carry out—land reform, or nationality rights, or workplace democracy. These, as much as the emancipation of women and the guaranteeing of reproductive rights, are part of the programme of post-revolutionary regimes, but all equally require certain conditions to be met before they can be successfully implemented. Precisely because they challenge existing power relations and widely held ideologies, including ones introjected by the social category subordinated within oppressive power relations, they can only be successful if the ground for contest is adequately prepared. A land reform decreed against a landowning class that still retains widespread power in the countryside, and in the name of a peasantry that is not adequately mobilized, organized and supported to assume the rights given to it by the reform, can end in disaster—landlord sabotage and revolts, widespread harvest failures and shortages and, in many cases, counter-revolutionary mobilizations of the peasantry.

For all the differences that exist, some parallels with the position of women can also apply; the very deep-rootedness of the oppression of women, its tenacious and at times violent defence by men, and the often ingrained acquiescence in it by some women, make it something that cannot simply be abolished by decree, but most also be prepared for. Women's emancipation requires a determined challenge to the structures of power—with specific emphasis on gender relations and the Catholic Church; a programme of education amongst women and their mobilization and organization in support of reform; and a decisive and united action by the revolutionary State.

It is therefore to under-estimate the entrenched nature of women's subordination to suggest that a programme of emancipation can be decreed and implemented immediately in any society. Revolutions can accelerate the rate of change and strike at established practices. All such changes involve struggle but they still take place within the constraints of opposition and support existing in their societies. The course of other revolutions indicates that Nicaragua is not alone in facing this problem. If Cuba is not a suitable point of comparison, because of the different conditions prevailing there, a more approriate comparison may be that of Mexico, a revolution that did, in the 1930s under Cardenas, confront the Catholic Church head on. Yet it is significant that even in Mexico, where Cardenas tried to mobilize women, the issue of reproductive freedom was not raised and that, later, the feminist component within the revolution was suppressed. Women did not get the vote in Mexico until 1953, two years before Nicaragua, and today the legal position on abortion and its consequences is similar to that in Nicaragua. (According to the UN Fund for Population Activities), in Mexico City the hospitalization rate for abortion complications is now some 40 per cent per 1,000 women of reproductive age.

The abortion issue in Nicaragua therefore sums up many of the tensions that exist between socialism and feminism, ones which are accentuated in the conditions of extreme precariousness, both political and economic, which have been a particular feature of this revolution. It is clear that to do nothing entails the continuation of the catalogue of injustices and misery which the present situation inflicts upon women; yet to do anything substantial entails political risks on the one hand and considerable economic outlay on the other. Ultimately such measures as need to be taken can only be arrived at with the political will to address the problem with solutions appropriate to the political, social and economic constraints which Nicaragua faces. That political will, however, may only emerge with sufficient conviction when there are enough voices within the leadership, or positions of influence within the society more generally, that are prepared to press the case and come up with workable answers.

What those answers are to be will depend both upon the overall course of the Nicaraguan revolution in the difficult months and years ahead, and on the specific outcome of the debate between different schools of thought on women's emancipation within the FSLN and outside it. If there are reasons for accepting that an immediate policy of full reproductive rights is neither prudent nor capable of implementation, it is equally evident that the FSLN could do more than it has hitherto achieved in this area. The outcome will depend to a considerable extent on what Nicaraguan women themselves, including those who have suffered under the present legislation, can demand and enforce.

NOTES

1. Interview supplied by Nicaragua Health Fund, spring 1987.
2. Speech reported in *The Militant* 19.11.87.
3. Abortion is legal in most of the self-proclaimed

socialist states, and in a substantial number is available on demand for social as well as medical reasons. However, it was made illegal by Stalin in the USSR in 1937 and was only legalized again in 1955. It is severely restricted in Romania and Albania and absolutely illegal in the first "Third World" socialist republic, Mongolia, where it is officially outlawed on the grounds that the population is too small at 1½ million. "Socialist" is used here in the broadest sense to include the "existing socialism" of Soviet-type states, as well as progressive governments such as Nicaragua's which preside over societies and states quite different in type, but which endeavour to implement policies which are broadly socialist in character and orientation. The FSLN tends not to call itself socialist but "popular" and "democratic" because its policies "respond to the needs of the masses."

4. By reproductive rights is meant women's legal capacity to exercise choice over conception and childbearing. This includes the right to use and obtain contraceptives, abortions and sterilizations, or other safe methods of fertility control; it necessarily entails the loss of rights others might exercise over a woman's person.
5. See the South Yorkshire supporters of Socialist Action dossier of Nicaraguan press articles on abortion in Nicaragua. The translations first appeared in issues 1 and 3 of *Intercontinental Press* in 1986.
6. This is in accordance with regional trends. Catholic Latin American countries have seen a rise in abortion rates. In the mid-1970s it was estimated that there were 65 abortions per 1,000 women of reproductive age, or almost 30 per cent of known pregnancies.
7. Accounts of Sandinista policies on women and their results can be found in the following: Harris (1987); Harris (1998); Molyneux (1985a and 1985b); and in *Nicaragua Today*, the periodical of the Nicaragua Solidarity Campaign. For good quantitative material see Angel and Macintosh (1987) and Rooper (1987).
8. This acronym stands for the Luisa Amanda Espinosa Women's Association, bearing the name of the first woman Sandinista to fall in the fighting against Somoza.
9. Author's interviews in Nicaragua. The "theology of liberation" has been silent on these questions in general.
10. The term "feminist" is used in Nicaragua, both as a pejorative by those who are against its demands, but also by Nicaraguan women's rights activists. Officials, too, may use the term approvingly as in the following remarks by the head of AMNLAE, Lea Guido: "Through its participation in a popular revolution, the Nicaraguan women's movement has evolved from a patriotic, anti-imperialist and anti-dictatorial orientation to a strong feminist position" (*Women in Central America*, 1987). As in western feminism there are different conceptions of what constitutes a feminist position or practice.
11. These were Tomás Borge, Luis Carrión, Bayardo Arce and Carlos Nuñez .
12. This simply confirmed what had already been agreed in principle at earlier congresses. There was, however, some opposition to what was seen as the weakening of the institutionalized capacity of the movement.
13. I am grateful to Ruth Pearson for this point.
14. Yet the degree of acceptance of Catholic teaching on this issue varies enormously between countries. The majority of women oppose abortion in Ireland for example (Mahon, 1987) but in Poland political support for the Church is contrasted to widespread disregard for orthodox teachings on the family. Nicaragua would appear to be somewhere between the Polish and Irish cases.

REFERENCES

Angel, A. and Macintosh, F. (1987) editors, *The Tiger's Milk* London: Virago Press.

Barricada (1987) (9 December).

Barricada International (1987) Vol. 7, No. 251 (27 August).

Deighton, J. et al. *Sweet Ramparts* London: War on Want/Nicaragua Solidarity Campaign.

FSLN (1987) *Women and the Sandinista Revolution* Managua: Vanguardia.

Harris, H. Introduction to *The Tiger's Milk* in Angel and Macintosh.

Harris, H. (1998) "Women and War: the Case of Nicaragua" in Isaksson.

Isaksson, E. (1998) editor, *Women and the Military System* [New York: St. Martin's].

Mahon, E. (1987) "Women's Rights and Catholicism in Ireland" *New Left Review* no. 166.

Mass, B. (1975) *The Political Economy of Population Control in Latin America* Montreal: Women's Press.

Molyneux, M. (1985a) "Mobilisation without Emancipation? Women's Interests, the State and Revolution in Nicaragua" *Feminist Studies* Vol. 2, no. 2.

Molyneux, M. (1985b) "The Role of Women in the Revolution" in Walker (1985).

Perspectiva Mundial (1987) Vol. 2, no. 7 (July).

Oficina de la Mujer (1987) "Informes: Diéz años de investigaciónes sobre la mujer en Nicaragua 1976-1986" Managua.

Pensamiento Proprio (1985) November/December.

Rooper, A. (1987) *Fragile Victory: A Nicaraguan Community at War* London: Weidenfeld & Nicolson.

Vilas, C. M. (1986) "The Mass Organisations in Nicaragua" *Monthly Review* Vol. 38 (November) pp. 20-31.

Walker, T. (1985) editor, *Nicaragua: The First Five Years* New York: Praeger.

Women in Central America (1987) Year 1, no. 2, 2 March.

World Bank (1985) *Development Report* Oxford: Oxford University Press.

STUDY QUESTIONS

1. Why does Marquis describe the debate between the anti-abortionist and the pro-choicer as at a standoff on the question of the status of the fetus? How does Marquis resolve this standoff?
2. Do you think Marquis succeeds in defending the moral impermissibility of abortion by arguing that the fetus has a "future-like-ours"? Does he succeed in his claim that his argument avoids the usual equivocations on 'human life', 'human being', or 'person'? Provide reasons for your answers.
3. Why does Cudd raise objections to Marquis's identification of the status of the fetus as the only issue in the abortion debate? What other considerations should be given weight and why?
4. According to Porter, what is the distinction between formal and substantive equality? Why do these options reflect the inadequacies of a liberal framework with respect to the question of a woman's right to choose in the case of abortion?
5. How, according to Porter, does avoiding the "abstract, ahistorical, individualistic connotations of liberal rights" redefine and give substance to women's need for the "special right" of abortion?
6. Does Porter avoid the impasse of how to settle the conflicting rights to life and to choice evident in the Marquis and Cudd interchange? Why or why not?
7. Does Porter's account of moral praxis incorporate both individual rights and social responsibilities? Can her account play a role in resolving the issue of abortion for women differentially situated and in contexts other than our own? Provide reasons for your answers.
8. Why, according to Roberts, are feminists critical of new reproductive technologies? What reasons does Roberts give for questioning the belief that new reproductive technologies enhance human freedom by expanding procreative options?
9. What evidence does Roberts give for her claim that race and racism are factors in the availability of new reproductive technologies? What is the liberal response to this and why is it rejected by Roberts?
10. In light of the concerns raised by Roberts, do you think restrictions should be placed on the use of new reproductive technologies? If so, in what cases? If not, why not?
11. Molyneux explains that Nicaragua's Sandinistan government's progressive socialist commitment to women's emancipation is in tension with certain other movements and conditions in Nicaragua. Do you think that the particular social and political conditions in Nicaragua as described by Molyneux justify the suspension of or delay in implementing reproductive rights for women? Why or why not?
12. Do you think that women's emancipation requires the full implementation of reproductive rights? Should an answer to this question depend on an analysis of social and political conditions in particular contexts? Formulate your answer by evaluating how Roberts, Porter, and Molyneux would respond to these questions.

SUGGESTED READINGS

Callahan, Daniel. "How Technology is Reframing the Abortion Debate." *Hastings Center Report*, v. 16, no. 1 (1986): 33-42.

Daniels, Cynthia R. "Between Fathers and Fetuses: The Social Construction of Male Reproduction and the Politics of Fetal Harm." *Signs*, v. 22, no. 3 (1997): 579-616.

Donchin, Anne. "The Future of Mothering: Reproductive Technology and Feminist Theory." *Hypatia*, v. 1, no. 2 (Fall 1986): 121-137.

English, Jane. "Abortion and the Concept of a Person." *Canadian Journal of Philosophy*, v. 5, no. 2 (October 1975): 233-243.

Greenhalgh, Susan and Jiali Li. "Engendering Reproductive Policy and Practice in Peasant China: For a Feminist Demography of Reproduction." *Signs*, v. 20, no. 3 (1995): 601-641.

Kymlicka, Will. "Moral Philosophy and Public Policy: The Case of NRTs." *Bioethics*, v. 7, no. 1 (1993): 1-26.

Li, Xiaorong. "Two Concepts of Reproductive Rights." *Report from the Institute for Philosophy & Public Policy*, v. 13, no. 4 (Fall 1993): 22-23.

Morgan, Lynn M. "Fetal Relationality in Feminist Philosophy: An Anthropological Approach." *Hypatia*, v. 11, no. 3 (Summer 1996): 47-70.

Nedelsky, Jennifer. "Property in Potential Life? A Relational Approach to Choosing Legal Categories." *Canadian Journal of Law and Jurisprudence*, v. 7, no. 2 (1994): 343-365.

Overall, Christine. *Ethics and Human Reproduction: A Feminist Analysis.* Boston: Unwin Hyman, 1987.

Palmer-Fernandez, Gabriel and James E. Reagan. "Human Fetal Tissues Transplantation Research and Elective Abortion." *Journal of Social Philosophy*, v. 29, no. 1 (Spring 1998): 5-19.

Riley, Nancy E. "American Adoptions of Chinese Girls: The Socio-Political Matrices of Individual Decisions." *Women's Studies International Forum* 20:1 (1997): 87-102.

Sherwin, Susan. "Abortion Through a Feminist Ethics Lens." In *No Longer Patient: Feminist Ethics and Health Care*. Philadelphia: Temple University Press, 1992.

Sumner, L. W. "The Morality of Abortion." In *Abortion and Moral Theory*. Princeton: Princeton University Press, 1981.

Thomson, Judith Jarvis. "A Defense of Abortion." *Philosophy & Public Affairs*, v. 1, no. 1 (Fall 1971): 47-66.

Tooley, Michael. "Abortion and Infanticide." *Philosophy & Public Affairs*, v. 2, no. 1 (1972): 37-65.

Warren, Mary Anne. "On the Moral and Legal Status of Abortion." *The Monist*, v. 57, no. 1 (1973): 43-61.

CHAPTER ELEVEN

EUTHANASIA, ASSISTED SUICIDE, AND HEALTH CARE

The right to life and the right to choose and the weighing of these rights are as central to discussions about euthanasia and health care as they are to reproductive issues. Euthanasia, sometimes referred to as mercy killing, asks us to consider whether it is ever morally justified to end the life of someone who is incurably ill and suffering. It is important to begin by laying out a number of distinctions. Active versus passive euthanasia is the distinction, if there is one, between actively or directly taking measures to end the life of a patient by administering a drug, for example, and letting or allowing the patient to die by withholding or withdrawing treatment. Voluntary and involuntary euthanasia is the difference between cases in which the patient voluntarily expresses a desire to have his or her life ended and those in which patients are unable to make such a wish, either because they are infants or because they have lost the capacity to express desires or make decisions. Lastly, there is the distinction between suicide, the taking of one's own life, and being assisted by another, such as a doctor or agency. Theorists make use of these distinctions in their arguments about whether euthanasia can be morally justified and in what instances.

When the issue of euthanasia is placed in a broader social and political context, additional and complex issues of health care in general are raised. Is autonomy enhanced or diminished in contexts where health care is taken to be an individual rather than a state matter? If it is diminished, what does this mean for the right to make decisions about our own lives? Are decisions about resources, the availability of medical technologies, and terminating treatment affected by factors such as disability, age, gender, and race? If so, what does this tell us about conceptions of equality and arguments for universal health care? Should the vast disparities in wealth between countries affect our thinking about the right to health care or our obligations to provide care to those in less fortunate circumstances? How should we respond to the increased demand for and traffic in organs from people in poor and developing countries to those in rich and developed countries?

Adrienne Asch and Michelle Fine point to an apparent contradiction in their position: they defend both a woman's right to abortion for any reason and the right of newborns with disabilities to medical treatment. Defending the right to abortion for any reason has the consequence that fetuses with disabilities are aborted; this seems inconsistent with defending the right to medical treatment for newborns with disabilities. Both sets of rights are currently protected by statute in the United States, but continue to be under attack: the right to abortion by those on the right and the right to medical treatment by those on the left. Asch and Fine argue that both sets of rights are essential and compatible from a leftist, feminist perspective and that attention to the realities of insufficient financial and social support highlights how both these rights are empty for those who need them most.

Those who argue against the right to medical treatment for newborns with disabilities point out that sometimes life with a disability is not worth living and too costly to the family and the rest of non-disabled society. Fear, revulsion, and ignorance are characteristic of the sorts of discrimination faced by persons with disabilities and play a large role in judgments by doctors, parents, and society in general about the worthlessness and hopelessness of these lives. In the context of these sorts of judgments, arguments about limited resources, inadequate services, and dismal future prospects need to be questioned. Asch and Fine allow, however, that a woman's decision to abort a fetus with Down Syndrome is often shaped by the same stereotypes of persons with disabilities. They defend the right to abortion by arguing that birth is a relevant line marking personhood, delineating rights held by a woman prior to the birth of her child and those held by the child after birth. After birth, parents do not have the right to withhold treatment and nourishment from an infant with a disability, and the state has the responsibility to protect them. They outline several policy implications of the right to medical treatment for newborns with disabilities. The state should absorb medical expenses associated with treatment, give parents extensive information about disabilities, provide care when parents decide to put their infant up for adoption or foster care, and be responsible for assisting disabled children and their families throughout life. Asch and Fine argue that these policies can begin to eliminate the role of discrimination in decisions regarding medical treatment for persons with disabilities.

Asch and Fine's discussion of the high cost of medical treatment and of the allocation of resources raises the general theoretical question about whether health care is a basic social good owed by the state to its citizens. In the second reading, Michael Stingl explores answers to this question in the context of examining health care in Canada, where provision of health care is publicly funded through taxation and available to everyone. Stingl discusses the two social values of equality and efficiency at issue in the debate and the ways in which they coincide and collide in discussions about health care. He begins by applying the two liberal conceptions of equality to the different approaches to health care in Canada and the United States.

For formal equality theorists, or what Stingl refers to as libertarianism, state authority exists to enforce rules of non-interference between individuals, each of whom is then free to pursue the goals that give meaning and structure to their lives, enter into relationships of exchange of goods or services, and acquire material and social goods. Stingl takes the health care system of the United States to be closely aligned with libertarianism in that it gives individuals freedom to purchase private insurance plans in the free market and extends public insurance only to those who fall below a certain economic baseline. Liberal egalitarians, or substantive equality theorists, also value individual liberty, but recognize how it is limited in advance for some people in ways that result in diminished life prospects and unequal opportunities. Stingl argues that something like liberal egalitarianism is behind the single-tiered structure of the current Canadian health care system, the justification being that because health is a good important to each person's ability to pursue projects and goals, justice demands equal health care benefits for everyone. He applies this discussion of equality to proposals for reforming Canada's health care system, arguing that a two-tiered system based on a distinction between basic and non-basic medical services undermines equality because it cannot ensure that decisions about what counts as medically necessary are not based on factors such as age, gender, and race. Reforms, he argues, need to take place in the areas of reconceiving efficiency so that unequal access for some is eliminated, preventative rather then curative health services are put in place, and social programs are strengthened rather than undermined.

The debate about public versus privately funded health care takes on added complexity in a global context in which transplanting human organs has become so successful that few countries have sufficient organs to meet their needs. The increase in organ transplants and the growth of clinics around the world now makes it possible for Italians, Israelis or Americans, for example, to travel to Turkey or India to buy organs and get transplants. The low supply of organs in countries like Israel, Italy, and the United States is explained by religious and cultural taboos and the lack of success of public education campaigns to increase the number of people willing to donate organs at death. The low supply is met by other countries with a surplus of organs. India allows harvesting of and payment for the second kidney of those who are desperately poor for transplantation in patients from other countries who are willing to pay for the organ and surgery in India. China has a secret policy of allowing the harvesting of the organs of executed prisoners. The motive for all these practices is money. Europeans, Middle Easterners, and Asians who travel to India, China, and other countries pay high prices to doctors and hospitals for the organs and transplants. David Rothman's examination of the international traffic in organs raises moral questions about the methods used by countries with low rates of organ donation to obtain organs, the resources developing countries direct to costly technology to meet the demand for organs by rich people and rich countries, and the lack of international regulation in this area.

In the fourth reading, Margaret Battin analyzes the moral justifiability of euthanasia and assisted suicide by discussing end-of-life dilemmas in the Netherlands, Germany, and the USA, three advanced industrial democracies with sophisticated medical technology, high life expectancy, and a higher percentage of deaths by cancer and organ disease than by parasitic or infectious diseases. She uses this examination to reveal the background assumptions underlying each society's set of practices and to shed light on policy considerations for the United States.

The United States has developed a body of case law and state statute that permits a framework of passive euthanasia, the determination to withhold or withdraw treatment when there is no medical or moral point in going on. Although voluntary active euthanasia is prohibited by law in the Netherlands, it is legally tolerated and defended in court decisions that protect physicians who perform it. The protection covers doctors who follow specific guidelines, the most important of which is that the patient's request be voluntary. Germany's history of Nazism has resulted in an understandable distrust of doctors by the German public and has generated opposition to active euthanasia. However, assisting suicide is not a violation of the law and a private organization, German Society for Humane Dying (DGHS), helps those who choose suicide as an alternative to terminal illness by providing the means for ending one's life. Battin raises objections to each of these practices and considers the similarities and differences between the three countries. She cites advances with respect to women's rights, a confrontational public, a tendency for personal self-analysis, and a resistance to authority as differences that justify physician-assisted suicide as a practice that best suits the United States.

The description of Americans as "independent, confrontational, self-analyzing, do-it-yourself, authority-resisting" would seem to clinch the case for voluntary euthanasia as respectful of autonomous capacities so valued in liberal theory. Daniel Callahan argues that euthanasia undermines rather than respects autonomy. He examines four general arguments for euthanasia and raises objections to each. He argues that the moral claim of individual self-determination might apply in the case of suicide, but not in the case of euthanasia because self-determination is not the sort of right that can be waived or given to another. He rejects the argument that there is no moral difference between active and passive euthanasia. With a lethal injection we both cause death and are morally responsible. When we decide to stop treatment that no longer benefits a patient, we do not cause death even if we may be judged morally responsible. He counters the claim that active euthanasia has no harmful consequences by arguing that data from the Netherlands show abuses of the law and the difficulty of formulating and enforcing it. Finally, Callahan argues that euthanasia and assisted suicide are incompatible with the aims of medicine. Medicine should try to relieve human suffering, but only that suffering brought on by illness and dying as biological phenomena, not that brought on from anguish or despair about the human condition.

Some of the concerns raised by Callahan in his rejection of the idea that self-determination is enhanced when doctors end the lives of those who request it are made concrete in the final reading by Nathan Brett. Brett begins with the story of Margo, an Alzheimer's patient and a citizen of the Netherlands, who has signed a living will giving advance directives to her caretakers to end her life in the event that she suffers substantial loss of memory and other mental capacities. Now Margo is in that condition, but appears to be generally happy, gives no indication of wanting to die, and every indication of being fearful that her caretakers will harm her. Brett asks, Is there a case for saying that her life should be ended anyway? If so, how good is the case? Brett explores answers to this question through a discussion of Ronald Dworkin's account of critical interests.

Critical interests describe the structure, consistency, coherence, and meaning given to whole lives. To respect Margo as an autonomous agent is to respect her competent decisions about her life and the way she makes sense of it. If we assume that Margo's reflection about her life and prospects concerning the Alzheimer's was not based on misinformation and that her decision is not out of character, then it would seem to be in her critical interests to end her life sooner rather than after years of dementia. While Brett finds these arguments plausible, he thinks that ending Margo's life is problematic. Brett argues that the demented Margo is not the same person as the one who wrote the advance directive, and she cannot use a living will to end the life of someone different from herself. Margo has a simple, child-like perspective on the world and lacks any connection with the author of the orders for her death. Margo's life has ended and been replaced by someone who can experience pain and pleasure and has needs and desires. Brett argues that the satisfaction of these interests is a source of value and makes demands on our compassion in the same way that human beings who are infants or infantile demand our compassion.

SHARED DREAMS: A LEFT PERSPECTIVE ON DISABILITY RIGHTS AND REPRODUCTIVE RIGHTS

Adrienne Asch and Michelle Fine

Adrienne Asch teaches psychology and has the Henry R. Luce Chair of Biology, Ethics, and the Politics of Human Reproduction at Wellesley College. She is also Chair of the Society for Disability Studies, School of Social Sciences at the University of Texas at Dallas. She is co-editor with Michelle Fine of Women with Disabilities: Essays in Psychology, Policy, and Politics *(Temple, 1988).*

Michelle Fine is Professor of Psychology at City University of New York Graduate School and Senior Consultant at the Philadelphia Schools Collaborative. She is the author of Disruptive Voices: The Possibilities of Feminist Research *(Michigan, 1992); co-author of* Becoming Gentlemen: Women, Law School, and Institutional Change *(Beacon, 1997); and co-editor of* Beyond Silenced Voices: Class, Race and Gender in United States Schools *(SUNY, 1993) and* Off White: Readings on Race, Power, and Society *(Routledge, 1997).*

Asch and Fine use a leftist, feminist perspective to defend both a woman's right to have an abortion for any reason and the right of newborns with disabilities to medical treatment. They reject the view of those on the right and left that these rights are incompatible. A woman's right to control her own body needs to be protected even if one consequence is that fetuses with disabilities may be aborted. They argue, however, that parents should not have the right to withhold medical treatment from newborns with severe disabilities. Such choices are often the result of pressures, misinformation, and stereotypes by family members, doctors, and institutions. In both cases, directing resources to providing better information about disabilities and caring for persons with disabilities and to state assistance for disabled children and their families would affect the choices that women and parents make about abortion and caring for newborns with disabilities.

Women have the right to abortion for any reason they deem appropriate. Newborns with disabilities have the right to medical treatment whether or not their parent(s) wishes them to be treated. Both rights are unequivocal, consistent and currently protected by statute. Both sets of rights are, however, under severe attack—the former from the right and the latter from the left. And together they have been juxtaposed as a contradiction. We argue here that both sets of rights are essential to preserve, and are compatible from a leftist, feminist perspective. In fact, this compatibility forces us to struggle with the reality that in each case, with women's right to abortion and disabled infant's right to treatment, the institutions and services that translate these rights into realities are currently denied appropriate levels of financial and social support—often rendering these rights hollow and irrelevant for those who most need them.

Rights of women to abortion and of newborns with disabilities to medical treatment are, in fact, separate rights which have been linked by the Right in an anti-feminist and allegedly "pro-family" position, and by the Left out of ignorance of the meaning and politics of disability. In this article we review some of the recent controversies over disability rights as it relates to women's right to abortion, amniocentesis and more generally a left politic. To make our argument, we cover three topics: (1) the bias against people with disabilities inherent in most

Reprinted with permission of the publisher from *Radical America* 18:4 (1984): 51–58.

of the reasons offered for non-treatment of infants with disabilities; (2) the bias against women and a woman's right to control her own body inherent in the arguments against amniocentesis and abortion of fetuses with disabilities, and (3) the continuing problematic nature of the distinction between a fetus residing in the body of a woman and a newborn infant, as it relates to the question, whose body is it anyway? Because the only voices from the Left—including feminist organizations—which have spoken for the rights of disabled newborns to treatment have been those publicly identified with the disability rights movement, we turn first to the issues of infants with disabilities. Unfortunately, these voices have been relatively ignored thus far and must be given serious weight in this debate.

In our earlier writing on this subject[1], we challenged the prevailing assumption in the reproductive rights movement that any women *would* have an abortion if she were diagnosed as carrying a fetus with a disability. We urged that the reproductive rights movement and other feminists not presume nor prescribe any reason, e.g. "the Tragedy of the 'defective fetus'" for an abortion. As we would not advocate the "tragedy for a female fetus" as a legitimate reason for an abortion—although many of us abhor the use of abortion for sex selection—activists can not continue to exploit the disabled fetus as the good or compelling reason to keep abortion, safe, legal and funded. On the basis of women's rights, alone, abortion must be safe, legal and funded—not to rid our society of some of its "defective" members.

Recently the controversy has emerged in all its complexity: Baby Jane Doe, and infant born on Long Island with a series of disabling conditions including spina bifida and microencephaly, was denied an operation by her physician and parents acting jointly. Earlier, a Bloomington, Indiana boy was born with a diagnosis of Down Syndrome and an esophagus unattached to his stomach. Routinely an infant's open esophagus is corrected by surgery but Baby Doe's parents decided against surgery based on the diagnosis of his mental retardation. Despite some dozen offers of couples to adopt him, Baby Doe died at six days old of starvation. Even more recently and less well known, an infant girl was born in Illinois with a heart problem, and a "hand like a claw." Her father, a well known veterinarian, was handed the baby in the delivery room. On seeing the child he threw it to the floor, killing her. The community has rallied around this man claiming that everyone has a psychological threshold beyond which s/he is not responsible. For him it was the presumed tragedy of having a disabled child.

The reasons used to justify denial of medical treatment to these infants have been the reasons given by people who believe that living with a disability is either not worth living, too costly to the family, or too costly to the rest of nondisabled society. But no one ever questions the use of costly treatments to ameliorate or cure all sorts of neonatal medical problems if those procedures result in a perfect, "normal" child. The question arises only when no amount of medical treatment will relieve all of an infant's medical or mental problems, and that infant will remain throughout its life as a person with some level of disability. At that point, Leftists and feminists have, for the most part, joined in the arguments that such treatment wastes limited societal resources, harms nondisabled parents and siblings, harms society and does not benefit the child. All these arguments arise from confusing what is inherent in disability with the problems imposed on disabled people by a discriminating society—one without national health insurance, adequate financial and social supports for persons with disabilities, one which prizes profit over human needs and persists in discriminating at the level of medical treatment, education and employment opportunities and housing.

Unacknowledged by those who would deny treatment is this discrimination against people with disabilities. Such prejudice is found throughout the population and thus it is no surprise although quite dismaying to see people who decry discrimination on the basis of race, ethnicity, gender, sexual orientation or social class urging that public policy embody their fears, terrors, revulsion and ignorance of disability and people with disabilities. Millions of citizens with biological limitations would assert that their main obstacles to fulfilling lives stem not from these limitations but from a society which stresses mental and physical perfection and rugged individualism, that often rejects, isolates and segregates them, assuming that disabled people are unpleasant, unhappy, helpless, hopeless and burdensome.

Such stereotypes lead inevitably to the first of three major arguments given for non-treatment: that the child's quality of life will be intolerable. We ask: Intolerable to whom? How do we know? And, if that child's quality of life is less than someone else's, how much do we as a society contribute to its impoverishment by denying needed health care, education, independent living, rehabilitation and social supports to ensure a better life? We do not know what the lives of any children will be when they are born. People who decide that Down Syndrome or spina bifida automatically renders children or adults "vegetables" or "better off dead" simply know nothing about the lives of such people today—much less what those lives could be in a more inclusive, person oriented society.

Persons with Down Syndrome or spina bifida represent a broad range of potential. Many lead intellectually, economically, socially and sexually fulfilling lives. Others don't. We don't know how they would live in a society that did not systematically deprive children of opportunity if they do not meet norms of appearance, intelligence and autonomy. Some parents, who gave their children with Down Syndrome cosmetic surgery, have found that their children's social and intellectual skills improved once they no longer carried the stigma of the "Mongoloid" appearance. We can not separate the essence of disability from the social construction of disability, and must continue to struggle to insure a life free of the kinds of oppressions we have described so that disability can refer to the physical or mental limitation alone.

Others who recommend against treatment contend that even if the child could have a "meaningful" life, its presence would unduly burden or deprive nondisabled family members. Some feminists have argued that deinstitutionalising disabled people and saving disabled newborns constitute yet another means by the Right to keep women in their homes, bearing the "double burden" of the pathetic disabled child. Women, it is argued, are oppressed by deinstitutionalisation and medical treatment to insure life for infants with disabilities, and siblings will resent the attention and emotional and financial resources given to the disabled child.

Such argument is based on the assumption that disabled children contribute nothing to family life, which even in today's society can be denied by thousands of parents and siblings who attest to the pleasures as well as the problems of living with disabled people. Moreover it blames the disabled child and suggests eliminating that child, rather than blaming society for causing problems of inadequate resources for all. In the U.S. it is, often, quite expensive to care for a child with a disability. But sometimes it is not. When it is, we must struggle politically for funded medical, social and caretaking public programs. We can neither locate the problem inside the child with the disability nor the solution with the individual mother of that child. In Sweden, national health care and a full range of social services enable parents of disabled children to easily partake in infant stimulation programs, integrated daycare and schools, respite care and a host of other services that contribute to their lives and their children's lives. Adult relationships do not founder; siblings without disabilities are not neglected. A supportive context diminishes the alleged negative impact—which we contend is massively overestimated—of having a child with a disability. We would also argue, however, that a parent(s) unable or unwilling today to care for a child with a disability be offered the option of placing the child up for adoption or in foster care temporarily, and agitate for adoption agencies to recruit actively and aggressively support adults interested in adopting or providing foster care for a child with a disability.

We come to the last argument against treating newborns with disabilities: Society's resources are limited already and should thus not be spent on people who cannot measure up to the standards of what we think people should be. Obviously this argument rests on our first point—that disabled people cannot have a valuable existence. It also takes as given that society's resources are limited rather than misallocated. We know that under current political arrangements, military spending grossly overshadows spending for social programs. Saying that we should not treat disabled children because resources are scarce, existing services inadequate and futures uncertain is like saying that poor people and black people should not have children because society is hostile to poverty and deeply racist. No progressive would accept that. Nor should it be accepted where children with disabilities are concerned. We should all fight to transform social arrangements and allocation of resources so that needs are better met for all of us.

Progressives should fight not against deinstitutionalising disabled people as some have, and not against treatment for Baby Janes, as many have, but for community based residential centers, independent living policies, educational and employment opportunities and the civil rights of all disabled children and adults. All these arguments against treatment rest on the assumption that disabled people are less than human. That should be questioned, and not the rights of these children and adults to the societal goods to which the nondisabled members of the community are entitled.

If we believe, as we do, that all children with disabilities deserve treatment regardless of parental wishes, how can we support a woman's unquestioned right to an abortion if that abortion may stem from learning that a fetus being carried has a disability? We do so because we believe that abortion of a fetus and killing an infant are fundamentally different acts.

Women have won the right to abortion as a part of the right to control their bodies. As a society we have decided that women are not simply vessels to reproduce the species. While a fetus resides within her, a woman must retain the right to decide what happens to her body and her life. Otherwise we ask that women bear not just unwanted children but also unnecessary physical and psychic burdens of sexual acts which men do not. Since we have decided that each heterosexual act need not be linked in mind or fact to reproduction we must permit women to decide what becomes of their bodies and lives during a pregnancy.

When a woman decides that she wants to abort, rather than carry to term, a fetus with Down Syndrome, this represents a statement about how she perceives such a child would affect her life and what she wants from raising a child. Every woman has the right to make this decision in whatever way she needs. But the more information she has, the better her decision can be. Genetic counselors, physicians and all others involved with assisting women during amniocentesis should gain and provide far more and very different information about life with disabilities than is customarily available. Given proper information about how disabled children and adults live, many women might not choose to abort. And many will still choose to abort. While a fetus resides within her, a woman has the right to decide about her body and her life and to terminate a pregnancy for this or any other reason.

May we argue that a woman has a right to abort a fetus diagnosed with Down Syndrome but also that an infant with Down Syndrome has a right to treatment despite her/his parent's desires? Yes, we can and do. We must recognize the crucial "line" separating the fetus—residing in the body of her mother—and the infant, viable outside the womb. The fetus depends on the mother for sustenance and nourishment. We argue that the "line" of birth makes an enormous difference. Once that living being survives outside the mother, that mother cannot eliminate it because it does not meet her physical and mental specifications. As a society, our constitution accepts personhood as starting at birth. We cannot simply decide that "defective" persons are not really persons and not entitled to all the care and protection we grant other citizens.

The existing laws against murder, the recently passed Child Abuse Amendments of 1984, as well as the provisions of Section 504 of the Rehabilitiation Act, prohibit institutions and parents from withholding treatment to persons merely because those persons have disabilities. If parents and doctors would use the disability of a newborn as a reason to withhold treatment and nourishment, and if such treatment and nourishment would permit life for that infant—not a dying infant but an infant with a disability—the social collective and not the individual parent(s) bears the responsibility for that infant's protection. Parents do not today have unlimited rights over their children. Children are not their property. As state and federal laws now protect children from abuse of their parents and as courts have intervened to insist upon medical care and education for minor children when their parents oppose these for religious reasons, the federal government can appropriately intervene to protect newborns from being killed because their parents and doctors find them inconvenient, distasteful and/or burdensome.

Some will say that the government should not intervene in this private family matter—contending that parents are suffering a tragedy, that they are already going through a terrible time and that they should be left alone. Socialist feminists have learned to be wary of such privacy of the family arguments, aware that the family as we've known it has long been abusive to women and children. Grief stricken, shocked and anxious parents who may seek to end the lives of their "imperfect" infants should be counseled, educated and told that the child will receive treatment whether or not the parent(s) agrees. We should work toward a policy in which the government picks up the medical expenses associated with such treatment; that parents be given extensive information about what it means to have a disability, have access to disability rights organizations, and parents' groups, and assured of informed consent in which they are informed that should they wish they can put their infant up for adoption or foster care. Parents therefore may be removed *if they so desire* from responsibility, at which point the state acts to protect the infants. If nontreatment is contemplated when treatment would benefit the child, it should be rendered. If state intervention is necessary to ensure it, then we should opt for state intervention. We already opt for state intervention in all manner of other situations where one person's or group's rights are infringed upon by another. Denial of treatment means denial of life, the most basic right of all.

But this argument for treatment of newborns is not the same as that of the Reagan Administration nor the "Right to Life" movement. Unlike these supporters of the disabled who care about them only when they are in the intensive care nursery and who slash budgets for needed educational programs for them and try to deny them civil rights to education, housing and employment once out of the nursery, we believe that the government has major responsibility for assisting disabled children and their families throughout life. Not only does the government have the obligation to absorb the medical and social service expenses that children with disabilities entail. It has the obligation to provide parents with extensive information about life with a disability. Additionally the government must assist these parents in finding alternative homes for these children if parents do not feel prepared to raise them.

Such information about disabilites must include that provided by parents of similarly disabled children and that obtained through contact with advocacy groups of disabled adults. It can not merely consist of medical, diagnostic or prognostic information without including facts of the social meaning of disability and the ways people manage it in today's world. Disabled adults are among the most important advocates for disabled children and must participate in any decisions about the lives and policies affecting the lives of these children.

Like feminism, the disability rights movement entails a commitment to self determination and a shared sense of community, recognizing that self determination is meaningless without a sense of community. Thus as disabled adults increasingly advocate for the rights of children with disabilities they seek to ally with feminists and others on the Left to grapple with remaining questions posed and to put forward a shared dream of a just and inclusive society.

When disability rights groups and the American Academy of Pediatrics put forward a statement on the rights of newborns to treatment in November 1983, no known progressive or feminist groups signed the document. We urge that all of us on the Left rethink positions taken out of deep seated terror and repugnance of disability and out of almost equally deep seated—but in this case knee-jerk—opposition to the Right's attack on women and the pro-choice movement. We have conceded the issue of disability to the Right. We can and must commit ourselves to the lives of newborns with disabilities while protecting our hard-won gains as women.

New political contradictions will emerge in this struggle: e.g. how to mobilize against physicians and medical researchers who systematically prolong the lives of dying infants in order to afford expensive equipment, research laboratories and sophisticated technology at the expense of the pain and finances of parent(s) involved; how to deal with late abortions, viable disabled infants who survive abortion procedures or could be kept alive with new technological interventions; or how to deal with infant disabilities which may arise because a woman refused some form of medical intervention during delivery (for example a woman recently refused a Cesarian section recommended because of active vaginal herpes sore, producing a now blind infant)? Such questions can not halt us but must be incorporated into our political struggles as contradictions have always been. Indeed if we can create a society that supports the newborn with a disability, perhaps the most defenseless of all citizens, we can create a society humane and just for us all.

NOTES

1. Fine and Asch, from: *Reproductive Rights National Newsletter*, November 1982.

EQUALITY AND EFFICIENCY AS BASIC SOCIAL VALUES

Michael Stingl

Michael Stingl is an Associate Professor in the Department of Philosophy at the University of Lethbridge, Alberta. He teaches and writes in the area of ethics. In 1995 he served as the Chair of the Ethics Committee of the Lethbridge Regional Hospital.

Stingl frames the recent discussion of health care reform in Canada in terms of an examination of the two conceptions of equality in the liberal tradition: libertarianism and liberal egalitarianism. Canada's health care system can be said to fit the liberal egalitarianism found in Rawls. Because health is a good each of us needs to pursue life plans at all, we are treated as moral equals only if we are each given an equal amount of health insurance. Stingl argues that the current health system of the United States reflects the libertarian rejection of state interference and the defence of an individual's freedom to purchase private insurance plans. However, health care raises particularly complex issues of efficiency that tend to undermine a strict liberal egalitarian justification for equal health care and justify inequalities in terms of costs and available resources. Stingl argues that introducing additional inequalities into Canada's health system is neither reasonable nor fair.

Social Values and Political Choices

Equality and efficiency are two key terms in the growing national debate over reforming the Canadian health system. Both are widely understood to refer to values basic to the structure and identity of Canadian society. But this is true only on a loose understanding of both terms; in the debate over health reform, both terms mean different things to different people. As long as equality and efficiency remain widely but only loosely understood, the likelihood increases that this debate will become politically intractable and socially divisive.

In this paper, I examine some of the different things that those participating in the debate often mean by equality and efficiency. Taking stock of these different meanings, I distinguish several points of potential reform where we can expect the two values to coincide, as well as several where we can expect them to collide. It is this latter possibility, of course, that is the more ethically interesting and troubling: the fact that in reforming the health system, having more of the one value will sometimes mean having less of the other.

Basic social values guide public policy, and more generally, determine the conditions and limits of social interaction between individuals, groups, and institutions within Canada. They provide the shared social framework within which each of us defines his or her own life. When such values collide, we are individually and collectively faced with a social choice. On the one hand, we might allow our social values to shift in ways that, at least on the surface, avoid conflict; on the other hand, we might simply accept the fact that social values will sometimes collide, and when this happens, face the difficult choice of which value ought to give way to which. In either case, we need to be clear about who the "we" is that is determining the course of social change. Choices regarding basic social values must not be hidden away within governmental bureaucracies, but debat-

Reprinted with permission of Michael Stingl from *Efficiency versus Equality* (Halifax: Fernwood, 1996): 7–19.

ed publicly and openly within the larger political context of Canadian society as a whole. In a modern liberal society, determining the basic conditions of our social network with one another is an important right and an important responsibility, for again, basic social values not only determine the structure and identity of Canadian society, but as well, the structure and identity of our lives as individual Canadians.

Determining which basic social value should give way to which is thus a political choice in the broadest sense of the term. What is required to make such choices is public debate and government action. And this is what we are now seeing in varying degrees across Canada: public debate about the importance and possible limits of the Canadian health system and Canadian social services more generally, and government initiatives to make these services more responsive to deficit and debt as well as the needs of all Canadians. To evaluate these initiatives, and to make the social choices they represent wisely, we need a clear public understanding of what the terms equality and efficiency really mean.

Two Different Meanings of Equality

In the debate over health reform it is necessary to distinguish between two very different ways of thinking about human society. On the one hand, we might see society as providing nothing more than the institutional framework necessary for humans to organize the individual pursuit of their own separate ends, as they personally choose to define them. On this picture of society, it is the individual who is of fundamental value; society exists only as a set of formalized arrangements to better enable each individual to pursue his or her own personal good. This is the libertarian view of society.

On the other hand, we might see society as a joint, cooperative venture, participation in which creates the sense of a greater, social good that grounds and gives context to everyone's own personal good. On this second picture of human society individuals will still be fundamentally important, but so too will society. Personal goods may be pursued, but only as part of a larger, cooperative enterprise that works fairly and equally for the good of everyone. This second sort of view might be called liberal egalitarianism, "liberal" because it values the liberty to pursue one's own personal good, but "egalitarian" because it is prepared to limit such liberty for the good of others.[1]

Each of the two different ways of thinking about human society leads to its own idea of what it means to treat persons equally. To understand these two different meanings of equality, we need to examine more fully the views of society on which they are based.[2]

Let us start with what is common between the two views: the value of individual liberty. What makes human beings the interesting, valuable creatures that they are is the fact that they are able to think about and choose the ends towards which they will act. At the most general level, these ends may include such diverse things as material wealth, love and friendship, knowledge, or social power and prestige. Whatever particular mix of such ends a person might choose to pursue, the important thing about people is that they are able to make such choices; they are able, that is, to determine the goals and aims that give structure and meaning to their individual lives.

Acting alone, however, no one individual is likely to get very far towards any of the more interesting or complex ends that make our lives richly of fully human. For the goods that matter most to us, like having children or embarking on a career, we need the help of other people, or at the very least, their non-interference. This, then, is one minimal role that society might play in human life: to insure that no one individual unfairly interferes with the independent choices of another.

This libertarian view of society is developed at length by the philosopher Robert Nozick in his book *Anarchy, State and Utopia*.[3] According to Nozick, legitimate state authority exists only to enforce rules of non-interference between individual citizens, rules that outlaw things like lying, cheating, stealing, or reneging on promises. Regulating such actions allows a free market to develop between individuals that enables them to trade goods and service in ways that are mutually beneficial. On this free market view of human society, any trade that is consented to is fair, as long as the consent is not the result of coercion; as long, that is, as it is not the result of anything like lying, cheating, or any of the other forms of illicit interference in the life of another. The function of the state is not to create a market of exchanges, but rather to create the social conditions that freely allow such markets to develop and flourish. The markets themselves are nothing more than the separately motivated choices of individuals to enter into trading arrangements with one another.

According to this first view of society, people are ultimately separate from one another, and relationships of interchange and benefit require mutual agreement. Beyond non-interference, no one owes anyone anything. Each may enter into a free market of exchanges to derive whatever goods or services others agree to trade, but no one is obliged to participate in whatever markets might otherwise develop between others, nor to benefit in any way those who are for some reason unable to participate in such markets. Out of charity one might choose to help such a person, but no one is in any way morally obliged to render aid. The motto of this view is that I have my life, and you have yours: and just as I might choose to enter freely into an exchange of goods or services with you, I might just as freely choose not to.

The second way of thinking about human society and human life is not a simple reversal of libertarianism. It does not move to the opposite extreme of declaring that it is society that is of fundamental or primary importance, and individuals of mere derivative value. Liberal egalitarianism, like libertarianism, values individual choice. But unlike libertarianism, it gives independent value to the ongoing social relationships that link the choices of one person to those of the next. It recognizes that although each of us may choose the course of our own life, none of us chooses the background of ongoing social cooperation that makes such a choice possible. Where libertarianism sees society as nothing more than a series of individual agreements, the second conception sees society as having an independent existence and value of its own.

This second view of society is developed at length by the philosopher John Rawls in his book *A Theory of Justice*.[4] According to Rawls, a society is fairly arranged only when it is reasonable for any and all its members to consent to being part of it. Because the rich, full lives that matter most to humans require the shared cooperation of others, some social arrangement will be preferable to no social arrangement in all but the most dire circumstances. The problem is that different arrangements will offer different benefits to different people. A social arrangement that benefits some individuals more will benefit others less, depending on whose natural talents are in greater demand and generate greater social and individual rewards. Moreover, just as some individuals will suffer accidents that diminish whatever opportunities they would have had for developing their talents or lives in ways they might otherwise have chosen, some individuals will be born in ways that similarly limit the range of opportunities available to them.

So the question is, what sort of social arrangement would it be reasonable to enter into, regardless of one's plans, talents, or infirmities? According to Rawls, the only society it would be reasonable for each of us to enter into is one that guarantees every individual the same equal chance to pursue whatever life plan he or she might choose. People being people, such plans will of course vary greatly, some plans requiring more social resources, some fewer. But Rawls' idea is that whatever sort of life we might choose to lead, two basic sorts of goods will be important to us: civil liberties, like freedom of speech, association, and conscience, and material resources, like income and wealth. Since there is no way that those with fewer civil liberties could ever be advantaged by a social system that distributed such liberties unequally, the first principle of a just society is equal liberty for all. But with regard to material resources, Rawls claims that the situation is markedly different: if more productive individuals are allowed economic incentives, the social pie as a whole will be greater, and so those with lower incomes will have more material resources than they would under a system which distributed income and wealth in a strictly egalitarian fashion. To the extent that those with less material wealth are more advantaged than they otherwise would be, unequal levels of material wealth will be reasonable in a fair and just society.

We will return to Rawls' two principles in the next section, the first governing the fair distribution of basic liberties, and the second governing the fair distribution of material wealth. The question there will be whether health care, or health more generally, is a good more like liberty or more like wealth.

The point here is that just as there are two different ideals of modern society, there are also two different conceptions of equality. For the libertarian, each individual is treated equally by a state that guarantees no more than non-interference between individuals. The state itself treats individuals unequally when it interferes in the lives of its citizens to transfer between them material resources that were initially acquired through free exchange. Enforced charity, by means of a taxation scheme, for example, that transfers resources from those with more to those with less, is not fair or just according to the libertarian view of human life and society. Again, those with more may freely choose to help those with less, but they may just as freely choose not to.

For Rawls, on the other hand, transfers between individuals are required to ensure that each has an equal opportunity to lead whatever life he or she might choose. Since more productive individuals are allowed greater material resources only so far as this is required as an economic incentive to produce more goods and services overall, taxation is just up to the point that the social product as a whole would begin to diminish. Taxation is fair, that is, up to the point that the economic incentives for the better off would cease to motivate them to be more productive.

Something like this second notion of equality is arguably behind the single-tiered structure of the current Canadian health system.[5] The general form of the argument would be that because our health is equally important to all of us regardless of what sort of life we might choose to pursue, taxation schemes that provide equal health benefits to everyone represent a fair and just social arrangement, one that it would be reasonable for all individuals to enter into no matter what their talents of infirmities. Because of the kind of good that health is, each of us is treated as a moral equal only if we are each given an equal amount of health insurance.

In contrast, the current health system of the United States is more nearly libertarian, since individuals are guaranteed only as much health insurance as they are able to purchase in the free market of private insurance plans. This system is not perfectly libertarian, however, because public insurance is provided for people falling below a certain economic baseline or over a certain age limit. Even so, public insurance plans in the U.S. are extremely limited in their coverage, and there are a significant number of Americans above the economic baseline for public insurance who can nevertheless afford little or no private insurance.[6] It is thus unclear to what extent public insurance plans in the U.S. represent charity or justice for those unable to afford adequate private insurance.

More interesting than the U.S. system, and more conceptually problematic, is the sort of hybrid, two-tiered system of health insurance advocated by some Canadian health reformers.[7] Unlike public insurance plans in the United States, all medically necessary services would be covered for all Canadians. But for services deemed not to be medically necessary, or for faster or better quality service, access would be available only to people able to afford additional insurance or direct payment. As we shall see in the next section, it is hard to determine whether the idea of equality presupposed by this sort of two-tiered health system is a coherent one.

Health as a Basic Social Good

Just as there are two importantly different ways in which we might think about society, and hence equality, there are two importantly different ways in which we might think about the value of health services.

On the one hand, we might think of health services as services like any others: just as we might avail ourselves of the services of a travel agent or hair dresser, we might also avail ourselves of the services of a doctor, nurse, or any other health professional. On the other hand we might think of health services as having a direct tie to health, which alongside political liberty and material wealth we might consider a basic social good.[8]

If we follow Rawls in defining basic goods as those things that are likely to matter to us whatever our life plan might be, health seems an obvious addition to the list. Some people, however, seem entirely prepared to trade off at least portions of their health for other goods, such as the pleasures of smoking or high cholesterol diets. Although this does not change the fact that certain levels of health are needed to lead human lives however they might be defined by the individuals leading them, it does raise the possibility of a mixed understanding of the good of health, and hence, of health services. Perhaps only some health services, but not all, need to be understood as integral to the basic good of health. The health services that are not tied directly to the level of health needed to lead a good life, however one might define it, might then be understood as services like any others, commodities to be sought out and paid for by those who desire them.

Let us return here to Rawls' two principles for distributing basic goods. The first principle, the one regarding liberty, is strictly egalitarian. Because of the kind of basic good civil liberties represent, people are treated equally only if they receive equal amounts of this particular good. Here we need to remember the leading idea of Rawls' two principles, that it is equally reasonable for all to participate in a given social arrangement only if that arrangement gives everyone an equal opportunity to pursue their life plans however they might choose to define them. In general, this conception of society requires basic social goods to be distributed equally; the only exception is when distributing a good unequally means more of that same good for all. This is the situation, Rawls says, with material wealth: all do better than they otherwise would if some are given economic incentives to be more productive.

Considered alongside the basic goods of liberty and material wealth, health would seem to be a good more like the former than the latter. Allowing different levels of health does not in any immediate sort of way make those will less health better off than they would otherwise be, and so in this important respect, health seems to have more in common with political liberty than material wealth. If there are no other important differences between them, then it would seem that health ought to be distributed like liberty: in a strictly egalitarian way.

But there are a number of important differences between health services and the sorts of social arrangements needed to guarantee our civil liberties. First, health services can increase in number, kind, and cost. Civil liberties, on the other hand, are limited in number, and tend to be all or nothing. Were a state, for example, to guarantee political but not religious freedom, we would not think it a state that guaranteed freedom of speech, association, and conscience. But it does not seem in principle wrong that a state might provide antibiotics for everyone who needed them, but not artificial hearts. Moreover, certain choices of what sort of a life one is going to lead seem legitimately to require or to allow trade-offs involving increased health risks. So while a state can guarantee through its laws and political institutions equal liberty, it cannot through its health services guarantee anything approaching equal health, whatever technologies might be available to it.

Finally, it may be that by allowing a second tier of health services to develop, those with only publicly provided, first-tier services available to them will do better than they otherwise might. There are several ways this might happen, such as less waiting time or innovative treatment options that are developed at and filter down from the more expensive, privately purchased second tier of services. But there are also reasons for supposing that things will not be better for those who find themselves limited to first-tier services, as resources, personnel, and finally funding are increasingly drawn away from the first tier to the second. What would in fact happen were the Canadian system to go from one tier to two is far from clear.

Taken together, these differences between liberty and health suggest that health services might be more appropriately distributed in accord with something like Rawls' second principle of justice, the one regarding material wealth. The most straightforward way of doing this would be to incorporate their distribution directly into the second principle's distribution of material wealth. Assume, that is, that income and wealth were distributed in such a way that whatever inequalities existed made those with less as well off as they could be. To give those with less any more would be to decrease the incentives to the more productive members society below the level at which they will continue to be as productive as they are.[9] It might then seem to be fair to allow people to purchase as much or as little as they wanted. What rankles about this suggestion given the current free market method of distributing health services in the U.S. is that material wealth is clearly not distributed in accord with Rawls' second principle in either the U.S. or Canada; one result in the U.S., of course, is that a significant number of Americans are unable to purchase health insurance that would be considered in any way adequate or affordable by Canadian standards. But suppose wealth were distributed in a more equal fashion; why not let people spend their money on as much or as little as they wanted?

One practical problem with this market approach to the distribution of health services is that it would seem to require private insurance schemes, which are economically inefficient.[10] A second problem is that preventative services are in some ways more efficient than curative services, and it is not immediately clear how or why people would choose to insure themselves in ways that might allow full realization of the advantages of preventative medicine.[11]

These sorts of practical problems might be resolved with the right sort of public insurance plan, and the right sort of political will to establish and maintain such a plan. But this suggests an even more insurmountable problem for any proposal tying the distribution of health services to a more equal distribution of material wealth: to the extent that the struggle in both Canada and the U.S. for more egalitarian health systems has been uphill, the struggle for greater economic equality has faced a more nearly vertical climb.

This being so, we might wonder whether Rawls' theory of justice has any relevance for the current debate over Canadian health reform. Whatever we might want to say about the overall distribution of material wealth in Canada, all health services are currently available to all Canadians, at least in principle. But this very principle is itself one significant aspect of the Canadian health system that is now being threatened by governmental responses to increasing deficits and debts. Thinking about universality in the context of Rawls' two principles of justice may yet help clarify some of the larger social issues that are at stake in initiatives to trim deficits by trimming health services.

For example, one direct response to the problems involved in tying health services to the principle for distributing material wealth is to insist that health is ultimately more like liberty than not; despite the differences listed above, health services, like liberty, ought to be distributed in a strictly equal fashion. This would respond well to the idea that like liberty, having a certain level of health is central to our having any life plans at all. But we must still recognize at least this one important difference between the two goods: health services can escalate in cost and number in a way that the institutional arrangements guaranteeing equal liberty cannot. This difference could be met, however, by limiting the comprehensiveness of services provided rather than their universal provision. That cost containment should be focused on comprehensiveness rather than universality is suggested by the idea that health is more like liberty than material wealth.

Limiting the comprehensiveness of the public health plan raises a second interesting question regarding current proposals for reforming the health system. Would it be fair to all Canadians to tie basic, medically necessary services to the strictly egalitarian sort of principle appropriate to liberty, and then, in addition, piggyback the accessibility of all other services onto something like Rawls' second principle? This would preserve universal medical coverage for those services determined to be medially necessary, and allow people with more income or wealth to purchase whatever additional services they wanted to. The underlying idea would be that it is only basic health services that are like liberty; whatever life a person might choose to lead, certain basic health services, like liberty, are equally important to everyone. Additional health services, though, are like material wealth: some people will want to pursue more, some people less, depending on the different kinds of lives they choose to lead. Unequal access to additional health services, like unequal levels of material wealth, will be a fair social arrangement just so long as those who have less benefit more than they otherwise would have, given a completely equal arrangement.

Arguments of precisely this kind were aired at the 1995 annual general meeting of the Canadian Medical Association.[12] Some doctors, agreeing that equality requires all basic health services be provided to all Canadians, suggested that there was nothing wrong with providing additional services to those who were willing to pay for them. They argued that in allowing this second tier of services to develop, the first tier of basic services would in fact be strengthened.

Again, it is an open question whether this last claim is true. But even ignoring the question of how a second tier of health services might in fact impact on the quality of the first tier of publicly funded services, and ignoring, as well, the question of whether material wealth is itself fairly distributed in Canadian society, there is a deeper conceptual problem with this two-tiered sort of approach to reforming the health system. How are we to distinguish between basic and non-basic services? In some few cases, the distinction may appear to be quite clear: face lifts are not a medical necessity, however much one might plan one's life around the availability of such a service. But this is hardly the sort of service that is causing any cost problems for the health system, especially since it is not now included in any public health insurance plan. More relevant in this regard are newly developing life-saving technologies, many of which are costly and publicly available. For the individuals directly affected by them, such technologies will certainly appear to be medically necessary. The problem facing a publicly funded health system, however, is what happens when services of this kind begin to overreach the public's ability to pay for them? What happens when we can't afford to provide life-saving technologies to all those whose lives could thus be saved? Talking about basic versus non-basic services does nothing to resolve this problem.

We might, of course, try to avoid the problem by reinterpreting basic to refer only to those services that could be provided to all who need them, given the limitations of an antecedently determined budget, one that balanced the costs of the health against those of other public goods, such as defense, education, social assistance, and economic development. But what this means is that some individuals with the life-threatening conditions will be saved, while other individuals, with other life-threatening conditions, will not. Are those who are not saved treated equally to those who are? Even in a single-tiered system, one which accepts the economic necessity of limitations on comprehensiveness, this is a question that would have to be faced. But it is an even more difficult question if we allow those who can afford it to purchase life-saving treatments privately. The problem of what it means to call some services but not others part of the basic package of health insurance owed equally to every member of Canadian society is exacerbated by the fact that in a two-tiered system, those who would find themselves unable to purchase the additional treatments available to the economically advantaged would be even more disadvantaged by the advent of their ill health than they already are. Worse yet, those individuals least able to afford to purchase additional services would be the same ones most likely to need to.[13]

It is thus far from clear whether any proposal for two-tiered health reform based on a distinction between basic and non-basic services is workable or coherent. What this suggests, from the perspective of a liberal egalitarian theory of justice, is that the only fair health system is one that is single-tiered.

Conflicts Between Equality and Efficiency

Complicating questions about equality is the ambiguity of its companion term in the health reform debate, efficiency. Everyone seems to agree, in a vague, general sort of way, that the health system can and should be more efficiently organized and operated. The differences of opinion are over what exactly this means.

In its simplest use, pursuing greater efficiency means doing what we now do better. Better utilization of the services now available, it is claimed, will cost governments less and at the same time respond more fully to the actual health needs of all Canadians. The argument is that many tests, treatments, and services are currently being provided to those who do not need them or in ways that have not been proven to be generally effective and that may be even harmful.[14]

Regardless of the extent to which this is in fact true, problems regarding equality arise on even this simplest understanding of efficiency. For example, while the current system overtreats individuals consulting their doctors with nothing more than a common cold, other individuals, such as pregnant women who are economically or otherwise disadvantaged, go without appropriate medical care.

Merely eliminating the waste in the health system as it currently exists will do nothing by itself to respond to this second sort of problem, which bears directly on the question of the extent to which the current system is responding equally to the health needs of all Canadians. Achieving better treatment for disadvantaged individuals is, however, one important area of health reform where equality and efficiency might coincide, were the right sorts of reforms to be pursued. Current data suggests that a great many costly medical conditions arise out of early deficiencies in prenatal and childhood nutrition and care. Thus, ensuring that all Canadian fetuses and children receive sufficient nutrition and care is not just a question of greater social equality, but greater economic efficiency as well.

This leads us to a second meaning of efficiency, one that emphasizes preventative over curative health services. The argument here is that it is cheaper to prevent illness rather than to treat it once it has arisen. So far as those who are the most economically disadvantaged are also among the sickest, this is a second important area of health reform where considerations of equality and efficiency might coincide. The extent to which this is so, however, will depend on the extent to which the health statuses of those who are economically less advantaged are tied to social conditions that go beyond the purview of the health system. If a low income job, for example, is bad for your health, it is not clear what the health system can or should do about this fact.

Equality and efficiency are also less clearly connected in a third sense of efficiency, the one at issue in the discussion of the preceding section. Given the ever expanding horizon of medical possibility, we will soon be at that point, if we are not indeed already there, of not being able to afford to provide every possible medical service to every Canadian who might benefit from it. If we can't provide every service to everyone who might need it, what might it mean to provide as many services to as many people as we can? How are we to measure the efficiency of responding to the health needs of some Canadians, but not others?[15] Even supposing we felt able to answer such questions about efficiency, there is no reason to assume that the most efficient use of services would necessarily be the most equal.

Suppose, for example, that considerations regarding the most efficient use of health services led us to offer hip surgery to those younger than seventy-five but not to those over seventy- five. Would such a policy represent equal treatment for younger and older people, or is it in some sense ageist? Or suppose we were to treat less serious but more prevalent conditions at the expense of more serious but less prevalent conditions; are those affected by the more serious conditions and those affected by the less serious conditions treated as true equals? These sorts of questions are again exacerbated by the data that suggest that those individuals with less advantaged economic backgrounds are likely to experience more, and more serious, medical conditions.

A fourth and final meaning of efficiency involves reforms to the health system that reduce the cost to governments of providing services, but increase the cost to consumers of these services in either time or money. One example of such a reform is shortened hospital stays, which cost the hospital and hence the government less, but cost the consumer more in paying for home care or in relying on the time and energy of family members of friends. Assuming the current tax system to be more or less equal, the question is whether transferring such costs from the citizen as taxpayer to the citizen as consumer of health services introduces more or less equality into Canadian society. Looking back to the discussion of the second section of this paper, we might say, if we were libertarians, that those who are healthy have no social obligation to pay for those who are not. If some people get sick, this is their problem; those of us who are healthy might choose to help those of us who are sick out of charity, but the state should not compel such help by transferring money from the healthy to the sick through taxation.

On the liberal egalitarian conception of society, however, we must ask ourselves whether it would be reasonable to enter into a society that does not provide equal care for its sick and injured, regardless of their individual ability to pay for health services. For just as any one of us might find ourselves sick or injured, any one of us might experience a dramatic change in our ability to pay for whatever health services we might need. This sort of situation is prevalent in the United States, where for many people, losing either their jobs or their health means losing their health insurance.[16]

One way of responding to this problem is the health system adopted by Canada, universally available to all and publicly funded through taxation. Compared to the European Union, taxes in both Canada and the U.S. are low; yet in the U.S., and increasingly in Canada, there is much concern that taxes are too high. There is also concern in the European Union over high taxes, but it exists alongside concern for preserving the basic structure of the egalitarian sort of society that these taxes support. One German, a corporate manager facing a tax rate of nearly 60 percent, puts the point this way:

> The European knows that if he gets sick he can go to a good hospital and it won't bankrupt him ... he knows that if his old parents get sick ... they're protected. To Americans, these can be financially disastrous. But we don't fear them. That is shy we keep paying. That is why we say we don't like it but the taxes are necessary.[17]

This point returns us the idea that the current health reform debate in Canada is not just about the kind of health system we want for ourselves and our family members. At a deeper and more far-reaching level, it is about the kind of society we want to live in, one that feels an obligation to care for its sick and injured or one that does not. Economic inequalities may be part of a fair and reasonable society, as both libertarians and liberal egalitarians seem to agree. But unless we are willing to adopt the libertarian view of what a modern, liberal society should be, introducing additional inequalities into our health system does not appear to be either reasonable or fair.

NOTES

1. This is the term used, for example, by Will Kymlicka in *Contemporary Political Philosophy: An Introduction* (Oxford University Press, 1990). Some commentators on the health reform debate call the second view of society communitarianism, but this term has quite a different meaning in contemporary political debate. For a thorough discussion of the main differences between communitarianism and liberal egalitarianism, see Kymlicka, Chapter 6.
2. For further discussion of these different approaches to equality, as well as some of their implications for the just distribution of health care services, see Allen Buchanan, "Justice: A Philosophical Review" in *Justice and Health Care*, ed. Earl Shelp (Dordrecth: Reidel, 1981), 3-21.
3. Robert Nozick, *Anarchy, State, and Utopian* (New York: Basic Books, 1974).
4. John Rawls, *A Theory of Justice* (Cambridge: Harvard University Press, 1971).
5. For such an argument see Kai Nielsen, "Autonomy, Equality and a Just Health Care System," *The International Journal of Applied Philosophy* 4 (Spring 1989): 39-44.
6. Robert G. Evans, "Less is More: Contrasting Styles in Health Care," in *Canada and the United States: Differences that Count*, ed. David Thomas (Peterborough: Broadview, 1993), 21-41. For a glimpse into what the statistics mean for the everyday lives of affected Americans, see Eleanor D. Kinney and Suzanne K. Steinmetz, "Notes from the Insurance Underground: How the Chronically Ill Cope," *Journal of Health Politics, Policy and Law* 19, 3 (1994): 633-642.
7. Patrick Sullivan, "Private Health Care Dominates Meeting as General Council Calls for National Debate on Issue," *Canadian Medical Association Journal* 153, 6 (1995): 801-803.
8. For a more extended effort to include health in Rawls' theory of justice, see Norman Daniels, *Just Health Care* (Cambridge: Cambridge University Press, 1985). An interesting alternative to Daniels approach, closer to the one suggested here, is provided in Ronald M. Green, "The Priority of Health Care," *Journal of Medicine and Philosophy* 9 (1983): 373-379. Recent work on the social determinants of health (see note 13) suggests, however, that we might regard health itself, and not just health care services or health more generally, as a primary social good; this is the view I begin to develop here.
9. Again, the idea here is that if the general level of productivity in a society goes down there is less for everybody, those who are less advantaged together with those who are more advantaged. The underlying assumption is that financial incentives, and hence

inequalities in the distribution of wealth, are necessary for high levels of productivity in any modern, industrial society. Social programs whose costs cut too deeply into these incentives will thus have less funding available to them that they otherwise might due to a diminished GDP in the society in question. True or not, the underlying assumption of this line of thought is generally accepted among liberal egalitarians.

10. Evans.
11. One important option here is the idea of health maintenance organizations. For the preventative and health promotional potential of this sort of insurance and delivery arrangement, see Michael Rachlis and Carl Kushner, *Strong Medicine: How to Save Canada's Health Care System* (Toronto: Harper Collins 1994), 248-252, and H. H. Schauffler and T. Rodriguez, "The Availability and Utilization of Health Promotion Programs and Satisfaction with health Plan," *Medical Care* 32, 12 (1994): 1182-1196. But for concomitant problems relating to equal access to all provided services, see H.B. Fox, L. B. Wicks, and P. W. Newacheck, "Health Maintenance Organizations and Children with Special Health Needs: A Suitable Match?" *American Journal of Diseases of Children* 147, 5 (1993): 546-552.
12. Sullivan.
13. There is a fast-growing literature on the linkages between health and social position. An early work is Michael Marmot and Tores Theorell, "Social Class and Cardiovascular Disease: The Contribution of Work," *International Journal of Health Science* 18, 4 (1988): 659-674. Recent collections are Robert G. Evans, M. L. Barer, and T. R. Marmor, eds., *Why are Some People Healthy and Others Not? The Determinants of Health of Populations* (New York: Aldine de Gruyter, 1994) together with the fall 1994 issue of *Daedalus*. Especially interesting with regard to the version of liberal egalitarianism explored above is Richard G. Wilkinson, "National Mortality Rates: the Impact of Inequality?" *American Journal of Public Health* 82, 8 (1992): 1082-1084, and Richard G. Wilkinson, "Income Distribution and Life Expectancy," *British Medical Journal* 304, 6820 (1992): 165-168.
14. Rachlis and Kushner.
15. Health economists have, of course, developed an extensive literature devoted to the question of how we might measure the efficiency of different treatment or service options. But whether such precise, technical definitions of efficiency capture what we really ought to mean by the term remains an open question, depending, in part, on how acceptable we find the simplifying assumptions that are necessary to produce precise, technical definitions of such a multifaceted and complex idea. In the debate over health reform, efficiency is in many ways a much more slippery term than equality. For a recent challenge to economic notions of efficiency as they relate to health reform, see Erik Nord, Jeff Richardson, Andrew Street, Helga Kuhse, and Peter Singer, "Who Cares about Cost? Does Economic Analysis Impose or Reflect Social Values?" *Health Policy* 34, 2 (1995): 79-94, and Alastair V. Campbell, "Defining Core Health Services: The New Zealand Experience," *Bioethics* 9, 3/4 (1995): 252-258.
16. Evans.
17. Nathaniel C. Nash, "Europeans Brace Themselves for Higher Taxes," *Globe and Mail*, 25 February 1995, 4 (D).

THE INTERNATIONAL ORGAN TRAFFIC

David J. Rothman

David J. Rothman is Professor of History, Bernard Schoenberg Professor of Medicine, and Director of the Center for the Study of Society and Medicine at the Columbia College of Physicians and Surgeons at Barnard. He is the author of Beginnings Count: The Technological Imperative in American Health Care (Oxford, 1997) and Strangers at the Bedside: A History of How Law and Bioethics Transformed Medical Decision Making *(Basic, 1991). He is also co-editor of* Medicine and Western Civilization *(Rutgers, 1995) and* The Oxford History of the Prison: The Practice of Punishment in Western Society *(Oxford, 1995).*

Rothman argues that advances in medical technology have made it possible for people with resources in developed countries to harvest the organs of people in various developing countries to meet the increased demand created by the technology and the shortage of donor organs. Rothman describes practices in various countries in the world that have been created by this international traffic in organs. He points out that there are no policies for controlling this traffic and calls for the creation of an international body for monitoring and setting policies in this area.

Over the past fifteen years, transplanting human organs has become a standard and remarkably successful medical procedure, giving new life to thousands of people with failing hearts, kidneys, livers, and lungs. But very few countries have sufficient organs to meet patients' needs. In the United States, for example, some 50,000 people are on the waiting list for a transplant; fifteen percent of patients who need a new heart will die before one becomes available. The shortages are even more acute throughout the Middle East and Asia.

This lack of available organs arouses desperation and rewards greed. Would-be recipients are willing to travel far to get an organ and many surgeons, brokers, and government officials will do nearly anything to profit from the shortage. In India well-to-do people and their doctors buy kidneys from debt-ridden Indian villagers; in China officials profitably market organs of executed Chinese prisoners. The international commerce in organs is unregulated, indeed anarchic. We know a good deal about trafficking in women and children for sex. We are just beginning to learn about the trafficking in organs for transplantation.

Reprinted with permission from *The New York Review of Books* (26 March 1998): 14–17.

1.

The routes that would-be organ recipients follow are well known to both doctors and patients. Italians (who have the lowest rate of organ donation in Europe) travel to Belgium to obtain their transplants; so do Israelis, who lately have also been going to rural Turkey and bringing their surgeon along with them. Residents of the Gulf States, Egyptians, Malaysians, and Bangladeshis mainly go to India for organs. In the Pacific, Koreans, Japanese, and Taiwanese, along with the residents of Hong Kong and Singapore, fly to China. Less frequently, South Americans go to Cuba and citizens of the former Soviet Union go to Russia. Americans for the most part stay home, but well-to-do foreigners come to the

United States for transplants, and some centers allot up to 10 percent of their organs to them.

All of these people are responding to the shortages of organs that followed on the discovery of cyclosporine in the early 1980s. Until then, transplantation had been a risky and experimental procedure, typically a last-ditch effort to stave off death; the problem was not the complexity of the surgery but the body's immune system, which attacked and rejected the new organ as though it were a foreign object. Cyclosporine moderated the response while not suppressing the immune system's reactions to truly infectious agents. As a result, in countries with sophisticated medical programs, kidney and heart transplantation became widely used and highly successful procedures. Over 70 percent of heart transplant recipients were living four years later. Ninety-two percent of patients who received a kidney from a living donor were using that kidney one year later; 81 percent of the cases were doing so four years later, and in 40 to 50 percent of the cases, ten years later.[1]

Transplantation spread quickly from developed to less developed countries. By 1990, kidneys were being transplanted in nine Middle Eastern, six South American, two North African, and two sub-Saharan African countries. Kidney transplants are by far the most common, since kidney donors can live normal lives with one kidney, while kidneys are subject to disease from a variety of causes, including persistent high blood pressure, adult diabetes, nephritis (inflammation of vessels that filter blood), and infections, which are more usually found in poor countries. (It is true that the donor runs the risk that his remaining kidney will become diseased, but in developed countries, at least, this risk is small.) The transplant techniques moreover, are relatively simple. Replacing one heart with another, for example, is made easier by the fact that the blood-carrying vessels that must be detached from the one organ and reattached to the other are large and relatively easy to handle. (A transplant surgeon told me that if you can tie your shoes, you can transplant a heart.)

Fellowships in American surgical programs have enabled surgeons from throughout the world to master the techniques and bring them home. Countries such as India and Brazil built transplant centers when they might have been better advised to invest their medical resources in public health and primary care. For them the centers are a means for enhancing national prestige, for persuading their surgeons not to leave the country, and for meeting the needs of their own middle class citizens.

In China, more than fifty medical centers report they perform kidney transplants, and in India hundreds of clinics are doing so. Reliable information on the success of these operations is hard to obtain, and there are reports that hepatitis and even AIDS have followed transplant operations. But according to physicians I have talked to whose patients have traveled to India or China for a transplant, and from published reports within these countries, some 70 to 75 percent of the transplants seem to have been successful.[2]

With patient demand for transplantation so strong and the medical capacity to satisfy it so widespread, shortages of organs were bound to occur. Most of the doctors and others involved in early transplants expected that organs would be readily donated as a gift of life from the dead, an exchange that cost the donor nothing and brought the recipient obvious benefits. However, it turns out that powerful cultural and religious taboos discourage donation, not only in countries with strong religious establishments but in more secular ones as well. The issue has recently attracted the attention of anthropologists, theologians, and literary scholars, and some of their findings are brought together in the fascinating collection of essays, *Organ Transplantation: Meanings and Realities*.[3]

In the Middle East, it is rare to obtain organs from cadavers. Islamic teachings emphasise the need to maintain the integrity of the body after death, and although some prominent religious leaders make an exception for transplants, others refuse. An intense debate occurred last spring in Egypt when the government-appointed leader of the most important Sunni Muslim theological faculty endorsed transplantation as an act of altruism, saying that permitting it was to accept a small harm in order to avoid a greater harm—the same rationale that allows a Muslim to eat pork if he risks starvation. But other clerics immediately objected, and there is no agreement in favor of donation.

In Israel, Orthodox Jewish precepts define death exclusively as the failure of the heart to function, not the cessation of brain activity, a standard that makes it almost impossible to retrieve organs. The primary purpose of statutes defining death as the absence of brain activity is to ensure that organs to be transplanted are continuously supplied with oxygen and nutrients; in effect, the patient is declared dead, and a respirator keeps the heart pumping and the circulatory system working until the organs have been removed, whereupon the respirator is disconnected. Some rabbis give precedence to saving a life and would therefore accept the standard of brain death for transplantation. But overall rates of donation in Israel are very low. The major exceptions are kibbutz members, who tend to be community-minded, as well as other secular Jews.

In much of Asia, cultural antipathy to the idea of brain death and, even more important, conceptions of the respect due elders, have practically eliminated organ transplantation. For all its interest in new technology and its traditions of gift-giving, Japan has only a minuscule program, devoted almost exclusively to transplanting kidneys from living related donors. As the anthropologist Margaret Lock writes: "The idea of having a deceased relative whose body is not complete prior to burial or cremation is associated with misfortune, because in this situation suffering in the other world never terminates."[4] For tradition-minded Japanese, moreover, death does not take place at a specific moment. The process of dying involves not only the heart and brain but the soul, and it is not complete until services have been held on the seventh and forty-ninth days after bodily death. It takes even longer to convert a deceased relative into an ancestor, all of which makes violating the integrity of the body for the sake of transplantation unacceptable.

Americans say they favor transplantation but turn out to be very reluctant to donate organs. Despite countless public education campaigns, organ donation checkoffs on drivers' licenses, and laws requiring health professionals to ask families to donate the organs of a deceased relative, the rates of donation have not risen during the past five years and are wholly inadequate to the need. As of May 1997, according to the United Network for Organ Sharing, 36,000 people were awaiting a kidney transplant, 8,000 a liver transplant, and 3,800 a heart transplant.[5] One recent study found that when families were asked by hospitals for permission to take an organ from a deceased relative, 53 percent flatly refused.

The literary critic Leslie Fiedler suggests that the unwillingness of Americans to donate organs reflects an underlying antipathy to science and a fear of artificially creating life, a fear exploited, he suggests, in the many Hollywood remakes of the Frankenstein story. Moreover, donation would force Americans to concede the finality of death, which Fiedler is convinced they are reluctant to do.[6] I suspect, however, that the underlying causes are less psychological than social, Americans are unaccustomed to sharing resources of any kind when it comes to medicine. Since Americans refuse to care for one another in life—as witness the debacle of national health insurance—why would they do so in death? Receiving help is one thing, donating is another.

2.

If organs are in such short supply, how do some countries manage to fill the needs of foreigners? The answers vary. Belgium has a surplus of organs because it relies upon a "presumed consent" statute that probably would be rejected in every American state. Under its provisions, you must formally register your unwillingness to serve as a donor; otherwise, upon your death, physicians are free to transplant your organs. To object you must go to the town hall, make your preference known, and have your name registered on a national computer roster; when a death occurs, the hospital checks the computer base, and unless your name appears on it, surgeons may use your organs, notwithstanding your family's objections. I was told by health professionals in Belgium that many citizens privately fear that if they should ever need an organ, and another patient simultaneously needs one as well, the surgeons will check the computer and give the organ to the one who did not refuse to be a donor. There is no evidence that surgeons actually do this; still many people feel it is better to be safe than sorry, and so they do not register any objections.

One group of Belgian citizens, Antwerp's Orthodox Jews, have nonetheless announced they will not serve as donors, only as recipients, since they reject the concept of brain death. An intense, unresolved rabbinic debate has been taking place over the ethics of accepting but not giving organs. Should the Jewish community forswear accepting organs? Should Jews ask to be placed at the bottom of the waiting list? Or should the Jewish community change its position so as to reduce the prospect of fierce hostility or even persecution?

Because its system of presumed consent has worked so well, Belgium has a surplus of organs and will provide them to foreigners. However, it will not export them, say, to Milan or Tel Aviv, which would be entirely feasible. Instead, it requires that patients in need of a transplant come to Belgium, which then benefits from the surgical fees paid to doctors and hospitals.

Not surprisingly, money counts even more in India, which has an abundant supply of kidneys because physicians and brokers bring together the desperately poor with the desperately ill. The sellers include impoverished villagers, slum dwellers, power-loom operators, manual laborers, and daughters-in-law with small dowries. The buyers come from Egypt, Kuwait, Oman, and other Gulf States, and from India's enormous middle class (which numbers at least 200 million). They readily pay between $2,500 and $4,000 for a kidney (of which the donor, if he is not cheated, will receive between $1,000 and $1,500) and perhaps two times that for the surgery. From the perspective of patients with end-stage renal disease, there is no other choice. For largely cultural reasons, hardly any organs are available from cadavers; dialysis centers are scarce and often a source of infection, and only a few people are able to administer dialysis to themselves at home (as is also the case in the US). Thus it is not surprising that a flourishing transplant business has emerged in such cities as Bangalore, Bombay, and Madras.

The market in organs has its defenders. To refuse the sellers a chance to make the money they need, it is said, would be an unjustifiable form of paternalism. Moreover, the sellers may not be at greater risk living with one kidney, at least according to US research. A University of Minnesota transplant team compared seventy-eight kidney donors with their siblings twenty years or more after the surgery took place, and found no significant differences between them in health; indeed, risk-conscious insurance companies do not raise their rates for kidney donors.[7] And why ban the sale of kidneys when the sale of other body parts, including semen, female eggs, hair, and blood, is allowed in many countries? The argument that these are renewable body parts is not persuasive if life without a kidney does not compromise health. Finally, transplant surgeons, nurses, and social workers, as well as transplant retrieval teams and the hospitals, are all paid for their work. Why should only the donor and the donor's family go without compensation?

But because some body parts have already been turned into commodities does not mean that an increasing trade in kidneys and other organs is desirable. To poor Indians, as Margaret Radin, professor of law at Stanford, observes, "Commodification worries may seem like a luxury. Yet, taking a slightly longer view, commodification threatens the personhood of everyone, not just those who can now afford to concern themselves about it." Many of the poor Indians who sell their organs clearly feel they have had to submit to a degrading practice in order to get badly needed sums of money. They would rather not have parts of their body cut out, an unpleasant experience at best, and one that is probably more risky in Bombay than in Minnesota. Radin concludes: "Desperation is the social problem that we should be looking at, rather than the market ban. ... We must rethink the larger social context in which this dilemma is embedded."[8]

In 1994, perhaps for reasons of principle or because of public embarrassment—every world medical organization opposes the sale of organs—a number of Indian states, including the regions of Bombay, Madras, and Bangalore, outlawed the practice, which until then had been entirely legal. But the laws have an egregious loophole so that sales continue almost uninterrupted. A detailed and persuasive report in the December 26, 1997, issue of *Frontline*, one of India's leading news magazines, explains how the new system works.[9] The legislation permits donations from persons unrelated to the recipient if the donations are for reasons of "affection or attachment," and if they are approved by "authorization committees." These conditions are easily met. Brokers and buyers coach the "donors" on what to say to the committee—that he is, for example, a cousin and that he has a (staged) photograph of a family gathering to prove it, or that he is a close friend and bears great affection for the potential recipient. Exposing these fictions would be simple enough, but many committees immediately approve them, unwilling to block transactions that bring large sums to hospitals, surgeons, and brokers.

Accurate statistics on kidney transplantation in India are not available, but *Frontline* estimates that about one third of transplants come from living, unrelated donors; four years after the new law went into effect, the rate of transplantation has returned to its earlier levels. It is true that not every hospital participates in the charade, that the market in kidneys is less visible than it was, and it may well be that fewer foreigners are coming to India for a transplant. But the lower classes and castes in India, already vulnerable to so may other abuses, continue to sell their organs. As *Frontline* reports, many donors who sell their organs do so because they are badly in debt; and before long they are again in debt.

3.

China is at the center of the Pacific routes to organ transplantation because it has adopted the tactic of harvesting the organs of executed prisoners. In 1984, immediately after cyclosporine became available, the government issued a document entitled "Rules Concerning the Utilization of Corpses or Organs from the Corpses of Executed Prisoners." Kept confidential, the new law provided that organs from executed prisoners could be used for transplants if the prisoner agreed, if the family agreed, or if no one came to claim the body. (Robin Munro of Human Rights Watch/Asia brought the law to light.) That the law lacks an ethical basis according to China's own values is apparent from its stipulations. "The use of corpses or organs of executed prisoners must be kept strictly secret," it stated, "and attention must be paid to avoiding negative repercussions." The cars used to retrieve organs from the execution grounds cannot bear health department insignia; the people involved in obtaining organs are not permitted to wear white uniforms. In my own interviews with Chinese transplant surgeons, none would admit to the practice; when I showed them copies of the law, they shrugged and said it was news to them.

But not to other Asian doctors. Physicians in Japan, Hong Kong, Singapore, and Taiwan, among other countries, serve as travel agents, directing their patients to hospitals in Wuhan, Beijing, and Shanghai. The system is relatively efficient. Foreigners do not have to wait days or weeks for an organ to be made available; executions can be timed to meet market needs and the supply is more than adequate. China keeps the exact number of executions secret but Amnesty International calculates on the basis of executions reported in newspapers that there are at least 4,500 a year, and perhaps three to four times as many. Several years ago a heart transplant surgeon told me that he had just been invited to China to perform a transplant; accustomed to long waiting periods in America, he asked how he could be certain that a heart would be available when he arrived. His would-be hosts told him they would schedule an execution to fit with his travel schedule. He turned down the invitation. In February the FBI arrested two Chinese nationals living in New York for allegedly soliciting payment for organs from executed prisoners to be transplanted in China.

China's system also has its defenders. Why waste the organs? Why deprive prisoners of the opportunity to do a final act of goodness? But once again, the objections should be obvious. The idea that prisoners on death row—which in China is a miserable hovel in a local jail—can give informed consent to their donations is absurd. Moreover, there is no way of ensuring that the need for organs might not influence courtroom verdicts. A defendant's guilt may be unclear, but if he has a long criminal record, why not condemn him so that a worthy citizen may live?

To have physicians retrieve human organs at an execution, moreover, subverts the ethical integrity of the medical profession. There are almost no reliable eyewitness accounts of Chinese practices, but until 1994, Taiwan also authorized transplants of organs from executed prisoners, and its procedures are probably duplicated in China. Immediately before the execution, the physician sedates the prisoner and then inserts both a breathing tube in his lungs and a catheter in one of his veins. The prisoner is then executed with a bullet to his head; the physician immediately moves to stem the blood flow, attach a respirator to the breathing tube, and inject drugs into the catheter so as to increase blood pressure and cardiac output. With the organs thus maintained, the body is transported to a hospital where the donor is waiting and the surgery is performed. The physicians have become intimate participants in the executions; instead of protecting life, they are manipulating the consequences of death.

The motive for all such practices is money. The Europeans, Middle Easterners, and Asians who travel to China, India, Belgium, and other countries pay handsomely for their new organs and in hard currencies. Depending on the organization of the particular health care system and the level of corruption, their fees will enrich surgeons or medical centers, or both. Many of the surgeons I interviewed were quite frank about how important the income from transplants was to their hospitals, but they were far more reluctant to say how much of it they kept for themselves. Still, a leading transplant surgeon in Russia is well known for his vast estate and passion for horses. His peers in India and China may be less ostentatious but not necessarily less rich. They will all claim to be doing good, rescuing patients from near death.

4.

The international trade in organs has convinced may of the poor, particularly in South America, that they or their children are at risk of being mutilated and murdered. Stories are often told of foreigners who arrive in a village, survey the scene, kidnap and murder several children, remove their organs for sale aborad, and leave the dissected corpses exposed in the graveyard. In Guatemala in 1993 precisely such fears were responsible for one innocent American woman tourist being jailed for a month, and another being beaten to death.

Villagers' anxieties are shared by a number of outside observers who believe that people are being murdered for their organs. The author of the report of a transplant committee of the European Parliament unequivocally asserted that

> Organized trafficking in organs exists in the same way as trafficking in drugs. It involved killing people to remove organs which can be sold at a profit. To deny the existence of such trafficking is comparable to denying the existence of ovens and gas chambers during the last war.[10]

So, too, the rapporteur of a UN committee on child welfare circulated a questionnaire asserting that "the sale of children is mainly carried out for the purpose of organ transplantation." It then asked: "To what extent and in what ways and forms do these violations of children's rights exist in your country? Please describe."[11]

The stories of organ snatching have an American version. I have heard it from my students, read about it on e-mail, been told about it with great conviction by a Moscow surgeon, and been asked about it by more than a dozen journalists. According to the standard account, a young man meets an attractive woman in a neighborhood bar; they have a few drinks, go back to her place, whereupon he passes out and then wakes up the next morning to find a sewn-up wound on his side. When he seeks medical attention, he learns that he is missing a kidney.

Although there have been sporadically reported stories of robberies of kidneys from people in India, I have not found a single documented case of abduction, mutilation, or murder for organs, whether in North or South America. I was in Guatemala in 1993 when the atrocities are alleged to have occurred, and heard seemingly reliable people say there was convincing evidence for them. I stayed long enough to see every claim against the two American women tourists proven false. Nevertheless, as the anthropologist Nancy Scheper-Hughes argues, the villagers' fears and accusations are understandable in the light of their everyday experience. The bodies of the poor are ordinarily treated so contemptuously that organ snatching does not seem out of character. In Guatemala, babies are regularly kidnapped for sale abroad in the adoption market. Local doctors and health workers admitted to me that "fattening houses" have been set up so that kidnapped babies would be more attractive for adoption.

But it is extremely dangerous to investigate the adoption racket, since highly placed officials in the government and military take a cut of the large sums of money involved. Moreover, Scheper-Hughes continues, if street children in Brazil can be brazenly murdered without recrimination, it is not far-fetched for slum dwellers to believe that the organs of the poor are being removed for sale abroad. And since girls and boys can be kidnapped with impunity to satisfy an international market in sex, why not believe they are also kidnapped to satisfy an international market for organs?[12]

In truth, medical realities make such kidnappings and murder highly unlikely. The rural villages and the urban apartments in which transplants are alleged to secretly take place do not have the sterile environment necessary to remove or implant an organ. Organs from children are too small to be used in adults. And however rapacious health care workers may seem, highly trained and medically sophisticated teams of surgeons, operating room nurses, anesthesiologists, technicians, and blood transfusers are not likely to conspire to murder for organs or accept them off the street. Had they done so, at least one incident would have come to light during the past fifteen years.

5.

The well-documented abuses are bad enough. Is there some way of diminishing them? The Bellagio Task Force, an international group including transplant surgeons, human rights activists, and social scientists, has made several proposals that might be effective if they could be carried out.[13]

Almost all major national and international medical bodies have opposed the sale of organs and the transplantation of organs from executed prisoners; but none of the medical organizations has been willing to take action to enforce their view. The World Medical Association in 1984, 1987, and 1994 condemned "the purchase and sale of human organs for transplantation." But it asks "governments of all countries to take effective steps," and has adopted no measures of its own. It has also criticized the practice of using organs from executed prisoners without their consent; but it fails to ask whether consent on death row can be meaningful. The association leaves it to national medical societies to "severely discipline the physicians involved." Neither it nor any other medical organization has imposed sanctions on violators.

The Bellagio Task Force has posed several challenges to the international medical societies. What would happen if they took their proclaimed principles seriously, established a permanent monitoring body, and kept close surveillance on organ donation practices? What if they threatened to withhold training fellowships from countries which tolerated exploitative practices? What if they refused to hold international meetings in those countries, and, as was the case with South Africa under apartheid, did not allow physicians from those countries to attend their meetings? Why, moreover, couldn't the Novartis company, the manufacturer of cyclosporine, insist that it would sell its product only to doctors and hospitals that meet strict standards in obtaining organs? Such measures would be likely to have a serious effect, certainly in India, probably even in China. But as with the organs themselves, the willingness of doctors to use the moral authority of medicine as a force for change has, so far, been in short supply.

NOTES

1. The data is from the United Network for Organ Sharing (UNOS) Scientific Registry, as of July 5, 1997.
2. Xia Sui-sheng. "Organ Transplantation in China: Retrospect and Prospect," *Chinese Medical Journal*, 105 (1992) pp. 430-432.
3. Edited by Stuart J. Youngner, Renée C. Fox, and Laurence J. O'Connell (University of Wisconsin Press, 1996).
4. "Deadly Disputes: Ideologies and Brain Death in Japan," in Youngner et al., *Organ Transplantation*, pp. 142-167.
5. According to a recent report on CNN's Headline News, there are only 4,000 livers a year being donated. In response to the shortage, the UCLA Medical Center has developed a procedure for dividing livers taken from the cadavers of donors, so that two recipients can share it.
6. "Why Organ Transplant Programs Do Not Succeed," in Youngner et al., *Organ Transplantation*, pp. 56-65.
7. John S. Najarian, Blanche M. Chavers, Lois E. McHugh, and Arthur J. Matas, "20 Years or More of

Follow-Up of Living Kidney Donors," *Lancet*, 340 (October 3, 1992), pp. 807-809.

8. Margaret Jane Radin, *Contested Commodities* (Harvard University Press, 1996), p. 125.
9. "Kidneys Still for Sale," *Frontline*, 14 (December 13-26, 1997), pp. 64-79.
10. This and other examples of lending credence to the rumors may be found in the United States information Agency Report of December 1994. "The Child Organ Trafficking Rumor," written by Todd Leventhal.
11. Vitit Muntarbhorn, "Sale of Children." Report of the Special Rapporteur to the United Nations Commission on Human Rights, January 12, 1993.
12. Nancy Scheper-Hughes, "Theft of Life: The Globalization of Organ Stealing Rumours," *Anthropology Today*, 12 (June 1996), pp. 3-11.
13. D.J. Rothman, E. Rose, et al., "The Bellagio Task Force Report on Transplantation, Bodily Integrity, and the International Traffic in Organs," *Transplantation Proceedings*, 29 (1997), pp. 2739-2745. I am currently serving as chair of the Bellagio group.

EUTHANASIA: THE WAY WE DO IT, THE WAY THEY DO IT

Margaret Battin

Margaret Battin is Professor of Philosophy and adjunct professor of internal medicine, Division of Medical Ethics, University of Utah. She is the author of numerous books including Ethical Issues in Suicide *(Prentice, 1982),* Ethics in the Sanctuary: Examining the Practices of Organized Religion *(Yale, 1990) and* Least Worst Death: Essays in Bioethics on the End of Life *(Oxford, 1994). She is also co-editor of* Changing to National Health Care: Ethical and Policy Issues *(Utah, 1992) and* Physician Assisted Suicide: Expanding the Debate *(Routledge, 1998).*

Battin discusses the morality of euthanasia by providing a critical examination of euthanasia practices in three different societies: Holland, which allows active euthanasia, Germany, which allows assisted suicide but not active euthanasia, and the United States, which allows neither active euthanasia nor assisted suicide. Based on her analysis of these practices situated in their particular contexts of beliefs, values, and social conditions, she concludes that the United States should allow "physician-assisted-suicide."

Introduction

Because we tend to be rather myopic in our discussions of death and dying, especially about the issues of active euthanasia and assisted suicide, it is valuable to place the question of how we go about dying in an international context. We do not always see that our own cultural norms may be quite different from those of other nations, and that our background assumptions, and actual practices, differ dramatically. Thus, I would like to examine the perspectives on end-of-life dilemmas in three countries, the Netherlands, Germany, and the USA.

The Netherlands, Germany, and the United States are all advanced industrial democracies. They all have sophisticated medical establishments and life expectancies over 70 years of age; their populations are all characterized by an increasing proportion of older persons. They are all in what has been called the fourth stage of the epidemiologic transition[1]—that stage of societal development in which it is no longer the case that most people die of acute parasitic or infectious diseases. In this stage, most people do not die of diseases with rapid, unpredictable onsets and sharp fatality curves; rather, the majority of the population—as much as perhaps 70%-80%—dies of degenerative diseases, especially delayed degenerative diseases, that are characterized by late, slow onset and extended decline. Most people in highly industrialized countries die from cancer, atherosclerosis, heart disease (by no means always suddenly fatal), chronic obstructive pulmonary disease, liver, kidney or other organ disease, or degenerative neurological disorders. Thus, all three of these countries are alike in facing a common problem: how to deal with the characteristic new ways in which we die.

Dealing with Dying in the United States

In the United States, we have come to recognize that the maximal extension of life-prolonging treatment in these late-life degenerative conditions is often

---

Reprinted with permission of Elsevier Science from *Journal of Pain and Symptom Management* 6:5 (1991): 298–305.

inappropriate. Although we could keep the machines and tubes—the respirators, intravenous lines, feeding tubes—hooked up for extended periods, we recognize that this is inhumane, pointless, and financially impossible. Instead, as a society we have developed a number of mechanisms for dealing with these hopeless situations, all of which involve withholding or withdrawing various forms of treatment.

Some mechanisms for withholding or withdrawing treatment are exercised by the patient who is confronted by such a situation or who anticipates it; these include refusal of treatment, the patient-executed DNR order, the Living Will, and the Durable Power of Attorney. Others are mechanisms for decision by second parties about a patient who is no longer competent or never was competent. The latter are reflected in a long series of court cases, including *Quinlan, Saikewicz, Spring, Eichner, Barber, Barling, Conroy, Brophy,* the trio *Farrell*, *Peter* and *Jobes*, and *Cruzan*. These are cases that attempt to delineate the precise circumstances under which it is appropriate to withhold or withdraw various forms of therapy, including respiratory support, chemotherapy, antibiotics in intercurrent infections, and artificial nutrition and hydration. Thus, during the past 15 years or so, roughly since *Quinlan* (1976), we have developed an impressive body of case law and state statute that protects, permits, and facilitates our characteristic American strategy of dealing with end-of-life situations. These cases provide a framework for withholding or withdrawing treatment when we believe there is no medical or moral point in going on. This is sometimes termed *passive euthanasia*; more often, it is simply called *allowing to die*, and is ubiquitous in the United States.

For example, a recent study by Miles and Gomez indicates that some 85% of deaths in the United States occur in health-care institutions, including hospitals, nursing homes, and other facilities, and of these, about 70% involve electively withholding some form of life-sustaining treatment.[2] A 1989 study cited in the *Journal of the American Medical Association* claims that 85%-90% of critical care professionals state that they are withholding and withdrawing life-sustaining treatments from patients who are "deemed to have irreversible disease and are terminally ill."[3] Still another study identified some 115 patients in two intensive-care units from whom care was withheld or withdrawn; 110 were already incompetent by the time the decision to limit care was made. The 89 who died while still in the intensive care unit accounted for 45% of all deaths there.[4] It is estimated that 1.3 million American deaths a year follow decisions to withhold life support;[5] this is a majority of the just over 2 million American deaths per year. Withholding and withdrawing treatment is the way we in the USA go about dealing with dying, and indeed "allowing to die" is the only legally protected alternative to maximal treatment recognized in the United States. We do not legally permit ourselves to actively cause death.

Dealing with Dying in the Netherlands

In the Netherlands, voluntary active euthanasia is also an available response to end-of-life situations. Although active euthanasia remains prohibited by statutory law, it is protected by a series of lower and supreme court decisions and is widely regarded as legal, or, more precisely, *gedoeken*, legally "tolerated." These court decisions have the effect of protecting the physician who performs euthanasia from prosecution, provided the physician meets a rigorous set of guidelines.

These guidelines, variously stated, contain five central provisions:

1. that the patient's request be voluntary;
2. that the patient be undergoing intolerable suffering;
3. that all alternatives acceptable to the patient for relieving the suffering have been tried;
4. that the patient have full information;
5. that the patient consult with a second physician whose judgment can be expected to be independent.

Of these criteria, it is the first which is central: euthanasia may be performed only at the voluntary request of the patient. This criterion is also understood to require that the patient's request be a stable, enduring, reflective one—not the product of a transitory impulse. Every attempt is to be made to rule out depression, psychopathology, pressures from family members, unrealistic fears, and other factors compromising voluntariness.

Putting an end to years of inflammatory discussion in which speculation about the frequency of euthanasia had ranged from 2,000 (close to correct) to 20,000 cases a year, a comprehensive study requested by the Dutch government was published in late 1991; an English version appeared in *The Lancet*.[6] Popularly known as the Remmelink Commission report, this study provided the first objective data about the incidence of euthanasia as well as a wider range of medical practices at the end of life: the withholding or withdrawal of treatment, the use of life-shortening doses of opioids for the control of pain, and direct termination, including active euthanasia, physician-assisted suicide, and life-ending procedures not termed euthanasia. This study was supplemented by a second empirical examination, focusing particularly carefully on the characteristics of patients and the nature of their euthanasia requests.[7]

About 130,000 people die in the Netherlands every year, and of these deaths, about 30% are acute and unexpected; 70% are predictable and foreseen, usually the result of degenerative illnesses comparatively late in life. Of the total deaths in the Netherlands, the Remmelink Commissions's study found, about 17.5% involved decisions to withhold or withdraw treatment although continuing treatment would probably have prolonged life; another 17.5% involved the use of opioids to relieve pain but in dosages probably sufficient to shorten life. A total of 2.9% of all deaths involved euthanasia and related practices.

About 2,300 people, 1.8% of the total deaths in the Netherlands, died by euthanasia, understood as the termination of the life of the patient at the patient's explicit and persistent request. Another 400 people, 0.03% of the total, chose physician-assisted suicide. About 1,000 additional patients died as the result of "life-terminating procedures," not technically called euthanasia, in virtually all of which euthanasia had either been previously discussed with the patient or the patient had expressed in a previous phase of the disease a wish for euthanasia if his or her suffering became unbearable, or the patient was near death and clearly suffering grievously, yet verbal contact had become impossible.

Although euthanasia is thus not frequent—a small fraction of the total annual mortality—it is nevertheless a conspicuous option in terminal illness, well known to both physicians and the general public. There has been very widespread public discussion of the issues in euthanasia during the last several years, especially as the pros and cons of full legalization have been debated, and surveys of public opinion show that the public support for a liberal euthanasia policy has been growing: from 40% in 1966 to 81% in 1988.[8] Doctors too support this practice, and although there is a vocal opposition group, the opposition is in the clear minority. Some 54% of Dutch physicians said that they performed euthanasia or provided assistance in suicide; including 62% of *huisarts* or general practitioners, and an additional 34% said that although they had not actually done so, they could conceive of situations in which they would be prepared to do so. Thus, although many who had practiced euthanasia mentioned that they would be most reluctant to do so again and that "only in the face of unbearable suffering and with no alternatives would they be prepared to take such action,"[9] some 88% of Dutch physicians appear to accept the practice in some cases. As the Remmelink Commission commented, " ... a large majority of physicians in the Netherlands see euthanasia as an accepted element if medical practice under certain circumstances."[10]

In general, pain alone is not the basis for euthanasia, since pain can, in most cases, be effectively treated. Rather, "intolerable suffering," among the criteria for euthanasia, is understood to mean suffering that is intolerable in the patient's (rather than the physician's) view, and can include a fear of or unwillingness to endure *entluisterung*, that gradual effacement and loss of personal identity that characterizes the end stages of many terminal illnesses. In a year, about 25,000 patients seek reassurance from their physicians that they will be granted euthanasia if their suffering becomes severe; there are about 9,000 explicit requests, and more than two-thirds of these are turned down, usually on the grounds that there is some other way of treating the patient's suffering, and in just 14% on the grounds of psychiatric illness.

In Holland, many hospitals now have protocols for the performance of euthanasia; these serve to ensure that the court-established guidelines have been met. However, euthanasia is often practiced in the patient's home, typically by the *huisarts* or general practitioner who is the patient's long-term family physician. Euthanasia is usually performed after aggressive hospital treatment has failed to arrest the patient's terminal illness; the patient has come home to die, and the family physician is prepared to ease this passing. Whether practiced at home or in the hospital, it is believed that euthanasia usually takes place in the presence of the family members, perhaps the visiting nurse, and often the patient's pastor or priest. Many doctors say that performing euthanasia is never easy, but that it is something they believe a doctor ought to do for his or her patient, when nothing else can help.

Thus, in Holland a patient facing the end of life has an option not openly practiced in the United States: to ask the physician to bring his or her life to an end. Although not everyone does so—indeed, about 97% of people who die in a given year do not—it is a choice widely understood as available.

Facing Death in Germany

In part because of its very painful history of Nazism, Germany appears to believe that doctors should have no role in causing death. Although societal generalizations are always risky, it is fair, I think, to say that there is vigorous and nearly universal opposition in Germany to the notion of active euthanasia. Euthanasia is viewed as always wrong, and the Germans view the Dutch as stepping out on a dangerously slippery slope.

However, it is an artifact of German law that, whereas killing on request (including voluntary euthanasia) is prohibited, assisting suicide is not a violation of the law, provided the person is *tatherrschaftsfähig*, capable of exercising control over his or her actions, and also acting out of *freiverantworliche Wille*, freely responsible choice. Responding to this situation, there has developed a private organization, the *Deutsche Gesellschaft für Humanes Sterben (DGHS)*, or German Society for Humane Dying, which provides support to its very extensive membership (over 50,000 persons) in choosing suicide as an alternative to terminal illness.

After a person has been a member of the DGHS for at least a year, and provided that he or she has not received medical or psychotherapeutic treatment for depression or other psychiatric illness during the last two years, he or she may request a copy of DGHS's booklet *Menschenwürdiges und selbstverantworliches Sterben*, or "Dignified and Responsible Death." This booklet provides a list of about ten drugs available by prescription in Germany, together with the specific dosages necessary for producing a certain, painless death. (The DGHS no longer officially recommends cyanide, though its president, Hans Henning Atrott, was recently charged with selling it.) DGHS recommends that the members approach a physician for a prescription for the drug desired, asking, for example, for a barbiturate to help with sleep, or chloroquine for protection against malaria on a trip to India. If necessary, the DGHS may also arrange for someone to obtain drugs from neighboring countries, including France, Italy, Spain, Portugal, and Greece, where they may be available without prescription. In unusual cases, the DGHS will also provide what it calls *Sterbebegleitung* or "accompaniment in dying," providing a companion to remain with the person during the often extended period that is required for the lethal drug to take full effect. However, the *Sterbebegleiter* is typically a layperson, not someone medically trained, and physicians play no role in assisting in these cases of suicide. To preclude suspicion by providing evidence of the person's intentions, the DGHS also provides a form—printed on a single sheet of distinctive pink paper—to be signed once when joining the organization, expressing the intention to determine the time of one's own death, and to be signed again at the time of the suicide and left beside the body.

Because assisting suicide is not illegal in Germany, provided the person is competent and in control of his or her own will, there is no legal risk for family members, *Sterbebegleiter*, or others in reporting information about the methods and effectiveness of suicide attempts, and the DGHS encourages its network of regional bureaus (five, in major cities throughout the country) to facilitate feedback. On this basis, it regularly updates and revises the drug information it provides. It claims some 2,000-3,000 suicides per year among its members.

To be sure, assisted suicide is not the only option open to the terminally ill patient in Germany, nor is there clear evidence concerning its frequency either within the DGHS or in non-reported cases outside it. There is increasing emphasis on help in dying that does not involve direct termination, and organizations like Ormega, offering hospice-style care and an extensive program of companionship, are attracting increasing attention. Furthermore, there has been recent scandal directed towards the founder and president of the DGHS, Hans Henning Attrott, accused in late 1991 of selling cyanide to an attorney hospitalized for mental illness; in May 1992 police raided his office, finding capsules of cyanide, barbiturates, and a large amount of cash. What the outcome of this event will be remains at this writing to be seen, though it is clear that the scandal focuses on Atrott's alleged profiteering and assisting a mentally ill person, rather than with the DGHS's regular practice of assisting competent terminally ill individuals in suicide. Furthermore, the DGHS is a conspicuous, widely known organization, and many Germans appear to be aware that assisted suicide is available even if they do not use the services of the DGHS.

Objections to the Three Models of Dying

In response to the dilemmas raised by the new circumstances of death, in which the majority of the population in each of the advanced industrial nations dies of degenerative diseases after an extended period of terminal deterioration, different countries develop different practices. The United States legally permits only withholding and withdrawal of treatment, though of course active euthanasia and assisted suicide do occur. Holland also permits voluntary active euthanasia, and although Germany rejects euthanasia, it tolerates assisted suicide. But there are serious moral objections to be made to each of these practices, objections to be considered before resolving the issue of which practice our own culture ought to adopt.

Objections to the German Practice

German law does not prohibit assisting suicide, but postwar German culture discourages physicians from taking any active role in death. This gives rise to distinctive moral problems. For one thing, it appears that there is little professional help or review provided for patients' choices about suicide; because the patient makes this choice essentially outside the medical establishment, medical professionals are not in a position to detect or treat impaired judgment on the part of the patient, especially judgment impaired by depression. Similarly, if the patient must commit suicide assisted only by persons outside the medical profession, there are risks that the patient's diagnosis and prognosis are inadequately confirmed, that the means chosen for suicide will be unreliable or inappropriately used, that the means used for suicide will fall into the hands of other persons, and that the patient will fail to recognize or be able to resist intrafamilial pressures and manipulation. The DGHS policy for providing assistance requires that the patient be terminally ill and have been a member of the DGHS for at least one year in order to make use of its services, the latter requirement is intended to provide evidence of the stability of such a choice. However, these minimal requirements are hardly sufficient to answer the charge that suicide decisions, which are made for medical reasons but must be made without medical help, may be rendered under less than ideally informed and voluntary conditions.

Objections to the Dutch Practice

The Dutch practice of physician-performed active voluntary euthanasia also raises a number of ethical issues, many of which have been discussed vigorously both in the Dutch press and in commentary on the Dutch practices from abroad. For one thing, it is sometimes said that the availability of physician-performed euthanasia creates a disincentive for providing good terminal care. I have seen no evidence that this is the case; on the contrary, Peter Admiraal, the anesthesiologist who is perhaps Holland's most vocal proponent of voluntary active euthanasia, insists that pain should rarely or never be the occasion for euthanasia, as pain (in contrast to suffering) is comparatively easily treated.[11] Instead, it is a refusal to endure the final stages of deterioration, both mental and physical, that motivates requests.

It is also sometimes said that active euthanasia violates the Hippocratic Oath. Indeed, it is true that the original Greek version of the Oath prohibits the physician from giving a deadly drug, even when asked for it; but the original version also prohibits performing surgery and taking fees for teaching medicine, neither of which prohibitions has survived into contemporary medical practice. Dutch physicians often say that they see performing euthanasia—where it is genuinely requested by the patient and nothing else can be done to relieve the patient's condition—as part of their duty to the patient, not as a violation of it.

The Dutch are also often said to be at risk of starting down the slippery slope, that is, that the practice of voluntary active euthanasia for patients who meet the criteria will erode into practicing less-than-voluntary euthanasia on patients whose problems are not irremediable, and perhaps by gradual degrees develop into terminating the lives of people who are elderly, chronically ill, handicapped, mentally retarded, or otherwise regarded as undesirable. This risk is often expressed in vivid claims of widespread fear and wholesale slaughter, claims that are repeated in the right-to-life press in both the Netherlands, and the USA, though there is no evidence for these claims. However, the Dutch are now beginning to agonize over the problems of the incompetent patient, the mentally ill patient, the newborn with serious deficits, and other patients who cannot make voluntary choices, though these are largely understood as issues about withholding or withdrawing treatment, not about direct termination.[12]

What is not often understood is that this new and acutely painful area of reflection for the Dutch—withholding and withdrawing treatment from incompetent patients—has already led in the United States to the development of a vast, highly developed body of law: namely that series of cases just cited, beginning with *Quinlan* and culminating in *Cruzan*. Americans have been discussing these issues for a long time, and have developed a broad set of practices that are regarded as routine in withholding and withdrawing treatment. The Dutch see Americans as much further out on the slippery slope than they are, because Americans have already become accustomed to second-party choices about other people. Issues involving second-party choices are painful to the Dutch in a way they are not to us precisely because *voluntariness* is so central in the Dutch understanding of choices about dying. Concomitantly, the Dutch see the Americans' squeamishness about first-party choices—voluntary euthanasia, assisted suicide—as evidence that we are not genuinely committed to recognizing *voluntary* choice after all. For this reason, many Dutch commentators believe that the Americans are at a much greater risk of sliding down the slippery slope into involuntary killing than they are. I fear, I must add, that they are right about this.

Objections to the American Practice

There may be moral problems raised by the German and the Dutch practices, but there are also moral problems raised by the American practice of relying on withholding and withdrawal of treatment in end-of-life situations. The German, Dutch, and American practices all occur within similar conditions—in industrialized nations with highly developed medical systems, where a majority of the population dies of illnesses exhibiting characteristically extended downhill courses—but the issues raised by our own response to this situation may be even more disturbing than those of the Dutch or the Germans. We often assume that our approach is "safer" because it involves only letting someone die, not killing him or her; but it too raises very troubling questions.

The first of these issues is a function of the fact that withdrawing and especially withholding treatment are typically less conspicuous, less pronounced, less evident kinds of actions than direct killing, even though they can equally well lead to death. Decisions about nontreatment have an invisibility that decisions about directly causing death do not have, even though they may have the same result, and hence there is a much wider range of occasions in which such decisions can be made. One can decline to treat a patient in many different ways, at many different times—by not providing oxygen, by not instituting dialysis, by not correcting electrolyte imbalances, and so on—all of which will cause the patient's death; open medical killing also brings about death, but is a much more overt, conspicuous procedure. Consequently, letting die also invites many fewer protections. In contrast to the standard slippery slope argument which sees killing as riskier than letting die, the more realistic slippery slope argument warns that because our culture relies primarily on decisions about nontreatment, grave decisions about living or dying are not as open to scrutiny as they are under more direct life-terminating practices, and hence, are more open to abuse.

Second, and closely related, reliance on withholding and withdrawing treatment invites rationing in an extremely strong way, in part because of the comparative invisibility of these decisions. When a health care provider does not offer a specific sort of care, it is not always possible to discern the motivation; the line between believing that it would not provide benefit to the patient and that it would not provide benefit worth the investment of resources in the patient can be very thin. This is a particular problem where health care financing is highly decentralized, as in the United States, and where rationing decisions without benefit of principle are not always available for easy review.

Third, relying on withholding and withdrawal of treatment can often be cruel. It requires that the patient who is dying from one of the diseases that exhibits a characteristic extended, downhill course (as the majority of patients in the Netherlands, Germany and the U.S. do) must in effect wait to die until the absence of a certain treatment will cause death. For instance, the cancer patient who foregoes chemotherapy or surgery does not simply die from this choice; he or she continues to endure the downhill course of cancer until the tumor finally destroys some crucial bodily function or organ. The patient with amyotrophic lateral sclerosis who decides in advance to decline respiratory support does not die at the time the choice is made, but continues to endure increasing paralysis until breathing is impaired and suffocation occurs. We often try to ameliorate these situations by administering pain medication or symptom control at the same time we are withholding treatment, but these are all ways of disguising the fact that we are letting the disease kill the patient rather than directly bringing about death. But the ways diseases kill people are far more cruel than the ways physicians kill patients when performing euthanasia or assisting in suicide.

The Problem: A Choice of Cultures

Thus we see three similar cultures and countries and three similar sets of circumstances, but three different basic practices in approaching death. All three of these practices generate moral problems; none of them, nor any others we might devise, is free of moral difficulty. But the question that faces us is this: which of these practices is best?

It is not possible to answer this question in a less-than-ideal world without some attention to the specific characteristics and deficiencies of the society in question. In asking which of these practices is best, we must ask which is best *for us*. That we currently employ one set of these practices rather than others does not prove that it is best for us; the question is, would practices developed in other cultures or those not yet widespread in any be better for our own culture than that which has developed here? Thus, it is necessary to consider the differences between our society and these European cultures that have real bearing on which model of approach to dying we ought to adopt.

First, notice that different cultures exhibit different degrees of closeness between physicians and patients—different patterns of contact and involvement. The German physician is sometimes said to be more distant and more authoritarian than the American physician; on the other hand, the Dutch physician is sometimes said to be closer to his or her patients than either the American or the German is. In the Netherlands, basic primary care is provided by the *huisarts*, the general practitioner or family physician, who typically lives in the neighborhood, makes house calls frequently, and maintains an office in his or her own home. The *huisarts* is usually the physician for other members of the patient's family, and will remain the family's physician throughout his or her practice. Thus, the patient for whom euthanasia becomes an issue—say, the terminal cancer patient who has been hospitalized in the past but who has returned home to die—will be cared for by the trusted family physician on a regular basis. Indeed, for a patient in severe distress, the physician, supported by the visiting nurse, may make house calls as often as once a day, twice a day, or more (after all, it is right in the neighborhood), and is in continuous contact with the family. In contrast, the traditional American institution of the family doctor who makes house calls is rapidly becoming a thing of the past, and although some patients who die at home have access to hospice services and house-calls from their long-term physician, many have no such long-term care and receive most of it from staff at a clinic or housestaff rotating through the services of a hospital. The degree of continuing contact the patient can have with a familiar, trusted physician clearly influences the nature of his or her dying, and also plays a role in whether physician-performed active euthanasia, assisted suicide, and/or withholding and withdrawing treatment is appropriate.

Second, the United States has a much more volatile legal climate than either the Netherlands of Germany; our medical system is increasingly litigious, much more so than that of any other country in the world. Fears of malpractice action or criminal prosecution color much of what physicians do in managing the dying of their patients. We also tend to evolve public policy through court decisions, and to assume that the existence of a policy puts an end to any moral issue. A delicate legal and moral balance over the issue of euthanasia, as is the case in the Netherlands, would not be possible here.

Third, we in the United States have a very different financial climate in which to do our dying. Both the Netherlands and Germany, as well as every other industrialized nation except South Africa, have systems of national health insurance or national health care. Thus the patient is not directly responsible for the costs of treatment, and consequently the patient's choices about terminal care and/or euthanasia need not take personal financial considerations into account. Even for the patient who does have health insurance in the United States, many kinds of services are not covered, whereas the national health care or health insurance programs of many other countries variously provide many sorts of relevant services, including at-home physician care, home nursing care, home respite care, care in a nursing-home or other long-term facility, dietitian care, rehabilitation care, physical therapy, psychological counseling, and so on. The patient in the United States needs to attend to the financial aspects of dying in a way patients in many other countries do not, and in this country both the patient's choices and the recommendations of the physician are very often shaped by financial considerations.

There are many other differences between the USA on the one hand and the Netherlands and Germany, with their different models of dying, on the other. There are differences in degrees of paternalism in the medical establishment and in racism, sexism, and ageism in the general cultures, as well as awareness of a problematic historical past, especially Nazism. All of these and the previous factors influence the appropriateness or inappropriateness of practices such as active euthanasia and assisted suicide. For instance, the Netherlands' tradition of close physician/patient contact, its absence of malpractice-motivated medicine, and its provision of comprehensive health insurance, together with its comparative lack of racism and ageism and its experience in resistance to Nazism, suggest that this culture is able to permit the practice of voluntary active euthanasia, performed by physicians, without risking abuse. On the other hand, it is sometimes said that Germany still does not trust its physicians, remembering the example of Nazi experimentation, and given a comparatively authoritarian medical climate in which contact between physician and patient is quite distanced, the population could not be comfortable with the practice of active euthanasia. There, only a wholly patient-controlled response to terminal situations, as in non-physician-assisted suicide, is a reasonable and prudent practice.

But what about the United States? This is a country where (1) sustained contact with the personal physician is decreasing, (2) the risk of malpractice action is increasing, (3) much medical care is not insured, (4) many medical decisions are financial decisions as well, (5) racism is on the rise, and (6) the public is naive about direct contact with Nazism or similar totalitarian movements. Thus, the United States is in many respects an untrustworthy candidate for practicing active euthanasia. Given the pressures on individuals in an often atomized society, encouraging solo suicide, assisted if at all only by nonprofessionals, might well be open to considerable abuse too.

However, there are several additional differences between the United States and both Holland and Germany that seem relevant here.

So far, the differences cited between the U.S. and both the Netherlands and Germany are negative ones, ones in which the U.S. falls far short. But there are positive differences as well, differences in which distinctive aspects of American culture are more favorable than those of Holland or Germany to the practice of euthanasia and assisted suicide. For example:

First, although the U.S. is indeed afflicted by a great deal of racism and sexism, it is also developing an increasingly strong tradition of independence in women. In many other countries, especially the Far East and the Islamic countries, the role of women still involves much greater disempowerment and expectations of subservience; in contrast, the U.S. is particularly advanced—though, of course, it has a long way to go. The U.S. may even be ahead of the Netherlands and perhaps Germany in this respect. Whatever the case, this issue is of particular importance with respect to euthanasia, especially among elderly persons, because it is women whose life expectancies are longer than those of men and hence are more likely to be confronted with late-life degenerative terminal conditions.

Second, American culture is more confrontational than many others, including Dutch culture. While the Netherlands prides itself rightly on a long tradition of rational discussion of public issues and on toleration of others' views and practices, the U.S. (and to some degree, also Germany) tends to develop highly partisan, moralizing oppositional groups. In general, this is a disadvantage; but in the case of euthanasia it may serve to alert a public to issues and possibilities it might not otherwise consider, and especially to the risks of abuse.

Third, though this may at first seem to be a trivial difference, it is Americans who are particularly given to personal self-analysis. This tendency is evident not only in America's high rate of utilization of counseling services, including religious counseling, psychological counseling, and psychiatry, but is even more clearly evident in its popular culture: its diet of soap operas, situation comedies, and pop psychology books. It is here that the ordinary American absorbs models for analyzing his or her own personal relationships and individual psychological characteristics. While of course things are changing and our cultural tastes are widely exported, the fact remains that the ordinary American's cultural diet contains more in the way of both professional and do-it-yourself amateur psychology and self-analysis than anyone else's. This long tradition of self-analysis may put us in a better position for certain kinds of end-of-life practices than many other cultures—despite whatever other deficiencies we have, just because we live in a culture that encourages us to inspect our own motives, anticipate the impact of our actions on others and scrutinize our own relationships with others, including our physicians. This disposition is of importance in euthanasia contexts because euthanasia is the kind of fundamental choice about which one may have somewhat mixed motives, be subject to various interpersonal and situational pressures, and so on. If the voluntary character of these choices is to be protected, it may be a good thing to inhabit a culture in which self-inspection of one's own mental habits and motives is encouraged.

Finally, the U.S. is also characterized by a kind of "do-it-yourself" ethic, an ethic that does not rely on others to direct you or provide for you, but encourages individual initiative and responsibility. (To be sure this feature has been somewhat eclipsed in recent years, and is little in evidence in the series of court cases cited earlier, but it is still part, I think, of the American character.) This is coupled with a sort of resistance to authority that is sometimes also said to be basic to the American temperament. If these things are the case, it would seem to suggest that Americans would seek a style of end-of-life practices which would emphasize these characteristics rather than others.

These, of course, are all mere conjectures about features of American culture which would have a positive effect on the practice of euthanasia, or assisted suicide. These are the features that one would want to reinforce, should these practices become general, in part to minimize the effects of the negative features. But, of course, these positive features will differ from one country and culture to another, just as negative features do. In each country, a different architecture of antecedent assumptions and cultural features develops around the issues of the end of life, and in each country the practice of euthanasia, if it is to be free from abuse at all, must be adapted to the culture in which it takes place.

What, then, is appropriate for our own cultural situation? Physician-performed euthanasia, though not in itself morally wrong, is morally jeopardized where the legal, time, and especially financial pressures on both patients and physicians are severe; thus it is morally problematic in our culture in a way that it is not in the Netherlands. Solo suicide outside the institution of medicine (as in Germany) may be problematic in a culture (like the United States) that is increasingly alienated, offers deteriorating and uneven social services, is increasingly racist, and in other ways imposes unusual pressures on individuals despite opportunities for self-analysis. Reliance only on withholding and withdrawing treatment (as in the United States) can be, as we've seen, cruel, and its comparative invisibility invites erosion under cost containment and other pressures. These are the three principal alternatives we've considered; but none of them seems wholly suited to our actual situation for dealing with the new fact that most of us die of extended-decline, deteriorative diseases. However, permitting physicians to supply patients with the means for ending their own lives grants physicians some control over the circumstances in which this can happen—only, for example, when the prognosis is genuinely grim and the alternatives for symptom control are poor—but leaves the fundamental decision about whether to use these means to the patient alone. It is up to the patient then—the independent, confrontational self-analyzing, do-it-yourself, authority-resisting patient—and his or her advisors, including family, clergy, physician, other health-care providers, and a raft of pop-psychology books, to be clear about whether he or she really wants to use these means or not. Thus, the physician is involved, but not directly; and it is the patient's choice, but the patient is not alone in making it. We live in a quite imperfect world, but, of the alternatives for facing death—which we all eventually must—I think the practice of permitting physician-assisted suicide is the one most nearly suited to the current state of our own somewhat flawed society. This is a model not yet central in any of the three countries examined here—the Netherlands, Germany, or the United States—but it is the one I think suits us best.

NOTES

1. Olshansky S.J., Ault A.B. The fourth stage of the epidemiological transition: the age of delayed degenerative diseases. *Milbank Memorial Fund Quarterly/ Health and Society* 1986;64:355-391.
2. Miles S., Gomez C. *Protocols for elective use of life-sustaining treatment.* New York: Springer-Verlag. 1988.
3. Sprung C.L. Changing attitudes and practices in foregoing life-sustaining treatments. *JAMA* 1990; 263:2213.
4. Smedira N.G. et al. Withholding and withdrawal of life support from the critically ill. *N.Engl J Med* 1990; 322:309-315.
5. *New York Times*, July 23, 1990, p. A13.
6. Paul J. Van der Maas, Johannes J.M. vanDelden, Loes Pijnenborg, and Casper W.N. Looman, "Euthanasia and Other Medical Decisions Concerning the End of Life," *The Lancet* 338 (Sept. 14 1991): 669-674.
7. G. Van der Wal, J.Th. M. Van Eijk, H.J.J. Leenen and C. Spreeuwenberg, "Euthanasie en hulp bij selfdoding door artsen in the thuissituatie. I. Diagnosen, leeftijd en geslacht van de patienten," *Nederlands Tijdschrift voor Geneesekunde* 135 (1991): 1593-1598: and II. "Lijden van de patienten," 1500-1603.
8. Else Borst-Eilers, paper delivered at the conference "Controversies in the Care of Dying Patients," University of Florida, Orlando, Feb. 14-16, 1991.
9. Van der Maas, p. 673.
10. Van der Maas, p. 671.
11. Admiraal P. *Euthanasia in a general hospital.* Address to the Eighth World Congress of the International Federation of Right-To-Die Societies, Maastricht. Holland. June 8, 1990.
12. Ten Have, H. "Coma: controversy and consensus." *Newsletter of the European Society for Philosophy of Medicine and Health Care* (May 1990) 8:19-20.

WHEN SELF-DETERMINATION RUNS AMOK

Daniel Callahan

Daniel Callahan is President of The Hastings Center. He is the author of Setting Limits: Medical Goals in an Aging Society *(Schuster, 1987) and* What Kind of Life: the Limits of Medical Progress *(Schuster, 1990) and co-editor of* What Price Mental Health? The Ethics and Politics of Setting Priorities *(Georgetown, 1995) and* A World of Growing Old: The Coming Health Care Challenges *(Georgetown, 1995).*

Callahan considers and rejects four kinds of arguments in favor of active euthanasia. First, he argues that the notion that one person can end the life of another by appeal to a private view of the good life demeans rather than respects the notions of self-determination and autonomy. Second, he raises objections to the argument that there is no moral difference between killing and allowing to die. Third, he argues against those who claim that there is little evidence to show that likely harmful consequences will result from legalizing euthanasia. Lastly, he criticizes the view that euthanasia and assisted suicide are compatible with the aims of medicine.

The euthanasia debate is not just another moral debate, one in a long list of arguments in our pluralistic society. It is profoundly emblematic of three important turning points in Western thought. The first is that of the legitimate conditions under which one person can kill another. The acceptance of voluntary active euthanasia would morally sanction what can only be called "consenting adult killing." By that term I mean the killing of one person by another in the name of their mutual right to be a killer and killed if they freely agree to play those roles. This turn flies in the face of a longstanding effort to limit the circumstances under which one person can take the life of another, from efforts to control the free flow of guns and arms, to abolish capital punishment, and to more tightly control warfare. Euthanasia would add a whole new category of killing to a society that already has too many excuses to indulge itself in that way.

The second turning point lies in the meaning and limits of self-determination. The acceptance of euthanasia would sanction a view of autonomy holding that individuals may, in the name of their own private, idiosyncratic view of the good life, call upon others, including such institutions as medicine, to help them pursue that life, even at the risk of harm to the common good. This works against the idea that the meaning and scope of our own right to lead our own lives must be conditioned by, and be compatible with, the good of the community, which is more than an aggregate of self-directing individuals.

The third turning point is to be found in the claim being made upon medicine: it should be prepared to make its skills available to individuals to help them achieve their private vision of the good life. This puts medicine in the business of promoting the individualistic pursuit of general human happiness and well-being. It would overturn the traditional belief that medicine should limit its domain to promoting and preserving human health, redirecting it instead to the relief of that suffering which stems from life itself, not merely from a sick body.

Reprinted with permission of The Hastings Center from *Hastings Center Report* (March–April 1992): 52–55.

I believe that, at each of these three turning points, proponents of euthanasia push us in the wrong direction. Arguments in favor of euthanasia fall into four general categories, which I will take up in turn: (1) the moral claim of individual self-determination and well-being; (2) the moral irrelevance of the difference between killing and allowing to die; (3) the supposed paucity of evidence to show likely harmful consequences of legalized euthanasia; and (4) the compatibility of euthanasia and medical practice.

Self-Determination

Central to most arguments for euthanasia is the principle of self-determination. People are presumed to have an interest in deciding for themselves, according to their own beliefs about what makes life good, how they will conduct their lives. That is an important value, but the question in the euthanasia context is, What does it mean and how far should it extend? If it were a question of suicide, where a person takes her own life without assistance from another, that principle might be pertinent, at least for debate. But euthanasia is not that limited a matter. The self-determination in that case can only be effected by the moral and physical assistance of another. Euthanasia is thus no longer a matter only of self-determination, but of a mutual, social decision between two people, the one to be killed and the other to do the killing.

How are we to make the moral move from my right of self-determination to some doctor's right to kill me—from *my* right to *his* right? Where does the doctor's moral warrant to kill come from? Ought doctors to be able to kill anyone they want as long as permission is given by competent persons? Is our right to life just like a piece of property, to be given away or alienated if the price (happiness, relief of suffering) is right? And then to be destroyed with our permission once alienated?

In answer to all those questions, I will say this: I have yet to hear a plausible argument why it should be permissible for us to put this kind of power in the hands of another, whether a doctor or anyone else. The idea that we can waive our right to life, and then give to another the power to take that life, requires a justification yet to be provided by anyone.

Slavery was long ago outlawed on the ground that one person should not have the right to own another, even with the other's permission. Why? Because it is a fundamental moral wrong for one person to give over his life and fate to another, whatever the good consequences, and no less a wrong for another person to have that kind of total, final power. Like slavery, dueling was long ago banned on similar grounds: even free, competent individuals should not have the power to kill each other, whatever their motives, whatever the circumstances. Consenting adult killing, like consenting adult slavery or degradation, is a strange route to human dignity.

There is another problem as well. If doctors, once sanctioned to carry out euthanasia, are to be themselves responsible moral agents—not simply hired hands with lethal injections at the ready—then they must have their own *independent* moral grounds to kill those who request such services. What do I mean? As those who favor euthanasia are quick to point out, some people want it because their life has become so burdensome it no longer seems worth living.

The doctor will have a difficulty at this point. The degree and intensity to which people suffer from their diseases and their dying, and whether they find life more of a burden than a benefit, has very little directly to do with the nature or extent of their actual physical condition. Three people can have the same condition, but only one will find the suffering unbearable. People suffer, but suffering is as much a function of the values of individuals as it is of the physical causes of that suffering. Inevitably in that circumstance, the doctor will in effect be treating the patient's values. To be responsible, the doctor would have to share those values. The doctor would have to decide, on her own, whether the patient's life was "no longer worth living."

But how could a doctor possibly know that or make such a judgment? Just because the patient said so? I raise this question because, while in Holland at the euthanasia conference reported by Maurice the Wachter elsewhere in this issue, the doctors present agreed that there is no objective way of measuring or judging the claims of patients that their suffering is unbearable. And if it is difficult to measure suffering, how much more difficult to determine the value of a patient's statement that her life is not worth living?

However one might want to answer such questions, the very need to ask them, to inquire into the physician's responsibility and grounds for medical and moral judgment, points out the social nature of the decision. Euthanasia is not a private matter of self-determination. It is an act that requires two people to make it possible, and a complicit society to make it acceptable.

Killing and Allowing to Die

Against common opinion, the argument is sometimes made that there is no moral difference between stopping life-sustaining treatment and more active forms of killing, such as lethal injection. Instead I would content that the notion that there is no morally significant difference between omission and commission is just wrong. Consider in its broad implications what the eradication of the distinction implies: that death from disease has been banished, leaving only the actions of physicians in terminating treatment as the cause of death. Biology, which used to bring about death, has apparently been displaced by human agency. Doctors have finally, I suppose, thus genuinely become gods, now doing what nature and the deities once did.

What is the mistake here? It lies in confusing causality and culpability, and in failing to note the way in which human societies have overlaid natural causes with moral rules and interpretations. Causality (by which I mean the direct physical causes of death) and culpability (by which I mean our attribution of moral responsibility to human actions) are confused under three circumstances.

They are confused, first, when the action of a physician in stopping treatment of a patient with an underlying lethal disease is construed as *causing* death. On the contrary, the physician's omission can only bring about death on the condition that the patient's disease will kill him in the absence of treatment. We may hold the physician morally responsible for the death, if we have morally judged such actions wrongful omissions. But it confuses reality and moral judgment to see an omitted action as having the same causal status as one that directly kills. A lethal injection will kill both a healthy person and a sick person. A physician's omitted treatment will have no effect on a healthy person. Turn off the machine on me, a healthy person, and nothing will happen. It will only, in contrast, bring the life of a sick person to an end because of an underlying fatal disease.

Causality and culpability are confused, second, when we fail to note that judgments of moral responsibility and culpability are human constructs. By that I mean that we human beings, after moral reflection, have decided to call some actions right or wrong, and to devise moral rules to deal with them. When physicians could do nothing to stop death, they were not held responsible for it. When, with medical progress, they began to have some power over death—but only its timing and circumstances, not its ultimate inevitability—moral rules were devised to set forth their obligations. Natural causes of death were not thereby banished. They were, instead, overlaid with a medical ethics designed to determine moral culpability in deploying medical power.

To confuse the judgments of this ethics with the physical causes of death—which is the connotation of the word *kill*—is to confuse nature and human action. People will, one way or another, die of some disease; death will have dominion over all of us. To say that a doctor "kills" a patient by allowing this to happen should only be understood as a moral judgment about the licitness of his omission, nothing more. We can, as a fashion of speech only, talk about a doctor *killing* a patient by omitting treatment he should have provided. It is a fashion of speech precisely because it is the underlying disease that brings death when treatment is omitted; that is its cause, not the physician's omission. It is a misuse of the work *killing* to use it when a doctor stops a treatment he believes will no longer benefit the patient—when, that is, he steps aside to allow an eventually inevitable death to occur now rather than later. The only deaths that human beings invented are those that come from direct killing—when, with a lethal injection, we both cause death and are morally responsible for it. In the case of omissions, we do not cause death even if we may be judged morally responsible for it.

This difference between causality and culpability also helps us see why a doctor who has omitted a treatment he should have provided has "killed" that patient while another doctor—performing precisely the same act of omission on another patient in different circumstances—does not kill her, but only allows her to die. The difference is that we have come, by moral convention and conviction, to classify unauthorized or illegitimate omissions as acts of "killing." We call them "killing" in the expanded sense of the term: a culpable action that permits the real cause of death, the underlying disease, to proceed to its lethal conclusion. By contrast, the doctor who, at the patient's request, omits or terminates unwanted treatment does not kill at all. Her underlying disease, not his action, is the physical cause of death; and we have agreed to consider actions of that kind to be morally licit. He thus can truly be said to have "allowed" her to die.

If we fail to maintain the distinction between killing and allowing to die, moreover, there are some disturbing possibilities. The first would be to confirm many physicians in their already too powerful belief that, when patients die or when physicians stop treatment because of the futility of continuing it, they are somehow both morally and physically responsible for the deaths that follow. That notion needs to be abolished, not strengthened. It needlessly and wrongly burdens the physician, to whom should not be attributed the powers of the gods. The second possibility would be that, in every case where a doctor judges medical treatment no longer effective in prolonging life, a quick and direct killing of the patient would be seen as the next, most reasonable step, on grounds of both humaneness and economics. I do not see how that logic could easily be rejected.

Calculating the Consequences

When concerns about the adverse social consequences of permitting euthanasia are raised, its advocates tend to dismiss them as unfounded and overly speculative. On the contrary, recent data about the Dutch experience suggests that such concerns are right on target. From my own discussions in Holland, and from the articles on that subject in this issue and elsewhere, I believe we can now fully see most of the *likely* consequences of legal euthanasia.

Three consequences seem almost certain, in this or any other country: the inevitability of some abuse of the law; the difficulty of precisely writing, and then enforcing, the law; and the inherent slipperiness of the moral reasons for legalizing euthanasia in the first place.

Why is abuse inevitable? One reason is that almost all laws on delicate, controversial matters are to some extent abused. This happens because not everyone will agree with the law as written and will bend it, or ignore it, if they can get away with it. From explicit admissions to me by Dutch proponents of euthanasia, and from the corroborating information provided by the Remmelink Report and the outside studies of Carlos Gomez and John Keown, I am convinced that in the Netherlands there are a substantial number of cases of nonvoluntary euthanasia, that is, euthanasia undertaken without the explicit permission of the person being killed. The other reason abuse is inevitable is that the law is likely to have a low enforcement priority in the criminal justice system. Like other laws of similar status, unless there is an unrelenting and harsh willingness to pursue abuse, violations will ordinarily be tolerated. The worst thing to me about my experience in Holland was the casual, seemingly indifferent attitude toward abuse. I think that would happen everywhere.

Why would it be hard to precisely write, and then enforce, the law? The Dutch speak about the requirement of "unbearable" suffering, but admit that such a term is just about indefinable, a highly subjective matter admitting of no objective standards. A requirement for outside opinion is nice, but it is easy to find complaisant colleagues. A requirement that a medical condition be "terminal" will run aground on the notorious difficulties of knowing when an illness is actually terminal.

Apart from those technical problems there is a more profound worry. I see no way, even in principle, to write or enforce a meaningful law that can guarantee effective procedural safeguards. The reason is obvious yet almost always overlooked. The euthanasia transaction will ordinarily take place within the boundaries of the private and confidential doctor-patient relationship. No one can possibly know what takes place in that context unless the doctor chooses to reveal it. In Holland, less than 10 percent of the physicians report their acts of euthanasia and do so with almost complete legal impunity. There is no reason why the situation should be any better elsewhere. Doctors will have their own reasons for keeping euthanasia secret, and some patients will have no less a motive for wanting it concealed.

I would mention, finally, that the moral logic of the motives for euthanasia contain within them the ingredients of abuse. The two standard motives for euthanasia and assisted suicide are said to be our right of self-determination, and our claim upon the mercy of others, especially doctors, to relieve our suffering. These two motives are typically spliced together and presented as a single justification. Yet if they are considered independently—and there is no inherent reason why they must be linked—they reveal serious problems. It is said that a competent, adult person should have a right to euthanasia for the relief of suffering. But why must the person be suffering? Does not that stipulation already compromise the principle of self-determination? How can self-determination have any limits? Whatever the person's motives may be, why are they not sufficient?

Consider next the person who is suffering but not competent, who is perhaps demented or mentally retarded. The standard argument would deny euthanasia to that person. But why? If a person is suffering but not competent, then it would seem grossly unfair to deny relief solely on the grounds of incompetence. Are the incompetent less entitled to relief from suffering than the competent? Will it only be affluent, middle-class people, mentally fit and savvy about working the medical system, who can qualify? Do the incompetent suffer less because of their incompetence?

Considered from these angles, there are no good moral reasons to limit euthanasia once the principle of taking life for that purpose has been legitimated. If we really believe in self-determination, then any competent person should have a right to be killed by a doctor for any reason that suits him. If we believe in the relief of suffering, then it seems cruel and capricious to deny it to the incompetent. There is, in short, no reasonable or logical stopping point once the turn has been made down the road to euthanasia, which could soon turn into a convenient and commodious expressway.

Euthanasia and Medical Practice

A fourth kind of argument one often hears both in the Netherlands and in this country is that euthanasia and assisted suicide are perfectly compatible with the aims of medicine. I would note at the very outset that a physician who participates in another person's suicide already abuses medicine. Apart from depression (the main statistical cause of suicide), people commit suicide because they find life empty, oppressive, or meaningless. Their judgment is a judgment about the value of continued life, not only about health (even if they are sick). Are doctors now to be given the right to make judgments about the kinds of life worth living and to give their blessing to suicide for those they judge wanting? What conceivable competence, technical or moral, could doctors claim to play such a role? Are we to medicalize suicide, turning judgments about its worth and value into one more clinical issue? Yes, those are rhetorical questions.

Yet they bring us to the core of the problem of euthanasia and medicine. The great temptation of modern medicine, not always resisted, is to move beyond the promotion and preservation of health into the boundless realm of general human happiness and well-being. The root problem of illness and mortality is both medical and philosophical or religious. "Why must I die?" can be asked as a technical, biological question or as a question about the meaning of life. When medicine tries to respond to the latter, which it is always under pressure to do, it moves beyond its proper role.

It is not medicine's place to lift from us the burden of that suffering which turns on the meaning we assign to the decay of the body and its eventual death. It is not medicine's place to determine when lives are not worth living or when the burden of life is too great to be borne. Doctors have no conceivable way of evaluating such claims on the part of patients, and they should have no right to act in response to them. Medicine should try to relive human suffering, but only that suffering which is brought on by illness and dying as biological phenomena, not that suffering which comes from anguish or despair at the human condition.

Doctors ought to relieve those forms of suffering that medically accompany serious illness and the threat of death. They should relive pain, do what they can to allay anxiety and uncertainty, and be a comforting presence. As sensitive human beings, doctors should be prepared to respond to patients who ask why they must die, or die in pain. But here the doctor and the patient are at the same level. The doctor may have no better an answer to those old questions than anyone else; and certainly no special insight from his training as a physician. It would be terrible for physicians to forget this, and to think that in a swift, lethal injection, medicine has found its own answer to the riddle of life. It would be a false answer, given by the wrong people. It would be no less a false answer for patients. They should neither ask medicine to put its own vocation at risk to serve their private interests, nor think that the answer to suffering is to be killed by another. The problem is precisely that, too often in human history, killing has seemed the quick, efficient way to put aside that which burdens us. It rarely helps, and too often simply adds to one evil still another. That is what I believe euthanasia would accomplish. It is self-determination run amok.

DEMENTIA, CRITICAL INTERESTS, AND EUTHANASIA

Nathan Brett

Nathan Brett teaches Philosophy at Dalhousie University in Nova Scotia. His publications in legal and social philosophy include discussions of equality, rights, mercy, and consent.

An Alzheimer's patient (Margo) has left an advance directive requesting euthanasia if her disease leaves her demented. Four years later it has in fact left her severely demented. However, she now appears to be enjoying life. How good is the case for following her directive and ending her life? The first section of the paper defends Ronald Dworkin's view that both the principle of autonomy and the "best interests" standard provide reasons for following Margo's advance directive. But, Part II raises doubts about killing Margo by raising questions about personal identity.

> The apartment had many locks to keep Margo from slipping out at night and wandering in the park in her nightgown, which she had done before.... She said she was reading mysteries, but [the psychologist who was studying her] 'noticed that her place in the book jumps randomly from day to day; dozens of pages are dog-eared at any given moment. Maybe she feels good just sitting and humming to herself, rocking back and forth slowly, nodding off liberally, occasionally turning to a fresh page.' Margo attended an art class for Alzheimer's victims—they all, including her, painted pretty much the same picture every time, except near the end, just before death, when they became more primitive.
>
> [The psychologist reported that] '...Margo is undeniably one of the happiest people I have ever known.' He noted particularly her pleasure at eating peanut butter and jelly sandwiches.[1]

To this account of the life of an Alzheimer's patient, I want to add a few details which do not in fact belong to Margo's case, though they could easily have been a feature of other cases involving Alzheimer's patients. Margo, a citizen of Holland, has signed a living will giving an advance directive to her caretakers. If the disease has resulted in a substantial loss of memory and other mental capacities when she is evaluated on her 60th birthday, her life is to be ended through an overdose of painkillers.[2] This advance directive was written when Margo was 56, shortly after she received the diagnosis that she had Alzheimer's, and before the condition became advanced enough to undermine her powers of reason. In fact, it was precisely because she dreaded the prospect of living for some time in the condition of dementia which she is now in, that Margo had drawn up this directive.

Needless to say, the hospital committee charged with the examination of this case is troubled. Not only does Margo appear now to be generally happy, on the occasions when something does upset her, she gives every indication of being fearful that her caretakers will harm her. Moreover, she now gives no indication of wanting to die. Is there any case for saying that her life should be ended anyway? If so, how good is the case?

My discussion of this problem is in two parts. Part I examines the case that Ronald Dworkin, who originally posed the problem, provides for ending Margo's life. Dworkin's theory of "critical interests," that is, interests considered in relation to people's lives as a whole, will be central to this argument. I will defend the view that both the principle of auton-

---

Published with permission of Nathan Brett.

omy and the "best interests" standard provide reasons for following Margo's advance directive. But Part II raises doubts about killing Margo by raising questions about personal identity. I argue that if the living will is not based on beliefs or principles or even memories that belong to the demented Margo, then it cannot be legitimate to apply its directives to her.

Part I

1. *Critical Interests*

To understand the problem, at least as Dworkin sees it, we need to begin by distinguishing two sorts of interests that people can have.[3] In the first place we have interests that are "experiential." Everyone, including Margo, has preferences connected with their experience of the world. I think Gary Larson's cartoons are fun, for example, and like Margo, I like peanut butter sandwiches. I would enjoy painting under some circumstances, but would not like to paint the same picture over and over as Margo does. Margo (and just about everyone else) is eager to avoid pain; and (perhaps like Margo) nearly everyone is anxious to avoid situations that make them insecure, e.g., because they threaten harm.

Experiential interests, of course, presuppose consciousness, though not necessarily *self-consciousness* (this depends upon the object). Experiential interests presuppose the ability to react positively or negatively to what is experienced or anticipated. All sentient creatures have interests in this sense. Dworkin also refers to such interests as "volitional,"[4] presumably because they are sources of voluntary behaviour. Interests in this sense are necessarily connected with dispositions to pursue or avoid the objects in question, though of course such dispositions need not be sufficient to yield action.

Critical interests, on the other hand, are not (at least not directly) a function of desires and aversions or preferences for certain experiences. In Dworkin's view, the best lives (in a non-moral sense) are lives characterized by the virtue of *integrity*, and critical interests must be understood in relation to this virtue. To understand this, we can exploit two analogies that Dworkin suggests in thinking about integrity and its connection to our critical interests. On the one hand, there is the old comparison between leading a good life and writing a good novel (or producing a good film—one might label this the "film critic" model of the good life). There is some structure, some constancy of theme (or themes) in a good novel. It cannot just proceed randomly and succeed. Even if a "stream of consciousness" constitutes all or part of a novel, it will not be good if it is just a random collage of reported experience. Its real success will depend upon thematic undercurrents (or overtures) which give it a "meaning" that is not a mere aggregative function of the episodes to which the reader is exposed. Anyone who has written even an essay in philosophy has probably experienced the difficulty of getting from the point at which one has a subject and some ideas to the point at which there is a line of thought that has a "trajectory" which carries one forward. Such a line of thought gives one's paper a kind of integrity. Lives can have a structure similar to this; and (arguably) meaningful lives do have something analogous to the trajectory that is established as one moves (either as reader or writer) through a written work. Judgments about integrity in the life of a person are made with reference to the sort of consistency of pursuit or motivation that gives this life coherence. On this view, the fundamental commitments in a life provide a basis for establishing the critical interests of a person, just as the lines of plot and theme provide a basis for judgments about what fits and what is "out of character" in the selection of the next moves in a novel.[5]

There is a misinterpretation of this "film critic" model of the critical interests (and the good life) that should be avoided. Dworkin does not think that the best lives are ones in which everything happens according to an elaborately worked out exercise in self-reflection. If this were a necessary condition of the intrinsic good that Dworkin is talking about, it would be missing from the lives of most persons. But the reflective articulation of a plot line is not a feature of most novel writing either. The connections of theme, which are actually developing as the "trajectory" of a novel, may not be articulated, or may only be spelled out later (and not necessarily by the author). The fact that lives are often led without any articulated vision—that unexamined lives are often worth living—does not undercut the claim that good lives are ones that have connections of goal and principle.[6]

A particularly Dworkinian analogue of integrity in a life is the sort of coherence which can and should exist in a legal system. Dworkin devotes hundreds of pages of *Laws Empire* to the development of an ideal of legal integrity, but the basic ideas are relatively simple. Judges must look in two directions in deciding the cases that come before them, including the hard cases which the black letter of statute and precedent appear to leave open. On the one hand, there is the ideal answer to the question that abstract (moral) justice demands. On the other hand, there are the facts of institutional history that have generated a specific legal system that has embedded certain normative commitments. Judges cannot ignore the latter—the commitments of these institutions—without at least creating injustice across time. Like cases will not be treated alike. But, on the other hand, even a cursory reflection on what previous decision makers—legislators and judges—were trying to do, would reveal the emptiness of a completely "black letter" approach. For, previous decision-makers cannot be assumed to be discovering *only* what other decision-makers have decided (*ad infinitum*). We must assume that they took their task to be (in part) that of doing justice in a substantive sense.

Now, integrity in the life of a person is analogous to this in having an historical as well as an ideal basis. A person cannot take seriously the question "What should I do?" and at the same time suppose that it really doesn't matter. However, if a person is to lead a *life*, if she is to have an identity as an agent, she can't be indifferent to the way in which new decisions connect with those that have come before.[7] Judgments about what is in the "critical interests" of a person are made in a way that is relative to the integrity of that person's life taken as a whole. Thus, they are not just judgments as to how best to satisfy the person's existing and predicted preferences. The concept of critical interests is normative, not only because it assumes that there are some things which we ought to care about because we are human beings and persons, but also because there are some things I should want (and thus some interests I have) because I am *this* person with *these* commitments.

2. Autonomy and Critical Interests

On the basis of serious reflections about her life and her prospects (given the Alzheimer's diagnosis) Margo has decided that she does not want to live for any considerable time in a demented state. We will suppose that her mind was not already warped, and that her decision was not based on misinformation (e.g., about the prospects for recovery of her abilities). We shall further suppose that Margo's decision is not out of character. It does fit with or flow from her basic principles, so that from the point of view established by reflections on integrity, it is in her critical interests that her life end sooner rather than after years of dementia. The film analogy might be useful here. A Harrison Ford high impact action film would not be improved, but worsened, perhaps ruined, by ending it with the addition of several hours from an Andy Warhol film of the bricks in a wall. Moreover, shifting to the legal analogy, Margo may have reasons of principle that connect with her belief in self-sufficiency for her refusal to impose a burden upon others.[8] I will consider two arguments for respecting Margo's directive to end her life, one involving the protection of autonomy, the other beneficence, or the attempt to do what is in her best interests.

In the first place, following the directive seems most consistent with the full recognition of Margo's autonomy. Note that we *do* implement such decisions, where the request is not to be sustained in a permanently vegetative state. To give Margo respect as an autonomous agent is to respect her competent decisions about her life and her way of making the best sense of it that she can. Margo's prior decision is a clear and decisive attempt to control the way in which this life ends. It was made prior to the demise of her capacity for critical reflection, and made on the basis of reflections on her life as a whole. It thus represents what she deems to be in her critical interests; and by hypothesis (in this argument) we are taking her to be right, not mistaken, about this. In her present state she is incapable of revising that judgment. Thus, the only decision that respects her autonomy is the one that implements her own will as to the way her life should end.[9]

But why should it be a matter of great importance to protect a person's own decisions about their lives?

Dworkin considers two answers to this question. In the first place, there is the "evidentiary view," the answer given by John Stuart Mill. Individuals are generally in the best position to know what their own preferences are. Others are frequently wrong in thinking that they know better. Thus, a general rule that gives to individuals the final say in matters which relate specifically to their own lives is one that will in the long run do best in promoting human welfare. This evidentiary view is thus supported by a generalization about the access we have to knowledge of our interests, supplemented by a generalization concerning the effects of busybody paternalism. A right to autonomy is really a device that protects us from the negative effects of poorly informed interventions in our lives. Now, if this is the rationale for the right to autonomy, then that rationale itself will support some general categories of exceptions; and these exceptions also have to be recognized. We have good reason to suppose that those in their infancy and the insane or demented are not the best judges of their own interests. There is no reason, therefore, to suppose that protection of autonomy should extend to these categories of persons.

Was Margo in a good position to know the interests of the person she will become? Did she base her decision on adequate information? It has been argued that the autonomy model produces distortions when it is applied to dementia cases precisely because we do not have adequate access to "what it is like to be" in this state.[10] It is arguable that an individual who writes an advance directive such as Margo's cannot be well informed about the condition she will enter and the interests she will have. Later caregivers who can base their answers to these questions on concrete information about the relative happiness or misery of their patient may actually be in a much better position to assess Margo's interests than she was, years ahead of time, basing her views on a prognosis which may or may not be accurate. Not only is there a relative lack of information for this early decision, there is also a radical difference between the perspective of the competent person writing the advance directive and the incompetent patient who will be subject to it. Finally, the author of the advance directive will often be working from stereotyped views of the condition she will enter, views which inadequately represent the interests of the patient she will become. It is not implausible to argue, as Rebecca Dresser does in defending paternalistic intervention,[11] that those caregivers who are in day-to-day contact with Margo have much better evidence of her interests than Margo would have had in making her judgment under very different conditions several years earlier. This judgment about one's future is, in fact, very much like a judgment about another human being—and not a human being that is very much like oneself.

There is no question that these are important considerations. But it should also be clear that the evidentiary view does not capture everything that we want to say about autonomy. There is often a conflict between prudence and autonomy. Individuals autonomously take huge risks, for example, refusing relatively safe operations because of their Christian Science or Jehovah's Witness beliefs. As these and a myriad of other cases indicate, the protection of autonomy is not simply the best strategy for maximizing the satisfaction of a person's experiential interests. We protect autonomy in the liberal state as a way of protecting the individual's capacity to choose a life for herself. Autonomy involves self-selection and self-endorsement. But to understand these conceptions we must understand what it is for a *self* to choose. It is in accounting for this that we are led back to the ideal of integrity, to an ideal that respects the goals and principles through which individuals make coherent sense of their own lives. If Margo's intent in drawing up an advance directive were simply to see that her later preferences were well served, then this is not a matter about which we can reasonably expect her to be more expert than her later caregivers. But that is not the point of the protection of autonomy. We need to return to the idea of her *critical* interests – the interests that express what her life is about – in order to understand what the protection of autonomy involves in this situation. In her advance directive, Margo has attempted to integrate the manner of her death with the way in which she has led her life. On Dworkin's view, it is precisely this type of decision that the principle of autonomy aims to protect.

3. Understanding Best Interests Critically

In the above argument, I have assumed that Margo is aware of the possibility that her directive may conflict with the preferences that she will have at a later time, when she is demented. How should we relate these later preferences to Margo's *interests*? In this section I will argue that only those preferences which are in accord with a person's critical interests can be said to be genuinely in that person's interests. If this is correct, then we can agree with Dworkin that not only autonomy, but also beneficence (or the best interests standard) support the decision to end Margo's life.

Assuming that Margo has correctly articulated what is in her *critical* interests, we are in a state of conflict of a sort that characterizes "Ulysses contracts" where, with foresight, one has bound another to constrain her from some expected temptation.[12] The demented Margo's current experiential interests provide a basis for continued care. She clearly enjoys eating peanut butter sandwiches and randomly turning pages in the book she is "reading." But if her advance directive does articulate her critical interests (as we have supposed) then it requires that these simple activities be brought to an end. Of course, not all cases will be of this sort. Some patients with her disease give evidence that their mental lives are ones of inescapable torment. But our concern is with the cases in which critical and experiential interests seem to pull us in opposite directions. In these cases Dworkin clearly assumes that the answer to our dilemma is obvious: the person's critical interests must dominate.

We can provide some argument for this way of interpreting the situation (as a conflict of two types of interests) by looking at other circumstances in which such conflicts occur. A person's appetite for soap operas may conflict with her desire to finish her degree—a goal that is a part of her aspiration to become a university professor. Another person with a powerful desire to drink may correctly regard the satisfaction of this desire as antithetical to his critical interests in saving his job and marriage. In such cases it seems plausible to say that critical interests should dominate. Of course, in these cases there is always the possibility that the conflicts can be translated into conflicts between the long and short run satisfaction of experiential interests. But they need not be reducible to this. Suppose that the life possible for this person as a university teacher is actually more filled with moments of tedium and dread (etc.) than an alternative life as a telephone sales clerk, a life that is compatible (we will suppose) with far more hours of (vicarious) soap opera. It *still* seems plausible (to me) that her critical interests take precedence.

But this model of conflict between critical and experiential interests (with the former taking precedence) may not be appropriate to account for what is going on in the cases described. If it were the appropriate model, it would be highly unclear as to how the utilities should be calculated. Should we suppose that no amount of pleasure associated with satisfying experiential interests (or no escape from pain) is sufficient to justify even the smallest degradation of one's life plans? This seems preposterous. If the tedium involved in the teaching career would be massive, or if it is a life of nearly perpetual panic, this will surely count as grounds for abandoning even the well-established and highly-prized goal of university teaching which has the support of a person's principles and fits the "narrative" structure of her life. What (if anything) is wrong with this picture of conflict between critical and experiential interests?

On the interpretation that I want to advance, there are several things wrong with it. Note, in the first place, we were talking about the conditions of good or meaningful lives when we introduced the discussion of critical interests. A life plan that ignored one's experiential interests, which paid no attention to "simple" pleasure and pain would be a "preposterous" life, as Dworkin himself says.[13] Thus, the successful life plans of human beings will not be ones that reflect a complete indifference to their experiential interests. Secondly, it is a mistake to suppose, for example, that anything that is pleasurable must *ipso facto* count as something in an individual's experiential interests, and that if it is shunned, then this can only be because it is outweighed by some other negative states. Consider a fictional case in which intense bodily pleasure is caused in the course of a sexual assault (by a mad scientist, say). On my view, this pleasure does not add something of value that is outweighed by the pain on the other side of a utility balance sheet. Lacking any endorsement, an affront to this person's integrity, the pleasure does not count as a satisfaction of any *interest* of the person. On the contrary, because it is at odds with the critical interests of the person, the experience of pleasure can itself be taken as a *harm*. The opposite sort of case (involving pain as something in a person's interest) is also possible. Suffering from cold, from exhaustion, etc., states which nature and experience dispose us to avoid, can be aspects of *satisfying* the critical interests of persons. The goals of mountain climbing and long distance running (and a million other things) confer value on endurance in the face of suffering, and this suffering is an aspect of what makes the activities worthwhile.

These examples suggest a different model of the way in which critical and experiential interests are related in the life of a person. On this view, it is not the case that critical and experiential interests directly compete with one another. When we are talking about the interests of *persons*, the category of critical interests is always relevant. And whether or not a particular experience is really in one's interests depends upon whether it can be normatively integrated within the life of the person in question. It is normal for human beings to accommodate their lives to the experiential preferences that they happen to have. But, as the above examples indicate, it is perfectly possible that what nature and experience dispose a person to prefer is contrary to that person's interests. Thus, on this way of reading the dichotomy, the only genuine interests of persons are critical interests, and experiential interests are the interests of persons only because and to the extent that they receive endorsement in their lives.

Consider the implications of this interpretation for Margo's case. What appeared to be a conflict between Margo's critical and her experiential interests is not that. We have assumed that she was able to contemplate ahead of time (at least as one possibility) this dependent life of peanut butter sandwiches and leafing through books. She knowingly rejected it. This life of simple pleasures was deemed an affront to what her life had "stood for." So, it is not in her interest *at all*—but contrary to it—that she continue in a state in which she has lost control and is reduced to these simple pleasures. There may even be a small analogy with the assault case mentioned above: the pleasure Margo derives from these things may itself be an aspect of harm which is done to her if her life is preserved. If this is the case, then both autonomy and the best interests standard demand that we accept her directive and end her life, for Margo's genuine interests are inseparable from the critical interests which are a function of her life taken as a whole.

Part II

4. *The Identity Problem:* Whose *Interests?*

Though I find some plausibility to these arguments for ending Margo's life I am also troubled by them. I would not do it. And I am not convinced that this is just weakness of will. In the remainder of this discussion, I will explore an objection to Dworkin's solution; it is an objection that does not depend on questioning the above theory about autonomy and critical interests.[14]

Margo is no longer endowed with the capacity to reflect on the course her life is taking. So, it might be argued, she no longer has critical interests. Margo has lost the capacity to put herself together, to make choices that belong to a life that has narrative structure. If having such a life is an aspect of what it is to be a person, the life of this person has ended. What is happening now to what used to be Margo only belongs to Margo because we continue to put her together, because we continue the narrative. That is to say, the preservation of her identity is a fiction of ours. But, if this is so, then it seems she no longer has a critical interest in having her life ended. And without such interest we don't have a case for ending a life that is comprised largely of pleasurable experiences. Given that she is generally happy but occasionally fearful that she will be harmed, it could hardly be said that this would be a *mercy* killing. Moreover, it is one of our virtues that we respond with compassion to such lives, just as it is a virtue to respect the pre-reflective life of a child.

To this, it could be replied, however, that the basis for supposing that Margo's critical interests are gone assumes what is not true, viz., that one can only have an interest in some outcome if one can desire this outcome and be satisfied by its achievement. But many of our interests persist even in the absence of any desire; and many are *not* such that one must be conscious of their satisfaction. The most obvious example (in the literature on interests) is the interest in the fidelity of one's spouse. It seems very implausible to suppose that this is reducible to the interest in not knowing of (or being otherwise affected by) unfaithful acts. But there are less controversial examples. My concern for the welfare of my grandchildren really aims at *their thriving*, not at my awareness of it. Thus, it seems that the interests of persons can outlive them. When a person makes a will or gives instructions as to what is to be done with his body, we do not suppose (absurdly) that we are released from the obligation that it sets up as soon as the person is dead. On the contrary, we often suppose that it is of the utmost importance that the person's will be done; and this seems to presuppose that the relevant interests persist. Moreover, respect for such decisions of living, reflective persons could hardly be genuine if it were not accompanied by an intention to carry out the person's will. Thus, there seem to be reasons for thinking that Margo's critical interests can survive her demise as a being capable of reflecting on and integrating the moments of her life.

That interests can survive the persons they belong to is a troublesome idea. But so is its denial. For it has led some to the conclusion that, if one thinks this through, one arrives at the view that death cannot be a harm (to a person) since there is no surviving person to be harmed. Here, I want to accept as plausible the claim that Margo's critical interests could survive dementia and even death. The objection I want to raise involves questioning whether the demented Margo is the same person as the author of the advance directive. The Margo who drew up the advance directive cannot have a continuing interest in having her life ended if it already has ended. And Margo cannot legitimately utilize a living will to take out a contract on someone different from herself.

But has Margo's life ended? By hypothesis, the demented Margo no longer exists as an autonomous agent. She lacks the capacity to generate any narrative that knits together the day-to-day experiences of her life. There is no longer any structure of norms that can provide the normative core of self-identity that we considered in Part I. In addition to this, memory loss leaves her without psychological connection to the person who drafted the advance directive. But if this is correct, then Margo's earlier decision, represented in her advance directive, was itself based on an error. She had assumed that the demented person left after Alzheimer's disease had removed her critical faculties would be continuing to lead her life. But without the capacities necessary to establish psychological and normative continuities, that life and that self are gone.

Consider a parallel case. A man may have so structured his life that the very idea of the continuation of his spouse after his demise is an affront to what he has stood for. What was *deemed to be* properly a part of his life would be outside his control. But if a man declares that his wife is to be thrown onto his funeral pyre, he demands what he should not, although for centuries some legal systems enforced (or at least tolerated) such wills. Notice that such a person need not be making a mistake about the structure of his own identity or the critical interests that relate to this identity. It could be of central importance to him that his spouse does not survive. On the other hand, he would be making a mistake if he supposed that this other person is a mere extension of himself, is *just* an aspect of his own life. He would have illegitimately extended the boundaries of his self.

Now it would be incorrect to take this example to be *fully* analogous to Margo's situation, to suppose that Margo's advance directive has called for execution of another person. For the disease may have removed not only the psychological connections necessary for identity, but also the very conditions necessary for being a person.[15] Margo's narrative has ended (except insofar as it is taken up by *others*). But even if this is the case, a conscious and child-like human creature remains; and that human being clearly does have needs and desires. She is capable of experiencing pleasure and pain and capable of some rudimentary forms of communication. Other things being equal, the satisfaction of these interests is itself a source of value and a proper source of demands on our compassion.

5. Dworkin and the Identity Problem

In a work on the rights of those with senile dementia, Dworkin has considered the question of identity that the above objection depends upon. This condition he describes as follows:

> Someone seriously demented loses intellectual and emotional continuity with past stages of "his" life. He suffers total disintegration of personality, so that none of the beliefs, convictions and projects he may have can be seen as mainly fixed by earlier ones and he has total amnesia of prior experiences, identity and attachments.[16]

In this earlier work Dworkin defends the view that personal identity is *not* removed even by this sort of serious permanent dementia which has been the focus of our concern.[17] If this is correct, then the above objection misses the mark. We thus need to consider Dworkin's reasons for taking this view of personal identity.

There is a vast literature in which philosophers have sought amongst the properties of human beings a criterion that gives the identity conditions of persons and establishes what changes are sufficient to constitute loss of identity. The main contenders, of course, have involved the physical continuity of a (living) body, on the one hand, and on the other, some facts about psychological connection involving continuity of memory (and character) or a combination of these. But there is also (at least since Wittgenstein) a fairly standard objection to this way of proceeding. Should we suppose that there is any such criterion, e.g., that there are some necessary conditions which are jointly sufficient for the identity of a person? Dworkin sides with those who discard this analytical ideal (at least in relation to personal identity). Ascriptions of personal identity depend upon an array of characteristics that *do not* combine neatly to provide such a test. Moreover, what is central to such ascriptions can differ from one context to another. Across a wide set of judgments, bodily identity (established by fingerprints, DNA "signatures," etc., we may suppose) is sufficient for personal identity claims. Other contexts (e.g., those involving multiple personality) make personal identity depend upon continuity of memory and character. Puzzle cases—e.g., the present one about dementia—introduce problems that our classificatory systems are not completely equipped to handle. While some philosophers have supposed that there is some right answer to these questions discoverable in the criteria that we are assumed to utilize in more ordinary contexts, on the view Dworkin adopts, this assumption is false. Such cases present themselves as matters for *decision*. The best we can do in deciding these cases is, first, proceed in a way that does as little violence as possible to the clear cases that are similar; and second, we need to apply a directly normative test. Is there, for example, some reason to suppose that regarding this being as the same person will yield an avoidable injustice?

What should we say then (on Dworkin's view) about personal identity in the dementia cases? First, we ordinarily speak as if (total) dementia were a possible outcome for a person. I can contemplate the possibility of falling into dementia. And when I think (and write) about Margo, I think (and write) of the gradual demise of memory and other capacities of a single person. We *could* (guided by some theory) shed this way of thinking and conceive instead of a kind of metamorphosis that results in a *different* person (or quasi-person). However, it seems that the most intuitively plausible solution involves thinking of Margo as the same person throughout the progression into dementia.

But what should we say about the directly normative question? Dworkin's answer to this is clearly the opposite of the one I have given above. Nothing of significant value is sacrificed by the supposition that identity is preserved all the way into dementia. Respect for the author of an advance directive gives us a basis for decisions about the borderline case—demented Margo. It is true that we must in these cases rely on bodily continuity for the assignment of personal identity; and it is true as well that this test will not always work. But that's just a matter of facing the reality that our categories must sometimes be adapted to fit the world, and adapted in ways that seem at first *ad hoc*.

6. *Some Final Doubts*

In this account, Dworkin seems to strike a nice balance between philosophical theory and its real world application. Nonetheless, I find myself with some remaining doubts. In the first place, even if personal identity *is* best thought through without the assumption that there is a single criterion of personal identity that is applicable in all contexts, it does not follow that there are no *necessary* conditions of personal identity. Dworkin's arguments have not convinced me to drop the view that some minimum of psychological continuity is such a condition. Secondly, doubts can be raised about the normative claim that there is nothing wrong with this way of assimilating cases.

Psychological Continuity: The human being who is subject to the advance directive we have been considering can remember nothing of it and does not organize her life in a way that makes the directive seem appropriate. It is true that I continue to refer to her as "Margo," and have no doubt as to what human being the living will was directed toward. However, we should notice that the same point about ordinary usage could be made with regard to "Margo" if she had become irreversibly comatose or were now dead. But though we know exactly what "person" is referred to in directives regarding the permanently vegetative or dead Margo, we do not need to make the unlikely inference that this is because personal identity has been preserved. Human remains do not constitute a person or preserve personal identity in any meaningful sense. We do not need to suppose that someone making decisions about how much to set aside from her income to cover her own funeral expenses has made a mistake or has some extravagant theory of personal identity. Likewise, we do not need to suppose that setting aside money to cover the expenses of becoming demented requires the supposition that I could "suffer total disintegration of personality" and still retain my identity as a person.

The Normative Question: There is a significant issue that remains, however. As we have seen, Dworkin is working with a conception of a person's life taken as a whole in thinking these problems through. He would claim that what happens, not only to the demented, but also to the comatose and dead are matters that are relevant to questions about the value of the life, considered from this perspective. The fact that Margo can't possibly be aware that her advance directive is being followed when she is demented or comatose or dead does not prevent her treatment from having an impact on her critical interests, on her life considered as a whole. There is an interest in a certain narrative reputation—an interest in being remembered in a certain way—which is at stake in this situation. However, there is an obvious shift from the first to the third person that is involved when we consider this question in terms of such critical interests. Normally, there is no conflict between the dictates of these two viewpoints. But, the question that has been central to our discussion concerns a case where there is such a conflict. The fact that there is no psychological continuity between this being and the author of the directive – that self-identity is not present from the *inside* – does become relevant in just this case.

To see this, consider for a moment the fate of a person who suffers from amnesia, but *not* from dementia, and who is otherwise in Margo's circumstances. Now imagine that this person is you. You can remember none of the details of the life which others say you have led. You learn that someone has expressed an interest in ending your life. That person, you are told, still has this interest. You are surprised to discover that others whom you have relied on for help now believe they have an obligation to assist this person by acting for her in bringing about your death. They also report that this person's interests *are* yours, because, though you don't realize it, she *is* you. From the inside none of this makes sense. From your point of view, the person with homicidal motives seems as alien as any stranger whose case you might read about in the newspaper. Her motive for wanting you dead—that this fits best the plan of her life—is unintelligible to you.

Admittedly, this is not the perspective from which Margo sees the world, for she has not just lost psychological continuity. She is demented. She could not understand these reports of others about her situation. Nonetheless Margo is conscious. There is something that it is like to be Margo. She has a simple, child-like perspective on the world, and from this perspective she lacks any connection with the author of the orders for her death. That connection is maintained, not by her, but by others. It is a product of the physical continuity that usually guides our ascriptions of identity.

The problem is complicated by the fact that Margo, in drawing up the directive, was making a first person projection of what it would be like to be in this demented state. We have stipulated for the purpose of this paper that she was not mistaken in her estimate of what this state would be like. But the fact that Margo would not be psychologically continuous with this child-like being makes a difference to this projection. If Margo takes proper account of this fact in drawing up her directive, then she can no longer view the problem from a purely prudential viewpoint. The directive she has drawn up demands the death of a conscious subject who is completely unaware of her own life and aspirations. To think this through properly, she must adopt a moral point of view from which concern for another human being becomes appropriate. We have thus found some reason to suppose that there is a moral "cost" involved in Dworkin's use of bodily continuity as the test of personal identity in this type of case. Inevitably, it forces us to look at the problem from the third-person perspective.

It might be replied, however, that the directive asking for death is acceptable precisely because the events that have removed first-person personal identity (with the Margo who wrote the advance directive) have also taken away the necessary conditions of being *any* person. Allen Buchanan has used this convergence—loss of identity and loss of personhood—to defend the view that we should adhere to advance directives in this type of case.[18] He agrees with the claim that it would be wrong to impose "euthanasia" on one person because this was the will of another. He agrees as well that the loss of psychological continuity brought about by dementia of the sort under discussion would, indeed, remove personal identity. But, Buchanan argues, since these psychological incapacities also remove the conditions of personhood, it is permissible to end the life that remains. Respect for the autonomy of the former person gives us an obligation to do just this.

I cannot deny that this is an important argument or respond to it fully here. Still, I am not convinced. In general we do not (and in my view *should* not) treat (biologically) human beings who are infants or infantile as if they were disposable. Why do we seriously contemplate making an exception in this type of case? Clearly, it is the belief that we are acting on behalf of the person who has asked to die that leads us to take the option seriously under these circumstances. But, if the argument I have given is right, the loss of personal identity removes this special justification for euthanasia. This case is not analogous to that in which we respect a person's will to allow the biological death of their permanently vegetative body. It is not analogous precisely because the demented Margo is a conscious subject. Of course, there could be good reasons to end her life.[19] But, given the description of her inner life with which we began (a simple but remarkably happy life), and given that personal identity has been lost, we can hardly say that it is in her interest to die.

But perhaps if Margo is no longer a person, we should not take seriously the conscious life that remains. I will end by reversing the central features of Margo's case as a way of responding to this suggestion. Let's suppose that Margo had lived a different life and drawn up a will that was the reverse of the one we have considered so far. Instead of euthanasia, she had expressed her will to be resuscitated and kept alive through aggressive therapy for as long as possible. But let's suppose that the outcome of the disease was not the happy being that we have been discussing. Instead, Margo's condition is excruciatingly painful and tormented. Should we let the present patient's experiential interests play a role in our decisions about treatment? On my view we should do so even if it had been Margo's intention to endure this suffering. This is because Margo would not have been justified in inflicting this condition on the child-like person that would remain after the dementia had taken its course. Here it is appropriate for us to act with compassion in not adding to this torment even though it means setting aside the advance directive. In the absence of psychological continuity, that directive would lack the authority to command this fate.

AUTHOR'S NOTE

I would like to thank Sue Campbell, John Hubert, Duncan Macintosh, Susan Sherwin, Michael Milde, and Sheldon Wein for their helpful comments on earlier drafts of this paper and thank Mary Lou Ellerton and Christine Koggel for help in preparing the manuscript for publication.

NOTES

1. Margo's case is noted by Ronald Dworkin in *Life's Dominion* (Random House: N.Y., 1994). See Chapter 8, p. 220ff. He cites it from Andrew D. Ferlick, "Margo's Logo" 265 *Journal of the American Medical Association* (1991) p. 201. Dworkin utilizes his own embellishments of this case in presenting the problem addressed in this paper.
2. This version of the case is meant to present a dilemma in its starkest form by putting it in a context where active euthanasia will not be prosecuted. But if this feature of the case is too distracting (because it gets us into the questions about killing and letting die) one can reconstruct it so that only passive euthanasia is at issue: Margo's advance directive specifies that she is not to be given treatment for quite treatable life-threatening conditions which arise. This second scenario may, of course, involve additional dilemmas as Margo's condition deteriorates and becomes painful. The problems to be raised in this paper are independent of the issues relating to possible differences between acts and omissions.
3. The distinction is first advanced in the *Tanner Lecture: XI* entitled "Foundations of Liberal Equality" (Salt Lake City: University of Utah, 1990) section V, pp. 42-7. It is then applied to the problems of euthanasia in the final chapters of *Life's Dominion*. The importance of this distinction goes well beyond the esoteric sort of case that I have just introduced, if Dworkin is right, and we cannot understand many of the judgments we make within ethics and about human lives without taking it into account.
4. In "The Foundations of Liberal Equality," *ibid.*, Dworkin uses a contrast between "volitional" and critical interests. In this discussion I will assume that this is the same distinction.
5. Dworkin would agree, of course, that this cannot be the whole of the account of meaningful lives, any more than consistency can be sufficient within epistemology. It is possible to make consistent choices in relation to what is not itself choiceworthy, possible to lead a consistent but awful life. One might spend a life or a sizable portion of it, say, adjusting the thermostat in one's room to maintain a certain level of comfort (or painting the same image over and over). The consistency of one's dedication to these pursuits could hardly be said to give real value to such a life. Thus, the coherence of a life, is (at most) a necessary condition of its meaningfulness. That something is consistent with what I have done does not entail that it is in my critical interests.
6. Christine Korsgaard has written about this under the description of "practical identity" in *The Sources of Normativity* (Cambridge: Cambridge University Press, 1996). See especially Chapter Three.
7. The analogy between lives and legal systems is imperfect, of course. It is often true that *arbitrary* commitments, e.g., arbitrarily adopted goals are the source of worthwhile pursuits in the lives of individuals. Solving the four color problem, climbing K-2, discovering hitherto unknown properties of sub-atomic particles—each of these has provided inspiration and continuity in the lives of some people, though these are arbitrarily adopted goals. But there seems to be a contrast here. The function of legal systems in relation to justice might appear to leave little room—or none at all—for arbitrarily chosen pursuits; and good legal systems will converge upon highly similar decisions. But the contrast is not as sharp as this makes it seem. In the first place, persons leading good lives will find themselves converging upon many matters of moral principle. And, secondly, there are more or less arbitrary features of legal system, both at the level of specific conventions, (how many signatures are required for wills) and the goals which end up being given legal implementation, e.g., supporting the massive infrastructure necessary to get to the moon, or subsidizing a steel company.
8. We should note that, of course, given a different background her autonomous decision might have been the opposite. After a life filled with responsibilities one might decide that one was entitled to a "retirement" freed from all this—or religious beliefs might forbid one to "play God" even with respect to oneself. Thus,

either decision (for or against help in ending her life) could be a manifestation of integrity, though a given person with a particular biography may only be able to choose one of these options if she is to preserve her integrity.

9. A puzzle arises if we suppose that Margo can make a mistake about her critical interests. It seems obvious that a person could exercise bad judgment in making such a decision, just as a director could choose to end a film in a way that destroys it. The puzzle is this. Would we be recognizing Margo's autonomy if the advance directive were actually based on such a bad judgment? Suppose that Margo's life has been a life of never "playing God." Everything she stood for seems to be undermined by her "last will" as to the way her life should end. What do we say then? Notice that we often do have conflicts between the autonomy of a person and the protection of interests over all. A decision to take up smoking can be an autonomous one despite the fact that it is foolish. Is there a parallel exercise of autonomy in which one's own *critical* interests are flouted? Dworkin's answer to this question seems to be negative. The point of autonomy rights he argues is to protect a person's critical interests. And, one cannot just "exercise" autonomy through any random choice, a choice that cannot be connected with one's life. Some consistency of self and hence of choice (i.e., some integrity) is necessarily involved in any autonomous decisions on this view. Now, if this is right, then there can be occasions in which the advance directive is not a genuine reflection of autonomy, and hence protection of autonomy will not support its enforcement. One of the problems for this account is that it rules out some types of radical change in the self-chosen life of a person.
10. Rebecca Dresser, "Missing Persons: Legal Perceptions of Incompetent Patients," *Rutgers Law Review* 46:2 (1994) pp. 609-719. See also "Dworkin on Dementia: Elegant Theory, Questionable Policy," *Hastings Center Report* 26:6 (1995) pp. 32-38.
11. "[I]f honoring an advance directive required others to compromise the clear welfare interests of the patient now before them, the directive should be disregarded. Our affection for autonomy should not be permitted to sanction the inhumane treatment of people who have lost the capacity to appreciate the forces that drove their earlier choices, but not the capacity to be harmed by those choices" Dresser (1994) p. 715.
12. This description begs some of the questions about capacity and identity that I will raise later.
13. "It seems plain that each of these—pleasurable experiences and the satisfaction of [critical interests]—must find some place in any acceptable overall philosophical account of well being…" (*The Foundations of Liberal Equality*, p. 43). To be sure, there are lives that move fairly far in this direction, those of the ascetic or Puritan come to mind. Dworkin can make some sense of these lives, by stressing the way in which they (like scaling Mt. Everest) can manifest success in relation to a self-imposed challenge. But to most of us it seems plausible to say that these are not ideal human lives.
14. Rebecca Dresser (*supra*, note 10) has developed arguments against Dworkin's policy recommendations in "Dworkin on Dementia: Elegant Theory, Questionable Policy" which do involve questioning the protection of autonomy as the basis for decision in cases involving dementia.
15. Allen Buchanan, "Advance Directives and the Problem of Personal Identity," *Philosophy and Public Affairs*: 17 (1988) pp. 277-302.
16. Ronald Dworkin, "Philosophical Issues Concerning the Rights of Patients Suffering Permanent Dementia," (Springfield, VA: US Office of Technology Assessment, 1987) Section 7, pp. 85-108.
17. *Ibid.*, p. 86.
18. See Allen Buchanan (supra note 15). The argument is similar to that of Michael Tooley in "In Defense of Abortion and Infanticide," in Jan Narveson, *Moral Issues* (Oxford: Oxford University Press, 1984) pp. 215-33.
19. If Alzheimer's patients became "utility monsters" because of their drain on health resources, ending such lives *might* be justified by the need to prevent the destruction of the health care system. However, this justification raises questions that are not the subject of this paper. It depends in no way on the protection of autonomy or critical interests through the dictates of an advance directive.

STUDY QUESTIONS

1. Asch and Fine note that there is a tendency to construe women's right to have an abortion for any reason and the right of newborns with disabilities to medical treatment as contradictory. How do they defend both rights and argue for their compatibility?
2. Should parents have the right to withhold medical treatment from newborns with severe disabilities? Are Asch and Fine correct to suggest that this right can only be evaluated in the context of showing how such choices are often the result of misinformation about and stereotypes of disability and of pressure by family members, doctors, and institutions? Provide reasons for your answers.
3. Would the recommendations by Asch and Fine about the right of newborns with disabilities to medical treatment impose too severe a burden on society's resources? How would utilitarians answer this question? How would Stingl answer this question?
4. Stingl identifies two conceptions of equality within the liberal tradition. Outline these conceptions and show how Stingl applies them to an analysis of the different approaches to health care in Canada and the United States.
5. Has what you learned from Rothman about the international traffic in organ donation influenced your thoughts about an individual's right to medical treatment? Has it challenged your beliefs about basing the question of medical treatment on an individual's ability to pay? Provide reasons for your answers.
6. Do you think that harvesting the organs of those prisoners on death row who have been executed can be morally justified? Should China be allowed to continue this policy? Who should decide?
7. Do you think that there should be an international monitoring body that prevents the harvesting of organs in developing countries or that develops policies for controlling the traffic in organs? Give reasons for your answers.
8. According to Battin, what is gained by placing the issue of euthanasia in an international context and examining the norms and practices in other places? Why study the norms and practices in the three countries of United States, Holland, and Germany?
9. Outline the different practices with respect to euthanasia in Holland, Germany and the United States and evaluate the objections that Battin raises to the practices of each country.
10. What conclusions does Battin draw with respect to the question of the permissibility of assisted suicide in the United States? Do you agree with her analysis of the differences between the United States and Holland and would it justify changing the policy in the United States? Why or why not?
11. Identify the areas of disagreement between Callahan and Battin with respect to their respective analyses of self-determination and of the consequences of allowing assisted suicide. Whose arguments are more persuasive and why? Is your answer influenced by what you have learned about practices and norms in other countries? Why or why not?
12. What is the distinction between critical and experiential interests in Brett's account meant to capture? Is this distinction useful for evaluating Callahan's account of self-determination? Why or why not?
13. Should Margo's living will be carried out and the life of the person with Alzheimer's be ended? Formulate your answer to this question by outlining and evaluating Brett's answer to this question.

SUGGESTED READINGS

Asch, Adrienne and Gail Geller. "Feminism, Bioethics, and Genetics." In *Feminism & Bioethics: Beyond Reproduction* edited by Susan M. Wolf. New York: Oxford University Press, 1996: 318-350.

Bayles, Michael D. "Allocation of Scarce Medical Resources." *Public Affairs Quarterly*, v. 4, no. 1 (January 1990): 1-16.

Beauchamp, Dan E. "Public Health as Social Justice." *Inquiry*, v. 13 (March 1976): 3-14.

Brock, Dan. "Quality of Life Measures in Health Care and Medical Ethics." In *The Quality of Life* edited by Martha C. Nussbaum and Amartya Sen. Oxford: Clarendon Press, 1992: 95-132.

— . "Voluntary Active Euthanasia: An Overview and Defense." *Hastings Center Report*, v. 22 (March/April 1992): 10-22.

Buchanan, Allen E. "The Right to a Decent Minimum of Health Care." *Philosophy & Public Affairs* (Winter 1984): 55-78.

Callahan, Daniel. *What Kind of Life?* New York: Simon & Schuster, 1990.

Daniels, Norman. "Health Care Needs and Distributive Justice." In *In Search of Equity: Health Needs and the Health Care System* edited by Ronald Bayer, Arthur Caplan, and Norman Daniels. New York: Plenum Press, 1983: 1-41.

— . *Just Health Care.* Cambridge: Cambridge University Press, 1985.

Rachels, James. "Active and Passive Euthanasia." *The New England Journal of Medicine*, v. 292 (1975): 78-80.

Roberts, Dorothy E. "Reconstructing the Patient: Starting with Women of Color." In *Feminism & Bioethics: Beyond Reproduction* edited by Susan M. Wolf. New York: Oxford University Press, 1996: 116-143.

Rumsey, Jean P. "Justice, Care, and Questionable Dichotomies." *Hypatia*, v. 12, no. 1 (Winter 1997): 99-113.

Sherwin, Susan. "Gender, Race, and Class in the Delivery of Health Care." In *No Longer Patient: Feminist Ethics and Health Care*. Philadelphia: Temple University Press, 1992: 222-240.

Steinbock. Bonnie. "The Intentional Termination of Life." *Ethics in Science and Medicine*, v. 6, no. 1 (1979): 59-64.

Wolf, Susan. "Gender, Feminism, and Death: Physician-Assisted Suicide and Euthanasia." In *Feminism & Bioethics: Beyond Reproduction* edited by Susan M. Wolf. New York: Oxford University Press, 1996: 282-317.

CHAPTER TWELVE

PORNOGRAPHY AND HATE SPEECH

In liberal societies, liberty rights are central to questions about whether the state is ever justified in censoring material from its citizens. John Stuart Mill provides a defense of freedom of speech that has become foundational. He argued that people should be free to express their beliefs and to have access to beliefs because this freedom is essential to the free flow, interchange, and debate of ideas from which truth can emerge. On this account, an individual's right to freedom of expression should only be restricted if it causes clear and direct harm to other individuals. This position has shaped the debate in liberal societies about pornography and hate speech, where much of the discussion has centered on the value of individual freedom and the justifications for limiting it. Turning our attention to a global context and to issues of multiculturalism raises a different set of questions with the issue of censorship, as it did with other moral issues. What does the free flow of ideas mean in a global context in which information is so readily available through the media and the internet and accessible to people in all parts of the world? How are we to analyze what constitutes harm in a context in which Western liberal notions of freedom from state interference are being challenged by feminists and race theorists as well as non-Westerners? Does an analysis of discrimination and the harm to members of traditionally disadvantaged groups challenge liberal accounts of individual freedom, freedom of speech, the free flow of ideas, and social responsibility?

The chapter opens with an article by Ronald Dworkin, who provides a critical analysis of Catharine MacKinnon's feminist account of pornography and defense of state regulation of it. Dworkin argues that the feminist movement has given new form to campaigns once dominated by conservatives to outlaw pornography in the United States. According to Dworkin, feminists such as MacKinnon concentrate on pornography to the exclusion of other issues because pornography is the clearest expression of the message that women exist primarily to provide sexual service to men. Furthermore, it is offensive and makes no contribution to political or intellectual debate. It would seem then that liberals should be uncomfortable about defending it and that society would lose nothing if pornography were banned. Dworkin identifies this as MacKinnon's position and sets out to raise objections to it.

Dworkin rejects MacKinnon's argument that because pornography silences women by making it difficult for them to speak and be heard, women and not pornographers need First Amendment protection. However, Dworkin is most interested in a new argument of MacKinnon's: even if the publication of literature degrading to women is protected by the First Amendment, this material violates the competing constitutional value of the equal protection clause of the Fourteenth Amendment. The courts, argues MacKinnon, should resolve the conflict in favor of equality and censorship because pornography undermines women's equality and contributes nothing of any importance to political debate. In this account, censoring pornography should be regarded like other kinds of institutional policies designed to create genuine equality of opportunity, policies such as prohibiting discrimination against women and blacks in employment and education or university regulations regarding hate speech. Dworkin claims that this argument has broad and devastating implications because it would allow national and state governments to censor any expression that might reasonably be thought to sustain or exacerbate the unequal positions of women or racial, ethnic, and other minorities.

Dworkin argues that free speech contributes to political equality. It exposes corruption, generates new ideas, and refutes old ones through public debate. Dworkin argues that the ideals of political equality demand that no one be prevented from influencing the shared moral environment. Odious views cannot be locked out in advance by criminal law, but instead should be discredited by the disgust, outrage, and ridicule of other people. Dworkin concludes that the United States should not follow the lead of other countries in demoting freedom of speech as an elitist, inegalitarian ideal that has been of little value to women, blacks, and others without power. To follow that lead is to allow a majority to define some people as too corrupt, offensive, or radical to join in the informal moral life of the nation.

Dworkin criticizes many of the feminist arguments on the side of censoring pornography and/or hate speech. In the other readings in this chapter, some authors support him and others challenge him. Like Dworkin, Marvin Glass examines feminist arguments, but he focuses on disagreements among them. Glass concentrates on two specific arguments by anti-censorship feminists and raises objections to each: feminists who argue that feminists cannot trust the state to be a vehicle for their liberation and feminists who argue that a free market in sexual imagery is currently in women's best interests. Feminists who defend the first argument point out that a police and judiciary controlled primarily by sexist and homophobic men are more likely to suppress lesbian sexual representations or even feminist literature than that material which is offensive and degrading to women. Glass agrees that feminist politics will not succeed in transforming the state into a pro-woman institution, but argues that a realistic feminist political agenda is to add a strategy of fighting for feminist-inspired anti-pornography legislation to existing campaigns for pay equity and affirmation action and against sexual harassment, sexual violence, and rape. All of these strategies make use of state institutions and apparatus to further the goals of feminism. Feminists who defend the second argument endorse a strategy of increasing funding so that there is more speech, literature, and imagery with positive and liberating portrayals of women's sexuality. Glass argues that leaving the ownership and control of pornography to market forces is unlikely to empower women or ensure feminist sexual expression a prominent place in an increasingly concentrated and powerful global market. While civil and/or criminal laws may not succeed in censoring only that which degrades and exploits women, the losses in the arena of sexual expression are offset by the greater losses incurred in campaigning against the multi-billion dollar pornography industry in the marketplace.

In the next reading, Ann Snitow also examines debates within feminism about the issue of censorship. She defends the second of the two arguments Glass outlines by arguing that concentrating energy on anti-pornography campaigns is not in the best interests of women. However, she disputes Glass's claim that feminists agree about the messages concerning women's sexuality that are depicted and endorsed in pornography. Snitow finds agreement among feminists in the desire to own their own sexuality and to express their sexuality in images of their own choosing. She maintains, however, that rather than advancing feminist thinking about sexuality, anti-pornography campaigns perpetuate distortions by collapsing a wide range of sexually explicit images into portrayals of a universal and timeless male sexual brutality and of women as victims of that brutality.

Snitow argues that pornography not only includes violence, hatred, and fear of women but also elements of play, thrilling danger, and defiance of authority; women can engage in fantasies of power and powerlessness without having these affect beliefs and intentions. She argues that to accept rather than struggle against the idea that sex is dangerous and oppressive is to reject a realm of pornographic sexual fantasy that can be empowering for women. We do injury, she argues, to conflate sex with violence and victimhood because we deny women agency and present false accounts of what women's sexuality is all about. Snitow advocates that feminists turn their attention to exploring the elements of power and arousal in sexual relations and the full range of sexuality and sexual practices.

In the first reading, Dworkin evaluates an argument by MacKinnon that women need First Amendment protection in a context in which pornography limits their freedom to speak and be heard. He rejects this argument because it assumes an unacceptable account of free speech as including the right to be heard and to have what one says respected by others. In the fourth reading, Lisa Heldke develops precisely this sort of account of free speech as an alternative to a liberal conception that, she argues, fails to address certain free speech issues. The liberal conception of people as independent self-legislating beings is integrally tied to an account of free speech as the unconstrained utterances of individuals. Heldke reviews two arguments for the values that are said to be protected and promoted in an atmosphere of unconstrained utterances. The argument from individual rights states that free speech promotes individual self-fulfillment. It rests on the idea that human development is a solitary project and highly individual enterprise and that expressing ideas is an essential part of developing independence, autonomy, and maturity. The argument from utility states that free speech is needed to arrive at truths, and that the best way for us to arrive at the truth is for there to be as many ideas as possible for us to challenge and confront.

Heldke advances a conception of free speech that is based on the view that individuals are constituted as persons by and through relations with others. This view of persons motivates a conception of speaking as an activity that takes place among people and involves their participation as both speakers and listeners. Free speech is not attributable to individuals, but to individuals as members of a particular community. This view switches the question from "Is this speaker free?" to "Is the talk in this situation free?" Heldke argues that a relational collectivist conception of free speech is better equipped to explain how the interactive nature of speech shapes individual growth and maturity. It can show why preventing someone from using sexist language works to increase the level of freedom in a community. For a male professor to speak in ways that humiliate women, for example, is to lend support to systems that subordinate women and to curtail and diminish the freedom of some to speak freely. Heldke does not advocate implementing laws restricting speech, but changing behavior through critical thinking about the effects of our speech on others.

In the final reading in this chapter, Mari Matsuda explores the tension between the stories told by victims of racist speech and the First Amendment story of free speech. Victims are restricted in their personal freedom because they may need to quit jobs, leave their homes, avoid certain public places, curtail their own speech, and modify their behavior to avoid receiving hate messages. The effect on one's self-esteem and sense of personal security of being hated and despised can be devastating. Matsuda argues that these victim stories present perspectives of what it is to live with fear and be effected by racist messages, but these stories are absent in the legal domain where judges and lawyers cannot imagine a life diminished by hate propaganda. When victims of racist speech are ignored, we burden one group, a traditionally disadvantaged one, with a disproportionate share of the costs of absolutist free speech principles.

Matsuda points out that the current trend in the international community, evident in Article 4 of the International Convention on the Elimination of All Forms of Racial Discrimination, the Race Relations Act in the United Kingdom, and Sections of the Canadian Criminal Code, is to outlaw racist hate propaganda. But the United States is out of step with these international developments and continues to defend the primacy of First Amendment values of free speech, values that are so entrenched as to seem irreconcilable with the values of equality and full participation asserted in the laws prohibiting racist speech in other countries. Matsuda argues that in a society that expresses moral judgments through the law and in which the use of law is a characteristic response to many social phenomena, the absence of laws against racist speech in the United States is telling. She advocates that Americans draw from the international standard, adapt existing law, and create new law to limit hate propaganda.

WOMEN AND PORNOGRAPHY

Ronald Dworkin

Ronald Dworkin is Professor of Jurisprudence at Oxford University and Professor of Law and of Philosophy at New York University. He is the author of Freedom's Law: The Moral Reading of the American Constitution *(Harvard, 1996),* Life's Dominion: An Argument about Abortion, Euthanasia, and Individual Freedom *(Knopf, 1993),* Taking Rights Seriously *(Harvard, 1978), and* A Matter of Principle *(Harvard, 1985).*

Dworkin is critical of the feminist movement's reasons for censoring pornography and focuses his attention on the particular arguments in favor of censorship provided by Catharine MacKinnon in Only Words. Dworkin raises objections to MacKinnon's argument that the constitutional guarantees of free speech and press in the First Amendment are justifiably overridden in the case of pornography, which in contributing to the general subordination of women violates the competing constitutional value of equality embedded in the equal protection clause of the Fourteenth Amendment. He argues instead that liberals defend pornography on the basis of the First Amendment precisely because this protects equality in all the processes through which moral and political views are shaped.

1.

People once defended free speech to protect the rights of firebrands attacking government, or dissenters resisting an established church, or radicals campaigning for unpopular political causes. Free speech was plainly worth fighting for, and it still is in many parts of the world where these rights hardly exist. But in America now, free-speech partisans find themselves defending mainly racists shouting "nigger" or Nazis carrying swastikas or—most often—men looking at pictures of naked women with their legs spread open.

Conservatives have fought to outlaw pornography in the United States for a long time: for decades the Supreme court has tried, though without much success, to define a limited category of "obscenity" that the Constitution allows to be banned. But the campaign for outlawing all forms of pornography has been given new and fiercer form, in recent years, by the feminist movement. It might seem odd that feminists have devoted such energy to that campaign: other issues, including abortion and the fight for women's equality in employment and politics seem so much more important. No doubt mass culture is in various ways an obstacle to sexual equality, but the most popular forms of that culture—the view of women presented in soap operas and commercials, for example—are much greater obstacles to that equality than the dirty films watched by a small minority.

But feminists' concentration on pornography nevertheless seems easy to explain. Pornographic photographs, films, and videos are the starkest possible expression of the idea feminists most loath: that women exist principally to provide sexual service to men. Advertisements, soap operas, and popular fiction may actually do more to spread that idea in our culture, but pornography is the rawest, most explicit symbol of it. Like swastikas and burning crosses, pornography is deeply offensive in itself, whether or not it causes any other injustice or harm. It is also

---

Reprinted with permission from *The New York Review of Books* (21 October 1993): 36–42.

particularly vulnerable politically: the religious right supports feminist on this issue, though on few others, so feminists have a much greater chance to win political campaigns for censorship than any of the other campaigns they fight.

And pornography seems vulnerable on principle as well. The conventional explanation of why freedom of speech is important is Mill's theory that truth is most likely to emerge from a "marketplace" of ideas freely exchanged and debated. But most pornography makes no contribution at all to political or intellectual debate: it is preposterous to think that we are more likely to reach truth about anything at all because pornographic videos are available. So liberals defending a right to pornography find themselves triply on the defensive: their view is politically weak, deeply offensive to many women, and intellectually doubtful. Why, then, should we defend pornography? Why should we care if people can no longer watch films of people copulating for the camera, or of women being whipped and enjoying it? What would we lose, except a repellent industry?

Professor Catharine MacKinnon's new book of three short essays, *Only Words*, offers a sharp answer to the last of these questions: society would lose nothing if all pornography were banned, she says, except that women would lose their chains. MacKinnon is the most prominent of the feminists against pornography. She believes that men want to subordinate women, to turn them into sexual devices, and that pornography is the weapon they use to achieve that result. In a series of highly charged articles and speeches, she has tried to talk or shock other women into that view. In 1986, she wrote that

> Pornography constructs what a woman is as what men want from sex. This is what pornography means. ... It institutionalizes the sexuality of male supremacy, fusing the eroticization of dominance and submission with the social construction of male and female. ... Pornography is a harm of male supremacy made difficult to see because of its pervasiveness, potency, and principally, because of its success in making the world a pornographic place.[1]

Only Words is full of language apparently intended to shock. It refers repeatedly to "penises slamming into vaginas," offers page after page of horrifying descriptions of women being whipped, tortured, and raped, and begins with this startling passage:

> You grow up with your father holding you down and covering your mouth so that another man can make a horrible, searing pain between your legs. When you are older, your husband ties you to the bed and drips hot wax on your nipples and brings in other men to watch and makes you smile through it. Your doctor will not give you drugs he has addicted you to unless you suck his penis.

The book offers arguments as well as images, however, and these are presented as a kind of appeal, to the general public, from a judicial decision MacKinnon lost. In 1983, she and a feminist colleague, Andrea Dworkin, drafted an ordinance that outlawed or attached civil penalties to all pornography, defined as the "graphic sexually explicit subordination of women through pictures and/or words" that meet one or more of a series of tests (some of which are impossibly vague) including: "women are presented dehumanized as sexual object, things, or commodities"; or "women are presented as sexual objects experiencing sexual pleasure in rape, incest, or other sexual assaults"; or "in positions of sexual submission, servility, or display"; or "women's body parts—including but not limited to vaginas, breasts, or buttocks—are exhibited such that women are reduced to those parts."

In 1984, largely through their efforts, a similar ordinance was adopted by the Indianapolis legislature. The ordinance included no exception for literary or artistic value, and it could plausibly be interpreted to outlaw not only classic pornography like John Cleland's *Memoirs of a Woman of Pleasure*, but a great deal else, including, for example, D.H. Lawrence's novels and Titian's *Danae*. In 1985, the Seventh Circuit Court of Appeals held the ordinance unconstitutional on the grounds that it violated the First Amendment's guarantees of free speech and press, and in 1986, the Supreme court declined to overrule the Seventh Circuit's decision.[2]

Only Words offers several arguments in favor of the Indianapolis ordinance and against the Seventh

Circuit's ruling, though some of these are run together and must be disentangled to make sense. Some of MacKinnon's arguments are old ones that I have already considered in these pages.[3] But she devotes most of the book to a different and striking claim. She argues that even if the publication of literature degrading to women is protected by the First Amendment, as the Seventh circuit declared, such material offends another, competing constitutional value: the ideal of equality embedded in the equal protection clause of the Fourteenth Amendment, which declares that no state may deprive any person of the equal protection of the laws. If so, she says, then the courts must balance the two constitutional values, and since pornography contributes nothing of any importance to political debate, they should resolve the conflict in favor of equality and censorship.

Unlike MacKinnon's other arguments, this claim has application far beyond the issue of pornography. If her analysis is right, national and state governments have much broader constitutional powers than most lawyers think to prohibit or censor any "politically incorrect" expression that might reasonably be thought to sustain or exacerbate the unequal positions of women or of racial, ethnic, or other minorities. I shall therefore concentrate on this new argument, but I shall first comment briefly on MacKinnon's more conventional points.

2.

In *Only Words*, she repeats the now familiar claim that pornography significantly increases the number of rapes and other sexual crimes. If that claim could be shown to be even probable, through reliable research, it would provide a very strong though not necessarily decisive argument for censorship. But in spite of MacKinnon's fervent declarations, no reputable study has concluded that pornography is a significant cause of sexual crime: many of them conclude, on the contrary, that the causes of violent personality lie mainly in childhood, before exposure to pornography can have had any effect, and that desire for pornography is a symptom rather than a case of deviance.[4] MacKinnon tries to refute these studies, and it is important to see how weak her arguments are. One of them, though repeated several times, is only a metaphysical sleight-of-hand. She several times insists that pornography is not "only words" because it is a "reality." She says that because it is used to stimulate a sexual act—masturbation —it is sex, which seems to suggest that a film or description of rape is itself a kind of rape. But obviously that does not help to show that pornography causes rape in the criminal sense, and it is only the latter claim that can count as a reason for outlawing it.

Sometimes MacKinnon relies on breathtaking hyperbole disguised as common sense. "Sooner of later," she declares, "in one way or another, the consumers want to live out the pornography further in three dimensions. Sooner or later, in one way or another, they do. *It* does make them want to; when they believe they can, when they feel they can get away, *they* do." (Confronted with the fact that many men who read pornography commit no rapes, she suggests that their rapes are unreported.)[5] Elsewhere she appeals to doubtful and unexamined correlations: In a recent article, for example, she declares that "pornography saturated Yugoslavia before the war," and suggests that pornography is therefore responsible for the horrifying and widely reported rapes of Croatian and Muslim women by Serbian soldiers.[6] But, as George Kennan has noted in these pages, rape was also "ubiquitous" in the Balkan wars of 1913, well before any "saturation" by pornography had begun.[7]

Her main arguments, however, are anecdotal: she cites examples of rapists and murderers who report themselves as having been consumers of pornography, like Thomas Shireo, who was sentenced to death in 1981 in Indiana for raping and then killing a young woman (and copulating with her corpse) and who pleaded that he was not responsible because he was a lifelong pornography reader. Such evidence is plainly unreliable, however, not just because it is so often self-serving, but because, as the feminists Deborah Cameron and Elizabeth Fraser have pointed out, criminals are likely to take their views about their own motives from the folklore of their community, whether it is sound or not, rather than from serious analysis of their motives. (Cameron and Fraser, who favor banning pornography on other grounds, concede that "arguments that pornography 'causes' violent acts are, indeed, inadequate.")[8]

MacKinnon's second argument for censorship is a radically different one: that pornography should be banned because it "silences" women by making it more difficult for them to speak and less likely that others will understand what they say. Because of pornography, she says,

> You learn that language does not belong to you. ... You learn that speech is not what you say but what your abusers do to you. ... You develop a self who is ingratiating and obsequious and imitative and aggressively passive and silent.[9]

In an earlier work she put the point even more graphically:

> Who listens to a woman with a penis in her mouth?. ... Anyone who cannot walk down the street or even lie down in her own bed without keeping her eyes cast down and her body clenched against assault is unlikely to have much to say about the issues of the day. ... Any system of freedom of expression that does not address a problem where the free speech of men silences the free speech of women.... is not serious about securing freedom of expression.[10]

On this view, which has been argued more elaborately by others,[11] it is women not pornographers who need First Amendment protection, because pornography humiliates or frightens them into silence and conditions men to misunderstand what they say. (It conditions them to think, for example—as some stupid judges have instructed juries in rape trials—that when a woman says no she sometimes means yes.) Because this argument cites the First Amendment as a reason for banning, not for protecting, pornography, it has the appeal of paradox. But it is premised on an unacceptable proposition: that the right to free speech includes a right to circumstances that encourage one to speak, and a right that others grasp and respect what one means to say.

These are obviously not rights that any society can recognize or enforce. Creationists, flat-earthers, and bigots, for example, are ridiculed in many parts of America now; that ridicule undoubtedly dampens the enthusiasm many of them have for speaking out and limits the attention others pay to what they say. Many political and constitutional theorists, it is true, insist that if freedom of speech is to have any value, it must include some right to the opportunity to speak: they say that a society in which only the rich enjoy access to newspapers, television, or other public media does not accord a genuine right to free speech. But it goes far beyond that to insist that freedom of speech includes not only opportunity to speak to the public but a guarantee of a sympathetic or even competent understanding of what one says.

MacKinnon's third argument centers on the production rather than the distribution or consumption of pornography: she argues that women who act in pornographic films suffer actual, direct sexual subordination, compounded by the fact that their degradation is recorded for posterity. She points out that some women are coerced or tricked into making pornographic films, and mentions the notorious "snuff" films which are said to record the actual murder of women. But of course all these crimes can be prosecuted without banning pornography, and, as MacKinnon herself concedes, it would be wrong to "rely on the fact that some pornography is made through coercion as a legal basis for restricting all of it." Laws banning child pornography are indeed justified on the grounds that children may be damaged by appearing in pornographic films. But these laws, like many others that treat children differently, suppose that they are not competent to understand and consent to acts that may well be against their present and future interests.

It would plainly be a mistake to assume that women (or men) who appear in pornographic films do so unwillingly. Our economic system does, it is true, make it difficult for may women to find satisfactory, fulfilling employment, and may well encourage some of them to accept roles in pornographic films they would otherwise reject. The system, as MacKinnon grimly notes, works to the benefit of the pornographers. But it also works to the benefit of many other employers—fast-food chains, for example—who are able to employ women at low wages. There is great economic injustice in America, but that is not reason for depriving poor women of an economic opportunity some of them may prefer to the available alternatives.

I should mention a fourth consideration that MacKinnon puts forward, though it is difficult to find an argument in it. She says that much pornography is not just speech—it is not "only words"—because it produces erections in men and provides them with masturbatory fantasies. (She warns her readers never to "underestimate the power of an erection.") Her view of the psychology of sexual arousal is mechanical—she thinks men who read pornography "are sexually habituated to its kick, a process that is largely unconscious and works as primitive conditioning, with pictures and words as sexual stimuli." In any case, she thinks that pornography's physiological power deprives it of First Amendment protection: "An orgasm is not an argument," she says, "and cannot be argued with. Compared with a thought, it raises far less difficult speech issues, if it raises any at all." But that seems a plain non sequitur: a piece of music or a work of art or poetry does not lose whatever protection the First Amendment affords it when some people find it sexually arousing, even if that effect does not depend on its argumentative or aesthetic merits, or whether it has any such merits at all.

3.

The continued popularity of bad arguments such as those in *Only Words* testifies to the strength of the real but hidden reason why so many people despise pornography, and want to ban it. The sado-masochistic genre of pornography particularly, is so comprehensibly degrading that we are appalled and shamed by its existence. Contrary to MacKinnon's view, almost all men, I think, are as disgusted by it as almost all women. Because those who want to forbid pornography know that offensiveness alone does not justify censorship, however, they disguise their repulsion as concern that pornography will cause rape, or silence women, or harm the women who make it.

In the most interesting parts of *Only Words*, MacKinnon offers a new argument that is also designed to transcend mere repulsion. She says that the way in which pornography is offensive—that it portrays women as submissive victims who enjoy torture and mutilation—contributes to the unequal opportunities of women in American society, and therefore contradicts the values meant to be protected by the equal protection clause. She concedes, for the sake of this argument, that in spite of its minimal contribution to intellectual or political debate, pornography is protected under the First Amendment. But that First Amendment protection must be balanced, she says, against the Fourteenth Amendment's requirement that people be treated equally. "The law of equality and the law of freedom of speech are on a collision course in this country," she says, and she argues that the balance, which has swung too far toward liberty, must now be redressed.

The censorship of pornography, she says, should be regarded as like other kinds of government action designed to create genuine equality of opportunity. It is now accepted by almost everyone that government may properly prohibit discrimination against blacks and women in employment and education, for example. But such discrimination may take the form, not merely of refusing them jobs or university places, but of subjecting those who do manage to find jobs or places to an environment of insult and prejudice that makes work or education less attractive or even impossible. Government prohibits racial or sexual harassment at work—it punishes employers who subject blacks to racial insult or women to sexual pressures, in spite of the fact that these objectionable practices are carried out through speech—and many universities have adopted "speech codes" that prohibit racial insults in classrooms or on campus.

Banning or publishing pornography, MacKinnon suggests, should be regarded as a more general remedy of the same kind. If pornography contributes to the general subordination of women by picturing them as sexual or servile objects, as she believes it does, then eliminating pornography can also be defended as serving equality of opportunity even though it restricts liberty.[12] The "egalitarian" argument for censorship is in many ways like the "silencing" argument I described earlier: it supposes not that pornography significantly increases sexual crimes of violence, but that it works more insidiously to damage the standing and power of women within the community. But the "egalitarian" argument is in two ways different and apparently more cogent.

First, it claims not a new and paradoxical conflict within the idea of liberty, as the silencing argument does, but a conflict between liberty and equality, two ideals that many political philosophers think more often in conflict. Second, it is more limited in its scope. The "silencing" argument supposes that everyone—the bigot and the creationist as well the social reformer—has a right to whatever respectful attention on the part of others is necessary to encourage him to speak his mind and to guarantee that he will be correctly understood; and that is absurd. The "egalitarian" argument, on the contrary, supposes only that certain groups—those that are victims of persisting disadvantage in our society—should not be subjected to the kind of insult, harassment, or abuse that has contributed to that disadvantage.

But the "egalitarian" argument is nevertheless much broader and more dangerous in its scope than might first appear. The analogies MacKinnon proposes—to sexual harassment laws and university speech codes—are revealing, because though each of these forms of regulation might be said to serve a general egalitarian purpose, they are usually defended on much more limited and special grounds. Laws against sexual harassment are designed to protect women not from the diffuse effects of whatever derogatory opinions about them are part of the general culture, but from direct sexual taunts and other degrading language in the workplace.[13] University speech codes are defended on a different ground: they are said to serve an educational purpose by preserving the calm and reflective atmosphere of mutual respect and of appreciation for a diversity of cultures and opinions that is essential for effective teaching and research.

I do not mean that such regulations raise no problems about free speech. They do. Even if university speech codes, for example, are enforced fairly and scrupulously (and in the charged atmosphere of university politics they often are not) they sometimes force teachers and students to compromise or suppress their opinions by erring on the side of safety, and some speech codes may actually be unconstitutional. I mean only that constraints on speech at work and on the campus can be defended without appealing to the frightening principle that considerations of equality require that some people not be free to express their tastes or convictions or preferences anywhere. MacKinnon's argument for banning pornography from the community as a whole does presuppose this principle, however, and accepting her argument would therefore have devastating consequences.

Government could then forbid the graphic or visceral or emotionally charged expression of any opinion or conviction that might reasonably offend a disadvantaged group. It could outlaw performances of *The Merchant of Venice*, or films about professional women who neglect their children, or caricatures or parodies of homosexuals in nightclub routines. Courts would have to balance the value of such expression, as a contribution to public debate or learning, against the damage it might cause to the standing or sensibilities of its targets. MacKinnon thinks that pornography is different from other forms of discriminatory or hostile speech. But the argument she makes for banning it would apply to much else. She pointedly decares that freedom of speech is respected too much by Americans and that the Supreme Court was right in 1952 when it sustained a prosecution of anti-Semitic literature—a decision it has since abandoned[14]—and wrong in 1978 when it struck down an ordinance banning a Nazi march in Illinois.[15]

So if we must make the choice between liberty and equality that MacKinnon envisages—if the two constitutional values really are on a collision course—we should have to choose liberty because the alternative would be the despotism of thought-police.

But is she right that the two values do conflict in this way? Can we escape despotism only by cheating on the equality the constitution also guarantees? The most fundamental egalitarian command of the Constitution is for equality throughout the political process. We can imagine some compromises of political equality that would plainly aid disadvantaged groups—it would undoubtedly aid blacks and women, for example, if citizens who have repeatedly expressed racist or sexist or bigoted views were denied the vote altogether. That would be unconstitutional, of course; the Constitution demands that everyone be permitted to play an equal part in the formal process of choosing a president, a Congress, and other officials, that no one be excluded on the ground that his opinions or tastes are too offensive or unreasonable or despicable to count.

Elections are not all there is to politics, however, Citizens play a continuing part in politics between elections, because informal public debate and argument influences what responsible officials—and officials anxious for re-election—will do. So the First Amendment contributes a great deal to political equality: it insists that just as no one may be excluded from the vote because his opinions are despicable, so no one may be denied the right to speak or write or broadcast because what he will say is too offensive to be heard.

That amendment serves other goals as well, of course: free speech helps to expose official stupidity and corruption, and it allows vigorous public debate that sometimes generates new ideas and refutes old ones. But the First Amendment's egalitarian role is independent of these other goals: it forbids censoring cranks or neo-Nazis not because anyone thinks that their contributions will prevent corruption or improve public debate, but just because equality demands that everyone, no matter how eccentric or despicable, have a chance to influence policies as well as elections. Of course it does not follow that government will in the end respect everyone's opinion equally, or that official decisions will be equally congenial to all groups. Equality demands that everyone's opinion be given a chance for influence, not that anyone's opinion will triumph or even be represented in what government eventually does.

The First Amendment's egalitarian role is not confined, however, to political speech. People's lives are affected not just by their political environment—not just by what their presidents and legislators and other public officials do—but even more comprehensively by what we might call their moral environment. How others treat me—and my own sense of identity and self-respect—are determined in part by the mix of social conventions, opinions, tastes, convictions, prejudices, life styles, cultures that flourish in the community in which I live. Liberals are sometimes accused of thinking that what people say or do or think in private has no impact on anyone except themselves, and that is plainly wrong. Someone to whom religion is of fundamental importance, for example, will obviously lead a very different and perhaps more satisfying life in a community in which most other people share his convictions than in a dominantly secular society of atheists for whom his beliefs are laughable superstitions. A woman who believes that explicit sexual material degrades her will likely lead a very different, and no doubt more satisfying, life among people who also despise pornography than in a community where others, including other women, think it liberating and fun.

Exactly because the moral environment in which we all live is in good part created by others, however, the question of who shall have the power to help shape that environment, and how, is of fundamental importance, though it is often neglected in political theory. Only one answer is consistent with the ideals of political equality: that no one may be prevented from influencing the shared moral environment, through his own private choices, tastes, opinions, and example, just because these tastes or opinions disgust those who have the power to shut him up or lock him up. Of course, the ways in which anyone may exercise that influence must be limited in order to protect the security and interests of others. People may not try to mold the moral climate by intimidating women with sexual demands or by burning a cross on a black family's lawn, or by refusing to hire women or blacks at all, or by making their working conditions so humiliating as to be intolerable.

But we cannot count, among the kinds of interests that may be protected in this way, a right not to be insulted or damaged just by the fact that others have hostile or uncongenial tastes, or that they are free to express or indulge them in private. Recognizing that right would mean denying that some people—those whose tastes these are—have any right to participate in forming the moral environment at all. Of course it should go without saying that no one has a right to *succeed* in influencing others through his own private choices and tastes. Sexists and bigots have no right to live in a community whose ideology or culture is even partially sexist or bigoted: they have no right to any proportional representation for their odious views. In a genuinely egalitarian society, however, those views cannot be locked out, in advance, by criminal or civil law: they must instead be discredited by the disgust, outrage, and ridicule of other people.

MacKinnon's "egalitarian" argument for censorship is important mainly because it reveals the most important reason for resisting her suggestions, and also because it allows us to answer her charge that liberals who oppose her are crypto-pornographers themselves. She thinks that people who defend the right to pornography are acting out of self-interest, not principle—she says she has been driven to the conclusion that "speech *will* be defined so that men can have their pornography." That charge is based on the inadequacy of the conventional explanation, deriving from John Stuart Mill, that pornography must be protected so that truth may emerge. What is actually at stake in the argument about pornography, however, is not society's chance to discover truth, but its commitment to the very ideal of equality that MacKinnon thinks underrated in the American community. Liberals defend pornography, though most of them despise it, in order to defend a conception of the First Amendment that includes, as at least one of its purposes, protecting equality in the processes through which the moral as well as the political environment is formed. First Amendment liberty is not equality's enemy, but the other side of equality's coin.

MacKinnon is right to emphasize the connection between the fight over pornography and the larger, more general and important, argument about the freedom of Americans to say and teach what others think politically incorrect. She and her followers regard freedom of speech and thought as an elitist, inegalitarian ideal that has been of almost no value to woman, blacks, and others without power; they say America would be better off if it demoted that ideal as many other nations have. But most of her constituents would be appalled if this denigration of freedom should escape from universities and other communities where their own values about political correctness are now popular and take root in the more general political culture. Local majorities may find homosexual art or feminist theater just as degrading to women as the kind of pornography MacKinnon hates, or radical or separatist black opinion just as inimical to racial justice as crude racist epithets.

That is an old liberal warning—as old as Voltaire—and many people have grown impatient with it. They are willing to take that chance, they say, to advance a program that seems overwhelmingly important now. Their impatience may prove fatal for that program rather than essential to it, however. If we abandon our traditional understanding of equality for a different one that allows a majority to define some people as too corrupt or offensive or radical to join in the informal moral life of the nation, we will have begun a process that ends, as it has in so may other parts of the world, in making equality something to be feared rather than celebrated, a mocking, "correct" euphemism for tyranny.

NOTES

1. Catharine MacKinnon, "Pornography, Civil Rights and Speech," reprinted in Catherine Itzin, editor, *Pornography: Women, Violence and Civil Liberties, A Radical View* (Oxford University Press, 1992), page 456. (Quotations are from 461-463)
2. *American Booksellers Ass'n v. Hudnut*, 771 F. 2d 323 (1985), aff'd 475 US 1001 (1986). In a decision that MacKinnon discusses at length, a Canadian court upheld a similar Canadian statute as consistent with that nation's Charter of Rights and Freedoms, I discuss that decision in "The Coming Battle over Free Speech," *The New York Review*, June 11, 1992.
3. "Two Concepts of Liberty," in *Isaiah Berlin: A Celebration*, edited by Edna and Avishai Margalit (University of Chicago Press, 1991), and printed in *The New York Review of Books*, August 15, 1991.
4. Among the prestigious studies denying the causal link MacKinnon claims are the 1970 report of the National Commission on Obscenity and Pornography, appointed by Lyndon Johnson to consider the issue, the 1979 report of the Williams Commission in Britain, and a recent year-long British study which concluded that "the evidence does not point to pornography as a cause of deviant sexual orientation in offenders. Rather it seems to be used as part of that deviant sexual orientation." MacKinnon and other feminists cite the voluminous, two-volume report of the infamous Meese Commission, which was appointed by Reagan to contradict the findings of the

earlier Johnson-appointed group and was headed by people who had made a career of opposing pornography. The Meese Commission duly declared that although the scientific evidence was inconclusive, it believed that pornography (vast tracts of which were faithfully reprinted in its report) did indeed cause crime. But the scientists on whose work the report relied protested, immediately after its publication, that the commission had misunderstood and misused their work. (For a thorough analysis of all these and other studies, see Marcia Pally, *Sense and Censorship: The Vanity of Bonfires* [Americans for Constitutional Freedom, 1991]). MacKinnon also appeals to legal authority: she says, citing the Seventh Circuit opinion holding her antipornography statute unconstitutional, that "not even courts equivocate over [pornography's] carnage anymore." But this is disingenuous: that opinion assumed that pornography is a significant cause of sexual crime only for the sake of the argument it made, and it cited, among other material, the Williams Commission report, as support for the Court's own denial of any such demonstrated causal connection.

5. In "Pornography, Civil Rights and Speech," MacKinnon said,"It does not make sense to assume that pornography has no role in rape simply because little about its use or effects distinguishes convicted rapists from other men, when we know that a lot of those other men do rape women; they just never get caught." (page 475).
6. "Turning Rape Into Pornography: Postmodern Genocide," *Ms.*, July/August 1993, p. 28.
7. "The Balkan Crisis: 1913 and 1993," *The New York Review*, July 15, 1993.
8. Catherine Itzin, editor, *Pornography: Women, Violence and Civil Liberties*, p. 359. At one point MacKinnon offers a surprisingly timid formulation of her causal thesis: she says that "there is no evidence that pornography does no harm." The same negative claim can be made, of course, about any genre of literature. Ted Bundy, the serial murderer who said he had read pornography since his youth, and whom feminists often cite for that remark, also said that he had studied Dostoevsky's *Crime and Punishment*. Even MacKinnon's weak statement is controversial, moreover. Some psychologists have argued that pornography, by providing a harmless outlet for violent tendencies, may actually reduce that amount of such crime. See Patricia Gillian, "Therapeutic Uses of Obscenity," and other articles reprinted and cited in *Censorship and Obscenity*, edited by Rajeev Dhavan and Christie Davies (Rowman and Littlefield, 1978). And it is at least relevant that nations with the most permissive laws about pornography are among those with the least sexual crime (see Marjorie Heins, *Sex, Sin, and Blasphemy*, New Press, 1993, p. 152), though of course that fact might be explained in other ways.
9. MacKinnon's frequent rhetorical use of "you" and "your," embracing all female readers, invites every woman to see herself as a victim of the appalling sexual crimes and the abuses she describes, and reinforces an implicit suggestion that women are, in pertinent ways, all alike: all passive, innocent, and subjugated.
10. Reprinted in Catherine Itzin, editor *Pornography: Women, Violence and Civil Liberties*, p. 483-484.
11. See Frank I. Michelman, "Conceptions of Democracy in American Constitutional Argument: The Case of Pornography Regulation," *Tennessee Law Review* Vol. 56. No. 2 (1989), pp. 303-304.
12. Not all feminists agree that pornography contributes to the economic or social subordination of women. Linda Williams, for example, in the Fall, 1993 issue of the *Threepenny Review*, claims that "the very fact that today a variety of different pornographies are now on the scene in mass market videos is good for feminism, and that to return to the time of repressing pornographic sexual representations would mean the resurgence of at least some elements of an underground tradition ... of misogyny."
13. See Barbara Presley Noble, "New Reminders on Harassment," *The New York Times*, August 15, 1993, p. 25.
14. *Beauharnais v. Illinois*, 343 US 250 (1952), abandoned in *New York Times v. Sullivan*, 376 US 254 (1964) at 268-269.
15. See *Smith v. Collins*, 439 US 916 (1978).

FEMINIST ANTI-PORNOGRAPHY STRUGGLES: NOT THE CHURCH, BUT MAYBE THE STATE

Marvin Glass

Marvin Glass is an Associate Professor of Philosophy at Carleton University in Ottawa. He has published articles in ethics and social and political philosophy and is currently working on feminist ethics and children's rights. "Feminist Anti-Pornography Struggles" is from a manuscript entitled Feminism 'From Above': Pornography and State Censorship.

What are appropriate feminist politics in regard to pornography? Many respond: "Not censorship; women can't trust the patriarchal state to frame, pass, and enforce pro-feminist, anti-pornography legislation." But most pro-censorship feminists also rely on a model of the modern state which rules out such trust. Moreover, unlike their critics, they do not relegate to private market forces the determinants of words and pictures which will ultimately frame dominant ideas of women's sexuality. "But if pornography is censored, it will just go underground." Good!

> Whenever there is an ascendant class, a large portion of the morality of the country emanates from its class interests and its feelings of class superiority. The morality between Spartans and Helots, between planters and negroes, between princes and subjects, between nobles and returiers, between men and women, has been for the most part the creation of these class interests and feelings. ... (John Stuart Mill)[1]

> Pornography, in the feminist view, is a form of forced sex, a practice of sexual politics, an institution of gender inequality. ... The feminist critique of pornography ... proceeds from women's point of view, meaning the standpoint of the subordination of women to men. (Catharine MacKinnon)[2]

Although this paper begins with quotations from J.S. Mill and Catharine MacKinnon, my views on pornography and the state were not always so esoteric. Like most males of my generation, I first became interested in pornography in my early teens, about the same time that we also considered initiating ourselves into the equally illicit world of smoking. Parental prohibition of these activities was usually based on implausible claims to the effect that we were still too young to look at pictures of naked women or inhale cigarette smoke, and so my sceptical friends and I set out to acquire these desiderata. Lack of age being the basis of our supply problem, it was clear what had to be done. First, contribute collectively to the 35-cent cost of a package of cigarettes or the 50 cents needed for a copy of *Playboy*; second, designate the oldest-looking boy in the bunch as procurer; and finally, find a far-sighted storekeeper. Of course, this strategy eventually worked.

These episodes in the life and times of my little group, particularly the pornography escapade, were instrumental to the development of our adolescent male-bonding and consciousness-lowering. For example, should we invite a few girls we know to our pornography and tobacco sessions? You must be kidding! Is the centrefold looking at us? She must be; we're the only ones here. Many years later, I regret to say that I still smoke, though now I often do it in mixed company. But seriously, thanks to the wisdom

Published with permission of Marvin Glass.

and inspiration of feminists I have worked with and read, particularly Catherine MacKinnon in the latter category, my interest in contemporary commercial pornography is now predominantly political.

I first thought about freedom of speech when, in 1974, I noticed posters denouncing Nobel Prize-winning physicist William Shockley as a 'racist' and urging people to picket and obstruct, that is, censor, his Harvard University talk on alleged innate differences in intelligence between blacks and whites. Because I had never even entertained, let alone embraced, the idea that opposition to racism might be linked with opposition to free speech, I did not join the protesters. But, having some sabbatical time on my hands, I decided to investigate the matter. I read John Stuart Mill's *On Liberty* a few times, perused some commentaries, delved into a couple of books on racism, added a pinch or two of what I thought was historical materialism, neatly sidestepped the issue of censorship and the state and eventually produced a paper on the topic arguing for the moral permissibility of at least some such political protests.[3]

I first thought seriously about free speech in the context of modern pornography when, a year later, I read the aforementioned paper at a conference in Calgary to a group comprised mainly of leftist academics. Predictably, reaction was mixed, but there was one question for which I was totally unprepared. "If you are willing to censor racist language" a feminist in the audience asked, "are you also prepared to censor sexist images—*Playboy*, for example?" I had no idea how to respond, admitted as much, and said I would have to think about the matter. Almost twenty-five years later, I feel more-or-less ready to attempt an answer. This paper is part of that answer and it is a rejoinder to what is perhaps one of the most compelling anti-censorship arguments, one popular both with feminists who agree that pornography harms women and with feminists who think pornography has more benign effects, and thus concede its alleged harm only for the sake of argument. The concern that motivates this anti-censorship argument is best summed up in this rhetorical question posed by Lisa Duggan, Nan Hunter, and Carole Vance: "How can feminists be entrusting the patriarchal state with the task of legally distinguishing permissible from impermissible images?"[4] That is to say, although not as sexist as its predecessors, the modern state's strong prejudice against women's interests, including their sexual interests, would surely transform any genuine anti-pornography concepts and principles from feminist drawing boards into laws whose first target would be feminist representations of sexuality, especially lesbian ones.

The purposes of this paper are twofold. First, I want to answer some of the concerns that the state cannot be entrusted to deal with pornography by critically examining a number of feminist articulations of this distrust. Second, I want to undermine the privatization alternative to state censorship: the claim that a 'free market' in sexual imagery is currently in women's best interests. As regards particular pro-censorship tactics, this paper does not distinguish between criminal code sanctions against pornography and the civil rights strategy pioneered by Andrea Dworkin and Catherine MacKinnon. Elsewhere, however, I defend a feminist preference for the former approach.

Distrusting the State

At first sight, a strategy against misogynist representations of women's sexuality involving state bureaucrats and state mechanisms appears to be another misguided case of 'feminism from above,' that is, letting foxes stand guard over chicken coops or, as Audre Lorde might say, trying to use the master's tools to dismantle the master's house. Thus, Brats and Kok, in an article provocatively titled "Penal Sanctions as Feminist Strategy: A Contradiction in Terms?" urge women not to forget that: "by invoking the criminal justice, we are appealing to forces which are beyond our control and which, given the present political climate, may well get out of hand."[5] Erica Jong agrees: "Despite the ugliness of a lot of pornography ... I believe that censorship only springs back against the givers of culture—against authors, artists, and feminists, against anyone who wants to change society. Should censorship be imposed again, whether through the kind of legislation introduced in Minneapolis or Indianapolis, or through other means, feminists would be the first to suffer."[6] And Mariana Valverde and Lorna Weir believe that censoring pornography is not an appropriate strategy for feminists, particularly lesbian feminists, to pursue because "[l]egislation of this kind will only undermine our attempts to give birth to a lesbian culture. Under stricter pornography legislation, the sexist and anti-lesbian features in *Penthouse* might be prohibited—but such tougher laws could be applied equally to lesbian sexual representation."[7]

What political conclusions are to be drawn from the fact that all state institutions, particularly the police and the judiciary, are controlled primarily by men, many of whose attitudes are sexist (and racist and homophobic)? Is the question the choice between the wisdom of trusting the state to enact and enforce feminist-inspired, anti-pornography laws versus the willingness of anti-censorship feminists, such as ACLU president Nadine Strossen, "to trust our own voices—as well as those of our own anti-pornography sister feminists—to effectively counter misogynist expression, including misogynist sexual expression?"[8] If so, then history speaks clearly and consistently: women cannot trust this kind of state to be a vehicle for their liberation. But are there really feminists who embrace the contrary view, who explicitly or even implicitly place their *trust* in the modern state to effect progressive change for women?

Carol Smart thinks there are. At the end of her evaluation of the Catharine MacKinnon/Andrea Dworkin civil rights, anti-pornography strategy she warns "that there are major problems in transforming any feminist analysis of women's oppression into a legal practice, as if law were merely an instrument to be utilized by feminist lawyers with the legal skills to draw up statutes."[9] And what puzzles Pratiba Parmar "is how women who define men as the enemy can ask the 'patriarchal state' to intervene on their behalf and pass laws in the interest of women. Expecting the state to behave in a benevolent manner is naive."[10] Adrienne Rich joins the chorus: "I am less sure than Dworkin and MacKinnon that this is a time when further powers of suppression should be turned over to the state."[11] Even neo-conservative pundit George Will appears to grasp the problem: "For someone who so strenuously loathes American society, MacKinnon is remarkably eager to vest in this society's representative government vast powers to regulate expression."[12]

Are MacKinnon and Dworkin political pollyannas? After all, most feminists recognize structural sexism within modern legal systems. MacKinnon herself puts it this way: "The law sees and treats women the way men see and treat women. The liberal state coercively and authoritatively constitutes the social order in the interests of men as a gender".[13] And Dworkin claims that "[t]here is not a feminist alive who could possibly look to the male legal system for real protection from the systematized sadism of men."[14] These are not the words of two women afflicted with a terminal case of feminist political naivete, with the utopian view that the law can be entrusted, *carte blanche*, with representations of women's sexuality. Doubtless, as pro-censorship feminists they must believe that, for all its power, the patriarchal state is not omnipotent, that feminist-led coalitions are sometimes capable of pressuring it to enact and enforce some feminist-inspired laws. Are they entitled to believe this?

Not according to most of their critics. Nadine Strossen is just one of many commentators who characterize the Dworkin/MacKinnon analysis of sexism as a kind of patriarchal fatalism inconsistent with pro-censorship activism.

> The fundamental premise in the pro-censorship's philosophy—that our entire societal and legal system is patriarchal, reflecting and perpetuating the subordination of women—itself conclusively refutes their conclusion that we should hand over to that state additional power. The pro-censorship feminists cannot have it both ways. If, as they contend, government power is inevitably used to the particular disadvantage of relatively disempowered groups, it follows that women's rights advocates should oppose measures that augment that power, including Dworkin/MacKinnon type laws.[15]

But no quotation or even specific reference is offered in support of Strossen's claim that MacKinnon and Dworkin are committed to government power "inevitably" being used to the detriment of women. Moreover, claiming to see a few windows of opportunity for anti-pornography feminists here is consistent with believing that even modest censorship victories will be impossible without grass roots organizing, education, lobbying, vigilance, and good luck, followed by more such organizing, additional education, extra vigilance, etc. Thus, when Andrea Dworkin says that "[w]omen fight to reform male law ... because something is better than nothing," *trust* of the state has nothing to do with her politics.[16] Nor do she and MacKinnon believe that campaigns against pornography should be restricted solely to passing civil rights ordinances: "Feminists have been fighting pornography for ... years. Pickets, demonstrations, slide shows, debates, leaflets, civil disobedience, must all continue. ... Passing the ordinance *does not mean stopping* direct action, it means more of it."[17]

Myrna Kostash's views offer another illustration of how an anarchist approach can distort feminist political thinking about pornography.

> Some feminists argue that the issue is to, as the feminist newspaper *Broadside* has expressed it, 'regain control of the state's power by redefining and refining the definition of obscenity so that it meets our standards and needs.' But ... the state is hardly a neutral, let alone pro-woman institution that can be captured and directed towards our projects; it is specific to the development of capitalist patriarchy; its capture and transformation require a revolution.[18]

Aside from parting company with *Broadside* over the notion of women "regaining" state control—they never had it—I want to defend the spirit of their project to redefine and refine the definition of obscenity.

For the foreseeable future, feminist politics will involve neither the capture of the modern state nor its transformation into a pro-woman institution. To claim otherwise, to say that these are reasonable short or mid-term goals for feminism, assumes a near-impotent state and a large, highly organized, and militant women's movement. But neither of these presuppositions correspond to current or near-future reality. Instead, a realistic feminist political agenda would include pressuring an unsympathetic, often hostile state and to pass or retain legislation for pay equity and affirmative action and against sexual harassment, as well as to fund abortion and battered women's shelters. Why not include some feminist-inspired anti-pornography legislation on this list? To insist that this cannot be done without some kind of gender revolution flagrantly ignores the historical record of victories by oppressed groups, including women, where an increase in state control over some aspect of civil society has benefitted them. With all their warts and scars, publicly funded education and health care (more on these later), minimum wage and workers' safety legislation are good examples of such victories. Did the governments which reluctantly adopted these measures miraculously shed forever their traditional race, class, and gender skins? Of course not; indeed, much of the progressive legislation adopted in the past sixty years is currently being diluted and even reversed by liberal, conservative, and social-democratic governments throughout the world. But to deny that, at the time of enactment, these were at least minor victories and thus small steps forward is to denigrate both reforms and reformers.[19]

A more compelling version of the "women-can't-trust-the-patriarchal-state" anti-censorship argument has been developed by Lynn King. After reviewing the history of the "Family Law Reform Act" and equal pay legislation in Ontario, King concludes:

> We must always distinguish between laws that protect women's right to public resources, such as funding for day care or battered women's shelters, and those over which we have no control. These have been and will continue to be used to maintain women's second class status. ... [L]aws dealing with pornography and censorship ... are subject to interpretation by people who are selected by an anti-feminist system. ... For feminists who are concerned about sexism, sexuality, and sexual representation, legal reform is a trap. Let's leave it unsprung and move on to better ways.[20]

What better ways do anti-censorship feminists have in mind for those concerned about the current state of the sexual representation of women? Elizabeth Wilson's analysis of the shifting politics of sex and censorship leads her to conclude that "a truly feminist agenda on sex, sexuality, and representation would emphasize the need for sex education for children".[21] Varda Burstyn, after bemoaning the scarcity of television material produced by Planned Parenthood, feminist, gay, or even forward looking church groups, proposes that government fund art bodies at all levels. "In the area of sexuality, this means subsidizing feminist and gay cultural workers and their projects in particular."[22] These feminists adopt a Brandeisian 'more speech' response to pornography, that is, fighting 'bad' words and pictures with 'good' ones. Other non-censorship alternatives focus on job creation and law enforcement, with Ellis, O'Dair, and Talmar arguing that "[t]rue concern with violence against women would be expressed in demands as ... the rigorous enforcement of laws against rape,"[23] and Lynn Segal insisting that the only effective way of enabling women to avoid violence is "state funding for women refugees, anti-sexist, anti-violence educational initiatives, and above all empowering women through improved job prospects, housing and welfare facilities."[24]

First, the Brandeis strategy. In *Whitney v. California*, U.S. Supreme Court Justice Louis Brandeis said: "if there be time to expose through discussion the falsehood and fallacies, to avert the evil by the process of education, the remedy to be applied is *more speech, not enforced silence*."[25] Many (but not all) feminists who oppose censorship concede that there is an "evil" here, that is, they agree that the production and dissemination of pornography contribute to some extent to job discrimination, pay inequity, sexual harassment, sexual assault, and rape against women. Thelma McCormack, for example, claims that "a cultural milieu in which women are always perceived as sex objects contributes to the devaluation of women."[26] And Duggan, Hunter and Vance admit that "pornography magnifies the misogyny in society."[27] Varda Burstyn is equally candid: "we would never suggest that sexually explicit, sexist images do not harm [women] when we so strongly insist that sexist imagery of all kinds is a powerful course in our culture as a whole".[28] Well, given women's economic and political resources, suppose that the Brandeisian educational/anti-censorship approach, if it ever did succeed, took a hundred and fifty years longer than the MacKinnon/Dworkin strategy to achieve a significant reduction in the impact of misogynist pornography. According to what criteria would Judge Brandeis say that there was time to wait? What is reasonable progress here for those who continually suffer the evil, that is, for *women*? Invariably, like Brandeis, those who urge this strategy as an alternative to censorship are silent on this important question.

Secondly, there is a disturbing ambivalence to the modern state exhibited in these alternatives to legal regulation. Why is it deemed reasonable to expect pressure to bring about rigour in state enforcement of rape laws, but unreasonable to expect agitation to lead to the enforcement of moderately progressive anti-pornography laws? Why would such a state ideologically and financially underwrite progressive sex education programs, but refrain from replacing anachronistic obscenity laws with some feminist inspired anti-pornography legislation? Why would it be any more inclined to subsidize feminist cultural enterprises than it would be to appoint at least some pro-feminist censors or judges? Why could feminists compete successfully against the Christian Right for government funding but not for progressive anti-pornography laws? And why would a homophobic state—inclined, we are told, to distort irredeemably any feminist attempt to censor pornography—give lesbian and gay groups substantial funding to produce symbols of non-exploitative, non-heterosexual sexuality?

When Robin Morgan (often mistakenly characterized as pro-censorship solely on the basis of her famous quip that "pornography is the theory; rape is the practice") asserts that "a phallocentric culture is more likely to begin its censorship purges with books on pelvic self-examination for women or books containing lyrical peans to lesbianism than with *See Him Tear And Kill Her*," she is surely right.[29] But this is a tautology and therefore is of no help in comparative judgements about different strategies against pornography. Because 'phallocentrism' permeates *all* major institutions of society, feminist liberation struggles face one or two strikes against them *wherever* they turn. Thus, the sexist and homophobic forces which operate at the level of the state would be involved in both censorship *and* funding decisions. With regard to the latter, it is well-known that they almost always come with strings attached and are often restrained by boards of directors and executive committees not directly controlled by users and workers.[30] Does this mean that feminists should accept only *carte blanche* government cheques for the production of erotica? However high-minded and principled this approach may appear, it is certain to maximize the marginalization of feminist culture because such pristine cheques will, for the foreseeable future, be few and far between. Of course, one could naively revert to the old saw that in any struggle between cultural opposites—here state-untainted but vastly underfunded and minimally distributed feminist erotica vs. ubiquitous misogynist pornography—quality and truth always triumph. Instead, why not critically support both some less-than-perfect funding options and some equally flawed censorship legislation? That is, instead of rejecting out-of-hand the legislative approach, why not balance the chances of a particular piece of legislation being adopted and enforced, the frequency of misapplication and costs thereof, and the harm to women and girls the adoption and enforcement of such a law would prevent.

Trusting the Free Market

Anti-censorship feminism based on the distrust of the state is sometimes expounded in the name of both feminism and Marxism. I want to examine one such example to raise a second issue of trust—not of the state, but of the free market. Consider Sharon Smith's "Feminists For A Strong State?" In this review of MacKinnon's *Toward a Feminist Theory of the State*, Smith, after quoting Frederick Engels on the class nature of the state, concludes that:

> The state contributes to the oppression of women through its role as the enforcer of the prevailing level of class exploitation. Any strengthening of the state is a strengthening of the means of repression of the working class. ... The point for socialists—indeed for all those interested in women's liberation—is to weaken the hold of the state over worker's individual lives, not to strengthen it. Liberal democratic values such as freedom of speech, scorned by both MacKinnon and Brownmiller, strengthen the ability of the workers to organize against their exploitation and oppression. Lenin put this clearly in *State and Revolution*, when he wrote: 'We are in favour of a democratic republic as the best form of state for the proletariat under capitalism ....'[31]

The very brief quotation from Lenin is found in the context of his defense of Marx's critique of "a free people's state," a slogan which appeared in the *Gotha Program* of the German Social Democratic Party of the 1870's. But there is no mention of unlimited free speech, let alone endorsements of it, in either Marx's critique or Lenin's commentary, and arguably neither of them would reject legal sanctions against sexist pornography. Marx, for example, inveighed in more general terms against Sharon Smith's nineteenth century anti-statist precursors, followers of the anarchist (and extreme misogynist) Pierre Joseph Proudhon: "They scorn all ... action which can be carried through by political means (for instance, the legal shortening of the working day). Under the *pretext of freedom*, or of anti-governmentalism, or of anti-authoritarian individualism, these gentlemen ... actually preach ordinary bourgeois economy."[32] One doubts that Smith would oppose federal or state regulation of the length of the working day and instead, like their bosses, urge workers to exercise their "proletarian freedom from below" and negotiate such matters in individual labour contracts. Why then would women's interests best be served by her advice to feminists to abandon state regulation as part of an anti-pornography strategy?

Smith says the point for all those interested in women's liberation is "to weaken the state control over worker's [women's] lives." Well, we can at least agree that any such liberation means empowering women by making their lives safer. But, in the context of sexist pornography, this means weakening the *pornographer's* control over women lives. Yet privatization of pornography, that is, leaving its ownership and control to market forces—which is what, at least in the short run, her agenda amounts to—is unlikely to empower women or ensure feminist sexual expression a prominent place in our cultural landscape. Smith's strategy implicitly accepts the economic status quo and expects women to struggle there, thus relegating decisions about appropriate representations of sexuality to a sphere of society where profit, not justice for women, or women's welfare, or women's sexual interest is the litmus test for economic choice.

Today the market is near-ubiquitous, increasingly concentrated and powerful, and dripping red in tooth and claw. Its sexual component takes thirteen year old Thai and Filipino girls and serves them up as sexual delight on prostitution tours. It breaks their tiny backs in third-world sweat shops so that sneakers and slacks, after the appropriate inducement of multi-million dollar ad campaigns, can be sold in first-world countries. The global market feminizes poverty throughout the world. One generation of affirmative action for women is too much for it to bear. In the name of increasing personal choice, it makes desperate women guinea pigs for multinational drug companies and creates a class of reproductive prostitutes (so-called 'surrogate mothers'). It does this and much, much more to women, and it does it, as Smith's heroes, Marx and Engels, noted 150 years ago, "in the icy waters of egoistic calculation. It has resolved personal worth into exchange value."[33] These facts of the free market should have us question some of the feminist anti-pornography distrust of the state and the corresponding plethora of gloomy predictions of cultural losses for women should censorship be imposed.

The political relationship between feminist-inspired culture(s), the market, and the nature of the modern state may be illuminated by considering two analogies, one with health care and the other with schooling. Most feminists support publicly-funded health care over private plans where rich and poor alike are 'free' to subscribe or refrain from subscribing to the medical plan of their choice. And they endorse the former over the latter knowing that universal government medicare entails setting up "a vast state medical bureaucracy." This is not particularly problematic for them because such a bureaucracy would be an integral part of a system that includes some public, democratic control over doctors and drug and insurance conglomerates. The benefits of such control, including lower costs, are so obvious that it seems ludicrous to most feminists to suggest that women would be better off if only they could keep the state out of the hospitals and community health centres of their society. Why then would things improve for women if only they could keep the state out of the publishing firms, movie companies, and television networks of the nation? Few feminists would here respond that ideas about women's sexuality, but not their health, are socially constructed by the dominant gender and reflected by the policies of the modern patriarchal state.

Or consider modern education. Despite well-grounded criticisms of both its form and content, most feminists would be loathe to support the dissolution of all state-funded education or to wish that it had never come into existence. Although it has not been, nor is it now, the great liberal equalizer of opportunity for the underprivileged, it has, all things considered, been beneficial to the majority of society. Granted, it displays bias against unorthodox views, including feminism. Yes, much of its authoritarian structure is without rational justification. Nevertheless, it marks an historical advance over its predecessors, namely, church-dominated education, private education for the sons of the affluent, and little or no education for the poor. Analogously, a successful censorship strategy against pornography will entail some (temporary) losses in the arena of sexual expression. No feminist can guarantee that pristine anti-sexist legislation will govern the availability of sexual expression. To argue that civil and/or criminal laws can be framed, adopted and enforced so as to censor all and only that which degrades and exploits women is absolutely utopian. And worse, it is likely to induce cynicism when actual legislation falls short of this goal. But with all due respect for (and personal interest in) the siren call of erotica, are these losses the end of civilization as we know it? On the other hand, can anti-censorship feminists assure us that in a society in which there are no legal limits to degrading women through expressive liberty, where feminist artists fight it out only in the marketplace against the multi-billion dollar pornography industry, that there will not be significantly greater casualties for women?

A final note on the market and the effects of state censorship of pornography. Many have argued that even if some feminist-inspired anti-pornography laws are reluctantly passed by legislators, this will result only in pornography, like prostitution, being driven underground. Sarah Diamond, for example, claims that "[t]he elimination of the image is not the solution to misogyny, but a process that will make some images move underground to meet the continuing demand."[34] And there, others say, it "will take root out of the public eye,"[35] "could become even more profitable than it is already,"[36] and will be "all the more difficult to fight."[37] But, *contra* Diamond, one can defend a law, for example, against driving while intoxicated, without naively clinging to the hope that enforcement will *eliminate* the offending behaviour. Moreover, 'underground,' is not the name of a large chain of retail stores. Pro-censorship feminists are therefore not in the least embarrassed in wanting pornography to "take root out of the public eye" because this usually leads to diminished dissemination and therefore diminished profits. This likely consequence of state regulation of representations of sexuality, at least as much as their libertarian stance on freedom of expression, accounts for the universal opposition of pornocrats to any suggestion that content regulation should be applied to their products. Feminists, therefore, need not be as pessimistic as Sue George who, while conceding that pornography may oppress women and that censorship will reduce its availability, dismisses this tactic because it "has absolutely nothing to do with fighting women's oppression."[38] Absolutely *nothing*? Feminist anti-censorship hyperbole strikes again.

AUTHOR'S NOTE

I would like to thank Christine Koggel for comments on earlier drafts of this paper.

NOTES

1. John Stuart Mill, *On Liberty*, edited by Elizabeth Rapaport (Indianapolis: Hackett, 1978), p. 6.
2. Catharine MacKinnon, *Toward a Feminist Theory of the State* (Cambridge: Harvard University Press, 1989), p. 197.
3. The paper was later published as "Anti-Racism and Unlimited Freedom of Speech: An Untenable Dualism?" in the *Canadian Journal of Philosophy*, v. VIII, no. 3, Sept., 1978, pp. 559-575.
4. Lisa Duggan, Nan Hunter, and Carole S. Vance, "False Promises: Feminist Antipornography Legislation in the U.S." in Varda Burstyn, ed., *Women Against Censorship* (Vancouver: Douglas and McIntyre, 1985), p. 131.
5. C. Brants and E. Kok, "Penal Sanctions as a Feminist Strategy: a Contradiction in Terms?" in *International Journal of the Sociology of Law* v. 14, no. 3/4; pp. 269-286; quoted with approval in Carol Smart, *Feminism and the Power of Law* (London: Routledge, 1989), p. 136.
6. Erica Jong, "The Place of Pornography," *Harper's* (November, 1984), p. 33.
7. Mariana Valverde and Lorna Weir, "Thrills, Chills, and the 'Lesbian Threat,'" in Burstyn, *op. cit.*, p. 104.
8. Nadine Strossen, Defending Pornography (New York: Scribner, 1995), p. 48.
9. Smart, *op. cit.*, pp. 136-137. Pro-censorship feminists certainly see the law as instrumental. Are they then part of what Cossman and Bell describe as an "anti-pornography feminism which assumes the law is a simple instrument of change?" And are they ignoring the fact that "law is not an instrument, but a site of contradiction, where new discourses are superimposed on old?" No, to both questions. It is one thing to say that the law is neither a simple instrument nor simply an instrument, quite another to deny its instrumentality altogether. Why cannot pro-censorship feminism view the law as both a complex instrument and a site of contradiction? Moreover, the notion of a site of contradiction or struggle amongst various sectors of society (including gender, race, and class) for the *superimposition* of discourses makes law sound distinctly instrumental. See Brenda Cossman and Shannon Bell, "Introduction," in *Bad Attitude/s on Trial: Pornography, Feminism, and the Butler Decision* (Toronto: University of Toronto Press, 1997), p. 29.
10. Pratiba Parmar, "Rage and Desire: Confronting Pornography," in Gail Chester and Julienne Dickey, eds., *Feminism and Censorship: The Current Debate* (Dorset: Prism Press, 1988), p. 126.
11. Adrienne Rich, letter in off our backs XV: 6; quoted in Liz Kelly, "The US Ordinances: Censorship or Radical Law Reform," in Chester and Dickey, p. 60.
12. George Will, "Pornography Scare," *Washington Post*, October 28, 1993; quoted by Strossen, *op. cit.*, p. 218.
13. MacKinnon, *op. cit.*, p. 161-2.
14. Andrea Dworkin, "For Men, Freedom of Speech; for Women, Silence Please" in Laura Lederer, ed., *Take Back The Night: Women on Pornography* (New York: Bantam, 1982), p. 256.
15. Strossen, *op. cit.*, p. 217.
16. Dworkin, in Lederer, *op. cit.*

17. Andrea Dworkin and Catharine MacKinnon, *Pornography and Civil Rights* (Minneapolis: Organizing Against Pornography, 1988), p. 94.
18. Myrna Kostash, "Second Thoughts," in Burstyn, *op. cit.*, p. 37.
19. Consider, for example, Carol Smart's undocumented claim (*op. cit.*, p. 5) that "feminist 'legal theory' is immobilized in the face of the failure of feminism to affect law and the failure of law to transform the quality of women's lives." But Catherine MacKinnon's groundbreaking work on sexual harassment did affect the law and second-wave feminism struggled successfully in many countries for abortion rights and affirmative action. These changes to the law and the quality of women's lives did not bring about gender equality, but that's another matter.
20. Lynn King, "Censorship and Law Reform: Will Changing the Laws Mean a Change for the Better?" in Burstyn, *op. cit.*, p. 90.
21. Elizabeth Wilson, "Feminist Fundamentalism: The Shifting Politics of Sex and Censorship," in Lynn Segal and Mary McIntosh, eds., *Sex and Censorship: Sexuality and the Pornography Debate* (New Brunswick: Rutgers University Press, 1993), p. 28.
22. Varda Burstyn, "Positive Strategies," in Burstyn, *op. cit.*, p. 165.
23. Kate Ellis, Nan B. Hunter, and Abby Talmer, "Introduction," *Caught Looking*, Kate Ellis, Nan B. Hunter, Beth Jaker, Barbara O'Dair, and Abby Talmer (eds) (New York: Caught Looking Inc., 1986), p. 8.
24. Lynn Segal, "False Promises: Anti-Pornography Feminism," *Socialist Register*, edited by Ralph and Leo Panitch (London: Merlin Press, 1993), p. 100.
25. *Whitney v. California* (274 U.S. 357, 375-6, (1927), (Brandeis concurring); emphasis in original.
26. Thelma McCormack, "Making Sense of Research on Pornography," in Burstyn, *op.cit.*, p. 199.
27. Duggan, Hunter, and Vance, *op.cit.*, p. 145.
28. Burstyn, *op.cit.*, p. 181.
29. Robin Morgan, "Theory and Practice: Pornography and Rape," in Lederer, *op. cit.*, p. 137.
30. In an illuminating review of the women's health movement in South Australia in the 1970's and 80's, Jocelyn Auer concludes that while "there is constant tension in trying to maintain a commitment to feminist principles and goals while working within the state," and that while "[t]he acceptance of government funding entailed specific limitations on feminist goals and practices," it also "has given women some status and ability to seek reform there." See her "Encounters with the State: Co-option and Reform, A Case Study from Women's Health," in *Playing the State*, edited by Sophie Watson (London: Verso, 1990), p. 207-17.
31. Shannon Smith, "Feminists for a Strong State?" *International Socialism*, #51, Summer, 1991, p. 86.
32. Karl Marx, "Letter to Kugelman," Oct. 9, 1866, in *Marx, Engels, Lenin: Anarchism and Anarcho-Syndicalism*, (Moscow: Progress Publishers, 1972), p. 43.
33. Karl Marx and Frederick Engels, *Manifesto of the Communist Party*, in *Marx-Engels, Collected Works* (New York: International Publishers, 1976), Vol. VI, p. 487.
34. Sarah Diamond, "Pornography: Image and Reality," in Burstyn, *op. cit.*, p. 49.
35. Avedon Carol, *nudes, prudes, and attitudes* (Cheltenham: New Clarion Press, 1994), p. 2.
36. Alisa L. Carse, "Pornography: An Uncivil Liberty?" *Hypatia*, v. 10, no. 1 (Winter, 1995), p. 168.
37. Wendy Moore, "There should be a law against it ... shouldn't there?" In Chester and Dickey, *op. cit.*, p. 147.
38. Sue George, "Censorship and Hypocrisy: Some Issues Surrounding Pornography That Feminism Has Ignored," in Chester and Dickey, *op.cit.*, p. 115.

RETRENCHMENT VERSUS TRANSFORMATION: THE POLITICS OF THE ANTIPORNOGRAPHY MOVEMENT

Ann Snitow

Ann Snitow is Professor of Literature and Women's Studies at the New School for Social Research in New York. She is co-editor of Live, From Feminism: Memoirs of Women's Liberation *(Crown, 1998) and* Powers of Desire: The Politics of Sexuality *(Monthly Review Press, 1983).*

Snitow argues that the antipornography movement within feminism has generated divisiveness damaging to and not in the long-term best interests of the women's movement. Antipornography campaigns detract attention from other issues of women's inequality. Moreover, the monolithic tendency to present pornography as depicting violence, hatred, and fear of women assumes a view of women as victims and narrows the range of what counts as sexual pleasure for women. Snitow argues that elements in pornography of play, danger, fantasy, and defiance can expand and liberate women's sexuality.

This piece is drawn from a talk that was given to a number of groups between March and September 1983. Since that time, a whole new strategy for antipornography organizing has been developed in the U.S. by Andrea Dworkin and Catherine MacKinnon. Though I do not deal here with the specifics of the new laws they propose, much that I have written has critical bearing on their claim that "pornography is central in creating and maintaining the civil inequality of the sexes."

There is a storm brewing in the women's liberation movement over sexual politics. This is not to say the women's movement is by any means limited to the current debates about pornography but when a woman today goes searching for the feminism she's heard about, that has called her, she is likely to encounter the antipornography movement, with its definition of sex and sexual imagery as continuous zones of special danger to women. Of late, this has been one burning tip of feminism where energy and feeling collect.

These heated feelings recall the passions that fueled the early days of the present wave of feminism, that fueled the proabortion movement and the women's health movement—both also about that contested terrain, the female body. As a veteran of those years, I remember how empowering that anger was, how it opened the eyes and cleansed the blood. We must indeed act out of what we feel or be cut off from the deepest sources of energy and political authenticity.

Nonetheless, I want to argue here that we need to know more about these feelings, or else run the risk of creating a strategy likely to move us away from the very things we say we desire. I want to argue that, in general, today's antipornography campaigns achieve their energy by mobilizing a complex amalgam of female rage, fear and humiliation in strategic directions that are not in the long-term best interests of our movement. A politics of outrage—which can be valuable and effective—can also seriously fail women in our efforts to change the basic dynamics of the sex-gender system. ...

The antipornography movement has attracted women from many sectors of women's liberation. But this unity has a high price, for it requires that we

---

Reprinted with permission of Ann Snitow from *Women Against Censorship*, edited by Varda Burstyn (Vancouver: Douglas & McIntyre, 1985): 107–120 [edited].

oversimplify, that we hypothesize a monolithic enemy, a timeless, universal, male sexual brutality. When we create a "them," we perform a sort of ritual of purification: There are no differences among men or women—of power, class, race. All are collapsed into a false unity, the brotherhood of the oppressors, the sisterhood of the victims.

In this sisterhood, we can seem far closer than we are likely to feel when we discuss those more basic and problematic sources of sexual mores: ethnicity, church, school and family. We are bound to disagree once we confront the sexual politics implicit in these complex social institutions, but from just this sort of useful debate will come the substance of a nonracist feminist concept of sexual freedom. Sometimes, ironically, our drive toward a premature feminist unity through female outrage has led to scapegoating inside the women's movement, as if we were already agreed about which sexual practices belong beyond the feminist pale. I find such internal attacks particularly terrifying now at a time when sexual minorities are increasingly harassed by the state. Given the sexual ignorance, fear and oppression in a sex-negative society, it is a false hope that feminist unity can rely on a premature agreement on sexual expression.

What *are* the feminist grounds of unity in a discussion of pornography, or of women's sexual freedom in general? Feminists on all sides of this debate share the desire to "take back the night"; to own our sexual selves; to express these selves in images of our own choosing. We share a feminist anger about women's sexual exploitation and a desire to leave the impress of this feeling—our recognition of profound injustices that reach to the core of identity—upon the consciousness of the world.

We also share the belief that sex is primarily a social, not biological, construction; hence social power relations have everything to do with who can do what to whom sexually. Since sex is social, we agree that its symbolic representation is important, that the imagery of sex is worth feminist analytical attention. We agree, too, that in sex, as in everything, women are sometimes right to fear: misogyny permeates our social life and men dominate women. But finally, and significantly, we disagree about the best route to liberation—or even to safety.

Present antipornography theory, rather than advancing feminist thinking about sexuality, continues sexist traditions of displacement or distortion of sexual questions. Instead of enlarging the definition of sexual pleasure to include a formerly invisible female subjectivity, antipornography thinking perpetuates an all too familiar intellectual legacy, one that defines male arousal as intrinsically threatening to female autonomy. Once again, women's experience fades into the background while men fill the foreground. Antipornography theory limits this focus further by collapsing a wide range of sexually explicit images into only one thing: violence against women.

But feminists have little to gain from this narrowing idea of what pornographic imagery contains. A definition of pornography that takes the problem of analysis seriously has to include not only violence, hatred and fear of women, but also a long list of other elements, which may help explain why we women ourselves have such a mixture of reactions to the genre. (I have heterosexual porn in mind here, but some of this description applies to other types of pornography; generally, porn is a much more varied genre than antiporn activists acknowledge.)

Pornography sometimes includes elements of play, as if the fear women feel toward men had evaporated and women were relaxed and willing at last. Such a fantasy—sexual revolution as *fait accompli*—is manipulative and insensitive in most of the guises we know, but it can also be wishful, eager and utopian.

Porn can depict thrilling (as opposed to threatening) danger. Though some of its manic quality comes from women-hating, some seems propelled by fear and joy about breaching the always uncertain boundaries of flesh and personality.

Hostility haunts the genre, but as part of a psychodrama in which men often imagine themselves women's victims. Mother is the ultimate spectre and women, too, have moments of glee when she is symbolically brought low.

Some pornography is defiant and thumbs a nose at death, at the limitations of the body and nature, indeed at anything that balks the male (perhaps potentially the female?) will.

Porn offers men a private path to arousal, an arousal that may be all too easily routed by fear or shame.

Though pornography often centres emotionally on dramas of dominance and submission, anyone who has looked at the raging dependence or the imagined omnipotence of a one-year-old has reason to doubt that patriarchy is the only source of our species' love/hate relationship to the emotions of power and powerlessness. Pornography is infantile then, but "infantile" is a word we use as a simple negative at the risk of patronizing some of our own sources of deep feeling. In many of the guises we know, such infantile feelings give rise to images of the brutal or the coldly murderous; in others, however, childishness can be more innocently regressive, potentially renewing. As Kate Ellis and others have argued, we can indulge in fantasies of childish omnipotence without having these define the entire field of our consciousness or intentions. Particular deep feelings may be neither valuable or liberating, but they demand understanding; they cannot be sanitized through mere will.

Ridden with authoritarian fantasies as it is, pornography also flouts authority, which no doubt in part explains its appeal to young boys. Certainly while porn remains one of their few sources of sexual information we should not marvel at the importance of the genre. But porn as we know it is, of course, a miserably skewed source of information. While it does offer taboo, explicit images—however distorted—of the bodies of women, the male body usually remains invisible. Since men control porn, they can continue to conceal themselves from inquisitive female eyes.

The same people who want sex education removed from schools now join feminists in the fight against porn. If this odd alliance prospers, we will hear the crash of successive doors closing in the faces of curious but isolated children. In the present political context, pieties about protecting children are passive and reactive; we are not protecting them so much as abandoning them to silence. Pornography as we know it requires a social context of ignorance and shame that present feminist campaigns against it do nothing to alter.

Finally, antipornography theory's central complaint about pornography is that it is objectifying and fragmenting. The genre makes women into things for male pleasure and takes only that part of the woman that pleases without threat. Once again, the danger of objectification and fragmentation depend on context. Not even in my most utopian dreams can I imagine a state in which one recognizes all others as fully as one recognizes oneself (if one can even claim to recognize oneself, roundly, fully, without fragmentation). The real issue is a political one. Antipornography activists are right to see oppressive male power in the gaze of men at women: Women cannot gaze back with a similar, defining authority. But, while we all want the transformed sexuality that will be ours when we are neither dependent nor afraid, the antipornography campaign introduces misleading goals into our struggle when it intimates that in a feminist world we will never objectify anyone, never take the part for the whole, never abandon ourselves to mindlessness or the intensities of feeling that link sex with childhood, death, the terrors and pleasures of the oceanic. Using people as extensions of one's own hungry will is hardly an activity restrained within the boundaries of pornography, nor is there any proof that pornography is a cause rather than a manifestation of far more pervasive imbalances of power and powerlessness.

Antipornography activists argue that pornography is everywhere, both the source of woman hatred and its ultimate expression. This is an effort to have it both ways: woman-hating is everywhere, but the source of that hatred is specific, localized in pornography, the hate literature that educates men to degrade women. The internal contradiction here is plain. If misogyny is everywhere, why target its sexual manifestation? Or if misogyny collects around the sexual, why is this so? Why assume that the cordoning off of particular sexual images is likely to lessen women's oppression? This overemphasis placed on sex as cause is continuous with the very old idea that sex is an especially shameful, disturbing, guilt-provoking area of life. To accept rather than struggle against the idea that sex is dangerous and polluting is to fear ourselves as much as the men who rape and hurt. We need to be able to reject the sexism in porn without having to reject the realm of pornographic sexual fantasy as if that entire kingdom were without meaning or resonance for women.

Without history, without an analysis of complexity and difference, without a critical eye toward gender and its constant redefinitions, without some skepticism about how people ingest their culture, some recognition of the gap—in ideas and feelings—between the porn magazine and the man who reads it, we will only be purveying a false hope to those women whom we want to join us: that without porn, there will be far less male violence; that with less male violence that will be far less male power.

In the antipornography campaign, the thing we have most to fear is winning, for further legal control of pornography would, first, leave the oppressive structures of this society perfectly intact, even strengthened, and, second, leave us disappointed, since crimes against women are not particularly linked to pornography and indeed have many other highly visible sources.

Women will be victimized while we lack power. But even now we are not completely powerless. In fact, we are in the midst of complex power negotiations with men all the time. One of the basic themes of porn is the taming of the beast, Woman who if not bound, will grab; if not gagged, will speak. Pornography's fantasy penis is meant to tame the little bitch as it rarely can in real life.

However silenced and objectified we may be in the prevailing culture, we are not only silenced, not only objectified. Porn cannot fully define the situation in which we find ourselves. It symbolized some, but not all, of our experiences—with men, with sexuality, with culture. In the liberation struggles of the '60s, American radicals insisted that everything is connected: what was happening in Vietnam was connected to what was happening in imperialist America. In the analysis and rhetoric of the antipornography movement, this tendency is carried to a distorting extreme. Instead of seeing connections among very different elements in our culture, some antipornography activists conflate things, see them all running together down a slippery slope. Pornography leads to rape, which leads to the rape of the land, which leads to international imperialism.

I'm not arguing that these things are not connected, only that by connecting them too quickly, too seamlessly, through the evocative power of metaphor, we fail to see the all-important differences. We must make distinctions of kind and of degree. For it is in the places where things don't fit together neatly that we can best insert our political will toward change.

If we leave this discussion in the realm of moral absolutes, of slippery slopes on the road to sin, we have chosen a rhetorical strategy that can arouse and enrage but that cannot lead us to a position beyond the old moral categories of female righteousness.

Ironically enough, the slippery slope model isolates sex from all other issues, since all other issues collapse into sex, are only sex. Once again, differences, varieties of power and powerlessness, get lost in a false unity. A frame is drawn around women's sexual exploitation and we are told this is the whole picture, the essence, the core truth. Women's sexual suffering becomes women's sexuality itself.

We do particular injury to feminist work by conflating sex with violence. This is to cede precious territory to the political opponents of feminism. It may be the female legacy of shame and fear that makes us accept this equation so quickly. Is it in our interests—not to mention in the interest of truth—to say that because husbands often rape wives, all marriage is rape? Or to say that women who reject this equation have been brainwashed by patriarchy? This is to deny women any agency at all in the long history of heterosexuality.

It is hard to imagine good organizing that can emerge from this insulting presumption. In her book *Right Wing Women*, antipornography theorist Andrea Dworkin argues that there are but two models for women's roles in society: the farm model and the prostitution model. Women are either fields to be plowed, cows to be milked; or they are meat to be bought. This is a pornographic reductionism of the role of women in history.

The antipornography world view purports to solve several problems at once: it explains movement failure; it downplays what is unnerving in our successes; it reenergizes honorably weary activists; it reestablishes unity at a time when differences among women are increasingly visible and theoretically important. But, built on weak foundations, these political gains will not endure. When maleness is defined as a timeless quality, it becomes harder rather than easier to imagine how it can ever change. The politics of rage tapers off into a politics of despair—or of complacency—and gender, which at moments has seemed very fluid and variable, suddenly seems solid and reliable again. If, as Mary Daly generalized in *Gyn/Ecology*, footbinding in China and suttee in India and child molestation in Manitoba are all identical, seamless, essentially male acts, where is the break in this absolute tradition, the dynamic moment when female will can prevail?

Since one of the faults of antipornography theory is its misplaced concreteness, I can't be correspondingly specific about how I would go about working to alter the often limited rapacious or dreary sexual culture in which women—and also men—now live. There are a lot of questions to answer: Does a disproportionate amount of misogynistic feeling cluster around sex? Why? How deep does sexual phobia go? Is sex in fact an area of experience that will need to be seen as separate, with its own inner dynamic, even perhaps its won dialectic? If we reject the strategy of repression and banning, how *do* we raise self-consciousness and political consciousness about the aspects of porn that express sexual distress, derangement, hostility? (It does seem obvious to me that banning is a step in the opposite direction, away from learning, from unmasking, and toward a suppression that ignores meaning.) What is the actual content of porn and how is porn related to the broader questions of arousal? In other words, what makes something sexy, and what part does power play in the sexualization of a person or situation? Is it a feminist belief that without gender inequality all issues of power will wither away, or do we have a model for the future that will handle inequalities differently? Are there kinds of arousal we know and experience that are entirely absent in porn? How expressive is it of our full sexual range? How representative? How conventional and subject to its own aesthetic laws?

We must work to answer these questions, but we know a lot already. We know that women must have the right to abortion, to express freely our sexual preferences; that we must have the control of the structure and the economics of health care, day care, and our work lives in general. All these levels of private and social experience determine the degree of our sexual autonomy. The New Right is sure *it* knows what women's sexuality is all about. We must reject such false certainties—in both the feminist and New Right camps—while we set about building the nonrepressive sexual culture we hope for, one in which women's sexual expressiveness—and men's too—can flourish. In her essay "Why I'm against S/M Liberation" (in *Against Sadomasochism*), Ti Grace Atkinson says, "I do not know any feminist worthy of that name who, if forced to choose between freedom and sex, would choose sex." While women are forced to make such a choice we cannot consider ourselves free.

AUTHOR'S NOTE

I thank my coeditors of *Powers of Desire: The Politics of Sexuality* (Monthly Review Press), Christine Stansell and Sharon Thompson, and Carole Vance for many months of invaluable discussion. Nadine Taub helped me broaden and support my argument that disappointment is an unspoken theme of recent organizing, and Alice Echols was the first to develop the theme of false unities. Thanks, too, to members of my study group: Julie Abraham, Hannah Alderfer, Meryl Altman, Jan Boney, Frances Doughty, Kate Ellis, Faye Ginsburg, Diane Harriford, Beth Jaker, Barbara Kerr, Mary Clare Lennon, Marybeth Nelson, Paula Webster, Ellen Willis and Carole Vance.

This piece is a talk that was delivered to a number of groups during 1983. Thanks to the following sponsoring organizations: Calgary Status of Women; the San Francisco Socialist School and Women against Violence in Pornography and the Media; the Fourteenth National Conference: Women and the Law; Lavender Left and Philadelphia Reproductive Rights Organization; New York University Colloquium on Sex and Gender.

DO YOU MIND IF I SPEAK FREELY? RECONCEPTUALIZING FREEDOM OF SPEECH

Lisa Heldke

Lisa Heldke teaches philosophy at Gustavus Adolphus College. She is co-editor of Cooking, Eating, Thinking: Transformative Philosophies of Food *(Indiana, 1992) and has published articles in ethics and on sexual orientation.*

Heldke argues that the liberal conception of free speech as an individualized activity of speakers has proven ill-equipped to address free speech issues. In raising objections to two liberal justifications in terms of individual rights and utility for protecting speech, Heldke formulates an alternative conception of speech as a collective activity that involves both speaking and listening. By highlighting the relational aspects of speech in a community of speakers and listeners, Heldke mounts an argument that preventing someone from using sexist language, for example, does not constitute a violation of their free speech rights, but may in fact increase the level of freedom for all the various members of a community.

Introduction

In this paper, I develop a way to conceive of free speech that begins by redefining speech.[1] My definition affirms the fact that speaking is an activity that goes on *among* people in a community. Speaking, I will suggest, is an activity that involves not only the present speaker, but also others who act as listeners and potential speakers.

I contend that liberal conceptions of free speech have often proven ill-equipped to address certain free speech issues, precisely because they have tended to conceive of speech not as a collective activity in which participation involves both speaking and listening, but as an individualized activity in which only speakers and their utterances are relevant.[2]

The conception I develop defines speaking as collective, thereby illuminating the role played in it by listeners/potential speakers. In the bulk of activities that go under the name "speech," a community of "others" (listeners, potential listeners, "ignorers") plays some sort of role. Those instances of speaking in which there are no relevant others may be defined in terms of their relation to speech-with-listeners. That is, they are exceptions to the general cases, and their presence in the category "speaking" can be understood by reference to one of these general cases.

My original motivation for developing this conception of speech was to provide a way to illuminate those forms of sexual harassment that consist of sexist speech. I intend for the conception to characterize free speech in such a way that preventing someone from using sexist language does not (at least automatically) constitute a violation of their free speech rights, but in fact may increase the level of freedom of the community.

I develop my account by first providing a critical outline of one version of a liberal conception of free speech.[3] In the course of this outline, I examine two central liberal justifications for protecting speech; the argument from individual rights and the argument from utility. I conclude this section by making explicit my criticisms of this liberal conception.

Following this, I turn to develop an alternative collective conception of speaking and of free speaking.

Reprinted with permission from *Social Theory and Practice* 17:3 (Fall 1991): 349–368.

I argue that this conception is preferable for two reasons; first, because speaking is a collective activity, and to treat it otherwise is to mask its powers and disguise the benefit or harm it may bring to users. Second, a collective conception of speaking preserves the values of free speech advanced in liberal views better than does a liberal conception.

1.

To begin with a definition that will require some unpacking, I'll describe a liberal notion of free speech as speech that is unconstrained. Obviously two components of this definition require particular attention; what is meant by speech? and what does it mean to be unconstrained?

The liberal conception tends to focus on speech (as opposed to *speaking*), and treats speech as the utterances of an individual.[4] Indeed, the word "utterance" crops up in discussion of freedom of speech with some regularity. (Francis Canavan, for example, describes speech in the broadest sense to "include every kind of utterance and publication.")[5] The word "utterance"—a noun—conveys the notion that speaking is an activity that creates some "thing" that may be shared or traded with others.[6]

An essential feature of such speech is that it is the product of an individual. Speaking, on a liberal conception, is done by a single person. Only derivatively is it understood as conversing, corresponding, communicating *among* individuals. The community into which utterances are issued is relevant only secondarily.

This liberal conception of speech depends for its legitimacy and cogency upon a particular conception of the nature of the individual and of the relationship between the individual and society. On this conception the individual is unattached to others; it is not formed out of relations to others. Rather, it is an independently-created self that, for a variety of reasons, chooses or is constrained to enter into relations with others. At its core, this self is discrete, detached.

Emerging from this understanding of the individual is a conception of speech as the utterances of such an individual. Of course the liberal conception recognizes that speech may have an effect upon the individuals who hear it (just as it acknowledges that our development as individuals will be shaped by outside influences such as speech), but it regards that effect as extraneous to the speech itself. Speech is the act of discrete, independent individuals, and it too is discrete, independent, and individual.

This notion of the individual as detached, and of speech as the discrete utterances of the individual, motivates and supports a description of free speech as speech that is unconstrained. The reader will recall that this was the second component of the liberal definition I proposed that required some examination. "Unconstrained" here means that the individual speaker is in no way actively prevented, or coerced into refraining, from speaking.

On this view, assessing the freedom of any "piece" of speech requires determining who the speaker is, and whether his or her speech is being allowed to flow unrestrictedly. (The image that comes to mind is that of a river; free speech is a river that is allowed to flow from its mouth unimpeded by debris, dams, or diversionary measures.) No other concerns enter into the assessment at this stage; the only real consideration is whether the individual who would speak has been impeded in any way.

If an individual is restricted—if forced to cut out parts of speech, or call off a planned rally—then the speaker's speech is no longer unconstrained. Of course most people (though not everyone)[7] would argue that there are times when restrictions on freedom are appropriate or even necessary; that the unconstrained speech of individuals is not something always to be protected. But, whether the restriction be justified or unjustified, on this conception to restrict someone's speech is to limit his or her freedom. That is, while you might agree that those who would yell "Fire" in a crowded theater ought to be restricted from doing so—or prosecuted for doing so—what you are thereby agreeing is that speech ought not be entirely unconstrained, that its freedom ought not be unconditional.

On the liberal view as it is realized in U.S. Supreme Court decisions, free speech issues have tended to arise in the form of questions about whether or not the utterances of particular individuals ought to be limited in particular situations—whether, that is, our freedom to speak ought to have limitations. The history of free speech decisions by the Supreme Court is a history of stipulating if and when restriction is justified, when my freedom may legitimately be curbed, and when such a curb is an illegitimate constraint. Making these decisions, the Court suggests, generally requires looking beyond speech itself.[8] When speech is defined as utterance, any decision to restrict it because of its effect on others is a decision that requires taking into account issues that are not relevant to the concerns of free speech alone. (I shall say more about this later.)

As a result of the Supreme Court's decisions, an individual may not utter "fighting words" to another individual face-to-face, but a group of Nazis may hold a rally in a predominantly Jewish community, in which they vilify Jews.[9] Calling a police officer a "God damned racketeer" (the "fighting words" case) raises certain concerns that take precedence over an individual's right to speak—namely, concerns about the breach of peace likely to result when the insulted party retaliates. The white-supremacist rally does not involve such issues; in the case in question, the Court ruled that the presence in Skokie of many Jewish survivors of the Holocaust did not in itself constitute a compelling reason to restrict the free-speech rights of Nazi demonstrators. No ordinance forbidding their demonstrating there has been allowed to stand.

Of course this conception of freedom of speech recognizes that to protect an individual's utterances is to incur certain costs; it is understood that people may in fact be damaged either directly or indirectly by the speech of another. However, advocates of this conception argue that the benefits of protecting such speech generally outweigh the costs incurred in protecting it. Therefore, unless extenuating circumstances are sufficiently extreme, the utterances of the individual must be protected.[10]

A liberal defense of freedom of speech frequently focuses on two types of values or aims that it claims are best protected and promoted in an atmosphere of unconstrained utterances. They are individual self-fulfilment and the attainment of truth. In other language, they are the arguments from individual rights and utility; freedom of speech must be protected in order to safeguard/promote the rights of individuals, and in order to arrive at truths. I'll consider each claim briefly.

1. Thomas Emerson argues that

> The right to freedom of expression is justified first of all as the right of an individual purely in his capacity as an individual. It derives from the widely accepted premise of Western thought that the proper end of man is the realization of his character and potentialities as a human being.[11]

Free speech figures in here because

> every man—in the development of his own personality—has the right to form his own beliefs and opinions. And it also follows that he has the right to express these beliefs and opinions.... For expression is an integral part of the development of ideas, of mental exploration and of the affirmation of self.[12]

Emerson's rights-based defence of freedom of speech rests upon two notions that I've described as being part of a liberal conception of the individual and of speech. There is the idea that human (intellectual) development is a solitary project—one in which others' ideas can be of assistance to the individual, but which ultimately is a highly individual enterprise. And there is the emphasis on speech as a thing—an utterance or, for Emerson, an "expression." Emerson suggests that expressing our ideas—that is, speaking—is essential if the ideas are to have any significance.

Note that Emerson doesn't suggest that expression is necessary because humans and their ideas are social, and must have contact with other ideas in order to develop. Indeed, he seems to reject the idea that human intellectual development is inherently social. Instead, he argues that humans must express ideas as a way of developing/asserting independence, autonomy, and maturity. It is the act of issuing them to others that develops maturity in us. To suppress speech is to negate "man's essential nature."[13]

There is something slightly dizzying about such a defence of freedom of speech. On one level, it seems like a defense I would want to support—one that it would be almost blasphemous to reject—but on another level, I am left wondering just what is being defended. It is not the right to talk with others. It appears to be the right to express. Emerson defends the right to produce just what a liberal conception defines as speech—individual utterances or expressions.

But it isn't clear just how speech defined this way can contribute to our growth as individuals. What is it about expressing ideas that promotes our intellectual growth? In my discussion of an alternate conception of free speech, I'll show that this argument implicitly assumes that speaking goes on in a community. It's because we're talking *with* others who *respond* (or might) that expressing our ideas helps us mature.

2. For a characterization of the utilitarian defence of free speech, consider Mill: "[T]he peculiar evil of silencing the expression of an opinion is that it is robbing the human race [of a potentially correct opinion]...."[14] Mill's defence of freedom here assumes that speech is an activity through which we attempt to arrive at the truth, an assumption which quite clearly does not encompass all of the uses to which speech is put. But, setting that complication aside, what is Mill's defense?

Mill is arguing that the best way for us to arrive at the truth is for the community to be jammed with as many ideas as possible, and for all of these ideas to challenge and confront each other. Only if all possible views get articulated can we be reasonably sure that we haven't eliminated any true ones, and only if we perpetually subject our roughly-true ones to the criticism posed by other positions can we be sure that our most-valued ideas legitimately retain their status.

It seems to me that Mill's conception (even more than the individual rights notion) is collective at heart, for it recognizes the centrality of exchange and interchange.[15] Thus, this utilitarian defense of free speech implicitly acknowledges the collective nature of speech. Utilitarian values also would better be realized by a collective conception of speech.

I've been suggesting that liberal conceptions of free speech tend to be problematic because they treat speech as the utterances of an individual. This treatment obscures the fact that speaking is something we do *with* (or to) each other, that we are not solitary utterers of statements so much as participants in a collective activity. Because of this, a liberal notion of free speech is ill-equipped to analyze situations in which listeners are silenced or otherwise harmed by another's speech. For instance, it cannot analyze situations in which an utterance itself illegitimately restricts another's speech—in which speech restricts speech.

In the first place, a liberal conception of freedom of speech (which focuses on the present speaker) often makes it difficult even to articulate the fact that a listener may also become a speaker, thus obscuring the right that is violated when that person is prevented from speaking.[16] For example, in almost none of the cases in which the Supreme Court has ruled to restrict someone's right to speak has the restriction been applied because someone else was being kept silent. In the few cases in which the courts have seen fit to limit someone's speech in order to protect someone else's,[17] that this liberal conception was in force meant that such a ruling—which seems so commonsensical—could be reached only after some rather gymnastical thinking.

On a liberal conception, the most straightforward way I can see to understand such a guarantee-of-access case is as two separate freedom of speech cases. One involves the speaker, whose freedom is going to be curtailed if it is decided that his or her speaking prevents someone else's. The other case involves the party prevented from speaking, a party who tends to be invisible (which partly explains why so few cases of guarantees of access come before the courts).[18] The speech-as-utterance notion involves interpreting such a situation as one in which one party's speech is freed at the expense of the other's. The notion sets up a situation consisting of two parties with separate and competing interests. In this setting, (at least) one party must "lose."

Furthermore, a liberal conception makes no genuine acknowledgment of the fact that speech is an activity generally involving listeners; on this conception, evaluating the freedom of an individual's speech does not include evaluating the effects upon the community in which the speaking is done. Appealing to community concerns is something one might do—and perhaps even routinely does do in certain kinds of cases. (Treason, bribery, and conspiracy laws are examples of this.) But on a liberal conception, the moment you take such considerations into account, you go beyond the concerns or requirements of free speech proper. You assert that other concerns take precedence over the protection of speech. For example, in this country, the law that makes it a crime to advocate the violent overthrow of the government acknowledges that there are situations in which speech ought not be protected.[19]

In Part 2, I will attempt to show that if we conceive of speech as an activity that takes place among—and often *with*—other people, we can address such problems as access to speech and harm to listeners directly. We can do so because the larger situation isn't divided into separate, speaker-specific situations with competing concerns; and because speech, on this conception, is defined as an activity that involves listeners/potential speakers.

On such a conception, it is true that certain things we've come to regard as prima facie examples of protected speech may not turn out to be such. This may well be a cause for a certain amount of consternation. It is not my project here to suggest that certain views or certain people ought to be silenced, period. Rather, I am attempting to show that a liberal conception of speech already enables such silencing to go on, along with other kinds of harm as well—and it does so *in the service of protecting speech*. That a liberal conception actually facilitates certain kinds of silencing (to say nothing of other harm to listeners) provides a serious argument for reconceptualizing speech.[20]

2.

The conception of free speech set forth here is predicated upon the view that we are constituted as persons in part through our connections with others.[21] This is no accidental fact about us—although our relations with any particular "others" may be accidental.[22] This conception of persons as partially constituted by relations with others motivates a conception of speaking which understands it as an activity that takes place *among* people and involves their participation as both speakers and listeners.

For many of us, talking with other people is the kind of speaking in which we engage most often. Our days are filled with conversations with other people; intimate conversations, casual conversations, exchanges of information or pleasantries.[23] In all these cases, there is interaction among participants—individuals who are sometimes talkers, sometimes listeners.

Not all speech situations consist of actual exchanges among individuals; often someone speaks, but others do not or cannot respond. By defining speaking only as an activity that takes place among people rather than as communication per se I mean to include situations in which actual conversation cannot or does not take place. For even if the listener has no opportunity to respond to a speaker, he or she is connected to that speaker because he or she is or may be affected by that speech. Such an effect is not some accidental or secondary by-product of speech; speaking always holds at least the potential to affect those who receive it. (Indeed, conversation is one of the chief means by which we become the particular relational selves that we are.) I would argue that a definition of speech—and, consequently, of free speech—must recognize this. Unless you always talk only to yourself, whenever you speak you are entering into a relation with someone who stands to be affected by what you say.[24]

What happens if I apply this definition of speech which emphasizes relationality to a "hard case" like television, where I am physically prevented from responding to the speaker in person? Even this speech is relational, I would argue, because I the viewer am clearly affected by what is said; I am angered or pleased or offended or enlightened or bored. The same is true if I am part of a crowd listening to a speech. In this case, there is only a small chance that I will actually have an exchange with the speaker. But even if that doesn't happen, their talking affects me, and this effect is not extraneous to the speech itself. (To import the liberal vocabulary, the expression or utterance cannot be severed from its receipt; speaking involves both.) These examples serve to show that, while to define speech as communication makes too strong an assertion, we can claim that speech is relational, if we recognize that relations vary in intensity and are not always reciprocal.

Another qualification of the definition is required to address cases in which no listening goes on, for in many situations, the speaker intends to be listened to, but isn't. The "non-listening" may be passive (as when the listener's mind is elsewhere and he or she just isn't paying attention) or it may be active (as when an audience shouts down a speaker.) The important thing to note in most all such cases, though, is that despite the failure in being heard, the speaker did intend to be heard. Cases of failed hearings, I'd argue, still are best understood in relation to cases where speaking-and-hearing both go on.

To sum up, this conception of speaking views it as a connecting activity in which the role of listener/potential listener/ignorer is not derivative but partially constitutive of the activity. The situations I've outlined support and expand the claim that it is more useful as well as more accurate to understand speaking as a collective activity rather than to define speech as the product of an individual utterer. Ultimately, it is unhelpful and distorting to separate the "receiving" of speech from the "issuing" of it.[25]

Given a conception of individuals as constitutively relational and of speaking as an activity involving both speakers and listeners, it is also necessary to redefine free speech. This definition should acknowledge that it is not only the current speaker whose freedom may be curtailed; listeners/potential speakers may also suffer limitations on their freedom.[26] And, because their activity is part of speaking as defined here, limitations on such activity may also count as restrictions on freedom. Speaking in a particular situation is not free if my talking silences (or in other ways harms) another person through threat, intimidation, or oppressive generalization.[27]

Free speech on this view should be attributed not to the individual (or to communities that can be reduced to individuals) but to relevant community and to individuals only as members of that community. When I conceive of myself as a being in-relations-with-others, and of speech as an activity that places me in relations with particular others, I must also regard my speech as a thing that may build or disrupt those relations. In other words, I cannot consider my freedom-to-speak outside of the context in which I am speaking. In fact, it is only by reference to this context that I can adequately assess the freedom of any particular speech. In shifting attention away from the individual speaker, the question changes from "Is this speaker free to say what he or she wills?" to "Is the talk in this situation free—are all members of the group participating at a level that promotes, rather than prohibits, the speech of others." On the view I am constructing, the interests of listeners are a part of the very fabric of the speech. In determining whether the speech is free, their perspectives must routinely be considered.[28]

Sexist language is one pervasive variety of speech that empowers the speaker at the expense of the hearer. Such speech—conceived of as a community activity—is not free. The speech in a classroom is constrained if a professor speaks "freely" in a way that systematically debases a student or students. (The same is true for a student who debases others—student or teacher.) Thus, this conception makes it possible for someone's speaking quite literally to count as an instance of the violation of the community's free speaking. For instance, when a classics professor in his lectures consistently makes remarks that suggest that he thinks women are ill-suited to the study of classics, his remarks serve to limit the freedom of the classroom. By suggesting that women are not equipped to study classics, he is "inviting" certain members of the class *not* to speak.

This example may seem as though it counts as a restriction on free speech even from a liberal view, however, because it denies access to some. Consider instead a case in which a professor tells suggestive jokes that focus on women's sexuality. Here, the professor is not so clearly suggesting that women are not welcome in classroom conversation, so it seems less likely that it could be understood in terms of guarantee of access. However, such joke-telling would be likely to squelch women's willingness to participate in discussion (for fear it would call even more unwanted attention to them); it would move women into the "uncomfortable listeners" category. Thus, on my conception, such action would count as a violation of freedom of speech.

Furthermore, to consider an even harder case, even if this were a class in which student discussion played no role, I would still argue that the professor diminishes the freedom of speaking in this classroom, through humiliating (some of) his listeners. As you recall, my definition stipulates that the listener/potential listener is a part of the speaking situation, even in instances where he or she is not able to respond.[29] For a male professor to speak in ways that humiliate women students is to lend support to systems which subordinate women, to bolster the stratification of an already-stratified system.[30]

I describe the community as "already-stratified" because clearly, a classroom in which I am forbidden to speak is already a classroom where speech is not free. In fact, it may seem beside the point, even obfuscatory, to say that the freedom of speech of this community is further diminished by an instructor's singling out and degrading particular people or groups. Doesn't such a claim mask the *significant* suppression of free speech that is already present in a classroom where students aren't allowed to speak? And while we certainly should recognize the damage done to one who is forced to listen to sexist or racist talk, do we really want to call that a diminishment of the community's freeedom of speech?[31]

Indeed I do. It is important to recognize not only the speaking from which students are prohibited, but also the potential speaking, and active, engaged listening that is blocked in an atmosphere which dehumanizes them. With respect to potential speaking, consider that these students leave the classroom and enter other classes where talking is expected, perhaps even required. The experience of being harassed through sexist speech may make them reluctant to talk even when given the opportunity; as Tamara Root suggests, their "entitlement to speak" is curtailed.[32]

Furthermore, students' functioning as listeners is harmed in a context where they are denigrated. Listening and "listening-type activities" (like ignoring) are part of speaking. Even when listeners don't have opportuinty to talk, the freedom of speech of the community is further diminished when they are not treated as full humans.[33]

Recall my discussion of the two defenses offered of the liberal conception of freedom of speech. Here I shall attempt to make good the claim that these defenses are better served by a collective notion of speaking than by a liberal conception of speech.

The first defense was the argument from individual rights. I suggested that there was something slightly peculiar about such a defense, because it wasn't at all clear how speaking could promote intellectual growth when it was treated as a singularly individuallistic act. I asked how uttering—as opposed to talking- could foster intellectual growth. It is my experience that it is precisely when I am uttering, rather than talking-and-listening, that I am least likely to learn anything.

In contrast, a collective conception of speaking, by recognizing its interactive nature, and by acknowledging the potential effects that speakers and listeners can have on each other, gives us a clear way to understand the role of talk in an individual's intellectual growth. Consider, for example, the way one develops as a philosopher through one's training in graduate school.[34] One learns to formulate and understand arguments through interchange with one's graduate student peers, one's professors, the authors of one's texts, and so forth. Even when engaged in the seemingly solitary endeavor of writing a thesis, one is surrounded by other philosophers, in the form of texts, with whom one is engaged in philosophical debate and discussion. Speaking as discussion is central to one's mental maturation.

If we assume that our talk with others can affect their beliefs, and that their responses will in turn shape our thoughts, it follows that speaking in the community ought to be free, to enable persons to develop. It also follows that a definitiion of free speaking that treats objectifying, degrading, oppressive speech not as free but as destructive of freedom, is better equipped to enable free and full intellectual development than is a definition that suggests that the principles of "free speech" require us to listen to words that demoralize and silence us.[35]

Turning to the second liberal defense of freedom of speech, it can also be argued that this goal is best met by a collective concept of speaking as well. Recall that Mill's defense of free speech argues that we must keep our ideas circulating in public (through speech), if we are to have the best chance of developing true ideas. As our ideas are challenged, embellished, encouraged, refuted by others, they become stronger. Or they become weaker and we replace them.

Mill emphasizes the role of speech in the development of truth to the virtual exclusion of any other use it may have. Furthermore, he emphasizes that the community must allow all ideas, because we can never be sure an idea is really false. Such tenets clearly are not in keeping with the collective conception, where it is recognized that people talk and listen (or don't listen) for all sorts of reasons, and where it is suggested that certain ideas, when expressed, acutally undermine the freedom of the relevant community. The utilitarian goals are not in harmony with the goals of a collective notion of speaking.

Nonetheless, those goals can be achieved better on a collective than on a liberal conception. This, again, is simply because the collective conception begins with the assumption that speaking goes on among people. It is acknowledged from the outset that when we talk about an idea, somone might well listen—that's probably the reason we are saying it out loud in the first place. And in listening, they may be prompted to respond. Thus, while I reject many of the assumptions and the tactics of the utilitarian defense, I would argue that a defense of free speech that derives from the value of exchanging ideas is, in the end, a defense better served by a collective conception of speech than by a liberal individualist conception. (In some ways I think Mill would agree; as I have already suggested, his position is more cordial to a collective conception than is a postition like Emerson's.)

In sketching out a collective conception for free speaking, I have intended to show why it is more useful for thinking about speaking than is a liberal conception of free speech. In calling for a transformation in the ways we think about free speaking, I'm also calling for a change in the ways we act, particularly in the concrete situations we find ourselves, such as the classroom and the political meeting. (As I've already suggested, however, I am suspicious about the chances that externally-imposed regulations could bring about the kind of respect for the freedom of the community that this conception intends to promote. Thus this is not a call for enforcing action.)

On a collective conception of free speech, issues of power become paramount in importance. Those members of the community who, because of the construction of that community, are granted illegitimate power over other members must act to understand and to transform the ways that power figures into speaking in the community. On this view, we are responsible for the ways we perpetuate the silencing of others by talking in ways that support systems of domination and subordination, and that preserve illegitimate positions of power.

NOTES

1. Earlier versions of this paper were presented at the fall 1989 Midwest Society for Women in Philosophy Conference in Evanston, Illinois, and the New Feminist Scholarship Conference at SUNY, Buffalo, March 1990. I would also like to thank the members of a political philosophy reading group—Jeremy Iggers, Tamara Root, Corinne Bedecarre, Tom Atchison, and Nancy Potter—for an extremely helpful discussion of the paper; Peter Dalton and the anonymous reviewers from *Social Theory and Practice*, for their written comments; and Stephen Kellert, for many challenging conversations about the issues involved.
2. Of course not all liberal notions of speech are radically individualistic; a useful distinction might be made between "solipsistic" liberal models, and "two-or-more-person" models. The latter sort do ascribe some sort of role to those who hear and respond to speech. John Stuart Mill's arguments for the value of free speech, for example, display a significant emphasis on the role of the community. Mill's model emphasizes the importance of free debate and discussion as a means by which to improve one's ideas. One of his chief arguments in support of free speech is that collecting others' responses to one's speech enables one to develop clearer, stronger ideas. But such a view only addresses others' roles as speakers—as producers of ideas. My position recognizes an even broader role for these others; I shall suggest that listening/potential speaking are themselves aspects of speaking. Thus, others' interests do not become relevant (and eligible for protection) only when others themselves become speakers; the interests of listeners (and even "ignorers") as listeners must be taken into account in evaluating whether speech in a particular situation is free.
3. Obviously, there is more than one liberal model of free speech, and what I will say about this model is not true of every liberal model.
4. I think it not insignificant that discussions of the First Amendment tend to refer to "freedom of speech," and

not "free speaking." The former construction draws our attention to the product, while the latter focuses on the activity of speaking.

5. Francis Canavan, *Freedom of Expression* (Durham: Carolina Academic Press, 1984), p. 2.
6. Plato already could have told us that this was a bad way to think about speaking. In the *Protagoras*, he suggests that knowledge is not a substance you can take home in a bottle and inspect to see if it's safe. Knowledge goes directly into you (*Protagoras*, 314a-b). Although he is talking about knowledge here, his remarks are also relevant for the speech through which learning takes place.
7. Canavan cites U.S. Supreme Court Justices Hugo Black and William O. Douglas as two examples of those who regard freedom of speech to be a freedom that must never be abridged in any way (Canavan, p. 7).
8. "Looking beyond speech itself" often involves claiming that speech is not just speech, but is also action—illegal action at that. MacKinnon, in discussing this issue, says, "Consider for example that First Amendment bog, the distinction between speech and conduct. Most conduct is expressive as well as active; words are as often tantamount to acts as they are vehicles for removed cerebration" (*Feminism Unmodified* [Cambridge: Harvard University Press, 1987], p. 208). She points to laws against treason, bribery, and blackmail as illustrations of this fact.
9. Chaplinsky v. New Hampshire, 315 U.S. 568 (1942); and Smith v. Collin, 439 U.S. 916, 918 (1968).
10. Of course the question is "What constitutes sufficiently extreme circumstance?" and this is one of the questions the Court has been answering. It is not my project to summarize its answer here. In raising this discussion, I wish only to emphasize the way that the issue is formulated in the first place; to highlight the fact that, for the Court, any conditions that warrant restricting someone's speech are themselves regarded as extraneous to the (free) speech itself. (This is a particular illustration of my more general claim about a liberal conception of free speech—namely, that the roles of listeners, etc., are not regarded as being parts of the activity of speaking itself.)
11. Thomas Emerson, *Toward a General Theory of the First Amendment* (New York: Random House, 1966), p. 4.
12. Emerson, p. 4.
13. Emerson, p. 5.
14. John Stuart Mill, *On Liberty*, ed. Elizabeth Rapaport (Indianapolis: Hackett, 1978), p. 16.
15. As Tom Atchison suggests, Mill's model may be described as a "two-or-more-person" liberal model of free speech, for Mill does indeed acknowledge the role played by others in the community. It is through conversation that we improve our ideas. So it might be said that Mill is more immune to my criticisms than someone like Emerson, because he adopts a kind of community-based model. This is true, but as Corinne Bedecarre points out, Mill only recognizes part of the social context of speech. He still ends up focusing attention exclusively on the speaking part of speech—on what other speakers can add to my thought/speech. The receiving of speech is irrelevant to him. Thus, as I've already suggested, my position is not reducible to his. This fact will become more clear when I turn to explicate my position directly.
16. I would suggest that this is a rather conservative criticism, one which addresses the liberal conception on its own turf. That is, it criticizes the liberal conception for being less than thoroughgoing in its protection of speech, because it fails to recognize that some speech is suppressed even before it is started. As such, it is a criticism to which Mill's position is certainly less susceptible than some others'.
17. MacKinnon refers to such cases as "guarantees of access of speech" (MacKinnon, 208). One case MacKinnon points to as an example of affirmative guarantee of access to speech is the Red Lion decision (Red Lion Broadcasting Co. v. F.C.C., 395 U.S. 367 [1969]). "Because certain avenues of speech are inherently restricted—for instance, there are only so many broadcast frequencies ... some people's access has to be restricted in the interest of providing access to all. In other words, the speech of those who could buy up all the speech there is, is restricted" (MacKinnon, p. 208).
18. MacKinnon: "By contrast with those who wrote the First Amendment so they could keep what they had, those who didn't have it didn't get it. Those whose speech was silenced prior to law, prior to any operation of the state's prohibition of it, were not secured freedom of speech" (MacKinnon, p. 207). MacKinnon's analysis points to the fact that there are several

levels at which your speech may be restricted, and that it is important to focus an eye on each of those levels, to see the relations between them. My claim is a particular application of the more general claim that it's necessary for individuals to see their experience in the context of the larger social structures that shape their experience. In the case of speech, it is important for a woman who is denied access to speech to recognize her exclusion in relation to the historical denial of access to women.

19. An anonymous reviewer of this paper asks why this is an objection to the liberal model. "It is one thing to state what *constitutes* free speech; another to determine what value should be attached to it.... The liberal approach can take account of any and all effects of free speech when it comes to this evaluative question. The alternative account offered by the author seems to want to build the evaluation into the very conception of free speech itself ...." In response to this reviewer, I would agree that my account builds an evaluation into the conception of free speech—but so does the liberal conception. The difference between the two views is a difference over which aspects ("effects") of speaking one takes into account in determining its freedom—not between an account which builds evaluation into it and one which does not. My account calls into question the very legitimacy of calling someone's speech "free" when it perpetuates the silence of another.

20. It has frequently been asked whether my reconceptualization here is legal or moral. Although I illustrate my position with reference to Supreme Court decisions, and use the position of Catharine MacKinnon, a legal theorist, my project is primarily a moral or social one. This is because I have little confidence in the power of legislation to effect changes in the ways people think and act—and I have considerable suspicion about the ways such legislation would be enforced.

    I therefore regard my reconceptualization of speech as a tool for groups of people interested in rethinking/reshaping their ways of talking together—and for making policy decisions within that community. I think a college establishing policy against sexist or racist speech might exemplify its use—although showing whether and how this is so must be the projects of another paper.

21. My conception of individuals as relational has been shaped by Deane Curtin, Sarah Lucia Hoagland, Suzanne LaGrande, Maria Lugones, and Susan Heineman, among others.

22. In support of this claim, I would suggest, for example, that we really can't imagine what a human who grew up and lived entirely outside human culture would be like. Our difficulty in imagining this is not confined to our worry over how an infant could survive without a human parent. It extends to a genuine confusion about how such a being would behave, and what they would "be." To paraphrase Wittgenstein, even if a "human raised by lions" could speak, we wouldn't know what they were saying. (Wittgenstein, *Philosophical Investigations*, [New York: Macmillan, 1958], p. 223.) And if they weren't raised by anyone, we couldn't imagine them talking.

23. This description highlights another difference between the model I'm developing and the liberal model. Liberal theorists—one thinks especially of Mill here—consider speech only insofar as it is aimed at the acquisition of knowledge. But clearly that is not what all talking aims at; some of it aims at having fun with words, killing time, even preventing the acquisition of knowledge (as when I talk while you're trying to study).

24. Of course this is not to deny that your speech may have a very small (verging on nonexistent) effect on someone.

25. However, there is nothing in my definition that prevents treating certain acts of speech as genuine utterances. A liberal definition of speech may be more descriptive of some speech. But I would argue that such instances are the exceptions, and not the standards they are made to be. (I'm inclined to think that the sort of situation that is best described by a liberal model is one in which the speaker is utterly ignored by all potential listeners—or in which they are only talking to themselves. And of course in such situations, the problem of censorship is not likely to arise: if no one is paying attention to you, it is unlikely that they'll try to restrict you either.)

26. An anonymous reviewer worries that my definition makes speech unfree only if those whom it harms are present in the room with the speaker. Such a definition would exclude all-male "locker room" talk, for example. The reviewer writes, "I hope for a concep-

tion of free speech that excludes sexist talk whether or not women happen to be listening.... I concur with the desire for such a conception. And, though I will not develop the claim here, I would suggest that this desire could be met by understanding the notion of listener/potential listener as including persons who are not present (and perhaps never could be present) at the scene of the actual conversation, but are present for its aftermath. Women who bear the repercussions of conversations in which "men forge and strengthen their bonds with one another and their domination through misogynist talk" could then be regarded as potential listeners. This means of addressing the example uses a very broad notion of what counts as the relevant community.

Another way to address this example is to recognize that it is not only women who are harmed by sexist speech, though the harm to women is generally greater and more direct. Thus, men telling sexist jokes together in a locker room must also be understood as harming not only women, but also themselves through such practices (and thus, as not speaking freely). Sexist talk is harmful to the men who use it, and to the men who listen to it. This is true whether or not they recognize or acknowledge the harm as such.

27. I recognize that I run the danger of being perceived as advocating that everyone "be nice" to each other and never make anyone uncomfortable. This clearly is not my aim; in fact, my model virtually guarantees that those who talk in oppressive, arrogating ways will feel very uncomfortable when others in the group silence them. Although I will not develop the claim here, I suggest there is a difference between the discomfort you feel because you are the object of sexist or racist talk and the discomfort you feel because, as the perpetrator of such talk, you are subject to the criticism of others. (This is a variation on the familiar "toleration of the intolerant" issue.) Stated another way, just because you are uncomfortable doesn't automatically mean your freedom is being violated.
28. As Nancy Potter notes, this conception of responsibility bears certain similarities to the view Claudia Card develops in her paper "Intimacy and Responsibility: What Lesbians Do."

Jeremy Iggers also points out that taking into account the perspectives of hearers (or readers) could transform the notion of a "free press;" what if the perspective of newspaper readers were routinely considered in assembling a paper?

29. Again in response to the anonymous reviewer, I would suggest that even if women are not able to respond because they are not present (the locker room again, or a classroom in a men's college), this still constitutes a harm to women as potential listeners, and to men as actual listeners, whether they acknowledge it or not.
30. Again, I rush to emphasize that I do not intend to advocate everyone "tolerating" everyone else, or being nice to everyone else. I begin from the assumption that oppression, objectification, arrogation, are real features of classroom discussion, and that their presence ought to be addressed and dealt with just as routinely as would be an error in using *modus ponens*. (That this attitude sounds to many like a violation of academic freedom is, to me, an indication that there are some problems with this latter concept.) The question to be asked always is, "In what sense does this way of talking contribute to the freedom of the community?"
31. Thanks to Jeremy Iggers for drawing this to my attention.
32. In discussion.
33. Perhaps it would be easiest to show that harm to listeners is harm to freedom of speech if I could come up with a case in which all but one person were prohibited from speaking for "purely technical" reasons. I'm not sure there is such a case, however.
34. The example comes from Peter Dalton.
35. This model not only identifies such limiting speech, but also challenges the recipients of speech to work to make speech situations more free by eliminating it. That is, the model might call us to shout down someone giving a speech against civil rights for lesbians and gays, or to make lots of noise during a showing of a porn movie, in the name of free speech.

To take this notion of freedom seriously demands that we actively promote the speaking of those who are most systematically silenced—and work to eliminate speaking which silences them.

PUBLIC RESPONSE TO RACIST SPEECH: CONSIDERING THE VICTIM'S STORY

Mari J. Matsuda

Mari J. Matsuda teaches at the School of Law at Georgetown University, Washington, D.C. She is the author of Where is Your Body?: And Other Essays on Race, Gender and the Law *(Beacon, 1996) and co-author of* Words that Wound: Critical Race Theory, Assaultive Speech and the First Amendment *(Westview, 1993) and* We Won't Go Back: Making the Case for Affirmative Action *(Houghton, 1997).*

Matsuda tells victims' stories of the effects of racist hate messages as an entry point for defending legal sanctions against racist speech. Matsuda acknowledges the strength of arguments for first amendment values of free speech in the United States, but argues that this absolutist commitment to free speech conflicts with recent developments in other countries and in international law. International conventions declare a commitment to eliminating racism and many countries outside of the United States as well as international bodies are moving to create laws to restrict racist hate propaganda. Matsuda defines a special, narrow class of racist hate propaganda and applies it to various problem cases to defend her argument that the legal system in the United States needs to respond to the real harm of racist hate messages.

A Black family enters a coffee shop in a small Texas town. A white man places a card on their table. The card reads, "You have just been paid a visit by the Ku Klux Klan." The family stands and leaves.[1]

A law student goes to her dorm and finds an anonymous message posted on the door, a caricature image of her race, with a red line slashed through it.[2]

A Japanese-American professor arrives in an Australian city and finds a proliferation of posters stating "Asians Out or Racial War" displayed on telephone poles. She uses her best, educated inflection in speaking with clerks and cab drivers and decides not to complain when she is overcharged.[3]

These unheralded stories share company with the more notorious provocation of swastikas at Skokie, Illinois, and burning crosses on suburban lawns. The threat of hate groups like the Ku Klux Klan and the neo-Nazi skinheads goes beyond their repeated acts of illegal violence. Their presence and the active dissemination of racist propaganda means that citizens are denied personal security and liberty as they go about their daily lives....

[This paper] moves between two stories. The first is the victim's story of the effects of racist hate messages. The second is the first amendment story of free speech. The intent is to respect and value both stories. This bipolar discourse uses as its method what many outsider intellectuals do in silence: it mediates between different ways of knowing to determine what is true and what is just.

In calling for legal sanctions for racist speech, this chapter rejects an absolutist first amendment position. It calls for movement of the societal response to racist speech from the private to the public realm. The choice of public sanction, enforced by the state,

---

Reprinted with permission of Mari J. Matsuda from *Words That Wound: Critical Race Theory, Assaultive Speech, and the First Amendment*, edited by Mari J. Matsuda et al. (Boulder CO: Westview, 1993): 17–51 [edited].

is a significant one. The kinds of injuries historically left to private individuals to absorb and resist through private means are no accident. The places where the law does not go to redress harm have tended to be the places where women, children, people of color, and poor people live. This absence of law is itself another story with a message, perhaps unintended, about the relative value of different human lives. A legal response to racist speech is a statement that victims of racism are valued members of our polity.

The call for a formal, legal-structural response to racist speech goes against the long-standing and healthy America distrust of government power. It goes against an American tradition of tolerance that is precious in the sense of being both valuable and fragile.

Lee Bollinger, dean of the University of Michigan Law School, has concluded that a primary reason for the legal protection of hate speech is to reinforce our commitment to tolerance as a value.[4] If we can shore up our commitment to free speech in the hard and public cases, like *Skokie*,[5] perhaps we will internalize the need for tolerance and spare ourselves from regrettable error in times of stress. Given the real historical costs of state intolerance of minority views, the first amendment purpose Bollinger identifies is not one lightly set aside.

Recognizing both the real harm of racist speech and the need to strengthen our dangerously fickle collective commitment to freedom of discourse, I intend to feel and to work within the first amendment tension armed with stories from human lives. This chapter suggests that outsider jurisprudence—jurisprudence derived from considering stories from the bottom—will help resolve the seemingly irresolvable conflicts of value and doctrine that characterize liberal thought. I conclude that an absolutist first amendment response to hate speech has the effect of perpetuating racism: Tolerance of hate speech is not tolerance borne by the community at large. Rather, it is a psychic tax imposed on those least able to pay....

Racist Hate Messages: The Victim's Story

> The attempt of split bias from violence has been this society's most enduring rationalization.
>
> —Patricia Williams[6]

Who Sees What: Some Initial Stories

In writing this chapter I am forced to ask why the world looks so different to me from the way it looks to many of the civil libertarians whom I consider my allies. Classical thought labels ad hominem analysis a logical fallacy. The identity of the person doing the analysis often seems to make the difference, however, in responding to racist speech. In advocating legal restriction of hate speech, I have found my most sympathetic audience in people who identify with target groups, whereas I have often encountered incredulity, skepticism, and even hostility from others.

This split in reaction is also evident in case studies of hate speech. The typical reaction of target-group members to an incident of racist propaganda is alarm and immediate calls for redress. The typical reaction of non-members is to consider the incidents isolated pranks, the product of sick but harmless minds. This is in part a defensive reaction: a refusal to believe that real people, people just like us, are racists. This disassociation leads logically to the claim that there is no institutional or state responsibility to respond to the incident. It is not the kind of real and pervasive threat that requires the state's power to quell.

Here are some true "just kidding" stories:

> An African-American worker found himself repeatedly subjected to racist speech when he came to work. A noose was hanging one day in his work area; a dead animal and other threatening objects were placed in his locker. "KKK" references were directed at him, as well as other racist slurs and death threats. His employer discouraged him from calling the police, attributing the incidents to "horseplay."[7]
>
> In San Francisco, a swastika was placed near the desks of Asian-American and African-American inspectors in the newly integrated fire department. The official explanation for the presence of the swastika at the fire department was that it was presented several years earlier as a "joke" gift to the battalion chief, and that it was unclear why or how it ended up at the work stations of the minority employees.[8]
>
> In Jackson, Mississippi, African-American employees of Frito-Lay found their cars sprayed with "KKK"

inscriptions and were the targets of racist notes and threats. Local African Americans and Jews were concerned, but officials said the incidents were attributable to children.[9]

An African-American FBI agent was subject to a campaign of racist taunts by white coworkers. A picture of an ape was pasted over his child's photograph, and racial slurs were used. Such incidents were called "healthy" by his supervisor.[10]

In Seattle, a middle-management Japanese American was disturbed by his employer's new anti-Japanese campaign. As the employer's use of slurs and racist slogans in the workplace increased, so did the employee's discomfort. His objections were viewed as overly sensitive and uncooperative. He finally quit his job, and he was denied unemployment insurance benefits because his departure was "without cause."[11]

In Contra Costa County, California, Ku Klux Klan symbols were used to turn families looking for homes away from certain neighborhoods. The local sheriff said there was "nothing ... to indicate this is Klan activity."[12]

Similarly, a Hmong family in Eureka, California, was twice victimized by four foot-high crosses burning on their lawn. Local police dismissed this as "a prank."[13]

Why might anti-Japanese racial slurs mean something different to Asian and white managers? Here is a story of mine:

As a young child I was told never to let anyone call me a J-p. My parents, normally peaceable and indulgent folk, told me this in the tone reserved for dead-serious warnings. Don't accept rides from strangers. Don't play with matches. Don't let anyone call you that name. In their tone they transmitted a message of danger, that the word was a dangerous one, tied to violence.

Just as I grew up to learn the facts about the unspoken danger my parents saw in the stranger in the car, I learned how they connected the violence of California lynch mobs and Hiroshima atom bombs to racist slurs against Japanese Americans.

This early training in vigilance was reinforced by what I later learned about violence and Asian Americans: that people with features like mine are regular victims of violence tied to a wave of anti-Asian propaganda that stretches from Boston to San Francisco, from Calveston to Detroit.

The white managers who considered Mr. O. (the Japanese-American manager) an overly sensitive troublemaker and the unemployment board that determined there was no good cause for him to quit his job came from a different experience. They probably never heard of Vincent Chin, a twenty-seven-year-old Chinese American beaten to death by thugs wielding baseball bats who yelled, "It's because of you fucking J-ps that we're out of work!" They do not know about the Southeast-Asian-American children spat upon and taunted as they walk home from school in Boston; about the vigilante patrols harassing Vietnamese shrimpers in Texas. Nor do they know that the violence in all these cases is preceded by propaganda similar to that used in Mr. O.'s workplace: that those [racist slur for Asian groups] are taking over "our" country.

Stories of anti-Asian violence are regularly reported in the Asian-American press; just as stories of synagogue vandalism are regularly reported in the Jewish-American press; and anti-African-American violence, including the all-too-common phenomenon of "move-in" violence, is regularly reported in the African-American press. Members of target-group communities tend to know that racial violence and harassment are widespread, common, and life threatening; that, as one Georgia observer put it, "The youngsters who paint a swastika today may throw a bomb tomorrow."[14]

The mainstream press often ignores these stories, giving rise to the view of racist and anti-Semitic incidents as random and isolated and the corollary that isolated incidents are inconsequential. For informed members of the victim communities, however, it is logical to link together several thousand real life stories into one tale of caution....

The Specific Negative Effects of Racist Hate Messages

everywhere the crosses are burning,
sharp-shooting goose-steppers around every corner,
there are snipers in the schools ...

(I know you don't believe this.
You think this is nothing
but faddish exaggeration. But they
are not shooting at you.)

—Lorna Dee Cervantes[15]

Racist hate messages are rapidly increasing and are widely distributed in this country through a variety of low and high technologies, including anonymous phone calls and letters, posters, books, magazines and pamphlets, cable television, recorded phone messages, computer networks, bulk mail, graffiti, and leafleting. The negative effects of hate messages are real and immediate for the victims. Victims of vicious hate propaganda experience physiological symptoms and emotional distress ranging from fear in the gut to rapid pulse rate and difficulty in breathing, nightmares, post-traumatic stress disorder, hypertension, psychosis, and suicide. Patricia Williams has called the blow of racist messages "spirit murder" in recognition of the psychic destruction victims experience.[16]

Victims are restricted in their personal freedom. To avoid receiving hate messages, victims have to quit jobs, forgo education, leave their homes, avoid certain public places, curtail their own exercise of speech rights, and otherwise modify their behavior and demeanor. The recipient of hate messages struggles with inner turmoil. One subconscious response is to reject one's own identity as a victim-group member. As writers portraying the African-American experience have noted, the price of disassociating from one's own race is often sanity itself.

As much as one may try to resist a piece of hate propaganda, the effect on one's self-esteem and sense of personal security is devastating. To be hated, despised, and alone is the ultimate fear of all human beings. However irrational racist speech may be, it hits right at the emotional place where we feel the most pain. The aloneness comes not only from the hate message itself, but also from the government response of tolerance. When hundreds of police officers are called out to protect racist marchers, when the courts refuse redress for racial insult, and when racist attacks are officially dismissed as pranks, the victim becomes a stateless person. Target-group members must either identify with a community that promotes racist speech or admit that the community does not include them.

The effect on non-target-group members is also of constitutional dimensions. Associational and other liberty interests of whites are curtailed in an atmosphere rife with racial hatred. Hate messages, threats, and violence are often the price for whites of hiring, marrying, adopting, socializing with, and even jogging with people of color. In addition, the process of disassociation can affect the mental health of non-targets. Dominant-group members who rightfully, and often angrily, object to hate propaganda share a guilty secret: their relief that they are not themselves the target of the racist attack. Even as they reject the Ku Klux Klan, they may feel ambivalent relief that they are not African-American, Asian, or Jewish. Thus they are drawn into unwilling complicity with the Klan, spared from being the feared and degraded thing.

Just as when we confront human tragedy—a natural disaster, a plane crash—we feel the blessing of the fortunate that distances us from the victims, the presence of racist hate propaganda distances right-thinking dominant-group members from the victims, making it harder to achieve a sense of common humanity. Similarly, racist propaganda forces victim-group members to view all dominant-group members with suspicion. It forces well-meaning dominant-group members to use kid-glove care in dealing with outsiders. This is one reason why social relations across racial lines are so rare in the United States.

Research in the psychology of racism suggests a related effect of racist hate propaganda: At some level, no matter how much both victims and well-meaning dominant-group members resist it, racial inferiority is planted in our minds as an idea that may hold some truth.[17] The idea is improbable and abhorrent, but because it is presented repeatedly, it is there before us. "Those people" are lazy, dirty, sexualized, money grubbing, dishonest, inscrutable, we are told. We reject the idea, but the next time we sit next to one of "those people," the dirt message, the sex message, is triggered. We stifle it, reject it as wrong, but it is there, interfering with our perception and interaction with the person next to us. In conducting research for this chapter, I read an unhealthy number of racist statements. A few weeks after reading about a "dot busters" campaign against immigrants from India, I passed by an Indian woman on my campus. Instead of thinking, "What a beautiful sari," the first thought that came into my mind was "dot busters." Only after setting aside the hate message could I move on to my own thoughts. The propaganda I read had taken me one step back from casually treating a fellow brown-skinned human being as that, rather than as someone distanced from myself. For the victim, similarly, the angry rejection of the message of inferiority is coupled with absorption of the message. When a dominant-group member responds favorably, there is a moment of relief—the victims of hate messages do not always believe in their insides that they deserve decent treatment. This obsequious moment is degrading and dispiriting when the self-aware victim acknowledges it.

Psychologists and sociologists have done much to document the effects of racist messages on both victims and dominant-group members.[18] Writers of color have given us graphic portrayals of what life is like for victims of racist propaganda.[19] From the victim's perspective, racist hate messages cause real damage.

If the harm of racist hate messages is significant, and the truth value marginal, the doctrinal space for regulation of such speech becomes a possibility. An emerging international standard seizes this possibility.

International Law of Human Rights: The Emerging Acceptance of the Victim's Story

The international community has chosen to outlaw racist hate propaganda. Article 4 of the International Convention on the Elimination of All Forms of Racial Discrimination states:

> State Parties condemn all propaganda and all organizations which are based on ideas or theories of superiority of one race or group of persons of one colour or ethnic origin, or which attempt to justify or promote racial hatred and discrimination in any form, and undertake to adopt immediate and positive measures designed to eradicate all incitements to, or acts of, such discrimination and, to this end, with due regard to the principles embodied in the Universal Declaration of Human Rights and the rights expressly set forth in Article 5 of this Convention, *inter alia*:
>
> (a) Shall declare as an offence punishable by law all dissemination of ideas based on racial superiority or hatred, incitement to racial discrimination, as well as all acts of violence or incitement to such acts against any race or group of persons of another colour or ethnic origin, and also the provision of any assistance to racist activities, including the financing thereof;
>
> (b) Shall declare illegal and prohibit organizations, and also organized and all other propaganda activities, which promote and incite racial discrimination, and shall recognize participation in such organization or activities as an offence punishable by law; [and]
>
> (c) Shall not permit public authorities of public institutions, national or local, to promote or incite racial discrimination.[20]

Under this treaty, nation-states are required to criminalize racist hate messages. Prohibiting dissemination of ideas of racial superiority or hatred is not easily reconciled with U.S. concepts of free speech. The convention recognizes this conflict. Article 4 acknowledges the need for "due regard" for rights protected by the Universal Declaration of Human Rights and by Article 5 of the convention—including the rights of freedom of speech, association, and conscience.

Recognizing these conflicting values and nonetheless concluding that the right to freedom from racist hate propaganda deserves affirmative recognition represents the evolving international view. A U.S. lawyer, trained in a tradition of liberal thought, would read Article 4 and conclude immediately that it is unworkable. Acts of violence and perhaps imminent incitement to violence are properly prohibited, but the control of ideas is doomed to failure. This position was voiced continually in the debates preceding adoption of the convention,[21] leading to the view that Article 4 is both controversial and troublesome ....

The General Assembly debates on Article 4 focused on free speech. Although the issue was never clearly resolved, it is significant that no country, not even the United States, was willing to abandon the basic premise of Article 4. The article declares that parties "condemn all propaganda ... based on ideas or theories of superiority ... or which attempt[s] to justify or promote racial hatred and discrimination in any form."[22] Similarly, the preamble to the convention states explicitly that "any doctrine of superiority based on racial differentiation is scientifically false, morally condemnable, socially unjust and dangerous, and that there is no justification for racial discrimination.[23] The community of nations has thus made a commitment, with U.S. support, to eliminate racism. It has recognized that racist hate propaganda is illegitimate and is properly subject to control under the international law of human rights. The debate, then, centers around the limits of such control, not around the basic decision to control racism....

The convention is not the only expression of the emerging international view. The need to limit racist hate messages is implicit in basic human rights documents such as the UN Charter and the Universal Declaration of Human Rights. Both documents recognize the primacy of the right to equality and freedom from racism. Other human rights treaties, such as the European Convention for the Protection of Human Rights and Fundamental Freedoms[24] and the American Declaration of the Rights and Duties of Man,[25] also recognize this primacy. The United States is also a party to an international convention on genocide that forbids, *inter alia*, incitement to genocide.[26] Finally, the existing domestic law of several nations—including states that accept the Western notion of freedom of expression—has outlawed certain forms of racist speech.

The United Kingdom, for example, under the Race Relations Act, has criminalized incitement to discrimination and incitement to racial hatred.[27] The act criminalizes the publication or distribution of "threatening, abusive, or insulting" written matter or use of such language in a public place. The United Kingdom standard originally differed from the international standard in that it required proof of intent to incite to hatred. The intent requirement was later dropped.[28] The act is consistent with the international standard in that it recognizes that avoiding the spread of hatred is a legitimate object of the law and that some forms of racist expression are properly criminalized. The legislative history of the act suggests that the drafters were concerned with the spread of racist violence. Imminent violence, however, was not the only object of the act. The act recognized the inevitable connection between the general spread of race hatred and the spread of violence. Although commentators have suggested that the act is ineffective and capable of misuse,[29] the existence of the act supports the growing international movement toward outlawing racist hate propaganda.

Canada has similarly adopted a national statue governing hate propaganda. Sections 318 and 319 of the Canadian Criminal Code[30] outlaw advocacy of genocide, defined as *inter alia*, an act designed to kill a member of an identifiable group. Also outlawed are communications inciting hatred against any identifiable group where a breach of peace is likely to follow. The law further prohibits the expression of ideas inciting hatred if such expression is tied to a probable threat to order.

The new Canadian Bill of Rights incorporates strong protections for freedom of speech and association.[31] Conflict between the new Bill of Rights and the antihate legislation has not prevented actions to limit hate speech.

Australia and New Zealand also have laws restricting racist speech,[32] leaving the United States alone among the major common law jurisdictions in its complete tolerance of such speech. What the laws of these other countries and the UN convention have in common is that they specify a particularly egregious form of expression for criminalization. All expressions concerning differences between races is not banned. The definitive elements are discrimination, connection to violence, and messages of inferiority, hatred, or persecution. Thus the entire spectrum of what could be called racist speech is not prohibited. A belief in intellectual differences between the races, for instance, is not subject to sanctions unless it is coupled with an element of hatred or persecution. What the emerging global standard prohibits is the kind of expression that most interferes with the rights of subordinated-group members to participate equally in society and maintain their basic sense of security and worth as human beings.

The failure of U.S. law to accept this emerging standard reflects a unique first amendment jurisprudence. This jurisprudence is so entrenched in U.S. law that it at first seems irreconcilable with the values given primacy in Article 4, such as the values of equality and full participation....

Narrow Application and Protection of First Amendment Values

This chapter attempts to recognize and accommodate the civil libertarian position. The victim's perspective requires respect for the idea of rights, for it is those on the bottom who are most hurt by the absence of rights, and it is those on the bottom who have sustained the struggle for rights in U.S. history. The image of book burnings should unnerve us and remind us to argue long and hard before selecting a class of speech to exclude from the public domain. I am uncomfortable in making the suggestions in this section when others fall too easily into agreement.

A definition of actionable racist speech must be narrow in order to respect first amendment values. I believe racist speech is best treated as a sui generis category, presenting an idea so historically untenable, so dangerous, and so tied to perpetuation of violence and degradation of the very classes of human beings who are least equipped to respond that it is properly treated as outside the realm of protected discourse. The courts in the *Skokie* case[33] expressed doubt that principles were available to single out racist speech for public limitation. Here I attempt to construct a doctrinal and evidentiary world in which we might begin to draw the lines the *Skokie* courts could not imagine.

The alternative to recognizing racist speech as qualitatively different because of its content is to continue to stretch existing first amendment exceptions, such as the "fighting words" doctrine and the "content/conduct" distinction. This stretching ultimately weakens the first amendment fabric, creating neutral holes that remove protection for many forms of speech. Setting aside the worst forms of racist speech for special treatment is a non-neutral, value-laden approach that will better preserve free speech.

To distinguish the worst, paradigm example of racist hate messages from other forms of racist and nonracist speech, I offer three identifying characteristics:

1. The message is of racial inferiority
2. The message is directed against a historically oppressed group
3. The message is persecutory, hateful, and degrading.

Making each element a prerequisite to prosecution prevents opening of the dreaded floodgates of censorship.

The first element is the primary identifier of racist speech: Racist speech proclaims racial inferiority and denies the personhood of target-group members. All members of the target group are at one considered alike and inferior.

The second element attempts to further define racism by recognizing the connection of racism to power and subordination. Racism is more than race hatred or prejudice. It is the structural subordination of a group based on an idea of racial inferiority. Racist speech is particularly harmful because it is a mechanism of subordination, reinforcing a historical vertical relationship.

The final element is related to the "fighting words" idea. The language used in the worst form of racist speech is language that is, and is intended as, persecutory, hateful, and degrading.

The following section applies these three elements to hypothetical cases. Using these elements narrows the field of interference with speech. Under these narrowing elements, arguing that particular groups are genetically superior in a context free of hatefulness and without the endorsement of persecution is permissible. Satire and stereotyping that avoids persecutory language remains protected. Hateful verbal attacks upon dominant-group members by victims is permissible. These kinds of speech are offensive, but they are, in respect of first amendment principles, best subjected to the marketplace of ideas. This is not to suggest that we remain silent in the face of offensive speech of this type. Rather, the range of private remedies—including counterspeech, social approbation, boycott, and persuasion—should apply.

If the most egregious, paradigmatic racial hate messages are not properly left to private remedy, it is important to explain why. One way to explain this is to consider the difference between racist hate messages and Marxist speech. Marxist speech is the kind of unpopular political expression the first amendment is intended to protect. Marxist speech is, according to a once-prevalent view, the advocacy of overthrow of existing governments, inevitably leading to dictatorships and persecution of dissidents and capitalists. It is thus, it was argued, dangerous speech, properly censored. The legacy of this view was McCarthyism and the shattered lives of hundreds of decent citizens.

How can one argue for censorship of racist hate messages without encouraging a revival of McCarthyism? There is an important difference that comes from human experience, our only source of collective knowledge. We know, from our collective historical knowledge, that slavery was wrong. We know white minority rule in South Africa is wrong. This knowledge is reflected in the universal acceptance of the wrongness of the doctrine of racial supremacy. There is no nation left on this planet that submits as its national self-expression the view that Hitler was right....

At the universities, at the centers of knowledge of the international community, the doctrines of racial supremacy and racial hatred are again uniformly rejected. At the United Nations the same is true. We have fought wars and spilled blood to establish the universal acceptance of this principle. The universality of the principle, in a world bereft of agreement on many things, is a mark of collective human progress. The victim's perspective, one mindful of the lessons of history, thus accepts racist speech as sui generis and universally condemned.

Marxist speech, however, is not universally condemned. Marxism presents a philosophy for political organization, distribution of wealth and power, ordering of values, and promotion of social change. By its very content it is political speech going to the core of ongoing political debate. It is impossible to achieve world consensus either for or against this political view. Marxists teach in universities. Although Marxist ideas are rejected and abhorred by many, Marxist thought, like liberal thought, neoconservative economic theory, and other conflicting structures for understanding life and politics, is part of the ongoing efforts of human beings to understand their world and improve life in it.

What is argued here, then, is that we accept certain principles as the shared historical legacy of the world community. Racial supremacy is one of the ideas we have collectively and internationally considered and rejected. As an idea connected to continuing racism and degradation of minority groups, it causes real harm to its victims. We are not safe when these violent words are among us.

Treating racist speech as sui generis and universally condemned on the basis of its content and the harmful effect of its content is precisely the censorship that civil libertarians fear. I would argue, however, that explicit content-based rejection of narrowly defined racist speech is more protective of civil liberties than the competing-interests tests of the likely-to-incite-violence tests that can spill over to censor forms of political speech.

Looking to the emerging critical race theory, I derive basic principles: the need to fight racism at all levels, the value of explicit formal rules, and a fear of tyranny. These principles suggest the wisdom of legal intervention with only a narrowly defined class of racist hate propaganda.

A range of legal interventions, including the use of tort law and criminal law principles, is appropriate to combat racist hate propaganda. Although the value of free speech can guide the choice of procedure—including evidentiary rules and burdens of persuasion—it should not completely remove recourse to the institution of law to combat racist speech. Racism as an acquired set of behaviors can be disacquired, and law is the means by which the state typically provides incentives for changes in behavior.

Hard Cases

In order to get beyond racism, we must first take account of race. There is no other way.
—Harry Blackmun[34]

Of course I emphasize different things, Doctor, because history has treated my people differently from yours.
—Richard Delgado[35]

In this section I consider stories at the edge, a tentative discussion of problem cases that may arise under the definition of actionable racist speech discussed here. The connecting thread in these examples is the need for clarity about the historical context in which racist speech arises and attention to the degree of harm experienced by targets of different kinds of racist speech.

A Case of the Angry Nationalist

Expressions of hatred, revulsion, and anger directed against members of historically dominant groups by subordinated-group members are not criminalized by the definition of racist hate messages used here. Malcom X's "white devil" statements—which he later retracted—are an example. Some would find this troublesome, arguing that any attack on any person's ethnicity is harmful. In the case of the white devil, there is harm and hurt, but it is of a different degree. Because the attack is not tied to the perpetuation of racist vertical relationships, it is not the paradigm worst example of hate propaganda. The dominant-group member hurt by conflict with the angry nationalist is more likely to have access to a safe harbor of exclusive dominant-group interactions. Retreat and reaffirmation of personhood are more easily attained for members of groups not historically subjugated.

Although white-hating nationalist expressions are condemnable both politically and personally, I would interpret an angry, hateful poem by a person from a historically subjugated group as a victim's struggle for self-identity in response to racism. It is not tied to the structural domination of another group. Part of the special harm of racist speech is that it works in concert with other racist tools to keep victim groups in an inferior position. Should history change course, placing former victim groups in a dominant or equalized position, the newly equalized group will lose the special protection suggested here for expression of nationalist anger.

Critics of this proposal ask how one knows who is oppressed and who is not. Poor whites, ethnic whites, wealthy ethnics—the confusing examples and barriers to classification abound. The larger question is how anyone knows anything in life or in law. To conceptualize a condition called subordination is a legitimate alternative to denying that such a condition exists. In law we conceptualize. We take on mammoth tasks of discovery and knowing. We can determine when subordination exists by looking at social indicators: Wealth, mobility, comfort, health, and survival—or the absence of these—tend to mark the rise to the top and the fall to the depths. The rise and fall of group status is relevant even when an individual is a counterexample, because when the group is subordinated, even the lucky counterexample feels the downward tug. Luck is not the same as privilege.

In some cases, a group's social well-being may improve even as its victimization continues. Asians who experience economic success are often under employed relative to their talents. Jews who attain equality in employment still experience anti-Semitic vilification, harassment, and exclusion. Catholics are relatively free from discrimination is some communities and subject to vile bigotry in others. Evidence of the relative subjugation of various groups is available to fact finders.

In the same way that lawyers marshal evidence in an adversarial setting to find facts in other areas of law, we can learn to know the facts about subordination and to determine when hate speech is used as an instrument of that subordination.

First Variation: Anti-Semitism and Racism Within Subordinated Communities

What of hateful racist and anti-Semitic speech by people within subordinated communities? The phenomenon of one subordinated group inflicting racist speech upon another subordinated group is a persistent and touchy problem. Similarly, members of a subordinated group sometimes direct racist language at their own group. The victim's privilege becomes problematic when it is used by one subordinated person to lash out at another. I argue here for tolerance of hateful speech that comes from an experience of oppression, but when that speech is used to attack a subordinated-group member, using language of persecution and adopting a rhetoric of racial inferiority, I am inclined to prohibit such speech.

History and context are important in this case because the custom in a particular subordinated community may tolerate racial insults as a form of wordplay. Where this is the case, community members tend to have a clear sense of what is racially degrading and what is not. The appropriate standard in determining whether language is persecutory, hateful, and degrading is the recipient's community standard. We should beware lest by misunderstanding linguistic and cultural norms we further entrench structures of subordination.

Second Variation: Zionism

I reject the sweeping charge that Zionism is racism and argue instead for a highly contextualized consideration of Zionist speech. To the extent that any racial hostility expressed within a Zionist context is a reaction to historical persecution, it is protected under the doctrinal scheme suggested in this chapter. Should Zionists ever lose this historically based privilege? If Zionist speakers are white, do hateful, race-bound expressions of theirs necessarily reinforce historical conditions of white dominance over brown and black people? The analysis must turn on the particular context. If a Zionist's expression of anger includes a statement of generic white supremacy and persecution, the speaker chooses to ally with a larger, historically dominant group, and the privilege should not apply. On the other hand, angry, survivalist expression, arising out of the Jewish experience of persecution and without resort to the rhetoric of generic white supremacy, is protected under the contextualized approach. Again, it is important to add that the various subordinated communities are best equipped to analyze and condemn hate speech arising within their midst.

The Case of the Dead-Wrong Social Scientist

Another difficult case is that of the social scientist who makes a case for racial inferiority in an academic setting based on what is presented as scientific evidence. Various theories of genetic predisposition to violence, cultural lag, and a correlation between race and intelligence fall into this category. Critics note that these pseudoscientific theories are racist and ignorant.[36] This raises two separate questions. First, should such views receive an audience and a forum in an academic setting? Second, should we criminalize expressions of such views?

As to the first question, the answer may well be no. Not all views deserve the dignity of an academic forum. Poorly documented, racially biased work does not meet the professional standards required of academic writing. If a writer manages to come up with a theory of racial inferiority supported by evidence acceptable within the relevant discipline, that theory may deserve a forum. Under the principle of academic freedom, ignorant views need not be heard, but unpopular, academically tenable views should be.

As to the second question, outlawing this type of speech might be inappropriate. Assuming the dead-wrong social science theory of inferiority is free of any message of hatred and persecution, the ordinary, private solution is sufficient: Attack such theories with open public debate and with denial of a forum if the work is unsound in its documentation....

The Special Case of Universities

A marked rise of racial harassment, hate speech, and racially motivated violence marks the beginning of the 1990s. The epidemic of racist incidents on university campuses is a disturbing example of this. The application of the first amendment to racist speech, once discussed hypothetically in law schools, is now debated in classrooms where hate messages have actually appeared. The current judicial opinions tangling with hate speech and the first amendment often come from the universities.

The university case raises unique concerns. Universities are special places, charged with pedagogy and duty bound to a constituency with special vulnerabilities. Many of the new adults who come to live and study at the major universities are away from home for the first time and at a vulnerable stage of psychological development. The typical university student is emotionally vulnerable for several reasons. College is a time of emancipation from a preexisting home or community, of development of identity, of dependence-independence conflict, of major decisionmaking, and of formulation of future plans. The move to college often involves geographic relocation—a major life-stress event—and the forging of new peer ties to replace old ones. All of these stresses and changes render the college years critical in development of one's outlook on life. College students experiment with different passions, identities, and risks. A negative environmental response during this period of experimentation could mar for life an individual's ability to remain open, creative, and risk taking.[37] Students are particularly dependent on the university for community, for intellectual development, and for self-definition. Official tolerance of racist speech in this setting is more harmful than generalized tolerance in the community at large. It is harmful to student perpetrators in that it is a lesson in getting away with it that will have lifelong repercussions. It is harmful to targets, who perceive the university as taking sides through inaction and who are left to their own resources in coping with the damage wrought,. Finally, it is a harm to the goals of inclusion, education, development of knowledge, and ethics that universities exist and stand for. Lessons of cynicism and hate replace lessons in critical thought and inquiry.

The campus free speech issues of the Vietnam era and those evoked by the antiapartheid movement pit students against university administrators, multinational corporations, the U.S. military, and established governments. In the context of that kind of power imbalance, the free speech rights of students deserve particular deference. Unfortunately, as we know from our memory of four dead in Ohio, that deference is not always forthcoming.

Racist speech on campus occurs in a vastly different power context. Campus racism targets vulnerable students and faculty. Students of color often come to the university at risk academically, socially, and psychologically. Faculty of color—if they exist at all—are typically untenured, overburdened, and isolated.[38] The marginalized position of faculty of color further marginalizes students of color.

There is legal precedent for considering the status of the target in measuring the amount of freedom verbal attackers enjoy. In the law of defamation, private figures can more easily obtain damages for harm to their reputation than can public figures. This is based on the greater ability of public figures to launch an effective rebuttal and on their voluntary choice to enter the public eye. An additional implicit justification is that wealth, power, and fame provide ego support that helps one weather verbal abuse. If nothing else, the defamed movie star can retreat to Malibu.

The student, like the private figure, has fewer avenues of retreat. Living on or near campus, studying in the library, and interacting with fellow students are integral parts of university life. When racist propaganda appears on campus, target-group students experience debilitated access to the full university experience. This is so even when hate propaganda is directed at groups rather than at individuals.

Students are analogous to the captive audience that is afforded special first amendment consideration in other contexts. Similarly, students who support universities through tuition and who are encouraged to think of the university as their home are involuntarily forced into a position of complicity with racism when their campus is offered to hate groups as a forum.

A related and literally captive group deserves mention here. The majority of prison inmates in many communities are people of color. Prisons are also fertile grounds for spreading racist hate speech. Courts have protected the rights of hate groups in prisons. The physical vulnerability and inability to escape that characterize prison life make restriction of hate speech in prisons more important than in the population at large....

The Unintended Story: The Meaning of Legal Protection of Racist Hate Messages

The legal response to racist propaganda provides an interesting context for examination of the relation between law and racism. Legal protection of racism is seen in these doctrinal elements:

1. The limits of doctrinal imagination in creating first amendment exceptions for racist hate speech
2. The refusal to recognize the competing values of liberty and equality at stake in the case of hate speech
3. The refusal to view the protection of racist speech as a form of state action

The limits of the lawmaking imagination of judges, legislators, and other legal insiders who have considered proposals to outlaw hate propaganda are symptomatic of the position of privilege from which legal doctrine develops. Legal insiders cannot imagine a life disabled in a significant way by hate propaganda.

This limited imagination has not affected lawmakers faced with other forms of offensive speech. The law of defamation and privacy recognizes that certain forms of expression are qualitatively different from the kind of speech deserving absolute protection. The legal imagination is able to contemplate what it feels like to hear lies spread about one's professional competency or to have one's likeness used for commercial gain without consent. American law has even, at times, provided a tort remedy for white plaintiffs who are "insulted" by "imputation of association with persons of a race against which there is prejudice."[39] When the legal mind understands that reputational interests, which are analogized to the preferred interest in property, must be balanced against first amendment interests, it recognizes the concrete reality of what happens to people who are defamed. Their lives are changed. Their standing in the community, their opportunities , their self-worth, their free enjoyment of life are limited. Their political capital—their ability to speak and be heard—is diminished. To see this, and yet to fail to see that the very same things happen to the victims of racist speech, is selective vision.

The selective consideration of one victim's story and not another's results in unequal application of the law. Unlike the victims of defamation and other torts, the victims of racist speech are not representative of the population at large. In making typical legal concessions to the first amendment, we burden a range of victims. In the case of flag burning, we force flag lovers of all races and class positions to tolerate flag desecration as part of the price of freedom. In contrast, when victims of racist speech are left to assuage their own wounds, we burden a limited class: the traditional victims of discrimination. This class already experiences diminished access to private remedies such as effective counterspeech, and this diminished access is exacerbated by hate messages. As the feminist scholar Catharine MacKinnon notes, debasing speech discredits targets, further reducing their ability to have their speech taken seriously.[40] The application of absolutist free speech principles to hate speech, then, is a choice to burden one group with a disproportionate share of the costs of speech promotion. Tolerance of hate speech thus creates superregressivity—those least able to pay are the only ones taxed for this tolerance. The principle of equality is violated by such allocation. The more progressive principle of rectification or reparation—the obligation to repair effects of historical wrongs—is even more grossly violated....

The constitutional commitment to equality and the promise to abolish the badges and incidents of slavery are emptied of meaning when the target-group members must alter their behavior, change their choice of neighborhood, leave their jobs, and warn their children off the streets because of hate group activity. When the presence of the Klan deters employers from hiring target-group members, prevents citizens from socializing freely, and keeps parents from sending their children to integrated schools, the goal of nondiscrimination is moved farther away from present realities. When hate propaganda spreads attitudes of racism and desensitizes potential abusers to the wrongness of violence, other more obvious goals of safety and order are sacrificed.

The third doctrinal pillar supporting racist speech is the refusal to recognize that tolerance and protection of hate group activity by the government is a form of state action. Hate groups have operated openly in prisons, in the military, in law enforcement, and in other government institutions. To allow an organization known for violence, persecution, race hatred, and commitment to racial supremacy to exist openly and to provide police protection and access to public facilities, streets, and college campuses for such a group means that the state is promoting racist speech. But for such support, hate groups would decline in efficacy. The chilling sight of avowed racists in threatening regalia marching through our neighborhoods with full police protection is a statement of state authorization. The Klan marches because marching promotes the Klan and because of the terrorizing and inciting effect of its public displays. Open display conveys legitimacy. The government advances this effect when it protects these marches. In addition, the failure to provide a legal response limiting hate propaganda elevates the liberty interests of racists over the liberty interests of their targets. A member of the Georgia Bureau of Investigation, for example, once suggested to whites targeted for hate speech because of their association with African Americans that they should avoid being seen in cars with African Americans and cease inviting African Americans to their homes.[41]

The effect of racist propaganda is to devalue the individual and to treat masses of people in a degraded way with no measure of individual merit. This is precisely what civil libertarians oppose when the state acts. Because racist speech is seen as private, the connection to loss of liberty is not made. State silence, however, is public action where the strength of the new racist groups derives from their offering legitimation and justification for otherwise socially unacceptable emotions of hate, fear, and aggression. The need for a formal group, for a patriotic cause, and for an elevation of the doubting self are part of the traditional attraction of groups like the Klan. Government protection of the right of the Klan to exist publicly and to spread a racist message promotes the role of the Klan as a legitimizer of racism.

Further, the law's failure to provide recourse to persons who are demeaned by the hate messages is an effective second injury to that person. The second injury is the pain of knowing that the government provides no remedy and offers no recognition of the dehumanizing experience that victims of hate propaganda are subjected to. The governments's denial of personhood through its denial of legal recourse may be even more painful than the initial act of hatred. One can dismiss the hate group as an organization of marginal people, but the state is the official embodiment of the society we live in.

The legal realists and their progeny recognize that law formation is largely a matter of value.[42] There are no inevitable results; there is no controlling logic or doctrine that can make the hard choices for us. Reversion to discredited doctrinal absolutism carries a strong implication that racist activities are supported, albeit unintentionally, by the law. In a society that expresses its moral judgments through the law, and in which the rule of law and the use of law are characteristic responses to many social phenomena, this absence of laws against racist speech is telling.

We can defy the proposition that racism is part of law by opening our eyes to the reality of racism and making the decision to outlaw hate groups. We can draw from the international standard and acknowledge the competing interests at stake, adapting existing law and creating new law to limit hate group activities. It is not necessary to abandon first amendment values in order to do this. The analytical dexterity of legal thinkers offers many options for reconciling the U.S. position with the international goal of elimination of all forms of racial discrimination.

This chapter suggests that the stories of those who have experienced racism are of special value in defeating racism. It further suggests that we can, and have, chosen as a primary value freedom from racial oppression. Finally, in doing the awkward work of constructing doctrine, this chapter suggests a belief in the possibility and the necessity of creating a legal response to racist speech—not because it isn't really speech, not because it falls within a hoped-for neutral exception, but because it is wrong.

There is in every constitutional doctrine we devise the danger of misuse. For fear of falling, we are warned against taking a first step. Frozen at the first amendment bulkhead, we watch the rising tide of racial hatred wash over our schools and workplaces. Students victimized by racist speech turn to university administrators for redress and are told that the first amendment forecloses institutional action. We owe those students a more thoughtful analysis than absolutism. At the least, before we abandon the task of devising a legal response to racist speech, we should consider concretely the options available to us. The legal imagination is a fruitful one. That is the one hopeful message of the postmodern critique of law. Nothing inherent in law ties our hands, and lawyers through the ages have displayed abundant skills of invention.

Conclusion

Critical race theory uses the experience of subordination to offer a phenomenology of race and law. The victims' experience reminds us that the harm of racist hate messages is a real harm to real people. When the legal system offers no redress for that real harm, it perpetuates racism.

This chapter attempts to begin a conversation about the first amendment that acknowledges both the civil libertarian's fear of tyranny and the victims' experience of loss of liberty in a society that tolerates racist speech. It suggests criminalization of a narrow, explicitly defined class of racist hate speech to provide public redress for the most serious harm, leaving many forms of racist speech to private remedies. Some may feel that this proposal does not go far enough, leaving much hurtful speech to the uneven control of the marketplace of ideas. Others will cringe at what they perceive as a call for censorship. This is not an easy legal or moral puzzle, but it is precisely in these places where we feel conflicting tugs at heart and mind that we have the most work to do and the most knowledge to gain.

Ours is a law-bound culture. If law is where racism is, then law is where we must confront it. The doctrinal reconstruction presented here is tentative and subject to change as our struggle around this issue continues. However we choose to respond to racist speech, let us present a competing ideology, one that has existed in tension with racism since the birth of our nation: There is inherent worth in each human being, and each is entitled to a life of dignity.

NOTES

1. Incidents such as this are described in P. Sims, *The Klan* 167-72 (1978).
2. At the University of California Hastings College of the Law, someone defaced a Black History Month Display in just such a manner. "Racist Caricatures Anger Students," *Recorder* (San Francisco), Feb. 11, 1989, at 1.
3. Author's personal experience, Perth, Western Australia, July 1987, recounted in "Language as Violence v. Freedom of Expression: Canadian and American Perspectives on Group Defamation," 37 *Buffalo. L. Rev.* 337 (1989) (transcript of the James McCormick Mitchell Lecture, State University of New York at Buffalo School of Law, Nov. 4, 1988) [herinafter cited as *Language as Violence*].
4. L. Bollinger, *The Tolerant Society: Free Speech and Extremist Speech in America* (1986).
5. *Collin v. Smith*, 447 F. Supp. 676 (N.D. Ill.) Affd., 578 F. 2d 1197 (7th Cir.) cert. denied, 439 U.S. 916 (1978); *Village of Skokie v. National Socialist Party*, 51 Ill. App. 3d 279, 366 N.E. 2d 347 (1977), modified, 69 Ill. 2d 605, 373 N.E. 2d 21 (1978).
6. Williams, "Spirit-Murdering the Messenger: The Discourse of Fingerpointing as the Law's Response to Racism," 42 *Miami L. Rev.* 127, 139 (1987).
7. See *Critchen v. Firestone Steel Prods. Co.* Nos. 12,190—EM & 15,389—EM (Mich. Civ. Rts. Comm'n May 23, 1984) *reported in* 1984 Michigan Civ. Rts. Commission, Case Digest 13, 17-18.
8. "S.F. Fire Department Declared 'Out of Control,'" *Asian L. Caucus Rep.*, July/Dec. 1987, at 1, col. 1.
9. *Poverty Law Report*, Mar.-Apr. 1982, at 11, col. 2.
10. "Black F.B.I. Agents's Ordeal: Meanness That Never Let Up," *N.Y. Times*, Jan. 25, 1988, at 1, col.1.
11. Complaint at 3, *EEOC v. Hyster Co.*, Civ. No. 88-930—DA (D. Ore., filed Aug. 15, 1988) (alleging a hostile work environment created by racially objectionable advertisement campaign and use of racial slurs by management in work place). An answer denying those allegations was filed by the defendant.
12. "Racial Violence Belies Good Life in Contra Costa County," *L.A. Times*, Dec. 7, 1980, at 3, col. 5.
13. Asian and Pacific Islander Advisory Comm., Office of Attorney Gen. Cal. Dept. Of Justice, *Final Report* 45 (1988).
14. Ga. State Advisory Comm'n to the U.S. Comm'n on Civil Rights, Perceptions of Hate Group Activity in Georgia 3 (1983) (testimony of Stuart Lowengrub, Southeastern Regional Director, Anti-Defamation League of B'nai B'rith, Atlanta).
15. Cervantes, "Poem for the Young White Man Who Asked Me How I, An Intelligent Well Read Person could Believe in the War Between Races," *Emplumada* (1981).
16. Williams, *supra* note 6, at 129.
17. Greenberg and Pyszcynski, "The Effect of an Overheard Ethnic Slur on Evaluation of the Target: How to Spread a Social Disease," 21 *J. Experimental Soc. Psychology* 61, 70 (1985).
18. G. Allport, *The Nature of Prejudice* 461-78 (1954); H. Kitano, *Race Relations* 113-14 (1974); H. Schuman, C. Steeh & L. Bobo, *Racial Attitudes in America* 137 (1985).
19. See, eg., *Afro-American Writing* (R. Long & E. Collier eds. 1985).
20. International Convention on the Elimination of All

Forms of Racial Discrimination opened for signature Mar. 7, 1966, 660 U.N.T.S. 195 [hereinafter Racial Discrimination Convention].

21. See N. Lerner, *The U.N. Convention on the Elimination of All forms of Racial Discrimination* 43-53 (2nd ed. 1980).
22. Racial Discrimination Convention, *supra* note 20, at 218.
23. *Id.* At 214.
24. Council of Europe, *European Convention on Human rights: Collected Texts* §1 (7th ed. 1971).
25. Pan American Union, *Final Act of the Ninth International Conference of American States* 38 (1948)
26. The Convention on the Prevention and Punishment of the Crime of Genocide, art,. 3(c), *adopted* Dec.9, 1948, 78 U.N.T.S. 277, 280, requires member states to prohibit "[d]irect and public incitement to commit genocide." The convention was ratified by the U.S. Senate in 1986 with reservations noting that the U.S. Constitution would override any provisions of the convention, 132 Cong. Rec. 2349—50 (Feb. 19, 1986).
27. *Race Relations Act*, 1965, c. 73 §6 (1), amended in 1976 and 1986.
28. See *Race Relations Act*, of 1976, c. 74 §70.
29. I. MacDonald, Race Relations and Immigration Law 8 (1969).
30. *Can. Rev. Stat.* Ch. C-46 §318, 319 (1985).
31. *Constitution Act of 1982*, §2.
32. See, e.g., the proposed amendments to the New South Wales Racial Discrimination Act reported in Woomera, June/July 1987, at 1 (allowing group defamation actions for racial slurs). Violent racist groups are gaining in membership and visibility in Australia.
33. *Collin v. Smith*, 447 F. Supp. 676 (N.D. Ill.) Affd. 578 F. 2d 1197 (7th Cir.), cert. denied, 439 U.S. 916 (1978); *Village of Skokie v. National Socialist Party*, 51 Ill.App. 3d 279, 366 N.E. 2d 347 (1977), modified, 69 Ill. 2d 605, 373 N.E. 2d 21 (1978).
34. *Regents of the Univ. v. Bakke*, 438 U.S. 265, 407 (1978) (Blackmum, J., dissenting).
35. Delgado, "Derrick Bell and the Ideology of Racial Reform," 97 *Yale L.J.* 923, 937 (1988).
36. See "A Theory Goes on Trial," *Time*, Sept. 24, 1984, at 62 (Dr. Shockley, who admits to subscribing to the white supremacist publication Thunderbolt, is called "nearly incompetent" by trained geneticist).
37. I thank my colleague Dr. Chalsa Loo, a psychologist, college counselor, and specialist in multicultural interaction, for these insights.
38. See Delgado, "Minority Law Professors's Lives: The Bell-Delgado Survey," 24 *Harv. Civ. Rts.-Civ. Lib. L. Rev.* 407 (1989) (reporting on widespread effects of discrimination and high attrition rates among minority law teachers); Chused, "The Hiring and Retention of Minorities and Women on American Law School Faculties," 137 *U. Pa. L. Rev.* 537 (1988); Haines, "Minority Law Professors and the Myth of Sisyphus: Consciousness and Praxis Within the Special Teaching Challenges in American Law Schools," 10 *Nat'l Black L.J.* 247 (1988); McGee, "Symbol and Substance in the Minority Professoriat's Future," 3 *Harv. BlackLetter J.* 67 (1986) (special burdens and obligations of minority law professors).
39. Annotation, "Libel and Slander: Imputation of Association with Persons of Race or Nationality as to Which there Is Social Prejudice," 121 A.L.R. 1151, 1151 (1939) (citing *Sharp v. Bussey*, 137 Fla. 96, 187 So. 779 [1939]).
40. MacKinnon, "Not a Moral Issue," 2 *Yale L. & Pol'y. Rev.* 321 (1984).
41. Ga. State Advisory Comm'n to the U.S. Comm'n on Civil Rights, *supra* note 14, at 21.
42. Llewellyn, "Some Realism About Realism: Responding to Dean Pound," 44 *Harv. L. Rev.* 1222, 1236 (1931) ("The conception of law as a means to social ends and not an end in itself").

STUDY QUESTIONS

1. According to Dworkin, what are the two constitutional values that need balancing in the debate in the United States about censoring pornography? What arguments does Dworkin give for defending the primacy of the first amendment? What arguments does he provide for rejecting Catharine MacKinnon's resolution of the conflict of values in favour of the Fourteenth Amendment?
2. Is equality enhanced or threatened by censorship? Formulate your answer to this question by outlining and evaluating the contrasting views of equality defended by Dworkin and MacKinnon.
3. Did Glass's outline of feminist arguments for censorship raise questions for you about Dworkin's analysis of the arguments used by anti-pornography feminists? Why or why not?
4. Given the feminist analysis of the patriarchal nature of the state, how does Glass answer the charge that anti-pornography feminists place too much trust that the state will only censor material that is harmful to women?
5. According to Glass, anti-censorship feminists belie their distrust in the state by defending such things as public education and health care. Does their trust of the state in these areas contradict their distrust of the state in the case of censorship? Justify your answer.
6. Do you agree with Glass that the state should censor pornography even with the likelihood that the legislation will be applied to lesbian representations of sexuality, for example?
7. Why does Ann Snitow view the anti-pornography movement as a threat to the women's movement? According to Snitow, mainstream pornography depicts not only violence, hatred and fear of women but also elements of play, thrill, defiance, and fantasy. Do you agree with her that using these elements can be a positive strategy for flouting authority and exploring female sexuality? Why or why not?
8. Glass and Snitow have different views about what constitutes pornography and its harm to women. Can we define pornography so that legislation can succeed in targeting only that material that is morally objectionable? Defend your answer.
9. Why does Heldke redefine speech? How does this account of speech as relational work to reconceptualize liberal notions of freedom of speech?
10. According to Heldke, how does a collective conception of speech work to promote the very goals of a liberal conception of free speech as enhancing individual freedom and enabling free and full intellectual development?
11. In hearing the stories that Matsuda presents of the dissemination of racist speech and its effects on those targeted in the speech, has your thinking about the regulation of such speech changed? Why or why not?
12. According to Matsuda, the United States is out of step with moves in the international community to criminalize racist hate messages as is evident in the International Convention on the Elimination of All Forms of Racial Discrimination and in the human rights legislation of various countries. Is being out of step relevant to the question of which policies we should adopt for dealing with racist hate speech? How does Matsuda answer this question? How would you?
13. Matsuda attempts to define racist speech in a sufficiently narrow way to preserve First Amendment values in the United States and yet allow legal restrictions. Is her case convincing? Formulate your answer by discussing her analysis of some of the hard cases.

SUGGESTED READINGS

Burstyn, Varda (editor). *Women Against Censorship*. Vancouver: Douglas & McIntyre, 1985.

Clark, Chris. "Pornography Without Power?" *Changing Men Magazine* 1985. Feminist & Men's Publication, Inc.

Cohen, Cheryl H. "The Feminist Sexuality Debate: Ethics and Politics." *Hypatia*, v. 1, no. 2 (Fall 1986): 71-86.

Davies, Jacqueline MacGregor. "Pornographic Harms." In *Feminist Perspectives: Philosophical Essays on Method and Morals* edited by L. Code, S. Mullett, and C. Overall. Toronto: University of Toronto Press, 1988.

Diamond, Irene. "Reflections on a Nondogmatic Feminism: The Case of Pornography." *Humanities in Society*, v. 7 (Winter/Spring 1984): 77-86.

Duggan, Lisa, Nan Hunter and Carole Vance. "False Promises: Feminist Antipornography Legislation." In *Women Against Censorship* edited by Varda Burstyn. Toronto: Douglas and McIntyre, 1985: 130-151.

Dwyer, Susan (editor). *The Problem of Pornography*. Belmont: Wadsworth, 1995.

Dyzenhaus, David. "Pornography and Public Reason." *Canadian Journal of Law and Jurisprudence*, v. 7, no. 2 (1994): 261-281.

Fish, Stanley. "Boutique Multiculturalism, or Why Liberals are Incapable of Thinking about Hate Speech." *Critical Inquiry* 23 (Winter 1997): 378-395.

Garry, Ann. "Pornography and Respect for Women." *Social Theory and Practice*, v. 4 (1978): 395-421.

Hill, Judith M. "Pornography and Degradation." *Hypatia*, v. 2 (1987): 39-54.

Kimmel, Michael (editor). *Men Confront Pornography*. New York: Meridian, 1991.

Langton, Rae. "Whose Right? Ronald Dworkin, Women, and Pornographers." *Philosophy & Public Affairs*, v. 19, no. 4 (1990): 311-359.

Lederer, Laura (editor). *Take Back the Night: Women on Pornography*. New York: Morrow, 1980.

Longino, Helen. "Pornography, Oppression, and Freedom: A Closer Look." In *Take Back the Night: Women on Pornography* edited by Laura Lederer. New York: Morrow, 1980.

MacKinnon, Catharine. "Francis Biddle's Sister: Pornography, Civil Rights, and Speech." In *Feminism Unmodified: Discourses in Life and Law*. Cambridge, Mass.: Harvard University Press, 1987.

— . *Only Words*. Cambridge, Mass.: Harvard University Press, 1993.

Mahoney, Kathleen E. "Pornography and Violence Towards Women: Comparisons Between Europe, the United States and Canada." In *International Human Rights Law: Theory and Practice* edited by Irwin Cotler and F. Pearl Eliadis. Montreal: The Canadian Human Rights Foundation, 1992.

Matsuda, Mari, Charles R. Lawrence III, Richard Delgado, and Kimberlè Williams Crenshaw. *Words That Wound: Critical Race Theory, Assaultive Speech, and the First Amendment*. Boulder, CO: Westview, 1993.

Scoccia, Danny. "Can Liberals Support a Ban on Violent Pornography?" *Ethics*, v. 106 (July 1996): 776-799.

Stoltenberg, John. "Gays and the Pro-Pornography Movement: Having the Hots for Sex Discrimination." In *Men Confront Pornography* edited by Michael S. Kimmel. New York: Meridian, 1991.

CHAPTER THIRTEEN

SEXUAL VIOLENCE

In the last chapter, the connection (or lack thereof) between the consumption of pornography and incidences of sexual violence against women was examined. The authors in this chapter make no claims about this issue, but look at the phenomenon of sexual violence against women as ubiquitous and worldwide. Violence in general is a breakdown in moral response. The coercion and harm done to another through a violent response to conflict is a clear case of failing to treat others as autonomous beings deserving of respect and dignity. In this chapter, we examine violence that is sexual in nature and perpetrated by men against women.

The chapter opens with an analysis of how women are more fearful than men as a result of the prevalence of sexual violence against women. Keith Burgess-Jackson observes that theoretical accounts of distribution tend to focus on benefits such as opportunities, income, wealth, health care services, and rights to property rather than on burdens such as the payment of taxes, military service, and criminal punishment. He argues for extending the analysis to the neglected side of burdens by examining fear, a burden that the social-scientific literature shows to be unevenly distributed between men and women in identifiable and insidious patterns. While the fear of being a victim of criminal behavior is prevalent in the lives of many Americans, particularly the elderly, non-whites, those with low incomes, and those who live in urban areas, the most powerful predictor of fear of crime is gender. Data shows that fear of rape is a core fear for women, one that is more prevalent than fear of murder and underlies fears of being robbed, for example.

Fear, argues Burgess-Jackson, disrupts, debilitates, places restrictions on freedom and behavior, and leads to chronic anxiety, dependence on men, and a loss of self-confidence and self-respect. Fear is an issue for distributive justice because women are disproportionately burdened and because the fears they have are generated by social life itself. Burgess-Jackson argues that justice demands collective action through institutions such as law and education to reduce the overall level of fear in society and redistribute it so that women no longer bear the brunt of it. He offers several policy suggestions: taking steps to prevent rape through the criminal justice system, reducing or eliminating women's sense of vulnerability through self-defense training courses, increasing the number of police officers on the street and improving street lighting, and funding programs such as consciousness-raising groups for men.

The notion of collective responsibility for sexual violence is also explored by Larry May and Robert Strikwerda. They outline and reject four popular accounts of responsibility for rape. They dispute the first account that only the rapist is responsible since he committed the act by arguing that rape is not adequately understood in individualist terms because men receive strong encouragement to rape from the way they are socialized as men. The second account claims that no one is responsible because rape is a biological response to stimuli. However, evidence that rape is virtually nonexistent in some societies supports a sociological rather than biological account of rape. The socialization of men by men in their bonding groups and the view of women that is generated are the strongest cues for rates of rape. Those who defend the third account argue that women are equally responsible for the prevalence of rape and that the focus should be on violence rather than sex or gender. May and Strikwerda agree that some women do contribute to the patterns of socialization of men and women, but argue that it is a mistake to think that women share equal responsibility with men. The vast majority of rapists and murderers in our society are men and the condition of women is made worse off by the prevalence of rape. In the fourth account, patriarchy, not any person or group, is taken to be responsible for rape because patriarchy is a system that operates behind the backs of individual men.

May and Strikwerda argue that because patriarchy is based on common interests and benefits extending to all men in a particular culture, men are responsible both collectively and individually for the harms attributable to it. They argue that when rape is conjoined with war, it warrants the charge of being a crime against humanity because the victims are persecuted simply because they fall into a category of people who are perceived as ripe for assault. And insofar as men in a particular society contribute to the prevalence of rape, they participate in a crime against humanity for which men as individuals and in collectivities should take responsibility by re-socializing themselves and other men.

The argument by May and Strikwerda that rape should be considered a crime against humanity is questioned by Liz Philipose in the third reading. Philipose criticizes the widespread support by feminists for the proposal to have the Statute of the International Criminal Tribunal for the Former Yugoslavia (ICTY) include rape as such a crime. She points out that feminists have had some success using international bodies like the UN to highlight the kinds of violence to which women are uniquely subjected: domestic violence, genital mutilation, prostitution, pornography, and violence in the workplace. Feminist support for the ICTY has focused on its potential to acknowledge the gender specificity of rape and to enforce humanitarian protection for women's rights. Philipose has no argument with the claim that violence against women is systematic, pervasive, and a violation of the rights of women. Instead, she argues that the current laws of war are not appropriate mechanisms for the realization of human rights because they answer to military needs and have their meaning in a context that already sanctions violence and legitimates human rights violations.

Philipose questions whether prosecuting rape as a crime against humanity will advance women's human rights. The slogan "women's rights are human rights" captures the criticism that women's lives and rights are considered secondary to men's lives and human rights in general. Philipose argues that in advancing a prohibition against rape as a crime against humanity but as limited to a context of war and the more specific context of ethnic cleansing, the ICTY is not advancing a general statement of women's human rights or general prohibitions on the practice of rape. Philipose takes her analysis as a call for careful consideration of the ICTY's particular incorporation of rape as a crime against humanity and of criminal tribunals more generally because they operate with the prevailing assumption that we need laws *only to the extent* that they mitigate the ravages of war and protect civilians and states from unprovoked attack and violence.

In the final reading, Caldwell, Galster, and Steinzor place the discussion of sexual violence in a global context by examining the growing phenomenon of the trafficking of human beings in the international sex trade of prostitution, pornography, and arranged marriages. They investigate this trafficking in the context of the collapse of the Soviet Union, where the proliferation of criminal organizations and increased poverty and unemployment have led to the trafficking of women and children from Russia and the Newly Independent States to Asia, Western Europe, and the United States. The rapid socioeconomic decline in the post-communist transition after 1991 resulted in conditions of massive unemployment, increased poverty, and the collapse of social services, all of which had a disproportionate effect on women in the former Soviet Union. Caldwell, Galster, and Steinzor explain that in a context where there are no civil or labor laws against sexual harassment and only 5-10 percent of incidences of domestic violence and sexual assault gets reported, Russian women look to opportunities to work abroad as a way of bettering their lives. These opportunities, they argue, are controlled and organized by criminal groups who use deception and force to lure women and children into the international sex trade of prostitution, pornography, and arranged marriages. Caldwell, Galster, and Steinzor call for cooperative efforts between the "sending countries" of the former Eastern Bloc, Asia, Africa, and Latin America and the receiving, wealthy countries of North America and Western Europe so that policies for dealing with the sexual exploitation to which women and children are subjected can be implemented. In addition to pointing to the need to adhere to international standards and laws already in place, they advocate that countries develop policies for targeting criminal organizations and assisting victims of abuse.

JUSTICE AND THE DISTRIBUTION OF

Keith Burgess-Jackson

Keith Burgess-Jackson is Associate Professor of Philosophy at the University he teaches courses in logic, philosophy of law, moral philosophy, philosoph He is the author of Rape: A Philosophical Investigation *(Dartmouth Publishing, 19 ing M. Copi, of* Informal Logic *3rd ed. (Prentice Hall, 1996). He is also the editor of, and a multiple contributor to,* A Most Detestable Crime: New Philosophical Essays on Rape *(Oxford, 1999).*

Burgess-Jackson believes that philosophers have unduly neglected the distribution of socially created burdens, focusing instead on benefits (such as health care). He tries to rectify this omission by addressing the distribution of a particular burden, fearfulness. Social-scientific literature shows that fear of crime is distributed in patterns, not haphazardly. Women, for example, are significantly more fearful than men, in large part because women, but not men, are victimized by rape. Burgess-Jackson argues that this state of affairs is unjust and that, since the distribution of fear can be rectified by collective action, it must be. He considers and dismisses several objections to this argument.

> Rape operates as a social control mechanism to keep women in their "place" or put them there. The fear of rape, common to most women, socially controls them as it limits their ability to move about freely. As such, it establishes and maintains the woman in a position of subordination.[1]

Introduction

By default or by design, philosophical discussions of distributive justice concern the distribution of benefits rather than burdens. One influential philosopher, Stanley Benn, has gone so far as to say that "the problem [of distributive justice] is to allocate benefits."[2] The benefits in question are variable, taking the form of material objects (such as heart-lung machines), services (the provision of health care), opportunities (for example, to employment and education), rights (to property), income, wealth, offices, rewards, and other goods. Each benefit is supposed to be made possible by communal living and is, in the economist's sense, scarce—meaning that its supply is exceeded by aggregate demand. The problem of distributive justice, so conceived, is to state the principle(s) by which these benefits are to be allocated among individuals who desire or need them. The work of Rawls, Nozick, Walzer, and Ronald Dworkin exemplifies this class of normative theory.

But distributive justice is concerned with the burdens as well as the benefits of social living, Benn's characterization notwithstanding. These burdens take the form of unpleasant or undesirable things, obligations, and experiences,[3] such as labor, the payment of taxes, military service, and criminal punishment. By analogy to the case of benefits, we can say that each burden is made *necessary* by communal living. Each arises from the fact that human beings live in communities and have only partially overlapping interests and objectives....

My aim in this essay is to address an item on the neglected "burden" side of the ledger. What I want to explore are the normative implications of the distri-

---

Reprinted with permission from *The Southern Journal of Philosophy* 32 (Winter 1994): 367–391 [edited].

...cular socially created burden: fear- ...after "fear"). I begin by reciting facts ...m the social-scientific literature on fear, ...has become quite sophisticated. This literature ...ws unequivocally that fear of crime, far from being distributed uniformly or randomly throughout the population, is distributed in identifiable and insidious patterns.[4] Women, for example, are more fearful of crime than men. Why this is so is a matter of disagreement among social scientists, and since the answer to the explanatory question bears on the argument I go on to make as well as on some of the objections I consider, I state the most widely proffered explanations of why these patterns exist.

Having set out the facts and some explanations, I proceed to argue that while fear, or a certain amount and kind of fear, may be useful in keeping individuals safe from harm, it is, as a mental state, burdensome to those who experience it. Fear of crime in particular is a socially created burden. It follows that women bear a disproportionate share of this burden, a state of affairs that I argue in Part III is unjust in principle and, given its remediability through collective action (which I address in Part IV), unacceptable in practice. Justice, I maintain, requires that the state, employing institutions such as law and education and using the power of the purse, both reduce the overall level of fear in society and, more particularly, redistribute fear so that women no longer bear the brunt of it....

I. The Distribution of Fear

Let us begin with the facts. Any person, nonhuman animal, physical object, event, or state of affairs can, logically, be the object of fear, but one state of affairs that nearly everyone fears at one time or another in his or her life (albeit to different degrees), and one that nearly half of adult Americans have altered their lifestyle in some way to accommodate,[5] is victimization—being a victim of criminal behavior. But this fact, taken alone, is apt to mislead, for studies routinely show that fear of crime is distributed in patterns throughout society. For example, the elderly are more likely than the nonelderly to fear victimization. The same is true of nonwhites, those with low incomes, the comparatively uneducated, and those who live in urban areas, each of whom, as a class, is more fearful than its counterpart.[6] But the "most powerful predictor of fear of personal crimes" turns out to be not age, income, race, or class, but sex.[7] "[F]emales," a researcher writes, "exhibit higher fear than males for every offense,"[8] from being threatened with a knife, club, or gun to being murdered, having one's car stolen, or receiving an obscene telephone call.[9]

In one study men and women were asked "How safe do you feel being out alone in your neighborhood at night: very safe, reasonably safe, somewhat unsafe or very unsafe?"[10] More than 43 percent of the female respondents reported being either somewhat or very unsafe; but only 17.9 percent of the male respondents gave that answer. The disparity is even greater with respect to the response "very unsafe," with 22.8 percent of the women and 6.4 percent of the men giving that answer.[11] As for how often men and women reflect on their safety (or lack thereof), it has been found that "48 percent of the women, compared with 25 percent of the men, reported 'thinking of their own safety all or most of the time' or 'fairly often.'"[12] It appears from these and other studies that women, as compared to men, fear more different crimes, fear them to a greater degree, and fear them a greater proportion of the time.

That much is clear. What puzzles researchers is that, for most crime categories, "there are substantially lower victimization rates for women" than for men.[13] In other words, fear of crime does not track reality. If fear were a function solely of the likelihood of being victimized, then men, not women, should experience greater fear, for men are more often victimized. So why are women more fearful? One obvious explanation is that some or much of women's fear is unfounded.[14] But this explanation is implausible on its face and to this point at least lacks experimental confirmation. I address it in Part V. Another hypothesis is that men and women assign different degrees of seriousness to the various crimes, so that even if they agree on the *likelihood* of being victimized, they respond differently to the risk. As one researcher put it, men and women have "differential sensitivity to risk."[15] This hypothesis, unlike the first, *has* been experimentally confirmed;

"[f]emales," it has been discovered, "typically view each offence as more serious than males."[16] Yet another hypothesis concerns differential vulnerability, the suggestion being that women, the elderly, and other fearful individuals are, and take themselves to be, more vulnerable to crime (in the sense of being less able to defend themselves in case of attack), which gives rise to greater fear. Unfortunately, this hypothesis has not been rigorously tested and so has not been confirmed.

A fourth hypothesis, which *has* been confirmed, maintains that women are more fearful than men because only women are targets of sexual assault, "an especially terrifying form of personal violation."[17] Not only is rape particularly frightening to women, for obvious reasons, it is often accompanied by other crimes against person and property. "[A] high perceived probability of residential burglary," for example, "may provoke intense fear among many women because assault, rape, and even homicide are viewed as likely contemporaneous offenses."[18] One empirical study found that "fear of rape is significantly correlated ... with fear of all other offenses measured,"[19] which included threats, robbery, burglary while home, assault, murder, and loitering. The differential fear of crime experienced by women is explicable, at least in part, in terms of their fear of rape, which women as a class view as one of the most serious of offenses; if not *the* most serious. "Among women in each age group," sociologist Mark Warr writes, "the perceived serousness of rape is approximately equal to the perceived seriousness of murder."[20]

Rape (or sexual assault, I use the terms interchangeably) is a crime that almost all women but no men fear. For women between the ages of nineteen and thirty-five rape is the *most-feared crime*, more feared even than murder.[21] A team of researchers concludes that "virtually all adult women live at some level of consciousness with the fear and threat of sexual assault."[22] These researchers discovered that "67 percent of the women interviewed, when asked a direct question, said they were worried about sexual assault, while only 7 percent of the men interviewed said the same."[23]

The disparity between fear of rape and fear of other crimes has led social scientists to view rape as a "core" fear, a fear that "underlies" others, and as a "master offense."[24] Indeed, for younger women, "fear of crime *is* fear of rape."[25] While fear of sexual assault is not universal among women, all or most women "experience a period of routine or habitual fear at some point in their lives."[26] Warr concludes that "it is difficult to imagine many other social problems [besides rape] that affect so many people in such a direct way."[27]

II. The Burden of Fear

I use the word "burden" in the ordinary way, to refer to "something carried, a heavy load,"[28] the implication being that one would prefer not to have to carry the load. It is in this normatively loaded sense—the sense in which a benefit, by contrast, is *desired*—that fear is burdensome. But the burdens of fear are of different types as well as degrees. First, fear—the condition of being afraid—is an intrinsically unpleasant mental state.[29] This is true even when the mental state itself leads one to take self-protective action. We would not say in such a case that the fear was *pleasant*, or even affectively neutral, but that its *unpleasantness* served a useful purpose and was for that reason tolerable. Fear, in other words, can be functional. Moreover, like any strong emotion, fear can distract one's attention, disrupt otherwise operative mental processes, and displace or inhibit pleasant mental states. To be preoccupied with or overcome by fear is to be incapable of attending to other matters. At the extreme, fear can paralyze.

Second, fear debilitates. It can, and very often does, cause one to be feeble, weak, and vulnerable, with obvious detrimental effects on one's life plan. This is certainly true with respect to the fear of crime. Researchers have learned that fear of crime is correlated with limitations on liberty in general and mobility in particular. Since, as we have seen, women experience greater fear than men, especially in connection with rape, women suffer most from these debilitating effects. According to one research team, "78 percent of the men, compared with 32 percent of the women, reported they never avoid doing things they need to for fear of crime."[30]

To give some idea of the extent to which and ways in which women limit their behavior as a result of fear, consider that 25.3 percent of women, but only 2.9 percent of men, never walk alone in their neighborhood after dark. More than 68 percent of women, but only 5.4 percent of men, say they never go alone to bars or clubs after dark. Comparable differences exist with respect to going alone to movies after dark, going downtown alone after dark, and walking by parks or lots alone after dark.[31] As one group of researchers put it, "Our data suggest that women may have developed lifestyles that include restrictions on their freedom and behavior and that may keep them safe by limiting their chances of becoming victims."[32] Unfortunately, the lifestyles women adopt as a means of keeping them safe are not always successful; but even if they were, it would not make the costs of fear disappear and would not eliminate what I shall argue is the injustice of women's having to develop such lifestyles.

The costs of women's fear of rape, calculated both quantitatively and qualitatively, are enormous. They include the limitations on liberty just described[33] as well as the many reverberations from that constraint. One such reverberation is the reluctance of many women to assume positions of authority and public responsibility that might place them in dangerous situations or places. This consequence has immediate and obvious implications for distributive justice, for, as one feminist scholar has put it, "we cannot function as a true democracy as long as women's well-founded fear of rape inhibits our full participation in society."[34] A fearful woman is a woman drawn inward and kept on the defensive, not a woman focused on the sports arena, the economic marketplace, the laboratory, or the legislative chamber.

Other costs, some tangible and some not (although no less real for that), include: loss of self-confidence, self-respect, and self-esteem; nightmares and other sleep disorders; distrust and suspicion of strangers and acquaintances; chronic anxiety, stress,[35] and depression; inability to live alone (where that is desired);[36] and increased dependence on men for protection, which in turn undermines self-respect and self-confidence. Susan Sontag was not far off the mark, if at all, when she wrote many years ago that "Basically, a woman is only safe at 'home' or when protected by a man."[37] The fear of crime generally, and of rape in particular, may, according to Margaret Gordon and Stephanie Riger, "lead [women] to experience their whole environment as a dangerous place to be."[38] No criminal conspiracy, no organized patriarchal religion, no oppressive political regime could be as effective a means of social control.

I take it as established for purposes of this essay that fear is an unwelcome burden to be carried, however useful it may be (when properly focused and limited) in promoting personal safety. Fear is intrinsically unpleasant, distracting, disruptive, and debilitating; it is—and is universally experienced as—a cost to those who are in its grip. Nobody would voluntarily undertake to carry such a load without the prospect of a greater good. But the burdensomeness of fear alone, however great, does not implicate distributive justice. Distributive justice is implicated only when one *conjoins* to the burdensomeness of fear the fact that women, as a class, are significantly more fearful than men as a class—that women are *disproportionately* burdened. The questions then become (1) whether anything can be done about this state of affairs, and (2) if so, what justice requires to be done. It is to these and other normative matters that I now turn.

III. The Injustice of the Existing Distribution of Fear

There is no question that fear, as an unpleasant mental state, can and does have value. Its main value, as I have suggested, lies in the fact that it motivates individuals to take precautions against risks of harm to themselves and others. To that extent fear has instrumental value. But as I have shown, fear can also interfere with one's plan of life in drastic and deleterious ways. To that extent fear is a significant burden. Other things being equal, the less fear one experiences, the better off one is. Ideally, there would be only enough fear at any given time and place to motivate individuals to take precautions against harm. But what if certain fears, such as the fear of crime, are generated by social life itself; what if those fears fall disproportionately on certain individuals as defined by their membership in a class; and what if the class-defining characteristic is beyond individual control? Then we are in the realm of justice.

Some burdens of social living can be reduced or eliminated only by creating or increasing burdens on other individuals. There is in such a case, as economists are wont to say, no Pareto superior move—no move that makes some individuals better off without making at least one other individual worse off. Fear appears to be of this type. The newly imposed burdens can be of the same type as, or of a different type than, the existing burdens. For example, it may be that in order to reduce the burden of military service on one group of individuals (say, the poor), it is necessary to increase the burden of military service on another (the nonpoor). This would be the case if a certain level of military service must be maintained. But the burden of fear is not of this type. Nobody, least of all I, seriously suggests that in order to reduce the burden of fear on women, the elderly, and others, society should increase the burden on their counterparts. First, it's not clear how this could be done; but second, even if it could, it's not clear that it would be justified. What point would be served by increasing the fear of one group of individuals without decreasing the fear of anyone else?...

Some burdens can be reduced or eliminated only by increasing or creating different types of burdens on others. The burden of fear is of this type. While it would be nice if women's fear of crime could be reduced without imposing costs on them or on anyone else, this is not likely to be the case. More likely, such measures which reduce women's fear will be costly in the economist's sense; to achieve the desired results, other goods will have to be forgone. Since those who forgo these goods are not necessarily the same as those who benefit from the reduction or elimination of fear on the part of women, considerations of distributive justice come to the fore. The main question is one of principle—namely, whether justice requires that the existing distribution of fear be altered. I maintain that it does. Specifically, as I go on to argue, steps must be taken to reduce women's fear of crime, a significant part of which is women's fear of rape. A subsidiary question concerns who—that is, which class of individuals—ought to bear the cost of redistribution. In Part IV, I argue that since women's fear of crime is caused overwhelmingly by men as a class, men should bear all or most of the cost.

My argument is as follows. I assume that it is incompatible with justice for major benefits and burdens of social living to be distributed on the basis of irrelevant personal characteristics, by which I understand characteristics that are beyond a person's capacity to control or alter. This premise does not say which characteristics are *relevant*; it says only that if a particular characteristic is *irrelevant*, it cannot, consistently with justice, be the basis of distribution. Nor does the premise pre-suppose that we know or can specify in advance all of the characteristics that are relevant to each distribution. We can know that something is *irrelevant* to a distribution without knowing all the things that are relevant.[39] The second premise of the argument is the normative claim, defended above, that fear is a major burden of social living. Since sex, by hypothesis, is irrelevant to whether one should bear a particular benefit or burden—or rather, since sex is irrelevant to whether one should bear the burden of *fear*—fear may not be distributed on the basis of sex.[40] Unfortunately, as we have seen, it *is* distributed in just that way, so the existing distribution of fear is unjust.

I take it as uncontroversial that the state, as the instrument of the collective will, has an affirmative obligation to rectify injustice of all types, distributive and retributive, so it follows that the state has an affirmative obligation to reduce women's fear—even if the reduction comes at the expense of others, such as men, who do not stand to benefit, or do not stand to benefit to the same extent, from its actions. Like Rawls, I view justice as "the first virtue of social institutions,"[41] one that may not be subjugated to other virtues or values. But whereas Rawls explicitly limits justice to "laws and institutions," I include states of affairs that constitute, exemplify, or result from social interaction. To paraphrase Rawls, however "efficient and well-arranged" the existing distribution of fear, and however haphazardly it may have come into existence, it "must be reformed or abolished" if unjust.[42] The state, therefore, as the instrument of social justice, must use whatever means it has at its disposal to achieve this end.

IV. Rectifying the Injustice

I assume, then, that justice requires the redistribution of fear. But this claim is intolerably abstract. What concrete measures can be taken to reduce women's fear of crime, the bulk of which, as we have seen, consists in fear of sexual assault? First and foremost, the state can, through the criminal-justice system, take steps to prevent rape. We have seen that rape is fear-provoking in its own right and also that it is the source of much ancillary fear. If the incidence of rape is decreased, it stands to reason that a significant amount of women's fear will decrease as well.

But how can that be achieved? One way, which assumes that rape is a deterrable offense (there is no reason to think it is not),[43] is to increase the cost of rape to the prospective rapist. There are different ways to do this. The first and most obvious is to increase the magnitude of punishment for those convicted of rape. But this strategy, given prevailing attitudes, may have the perverse effect of *decreasing* the number of rape convictions, and thus lowering the expected punishment of the crime.[44] The problem is that jurors may be reluctant to convict men whom they believe to be guilty but who aren't seen as "deserving" of "severe" punishment.

A second and potentially more fruitful strategy is to increase the likelihood of apprehension, trial, and conviction of rapists while either leaving punishment as it is or reducing its magnitude. This would increase the expected punishment for the prospective rapist without encouraging or tempting jurors to ignore the law, and since we are assuming that rapists are rational and self-interested, it would have the salutary effect of deterring, and hence preventing, rape. It will take empirical research to discover which combination of punishment and likelihood of apprehension has the greatest deterrent effect. But in principle that is one action the state can take to reduce women's fear.

Apprehension, conviction, and punishment of rapists, while important components of an overall strategy to reduce women's fear of crime, are not the only components and may in the long run not be the most effective. It has been suggested that fear of crime is directly related to one's sense of vulnerability. This would explain why the elderly, for example, are more fearful than the nonelderly, for the elderly tend to experience themselves as weak and helpless. If that is so, then one way to reduce women's fear is to reduce or eliminate their sense of vulnerability. This can be done in many ways, foremost among which is to encourage women to learn self-defense techniques.[45] Studies show that "women who perceive themselves as less physically able are more likely to say they are afraid. However, after taking self-defense training courses, women reported feeling stronger, braver, more active, more in control, bigger, more efficacious in a variety of arenas—and less afraid."[46]

Related to this is a general sense of competence and control. Women traditionally have not been encouraged to participate—indeed, have been actively discouraged from participating—in athletic competition at either the individual or team level. Women have been "systematically instructed in the feminine virtues of ladylike behavior, particularly to be submissive to men."[47] As a result, many women reach adulthood without the most rudimentary of physical skills, such as running, jumping, kicking, striking a target, and fending off an attack. Criminologists Kurt Weis and Sandra Borges say that "Fearfulness and inhibition are core components of conventional femininity."[48] If they are right about this, and if fear of crime is to be reduced or eliminated, then conventional femininity must be supplanted or modified. The state can promote this objective by providing, subsidizing, or offering tax breaks for self-defense courses; insuring that women's athletics receive adequate funding at every age, grade, and skill level; and by altering or destroying socialization processes that cause girls and women to internalize a sense of inferiority, dependency, and vulnerability.[49] The state, using its power of the purse, club, and lectern, must break the cycle of socialized vulnerability and victimhood. This will go a long way toward alleviating women's fear of crime.

Two obvious but underestimated fear-reducing measures are increasing the number of police officers on the street and improving street lighting in neighborhoods and other public places, such as parks. Gordon and Riger write that "Many of the women we interviewed indicated that improved lighting in streets, alleys, and parks and/or more police on the streets would help to prevent rape, or at least make them feel less frightened."[50] Environmental psychologist Yvonne Bernard has found that "A well-lit place creates a warm, friendly atmosphere and reduces anxiety in people,"[51] particularly those, such as women, who are most afraid of crime. Yet another means is for the state to sponsor research on the etiology, nature, and consequences of sexual assault. The National Institute of Mental Health, for example, now includes a National Center for the Prevention and Control of Rape, which, among other things, funded the research by Gordon and Riger that culminated in the book *The Female Fear*.[52] Perhaps there should be a "war on fear" along lines of the recent "war on drugs" (although one hopes with greater success)....

This list of fear-reducing measures is not meant to be (and is not) exhaustive. It is suggestive. Anything that reduces the incidence of rape is likely to reduce women's fear of rape, not only for the obvious reason that a given woman's chances of being raped are thereby reduced, but because statistically speaking, fewer rape victims means fewer women who *know* a rape victim. Gordon and Riger discovered that one "major factor" in a woman's fear of rape is whether she knows someone who has been raped.[53] Women who know a rape victim, other things being equal, are more fearful than those who don't. The fear appears to be cyclical. Rape causes fear, which breeds more fear, which makes women draw inward for self-protection or to men for protection, which increases women's sense of vulnerability, which makes them better targets for rapists, which increases the likelihood of rape. This fear, I have argued, is an unjust burden for women to bear. I have tried to show, moreover, that there is much that can be done to lighten or eliminate the load. What exactly *should* be done, all things considered, is a matter of policy rather than principle.

There is one other matter of principle to be addressed, and that concerns who should bear the costs of fear-reducing measures. Ideally, since the overwhelming majority of rapes are by men of women, men should bear the cost. Men—not just rapists, but men as a class—are the source of women's fear of rape and of those crimes associated with rape. Male college students, for example, can be made to pay a surcharge while attending universities, the revenues to be used for self-defense classes for women, improved lighting, greater campus security, and other fear-reducing measures. Men's athletic programs and scholarships might be slashed or restructured, or additional tax monies collected, in order to create comparable programs and scholarships for women. All men can be required to participate in study groups or consciousness-raising sessions as a condition of receiving certain privileges, such as drinking alcoholic beverages or driving a motor vehicle, or to visit rape-crisis centers and hospitals to see the effects of rape on women. In areas with particularly high incidences of rape, there might be curfews for men. Men should pay higher taxes. Admittedly, these and other measures create practical and theoretical problems that must be solved. Precisely which measures should be adopted, and how their costs should be distributed, remains to be worked out. My philosophical point is that, for reasons of justice, the costs of fear-reducing measures should fall solely, or at least disproportionately, on men.

V. Objections and Replies

I have argued that the existing distribution of fear, in which women are disproportionately fearful, is unjust—and that the state, as the instrument of justice, has an affirmative obligation to rectify it. It might be objected that this claim is nonsensical, for no person or group of persons has *distributed* fear, either consciously or unconsciously. But if no person or group has distributed fear, then (so the objection goes) there is no obligation on the part of the state or anyone else to *re*distribute it. This objection has been made by F.A. Hayek in connection with the distribution of wealth in a market economy.[54] Hayek's argument is that since, strictly speaking, wealth is not *distributed*, and since distributive justice by definition concerns only *distributions*, distributive justice has nothing to say about wealth or any other good allocated in a market by market mechanisms.[55] An analogous objection might be made with respect to fear.

But as Tom Campbell has pointed out, Hayek "fails to make the important distinction between states of affairs which are consciously and deliberately brought about and those which *can* be intentionally altered, whatever their origin."[56] Why should justice concern only the former? As long as a particular "distribution" can be altered, it is an open question whether it should be. How the state of affairs came into existence may be relevant to the question of responsibility and to who should pay the cost of the alteration (see the discussion in Part IV), but it is irrelevant to whether alteration should be undertaken at all. If this is correct, and I believe it is, than *even if* fear is neither deliberately nor consciously distributed, its distribution—the patterns in which one finds it—can be unjust and rectifiable.[57]

This, however, may be to concede too much to the critic. Can it be said that women's fear of rape and other crimes *is* "consciously and deliberately brought about"? Susan Brownmiller claims that rape is and long has been "nothing more or less than a conscious process of intimidation by which all men keep all women in a state of fear."[58] Susan Griffin maintains that "rape is a form of mass terrorism,"[59] which implies consciousness, deliberation, and strategy on the part of many, most, or all men. Susan Rae Peterson writes that "rape is not merely an accidental series of individual events, but is institutionalized. It is a Rawlsian kind of 'practice': a 'form of activity specified by a system of rules which define offices, roles, moves, penalties, defences, and so on, and which give the activity its structure.'"[60] I quote these passages not to establish that fear of rape *is* deliberately created to serve male interests, a burden that I need not discharge here (and could not discharge by quotation anyway), but to suggest that it *might* be. And if it is, then even Hayekian critics must concede that it raises issues of distributive justice....

A third objection to my argument concerns the nature and extent of women's fear of crime, and in particular their fear of rape. Studies consistently show that women are victimized at a lesser rate than men, and yet women's fear of crime is greater and more widespread than that of men. In the case of rape, while "55 percent of American women are afraid of being raped ... the number of declared victims is very low (0.06 percent)."[61] These empirical findings suggest to some researchers that women's fear of crime is partly or wholly irrational—that it is without basis in fact. But the state, the objection goes, has no obligation rooted in justice to alleviate irrational fears. So justice does not require that steps be taken to reduce or eliminate women's fear of crime.

This objection confuses at least three points that ought to be kept separate: the first is women's greater fear vis-à-vis men; the second is the alleged disparity between women's fear of rape and their *own estimate* of the risk of rape; the third is the disparity between women's fear of rape (or of crime generally) and the *actual risk* of rape (crime). As for the first point, unless we take men's level of fear to be the norm of rationality, there is no reason to view women's greater fear as irrational. But even if men as a class were less fearful than women as a class, it would still be an open question which sex, if any, is irrational. If irrationality consists in a disproportion between fear and risk, then perhaps men rather than women are irrational; men, we might conclude, have too *little* fear. This much is clear: the mere fact that men and women have different levels of fear says nothing about who, if either of them, is irrational.

The second point, that women's fear of rape is disproportionate to their own estimate of the likelihood of being raped, and is on that account irrational, would be damaging if true, but lacks empirical support. In an extensive study of women's fear, researchers Gordon and Riger discovered that "women's fear [of rape] is proportionate to their own *estimates* of their own risks."[62] In other words, *given* a typical woman's perception of risk, however acquired, her level of fear is appropriate. Her fear tracks reality as she sees it. Therefore, if irrationality consists in disproportion between one's estimate of a given risk and the level of fear one experiences, women's fear of rape is not irrational.

Let us focus, then, on the third point. Let us suppose that women's fear of crime generally, and of rape in particular, *is* disproportionate to the actual risk. Does that alone undermine the state's obligation to reduce or eliminate fear? It seems not. If anything, it imposes a new and additional obligation: to educate women as to the real likelihood of being raped or otherwise victimized. The state's obligation to reduce fear, such as it is, is based on the burdensomeness of fear, and the burden exists whether the underlying fear is realistic or not. What constrains women, physically, psychologically, and socially, is their fear, not the risk to which they are exposed. Moreover, if the state's obligation is tied to risk rather than to fear, then those individuals (men, for example) who have less fear than is warranted by the risk would be entitled to greater resources than even they would view as necessary, which is puzzling if not absurd.

I believe that this is an adequate reply to the objection, but an even more powerful reply can be made. *Is* women's fear of rape irrational? That depends, of course, on how one conceives of rationality in this context. Warr has found that "age and sex differences in fear are largely a function of differential sensitivity to risk, meaning that the relation between fear and perceived risk varies among males and females, young and old.[63] For present purposes the important finding is that women are more sensitive than men to risk. This means that for a given level of perceived risk, women experience greater fear. Why? In studying differential sensitivity to risk, Warr discovered that it is a function of two variables: first, the perceived seriousness of the offense; and second, the presence of what he calls "perceptually contemporaneous offenses." Women as a class assign greater seriousness to the various criminal offenses, including rape, than do men. As we saw in Part I, a significant percentage of women view rape and murder as equally serious. Women are also more likely than men to see rape as part of a cluster of offenses to which they are exposed.

Suppose Warr is right about this—that women are more sensitive than men to the risk of victimization. Can it be said that women's greater fear is irrational? Only if one is prepared to say that, of two evaluations of the seriousness of rape, one is rational and the other not. But this is to adopt a substantive conception of rationality that is dubious at best and incoherent at worst. Ordinally we say that a particular attitude, belief, or response is rational *given* certain values. Given the high value I attach to my health, for example, my vegetarianism is rational; given the low value I attach to religion, my scorn for preachers and proselytizers is rational. Rationality is a relation between values (which are taken as given) and a particular response. The objection under consideration urges us to evaluate the values themselves. We are asked to say that women attach *too great* a value to their safety, bodily integrity, and lives—that the effects of rape and other crimes are not all *that* bad.[64] But it could just as easily be said, as I suggested above, that men attach too little value to these things.[65]

I conclude that women's fear of crime is not irrational in any sense that undermines the state's obligation to redistribute fear. That women fear crimes such as rape to a degree beyond what would be strictly necessary to protect them from harm suggests that women attach significant value to their lives, health, and well-being. This greater value manifests itself in a greater sensitivity to risk, which in turn manifests itself in greater fear of victimization. But I maintain that even if women's fear of crime were irrational (in the sense of unfounded), it would not follow that the state lacks an obligation to reduce or eliminate it. The objection is without merit.

A fourth and a final objection to my argument is that rectifying the injustice of women's disproportionate fear is the first step on a logical slippery slope to dystopia. There are two versions of this objection. One is that if, as I have argued, it is unjust for women to be disproportionately fearful, then, by parity of reasoning, it is unjust for the elderly, the poor, nonwhites, and urban residents to be disproportionately fearful—because these groups, too, as studies show, have greater fear than their counterparts. But it is absurd (says the objector) to think that there is so much injustice in society. Therefore, the state of affairs in which women are disproportionately fearful is not unjust. Put differently, either no fear differentials are unjust or all fear differentials are unjust, but not all fear differentials are unjust (for the reason given); therefore, none is.

This version of the objection is easily dismissed. Why, a priori, must there be only a certain amount of injustice in society? Can't a particular society be unjust through and through—to its core? Suppose a particular group of individuals, say middle-class white males, decides to oppress the poor, nonwhites, and females—and does so. Would we say that this is *impossible*, because too extensive? Surely not. What we would say is that the injustice has a common source, many faces, and must be combatted on many fronts. Far from being an embarrassment to my argument, the fact that other groups in society (such as the elderly) are disproportionately fearful shows the power of the argument. It shows that the argument is not ad hoc, that it rests on a moral principle of broad application. Admittedly, this essay concerns only the fear that women experience, but I could just as easily have focused on the fear of the elderly, the poor, or the comparatively uneducated. The state, I would maintain, has an obligation to redistribute fear in those cases as well, and for the same reasons.

The second version of the objection differs from the first in that it *concedes* the injustice of women's disproportionate fear of crime—and also that of other groups, such as the elderly. But it claims that rectifying those injustices would be too costly in terms of liberty and other values. It says, in effect, that either all injustices must be rectified or no injustices need be rectified, but rectification of all injustices is too costly; therefore, no rectification is necessary. This is reminiscent of (although not identical to) Nozick's[66] and Hayek's[67] claims that redistribution of wealth requires constant and unjust infringements of liberty. Since these thinkers assign great (one is tempted to say "absolute") value to liberty, and since in most cases of redistribution the aim is not to compensate for harm done, which would justify it, the redistribution (they say) is unjustified.

One need not deny the value of liberty to respond to this objection. All one needs to show is that the liberty in question results in significant harm to others, for even liberals such as Nozick concede that harm to others is a good reason to limit liberty.[68] I have argued in this essay that fear is a burden—a real harm—to individuals. Admittedly, it is difficult in most cases to identify the person causing the harm; but why is that a necessary condition of redistribution? If liberty may, consistently with justice, be infringed to protect others from significant harm, and if those being harmed and those creating the harm can be identified through group membership, as they are in the case of fear, it is at most a strategic matter how one goes about redistributing fear. It should be done at least cost to other values, of course, but it should be done. Justice requires it. Indeed, justice would not be the first virtue of social institutions, as Rawls maintains, if it could be easily overridden or outweighed by other considerations....[69]

NOTES

1. Kurt Weis and Sandra S. Borges, "Victimology and Rape: The Case of the Legitimate Victim," *Issues in Criminology* 8 (Fall 1973):94. See also Margaret T. Gordon and Stephanie Riger, *The Female Fear: The Social Cost of Rape* (Urbana and Chicago: University of Illinois Press, 1991), 118: "Feminist analyses of the effect of the threat of rape on women assert that it operates as an instrument of social control, encouraging women to restrict their behavior and keeping them in a state of continuous stress."
2. Stanley I. Benn, "Justice," *The Encyclopedia of Philosophy*, ed. Paul Edwards (New York: Macmillan, 1967; reprint ed. 1972), vol. 4, 298.
3. Here I borrow from Tom Campbell, *Justice* (Atlantic Highlands, NJ: Humanities Press International, 1988), 19; who writes: "With all these reservations, it remains illuminating to say that justice has to do with the distribution amongst persons of benefits and burdens, these being loosely defined so as to cover any desirable or undesirable thing or experience."
4. I do not imply that if it were distributed randomly, it would be morally acceptable—although, in that case, at least one ground of moral unacceptability would be absent.
5. See Mark Warr, "Fear of Victimization: Why Are Women and the Elderly More Afraid?," *Social Science Quarterly* 65 (September 1984):681.
6. See Terry L. Baumer, "Research on Fear of Crime in the United States," *Victimology: An International Journal* 3 (1978):256, 257; Stephanie Riger, Margaret T. Gordon, and Robert LeBailly, "Women's Fear of Crime: From Blaming to Restricting the Victim," *Victimology: An International Journal* 3 (1978):277; Allen E. Liska, Andrew Sanchirico, and Mark D. Reed, "Fear of Crime and Constrained Behavior Specifying and Estimating a Reciprocal Effects Model," *Social Forces* 66 (March 1988):828; Gordon and Riger, *The Female Fear*; 118; Yvonne Bernard, "North American and European Research on Fear of Crime," *Applied Psychology: An International Review* 41 (January 1992):70.
7. Baumer, "Research on Fear of Crime in the United States," 255; see also *ibid.*, 260; Margaret T. Gordon et al., "Crime, Women, and the Quality of Urban

Life," *Signs: Journal of Women in Culture and Society* 5 (Spring 1980); S144.

8. Warr, "Fear of Victimization," 687.
9. *Ibid.*, 685.
10. Riger, Gordon, and LeBailly, "Women's Fear of Crime," 276.
11. *Ibid.*, see also Gordon et al., "Crime, Women, and the Quality of Urban Life," 147.
12. Gordon *et al.*, "Crime, Women, and the Quality of Urban Life," 147.
13. Baumer, "Research on Fear of Crime in the United States," 255.
14. Many ordinary expressions reflect this. Fear is said to be misplaced, unnecessary, exaggerated, excessive, foolish, groundless, unjustified, baseless, unreasonable, unwarranted, and irrational. A phobia, popularly, is "a lasting abnormal fear or great dislike of something? Eugene Ehrlich et al., *Oxford American Dictionary* (New York: Oxford University Press, 1980), 501.
15. Warr, "Fear of Victimization," 698.
16. *Ibid.*, 696.
17. Baumer, "Research on Fear of Crime in the United States," 255; see also Warr, "Fear of Victimization," 682. It is interesting that Rodney King, the victim of a brutal beating by police officers that captured the attention of the nation, chose rape as his phenomenological model. He testified that after the beating "I felt like I had been raped ... I felt like I was going to die." Quoted in *The Dallas Morning News*, 29 March 1994, 5A.
18. Warr, "Fear of Victimization," 695.
19. *Ibid.*, 700.
20. *Ibid.*, 698; but compare Riger, Gordon, and LeBailly, "Women's Fear of Crime," 278: "Among women, the fear of rape ranks second only to murder" (citations omitted).
21. See Warr, "Fear of Victimization," 698.
22. Martha R. Burt and Rhoda E. Estep, "Apprehension and Fear: Learning a sense of Sexual Vulnerability," *Sex Roles* 7 (May 1981):512.
23. *Ibid.*, 520.
24. Warr, "Fear of Victimization," 698, 700.
25. *Ibid.*, 700 (italics in original).
26. Mark Warr, "Fear of Rape Among Urban Women," *Social Problems* 32 (February 1985):248.
27. *Ibid.*, 249.
28. Ehrlich et al., *Oxford American Dictionary*, 81.
29. *Ibid.*, 235: Fear is "an unpleasant emotion caused by the nearness of danger or expectation of pain etc." I refer here to the phenomenological aspect of fear (the way it feels "from the inside") rather than to its intentional aspect (what it is about). Even so-called cognitive theories of emotion, in which emotions involve or are caused by beliefs, allow room for this aspect. See, for example, Ronald Alan Nash, "Cognitive Theories of Emotion," *Noûs* 23 (September 1989):481-504; John Morreall, "Fear Without Belief," *The Journal of Philosophy* 90 (July 1993):359-366. Nothing in my essay hinges on accepting or rejecting a particular theory of the nature of fear, let alone a theory of the nature of emotion.
30. Gordon et al., "Crime, Women, and the Quality of Urban Life," 157-158; see also Warr, "Fear of Rape Among Urban Women," 248.
31. See Riger, Gordon, and LeBailly, "Women's Fear of Crime," 281.
32. Gordon et al., "Crime, Women, and the Quality of Urban Life," S158.
33. See Gordon and Riger, *The Female Fear*, 14, 15-18, 113-14, 121, 122; Warr, "Fear of Rape Among Urban women," 247-249.
34. Pauline B. Bart, review of *Intimate Violence: A Study of Injustice*, by Julie Blackman; *The Female Fear: The Social Cost of Rape*, by Margaret T. Gordon and Stephanie Riger; *Battered Women as Survivors*, by Lee Ann Hoff; *Women and Rape*, by Cathy Roberts; and *Fraternity Gang Rape: Sex, Brotherhood, and Privilege on Campus*, by Peggy Reeves Sanday, in *Signs: Journal of Women in Culture and Society* 19 (Winter 1994):530.
35. See Catharine A. MacKinnon, *Toward a Feminist Theory of the State* (Cambridge, MA: Harvard University Press, 1989), 149, 151.
36. See Andra Medea and Kathleen Thompson, *Against Rape* (New York: Farrar, Straus and Giroux, 1974), 146.
37. Susan Sontag, "The Third World of Women," *Partisan Review* 40 (1973):184; see also, in this connection, Sarah Lucia Hoagland " A Note on the Logic of Protection and Predation," *American Philosophical Association Newsletter on Feminism and Philosophy* 88 (November 1988):7-8.
38. Gordon and Riger, *The Female Fear*, 121. See also

Medea and Thompson, *Against Rape*, 5: "For women the luxury of going out for a walk alone, of getting away for a few minutes, is almost impossible. Every day of their lives, women learn to accept the fact that their freedom is limited in a way that a man's is not. There is a curfew on women in this country and it is enforced by rapists."

39. Cf. Benn, "Justice," 299: "It is not for a judge to decide the respects in which men are equal but to decide whether the respects in which they are unequal are relevant to the issues in the case."
40. Here I employ the principle that "Where no good ground can be shown for treating people differently, they ... ought to be treated alike." *Ibid.*, 301. By the way, I am not implying that sex is sometimes morally relevant, nor am I implying that it is never morally relevant. I concern myself only with the irrelevance of sex for the distribution of *fear*.
41. John Rawls, *A Theory of Justice* (Cambridge: Harvard University Press, 1971), 3.
42. *Ibid.*
43. According to Richard Posner, research conducted by Isaac Ehrlich "shows that rapists, like other criminals, respond to increases in the severity as well as probability of punishment." Richard A. Posner, *Sex and Reason* (Cambridge, MA: Harvard University Press, 1992), 394 (citation omitted).
44. *Ibid.*, 394. "The heavier the punishment for a particular crime is known to be, the more inclined a jury may be to resolve doubts in the defendants's favor." See also *ibid.*, 401: "[A]n increase in the severity of punishment may be offset by a reduction in the probability of conviction, leaving expected punishment costs (the product of the probability and the severity of punishment) unchanged or even lower."
45. For a discussion and illustration of such techniques, see Medea and Thompson, *Against Rape*, chap. 7, 73-96.
46. Gordon and Riger, *The Female Fear*, 54 (citation omitted). See also *ibid.*, 52, 115, 129, 135, 136. This is not to say that women will eagerly enroll in such courses. As Medea and Thompson point out, "Few people would object to a little boy's learning to defend himself, but in a group of women who had gathered together to work against rape, one woman worried about encouraging women to learn self-defense because, she said, it would be a 'brutalizing' experience. Most women have encountered that attitude before and have been affected by it." Medea and Thompson, *Against Rape*, 54. The authors trace this attitude to "the feminine ideal," which (they say) teaches that "Women are not supposed to take care of themselves, to be independent. They are taught that it is appealing to be weak, that it is attractive to be helpless." *Ibid.*
47. Weis and Borges, "Victimology and Rape," 83. See also Medea and Thompson, *Against Rape*, 22.
48. Weis and Borges, "Victimology and Rape," 81
49. Gordon and Riger write that "Perhaps more than anything else, the women who shared their stories [of rape] suggest that egalitarian views of women's roles and education are related to less fear, less isolation, and less restricted behavior." Gordon and Riger, *The Female Fear*, 123. This would suggest an obligation on the part of the state to undermine traditional sex roles rather than remain neutral with respect to them.
50. *Ibid.*, 135.
51. Bernard, "North American and European Research on Fear of Crime,"69.
52. See Gordon and Riger, *The Female Fear*, xiv. The Center suffered massive budget cuts and significant personnel turnover during the Reagan administration. See *ibid.*, 127.
53. See Gordon and Riger, *The Female Fear*, 112.
54. See F. A. Hayek, *Law, Legislation and Liberty: A New Statement of the Liberal Principles of Justice and Political Economy*, vol. 2: *The Mirage of Social Justice* (Chicago: The University of Chicago Press, 1976), chap. 9, 62-100.
55. Hayek says that "only human conduct can be called just or unjust. If we apply the terms to a state of affairs, they have meaning only in so far as we hold someone responsible for bringing it about or allowing it to come about. A bare fact, or a state of affairs which nobody can change, may be good or bad, but not just or unjust." *Ibid.*, 31.
56. Campbell, *Justice*, 15-16 (italics in original).
57. Hayek engages in persuasive definition when he insists that "only situations which have been created by human will can be called just or unjust." Hayek, *The Mirage of Social Justice*, 33. In fact, he admits as much. According to Hayek, "the manner in which the benefits and burdens are apportioned by the market mechanism would in many instances have to be

regarded as very unjust if it were the result of a deliberate allocation to particular people." *Ibid.*, 64 (emphasis in original). So it is only Hayek's decision not to use the word "unjust" for these instances that prevents such a distribution from being unjust. And Hayek's decision not to use the word rests on his ideological commitment to a laissez-faire economy.

58. Susan Brownmiller, *Against Our Will: Men, Women and Rape* (New York: Simon and Schuster, 1975), 15; see also *ibid.*, 209, 254, 309, 398-403.
59. Susan Griffin, "Rape: The All-American Crime," in *Feminism and Philosophy*, ed. Mary Vetterling-Braggin, Frederick A. Elliston, and Jane English (Totowa, NJ: Littlefield, Adams, 1977), 331. See also Robin Morgan, "Theory and Practice: Pornography and Rape," in *Take Back the Night: Women on Pornography*, ed. Laura Lederer (New York: William Morrow and Company, 1980), 135 ("Knowing our place is the message of rape—as it was for blacks the message of lynchings. Neither is an act of spontaneity or sexuality—they are both acts of political terrorism, designed consciously and unconsciously to keep an entire people in its place by continual reminders" (emphasis in original)); Claudia Card, "Rape As a Terrorist Institution," in *Violence, Terrorism, and Justice*, ed. R. G. Frey and Christopher W. Morris (Cambridge: Cambridge University Press, 1991), 296-319.
60. Susan Rae Peterson, "Coercion and Rape: The State as a Male Protection Racket," in Vetterling-Braggin, Elliston, and English, eds., *Feminism and Philosophy*, 360-361.
61. Bernard, "North American and European Research on Fear of Crime," 70.
62. Gordon and Riger, *The Female Fear*; 121 (emphasis in original).
63. Warr, "Fear of Victimization," 681.
64. Gordon and Riger give the following explanation of women's evaluation of the seriousness of rape: "Since women know the devastating emotional consequences of rape and know they are held responsible for preventing it, their heightened fear is a rational response." Gordon and Riger, *The Female Fear*, 47. It may be that men make lower estimates of, or ignore, these costs.
65. Warr concludes his essay as follows: "[D]ifferences in fear among individuals or groups must ultimately come down to normative differences (judgments about the value of one's person or property), and surely there is no universal metric by which such judgments can be deemed 'correct' or 'incorrect.'" Warr, "Fear of Victimization," 701. Perhaps women's fear of rape is viewed as irrational because (1) men determine what is rational and irrational, (2) men attach comparatively little value to women's lives and bodily integrity, and (3) men assume that women share their (men's) low evaluation of them (women).
66. See Robert Nozick, *Anarchy, State, and Utopia* (New York: Basic books, 1974), 160-164.
67. See Hayek, *The Mirage of Social Justice*, 82-85.
68. See, e.g., Joel Feinberg, *The Moral Limits of the Criminal Law*, vol. 1: *Harm to Others* (New York: Oxford University Press, 1984). Feinberg, a liberal (see *ibid.*, 15), defends what he calls "the harm principle, which states that "It is always a good reason in support of penal legislation that it would probably be effective in preventing (eliminating, reducing) harm to persons other than the actor (the one prohibited from acting) *and* there is probably no other means that is equally effective at no greater cost to other values." *Ibid.*, 26 (emphasis in original). Feinberg's concern in this and the other volumes of the tetralogy is the criminal law, but presumably he would be concerned to reduce or eliminate harm in noncriminal contexts as well. At any rate, that is *my* concern.
69. A slightly altered version of this essay will form a chapter of my book *Rape: A Philosophical Investigation* [Dartmouth Publishing, 1996].

This essay began life as an informal talk to an informal gathering sponsored by the Philosophy Club of the University of Texas at Arlington. The brainstorming that took place on that occasion was useful to me in developing my thoughts and ultimately in formulating my arguments. Steve Hiltz asked particularly good questions. The written version of that talk was presented, by invitation, to the Society for Philosophy and Public Affairs at the 1994 Pacific Division meeting of the American Philosophical Association in Los Angeles, California. The topic, on a panel chaired by Sally Haslanger, was "Justice and Sexual Violence." I thank Stanley French, Lois Pineau, Sally Haslanger, and several members of the audience for useful comments and criticism on that occasion. I also thank my partner, Lora Schmid-Dolan, for encouragement, insight, and for bringing home to me the heretofore unacknowledged privilege I have, qua male, of walking the streets without fear—or with less fear than I might otherwise have.

MEN IN GROUPS: COLLECTIVE RESPONSIBILITY FOR RAPE

Larry May and Robert Strikwerda

Larry May teaches philosophy at Washington University in St. Louis. He is the author of The Morality of Groups *(Notre Dame, 1987),* Sharing Responsibility *(Chicago, 1992), and* The Socially Responsive Self *(Chicago, 1996) and co-editor of* Applied Ethics: A Multicultural Approach, *(Prentice-Hall, 1998).*

Robert Strikwerda teaches philosophy at Indiana University at Kokomo. He is the author of articles in the areas of philosophy of social science and moral philosophy. He has also co-edited Rethinking Masculinity: Philosophical Explorations in Light of Feminism *with Larry May and Patrick Hopkins (Rowman & Littlefield, 1996).*

"We criticize the following views: only the rapist is responsible since only he committed the act; no one is responsible since rape is a biological response to stimuli; everyone is responsible since men and women contribute to the rape culture; and patriarchy is responsible but no person or group. We then argue that, in some societies, men are collectively responsible for rape since most benefit from rape and most are similar to the rapist."

As teenagers, we ran in a crowd that incessantly talked about sex. Since most of us were quite afraid of discovering our own sexual inadequacies, we were quite afraid of women's sexuality. To mask our fear, of which we were quite ashamed, we maintained a posture of bravado, which we were able to sustain through mutual reinforcement when in small groups or packs. Riding from shopping mall to fast food establishment, we would tell each other stories about our sexual exploits, stories we all secretly believed to be pure fictions. We drew strength from the camaraderie we felt during these experiences. Some members of our group would yell obscenities at women on the street as we drove by. Over time, conversation turned more and more to group sex, especially forced sex with women we passed on the road. To give it its proper name, our conversation turned increasingly to rape. At a certain stage, we tired of it all and stopped associating with this group of men, or perhaps they were in most ways still boys. The reason we left was not that we disagreed with what was going on but, if this decision to leave was reasoned at all, it was that the posturing (the endless attempts to impress one another by our daring ways) simply became very tiresome. Only much later in life did we think that there was anything wrong, morally, socially, or politically, with what went on in that group of adolescents who seemed so ready to engage in rape. Only later still did we wonder whether we shared in responsibility for the rapes that are perpetrated by those men who had similar experiences to ours.[1]

Catharine MacKinnon has recently documented the link between violence and rape in the war in Bosnia. Young Serbian soldiers, some with no previous sexual experience, seemed quite willing to rape Muslim and Croatian women as their reward for "winning" the war. These young men were often encouraged in these acts by groups of fellow soldiers, and even sometimes by their commanding officers. Indeed, gang rape in concentration camps, at least at the beginning of the war, seems to have

Reprinted with permission of the publisher, Larry May, and Robert Strikwerda from *Hypatia* 9:2 (Spring 1994): 134–151.

been common. (Post, et al., in *Newsweek*) The situation in Bosnia is by no means unique in the history of war (Brownmiller, 37). But rape historically has never been considered a war crime. MacKinnon suggests that this is because "Rape in war has so often been treated as extracurricular, as just something men do, as a product rather than a policy of war" (MacKinnon 1993, 30).

War crimes are collective acts taken against humanity; whereas rape has almost always been viewed as a despicable "private" act. In this paper we wish to challenge the view that rape is the responsibility only of the rapists by challenging the notion that rape is best understood as an individual, private act. This is a paper about the relationship between the shared experiences of men in groups, especially experiences that make rape more likely in western culture, and the shared responsibility of men for the prevalence of rape in that culture. The claim of the paper is that in some societies men are collectively responsible for rape in that most if not all men contribute in various ways to the prevalence of rape, and as a result these men should share in responsibility for rape.

Most men do very little at all to oppose rape in their societies; does this make them something like co-conspirators with the men who rape? In Canada, a number of men have founded the "White Ribbon Campaign." This is a program of fund-raising, consciousness raising, and symbolic wearing of white ribbons during the week ending on December 6th, the anniversary of the murder of 14 women at a Montreal engineering school by a man shouting "I hate feminists." Should men in U.S. society start a similar campaign? If they do not, do they deserve the "co-conspirator" label? If they do, is this symbolic act enough to diminish their responsibility? Should men be speaking out against the program of rape in the war in Bosnia? What should they tell their sons about such rapes, and about rapes that occur in their home towns? If men remain silent, are they not complicitous with the rapists?

We will argue that insofar as male bonding and socialization in groups contributes to the prevalence of rape in western societies, men in those societies should feel responsible for the prevalence of rape and should feel motivated to counteract such violence and rape. In addition, we will argue that rape should be seen as something that men, as a group, are collectively responsible for, in a way which parallels the collective responsibility of a society for crimes against humanity perpetrated by some members of their society. Rape is indeed a crime against humanity, not merely a crime against a particular woman. And rape is a crime perpetrated by men as a group, not merely by the individual rapist.

To support our claims we will criticize four other ways to understand responsibility for rape. First, it is sometimes said that only the rapist is responsible since he alone intentionally committed the act of rape. Second, it is sometimes said that no one is responsible since rape is merely a biologically oriented response to stimuli that men have little or no control over. Third, it is sometimes said that everyone, women and men alike, contribute to the violent environment which produces rape so both women and men are equally responsible for rape, and hence it is a mistake to single men out. Fourth, it is sometimes said that it is "patriarchy," rather than individual men or men as a group, which is responsible for rape.[2] After examining each of these views we will conclude by briefly offering our own positive reasons for thinking that men are collectively responsible for the prevalence of rape in western society

I. The Rapist as Loner or Demon

Joyce Carol Oates has recently described the sport of boxing, where men are encouraged to violate the social rule against harming one another, as "a highly organized ritual that violates taboo."

> The paradox of the boxer is that, in the ring, he experiences himself as a living conduit for the inchoate, demonic will of the crowd: the expression of their collective desire, which is to pound another human being into absolute submission. (Oates 1992, 60)

Oates makes the connection here between boxing and rape. The former boxing heavyweight champion of the world, Mike Tyson, epitomizes this connection both because he is a convicted rapist, and also because, according to Oates, in his fights he regularly used the pre-fight taunt "I'll make you into my girlfriend," clearly the "boast of a rapist." (Oates 1992, 61)

Just after being convicted of rape, Mike Tyson gave a twisted declaration of his innocence:

> I didn't rape anyone. I didn't hurt anyone—no black eyes, no broken ribs. When I'm in the ring, I break their ribs, I break their jaws. To me, that's hurting someone. (*St. Louis Post Dispatch*, March 27, 1992, 20A)

In the ring, Tyson had a license to break ribs and jaws; and interestingly he understood that this was a case of hurting another person. It was just that in the ring it was acceptable. He knew that he was not supposed to hurt people outside the ring. But since he didn't break any ribs or jaws, how could anyone say that he hurt his accuser, Desiree Washington? Having sex with a woman could not be construed as having hurt her, for Tyson apparently, unless ribs or jaws were broken.

Tyson's lawyer, attempting to excuse Tyson's behavior, said that the boxer grew up in a "male-dominated world." And this is surely true. He was plucked from a home for juvenile delinquents and raised by boxing promoters. Few American males had been so richly imbued with male tradition, or more richly rewarded for living up to the male stereotype of the aggressive, indomitable fighter. Whether or not he recognized it as a genuine insight, Tyson's lawyer points us toward the heart of the matter in American culture: misbehavior, especially sexual misbehavior of males toward females is, however mixed the messages, something that many men condone. This has given rise to the use of the term "the rape culture" to describe the climate of attitudes that exists in the contemporary American male-dominated world (see Griffin 1971).

While noting all of this, Joyce Carol Oates ends her *Newsweek* essay on Tyson's rape trial concluding that "no one is to blame except the perpetrator himself." She absolves the "culture" at large of any blame for Tyson's behavior. Oates regards Tyson as a sadist who took pleasure in inflicting pain both in and out of the boxing ring. She comes very close to demonizing him when, at the end of her essay, she suggests that Tyson is an outlaw or even a sociopath. And while she is surely right to paint Tyson's deed in the most horrific colors, she is less convincing when she suggests that Tyson is very different from other males in our society. In one telling statement in her essay, however, Oates opens the door for a less individualistic view of rape by acknowledging that the boxing community had built up in Tyson a "grandiose sense of entitlement, fueled by the insecurities and emotions of adolescence" (Oates 1992, 61).

Rape is normally committed by individual men; but, in our view, rape is not best understood in individualistic terms. The chief reasons for this are that individual men are more likely to engage in rape when they are in groups, and men receive strong encouragement to rape from the way they are socialized as men, that is, in the way they come to see themselves as instantiations of what it means to be a man. Both the "climate" that encourages rape and the "socialization" patterns which instill negative attitudes about women are difficult to understand or assess when one focuses on the isolated individual perpetrator of a rape. There are significant social dimensions to rape that are best understood as group-oriented.

As parents, we have observed that male schoolchildren are much more likely to misbehave (and subsequently to be punished by being sent to "time out") than are female schoolchildren. This fact is not particularly remarkable, for boys are widely believed to be more active than girls. What is remarkable is that school teachers, in our experience, are much more likely to condone the misbehavior of boys that the misbehavior of girls. "Boys will be boys" is heard as often today as it was in previous times. (See Robert Lipsyte's (1993) essay about the Glen Ridge, New Jersey rape trial where the defense attorney used just these words to defend the star high school football players who raped a retarded girl). From their earliest experience with authority figures, little boys are given mixed signals about misbehavior. Yes, they are punished, but they are also treated as if their misbehavior is expected, even welcome. It is for some boys, as it was for us, a "badge of honor" to be sent to detention or "time out." From older boys and from their peers, boys learn that they often will be ostracized for being "too goody-goody." It is as if part of the mixed message is that boys are given a license to misbehave.

And which of these boys will turn out to be rapists is often as much a matter of luck as it is a matter of choice. Recent estimates have it that in the first few months of the war "30,000 to 50,000 women, most of them Muslim" were raped by Serbian soldiers (Post et al., 1993, 32). The data on date rape suggest that young men in our society engage in much more rape than anyone previously anticipated. It is a serious mistake in psychological categorization to think that all of these rapes are committed by sadists. (Studies by Amir show that the average rapist is not psychologically "abnormal." [Cited in Griffin 1971, 178].) Given our own experiences and similar reports from others, it is also a serious mistake to think that those who rape are significantly different from the rest of the male population. (Studies by Smithyman indicate that rapists "seemed not to differ markedly from the majority of males in our culture." [Cited in Scully 1990, 75].) Our conclusion is that the typical rapist is not a demon or sadist, but, in some sense, could have been many men.

Most of those who engage in rape are at least partially responsible for these rapes, but the question we have posed is this: are those who perpetrate rape the *only* ones who are responsible for rape? Contrary to what Joyce Carol Oates contends, we believe that it is a serious mistake to think that only the perpetrators are responsible. The interactions of men, especially in all-male groups, contribute to a pattern of socialization that also plays a major role in the incidence of rape. In urging that more than the individual perpetrators be seen as responsible for rape, we do not mean to suggest that the responsibility of the perpetrator be diminished. When responsibility for harm is shared it need not be true that the perpetrators of harm find their responsibility relieved or even diminished. Rather, shared responsibility for harms merely means that the range of people who are implicated in these harms is extended. (More will be said on this point in the final section.)

II. The Rapist as Victim of Biology

The most recent psychological study of rape is that done by Randy Thornhill and Nancy Wilmsen Thornhill (1992), "The Evolutionary Psychology of Men's Coercive Sexuality." In this work, any contention that coercion or rape may be socially or culturally learned is derisively dismissed, as is any feminist argument for changing mens's attitudes through changing especially group-based socialization. The general hypothesis they support is that

> sexual coercion by men reflects a sex-specific, species-typical psychological adaptation to rape: Men have certain psychological traits that evolved by natural selection specifically in the context of coercive sex and made rape adaptive during human evolution. (363)

They claim that rape is an adaptive response to biological differences between men and women.

Thornhill and Thornhill contend that the costs to women to engage in sex ("nine months of pregnancy") greatly exceed the costs to men ("a few minutes of time and an energetically cheap ejaculate"). As a result women and men come very early in evolutionary time to adapt quite differently sexually.

> Because women are more selective about mates and more interested in evaluating them and delaying copulation, men, to get sexual access, must often break through feminine barriers of hesitation, equivocation, and resistance. (366)

Males who adapted by developing a proclivity to rape and thus who "solved the problem" by forcing sex on a partner, were able to "out-reproduce" other more passive males and gain an evolutionary advantage.

In one paragraph, Thornhill and Thornhill dismiss feminists who support a "social learning theory of rape" by pointing out that males of several "species with an evolutionary history of polygyny" are also "more aggressive, sexually assertive and eager to copulate." Yet, in "the vast majority of these species there is no sexual training of juveniles by other members of the group." This evidence, they conclude, thoroughly discredits the social learning theory and means that such theories "are never alternatives to evolutionary hypotheses about psychological adaptation" (364). In response to their critics, Thornhill and Thornhill go so far as to say that the feminist project of changing socialization patterns is pernicious.

> The sociocultural view does seem to offer hope and a simple remedy in that it implies that we need only fix the way that boys are socialized and rape will disappear. This naive solution is widespread.... As Hartung points out, those who feel that the social problem of rape can be solved by changing the nature of men through naive and arbitrary social adjustments should "get real about rape" because their perspective is a danger to us all. (416)

According to the Thornhills, feminists and other social theorists need to focus instead on what are called the "cues that affect the use of rape by adult males" (416).

The evolutionary biological account of rape we have rehearsed above would seemingly suggest that no one is responsible for rape. After all, if rape is an adaptive response to different sexual development in males and females, particular individuals who engage in rape are merely doing what they are naturally adapted to do. Rape is something to be controlled by those who control the "cues" that stimulate the natural rapist instincts in all men. It is for this reason that the Thornhills urge that more attention be given to male arousal and female stimulation patterns in laboratory settings (375). Notice that even on the Thornhill's own terms, those who provide the cues may be responsible for the prevalence of rape, even if the perpetrators are not. But Thornhill and Thornhill deny that there are any normative conclusions that follow from their research and criticize those who wish to draw out such implications as committing the "naturalistic fallacy" (see 407).

In contrast to the Thornhills, a more plausible sociobiological account is given by Lionel Tiger. Tiger is often cited as someone who attempted to excuse male aggression. In his important study he defines aggression as distinct from violence, but nonetheless sees violence as one possible outcome of the natural aggressive tendencies, especially in men.

> Aggression occurs when an individual or group see their interest, their honor, or their job bound up with coercing the animal, human, or physical environment to achieve their own ends rather than (or in spite of) the goals of the object of their action. Violence may occur in the process of interaction. (Tiger 1984, 158-59)

For Tiger, aggression is intentional behavior which is goal-directed and based on procuring something which is necessary for survival. Aggression is a "'normal' feature of the human biologically based repertoire" (159). Violence, "coercion involving physical force to resolve conflict," (159) on the other hand, is not necessarily a normal response to one's environment, although in some circumstances it may be. Thus, while human males are evolutionarily adapted to be aggressive, they are not necessarily adapted to be violent.

Tiger provided an account that linked aggression in males with their biological evolution.

> Human aggression is in part a function of the fact that hunting was vitally important to human evolution and that aggression is typically undertaken by males in the framework of a unisexual social bond of which participants are aware and with which they are concerned. It is implied, therefore, that aggression is 'instinctive' but also must occur within an explicit social context varying from culture to culture and to be learned by members of any community.... Men in continuous association aggress against the environment in much the same way as men and women in continuous association have sexual relations. (Tiger 1984, 159-60).

And while men are thus predisposed to engage in aggression, in ways that women are not, it is not true in Tiger's view that a predisposition to engage in violent acts is a normal part of this difference.

Thornhill and Thornhill fail to consider Tiger's contention that men are evolutionarily adapted to be aggressive, but not necessarily to be violent. With Tiger's distinction in mind it may be said that human males, especially in association with other males, are adapted to aggress against women in certain social environments. But this aggressive response need not lead to violence, or the threat of violence, of the sort epitomized by rape; rather it may merely affect noncoercive mating rituals. On a related point, Tiger argues that the fact that war has historically been "virtually a male monopoly" (81) is due to both male bonding patterns and evolutionary adaption. Evolutionary biology provides only part of the story since male aggressiveness need not result in such violent encounters as occur in war or rape. After all, many men do not rape or go to war; the cultural cues provided by socialization must be considered at least as important as evolutionary adaptation.

We side with Tiger against the Thornhills in focusing on the way that all-male groups socialize their members and provide "cues" for violence. Tiger has recently allied himself with feminists such as Catharine MacKinnon and others who have suggested that male attitudes need to be radically altered in order to have a major impact on the incidence of rape (see the preface to the second edition of *Men In Groups*). One of the implications of Tiger's research is that rape and other forms of male aggressive behavior are not best understood as isolated acts of individuals. Rather than simply seeing violent aggression as merely a biologically predetermined response, Tiger places violent aggressiveness squarely into the group dynamics of men's interactions—a result of his research not well appreciated.

In a preface to the second edition of his book, Tiger corrects an unfortunate misinterpretation of his work.

> One of the stigmas which burdened this book was an interpretation of it as an apology for male aggression and even a potential stimulus of it—after all, boys will be boys. However I clearly said the opposite: "This is not to say that ... hurtful and destructive relations between groups of men are inevitable.... It may be possible, as many writers have suggested, to alter social conceptions of maleness so that gentility and equivocation rather than toughness and more or less arbitrary decisiveness are highly valued." (Tiger 1984, 191)

If Tiger is right, and the most important "cues are those which young boys and men get while in the company of other boys and men, then the feminist project of changing in male socialization patterns may be seen as consistent with, rather than opposed to, the sociobiological hypotheses. Indeed, other evidence may be cited to buttress the feminist social learning perspective against the Thornhills. Different human societies have quite different rates of rape. In her anthropological research among the Minangkabau of West Sumatra, Peggy Reeves Sanday has found that this society is relatively rape-free. Rape does occur, but at such a low rate—28 per 3 million in 1981-82 for example—as to be virtually nonexistent (Sanday 1986, 85; also see Sanday, 1990 and Lepowsky). In light of such research, men, rather than women, are the ones who would need to change their behavior. This is because it is the socialization of men by men in their bonding-groups, and the view of women that is engendered, that provides the strongest cues toward rape. Since there may indeed be something that males could and should be doing differently that would affect the prevalence of rape, it does not seem unreasonable to continue to investigate the claim that men are collectively responsible for the prevalence of rape.

III. The Rapist as Victim of Society

It is also possible to acknowledge that men are responsible for the prevalence of rape in our society but nonetheless to argue that women are equally responsible. Rape is often portrayed as a sex crime perpetrated largely by men against women. But importantly, rape is also a crime of violence, and many factors in our society have increased the prevalence of violence. This prevalence of violence is the cause of both rape and war in western societies. Our view, that violence of both sorts is increased in likelihood by patterns of male socialization which then creates collective male responsibility, may be countered by pointing out that socialization patterns are created by both men and women, thereby seemingly implicating both men and women in collective responsibility for rape and war.

Sam Keen has contended that it is violence that we should be focusing on rather than sex or gender, in order to understand the causes and remedies for the prevalence of rape. According to Keen,

> Men are violent because of the systematic violence done to their bodies and spirits. Being hurt they become hurters. In the overall picture, male violence toward women is far less than male violence toward other males ... these outrages are a structural part of a warfare system that victimizes both men and women. (Keen 1991, 47)

Keen sees both men and women conspiring together to perpetuate this system of violence, especially in the way they impart to their male children an acceptance of violence.

Women are singled out by Keen as those who have not come to terms with their share of responsibility for our violent culture. And men have been so guilt-tripped on the issue of rape that they have become desensitized to it. Keen thinks that it is a mistake to single out men, and not women also, as responsible for rape.

> Until women are willing to weep for and accept equal responsibility for the systematic violence done to the male body and spirit by the war system, it is not likely that men will lose enough of their guilt and regain enough of their sensitivity to accept responsibility for women who are raped. (Keen 1191, 47)

Even though women are equally responsible for the rape culture, in Keen's view, women should be singled out because they have not previously accepted their share of responsibility for the creation of a violent society.

Keen is at least partially right insofar as he insists that issues of rape and war be understood as arising from the same source, namely the socialization of men to be violent in western cultures. We agree with Keen that rape is part of a larger set of violent practices that injure both men and women. He is right to point out that men are murdering other men in our society in increasing numbers, and that this incidence of violence probably has something to do with the society's general condoning, even celebrating, of violence, especially in war.

Keen fails to note though that it is men, not women, who are the vast majority of both rapists and murderers in our society. And even if some women do act in ways which trigger violent reactions in men, nevertheless, in our opinion this pales in comparison with the way that men socialize each other to be open to violence. As Tiger and others have suggested, aggressive violence results primarily from male-bonding experiences. In any event, both fathers and mothers engage in early childhood socialization. Men influence the rape culture both through early childhood socialization and through male-bonding socialization of older male children. But women only contribute to this culture, when they do, through individual acts of early childhood socialization. For this reason Keen is surely wrong to think that women share responsibility *equally* with men for our rape culture.

In our view, some women could prevent some rapes; and some women do contribute to the patterns of socialization of both men and women that increase the incidence of rape. For these reasons, it would not be inappropriate to say that women share responsibility for rape as well as men. But we believe that it is a mistake to think that women share equally in this responsibility with men. For one thing, women are different from men in that they are, in general, made worse off by the prevalence of rape in our society. As we will next see, there is a sense in which men, but not women, benefit from the prevalence of rape, and this fact means that men have more of a stake in the rape culture, and hence have more to gain by its continued existence.

In general, our conclusion is that women share responsibility, but to a far lesser extent than men, for the prevalence of rape. We do not support those who try to "blame the victim" by holding women responsible for rape because of not taking adequate precautions, or dressing seductively, etc. Instead, the key for us is the role that women, as mothers, friends and lovers, play in the overall process of male socialization that creates the rape culture. It should come as no surprise that few members of western society can be relieved of responsibility for this rape culture given the overwhelming pervasiveness of that culture. But such considerations should not deter us from looking to men, first and foremost, as being collectively responsible for the prevalence of rape. The women who do contribute to aggressive male-socialization do so as individuals; women have no involvement parallel to the male-bonding group.

IV. The Rapist as Group Member

Popular literature tends to portray the rapist as a demonic character, as the "Other." What we find interesting about the research of Thornhill and Thornhill is that it operates unwittingly to support the feminist slogan that "all men are rapists," that the rapist is not male "Other" but male "Self." What is so unsettling about the tens of thousands of rapes in Bosnia is the suggestion that what ordinary men have been doing is not significantly different from what the "sex-fiends" did. The thesis that men are adapted to be predisposed to be rapists, regardless of what else we think of the thesis, should give us pause and make us less rather than more likely to reject the feminist slogan. From this vantage point, the work of Tiger as well as Thornhill and Thornhill sets the stage for a serious reconsideration of the view that men are collectively responsible for rape.

There are two things that might be meant by saying that men are collectively reponsible for the prevalence of rape in western culture. First, seeing men as collectively responsible may mean that men as a group are responsible in that they form some sort of super-entity that causes, or at least supports, the prevalence of rape. When some feminists talk of "patriarchy," what they seem to mean is a kind of institution that operates through, but also behind the backs of, individual men to oppress women. Here it may be that men are collectively responsible for the prevalence of rape and yet no men are individually responsible. We call this nondistributive collective responsibility. Second, seeing men as collectively responsible may mean that men form a group in which there are so many features that the members share in common, such as attitudes or dispositions to engage in harm, that what holds true for one man also holds true for all other men. Because of the common features of the members of the group men, when one man is responsible for a particular harm, other men are implicated. Each member of the group has a share in the responsibility for a harm such as rape. We call this distributive collective responsibility (see May 1992, Ch. 2). In what follows we will criticize the first way of understanding men's collective responsibility, and offer reasons to support the second.

When collective responsibility is understood in the first (nondistributive) sense, this form of responsibility is assigned to those groups that have the capacity to act. Here there are two paradigmatic examples: the corporation and the mob (see May 1992. Chs. 2 and 4). The corporation has the kind of organizational structure that allows for the group to form intentions and carry out those intentions, almost as if the corporation were itself a person. Since men, qua men, are too amorphous a group to be able to act in an organized fashion, we will not be interested in whether they are collectively responsible in this way. But it may be that men can act in the way that mobs act, that is, not through a highly organized structure but through something such as like-mindedness. If there is enough commonality of belief, disposition and interest of all men, or at least all men within a particular culture, then the group may be able to act just as a mob is able to respond to a commonly perceived enemy.

It is possible to think of patriarchy as the oppressive practices of men coordinated by the common interests of men, but not organized intentionally. It is also productive to think of rape as resulting from patriarchy. For if there is a "collective" that is supporting or creating the prevalence of rape it is not a highly organized one, since there is nothing like a corporation that intentionally plans the rape of women in western culture. If the current Serbian army has engaged in the systematic and organized rape of Muslim women as a strategy of war, then this would be an example of nondistributive responsibility for rape. But the kind of oppression characterized by the prevalence of rape in most cultures appears to be systematic but not organized. How does this affect our understanding of whether men are collectively responsible for rape?

If patriarchy is understood merely as a system of coordination that operates behind the backs of individual men, then it may be that no single man is responsible for any harms that are caused by patriarchy. But if patriarchy is understood as something which is based on common interests, as well as common benefits, extended to all or most men in a particular culture, then it may be that men are collectively responsible for the harms of patriarchy in a way which distributes out to all men, making each man in a particular culture at least partially responsible for the harms attributable to patriarchy. This latter strategy is consistent with our own view of men's responsibility for rape. In the remainder of this essay we will offer support for this conceptualization of the collective responsibility of men for the prevalence of rape.

Our positive assessment, going beyond our criticism of the faulty responses in earlier sections of our paper, is that men in western culture are collectively responsible in the distributive sense, that is, they each share responsibility, for the prevalence of rape in that culture. This claim rests on five points: (1) Insofar as most perpetrators of rape are men, then these men are responsible, in most cases, for the rapes they committed. (2) Insofar as some men, by the way they interact with other (especially younger) men, contribute to a climate in our society where rape is made more prevalent, then they are collaborators in the rape culture and for this reason share in responsibility for rapes committed in that culture. (3) Also, insofar as some men are not unlike the rapist, since they would be rapists if they had the opportunity to be placed into a situation where their inhibitions against rape were removed, then these men share responsibility with actual rapists for the harms of rape. (4) In addition, insofar as many other men could have prevented fellow men from raping, but did not act to prevent these actual rapes, then these men also share responsibility along with the rapists. (5) Finally, insofar as some men benefit from the existence of rape in our society, these men also share responsibility along with the rapists.

It seems to us unlikely that many, if any, men in our society fail to fit into one or another of these categories. Hence, we think that it is not unreasonable to say that men in our society are collectively responsible (in the distributive sense) for rape. We expect some male readers to respond as follows:

> I am adamantly opposed to rape, and though when I was younger I might have tolerated rape-conducive comments from friends of mine, I don't now, so I'm not a collaborator in the rape culture. And I would never be a rapist whatever the situation, and I would certainly act to prevent any rape that I could. I'm pretty sure I don't benefit from rape. So how can I be responsible for the prevalence of rape?

In reply we would point out that nearly all men in a given western society meet the third and fifth conditions above (concerning similarity and benefit). But women generally fail to meet either of these conditions, or the first. So, the involvement of women in the rape culture is much less than is true for men. In what follows we will concentrate on these similarity and benefit issues.

In our discussion above, we questioned the view that rapists are "other." Diane Scully, in her study of convicted rapists, turns the view around, suggesting that it is women who are "other." She argues that rapists in America are not pathological, but instead

> that men who rape have something to tell us about the cultural roots of sexual violence.... They tell us that some men use rape as a means of revenge and punishment. Implicit in revenge rape is the collective liability of women. In some cases, victims are substitutes for significant women on whom men desire to take revenge. In other cases, victims represent all women.... In either case, women are seen as objects, a category, but not as individuals with rights. For some men, rape is an afterthought or bonus they add to burglary or robbery. In other words, rape is "no big deal".... Some men rape in groups as a male bonding activity—for them it's just something to do.... Convicted rapists tell us that in this culture, sexual violence is rewarding ... these men perceived rape as a rewarding, low-risk act. (Scully 1990, 162-63)

It is the prevalent perception of women as "other" by men in our culture that fuels the prevalence of rape in American society.

Turning to the issue of benefit, we believe that Lionel Tiger's work illustrates the important source of strength that men derive from the all-male groups they form. There is a strong sense in which men benefit from the all-male groups that they form in our culture. What is distinctly lacking is any sense that men have responsibility for the social conditions, especially the socialization of younger men which diminishes inhibitions toward rape, that are created in those groups. Male bonding is made easier because there is an "Other" that males can bond "against." And this other is the highly sexualized stereotype of the "female." Here is a benefit for men in these groups—but there is a social cost: from the evidence we have examined there is an increased prevalence of rape. Men need to consider this in reviewing their own role in a culture that supports so much rape.

There is another sense in which benefit is related to the issue of responsibility for rape. There is a sense in which many men in our society benefit from the prevalence of rape in ways many of us are quite unaware. Consider this example:

> Several years ago, at a social occasion in which male and female professors were present, I asked off-handedly whether people agreed with me that the campus was looking especially pretty at night these days. Many of the men responded positively. But all of the women responded that this was not something that they had even thought about, since they were normally too anxious about being on campus at night, especially given the increase in reported rapes recently.[3]

We men benefitted in that, relative to our female colleagues, we were in an advantageous position vis á vis travel around campus. And there were surely other comparative benefits that befell us as a result of this advantage concerning travel, such as our ability to gain academically by being able to use the library at any hour we chose.

In a larger sense, men benefit from the prevalence of rape in that many women are made to feel dependent on men for protection against potential rapists. It is hard to overestimate the benefit here for it potentially affects all aspects of one's life. One study found that 87% of women in a borough of London felt that they had to take precautions against potential rapists, with a large number reporting that they never went out at night alone (Radford 1987, 33). Whenever one group is made to feel dependent on another group, and this dependency is not reciprocal, then there is a strong comparative benefit to the group that is not in the dependent position. Such a benefit, along with the specific benefits mentioned above, support the view that men as a group have a stake in perpetuating the rape culture in ways that women do not. And just as the benefit to men distributes throughout the male population in a given society, so the responsibility should distribute as well.

V. Conclusions

When people respond to conflict with violence, they coerce one another and thereby fail to treat one another with respect as fellow autonomous beings. Rape and murder, especially in war, victimize members of various groups simply because they are group members. These two factors combine to create a form of dehumanization that can warrant the charge of being a crime against humanity. What makes an act of violence more than just a private individual act in wartime is that killing and rape are perpetrated not against the individual for his or her unique characteristics, but solely because the individual instantiates a group characteristic, for example, being Jewish, or Muslim, or being a woman. Such identification fails to respect what is unique about each of us.

Our point is not that all men everywhere are responsible for the prevalence of rape. Rather, we have been arguing that in western societies, rape is deeply embedded in a wider culture of male socialization. Those who have the most to do with sustaining that culture must also recognize that they are responsible for the harmful aspects of that culture (see Porter 1986, 222-23). And when rape is conjoined with war, especially as an organized strategy, then there is a sense that men are collectively responsible for the rapes that occur in that war,[4] just as groups of people are held responsible for the crimes of genocide, where the victims are persecuted simply because they fall into a certain category of low-risk people who are ripe for assault.

Rape, especially in times of war, is an act of violence perpetrated against a person merely for being an instantiation of a type. Insofar as rape in times of war is a systematically organized form of terror, it is not inappropriate to call rape a war crime, a crime against humanity. Insofar as rape in times of peace is also part of a pattern of terror against women to the collective benefit of men, then rape in times of peace is also a crime against humanity (see Card 1991). Rape, in war or in peace, is rarely a personal act of aggression by one person toward another person. It is an act of hostility and a complete failure to show basic human respect (see Shafer and Frye 1977). And more than this, rape is made more likely by the collective actions, or inactions, of men in a particular society. Insofar as men in a particular society contribute to the prevalence of rape, they participate in a crime against humanity for which they are collectively responsible.

The feminist slogan "all men are rapists" seems much stronger than the claim "all men contribute to the prevalence of rape." Is the feminist slogan merely hyperbole? It is if what is meant is that each time a rape occurs, every man did it, or that only men are ever responsible for rape. But, as we have seen, each time a rape occurs, there is a sense in which many men could have done it, or made it less likely to have occurred, or benefitted from it. By direct contribution, or by negligence or by similarity of disposition, or by benefitting, most if not all men do share in each rape in a particular society. This is the link between being responsible for the prevalence of rape and being responsible, at least to some extent, for the harms of each rape.

The purpose of these arguments has been to make men aware of the various ways that they are implicated in the rape culture in general as well as in particular rapes. And while we believe that men should feel some shame for their group's complicity in the prevalence of rape, our aim is not to shame men but rather to stimulate men to take responsibility for re-socializing themselves and their fellow men. How much should any particular man do? Answering this question would require another paper, although participating in the Canadian White Ribbon Campaign, or in anti-sexism education programs, would be a good first step.[5] Suffice it to say that the status quo, namely doing nothing, individually or as a group, is not satisfactory, and will merely further compound our collective and shared responsibility for the harms caused by our fellow male members who engage in rape.[6]

NOTES

1. This paragraph is based on Larry May's experiences growing up in an upper middle class suburban U.S. society. While our experiences differ somewhat in this respect, these experiences are so common that we have referred to them in the first person plural.
2. There is a fifth response, namely, that women alone are somehow responsible for being raped. This response will be largely ignored in our essay since we regard it as merely another case of "blaming the victim." See Scully (1990) for a critical discussion of this response. Undoubtedly there are yet other responses. We have tried to focus our attention on the most common responses we have seen in the literature on rape.
3. In his fascinating study of the climate of rape in American culture, Timothy Beneke also reports as one of his conclusions that the fear of rape at night "inhibits the freedom of the eye, hurts women economically, undercuts women's independence, destroys solitude, and restricts expressiveness." Such curtailments of freedom, he argues, "must be acknowledged as part of the crime" (Beneke 1982, 170).
4. The European community's preliminary investigation into the reports of widespread Bosnian rapes of Muslim women by Serbian soldiers concluded that "Rape is part of a pattern of abuse, usually perpetrated with the conscious intention of demoralizing and terrorizing communities, driving them from their homes and demonstrating the power of the invading forces. Viewed in this way, rape cannot be seen as incidental to the main purpose of the aggression but as serving a strategic purpose in itself" (*St. Louis Post-Dispatch*, January 9, 1993, 8A).
5. We would also recommend recent essays by philosophers who are trying to come to terms with their masculinity. See our essay on friendship as well as the essay by Hugh LaFollette in our anthology *Rethinking Masculinity* (1992).
6. We would like to thank Virginia Ingram, Jason Clevenger, Victoria Davion, Karen Warren, Duane Cady and Marilyn Friedman for providing us with critical comments on earlier drafts of this paper.

REFERENCES

Beneke, Timothy. 1982. *Men on rape.* New York: St. Martin's Press.

Brownmiller, Susan. 1993. Making female bodies the battlefield. *Newsweek* (January 4):37.

Card, Claudia. 1991. Rape as a terrorist institution. In *Violence, terrorism, and justice*, ed. R. G. Frey and Christopher Morris. New York: Cambridge University Press.

Griffin, Susan. 1971. Rape: The all-american crime. *Ramparts* (September) 26-35. Reprinted in *Women and values: Readings in feminist philosophy*, ed. Marilyn Pearsall. Belmont, CA: Wadsworth, 1986.

Keen, Sam. 1991. *Fire in the belly.* New York: Bantam Books.

LaFollette, Hugh. 1992. Real men. In *Rethinking masculinity*, ed. Larry May and Robert Strikwerda. Lanham, MD: Rowman & Littlefield.

Lepowsky, Maria. 1990. Gender in an egalitarian society. In *Beyond the second sex*, ed. Peggy Reeves Sanday and Ruth Gallagher Goodenough. Philadelphia: University of Pennsylvania Press.

Lipsyte, Robert. 1993. An ethics trial: Must boys always be boys? *The New York Times* (March 12): B-11.

MacKinnon, Catharine A. 1993. Turning rape into pornography: Postmodern genocide. *Ms.* (July/ August): 24-30.

May, Larry. 1987. *The morality of groups.* Notre Dame, IN: University of Notre Dame Press.

— . 1992. *Sharing responsibility.* Chicago: University of Chicago Press.

Oates, Joyce Carol. 1992. Rape and the boxing ring. *Newsweek* (February 24): 60-61.

Peterson, Susan Rae. 1977. Coercion and rape: The state as a male protection racket. In *Feminism and philosophy*, ed. Mary Vetterling-Braggin, Frederick Elliston, and Jane English. Totowa, NJ: Littlefield, Adams: 360-371.

Porter, Roy. 1986. Does rape have a historical meaning: In *Rape: An historical and social enquiry*, ed. Sylvana Tomaselli and Roy Porter. Oxford: Basil Blackwell.

Post, Tony et al. 1993. A pattern of rape. *Newsweek.* (January 4): 32-36.

Radford, Jill. 1987. Policing male violence, policing women. In *Women, violence and social control*, ed. Jalna Hanmer and Mary Maynard. Atlantic Highlands, NJ: Humanities Press.

Sanday, Peggy Reeves. 1986. Rape and the silencing of the feminine. In *Rape: An historical and social enquiry*, ed. Sylvana Tomaselli and Roy Porter. Oxford: Basil Blackwell.

— . 1990. Androcentric and matrifocal gender representation in minangkabau ideology. In *Beyond the second sex*, ed. Peggy Reeves Sanday and Ruth Gallagher Goodenough. Philadelphia: University of Pennsylvania Press.

Scully, Diana. 1990. *Understanding sexual violence.* Boston: Unwin Hyman.

Shafer, Carolyn M. And Marilyn Frye. 1977. Rape and respect. In *Feminism and philosophy*, ed. Mary Vetterling-Braggin. Frederick Elliston, and Jane English. Totowa, NJ: Littlefield Adams.

Strikwerda, Robert, and Larry May. 1992. Male friendship and intimacy. *Hypatia* 7(3): 110-25. Reprinted in *Rethinking masculinity*, ed. Larry May and Robert Strikwerda, Lanham, MD: Rowman & Littlefield.

Thornhill, Randy, and Nancy Wilmsen Thornhill. 1992. The evolutionary psychology of men's coercive sexuality. *Behavioral and Brain Sciences* 15: 363-75.

Tiger, Lionel. [1969] 1984. *Men in groups* 2nd ed. New York: Marion Boyars Publishers.

THE LAWS OF WAR AND WOMEN'S HUMAN RIGHTS

Liz Philipose

Liz Philipose teaches in the Atlantic Human Rights Centre, St. Thomas University, Fredericton, New Brunswick.

This is a review of historical developments in international criminal law leading up to the inclusion of rape as a "crime against humanity" in the current war crimes tribunal for the ex-Yugoslavia. In addition to the need to understand the specificity of events and their impact on women, the laws of war must also be understood in their specificity and the ways in which even the humanitarian provisions of those laws privilege military needs.

The recent establishment of war crimes tribunals has renewed interest in the laws of war and their effectiveness as a mechanism of humanitarian intervention, international peace and justice, and enforcer of human rights. Concurrent with the celebration of the Gulf War as a watershed event in this apparent new era of cooperation is a celebration of the return to legalism and the potential fulfillment of the original "peace and security" mandate of the United Nations (UN).[1] In international relations terms, because law is characterized in opposition to power politics, a return to legalism is at the same time seen to be a decline in the efficacy of violent conflict for the achievement of state interests. Boutros-Ghali has called the current period "a Grotian moment—one in which a renaissance of international law is needed ... in the process of building a new international system" (Boutros-Ghali 1995, 1609). He names the Security Council decision to establish *ad hoc* international criminal courts as a "monumental advance" on the road to "the democratization of international relations," breaking "new ground in international criminal law" and allowing the UN to achieve long-standing goals in the application of humanitarian law (Boutros-Ghali 1995, 1, 613). In the context of "new world ordering," the establishment of international tribunals to charge individuals for war crimes is seen to be multiply significant for the eventual consolidation of peace: marking a decline in the hegemony of realism in international relations theory and practice; the triumph of law and organizations, of liberal institutionalism, and idealist aspirations; a statement of international justice and morality; and a (re)new(ed) consensus about the acceptability of unjust wars and unjust acts in war.

Of interest to me is the inclusion of rape as a crime against humanity in the Statute of the International Criminal Tribunal for the Former Yugoslavia (ICTY),[2] which has been hailed as a timely and gender-sensitive response to acts of sexual violence committed against women in the course of armed conflict. While there is much evidence that women have been raped in many previous armed conflicts, the mass and systematic rapes in the former Yugoslavia have been widely publicized as particularly brutal and calculated acts. Theodor Meron argues that the widespread publicity has contributed to galvanizing an international commitment to prosecute individuals for the crime of rape (Meron 1993, 424).[3] Cynthia Enloe emphasizes the influence of women's organizations in bringing the tribunal to fruition by documenting the rapes in Bosnia, by providing analyses of warfare and its relationship to particular ideas about masculinity, and by arguing for human rights protection which include women

---

Reprinted with permission of the publisher and Liz Philipose from *Hypatia* 11:4 (Fall 1996): 46–62.

(Enloe 1994, 219). While commentators remain skeptical in some instances about the efficacy of this current tribunal, the general response has been laudatory, focusing on the potential to concretize international recognition of "women's rights as human rights" and the realization of "gender justice" (see Pratt and Fletcher 1994; Copelon 1994; MacKinnon 1994a and 1994b). Gender justice in this instance refers to the explicit acknowledgment, through criminal prosecutions, of what feminists have long argued—that women are targeted in gender-specific ways in the conduct of armed conflict (Copelon 1994). The suggestion that women's human rights and gender justice might be realized by this tribunal depends on two assumptions: that including women in the laws of war is equivalent to gender-specificity and perhaps more importantly, that the laws of war are continuous with human rights law.

My analysis suggests that the prohibition of rape by the ICTY is a prohibition only to the extent that rape is used in the service of ethnic cleansing, and as such is not a generalizable condemnation of the use of rape as a weapon of war. Further, the laws of war, while increasingly intertwined with human rights law, still remain tied to the fact of armed conflict, a context where military needs, not humanitarian concerns, are the priority. As presently constituted, the laws of war are not the appropriate mechanisms for the realization of human rights protection because the laws of war are only meaningful in a context of already sanctioned violence and legitimate human rights violations. In other words, the laws of war remain on the discursive terrain of war, necessarily sanctioning a certain level of violence and taking for granted realist and strategic assumptions about the world.[4] Presumably this is contrary to the intent of human rights norms and legislation which aim to prevent the abuse of individuals' fundamental rights to be free from violence, regardless of context, whether in war or peace.

This suggests that in remaining on the discursive terrain of war, the laws of war prohibit certain acts at the same time that they legitimate others, and that in fact, the laws of war, developed according to the dictates of military necessity, make war itself possible and legitimate. In this way, states' rights to wage war, a foundational principle of the realist state, is never challenged by international law, and is in fact concretized every time a war crime or war criminal is named.

I develop this analysis by considering the extent to which humanitarian law departs from human rights law with particular attention to the category "crimes against humanity," and feminist arguments for the recognition of women's human rights through the application of humanitarian law in the current war crimes tribunal. This analysis raises a further question as to the conditions which have invested the laws of war with the task of protecting people from the ravages of war. Starting with gender, this analysis raises doubts about the new world order return to legalism as a peacemaking measure and the efficacy of the laws of war in protecting civilians from wartime violence and abuse. Understanding the parameters of the current war crimes tribunal and the implications of naming rape as a crime against humanity is a first step towards understanding what can be expected for women's human rights and gender justice through the application of humanitarian law.

The International Criminal Tribunal for the Former Yugoslavia

A series of Security Council resolutions aimed at addressing "serious violations of international humanitarian law in the territory of the former Yugoslavia" preceded the decision to establish an international tribunal. With Resolution 771 (1992), the Security Council "expressed grave alarm" at the reports of widespread violations of international humanitarian law, especially within Bosnia and Herzegovina (UN 1993c, 3). The Security Council condemned the practices of, among others, mass forcible expulsion and deportation of civilians, imprisonment and abuse of civilians, deliberate attacks on noncombatants and wanton devastation of property, including the practice of ethnic cleansing, and demanded that parties to the conflict "cease and desist" (UN 1993c, 3). By February 1993, rape was included in the list of "grave breaches and other violations of international humanitarian law," along with willful killing, ethnic cleansing, torture and pillage (UN 1993c, 4). Resolution 808 (1993) was the decision to establish an international tribunal to "contribute to the restoration and maintenance of peace," and to put an end to the "mass killings and the continuation of the practice of 'ethnic cleansing'"(UN 1993c, 4).

The Statute of the ICTY, as recommended by the Report of the Secretary-General, was adopted without revisions by the Security council on May 25, 1993 (UN 1993b, 393). The Statute outlines the competence of the tribunal in Article 1:

> The International Tribunal shall have the power to prosecute persons responsible for serious violations of international humanitarian law committed in the territory of the former Yugoslavia since 1991 in accordance with provisions of the present Statute. (UN 1993b, 393)

Drawing on the Geneva Conventions of 1949, Additional Protocols I and II, the Nuremberg principles,[5] the Genocide Convention of 1948, and the Hague Convention of 1907, the Statute outlines the categories of prohibited acts over which the ICTY has jurisdiction. Article 2—"grave breaches of the Geneva Conventions of 1949"- includes willful killing, torture or inhuman treatment, willfully causing great suffering or serious injury to body or health, the unlawful deportation or transfer or unlawful confinement of a civilian, or taking civilians as hostages. Article 3 lists the "laws of war" provisions, which are largely concerned with the use of prohibited weapons and the wanton destruction of cities, towns, and public or private property, not warranted by military needs. Article 4 draws on the Genocide Convention, and grants the ICTY the power to prosecute persons committing genocide, which is defined as "acts committed with intent to destroy, in whole or in part, a national, ethnical, racial or religious group" (UN 1993b, 394).

Article 5, outlining crimes against humanity is the only provision of the Statute which explicitly names rape. The article states that the ICTY "shall have the power to prosecute persons for the following crimes when committed in armed conflict, whether international or internal in character, and directed against any civilian population" (UN 1993b, 395). In addition to naming rape as a crime against humanity, Article 5 lists murder, extermination, enslavement, deportation, imprisonment, torture, persecutions (on political, racial and religious grounds), and "other inhumane acts" (UN 1993b, 395). The Report of the Secretary-General refers to the Nuremberg principles as well as Control Council Law No. 10[6] as legal bases for this provision, and further defines crimes against humanity as inhuman acts "committed as part of a widespread or systematic attack against any civilian population on national, political, ethnic, racial or religious grounds" (UN 1993c, 13). As well, the Secretary General reports that in this conflict, "such inhuman acts have taken the form of so-called 'ethnic cleansing' and widespread and systematic rape and other forms of sexual assault, including enforced prostitution" (UN 1993c, 13).

Some arguments suggest that because the "grave breaches" provision is a nonexhaustive list, that rape could be interpreted as a grave breach, and thus a violation of rights considered to be nonderogable (Pratt and Fletcher 1994; Copelon 1994). While a number of the ICTY indictments have charged rape as a grave breach and thus a violation of nonderogable rights, this is an issue which will only be decided as prosecutions proceed.[7] For the moment, this paper is limited to a discussion of the implications of prosecuting rape as a crime against humanity as defined by this tribunal, for the advancement of women's human rights.

Women's Rights as Human Rights

Feminist scholars and activists have argued for some time that violence against women is pervasive and present in a wide range of contexts. Transcending boundaries of public and private, home and neighborhood, rich and poor, North and South, war and (so-called) peace, it is argued that violence against women is evidence of universal discrimination and misogyny, manifested in particular ways in particular contexts. Part of the analysis of violence against women focuses on the ways in which women are targeted specifically because they are women. As Catharine MacKinnon states, "women are violated in many ways in which men are violated. But women are also violated in ways men are not" (MacKinnon 1994b, 184).

The ways in which women are uniquely subject to violence form the core concerns of feminist scholars and activists. Joan Fitzpatrick's overview of international norms protecting women from violence outlines seven areas of violence against women included in the Convention of the Elimination of All Forms of Discrimination against Women (CEDAW) ratified by the General Assembly in September 1981. These areas are domestic violence; genital mutilation or traditional practices; police and security forces violence, including torture; violence against women during armed conflict; women refugees and asylum seekers; prostitution and pornography; and violence in the workplace. Under the general category of violence against women, these areas have been specified in existing treaties, intergovernmental resolutions, human rights and humanitarian law, and have been official subjects of debate amongst international organizations for some time. Fitzpatrick states that international recognition of abuses against women in these circumstances already exists as legitimate topics of concern. While valid, however, they have yet to become effective, and for Fitzpatrick, the implementation of existing norms ought to be the proper focus for women's rights activists (Fitzpatrick 1995).

Campaigns against violence against women are often expressed in liberal human rights terms, as violence against women contravenes women's human rights and the struggles are struggles for the national or international recognition of women's human rights. The slogan "women's rights *are* human rights," popularized by nongovernmental organizations during the 1993 Vienna World Conference on Human Rights, captures the criticism that internationally "'women's rights' and women's lives have been deemed secondary to the 'human rights' and lives of men," and "make(s) clear that widespread gender-based discrimination and abuse of women is a devastating reality as urgently in need of redress as other human rights violations" (Bunch and Rielly 1994, 3-4). To date, the application of human rights instruments have not included women. "What is done to women is either too specific to women to be seen as human or too generic to human beings to be seen as specific to women" (MacKinnon 1994b, 184). For this reason, international initiatives which specifically focus on the rights of women, such as CEDAW, are seen to be welcome advances for the cause of women's human rights. More significant, however, are those occasions when international laws and norms are enforced and applied.

A central concern of international organizations literature is with the possible enforcement of existing international laws and norms. Given the decentralized structure of the international system coupled with the right of states to be self-determining, enforcing international laws has proven to be a difficult and often untenable endeavor. To a large extent, one reason why the ICTY is celebrated by international relations commentators is because it is one of the rare occasions that the existing laws of war will be enforced through legitimate international mechanisms.[8] For feminist scholars, the ICTY is one of the only mechanisms to potentially enforce those laws of war which specifically protect women from rape and sexual assault in the course of war.

Feminist appraisals of the ICTY have focused on its potential to acknowledge the gender-specificity of particular violence as well as to enforce humanitarian protection for women's human rights.[9] Precedents exist in humanitarian law for the tribunal to concretize protection of women in armed conflict. Along with Fitzpatrick, many others have documented existing precedents in the laws of war, demonstrating that as presently constituted they already prohibit attacks on women's honor, dignity, and physical integrity in the course of armed conflict (see Pratt and Fletcher 1994; Khushalani 1982; Copelon 1994). According to the laws of war, including the Geneva Convention 1949 and the Additional Protocols, women are to be "especially protected" (along with children and the elderly) from inhumane treatment.[10] As such, precedents exist for the current tribunal to acknowledge that

> rape and gender-based violence contravene fundamental principles of humanitarian law and violate the most basic, non-derogable human rights guaranteed in times of conflict or peace—... the right to dignity, the right to bodily integrity and the right to be free form torture or other cruel, inhuman, or degrading treatment. (Pratt and Fletcher 1994, 78)

Because the ICTY draws on existing legislation for the protection of women, it is not initiating changes in the laws of war nor is it the first time that women have been "especially protected." What is new, however, is that the ICTY represents the first occasion that there appears to be an international commitment to charge individuals for the act of rape in war. In doing so, there appears to be a commitment to criminalize what is too often tolerated as an unfortunate but inevitable by-product of war. Arguments in favor of prosecutions for rape under humanitarian law state that the tribunal offers the historic opportunity for the explicit international acknowledgment that women's rights are human rights (MacKinnon 1994b, 195).

Because women's human rights activists have drawn connections between particular manifestations of gender-based violence, they too quickly assume that prohibitions against violence against women through the laws of war *will* constitute a recognition of women's human rights. My dispute is not with the claim that violence against women is a systematic and pervasive phenomenon that violates the rights of women; rather, the issue I am raising is the need to understand the context of armed conflict as it is defined, constrained, and constituted by the laws of war. Put another way, in addition to the need to understand the specificity of particular events and their impact on particular women, the laws of war must be understood in their specificity as well, in the ways in which even the humanitarian provision of the laws of war privilege military needs. What needs to be considered is whether there is a necessary convergence between humanitarian and human rights law. More precisely, what needs to be evaluated is the relationship between these two bodies of law as expressed by the current tribunal towards understanding the implications of rape as a crime against humanity.

Human Rights and Humanitarian Law

"Humanitarian law" is a relatively new term, coined in the 1950s by the International Committee of the Red Cross to distinguish the provisions of the Geneva Convention from broader laws of war (Schindler 1982, 935). Sometimes called the human rights provision of the laws of war, humanitarian law aims to ameliorate the adverse conditions of war for civilians and combatants, as well as to limit the level of destruction aimed at property, cities, and weapons (Montealegre 1982, 969). Historically, human rights law developed separately from the laws of war, differing significantly in terms of substance and jurisdiction. Human rights were seen to be essentially domestic matters, prohibiting the state from abusing its citizens, while the laws of war aimed to regulate war and to prevent abuse of enemy combatants and civilians which exceeded the needs of war (Schindler 1982, 936).

Since the Nuremberg Tribunal, debates have focused on the extent to which human rights law and the laws of war have converged, and there is some agreement that humanitarian and human rights law are increasingly intertwined, at least substantively. Disagreements about the convergence of these two bodies of law usually focus on jurisdiction, although jurisdiction is arguably becoming less relevant, as the gaps between combatant and noncombatant, international and internal conflicts, and state boundaries are challenged (see Schindler 1982; Bettauer 1982; Kennedy and Andreopoulos 1995; Khushalani 1982, 1-71; Howard 1995). One distinction that remains relevant is that humanitarian law is only applicable to acts committed in the context of war, whereas human rights law is applicable in war and peace. While humanitarian law applies to discrete, extreme, and unique circumstances of armed conflict, human rights law applies to both public emergencies and everyday circumstances. This means that human rights documents

> *speak in terms of absolute prohibitions on certain government actions against people*, while the law of war is premised on the existence of a belligerent situation in which high levels of violence will be directed by governments and their agents against people .... The question in the law of war, more often than not, is *what level of violence is reasonably necessary and proportional in the context*. (Reisman and Antoniou 1994, xxi; my emphasis)

To make the case that the tribunal is making a statement of women's human rights, rape as a crime against humanity must be understood as an expression of *absolute prohibitions* against the public act of rape.[11] This means that the rape of women must be condemned by this tribunal as acts which exceed a reasonably necessary and proportional level of violence in *all* circumstances of armed conflict. Although historical precedents exist for both the prosecution of rape and crimes against humanity as violations of basic human rights, Security Council has limited the crimes against humanity provision, and therefore rape, to particular acts committed in the conduct of this particular illegitimate war. The implications are that the ICTY is not a confirmation of absolute prohibitions against the act of rape in war, and is thus not a statement of women's human rights.

Crimes Against Humanity

The category of crimes against humanity, established by the London Charter of August 8, 1945 and prosecuted by the Nuremberg Tribunal[12], is the first codified convergence between human rights and the laws of war. In Egon Schwelb's words, by creating the category crimes against humanity, "the acknowledgment of fundamental human rights has taken place" (Schwelb 1947, 103). "Crimes against humanity" was designed to include those acts which did not come under the categories of "war crimes" or "crimes against peace," although there was significant overlap between the three categories (Schwelb 1946, 179-80). Article 6 of the Charter of the Nuremberg Tribunal specifies crimes against humanity as

> murder, extermination, enslavement, deportation, and other inhumane acts committed against any civilian population, before or during the war; or persecutions on political, racial, or religious grounds in execution of or in connection with any crime within the jurisdiction of the Tribunal, whether or not in violation of the domestic law of the country where perpetrated. (Schwelb 1946, 178)

The phrases "before or during the war" and "against any civilian populations" appeared to be "startling and controversial changes" in international law, meaning that crimes against humanity were prohibited in war and peace and included acts committed against citizens by their own states (Schwelb 1946, 178-79). In this way, it was argued that crimes against humanity bridged the gap between the laws of war and human rights law. However, the phrase "in connection with any crime within the jurisdiction of the Tribunal," noted by Schwelb, served to limit the meaning of crimes against humanity as acts committed as "a kind of by-product of war applicable only in time of war or in connection with war" (Schwelb 1946, 206).

In the first formulation then, crimes against humanity were not characterized as acts independent from the fact of war, but elements that contributed to the German and Japanese acts of waging aggressive war. In order for crimes against humanity to be a human rights law, it must be characterized as an offense independent from the context of war. Seen to be an "'accompanying' or an 'accessory' crime" (Schwelb 1946, 207), and "ancillary or subsidiary" crimes (Lauterpacht 1947, 102), the potential for crimes against humanity to be a law of human rights—transcending the boundary of war and peace—was denied. Limiting the jurisdiction and substance of crimes against humanity was deliberate and calculated and reflected the extent to which humanitarianism was a priority. This is evident from the statement made in 1948 by Lord Wright, chairman of the UN War Crimes Commission:

> The war just ended is what has been called the totalitarian war and has the peculiar feature that it was ushered in by the most brutal and blatant announcements, *not only that it aimed at aggression and world domination, but would be conducted with every possible atrocity in order to strike terror, and would include both national degradation of the vanquished and racial extermination of the Jews and others*. The war was to be not only aggressive and unjust, but was to be merciless. What was actually done by the Nazi Government and forces carried out the policy. (UNWCC 1948, 552; my emphasis)
>
> There is a close parallel between such crimes [referring to racial/religious extermination] and crimes against the peace. But *the plan of exterminating the Jews, though in one sense a war crime, was rather sec-*

ondary and ancillary to the actual war. (UNWCC 1948, 553; my emphasis)

While it may be the case that crimes against humanity introduced in a formal way the connection between humanitarianism and the laws of war, it is not the case that there was a commitment to condemn the extermination of Jews (and other civilians) as offenses independent from aggressive war. Rather, the charge of crimes against humanity characterized the massacred Jews as tools for the realization of illegitimate military ends. In this way, the illegitimacy of the goals in war determined the legality of the means employed to realize those goals, implying that the massacre of millions of people in a *just* and *legitimate* war is not necessarily prohibited by the law of crimes against humanity. Ultimately, as interpreted by the Nuremberg principles, crimes against humanity cannot be regarded as absolute prohibitions on certain acts, and thus, not as a law of human rights.

Rape as a Crime Against Humanity

Post-Nuremberg translations of crimes against humanity potentially eliminated the dependence of the category to the fact of armed conflict, largely through Control Council Law No. 10. Yougindra Khushalani argues that Control Council Law No.10 significantly expanded the scope of crimes against humanity by omitting the Nuremberg caveat that defined them as acts committed during the course of war. The implications of the Law No. 10 extension are that crimes against humanity no longer have to be linked to the conduct of war, as had been in the case of Nuremberg, and that international tribunals and national courts (where adopted) have jurisdiction to prosecute individuals accused of crimes against humanity in times of war or peace (Khushalani 1982, 23-27).

Moreover, discussions leading up to the statute of the ICTY acknowledged the relationship between human rights and humanitarian law in defining crimes against humanity. *The Interim Report of the commission of Expert*s states that crimes against humanity constitute "gross violations of fundamental rules of humanitarian and human rights law committed by persons demonstrably linked to a party to the conflict, as part of an official polity ... *irrespective of war*" (UN 1993a, 387-92; my emphasis). In addition, the Commission of Experts notes that the foundations of human rights law "often are materially identical to rules of the law of armed conflict" (UN 1993a, 388). In saying this, the commission of Experts demonstrated an adherence to the notion that crimes against humanity are human rights violations and as such, should be subject to absolute prohibitions.[13]

In 1982, Khushalani suggested that the implications of Law No. 10 remained controversial as to whether changes made in international law for domestic trials would be adopted by international trials (Khushalani 1982, 27). Since the ICTY is the first test of Law No. 10, it seems that the implications are clear. While the *Interim Report* indicated that the ICTY might prosecute crimes against humanity as independent offenses, the crimes against humanity provision in the Statute of the Tribunal is limited to acts "when committed in armed conflict." Further limitations are placed on the meaning of crimes against humanity by the Secretary-General's report, which condemns acts "when committed as part of a widespread or systematic attack against any civilian population" and as committed in the service of ethnic cleansing (UN 1993c, 13).

These limitations raise a number of implications for the ways in which rape is included by this particular tribunal. Since rape is not explicitly named in the other provisions of the tribunal, this particular characterization of rape—as a prohibited act when committed in armed conflict, when part of a widespread or systematic attack against a population, and when committed as part of ethnic cleansing—must be seen as deliberate and calculated jurisdictional limits. Just as the extermination of Jews in World War Two was characterized as a tool of aggressive war, the crime of rape is seen as merely *ancillary and secondary* to the illegitimate pursuit of ethnic cleansing. The broader implication is that rape, in this instance, remains a breach of the laws of war rather than a human rights violation. This means that international law is not placing absolute prohibitions on the practice of rape, rather, is prohibiting rape only to the extent that it is in the service of illegitimate military ends.

While it is the case that rape and other abuse of women, whether in war or peace, constitutes a violation of women's human rights according to existing legislation, it is not clear that the enforcement of the laws of war by this particular tribunal will result in international legal recognition of women's human rights. The present application of the laws of war and the inclusion of rape as a crime against humanity is a condemnation of rape as it is used to pursue policies of ethnic cleansing, but not a condemnation of rape as a violation of women's human rights. Rape is not prohibited in this instance as intrinsically illegitimate or illegal. What this implies then is that the condemnation of rape in this instance is *not suggesting that rape never serves a legitimate military purpose*, nor is it a generalizable condemnation of rape in war. As Rhonda Copelon states, "The danger, as always, is that extreme examples produce narrow principles" (Copelon 1994, 204). Ultimately, the tribunal is not acknowledging that rape and other gender-based violence are transgressions of women's fundamental human rights.

In the instance of the Statute of the ICTY, international law has confirmed what some feminists have long argued—that the rape of women serves purposes which are central to the enterprise of war-making. Women are raped in armed conflict on a regular basis, and "the rape of women, where permitted or systematized as 'booty' of war, is likewise an engine of war: it maintains the morale of soldiers, feeds their hatred and sense of superiority, and keeps them fighting" (Copelon 1994, 205). Raping enemy women is one measure in a series of measures to achieve victory in war. If it is the case that the tribunal for the former Yugoslavia has not prohibited rape as a human rights violation but as acts which *in the circumstances* exceed legitimate military needs, then a further question is raised: Under what conditions does rape serve legitimate military ends? Given the overwhelming evidence that women are raped in war regularly, the widely publicized rapes in the conflicts in the former Yugoslavia, the legal bases for charging rape as a human rights violation, and the historic opportunity the tribunal has to recognize that women are targeted in gender-specific ways in war, questions must be raised about the deliberately limited fashion that rape has been characterized.

In a broad sense, these questions are not so much about the acts which are prohibited by the laws of war, but more importantly, the acts which are sanctioned and legitimized and made possible by the laws of war. After all, these are the same laws which sanction "collateral damage" and "exemplary force" as matters of legitimate military strategy. In particular, the impact of military necessity on the laws of war must be interrogated as military necessity poses "perhaps the biggest challenge" to the "elusive quest for humanitarian norms" (Kennedy and Andreopoulos 1995, 218). While the attempt has been to establish certain nonderogable rights in humanitarian law, the need to always balance those with military necessity, which is very often a determination in the course of armed conflict, makes the enterprise problematic (Kennedy and Andreopoulos 1995, 218). As Telford Taylor points out, while the rules governing military necessity "read like absolute requirements ... circumstances arise where military necessity ... causes them to be disregarded" (Taylor 1971, 36).

The problem however, is not only when the humanitarian provisions of the laws of war are disregarded. In their critical history of the laws of war, Chris af Jochnick and Roger Normand demonstrate that, as presently constituted, the laws of war are not opposed to inhumane acts in war, and in fact, "through law, violence has been legitimated" (af Jochnick and Normand 1994, 50). Military necessity itself is enshrined in the laws of war, sanctioning inhuman and immoral acts that otherwise might qualify as illegitimate violence. The determining factor, of course, is whether the war is "just" (af Jochnick and Normand 1994).

Prevailing assumptions in international relations suggest that the laws of war can mitigate the ravages of war and protect civilians and states from unprovoked attack and violence. The Tokyo and Nuremberg Tribunals have been celebrated as events which marked breakthroughs in international law-making, a momentous refusal of barbarism, and a return to civility after a period of primordial violence.[14] The return of war crimes tribunals in the 1990s, to charge individuals responsible for illegal violence in the ex-Yugoslavia, is again celebrated as a humanitarian-inspired refusal of violence. This is a claim, I have suggested, that warrants careful consideration.

AUTHOR'S NOTE

Thanks to Davina Bhandar, Terry Hunt, and Sandra Whitworth for their helpful comments on earlier versions of this article.

NOTES

1. In part, this is what is meant by the "New World Order." New World Order debates are less debates and more simply declarations about the contemporary period. There are far more articles that begin with a statement of the New World Order than there is room to list here. Some examples are Russett and Sutterlin (1991); Lister (1990); Jacobson (1990).
2. The full name of the Tribunal, established by Security Council Resolution 827, on May 25, 1993, is the International Tribunal for the Prosecution of Persons Responsible for Serious Violations of International Humanitarian Law Committed in the Territory of the Former Yugoslavia since 1991.
3. As Meron states, "there is nothing new in atrocities.... What is new is the role of the media.... The rapid dissemination of knowledge about the continuing abuses [and] the public's broader sensitivity to human rights" (Meron 1993, 424).
4. Elshtain makes a similar argument in her discussion of the extent to which just war theory challenges "realism's discursive hegemony." Elshtain argues that because it takes for granted the discursive terrain of war, just war theory serves to reconfirm the discourse of war by distinguishing between legitimate and illegitimate collective violence (see Elshtain 1985).
5. The Nuremberg principles usually refer to the Charter and Judgements of the International Military Tribunal (Nuremberg).
6. Control Council Law No. 10 was a translation of the Nuremberg principles which states adopted for domestic trials of "lesser war criminals."
7. Indictments list all relevant law pertaining to particular acts alleged to have been committed by the accused and they indicate under what jurisdictional circumstances individuals will be brought to trial. It is not necessarily the case that all relevant law will be applied to individuals as cases proceed. See *Indictment 3*, amended on September 1, 1995, and again on December 14, 1995, against Dusko Tadic and Goran Borovnica. Counts 2-4 charge Tadic with "forcible sexual intercourse with 'F'," stating that "by these acts, Dusko Tadic committed: a Grave Breach recognized by Articles 2(b) (inhuman treatment) and 7 (1) of the Statute of the Tribunal; and ... a Violation of the Laws or Customs of War ... and .... a Crime Against Humanity" (International Criminal Tribunal for the Former Yugoslavia, *Indictment* 3, [amended], Tadic and Borovnica, 14 December 1995, 5).
8. The first trial of the ICTY began on May 7, 1996, hearing charges of crimes against humanity and war crimes against Dusko Tadic, a Serbian national who is accused with, among other atrocities, torturing prisoners at the Omarska camp in Eastern Bosnia. Since judgements have not been issued, the ICTY is yet to enforce the laws of war. In other ways, however, the ICTY has been enforcing the laws of war for at least a year, by issuing indictments and warrants for arrest and hearing charges against certain indicted individuals (under Rule 61 of the ICTY Rules of Procedure and Evidence) who are yet to be taken into custody. Since the Tadic trial was to be potentially decisive in determining the status of women and rape in war, I refer in this paper to the enforcement capacity of the ICTY in the future tense.

   Since writing this article, the potential of the first trial to enforce humanitarian protection of women has changed. On the opening day of the Tadic trial Counts 2-4 covering "forcible sexual intercourse with 'F'" were dropped by the prosecution, presumably because they could not produce the witness. Other indicted individuals however have also been charged with sexual assault so there will be future possibilities for the ICTY to render decisions on the protection of women in war.
9. Included among those who have offered feminist analyses of the tribunal are Catharine MacKinnon (1994a; 1994b), Kathleen Pratt and Laurel Fletcher (1994), Cynthia Enloe (1994), Joan Fitzpatrick (1995), and Rhonda Copelon (1994). While offering very different arguments in some cases, all agree *or at least leave unexamined* the assumption that the laws of war are able to recognize women's human rights and to make advances for gender justice if women/rape/sexual assault are appropriately charged by the tribunal.

MacKinnon is one of the more prolific commentators about rape and war and this particular tribunal. In addition, she is working as legal counsel for two Bosnian women ("Jane Doe I" and "Jane Doe II") who have brought civil suits to American courts against Radovan Karadzic and Ratko Mladic, seeking redress for their rape and torture at the hands of Serbian soldiers. Because she is one of the leading activists in these issues, I have drawn extensively on her characterization of the ICTY. While she has a tendency to universalize women's oppression without adequate attention to the specificities of women's experiences, none of the other feminist commentary about the ICTY has offered a corrective, focusing rather on the general implications of international humanitarian legislation for women in war, within the general category of concerns about violence against women and women's human rights.

10. The protection of women, children, and the elderly is in regard to the usual noncombatant status of these groups. It is more accurate to say that the protection of women from violence in war is largely a product of their usual civilian status rather than a product of the gender-specificity of the laws of war. The thinking is that in the course of war, there may not be occasion to determine which men are combatants and which are not. The laws of war allow the legal assumption that all men of combat age and ability are combatants (as well as the obverse), and thus not subject to civilian immunities. While the intent of noncombatant protection may not be an exercise in gender-specificity, the presence of such legislation opens spaces from which to develop gender-specific legislation.
11. The act of rape in war is seen to be a public act because individuals as combatants act on behalf of the state or another contracting party as representatives or agents rather than as private individuals (see MacKinnon 1994b, 194).
12. The category "crimes against humanity" was criticized as law which had no existing legal basis and thus was an illegitimate charge, an *ex post facto* application. The reasoning is that law must be transparent; parties should be apprised of their obligations prior to committing certain acts. Schwelb agrees that crimes against humanity had no technical precedents, but argues that "non-technical" precedents existed in the Hague Convention 1907, and the Preliminary Peace Conference, January 1919, in terms of the interests or laws of humanity (Schwelb 1946). Precedents existed, as "the laws of humanity' [are] ... one of the sources of the law of nations" (Schwelb 1946, 180). See also Lauterpacht (1947), and Radin (1946), for other discussions of the *ex post facto* charge.
13. The decision of the Appeals Chamber in *The Prosecutor v. Dusko Tadic* has further substantiated the point that there is no longer a necessary nexus between armed conflict and crimes against humanity. As the decision states:

    It is by now a settled rule of customary international law that crimes against humanity do not require a connection to international armed conflict. Indeed, as the Prosecutor points out, customary international law may not require a connection between crimes against humanity and any conflict at all. Thus, by requiring that crimes against humanity be committed neither internal or international armed conflict, the Security council may have defined the crime in Article 5 more narrowly than necessary under customary international law. (International Criminal Tribunal for the Former Yugoslavia, Appeals Chamber, 2 October 1995, 73)

    That said, the ICTY is bound by the Statute as it has been framed by the Security Council.
14. This is not to suggest that the Nuremberg and Tokyo Tribunals have not also been the subjects of extensive criticism. Commentators have enumerated a range of flaws: that they were examples of "victor's justice" rather than fair applications of international law; that the participation of the Soviet Union cast a pall of hypocrisy over the proceedings given their World War II atrocities; or that the application of international law was *ex post facto*, and thus illegitimate (see Davidson 1973; Fox 1993; Taylor 1992). Most critics are concerned with the particular technicalities of these tribunals however, and despite the flaws agree that the tribunals represent a positive breakthrough in international criminal law-making, codifying certain customary principles and, for the first time, reflecting an international consensus about the limits of tolerable violence.

REFERENCES

af Jochnick, Chris, and Roger Normand. 1994. The legitimation of violence: A critical history of the laws of war. *Harvard International Law Journal* 35(1): 49-95.

Bettauer, Ronald. 1982. Human rights and humanitarian law: Commentator. *American University Law Review* 31: 965-68.

Boutros-Ghali, Boutros. 1995. A Crotian moment. *Fordham International Law Journal* 18 (5): 1609-22.

Bunch, Charlotte, and Niamh Reilly. 1994. *Demanding accountability: The global campaign and Vienna Tribunal for women's human rights.* Brunswick, NJ: Rutgers University: The Centre for Women's Global Leadership.

Copelon, Rhonda. 1994. Surfacing gender: Reconceptualizing crimes against women in times of war. In *Mass rape: The war against women in Bosnia-Herzegovina.* See Stiglmayer 1994.

Davidson, Eugene. 1973. *The Nuremberg fallacy.* New York: MacMillan

Elshtain, Jean Bethke. 1985. Reflections on war and political discourse: Realism, just war, and feminism in a nuclear age. *Political Theory* 13 (1): 39-57.

Enloe, Cynthia. 1994. Have the Bosnian rapes opened a new era of feminist consciousness? In *Mass rape: The war against women in Bosnia-Herzegovina.* See Stiglmayer 1994.

Fitzpatrick, Joan. 1995. The use of international human rights norms to combat violence against women. In *Human rights of women: National and international perspectives*, ed. Rebecca J. Cook. Philadelphia: University of Pennsylvania Press.

Fox, Hazel. 1993. An international tribunal for war crimes: Will the UN succeed where Nuremberg failed? *The World Today* 49 (10): 194-97.

Gordon, Melissa 1995. Justice on trial: The efficacy of the international criminal tribunal for Rwanda. ILSA: *Journal of International and Comparative Law* 1 (1): 217-52.

Howard, Michael. 1995. Constraints on warfare. In *The laws of war: Constraints on warfare in the Western world*, ed. Michael Howard, George J. Andreopoulos, and Mark R. Shulman. New Haven: Yale University Press.

International Criminal Tribunal for the Former Yugoslavia (ICTY), *Indictment 3* Tadic and Borovnica (amended) 1 September 1995; (amended) 14 December 1995. Case No: IT-94-1-T.

— . Appeals Chamber. 2 October 1995. *The Prosecutor v. Dusko Tadic a/k/a "Dule."* Decision on the defence motion for interlocutory appeal on jurisdiction. UN Document IT-94-1-AR72.

Jacobson, Harold K. 1990. The United Nations system in the nineties: Opportunities and challenges. *International Journal* 45 (4): 765-95.

Kennedy, Paul and George J. Andreopoulos. 1995. The laws of war: Some concluding reflections. *The laws of war: Constraints on warfare in the western world*, ed. Michael Howard, George J. Andreopoulos, and Mark R. Shulman. New Haven: Yale University Press.

Khushalani, Yougindra. 1982. *Dignity and honour of women as basic and fundamental human rights.* The Hague: Martinus Nijhoff Publishers.

Lauterpacht, Hersch. 1947. The subjects of the law of nations. *The Law Quarterly Review* 63 (252): 438-60.

Lister, Frederick. 1990. The role of international organizations in the 1990s and beyond. *International Relations* 10(2): 101-16.

MacKinnon, Catharine. 1994a. Turning rape into pornography: Postmodern genocide. In *Mass rape: The war against women in Bosnia-Herzegovina.* See Stiglmayer 1994.

— . 1994b. Rape, genocide, and women's human rights. In *Mass rape: The war against women in Bosnia-Herzegovina.* See Stiglmayer 1994.

Meron, Theodor. 1994. War crimes in Yugoslavia and the development of international law. *American Journal of International Law* 88(1): 78-87.

— . 1993. Rape as a crime under international humanitarian law. *American Journal of International Law* 87 (3): 424-28.

Montealegre, Henri. 1982. Human rights and humanitarian law: Commentator. *American University Law Review* 13: 969-73.

O'Brien, James C. 1993. The international tribunal for violations of international humanitarian law in the former Yugoslavia. *American Journal of International Law* 87 (7): 635-55.

Pratt, Kathleen M., and Laurel E. Fletcher. 1994. Time for justice: The case for international prosecutions of rape and gender-based violence in the former Yugoslavia. *Berkeley Women's law Journal* 9: 77-102.

Radin, Max. 1946. International crimes. *Iowa Law Review* 32 (1): 32-50.

Reisman, W. Michael, and Chris T. Antoniou. 1994. Introduction. *The laws of war: A comprehensive collection of primary documents on international laws governing armed conflict*, ed. W. Michael Reisman and Chris T. Antoniou. New York: Random House.

Russett, Bruce and James Sutterlin. 1991. The U.N. in a new world order. *Foreign Affairs* 70(2): 227-35.

Schindler, Dietriech. 1982. Human rights and humanitarian law: Interrelationship of the laws. *American University Law Review* 31: 935-43.

Schwelb, Egon. 1946. Crimes against humanity. *The British Yearbook of International Law* 23: 178-226.

Stiglmayer, Alexandra ed. 1994. *Mass rape: The war against women in Bosnia-Herzegovina.* Lincoln: University of Nebraska Press.

Taylor, Telford. 1992. *The anatomy of the Nuremberg trials: A personal memoir.* New York: Knopf.

– . 1971. *Nuremberg and Vietnam: An American tragedy.* New York: Bantam.

United Nations War Crimes Commission (UNWCC). 1948. *History of the United Nations War Crimes Commission and the development of the laws of war.* London: Her Majesty's Stationery Office.

United Nations (UN). 1993a. Interim report of the Commission of Experts (UN Doc. S/25274, 2 January). In *The laws of war: A comprehensive collection of primary documents on international laws governing armed conflict*, ed. W. Michael Reisman and Chris T. Antoniou. New York: Random House.

— . 1993b. Statute of the International Tribunal (Security Council Resolution 827, 25 May). In *The laws of war: A comprehensive collection of primary documents on international laws governing armed conflict*, ed. W. Michael Reisman and Chris T. Antoniou. New York: Random House.

— . 1993c. Report of the Secretary-General pursuant to Paragraph 2 of the Security Council Resolution 808. UN Doc. S/25704, 3 May, 1-48.

CRIME & SERVITUDE: AN EXPOSÉ OF THE TRAFFIC IN WOMEN FOR PROSTITUTION FROM THE NEWLY INDEPENDENT STATES

Gillian Caldwell, Steven Galster, and Nadia Steinzor

Gillian Caldwell is Co-Director of the Global Survival Network. She is an attorney in the areas of international human rights, civil rights, and family law.

Steven Galster is the Executive Director of the Global Survival Network. He is a journalist who has conducted numerous undercover investigations in the United States, Africa, Asia, and Europe. His reports have appeared in journals such as TIME, BBC Wildlife, *and* Third World Quarterly.

Nadia Steinzor has held positions in research, education, and communications and has lectured and written on a range of subjects including human rights, women's development, international law, environmental policy, and ethnic conflict.

Caldwell, Galster, and Steinzor describe how the proliferation of criminal organizations and increased poverty and unemployment that followed the collapse of the Soviet Union has generated the trafficking of women and children from Russia and the former Eastern Bloc to Asia, Western Europe, and the United States. They argue that the sexual exploitation to which human beings are subjected in the international sex trade of prostitution, pornography, and arranged marriages demands responses both within countries and internationally. They end with a critical analysis of current policies regarding immigration and prostitution and provide a series of recommendations for addressing the growing commerce in human beings.

The United Nations estimates that four million people are trafficked throughout the world each year, resulting in illicit profits to criminal syndicates of up to seven billion dollars annually. One of the fastest growing trafficking businesses is the sex trade.

This ground-breaking report details the findings of a two-year investigation by the Global Survival Network into the trafficking of women from Russia and the Newly Independent States for prostitution. Each day, thousands of women and girls are lured into the international sex trade with promises of a better life and a lucrative job abroad. These false promises are especially appealing to the scores of unemployed and underemployed women struggling to survive in impoverished regions and in societies facing post-Communist transition.

They are transported by bus, plane, and train to Europe, Asia, the Middle East, and North America, where they unexpectedly find themselves forced into cruel sexual exploitation. They may be forced to work for months or years without earnings, and many endure deep physical and psychological trauma as a result of their experience. In the worst of cases, they may lose not only their freedom but also their lives.

Trafficking has been recognized by the United Nations as a form of slavery and violence against women. It has also been condemned by numerous international human rights documents, including the Convention on the Elimination of All Forms of Discrimination Against Women, the Convention for the Suppression of the Traffic in Persons and the

---

Reprinted with permission of the Global Survival Network, PO Box 73214, Washington DC 20009 (www.globalsurvival.net) [edited].

Exploitation of the Prostitution of Others, the Declaration on the Elimination of Discrimination Against Women, and the Convention on the Rights of the Child.

Despite the many prohibitions against trafficking, international networks that market women and children for prostitution continue to thrive. Their success can be attributed to several factors, including the global economic trends, the declining socioeconomic status of women, the enormous profitability of the business, government inaction, and, in the most egregious circumstances, government complicity.

It will not be possible to address the growing problem of trafficking without the collaboration of state institutions and non-governmental organizations, and both have their own challenges to meet. Governments must identify and remove corrupt public officials acting as accomplices of sex traders, and resist the pressure to attempt to address trafficking by restricting migration, which exacerbates the problem and leads to a violation of another fundamental human right, the freedom of movement.

For the human rights movement, trafficking extends beyond the familiar set of civil and political concerns. It is a multidimensional problem which demands comprehensive evaluation. Recommended responses must be informed by active cooperation between the traditional human rights community and the newer women's rights groups.

Moreover, because trafficking is a problem that transcends national borders, it demands a transnational response. Collaborative relationships must be formed between the "sending countries" of the former Eastern Bloc, Asia, Africa and Latin America, and "receiving countries" in the wealthier nations of North America and Western Europe....

2. Worldwide Trade in Humans: An Overview

> The Japanese will take anything, as long as she has a passport and she is Russian. Whether she is fat or skinny does not concern them. - "Vladimir," a Russian trafficker

Since the fall of the Berlin Wall in 1989 and the break-up of the Soviet Union after 1991, a growing commerce in human beings has arisen between Russia and the former Eastern Bloc, on the one hand, and Asia, Western Europe, and the United States, on the other. Russian women are in high demand in many countries because of their "exotic" nature and relative novelty in the sex market. Russia and the Newly Independent States, including Ukraine and Latvia, have become primary "sender" countries, supplementing and sometimes replacing previously significant sources of women from Asia and Latin America. In a recent study in the Netherlands, 75 percent of the trafficked women interviewed were from Central and Eastern Europe.

According to official records, 50,000 women leave Russia permanently every year. Unofficial estimates by non-governmental organizations and researchers indicate that perhaps hundreds of thousands of other women leave Russia annually in search of temporary work, with plans to return. The number of Russian women working in international sex industries is large and growing. According to Marco Gramegna of the International Organization for Migration, an estimated 500,000 women are trafficked each year into Western Europe, which was the first region to receive large numbers of women trafficked from Russia. Since few Russian women willing to travel abroad for work have the cash to purchase airline or train tickets, it is likely that many if not most of them are arriving via trafficking networks....

Trafficking in Children

One of the most disturbing trends in trafficking is the growing number of young women and children. For various reasons, including the AIDS epidemic, virgins are increasingly in demand and can fetch some of the highest prices in the international sex market. A telling statistic comes from the Netherlands, where the Foundation Against Traffic in Women reports that of the women it assisted in 1995 and 1996 who came from the Central and Eastern European Countries and the Newly Independent States, more than 75 percent were under the age of 25 and 57 percent were under 21.

The German Federal Department of Criminal Investigation estimates that five percent of the women trafficked from Eastern Europe are younger than 18 years of age. Solwodi (Solidarity with Women in Distress), a German non-governmental organization working with migrant prostitutes, estimates the actual number of underage migrant women working in German sex clubs is much higher. Many of the clients who seek legal assistance from counselors for trafficking victims in Germany are between 15 and 21 years old. Traffickers lure girls with promises of work as au-pairs, waitresses, or dancers, then transport them abroad to work as prostitutes with false passports which hide their actual age....

Why Women Go

Modern-day servitude usually begins with the best of motives: hope for a better life. A recent Russian study analyzed interviews with women standing in line at embassies in Moscow, and at the few state-registered firms that offer employment opportunities abroad, regarding their reasons for emigrating. Eighty-six percent of respondents said they were seeking higher earnings.

Women have special incentives to leave Russia and other Newly Independent States, owing to their rapid socioeconomic decline in the chaotic post-communist transition that ensued after 1991. This transition has brought massive social dislocation and uncertainty—along with new political freedoms for all and emerging economic opportunities for a few.

Even though inflation was brought down to a relatively reasonable level in 1996-97, economic activity in Russia continues to decline and the government owes its citizens billions of dollars in unpaid salaries. Many businesses and manufacturing plants have downsized or ceased operation altogether, as the government is not able to subsidize ineffective industries. Some experts estimate that 80 percent of those who have lost their jobs in recent years due to downsizing and economic shifts have been women. As thousands of unprofitable enterprises close down, and newly privatized companies continue to lay off workers, still higher unemployment levels among women will result. The development of small and medium sized businesses that could create new employment opportunities for millions of women has been halted due to excessive and irrational taxation, extortion from criminal groups and corrupted officials, and the lack of legal regulation and financial incentives for loans and leases. Retraining programs are virtually nonexistent, and unemployment compensation is symbolic.

Between 1991 and 1995, Russia's real gross domestic product fell 34 percent, while per capita annual income is currently a mere US$3,400. Almost one-quarter of the population lives below the poverty line. Women account for nearly two-thirds of people unemployed nationwide, but as much as 85 or 90 percent in some regions of the Russian Federation. In 1996, 87 percent of Russia's employed urban residents whose monthly income was less than 100,000 rubles (US$21) were women. According to Zoya Khotkina, a specialist in women and employment at the Moscow Center for Gender Studies, "Seventy percent of the women graduating from institutes of higher learning and from schools declare that they cannot find gainful employment."

In a society where an estimated 98 percent of the women are literate, and substantial numbers university educated, Human Rights Watch concluded in its 1995 report that: "Women in Russia face widespread employment discrimination that is practiced, condoned, and tolerated by the government." Jobs are often secured through personal connections to high-level managers, directors, or members of a mafiya group. Few women have such connections, forcing many highly trained female engineers, doctors, lawyers, teachers, and other professionals to look for jobs outside of their profession.

Sexual harassment often accompanies job discrimination. In many Russian businesses it is not considered out of the ordinary for a male boss to demand that his female secretary have sexual relations with him. In an analysis of the "help wanted" advertisements in Moscow newspapers, Zoya Khotkina has observed that an average of 75 percent of the women who advertised their availability to work as secretaries had to specify "no intimacy," meaning no sexual services provided. Furthermore, newspapers contain advertisements for secretarial positions which request women "without complexes," which is commonly understood to mean willing to have sex....

There are no civil or labor laws relating to sexual harassment in Russia. The relevant criminal provision for sexual coercion is rarely applied, and cases brought under it seldom reach a court. Syostri, a support center for survivors of domestic violence, rape and sexual assault in Moscow, reports receiving over 2,500 calls on its single crisis telephone hotline in the first three years of operation. Only 5-10 percent of the women subjected to domestic violence or sexual assault report their experience to police, which may be partly attributed to the fact that only one in five reports made to police are accepted and investigated.

Russian women have also suffered from a collapse of social services. Under the old system, they received up to three years of maternity leave with a guaranteed job upon their return and, like men, were guaranteed a modest pension. Furthermore, day care centers were provided for working women, and while the medical care system offered mediocre services, they were free. Since the transition to a market economy began, the state has withdrawn much of its social and economic support. Thousands of day care centers and preschools have closed, and health care and education systems are severely underfunded.

The plight of Russian women during the transition to a market economy has been exacerbated by the government's indifference to the problem. The Former Minister of Labor, Gennady Melikyan, stated in 1994 that the government would disregard female unemployment until the day arrives when all Russian men are employed. The appointment of a new Minister of Labor and of Deputy Prime Minister Oleg Sysuyev as the chair of the special Governmental commission charged with finding ways of improving the status of women in Russia may be a genuine attempt to find solutions to painful problems. But it remains to be seen whether real changes will ensue.

For women confronting unemployment, sexual harassment, and domestic violence, an offer of good pay for working abroad often seems like a magical escape to a better world. According to Elena Tiuriukanova of the Institute for Population Studies in Moscow, "although women's migration has great public resonance, there is practically no official policy aimed at stopping violence, sexual harassment, trafficking in women and other forms of human rights' violations in the field of female labor migration." As Marina Aristova, from the St. Petersburg Center for Gender Studies, has observed, "Women in Russia have a choice now: they can be prostitutes on the street, or they can be prostitutes in the office." Some women and girls conclude that they might as well take their chances abroad.

Few of the women have the experience or information to see the potential risks they may face abroad. The Tiuriukanova study revealed that most of the respondents were unaware that they might be preyed upon by traffickers. Among women interviewed in "high risk" categories of labor migration, such as entertainment, hotels, bars, and restaurants, 40 percent rejected the possibility of sexual exploitation altogether. Fifty-two percent accepted the possibility, but felt they would be able to avoid exploitation; only eight percent had fears or misgivings of sexual exploitation. Elena, a 21-year-old dancer, was interviewed while preparing to leave for Switzerland, and said: "In Russia there is also sexual exploitation at work with no legal protection for the girls. At least abroad I'll earn more money for this!"

Victims of their own hopes and illusions, most trafficked women leave their home country willingly to pursue a seemingly legitimate opportunity, and even those who know they may have to engage in the sex business assume that they will be treated humanely. But they often fall victim to the skilled deceptions of the traffickers and their agents, who force them into a life far worse than they imagined when they left Russia....

4. The Marriage Connection

> Why Russian ladies are SO desirable...Unlike Americans, they understand the realities of life all too well. They are unpretentious, down to earth, and their views of relationships have not been ruined by unreasonable expectations. - American marriage agency catalogue

> Who can differentiate who is a prostitute and who is a real bride? I do not have any legal responsibility.—Sergey (a Moscow pimp)

Many women from Russia, Eastern Europe, and the Newly Independent States pin their hopes of residency, work, and citizenship abroad on marriage to a man. Through its investigations, GSN found that some women enter foreign countries through marriages that are arranged by traffickers or by businesses commonly known as "mail-order bride" companies.

While international matchmaking agencies are considered legitimate businesses, they are almost completely unregulated. In Germany, for example, all that is required to establish a marriage business is a trading license and contacts in a "sender" country. Marriage agencies generally do not screen their male clients, some of whom have histories of domestic abuse or criminal records. Companies in the United States often print disclaimers on their mailing envelopes, stating that they do not knowingly mail catalogues to residents of penal institutions. One U.S. study concluded that many male clients of marriage agencies are considered "socially or physically unattractive in their own culture," hold chauvinistic attitudes, and have histories of abuse. Another result of the lack of regulation is that marriage agencies frequently advertise minors to their clients; one German agency advertising on the Internet offers Russian girls as young as 15 years old.

Marriage agencies catering to Europeans and Americans tout Russian women for their physical charms and their lack of a "feminist" perspective relative to Western women. "Russian women have a different outlook on life and marriage," claims the website of one marriage agency. "They are less materialistic than their American counterparts and more family-oriented. As wives, they desire to build a loving home, follow their husband's lead, and stick with the marriage, even when times get tough or things stop being 'fun.'" A concerted effort is made to appeal to clients' frustration with the "feminist" ideals and independence of "modern" Western women. Businesses that have historically marketed Asian and Latin American women now advertise "glasnost beauties" as ideal candidates for wives, and notes that Russian women are willing to marry older, divorced men....

5. The Mafiya Connection

> [Organized criminal groups] "kidnap, imprison, and force females into prostitution by the use of, at times, extreme violence and intimidation. These organized groups transcend police boundaries locally, nationally, and even internationally. This is truly organized crime on a major scale." - Dr. Willy Bruggeman, Europol Drugs Unit

Trafficking in Russia and throughout the world is organized by criminal groups. GSN investigations revealed that even in instances where they are not directly responsible for traffiking women overseas, Russian criminal groups provide a "krisha" ("roof"), or security and protection, for the operations, and that they have incorporated the traffic of women as an increasingly profitable part of their activities inside and outside the country.

This study considers an organized criminal group in Russia as "mafiya" if it is "characterized by profit-oriented criminal activity, uses violence or threat of violence, expends resources to discourage cooperation of its members with police, and corrupts legitimate government authority." Unlike the Italian mafia, which is organized hierarchically and often within families around a single "godfather," the Russian mafiya, or "organizatsiya," is generally divided into networks arranged along regional or ethnic lines....

The collapse of the Soviet Union and the consequent development of new state governments left a vacuum in activities related to the economy and law enforcement. This void has quickly been filled by organized criminal groups, which have capitalized on a legacy of corruption and underground networks. Many mafiya members are former employees of the national security agency, the KGB, which was replaced after 1991 by the FSB (the state intelligence bureau). This transition left thousands of people unemployed who were highly skilled in intelligence work and the use of force. Because security police often have political connections, access to weapons, and knowledge of the banking and business worlds, they are well-positioned to participate in international criminal activities.

Mafiya involvement in trafficking amounts to providing "protection" to sex businesses. More than 200 illegal sex businesses exist in Moscow alone, providing services ranging from escorts and prostitutes for Russian or foreign businessmen, to sending groups of women to other countries to work as prostitutes. Some companies also make inexpensive pornographic films which are sold within Russia or exported to European countries....

6. Mechanisms of Control

> I know about women who worked in an apartment. There was a camera in the bedroom, in the toilet, in the kitchen...and in one of the rooms was the pimp sitting, watching all the time what they were doing...These women stay for months without going on the streets. - Counselor, Amnesty for Women

Traffickers control women through various techniques of emotional and physical manipulation. They begin by isolating them from the surrounding local society. This is usually easy to do because of language differences and a common lack of legal status in the host country. Many brothel operators actually prefer foreign women precisely because of the ease of controlling them. A typical isolating strategy is to trick or coerce a woman into surrendering her passport, which makes her virtually a "nonperson."

Another technique is to compel the woman to work and live in the same place, and to forbid her from leaving the premises without permission. The brothel operator may keep the woman under constant surveillance and give her little opportunity to become connected to the society or to learn the language. In order to keep their business activities secret and to maintain control over their workers, sex club owners, pimps, and traffickers may also forbid women from receiving any form of legal or medical assistance.

Isolation makes a woman vulnerable to additional forms of control, such as withholding of pay, physical intimidation, and dependency on drugs or alcohol. A recent study in the Netherlands revealed that among more than 250 trafficked women interviewed, there were 177 reported instances of violence and extreme pressure, including cases of rape, passport confiscation, withholding of salaries and physical or psychological abuse by traffickers, pimps, and clients.

Through such actions, traffickers and brothel operators imprison women in a world of economic and sexual exploitation that imposes a constant fear of arrest and deportation, as well as of reprisals by the traffickers themselves, to whom the women must pay off accrued debts....

8. Stopping the Trade

> We must take part in a global effort to crack down on illegal trafficking in women and girls...If those who trafficked drugs should be punished severely...so should those who traffic in human beings. - Madeleine K. Albright, U.S. Secretary of State

The stories of all the women in this report provide a glimpse into the human tragedy of trafficking, but they do not offer remedies. In the final analysis, only governments have the authority and the means to significantly limit the scope of trafficking. Doing so effectively will require changes in international and national laws and political cooperation worldwide. Above all, mitigating the effects of trafficking will demand a rethinking about the position of the trafficked person in the receiving country.

In recent years, the international traffic in women has become a hot political topic. The governments and citizens of receiving countries are increasingly concerned about an influx of illegal immigrants and the growing presence of organized criminal networks. However, these interests, and the policies designed to satisfy them, often prove counterproductive for trafficked women and have failed to halt the growth of trafficking networks.

Governments have traditionally framed trafficking as an immigration question, and have treated people who are trafficked as violators of immigration laws because they often cross borders illegally and may work without proper papers. However, by defining trafficked persons primarily as illegal migrants, a state ensures that they are rendered powerless and that they lack a critical means for self-protection. In fact, as many of the stories recounted in this report show, tightening legal screws only gives traffickers a more prominent role in the migration flow. When potential migrants are denied the means of entering and remaining in a country independently, they are forced to turn to apparently legitimate organizations that offer to handle visas and passports. Even worse, once a government has made entry more restrictive, it may assume that it has no other obligation to those persons who have been trafficked.

Moreover, increased scrutiny and prosecution of illegal migrants by receiving states make women hesitant to report abuse to authorities; they know they will be treated as illegal migrants and summarily arrested, detained, and deported. This is particularly true for women working in prostitution, because prostitution or the associated activities of brothel-keeping and pimping are criminalized in most countries. An estimated 90 percent of the foreign women working illegally in German brothels, for example, are deported when discovered by authorities, while those who run illegal trafficking operations are rarely brought to justice. In contrast to individual women with illegal status, criminal networks are entrenched, organized, and well-connected economically and politically. Greater priority must be placed on weakening the scope and influence of organized crime, rather than on the particular actions of victimized women.

However, prosecution of traffickers is complicated by the fact that, even where stays of deportation are granted to women who are willing to testify, the risks for a woman (as well as her family at home) posed by thwarting traffickers are substantial. Witness protection and relocation programs are rarely offered for cases involving trafficking. Moreover, while the state may benefit from a woman's testimony because it can lead to a crackdown on organized crime, the benefits to the witness are minimal—perhaps, as in Belgium and the Netherlands, a stay of deportation for the duration of a trial, with no guarantee of residency after proceedings are completed.

What governments have failed to understand, or have chosen to ignore, is that trafficking is a contravention of basic human rights that has been condemned by an array of international conventions, treaties, and other instruments. Furthermore, practices routinely used by traffickers, such as debt bondage, threats, intimidation, and withholding of wages are illegal under national laws.

A trafficked person must be treated not as a criminal but as a fully empowered human being. If each government focused on these human rights abuses when they are inflicted on foreign women residing within their national borders, they would be addressing fundamental human rights violations associated with trafficking operations.

A broader, more consistent approach to stopping the traffic in women is clearly needed. State action in and of itself is only part of the solution, since the profitable trade in women depends greatly on the naivete and powerlessness of its victims. It is therefore important that any attempt to curb trafficking addresses not only law enforcement and immigration authorities, but the need to educate women worldwide—particularly young women and those who are economically vulnerable—about the patterns and dangers of trafficking. Knowledge is key to helping women avoid falling into the hands of traffickers.

The following recommendations provide an agenda for action that could dramatically alter the position of trafficked women by providing them with three things they do not now have. First, it would ensure that they have personal freedom as established in the many international treaties, covenants, and conventions that outlaw aspects of trafficking, such as intimidation and debt bondage. Second, the agenda provides protection from harm by providing education to both women and state officials, such as police and foreign service personnel, about the structure and ramifications of trafficking. Third, the agenda provides compensation and support for victims through laws that enable the state to seize the property of traffickers and use it to reimburse victims for wages withheld, and to provide the necessary legal, psychological, and medical services.

Recommendations

1. Adherence to international standards and laws

Governments of sending and receiving countries must reaffirm their adherence to all international treaties, conventions, and covenants that relate to issues of trafficking, and *should take steps to implement and enforce existing obligations*. Governments that have not ratified any of the relevant treaties should immediately do so.

Such instruments include the Slavery Convention of 1926; the 1956 Supplementary Convention on the Abolition of Slavery, the Slave Trade, and Institutions and Practices Similar to Slavery; International Labour Organization Conventions on Forced Labour (No. 29), Abolition of Forced Labour (No.105), On Freedom of Association (No. 87), and Protection of Wages (No. 95); United Nations Conventions on the Protection of the Rights of All Migrant Workers and Members of Their Families and on the Elimination of All Forms of Discrimination Against Women (CEDAW); the United Nations International Covenants on Civil and Political Rights (ICCPR) and on Economic, Social, and Cultural Rights (ICESCR); and the Universal Declaration of Human Rights.

2. National Laws, Practices, and Policies

a) Governments and Non-governmental organizations (NGOs), acting individually and together, should initiate broad-based, ongoing educational campaigns with the media to combat domestic and international trafficking. Public service announcements should be developed for television, radio, and newpapers. The education campaign should address issues such as the methods used by traffickers, basic elements of labor and contract law, the rights of migrants in a foreign country, and means of obtaining help if one's rights are violated.

b) Governments should train law enforcement officials at all levels regarding: issues of violence against women; how to recognize situations that may involve trafficking, including identification of "front" companies and groups; and the fact that trafficked persons are to be treated not as criminals or illegal migrants, but as victims of human rights abuses and of violations of national and international law.

c) Governments should institute stays of deportation and witness protection and relocation programs for victims of trafficking to facilitate testimony in criminal proceedings. Governments should also finance hotlines staffed with specially trained experts for receiving complaints and inquiries from victims of trafficking.

d) Governments should establish mechanisms of interagency and international cooperation to combat trafficking and assist its victims.

e) Governments should train their embassy staffs about illegal trafficking and instruct them to provide visa-seekers with materials about the dangers of trafficking and about non-governmental organizations that help victims of trafficking. Consulates and embassies of receiving countries should provide information to prospective migrants about their rights and legal options in cases of abuse.

f) Government agencies and offices should collaborate with grassroots organizations and NGOs to develop comprehensive national programs to assist victims of abuse during migration and in the workplace. This program should provide legal assistance, health care, job training, shelter, and financial assistance if required.

g) To facilitate these services, governments should develop legal mechanisms for confiscating the assets of traffickers and making them available as a special fund for the benefit of victims. In addition to reimbursing women for wages illegally confiscated and debts accrued through financial schemes, the fund should help pay for legal, medical, social and psychiatric services.

h) Governments should decriminalize prostitution in order to guarantee that women working in the sex industry have access to health care, as well as to the protection provided by labor and criminal regulations in cases of violence and abuse....

STUDY QUESTIONS

1 Is Burgess-Jackson correct to suggest that an unequal distribution of fear needs to be addressed in theories of distributive justice? Does the fact that fear is not a benefit but a burden make it difficult to provide an account of the distribution of fear? Provide reasons for your answers.

2 What evidence does Burgess-Jackson provide for the claim that women bear a much greater burden of fear than do men? Who should bear the cost of easing this burden and why?

3 Outline and evaluate the several objections to his own account that Burgess-Jackson raises and rejects.

4 On what grounds do May and Strikwerda reject the three main arguments that men are not responsible for rape: a) the rapist is a loner or demon, or b) the rapist is a victim of biological drives, or c) the rapist is a victim of society?

5 Evaluate the arguments May and Strikwerda provide to defend their claim that men are collectively responsible for rape. Is the qualification that collective responsibility is assignable "in some societies" important? If so, how?

6 Should sexual violence committed against women in the course of armed conflict be treated as crimes against humanity? What reservations does Philipose express with respect to this move in the international community to make rape a crime against humanity? Is her reasoning sound? Why or why not?

7 Caldwell, Galster, and Steinzor cast doubt on arguments that women from Russia and the Newly Independent States freely choose to engage in trafficking to improve conditions in their lives. What explanations do they offer?

8 Why are Caldwell, Galster, and Steinzor critical of current policies regarding immigration and prostitution? Given their analysis of the growing commerce in human beings, do you think that prostitution should be decriminalized? Why or why not?

9 Outline and evaluate the policies recommended in the report by the Global Survival Network for addressing sexual violence as it is manifested in the trafficking of women and children.

SUGGESTED READINGS

Archard, David. *Sexual Consent.* Boulder, CO: Westview Press, 1998.

Baber. H. E. "How Bad is Rape?" *Hypatia*, v. 2 (1987): 125-138.

Brett, Nathan. "Sexual Offenses and Consent." *The Canadian Journal of Law & Jurisprudence*, v. 11, no. 1 (1998): 69-88.

Brison Susan J. "Surviving Sexual Violence: A Philosophical Perspective." *Journal of Social Philosophy*, v. 24 (1993): 5-22.

Burgess-Jackson, Keith (editor). *A Most Detestable Crime: New Philosophical Essays on Rape.* New York: Oxford University Press, 1999.

— . "Wife Rape." *Public Affairs Quarterly*, v. 12, no. 1 (January 1998): 1-23.

— . "Statutory Rape: A Philosophical Analysis." *The Canadian Journal of Law & Jurisprudence*, v. 8, no. 1 (1995): 139-158.

Calhoun, Laurie. "On Rape: A Crime Against Humanity." *Journal of Social Philosophy*, v. 28 (1997): 101-109.

Card, Claudia. "Rape as a Weapon of War." *Hypatia*, v. 11 (1996): 5-18.

Clark, Lorenne and Debra Lewis. *Rape: The Price of Coercive Sexuality.* Toronto: The Women's Press, 1977.

Crenshaw, Kimberlè Williams. "Beyond Racism and Misogyny: Black Feminism and 2 Live Crew." In *Words That Wound: Critical Race Theory, Assaultive Speech, and the First Amendment*. Edited by M. Matsuda et al. Boulder CO: Westview, 1993.

Cuomo, Chris J. "War is Not Just an Event: Reflections on the Significance of Everyday Violence." *Hypatia*, v. 11 (1996): 30-45.

Davion, Victoria. "Rape, Group Responsibility and Trust." *Hypatia*, v. 10 (1995): 153-156.

Francis, Leslie (editor). *Date Rape: Feminism, Philosophy, and the Law.* University Park: Penn State Press, 1996.

French, Stanley, Wanda Teays and Laura Purdy (editors). *Violence Against Women: Philosophical Perspectives.* Ithaca, NY: Cornell University Press, 1998.

Heberle, Renee. "Deconstructive Strategies and the Movement Against Sexual Violence." *Hypatia*, v. 11, no. 4 (Fall 1996): 63-76.

LeMoncheck, Linda. *Dehumanizing Women: Treating Persons as Sex Objects.* Lanham, MD: Rowman & Littlefield, 1985.

MacKinnon, Catharine. *Sexual Harassment of Working Women* (New Haven, Conn.: Yale University Press, 1979.

May, Larry and Robert Strikwerda. "Reply to Victoria Davion's Comments on May and Strikwerda." *Hypatia*, v. 10 (1995): 157-158.

Narayan, Uma. "'Male-Order Brides: Immigrant Women, Domestic Violence and Immigration Law." *Hypatia*, v. 10, no. 1 (Winter 1995): 104-119.

O'Neill, Onora. "Between Consenting Adults." *Philosophy & Public Affairs*, v. 14 (1985): 252-277.

Pineau, Lois. "Date Rape: A Feminist Analysis." *Law and Philosophy* 8 (1989): 217-243.

Superson, Anita. "A Feminist Definition of Sexual Harassment." *Journal of Social Philosophy*, v. 24, no. 1 (1993): 46-64.

Tong, Rosemarie. "Rape." In *Women, Sex, and the Law*. Lanham, MD: Rowman & Littlefield, 1984.

CHAPTER FOURTEEN

ANIMALS AND THE ENVIRONMENT

So far, our discussion of moral theory and issues has centered on the interactions of human beings within and across societies. Part I explored human rights and questions about their meaning, universalizabilty, and the structures needed to respect them. Part II examined historical and social conditions of discrimination based on membership in traditionally disadvantaged groups. Part III investigated possible resolutions of moral dilemmas that people face in various social and political contexts. We touched on issues of non-human animals and the environment, but only by implication: first in liberal arguments that capacities unique to human beings give them inherent worth that justifies their privileged status over non-human entities and then in the questions raised about the effects of Eurocentrism on economic and political issues regarding developmental policies. In this chapter, we confront questions about our treatment of non-human animals and the environment and do so once again in a global context of differing values, practices, and policies. As well as examining responsibilities for protecting the rights of non-human entities and for maintaining resources, species, and the environment itself for future generations, we will explore the particular challenges that these issues have presented for traditional Western moral theory.

Peter Singer surveys the arguments underlying the principle of equality in various liberation movements. The principle of equality is not a description of an alleged actual equality: human beings come in different sizes and shapes, with different moral and intellectual capacities, and different capacities to feel pleasure and pain and to communicate with others. Singer defends a conception of equality as equal consideration and argues that what gives entities a right to equal consideration is the capacity for suffering, a capacity that is a prerequisite for having capacities at all. But speciesism, like racism and sexism, violates the principle of equal consideration because it is a prejudice or bias in favor of the interests of members of one's own species and against members of others. Singer chastises philosophers for taking suffering to be morally relevant in the case of human beings, yet failing to apply this simple principle to members of other species.

To avoid speciesism, argues Singer, we must allow that beings similar in relevant respects have a similar right to life and that mere membership in a biological category is not morally relevant. Concerning the sanctity of life, he argues that speciesism is at work when we preserve infants who have suffered irreparable brain damage, but kill non-human animals who surpass the brain-damaged infant in capabilities. It is not that there is some absolute prohibition on killing, but rather that consistency demands that we bring non-human animals within our sphere of moral concern and treatment and cease to treat their lives as expendable for whatever trivial purposes we have. Singer argues that the principle of minimizing suffering can tell us what our duties to animals are. In this reading, he applies this principle to the case for vegetarianism. Becoming a vegetarian is a practical and effective step toward ending the killing and infliction of suffering on animals. Because it is not possible to rear animals for food on a large scale without inflicting suffering, vegetarianism is a form of boycott that can succeed in reducing the number of animals raised in factory farms and slaughtered for food.

J. Baird Callicott questions aspects of Singer's strategy. Callicott distinguishes the individualistic approach, evident in Singer's account of equal consideration for non-human animals, from the holistic approach that he defends. He tells us in the 1994 preface to his 1980 article that he no longer believes the two approaches are irreconcilable to the extent he pronounced in his original harsh critique of animal liberation/rights strategies. What is important about the reading, he tells us, are the distinctions drawn between holistic environmental ethics, on the one hand, and individualistic "moral humanism" and "humane moralism," on the other, and the ways in which they can be seen as conflicting, converging, and mutually enforcing.

Moral humanists identify capacities unique to human beings that make them worthy of respect. Because non-human animals lack capacities such as rationality or linguistic abilities, they lack the criteria for ethical consideration and so can be treated as things or means. Humane moralists then point out that it is inconsistent for the moral humanist to be outraged by the idea that irrational or inarticulate infants, who do not have the capacities granting them moral consideration, can be used in medical experiments while maintaining that non-human animals can. Callicott argues that the strategy of drawing an increasing number of entities into the circle of beings worthy of moral consideration is severely limited as an environmental ethic. It cannot provide moral reasons for why rivers or mountains or ecosystems should be respected and presents no serious challenge to cherished first principles. Callicott outlines Aldo Leopold's land ethic as a third approach that provides that challenge.

The precept of the land ethic is that "a thing is right when it tends to preserve the integrity, stability, and beauty of the biotic community. It is wrong when it tends otherwise." Callicott takes Leopold's land ethic to be a holistic perspective that challenges the individualism of the two traditional approaches to animals and the environment. Holism presents a picture of the biotic community as a system of parts that are interdependent. It asks moral agents to respond in relation to that whole, a delicately complex, functioning social and organic system. Callicott gives examples of how the holistic approach of the land ethic generates moral imperatives distinct from individualist approaches. The humane moralist principle of equal consideration calls for the protection and preservation of individual non-human animals, but this is precisely the sort of practice that could be a threat to the environment. The humane moralist's call for the liberation of livestock would have devastating ecological consequences. In both these cases, the land ethic would seem to demand removal or destruction of that which threatens the integrity of the biotic community. Callicott retracts his earlier view that these are the consequences. In the preface, he uses the notion of community and membership in communities to sketch an account of duties and obligations to domestic animals, wild-fellow members, and to the biotic community as a whole.

Callicott's revisions to his own work reflect the complexity and difficulty of fashioning policies from moral theories and principles concerning animals and the environment. This is the topic of Kristin Shrader-Frechette's analysis of the practical implications of environmental ethics. Shrader-Frechette identifies two policy approaches to the environment. Soft environmental ethicists, of which Callicott is an example, begin with general goals and motivational ideals and use vague concepts like integrity to advocate protective attitudes to the biosphere. Hard environmental ethicists are scientists who begin with general principles for understanding nature, avoiding erroneous claims, and producing grand deductive theories. Shrader-Frechette argues that both soft and hard environmental ethics are inadequate to the task of providing an ordered set of norms that will withstand courtroom challenges and support precise claims. She raises criticisms of each of the two approaches on the road to defending a middle position that she refers to as practical ecology. Practical ecology is grounded on rules of thumb, rough generalizations, and case studies covering simple systems over a short period of time rather than on an uncertain general ecological theory or model.

Ramachandra Guha argues that deep ecology in the United States and radical environmental movements in places like Germany and India emerge from radically dissimilar cultural and social histories and that this is relevant to a critical analysis of the American version of deep ecology, which tends to depict itself in universalistic terms. While Guha applauds the check on human arrogance demanded by deep ecology, he argues that American discussions of the dichotomy between anthropocentric and biocentric perspectives are of little use in understanding such fundamental ecological problems as overconsumption by the industrialized world and by the urban elite of developing countries. He points out that deep ecologists' invocation of Eastern philosophies fails to appreciate the complex and differentiated traditions of Hinduism, Buddhism, and Taoism and romanticizes and simplifies human relations with nature. Lastly, Guha contends that preserving wilderness and creating parks fits with rather than challenges a consumer society that is rich, urban, and sophisticated. The preservation of unspoilt wilderness is harmful in places like India, which has a long history of agrarian populations achieving a finely balanced relationship with nature. Here, the central issue is taking control of nature away from the state and the industrial sector and placing it in the hands of rural communities who live within that environment. For these communities, the issues are equity, justice, and survival itself. Rural communities make fewer demands on the environment and can draw on a reservoir of cooperative social institutions and local ecological knowledge in managing and sustaining the environment in which they live.

Guha claims that it is a mistake to understand Eastern thinking as monolithic. There are a diversity of views within Eastern accounts of human relations with the environment. In the final reading, John Patterson argues that the Maori of New Zealand have maintained their tribal traditions of an ethics that encodes environmental virtues while appropriating and adapting to technological thinking introduced by Europeans. Patterson discusses aspects of these traditions as reflected in the largely oral narratives of the Maori passed on by ancestors and told today. These stories depict a Maori view of the place of humans in the natural world and describe human responsibilities and obligations in terms of particular virtues. The concept and practice of *tapu*, for example, involve the idea that the world is not ours and that we need to be a certain sort of person in that world, one that embraces unconditional responsibilities of care and protection. The concept *mauri* expresses the idea that all things have a life or nature of their own that must be respected and calls for an understanding of and sympathetic attitude toward the nature or special character of each item. The concept *whanaungatanga* reminds Maori to seek and implement ways of enhancing the welfare of the whole environment and all its members. It demands more than refraining from harming others and asks that all our activities contribute to making the whole environment better. *Mana* describes one's place in the world in terms of an acceptance that others have their place and mine is neither privileged nor exclusive of theirs. Patterson argues that Maori virtues challenge the anthropocentrism of the West and that the Maori display a successful environmental virtue ethic that is alive and working and can give us insights into what is needed in a contemporary technological world.

ALL ANIMALS ARE EQUAL ...

Or why the ethical principle on which human equality rests requires us to extend equal consideration to animals too

Peter Singer

Peter Singer is Professor of Philosophy and Director of the Center for Human Bioethics at Monash University in Australia. He is the author of many publications on animals and the nonhuman environment. He is also the editor of Practical Ethics *(Cambridge, 1993),* Applied Ethics *(Oxford, 1986), and* Ethics *(Oxford, 1994).*

Singer defines speciesism as prejudice towards the interests of members of one's own species and against those of members of other species and argues that it is analogous to racism and sexism. Just as it is unjust to discriminate against women and blacks by not considering their interests, so too is it unjust to ignore the interests of animals. Because avoidance of suffering is one interest that is shared by human and non-human animals, it is morally wrong to ignore the suffering of animals.

"Animal Liberation" may sound more like a parody of other liberation movements than a serious objective. The idea of "The Rights of Animals" actually was once used to parody the case for women's rights. When Mary Wollstonecraft, a forerunner of today's feminists, published her *Vindication of the Rights of Woman* in 1792, her views were widely regarded as absurd, and before long an anonymous publication appeared entitled *A Vindication of the Rights of Brutes*. The author of this satirical work (now known to have been Thomas Taylor, a distinguished Cambridge philosopher) tried to refute Mary Wollstonecraft's arguments by showing that they could be carried one stage further. If the argument for equality was sound when applied to women, why should it not be applied to dogs, cats, and horses? The reasoning seemed to hold for these "brutes" too; yet to hold that brutes had rights was manifestly absurd. Therefore the reasoning by which this conclusion had been reached must be unsound, and if unsound when applied to brutes, it must also be unsound when applied to women, since the very same arguments had been used in each case.

In order to explain the basis of the case for the equality of animals, it will be helpful to start with an examination of the case for the equality of women. Let us assume that we wish to defend the case for women's rights against the attack by Thomas Taylor. How should we reply?

One way in which we might reply is by saying that the case for equality between men and women cannot validly be extended to nonhuman animals. Women have a right to vote, for instance, because they are just as capable of making rational decisions about the future as men are; dogs, on the other hand, are incapable of understanding the significance of voting, so they cannot have the right to vote. There are many other obvious ways in which men and women resemble each other closely, while humans and animals differ greatly. So, it might be said, men and women are similar beings and should have similar rights, while humans and nonhumans are different and should not have equal rights.

Reprinted with permission of Peter Singer from *Animal Liberation*, by Peter Singer, 2nd ed. (New York: Random House, 1990). [Edited]

The reasoning behind this reply to Taylor's analogy is correct up to a point, but it does not go far enough. There are obviously important differences between humans and other animals, and these differences must give rise to some differences in the rights that each have. Recognizing this evident fact, however, is no barrier to the case for extending the basic principle of equality to nonhuman animals. The differences that exist between men and women are equally undeniable, and the supporters of Women's Liberation are aware that these differences may give rise to different rights. Many feminists hold that women have the right to an abortion on request. It does not follow that since these same feminists are campaigning for equality between men and women they must support the right of men to have abortions too. Since a man cannot have an abortion, it is meaningless to talk of his right to have one. Since dogs can't vote, it is meaningless to talk of their right to vote. There is no reason why either Women's Liberation or Animal Liberation should get involved in such nonsense. The extension of the basic principle of equality from one group to another does not imply that we must treat both groups in exactly the same way, or grant exactly the same rights to both groups. Whether we should do so will depend on the nature of the members of the two groups. The basic principle of equality does not require equal or identical *treatment*; it requires equal consideration. Equal consideration for different beings may lead to different treatment and different rights.

So there is a different way of replying to Taylor's attempt to parody the case for women's rights, a way that does not deny the obvious differences between human beings and nonhumans but goes more deeply into the question of equality and concludes by finding nothing absurd in the idea that the basic principle of equality applies to so-called brutes. At this point such a conclusion may appear odd; but if we examine more deeply the basis on which our opposition to discrimination on grounds of race or sex ultimately rests, we will see that we would be on shaky ground if we were to demand equality for blacks, women, and other groups of oppressed humans while denying equal consideration to nonhumans. To make this clear we need to see, first, exactly why racism and sexism are wrong. When we say that all human beings, whatever their race, creed, or sex, are equal, what is it that we are asserting? Those who wish to defend hierarchical, inegalitarian societies have often pointed out that by whatever test we choose it simply is not true that all humans are equal. Like it or not we must face the fact that humans come in different shapes and sizes; they come with different moral capacities, different intellectual abilities, different amounts of benevolent feeling and sensitivity to the needs of others, different abilities to communicate effectively, and different capacities to experience pleasure and pain. In short, if the demand for equality were based on the actual equality of all human beings, we would have to stop demanding equality.

Still, one might cling to the view that the demand for equality among human beings is based on the actual equality of the different races and sexes. Although, it may be said, humans differ as individuals, there are no differences between the races and sexes as such. From the mere fact that a person is black or a woman we cannot infer anything about that person's intellectual or moral capacities. This, it may be said, is why racism and sexism are wrong. The white racist claims that whites are superior to blacks, but this is false; although there are differences among individuals, some blacks are superior to some whites in all of the capacities and abilities that could conceivably be relevant. The opponent of sexism would say the same: a person's sex is no guide to his or her abilities, and this is why it is unjustifiable to discriminate on the basis of sex.

The existence of individual variations that cut across the lines of race or sex, however, provides us with no defense at all against a more sophisticated opponent of equality, one who proposes that, say, the interests of all those with IQ scores below 100 be given less consideration than the interests of those with ratings over 100. Perhaps those scoring below the mark would, in this society, be made the slaves of those scoring higher. Would a hierarchical society of this sort really be so much better than one based on race or sex? I think not. But if we tie the moral principle of equality to the factual equality of the different races or sexes, taken as a whole, our opposition to racism and sexism does not provide us with any basis for objecting to this kind of inegalitarianism.

There is a second important reason why we ought not to base our opposition to racism and sexism on any kind of factual equality, even the limited kind that asserts that variations in capacities and abilities are spread evenly among the different races and between the sexes: we can have no absolute guarantee that these capacities and abilities really are distributed evenly, without regard to race or sex, among human beings. So far as actual abilities are concerned there do seem to be certain measurable differences both among races and between sexes. These differences do not, of course, appear in every case, but only when averages are taken. More important still, we do not yet know how many of these differences are really due to the different genetic endowments of the different races and sexes, and how many are due to poor schools, poor housing, and other factors that are the result of past and continuing discrimination. Perhaps all of the important differences will eventually prove to be environmental rather than genetic. Anyone opposed to racism and sexism will certainly hope that this will be so, for it will make the task of ending discrimination a lot easier; nevertheless, it would be dangerous to rest the case against racism and sexism on the belief that all significant differences are environmental in origin. The opponent of, say, racism who takes this line will be unable to avoid conceding that if differences in ability did after all prove to have some genetic connection with race, racism would in some way be defensible.

Fortunately there is no need to pin the case for equality to one particular outcome of a scientific investigation. The appropriate response to those who claim to have found evidence of genetically based differences in ability among the races or between the sexes is not to stick to the belief that the genetic explanation must be wrong, whatever evidence to the contrary may turn up; instead we should make it quite clear that the claim to equality does not depend on intelligence, moral capacity, physical strength, or similar matters of fact. Equality is a moral idea, not an assertion of fact. There is no logically compelling reason for assuming that a factual difference in ability between two people justifies any difference in the amount of consideration we give to their needs and interests. *The principle of the equality of human beings is not a description of an alleged actual equality among humans: it is a prescription of how we should treat human beings.*

Jeremy Bentham, the founder of the reforming utilitarian school of moral philosophy, incorporated the essential basis of moral equality into his system of ethics by means of the formula: "Each to count for one and none for more than one." In other words, the interests of every being affected by an action are to be taken into account and given the same weight as the like interests of any other being. A later utilitarian, Henry Sidgwick, put the point in this way: "The good of any one individual is of no more importance, from the point of view (if I may say so) of the Universe, than the good of any other." More recently the leading figures in contemporary moral philosophy have shown a great deal of agreement in specifying as a fundamental presupposition of their moral theories some similar requirement that works to give everyone's interests equal consideration—although these writers generally cannot agree on how this requirement is best formulated.[1]

It is an implication of this principle of equality that our concern for others and our readiness to consider their interests ought not to depend on what they are like or on what abilities they may possess. Precisely what our concern or consideration requires us to do may vary according to the characteristics of those affected by what we do: concern for the well-being of children growing up in America would require that we teach them to read; concern for the well-being of pigs may require no more than that we leave them with other pigs in a place where there is adequate food and room to run freely. But the basic element—the taking into account of the interests of the being, whatever those interests may be—must, according to the principle of equality, be extended to all beings, black or white, masculine of feminine, human or nonhuman.

Thomas Jefferson, who was responsible for writing the principle of the equality of men into the American Declaration of Independence, saw this point. It led him to oppose slavery even though he was unable to free himself fully from his slaveholding background. He wrote in a letter to the author of a book that emphasized the notable intellectual achievements of Negroes in order to refute the then common view that they had limited intellectual capacities:

> Be assured that no person living wishes more sincerely than I do, to see a complete refutation of the doubts I myself have entertained and expressed on the grade of understanding allotted to them by nature, and to find that they are on a par with ourselves ... but whatever be their degree of talent it is no measure of their rights. Because Sir Isaac Newton was superior to others in understanding, he was not therefore lord of the property or persons of others.[2]

Similarly, when in the 1850s the call for women's rights was raised in the United States, a remarkable black feminist named Sojourner Truth made the same point in more robust terms at a feminist convention:

> They talk about this thing in the head; what do they call it? ["Intellect," whispered someone nearby.] That's it. What's that got to do with women's rights or Negroes' rights? If my cup won't hold but a pint and yours holds a quart, wouldn't you be mean not to let me have my little half-measure full?[3]

It is on this basis that the case against racism and the case against sexism must both ultimately rest; and it is in accordance with this principle that the attitude that we may call "speciesism," by analogy with racism, must also be condemned. Speciesism—the word is not an attractive one, but I can think of no better term—is a prejudice or attitude of bias in favor of the interests of members of one's own species and against those of members of other species. It should be obvious that the fundamental objections to racism and sexism made by Thomas Jefferson and Sojourner Truth apply equally to speciesism. If possessing a higher degree of intelligence does not entitle one human to use another for his or her own ends, how can it entitle humans to exploit nonhumans for the same purpose?[4]

Many philosophers and other writers have proposed the principle of equal consideration of interests, in some form or other, as a basic moral principle; but not many of them have recognized that this principle applies to members of other species as well as to our own. Jeremy Bentham was one of the few who did realize this. In a forward-looking passage written at a time when black slaves had been freed by the French but in the British dominions were still being treated in the way we now treat animals, Bentham wrote:

> The day *may* come when the rest of the animal creation may acquire those rights which never could have been withholden from them but by the hand of tyranny. The French have already discovered that the blackness of the skin is no reason why a human being should be abandoned without redress to the caprice of a tormentor. It may one day come to be recognized that the number of the legs, the villosity of the skin, or the termination of the *os sacrum* are reasons equally insufficient for abandoning a sensitive being to the same fate. What else is it that should trace the insuperable line? Is it the faculty of reason, or perhaps the faculty of discourse? But a full-grown horse or dog is beyond comparison a more rational, as well as a more conversable animal, than an infant of a day or a week or even a month, old. But suppose they were otherwise, what would it avail? The question is not, Can they *reason*? nor Can they *talk*? but, Can they *suffer*?[5]

In this passage Bentham points to the capacity for suffering as the vital characteristic that gives a being the right to equal consideration. The capacity for suffering—or more strictly, for suffering and/or enjoyment or happiness—is not just another characteristic like the capacity for language or higher mathematics. Bentham is not saying that those who try to mark "the insuperable line" that determines whether the interests of a being should be considered happen to have chosen the wrong characteristic. By saying that we must consider the interests of all beings with the capacity for suffering or enjoyment Bentham does not arbitrarily exclude from consideration any interests at all—as those who draw the line with reference to the possession of reason or language do. The capacity for suffering and enjoyment is *a prerequisite for having interests at all*, a condition that must be satisfied before we can speak of interests in a meaningful way. It would be nonsense to say that it was not in the interests of a stone to be kicked along the road by a schoolboy.

A stone does not have interests because it cannot suffer. Nothing that we can do to it could possibly make any difference to its welfare. The capacity for suffering and enjoyment is, however, not only necessary, but also sufficient for us to say that a being has interests—at an absolute minimum, an interest in not suffering. A mouse, for example, does have an interest in not being kicked along the road, because it will suffer if it is.

Although Bentham speaks of "rights" in the passage I have quoted, the argument is really about equality rather than about rights. Indeed, in a different passage, Bentham famously described "natural rights" as "nonsense" and "natural and imprescriptable rights" as "nonsense upon stilts." He talked of moral rights as a shorthand way of referring to protections that people and animals morally ought to have; but the real weight of the moral argument does not rest on the assertion of the existence of the right, for this in turn has to be justified on the basis of the possibilities for suffering and happiness. In this way we can argue for equality for animals without getting embroiled in philosophical controversies about the ultimate nature of rights.

In misguided attempts to refute the arguments of this book, some philosophers have gone to much trouble developing arguments to show that animals do not have rights.[6] They have claimed that to have rights a being must be autonomous, or must be a member of a community, or must have the ability to respect the rights of others, or must possess a sense of justice. These claims are irrelevant to the case for Animal Liberation. The language of rights is a convenient political shorthand. It is even more valuable in the era of thirty-second TV news clips than it was in Bentham's day; but in the argument for a radical change in our attitude to animals, it is in no way necessary.

If a being suffers there can be no moral justification for refusing to take that suffering into consideration. No matter what the nature of the being, the principle of equality requires that its suffering be counted equally with the like suffering—insofar as rough comparisons can be made—of any other being. If a being is not capable of suffering, or of experiencing enjoyment or happiness, there is nothing to be taken into account. So the limit of sentience (using the term as a convenient if not strictly accurate shorthand for the capacity to suffer and/or experience enjoyment) is the only defensible boundary of concern for the interests of others. To mark this boundary by some other characteristic like intelligence or rationality would be to mark it in an arbitrary manner. Why not choose some other characteristic, like skin color?

Racists violate the principle of equality by giving greater weight to the interests of members of their own race when there is a clash between their interests and the interests of those of another race. Sexists violate the principle of equality by favoring the interests of their own sex. Similarly, speciesists allow the interests of their own species to override the greater interests of members of other species. The pattern is identical in each case....

So far I have said a lot about inflicting suffering on animals, but nothing about killing them. This omission has been deliberate. The application of the principle of equality to the infliction of suffering is, in theory at least, fairly straightforward. Pain and suffering are in themselves bad and should be prevented or minimized, irrespective of the race, sex, or species of the being that suffers. How bad a pain is depends on how intense it is and how long it lasts, but pains of the same intensity and duration are equally bad, whether felt by humans or animals.

The wrongness of killing a being is more complicated. I have kept, and shall continue to keep, the question of killing in the background because in the present state of human tyranny over other species the more simple, straightforward principle of equal consideration of pain or pleasure is a sufficient basis for identifying and protesting against all the major abuses of animals that human beings practice. Nevertheless, it is necessary to say something about killing.

Just as most human beings are speciesists in their readiness to cause pain to animals when they would not cause a similar pain to humans for the same reason, so most human beings are speciesists in their readiness to kill other animals when they would not kill human beings. We need to proceed more cautiously here, however, because people hold widely differing views about when it is legitimate to kill humans, as the continuing debates over abortion and euthanasia attest. Nor have moral philosophers been able to agree on exactly what it is that makes it wrong to kill human beings, and under what circumstances killing a human being may be justifiable.

Let us consider first the view that it is always wrong to take an innocent human life. We may call this the "sanctity of life" view. People who take this view oppose abortion and euthanasia. They do not usually, however, oppose the killing of nonhuman animals—so perhaps it would be more accurate to describe this view as the "sanctity of *human* life" view. The belief that human life, and only human life, is sacrosanct is a form of speciesism. To see this, consider the following example.

Assume that, as sometimes happens, an infant has been born with massive and irreparable brain damage. The damage is so severe that the infant can never be any more than a "human vegetable," unable to talk, recognize other people, act independently of others, or develop a sense of self-awareness. The parents of the infant, realizing that they cannot hope for any improvement in their child's condition and being in any case unwilling to spend, or ask the state to spend, the thousands of dollars that would be needed annually for proper care of the infant, ask the doctor to kill the infant painlessly.

Should the doctor do what the parents ask? Legally, the doctor should not, and in this respect the law reflects the sanctity of life view. The life of every human being is sacred. Yet people who would say this about the infant do not object to the killing of nonhuman animals. How can they justify their different judgments? Adult chimpanzees, dogs, pigs, and members of many other species far surpass the brain-damaged infant in their ability to relate to others, act independently, be self-aware, and any other capacity that could reasonably be said to give value to life. With the most intensive care possible, some severely retarded infants can never achieve the intelligence level of a dog. Nor can we appeal to the concern of the infant's parents, since they themselves, in this imaginary example (and in some actual cases) do not want the infant kept alive. The only thing that distinguishes the infant from the animal, in the eyes of those who claim it has a "right to life," is that it is, biologically, a member of the species Homo-sapiens, whereas chimpanzees, dogs, and pigs are not. But to use *this* difference as the basis for granting a right to life to the infant and not to the other animals is, of course, pure speciesism.[7] It is exactly the kind of arbitrary difference that the most crude and overt kind of racist uses in attempting to justify racial discrimination.

This does not mean that to avoid speciesism we must hold that it is as wrong to kill a dog as it is to kill a human being in full possession of his or her faculties. The only position that is irredeemably speciesist is the one that tries to make the boundary of the right to life run exactly parallel to the boundary of our own species. Those who hold the sanctity of life view do this, because while distinguishing sharply between human beings and other animals they allow no distinctions to be made within our own species, objecting to the killing of the severely retarded and the hopelessly senile as strongly as they object to the killing of normal adults.

To avoid speciesism we must allow that beings who are similar in all relevant respects have a similar right to life—and mere membership in our own biological species cannot be a morally relevant criterion for this right. Within these limits we could still hold, for instance, that it is worse to kill a normal adult human, with a capacity for self-awareness and the ability to plan for the future and have meaningful relations with others, than it is to kill a mouse, which presumably does not share all of these characteristics; or we might appeal to the close family and other personal ties that humans have but mice do not have to the same degree; or we might think that it is the consequences for other humans, who will be put in fear for their own lives, that makes the crucial difference; or we might think it is some combination of these factors, or other factors altogether.

Whatever criteria we choose, however, we will have to admit that they do not follow precisely the boundary of our own species. We may legitimately hold that there are some features of certain beings that make their lives more valuable than those of other beings; but there will surely be some nonhuman animals whose lives, by any standards, are more valuable than the lives of some humans. A chimpanzee, dog, or pig, for instance, will have a higher degree of self-awareness and a greater capacity for meaningful relations with others than a severely retarded infant or someone in a state of advanced senility. So if we base the right to life on these characteristics we must grant these animals a right to life as good as, or better than, such retarded or senile humans.

This argument cuts both ways. It could be taken as showing that chimpanzees, dogs, and pigs, along with some other species, have a right to life and we commit a grave moral offense whenever we kill them, even when they are old and suffering and our intention is to put them out of their misery. Alternatively one could take the argument as showing that the severely retarded and hopelessly senile have no right to life and may be killed for quite trivial reasons, as we now kill animals.

Since the main concern of this book is with ethical questions having to do with animals and not with the morality of euthanasia I shall not attempt to settle this issue finally.[8] I think it is reasonably clear, though, that while both of the positions just described avoid speciesism, neither is satisfactory. What we need is some middle position that would avoid speciesism but would not make the lives of the retarded and senile as cheap as the lives of pigs and dogs now are, or make the lives of pigs and dogs so sacrosanct that we think it wrong to put them out of hopeless misery. What we must do is bring nonhuman animals within our sphere of moral concern and cease to treat their lives as expendable for whatever trivial purposes we may have. At the same time, once we realize that the fact that a being is a member of our own species is not in itself enough to make it always wrong to kill that being, we may come to reconsider our policy of preserving human lives at all costs, even when there is no prospect of a meaningful life or of existence without terrible pain.

I conclude, then, that a rejection of speciesism does not imply that all lives are of equal worth. While self-awareness, the capacity to think ahead and have hopes and aspirations for the future, the capacity for meaningful relations with others and so on are not relevant to the question of inflicting pain—since pain is pain, whatever other capacities, beyond the capacity to feel pain, the being may have—these capacities are relevant to the question of taking life. It is not arbitrary to hold that the life of a self-aware being, capable of abstract thought, of planning for the future, of complex acts of communication, and so on, is more valuable than the life of a being without these capacities. To see the difference between the issues of inflicting pain and taking life, consider how we would choose within our own species. If we had to choose to save the life of a normal human being or an intellectually disabled human being, we would probably choose to save the life of a normal human being; but if we had to choose between preventing pain in the normal human being or the intellectually disabled one—imagine that both have received painful but superficial injuries, and we only have enough painkiller for one of them—it is not nearly so clear how we ought to choose. The same is true when we consider other species. The evil of pain is, in itself, unaffected by the other characteristics of the being who feels the pain; the value of life is affected by these other characteristics. To give just one reason for this difference, to take the life of a being who has been hoping, planning, and working for some future goal is to deprive that being of the fulfillment of all those efforts; to take the life of a being with a mental capacity below the level needed to grasp that one is a being with a future—much less make plans for the future—cannot involve this particular kind of loss.[9]

Normally this will mean that if we have to choose between the life of a human being and the life of another animal we should choose to save the life of the human; but there may be special cases in which the reverse holds true, because the human being in question does not have the capacities of a normal human being. So this view is not speciesist, although it may appear to be at first glance. The preference, in normal cases, for saving a human life over the life of an animal when a choice *has* to be made is a preference based on the characteristics that normal humans have, and not on the mere fact that they are members of our own species. This is why when we consider members of our own species who lack the characteristics of normal humans we can no longer say that their lives are always to be preferred to those of other animals. In general, though, the question of when it is wrong to kill (painlessly) an animal is one to which we need give no precise answer. As long as we remember that we should give the same respect to the lives of animals as we give to the lives of those humans at a similar mental level, we shall not go far wrong.[10]

In any case, the conclusions that are argued for in this book flow from the principle of minimizing suffering alone. The idea that it is also wrong to kill animals painlessly gives some of these conclusions additional support that is welcome but strictly unnecessary. Interestingly enough, this is true even of the conclusion that we ought to become vegetarians, a conclusion that in the popular mind is generally based on some kind of absolute prohibition on killing....

Becoming a Vegetarian ...

Or how to produce less suffering and more food at a reduced cost to the environment

As a matter of strict logic, perhaps, there is no contradiction in taking an interest in animals on both compassionate and gastronomic grounds. If one is opposed to inflicting suffering on animals, but not to the painless killing of animals, one could consistently eat animals who had lived free of all suffering and been instantly, painlessly slaughtered. Yet practically and psychologically it is impossible to be consistent in one's concern for nonhuman animals while continuing to dine on them. If we are prepared to take the life of another being merely in order to satisfy our taste for a particular type of food, then that being is no more than a means to our end. In time we will come to regard pigs, cattle, and chickens as things for us to use, no matter how strong our compassion may be; and when we find that to continue to obtain supplies of the bodies of these animals at a price we are able to pay it is necessary to change their living conditions a little, we will be unlikely to regard these changes too critically. The factory farm is nothing more than the application of technology to the idea that animals are means to our ends. Our eating habits are dear to us and not easily altered. We have a strong interest in convincing ourselves that our concern for other animals does not require us to stop eating them. No one in the habit of eating an animal can be completely without bias in judging whether the conditions in which that animal is reared cause suffering.

It is not practically possible to rear animals for food on a large scale without inflicting considerable suffering. Even if intensive methods are not used, traditional farming involves castration, separation of mother and young, breaking up social groups, branding, transportation to the slaughterhouse, and finally slaughter itself. It is difficult to imagine how animals could be reared for food without these forms of suffering. Possibly it could be done on a small scale, but we could never feed today's huge urban populations with meat raised in this manner. If it could be done at all, the animal flesh thus produced would be vastly more expensive than animal flesh is today—and rearing animals is already an expensive and inefficient way of producing protein. The flesh of animals reared and killed with equal consideration for the welfare of animals while they were alive would be a delicacy available only to the rich.

All this is, in any case, quite irrelevant to the immediate question of the ethics of our daily diet. Whatever the theoretical possibilities of rearing animals without suffering may be, the fact is that the meat available from butchers and supermarkets comes from animals who were not treated with any real consideration at all while being reared. So we must ask ourselves, not: Is it *ever* right to eat meat? but: Is it right to eat *this* meat? Here I think that those who are opposed to the needless killing of animals and those who oppose only the infliction of suffering must join together and give the same, negative answer.

Becoming a vegetarian is not merely a symbolic gesture. Nor is it an attempt to isolate oneself from the ugly realities of the world, to keep oneself pure and so without responsibility for the cruelty and carnage all around. Becoming a vegetarian is a highly practical and effective step one can take toward ending both the killing of nonhuman animals and the infliction of suffering upon them....

The people who profit by exploiting large numbers of animals do not need our approval. They need our money. The purchase of the corpses of the animals they rear is the main support the factory farmers ask from the public (the other, in many countries, is big government subsidies). They will use intensive methods as long as they can sell what they produce by these methods; they will have the resources needed to fight reform politically; and they will be able to defend themselves against criticism with the reply that they are only providing the public with what it wants.

Hence the need for each one of us to stop buying the products of modern animal farming—even if we are not convinced that it would be wrong to eat animals who have lived pleasantly and died painlessly. Vegetarianism is a form of boycott. For most vegetarians the boycott is a permanent one, since once they have broken away from flesh-eating habits they can no longer approve of slaughtering animals in order to satisfy the trivial desires of their palates. But the moral obligation to boycott the meat available in butcher shops and supermarkets today is just as inescapable for those who disapprove only of inflicting suffering, and not of killing. Until we boycott meat, and all other products of animal factories, we are, each one of us, contributing to the continued existence, prosperity, and growth of factory farming and all the other cruel practices used in rearing animals for food.

It is at this point that the consequences of speciesism intrude directly into our lives, and we are forced to attest personally to the sincerity of our concern for nonhuman animals. Here we have an opportunity to do something, instead of merely talking and wishing the politicians would do something. It is easy to take a stand about a remote issue, but speciesists, like racists, reveal their true nature when the issue comes nearer home. To protest about bullfighting in Spain, the eating of dogs in South Korea, or the slaughter of baby seals in Canada while continuing to eat eggs from hens who have spent their lives crammed into cages, or veal from calves who have been deprived of their mothers, their proper diet, and the freedom to lie down with their legs extended, is like denouncing apartheid in South Africa while asking your neighbors not to sell their houses to blacks....

I have emphasized the boycott element of vegetarianism so much that the reader may ask whether, if the boycott does not spread and prove effective, anything has been achieved by becoming a vegetarian. But we must often venture when we cannot be certain of success, and it would be no argument against becoming a vegetarian if this were all that could be said against it, since none of the great movements against oppression and injustice would have existed if their leaders had made no efforts until they were assured of success. In the case of vegetarianism, however, I believe we do achieve something by our individual acts, even if the boycott as a whole should not succeed. George Bernard Shaw once said that he would be followed to his grave by numerous sheep, cattle, pigs, chickens, and a whole shoal of fish, all grateful at having been spared from slaughter because of his vegetarian diet. Although we cannot identify any individual animals whom we have benefited by becoming a vegetarian, we can assume that our diet, together with that of the many others who are already avoiding meat, will have some impact on the number of animals raised in factory farms and slaughtered for food. This assumption is reasonable because the number of animals raised and slaughtered depends on the profitability of this process, and this profit depends in part on the demand for the product. The smaller the demand, the lower the price and the lower the profit. The lower the profit, the fewer the animals that will be raised and slaughtered. This is elementary economics, and it can easily be observed in tables published by the poultry trade journals, for instance, that there is a direct correlation between the price of poultry and the number of chickens placed in broiler sheds to begin their joyless existence.

So vegetarianism is really on even stronger ground than most other boycotts or protests. The person who boycotts South African produce in order to bring down apartheid achieves nothing unless the boycott succeeds in forcing white South Africans to modify their policies (though the effort may have been well worth making, whatever the outcome); but vegetarians know that they do, by their actions, contribute to a reduction in the suffering and slaughter of animals, whether or not they live to see their efforts spark off a mass boycott of meat and an end to cruelty in farming.

NOTES

1. For Bentham's moral philosophy, see his *Introduction to the Principles of Morals and Legislation*, and for Sidgwick's see *The Methods of Ethics*, 1907 (the pas-

sage is quoted from the seventh edition; reprint, London: Macmillan, 1963), p. 382. As examples of leading contemporary moral philosophers who incorporate a requirement of equal consideration of interests, see R. M. Hare, *Freedom and Reason* (New York: Oxford University Press, 1963), and John Rawls, *A Theory of Justice* (Cambridge: Harvard University Press, Belknap Press, 1972). For a brief account of the essential agreement on this issue between these and other positions, see R. M. Hare, "Rules of War and Moral Reasoning," *Philosophy and Public Affairs* 1 (2) (1972).

2. Letter to Henry Gregoire, February 25, 1809.
3. Reminiscences by Francis D. Gage, from Susan B. Anthony, *The History of Woman Suffrage*, vol. 1; the passage is to be found in the extract in Leslie Tanner, ed., *Voices From Women's Liberation* (New York: Signet, 1970).
4. I owe the term "speciesism" to Richard Ryder. It has become accepted in general use since the first edition of this book, and now appears in *The Oxford English Dictionary*, second edition (Oxford: Clarendon Press, 1989).
5. *Introduction to the Principles of Morals and Legislation*, chapter 17.
6. See M. Levin, "Animal Rights Evaluated," *Humanist* 37: 14-15 (July/August 1977); M. A. Fox, "Animal Liberation: A Critique," *Ethics* 88: 134-138 (1978); C. Perry and G. E. Jones, "On Animal Rights," *International Journal of Applied Philosophy* 1: 39-57 (1982).
7. I am here putting aside religious views, for example the doctrine that all and only human beings have immortal souls, or are made in the image of God. Historically these have been very important, and no doubt are partly responsible for the idea that human life has a special sanctity....Logically, however, these religious views are unsatisfactory, since they do not offer a reasoned explanation of why it should be that all humans and no nonhumans have immortal souls. This belief too, therefore, comes under suspicion as a form of speciesism. In any case, defenders of the "sanctity of life" view are generally reluctant to base their position on purely religious doctrines, since these doctrines are no longer as widely accepted as they once were.
8. For a general discussion of these questions, see my *Practical Ethics* (Cambridge: Cambridge University Press, 1979), and for a more detailed discussion of the treatment of handicapped infants, see Helga Kuhse and Peter Singer, *Should the Baby Live?* (Oxford: Oxford University Press, 1985).
9. For a development of this theme, see my essay, "Life's Uncertain Voyage," in P. Pettit, R. Sylvan and J. Norman, eds., *Metaphysics and Morality* (Oxford: Blackwell, 1987), pp. 154-172.
10. The preceding discussion, which has been changed only slightly since the first edition, has often been overlooked by critics of the Animal Liberation movement. It is a common tactic to seek to ridicule the Animal Liberation position by maintaining that, as an animal experimenter put it recently, "Some of these people believe that every insect, every mouse, has as much right to life as a human." (Dr. Irving Weissman, as quoted in Katherine Bishop, "From Shop to Lab to Farm, Animal Rights Battle is Felt," *The New York Times*, January 14, 1989.) It would be interesting to see Dr. Weissman name some prominent Animal Liberationists who hold this view. Certainly (assuming only that he was referring to the right to life of a human being with mental capacities very different from those of the insect and the mouse) the position described is not mine. I doubt that it is held by many—if any—in the Animal Liberation movement.

ANIMAL LIBERATION: A TRIANGULAR AFFAIR

J. Baird Callicott

J. Baird Callicott is in the Department of Philosophy and Religious Studies at the University of North Texas. He is the author of In Defense of the Land Ethic: Essays in Environmental Philosophy *(SUNY, 1989) and* Earth's Insights: A Survey of Ecological Ethics from the Mediterranean Basin to the Australian Outback *(California, 1994) and co-editor of* Earth Summit Ethics: Toward a Reconstructive Postmodern Philosophy of Environmental Education *(SUNY, 1996) and* The Great New Wilderness Debate *(Georgia Press, 1998).*

Callicott identifies two main strategies in social movements aiming to extend rights to an increasing number of entities. "Ethical humanists" defend the view that there are fundamental properties that demand moral consideration be given to all human beings. "Humane moralists" extend moral consideration to non-human animals by identifying criteria shared by human and non-human animals. Callicott argues that these views are not equipped to allow extension of moral consideration to trees, rocks, or rivers, for example, or to species and ecosystems. Callicott turns to Aldo Leopold's land ethic as an approach that shifts from accounts of the intrinsic value of individuals in ethical humanism and humane moralism to ecosystems and the value of preserving the "integrity, stability, and beauty of the biotic community."

Preface (1994)

I wrote "A Triangular Affair" to sharply distinguish environmental ethics from animal liberation/rights when the former seemed to be overshadowed by the latter. Back in the late 1970s and early 1980s, when the piece was conceived and composed, many people seemed to conflate the two. In my youthful zeal to draw attention to the then unheralded Leopold land ethic, I made a few remarks that in retrospect appear irresponsible.

Most important, I no longer think that the land ethic is misanthropic. "All ethics so far evolved," Leopold wrote, "rest upon a single premiss: that the individual is a member of a community of interdependent parts....The land ethic simply enlarges the boundaries of the community to include soils, waters, plants, and animals, or collectively: the land." The biotic community and its correlative land ethic *does not replace* our several human communities and their correlative ethics—our duties and obligations to family and family members, to municipality and fellow-citizens, to country and countrymen, to humanity and human beings. Rather it *supplements* them. Hence the land ethic leaves our traditional human morality quite intact and pre-emptive.

Second in importance, I now think that we do in fact have duties and obligations—implied by the essentially communitarian premisses of the land ethic—to domestic animals, as well as to wild fellow-members of the biotic community and to the biotic community as a whole. Farm animals, work animals, and pets have long been members of what Mary Midgley calls the "mixed" community. They have entered into a kind of implicit social contract with us which lately we have abrogated. Think of it this way. Each of us belongs to several hierarchical-

---

"Preface" reprinted with permission of the publisher from *Environmental Ethics*, edited by Robert Elliot (Oxford: Oxford University Press, 1995): 29–30. "Animal Liberation" printed with permission of the publisher and J. Baird Callicott from *Environmental Ethics* 2:4 (Winter 1980): 311–338 [edited].

ly ordered human communities, each with its peculiar set of duties and obligations; to various mixed human-animal domestic communities, with their peculiar sets of duties and obligations; and to the biotic community, with its peculiar set of duties and obligations (which in sum Leopold called the land ethic). The land ethic no more eclipses our moral responsibilities in regard to domestic animals than it does our moral responsibilities in regard to other people.

Further, I now think that a vegetarian diet is indicated by the land ethic, no less than by the animal welfare ethics. Rainforests are felled to make pasture for cattle. Better for the environment if we ate forest fruits instead of beef. Livestock ruin watercourses and grasslands. And raising field crops for animal feed increases soil erosion and ground-water depletion.

Finally, though certainly I still wish there were far more bears than actually there are, a target ratio of one bear for every two people seems a bit extravagant.

"A Triangular Affair" clearly distinguishes between holistic environmental ethics, on the one hand, and individualistic "moral humanism" and "humane moralism," on the other. And that remains a serviceable distinction. Moralists of every stripe, however, must make common cause against the forces that are often simultaneously destroying human, mixed, and biotic communities. The differences between human, humane, and environmental concerns are real, and sometimes conflictive. But just as often they are convergent and mutually reinforcing. And all our ethical concerns can be theoretically unified, I am convinced, by a communitarian moral philosophy, thus enabling conflicts, when they do arise, to be adjudicated rationally.

Environmental Ethics and Animal Liberation

Partly because it is so new to Western philosophy (or at least heretofore only scarcely represented) *environmental ethics* has no precisely fixed conventional definition in glossaries of philosophical terminology. Aldo Leopold, however, is universally recognized as the father of founding genius of recent environmental ethics. His "land ethic" has become a modern classic and may be treated as the standard example, the paradigm case, as it were, of what an environmental ethic is. *Environmental ethics* then can be defined ostensively by using Leopold's land ethic as the exemplary type. I do not mean to suggest that all environmental ethics should necessarily conform to Leopold's paradigm, but the extent to which an ethical system resembles Leopold's land ethic might be used, for want of anything better, as a criterion to measure the extent to which it is or is not of the environmental sort.

It is Leopold's opinion, and certainly an overall review of the prevailing traditions of Western ethics, both popular and philosophical, generally confirms it, that traditional Western systems of ethics have not accorded moral standing to nonhuman beings.[1] Animals and plants, soils and waters, which Leopold includes in his community of ethical beneficiaries, have traditionally enjoyed no moral standing, no rights, no respect, in sharp contrast to human persons whose rights and interests ideally must be fairly and equally considered if our actions are to be considered "ethical" or "moral." One fundamental and novel feature of the Leopold land ethic, therefore, is the extension of *direct* ethical considerability from people to nonhuman natural entities.

At first glance, the recent ethical movement usually labeled "animal liberation" or "animal rights" seems to be squarely and centrally a kind of environmental ethics. The more uncompromising among the animal liberationists have demanded equal moral consideration on behalf of cows, pigs, chickens, and other apparently enslaved and oppressed nonhuman animals. The theoreticians of this new hyperegalitarianism have coined such terms as *speciesism* (on analogy with *racism* and *sexism*) and *human chauvinism* (on analogy with *male chauvinism*), and have made animal liberation seem, perhaps not improperly, the next and most daring development of political liberalism. Aldo Leopold also draws upon metaphors of political liberalism when he tells us that his land ethic "changes the role of *Homo sapiens* from conqueror of the land community to plain member and citizen of it."[2] For animal liberationists it is as if the ideological battles for equal rights and equal consideration for women and for racial minorities have been all but won, and the next and greatest challenge is to purchase equality, first theoretically and then practically, for all (actually only *some*) animals, regardless of species. This more rhetorically implied than fully articulated historical progression of moral rights from fewer to greater numbers of "persons" (allowing that animals may also be persons) as advocated by animal liberationists, also parallels Leopold's scenario in "The Land Ethic" of the historical extension of "ethical criteria" to more and more "fields of conduct" and to larger and larger groups of people during the past three thousand or so years.[3] As Leopold develops it, the land ethic is a cultural "evolutionary possibility," the next "step in a sequence."[4] For Leopold, however, the next step is much more sweeping, much more inclusive than the animal liberationists envision, since it "enlarges the boundaries of the [moral] community to include soils, waters, [and] plants ... " as well as animals.[5] Thus, the animal liberation movement *could* be construed as partitioning Leopold's perhaps undigestible and totally inclusive environmental ethic into a series of more assimilable stages: today animal rights, tomorrow equal rights for plants, and after that full moral standing for rocks, soil, and other earthy compounds, and perhaps sometime in the still more remote future, liberty and equality for water and other elementary bodies.

Put just this way, however, there is something jarring about such a graduated progression in the exfoliation of a more inclusive environmental ethic, something that seems absurd. A more or less reasonable case might be made for rights for some animals, but when we come to plants, soils, and waters, the frontier between plausibility and absurdity appears to have been crossed. Yet, there is no doubt that Leopold sincerely proposes that *land* (in his inclusive sense) be ethically regarded. The beech and chestnut, for example, have in his view as much "biotic right" to life as the wolf and the deer, and the effects of human actions on mountains and streams for Leopold is an ethical concern as genuine and serious as the comfort and longevity of brood hens.[6] In fact, Leopold to all appearances never considered the treatment of brood hens on a factory farm or steers in a feed lot to be a pressing moral issue. He seems much more concerned about the integrity of the farm *wood lot* and the effects of clear-cutting steep slopes on neighboring *streams*.

Animal liberationists put their ethic into practice (and display their devotion to it) by becoming vegetarians, and the moral complexities of vegetarianism have been thoroughly debated in the recent literature as an adjunct issue to animal rights. (No one however has yet expressed, as among Butler's Erewhonians, qualms about eating plants, though such sentiments might be expected to be latently present, if the rights of plants are next to be defended.) Aldo Leopold, by contrast did not even condemn hunting animals, let alone eating them, nor did he personally abandon hunting, for which he had had an enthusiasm since boyhood, upon becoming convinced that his ethical responsibilities extended beyond the human sphere. There are several interpretations for this behavioral peculiarity. One is that Leopold did not see that his land ethic actually ought to prohibit hunting, cruelly killing, and eating animals. A corollary of this interpretation is that Leopold was so unperspicacious as deservedly to be thought stupid—a conclusion hardly comporting with the intellectual subtlety he usually evinces in most other respects. If not stupid, then perhaps Leopold was hypocritical. But if a hypocrite, we should expect him to conceal his proclivity for blood sports and flesh eating and to treat them as shameful vices to be indulged secretively. As it is, bound together between the same covers with "The Land Ethic" are his unabashed reminiscences of killing and consuming *game*. This term (like *stock*) when used of animals, moreover, appears to be morally equivalent to referring to a sexually appealing young woman as a "piece" or to a strong, young black man as a "buck"—if animal rights, that is, are to be considered as on a par with women's rights and the rights of formerly enslaved races. A third interpretation of Leopold's approbation of regulated and disciplined sport hunting (and *a fortiori* meat eating) is that it is a form of human/animal behavior not inconsistent with the land ethic as he conceived it. A corollary of this interpretation is that Leopold's land ethic and the environmental ethic of the animal liberation movement rest upon very different theoretical foundations, and that they are thus two very different forms of environmental ethics.

The urgent concern of animal liberationists for the suffering of *domestic* animals, toward which Leopold manifests an attitude which can only be described as indifference, and the urgent concern of Leopold, on the other hand, for the disappearance of *species* of plants as well as animals and for soil erosion and stream pollution, appear to be symptoms not only of very different ethical perspectives, but profoundly different cosmic visions as well. The neat similarities, noted at the beginning of this discussion, between the environmental ethic of the animal liberation movement and the classical Leopoldian land ethic appear in light of these observations to be rather superficial and to conceal substrata of thought and value which are not at all similar. The theoretical foundations of the animal liberation movement and those of the Leopoldian land ethic may even turn out not to be companionable, complementary, or mutually consistent. The animal liberationists may thus find themselves not only engaged in controversy with the many conservative philosophers upholding *apartheid* between man and "beast," but also faced with an unexpected dissent from another, very different, system of environmental ethics. Animal liberation and animal rights may well prove to be a triangular rather than, as it has so far been represented in the philosophical community, a polar controversy.

Ethical Humanism and Humane Moralism

The orthodox response of "ethical humanism" (as this philosophical perspective may be styled) to the suggestion that nonhuman animals should be accorded moral standing is that such animals are not worthy of this high perquisite. Only human beings are rational, or capable of having interests, or possess *self*-awareness, or have linguistic abilities, or can represent the future, it is variously argued. These essential attributes taken singly or in various combinations make people somehow exclusively deserving of moral consideration. The so-called "lower animals," it is insisted, lack the crucial qualification for ethical considerability and so may be treated (albeit humanely, according to some, so as not to brutalize man) as things or means, not as persons or as ends.

The theoreticians of the animal liberation movement ("humane moralists" as they may be called) typically reply as follows. Not all human beings qualify as worthy of moral regard, according to the various criteria specified. Therefore, by parity of reasoning, human persons who do not so qualify as moral patients may be treated, as animals often are, as mere things or means (e.g., used in vivisection experiments, disposed of if their existence is inconvenient, eaten, hunted, etc., etc.). But the ethical humanists would be morally outraged if irrational and inarticulate infants, for example, were used in painful or lethal medical experiments, or if severely retarded people were hunted for pleasure. Thus, the double-dealing, the hypocrisy, of ethical humanism appears to be exposed. Ethical humanism, though claiming to discriminate between worthy and unworthy ethical patients on the basis of objective criteria impartially applied, turns out after all, it seems, to be *speciesism*, a philosophically indefensible prejudice (analogous to racial prejudice) against animals. The tails side of this argument is that some animals, usually the "higher" lower animals (cetaceans, other primates, etc.), as ethological studies seem to indicate, may meet the criteria specified for moral worth, although the ethical humanists, even so, are not prepared to grant them full dignity and the rights of persons. In short, the ethical humanists' various criteria for moral standing do not include all or only human beings, humane moralists argue, although in practice ethical humanism wishes to make the class of morally considerable beings coextensive with the class of human beings.

The humane moralists, for their part, insist upon *sentience* (*sensibility* would have been a more precise word choice) as the only relevant capacity a being need possess to enjoy full moral standing. If animals, they argue, are conscious entities who, though deprived of reason, speech, forethought or even *self*-awareness (however that may be judged), are capable of suffering, then their suffering should be as much a matter of ethical concern as that of our fellow human beings, or strictly speaking, as our very own. What, after all, has rationality or any of the other allegedly uniquely human capacities to do with ethical standing? Why, in other words, should beings who reason or use speech (etc.) qualify for moral status, and those who do not fail to qualify? Isn't this just like saying that only persons with white skin should be free, or that only persons who beget and not those who bear should own property? The criterion seems utterly unrelated to the benefit for which it selects. On the other hand, the capacity to suffer is, it seems, a more relevant criterion for moral standing because—as Bentham and Mill, notable among modern philosophers, and Epicurus, among the ancients, aver—pain is evil, and its opposite, pleasure and freedom from pain, good. As moral agents (and this seems axiomatic), we have a duty to behave in such a way that the effect of our actions is to promote and procure good, so far as possible, and to reduce and minimize evil. That would amount to an obligation to produce pleasure and reduce pain. Now pain is pain wherever and by whomever it is suffered. As a *moral* agent, I should not consider my pleasure and pain to be of greater consequence in determining a course of action than that of other persons. Thus, by the same token, if animals suffer pain—and among philosophers only strict Cartesians would deny that they do—then we are morally obliged to consider their suffering as much an evil to be minimized by conscientious moral agents as human suffering. Certainly actions of ours which contribute to the suffering of animals, such as hunting them, butchering and eating them, experimenting on them, etc., are on these assumptions morally reprehensible. Hence, a person who regards himself or herself as not aiming in life to live most selfishly, conveniently, or profitably, but rightly and in accord with practical principle, if convinced by these arguments, should, among other things, cease to eat the flesh of animals, to hunt them, to wear fur and leather clothing and bone ornaments and other articles made from the bodies of animals, to eat eggs and drink milk, if the animal producers of these commodities are retained under inhumane circumstances, and to patronize zoos (as sources of psychological if not physical torment of animals). On the other hand, since certain very simple animals are almost certainly insensible to pleasure and pain, they may and indeed should be treated as morally inconsequential. Nor is there any moral reason why trees should be respected or rivers or mountains or anything which is, though living or tributary to life processes, unconscious. The humane moralists, like the moral humanists, draw a firm distinction between those beings worthy of moral consideration and those not. They simply insist upon a different but quite definite cut-off point on the spectrum of natural entities, and accompany their criterion with arguments to show that it is more ethically defensible (granting certain assumptions) and more consistently applicable than that of the moral humanists.

The First Principle of the Land Ethic

The fundamental principle of humane moralism, as we see, is Benthamic. Good is equivalent to pleasure and, more pertinently, evil is equivalent to pain. The presently booming controversy between moral humanists and humane moralists appears, when all the learned dust has settled, to be essentially internecine; at least, the lines of battle are drawn along familiar watersheds of the conceptual terrain. A classical ethical theory, Bentham's, has been refitted and pressed into service to meet relatively new and unprecedented ethically relevant situations—the problems raised especially by factory farming and ever more exotic and frequently ill-conceived scientific research employing animal subjects. Then those with Thomist, Kantian, Lockean, Moorean (etc.) ethical affiliation have heard the bugle and have risen to arms. It is no wonder that so many academic philosophers have been drawn into the fray. The issues have an apparent newness about them; moreover, they are socially and politically *avant garde*. But there is no serious challenge to cherished first principles. Hence, without having to undertake any creative ethical reflection or exploration, or any reexamination of historical ethical theory, a fresh debate has been stirred up. The familiar historical positions have simply been retrenched, applied, and exercised.

But what about the third (and certainly minority) party to the animal liberation debate? What sort of reasonable and coherent moral theory would at once urge that animals (and plants and soils and waters) be included in the same class with people as beings to whom ethical consideration is owed and yet not object to some of them being slaughtered (whether painlessly or not) and eaten, others hunted, trapped, and in various other ways seemingly cruelly used? Aldo Leopold provides a concise statement of what might be called the categorical imperative or principal precept of the land ethic: "A thing is right when it tends to preserve the integrity, stability, and beauty of the biotic community. It is wrong when it tends otherwise."[7] What is especially note-worthy, and that to which attention should be directed in this proposition, is the idea that the good of the biotic *community* is the ultimate measure of the moral value, the rightness or wrongness, of actions. Thus, to hunt and kill a white-tailed deer in certain districts may not only be ethically permissible, it might actually be a moral requirement, necessary to protect the local environment, taken as a whole, from the disintegrating effects of a cervid population explosion. On the other hand, rare and endangered animals like the lynx should be especially nurtured and preserved. The lynx, cougar, and other wild feline predators, from the neo-Benthamite perspective (if consistently and evenhandedly applied) should be regarded as merciless, wanton, and incorrigible murderers of their fellow creatures, who not only kill, it should be added, but cruelly toy with their victims, thus increasing the measure of pain in the world. From the perspective of the land ethic, predators generally should be nurtured and preserved as critically important members of the biotic communities to which they are native. Certain plants, similarly, may be overwhelmingly important to the stability, integrity, and beauty of biotic communities, while some animals, such as domestic sheep (allowed perhaps by egalitarian and humane herdspersons to graze freely and to reproduce themselves without being harvested for lamb and mutton) could be a pestilential threat to the natural floral community of a given locale. Thus, the land ethic is logically coherent in demanding at once that moral consideration be given to plants as well as to animals and yet in permitting animals to be killed, trees felled, and so on. In every case the effect upon ecological systems is the decisive factor in the determination of the ethical quality of action....

The Land Ethic and the Ecologica View

... Since ecology focuses upon th between and among things, it incli toward a more holistic vision of the the rather recent emergence of ecology as a science the landscape appeared to be, one might say, a collection of objects, some of them alive, some conscious, but all the same, an aggregate, a plurality of separate individuals. With this "atomistic" representation of things it is no wonder that moral issues might be understood as competing and mutually contradictory clashes of the "rights" of separate individuals, each separately pursuing its "interests." Ecology has made it possible to apprehend the same landscape as an articulate unity (without the least hint of mysticism of ineffability). Ordinary organic bodies have articulated and discernible parts (limbs, various organs, myriad cells); yet, because of the character of the network of relations among those parts, they form in a perfectly familiar sense a second-order whole. Ecology makes it possible to see land, similarly, as a unified system of integrally related parts, as, so to speak, a third-order organic whole.

Another analogy that has helped ecologists to convey the particular holism which their science brings to reflective attention is that land is integrated as a human community is integrated. The various parts of the "biotic community" (individual animals and plants) depend upon one another *economically* so that the system as such acquires distinct characteristics of its own. Just as it is possible to characterize and define collectively peasant societies, agrarian communities, industrial complexes, capitalist, communist, and socialist economic systems, and so on, ecology characterizes and defines various biomes as desert, savanna, wetland, tundra, wood land, etc., communities, each with its particular "professions" "roles," or "niches."

Now we may think that among the duties we as moral agents have toward ourselves is the duty of self-preservation, which may be interpreted as a duty to maintain our own organic integrity. It is not uncommon in historical moral theory, further, to find that in addition to those peculiar responsibilities we e in relation both to ourselves and to other persons severally, we also have a duty to behave in ways that do not harm the fabric of society *per se*. The land ethic, in similar fashion, calls our attention to the recently discovered integrity—in other words, the unity—of the biota and posits duties binding upon moral agents in relation to that whole. Whatever the strictly formal logical connections between the concept of a social community and moral responsibility, there appears to be a strong psychological bond between that idea and conscience. Hence, the representation of the natural environment as, in Leopold's terms, "one humming community" (or, less consistently in his discussion, a third-order organic being) brings into play, whether rationally or not, those stirrings of conscience which we feel in relation to delicately complex, functioning social and organic systems.

The neo-Benthamite humane moralists have, to be sure, digested one of the metaphysical implications of modern biology. They insist that human beings must be understood continuously with the rest of organic nature. People are (and are only) animals, and much of the rhetorical energy of the animal liberation movement is spent in fighting a rear guard action for this aspect of Darwinism against those philosophers who still cling to the dream of a special metaphysical status for people in the order of "creation." To this extent the animal liberation movement is biologically enlightened and argues from the taxonomical and evolutionary continuity of man and beast to moral standing for some nonhuman animals. Indeed, pain, in their view the very substance of evil, is something that is conspicuously common to people and other sensitive animals, something that we as people experience not in virtue of our metasimian cerebral capabilities, but because of our participation in a more generally animal, limbic-based consciousness. *If* it is pain and suffering that it the ultimate evil besetting human life, and this not in virtue of our humanity but in virtue of our animality, then it seems only fair to promote freedom from pain for those animals who share with us in this mode of experience and to grant them rights similar to ours as a means to this end.

Recent ethological studies of other primates, cetaceans, and so on, are not infrequently cited to drive the point home, but the biological information of the animal liberation movement seems to extend no further than this—the continuity of human with other animal life forms. The more recent ecological perspective especially seems to be ignored by humane moralists. The holistic outlook of ecology and the associated value premium conferred upon the biotic community, its beauty, integrity, and stability may simply not have penetrated the thinking of the animal liberationists, or it could be that to include it would involve an intolerable contradiction with the Benthamite foundations of their ethical theory. Bentham's view of the "interests of the community" was bluntly reductive. With his characteristic bluster, Bentham wrote, "The community is a fictitious *body* composed of the individual persons who are considered as constituting as it were its *members*. The interest of the community then is, what?—the sum of the interests of the several members who compose it."[8] Bentham's very simile—the community is like a body composed of members—gives the lie to his reduction of its interests to the sum of its parts taken severally. The interests of a person are not those of his or her cells summed up and averaged out. Our organic health and well-being, for example, require vigorous exercise and metabolic stimulation which cause stress and often pain to various parts of the body and a more rapid turnover in the life cycle of our individual cells. For the sake of the person taken as whole, some parts may be, as it were, unfairly sacrificed. On the level of social organization, the interests of society may not always coincide with the sum of the interests of its parts. Discipline, sacrifice, and individual restraint are often necessary in the social sphere to maintain social integrity as within the bodily organism. A society, indeed, is particularly vulnerable to disintegration when its members become preoccupied totally with their own particular interest, and ignore those distinct and independent interests of the community as a whole. One example, unfortunately, our own society, is altogether too close at hand to be examined with strict academic detachment. The United States seems to pursue uncritically a social policy of reductive utilitarianism, aimed at promoting the happiness of all its members severally. Each special interest accordingly clamors more loudly to be satisfied while the community as a whole becomes noticeably more and more infirm economically, environmentally, and politically.

The humane moralists, whether or not they are consciously and deliberately following Bentham on this particular, nevertheless, in point of fact, are committed to the welfare of certain kinds of animals distributively or reductively in applying their moral concern for nonhuman beings. They lament the treatment of animals, most frequently farm and laboratory animals, and plead the special interests of these beings. We might ask, from the perspective of the land ethic, what the effect upon the natural environment taken as whole would be if domestic animals were actually liberated? There is, almost certainly, very little real danger that this might actually happen, but it would be instructive to speculate on the ecological consequences.

Ethical Holism

Before we take up this question, however, some points of interest remain to be considered on the matter of a holistic versus a reductive environmental ethic. To pit the one against the other as I have done without further qualification would be mistaken. A society is constituted by its members, an organic body by its cells, and the ecosystem by the plants, animals, minerals, fluids, and gases which compose it. One cannot affect a system as a whole without affecting at least some of its components. An environmental ethic which takes as it *summum bonum* the integrity, stability, and beauty of the biotic community is not conferring moral standing on something *else* besides plants, animals, soils, and waters. Rather, the former, the good of the community as a whole, serves as a standard for the assessment of the relative value and relative ordering of its constitutive parts and therefore provides a means of adjudicating the often mutually contradictory demands of the parts considered separately for equal consideration. If diversity does indeed contribute to stability (a classical "law" of ecology), then specimens of rare and endangered species, for example, have a *prima facie* claim to preferential consideration from the perspective of the land ethic. Animals of those species, which, like the honey bee, function in ways critically important to the economy of nature, moreover, would be granted a greater claim to moral attention than psychologically more complex and sensitive ones, say, rabbits and moles, which seem to be plentiful, globally distributed, reproductively efficient, and only routinely integrated into the natural economy. Animals and plants, mountains, rivers, seas, the atmosphere are the *immediate* practical beneficiaries of the land ethic. The well-being of the biotic community, the biosphere as a whole, cannot be logically separated from their survival and welfare.

Some suspicion may arise at this point that the land ethic is ultimately grounded in *human* interests, not in those of nonhuman natural entities. Just as we might prefer a sound and attractive house to one in the opposite condition so the "goodness" of a whole, stable, and beautiful environment seems rather to be of the instrumental, not the autochthonous, variety. The question of ultimate value is a very sticky one for environmental as well as for all ethics and cannot be fully addressed here. It is my view that there can be no value apart from an evaluator, that all value is as it were in the eye of the beholder. The value that is attributed to the ecosystem, therefore, is humanly dependent or (allowing that other living things may take a certain delight in the well-being of the whole of things, or that the gods may) at least dependent upon some variety of morally and aesthetically sensitive consciousness. Granting this, however, there is a further, very crucial distinction to be drawn. It is possible that while things may only have value because we (or someone) values them, they may nonetheless be valued for themselves as well as for the contribution they might make to the realization of our (or someone's) interests. Children are valued for themselves by most parents. Money, on the other hand, has only an instrumental or indirect value. Which sort of value has the health of the biotic community and its members severally for Leopold and the land ethic? It is especially difficult to separate these two general sorts of value, the one of moral significance, the other merely selfish, when something that may be valued in *both ways at once* is the subject of consideration. Are pets, for example, well-treated, like children, for the sake of themselves, or, like mechanical appliances, because of the sort of services they provide their owners? Is a healthy biotic community something we value because we are so utterly and (to the biologically well-informed) so obviously dependent upon it not only for our happiness but for our very survival, or may we also perceive it disinterestedly as having an independent worth? Leopold insists upon a noninstrumental value for the biotic community and *mutatis mutandis* for its constituents. According to Leopold, collective enlightened self-interest on the part of human beings does not go far enough; the land ethic in his opinion (and no doubt this reflects his own moral intuitions) requires "love, respect, and admiration for land, and a high regard for its value." The land ethic, in Leopold's view, creates "obligations over and above self-interest." And "obligations have no meaning without conscience, and the problem we face is the extension of the social conscience from people to land."[9] If, in other words, any genuine ethic is possible, if it is possible to value *people* for the sake of themselves, then it is equally possible to value *land* in the same way.

Some indication of the genuinely biocentric value orientation of ethical environmentalism is indicated in what otherwise might appear to be gratuitous misanthropy. The biospheric perspective does not exempt *Homo sapiens* from moral evaluation in relation to the well-being of the community of nature taken as a whole. The preciousness of individual deer, as of any other specimen, is inversely proportional to the population of the species. Environmentalists, however reluctantly and painfully, do not omit to apply the same logic to their own kind. As omnivores, the population of human beings should, perhaps, be roughly twice that of bears, allowing for differences of size. A global population of more than four billion persons and showing no signs of an orderly decline presents an alarming prospect to humanists, but it is at present a global disaster (the more *per capita* prosperity, indeed, the more disastrous it appears) for the biotic community. If the land ethic were only a means of managing nature for the sake of man, misleadingly phrased in moral terminology, then man would be considered as having an ultimate value essentially different from that of his "resources." The extent of misanthropy in modern environmentalism thus may be taken as a measure of the degree to which it is biocentric. Edward Abbey in his enormously popular *Desert Solitaire* bluntly states that he would sooner shoot a man than a snake.[10] Abbey may not be simply depraved; this is perhaps only his way of dramatically making the point that the human population has become so disproportionate from the biological point of view that if one had to choose between a specimen of *Homo sapiens* and a specimen of a rare even if unattractive species, the choice would be moot. Among academicians, Garrett Hardin, a human ecologist by discipline who has written extensively on ethics, environmental and otherwise, has shocked philosophers schooled in the preciousness of human life with his "lifeboat" and "survival" ethics and his "wilderness economics." In context of the latter, Hardin recommends limiting access to wilderness by criteria of hardiness and woodcraft and would permit no emergency roads or airborne rescue vehicles to violate the pristine purity of wilderness areas. If a wilderness adventurer should have a serious accident, Hardin recommends that he or she get out on his or her own or die in the attempt. Danger, from the strictly human-centered, psychological perspective, is part of the wilderness experience, Hardin argues, but in all probability his more important concern is to protect from mechanization the remnants of wild country that remain even if the price paid is the incidental loss of human life which, from the perspective once more of the biologist, is a commodity altogether too common in relation to wildlife and to wild landscapes....[11]

... Modern systems of ethics have, it must be admitted, considered the principle of the equality of persons to be inviolable. This is true, for example, of both major schools of modern ethics, the utilitarian school going back to Bentham and Mill, and the deontological, originating with Kant. The land ethic manifestly does not accord equal moral worth to each and every member of the biotic community; the moral worth of individuals (including, n.b., human individuals) is relative, to be assessed in accordance with the particular relation of each to the collective entity which Leopold called "land."...

Reappraising Domesticity

Among the last philosophical remarks penned by Aldo Leopold before his untimely death in 1948 is the following: "Perhaps such a shift of values [as implied by the attempt to weld together the concepts of ethics and ecology] can be achieved by reappraising things unnatural, tame, and confined in terms of things natural, wild and free."[12] John Muir, in a similar spirit of reappraisal, had noted earlier the difference between the wild mountain sheep of the Sierra and the ubiquitous domestic variety. The latter, which Muir described as "hooved locusts," were only, in his estimation, "half alive" in comparison with their natural and autonomous counterparts.[13] One of the more distressing aspects of the animal liberation movement is the failure of almost all its exponents to draw a sharp distinction between the very different plights (and rights) of wild and domestic animals. But this distinction lies at the very center of the land ethic. Domestic animals are creations of man. They are living artifacts, but artifacts nevertheless, and they constitute yet another mode of extension of the works of man into the ecosystem. From the perspective of the land ethic a herd of cattle, sheep, or pigs is as much or more a ruinous blight on the landscape as a fleet of four-wheel drive off-road vehicles. There is thus something profoundly incoherent (and insensitive as well) in the complaint of some animal liberationists that the "natural behavior" of chickens and bobby calves is cruelly frustrated on factory farms. It would make almost as much sense to speak of the natural behavior of tables and chairs.

Here a serious disanalogy (which no one to my knowledge has yet pointed out) becomes clearly evident between the liberation of blacks from slavery (and more recently, from civil inequality) and the liberation of animals from a similar sort of subordination and servitude. Black slaves remained, as it were, metaphysically autonomous: they were by nature if not by convention free beings quite capable of living on their own. They could not be enslaved for more than a historical interlude, for the strength of the force of their freedom was too great. They could, in other words, be retained only by a continuous counterforce, and only temporarily. This is equally true of caged wild animals. African cheetahs in American and European zoos are captive, not indentured, beings. But this is not true of cows, pigs, sheep, and chickens. They have been bred to docility, tractability, stupidity, and dependency. It is literally meaningless to suggest that they be liberated. It is, to speak in hyperbole, a logical impossibility.

Certainly it is a practical impossibility. Imagine what would happen if the people of the world became morally persuaded that domestic animals were to be regarded as oppressed and enslaved persons and accordingly *set free*. In one scenario we might imagine that like former American black slaves they would receive the equivalent of forty acres and a mule and be turned out to survive on their own. Feral cattle and sheep would hang around farm outbuildings waiting forlornly to be sheltered and fed, or would graze aimlessly through their abandoned and deteriorating pastures. Most would starve or freeze as soon as winter settled in. Reproduction which had been assisted over many countless generations by their former owners might be altogether impossible in the feral state for some varieties, and the care of infants would be an art not so much lost as never acquired. And so in a very short time, after much suffering and agony, these species would become abruptly extinct. Or, in another scenario beginning with the same simple emancipation from human association, survivors of the first massive die-off of untended livestock might begin to recover some of their remote wild ancestral genetic traits and become smaller, leaner, heartier, and smarter versions of their former selves. An actual contemporary example is afforded by the feral mustangs ranging over parts of the American West. In time such animals as these would become (just as the mustangs are now) competitors both with their former human masters and (with perhaps more tragic consequences) indigenous wildlife for food and living space.

Foreseeing these and other untoward consequences of immediate and unplanned liberation of livestock, a human population grown morally more perfect than at present might decide that they had a duty, accumulated over thousands of years, to continue to house and feed as before their former animal slaves (whom they had rendered genetically unfit to care for themselves), but not to butcher them or make other ill use of them, including frustrating their "natural" behavior, their right to copulate freely, reproduce, and enjoy the delights of being parents. People, no longer having meat to eat, would require more vegetables, cereals, and other plant foods, but the institutionalized animal incompetents would still consume all the hay and grains (and more since they would no longer be slaughtered) than they did formerly. This would require clearing more land and bringing it into agricultural production with further loss of wild life habitat and ecological destruction. Another possible scenario might be a decision on the part of people not literally to liberate domestic animals but simply to cease to breed and raise them. When the last livestock have been killed and eaten (or permitted to die "natural" deaths), people would become vegetarians and domestic livestock species would thus be rendered deliberately extinct (just as they had been deliberately created). But there is surely some irony in an outcome in which the beneficiaries of a humane extension of conscience are destroyed in the process of being saved.

The land ethic, it should be emphasized, as Leopold has sketched it, provides for the *rights* of nonhuman natural beings to a share in the life processes of the biotic community. The conceptual foundation of such rights, however, is less conventional than natural, based upon, as one might say, evolutionary and ecological entitlement. Wild animals and native plants have a particular place in nature, according to the land ethic, which domestic animals (because they are products of human art and represent an extended presence of human beings in the natural world) do not have. The land ethic, in sum, is as much opposed, though on different grounds, to commercial traffic in wildlife, zoos, the slaughter of whales and other marine mammals, etc., as is the humane ethic. Concern for animal (and plant) rights and well-being is as fundamental to the land ethic as to the humane ethic, but the difference between naturally evolved and humanly bred species is an essential consideration for the one, though not for the other.

The "shift of values" which results from our "reappraising things unnatural, tame, and confined in terms of things natural, wild, and free" is especially dramatic when we reflect upon the definitions of *good* and *evil* espoused by Bentham and Mill and uncritically accepted by their contemporary followers. Pain and pleasure seem to have nothing at all to do with good and evil if our appraisal is taken from the vantage point of ecological biology. Pain in particular is primarily information. In animals, it informs the central nervous system of stress, irritation, or trauma in outlying regions of the organism. A certain level of pain under optimal organic circumstances is indeed desirable as an indicator of exertion—of the degree of exertion needed to maintain fitness, to stay "in shape," and of a level of exertion beyond which it would be dangerous to go. An arctic wolf in pursuit of a caribou may experience pain in her feet or chest because of the rigors of the chase. There is nothing bad or wrong in that. Or, consider a case of injury. Suppose that a person in the course of a wilderness excursion sprains an ankle. Pain informs him or her of the injury and by its intensity the amount of further stress the ankle may endure in the course of getting to safety. Would it be better if pain were not experienced upon injury or, taking advantage of recent technology, anaesthetized? Pleasure appears to be, for the most part (unfortunately it is not always so) a reward accompanying those activities which contribute to organic maintenance, such as the pleasures associated with eating, drinking, grooming, and so on, or those which contribute to social solidarity like the pleasures of dancing, conversation, teasing, etc., or those which contribute to the continuation of the species, such as the pleasures of sexual activity and of being parents. The doctrine that life is the happier the freer it is from pain and that the happiest life conceivable is one in which there is continuous pleasure uninterrupted by pain is biologically preposterous. A living mammal which experienced no pain would be one which had a lethal dysfunction of the nervous system. The idea that pain is evil and ought to be minimized or eliminated is as primitive a notion as that of a tyrant who puts to death messengers bearing bad news on the supposition that thus his well-being and security is improved.

More seriously still, the value commitments of the humane movement seem at bottom to betray a world-denying or rather a life-loathing philosophy.

The natural world as actually constituted is one in which one being lives at the expense of others. Each organism, in Darwin's metaphor, struggles to maintain its own organic integrity. The more complex animals seem to experience (judging from our own case, and reasoning from analogy) appropriate and adaptive psychological accompaniments to organic existence. There is a palpable passion for self-preservation. There are desire, pleasure in the satisfaction of desires, acute agony attending injury, frustration, and chronic dread of death. But these experiences are the psychological substance of living. To live *is* to be anxious about life, to feel pain and pleasure in a fitting mixture, and sooner or later to die. That is the way the system works. If nature as a whole is good, then pain and death are also good. Environmental ethics in general require people to play fair in the natural system. The neo-Benthamites have in a sense taken the uncourageous approach. People have attempted to exempt themselves from the life/death reciprocities of natural processes and from ecological limitations in the name of a prophylactic ethic of maximizing rewards (pleasure) and minimizing unwelcome information (pain). To be fair, the humane moralists seem to suggest that we should attempt to project the same values into the nonhuman animal world and to widen the charmed circle—no matter that it would be biologically unrealistic to do so or biologically ruinous if, per impossible, such an environmental ethic were implemented.

There is another approach. Rather than imposing our alienation from nature and natural processes and cycles of life on other animals, we human beings could reaffirm our participation in nature by accepting life as it is given without a sugar coating. Instead of imposing artificial legalities, rights, and so on on nature, we might take the opposite course and accept and affirm natural biological laws, principles, and limitations in the human personal and social spheres. Such appears to have been the posture toward life of tribal peoples in the past. The chase was relished with its dangers, rigors, and hardships as well as its rewards: animal flesh was respectfully consumed; a tolerance for pain was cultivated; virtue and magnanimity were prized; lithic, floral, and faunal spirits were worshipped; population was routinely optimized by sexual continency, abortion, infanticide, and stylized warfare; and other life forms, although certainly appropriated, were respected as fellow players in a magnificent and awesome, if not altogether idyllic, drama of life. It is impossible today to return to the symbiotic relationship of Stone Age man to the natural environment, but the ethos of this by far the longest era of human existence could be abstracted and integrated with a future human culture seeking a viable and mutually beneficial relationship with nature. Personal, social, and environmental *health* would, accordingly, receive a premium value rather than comfort, self-indulgent pleasure, and anaesthetic insulation from pain. Sickness would be regarded as a worse evil than death. The pursuit of health or wellness at the personal, social, and environmental levels would require self-discipline in the form of simple diet, vigorous exercise, conservation, and social responsibility.

Leopold's prescription for the realization and implementation of the land ethic—the reappraisal of things unnatural, tame, and confined in terms of things natural, wild, and free—does not stop, in other words, with a reappraisal of nonhuman domestic animals in terms of their wild (or willed) counterparts; the human ones should be similarly reappraised. This means, among other things, the reappraisal of the comparatively recent values and concerns of "civilized" *Homo sapiens* in terms of those of our "savage" ancestors. Civilization has insulated and alienated us from the rigors and challenges of the natural environment. The hidden agenda of the humane ethic is the imposition of the antinatural prophylactic ethos of comfort and soft pleasure on an even wider scale. The land ethic, on the other hand, requires a shrinkage, if at all possible, of the domestic sphere; it rejoices in a recrudescence of wilderness and a renaissance of tribal cultural experience.

The converse of those goods and evils, axiomatic to the humane ethic, may be illustrated and focused by the consideration of a single issue raised by the humane morality: a vegetarian diet. Savage people seem to have had, if the attitudes and values of surviving tribal cultures are representative, something like an intuitive grasp of ecological relationships and certainly a morally charged appreciation of eating. There is nothing more intimate than eating, more symbolic of the connectedness of life, and more mysterious. What we eat and how we eat is by no means an insignificant ethical concern.

From the ecological point of view, for human beings universally to become vegetarians is tantamount to a shift of trophic niche from omnivore with carnivorous preferences to herbivore. The shift is a downward one on the trophic pyramid, which in effect shortens those food chains terminating with man. It represents an increase in the efficiency of the conversion of solar energy from plant to human biomass, and thus, by bypassing animal intermediates, increases available food resources for human beings. The human population would probably, as past trends overwhelmingly suggest, expand in accordance with the potential thus afforded. The net result would be fewer nonhuman beings and more human beings, who, of course, have requirements of life far more elaborate than even those of domestic animals, requirements which would tax other "natural resources" (trees for shelter, minerals mined at the expense of topsoil and its vegetation, etc.) More than under present circumstances. A vegetarian human population is therefore *probably* ecologically catastrophic.

Meat eating as implied by the foregoing remarks may be more *ecologically* responsible than a wholly vegetable diet. Meat, however, purchased at the supermarket, externally packaged and internally laced with petrochemicals, fattened in feed lots, slaughtered impersonally, and, in general, mechanically processed from artificial insemination to microwave roaster, is an affront not only to physical metabolism and bodily health but to conscience as well. From the perspective of the land ethic, the immoral aspect of the factory farm has to do far less with the suffering and killing of nonhuman animals than with the monstrous transformation of living things from an organic to a mechanical mode of being. Animals, beginning with the Neolithic Revolution, have been debased through selective breeding, but they have nevertheless remained animals. With the Industrial Revolution an even more profound and terrifying transformation has overwhelmed them. They have become, in Ruth Harrison's most apt description, "animal machines." The very presence of animals, so emblematic of delicate, complex organic tissue, surrounded by machines, connected to machines, penetrated by machines in research laboratories or crowded together in space-age "production facilities" is surely the more real and visceral source of our outrage at vivisection and factory farming than the contemplation of the quantity of pain that these unfortunate beings experience. I wish to denounce as loudly as the neo-Benthamites this ghastly abuse of animal life, but also to stress that the pain and suffering of research and agribusiness animals is not greater than that endured by free-living wildlife as a consequence of predation, disease, starvation, and cold—indicating that there is something immoral about vivisection and factory farming which is not an ingredient in the natural lives and deaths of wild beings. That immoral something is the transmogrification of organic to mechanical processes.

Ethical vegetarianism to all appearances insists upon the human consumption of plants (in a paradoxical moral gesture toward those animals whose very existence is dependent upon human carnivorousness), even when the tomatoes are grown hydroponically, the lettuce generously coated with chlorinated hydrocarbons, the potatoes pumped up with chemical fertilizers, and the cereals stored with the help of chemical preservatives. The land ethic takes as much exception to the transmogrification of plants by mechanico-chemical means as to that of animals. The important thing, I would think, is not to eat vegetables as opposed to animal flesh, but to resist factory farming in all its manifestations, including especially its liberal application of pesticides, herbicides, and chemical fertilizers to maximize the production of *vegetable* crops.

The land ethic, with its ecological perspective, helps us to recognize and affirm the organic integrity of self and the untenability of a firm distinction between self and environment. On the ethical question of what to eat, it answers, not vegetables instead of animals, but organically as opposed to mechanico-chemically produced food. Purists like Leopold prefer, in his expression, to get their "meat from God," i.e., to hunt and consume wildlife and to gather wild plant foods, and thus to live within the parameters of the aboriginal human ecological niche. Second best is eating from one's own orchard, garden, henhouse, pigpen, and barnyard. Third best is buying or bartering organic foods from one's neighbors and friends.

Conclusion

Philosophical controversy concerning animal liberation/rights has been most frequently represented as a polar dispute between traditional moral humanists and seemingly *avant garde* humane moralists. Further, animal liberation has been assumed to be closely allied with environmental ethics, possibly because in Leopold's classical formulation moral standing and indeed rights (of some unspecified sort) is accorded nonhuman beings, among them animals. The purpose of this discussion has been to distinguish sharply environmental ethics from the animal liberation/rights movement both in theory and practical application and to suggest, thereupon, that there is an underrepresented, but very important, point of view respecting the problem of the moral status of nonhuman animals. The debate over animal liberation, in short, should be conceived as triangular, not polar, with land ethics or environmental ethics, the third and, in my judgment, the most creative, interesting, and practicable alternative. Indeed, from this third point of view moral humanism and humane moralism appear to have much more in common with one another than either have with environmental or land ethics. On reflection one might even be led to suspect that the noisy debate between these parties has served to drown out the much deeper challenge to "business-as-usual" ethical philosophy represented by Leopold and his exponents, and to keep ethical philosophy firmly anchored to familiar modern paradigms.

Moral humanism and humane moralism, to restate succinctly the most salient conclusions of this essay, are *atomistic* or distributive in their theory of moral value, while environmental ethics (again, at least, as set out in Leopold's outline) is *holistic* or collective. Modern ethical theory, in other words, has consistently located moral value in individuals and set out certain metaphysical reasons for including some individuals and excluding others. Humane moralism remains firmly within this modern convention and centers its attention on the competing criteria for moral standing and rights holding, while environmental ethics locates ultimate value in the "biotic community" and assigns differential moral value to the constitutive individuals relatively to that standard. This is perhaps the most fundamental theoretical difference between environmental ethics and the ethics of animal liberation.

Allied to this difference are many others. One of the more conspicuous is that in environmental ethics, plants are included within the parameters of the ethical theory as well as animals. Indeed, inanimate entities such as oceans and lakes, mountains, forests, and wetlands are assigned a greater value than individual animals and in a way quite different from systems which accord them moral considerability through a further multiplication of competing individual loci of value and holders of rights.

There are intractable practical differences between environmental ethics and the animal liberation movement. Very different moral obligations follow in respect, most importantly, to domestic animals, the principal beneficiaries of the humane ethic. Environmental ethics sets a very low priority on domestic animals as they very frequently contribute to the erosion of the integrity, stability, and beauty of the biotic communities into which they have been insinuated. On the other hand, animal liberation, if pursued at the practical as well as rhetorical level, would have ruinous consequences on plants, soils, and waters, consequences which could not be directly reckoned according to humane moral theory. As this last remark suggests, the animal liberation/animal rights movement is in the final analysis utterly unpracticable. An imagined society in which all animals capable of sensibility received equal consideration or held rights to equal consideration would be so ludicrous that it might be more appropriately and effectively treated in satire than in philosophical discussion. The land ethic, by contrast, even though its ethical purview is very much wider, is nevertheless eminently practicable, since, by reference to a single good, competing individual claims may be adjudicated and relative values and priorities assigned to the myriad components of the biotic community. This is not to suggest that the implementation of environmental ethics as social policy would be easy. Implementation of the land ethic would require discipline, sacrifice, retrenchment, and massive economic reform, tantamount to a virtual revolution in prevailing attitudes and life styles. Nevertheless, it provides a unified and coherent practical principle and thus a decision procedure at the practical level which a distributive or atomistic ethic may achieve only artificially and so imprecisely as to be practically indeterminate.

NOTES

1. Aldo Leopold, *A Sand County Almanac* (New York: Oxford University Press, 1949), pp. 202-203.
2. Ibid., p. 204.
3. Ibid., pp. 201-203.
4. Ibid., p. 203.
5. Ibid., p. 204.
6. Ibid., p. 221 (trees); pp. 129-133 (mountains); p. 209 (streams).
7. Ibid., pp. 224-225.
8. *An Introduction to the Principles of Morals and Legislatio*n (Oxford: Oxford University Press, 1823), chap. 1, sec. 4.
9. Leopold, *Sand County Almanac*, pp. 223 and 209.
10. Edward Abbey, *Desert Solitaire* (New York: Ballantine Books, 1968), p. 20.
11. Garrett Hardin, "The Economics of Wilderness," *Natural History* 78 [1969]: 173-177. Hardin is blunt: "Making great and spectacular efforts to save the life of an individual makes sense only when there is a shortage of people. I have not lately heard that there is a shortage of people" (p. 176).
12. Leopold, *Sand County Almanac*, p. ix.
13. See John Muir, "The Wild Sheep of California," *Overland Monthly* 12 (1874): 359.

PRACTICAL ECOLOGY AND FOUNDATIONS FOR ENVIRONMENTAL ETHICS

Kristin Schrader-Frechette

Kristin Shrader-Frechette is Professor in Philosophy and in Environmental Sciences and Policy at the University of South Florida. She is the author of Risk and Rationality: Philosophical Foundations for Populist Reforms *(California, 1991) and co-editor of* Technology and Values *(Rowman & Littlefield, 1997).*

Shrader-Frechette defends a middle ground between the two options of what she refers to as soft and hard environmental ethics. She identifies Callicott as an example of a soft environmental ethicist and argues that while this approach has inspirational power, it fails to generate environmental policies that can resolve controversy. Hard environmental ethicists have scientific credibility, but because they are too general and conservative they have provided theories that have limited practical value in protecting the environment. Shrader-Frechette calls for a "practical ecology" that is based largely on case studies and rules of thumb.

What you take as your starting point depends on where you want to go. If you want to sail due south to the Dry Tortugas, then you start with plenty of fresh water, some food, a good navigational system, and arguably a ship-to-shore radio for the long trip. But if you want to sail due West to nearby John's Pass, then you might need some fresh water, but no food, no sophisticated navigational system, and no radio. How you begin a journey depends on where you want to go. So it is with environmental ethics.

How you begin your environmental ethics depends on where you want them to go—whether you want them to guide naturalists or instead scientists or perhaps policy makers. If you want naturalists to use environmental ethics to encourage protective attitudes toward the biosphere, then you might begin with general goals and motivational ideals. These principles will inspire backpackers and birders, sailors and scuba divers, but they will have limited practical value in resolving environmental controversies. What such ethics gain because of their appeal and accessibility, they lose because of their generality and inapplicability. They are soft environmental ethics.

If you want scientists to use your environmental ethics to encourage accurate understanding of nature, then you might begin with general principles for avoiding erroneous claims. Such principles might enable experimenters to reduce false positives and to avoid claiming environmental effects where there are none, but they also will have limited practical value in protecting the environment. Because the most serious environmental conflicts concern situations of factual and probabilistic uncertainty, following scientific norms of avoiding false positives, in a context of uncertainty, often encourages false negatives, failing to recognize environmental damage when it occurs.[1] What such ethics gain because of their scientific credibility, they lose because of their generality. What they gain because of their epistemological conservatism, they lose because of their inadequate environmental protectionism. They are hard environmental ethics.

I shall argue that neither soft nor hard environmental ethics will take you where you want to go, if your destination is an ordered system of norms which will withstand courtroom challenges and

---

Reprinted with permission from *The Journal of Philosophy* XCII (December 1995): 621–35.

which will support precise, often disputed claims over wetlands protection or development rights. The argument is that soft ethics—such as those of J. Baird Callicott, Aldo Leopold, Paul Taylor, Holmes Rolston, and Laura Westra[2]—have great heuristic and inspirational power, but they are more useful in preaching to the converted than in resolving controversy. Because they are so general, they fail to include precise second- and higher-order ethical principles that would make them operationalizable in decision making. Hard ethics—such as those of Dan Simberloff and Robert Henry Peters[3]—have great scientific credibility, but they are more useful in avoiding false claims than in discovering true ones. Instead, the ethics needed in practical policy making must be not only inspirational, but also complex and precise enough to help resolve controversy. They must be not only scientifically conservative, but also protective and specific enough to support particular environmental policies. They must avoid the philosophical ivory tower of soft ethics and the scientific ivory tower of hard ethics.

Although both hard and soft approaches are valuable in environmental ethics, their proponents appear to think that they are sufficient, not merely necessary, for solving environmental problems. In so doing, Rolston and others appeal to "soft ecology" to support their ethics based on inspiration rather than argument, preaching rather than offering second- and higher-order ethical analyses that are capable of helping to adjudicate environmental controversies. Likewise, Peters and others follow "hard ecology" and search for grand, deductive ecological theories rather than modest rules of thumb that are operationalizable and applicable. My argument is that the science necessary to undergird practical environmental ethics requires that we avoid the extremes of either soft or hard ecology. Sound environmental ethics, at least at present, require a "practical ecology" based largely on case studies and rules of thumb.

A practical scientific foundation for environmental ethics must chart a middle course between the "hard," hypothetico-deductive ecology of persons like Peters and the "soft," largely qualitative ecology espoused by persons—such as Westra or Rolston[4]—who propose concepts such as ecosystem and integrity as the foundation for environmental policy making. The problem with using these concepts, as a proposed scientific foundation for environmental ethics, is that they underestimate ecological uncertainty and thus demand too little of ecology. Likewise, the more deductive concepts of Peters overestimate ecological uncertainty and thus demand too much of ecology. I shall show where both go wrong and propose an alternative.

I. Problems with Deductive Theories and "Hard Ecology"

In an analysis that is both tough-minded and controversial, Peters argues that ecology is a "weak science" (*op.cit.*, p. 11). He claims that the primary way to correct this weakness is to judge every ecological theory "on the basis of its ability to predict" (*op.cit.*, p. 290). Peters's argument, that the main criterion for ecological theorizing ought to be its predictive power, is somewhat correct in at least two senses. Prediction often is needed for applying ecology to environmental problem solving. Peters also is right to emphasize prediction because, if scientists did not seek this goal, at least in some cases, they likely would foreclose the possibility of ever having any predictive scientific theories.

Despite the value of prediction in science, Peters's argument is misguided in at least four ways. For one thing, he is wrong to use prediction as a *criterion for*, rather than a *goal of*, ecological theorizing. Not all sciences are equally predictive. Economics and sociology, for example, are both more explanatory than predictive, yet it is not obvious that they are nonscientific by virtue of being so. Likewise, many geological phenomena—such as whether a given rock formation will be intact in 100,000 years—are not susceptible to precise, long-term prediction. We conclude from this predictive imprecision neither that geology is unscientific nor that we should reject the goal of precise geological prediction, but rather that geology probably deals with long-term phenomena that are less deterministic than those in other sciences. In overemphasizing the importance of *prediction* in ecology and science generally, Peters has erred in underemphasizing the role of *explanation*.

Peters's overemphasis on prediction and hypothesis deduction is also highly questionable in the light of the last three decades of research in philosophy of science, much of which has identified fundamental flaws in the positivistic, hypothetico-deductive paradigm for science. Thomas Kuhn[5]—and other critics of the positivist paradigm—have argued that science is likely based more on retroduction and good reasons than on deduction alone. One of the fundamental reasons that no sciences can be perfectly deductive in method is that they depend on methodological value judgments—about whether certain data are sufficient, about whether a given model fits the data, about whether nontestable predictions are reliable, and so on. Because such value judgments render strict deduction impossible, falsification and confirmation of hypotheses are always questionable, at least to some degree. Moreover, though all sciences depend on such value judgments, this dependence is particularly acute for ecology, because ecology is more empirically and theoretically underdetermined than many other sciences. In island biogeography, for example, there are many areas of underdetermination that require one to make choices among different methodological value judgments. These choices concern how to interpret data, how to practice good science, and how to apply theory in given situations, such as determining the best design for nature reserves. Such choices are evaluative because they are never wholly determined by the data.

Consider how value judgments are necessary in using the ecological theory of island biogeography in the nature reserve case. Ecologists must decide whether ethical and conservation priorities require protecting an individual species, an ecosystem, or biodiversity, when not all can be protected at once. Different design choices usually are required to protect a particular species of interest, as opposed to preserving a specific ecosystem of biotic diversity.[6] Also, ecologists often must choose between maximizing present and future biodiversity. Currently, they are able to determine only which types of reserves, for example, contain the most species at present, not which ones will contain the most over the long term.[7] Moreover, in the absence of adequate empirical data on particular taxa and their specific autecology, ecologists frequently must decide how to evaluate the worth of general ecological theory in dictating a preferred reserve design for a particular case.[8] They also are often forced to assess subjectively the value of different reserve shapes. Besides, reserve shape, as such, may not explain variation in species number.[9] Ecologists likewise must frequently rely on subjective estimates and methodological value judgments whenever the "minimum viable population" size is not known in a precise area."[10] One of the most fundamental sources of value judgments in ecology is the fact that the island-biogeographical theory underlying current paradigms regarding reserve design has rarely been tested[11] and is dependent primarily on ornithological data,[12] on correlations rather than causal explanations (*ibid.*, p. 13), on assumptions about homogeneous habitats,[13] and on unsubstantiated turnover rates and extinction rates.[14] Hence, whenever ecologists apply this theory, they must make a variety of methodological—and sometimes ethical—value judgments. Some of these value judgments concern the importance of factors other than those dominant in island biogeography (for example, maximum breeding habitat), factors that often have been shown to be superior predictors of species number.[15] Making value judgments regarding reserve design is also difficult because corridors (an essential part of island biogeographic theory) have questionable overall value for species preservation.[16] Recommending use of corridors thus requires ecologists to evaluate subjectively their effectiveness in particular situations. Also, owing to the large variance about species-area relationships,[17] those who use island biogeographical theory are often forced to make subjective evaluations of nontestable predictions. Some of these subjective evaluations arise because islands are disanalogous in important ways with nature reserves.[18] As a result, ecologists who apply data about islands to problems of reserve design must make a number of value judgments about the representativeness and importance of their particular data.

Because of the empirical and theoretical underdetermination exhibited by ecological theories like island biogeography, and because of the resultant methodological value judgments necessary to interpret and apply it in specific cases, ecology does not appear to be fully amenable to hypothesis deduction. The included value judgments break the deductive connections of the theory. Of course, there are rough generalizations that can aid problem solving in specific ecological situations, as a prominent National Academy of Sciences Committee recognized (*op.cit.*). Nevertheless, it is unlikely that we shall be able to find many (if any) simple, general, hypothetico-deductive (HD) laws that we can easily apply to a variety of particular communities or species. A second reason—in addition to the under-determined, value-laden theory—that such laws are unlikely is that fundamental ecological terms (like "community" and "stability") are imprecise and vague, and therefore unable to support precise empirical laws.[19] Likewise, though the term "species" has a commonly accepted meaning, and though evolutionary theory gives a precise technical sense to the term, there is no general agreement in biology on an explicit definition of "species." There is consensus neither on what counts as causally sufficient or necessary conditions for a set of organisms to be a species, nor on whether species are individuals. Phenetic taxonomy has failed to generate a workable taxonomy, perhaps because species are not natural kinds and because facts cannot be carved up and rearranged in accord with the hopes of numerical taxonomists.[20]

Simple, general, hypothetico-deductive laws are also unlikely in ecology because of the uniqueness of ecological phenomena. If an event is unique, it is typically difficult to specify the relevant initial conditions for it and to know what counts as relevant behavior. One must often have extensive historical information in order to do so.[21] Hence, from an empirical point of view, complexity and uniqueness hamper the elaboration of a simple, general set of hypothetico-deductive laws to explain most or all ecological phenomena. And if so, then the "hard ecology" of Peters is not a reasonable foundation for environmental ethics because it does not appear achievable. HD may be an important ideal but, at present, it appears to demand too much of ecology and to overestimate its potential for certainty.

II. Problems with Ecosystem Integrity and "Soft Ecology"

At the other extreme of proposed scientific foundations for environmental policy making, concepts like "integrity" demand too little of ecology because they are qualitative, unclear, and vague. They underestimate the ecological uncertainty associated with such fuzzy terms. Arne Naess[22] recognized this point when he claimed that the normative foundations provided by ecology are "basic intuitions." The problem with intuitions is not only that they are vague and qualitative but also that one either has them or does not. They are not the sort of things amenable even to intelligent debate, much less to scientific confirmation or falsification. Hence, intuitions ask too little of ecology; their uncertainty causes us to come up short when ecologists need to defend their conclusions in an environmental courtroom.

To illustrate the difficulties with "soft ecology," consider some of the problems associated both with the scientific foundations of the concept of ecosystemic integrity and with its philosophical applications. Much of the scientific and ethical interest in integrity arose as a result of Leopold's famous 1949 environmental precept: "A thing is right when it tends to preserve the integrity, stability, and beauty of the biotic community. It is wrong when it tends otherwise" (*op.cit*, pp. 224-25). Numerous persons—such as Callicott, J. D. Heffernan, Leopold, Rolston, Mark Sagoff, and Westra[23]—have done insightful analyses of the philosophical concept of integrity, but unfortunately these studies rely on problematic science or soft ecology. One of the major problems with the scientific concept of integrity is that one of the leading experts on integrity, Henry Regier,[24] has admitted that the term has been explicated in a variety of ways: to refer to open-system thermodynamics, to networks, to Bertalanffian general systems, to trophic systems, to hierarchical organizations, to harmonic communities, and so on. Obviously, a clear, operational scientific concept cannot be explicable in a multiplicity of ways, some of which are mutually incompatible, if one expects the concept to do explanatory and predictive duty for field ecologists and therefore philosophical and political duty for attorneys, policy makers, and citizens involved in environmental controversies.

A second problem with the integrity concept is that when persons attempt to define it precisely, often the best they can do is to specify necessary conditions, such as the presence of "indicator species" for ecosystem integrity. For example, the 1987 Protocol to the 1978 Great Lakes Water Quality Agreement formally specified lake trout as an indicator of a desired state of oligotrophy (*ibid.*). One difficulty—with using such species to indicate environmental integrity—is in part that tracking the presence or absence of an indicator species is imprecise and inadequately quantitative. A better idea might be to track the change in species number or taxonomic composition. Another recognized problem is that the presence or absence of an indicator species alone presumably is not sufficient to characterize everything that might be meant by "integrity"; otherwise, persons would not speak of "ecosystem integrity" but merely of "ecosystem presence of lake trout." Hence, though the meaning of "integrity" is not clear, defining the term via several indicator species appears both crude and inadequately attentive to the underlying processes likely contributing to the presence or absence of certain species and to the larger processes presumably possessing integrity.

The definition of "integrity" is also methodologically suspect because it is based merely on opinions rather than on confirmed ecological theories or empirical generalizations. As Regier admits, though the aggregated form of the index of biological integrity (IBI) avoids reliance on a single indicator species, it provides an arbitrary definition of "integrity." It

> does not relate directly to anything that is observable by the nonexpert, nor to any encompassing theoretical or empirical synthesis. As a conceptual mixture put together according to judgments of knowledgeable observers, it is not "understandable" in a theoretical sense. It is conceptually opaque in that it provides only a number on a scale; this number is then interpreted as bad or good according to practical considerations (*ibid.*, p. 191).

Indeed, the whole concept of ecosystem integrity seems to be conceptually opaque and vague. Regier admits, for example, that "general, qualitative, developmental tendencies of healthy organic systems ... provide a basis for practical understanding measurement, and management of *ecosystem integrity*" (*ibid.*, p. 191). But if general, qualitative judgments provide the basis for understanding, ecosystem integrity, then it is arguable that they are likely to be insufficiently precise and quantitative to do the environmental work required of them if they are challenged in court by developers, polluters, or citizens asked to pay for cleanup. Also, if only experts can recognize integrity, and if "integrity" is not tied to any publicly recognizable criteria, then the term seems incapable of uncontroversial operationalization. Hence, concepts like ecosystem integrity may be closer to "soft ecology"—or as Simberloff would put it, "theological ecology"—that preaches only to the converted (*ibid.*, p. 194). Soft ecology may be too uncertain to provide a firm foundation for the precise norms often required in environmental ethics and policy.

Admittedly, at least one branch of theory regarding ecosystems integrity—James Kay and Eric Schneider's[25] nonequilibrium thermodynamic account—is not "soft ecology" in the sense that it is not general, qualitative, and vague. Rather, it is specific, quantitative, and precise. It also yields a number of insights about ecosystem behavior. The thermodynamic version, however, assuming it might provide a correct definition of "integrity," appears to be "soft ecology" in several other damaging senses. For one thing, the account is based on *defining* ecological phenomena in terms of a thermodynamic model rather than on discovering, confirming, or falsifying specific hypotheses about ecological phenomena. Because this account relies on definition rather than discovery, and because it does not show how at least two independent avenues function in advancing our explanation of ecological phenomena, the thermodynamic account appears to provide merely a stipulative definition, rather than a causal explanation, of ecological phenomena.

The thermodynamic account of integrity is also definitionally problematic in a second sense. On the thermodynamic model, ecosystem organization tends to increase degradation of energy, and measures of this organization rely in part on measures of energy utilization in the food web. Yet, because it is often difficult to assign organisms to a particular trophic level, it is difficult to measure ecosystem organization accurately. Linking the integrity of an ecosystem to its ability to maintain its organization, Kay and Schneider argue that there are certain situations in which an ecosystem would not maintain its organization. One such example is an ecosystem that is stressed by exposure to a 6°C increase in temperature of the water effluent from a nuclear power station.[26] If, as a result of this thermal stress, the size of the ecosystem were diminished, its trophic levels were decreased, it recycled less, and it leaked nutrients and energy, then Kay and Schneider claim that the ecosystem would not have maintained its organization. They claim that such effects are signs of "disorganization and a step backward in development."[27]

One problem with their argument is that there are many ecosystem responses to stress, and complex systems have multiple steady states. After stress, (1) the system could eventually continue to operate as before, or (2) it could operate with a reduction or increase in species number, or (3) it could exhibit new paths in the food web, or (4) it could take on a largely different structure with different species and food webs (cf. note 25). Because of the multiple steady states of complex ecosystems, a third definitional problem is that the thermodynamic model, as Kay and Schneider recognize, does not indicate which (if any) of these four changes is more or less natural or acceptable, in terms of maintaining integrity. Hence, the thermodynamic account, in itself, indicates different ways in which ecosystems respond to stress, but not which responses constitute a lack of integrity. And here is the rub. Either we must say, first, that any system maintaining itself at any optimum operating point has integrity—with the consequence that virtually any environmental change anywhere anytime is said to be consistent with integrity. This first position likely would cause environmental catastrophe and would delight many developers and polluters. Or we must say, second, that a system has integrity if it resists permanent ecosystem change—a position that does not fit the facts of dynamic and evolutionary ecosystems. This second position is inapplicable to the real world. Or, third, we must define, independently of the thermodynamic account, some type of change as a loss of integrity. Hence, the thermodynamic model reduces us, when using it for environmental policy making, to using science that is either (1) incapable of defining integrity in an environmentally protective way, or (2) inconsistent with evolution, or (3) dependent on some nonthermodynamic (arguably subjective) account of community structure. Thus, the thermodynamic model, despite its heuristic power, is definitional in at least three senses. It does not provide two independent avenues for explanation; it assigns organisms to trophic levels in a question-begging way; and it requires one to stipulate some change as a loss of integrity. For all these reasons, the account is fundamentally uncertain. It is obviously not an adequate ecological basis for environmental policy making. At best, it provides necessary, but not sufficient, scientific grounds for environmental ethics and policy. Insofar as it is uncertain and requires us to fill in our knowledge gaps with subjective judgments, it leads to incomplete and soft ecology.

The objection, of course, is not to philosophical or ethical concepts of integrity which obviously may have heuristic and political power. Rather, the argument is that philosophers and soft ecologists do not call a spade a spade. They do not call soft science "soft" when it is soft, and they appear not to realize that soft science, in the absence of an environmental political consensus, is unlikely to be robust enough to support precise environmental policy decisions. When a consensus supports particular environmental values, then soft ecology is obviously valuable and heuristically useful. But situations of consensus regarding environmental values are not those in which we most need ecology.

III. A Middle Path

Given widespread controversy over environmental ethics and policy, soft ecology is unable to ground biocentric ethics on mere stipulative definition, just as hard ecology is unable to provide hypothetico-deductive theories to resolve environmental controversies. Because both types of ecology are uncertain, anyone who does environmental ethics needs both (1) a procedure for making ethical decisions under conditions of ecological uncertainty and (2) a method for using ecology, in a practical sense, to direct environmental policy. One procedure for dealing with ecological uncertainty, a procedure defended elsewhere,[28] is to minimize type II, rather than type I, statistical errors when both cannot be avoided. Contrary to current scientific norms, this rule of thumb places the burden of proof not on anyone who posits an effect, but on anyone who argues that there will be no damaging effect from a particular environmental action. One can defend this rule, despite its reversal of the norms of statistical practice, on straightforward grounds of protecting human welfare. Because of the uncertainty of both soft and hard ecology, one does not have the luxury of using them to ground purely biocentric arguments (not based on human welfare) for particular environmental decisions.

Another means of avoiding the scientific uncertainty of both soft and hard ecology is to develop a more reliable middle path, practical ecology. Based neither on stipulatively defined concepts nor on general theories lacking precise predictive power, practical ecology is grounded on rules of thumb (like the norm regarding types I and II statistical error), on rough generalizations, and on case studies about individual organisms. A recent National Academy of Sciences (NAS) committee illustrated how case-specific, empirical, ecological *knowledge*, rather than an uncertain general ecological *theory* or *model*, might be used in environmental problem solving (*op.cit.*, pp. 1, 5). According to the NAS committee, ecology's greatest predictive successes occur in cases that involve only one or two species, perhaps because ecological generalizations are most fully developed for relatively simple systems. This is why, for example, ecological management of game and fish populations through regulation of hunting and fishing can often be successful (*op.cit.*, p.8). Applying this insight to our discussion, ecology might be most helpful in undergirding environmental ethics and policy making when it does not try to predict complex interactions among many species, but instead avoids the uncertainties of both soft and hard ecology and attempts to predict what will happen for only one or two taxa in a particular case. Predictions for one or two taxa are often successful because, despite the problems with general ecological theory, there are numerous lower-level theories in ecology that provide reliable predictions. Application of lower-level theory about the evolution of cooperative breeding, for example, has provided many successes in managing red-cockaded woodpeckers.[29] In this case, successful management and predictions appear to have come from specific information, such as data about the presence of cavities in trees that serve as habitat *(ibid.*, pp. 506ff.).

Examples like that of the woodpecker suggest that, if the case studies used in the NAS report are representative, then some of the most successful ecological applications arise when (and because) scientists have a great deal of knowledge about the specific organisms investigated in a particular case study (*op.cit.*, p. 13). As the authors of the NAS report put it, "the success of the cases described ... depended on such information" (*op.cit.*, p. 16). The vampire-bat case study, for instance, is an excellent example of the value of specific information when ecologists are interested in practical environmental problem solving (*op.cit.*, p. 28). The goal in the bat study was to find a control agent that affected only the "pest" species of concern, the vampire bat. The specific information that was useful in finding and using a control, diphenadione, included the facts that the bats are much more susceptible than cattle to the action of anticoagulants; that they roost extremely closely to each other; that they groom each other; that their rate of reproduction is low; that they do not migrate; and that they forage only in the absence of moonlight.[30] Using this information, ecologists were able to provide a case study as a firm foundation for policy about controlling vampire bats and for the ethics of doing so. Rather than attempt to apply some general ecological theory "top down"—as hard ecologists might do—they scrutinized a particular case, "bottom up," in order to gain explanatory insights. Their case-study explanation was local or "bottom up" in the sense that it showed how particular occurrences come about. It explained particular phenomena in terms of collections of causal processes and interactions.[31] Their explanations do not mean, however, that general laws play no role in ecological explanations, because the mechanisms discussed in the vampire-bat study operate in accord with general laws of nature. Nor do they mean that all explanations are of particular occurrences, because we can often provide causal accounts of regularities. Rather, their case-study explanations, like the accounts of practical ecology that we wish to emphasize, are more inductive or "bottom-up" in that they appeal to the underlying microstructure of the phenomena being explained. They avoid both the hard ecology of more deductive or "top-down" explanation,[32] as well as the soft ecology based on stipulative definition of desired states.

IV. Conclusion

The success of the NAS case study, with its "bottom-up" approach to scientific explanation, suggests that—whenever ecology is needed to resolve environmental controversies—ecological method needs to avoid the uncertain and stipulative concepts of soft ecology, like integrity and stability. It also needs to avoid the equally uncertain, grand deductive theories of hard ecology. Reliable environmental actions seem to require case studies and autecology. Such a recipe for grounding environmental ethics and policy, however, provides no basis for purely biocentric concepts, laws, or theories. Rather, the modest practical ecology for which we have argued appears to rely on the practice of ecologists and on their individual cases. Genuinely biocentric ethics seem to require more certainty about underlying ecological concepts and theories than is currently available in the modest rules of thumb characterizing case studies and practical ecology.

Practical ecology is particularly needed in unique situations, like most of those in community ecology, where we cannot replicate singular events. If we can use the vampire-bat study as a model for future ecological research, and if the NAS committee is correct, then both suggest that accounts of ecological method might do well to focus on practical applications and on unavoidably human, but well substantiated and nonstipulative judgments about environmental management. Moreover, if ecology turns out to be a science of case studies, practical applications, and human-directed environmental management, it is not obvious that this is a defect. Ecology may not be flawed because it must sacrifice universality for utility and practicality, or because it must sacrifice generality for the precision gained through case studies.

Even with its case-study knowledge, ecology often can provide the insights necessary for sound preservation and environmental policy. This practical and precise knowledge, coupled with conceptual and methodological analysis, is a critical departure from the hypothetical deductive and general mathematical models of hard ecology and the untestable, definitional, or incomplete principles of soft ecology. Both soft ecology and hard ecology seem to fail to address the uniqueness, particularity, and historicity of many ecological phenomena. As a consequence, it likely will be difficult for either of them to provide clear directions for how to preserve the environment or how to guide environmental ethics and policy. For this we need a middle path—dictated in part by humans, not merely by biocentric theory. We need the practical ecology of case studies.

NOTES

1. Earl D. McCoy and my *Method in Ecology: Strategies for Conservation Problems* (New York: Cambridge, 1993), pp. 149-97; and "Statistics, Costs, and Rationality in Ecological Inference," *Trends in Evolution and Ecology*, VII, 3 (March 1992): 96-99.
2. See Callicott, *In Defense of the Land Ethic* (Albany: SUNY, 1989); Leopold, *A Sand County Almanac and Sketches Here and There* (New York: Oxford, 1968); Rolston, *Environmental Ethics* (Philadelphia: Temple, 1988); Taylor, *Respect for Nature* (Princeton: University Press, 1986); Westra, *An Environmental Proposal for Ethics: The Principle of Integrity* (Lanham, MD: Rowman and Littlefield, 1994). See also note 27.
3. Simberloff, "Simplification, Danger, and Ethics in Conservation Biology," *Bulletin of the Ecological Society of America*, LXVIII (1987): 156-57; and Peters, *A Critique for Ecology* (New York: Cambridge, 1991).
4. Westra, *op.cit.*; Rolston, op.cit., "Duties to Ecosystems," in Callicott, ed., *Companion to "A Sand County Almanac"* (Madison: Wisconsin UP, 1987), pp. 246-74, and *Philosophy Gone Wild* (Buffalo: Prometheus, 1986). For a discussion of ecologists who believe that ecosystem or community concepts

and stability concepts can be used to ground environmental ethics and policy, see *Method in Ecology*, ch. 3.

5. *The Structure of Scientific Revolutions* (Chicago: University Press, 1970).
6. C. Margules, A. Higgs, and R. Rafe, "Modern Biogeographic Theory: Are There Any Lessons for Nature Reserve Design?" *Biological Conservation*, XXIV, 2 (October 1982): 115-28, here p. 116; M. Soulé and D. Simberloff, "What Do Genetics and Ecology Tell Us About the Design of Nature Reserves?" *Biological Conservation*, XXXV, 1 (1986): 19-40; M. Williamson, "Are Communities Ever Stable?" *Symposium of the British Ecological Society*, XXVI (1987): 353-70, here p. 367; B. Zimmerman and R. Bierregaard, "Relevance of the Equilibrium Theory of Island Biogeography and Species-area Relations to Conservation with a Case from Amazonia," *Journal of Biogeography*, XIII, 2 (March 1986): 133-43, here p. 134.
7. Soulé and Simberloff, pp. 24ff.
8. W. J. Boecklen and Simberloff, "Area-Based Extinction Models in Conservation," in D. Elliot, ed., *Dynamics of Extinction* (New York: Wiley, 1987), pp. 247-76; Margules, Higgs, and Rafe, p. 124; Simberloff and J. Cox, "Consequences and Costs of Conservation Corridors," *Conservation Biology*, I, 1 (May 1987): 63-71; Soulé and Simberloff, pp. 25ff.; see Zimmerman and Bierregaard, p. 135.
9. M. Blouin and E. Connor, "Is There a Best Shape for Nature Reserves?" *Biological Conservation*, XXXII, 3 (1985): 277-88.
10. Boecklen and Simberloff, pp. 252-55; Soulé and Simberloff, pp. 26-32; G.H. Orians, Committee on the Applications of Ecological Theory to Environmental Problems, *Ecological Knowledge and Environmental Problem Solving* (Washington, DC: National Academy, 1986), p. 231.
11. See Margules, Higgs, and Rafe, p. 117; Zimmerman and Bierregaard, p. 134.
12. See Zimmerman and Bierregaard, pp. 130-39.
13. Margules, Higgs, and Rafe, p. 117.
14. Boecklen and Simberloff, pp. 248-49, here p. 257.
15. *Ibid.*, p. 272; see Simberloff and Cox, pp. 63-71; Margules, Higgs, and Rafe, p. 120; Zimmerman and Bierregaard, pp. 136ff.
16. Simberloff and Cox, pp. 63-71; see Orians, p. 32; H. Salwasser, "Conserving a Regional Spotted Owl Population," in *Ecological Knowledge and Environmental Problem Solving*, pp. 227-47.
17. Boecklen and Simberloff, pp. 261-72; E. F. Connor and McCoy, "The Statistics and Biology of the Species-area Relationship." *American Naturalist*, CXIII, 6 (June 1979): 791-833; McCoy, "The Application of Island Biogeography to Forest Tracts: Problems in Determination of Turnover Rates," *Biological Conservation*, XXII, 3 (March 1982): 217-27, and "The Application of Island Biogeographic Theory to Patches of Habitat: How Much Land is Enough?" *Biological Conservation*, XXV, 1 (January 1983): 53-61.
18. Margules, Higgs, and Rafe, p. 118.
19. See *Method in Ecology*, ch. 2.
20. A. Rosenberg, *The Structure of Biological Science* (New York: Cambridge, 1985), pp. 182-87; P. Sokal and P. Sneath, *Principles of Numerical Taxonomy* (San Francisco: Freeman, 1963); D. Hull, *Science as a Process* (Chicago: University Press, 1988), pp. 102ff.
21. See A. Kiester, "Natural Kinds, Natural History, and Ecology," in E. Saarinen, ed., *Conceptual Issues in Ecology* (Boston: Reidel, 1982), pp. 355ff; James H. Fetzer, "On the Historical Explanation of Unique Events," *Theory and Decision*, VI, 1 (February 1975): 87-97.
22. "The Shallow and the Deep, Long-range Ecology Movements: A Summary." *Inquiry*, XVI (1973): 95-100.
23. Callicott, *Companion to "A Sand County Almanac"*; Heffernan, "The Land Ethic: A Critical Appraisal," *Environmental Ethics*, IV, 3 (Fall 1982): 235-47: Leopold, pp. 224-55; Rolston, "Is There an Ecological Ethic?" *Ethics*, LXXXV, 2 (January 1975): 103-09; Sagoff, "Fact and Value in Ecological Science," *Environmental Ethics*, VII, 2 (Summer 1985):99-116; Westra, "'Respect', 'Dignity', and 'Integrity': An Environmental Proposal for Ethics," *Epistemologia*, XII, 1 (1989): 91-124.
24. "Indicators of Ecosystem Integrity," in D. H. McKenzie, D. E. Hyatt, and V. J. McDonald, eds., *Ecological Indicators* (Ft. Lauderdale, FL: Elsevier, 1992), pp. 183-200.
25. "Thermodynamics and Measures of Ecological Integrity," in *Ecological Indicators*, pp. 159-82, and

"Life as a Manifestation of a Second Law of Thermodynamics," in *Advances in Mathematics and Computers in Medicine* (Waterloo, Ontario: Waterloo UP, 1993); Kay, "On the Nature of Ecological Integrity," in S. Woodley, J. Francis, Kay, eds., *Ecological Integrity and the Management of Ecosystems* (Del Ray Beach, FL: St. Lucie, 1993), pp. 201-14, and "A Nonequilibrium Thermodynamic Framework for Discussing Ecosystem Management," *Environmental Management*, XV (1991): 483-95; Peter A. Victor, Kay, and H. J. Ruitenbeek, *Economic, Ecological, and Decision Theories: Indicators of Ecologically Sustainable Development* (Ottawa: Canadian Environmental Advisory Council, 1991).

26. R. E. Ulanowicz, "Community Measures of Marine Food Networks and Their Possible Applications," in M. J. R. Fasham, ed., *Flows of Energy and Material in Marine Ecosystems* (London: Plenum, 1985), pp. 23-47.
27. "Life as a Manifestation of a Second Law of Thermodynamics," p. 21.
28. McCoy and my "Statistics, Costs, and Rationality in Ecological Inference"; see also our *Method in Ecology*.
29. J. R. Walters, "Application of Ecological Principles to the Management of Endangered Species: The Case of the Red-Cockaded Woodpecker," *Annual Review of Systematics*, XXII (1991): 505-23, here p. 518.
30. C. G. Mitchell, "Vampire Bat Control in Latin America," in *Ecological Knowledge and Environmental Problem Solving*, pp. 151-64.
31. McCoy and my "Applied Ecology and the Logic of Case Studies," *Philosophy of Science*, LXI, 1 (June 1994): 228-49.
32. W. Salmon, "Four Decades of Scientific Explanations," in P. Kitcher and Salmon, eds., *Scientific Explanation* (Minneapolis: Minnesota UP, 1989), pp. 3-219.

RADICAL AMERICAN ENVIRONMENTALISM AND WILDERNESS PRESERVATION: A THIRD WORLD CRITIQUE

Ramachandra Guha

Ramachandra Guha is a Professorial Fellow at the Nehru Memorial Museum and Library, New Delhi. He is the author of The Unquiet Woods: Ecological Change and Peasant Resistance in the Himalaya *(California, 1990); co-author with Madhav Gadgil of* This Fissured Land: An Ecological History of India *(California, 1993) and of* Ecology and Equity: The Use and Abuse of Nature in Contemporary India *(Routledge, 1995); and co-editor of* Nature, Culture, Imperialism: Essays on the Environmental History of South Asia *(Oxford, 1995).*

"I present a Third World critique of the trend in American environmentalism known as deep ecology, analyzing each of deep ecology's central tenets: the distinction between anthropocentrism and biocentrism, the focus on wilderness preservation, the invocation of Eastern traditions, and the belief that it represents the most radical trend within environmentalism. I argue that the anthropocentrism/biocentrism distinction is of little use in understanding the dynamics of environmental degradation, that the implementation of the wilderness agenda is causing serious deprivation in the Third World, that the deep ecologist's interpretation of Eastern traditions is highly selective, and that in other cultural contexts (e.g., West Germany and India) radical environmentalism manifests itself quite differently, with a far greater emphasis on equity and the integration of ecological concerns with livelihood and work. I conclude that despite its claims to universality, deep ecology is firmly rooted in American environmental and cultural history and is inappropriate when applied to the Third World."

Even God dare not appear to the poor man except in the form of bread.

—Mahatma Gandhi

I. Introduction

The respected radical journalist Kirkpatrick Sale recently celebrated "the passion of a new and growing movement that has become disenchanted with the environmental establishment and has in recent years mounted a serious and sweeping attack on it—style, substance, systems, sensibilities and all."[1] The vision of those whom Sale calls the "New Ecologists"—and what I refer to in this article as deep ecology—is a compelling one. Decrying the narrowly economic goals of mainstream environmentalism, this new movement aims at nothing less than a philosophical and cultural revolution in human attitudes toward nature. In contrast to the conventional lobbying efforts of environmental professionals based in Washington, it proposes a militant defence of "Mother Earth," an unflinching opposition to human attacks on undisturbed wilderness. With their goals ranging from the spiritual to the political, the adherents of deep ecology span a wide spectrum of the American environmental movement. As Sale correctly notes, this emerging strand has in a matter of a few years made its presence felt in a number of fields: from academic philosophy (as in the journal

Reprinted with permission of the publisher and Ramachandra Guha from *Environmental Ethics* 11 (Spring 1989): 71–83.

Environmental Ethics) to popular environmentalism (for example, the group Earth First!).

In this article I develop a critique of deep ecology from the perspective of a sympathetic outsider. I critique deep ecology not as a general (or even a foot soldier) in the continuing struggle between the ghosts of Gifford Pinchot and John Muir over control of the U.S. environmental movement, but as an outsider to these battles. I speak admittedly as a partisan, but of the environmental movement in India, a country with an ecological diversity comparable to the U. S., but with a radically dissimilar cultural and social history.

My treatment of deep ecology is primarily historical and sociological, rather than philosophical, in nature. Specifically, I examine the cultural rootedness of a philosophy that likes to present itself in universalistic terms. I make two main arguments: first, that deep ecology is uniquely American, and despite superficial similarities in rhetorical style, the social and political goals of radical environmentalism in other cultural contexts (e.g., West Germany and India) are quite different; second, that the social consequences of putting deep ecology into practice on a worldwide basis (what its practitioners are aiming for) are very grave indeed.

II. The Tenets of Deep Ecology

While I am aware that the term *deep ecology* was coined by the Norwegian philosopher Arne Naess, this article refers specifically to the American variant.[2] Adherents of the deep ecological perspective in this country, while arguing intensely among themselves over its political and philosophical implications, share some fundamental premises about human-nature interactions. As I see it, the defining characteristics of deep ecology are fourfold:

First, deep ecology argues, that the environmental movement must shift from an "anthropocentric" to a "biocentric" perspective. In many respects, an acceptance of the primacy of this distinction constitutes the litmus test of deep ecology. A considerable effort is expended by deep ecologists in showing that the dominant motif in Western philosophy has been anthropocentric—i.e., the belief that man and his works are the center of the universe—and conversely, in identifying those lonely thinkers (Leopold, Thoreau, Muir, Aldous Huxley, Santayana, etc.) who, in assigning man a more humble place in the natural order, anticipated deep ecological thinking. In the political realm, meanwhile, establishment environmentalism (shallow ecology) is chided for casting its arguments in human-centered terms. Preserving nature, the deep ecologists say, has an intrinsic worth quite apart from any benefits preservation may convey to future human generations. The anthropocentric-biocentric distinction is accepted as axiomatic by deep ecologists, it structures their discourse, and much of the present discussion remains mired within it.

The second characteristic of deep ecology is its focus on the preservation of unspoilt wilderness—and the restoration of degraded areas to a more pristine condition—to the relative (and sometimes absolute) neglect of other issues on the environmental agenda. I later identify the cultural roots and portentous consequences of this obsession with wilderness. For the moment, let me indicate three distinct sources from which it springs. Historically, it represents a playing out of the preservationist (read *radical*) and utilitarian (read *reformist*) dichotomy that has plagued American environmentalism since the turn of the century. Morally, it is an imperative that follows from the biocentric perspective; other species of plants and animals, and nature itself, have an intrinsic right to exist. And finally, the preservation of wilderness also turns on a scientific argument—viz., the value of biological diversity in stabilizing ecological regimes and in retaining a gene pool for future generations. Truly radical policy proposals have been put forward by deep ecologists on the basis of these arguments. The influential poet Gary Snyder, for example, would like to see a 90 percent reduction in human populations to allow a restoration of pristine environments, while others have argued forcefully that a large portion of the globe must be immediately cordoned off from human beings.[3]

Third, there is a widespread invocation of Eastern spiritual traditions as forerunners of deep ecology. Deep ecology, it is suggested, was practiced both by major religious traditions and at a more popular level by "primal" peoples in non-Western settings. This complements the search for an authentic lineage in Western thought. At one level, the task is to recover those dissenting voices within the Judeo-Christian tradition; at another, to suggest that religious traditions in other cultures are, in contrast, dominantly if not exclusively "biocentric" in their orientation. This coupling of (ancient) Eastern and (modern) ecological wisdom seemingly helps consolidate the claim that deep ecology is a philosophy of universal significance.

Fourth, deep ecologists, whatever their internal differences, share the belief that they are the "leading edge" of the environmental movement. As the polarity of the shallow/deep and anthropocentric/biocentric distinctions makes clear, they see themselves as the spiritual, philosophical, and political vanguard of American and world environmentalism.

III. Toward a Critique

Although I analyze each of these tenets independently, it is important to recognize, as deep ecologists are fond of remarking in reference to nature, the interconnectedness and unity of these individual themes.

(1) Insofar as it has begun to act as a check on man's arrogance and ecological hubris, the transition from an anthropocentric (human-centered) to a biocentric (humans as only one element in the ecosystem) view in both religious and scientific traditions is only to be welcomed.[4] What is unacceptable are the radical conclusions drawn by deep ecology, in particular, that intervention in nature should be guided primarily by the need to preserve biotic integrity rather than by the need of humans. The latter for deep ecologists is anthropocentric, the former biocentric. This dichotomy is, however, of very little use in understanding the dynamics of environmental degradation. The two fundamental ecological problems facing the globe are (i) overconsumption by the industrialized world and by urban elites in the Third World and (ii) growing militarization, both in a short-term sense (i.e., ongoing regional wars) and in a long-term sense (i.e., the arms race and the prospect of nuclear annihilation). Neither of these problems has any tangible connection to the anthropocentric-biocentric distinction. Indeed, the agents of these processes would barely comprehend this philosophical dichotomy. The proximate causes of the ecologically wasteful characteristics of industrial society and of militarization are far more mundane: at an aggregate level, the dialectic of economic and political structures, and at a micro-level, the life style choices of individuals. These causes cannot be reduced, whatever the level of analysis, to a deeper anthropocentric attitude toward nature; on the contrary, by constituting a grave threat to human survival, the ecological degradation they cause does not even serve the best interests of human beings! If my identification of the major dangers to the integrity of the natural world is correct, invoking the bogy of anthropocentricism is at best irrelevant and at worst a dangerous obfuscation.

(2) If the above dichotomy is irrelevant, the emphasis on wilderness is positively harmful when applied to the Third World. If in the U.S. the preservationist/utilitarian division is seen as mirroring the conflict between "people" and "interest," in countries such as India the situation is very nearly the reverse. Because India is a long settled and densely populated country in which agrarian populations have a finely balanced relationship with nature, the setting aside of wilderness areas has resulted in a direct transfer of resources from the poor to the rich. Thus, Project Tiger, a network of parks hailed by the international conservation community as an outstanding success, sharply posits the interests of the tiger against those of poor peasants living in and around the reserve. The designation of tiger reserves was made possible only by the physical displacement of existing villages and their inhabitants; their management requires the continuing exclusion of peasants and livestock. The initial impetus for setting up parks for the tiger and other large mammals such as the rhinoceros and elephant came from two social groups, first, a class of ex-hunters turned conservationists belonging mostly to the declining Indian feudal elite and second, representatives of international agencies, such as the World Wildlife Fund (WWF) and the International Union for the Conservation of Nature and Natural Resources (IUCN), seeking to transplant the American system of national parks onto Indian soil. In no case have the needs of the local population been taken into account, and

as in many parts of Africa, the designated wildlands are managed primarily for the benefit of rich tourists. Until very recently, wildlands preservation has been identified with environmentalism by the state and the conservation elite; in consequence, environmental problems that impinge far more directly on the lives of the poor—e.g., fuel, fodder, water shortages, soil erosion, and air and water pollution—have not been adequately addressed.[5]

Deep ecology provides, perhaps unwittingly, a justification for the continuation of such narrow and inequitable conservation practices under a newly acquired radical guise. Increasingly, the international conservation elite is using the philosophical, moral, and scientific arguments used by deep ecologists in advancing their wilderness crusade. A striking but by no means atypical example is the recent plea by a prominent American biologist for the takeover of large portions of the globe by the author and his scientific colleagues. Writing in a prestigious scientific forum, the *Annual Review of Ecology and Systematics*, Daniel Janzen argues that only biologists have the competence to decide how the tropical landscape should be used. As "the representatives of the natural world," biologists are "in charge of the future of tropical ecology," and only they have the expertise and mandate to "determine whether the tropical agroscape is to be populated only by humans, their mutualists, commensals, and parasites, or whether it will also contain some islands of the greater nature—the nature that spawned humans, yet has been vanquished by them." Janzen exhorts his colleagues to advance their territorial claims on the tropical world more forcefully, warning that the very existence of these areas is at stake: "if biologists want a tropics in which to biologize, they are going to have to buy it with care, energy, effort, strategy, tactics, time, and cash."[6]

This frankly imperialist manifesto highlights the multiple dangers of the preoccupation with wilderness preservation that is characteristic of deep ecology. As I have suggested, it seriously compounds the neglect by the American movement of far more pressing environmental problems within the Third World. But perhaps more importantly, and in a more insidious fashion, it also provides an impetus to the imperialist yearning of Western biologists and their financial sponsors, organizations such as the WWF and IUCN. The wholesale transfer of a movement culturally rooted in American conservation history can only result in the social uprooting of human populations in other parts of the globe.

(3) I come now to the persistent invocation of Eastern philosophies as antecedent in point of time but convergent in their structure with deep ecology. Complex and internally differentiated religious traditions—Hinduism, Buddhism, and Taoism—are lumped together as holding a view of nature believed to be quintessentially biocentric. Individual philosophers such as the Taoist Lao Tzu are identified as being forerunners of deep ecology. Even an intensely political, pragmatic, and Christian influenced thinker such as Gandhi has been accorded a wholly undeserved place in the deep ecological pantheon. Thus the Zen teacher Robert Aitken Roshi makes the strange claim that Gandhi's thought was not human-centered and that he practiced an embryonic form of deep ecology which is "traditionally Eastern and is found with differing emphasis in Hinduism, Taoism and in Theravada and Mahayana Buddhism."[7] Moving away from the realm of high philosophy and scriptural religion, deep ecologists make the further claim that at the level of material and spiritual practice "primal" peoples subordinated themselves to the integrity of the biotic universe they inhabited.

I have indicated that this appropriation of Eastern traditions is in part dictated by the need to construct an authentic lineage and in part a desire to present deep ecology as a universalistic philosophy. Indeed, in his substantial and quixotic biography of John Muir, Michael Cohen goes so far as to suggest that Muir was the "Taoist of the [American] West."[8] This reading of Eastern traditions is selective and does not bother to differentiate between alternate (and changing) religious and cultural traditions; as it stands, it does considerable violence to the historical record. Throughout most recorded history the characteristic form of human activity in the "East" has been a finely tuned but nonetheless conscious and dynamic manipulation of nature. Although mystics such as Lao Tzu did reflect on the spiritual essence of human relations with nature, it must be recognized that such ascetics and their reflections were supported by a society of cultivators whose relationship with nature was a far more *active* one. Many agricultural communities do have a sophisticated knowledge of the natural environment that may equal (and sometimes surpass) codified "scientific" knowledge; yet, the elaboration of such traditional ecological knowledge (in both material and spiritual contexts) can hardly be said to rest on a mystical affinity with nature of a deep ecological kind. Nor is such knowledge infallible: as the archaeological record powerfully suggests, modern Western man has no monopoly on ecological disasters.

In a brilliant article, the Chicago historian Ronald Inden points out that this romantic and essentially positive view of the East is a mirror image of the scientific and essentially pejorative view normally upheld by Western scholars of the Orient. In either case, the East constitutes the Other, a body wholly separate and alien from the West; it is defined by a uniquely spiritual and nonrational "essence," even if this essence is valorized quite differently by the two schools. Eastern man exhibits a spiritual dependence with respect to nature—on the one hand, this is symptomatic of his prescientific and backward self, on the other, of his ecological wisdom and deep ecological consciousness. Both views are monolithic, simplistic, and have the characteristic effect—intended in one case, perhaps unintended in the other—of denying agency and reason to the East and making it the privileged orbit of Western thinkers.

The two apparently opposed perspectives have then a common underlying structure of discourse in which the East merely serves as a vehicle for Western projections. Varying images of the East are raw material for political and cultural battles being played out in the West; they tell us far more about the Western commentator and his desires than about the "East." Inden's remarks apply not merely to Western scholarship on India, but to Orientalist constructions of China and Japan as well:

> Although these two views appear to be strongly opposed, they often combine together. Both have a similar interest in sustaining the Otherness of India. The holders of the dominant view, best exemplified in the past in imperial administrative discourse (and today probably by that of "development economics"), would place a traditional, superstition-ridden India in a position of perpetual tutelage to a modern, rational West. The adherents of the romantic view, best exemplified academically in the discourses of Christian liberalism and analytic psychology, concede the realm of the public and impersonal to the positivist. Taking their succour not from governments and big business, but from a plethora of religious foundations and self-help institutes, and from allies in the "consciousness industry," not to mention the important industry of tourism, the romantics insist that India embodies a private realm of the imagination and the religious which modern, western man lacks but needs. They, therefore, like the positivists, but for just the opposite reason, have a vested interest in seeing that the Orientalist view of India as "spiritual," "mysterious," and "exotic" is perpetuated.[9]

(4) How radical, finally, are the deep ecologists? Notwithstanding their self-image and strident rhetoric (in which the label "shallow ecology" has an opprobrium similar to that reserved for "social democratic" by Marxist-Leninists), even within the American context their radicalism is limited and it manifests itself quite differently elsewhere.

To my mind, deep ecology is best viewed as a radical trend within the wilderness preservation movement. Although advancing philosophical rather than aesthetic arguments and encouraging political militancy rather than negotiation, its practical emphasis—viz., preservation of unspoilt nature—is virtually identical. For the mainstream movement, the function of wilderness is to provide a temporary antidote to modern civilization. As a special institution within an industrialized society, the national park "provides an opportunity for respite, contrast, contemplation, and affirmation of values for those who live most of their lives in the workaday world."[10] Indeed, the rapid increase in visitations to the national parks in postwar America is a direct consequence of economic expansion. The emergence of a popular interest in wilderness sites, the historian Samuel Hays points out, was "not a throwback to the primitive, but an integral part of the modern standard of living as people sought to add new 'amenity' and 'aesthetic' goals and desires to their earlier preoccupation with necessities and conveniences."[11]

Here, the enjoyment of nature is an integral part of the consumer society. The private automobile (and the life style it has spawned) is in many respects the ultimate ecological villain, and an untouched wilderness the prototype of ecological harmony; yet, for most Americans it is perfectly consistent to drive a thousand miles to spend a holiday in a national park. They possess a vast, beautiful, and sparsely populated continent and are also able to draw upon the natural resources of large portions of the globe by virtue of their economic and political dominance. In consequence, America can simultaneously enjoy the material benefits of an expanding economy and the aesthetic benefits of unspoilt nature. The two poles of "wilderness" and "civilization" mutually coexist in an internally coherent whole, and philosophers of both poles are assigned a prominent place in this culture. Paradoxically as it may seem, it is no accident that Star Wars technology and deep ecology both find their fullest expression in that leading sector of Western civilization, California.

Deep ecology runs parallel to the consumer society without seriously questioning its ecological and socio-political basis. In its celebration of American wilderness, it also displays an uncomfortable convergence with the prevailing climate of nationalism in the American wilderness movement. For spokesmen such as the historian Roderick Nash, the national park system is America's distinctive cultural contribution to the world, reflective not merely of its economic but of its philosophical and ecological maturity as well. In what Walter Lippman called the American century, the "American invention of national parks" must be exported worldwide. Betraying an economic determinism that would make even a Marxist shudder, Nash believes that environmental preservation is a "full stomach" phenomenon that is confined to the rich, urban, and sophisticated. Nonetheless, he hopes that "the less developed nations may eventually evolve economically and intellectually to the point where nature preservation is more than a business."[12]

The error which Nash makes (and which deep ecology in some respects encourages) is to equate environmental protection with the protection of wilderness. This is a distinctively American notion, borne out of a unique social and environmental history. The archetypal concerns of radical environmentalists in other cultural contexts are in fact quite different. The German Greens, for example, have elaborated a devastating critique of industrial society which turns on the acceptance of environmental limits to growth. Pointing to the intimate links between industrialization, militarization, and conquest, the Greens argue that economic growth in the West has historically rested on the economic and ecological exploitation of the Third World. Rudolf Bahro is characteristically blunt:

> The working class here [in the West] is the richest lower class in the world. And if I look at the problem from the point of view of the whole of humanity, not just from that of Europe, then I must say that the metropolitan working class is the worst exploiting class in history.... What made poverty bearable in eighteenth or nineteenth-century Europe was the prospect of escaping it through exploitation of the periphery. But this is no longer a possibility, and continued industrialism in the Third World will mean poverty for whole generations and hunger for millions.[13]

Here the roots of global ecological problems lie in the disproportionate share of resources consumed by the industrialized countries as a whole *and* the urban elite within the Third World. Since it is impossible to reproduce an industrial monoculture worldwide, the ecological movement in the West must begin by cleaning up its own act. The Greens advocate the creation of a "no growth" economy, to be achieved by scaling down current (and clearly unsustainable) consumption levels.[14] This radical shift in consumption and production patterns requires the creation of alternate economic and political structures—smaller in scale and more amenable to social participation—but it rests equally on a shift in cultural values. The expansionist character of modern Western man will have to give way to an ethic of renunciation and self-limitation, in which spiritual and communal values play an increasing role in sustaining social life. This revolution in cultural values, however, has as its point of departure an understanding of environmental processes quite different from deep ecology.

Many elements of the Green program find a strong resonance in countries such as India, where a history of Western colonialism and industrial development has benefited only a tiny elite while exacting tremendous social and environmental costs. The ecological battles presently being fought in India have as their epicenter the conflict over nature between the subsistence and largely rural sector and the vastly more powerful commercial-industrial sector. Perhaps the most celebrated of these battles concerns the Chipko (Hug the Tree) movement, a peasant movement against deforestation in the Himalayan foothills. Chipko is only one of several movements that have sharply questioned the nonsustainable demand being placed on the land and vegetative base by urban centers and industry. These include opposition to large dams by displaced peasants, the conflict between small artisan fishing and large-scale trawler fishing for export, the countrywide movements against commercial forest operations, and opposition to industrial pollution among downstream agricultural and fishing communities.[15]

Two features distinguish these environmental movements from their Western counterparts. First, for the sections of society most critically affected by environmental degradation—poor and landless peasants, women, and tribals—it is a question of sheer survival, not of enhancing the quality of life. Second, and as a consequence, the environmental solutions they articulate deeply involve questions of equity as well as economic and political redistribution. Highlighting these differences, a leading Indian environmentalist stresses that "environmental protection per se is of least concern to most of these groups. Their main concern is about the use of the environment and who should benefit from it."[16] They seek to wrest control of nature away from the state and the industrial sector and place it in the hands of rural communities who live within that environment but are increasingly denied access to it. These communities have far more basic needs, their demands on the environment are far less intense, and they can draw upon a reservoir of cooperative social institutions and local ecological knowledge in managing the "commons"—forests, grasslands, and the waters—on a sustainable basis. If colonial and capitalist expansion has both accentuated social inequalities and signaled a precipitous fall in ecological wisdom, an alternate ecology must rest on an alternate society and polity as well.

This brief overview of German and Indian environmentalism has some major implications for deep ecology. Both German and Indian environmental traditions allow for a greater integration of ecological concerns with livelihood and work. They also place a greater emphasis on equity and social justice (both within individual countries and on a global scale) on the grounds that in the absence of social regeneration environmental regeneration has very little chance of succeeding. Finally, and perhaps most significantly, they have escaped the preoccupation with wilderness preservation so characteristic of American cultural and environmental history.[17]

IV. A Homily

In 1958, the economist J.K. Galbraith referred to overconsumption as the masked question of the American conservation movement. There is a marked selectivity, he wrote, "in the conservationist's approach to materials consumption. If we are concerned about our great appetite for materials, it is plausible to seek to increase the supply, to decrease waste, to make better use of the stocks available, and to develop substitutes. But what of the appetite itself? Surely this is the ultimate source of the problem. If it continues its geometric course, will it not one day have to be restrained? Yet in the literature of the resource problem this is the forbidden question. Over it hangs a nearly total silence."[18]

The consumer economy and society have expanded tremendously in the three decades since Galbraith penned these words; yet his criticisms are nearly as valid today. I have said "nearly," for there are some hopeful signs. Within the environmental movement several dispersed groups are working to develop ecologically benign technologies and to encourage less wasteful life styles. Moreover, outside the self-defined boundaries of American environmentalism, opposition to the permanent war economy is being carried on by a peace movement that has a distinguished history and impeccable moral and political credentials.

It is precisely these (to my mind, most hopeful) components of the American social scene that are missing from deep ecology. In their widely noticed book, Bill Devall and George Sessions make no mention of militarization or the movements for peace, while activists whose practical focus is on developing ecologically responsible life styles (e.g., Wendell Berry) are derided as "falling short of deep ecological awareness."[19] A truly radical ecology in the American context ought to work toward a synthesis of the appropriate technology, alternate life style, and peace movements.[20] By making the (largely spurious) anthropocentric-biocentric distinction central to the debate, deep ecologists may have appropriated the moral high ground, but they are at the same time doing a serious disservice to American and global environmentalism.[21]

AUTHOR'S NOTE

This essay was written while the author was a visiting lecturer at the Yale School of Forestry and Environmental Studies. He is grateful to Mike Bell, Tom Birch, Bill Burch, Bill Cronon, Diane Mayerfeld, David Rothenberg, Kirkpatrick Sale, Joel Seton, Tim Weiskel, and Don Worster for helpful comments.

NOTES

1. Kirkpatrick Sale, "The Forest for the Trees: Can Today's Environmentalists Tell the Difference," *Mother Jones* 11, no. 8 (November 1986): 26.
2. One of the major criticisms I make in this essay concerns deep ecology's lack of concern with inequalities *within* human society. In the article in which he coined the term *deep ecology*, Naess himself expresses concerns about inequalities between and within nations. However, his concern with social cleavages and their impact on resource utilization patterns and ecological destruction is not very visible in the later writings of deep ecologists. See Arne Naess, "The Shallow and the Deep, Long-Range Ecology Movement: A Summary," *Inquiry* 16 (1973): 96 (I am grateful to Tom Birch for this reference).
3. Gary Snyder, quoted in Sale, "The Forest for the Trees," p. 32. See also Dave Foreman, "A Modest Proposal for a Wilderness System," *Whole Earth Review*, no. 53 (Winter 1986-87): 42-45.
4. See, for example, Donald Worster, *Nature's Economy: The Roots of Ecology* (San Francisco, Sierra Club Books, 1977).
5. See Centre for Science and Environment, *India: The State of the Environment 1982: A Citizens Report* (New Delhi: Centre for Science and Environment, 1982); R. Sukumar, "Elephant-Man Conflict in Karnataka," in Cecil Saldanha, ed., *The State of Karnataka's Environment* (Bangalore: Centre for Taxonomic Studies, 1985). For Africa, see the brilliant analysis by Helge Kjekshus, *Ecology Control and Economic Development in East African History* (Berkeley: University of California Press, 1977).
6. Daniel Janzen, "The Future of Tropical Ecology," *Annual Review of Ecology and Systematics* 17 (1986): 305-06; emphasis added.
7. Robert Aitken Roshi, "Gandhi, Dogen, and Deep Ecology," reprinted as appendix C in Bill Devall and George Sessions, *Deep Ecology: Living as if Nature Mattered* (Salt Lake City: Peregrine Smith Books, 1985). For Gandhi's own views on social reconstruction, see the excellent three volume collection edited by Raghavan Iyer, *The Moral and Political Writings of Mahatma Gandhi* (Oxford: Clarendon Press, 1986-87).
8. Michael Cohen, *The Pathless Way* (Madison: University of Wisconsin Press, 1984), p. 120.
9. Ronald Inden, "Orientalist Constructions of India," *Modern Asian Studies* 20 (1986): 442. Inden draws inspiration from Edward Said's forceful polemic, *Orientalism* (New York: Basic Books, 1980). It must be noted, however, that there is a salient difference between Western perceptions of Middle Eastern and Far Eastern cultures respectively. Due perhaps to the long history of Christian conflict with Islam, Middle Eastern cultures (as Said documents) are consistently presented in pejorative terms. The juxtaposition of hostile and worshiping attitudes that Inden talks of applies only to Western attitudes toward Buddhist and Hindu societies.
10. Joseph Sax, *Mountains Without Handrails: Reflections on the National Parks* (Ann Arbor, University of Michigan Press, 1980), p. 42. Cf. also Peter Schmitt, *Back to Nature: The Arcadian Myth in Urban America* (New York: Oxford University Press, 1969), and Alfred Runte, *National Parks: The American Experience* (Lincoln: University of Nebraska Press, 1979).
11. Samuel Hays, "From Conservation to Environment: Environmental Politics in the United States since World War Two," *Environmental Review* 6 (1982): 21.

See also the same author's book entitled *Beauty, Health and Permanence: Environmental Politics in the United States, 1955-85* (New York: Cambridge University Press, 1987).

12. Roderick Nash, *Wilderness and the American Mind*, 3rd ed. (New Haven: Yale University Press, 1982).
13. Rudolf Bahro, *From Red to Green* (London: Verso Books, 1984).
14. From time to time, American scholars have themselves criticized these imbalances in consumption patterns. In the 1950s, William Vogt made the charge that the United States, with one-sixteenth of the world's population, was utilizing one-third of the globe's resources. (Vogt, cited in E. F. Murphy, *Nature, Bureaucracy and the Rule of Property* [Amsterdam: North Holland, 1977, p. 29]). More recently, Zero Population Growth has estimated that each American consumes thirty-nine times as many resources as an Indian. See *Christian Science Monitor*, 2 March 1987.
15. For an excellent review, see Anil Agarwal and Sunita Narain, eds., *India: The State of the Environment 1984-85: A Citizens Report* (New Delhi: Centre for Science and Environment, 1985). Cf. also Ramachandra Guha, *The Unquiet Woods: Ecological Change and a Peasant Resistance in the Indian Himalaya* (Berkeley: University of California Press, 1990).
16. Anil Agarwal, "Human-Nature Interactions in a Third World Country," *The Environmentalist* 6, no.3 (1986): 167.
17. One strand in radical American environmentalism, the bioregional movement, by emphasizing a greater involvement with the bioregion people inhabit, does indirectly challenge consumerism. However, as yet bioregionalism has hardly raised the questions of equity and social justice (international, intranational, and intergenerational) which I argue must be a central plank of radical environmentalism. Moreover, its stress on (individual) experience as the key to involvement with nature is also somewhat at odds with the integration of nature with livelihood and work that I talk of in this paper. Cf. Kirkpatrick Sale, *Dwellers in the Land: The Bioregional Vision* (San Francisco: Sierra Club Books, 1985).
18. John Kenneth Galbraith, "How Much Should a Country Consume?" in Henry Jarrett, ed., *Perspectives on Conservation* (Baltimore: Johns Hopkins Press, 1958), pp. 91-92.
19. Devall and Sessions, *Deep Ecology*, p. 122. For Wendell Berry's own assessment of deep ecology, see his "Amplications: Preserving Wildness," *Wilderness* 50 (Spring 1987): 39-40, 50-54.
20. See the interesting recent contribution by one of the most influential spokesmen of appropriate technology—Barry Commoner, "A Reporter at Large: The Environment," *New Yorker*, 15 June 1987. While Commoner makes a forceful plea for the convergence of the environmental movement (viewed by him primarily as the opposition to air and water pollution and to the institutions that generate such pollution) and the peace movement, he significantly does not mention consumption patterns, implying that "limits to growth" do not exist.
21. In this sense, my critique of deep ecology, although that of an outsider, may facilitate the reassertion of those elements in the American environmental tradition for which there is a profound sympathy in other parts of the globe. A global perspective may also lead to a critical reassessment of figures such as Aldo Leopold and John Muir, the two patron saints of deep ecology. As Donald Worster has pointed out, the message of Muir (and, I would argue, of Leopold as well) makes sense only in an American context; he has very little to say to other cultures. See Worster's review of Stephen Fox's *John Muir and His Legacy*, in *Environmental Ethics* 5 (1983): 277-81.

MAORI ENVIRONMENTAL VIRTUES

John Patterson

John Patterson is Senior Lecturer in the School of Historical & Philosophical Studies at Massey University in New Zealand. His areas of interest are in Maori Philosophy, Daoist Philosophy, aesthetics, environmental ethics and critical thinking. He is the author of Exploring Maori Values *(Dunmore, 1992).*

"The standard sources for Maori ethics are the traditional narratives. These depict all things in the environment as sharing a common ancestry, and as thereby required, ideally, to exhibit certain virtues of respect and responsibility for each other. These environmental virtues are expressed in terms of distinctively Maori concepts: respect for mauri *and* tapu, kaitiakitanga, whanaungatanga, manaakitanga, *and environmental balance. I briefly explore these Maori environmental virtues, and draw from them some messages of the world at large."*

Maori Traditions and Maori Philosophy

The Maori were the first people to settle in New Zealand, arriving from the islands to the north some 1,000 years ago. They are closely related to the other Polynesian peoples of the Pacific in language, culture, practices, and beliefs. Although until the fairly recent arrival of Europeans in New Zealand, Maori technology was simple, they have been quick to adapt European techniques and concepts to their needs, and now, after some two centuries of contact with Europeans, Maori manage to maintain a dynamic balance between traditional and technological living and thinking.

Despite their ability to adopt and adapt to European ways, Maori ethics is in important respects a traditional ethics. For example, the traditional narratives that encode central Maori environmental virtues are *tribal* traditions, varying significantly from tribe to tribe. In addition, they are *living* traditions—they have no doubt changed in some respects in the last two centuries. While there is widespread interest among Europeans in the state of the Maori before they came into contact with Europeans, I want to point out that my interest is in the *living* traditions of the Maori, as found in the versions and interpretations of their traditions that are encountered *today*.

Maori traditions are also largely *oral* traditions, even today. Much has been written down, but a lot has not and may never be committed to paper.[1] What is more, the written versions have no special standing among Maori. Much no doubt will never be written down because the traditions are seen as being *tapu*. This concept is one of several distinctively Maori concepts that feature prominently in Maori environmental ethics, and which do not translate at all closely into English. Ideally, to come to understand any unfamiliar ethics we should come to understand the unfamiliar and possibly untranslatable concepts involved, and as a first step, we should try to familiarize ourselves with the typical contexts within which they are used. It is for this reason that I keep close to the narratives in exploring Maori environmental virtues. These narratives are regularly appealed to by Maori when ethical problems arise and provide living examples of the contexts in which concepts such as *tapu* are employed.

Reprinted with permission of the publisher and John Patterson from *Environmental Ethics* 16 (Winter 1994): 397–409.

Although they are often or even typically presented in the form of historical narrative, Maori traditions also typically bear a range of *ethical* messages, and in particular as depicting the Maori *virtues*.[2] As should be expected, considering their role in expressing a living and complex environmental ethic, Maori traditional narratives can bear a range of rather different *interpretations*: they can be and are told in different ways to make different ethical points.

Finally, the historical and ethical aspects of Maori narrative are connected through the ethical importance to Maori of *ancestral precedent*. That is, the traditions relating to the deeds of the ancestors provide ethical models for behavior today.[3]

First Narrative: Rata and His Canoe

Here is the first of five brief narratives I wish to present, each of which contains elements of Maori environmental philosophy:

> A man named Rata proposes to make a journey in order to avenge the death of his father, and needs a canoe in which to travel. He goes into the forest and fells a suitable tree, but neglects to recite the traditional *karakia* (incantations) to the forest god Tane-mahuta, seeking permission to take a tree. So, when he goes home after his day's work, the *kaitiaki* or spiritual guardians of the forest (in the form of birds) restore the felled tree to life, replacing all the wood-chips removed by Rata's axe. When he returns in the morning, Rata is amazed to find no sign of the log he prepared the day before. Again he fells the tree. Again at night the *kaitiaki* restore the tree. On the third day, after felling the tree yet again, Rata pretends to go home but hides nearby. When the forest guardians start again to erect the fallen tree he comes out of hiding and upbraids them for interfering with his work. They respond by accusing him of taking a tree without obtaining permission from their master Tane-mahuta. Rata is overcome with shame. But the story has a happy ending, for Rata at least: he explains his project, and the *kaitiaki* realize that it is a worthy one. Instead of restoring the tree once more, they hollow it out and shape it into the canoe that Rata needs to avenge the death of his father.

Two distinguished Maori scholars comment on this narrative: Ranginui Walker says that the propitiatory rites ensure "that nature is not treated wantonly but with care and respect,"[4] and Te Rangi Hiroa comments that recognition of Tane's *parenthood* had to be made by Rata.[5] The forests are under the *mana* of a great god, and so are *tapu*. This *tapu* is enforced by agents appointed by Tane—the forest guardians of *kaitiaki*. In Maori tradition, Tane is ancestor of both trees and humans. Thus, the trees are (distant) cousins of the Maori. Maori are expected to respect Tane as their "godly" ancestor, and to respect trees as their kin and as children of Tane. The Rata narrative thus depicts a Maori view of the place of humans in the natural world: the environment is not simply a collection of resources to be exploited but a community of related beings, all of them linked to human beings by ties of kinship, all of them important in themselves, all of them needing protection (through *kaitiaki* or guardians) and demanding respect (through *tapu* and *karakia*).

Second Narrative: Tane Separates His Parents

> In the beginning Papa the Earth Mother and Rangi the Sky Father are close together in a loving embrace, so close that their children are cramped and unable to develop properly. A group of the children decide to separate their parents. After some of them have tried and failed, Tane places his head on his mother and his feet against his father and with the power of growth prizes his father up and away from his mother, admitting light into the world. This act allows Tane and his brothers to live their own lives fully, unencumbered by parental restriction. Nevertheless, Tane takes pity on his unadorned and unprotected parents, and proceeds to clothe his mother Papa the Earth with trees, plants, and birds, and to adorn his father Rangi the Sky with stars and comets, clouds and rainbows.

Here, early in the "creation" traditions, we find a tension in Maori environmental philosophy between the demands of kinship and the need for survival and growth. Although Tane breaks the intimate bonds of love that unite his parents so that he and his brothers can flourish, in return he takes responsibility for his parents' physical and aesthetic welfare by protecting and decorating them. Likewise, we are expected to take responsibility for the environment that nurtures us, to make sure that it is protected and enhanced. This concern is not only a matter of "negative" respect, of making sure that we do no harm. Indeed, as Tane discovered, we may well have to do harm to the environment in which we live, if we are to live at all well. Nonetheless, we are to interact in a positive and *creative* way, making up for the harm we do by enhancing the environment in appropriate ways, as Tane did with his parents.

Also, Tane's separation of earth and sky is not to be seen only as a historical event, over and done with. It must be constantly reenacted. That is, the very possibility of life and growth on the planet is seen as depending upon the children of Tane—the forests—continuing to separate earth and sky. Remove the forests, and the proper order of the world collapses. Here then is an up-to-date, familiar, and urgent message—that the forests must be protected—contained in the ancient traditions of the Maori.

Third Narrative: Tane and His Human Children

> In order to produce the Maori people, Tane fashions a female being (Hine-ahu-one) from earth, breathes life into her, and mates first with her and later with their daughter Hine-titama. When Hine-titama discovers that her husband is also her father, she descends to the world of darkness (as Hine-nui-te-po). Tane follows her, but Hine tells him that she will dwell in the world of darkness and take care of their children after they have died, while Tane must return to the world of light and foster their living offspring.

This narrative illustrates the Maori virtues of *whanaungatanga* and *manaakitanga*—our obligations to support our kin. In particular it provides part of the traditional basis for the obligations we have toward our *environmental* kin. These obligations are, of course, one aspect of a two-way responsibility: our ancestors must foster us; we must foster them. Kinship obligations of respect and enhancement work in both directions.

Fourth Narrative: Tangaroa and His Brothers

> One of the children of Rangi the Sky Father, Tawhiri god of winds, becomes angry with his half-brothers who have deprived Rangi of his partner Papa. He therefore attacks them with his winds, causing great devastation (to forests, crops, etc.). One of the brothers, Tangaroa the ancestor of fishes, becomes angered when some of his children—the reptiles—desert him, seeking shelter from Tawhiri's onslaught in the forests of his brother Tane. He therefore attacks not Tawhiri, who caused his children to leave him, but Tane the god of forests.

It is appropriate in Maori thought for Tangaroa to take issue with Tane. Because the forests are under the *mana* of Tane, he is regarded as being responsible for everything that occurs in them, *whatever the cause*. This narrative points to a difference between Maori and Pakeha conceptions of responsibility. In Maori terms, we are often held to be responsible for states of affairs that we have *not* brought about.[6] As a result, it is no use trying to evade our environmental responsibilities by claiming that we have not caused the present sorry state of the planet. In particular, if we are to claim any *mana* over our environment—and without *mana* we have no standing, no place, no access to "resources"—we must accept the associated, unconditional responsibilities of care and protection.

Fifth and Final Narrative: Tu and His Brothers

> Of the sons of Rangi and Papa, only Tu, the warlike ancestor of the Maori, succeeds in resisting the attacks of Tawhiri, and he in turn attacks his brothers for not supporting him against Tawhiri. He is described as killing and eating his brothers—the ancestors of trees, plants, and animals—thus, destroying their *tapu* and making them available for everyday use as food, timber and so on.

This narrative can be seen as licensing the Maori's use of the children of these brothers—the plants, birds, and fish—for food and other needs. Without this precedent, all of the children of the great gods, all of the animals and plants, would be highly *tapu* and therefore too dangerous to use. Because of Tu's actions, the *tapu* can now be removed by performing the ritual *karakia* laid down by Tu when he overcame the *mana* of his brothers. That is, by uttering the *karakia*, by reenacting Tu's recitation, his descendants can reenact his acts of desecration, can remove the *tapu* or godly *mana* from the food and materials they need. It was, of course, precisely this ritual reenactment that Rata omitted when he felled one of the children of Tane to make his canoe.

Respect for *Tapu* and *Mauri*

The concept and practice of *tapu*—as in the Rata narrative—involve the idea that the *world is not ours*. Although this idea is part of what some people mean when they say that the world is sacred,[7] the Maori concept is not exactly that of being "set apart"—we are *one with* the world in which we live, ultimately, on a Maori view. To respect *tapu* is thus an environmental *virtue*: rather than seeing a respect for *tapu* as a matter of *following rules*, see it as *being a certain sort of person*. In Maori, the right to make use of the "resources" of the world in which one lives has to be established, and is conditional. The Tu narrative establishes the right in general terms, and kinship and *tapu* underlie those conditions.[8] We often need to be *reminded* of the need to respect the environment—that the world is not ours—both in general, and in particular cases—where part of the environment is imperiled, and where part of the world endangers us. The concept and practice of *tapu*[9] thus serve as constant reminders to the Maori that we must always respect the natural environment in which we live.

I want to emphasize the importance of *symbolism* in this exposition, and downplay the part of metaphysics. The narratives can be seen as *symbolic* statements of *ethical* messages rather than *literal* statements of *metaphysical* "truths."[10] The virtue of respect for *tapu* can thus be seen as respect for the *inherent worth* of all items in the environment, as being prepared to balance our customary *egocentric* position with an *ecocentric* one.

The environmental virtue of respect for all things is frequently expressed in terms of the concept of *mauri*. For example, the weaver Erenora Puketapu-Hetet says that she respects the material with which she weaves by giving another dimension to its *mauri* or life force, by making sure that what is produced is a thing of beauty, by trying to live in harmony with the natural world, by trying to be at one with the environment.[11] The carver Rangi Hetet says that the materials he uses are not simply materials—they have a spiritual nature, being descended from Tane. A carver should show respect for Tane by not carving in too flamboyant a manner; he should, of course, inject his own *mauri* into the work, but should do so for the sake of the work, not for his own sake. Hetet tries to use raw timber rather than milled timber, so as to be able to show respect by following the nature character of the timber.[12]

This idea enters Maori tradition early in the "creation story," where *mauri* is represented as emerging from an original chaos—*Te Korekore*.[13] The word *mauri* is commonly translated into English as "life force," but our examples suggest that, in the context of environmental virtue ethics, it is perhaps better thought of as "character" or "nature." However it is translated, the central idea here is that *all* things have a *mauri*—a life or nature or character of their own—which must be respected. This respect applies not only to obviously living things—humans, animals, plants—but also to such things as houses, villages, meetings, and rivers. Because everything has a *mauri*, which must be respected, nothing is to be regarded as a mere means to our ends. Use of a material, for example, must be justified—the product must be worthy of the material.

We should not, however, be coldly analytical here. Although on the account that we have so far, *mauri* and *tapu* seem to be distinct, no less an authority than John Rangihau considers that the words may be interchangeable.[14] We may, therefore, be wise to consider the messages relating to *mauri* and *tapu* as a whole. Personally, I tend to associate the idea of *tapu* with the negative or restrictive aspect—that other items in the world have not been put there for my benefit. Moreover, I associate the idea of *mauri* with the positive or permissive aspect—that my relations and interactions with other items in the world should be understanding, sympathetic, and creative—understanding of and sympathetic toward the nature or special character of each item, and dealing with it creatively.

Whanaungatanga

Another Maori ethical concept that features in an explanation of the traditional narratives is *whanaungatanga*. The term derives from *whanaunga*, meaning "relative" or "blood relation," and is now used to refer to the way in which kin should interact with each other.[15] As an environmental virtue, *whanaungatanga* highlights the point that to be destructive of the environment is inappropriate for environmental kin. And failure to provide necessary *protection* is environmentally hostile.

The other side of that coin is that kin should interact *creatively*, as illustrated by Tane decorating his parents. Of course, kin should not be destructive of one another; in addition, however, they should actively promote each other's interests. Thus, in relation to the environment, *whanaungatanga* reminds Maori to seek and implement ways of enhancing the welfare of the whole environment and all its members, rather than simply abstaining from harming them. Of course, destructiveness and wastefulness are environmental vices; however, simply to refrain from them is not enough. Just as those engaged in the crafts try to make creative use of their materials, all of us in all of our activities should do what we can to make the whole environment better, and in particular, do what we can to heal environmental injuries, whoever caused them.

Another Maori concept that features in the explanation of such narratives as Tane protecting and decorating his separated parents is *aroha*. Commonly translated as "love," this word expresses the ways in which kin should act and feel toward each other. If humans really are to see themselves as kin to the whole natural world, we should show the appropriate forms and degrees of *aroha* toward all natural items.

At this point, the skeptic is likely, and entitled, to recall some rather insipid or woolly ideas of "loving nature." There is, however, quite a range of concepts of love available here, not all of them woolly or insipid. For example, there is the hardheaded view that real love entails a willingness to sacrifice one's personal interests, even one's life, and this willingness is certainly a requirement of *aroha*, at least among close kin. Another quality that distinguishes *aroha* from the woollier varieties of "love of nature" is the fact that, traditionally, *aroha* is not a universal "right." There is a proverb to the effect that it has to be earned and reciprocated: "*Aroha mai, aroha atu*"—"Love toward us, love going out from us."[16] Although many Maori nowadays accept Christian ideas of universal love, and express it in terms of *aroha*, the idea that *aroha* has to be earned and repaid is also alive and well.[17]

This reciprocity and balance of *aroha* is prominent in the idea of Papa or Mother Earth. The idea of a two-way love between earth and humans forms a natural basis for an environmental philosophy. Our obligation to show *aroha* to Papa is based upon the *aroha* she shows to us, in feeding and sheltering us.[18]

Manaakitanga

When the children of Tangaroa seek refuge in Tane's forests, he is hospitable and generous toward them. These virtues are implicit in the Maori concept of *manaakitanga*.[19] The question of whether the children deserve or have a right to this generosity does not arise (although they will be expected to repay it if the occasion arises). The forests are under the *mana* of Tane; those who enter them are, therefore, under his *mana* and can expect to be treated well. If they are not received with the best of hospitality, that *mana* would immediately suffer.[20]

Just as Tane's *mana* over the forests requires him to *manaaki* or care for anyone who enters, or at least anyone who enters peacefully, without challenging his *mana*, if I am to claim mana over the environment in which I live, I am seen from a Maori point of view as responsible for the welfare of all creatures within that environment, within the sphere of my *mana*. A central theme of environmental ethics is the move away from the ridiculous and dangerous idea that "I" am the center of the universe. By exhibiting the virtue of *manaakitanga* in my dealings with my environment, I accept that others also have their place, right here where I am, that my *mana* does not exclude theirs. Thus, environmental *manaakitanga* involves the idea that we should identify with our environmental kin, as parts of a larger whole and as children of common ancestors.

The important concept of *mana*, which underlies *manaaki*, features prominently in the narratives. The *mana* of an ancestor passes on to the descendants, other things being equal. To treat descendants with disrespect is, therefore, to trample on their *mana*, which is their ancestors' *mana*. Respect for *mana* is especially important when it is the *mana* of an *atua*, such as Tane, because such *mana* amounts to *tapu*.[21] The behavior of the forest *kaitiaki* in the Rata narrative illustrates the place of *mana* in a Maori concept of environmental responsibility. All of us are responsible for the areas that come under our *mana* individually or collectively. To the Maori, that includes the lands and waters with which we are associated, and all their inhabitants and natural features.

Kaitiakitanga

I started with a narrative about *kaitiaki* or guardians. Traditionally, the *kaitiaki* of a place or resource are seen as having been appointed by whatever person, tribe, or being has the appropriate *mana*. Because forests come under the *mana* of Tane, he appoints the forest *kaitiaki*. Likewise, Tangaroa appoints *kaitiaki* for the seas. However, there will also be more local and often human *kaitiaki*: a particular fishing ground, for example, will have *kaitiaki* appointed from among the people who have traditional fishing rights. In all cases, the *mana* of the *kaitiaki* is, as it were, delegated. While to democratized Europeans the concept of a guardian might suggest a sort of authority and authoritarianism that is perhaps out of place in Western environmental philosophy, in Maori terms, environmental guardians both have and need to have *mana*. Without such *mana*, the forest *kaitiaki* would have been powerless against Rata. However, this *mana* does not have to be seen as an authority over a part of the environment so much as an authority over other beings in relation to that part of the environment.

Thus, although from a traditional Maori perspective, *kaitiakitanga* over the environment may not be open to outsiders, there is another sense in which all of us can be *kaitiaki* of the systems in which we live, work, and play. Rather than traditionally appointed guardians, we can be voluntary caretakers, individually and collectively. In this sense, *kaitiakitanga* is an environmental virtue that any of us can practice, daily. Indeed, it is a virtue that many do practice: all who take it upon themselves to care for ecosystems are practicing the environmental virtue of *kaitiakitanga*.[22]

Balance as an Environmental Virtue

If we attend only to distinctively Maori concepts such as *tapu*, *mana*, *manaakitanga*, *whanaungatanga*, and *kaitiakitanga*, we might overlook an important aspect of Maori environmental virtues—*balance*. Although there is no "important" Maori word for balance, the concept is central in Maori ethics and metaphysics (as in Chinese), and a concept of balance is built into the very structure of the Maori language.[23]

The idea of environmental balance is incorporated in many of the traditional narratives. At the beginning, there is a state of balance (e.g., Rangi and Papa united), but then something happens that upsets the balance (Tane separates them), which requires some new balancing action (Tane protects and decorates them). Thus, balance is presented, if only implicitly, as an environmental virtue in the interactions between Rangi and Papa and their children, and among the children. Seeking balance from a different point of view: rather than kill the parents, or leave them close together, Tane achieves a new balance in their separation. The children can thus grow and flourish, and the parents can continue to express their love for one another and for their children, although not in the way they used to. Among the children, balance is achieved, for example, each time the human children of Tu continue to overcome those of Tane, etc. (the plants and animals), but subject to balancing constraints of respect for the *tapu* of the descendants of the original children of earth and sky. It is always important in Maori thought and practice to recognize conflicting demands, and to devise procedures that restore balance when there is trouble. Of course, "restoring balance" is rarely a matter of returning precisely to the initial state; environmental balance is typically dynamic rather than static.

This emphasis on balance reflects a fundamental aspect of a Maori world view: the universe is seen as consisting of polar pairs—male and female, *tapu* and *noa* (common, available), light and dark, life and death, and so on. These pairs in themselves are neither good nor evil. There is no unattainable ideal state; the ideal in Maori ethics is not to stamp out one member of a polar pair and foster the other, but to seek an appropriate *balance* between the polar pairs.[24] Although there is no unconditional dualism in such a world, from any perspective there are likely to be items that are friendly and items that are hostile (as well as vast indifference). This situation is to be expected in terms of the natural properties of the items concerned, and is a contingent matter, perhaps even changeable.

This contingency influences the way I conceive of myself in relation to the environment. Mine is not the only valid perspective. While I am entitled through precedent and ritual to satisfy my needs, so too are others. Environmentally, this polar-complementary perspective encourages me to distinguish my needs from mere wants, and thus adopt an ecocentric view of the world. It contrasts with a dualistic perspective that divides the world into the good and the evil, and views hostile items as items to be eliminated. Maori environmental philosophy neatly avoids this unfounded and environmentally unfriendly idea.

Conclusions

The environment is seen in Maori tradition not simply as resources to be exploited, but as a community of kin, other members of which are normally *tapu*, but which can be made available for justified use. This kinship between humans and the environment, as it is expressed in Maori traditions, has familiar parallels in science; the Maori traditions can thus be presented and interpreted as symbolic representations of ecological principles—the trees, for example, separate earth and sky and thus foster the proper development of all organisms, including humans.

The narratives also express a tension between the demands of kinship and the need for survival and growth. Our place in the world is a matter of *mana*. If we are to claim any mana over our environment—without which we have no place in it, and no access to "resources"—we must accept the associated strict or unconditional responsibilities of care and protection; we must respect the environment positively or creatively. Non-technological peoples have always depended for their survival on a detailed understanding (and enforcement) of principles of ecology. Maori environmental ethics serves to remind us of this requirement, in principle and in detail. Of course, for a short period in Western history, technology seemed to change all that, seemingly making us independent of our "environment," and permitting many of us to forget the principles of ecology. We now know that we must learn once more to live in harmony with the whole natural world. The Maori give us one insight (among many) of what is needed, showing us a successful environmental virtue ethic, alive and working in a contemporary technological world.

If I were a Maori speaker and this paper were a Maori *korero* or speech, I would be expected to conclude with a *waiata* or song, that captures the essence of what I have been saying. As it happens, I am not and this conclusion is not. Instead, I leave you with an image that recalls Rata and his environmental significance. If you are lucky enough to be in the right place at the right time, in the remaining New Zealand forests, you will be greeted by a mass of brilliant red flowers lighting up the forest. These are the flowers of Rata, in his present form as a forest tree.[25] Knowing as we do the narrative about Rata and his canoe, and understanding as we do its environmental significance, these flowers remind us of the ways in which, according to Maori tradition and practice, we should relate to the other creatures in the world in which we live.

Glossary[26]

aroha: love, pity
atu: away from the speaker
atua: god, supernatural
hine-ahu-one: Earth-formed maid
hine-nui-te-po: Great daughter of darkness
hine-titama: daughter of Tane and Hine-ahu-one
kaitiaki: guardian
kaitiakitanga: guardianship
karakia: prayer, incantation

korero: speech
mai: toward the speaker
mana: influence, power
manaaki: entertain, befriend
manaakitanga: hospitality
mauri: life force, character
noa: free from tapu
Papa-tuanuku: Earth Mother
raahui: ban, reserve
rangatira: chief, leader
rangatiratanga: sovereignty
Rangi: Sky Father
Rata: the canoe builder, a forest tree
Tane-mahuta: god of trees and birds
Tangaroa: god of fishes
tapu: sacred, forbidden
Tawhiri-matea: god of winds and rain
Te Korekore: original void or chaos
Tu-mata-uenga: warlike ancestor of Maori
waiata: song
whanaungatanga: kinship solidarity

NOTES

1. The traditional narratives that feature in this paper, though, are all freely available in a number of published sources, the most convenient for the English reader being Antony Alpers, *Maori Myths and Tribal Legends* (Auckland: Longman Paul, 1964). Maori language texts of the narratives presented below may be found in George Grey, *Nga Mahi a nga Tuupuna* (Wellington: A. H. & A. W. Reed, 1971), pp. 1-2 (Separation); pp. 2-4 (Tangaroa); pp. 4-5 (Tu); pp. 46-49 (Rata) and in John White, *The Ancient History of the Maori* (Wellingon: Government Printer, 1887), vol. 1, pp. 117-78 (Tane and Hine). The versions that appear in this paper are in the author's words. For translations of key terms, see the glossary at the end of this paper.
2. The view that Maori ethics is best thought of as a virtue ethics is defended in Roy Perrett and John Patterson, "Virtue Ethics and Maori Ethics," *Philosophy East and West* 41 (1991): 185-202.
3. This relationship is reflected, for example, in the concept of *tika*, which translates into English variously as customary, correct, or lawful. Where tradition is the primary source of ethics, a distinction between the customary and the lawful is not so obvious as it is elsewhere.
4. Ranginui Walker, "The Relevance of Maori Myths and Tradition," Michael King, ed., *Tihe Mauri Ora: Aspects of Maoritanga* (New Zealand: Methuen, 1978), p. 29.
5. Te Rangi Hiroa (Peter Buck), *The Coming of the Maori* (Wellington: Maori Purposes Fund Board, 1950), p. 455.
6. John Patterson, "A Maori Concept of Collective Responsiblity," in Graham Oddie and Roy Perrett, eds., *Justice, Ethics and New Zealand Society* (Auckland: Oxford University Press, 1992), pp. 20-22.
7. Indeed, *tapu* is the standard word for "sacred" in Maori Christianity.
8. Compare a familiar (if challenged) interpretation of Hebrew and Christian traditions, where the world can be seen as being under our dominion, to use as we see fit.
9. And the associated concept and practice of *raahui.*
10. Detailed examples of ethical interpretation of one Maori "metaphysical" concept are provided in John Patterson, *Exploring Maori Values* (Palmerston North: Dunmore Press, 1992), pp. 28-33.
11. Erenora Puketapu-Hetet, *Maori Weaving* (Auckland; Pitman, 1989).
12. Rangi Hetet, interview in Darcy Nicholas, ed., *Seven Maori Artists* (Wellington: Government Printer, 1986), p. 29.
13. Maori Marsden, "God, Man and Universe: A Maori View," in Michael King, ed., *Te Ao Hurihuri: The World Moves On* (New Zealand: Hicks Smith and Methuen, 1977), p. 147.
14. John Rangihau, "Learning and *Tapu*" in King, *Te Ao Hurihuri*, p. 11.
15. Perhaps *whanaungatanga* is a rather recent term, as it does not appear in some dictionaries. Nevertheless, it is given a central place by contemporary writers such as Rangimarie Rose Pere, *Ako, Concepts and Learning in the Maori Tradition* (Hamilton: Department of Sociology, University of Waikato, 1982). See also Joan Metge, "Te Rito o te Harakeke: Conceptions of the *Whaanau,*" *Journal of the Polynesian Society* 99 (1990): 55-92.
16. T. S. Karetu, A. E. Brougham, and A. W. Reed, *Maori Proverbs* (Auckland: Reed Methuen, 1987), p. 61.
17. Tilly Te Koingo Reedy, "The Maori in the Future: A

Woman's View," in *He Maataapuna: Some Maori Perspectives* (Wellington: New Zealand Planning Council, 1979), p. 47.

18. Again we do not have to take the narratives as literal and metaphysical—they can be taken as symbolic expressions of ethical messages. As in the case of the Gaia hypothesis, we do not literally have to believe that Papa has *feelings* of *aroha* towards us; only that she (or "she") behaves (or "behaves") in an appropriate way.
19. They are also implicit in the idea of *rangatiratanga*, the qualities shown by a *rangatira* or leader.
20. Lao Tzu: "Those who are good I treat as good. Those who are not good I also treat as good. In so doing I gain in goodness"—D. C. Lau, trans., *Lao Tzu: Tao Te Ching* (London; Penguin, 1963), chap. 49. A Maori parallel might run: "Those who have *mana I manaaki*; those who do not have *mana* I also *manaaki*; in so doing I gain in *mana*."
21. A proverb: "*Ko te tapu te mana o nga atua—Tapu* is the *mana* of the spiritual powers"—Moana Jackson, *The Maori and the Criminal Justice System: He Whaipanga Hou—A New Perspective* (Wellington: Department of Justice, 1988), p. 43.
22. In these days of catastrophic human overpopulation we might adopt environmental *kaitiakitanga* as a substitute for *reproducing*. Rather than trying to gain fulfillment through bringing up human offspring, we might chose to become foster parents of *nonhumans*, taking responsibility for the well-being of parts of the ecosystems which sustain us.
23. A proverb we have already met—*Aroha mai, aroha atu*—illustrates this feature of balanced sentence construction in Maori. For an extended example of the place of balance in Maori ethics, see John Patterson, "Utu, Revenge and *Mana*," *British Review of New Zealand Studies* 2 (1989): 51-61.
24. Roughly, an Aristotelian rather than a Platonic ethics, a Chinese rather than a European one.
25. *Metrosideros umbellata*, the southern rata, and *M. Robusta*, the northern rata.
26. These glosses are a rough guide only. Many of these words do not translate at all accurately into simple English phrases, and some of them are used rather differently by different speakers.

STUDY QUESTIONS

1 What does Singer mean when he says: "The principle of the equality of human beings is not a description of an alleged actual equality among humans: it is a prescription of how we should treat human beings"? How does Singer use this understanding of equality to argue that "all animals are equal"?

2 What arguments does Singer mount in favor of vegetarianism? If you are not already a vegetarian, has Singer convinced you to become one? If you are, are Singer's arguments the ones you would use? Why or why not?

3 What does Callicott mean by the terms "ethical humanism" and "humane moralism"? According to Callicott, what is problematic about Singer's strategy of extending moral consideration to non-human animals?

4 What is the land ethic and why does Callicott claim that it represents a shift in the way the environment and our treatment of it is conceived?

5 Do you find Singer's or Callicott's account of the way we ought to treat non-human animals more convincing? Give reasons for your answer.

6 Shrader-Frechette identifies Callicott's account as a "soft environmental ethics." What does she mean by this and why does she reject this approach to environmental issues?

7 According to Shrader-Frechette, what is hard environmental ethics and why does she say that this approach cannot address issues of policy with respect to the environment?

8 Does Shrader-Frechette succeed in her attempt to find a middle path between soft and hard environmental ethics? In your view, would her proposal succeed in providing clear directions for how to preserve the environment and guide environmental policy? Provide reasons for your answers.

9 According to Guha, what is deep ecology? What are the similarities and differences between deep ecology and Callicott's land ethic or ethical holism?

10 What objections does Guha raise to the version of deep ecology defended by American environmentalists? How does this differ from the versions of radical environmentalism in other cultural contexts such as Germany and India?

11 According to Guha, why has deep ecology become rooted in the specific context of American environmentalism? Why is it an inappropriate model to apply to the Third World? Do you agree? Why or why not?

12 From what you learned through Maori traditional narratives in Patterson's account, in what ways do Maori environmental values differ from Western values? Can we apply lessons about Maori environmental philosophy to environmental issues in other parts of the world? Why or why not?

SUGGESTED READINGS

Barry, Brian. "Intergenerational Justice in Energy Policy." In *Energy and the Future* edited by Douglas MacLean and Peter Brown. Lanham, MD: Rowman & Littlefield, 1983.

Burgess-Jackson, Keith. "Doing Right by Our Animal Companions." *The Journal of Ethics*, v. 2 (1998): 159-85.

Donovan, Josephine. "Attention to Suffering: A Feminist Caring Ethic for the Treatment of Animals." *Journal of Social Philosophy*, v. 27, no. 1 (1996): 81-102.

Grossman, Karl. "Environmental Racism." In *The 'Racial' Economy of Science: Toward a Democratic Future* edited by Sandra Harding. Bloomington: Indiana University Press, 1993: 326-334.

Katz, Eric and Lauren Oechsli. "Moving Beyond Anthropocentrism: Environmental Ethics, Development, and the Amazon." *Environmental Ethics*, v. 15 (1993): 49-59.

Lahar, Stephanie. "Ecofeminist Theory and Grassroots Politics." *Hypatia*, v. 6, no. 1 (Spring 1991): 28-45.

Leopold, Aldo. "The Land Ethic." In *A Sand County Almanac: And Sketches Here and There*. New York: Oxford University Press, 1949.

Nickel, James W. and Eduardo Viola. "Integrating Environmentalism and Human Rights." *Environmental Ethics*, v. 16 (1994): 265-273.

Regan, Tom. *The Case for Animal Rights.* Berkeley: University of California Press, 1983.

Shiva, Vandana. "Colonialism and the Evolution of Masculinist Forestry." In *The 'Racial' Economy of Science: Toward a Democratic Future* edited by Sandra Harding. Bloomington: Indiana University Press, 1993: 303-314.

— . "Development, Ecology and Women." In *Staying Alive: Women, Ecology and Development*. Zed Books, 1988.

Slicer, Deborah. "Your Daughter or Your Dog? A Feminist Assessment of the Animal Research Issue." *Hypatia*, v. 6, no. 1 (Spring 1991): 108-124.

Warren, Karen. "The Power and the Promise of Ecological Feminism." *Environmental Ethics*, v. 12 (1990): 125-146.